Social & Developmental Psychology 249PY

Social & Developmental Psychology 249PY

Compiled from:

Social Psychology
Seventh Edition
Michael A. Hogg and Graham M. Vaughan

Developmental Psychology
Rachel Gillibrand, Virginia Lam, and Victoria L. O'Donnell

Harlow, England • London • New York • Boston • San Francisco • Toronto • Sydney • Auckland • Singapore • Hong Kong
Tokyo • Seoul • Taipei • New Delhi • Cape Town • Sao Paulo • Mexico City • Madrid • Amsterdam • Munich • Paris • Milan

Pearson Education Limited
Edinburgh Gate
Harlow
Essex CM20 2JE

And associated companies throughout the world

Visit us on the World Wide Web at:
www.pearson.com/uk

Compiled from:

Social Psychology
Seventh Edition
Michael A. Hogg, and Graham M. Vaughan
ISBN 978-0-273-76459-5
© Pearson Education Limited 2014 (print and electronic)

Developmental Psychology
Rachel Gillibrand, Virginia Lam, and Victoria L. O'Donnell
ISBN 978-0-13-205259-7
© Pearson Education Limited

ISBN 978-1-78447-955-8

Printed and bound in Great Britain by Ashford Colour Press, Gosport, Hampshire.

Contents

Section I

CHAPTER 1
Introducing social psychology

Chapter contents

Focus questions

1   Would it ever be ethically acceptable to conceal aspects of the true purpose and nature of a psychology experiment from someone volunteering to take part?

2   How complete an explanation of social behaviour do you think evolution provides? In Chapter 1 of MyPsychLab at www.mypsychlab.com (watch *Choosing a mate*) students describe attributes with evolutionary significance that they would look for in a mate.

3   Social psychology texts often convey the impression that social psychology is primarily an American discipline. Do you have a view on this?

will use which involves getting you to decide to buy a car by giving you a very low price

Go to MyPsychLab to explore video and test your understanding of key topics addressed in this chapter.

MyPsychLab

Use MyPsychLab to refresh your understanding with interactive summaries, explore topics further with video and audio clips and assess your progress with quick test and essay questions. To buy access or register your code, visit www.mypsychlab.com. You will also need a course ID from your instructor.

What is social psychology?

Social psychology
Scientific investigation of how people's thoughts, feelings and behaviour are influenced by the actual, imagined or implied presence of others.

Social psychology has been defined as 'the scientific investigation of how the thoughts, feelings and behaviours of individuals are influenced by the actual, imagined or implied presence of others' (G. W. Allport, 1954a, p. 5). But what does this mean? What do social psychologists actually do, how do they do it, and what do they study?

Social psychologists are interested in explaining *human* behaviour and generally do not study animals. Some general principles of social psychology may be applicable to animals, and research on animals may provide evidence for processes that generalise to people (e.g. social facilitation – **see Chapter 8**). Furthermore, certain principles of social behaviour may be general enough to apply to humans and, for instance, other primates (e.g. Hinde, 1982). As a rule, however, social psychologists believe that the study of animals does not take us very far in explaining human social behaviour, unless we are interested in its evolutionary origins (e.g. Neuberg, Kenrick and Schaller, 2010; Schaller, Simpson and Kenrick, 2006).

Behaviour
What people actually do that can be objectively measured.

Social psychologists study behaviour because behaviour can be observed and measured. However, behaviour refers not only to obvious motor activities (such as running, kissing, driving) but also to more subtle actions such as a raised eyebrow, a quizzical smile or how we dress, and, critically important in human behaviour, what we say and what we write. In this sense, behaviour is publicly verifiable. However, the meaning attached to behaviour is a matter of theoretical perspective, cultural background or personal interpretation.

Social psychologists are interested not only in behaviour, but also in feelings, thoughts, beliefs, attitudes, intentions and goals. These are not directly observable but can, with varying degrees of confidence, be inferred from behaviour; and to a varying extent may influence or even determine behaviour. The relationship between these unobservable processes and overt behaviour is in itself a focus of research; for example, in research on attitude–behaviour correspondence (**see Chapter 5**) and research on prejudice and discrimination (**see Chapter 10**). Unobservable processes are also the psychological dimension of behaviour, as they occur within the human brain. However, social psychologists almost always go one step beyond relating social behaviour to underlying psychological processes – they almost always relate psychological aspects of behaviour to more fundamental cognitive processes and structures in the human mind and sometimes to neuro-chemical processes in the brain (**see Chapter 2**).

What makes social psychology *social* is that it deals with how people are affected by other people who are physically present (e.g. an audience – **see Chapter 8**) or who are imagined to be present (e.g. anticipating performing in front of an audience), or even whose presence is implied. This last influence is more complex and addresses the fundamentally social nature of our experiences as humans. For instance, we tend to think with words; words derive from language and communication; and language and communication would not exist without social interaction (**see Chapter 15**). Thought, which is an internalised and private activity that can occur when we are alone, is thus clearly based on implied presence. As another example of implied presence, consider that most of us do not litter, even if no one is watching and even if there is no possibility of ever being caught. This is because people, through the agency of society, have constructed a powerful social convention or norm that proscribes such behaviour. Such a norm implies the presence of other people and 'determines' behaviour even in their absence (**see Chapters 7 and 8**).

Science
Method for studying nature that involves the collecting of data to test hypotheses.

Theory
Set of interrelated concepts and principles that explain a phenomenon.

Data
Publicly verifiable observations.

Social psychology is a science because it uses the scientific method to construct and test theories. Just as physics has concepts such as electrons, quarks and spin to explain physical phenomena, social psychology has concepts such as dissonance, attitude, categorisation and identity to explain social psychological phenomena. The scientific method dictates that no theory is 'true' simply because it is logical and seems to make sense. On the contrary, the validity of a theory is based on its correspondence with fact. Social psychologists construct theories from data and/or previous theories and then conduct empirical research, in which data are collected to test the theory (see below).

Social psychology and its close neighbours

Social psychology is poised at the crossroads of a number of related disciplines and subdisciplines (see Figure 1.1). It is a subdiscipline of general psychology and is therefore concerned with explaining human behaviour in terms of processes that occur within the human mind. It differs from individual psychology in that it explains *social* behaviour, as defined in the previous section. For example, a general psychologist might be interested in perceptual processes that are responsible for people overestimating the size of coins. However, a social psychologist might focus on the fact that coins have value (a case of implied presence, because the value of something generally depends on what others think), and that perceived value might influence the judgement of size. A great deal of social psychology is concerned with face-to-face interaction between individuals or among members of groups, whereas general psychology focuses on people's reactions to stimuli that do not have to be social (e.g. shapes, colours, sounds).

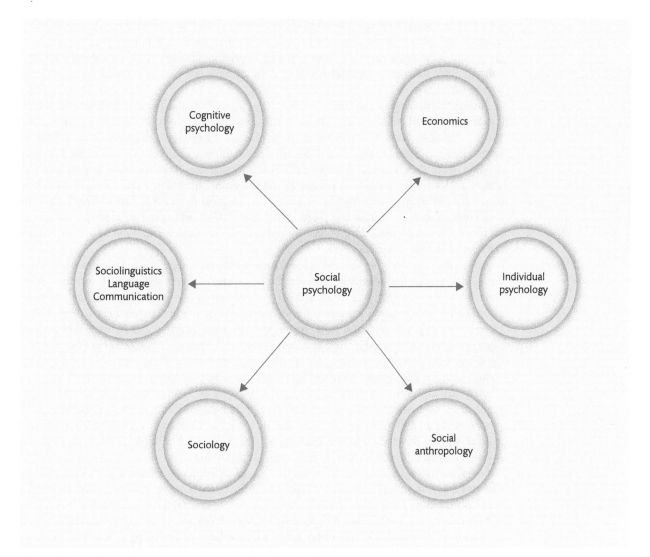

Figure 1.1 Social psychology and some close scientific neighbours

Social psychology draws on a number of subdisciplines in general psychology for concepts and methods of research. It also has fruitful connections with other disciplines, mostly in the social sciences

The boundary between individual and social psychology is approached from both sides. For instance, having developed a comprehensive and highly influential theory of the individual human mind, Sigmund Freud set out, in his 1921 essay 'Group psychology and the analysis of the ego', to develop a social psychology. Freudian, or psychodynamic, notions have left an enduring mark on social psychology (Billig, 1976), in particular in the explanation of prejudice **(see Chapter 10)**. Since the late 1970s, social psychology has been strongly influenced by cognitive psychology, in an attempt to employ its methods (e.g. reaction time) and its concepts (e.g. memory) to explain a wide range of social behaviours. In fact, what is called social cognition **(see Chapter 2)** is the dominant approach in contemporary social psychology (Fiske and Taylor, 2008; Moskowitz, 2005; Ross, Lepper and Ward, 2010), and it surfaces in almost all areas of the discipline (Devine, Hamilton and Ostrom, 1994). In recent years the study of brain biochemistry and neuroscience (Gazzaniga, Ivry and Mangun, 2009) has also influenced social psychology (Lieberman, 2010).

Social psychology also has links with sociology and social anthropology; mostly in studying groups, social and cultural norms, social representations, and language and intergroup behaviour. In general, sociology focuses on how groups, organisations, social categories and societies are organised, how they function and how they change. The unit of analysis (i.e. the focus of research and theory) is the group as a whole rather than the individual people who make up the group. Sociology is a *social science* whereas social psychology is a *behavioural science* – a disciplinary difference with far-reaching consequences for how one studies and explains human behaviour.

Social anthropology is much like sociology but historically has focused on 'exotic' societies (i.e. non-industrial tribal societies that exist or have existed largely in developing countries). Social psychology deals with many of the same phenomena but seeks to explain how individual human interaction and human cognition influence 'culture' and, in turn, are influenced or constructed by culture (Heine, 2012; Smith, Bond and Kağitçibaşi, 2006; **see also Chapter 16**). The unit of analysis is the individual person within the group. In reality, some forms of sociology (e.g. microsociology, psychological sociology, sociological psychology) are closely related to social psychology (Delamater and Ward, 2013). There is, according to Farr (1996), a sociological form of social psychology that has its origins in the *symbolic interactionism* of G. H. Mead (1934) and Herbert Blumer (1969).

Just as the boundary between social and individual psychology has been approached from both sides, so has the boundary between social psychology and sociology. From the sociological side, for example, Karl Marx's theory of cultural history and social change has been extended to incorporate a consideration of the role of individual psychology (Billig, 1976). From the social psychological side, intergroup perspectives on group and individual behaviour draw on sociological variables and concepts (Hogg and Abrams, 1988; **see also Chapter 11**). Contemporary social psychology also abuts sociolinguistics and the study of language and communication (Giles and Coupland, 1991; **see also Chapter 15**) and even literary criticism (Potter, Stringer and Wetherell, 1984). It also overlaps with economics, where behavioural economists have recently 'discovered' that economic behaviour is not rational, because people are influenced by other people – actual, imagined or implied (Cartwright, 2011). Social psychology also draws on and is influenced by applied research in many areas, such as sports psychology, health psychology and organisational psychology.

Social psychology's location at the intersection of different disciplines is part of its intellectual and practical appeal. However, it is also a cause of debate about what precisely constitutes social psychology as a distinct scientific discipline. If we lean too far towards individual cognitive processes, then perhaps we are pursuing individual psychology or cognitive psychology. If we lean too far towards the role of language, then perhaps we are being scholars of language and communication. If we overemphasise the role of social structure in intergroup relations, then perhaps we are being sociologists. The issue of exactly what constitutes social psychology provides an important and ongoing metatheoretical debate (i.e. a debate about what sorts of theory are appropriate for social psychology), which forms the background to the business of social psychology (see below).

Topics of social psychology

One way to define social psychology is in terms of what social psychologists study. This book is a comprehensive coverage of the main phenomena that social psychologists study now and have studied in the past. As such, social psychology can be defined by the contents of this and other books that present themselves as social psychology texts. A brief look at the contents of this book will give a flavour of the scope of social psychology. Social psychologists study an enormous range of topics, including conformity, persuasion, power, influence, obedience, prejudice, prejudice reduction, discrimination, stereotyping, bargaining, sexism and racism, small groups, social categories, intergroup relations, crowd behaviour, social conflict and harmony, social change, overcrowding, stress, the physical environment, decision making, the jury, leadership, communication, language, speech, attitudes, impression formation, impression management, self-presentation, identity, the self, culture, emotion, attraction, friendship, the family, love, romance, sex, violence, aggression, altruism and prosocial behaviour (acts that are valued positively by society).

One problem with defining social psychology solely in terms of its topics is that this does not properly differentiate it from other disciplines. For example, 'intergroup relations' is a focus not only of social psychologists but also of political scientists and sociologists. The family is studied not only by social psychologists but also by clinical psychologists. What makes social psychology distinct is a combination of *what* it studies, *how* it studies it and what *level of explanation* is sought.

Conformity
Norms govern the attitudes and behaviour of group members. Norms shared by these punks in Dublin include their dress, hair style, music and a love of Oscar Wilde witticisms

Methodological issues

Scientific method

Social psychology employs the scientific method to study social behaviour (Figure 1.2). Science is a *method* for studying nature, and it is the method – not the people who use it, the things they study, the facts they discover or the explanations they propose – that distinguishes science from other approaches to knowledge. In this respect, the main difference between social psychology and, say, physics, chemistry or biology is that the former studies human social behaviour, while the others study non-organic phenomena and chemical and biological processes.

Science involves the formulation of **hypotheses** (predictions) on the basis of prior knowledge, speculation and casual or systematic observation. Hypotheses are formally stated predictions about what factor or factors may cause something to occur; they are stated in such a way that they can be tested empirically to see if they are true. For example, we might hypothesise that ballet dancers perform better in front of an audience than when dancing alone. This hypothesis can be tested empirically by assessing their performance alone and in front of an audience. Strictly speaking, empirical tests can falsify hypotheses (causing the investigator to reject the hypothesis, revise it or test it in some other way) but not prove them (Popper, 1969). If a hypothesis is supported, confidence in its veracity increases and one may generate more finely tuned hypotheses. For example, if we find that ballet dancers do indeed perform better in front of an audience, we might then hypothesise that this only occurs when the dancers are already well-rehearsed; in science-speak we have hypothesised that the effect of the presence of an audience on performance is conditional on (moderated by) amount of prior rehearsal. An important feature of the scientific method is replication: it guards against the possibility that a finding is tied to the circumstances in which a test was conducted. It also guards against fraud.

The alternative to science is dogma or rationalism, where understanding is based on authority: something is true because an authority (e.g. the ancient philosophers, religious scriptures,

Hypotheses
Empirically testable predictions about what co-occurs with what, or what causes what.

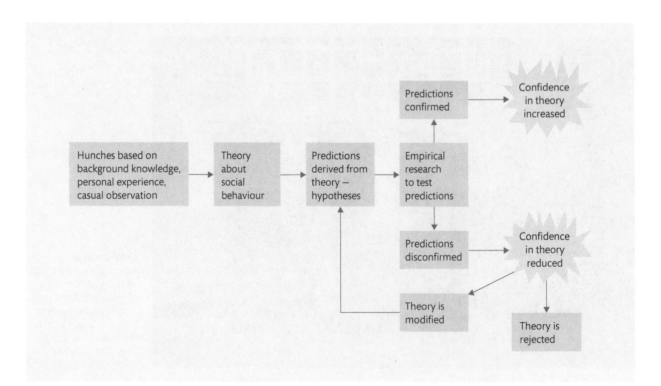

Figure 1.2 A model of the scientific method employed by social psychologists

charismatic leaders) says it is so. Valid knowledge is acquired by pure reason and grounded in faith: that is, by learning well, and uncritically accepting and trusting, the pronouncements of authorities. Even though the scientific revolution, championed by such people as Copernicus, Galileo and Newton, occurred in the sixteenth and seventeenth centuries, dogma and rationalism still exist as influential alternative paths to knowledge.

As a science, social psychology has at its disposal an array of different methods for conducting empirical tests of hypotheses. There are two broad types of method, *experimental* and *non-experimental*: each has its advantages and its limitations. The choice of an appropriate method is determined by the nature of the hypothesis under investigation, the resources available for doing the research (e.g. time, money, research participants) and the ethics of the method. Confidence in the validity of a hypothesis is enhanced if the hypothesis has been confirmed a number of times by different research teams using different methods. Methodological pluralism helps to minimise the possibility that the finding is an artefact of a particular method, and replication by different research teams helps to avoid confirmation bias – a tendency for researchers to become so personally involved in their own theories that they lose objectivity in interpreting data (Greenwald and Pratkanis, 1988; Johnson and Eagly, 1989).

Experiments

An experiment is a hypothesis test in which something is done to see its effect on something else. For example, if I hypothesise that my car greedily guzzles too much petrol because the tyres are under-inflated, then I can conduct an experiment. I can note petrol consumption over an average week, then I can increase the tyre pressure and again note petrol consumption over an average week. If consumption is reduced, then my hypothesis is supported. Casual experimentation is one of the commonest and most important ways in which people learn about their world. It is an extremely powerful method because it allows us to identify the causes of events and thus gain control over our destiny.

Not surprisingly, systematic experimentation is the most important research method in science. Experimentation involves *intervention* in the form of *manipulation* of one or more **independent variables**, and then measurement of the effect of the treatment (manipulation)

Independent variables
Features of a situation that change of their own accord, or can be manipulated by an experimenter to have effects on a dependent variable.

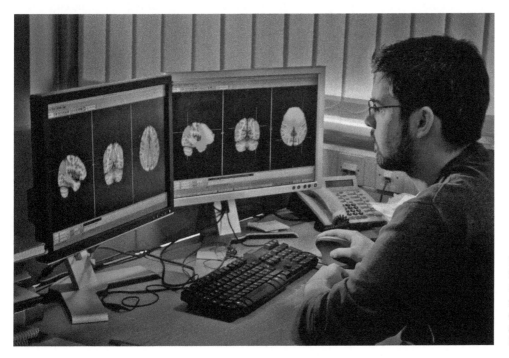

Brain imaging
Social neuroscientists are using new techniques, such as fMRI, to establish correlates, consequences and causes of social behaviour

Dependent variables
Variables that change as a consequence of changes in the independent variable.

on one or more focal **dependent variables**. In the example above, the independent variable is tyre inflation, which was manipulated to create two experimental conditions (lower versus higher pressure), and the dependent variable is petrol consumption, which was measured on refilling the tank at the end of the week. More generally, independent variables are dimensions that the researcher hypothesises will have an effect and that can be varied (e.g. tyre pressure in the present example, and the presence or absence of an audience in the ballet-dancing example). Dependent variables are dimensions that the researcher hypothesises will vary (petrol consumption or quality of the ballet dancer's performance) as a consequence of varying the independent variable. Variation in the dependent variable is *dependent* on variation in the independent variable.

Social psychology is largely experimental, in that most social psychologists would prefer to test hypotheses experimentally if at all possible, and much of what we know about social behaviour is based on experiments. Indeed, one of the most enduring and prestigious scholarly societies for the scientific study of social psychology is the *Society of Experimental Social Psychology*.

A typical social psychology experiment might be designed to test the hypothesis that violent television programmes increase aggression in young children. One way to do this would be to assign twenty children randomly to two conditions in which they individually watch either a violent or a non-violent programme, and then monitor the amount of aggression expressed immediately afterwards by the children while they are at play. Random assignment of participants (in this case, children) reduces the chance of systematic differences between the participants in the two conditions. If there were any systematic differences, say, in age, sex or parental background, then any significant effects on aggression might be due to age, sex or background rather than to the violence of the television programme. That is, age, sex or parental background would be *confounded* with the independent variable. Likewise, the television programme viewed in each condition should be identical in all respects except the degree of violence. For instance, if the violent programme also contained more action, then we would not know whether subsequent differences in aggression were due to the violence, the action, or both. The circumstances surrounding the viewing of the two programmes should also be identical. If the violent programmes were viewed in a bright red room and the non-violent programmes in a blue room, then any effects might be due to room colour, violence, or both. It is critically important in experiments to avoid **confounding**: the conditions must be identical in all respects except for those represented by the manipulated independent variable.

Confounding
Where two or more independent variables covary in such a way that it is impossible to know which has caused the effect.

We must also be careful about how we measure effects: that is, the dependent measures that assess the dependent variable. In our example it would probably be inappropriate, because of the children's age, to administer a questionnaire measuring aggression. A better technique would be unobtrusive observation of behaviour, but then what would we code as 'aggression'? The criterion would have to be sensitive to changes: in other words, loud talk or violent assault with a weapon might be insensitive, as all children talk loudly when playing (there is a *ceiling effect*), and virtually no children violently assault one another with a weapon while playing (there is a *floor effect*). In addition, it would be a mistake for whoever records or codes the behaviour to know which experimental condition the child was in: such knowledge might compromise objectivity. The coder(s) should know as little as possible about the experimental conditions and the research hypotheses.

The example used here is of a simple experiment that has only two levels of only one independent variable – called a one-factor design. Most social psychology experiments are more complicated than this. For instance, we might formulate a more textured hypothesis that aggression in young children is increased by television programmes that contain *realistic* violence. To test this hypothesis, a two-factor design would be adopted. The two factors (independent variables) would be (1) the violence of the programme (low versus high) and (2) the realism of the programme (realistic versus fantasy). The participants would be randomly assigned across four experimental conditions in which they watched (1) a non-violent fantasy programme, (2) a non-violent realistic programme, (3) a violent fantasy programme or (4) a violent realistic programme. Of course, independent variables are not restricted to two levels. For instance, we might predict that aggression is increased by moderately violent programmes, whereas extremely violent programmes are so distasteful that aggression is actually suppressed. Our independent variable of programme violence could now have three levels (low, moderate, extreme).

The laboratory experiment

The classic social psychology experiment is conducted in a laboratory in order to be able to control as many potentially confounding variables as possible. The aim is to isolate and manipulate a single aspect of a variable, an aspect that may not normally occur in isolation outside the laboratory. Laboratory experiments are *intended* to create artificial conditions. Although a social psychology laboratory may contain computers, wires and flashing lights, or even medical equipment and sophisticated brain imaging technology, often it is simply a room containing tables and chairs. For example, our ballet hypothesis could be tested in the laboratory by formalising it to one in which we predict that someone performing any well-learnt task performs the task more quickly in front of an audience. We could unobtrusively time individuals for example taking off their clothes and then putting them back on again (a well-learnt task) either alone in a room or while being scrutinised by two other people (an audience). We could compare these speeds with those of someone dressing up in unusual and difficult clothing (a poorly learnt task). This method was actually used by Markus (1978) when she investigated the effect of an audience on task performance **(see Chapter 8 for details)**.

Social psychologists have become increasingly interested in investigating the bio-chemical and brain activity correlates, consequences and causes of social behaviour. This has generated an array of experimental methods that make social psychology laboratories look more like biological or physical science laboratories. For example, a psychologist might wish to know how stress or anxiety might sometimes occur when we interact with other people, and so measures change in our level of the hormone cortisol in our saliva (e.g. Blascovich and Seery, 2007; Townsend, Major, Gangi and Mendes, 2011).Research in social neuroscience using functional magnetic resonance imaging (fMRI) has become popular. This involves participants being placed in a huge and very expensive magnetic cylinder to measure their electro-chemical brain activity (Lieberman, 2010).

Laboratory experiments allow us to establish cause–effect relationships between variables. However, laboratory experiments have a number of drawbacks. Because experimental conditions are artificial and highly controlled, particularly social neuroscience experiments, laboratory findings cannot be generalised directly to the less 'pure' conditions that exist in the 'real' world outside the laboratory. However, laboratory findings address *theories* about human social behaviour, and on the basis of laboratory experimentation we can generalise these theories to apply to conditions other than those in the laboratory. Laboratory experiments are intentionally low on external validity or mundane realism (i.e. how similar the conditions are to those usually encountered by participants in the real world) but should always be high on internal validity or experimental realism (i.e. the manipulations must be full of psychological impact and meaning for the participants) (Aronson, Ellsworth, Carlsmith and Gonzales, 1990).

Laboratory experiments can be prone to a range of biases. There are subject effects that can cause participants' behaviour to be an artefact of the experiment rather than a spontaneous and natural response to a manipulation. Artefacts can be minimised by carefully avoiding demand characteristics (Orne, 1962), *evaluation apprehension* and *social desirability* (Rosenberg, 1969). Demand characteristics are features of the experiment that seem to 'demand' a particular response: they give information about the hypothesis and thus inform helpful and compliant participants about how to react to confirm the hypothesis. Participants are thus no longer naive or *blind* regarding the experimental hypothesis. Participants in experiments are real people, and experiments are real social situations. Not surprisingly, participants may want to

Laboratory
A place, usually a room, in which data are collected, usually by experimental methods.

fMRI (functional Magnetic Resonance Imaging)
A method used in social neuroscience to measure where electrochemical activity in the brain is occurring.

External validity or Mundane realism
Similarity between circumstances surrounding an experiment and circumstances encountered in everyday life.

Internal validity or Experimental realism
Psychological impact of the manipulations in an experiment.

Subject effects
Effects that are not spontaneous, owing to demand characteristics and/ or participants wishing to please the experimenter.

Demand characteristics
Features of an experiment that seem to 'demand' a certain response.

project the best possible image of themselves to the experimenter and other participants present. This can influence spontaneous reactions to manipulations in unpredictable ways. There are also experimenter effects. The experimenter is often aware of the hypothesis and may inadvertently communicate cues that cause participants to behave in a way that confirms the hypothesis. This can be minimised by a double-blind procedure, in which the experimenter is unaware of which experimental condition they are running.

Since the 1960s, laboratory experiments have tended to rely on psychology undergraduates as participants (Sears, 1986). The reason is a pragmatic one – psychology undergraduates are readily available in large numbers. In almost all major universities there is a research participation scheme, or 'subject pool', whereby psychology students act as experimental participants in exchange for course credits or as a course requirement. Critics have often complained that this over-reliance on a particular type of participant may produce a somewhat distorted view of social behaviour – one that is not easily generalised to other sectors of the population. In their defence, experimental social psychologists point out that theories, not experimental findings, are generalised, and that replication and methodological pluralism ensures that social psychology is about people, not just about psychology students.

The field experiment

Social psychology experiments can be conducted in more naturalistic settings outside the laboratory. For example, we could test the hypothesis that prolonged eye contact is uncomfortable and causes 'flight' by having an experimenter stand at traffic lights and either gaze intensely at the driver of a car stopped at the lights or gaze nonchalantly in the opposite direction. The dependent measure would be how fast the car sped away once the lights changed (Ellsworth, Carlsmith and Henson, 1972; **see also Chapter 15**). Field experiments have high external validity and, as participants are usually completely unaware that an experiment is taking place, are not reactive (i.e. no demand characteristics are present). However, there is less control over extraneous variables, random assignment is sometimes difficult, and it can be difficult to obtain accurate measurements or measurements of subjective feelings (generally, overt behaviour is all that can be measured).

Non-experimental methods

Systematic experimentation tends to be the preferred method of science, and indeed it is often equated with science. However, there are all sorts of circumstances where it is simply impossible to conduct an experiment to test a hypothesis. For instance, theories about planetary systems and galaxies can pose a real problem: we cannot move planets around to see what happens! Likewise, social psychological theories about the relationship between biological sex and decision making are not amenable to experimentation, because we cannot manipulate biological sex experimentally and see what effects emerge. Social psychology also confronts ethical issues that can proscribe experimentation. For instance, hypotheses about the effects on self-esteem of being a victim of violent crime are not easily tested experimentally – we would not be able to assign participants randomly to two conditions and then subject one group to a violent crime and see what happened!

Where experimentation is not possible or not appropriate, social psychologists have a range of non-experimental methods from which to choose. Because these methods do not involve the manipulation of independent variables against a background of random assignment to condition, it is almost impossible to draw reliable causal conclusions. For instance, we could compare the self-esteem of people who have been victims of violent crime with those who have not. Any differences could be attributed to violent crime but could also be due to other uncontrolled differences between the two groups. We can only conclude that there is a correlation between self-esteem and being the victim of violent crime. There is no evidence that one causes the other (i.e. being a victim may lower self-esteem or having lower self-esteem may increase

Experimenter effects
Effect that is produced or influenced by clues to the hypotheses under examination, inadvertently communicated by the experimenter.

Double-blind
Procedure to reduce experimenter effects, in which the experimenter is unaware of the experimental conditions.

Correlation
Where changes in one variable reliably map on to changes in another variable, but it cannot be determined which of the two variables *caused* the change.

the likelihood of becoming a victim). Both could be *correlated* or co-occurring effects of some third variable, such as chronic unemployment, which independently lowers self-esteem *and* increases the probability that one might become a victim. In general, non-experimental methods involve the examination of correlation between naturally occurring variables and as such do not permit us to draw causal conclusions.

Archival research

Archival research is a non-experimental method that is useful for investigating large-scale, widely occurring phenomena that may be remote in time. The researcher assembles data collected by others, often for reasons unconnected with those of the researcher. For instance, Janis (1972) used an archival method to show that overly cohesive government decision-making groups may make poor decisions with disastrous consequences because they adopt poor decision-making procedures (called 'groupthink'; **see Chapter 9**). Janis constructed his theory on the basis of an examination of biographical, autobiographical and media accounts of the decision-making procedures associated with, for example, the 1961 Bay of Pigs fiasco, in which the United States futilely tried to invade Cuba. Other examples of archival research include Fogelson's (1970) archival analysis of the 1960s urban riots in the United States and Simonton's (1980) archival and secondary data analyses of battles **(see Chapter 8)**.

Archival methods are often used to make comparisons between different cultures or nations regarding things such as suicide, mental health or child-rearing strategies. Archival research is not reactive, but it can be unreliable because the researcher usually has no control over the primary data collection, which might be biased or unreliable in other ways (e.g. missing vital data). The researcher has to make do with whatever is there.

Archival research
Non-experimental method involving the assembly of data, or reports of data, collected by others.

Case studies

The case study allows an in-depth analysis of a single case (either a person or a group) or a single event. Case studies often employ an array of data collection and analysis techniques involving structured and open-ended interviews and questionnaires, and the observation of behaviour. Case studies are well suited to the examination of unusual or rare phenomena that could not be created in the laboratory: for instance, bizarre cults, mass murderers or disasters. Case studies are useful as a source of hypotheses, but findings may suffer from researcher or subject bias (the researcher is not blind to the hypothesis, there are demand characteristics and participants suffer evaluation apprehension), and findings may not easily be generalised to other cases or events.

Case study
In-depth analysis of a single case (or individual).

Qualitative research and discourse analysis

Closely related to case studies is a range of non-experimental methodologies that analyse largely naturally occurring behaviour in great detail. Among these are methods that meticulously unpack discourse, what people say to whom and in what context, in order to identify the underlying narrative that may reveal what people are thinking, what their motivations are and what the discourse is intended to do. Discourse analysis (Edwards, 1997; Potter and Wetherell, 1987; Wetherell, Taylor and Yates, 2001), draws on literary criticism and the notion that language is a performance (e.g. Hall, 2000) and is often grounded in a generally critical orientation towards mainstream social psychology (cf. Billig, 2008). Discourse analysis is both a language-based and communication-based methodology and approach to social psychology **(see Chapter 15)** that has proven particularly useful in a number of areas including the study of prejudice (e.g. Van Dijk, 1987; Verkuyten, 2010).

Discourse
Entire communicative event or episode located in a situational and sociohistorical context.

Discourse analysis
A set of methods used to analyse text – in particular, naturally occurring language – in order to understand its meaning and significance.

Survey research

Another non-experimental method is data collection by *survey*. Surveys can involve structured interviews, in which the researcher asks participants a number of carefully chosen questions and notes the responses, or a questionnaire, in which participants write their own responses to written questions. In either case the questions can be open-ended (i.e. respondents can give as much or as little detail in their answers as they wish) or closed-ended (where there is a limited number of predetermined responses, such as circling a number on a nine-point scale). For instance, to investigate immigrant workers' experiences of prejudice one could ask respondents a set of predetermined questions and summarise the gist of their responses or assign a numerical value to their responses. Alternatively, respondents could record their own responses by writing a paragraph, or by circling numbers on scales in a questionnaire.

Surveys can be used to obtain a large amount of data from a large sample of participants; hence generalisation is often not a problem. However, it is a method that, like case studies and qualitative methods, is subject to experimenter bias, subject bias and evaluation apprehension. Anonymous and confidential questionnaires may minimise experimenter bias, evaluation apprehension and some subject biases, but demand characteristics may remain. In addition, poorly constructed questionnaires may obtain biased data due to 'response set' – that is, the tendency for some respondents to agree unthinkingly with statements, or to choose mid-range or extreme responses.

Field studies

The final non-experimental method is the field study. We have already described the field experiment: the field study is essentially the same but without any interventions or manipulations. Field studies involve the observation, recording and coding of behaviour as it occurs. Most often, the observer is non-intrusive by not participating in the behaviour, and 'invisible' by not having an effect on the ongoing behaviour. For instance, one could research the behaviour of students in the student cafeteria by concealing oneself in a corner and observing what goes on. Sometimes 'invisibility' is impossible, so the opposite strategy can be used – the researcher becomes a full participant in the behaviour. For instance, it would be rather difficult to be an invisible observer of gang behaviour. Instead, you could study the behaviour of a street gang by becoming a full member of the gang and surreptitiously taking notes (e.g. Whyte, 1943; **see also Chapter 8**). Field studies are excellent for investigating spontaneously occurring behaviour in its natural context but are particularly prone to experimenter bias, lack of objectivity, poor generalisability and distortions due to the impact of the researcher on the behaviour under investigation. Also, if you join a gang there is an element of personal danger!

Data and analysis

Social psychologists love data, and are prepared to collect it in a variety of different ways. Recently, the internet has provided a wonderful new opportunity for data collection that is becoming increasingly popular because it is an inexpensive, fast and efficient way to collect data from a large and diverse population. One particularly popular web-based resource is Amazon's mechanical turk (MTurk), which if used carefully allows a range of methods that can generate high-quality data (Buhrmeister, Kwang and Gosling, 2011; Mason and Suri, 2012; Paolacci, Chandler and Ipeirotis, 2010).

Research provides data, which are analysed to draw conclusions about whether hypotheses are supported. The type of analysis undertaken depends on at least:

- *The type of data obtained* – for example, binary responses such as 'yes' versus 'no', continuous variables such as temperature or response latency, defined positions on nine-point scales, rank ordering of choices and open-ended written responses (text).
- *The method used to obtain data* – for example, controlled experiment, open-ended interview, participant observation, archival search.
- *The purposes of the research* – for example, to describe in depth a specific case, to establish differences between two groups of participants exposed to different treatments, to investigate the correlation between two or more naturally occurring variables.

Statistics
Social psychological data are often quantitative, requiring statistical analysis to find patterns that give meaning to the numbers

Overwhelmingly, social psychological knowledge is based on statistical analysis of quantitative data. Data are obtained as, or are transformed into, numbers (i.e. quantities), and these numbers are then compared in various formalised ways (i.e. by statistics). For example, to decide whether women are more friendly interviewees than are men, we could compare transcripts of interviews of both men and women. We could then code the transcripts to count how often participants made positive remarks to the interviewer, and compare the mean count for, say, twenty women with the mean for twenty men. In this case, we would be interested in knowing whether the difference between men and women was 'on the whole' greater than the difference among men and among women. To do this, we could use a simple statistic called the *t* test, which computes a number called the *t* statistic that is based on both the difference between the women's and men's mean friendliness scores and the degree of variability of scores within each sex. The larger the value of *t,* the larger the between-sex difference relative to within-sex differences.

The decision about whether the difference between groups is psychologically significant depends on its statistical significance. Social psychologists adhere to the arbitrary convention that if the obtained value of *t* has less than a 1 in 20 (i.e. 0.05) probability of occurring simply by chance (that is, if we randomly selected 100 groups of ten males and ten females, only five times or fewer would we obtain a value of *t* as great as or greater than that obtained in the study), then the obtained difference is statistically significant and there really is a difference in friendliness between male and female interviewees (see Figure 1.3).

The *t* test is very simple. However, the principle underlying the *t* test is the same as that underlying more sophisticated and complex statistical techniques used by social psychologists to test whether two or more groups differ significantly. The other major method of data analysis used by social psychologists is correlation, which assesses whether the co-occurrence of two or more variables is significant. Again, although the example below is simple, the underlying principle is the same for an array of correlational techniques.

To investigate the idea that rigid thinkers tend to hold more politically conservative attitudes (Rokeach, 1960; **see also Chapter 10**), we could have thirty participants answer a questionnaire measuring cognitive rigidity (dogmatism: a rigid and inflexible set of attitudes) and political conservatism (e.g. endorsement and espousal of right-wing political and social

Statistics
Formalised numerical procedures performed on data to investigate the magnitude and/or significance of effects.

***t* test**
Statistical procedure to test the statistical significance of an effect in which the mean for one condition is greater than the mean for another.

Statistical significance
An effect is statistically significant if statistics reveal that it, or a larger effect, is unlikely to occur by chance more often than 1 in 20 times.

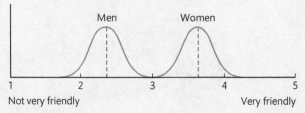

CASE 1. *A significant difference*: The *t* statistic is relatively large because the difference between means is large and the variation within sex groups is small.

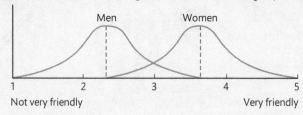

CASE 2. *Not a significant difference*: The *t* statistic is relatively small because, although the difference between means is still large, the variation within sex groups is much larger.

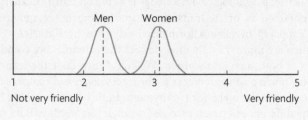

CASE 3. *A significant difference*: The *t* statistic is large because, although the difference between means is smaller, the variation within sex groups is small.

Figure 1.3
Distribution of friendliness scores for twenty male and twenty female interviewees: using the *t* statistic

policies). If we rank the thirty participants in order of increasing dogmatism and find that conservatism also increases, with the least dogmatic person being the least conservative and the most dogmatic the most conservative, then we can say that the two variables are positively correlated (see Figure 1.4, in which dots represent individual persons, positioned with respect to their scores on both dogmatism and conservatism scales). If we find that conservatism systematically decreases with increasing dogmatism, then we say that the two variables are negatively correlated. If there seems to be no systematic relationship between the two variables, then they are uncorrelated – there is zero correlation. A statistic can be calculated to represent correlation numerically: for instance, the statistical measure known as Pearson's *r* varies from −1 for a perfect negative to +1 for a perfect positive correlation. Depending on, among other things, the number of persons, we can also know whether the correlation is statistically significant at the conventional 5 per cent level.

Although statistical analysis of quantitative data is the bread and butter of social psychology, some social psychologists find that this method is unsuited to their purposes and prefer a more *qualitative* analysis. For example, analysis of people's explanations for unemployment or prejudice may sometimes benefit from a more discursive, non-quantitative analysis in which the researcher tries to unravel what is said in order to go beyond surface explanations and get to the heart of the underlying beliefs and reasons. One form of qualitative analysis is *discourse analysis* (e.g. Potter and Wetherell, 1987; Tuffin, 2005; Wetherell, Taylor and Yates,

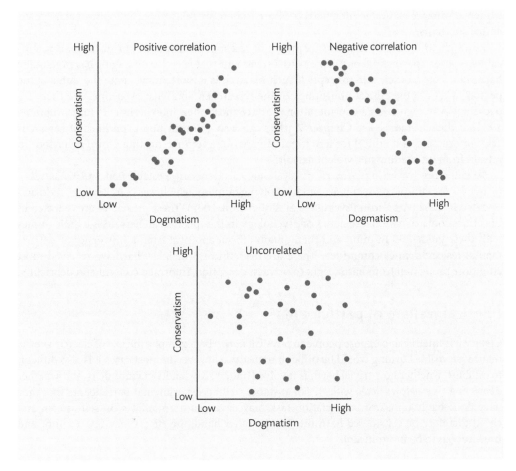

Figure 1.4 Correlation between dogmatism and conservatism for thirty respondents: using Pearson's correlation coefficient

2001). Discourse analysis treats all 'data' as 'text' – that is, as a communicative event that is replete with multiple layers of meaning but that can be interpreted only by considering the text in its wider social context. For example, discourse analysts believe that we should not take people's responses to attitude statements in questionnaires at face value and subject them to statistical analysis. They believe, instead, that we should interpret what is being communicated. This is made possible only by considering the response as a complex conjunction of social-communicative factors embedded in both the immediate and wider sociohistorical context. However, discourse analysis is more than a research method: it is also a systematic critique of 'conventional' social psychological methods and theories (see below).

Research ethics

As researchers, social psychologists confront important ethical issues. Clearly, it is unethical to fake data or to report results in a biased or partial manner that significantly distorts what was done, what was found, and how the hypotheses and theory under examination now fare. As in life, scientists do sometimes cheat, and this not only impedes scientific progress and damages the reputation of the discipline, but has dreadful career and life consequences for those involved. However, cheating is very rare and equally rare across both the psychological and biomedical sciences (Stroebe, Postmes and Spears, 2012). In the case of social psychology, the largely team-based nature of research helps prevent academics and their postgraduate students, who are all under enormous pressure to publish, take, to put it euphemistically, scientific shortcuts.

Research ethics is also all about treatment of research participants. For instance, is it ethical to expose experimental participants to a treatment that is embarrassing or has potentially harmful effects on their self-concept? If such research is important, what are the rights of the person, what are the ethical obligations of the researcher, and what guidelines are there for deciding? Although ethical considerations surface most often in experiments (e.g. Milgram's 1974 obedience studies; **see Chapter 7**) they can also confront non-experimental researchers. For example, is it ethical for a non-participant observer investigating crowd behaviour to refrain from interceding in a violent assault?

To guide researchers, the American Psychological Association established, in 1972, a set of principles for ethical conduct in research involving humans, which was completely revised and updated in 2002 (American Psychological Association, 2002). These principles are reflected in the ethics codes of national societies of psychology in Europe. Researchers design their studies with these guidelines in mind and then obtain official approval from a university or departmental research ethics committee. There are five ethical principles that have received most attention: protection from harm, right to privacy, deception, informed consent and debriefing.

Physical welfare of participants

Clearly it is unethical to expose people to physical *harm*. For example, the use of electric shocks that cause visible burning would be difficult to justify. However, in most cases it is also difficult to establish whether non-trivial harm is involved and, if so, what its magnitude is, and whether debriefing (see below) deals with it. For instance, telling experimental participants that they have done badly on a word-association task may have long-term effects on self-esteem and could therefore be considered harmful. On the other hand, the effects may be so minor and transitory as to be insignificant.

Respect for privacy

Social psychological research often involves invasion of *privacy*. Participants can be asked intimate questions, can be observed without their knowledge and can have their moods, perceptions and behaviour manipulated. It is sometimes difficult to decide whether the research topic justifies invasion of privacy. At other times it is more straightforward – for example, intimate questions about sexual practices are essential for research into behaviour that may put people at risk of contracting HIV and developing AIDS. Concern about privacy is usually satisfied by ensuring that data obtained from individuals are entirely *confidential*: that is, only the researcher knows who said or did what. Personal identification is removed from data (rendering them *anonymous*), research findings are reported as means for large groups of people, and data no longer useful are usually destroyed.

Use of deception

Laboratory experiments, as we have seen, involve the manipulation of people's cognition, feelings or behaviour in order to investigate the spontaneous, natural and non-reactive effect of independent variables. Because participants need to be naive regarding hypotheses, experimenters commonly conceal the true purpose of the experiment. A degree of *deception* is often necessary. Between 50 and 75 per cent of published experiments involve some degree of deception (Adair, Dushenko and Lindsay, 1985; Gross and Fleming, 1982). Because the use of deception seems to imply 'trickery', 'deceit' and 'lying', it has attracted a frenzy of criticism – for example, Baumrind's (1964) attack on Milgram's (1963, 1974) obedience studies **(see Chapter 7)**. Social psychologists have been challenged to abandon controlled experimental research in favour of role playing or simulations (e.g. Kelman, 1967) if they cannot do experiments without deception.

This is probably too extreme a request, as social psychological knowledge has been enriched enormously by classic experiments that have used deception (many such experiments are described in this book). Although some experiments have used an amount of deception that seems excessive, in practice the deception used in the overwhelming majority of social psychology experiments is trivial. For example, an experiment may be introduced as a study of group decision making when in fact it is part of a programme of research into prejudice and stereotyping. In addition, there has been no evidence of any long-term negative consequences of the use of deception in social psychology experiments (Elms, 1982), and experimental participants themselves tend to be impressed, rather than upset or angered, by cleverly executed deceptions, and they view deception as a necessary withholding of information or a necessary ruse (Christensen, 1988; Sharpe, Adair and Roese, 1992; Smith, 1983). How would you address the first focus question at the beginning of this chapter?

Informed consent

A way to safeguard participants' rights in experiments is to obtain their *informed consent* to participate. In principle, people should give their consent freely (preferably in writing) to participate on the basis of full information about what they are consenting to take part in, and they must be entirely free to withdraw without penalty from the research whenever they wish. Researchers cannot lie or withhold information in order to induce people to participate; nor can they make it 'difficult' to say 'no' or to withdraw (i.e. via social pressure or by exercise of personal or institutionalised power). In practice, however, terms such as 'full information' are difficult to define, and, as we have just seen, experiments often require some deception in order that participants remain naive.

Debriefing

Participants should be fully *debriefed* after taking part in an experiment. Debriefing is designed to make sure that people leave the laboratory with an increased respect for and understanding of social psychology. More specifically, debriefing involves a detailed explanation of the experiment and its broader theoretical and applied context. Any deceptions are explained and justified to the satisfaction of all participants, and care is taken to make sure that the effects of manipulations have been undone. However, strong critics of deception (e.g. Baumrind, 1985) believe that no amount of debriefing puts right what they consider to be the fundamental wrong of deception that undermines basic human trust.

Social psychologists often conduct and report research into socially sensitive phenomena, or research that has implications for socially sensitive issues: for example, stereotyping, prejudice and discrimination **(see Chapters 10, 11 and 15)**. In these cases the researcher has to be especially careful that both the conducting and reporting of research are done in such a way that they are not biased by personal prejudices and are not open to public misinterpretation, distortion or misuse. For example, early research into sex differences in conformity found that women conformed more than men. This finding is, of course, fuel to the view that women are more dependent than men. Later research discovered that men and women conform equally, and that whether one conforms or not depends largely on how much familiarity and confidence one has with the conformity task. Early research used tasks that were more familiar to men than to women, and many researchers looked no further because the findings confirmed their assumptions **(Chapters 7 and 10)**.

Theoretical issues

Social psychologists construct and test theories of human social behaviour. A social psychological theory is an integrated set of propositions that explains the causes of social behaviour, generally in terms of one or more social psychological processes. Theories rest on explicit assumptions about social behaviour and contain a number of defined concepts and formal statements about the relationship between concepts. Ideally, these relationships are causal ones that are attributed to the operation of social and/or psychological processes. Theories are framed in such a way that they generate hypotheses that can be tested empirically. Social psychological theories vary greatly in terms of their rigour, testability and generality. Some theories are short-range mini-theories tied to specific phenomena, whereas others are broader general theories that explain whole classes of behaviour. Some even approach the status of 'grand theory' (such as evolutionary theory, Marxism, general relativity theory and psychodynamic theory) in that they furnish a general perspective on social psychology.

Social identity theory (e.g. Tajfel and Turner, 1979; **see Chapters 4 and 11**) is a good example of a relatively general mid-range social psychological theory. It is an analysis of the behaviour of people in groups and how this relates to their self-conception as group members. The theory integrates a number of compatible (sub)theories that deal with and emphasise (see Abrams and Hogg, 2010; Hogg, 2006):

- intergroup relations and social change;
- motivational processes associated with group membership and group behaviour;
- social influence and conformity processes within groups;
- cognitive processes associated with self-conception and social perception.

These, and other associated processes, operate together to produce group behaviour, as distinct from interpersonal behaviour. This theory generates testable predictions about a range of group phenomena, including stereotyping, intergroup discrimination, social influence in groups, group cohesiveness, social change and even language and ethnicity.

Social identity
Hoodies belong to groups too. They dress to emphasise group membership and social identity

Theories in social psychology

Theories in social psychology can generally be clustered into types of theory (Van Lange, Kruglanski and Higgins, 2013), with different types of theory reflecting different *metatheories*. Just as a theory is a set of interrelated concepts and principles that explain a phenomenon, a metatheory is a set of interrelated concepts and principles about which theories or types of theory are appropriate. Some theories can be extended by their adherents to account for almost the whole of human behaviour – the 'grand theories' mentioned above. In this section, we discuss several major types of theory that have had an impact on social psychology.

Metatheory
Set of interrelated concepts and principles concerning which theories or types of theory are appropriate.

Behaviourism

Behaviourist or learning perspectives derive originally from Ivan Pavlov's early work on conditioned reflexes and B. F. Skinner's work on operant conditioning. Radical behaviourists believe that behaviour can be explained and predicted in terms of reinforcement schedules – behaviour associated with positive outcomes or circumstances grows in strength and frequency. However, more popular with social psychologists is neo-behaviourism, which maintains that one needs to invoke unobservable intervening constructs (e.g. beliefs, feelings, motives) to make sense of behaviour.

Radical behaviourist
One who explains observable behaviour in terms of reinforcement schedules, without recourse to any intervening unobservable (e.g. cognitive) constructs.

Neo-behaviourism
One who attempts to explain observable behaviour in terms of contextual factors and unobservable intervening constructs such as beliefs, feelings and motives.

The behaviourist perspective in social psychology produces theories that emphasise the role of situational factors and reinforcement/learning in social behaviour. One example is the *reinforcement–affect model of interpersonal attraction* (e.g. Lott, 1961; **Chapter 14**): people grow to like those people with whom they associate positive experiences (e.g. we like people who praise us). Another more general example is *social exchange theory* (e.g. Kelley and Thibaut, 1978; **Chapter 14**): the course of social interactions depends on subjective evaluation of the rewards and costs involved. *Social modelling* is another broadly behaviourist perspective: we imitate behaviour that is reinforced in others, and thus our behaviour is shaped by vicarious learning (e.g. Bandura, 1977; **Chapter 12**). Finally, *drive theory* (Zajonc, 1965; **Chapter 8**) explains improvement and deterioration of task performance in front of an audience in terms of the strength of a learnt response.

Cognitive psychology

Critics have argued that behaviourist theories exaggerate the extent to which people are passive recipients of external influences. Cognitive theories redress the balance by focusing on how people actively interpret and change their environment through the agency of cognitive processes and cognitive representations. Cognitive theories have their origins in Kurt Koffka and Wolfgang Köhler's *Gestalt* psychology of the 1930s, and in many ways social psychology has always been very cognitive in its perspective (Landman and Manis, 1983; Markus and Zajonc, 1985). One of social psychology's earliest cognitive theories was Kurt Lewin's (1951) field theory, which dealt, in a somewhat complicated manner, with the way in which people's cognitive representations of features of the social environment produce motivational forces to behave in specific ways. Lewin is generally considered the father of experimental social psychology.

Cognitive theories
Explanations of behaviour in terms of the way people actively interpret and represent their experiences and then plan action.

In the 1950s and 1960s, cognitive consistency theories dominated social psychology (Abelson et al., 1968). These theories assumed that cognitions about ourselves, our behaviour and the world, which were contradictory or incompatible in other ways, produced an uncomfortable state of cognitive arousal that motivated people to resolve the cognitive conflict. This perspective has been used to explain attitude change (e.g. Aronson, 1984; **Chapter 6**). In the 1970s, attribution theories dominated social psychology. Attribution theories focus on the way in which people explain the causes of their own and other people's behaviour, and on the consequences of causal explanations (e.g. Hewstone, 1989; **Chapter 3**). Finally, since the late 1970s, social cognition has been the dominant perspective in social psychology. This is a perspective that subsumes a number of theories dealing with the way in which cognitive processes (e.g. categorisation) and cognitive representations (e.g. schemas) are constructed and influence behaviour (e.g. Fiske and Taylor, 2008; **Chapter 2**).

Neuroscience and biochemistry

Social neuroscience
Exploration of brain activity associated with social cognition and social psychological processes and phenomena.

A recent development or offshoot of social cognition is a focus in social psychology on neurological and biochemical correlates of social behaviour. Called social neuroscience, or social cognitive neuroscience, this approach is predicated on the view that because psychology happens in the brain, cognition must be associated with electro-chemical brain activity (e.g. Harmon-Jones and Winkielman, 2007; Lieberman, 2010; Ochsner, 2007; Ochsner and Lieberman, 2001; **see Chapter 2**). Social neuroscience uses brain imaging methodologies, for example fMRI (functional Magnetic Resonance Imaging), to detect and locate brain activity associated with social thinking and social behaviour. This general idea that we are biological entities and that therefore social behaviour has neuro- and bio-chemical correlates surfaces in other theorising that focuses more on biochemical markers of social behaviour – for example, measures of the hormone cortisol in people's blood or saliva as a marker of stress (see Blascovich and Seery, 2007).

Evolutionary social psychology

Evolutionary social psychology
An extension of evolutionary psychology that views complex social behaviour as adaptive, helping the individual, kin and the species as a whole to survive.

Evolutionary psychology
A theoretical approach that explains 'useful' psychological traits, such as memory, perception or language, as adaptations through natural selection.

Another theoretical development is evolutionary social psychology (Caporael, 2007; Kenrick, Maner and Li, 2005; Neuberg, Kenrick and Schaller, 2010; Schaller, Simpson and Kenrick, 2006; Simpson and Kenrick, 1997). Drawing on nineteenth-century Darwinian theory, modern evolutionary psychology and sociobiology (e.g. Wilson, 1975, 1978), evolutionary social psychologists argue that much of human behaviour is grounded in the ancestral past of our species. Buss and Reeve (2003, p. 849) suggest that evolutionary processes have shaped 'cooperation and conflict within families, the emergence of cooperative alliances, human aggression, acts of altruism . . .' These behaviours had survival value for the species and so, over time, became a part of our genetic make-up.

A biological perspective can be pushed to extremes and used as a sovereign explanation for most, even all, behaviour. However, when the human genome had finally been charted in 2003, researchers felt that the 20,000–25,000 genes and 3 billion chemical base pairs making up human DNA were insufficient to account for the massive diversity of human behaviour – context and environment play a significant role (e.g. Lander et al., 2001). This is of course where social psychology steps in. Nevertheless, evolutionary social psychology has relevance for several topics covered in this book – for example, leadership (**Chapter 9**), aggression (**Chapter 12**), prosocial behaviour (**Chapter 13**), interpersonal attraction (**Chapter 14**), and non-verbal and human spatial behaviour (**Chapter 15**).

Personality

Social psychologists have often tried to explain social behaviour in terms of enduring (sometimes innate) personality attributes. For instance, good leaders have charismatic personalities (**Chapter 9**), people with prejudiced personalities express prejudice (**Chapter 10**), and people who conform too much have conformist personalities (**Chapter 7**). In general, social psychologists now consider personality to be at best a partial explanation, at worst an inadequate re-description, of social phenomena. There are at least two reasons for this:

1 There is actually very little evidence for stable personality traits. People behave in different ways at different times and in different contexts – they are influenced by situation and context.

2 If personality is defined as behavioural consistency across contexts, then rather than being an explanation of behaviour, personality is something to be explained. Why do some people resist social and contextual influences on behaviour? What is it about their interpretation of the context that causes them to behave in this way?

Overall most contemporary treatments of personality see personality as interacting with many other factors to impact behaviour (e.g. Funder and Fast, 2010; Snyder and Cantor, 1998).

Collectivist theories

Personality theories can be contrasted with collectivist theories. Collectivist theories focus on the way in which people are socially constituted by their location in the matrix of social categories and groups that make up society. People behave as they do, not because of personality or individual predispositions, but because they internally represent socially constructed group norms that influence behaviour in specific contexts. An early collectivist viewpoint was William McDougall's (1920) theory of the 'group mind' (**Chapter 11**). In groups, people change the way they think, process information and act, so that group behaviour is quite different from interpersonal behaviour – a group mind emerges.

More recently, this idea has been significantly elaborated and developed by European social psychologists seeking a perspective on social behaviour that emphasises the part played by the wider social context of intergroup relations in shaping behaviour (e.g. Tajfel, 1984). Of these, social identity theory is perhaps the most developed (Tajfel and Turner, 1979; **Chapter 11**). Its explanation of the behaviour of people in groups is strongly influenced by an analysis of the social relations between groups. Collectivist theories adopt a 'top-down' approach, in which individual social behaviour can be properly explained only with reference to groups, intergroup relations and social forces. Individualistic theories, in contrast, are 'bottom-up': individual social behaviour is constructed from individual cognition or personality.

It is important to recognise that many social psychological theories contain elements of two or more different perspectives, and also that these and other perspectives often merely lend emphasis to different theories. Metatheory does not usually intentionally reveal itself with prodigious fanfare (but see Abrams and Hogg, 2004).

Social psychology in crisis

Social psychology occurs against a background of, often latent, metatheoretical differences. In many respects this is an intellectually engaging feature of the discipline. From time to time these differences come to the fore and become the focus of intense public debate. The most recent occurrence was in the late 1960s and early 1970s, when social psychology appeared to many to have reached a crisis of confidence (e.g. Elms, 1975; Israel and Tajfel, 1972; Rosnow, 1981; Strickland, Aboud and Gergen, 1976). There were two principal worries about social psychology:

1 It was overly *reductionist* (i.e. by explaining social behaviour mainly in terms of individual psychology it failed to address the essentially social nature of the human experience).

2 It was overly *positivistic* (i.e. it adhered to a model of science that was distorted, inappropriate and misleading).

Reductionism and levels of explanation

Reductionism is the practice of explaining a phenomenon with the language and concepts of a lower level of analysis. Society is explained in terms of groups, groups in terms of interpersonal processes, interpersonal processes in terms of intrapersonal cognitive mechanisms, cognition in terms of neuropsychology, neuropsychology in terms of biology, and so on. A problem of reductionist theorising is that it can leave the original scientific question unanswered. For example, the act of putting one's arm out of the car window to indicate an intention to turn can be explained in terms of muscle contraction, or nerve impulses, or understanding of and adherence to social conventions, and so on. If the level of explanation does not match the level of the question, then the question remains effectively unanswered. In researching interpersonal relations, to what extent does an explanation in terms of social neuroscience really explain interpersonal relations?

Reductionism
Explanation of a phenomenon in terms of the language and concepts of a lower level of analysis, usually with a loss of explanatory power.

Level of analysis (or explanation)
The types of concepts, mechanisms and language used to explain a phenomenon.

Although a degree of reductionism is possibly necessary for theorising, too great a degree is undesirable. Social psychology has been criticised for being inherently reductionist because it tries to explain social behaviour in terms of asocial intrapsychic cognitive and motivational processes (e.g. Moscovici, 1972; Pepitone, 1981; Sampson, 1977; Taylor and Brown, 1979). The recent trends towards social cognitive neuroscience and evolutionary social psychology, explaining behaviour in terms of neural activity and genetic predisposition, can be criticised on the same grounds (cf. Dovidio, Pearson and Orr, 2008). Reflect now on the second focus question.

The problem is most acute when social psychologists try to explain group processes and intergroup relations. By tackling these phenomena exclusively in terms of personality, interpersonal relations or intrapsychic processes, social psychology may leave some of its most important phenomena inadequately explained – for example, prejudice, discrimination, stereotyping, conformity and group solidarity (Billig, 1976; Hogg and Abrams, 1988; Turner and Oakes, 1986). Or worse – reductionist explanations of societally constructed perceptions and behaviours can have undesirable sociopolitical consequences. Fine has levelled this charge at social neuroscience; arguing that some fMRI research reinforces gender stereotypes (Fine, 2010).

Willem Doise (1986; Lorenzi-Cioldi and Doise, 1990) has suggested that one way around this problem is to accept the existence of different levels of explanation but to make a special effort to construct theories that formally integrate (Doise uses the French term 'articulate') concepts from different levels (see Box 1.1). This idea has been adopted, to varying degrees, by many social psychologists (see Tajfel, 1984). One of the most successful attempts is social identity theory (e.g. Tajfel and Turner, 1979; **see Chapter 11**), which formally articulates individual cognitive processes with large-scale social forces to explain group behaviour. Doise's ideas have also been employed to reinterpret group cohesiveness (Hogg, 1992, 1993), attribution theories (Hewstone, 1989) and social representations (e.g. Doise, Clémence and Lorenzi-Cioldi, 1993; Lorenzi-Cioldi and Clémence, 2001). Organisational psychologists have also advocated articulation of levels of analysis – they use the term cross-level research, but the debate is less developed than in social psychology and little research has been done (Wilpert, 1995; but see Haslam, 2004).

Positivism

Positivism
Non-critical acceptance of science as the only way to arrive at true knowledge: science as religion.

Positivism is the non-critical acceptance of scientific method as the only way to arrive at true knowledge. Positivism was introduced in the early nineteenth century by the French mathematician and philosopher Auguste Comte and was enormously popular until the end of that century. The character Mr Gradgrind in Charles Dickens's 1854 novel *Hard Times* epitomises positivism: science as a religion.

Social psychology has been criticised for being positivistic (e.g. Gergen, 1973; Henriques et al., 1984; Potter, Stringer and Wetherell, 1984; Shotter, 1984). It is argued that because social psychologists are ultimately studying themselves they cannot achieve the level of objectivity of, say, a chemist studying a compound or a geographer studying a landform. Since complete objectivity is unattainable, scientific methods, particularly experimental ones, are simply not appropriate for social psychology. Social psychology can only masquerade as a science – it cannot be a true science. Critics argue that what social psychologists propose as fundamental causal mechanisms (e.g. categorisation, attribution, cognitive balance, self-concept) are only 'best-guess' concepts that explain some historically and culturally restricted data – data that are subject to unavoidable and intrinsic bias. Critics also feel that by treating humans as objects or clusters of variables that can be manipulated experimentally we are not only cutting ourselves off from a rich reservoir of subjective or introspective data, we are also dehumanising people.

These criticisms have produced some quite radical alternatives to traditional social psychology. Examples include social constructionism (Gergen, 1973), humanistic psychology (Shotter, 1984), ethogenics (Harré, 1979), discourse analysis or discursive psychology (Edwards, 1997; Potter and Wetherell, 1987) critical psychology (Billig, 2008), and poststructuralist perspectives (Henriques et al., 1984). There are marked differences between some of these alternatives, but they share a broad emphasis on understanding people as whole human beings who are constructed historically and who try to make sense of themselves and their world. Research methods tend to emphasise in-depth subjective analysis (often called *deconstruction*) of the relatively spontaneous accounts that people give of their thoughts, feelings and actions. Subjectivity is considered a virtue of, rather than an impediment to, good research. More recently, some authors who have noted that discursive psychology is fundamentally incommensurate with 'mainstream' social psychology have taken a position of relative tolerance (e.g. Tuffin, 2005), and have sought avenues of cooperative research (e.g. Rogers, 2003).

However, most mainstream social psychologists respond to the problem of positivism in a less dramatic manner, which does not involve abandoning the scientific method. Instead, they deal with the pitfalls of positivism by being rigorous in the use of appropriate scientific methods of research and theorising (e.g. Campbell, 1957; Jost and Kruglanski, 2002; Kruglanski, 1975; Turner, 1981a). Included in this is an awareness of the need for operational definitions of social processes such as aggression, altruism and leadership. Operationalism is a product of positivism and refers to a plea that theoretical terms in science be defined in a manner that renders them susceptible to measurement. As scientists, we should be mindful of our own subjectivity, and should acknowledge and make explicit our biases. Our theories should be sensitive to the pitfalls of reductionism and, where appropriate, articulate different levels of analysis. We should also recognise that experimental participants are real people who do not throw off their past history and become unidimensional 'variables' when they enter the laboratory. On the contrary, culture, history, socialisation and personal motives are all present in the laboratory – experiments are social situations (Tajfel, 1972). Finally, attention should be paid to language, as that is perhaps the most important way in which people represent the world, think, plan action and manipulate the world around them **(Chapter 15)**. Language is also the epitome of a social variable: it is socially constructed and internalised to govern individual social cognition and behaviour.

Operational definition
Defines a theoretical term in a way that allows it to be manipulated or measured.

Theory 1.1
Levels of explanation in social psychology

I Intrapersonal

Analysis of psychological processes to do with individuals' organisation of their experience of the social environment (e.g. research on cognitive balance).

II Interpersonal and situational

Analysis of interindividual interaction within circumscribed situations. Social positional factors emanating from outside the situation are not considered. The object of study is the dynamics of relations established at a given moment by given individuals in a given situation (e.g. some attribution research, research using game matrices).

III Positional

Analysis of interindividual interaction in specific situations, but with the role of social position (e.g. status, identity) outside the situation taken into consideration (e.g. some research into power and social identity).

IV Ideological

Analysis of interindividual interaction that considers the role of general social beliefs, and of social relations between groups (e.g. some research into social identity, social representations and minority influence; studies considering the role of cultural norms and values).

Source: taken from material in Hogg (1992, p. 62) and based on Lorenzi-Cioldi and Doise (1990, p. 73) and Doise (1986, pp. 10–16).

Historical context

Social psychology, as we have described it, is not a static science. It has a history, and it is invaluable to consider a science in its proper historical context in order to understand its true nature. Here we give an overview of the history of social psychology. Although ancient forms of social and political philosophy considered such questions as the nature–nurture controversy, the origins of society and the function of the state, it was mostly a speculative exercise and devoid of fact gathering (Hollander, 1967). An empirical approach to the study of social life did not appear until the latter part of the nineteenth century.

Social psychology in the nineteenth century

Anglo-European influences

An important precursor to the development of social psychology as an independent discipline was the work of a number of scholars in Germany known as the *folk psychologists*. In 1860, a journal devoted to *Völkerpsychologie* was founded by Steinthal and Lazarus. It contained both theoretical and factual articles. In contrast to general psychology (elaborated later by Wundt) which dealt with the study of the individual mind, folk psychology, which was influenced by the philosopher Hegel, dealt with the study of the *collective* mind. This concept of collective mind was interpreted in conflicting ways by Steinthal and Lazarus, meaning on the one hand a societal way of thinking within the individual and on the other a form of super-mentality that could enfold a whole group of people.

Völkerpsychologie
Early precursor of social psychology, as the study of the collective mind, in Germany in the mid- to late nineteenth century.

This concept, of a *group mind*, became, in the 1890s and early 1900s, a dominant account of social behaviour. An extreme example of it can be found in the work of the French writer Gustav LeBon (1896/1908). LeBon argued that crowds often behave badly because the behaviour of the individual becomes subject to the control of the *group mind*. Likewise, the English psychologist William McDougall (1920) subscribed to the group mind explanation when he dealt with collective behaviour, devoting an entire book to the topic. Much later, Solomon Asch (1951) observed that the basic issue that such writers wanted to deal with has not gone away: that to understand the complexities of an individual's behaviour requires us to view the person in the context of group relations.

Early texts

At the turn of the century there were two texts dealing with social psychology, by Bunge (1903) and Orano (1901). Because they were not in English, they received little attention in Britain and the United States. Even earlier, an American, Baldwin (1897), touched on social psychology in a work that dealt mainly with the social and moral development of the child. A book by the French sociologist Gabriel Tarde (1898) had clear implications for the kind of data and the level of explanation that social psychology should adopt. He adopted a bottom-up approach, which was offered in debate with Emile Durkheim. Whereas Durkheim argued that the way people behave is determined by social laws that are fashioned by society, Tarde proposed that a science of social behaviour must derive from laws that deal with the individual case. His conception of social psychology is closer in flavour to most current thinking than any of the other early texts (Clark, 1969).

The two early texts that caught the attention of the English-speaking world were written by McDougall (1908) and the American sociologist E. A. Ross (1908). Neither looks much like a modern social psychology text, but we need to remember that living scientific disciplines continue to be redefined. The central topics of McDougall's book, for example, were the principal instincts, the primary emotions, the nature of sentiments, moral conduct, volition, religious conceptions and the structure of character. Compare these with the chapter topics of the present textbook.

The rise of experimentation

An influential textbook by Floyd Allport (1924) provided an agenda for social psychology that was quickly and enduringly followed by many teachers in psychology departments for years to come. Following the manifesto for psychology as a whole laid out by the behaviourist John Watson (1913), Allport argued strongly that social psychology would flourish only if it became an experimental science. A little later, Gardner Murphy and Lois Murphy (1931/1937) felt justified in producing a book proudly entitled *Experimental social psychology*. Not all of the studies reviewed were true experiments, but the authors' intentions for the discipline were clear.

Although the earlier texts had not shown it, the closing decade of the nineteenth century had set an agenda in which social psychology would be inextricably entwined with the broader discipline of general psychology. As such, social psychology's subsequent development reflects the way in which psychology was defined and taught in university departments of psychology, particularly in the United States which rapidly replaced Germany as the leading nation for psychological research. Just as the psychological laboratory at Leipzig founded by Wilhelm Wundt in 1879 had provided an experimental basis for psychology in Germany, the laboratories set up at American universities did likewise in the United States. In the period 1890–1910, the growth of laboratories devoted to psychological research was rapid (Ruckmick, 1912). Thirty-one American universities established experimental facilities in those twenty years. The subject taught in these departments was clearly defined as an experimental science. In the United States, therefore, it is not surprising that social psychology should quite early on view the experimental method as a touchstone. By the time Allport produced his 1924 text, this trend was well established.

Experimental method
Intentional manipulation of independent variables in order to investigate effects on one or more dependent variables.

When was social psychology's first experiment?

This is a natural question to ask, but the answer is clouded. One of the oldest psychological laboratories was at Indiana University. It was here that Norman Triplett (1898) conducted a study that some modern textbooks have cited as the first experiment in social psychology (e.g. Lippa, 1990; Penrod, 1983; Sears, Peplau and Taylor, 1991) and have listed as an experiment on social facilitation (e.g. Baron and Byrne, 1994; Brigham, 1991; Deaux and Wrightsman, 1988; **see also Chapter 8**). Gordon Allport (1954a) implied that what Wundt did in Leipzig for

Social facilitation
These pictures represent an idea that caught Triplett's attention. Gold medallist Bradley Wiggins competed in the time trial and the road race at the London Olympics. Would he ride faster when competing alone or with others? Why?

experimental psychology Triplett did in Indiana for a scientific social psychology. A different picture emerges in the literature of that time.

Norman Triplett was a mature teacher who returned to postgraduate study to work on his master's thesis, published in 1898. His supervisors were two experimental psychologists and the research was conducted in a laboratory that was one of the very best in the world. His interest had been stimulated by popular wisdom that competitive cyclists go faster when racing or being paced, than when riding alone. Cycling as an activity had increased dramatically in popularity in the 1890s and had spectacular press coverage. Triplett listed possible explanations for superior performance by cyclists who were racing or being paced:

- The pacer in front provided suction that pulled the following rider along, helping to conserve energy; or else the front rider provided shelter from the wind.
- A popular 'brain worry' theory predicted that solitary cyclists did poorly because they worried about whether they were going fast enough. This exhausted their brain and muscles, numbing them and inhibiting motor performance.
- Friends usually rode as pacers and no doubt encouraged the cyclists to keep up their spirits.
- In a race, a follower might be hypnotised by the wheels in front and so rode automatically, leaving more energy for a later, controlled burst.
- A dynamogenic theory – Triplett's favourite – proposed that the presence of another person racing aroused a 'competitive instinct' that released 'nervous energy', similar to the modern idea of arousal. The sight of movement in another suggested more speed, inspired greater effort, and released a level of nervous energy that an isolated rider cannot achieve alone. The energy of the cyclist's movement was in proportion to the idea of that movement.

In the most famous of Triplett's experiments, schoolchildren worked in two conditions, alone and in pairs. They worked with two fishing reels that turned silk bands around a drum. Each reel was connected by a loop of cord to a pulley two metres away, and a small flag was attached to each cord. To complete one trial, the flag had to travel four times around the pulley. Some children were slower and others faster in competition, while others were little affected. The faster ones showed the effects of both 'the arousal of their competitive instincts and the idea of a faster movement' (Triplett, 1898, p. 526). The slower ones were overstimulated and 'going to pieces' – a rather modern turn of phrase!

In drawing on the *dynamogenic theory* of his day, Triplett focused on ideo-motor responses – that is, one competitor's bodily movements acted as a stimulus for the other competitor. Essentially, Triplett highlighted *non-social* cues to illustrate the idea of movement being used as a cue by his participants.

The leading journals in the decade after Triplett's study scarcely referred to it. It was catalogued in general sources, but not under any headings with a 'social' connotation. Clearly, Triplett was neither a social psychologist nor considered to be one. If we adopt a revisionist view of history, then the spirit of his experiment emerges as a precursor to the theme of social facilitation research. The search for a founding figure, or a first idea, is not a new phenomenon in the history of science or, indeed, in the history of civilisation. The Triplett study has the trappings of an origin myth. There were other, even earlier, studies that might just as easily be called the 'first' in social psychology (Burnham, 1910; Haines and Vaughan, 1979). Vaughan and Guerin (1997) point out that sports psychologists have claimed Triplett as one of their own.

Later influences

Behaviourism
An emphasis on explaining observable behaviour in terms of reinforcement schedules.

Social psychology's development after the early impact of behaviourism was redirected by a number of other important developments, some of which came from beyond mainstream psychology.

Attitude scaling

One of these developments was the refinement of several methods for constructing scales to measure attitudes (Bogardus, 1925; Likert, 1932; Thurstone, 1928; **see Chapter 5**), two of which were published in sociology journals. Sociology has often championed approaches to social psychology that have been critical of an individual-behaviour level of analysis. Thomas and Znaniecki (1918), for example, defined social psychology as the scientific study of attitudes rather than of social behaviour.

Studies of the social group

Central to social psychology is an abiding interest in the structure and function of the social group (**see Chapters 8, 9 and 11**). Kurt Lewin, considered the 'father' of experimental social psychology, put much of his energy into the study of group processes (Marrow, 1969). For example, one of Lewin's imaginative studies was an experiment on the effect of leadership style on small-group behaviour (Lewin, Lippitt and White, 1939; **see also Chapter 9**), and by 1945 he had founded a research centre devoted to the study of group dynamics (which still exists, in a different guise and now at the University of Michigan).

Another important thread in research on the social group came from industrial psychology. A key study carried out in a factory setting showed that work productivity can be more heavily influenced by the psychological properties of the work group and the degree of interest that management shows in its workers (Roethlisberger and Dickson, 1939) than by mere physical working conditions. A significant outcome of research of this kind was consolidation of an approach to social psychology in which theory and application can develop together. Indeed, Lewin is often quoted as saying 'there is nothing so practical as a good theory'. He was a passionate advocate of what he called 'full cycle' research, where symbiosis exists between basic and applied research.

Popular textbooks

The 1930s marked several quite different themes that had a striking impact on the continuing development of the discipline. Carl Murchison (1935) produced the first handbook, a weighty tome that proclaimed that here was a field to be taken seriously. A later, expanded edition of the Murphy and Murphy text (1931/1937) appeared that summarised the findings of more than 1,000 studies, although it was used mainly as a reference work. Perhaps the most widely used textbook of this period was written by LaPiere and Farnsworth (1936). Another by Klineberg

Role transition
Birthdays can mark important life changes. In Latin America, quinceañera marks a fifteen-year-old girl's transition from childhood to womanhood – a great opportunity to have fun!

(1940) was also popular; it featured contributions from cultural anthropology and emphasised the crucial role played by culture in the development of a person's personality. Just after the Second World War, Krech and Crutchfield (1948) published an important text that emphasised a *phenomenological approach* to social psychology: that is, an approach focusing on the way in which people actually experience the world and account for their experiences.

In the 1950s and thereafter, the number of textbooks appearing on the bookshelves increased exponentially. Most have been published in the United States, with a heavy reliance on both American data and American theory.

Famous experiments

For different reasons, several experiments stand out over the years that have fascinated teachers and students alike. The following have had an impact beyond the immediate discipline, reaching out to the wider perspective of general psychology, and some out further, to other disciplines. We will not go into detail about these studies here, as they are described in later chapters.

Muzafer Sherif (1935) conducted an experiment on *norm formation,* which caught the attention of psychologists eager to pinpoint what could be 'social' about social psychology (**Chapter 7**). Solomon Asch (1951) demonstrated the dramatic effect that *group pressure* can have in persuading an individual to conform (**Chapter 7**). Muzafer and Carolyn Sherif (Sherif and Sherif, 1953) examined the role that competition for resources can have on intergroup conflict (**Chapter 11**). Leon Festinger (1957) used his theory of *cognitive dissonance* to show that a smaller reward can change attitudes more than can a larger reward (Festinger and Carlsmith, 1959), a finding that annoyed the orthodox reinforcement theorists of the time (**Chapters 5 and 6**). Stanley Milgram's (1963) study of *destructive obedience* highlighted the dilemma facing a person ordered by an authority figure to perform an immoral act, a study that unwittingly became one focus of critics who questioned the future of the experimental method in social psychology (**Chapter 7**). Henri Tajfel (1970; Tajfel, Billig, Bundy and Flament, 1971) conducted a watershed experiment to show that merely being categorised into groups was sufficient to generate *intergroup discrimination* (**Chapter 11**).

Finally, Phil Zimbardo (1971) set up a simulated prison in the basement of the Stanford University psychology department to study *deindividuation* and the reality of and extremity of *roles* (**Chapter 8**). This study has caught the imagination of a reality-TV oriented society; to the extent that two prominent British social psychologists, Alex Haslam and Stephen Reicher, were commissioned as consultants on a 2002 BBC TV programme re-running the experiment (Reicher and Haslam, 2006).

Famous programmes

One way of viewing the way in which a discipline develops is to focus on social networks and ask the question 'Who's who?' and then 'Who influenced whom?' Looked at in this way, the group-centred research of the charismatic Kurt Lewin (Marrow, 1969) had a remarkable impact on other social psychologists in the United States. One of his students was Leon Festinger, and one of Festinger's students was Stanley Schachter. The latter's work on the cognitive labelling of emotion is a derivative of Festinger's notion of social comparison (i.e. the way in which individuals use other people as a basis for assessing their own thoughts, feelings and behaviour).

There have been other groups of researchers whose impact is more obvious by the nature of the concepts emerging from their programmes. There were two influential groups whose research concerned questions raised and made urgent by events during and surrounding the Second World War. One group studied the *authoritarian personality* (Adorno, Frenkel-Brunswik, Levinson and Sanford, 1950). Inspired by the possibility that an explanation for the rise of German autocracy resided in the personality and child-rearing practices of a nation, the researchers embarked on an ambitious cross-cultural study of authoritarianism in the United States (**Chapter 10**). Another group studied how to change people's attitudes. The Yale *attitude change* programme, led by Carl Hovland, was designed to uncover the theory and techniques of propaganda (Hovland, Janis and Kelley, 1953; **see also Chapter 6**).

John Thibaut and Harold Kelley (1959) developed an influential approach to the study of interpersonal relationships, based on an economic model of *social exchange* (**Chapter 14**), which continued to stimulate theories into the 1980s. Likewise, Morton Deutsch's (Deutsch and Krauss, 1960) application of exchange theory to interpersonal bargaining subsequently attracted enormous research interest and activity form psychologists. Once again, the long arm of Lewin is clearly evident – all of these innovators (Thibaut, Kelley, Deutsch) were his students.

The modern period has been dominated by cognitive approaches. *Attribution theory* was set on its path by Ned Jones (Jones and Davis, 1965), who focused attention on the ordinary person's ideas about causality (**Chapter 3**). Darley and Latané (1968) employed an innovative cognitive model to research *prosocial behaviour* by throwing light on the way in which people interpret an emergency and sometimes fail to help a victim (**Chapter 13**).

Following earlier work by Fritz Heider (1946) and Solomon Asch (1946) in a field loosely described as social perception, a major restructuring reconfigured this field into modern *social cognition* (**see Chapter 2**). Several researchers made major contributions to this development, including Walter Mischel (Cantor and Mischel, 1977), who explored the way that perceived behaviour traits can function as prototypes, and Richard Nisbett and Lee Ross (1980), who explored the role of cognitive heuristics (mental short-cuts) in social thinking.

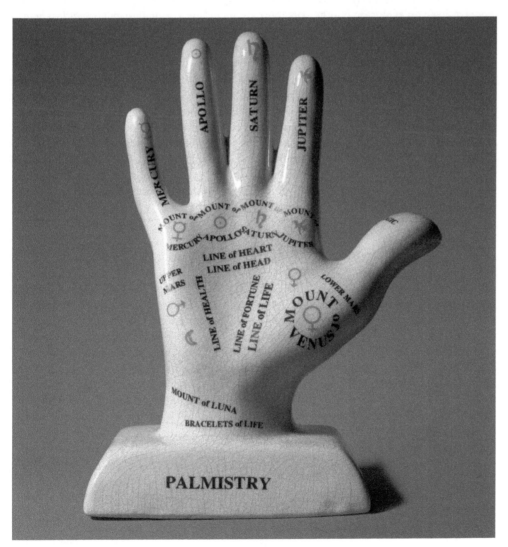

Attribution
People try to make sense of their lives in many different ways. We can try palmistry, or more mundanely examine the immediate causes of our experiences

The journals

Journals are critical in science as they are the key forum for scientists to exchange ideas and communicate ideas and findings. Early journals that were important up to the 1950s were the *Journal of Abnormal and Social Psychology* and the *Journal of Personality*. A sociological journal, *Sociometry,* also catered for social psychological work.

From the 1960s there was increased demand for outlets. This reflected not only growth in the number of social psychologists around the world but also a demand for regional representation. The *Journal of Abnormal and Social Psychology* divided into two, one part devoted to abnormal psychology and the other titled the *Journal of Personality and Social Psychology* (founded in 1965). *Sociometry* was re-titled *Social Psychology Quarterly* (1979) to reflect more accurately its heavy social psychological content. Anglo-European interests were represented by the *British Journal of Social and Clinical Psychology* (1963) (which split in about 1980 to spin off the *British Journal of Social Psychology*), and the *European Journal of Social Psychology* (1971). Demand for a second, American, journal dedicated to experimental research was realised by the *Journal of Experimental Social Psychology* (1965), and then in 1975 a third major American social psychology journal was launched, *Personality and Social Psychology Bulletin.* Other journals devoted to the area include *Journal of Applied Social Psychology* (1971), *Social Cognition* (1982) and *Journal of Social and Personal Relationships* (1984). In the last fifteen years there has been an explosion of other key journals, including *Personality and Social Psychology Review, Social Psychological and Personality Science, Group Processes and Intergroup Relations, Group Dynamics, Social Cognition* and *Self and Identity.*

From the point of view of articles published, therefore, there was huge growth of interest in the subject during the decade bridging the 1960s and the 1970s.Since then publication has accelerated. The past decade or two have witnessed a journal crisis in social psychology, and psychology more generally. There is so much published that the task of deciding what to read can seem overwhelming. One important criterion is the quality of the journal (its impact factor and the calibre of its editorial board), but there are now so many journals and such huge volume of articles submitted that the editorial review process that is essential to quality is creaking under the load. This, in conjunction with the massive potential of electronic access to research, has led to a fiery debate about alternative forms of scientific communication and publication (Nosek and Bar-Anan, 2012).

Social psychology in Europe

Although, as our historical overview has shown, the beginnings of social psychology, and indeed psychology as a whole, were in Europe, America quickly assumed leadership in terms not only of concepts but also of journals, books and organisations. One important reason for this shift in hegemony was the rise of fascism in Europe in the 1930s. For instance, in Germany in 1933 Jewish professors were dismissed from the universities, and from then until the end of the Second World War the names of Jewish authors were expunged from university textbooks in the name of National Socialism and to promulgate Aryan doctrine (Baumgarten-Tramer, 1948). This led, during the immediate pre-war period, to a massive exodus of European social psychologists and other scholars to the United States. By 1945, social psychology in Europe had been significantly weakened, particularly when compared with the rapid development of the field in the United States. By 1945, very little European social psychology remained.

From 1945 into the 1950s the United States provided resources (e.g. money and academic links) to (re-)establish centres of European social psychology. Although partly a scientific gesture, this was also part of a wider Cold War strategy to provide an intellectual environment in Western Europe to combat the potential encroachment of communism. These centres were linked to the United States rather than to one another. In fact, there were very few links among European social psychologists, who were often unaware of one another and who tended instead to have lines of communication with American universities. Europe, including Britain, was largely an outpost of American social psychology. In the period from 1950 to the end of the 1960s, social psychology in Britain was largely based on American ideas. Likewise in The Netherlands, Germany, France and Belgium, most work was influenced by American thinking (Argyle, 1980).

Gradually, however, European social psychologists became more conscious of the hegemony of American ideas and of the intellectual, cultural and historical differences between Europe and America. For instance, at that time the recent European experience was of war and conflict, while America's last major conflict within its own borders was its Civil War in the 1860s. Not surprisingly, Europeans considered themselves to be more concerned with intergroup relations and groups, while Americans were perhaps more interested in interpersonal relations and individuals. Europeans pushed for a more *social* social psychology. There was a clear need for better communication channels among European scholars and some degree of intellectual and organisational independence from the United States.

The first step along this road was initiated in the early 1950s by Eric Rinde in Norway, who, in collaboration with the American David Krech, brought together several American and more than thirty European social psychologists to collaborate on a cross-national study of threat and rejection. The wider goal was to encourage international collaboration and to increase training facilities for social scientists in Europe. Building on this project, the next step was a *European conference on experimental social psychology* organised by John Lanzetta and Luigi Petrullo, both from the United States, held in Sorrento in 1963. Among the twenty-eight participants were five Americans and twenty-one Europeans from eight countries. The organising committee (Mulder, Pages, Rommetveit, Tajfel and Thibaut) was also charged with preparing a proposal for the development of experimental social psychology in Europe.

It was decided to hold a second European conference, and a summer school (held later in Leuven in 1967). The conference was held in Frascati in 1964, and it elected a 'European planning committee' (G. Jahoda, Moscovici, Mulder, Nuttin and Tajfel) to explore further a formal structure for European social psychology. A structure was approved at the third European conference, held in 1966 at Royaumont near Paris: thus was formally born the *European Association of Experimental Social Psychology* (EAESP). Moscovici was the foundation president, and there were approximately forty-four members.

EAESP, which was renamed the *European Association of Social Psychology* (EASP) in 2008 has been the enormously successful focus for the development of European social psychology for almost fifty years, and currently has more than 1,250 members. Most members by far are from The Netherlands, UK and Germany (in that order), followed by Italy, France and then the US. It is a dynamic and integrative force for social psychology that for many years now has reached outside Europe with strong links with the leading international social psychology organisations (*Society for Personality and Social Psychology, Society of Experimental Social Psychology, Society for the Psychological Study of Social Issues*) – its last triennial conference, the 16th general meeting, held in Stockholm in July 2011 (the previous five conferences were held in Lisbon, Gmunden, Oxford, San Sebastián, Würzburg, and Opatija) had 1,300 delegates from 42 countries across Europe and the rest of the world.

European journals and textbooks have provided additional focus for European social psychology. The *European Journal of Social Psychology* was launched in 1971, and the *European Review of Social Psychology* in 1990 – both are considered among the most prestigious social psychology journals in the world. Textbooks used in Europe have largely been American or, more recently, European adaptations of American books. But there have been notable European texts, probably beginning with Moscovici's *Introduction à la psychologie sociale* (1973), followed by Tajfel and Fraser's *Introducing social psychology* (1978) and then Moscovici's *Psychologie sociale* (1984). Aside of course from our own, the most recent other European text is Hewstone, Stroebe and Jonas's *Introduction to social psychology*, which is now in its fifth edition (2012).

Since the early 1970s, then, European social psychology has undergone a powerful renaissance (Doise, 1982; Jaspars, 1980, 1986). Initially, it self-consciously set itself up in opposition to American social psychology and adopted an explicitly critical stance. However, since the late 1980s European social psychology, although not discarding its critical orientation, has attained substantial self-confidence and international recognition. Its impact on American social psychology, and thus on international perspectives, is significant and acknowledged (e.g. Hogg and Abrams, 1999). Moreland, Hogg and Hains (1994) documented how an upsurge in research into group processes (as evidenced from publication trends over the previous twenty years in the three major American social psychology journals) was almost exclusively due to European research and perspectives. It is, perhaps, through work on social representations (**Chapter 3**), social identity and intergroup behaviour (**Chapter 11**), minority influence (**Chapter 7**) and more recently social cognition (**Chapter 2**) that Europe has had and continues to have its most visible and significant international impact. Now revisit the third focus question.

Europe is a continent of many languages and a historical diversity of national emphases on different aspects of social psychology: for example, social representations in France, political psychology and small-group processes in Germany, social justice research and social cognition in The Netherlands, social development of cognition in French-speaking Switzerland, goal-oriented action in German-speaking Switzerland, and applied and social constructionist approaches in Scandinavia. A 2010 international benchmarking review of British psychology identified British social psychology as being strongly invested in research on social identity, prejudice and discrimination, attitudes, health behaviour, and discourse analysis and critical psychology. A great deal of research is published in national social psychology journals. However, in recognition of the fact that English is the global language of science, European social psychologists publish in English so that their ideas might have the greatest impact both internationally and within Europe: most major European journals, series and texts publish in English.

Historically, there are two figures that have particularly shaped European social psychology: Henri Tajfel and Serge Moscovici. Tajfel (1974), at the University of Bristol, revolutionised how we think about intergroup relations. His *social identity theory* focused on how a person's identity is grounded in belonging to a group, and how such *social* identity shapes intergroup behaviour. It questioned Sherif's argument that an objective clash of interests was the necessary ingredient for intergroup conflict (**Chapter 11**). Moscovici (1961), at the Maison des Sciences de l'Homme in Paris, resuscitated an interest in the work of the nineteenth-century sociologist Durkheim with his idea of social representations (**Chapter 3**). In addition, he initiated a radical new interpretation of conformity processes – developing an entirely new focus on how minorities can influence majorities and thus bring about social change (**Chapter 7**).

About this book

We have written this introductory text, now in its seventh edition, to reflect contemporary European social psychology: a social psychology that smoothly integrates American and European research but with a distinct emphasis that is framed by European, not American, intellectual and sociohistorical priorities. Students of social psychology in Britain and Europe tend to use a mixture of American and European texts. American texts are comprehensive, detailed and well produced, but are pitched too low for British and European universities, do not cover European topics well or at all, and quite understandably are grounded in the day-to-day cultural experiences of Americans. European texts, which are generally edited collections of chapters by different authors, address European priorities but tend to be idiosyncratic, uneven and less well produced, and incomplete in their coverage of social psychology. Our text satisfies the need for a single comprehensive introduction to social psychology for British and European students of social psychology.

Our aim has been to write an introduction to social psychology for undergraduate university students of psychology. Its language caters to intelligent adults. However, since it is an *introduction* we pay careful attention to accessibility of specialist language (i.e. scientific or social psychological jargon). It is intended to be a comprehensive introduction to mainstream social psychology, with no intentional omissions. We cover classic and contemporary theories and research, generally adopting a historical perspective that most accurately reflects the unfolding of scientific inquiry. The degree of detail and scope of coverage are determined by the scope and intensity of undergraduate social psychology courses in Britain and Europe. We have tried to write a text that combines the most important and enduring features of European and American social psychology. As such, this can be considered an international text, but one that specifically caters for the British and European intellectual, cultural and educational context.

Many social psychology texts separate basic theory and research from applied theory and research, generally by exiling to the end of the book 'applied' chapters that largely address health, organisations, justice or gender. Much like Kurt Lewin's view that there is nothing so practical as a good theory, our philosophy is that basic and applied research and theory are intertwined or best treated as intertwined: they are naturally interdependent. Thus, applied topics are interwoven with basic theory and research. Currently, some significant areas of application of social psychology include human development (e.g. Bennett and Sani, 2004; Durkin, 1995), health (e.g. Rothman and Salovey, 2007; Stroebe, 2011; Taylor, 2003), gender (e.g. Eagly, Beall and Sternberg, 2005), organisations (e.g. Haslam, 2004; Thompson and Pozner, 2007), law and criminal justice (e.g. Kovera and Borgida, 2010; Tyler and Jost, 2007), political behaviour (e.g. Krosnick, Visser and Harder, 2010; Tetlock, 2007) and culture (e.g. Heine, 2010, 2012; Smith, Bond andKağitçibaşi, 2006). The latter, culture, is now an integral part of contemporary social psychology (**see Chapter 16**); and language and communication (e.g., Holtgraves, 2010), which is central to social psychology but is often treated as an application, has its own chapter (**Chapter 15**).

The book is structured so that Chapters 2 to 5 deal with what goes on in people's head – cognitive processes and cognitive representations, including how we conceive of ourselves and how our attitudes are structured. Chapter 6 continues the attitude theme but focuses on how attitudes change and how people are persuaded. This leads directly into Chapter 7, which discusses more broadly how people influence one another. Because groups play a key role in social influence, Chapter 7 flows logically into Chapters 8 and 9, which deal with group processes including leadership. Chapters 10 and 11 broaden the discussion of groups to consider what happens between groups – prejudice, discrimination, conflict and intergroup behaviour. The sad fact that intergroup behaviour so often involves conflict invites a discussion of human aggression, which is dealt with in Chapter 12.

Lest we become disillusioned with our species, Chapter 13 discusses how people can be altruistic and can engage in selfless prosocial acts of kindness and support. Continuing the general emphasis on more positive aspects of human behaviour, Chapter 14 deals with interpersonal relations, including attraction, friendship and love, but also with breakdowns in relationships. At the core of interpersonal interaction lies communication, of which spoken language is the richest form: Chapter 15 explores language and communication. Chapter 16 discusses the cultural context of social behaviour – an exploration of cultural differences, cross-cultural universals, and the significance of culture in contemporary multicultural society.

Each chapter is self-contained, although integrated into the general logic of the entire text. There are plentiful cross-references to other chapters, and at the end of each chapter are references to further, more detailed coverage of topics covered by the chapter. We also suggest classic and contemporary literature, films and TV programmes that deal with subject matter that is relevant to the chapter topic.

Many of the studies referred to in this book can be found in the social psychology journals that we have already noted in the historical section – check new issues of these journals to learn about up-to-date research. In addition, there are three social psychology journals that are dedicated to scholarly state-of-the-art summaries and reviews of topics in social psychology: *Advances in Experimental Social Psychology, Personality and Social Psychology Review* and

European Review of Social Psychology. Topics in social psychology are also covered in general psychology theory and review journals such as *Annual Review of Psychology, Psychological Bulletin,* and *Psychological Review.*

For a short general introduction to social psychology, see Hogg's (2000a) chapter in Pawlik and Rosenzweig's (2000) *International Handbook of Psychology.* For a stripped-down simple introductory European social psychology text that focuses on only the very essentials of the subject see Hogg and Vaughan's (2010) *Essentials of Social Psychology.* In contrast, the most authoritative and detailed sources of information about social psychology are undoubtably the current handbooks of social psychology, of which there are four: (1) Fiske, Gilbert and Lindzey's (2010) *Handbook of Social Psychology,* which is currently in its fifth edition; (2) Hogg and Cooper's (2007) *The SAGE Handbook of Social Psychology: Concise Student Edition;* (3) Kruglanski and Higgins's (2007) *Social Psychology: Handbook of Basic Principles,* which is in its second edition; and (4) Hewstone and Brewer's four-volume *Blackwell Handbook of Social Psychology,* each volume of which is a stand-alone book with a different pair of editors: *Intraindividual Processes* by Tesser and Schwartz (2001), *Interpersonal Processes* by Fletcher and Clark (2001), *Group Processes* by Hogg and Tindale (2001) and *Intergroup Processes* by Brown and Gaertner (2001).

A wonderful source of shorter overview pieces is Baumeister and Vohs's (2007) two-volume 1020-page *Encyclopedia of Social Psychology* – there are more than 550 entries written by an equal number of the leading social psychologists from around the world. Two other similar but topic-specific encyclopedias are Reis and Sprecher's (2009) *Encyclopedia of Human Relationships,* and Levine and Hogg's (2010) *Encyclopedia of Group Processes and Intergroup Relations.* Finally, Hogg's (2003b) *SAGE Benchmarks in Psychology: Social Psychology* is a four-volume edited and annotated collection of almost 80 benchmark research articles in social psychology – it contains many of the discipline's most impactful classic works. The volumes are divided into sections with short introductions.

Summary

- Social psychology can be defined as the scientific investigation of how the thoughts, feelings and behaviour of individuals are influenced by the actual, imagined or implied presence of others. Although social psychology can also be described in terms of what it studies, it is more useful to describe it as a way of looking at human behaviour.

- Social psychology is a science. It employs the scientific method to study social behaviour. Although this involves a whole range of empirical methods to collect data to test hypotheses and construct theories, experimentation is usually the preferred method as it is the best way to reveal causal processes. Nevertheless, methods are matched to research questions, and methodological pluralism is highly valued.

- Social psychological data are usually transformed into numbers, which are analysed by a range of formal numerical procedures – that is, statistics. Statistics allow conclusions to be drawn about whether a research observation is a true effect or some chance event.

- Social psychology is enlivened by fierce and invigorating debates about the ethics of research methods, the appropriate research methods for an understanding of social behaviour, the validity and power of social psychology theories, and the type of theories that are properly social psychological.

- Although having origins in nineteenth-century German folk psychology and French crowd psychology, modern social psychology really began in the United States in the 1920s with the adoption of the experimental method. In the 1940s, Kurt Lewin provided significant impetus to social psychology, and the discipline has grown exponentially ever since.

- Despite its European origins, social psychology quickly became dominated by the United States – a process greatly accelerated by the rise of fascism in Europe during the 1930s. However, since the late 1960s there has been a rapid and sustained renaissance of European social psychology, driven by distinctively European intellectual and sociohistorical priorities to develop a more *social* social psychology with a greater emphasis on collective phenomena and group levels of analysis. European social psychology is now a dynamic and rapidly growing discipline that is an equal but complementary partner to the United States in social psychological research.

Key terms

Archival research
Behaviour
Behaviourism
Case study
Cognitive theories
Confounding
Correlation
Data
Demand characteristics
Dependent variables
Discourse
Discourse analysis
Double-blind
Evolutionary social psychology

Experimental method
Experimental realism
Experimenter effects
External validity
fMRI
Hyphotheses
Independent variables
Internal validity
Laboratory
Level of explanation
Metatheory
Mundane realism
Neo-behaviourism
Operational definition

Positivism
Radical behaviourist
Reductionism
Science
Social neuroscience
Social psychology
Statistical significance
Statistics
Subject effects
t test
Theory
Völkerpsychologie

Literature, film and TV

The Wave (*Die Welle*)

This 2008 German film builds on Zimbardo's research and shows how science can go wrong. A schoolteacher's attempt to demonstrate to his class what life is like under a dictatorship spins horribly out of control as the class takes on a life of its own. In a similar vein, *Das Experiment* is an earlier, 2001, Oliver Hirschbiegel film (German with English subtitles). It opens with a fairly accurate treatment of Zimbardo's Stanford prison experiment. It engages with ethical issues associated with the research, but deteriorates rapidly into a dramatisation that would do Hollywood proud. This is a good example of how the popular media can distort science and scientific issues and debates.

The Double Helix

1968 book by James Watson. It is an account of how Francis Crick and James Watson identified the structure of DNA, for which they won the Nobel Prize. The book is readable, engrossing and even thrilling. It shows how science is

conducted – the rivalries, the squabbles, the competition, set against the backdrop of great minds and great discoveries. It captures the excitement of doing science.

Bad Science

A weekly column in *The Guardian* in which the physician and academic Ben Goldacre skewers those who distort and misrepresent science for the sake of spin, promotion or a headline. Goldacre has also published a 2009 book entitled *Bad Science*, published by Fourth Estate, and a more recent 2012 book entitled *Bad Pharma* which focuses on how the pharmaceutical industry influences and distorts science in order to sell drugs and, ultimately, make a profit.

Lord of the Flies

William Golding's (1954) classic novel about the disintegration of civilised social norms among a group of boys marooned on an island. A powerful portrayal of a whole range of social psychological phenomena, including leadership, intergroup conflict, norms and cultures, conformity, deviance, aggression and so forth. A very social psychological book.

War and Peace

Leo Tolstoy's (1869) masterpiece on the impact of society and social history on people's lives. It does a wonderful job of showing how macro- and micro-levels of analysis influence one another, but cannot be resolved into one another. A wonderful literary work of social psychology – how people's day-to-day lives are located at the intersection of powerful interpersonal, group and intergroup processes. Other classic novels of Leo Tolstoy, Emile Zola, Charles Dickens and George Eliot accomplish much the same social psychological analysis.

Les Misérables

Victor Hugo's (1862) magnum opus and classic literary masterpiece of the nineteenth century. It explores everyday life and relationships against the background of conventions, institutions and historical events in Paris over a 17-year period (1815–1832). Those of you who enjoy musicals will know that it has been adapted into an eponymous 2012 musical film directed by Tom Hooper, and starring Hugh Jackman (as the central character, Jean Valjean), Russell Crowe, Anne Hathaway and Amanda Seyfried.

Gulliver's Travels

Jonathan Swift's 1726 satirical commentary on the nature of human beings. This book is relevant to virtually all the themes in our text. The section on Big-Endians and Little-Endians is particularly relevant to Chaper 11, on intergroup behaviour. Swift provides a hilarious and incredibly full and insightful description of a society that is split on the basis of whether people open their boiled eggs at the big or the little end – relevant to the minimal group studies in Chapter 11 but also to the general theme of how humans can read so much into subtle features of their environment.

Guided questions

1 What do social psychologists study? Can you give some examples of interdisciplinary research?

2 Sometimes experiments are used in social psychological research. Why?

3 What do you understand by levels of explanation in social psychology? What is meant by reductionism?

4 If you or your lecturer were to undertake research in social psychology you would need to gain ethical approval. Why is this, and what criteria would be required?

MyPsychLab

5 If the shock level 'administered' in Milgram's obedience study had been 150 volts instead of the maximum 450 volts, would this have made the experiment more ethical? Watch the video illustrating this pivotal research in Chapter 1 of MyPsychLab at www.mypsychlab.com (watch *Milgram's obedience study*).

Learn more

Allport, G. W. (1954). The historical background of modern social psychology. In G. Lindzey (ed.), *Handbook of social psychology* (Vol. 1, pp. 3–56). Reading, MA: Addison-Wesley. Classic and often-cited account of the history of social psychology, covering the period up to the 1950s.

Aronson, E., Ellsworth, P. C., Carlsmith, J. M., and Gonzales, M. H. (1990). *Methods of research in social psychology* (2nd edn). New York: McGraw-Hill. Detailed, well-written and now classic coverage of research methods in social psychology.

Crano, W. D., and Brewer, M. B. (2002). *Principles and methods of social research* (2nd edn). Mahwah, NJ: Erlbaum. A detailed but very readable overview of research methods in social psychology.

Dawkins, R. (2011). *The magic of reality: How we know what's really true*. London: Bantam Press. Ethologist and evolutionary biologist, Richard Dawkins argues that science does indeed aim to uncover what is real – whether it be an earthquake, a supernova, DNA, or the nature of jealousy.

Denzin, N. K., and Lincoln, Y. S. (eds) (2005). *The SAGE handbook of qualitative research* (3rd edn). Thousand Oaks, CA: SAGE. This academic bestseller is considered the gold standard for qualitative research methods.

Ellsworth, P. C., and Gonzales, R. (2007). Questions and comparisons: Methods of research in social psychology. In M. A. Hogg, and J. Cooper (eds), *The SAGE handbook of social psychology: Concise student edition* (pp. 24–42). London: SAGE. A concise and readable overview of how one moves from research question to research itself in social psychology, and how one makes choices about methods.

Farr, R. M. (1996). *The roots of modern social psychology: 1872–1954*. Oxford, UK: Blackwell. A scholarly and provocative discussion of the intellectual roots of modern social psychology. Farr is a renowned historical commentator on social psychology.

Goethals, G. R. (2007). A century of social psychology: Individuals, ideas, and investigations. In M. A. Hogg, and J. Cooper (eds), *The SAGE handbook of social psychology* (pp. 3–23). London: SAGE. A very readable, comprehensive and inclusive coverage of the history of social psychology.

Howell, D. C. (2007). *Statistical methods for psychology* (6th edn). Belmont, CA: Duxbury. Highly respected and often-used basic introduction to psychological statistics. With the usual equations and formulae that we all love so much – it is also easy to read.

Jones, E. E. (1998). Major developments in five decades of social psychology. In D. T. Gilbert, S. T. Fiske, and G. Lindzey (eds), *The handbook of social psychology* (4th edn, Vol. 1, pp. 3–57). Boston, MA: McGraw-Hill. This treatment overlaps with and moves on from Allport's (1954a) treatment, covering the period from 1935 to 1985. In addition to classical developments, it also covers the growth of research on social comparison, cognitive dissonance, attitude change, conformity, person perception and attribution.

Rosnow, R. L., and Rosenthal, R. (1997). *People studying people: Artifacts and ethics in behavioral research*. New York: Freeman. An introduction to the major biases that can distort research on human behaviour. There is also coverage of ethical issues.

Ross, L., Lepper, M., and Ward, A. (2010). History of social psychology: Insights, challenges, and contributions to theory and application. In S. T. Fiske, D. T. Gilbert, and G. Lindzey (eds), *Handbook of social psychology* (5th edn, Vol. 1, pp. 3–50). New York: Wiley. The most recent overview and account of the history of social psychology.

Sansone, C., Morf, C. C., and Panter, A. T. (eds) (2004). *The SAGE handbook of methods in social psychology*. Thousand Oaks, CA: SAGE. At over 500 pages and 22 chapters this is a comprehensive coverage of quantitative and qualitative research methods in social psychology, including discussion of research ethics, programme development, cultural sensitivities, and doing interdisciplinary and applied research.

Tabachnik, B. G., and Fidell, L. S. (1989). *Using multivariate statistics* (2nd edn). New York: HarperCollins. The acknowledged 'bible' for doing, interpreting and reporting multivariate statistics in psychology.

Van Lange, P. A. M., Kruglanski, A. W., and Higgins, E. T. (eds) (2013). *Handbook of theories of social psychology*. Thousand Oaks, CA: SAGE. All the major theories in social psychology are here, described clearly and concisely, in a completely up-to-date form by experts in the theory or by the theorists themselves.

CHAPTER 3
Attribution and social explanation

Chapter contents

Focus questions

1. Helen is angry with her husband Lewis who avoids approaching his boss for a pay rise. Lewis argues that the timing is not right. Helen says he simply fails to face up to people. How are these attributions different in kind? Watch Helen and Lewis debate this issue in Chapter 3 of MyPsychLab at www.mypsychlab.com (watch *Social perception*).

2. You read a newspaper report about a rape case in which the defence lawyer pointed out that the young woman who was the victim was dressed provocatively. What attributional error is involved here?

3. The job market was tight and Rajna began to worry that she might be made redundant. Then she heard a rumour that the worst had come – several staff were about to be fired. She was itching to pass this on to the next colleague that she saw. Why would Rajna want to spread the rumour further?

will use which involves getting you to decide to buy a car by giving you a very low price

Go to MyPsychLab to explore video and test your understanding of key topics addressed in this chapter.

MyPsychLab

Use MyPsychLab to refresh your understanding with interactive summaries, explore topics further with video and audio clips and assess your progress with quick test and essay questions. To buy access or register your code, visit www.mypsychlab.com. You will also need a course ID from your instructor.

Seeking the causes of behaviour

People are preoccupied with seeking, constructing and testing explanations of their experiences. We try to understand our world to make it orderly and meaningful enough for adaptive action, and we tend to feel uncomfortable if we do not have such an understanding. In particular we need to understand people. Through life most of us gradually construct adequate explanations (i.e. theories) of why people behave in certain ways; in this respect, we are all 'naive' or lay psychologists. This is extraordinarily useful, because it allows us (with varying accuracy) to predict how someone will behave, and possibly to influence whether someone will behave in that way or not. Thus, we gain some control over our destiny.

People construct explanations for both physical phenomena (e.g. earthquakes, the seasons) and human behaviour (e.g. anger, a particular attitude), and in general such explanations are *causal* explanations, in which specific conditions are attributed a causal role. Causal explanations are particularly powerful bases for prediction and control (Forsterling and and Rudolph, 1988).

In this chapter, we discuss how people make inferences about the causes of their own and other people's behaviour, and the antecedents and consequences of such inferences. Social psychological theories of causal inference are called *attribution theories* (Harvey and Weary, 1981; Hewstone, 1989; Kelley and Michela, 1980; Ross and Fletcher, 1985). There are seven main theoretical emphases that make up the general body of **attribution** theory:

Attribution
The process of assigning a cause to our own behaviour, and that of others.

1 Heider's (1958) theory of naive psychology;
2 Jones and Davis's (1965) theory of correspondent inference;

In search of the meaning of life
Religions are one expression of our most basic need to understand the world we live in. Millions of Catholics hope that their new Pope will satisfy this need

3 Kelley's (1967) covariation model;

4 Schachter's (1964) theory of emotional lability;

5 Bem's (1967, 1972) theory of self-perception;

6 Weiner's (1979, 1985) attributional theory; and

7 Deschamps's (1983), Hewstone's (1989) and Jaspars's (Hewstone and Jaspars, 1982, 1984) intergroup perspective.

We discuss the first six of these below and then deal with intergroup attribution by itself in greater detail later in the chapter.

How people attribute causality

People as naive psychologists

Fritz Heider (1958) believed it was crucially important for social psychologists to study people's naive, or common sense, psychological theories, because such theories influenced ordinary people's everyday perceptions and behaviour. For example, people who believe in astrology are likely to have different expectations and are likely to act in different ways from those who do not. Heider believed that people are intuitive psychologists who construct causal theories of human behaviour, and because such theories have the same form as systematic scientific social psychological theories, people are actually intuitive or naive psychologists.

Heider based his ideas on three principles:

1 Because we feel that our own behaviour is motivated rather than random, we tend to look for the causes and reasons for other people's behaviour in order to discover their motives. The search for causes does seem to pervade human thought, and indeed it can be difficult to explain or comment on something without using causal language. Heider and Simmel (1944) demonstrated this in an ingenious experiment in which people who were asked to describe the movement of abstract geometric figures described them as if they were humans with intentions to act in certain ways. Nowadays, we can witness the same phenomenon in people's often highly emotional ascription of human motives to inanimate figures in video and computer games. The pervasive need that people have for causal explanation reveals itself most powerfully in the way that almost all societies construct an origin myth, an elaborate causal explanation for the origin and meaning of life that is often a centrepiece of a religion.

2 Because we construct causal theories in order to be able to predict and control the environment, we tend to look for stable and enduring properties of the world around us. We try to discover personality traits and enduring abilities in people, or stable properties of situations, that cause behaviour.

3 In attributing causality for behaviour, we distinguish between personal factors (e.g. personality, ability) and environmental factors (e.g. situations, social pressure). The former are examples of an internal (or dispositional) attribution and the latter of an external (or situational) attribution. So, for example, it might be useful to know whether someone you meet at a party who seems aloof and distant is an aloof and distant person or is acting in that way because she is not enjoying that particular party. Heider believed that because internal causes, or intentions, are hidden from us, we can only infer their presence if there are no clear external causes. However, as we see below, people tend to be biased in preferring internal to external attributions even in the face of evidence for external causality. It seems that we readily attribute behaviour to stable properties of people. Scherer (1978), for example, found that people made assumptions about the stable personality traits of complete strangers simply on the basis of hearing their voices on the telephone.

Naive psychologist (or scientist)
Model of social cognition that characterises people as using rational, scientific-like, cause–effect analyses to understand their world.

Internal (or dispositional) attribution
Process of assigning the cause of our own or others' behaviour to internal or dispositional factors.

External (or situational) attribution
Assigning the cause of our own or others' behaviour to external or environmental factors.

Heider identified the major themes and provided the insight that forms the blueprint for all subsequent, more formalised, theories of attribution.

From acts to dispositions

Correspondent inference
Causal attribution of behaviour to underlying dispositions.

Ned Jones and Keith Davis's (1965; Jones and McGillis, 1976) theory of **correspondent inference** explains how people infer that a person's behaviour corresponds to an underlying disposition or personality trait – how we infer, for example, that a friendly action is due to an underlying disposition to be friendly. People like to make correspondent inferences (attribute behaviour to underlying disposition) because a dispositional cause is a stable cause that renders people's behaviour predictable and thus increases our own sense of control over our world.

To make a correspondent inference, we draw on five sources of information, or cues (see Figure 3.1):

1 *Freely chosen* behaviour is more indicative of a disposition than is behaviour that is clearly under the control of external threats, inducements or constraints.

Non-common effects
Effects of behaviour that are relatively exclusive to that behaviour rather than other behaviours.

Outcome bias
Belief that the outcomes of a behaviour were intended by the person who chose the behaviour.

2 Behaviour with effects that are relatively exclusive to that behaviour rather than common to a range of other behaviour (i.e. behaviour with **non-common effects**) tells us more about dispositions. People assume that others are aware of non-common effects and that the specific behaviour was performed intentionally to produce the non-common effect – this tendency has been called **outcome bias** (Allison, Mackie and Messick, 1996). So, for example, if a person has to choose between behaviour A and behaviour B, and both produce roughly the same effects (i.e. no non-common effects) or a very large number of different effects (i.e. many non-common effects), the choice tells us little about the person's disposition. However, if the behaviours produce a small number of different effects (i.e. few non-common effects – e.g. behaviour A produces only terror and behaviour B produces only joy), then the choice does tell us something about that person's disposition.

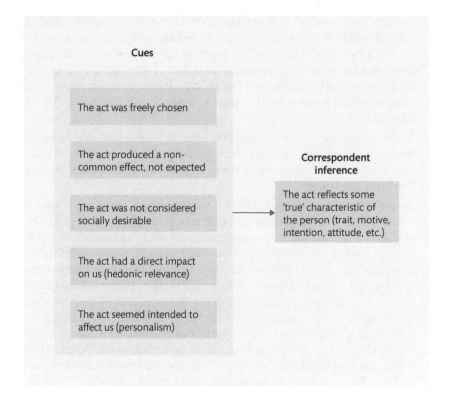

Figure 3.1 How we make a correspondent inference

To make an inference that a person's behaviour corresponds to an underlying disposition, we draw on five sources of information

3 *Socially desirable* behaviour tells us little about a person's disposition, because it is likely to be controlled by societal norms. However, socially undesirable behaviour is generally counter-normative and is thus a better basis for making a correspondent inference.

4 We make more confident correspondent inferences about others' behaviour that has important consequences for ourselves: that is, behaviour that has **hedonic relevance**.

5 We make more confident correspondent inferences about others' behaviour that seems to be directly intended to benefit or harm us: that is, behaviour that is high in **personalism**.

Experiments testing correspondent inference theory provide some support. Jones and Harris (1967) found that American students making attributions for speeches made by other students tended to make more correspondent inferences for freely chosen socially unpopular positions, such as freely choosing to make a speech in support of Cuba's President at the time, Fidel Castro.

In another experiment, Jones, Davis and Gergen (1961) found that participants made more correspondent inferences for out-of-role behaviour, such as friendly, outer-directed behaviour by someone who was applying for an astronaut job, in which the required attributes favour a quiet, reserved, inner-directed person.

Correspondent inference theory has some limitations and has declined in importance as an attribution theory (Hewstone, 1989; Howard, 1985). For instance, the theory holds that correspondent inferences depend to a great extent on the attribution of intentionality, yet unintentional behaviour (e.g. careless behaviour) can be a strong basis for a correspondent inference (e.g. that the person is a careless person).

There is also a problem with the notion of non-common effects. While correspondent inference theory maintains that people assess the commonality of effects by comparing chosen and non-chosen actions, other research indicates that people simply do not attend to non-occurring behaviours and so would not be able to compute the commonality of effects accurately (Nisbett and Ross, 1980; Ross, 1977). More generally, although we may correct dispositional attributions in the light of situational factors, this is a rather deliberate process, whereas correspondent inferences themselves are relatively automatic (Gilbert, 1995).

People as everyday scientists

The best-known attribution theory is Harold Kelley's (1967, 1973) **covariation model**. Kelley believed that in trying to discover the causes of behaviour people act much like scientists. They identify what factor covaries most closely with the behaviour and then assign that factor a causal role. The procedure is similar to that embodied by the statistical technique of analysis of variance (ANOVA), and for this reason Kelley's model is often referred to as an ANOVA model. People use this covariation principle to decide whether to attribute a behaviour to internal dispositions (e.g. personality) or external environmental factors (e.g. social pressure).

In order to make this decision, people assess three classes of information associated with the co-occurrence of a certain action (e.g. laughter) by a specific person (e.g. Tom) with a potential cause (e.g. a comedian):

1 **Consistency information** – does Tom always laugh at this comedian (high consistency) or only sometimes laughs at this comedian (low consistency)?

2 **Distinctiveness information** – does Tom laugh at everything (low distinctiveness) or only at the comedian (high distinctiveness)?

3 **Consensus information** – does everyone laugh at the comedian (high consensus) or is it only Tom who laughs (low consensus)?

Where consistency is low, people **discount** the potential cause and search for an alternative (see Figure 3.2). If Tom sometimes laughs and sometimes does not laugh at the comedian, then presumably the cause of the laughter is neither the comedian nor Tom but some other

Hedonic relevance
Refers to behaviour that has important direct consequences for self.

Personalism
Behaviour that appears to be directly intended to benefit or harm oneself rather than others.

Covariation model
Kelley's theory of causal attribution – people assign the cause of behaviour to the factor that covaries most closely with the behaviour.

Consistency information
Information about the extent to which a behaviour Y always co-occurs with a stimulus X.

Distinctiveness information
Information about whether a person's reaction occurs only with one stimulus, or is a common reaction to many stimuli.

Consensus information
Information about the extent to which other people react in the same way to a stimulus X.

Discount
If there is no consistent relationship between a specific cause and a specific behaviour, that cause is discounted in favour of some other cause.

Consensus information
Everyone in this audience is reacting in the same way to a stand-up comedian. Clearly, his routine has worked!

covarying factor: for example, whether or not Tom smoked marijuana before listening to the comedian or whether or not the comedian told a funny joke or not (see McClure, 1998, for a review of the conditions under which discounting is most likely to occur). Where consistency is high, and distinctiveness and consensus are also high, one can make an external attribution to the comedian (the cause of Tom's laughter was the comedian), but where distinctiveness and consensus are low, one can make an internal attribution to Tom's personality (Tom laughed at the comedian because Tom is simply the sort of person who tends to laugh a lot).

McArthur (1972) tested Kelley's theory by having participants make internal or external attributions for a range of behaviours, each accompanied by one of the eight possible configurations of high or low consistency, distinctiveness and consensus information. Although the

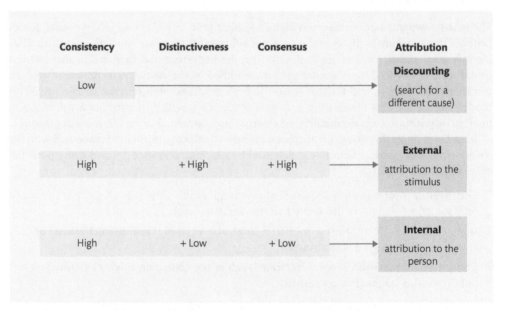

Figure 3.2 Kelley's attribution theory
Kelley's covariation model states that people decide what attributions to make after considering the consistency, distinctiveness and consensus of a person's behaviour

theory was generally supported (see review by Kassin, 1979), there was a tendency for people to under-use consensus information. There are also some general issues worth considering:

- Just because people can use pre-packaged consistency, distinctiveness and consensus information to attribute causality (the case in experimental tests of Kelley's model), this does not mean that in the normal course of events they do.
- There is evidence that people are actually poor at assessing the covariation of different events – they are poor statisticians (Alloy and Tabachnik, 1984).
- There is no guarantee that people are using the covariation principle – they may attribute causality to the most salient feature or to whatever causal agent appears to be similar to the effect (Nisbett and Ross, 1980).
- If people do attribute causality on the basis of covariance or correlation, then they certainly are *naive* scientists (Hilton, 1988) – covariation is not causation.

Another drawback of the covariation model is that consistency, distinctiveness and consensus information require multiple observations. Sometimes we have this information: we may know that Tom does indeed laugh often at almost anything (low distinctiveness), and that others do not find the comedian particularly amusing (low consensus). At other times, we may have, at best, incomplete information or even no information from multiple observations. How do we attribute causality under these circumstances? To deal with this, Kelley (1972a) introduced the notion of **causal schemata** – beliefs or preconceptions, built up from experience, about how certain kinds of cause interact to produce a specific effect. One such schema is that a particular effect requires at least two causes (called the 'multiple necessary cause' schema): for example, someone with a drink-driving record must have consumed a certain amount of alcohol and have been in control of a vehicle. Although the notion of causal schemata does have some empirical support (Kun and Weiner, 1973) and does help to resolve attributional problems raised by the case of a single observation, it is by no means uncritically accepted (Fiedler, 1982).

Causal schemata
Experience-based beliefs about how certain types of cause interact to produce an effect.

Extensions of attribution theory

Explaining our emotions

Causal attribution may play a central role in how we experience emotions. Stanley Schachter (1964, 1971; for review see Reisenzein, 1983) has suggested that emotions may have two distinct components: an undifferentiated state of physiological *arousal*, and *cognitions* that label the arousal and determine which emotion is experienced. Usually the arousal and label go hand-in-hand and our thoughts can generate the associated arousal (e.g. identifying a dog as a Rottweiler may produce arousal that is experienced as fear). However, in some cases there is initially unexplained arousal that could be experienced as different emotions depending on what kind of attributions we make for what we are experiencing. This intriguing possibility of 'emotional lability' was the focus of a classic study by Schachter and Singer (1962) – see Box 3.1 and Figure 3.3.

For a time, the most significant implication of Schachter's work was the possibility that it might be applied in therapy (Valins and Nisbett, 1972). If emotions depend on what cognitive label is assigned, through causal attribution to undifferentiated arousal, then it might, for example, be possible to transform depression into cheerfulness simply by reattributing arousal. A paradigm was devised to test this idea – called the misattribution paradigm (Valins, 1966). People who feel anxious and bad about themselves because they attribute arousal internally are encouraged to attribute arousal to external factors. For example, someone who is shy can be encouraged to attribute the arousal associated with meeting new people to ordinary environmental causes rather than to personality deficiencies and thus no longer feel shy. A number of experiments have employed this type of intervention with some success (e.g. Olson, 1988; Storms and Nisbett, 1970; for critical reviews of clinical applications of attribution theory, see Buchanan and Seligman, 1995; Forsterling, 1988).

Research classic 3.1
Context can affect how we label an emotion

In the late nineteenth century the famous psychologist William James turned the usual account of how we experience an emotion on its head. As ordinary folk, we might believe that our mental images cause the body to react, and define our feelings as an emotion. However, James argued that the body first responds automatically to a stimulus, and then we interpret our bodily responses on the basis of what is going on around us: if we see a bear, we run, and a little later our pounding heart tells us that we are afraid.

One of Stanley Schachter's experiments dealing with 'emotional lability' brought this idea into the laboratory and gave it an attributional flavour (Schachter and Singer, 1962). Male students were given an injection of either adrenalin (the drug epinephrine), or a placebo (salt water) that provided a control condition. Students who had been administered the drug were then allocated to one of three conditions: (1) they were correctly informed that this would cause symptoms of arousal (e.g. rapid breathing, increased heart rate); (2) they were given no explanation;

or (3) they were misinformed that they might experience a slight headache and some dizziness. All participants then waited in a room with a confederate to complete some paperwork. For half the participants, the confederate behaved euphorically (engaging in silly antics and making paper aeroplanes), and for the other half angrily (ripping up the papers and stomping around).

Schachter and Singer predicted that the 'drug-uninformed' participants would experience arousal and would search for a cause in their immediate environment (see Figure 3.3). The behaviour of the confederate would act as the salient cue, encouraging participants in the 'euphoric' condition to feel euphoric and those in the 'angry' condition to feel angry. The emotions of the other two drug groups and the control group would be unaffected by the behaviour of the confederate: the control participants had experienced no arousal from the drug, and the correctly informed and misinformed participants already had an explanation for their arousal. The results of the experiment largely supported these predictions.

However, initial enthusiasm for emotional lability and the clinical application of misattribution waned in the light of subsequent criticisms (Reisenzein, 1983):

- Emotions may be significantly less labile than was originally thought (Maslach, 1979). Environmental cues are not readily accepted as bases for inferring emotions from unexplained arousal, and because unexplained arousal is intrinsically unpleasant, people have a propensity to assign it a negative label.

- The misattribution effect seems to be limited (Parkinson, 1985). It is largely restricted to laboratory investigations and is unreliable and short-lived. It is not clear that the effect is

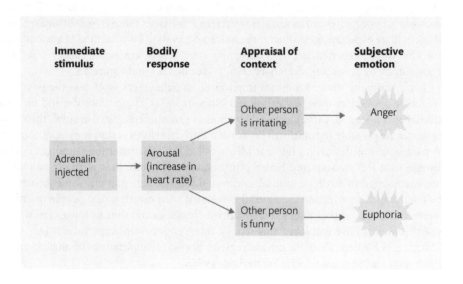

Figure 3.3 Attributing a likely cause to an experimentally induced emotion

mediated by an attribution process, and in any case it is restricted to a limited range of emotion-inducing stimuli.

The more general idea that cognition, in particular cognitive appraisals of the surrounding situation, plays an important role in generation and experience of emotion has, however, fed into the contemporary revival of research on affect and emotion (e.g. Blascovich, 2008; Forgas, 2006; Keltner and Lerner, 2010; **see Chapter 2**). Indeed, attribution theory was the conceptual springboard for the later exploration of the concept of appraisal (e.g. Lazarus, 1991).

Attributions for our own behaviour

One far-reaching implication of treating emotion as cognitively labelled arousal is that people may make more general attributions for their *own* behaviour. This idea has been elaborated by Daryl Bem (1967, 1972) in his self-perception theory. **(Because this is an account of how people construct their self-concept, we describe it in Chapter 4 which explores the nature of self and identity.)**

Self-perception theory
Bem's idea that we gain knowledge of ourselves only by making self-attributions: for example, we infer our own attitudes from our own behaviour.

Task performance attributions

Attributional dimensions of task achievement are the focus of another extension of attribution theory, by Bernard Weiner (1979, 1985, 1986). Weiner was interested in the causes and consequences of the sorts of attribution made for people's success or failure on a task – for example, success or failure in a social psychology examination. He believed that in making an achievement attribution, we consider three performance dimensions:

1 *Locus* – is the performance caused by the actor (internal) or the situation (external)?
2 *Stability* – is the internal or external cause a stable or unstable one?
3 *Controllability* – to what extent is future task performance under the actor's control?

These produce eight different types of explanation for task performance (see Figure 3.4). For example, failure in a social psychology examination might be attributed to 'unusual –hindrance

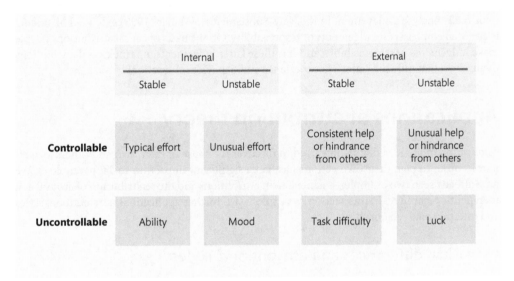

Figure 3.4 Achievement attributions as a function of locus, stability and controllability
How we attribute someone's task achievement depends on:

• *Locus* – is the performance caused by the actor (internal) or the situation (external)?
• *Stability* – is the internal or external cause a stable or unstable one?
• *Controllability* – to what extent is future task performance under the actor's control?

Achievement attribution
Isn't she lovely? Will Miss World attribute her new crown to her hard work, her physical beauty, biased judges – or perhaps to luck?

from others' (the top right-hand box in Figure 3.4) if the student was intelligent (therefore, failure is external) and was disturbed by a nearby student sneezing from hay fever (unstable and controllable, because in future examinations the sneezing student might not be present or have taken an antihistamine, and/or one could choose to sit in a place away from the sneezing student).

Weiner's model is a dynamic one, in that people first assess whether someone has succeeded or failed and accordingly experience positive or negative emotion. They then make a causal attribution for the performance, which produces more specific emotions (e.g. pride for doing well due to ability) and expectations that influence future performance.

The model is relatively well supported by experiments that provide participants with performance outcomes and locus, stability and controllability information, often under role-playing conditions (e.g. de Jong, Koomen and Mellenbergh, 1988; Frieze and Weiner, 1971). However, critics have suggested that the controllability dimension may be less important than was first thought. They have also wondered to what extent people outside controlled laboratory conditions really analyse achievement in this way. Subsequently, Weiner (1995) extended his model to place an emphasis on judgements of responsibility. On the basis of causal attributions people make judgements of responsibility, and it is these latter judgements, not the causal attributions themselves, that influence affective experience and behavioural reactions.

Applications of attribution theory

Application of the idea that people need to discover the cause of their own and others' behaviour in order to plan their own actions has had a significant impact on social psychology. We have already seen two examples – achievement attributions and the reattribution of arousal as a therapeutic technique. In this section, we explore two further applications: attributional styles and interpersonal relationships.

Individual differences and attributional styles

Attributional style
An individual (personality) predisposition to make a certain type of causal attribution for behaviour.

Research suggests there are enduring individual differences in the sorts of attributions that people make: their **attributional style**. Julian Rotter (1966) believes that people differ in the amount of control they feel they have over the reinforcements and punishments they receive. *Internals* believe they have significant personal control over their destiny – things happen because they make them happen. *Externals* are more fatalistic: they believe that they have little control over what happens to them – things simply occur by chance, luck or the actions of powerful external agents. To measure people's locus of control Rotter devised a 29-item scale. This scale has been used to relate locus of control to a range of behaviours, including political beliefs, achievement behaviour and reactions to illness. One problem with the scale is that it may not measure a unitary construct (i.e. a single personality dimension) but, rather, a number of relatively independent beliefs to do with control (Collins, 1974).

A number of other questionnaires have been devised to measure attributional styles – a tendency for individuals to make particular kinds of causal inference, rather than others, over time and across different situations (Metalsky and Abramson, 1981). Of these, the attributional style questionnaire or ASQ (Peterson et al., 1982; Seligman, Abramson, Semmel and von Baeyer, 1979) is perhaps the most widely known. It measures the sorts of explanation that people give for aversive (i.e. unpleasant) events on three dimensions: internal/external, stable/ unstable, global/specific. The global/specific dimension refers to how wide or narrow a range of effects a cause has – 'the economy' is a global explanation for someone being made redundant, whereas the closing of a specific company is a specific explanation. People who view aversive events as being caused by internal, stable, global factors have a 'depressive attributional style' (i.e. the glass is half empty), which may promote helplessness and depression and may have adverse health consequences (Abramson, Seligman and Teasdale, 1978; Crocker, Alloy and Kayne, 1988).

Another slightly different scale, called the attributional complexity scale (ACS), has been devised by Fletcher et al. (1986) to measure individual differences in the complexity of the attributions that people make for events.

The notion of attributional style as a personality trait is not without problems: for instance, the ASQ and the ACS provide only limited evidence of cross-situational individual consistency in causal attribution (e.g. Cutrona, Russell and Jones, 1985). Also not without problems is the important link between attributional style, learnt helplessness and clinical depression. Although more than 100 studies involving about 15,000 participants confirm an average correlation of 0.30 between attributional style and depression (Sweeney, Anderson and Bailey, 1986), this does not prove causation – it is a correlation in which one factor explains 9 per cent of variance in the other.

More useful are diachronic studies, which show that attributional style measured at one time predicts depressive symptoms at a later date (Nolen-Hoeksma, Girgus and Seligman, 1992), but again causality is not established. Causality is difficult to establish because it is of course unethical to induce clinical depression in experimental settings. We are largely left with experimental evidence from studies of transitory mood, which is a rather pale analogue of depression. Is it justified to generalise from feelings about doing well or poorly on a trivial laboratory task to full-blown clinical depression?

Interpersonal relationships

Attributions play an important role in interpersonal relationships **(see Chapter 14)**; particularly close interpersonal relationships (e.g. friendship and marriage) where attributions are *communicated* to fulfil a variety of functions: for instance, to explain, justify or excuse behaviour, as well as to attribute blame and instil guilt (Hilton, 1990).

Harvey (1987) suggests that interpersonal relationships go through three basic phases: formation, maintenance and dissolution (see also Moreland and Levine's (1982, 1984) model of group socialisation **in Chapter 8**). Fincham (1985) explains that during the formation stage, attributions reduce ambiguity and facilitate communication and an understanding of the relationship. In the maintenance phase, the need to make attributions wanes because stable personalities and relationships have been established. The dissolution phase is characterised by an increase in attributions in order to regain an understanding of the relationship.

A notable feature of many interpersonal relationships is attributional conflict (Horai, 1977), in which partners proffer divergent causal interpretations of behaviour and disagree over what

Attributing blame
Couples sometimes cannot agree on what is cause and what is effect. For example, does nagging cause withdrawal or withdrawal cause nagging?

attributions to adopt. Often partners cannot even agree on a cause–effect sequence, one exclaiming, 'I withdraw because you nag', the other, 'I nag because you withdraw'. From research mainly on heterosexual couples, attributional conflict has been shown to be correlated strongly with relationship dissatisfaction (Kelley, 1979; Orvis, Kelley and Butler, 1976; Sillars, 1981).

However, the main thrust of research has focused on the role of attributions in heterosexual marital satisfaction (e.g. Fincham and Bradbury, 1991; Fletcher and Thomas, 2000; Noller and Ruzzene, 1991). An important aim has been to distinguish between distressed and non-distressed spouses in order to provide therapy for dysfunctional marital relationships. Correlational studies (e.g. Fincham and O'Leary, 1983; Holtzworth-Munroe and Jacobson, 1985) reveal that happily married (or non-distressed) spouses tend to credit their partners for positive behaviour by citing internal, stable, global and controllable factors to explain them. Negative behaviour is explained away by ascribing it to causes viewed as external, unstable, specific and uncontrollable. Distressed couples behave in exactly the opposite way.

While women tend fairly regularly to think in causal terms about the relationship, men do so only when the relationship becomes dysfunctional. In this respect, and contrary to popular opinion, men may be the more diagnostic barometers of marital dysfunction – when men start analysing the relationship alarm bells should ring!

Do attributional dynamics produce dysfunctional marital relationships, or do dysfunctional relationships distort the attributional dynamic? This important causal question has been addressed by Fincham and Bradbury (1987; see overview by Hewstone, 1989), who obtained responsibility attributions, causal attributions and marital satisfaction measures from 39 married couples on two occasions 10–12 months apart. Attributions made on the first occasion were found reliably to predict marital satisfaction 10–12 months later, but only for wives.

Another longitudinal study (although over only a two-month period) confirmed that attributions do have a causal impact on subsequent relationship satisfaction (Fletcher, Fincham, Cramer and Heron, 1987). Subsequent, more extensive and better-controlled longitudinal studies have replicated these findings for both husbands and wives (Fincham and Bradbury, 1993; Senchak and Leonard, 1993).

Attributional biases

The attribution process, then, is clearly subject to bias: for example, it can be biased by personality, biased by interpersonal dynamics or biased to meet communication needs. We do not approach the task of attributing causes for behaviour in an entirely dispassionate, disinterested and objective manner, and the cognitive mechanisms that are responsible for attribution may themselves be subject to imperfections that render them suboptimal.

Accumulating evidence for attributional biases and 'errors' occasioned a shift of perspective. Instead of viewing people as naive scientists or even statisticians (in which case biases were largely considered a theoretical nuisance), we now think of people as cognitive misers or motivated tacticians (Moskowitz, 2005; Fiske and Taylor, 2008; **see also Chapter 2**). People use cognitive short-cuts (called heuristics) to make attributions that, although not objectively correct all the time, are quite satisfactory and adaptive. Sometimes the choice of short-cut and choice of attribution can also be influenced by personal motives.

Biases are entirely adaptive characteristics of ordinary, everyday social perception (Fiske and Taylor, 2008; Nisbett and Ross, 1980; Ross, 1977). In this section, we discuss some of the most important attributional biases.

Correspondence bias and the fundamental attribution error

One of the best-known attribution biases is correspondence bias – a general tendency for people to overly attribute behaviour to stable underlying personality dispositions (Gilbert and Malone, 1995). This bias was originally called the fundamental attribution error, and although the correspondence bias and fundamental attribution errors are not identical (Gawronski, 2004), the terms are often used interchangeably – the change in the preferred label mainly reflects accumulating evidence that this bias or error may not be quite as 'fundamental' as originally thought (see below).

The fundamental attribution error, originally identified by Ross (1977), refers to a tendency for people to make dispositional attributions for others' behaviour, even when there are clear external/environmental causes. For example, in the Jones and Harris (1967) study mentioned earlier, American participants read speeches about Cuba's President Fidel Castro ostensibly written by fellow students. The speeches were either pro-Castro or anti-Castro, and the writers had ostensibly either freely chosen to write the speech or been instructed to do so. Where there was a choice, participants not surprisingly reasoned that those who had written a pro-Castro speech were in favour of Castro, and those who had written an anti-Castro speech were against Castro – an internal, dispositional attribution was made (see Figure 3.5).

However, a dispositional attribution was also made even when the speech writers had been *instructed* to write the speech. Although there was overwhelming evidence for an

Cognitive miser
A model of social cognition that characterises people as using the least complex and demanding cognitions that are able to produce generally adaptive behaviours.

Motivated tactician
A model of social cognition that characterises people as having multiple cognitive strategies available, which they choose among on the basis of personal goals, motives and needs.

Correspondence bias
A general attribution bias in which people have an inflated tendency to see behaviour as reflecting (corresponding to) stable underlying personality attributes.

Fundamental attribution error
Bias in attributing another's behaviour more to internal than to situational causes.

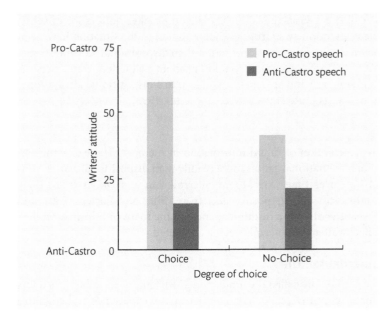

Figure 3.5 The fundamental attribution error: attributing speech writers' attitudes on the basis of their freedom of choice in writing the speech

- Students who freely chose to write a pro- or an anti-Castro speech were attributed with a pro- or anti-Castro attitude respectively.
- Although less strong, this same tendency to attribute the speech to an underlying disposition (the fundamental attribution error) prevailed when the writers had no choice and were simply instructed to write the speech.

Source: Based on data from Jones and Harris (1967)

exclusively external cause, participants seemed largely to overlook this and to still prefer a dispositional explanation – the fundamental attribution error. (Bearing these points in mind, how would you account for the different views held by Helen and Lewis? See the first focus question.)

Other studies furnish additional empirical evidence for the fundamental attribution error (Jones, 1979; Nisbett and Ross, 1980). Indeed, the fundamental attribution error, or correspondence bias, has been demonstrated repeatedly both inside and outside the social psychology laboratory (Gawronski, 2004; Gilbert, 1998; Jones, 1990). Correspondence bias may also be responsible for a number of more general explanatory tendencies: for example, the tendency to attribute road accidents unduly to the driver rather than to the vehicle or the road conditions (Barjonet, 1980); and the tendency among some people to attribute poverty and unemployment to the person rather than to social conditions (see below).

Pettigrew (1979) has suggested that the fundamental attribution error may emerge in a slightly different form in intergroup contexts where groups are making attributions about ingroup and outgroup behaviour – he calls this the *ultimate attribution error* (see below). Correspondence bias and the fundamental attribution error are closely related to two other biases: the *outcome bias* (e.g. Allison, Mackie and Messick, 1996) in which people assume that a person behaving in some particular way intended all the outcomes of that behaviour; and essentialism (Haslam, Rothschild and Ernst, 1998; Medin and Ortony, 1989), in which behaviour is considered to reflect underlying and immutable, often innate, properties of people or the groups they belong to.

> **Essentialism**
> Pervasive tendency to consider behaviour to reflect underlying and immutable, often innate, properties of people or the groups they belong to.

Essentialism can be particularly troublesome when it causes people to attribute stereotypically negative attributes of outgroups to essential and immutable personality attributes of members of that group (e.g. Bain, Kashima and Haslam, 2006; Haslam, Bastian, Bain and Kashima, 2006; Haslam, Bastian and Bissett, 2004). Indeed there is evidence that groups can use essentialism strategically to discriminate against outgroups (Morton, Hornsey and Postmes, 2009). For example, the stereotype of an outgroup as being laid-back, liberal and poorly educated becomes more pernicious if these attributes are considered immutable, perhaps genetically induced, properties of the group's members – the people themselves are considered to have personalities that are immutably lazy, immoral and stupid.

Different explanations of the fundamental attribution error have been proposed:

Focus of attention

The actor's behaviour attracts more attention than the background: it is disproportionately salient in cognition, stands out as the figure against the situational background, and is therefore overrepresented causally (Taylor and Fiske, 1978). Thus the actor and the actor's behaviour form what Heider (1958) called a 'causal unit'. This explanation makes quite a lot of sense. Procedures designed to focus attention away from the actor and on to the situation have been shown to increase the tendency to make a situational rather than dispositional attribution (e.g. Rholes and Pryor, 1982). When people really want to find out about a situation from a person's behaviour, they focus on the situation and are less likely to leap to a dispositional attribution – the fundamental attribution error is muted or reversed (e.g. Krull, 1993).

Differential forgetting

Attribution requires the representation of causal information in memory. There is some evidence that people tend to forget situational causes more readily than dispositional causes, thus producing a dispositional shift over time (e.g. Moore, Sherrod, Liu and Underwood, 1979; Peterson, 1980). Other studies show the opposite effect (e.g. Miller and Porter, 1980), and Funder (1982) has argued that the direction of shift depends on the focus of information processing and occurs immediately after the behaviour being attributed.

Cultural and developmental factors

The correspondence bias was originally called the fundamental attribution error because it was considered to be an automatic and universal outcome of perceptual experience and cognitive activity (e.g. McArthur and Baron, 1983). However, there is evidence that both developmental factors and culture may affect the correspondence bias. For example, in Western cultures, young children explain action in concrete situational terms and learn to make dispositional attributions only in late childhood (Kassin and Pryor, 1985; White, 1988). Furthermore, this developmental sequence itself may not be universal. Miller (1984; see Figure 3.7) reports data showing that Hindu Indian children do not drift towards dispositional explanations at all, but rather towards increasingly situational explanations.

These differences quite probably reflect different cultural norms for social explanation, or more basic differences between Western and non-Western conceptions of self – the autonomous and independent Western self and the interdependent non-Western self (Chiu and Hong, 2007; **see Chapters 4 and 16**). The fundamental attribution error is a relatively ubiquitous and socially valued feature of Western cultures (Beauvois and Dubois, 1988; Jellison and Green, 1981), but, although present, it is less dominant in non-Western cultures (Fletcher and Ward, 1988; Morris and Peng, 1994).

The fundamental attribution error may not be as fundamental as was first thought. It may, to some extent, be a normative way of thinking (**see discussion of norms in Chapters 7 and 8**). This is one reason why Gilbert and colleagues (e.g. Gilbert and Malone, 1995) recommend that the term 'correspondence bias' be used in preference to the term 'fundamental attribution error'. Indeed, according to Gawronski (2004) the two constructs are subtly different: technically, he argues, the fundamental attribution error is the tendency to underestimate the impact of situational factors; and the correspondence bias is the tendency to draw correspondent dispositional inferences from behaviour that is constrained by the situation.

Linguistic factors

One final, rather interesting, observation by Nisbett and Ross (1980) is that the English language is so constructed that it is usually relatively easy to describe an action and the actor in the same terms, and much more difficult to describe the situation in the same way. For example, we can talk about a kind or honest person, and a kind or honest action, but not a kind or honest situation. The English language may facilitate dispositional explanations (Brown and Fish, 1983; Semin and Fiedler, 1991).

The actor–observer effect

Imagine the last time a shop assistant was rude to you. You probably thought, 'What a rude person!' though perhaps put less politely – in other words, you made an internal attribution to the shop assistant's enduring personality. In contrast, how did you explain the last time *you* snapped at someone? Probably not in terms of your personality, more likely in terms of external factors such as time pressure or stress. The actor–observer effect (or the self–other effect) is really an extension of the correspondence bias. It refers to the tendency for people to attribute others' behaviour internally to dispositional factors and their own behaviour externally to environmental factors (Jones and Nisbett, 1972). Twenty years of research has provided substantial evidence for this effect (Watson, 1982), and some extensions and qualifications. For example, not only do we tend to attribute others' behaviour more dispositionally than our own, but we also tend to consider their behaviour to be more stable and predictable than our own (Baxter and Goldberg, 1988).

Actor–observer effect
Tendency to attribute our own behaviours externally and others' behaviours internally.

A number of factors can influence the actor–observer effect. People tend to make more dispositional attributions for socially desirable than socially undesirable behaviour, irrespective of who the actor is (e.g. Taylor and Koivumaki, 1976), and there is a tendency for actors to be more dispositional in attributing positive behaviour and more situational in attributing negative behaviour than are observers (e.g. Chen, Yates and McGinnies, 1988).

The actor–observer effect can be inverted if the actor knows that his or her behaviour is dispositionally caused. For example, you may 'adopt' an injured hedgehog in the full knowledge that you are a sucker for injured animals and you have often done this sort of thing in the past

(Monson and Hesley, 1982). Finally, the actor–observer effect can be abolished or reversed if the actor is encouraged to take the role of the observer regarding the behaviour to be attributed, and the observer the role of the actor. Under these circumstances, the actor becomes more dispositional and the observer more situational (e.g. Frank and Gilovich, 1989).

There are two main explanations for the actor–observer effect:

1 *Perceptual focus.* This explanation is almost identical to the 'focus of attention' explanation for the correspondence bias (see above). For the observer, the actor and the actor's behaviour are figural against the background of the situation. However, an actor cannot 'see' him/herself behaving, so the background situation assumes the role of figure against the background of self. The actor and the observer quite literally have different perspectives on the behaviour and thus explain it in different ways (Storms, 1973). Perceptual salience does indeed seem to have an important role in causal explanation. For example, McArthur and Post (1977) found that observers tended to make more dispositional attributions for an actor's behaviour when the actor was strongly illuminated than when dimly illuminated.

2 *Informational differences.* Another reason why actors tend to make external attributions and observers internal ones is that actors have a wealth of information to draw on about how they have behaved in other circumstances. They may actually know that they behave differently in different contexts and thus quite accurately consider their behaviour to be under situational control. Observers are not privy to this autobiographical information. They tend simply to see the actor behaving in a certain way in one context, or a limited range of contexts, and have no information about how the actor behaves in other contexts. It is therefore not an unreasonable assumption to make a dispositional attribution. This explanation, first suggested by Jones and Nisbett (1972), does have some empirical support (Eisen, 1979; White and Younger, 1988).

The false consensus effect

Kelley (1972b) identified consensus information as being one of the three types of information that people used to make attributions about others' behaviour (see above). One of the first cracks in the naive scientist model of attribution was McArthur's (1972) discovery that attributors in fact underused or even ignored consensus information (Kassin, 1979).

False consensus effect
Seeing our own behaviour as being more typical than it really is.

Subsequently, it became apparent that people do not ignore consensus information but rather provide their own consensus information. People see their own behaviour as typical and assume that under similar circumstances others would behave in the same way. Ross, Greene and House (1977) first demonstrated this false consensus effect. They asked students if they would agree to walk around campus for 30 minutes wearing a sandwich board carrying the slogan 'Eat at Joe's'. Those who agreed estimated that 62 per cent of their peers would also have agreed, while those who refused estimated that 67 per cent of their peers would also have refused.

There are well over 100 studies that bear testimony to the robust nature of the false consensus effect (Marks and Miller, 1987; Mullen, Atkins, Champion, Edwards, Hardy, Story and Vanderklok, 1985; Wetzel and Walton, 1985). The effect can arise in several ways:

- we usually seek out similar others and so should not be surprised to find that other people are similar to us;
- our own opinions are so salient to us, at the forefront of our consciousness, that they eclipse the possibility of alternative opinions;
- we are motivated to ground our opinions and actions in perceived consensus in order to validate them and build a stable world for ourselves.

Other research indicates that the false consensus effect is stronger for important beliefs, ones that that we care a great deal about (e.g. Granberg, 1987), and for beliefs about which we are very certain (e.g. Marks and Miller, 1985). External threat, positive qualities, the perceived similarity of others and minority group status all also inflate perceptions of consensus (e.g. Sanders and Mullen, 1983; Sherman, Presson and Chassin, 1984; van der Pligt, 1984).

The false consensus effect
This mid-winter arctic dipper discovers an attributional bias. Who else would swim here before breakfast?

Self-serving biases

In keeping with the motivated tactician model of social cognition (Fiske and Taylor, 1991) discussed earlier **in this chapter (also see Chapter 2)**, attribution is influenced by our desire for a favourable image of ourselves **(see Chapter 4)**. We are very good at producing self-serving biases. Overall, we take credit for our positive behaviours and successes as reflecting who we are and our intention and effort to do positive things (the *self-enhancing bias*). At the same time, we explain away our negative behaviours and failures as being due to coercion, normative constraints and other external situational factors that do not reflect who we 'really' are (the *self-protecting bias*). This is a robust effect that holds across many cultures (Fletcher and Ward, 1988).

Self-serving biases are clearly ego-serving (Snyder, Stephan and Rosenfield, 1978). However, Miller and Ross (1975) suggest that there may also be a cognitive component, particularly for the self-enhancing aspect. People generally expect to succeed and therefore accept responsibility for success. If they try hard to succeed, they associate success with their own effort, and they generally exaggerate the amount of control they have over successful performances. Together, these cognitive factors might encourage internal attribution of success. In general, however, it seems likely that both cognitive and motivational factors have a role (Anderson and Slusher, 1986; Tetlock and Levi, 1982) and that they are difficult to disentangle from one another (Tetlock and Manstead, 1985; Zuckerman, 1979).

Self-enhancing biases are more common than self-protecting biases (Miller and Ross, 1975) – partly because people with low self-esteem tend not to protect themselves by attributing their failures externally; rather, they attribute them internally (Campbell and Fairey, 1985). However, self-enhancement and self-protection can sometimes be muted by a desire not to be seen to be boasting over our successes and lying about our failures (e.g. Schlenker, Weingold and Hallam, 1990) – but not totally extinguished (Riess, Rosenfield, Melburg and Tedeschi, 1981). A fascinating self-serving bias, which most of us have used from time to time, acts in anticipation – self-handicapping, a term described by Jones and Berglas:

> The self-handicapper, we are suggesting, reaches out for impediments, exaggerates handicaps, embraces any factor reducing personal responsibility for mediocrity and enhancing personal responsibility for success.
>
> Jones and Berglas (1978, p. 202)

Self-serving biases
Attributional distortions that protect or enhance self-esteem or the self-concept.

Self-handicapping
Publicly making advance external attributions for our anticipated failure or poor performance in a forthcoming event.

People use this bias when they anticipate failure, whether in their job performance, in sport, or even in therapeutic settings when being 'sick' allows one to drop out of life. What a person often will do is to intentionally and publicly make external attributions for a poor showing even before it happens. Check the experiment about choosing between drugs in Box 3.2 and Figure 3.6.

Another self-serving instance is the attribution of responsibility (Weiner, 1995), which is influenced by an outcome bias (Allison, Mackie and Messick, 1996). People tend to attribute greater responsibility to someone who is involved in an accident with large rather than small consequences (Burger, 1981; Walster, 1966). For example, we would attribute greater responsibility to the captain of a tanker that spills millions of litres of oil than to the captain of a small

Research highlight 3.2
Self-handicapping: Explaining away your failure

Imagine that you are waiting to take an examination in a subject you find difficult and that you fully anticipate failing. You might well make sure that as many people as possible know that you have done no revision, are not really interested in the subject and have a mind-numbing hangover to boot. Your subsequent failure is thus externally attributed without it seeming that you are making excuses to explain away your failure.

To investigate this idea, Berglas and Jones (1978) had introductory psychology students try to solve some problems where the problems were either solvable or not solvable. They were told that they had done very well, and

before continuing with a second problem-solving task they were given the choice of taking either a drug called 'Actavil', which would ostensibly improve intellectual functioning and performance, or 'Pandocrin', which would have the opposite effect. As predicted, those students who had succeeded on the solvable puzzles felt confident about their ability and so chose Actavil in order to improve further (see Figure 3.6). Those who had succeeded on the not-solvable puzzles attributed their performance externally to luck and chose Pandocrin in order to be able to explain away more easily the anticipated failure on the second task.

Source: Based on data from Berglas and Jones (1978).

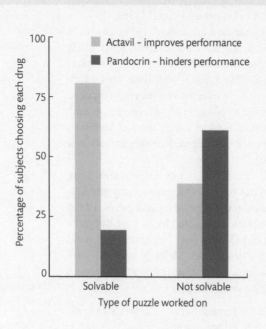

Figure 3.6 Self-handicapping: choosing a drug depends on a puzzle's solvability

- Students who had done well on a solvable puzzle could attribute their performance internally (e.g. to ability): anticipating an equally good performance on a second similar task, they chose a performance-enhancing drug, Actavil, rather than a performance-impairing drug, Pandocrin.

- Students who had done well on a not-solvable puzzle could only attribute their performance externally (e.g. to luck): with the prospect of an equivalent performance on the second task they chose the performance-impairing drug, as the self-handicapping option.

Source: Based on data from Berglas and Jones (1978)

fishing boat that spills only a few litres, although the degree of responsibility may actually be the same.

We can link this effect to the tendency for people to cling to an **illusion of control** (Langer, 1975) by believing in a *just world* (Furnham, 2003; Lerner, 1977). People like to believe that bad things happen to 'bad people' and good things to 'good people' (i.e. people get what they deserve), and that people have control over their outcomes. This pattern of attributions makes the world seem a controllable and secure place in which we can determine our own destiny.

The **belief in a just world** can result in a general pattern of attribution in which victims are deemed responsible for their misfortune – poverty, oppression, tragedy and injustice all happen because victims deserve it. Examples of the just world hypothesis in action are such views as the unemployed are responsible for being out of work, and rape victims are responsible for the violence against them. Another example is the belief, still held by some people, that the 6 million Jewish victims of the Holocaust were responsible for their own fate – that they deserved it (Davidowicz, 1975). Refer back to the second focus question. Just world beliefs are also an important component of many religious ideologies (Hogg, Adelman and Blagg, 2010).

The belief in a just world may also be responsible for self-blame. Victims of traumatic events such as incest, debilitating illness, rape and other forms of violence can experience a strong sense that the world is no longer stable, meaningful, controllable and just. One way to reinstate an illusion of control is, ironically, to take some responsibility for the event (Miller and Porter, 1983).

Illusion of control
Belief that we have more control over our world than we really do.

Belief in a just world
Belief that the world is a just and predictable place where good things happen to 'good people' and bad things to 'bad people'.

Intergroup attribution

Attribution theories are concerned mainly with how people make dispositional or situational attributions for their own and others' behaviour, and the sorts of bias that distort this process. The perspective is very much tied to interpersonal relations: people as unique individuals make attributions for their own behaviour or the behaviour of other unique individuals. However, there is another attributional context – intergroup relations – where individuals as group members make attributions for the behaviour of themselves as group members and others as either ingroup or outgroup members (Deschamps, 1983; Hewstone, 1989; Hewstone and Jaspars, 1982, 1984).

Examples of **intergroup attributions** abound. One example is the attribution of economic ills to minority outgroups (e.g. North African immigrants and refugees in Italy, Romani

Intergroup attributions
Process of assigning the cause of one's own or others' behaviour to group membership.

Intergroup attribution
This woman commemorates a young gang member who was stabbed to death. Retribution against the outgroup is likely

immigrants in France). Another is the explanation of behaviour in terms of stereotypical properties of group membership – for example, attributions for performance that are consistent with sex-stereotypes (Deaux, 1984), or racial stereotypes (Steele, Spencer and Aronson, 2002).

Intergroup attributions serve two functions, the first relating to ingroup bias and the second to self-esteem.

We have noted in the preceding section several attributional biases that are self-serving. By extension and by taking an intergroup perspective, we can now view ethnocentrism as an ingroup-serving bias. Socially desirable (positive) behaviour by ingroup members and socially undesirable (negative) behaviour by outgroup members are internally attributed to dispositions, and negative ingroup and positive outgroup behaviour are externally attributed to situational factors (Hewstone and Jaspars, 1982; Hewstone, 1989, 1990). This effect is more prevalent in Western than in non-Western cultures (Fletcher and Ward, 1988). It is common in team sports contexts, where the success of one's own team is attributed to internal stable abilities rather than effort, luck or task difficulty – we are skilful, they were lucky. This *group-enhancing* bias is stronger and more consistent than the corresponding *group-protective* bias (Mullen and Riordan, 1988; Miller and Ross, 1975).

Pettigrew (1979) has described a related bias, called the ultimate attribution error. This is an extension of Ross's (1977) fundamental attribution error, and takes us into the domain of attributions for outgroup behaviour. Pettigrew argued that negative outgroup behaviour is dispositionally attributed, whereas positive outgroup behaviour is externally attributed or explained away so that we preserve our unfavourable outgroup image. The ultimate attribution error refers to attributions made for outgroup behaviour only, whereas broader intergroup perspectives focus on ingroup attributions as well.

Taylor and Jaggi (1974) conducted an early study of intergroup attributions in southern India against a background of intergroup conflict between Hindus and Muslims. Hindu participants read vignettes describing Hindus or Muslims acting in a socially desirable way (e.g. offering shelter from the rain) or socially undesirable way (e.g. refusing shelter) towards them, and then chose one of a number of explanations for the behaviour. The results were as predicted. Hindu participants made more internal attributions for socially desirable than socially undesirable acts by Hindus (ingroup). This difference disappeared when Hindus made attributions for Muslims (outgroup).

Hewstone and Ward (1985) conducted a more complete and systematic follow-up, with Malays and Chinese in Malaysia and Singapore. Participants made internal or external attributions for desirable or undesirable behaviour described in vignettes as being performed by Malays or by Chinese. In Malaysia, Malays showed a clear ethnocentric attribution bias – they attributed a positive act by a Malay more to internal factors than a similar act by a Chinese, and a negative act by a Malay less to internal factors than a similar act by a Chinese (see Figure 3.7). The ingroup enhancement effect was much stronger than the outgroup derogation effect. The Chinese participants showed no ethnocentric bias – instead, they showed a tendency to make similar attributions to those made by Malays. In Singapore, the only significant effect was that Malays made internal attributions for positive acts by Malays.

Hewstone and Ward explain these findings in terms of the nature of intergroup relations in Malaysia and Singapore. In Malaysia, Malays are the clear majority group and Chinese an ethnic minority. Furthermore, relations between the two groups were tense and relatively conflictual at the time, with Malaysia pursuing a policy of ethnic assimilation. Both Malays and Chinese generally shared an unfavourable stereotype of Chinese and a favourable stereotype of Malays. In contrast, Singapore has been ethnically more tolerant. The Chinese are in the majority, and ethnic stereotypes are markedly less pronounced.

The important implication of this analysis is that ethnocentric attribution is not a universal tendency that reflects asocial cognition; rather, it depends on intergroup dynamics in a sociohistorical context. The sorts of attribution that group members make about ingroup and outgroup behaviour are influenced by the nature of the relations between the groups.

Ethnocentrism
Evaluative preference for all aspects of our own group relative to other groups.

Ultimate attribution error
Tendency to attribute bad outgroup and good ingroup behaviour internally, and to attribute good outgroup and bad ingroup behaviour externally.

Stereotype
Widely shared and simplified evaluative image of a social group and its members.

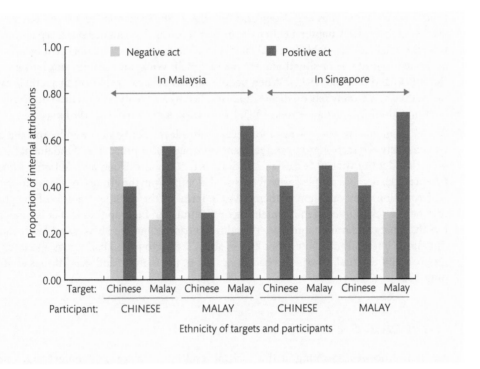

Figure 3.7 Internal attribution of positive and negative acts by Malays or Chinese as a function of attributor ethnicity

Malays showed an ethnocentric attributional bias in which a positive act was more internally attributed to a Malay than a Chinese, and a negative act less internally attributed to a Malay than a Chinese: the effect was more pronounced in Malaysia, where Malays are the dominant group and Chinese the ethnic minority, than in Singapore. Chinese did not show an ethnocentric attribution bias

Source: Based on data from Hewstone and Ward (1985)

This is consistent with Hewstone's (1989) argument that a proper analysis of attribution, more accurately described as social explanation, requires a careful articulation (i.e. theoretical integration or connection) of different **levels of analysis (or explanation)** (see Doise, 1986; **see also Chapter 1**). In other words, we need to know how individual cognitive processes, interpersonal interactions, group membership dynamics and intergroup relations all affect, are affected by and are interrelated with one another.

Further evidence for ethnocentric intergroup attributions comes from studies of inter-racial attitudes in educational settings in the United States (Duncan, 1976; Stephan, 1977); from studies of inter-ethnic relations between Israelis and Arabs (Rosenberg and Wolfsfeld, 1977) and between Hindus and Muslims in Bangladesh (Islam and Hewstone, 1993); and from studies of race, sex and social class-based attributions for success and failure (Deaux and Emswiller, 1974; Feather and Simon, 1975; Greenberg and Rosenfield, 1979; Hewstone, Jaspars and Lalljee, 1982).

More recently, Mackie and Ahn (1998) found that the *outcome bias,* the assumption that the outcomes of behaviour were intended by the person who chose the behaviour, is affected by whether the actor is a member of your group or not, and whether the outcome was desirable or not. Mackie and Ahn found that there was an outcome bias in the case of an ingroup member and a desirable outcome but not when the outcome was undesirable.

There are at least two processes that may be responsible for ethnocentric intergroup attributions:

1 *A cognitive process*: Social categorisation generates category-congruent expectations in the form of expectancies (Deaux, 1976), schemas (e.g. Fiske and Taylor, 1991), or group

Level of analysis (or explanation)
The types of concepts, mechanisms and language used to explain a phenomenon.

prototypes or stereotypes (e.g. Hogg and Abrams, 1988; Turner, Hogg, Oakes, Reicher and Wetherell, 1987; **see Chapter 11**).Behaviour that is consistent with our stereotypes or expectancies is attributed to stable internal factors, whereas expectancy-inconsistent behaviour is attributed to unstable or situational factors (e.g. Bell, Wicklund, Manko and Larkin, 1976; Rosenfield and Stephan, 1977). When people explain behaviour that confirms their expectancy, they may simply rely on dispositions implied by a stereotype, with little or no effort to consider additional factors (Kulik, 1983; Pyszczynski and Greenberg, 1981).

2 *A self-esteem process*: People's need for secure self-esteem can be nurtured by making comparisons between their ingroup and relevant outgroups. This process is a fundamental aspect of social identity theory (e.g., Tajfel and Turner, 1979; also Hogg and Abrams, 1988; **see Chapter 11**). Because people derive their social identity from the groups to which they belong (a description and evaluation of themselves in terms of the defining features of the group), they have a vested interest in maintaining or obtaining an ingroup profile that is more positive than that of relevant outgroups. The ethnocentric attributional bias quite clearly satisfies this aim: it internally attributes good things about the ingroup and bad things about the outgroup, and it externally attributes bad things about the ingroup and good things about the outgroup.

Social identity theory
Theory of group membership and intergroup relations based on self-categorisation, social comparison and the construction of a shared self-definition in terms of ingroup-defining properties.

Attribution and stereotyping

Attribution processes operating at the societal level in an intergroup context may play an important role in shaping the profile and dominance of the stereotypes we have of specific groups. Stereotyping is not only an individual cognitive activity **(see Chapter 2)**; it can also serve ego-defensive functions (making one feel good in contrast to others) and social functions (allowing one to fit in with other people's world views) (Snyder and Miene, 1994).

According to Tajfel (1981a), social groups may activate or accentuate existing stereotypes in order to attribute large-scale distressing events to the actions of specific outgroups – that is, scapegoats. For instance, during the 1930s in Germany the Jews were blamed for the economic crisis of the time. It was convenient to activate the 'miserly Jew' stereotype to explain in simplistic terms the lack of money: there is no money because the Jews are hoarding it. Stereotypes may also be elaborated to justify actions committed or planned against an outgroup (e.g. Crandall, Bahns, Warner and Schaller, 2011). For instance, a group might develop a stereotype of an outgroup as dull-witted, simple, lazy and incompetent in order to explain or justify the economic and social exploitation of that group.

Social knowledge and societal attributions

People do not wake up every morning and causally reconstruct their world anew. In general, we rely on well-learnt causal scripts (Abelson, 1981) and general causal schemata. We stop, think and make causal attributions only when events are unexpected or inconsistent with expectations (e.g. Hastie, 1984; Langer, 1978; Pyszczynski and Greenberg, 1981), when we are in a bad mood (Bohner, Bless, Schwarz and Strack, 1988), when we feel a lack of control (Liu and Steele, 1986), or when attributions are occasioned by conversational goals: for example, when we want to offer a particular explanation or justification of behaviour to someone with whom we are conversing (Hewstone and Antaki, 1988; Lalljee, 1981; Tetlock, 1983). Usually, we rely on a wealth of acquired and richly textured cultural knowledge that automatically explains what is going on around us. This knowledge resides in cultural beliefs, social stereotypes, collective ideologies and social representations (see Box 3.3).

Social representations
Collectively elaborated explanations of unfamiliar and complex phenomena that transform them into a familiar and simple form.

Real world 3.3
A very strange custom: The cultural context of causal attribution

Gün Semin tells a fictitious story about a Brazilian aborigine who visits Rio de Janeiro and then returns home to his tribe deep in the Amazonian rainforest to give an account of the visit (Semin, 1980, p. 292).

> On particular days more people than all those you have seen in your whole lifetime roam to this huge place of worship, an open hut the size of which you will never imagine. They come, chanting, singing, with symbols of their gods and once everybody is gathered the chanting drives away all alien spirits. Then, at the appointed time the priests arrive wearing colourful garments, and the chanting rises to war cries until three high priests, wearing black, arrive. All priests who were running around with sacred round objects leave them and at the order of the high priests be-

gin the religious ceremony. Then, when the chief high priest gives a shrill sound from himself they all run after the single sacred round object that is left, only to kick it away when they get hold of it. Whenever the sacred object goes through one of the two doors and hits the sacred net the religious followers start to chant, piercing the heavens, and most of the priests embark on a most ecstatic orgy until the chief priest blows the whistle on them.

This is, of course, a description of a football match by someone who does not know the purpose or rules of the game. It illustrates an important point. For causal explanations to be meaningful they need to be part of a highly complex general interpretative framework that constitutes our socially acquired cultural knowledge.

Social representations

One way in which cultural knowledge about the causes of things may be constructed and transmitted is described by Moscovici's theory of social representations (e.g. Farr and Moscovici, 1984; Lorenzi-Cioldi and Clémence, 2001; Moscovici, 1961, 1981, 1988; Purkhardt, 1995). **(See Chapter 5 for a discussion of the relationship between social representations and attitudes.)** Social representations are consensual understandings shared among group members. They emerge through informal everyday communication. They transform the unfamiliar and complex into the familiar and straightforward, and thus provide a common sense framework for interpreting our experiences.

An individual or a specialist interest group develops a sophisticated, non-obvious, technical explanation of a commonplace phenomenon (e.g. explaining mental illness in terms of biological or social factors rather than spiritual forces). This attracts public attention and becomes widely shared and popularised (i.e. simplified, distorted and ritualised) through informal discussion among non-specialists. It is now a social representation – an accepted, unquestioned common sense explanation that ousts alternatives to become the orthodox explanation.

Moscovici's original formulation focused on the development of the theory of psychoanalysis, but it is just as applicable to other formal theories and complex phenomena that have been transformed and simplified to become part of popular consciousness: for example, evolutionary theory, relativity theory, dietary and health theories, Marxist economics and AIDS. The theory of social representations has come under some criticism, often for the rather imprecise way in which it is formulated (e.g. Augoustinos and Innes, 1990). Nonetheless, it does suggest a way in which ordinary social interaction in society constructs commonsense or 'naïve' causal theories that are widely used to explain events (Heider, 1958).

One source of criticism is that it has been difficult to know how to analyse social representations quantitatively. However, steps have been taken towards the development of appropriate quantitative techniques (Doise, Clémence and Lorenzi-Cioldi, 1993), and Breakwell and Canter (1993) have assembled a collection of chapters describing in practical terms the variety of ways that different researchers have approached the measurement of social representations. These methods include qualitative and quantitative analyses of interviews, questionnaires, observational data and archival material. A good example of this methodological pluralism is Jodelet's (1991) classic description of social representations of mental illness in the small French community of Ainay-le-Chateau, in which questionnaires, interviews and ethnographic observation were all used.

Social representations, like norms **(see Chapters 7 and 8)**, tend to be grounded in groups and differ from group to group, such that intergroup behaviour can often revolve around a clash of social representations (Lorenzi-Cioldi and Clémence, 2001). For example, in Western countries attitudes and behaviour that promote healthy lifestyles are associated with higher social status, and health promotion messages tend to emanate from middle-class professional groups (Salovey, Rothman and Rodin, 1998). A social representations analysis suggests that these messages are relatively ineffective in promoting healthy lifestyles for non-middle-class people because they are inconsistent with the wider representational framework of a good life for such people.

The development of the European Union (EU) has provided fertile ground for social representation research (e.g. Chryssochoou, 2000) that connects with the study of European identity dynamics (e.g. Cinnirella, 1997; Huici, Ros, Cano, Hopkins, Emler and Carmona, 1997). The EU is, in many respects, a prototypical social representation. A relatively new and quite technical idea that has its roots in complex economic matters such as free trade and subsidies. But the EU is now an accepted and commonplace part of European discourse which often emphasises more emotive issues of national and European identity – although the recent global and European economic crises have refocused attention on economic and trade issues associated with the single currency and the concept of a European Central Bank.

Rumour

The process through which social representations are constructed has more than a passing resemblance to the way in which rumours develop and are communicated (Allport and Postman, 1947; DiFonzo and Bordia, 2007). One of the earliest studies of rumour was conducted by Allport and Postman (1945), who found that if experimental participants described a photograph to someone who had not seen the photo, and then this person described it to another person, and so on, only 30 per cent of the original detail remained after five retellings. Allport and Postman identified three processes associated with rumour transmission:

1 *Levelling* – the rumour quickly becomes shorter, less detailed and less complex.

2 *Sharpening* – certain features of the rumour are selectively emphasised and exaggerated.

3 *Assimilation* – the rumour is distorted in line with people's pre-existing prejudices, partialities, interests and agendas.

More naturalistic studies have found rather less distortion as a consequence of rumour transmission (e.g. Caplow, 1947; Schachter and Burdeck, 1955).

Whether or not rumours are distorted, and even whether rumours are transmitted at all, seems to depend on the anxiety level of those who hear the rumour (Buckner, 1965; Rosnow, 1980). Uncertainty and ambiguity increase anxiety and stress, which leads people to seek out information with which to rationalise anxiety, which in turn enhances rumour transmission. (Check the third focus question. Here is one reason why Rajna wanted to pass a rumour on.) Whether the ensuing rumour is distorted or becomes more precise depends on whether people approach the rumour with a critical or uncritical orientation. In the former case the rumour becomes refined, while in the latter (which often accompanies a crisis) the rumour becomes distorted.

Rumours always have a source, and often this source purposely elaborates the rumour for a specific reason. The stock market is a perfect context for rumour elaboration – and of course the consequences for ordinary people's everyday lives can be enormous. At the end of the 1990s, rumour played a clear role in inflating the value of 'dot-com' start-up companies, which then crashed in the NASDAQ meltdown early in 2000. More recently there was enormous build-up and hype surrounding the launching of Facebook as a public company on the stock market in May 2012 – Facebook shares lost 25 per cent of their value in the two weeks following the launch. Rumour also played a significant role in the global stock market crash at the end of 2008 and beginning of 2009 (the market lost more than half its value), and in reports about Greek economic collapse that depressed the stock market in August 2011 and May 2012.

Another reason why rumours are purposely elaborated is to discredit individuals or groups. An organisation can spread a rumour about a competitor in order to undermine the competitor's market share (Shibutani, 1966), or a group can spread a rumour to blame another group for a widespread crisis. A good example of this is the fabrication and promulgation of conspiracy theories (Graumann and Moscovici, 1987).

Conspiracy theories

Conspiracy theories are simplistic and exhaustive causal theories that attribute widespread natural and social calamities to the intentional and organised activities of certain social groups that are seen to form conspiratorial bodies set on ruining and then dominating the rest of humanity. One of the best-documented conspiracy theories is the myth, dating from the Middle Ages, of the Jewish world conspiracy (Cohn, 1966), which surfaces periodically and often results in massive systematic persecution. Other conspiracy theories include the belief that immigrants are intentionally plotting to undermine the economy, that homosexuals are intentionally spreading HIV, and that witches (in the Middle Ages) and Al-Qaida (most recently) are behind virtually every world disaster you care to mention (e.g. Cohn, 1975). Research suggests that it is people who show a personal willingness to conspire who tend to endorse conspiracy theories most readily (Douglas and Sutton, 2011).

Conspiracy theories wax and wane in popularity. They were particularly popular from the mid-seventeenth to the mid-eighteenth century:

> Everywhere people sensed designs within designs, cabals within cabals; there were court conspiracies, backstairs conspiracies, ministerial conspiracies, factional conspiracies, aristocratic conspiracies, and by the last half of the eighteenth century even conspiracies of gigantic secret societies that cut across national boundaries and spanned the Atlantic.
>
> Wood (1982, p. 407)

Conspiracy theory
Explanation of widespread, complex and worrying events in terms of the premeditated actions of small groups of highly organised conspirators.

The accomplished conspiracy theorist can, with consummate skill and breath-taking versatility, explain even the most arcane and puzzling events in terms of the devious schemes and inscrutable machinations of hidden conspirators. Billig (1978) believes it is precisely this that can make conspiracy theories so attractive – they are incredibly effective at reducing uncertainty (Hogg, 2007b, 2012). They provide a causal explanation in terms of enduring dispositions that can explain a wide range of events, rather than complex situational factors that are less widely applicable. Furthermore, worrying events become controllable and easily remedied because they are caused by small groups of highly visible people rather than being due to complex sociohistorical circumstances (Bains, 1983).

Not surprisingly, conspiracy theories are almost immune to disconfirming evidence. For example, in December 2006 the outcome of a three-year, 3.5 million pound enquiry into the death in 1997 of Princess Diana was reported – although there was absolutely no evidence that the British Royal family conspired with the British government to have her killed to prevent her marrying an Egyptian Muslim, this conspiracy theory still persists. There are also conspiracy theories about the 9/11 terrorist attacks in the United States in 2001 – some Americans are absolutely convinced it was the doing of the US government, and in parts of the Muslim world many people believe it was perpetrated by Israel (Lewis, 2004). A recent conspiracy theory has

Real world 3.4
Barack Obama is black and not really an American

Why is Barack Obama – the child of a Midwestern mother 'white as milk' and a Kenyan father 'black as pitch' (Obama, 2004, p. 10) – considered an African American, but never White?

Halberstadt, Sherman and Sherman (2011, p. 29)

This is an example of *hypodescent* – a tendency to categorise children whose parents come from different status groups, usually ethnic, into the subordinate group. Jamin Halberstadt and his colleagues have argued that hypodescent is a bias in the way we compare and classify features of majority and minority group members, and the importance that we give to distinctive features of the minority. **(See Chapter 2 for a detailed discussion of salient or attention-capturing stimuli.)**

In the case of Obama, the bias of hypodescent has been elaborated into a conspiracy myth. In the United States,

a full quarter of adult Americans, mainly right-wing social and religious conservatives, are 'birthers'. They believe that President Barak Obama was not born in America and thus is ineligible to be President and that there is a Democratic conspiracy to conceal this.

Even though there is overwhelming and incontrovertible proof that Obama was born in Hawaii (his official birth certificate was made public in 2008 and again in April 2011) birthers were not fazed – a 13 May 2011 Gallup poll showed that 23 per cent of Republican supporters remain birthers. Conspiracy theorists are tenacious. As it became increasingly difficult to sustain the belief that Obama was foreign-born, some birthers became 'schoolers' who believe that because Obama is black there is no way he could have gained entry to Harvard without cheating and receiving special favours, and that, wait for it, the Democrats have a conspiracy going to conceal this.

it that President Barack Obama is not only black, and presumably not white, but not really an American at all! (See Box 3.4.)

Societal attributions

The emphasis on attributions as social knowledge finds expression in research on the explanations that people give for large-scale social phenomena. In general, this research supports the view that causal attributions for specific phenomena are located within and shaped by wider, socially constructed belief systems.

For example, research into explanations for poverty reveals that both the rich and the poor tend to explain poverty in terms of poor people's behaviour rather than the situation that those people find themselves in (e.g. Feagin, 1972; Feather, 1974). This individualistic tendency is not so strong for people with a more left-wing or liberal ideology, or for people living in developing countries, where poverty is widespread (Pandey, Sinha, Prakash and Tripathi, 1982).

Explanations for wealth tend to depend on political affiliation. In Britain, Conservatives often ascribe it to positive individual qualities of thrift and hard work, while Labour supporters attribute it to the unsavoury individual quality of ruthless determination (Furnham, 1983). Not surprisingly, there are also cross-cultural differences: for example, individualistic explanations are very common in Hong Kong (Forgas, Morris and Furnham, 1982; Furnham and Bond, 1986).

Similarly, the sorts of explanation given for unemployment are influenced by people's wider belief and value systems (**Chapter 5**). Feather (1985) had Australian students give their explanations of unemployment on a number of dimensions. They preferred societal over individualistic explanations: for example, defective government, social change and economic recession were seen as more valid causes of unemployment than lack of motivation and personal handicap (see also Feather and Barber, 1983; Feather and Davenport, 1981). However, students who were politically more conservative tended to place less emphasis on societal explanations. Studies conducted in Britain also reveal that societal explanations are more prominent than individualistic explanations, and that there is a fair amount of agreement between employed and unemployed respondents (Furnham, 1982; Gaskell and Smith, 1985; Lewis, Snell and Furnham, 1987).

Other research has focused on the sorts of explanation that people give for riots (**social unrest, collective behaviour and riots are discussed in detail in Chapter 11**). Riots are enormously complicated social phenomena where there are both proximal and distal causes – a specific event or action might trigger the riot, but only because of the complex conjunction of wider conditions. For instance, the proximal cause of the 1992 Los Angeles riot may have been the acquittal of white police officers charged with the beating of a black motorist, Rodney King (see Box 11.1); however, this alone would have been unlikely to promote a riot without the background of racial unrest and socio-economic distress in the United States at the time.

As with explanations of poverty, wealth and unemployment, the sorts of explanation that people give for a specific riot seem to be influenced by the person's sociopolitical perspective (e.g. Litton and Potter, 1985; Reicher, 1984, 2001; Reicher and Potter, 1985; Schmidt, 1972). More conservative members of the establishment tend to identify deviance, or personal or social pathology, while people with more liberal social attitudes tend to identify social circumstances.

For example, Schmidt (1972) analysed printed media explanations of the spate of riots that occurred in American cities during 1967. The explanations could be classified on three dimensions:

1 legitimate–illegitimate

2 internal–external cause

3 institutional–environmental cause.

The first two dimensions were strongly correlated, with legitimate external causes (e.g. urban renewal mistakes, slum conditions) going together and illegitimate internal causes (e.g. criminal intent, belief that violence works) going together. Media sources on the political right tended to identify illegitimate internal causes, whereas those classified as 'left–centre' (i.e. liberal) emphasised legitimate external causes.

Finally, Sniderman, Hagen, Tetlock and Brady (1986) investigated the way in which people give explanations for racial inequality and have preferences for different government policies. They used a national sample of whites in the United States (in 1972) and were interested in investigating the influence of level of education. They found that less-educated whites employed an 'affect-driven' reasoning process. They started with their (mainly negative) feelings about blacks, then proceeded directly to advocate minimal government assistance. Having done this, they 'doubled back' to fill in the intervening link to justify their advocacy – namely that blacks were personally responsible for their own disadvantage. In contrast, better-educated whites adopted a 'cognition-driven' reasoning process, in which they reasoned both forwards and backwards. Their policy recommendations were based on causal attributions for inequality, and in turn their causal attributions were influenced by their policy preference.

Culture's contribution

The casual attributions and explanations that people proffer for events and behaviours are influenced not only by the nature of the information available, but also by people's wider belief and value systems. We have already seen, for example, the influence of sociopolitical values, educational status, group membership and ethnicity; and some evidence for the impact of culture.

People from different cultures often make very different attributions, make attributions in different ways or approach the entire task of social explanation in different ways (Chiu and Hong, 2007; Heine, 2012; Smith, Bond andKağitçibaşi, 2006). Consequently, the potential for cross-cultural interpersonal misunderstanding is enormous. For example, the Zande people of West Africa have a dual theory of causality, where common sense proximal causes operate

Culture and attribution

Is the puppet responsible for its own actions? Easterners are less likely than Westerners to make dispositional attributions about people – let alone puppets!

within the context of witchcraft as the distal cause (Evans-Pritchard, 1937; see also Jahoda, 1979) – which is, ironically, not really that different to moderate Christians' belief in the proximal operation of scientific principles within the context of God as the distal cause. For the Zande, an internal–external distinction would make little sense.

Another example: Lévy-Bruhl (1925) reported that the natives of Motumotu in New Guinea attributed a pleurisy epidemic to the presence of a specific missionary, his sheep, two goats and, finally, a portrait of Queen Victoria. Although initially quite bizarre, these sorts of attribution are easily explained as social representations. How much more bizarre are they than, for example, the postulation in physics of other universes and hypothetical particles shaped like strings or membranes as part of a unified theory to explain the origin and structure of the cosmos (Hawking, 1988; Hawking and Mlodinow, 2010) – Horgan exclaimed that 'This isn't physics any more. It's science fiction with mathematics' (Horgan, 2011, p. B7).

One area of cross-cultural attribution research is the correspondence bias (see above). We have seen that in Western cultures people tend to make dispositional attributions for others' behaviour (Gilbert and Malone, 1995; Ross, 1977). There is also evidence that such dispositional attributions become more evident over ontogeny (e.g. Pevers and Secord, 1973). In non-Western cultures, however, people are less inclined to make dispositional attributions (Carrithers, Collins and Lukes, 1986; Morris and Peng, 1994). This is probably partly a reflection of the more pervasive and all-enveloping influence of social roles in more collectivist non-Western cultures (Fletcher and Ward, 1988; Jahoda, 1982) and partly a reflection of a more holistic worldview that promotes context-dependent, occasion-bound thinking (Shweder and Bourne, 1982).

To investigate further the role of culture in dispositional attributions, Miller (1984) compared middle-class North Americans and Indian Hindus from each of four age groups (adults, and 15-, 11- and 8-year-olds). Participants narrated prosocial and antisocial behaviour and gave their own spontaneous explanations of the causes of this behaviour. Miller coded responses to identify the proportion of dispositional and contextual attributions that participants made. Among the youngest children there was little cross-cultural difference (see Figure 3.8). As age increased, however, the two groups diverged, mainly because the Americans increasingly adopted dispositional attributions. For context attributions the results were reversed.

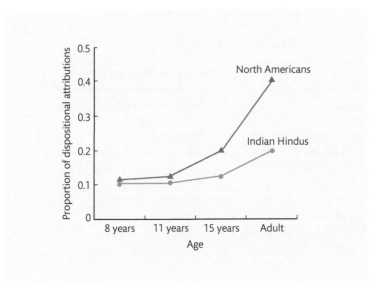

Figure 3.8 Dispositional attributions as a function of age and cultural background

North Americans and Indian Hindus initially do not differ in the proportion of dispositional attributions made for behaviour. However, by the age of 15 there is a clear difference that strengthens in adulthood, with Americans being significantly more dispositional than Indians in their attributions

Source: Based on data from Miller (1984)

The important lesson this study teaches us is that cultural factors have a significant impact on attribution and social explanation. **We return to the role of culture in social behaviour in Chapter 16.**

Summary

- People are naive psychologists seeking to understand the causes of their own and other people's behaviour.
- Much like scientists, people take account of consensus, consistency and distinctiveness information in deciding whether to attribute behaviour internally to personality traits and dispositions, or externally to situational factors.
- The attributions that we make can have a profound impact on our emotions, self-concept and relationships with others. There may be individual differences in propensities to make internal or external attributions.
- People are actually poor scientists when it comes to making attributions. They are biased in many different ways, the most significant of which are a tendency to attribute others' behaviour dispositionally and their own behaviour externally, and a tendency to protect the self-concept by externally attributing their own failures and internally attributing their successes.
- Attributions for the behaviour of people as ingroup or outgroup members are ethnocentric and based on stereotypes. However, this bias is affected by the real or perceived nature of intergroup relations.
- Stereotypes may originate in a need for groups to attribute the cause of large-scale distressing events to outgroups that have (stereotypical) properties that are causally linked to the events.
- People resort to causal attributions only when there is no readily available social knowledge (e.g. scripts, causal schemata, social representations, cultural beliefs) to explain things automatically.
- Social representations are simplified causal theories of complex phenomena that are socially constructed through communication contextualised by intergroup relations. Rumour may play a key role in social representations.
- Conspiracy theories are one particularly bizarre but sadly prevalent type of causal theory that often persists in the face of overwhelming evidence that the theory is wrong.

Key terms

Actor–observer effect
Attribution
Attributional style
Belief in a just world
Causal schemata
Cognitive miser
Consensus information
Consistency information
Conspiracy theory
Correspondence bias
Correspondent inference
Covariation model

Discount
Distinctiveness information
Essentialism
Ethnocentrism
External (or situational) attribution
False consensus effect
Fundamental attribution error
Hedonic relevance
Illusion of control
Intergroup attributions
Internal (or dispositional) attribution
Level of analysis (or explanation)

Motivated tactician
Naive psychologist (or scientist)
Non-common effects
Outcome bias
Personalism
Self-handicapping
Self-perception theory
Self-serving bias
Social representations
Societal identity theory
Stereotype
Ultimate attribution error

Literature, film and TV

JFK

1991 film by Oliver Stone. It stars Kevin Costner as a New Orleans district attorney who reopens the case to find out who really assassinated JFK on 22 November 1963, in Dallas, and what the process/plot behind it was. This is a wonderful encounter with conspiracy theories and people's need to construct a causal explanation, however bizarre, of a disturbing event. The film also stars Tommy Lee Jones and Sissy Spacek.

The Devils

Based on Aldous Huxley's 1952 book, *The Devils of Loudun*, this is a very harrowing 1971 Ken Russell cult classic, starring Vanessa Redgrave and Oliver Reed, about the inquisition and political intrigue in the church/state. The scenes are grotesque, evocative of the paintings of Hieronymus Bosch. It shows the awful lengths to which a group can go to protect its ultimate causal explanation – any divergence is seen as heresy or blasphemy, and is severely and cruelly punished in order to make sure that everyone believes in its explanation of the nature of things.

Macbeth

Shakespeare's 1606/07 tragedy in which three witches prophesise a string of evil deeds committed by Macbeth during his bloody rise to power, including the murder of the Scottish king Duncan. The causal question is whether the prophecy caused the events – or was there some other complex of causes.

Legally Blonde

2001 ward-winning comedy directed by Robert Luketic and starring Reese Witherspoon. Witherspoon plays Elle Woods, a stereotypically breathless self-confident blonde southern California sorority girl – sounds pretty much one of a million such films, but this one is actually funny, relatively clever and has more going on. It is a nice vehicle for exploring the way that people construct someone's personality from the way they appear and behave, and then it can be difficult for the target to break free of the pigeon hole. Elle, like most people, is a more complex and less superficial character than her appearance and some of her behaviour leads one to think. But as she tries to be taken seriously as a law student and a person, she finds that those around her continually construct her personality on the basis of superficial cues.

Guided questions

MyPsychLab

1 What is meant by *locus of control*? Compare the contributions that are made by people's efforts to their chances of success in life with those made by fate or by circumstances. See what other students think about these issues in Chapter 6 of MyPsychLab at **www.mypsychlab.com** (watch *IT video: Where is your locus of control?*).

2 Do attributional dynamics lead to problems in close relationships, or vice versa?

3 Sometimes our mental short-cuts lead us into error. One of these is *correspondence bias*. Describe and illustrate this concept.

4 What is meant by self-handicapping? Provide a real-world setting in which it can be applied.

5 The term *conspiracy theory* has entered everyday language. Can social psychology help us understand what purpose these theories serve?

Learn more

Fiske, S. T., and Taylor, S. E. (2008). *Social cognition: From brains to culture*. New York: McGraw-Hill. This is the third edition of Fiske and Taylor's classic social cognition text – it is comprehensive, detailed and well written, and covers the recent development of social neuroscience.

Fletcher, G., and Fincham, F. D. (eds) (1991). *Cognition in close relationships*. Hillsdale, NJ: Erlbaum. A collection of leading scholars provide detailed chapters on attribution and other sociocognitive approaches to close relationships.

Hewstone, M. (1989). *Causal attribution: From cognitive processes to collective beliefs*. Oxford: Blackwell. A comprehensive and detailed coverage of attribution theory and research, which also includes coverage of European perspectives that locate attribution processes in the context of society and intergroup relations.

Hilton, D. J. (2007). Causal explanation: From social perception to knowledge-based causal attribution. In A. W. Kruglanski, and E. T. Higgins (eds), *Social psychology: Handbook of basic principles* (2nd edn, pp. 232–53). New York: Guilford. A comprehensive coverage of research on causal attribution processes and social explanation.

Macrae, C. N., and Quadflieg, S. (2010). Perceiving people. In S. T. Fiske, D. T. Gilbert, and G. Lindzey (eds), *Handbook of social psychology* (5th edn, Vol. 1, pp. 428–63). New York: Wiley. Comprehensive coverage of what we know about person perception – how we form and use our cognitive representations of people.

McClure, J. (1991). *Explanations, accounts, and illusions: A critical analysis*. Cambridge, UK: Cambridge University Press. A critical, wide-ranging and eclectic discussion of attribution as social explanation.

Moskowitz, G. B. (2005). *Social cognition: Understanding self and others*. New York: Guilford. A relatively recent comprehensive social cognition text that is written in an accessible style as an introduction to the topic.

Smith, E. R. (1994). Social cognition contributions to attribution theory and research. In P. G. Devine, D. L. Hamilton, and T. M. Ostrom (eds), *Social cognition: Impact on social psychology* (pp. 77–108). San Diego, CA: Academic Press. A focused coverage of social cognitive dimensions of attribution processes.

Trope, Y., and Gaunt, R. (2007). Attribution and person perception. In M. A. Hogg, and J. Cooper (eds), *The SAGE handbook of social psychology: Concise student edition* (pp. 176–94). London: SAGE. A relatively recent, comprehensive and above all readable overview of attribution research.

Weary, G., Stanley, M. A., and Harvey, J. H. (1989). *Attribution*. New York: Springer-Verlag. A discussion of applications of attribution theory and the operation of attribution processes in clinical settings and everyday life outside the laboratory.

MyPsychLab

Use MyPsychLab to refresh your understanding, assess your progress and go further with interactive summaries, questions, podcasts and much more. To buy access or register your code, visit **www.mypsychlab.com.**

CHAPTER 7
Social influence

Chapter contents

Focus questions

1   While serving in the army on combat duty, Private Jones is ordered to set booby traps in a neighbourhood that is also used as a playground by small children. Although he feels very distressed about doing this, he sees that other members of his unit are already obeying the order. What is Private Jones likely to do and how will he feel about it? What factors might make it easier for him to disobey this order?

2   Tom entered an elevator with several people already in it. Like them, he positioned himself to face the door. At the next floor, a few more people entered, and stood immediately in front of him. As the elevator moved off, they all turned to face the rear. Tom thought this was strange, even stupid. Why did they do this? Should he do the same? (Watch *The Asch Experiment: Hilarious! Or Is It?* – http://www.youtube.com/watch?v=uuvGh_n3I_M)

3   While playing Trivial Pursuit®, Sarah simply agrees with Paul and John when they decide which plane first broke the sound barrier. They say she is a typical conformist female. What do you say?

4   Aleksei and Ivan work for a large multinational corporation. They agree that many conditions of their employment are highly exploitative. Aleksei wants to take the corporation on, but Ivan exclaims, 'How can we possibly succeed? There are only two of us up against the system!' What tips would you give Aleksei and Ivan to improve their chance of success?

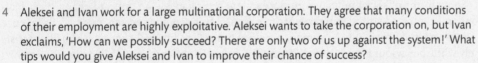
will use which involves getting you to decide to buy a car by giving you a very low price

Go to MyPsychLab to explore video and test your understanding of key topics addressed in this chapter.

Types of social influence

Social psychology was defined by Gordon Allport as 'an attempt to understand and explain how the thoughts, feelings, and behaviours of individuals are influenced by the actual, imagined, or implied presence of others' (1954a, p. 5). This widely accepted and often quoted definition of social psychology (**see Chapter 1**) identifies a potential problem for the study of social influence – how does the study of social influence differ from the study of social psychology as a whole? There is no straightforward answer. Instead, we will look at the kinds of issues that are researched by social psychologists who claim to be studying social influence.

Social life is characterised by argument, conflict and controversy in which individuals or groups try to change the thoughts, feelings and behaviour of others by persuasion, argument, example, command, propaganda or force. People can be quite aware of influence attempts and can form impressions of how affected they and other people are by different types of influence (**see Chapter 6**).

Social life is also characterised by norms: that is, by attitudinal and behavioural uniformities among people, or what Turner has called 'normative social similarities and differences between people' (1991, p. 2). One of the most interesting sets of issues in social influence, perhaps even in social psychology, is how people construct norms, how they conform to or are regulated by those norms, and how those norms change. Since norms are very much group phenomena, we discuss their structure, their origins and some of their effects later in the text (**Chapter 8**), reserving for this chapter discussion of the processes of conformity and resistance to norms.

Leaders play a key role in the construction of norms and, more broadly, in processes of influence and persuasion. Leadership is thus an influence process (Hogg, 2010), but it is also a group process because norms are emergent properties of groups, and where there are leaders there are followers. For this reason, and because leadership is so central to the human condition, we discuss leadership in detail later in the text (**see Chapter 9**).

Compliance, obedience, conformity

We are all familiar with the difference between yielding to direct or indirect pressure from a group or an individual, and being genuinely persuaded. For example, you may simply agree publicly with other people's attitudes, comply with their requests or go along with their behaviour, yet privately not feel persuaded at all. On other occasions, you may privately change your innermost beliefs in line with their views or their behaviour. This has not gone unnoticed by social psychologists, who find it useful to distinguish between coercive compliance on the one hand and persuasive influence on the other.

Some forms of social influence produce public compliance – an outward change in behaviour and expressed attitudes in response to a request from another person, or as a consequence of persuasion or coercion. As compliance does not reflect internal change, it usually persists only while behaviour is under surveillance. For example, children may obey parental directives to keep their room tidy, but only if they know that their parents are watching! An important prerequisite for coercive compulsion and compliance is that the source of social influence is perceived by the target of influence to have power; power is the basis of compliance (Moscovici, 1976).

However, because evidence for internal mental states is gleaned from observed behaviour it can be difficult to know whether compliant behaviour does or does not reflect internalisation (Allen, 1965) – although some recent neuroscience studies have begun to chart brain activity differences associated with compliant behaviour versus more deep-seated cognitive changes (cf. Berns, Chappelow, Zink, Pagnoni, Martin-Skurski and Richard, 2005). People's strategic

Social influence
Process whereby attitudes and behaviour are influenced by the real or implied presence of other people.

Norms
Attitudinal and behavioural uniformities that define group membership and differentiate between groups.

Compliance
Superficial, public and transitory change in behaviour and expressed attitudes in response to requests, coercion or group pressure.

control over their behaviour for self-presentation and communication purposes can amplify this difficulty. Research into compliance with direct requests has generally been conducted within an attitude-change and persuasion framework (**see Chapter 6**).

In contrast to compliance, other forms of social influence produce private acceptance and internalisation. There is subjective acceptance and conversion (Moscovici, 1976), which produces true internal change that persists in the absence of surveillance. Conformity is not based on power but rather on the subjective validity of social norms (Festinger, 1950): that is, a feeling of confidence and certainty that the beliefs and actions described by the norm are correct, appropriate, valid and socially desirable. Under these circumstances, the norm becomes an internalised standard for behaviour, and thus surveillance is unnecessary. However, in making determinations about the validity and self-relevance of group norms we often turn to leaders we trust as members of our group – and this can cause us to perceive them as having charisma (e.g., Platow, van Knippenberg, Haslam, van Knippenberg and Spears, 2006) and power (Turner, 2005).

Harold Kelley (1952) has made a valuable distinction between reference group and membership group. Reference groups are groups that are psychologically significant for people's attitudes and behaviour, either in the positive sense that we seek to behave in accordance with their norms, or in the negative sense that we seek to behave in opposition to their norms. Membership groups are groups to which we belong (which we are *in*) by some objective criterion, external designation or social consensus. A positive reference group is a source of conformity (which will be socially validated if that group also happens to be our membership group), while a negative reference group that is also our membership group has enormous coercive power to produce compliance. For example, if I am a student but I despise all the attributes of being a student, and if I would much rather be a lecturer because I value lecturer norms so much more, then 'student' is my membership group and is also a negative reference group, while 'lecturer' is a positive reference group but not my membership group. I will comply with student norms but conform to lecturer norms.

The general distinction between coercive compliance and persuasive influence is a theme that surfaces repeatedly in different guises in social influence research. The distinction maps on to a general view in social psychology that two quite separate processes are responsible for social influence phenomena. Thus Turner and colleagues refer to traditional perspectives on social influence as representing a dual-process dependency model (e.g. Turner, 1991). This dual-process approach is currently perhaps most obvious in Petty and Cacioppo's (1986b) elaboration–likelihood model and Chaiken's (Bohner, Moskowitz and Chaiken, 1995) heuristic–systematic model of attitude change (**see Chapter 6**; Eagly and Chaiken, 1993).

Power and influence

We have noted that compliance tends to be associated with power relations, whereas conformity is not. Compliance is affected not only by the persuasive tactics that people use to make requests but also by how much power they are perceived to have. Power can be interpreted as the capacity or ability to exert influence; and influence is power in action. For example, John French and Bert Raven (1959) identified five bases of social power, and later Raven (1965, 1993) expanded this to six: reward power, coercive power, informational power, expert power, legitimate power and referent power (see Figure 7.1).

Because it is almost a truism in psychology that the power to administer reinforcements or punishments should influence behaviour, there have been virtually no attempts to demonstrate reward and coercive power (Collins and Raven, 1969).One general problem is that reinforcement formulations, particularly of complex social behaviour, tend to strike enormous difficulty in specifying in advance what are rewards and what are punishments, yet find it very

Reference group
Kelley's term for a group that is psychologically significant for our behaviour and attitudes.

Membership group
Kelley's term for a group to which we belong by some objective external criterion.

Dual-process dependency model
General model of social influence in which two separate processes operate – dependency on others for social approval and for information about reality.

Power
Capacity to influence others while resisting their attempts to influence.

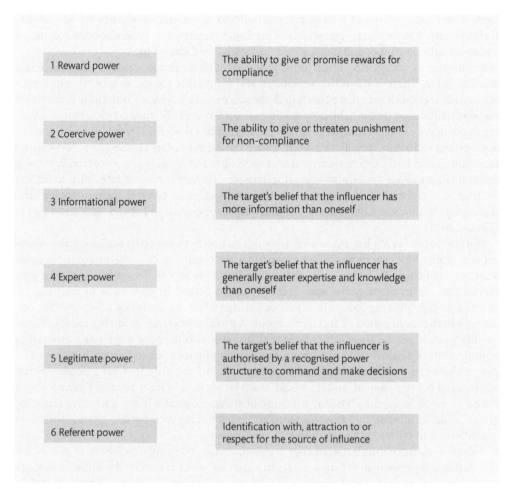

1 Reward power	The ability to give or promise rewards for compliance
2 Coercive power	The ability to give or threaten punishment for non-compliance
3 Informational power	The target's belief that the influencer has more information than oneself
4 Expert power	The target's belief that the influencer has generally greater expertise and knowledge than oneself
5 Legitimate power	The target's belief that the influencer is authorised by a recognised power structure to command and make decisions
6 Referent power	Identification with, attraction to or respect for the source of influence

Figure 7.1 There are many different sources of power that people can access to persuade others
Source: Based on Raven (1965)

easy to do so after the event. Thus reinforcement formulations tend to be unfalsifiable, and it may be more useful to focus on the cognitive and social processes that cause specific individuals in certain contexts to treat some things as reinforcement and others as punishment.

While information may have the power to influence, it is clearly not true that all information has such power. If we were earnestly to tell you that we had knowledge that pigs really do fly, it is very unlikely that you would be persuaded. For you to be persuaded, other influence processes would also have to be operating: for instance, the information might have to be perceived to be consistent with normative expectations, or coercive or reward power might have to operate.

However, information can be influential when it originates from an expert source. Bochner and Insko (1966) provided a nice illustration of expert power. They found that participants more readily accepted information that people did not need much sleep when the information was attributed to a Nobel Prize-winning physiologist than to a less prestigious source. The information lost the power to influence only when it became intrinsically implausible – stating that almost no sleep was needed (see Figure 6.2 **in Chapter 6**).

Legitimate power is based in authority and is probably best illustrated by a consideration of obedience (see below). Referent power may operate through a range of processes (see also Collins and Raven, 1969), including consensual validation, social approval and group identification (all of which are discussed below in the section on conformity). Focusing on legitimacy and power, Galinsky and his colleagues have pursued a line of research showing, among other things that people who believe they have legitimate power are more likely to take action to pursue goals – they feel empowered (Galinsky, Gruenfeld and Magee, 2003), and that people who do not feel their power is legitimate or associated with status can be extremely destructive (Fast, Halevy and Galinsky, 2012).

In addition to power as the ability to influence, there are other perspectives on social power (Fiske and Berdahl, 2007; Keltner, Gruenfeld and Anderson, 2003; Ng, 1996). For example, Fiske (1993b; Fiske and Dépret, 1996; Goodwin, Gubin, Fiske and Yzerbyt, 2000) presents a social cognitive and attributional analysis of power imbalance within a group (**see Chapter 9**). Serge Moscovici (1976) actually contrasts power with influence, treating them as two different processes. Power is the control of behaviour through domination that produces compliance and submission: if people have power, in this sense, they do not need influence; and if they can influence effectively, they need not resort to power. There is also a significant literature on intergroup power relations (e.g. Hornsey, Spears, Cremers and Hogg, 2003; Jost and Major, 2001; **see Chapter 11**).

Power can also be considered as a role within a group that is defined by effective influence over followers: that is, as a leadership position. However, as we shall see **in Chapter 9,** the relationship between power and leadership is not clear-cut. Some leaders certainly do influence by the exercise of power through coercion – they are the all-too-familiar autocratic or dictatorial leaders who may cajole and use ideological methods to keep their power elite in line, but most certainly exercise raw power over the masses (e.g. Moghaddam, in press). However, most leaders influence by persuasion and by instilling their vision in the rest of the group. Groups tend to permit their leaders to be idiosyncratic and innovative (Abrams, Randsley de Moura, Marques and Hutchison, 2008; Hollander, 1985), and they see their leaders as being charismatic (Avolio and Yammarino, 2003) and, in many cases, as having legitimate authority (Tyler, 1997).

Legitimate power
You may want the leader of a powerful nation to have expertise, charisma and to be greeted with respect. Does a buffed pose do it for you?

Generally, leadership researchers distinguish leadership from power (e.g. Chemers, 2001; Lord, Brown and Harvey, 2001). Leadership is a process of influence that enlists and mobilises others in the attainment of collective goals; it imbues people with the group's attitudes and goals, and inspires them to work towards achieving them. Leadership is not a process that requires people to exercise power over others in order to gain compliance or, more extremely, in order to coerce or force people. Leadership may actually be more closely associated with conformity processes than power processes and power may be social construct rather than a cause of effective leadership (Hogg, 2010; Hogg and van Knippenberg, 2003; Hogg, van Knippenberg and Rast, 2012; Reid and Ng, 1999).

John Turner (2005) has critiqued traditional perspectives on power and influence. The traditional perspective is that power rests on control of resources, and that power is the basis of influence that psychologically attaches people to groups. In contrast, Turner argues that attachment to and identification with a group is the basis of influence processes. Those who are influential are invested with power, and power allows control of resources. Turner's approach is a social identity analysis **(see Chapter 11)**. It invokes social identity theory's conceptualisation of influence in groups (e.g. Turner, 1981b; see below) and of leadership in groups (e.g. Hogg and van Knippenberg, 2003; **see Chapter 9**).

Obedience to authority

In 1951 Solomon Asch published the results of a now classic experiment on conformity, in which student participants conformed to erroneous judgements of line lengths made by a numerical majority (see later in this chapter for details). Some critics were simply unimpressed by this study: the task, judging line length, was trivial, and there were no significant consequences for self and others of conforming or resisting.

Stanley Milgram (1974, 1992) was one of these critics; he tried to replicate Asch's study, but with a task that had important consequences attached to the decision to conform or remain independent. He decided to have experimental confederates apparently administer electric shocks to another person to see whether the true participant, who was not a confederate, would conform. Before being able to start the study, Milgram needed to run a control group to obtain a base rate for people's willingness to shock someone *without* social pressure from confederates. For Milgram, this almost immediately became a crucial question in its own right. In fact, he never actually went ahead with his original conformity study, and the control group became the basis of one of social psychology's most dramatic research programmes.

A wider social issue influenced Milgram. Adolf Eichmann was the Nazi official most directly responsible for the logistics of Hitler's 'Final Solution', in which 6 million Jews were systematically slaughtered. Hannah Arendt (1963) reported his trial in her book *Eichmann in Jerusalem*, bearing the riveting subtitle *A report on the banality of evil*. This captures a scary finding, one that applied to Eichmann and later to other war criminals who have been brought to trial. These 'monsters' may not have been monsters at all. They were often mild-mannered, softly spoken, courteous people who repeatedly and politely explained that they did what they did not because they hated Jews (or Muslims, etc.) but because they were ordered to do it – they were simply obeying orders. Looks can, of course, be deceiving. Peter Malkin, the Israeli agent who captured Adolf Eichmann in 1960, discovered that Eichmann knew some Hebrew words, and he asked:

> 'Perhaps you're familiar with some other words,' I said. '*Aba. Ima.* Do those ring a bell?'
> 'Aba, Ima,' he mused, trying hard to recall. 'I don't really remember. What do they mean?'
> 'Daddy, Mommy. It's what Jewish children scream when they're torn from their parents' arms.' I paused, almost unable to contain myself. 'My sister's boy, my favorite playmate, he was just your son's age. Also blond and blue-eyed, just like your son. And you killed him.'

Genuinely perplexed by the observation, he actually waited a moment to see if I would clarify it. 'Yes,' he said finally, 'but he was Jewish, wasn't he?'

Malkin and Stein (1990, p. 110)

Milgram brought these strands together in a series of experiments with the underlying feature that people are socialised to respect the authority of the state (Milgram, 1963, 1974; see Blass, 2004). If we enter an **agentic state**, we can absolve ourselves of responsibility for what happens next. Participants in his experiments were recruited from the community by advertisement and reported to a laboratory at Yale University to participate in a study of the effect of punishment on human learning. They arrived in pairs and drew lots to determine their roles in the study (one was the 'learner', the other the 'teacher'). See Box 7.1 for a description of what happened next, and check how the shock generator looked in Figure 7.2.

Agentic state
A frame of mind thought by Milgram to characterise unquestioning obedience, in which people as agents transfer personal responsibility to the person giving orders.

Factors influencing obedience

Milgram (1974) conducted eighteen experiments, in which he varied different parameters to investigate factors influencing obedience. In all but one experiment the participants were 20–50-year-old males, not attending university, from a range of occupations and socioeconomic levels. In one study in which women were the participants, exactly the same level of obedience was obtained as with male participants. In an attempt to see if twenty-first-century Americans would be obedient like their 1970s counterparts, Burger (2009) conducted a partial replication of the original Milgram studies (a full replication was not possible due to research ethics concerns – see below). Burger discovered only slightly lower levels of obedience than in the original 1970s studies.

Milgram's experiment has been replicated in Italy, Germany, Australia, Britain, Jordan, Spain, Austria and The Netherlands (Smith, Bond and Kağıtçıbaşı, 2006). Complete obedience ranged from over 90 per cent in Spain and The Netherlands (Meeus and Raaijmakers, 1986), through over 80 per cent in Italy, Germany and Austria (Mantell, 1971), to a low of 40 per cent among Australian men and only 16 per cent among Australian women (Kilham and Mann, 1974). Some studies have also used modified settings: for example, Meeus and Raaijmakers (1986) used an administrative obedience setting in which an 'interviewer' was required to harass a 'job applicant'.

One reason why people continue to administer electric shocks may be that the experiment starts very innocuously with quite trivial shocks. Once people have committed themselves to a course of action (i.e. to give shocks), it can be difficult subsequently to change their mind. The process, which reflects the psychology of sunk costs in which once committed to a course of action people will continue their commitment even if the costs increase dramatically (Fox and Hoffman, 2002), may be similar to that involved in the foot-in-the-door technique of persuasion (Freedman and Fraser, 1966; **see Chapter 6**).

An important factor in obedience is *immediacy of the victim* – how close or obvious the victim is to the participant. Milgram (1974) varied the level of immediacy across a number of experiments. We have seen above that 65 per cent of people 'shocked to the limit' of 450 V when the victim was unseen and unheard except for pounding on the wall. In an even less immediate condition in which the victim was neither seen nor heard at all, 100 per cent of people went to the end. The baseline condition (the one described in detail above) yielded 62.5 per cent obedience. As immediacy increased from this baseline, obedience decreased: when the victim was visible in the same room, 40 per cent obeyed to the limit; and when the teacher actually had to hold the victim's hand down on to the electrode to receive the shock, obedience dropped to a still frighteningly high 30 per cent.

Immediacy may prevent dehumanisation of the victim (cf. Haslam, 2006; Haslam, Loughnan and Kashima, 2008), making it easier to view a victim as a living and breathing

Research classic 7.1
Milgram's procedure in an early study of obedience to authority

Together with the experimenter in the Yale laboratory, there was a teacher (the real participant) and a learner (actually, a confederate).

The learner's role was to learn a list of paired associates, and the teacher's role was to administer an electric shock to the learner every time the learner gave a wrong associate to the cue word. The teacher saw the learner being strapped to a chair and having electrode paste and electrodes attached to his arm. The teacher overheard the experimenter explain that the paste was to prevent blistering and burning, and overheard the learner telling the experimenter that he had a slight heart condition. The experimenter also explained that although the shocks might be painful, they would cause no permanent tissue damage.

The teacher was now taken into a separate room housing a shock generator (see Figure 7.2). He was told to administer progressively larger shocks to the learner every time the learner made a mistake – 15 V for the first mistake, 30 V for the next mistake, 45 V for the next, and so on. An important feature of the shock generator was the descriptive labels attached to the scale of increasing voltage. The teacher was given a sample shock of 45 V, and then the experiment commenced.

The learner got some pairs correct but also made some errors, and very soon the teacher had reached 75 V, at which point the learner grunted in pain. At 120 V the learner shouted out to the experimenter that the shocks were becoming painful. At 150 V the learner, or now more accurately the 'victim', demanded to be released from the experiment, and at 180 V he cried out that he could stand it no longer. The victim continued to cry out in pain at each shock, rising to an 'agonised scream' at 250 V. At

300 V the victim ceased responding to the cue words; the teacher was told to treat this as a 'wrong answer'.

Throughout the experiment, the teacher was agitated and tense, and often asked to break off. To such requests, the experimenter responded with an ordered sequence of replies proceeding from a mild 'please continue', through 'the experiment requires that you continue' and 'it is absolutely essential that you continue', to the ultimate 'you have no other choice, you must go on'.

A panel of 110 experts on human behaviour, including 39 psychiatrists, were asked to predict how far a normal, psychologically balanced human being would go in this experiment. These experts believed that only about 10 per cent would exceed 180 V, and no one would obey to the end. These predictions, together with the actual and the remarkably different behaviour of the participants are shown schematically in Figure 7.3).

In a slight variant of the procedure described above, in which the victim could not be seen or heard but pounded on the wall at 300 V and 315 V and then went silent, almost everyone continued to 255 V, and 65 per cent continued to the very end – administering massive electric shocks to someone who was not responding and who had previously reported having a heart complaint!

The participants in this experiment were quite normal people – forty 20–50-year-old men from a range of occupations. Unknown to them, however, the entire experiment involved an elaborate deception in which they were always the teacher, and the learner/victim was actually an experimental stooge (an avuncular-looking middle-aged man) who had been carefully briefed on how to react. No electric shocks were actually administered apart from the 45 V sample shock to the teacher.

Note: See extracts from Milgram's work at **http://www.panarchy.org/milgram/obedience.html**.

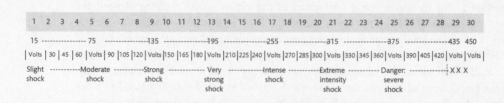

Figure 7.2 Milgram's shock generator
Participants in Milgram's obedience studies were confronted with a 15–450 Volt shock generator that had different descriptive labels, including the frighteningly evocative 'XXX', attached to the more impersonal voltage values
Source: Milgram (1974)

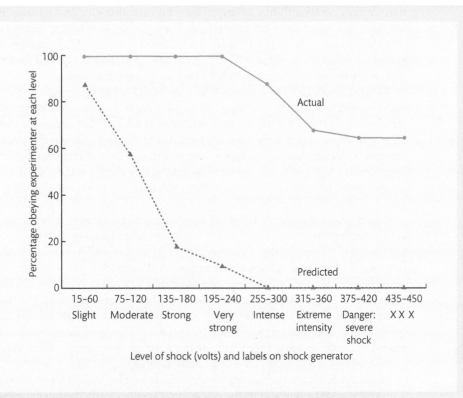

Figure 7.3 Predicted versus actual levels of shock given to a victim in Milgram's obedience-to-authority experiment

'Experts' on human behaviour predicted that very few normal, psychologically balanced people would obey orders to administer more than a 'strong' electric shock to the 'incompetent' learner in Milgram's experiment – in actual fact 65 per cent of people were obedient right to the very end, going beyond 'danger: severe shock', into a zone labelled 'XXX'

Source: Based on data from Milgram (1974)

Obedience to authority
This guard's uniform symbolises complete unquestioning obedience to the British Monarch as a legitimate authority

person like oneself and thus to empathise with their thoughts and feelings. Hence, pregnant women express greater commitment to their pregnancy after having seen an ultrasound scan that clearly reveals body parts (Lydon and Dunkel-Schetter, 1994); and it is easier to press a button to wipe out an entire village from 12,000 metres or from deep under the ocean in a submarine than it is to shoot an individual enemy from close range.

Another important factor is *immediacy of the authority figure*. Obedience was reduced to 20.5 per cent when the experimenter was absent from the room and relayed directions by telephone. When the experimenter gave no orders at all, and the participant was entirely free to choose when to stop, 2.5 per cent still persisted to the end. Perhaps the most dramatic influence on obedience is group pressure. The presence of two disobedient peers (i.e. others who appeared to revolt and refused to continue after giving shocks in the 150–210 V range) reduced complete obedience to 10 per cent, while two obedient peers raised complete obedience to 92.5 per cent.

Group pressure probably has its effects because the actions of others help to confirm that it is either legitimate or illegitimate to continue administering the shocks. Another important factor is the legitimacy of the authority figure, which allows people to abdicate personal responsibility for their actions. For example, Bushman (1984, 1988) had confederates, dressed in uniform, neat attire or a shabby outfit stand next to someone fumbling for change for a parking meter. The confederate stopped passers-by and 'ordered' them to give the person change for the meter. Over 70 per cent obeyed the uniformed confederate (giving 'because they had been told to' as the reason) and about 50 per cent obeyed a confederate who was either neatly attired or shabbily dressed (generally giving altruism as a reason). These studies suggest that mere emblems of authority can create unquestioning obedience.

Milgram's original experiments were conducted by lab-coated scientists at prestigious Yale University, and the purpose of the research was quite clearly the pursuit of scientific knowledge. What would happen if these trappings of legitimate authority were removed? Milgram ran one experiment in a run-down inner-city office building. The research was ostensibly sponsored by a private commercial research firm. Obedience dropped, but to a still remarkably high 48 per cent.

Milgram's research addresses one of humanity's great failings – the tendency for people to obey orders without first thinking about (1) what they are being asked to do and (2) the consequences of their obedience for other living beings. However, obedience can sometimes be beneficial: for example, many organisations would grind to a halt or would be catastrophically dysfunctional if their members continually painstakingly negotiated orders (think about an emergency surgery team, a flight crew, a commando unit). (Now consider the first focus question.) However, the pitfalls of blind obedience, contingent on immediacy, group pressure, group norms and legitimacy, are also many. For example, American research has shown that medication errors in hospitals can be attributed to the fact that nurses overwhelmingly defer to doctors' orders, even when metaphorical alarm bells are ringing (Lesar, Briceland and Stein, 1977).

In another study focusing on organisational obedience, 77 per cent of participants who were playing the role of board members of a pharmaceutical company advocated continued marketing of a hazardous drug merely because they felt that the chair of the board favoured this decision (Brief, Dukerich and Doran, 1991).

Before closing this it is worth noting that reservations have been expressed over the connection between destructive obedience as Milgram conceived it on one hand, and the Holocaust itself on the other. Cialdini and Goldstein (2004), in their review of social influence research, have pointed out that:

- Milgram's participants were troubled by the orders they were given, whereas many of the perpetrators of Holocaust atrocities obeyed orders willingly and sometimes sadistically.
- Although the Nazi chain of command and the experimenter in Milgram's studies had apparent legitimate authority, the experimenter had expert authority as well.

The ethical legacy of Milgram's experiments

One enduring legacy of Milgram's experiments is the heated debate that it stirred up (research ethics (Baumrind, 1964; Rosnow, 1981). Recall that Milgram's participants r believed they were administering severe electric shocks that were causing extreme pa another human being. Milgram was careful to interview and, with the assistance of a psychiatrist, to follow up the more than 1,000 participants in his experiments. There was no evidence of psychopathology, and 83.7 per cent of those who had taken part indicated that they were glad, or very glad, to have been in the experiment (Milgram, 1992, p. 186). Only 1.3 per cent were sorry or very sorry to have participated.

The ethical issues really revolve around three questions concerning the ethics of subjecting experimental participants to short-term stress:

1 Is the research important? If not, then such stress is unjustifiable. However, it can be difficult to assess the 'importance' of research objectively.

2 Is the participant free to terminate the experiment at any time? How free were Milgram's participants? In one sense they were free to do whatever they wanted, but it was never made explicit to them that they could terminate whenever they wished – in fact, the very purpose of the study was to persuade them to remain!

3 Does the participant freely consent to being in the experiment in the first place? In Milgram's experiments the participants did not give fully informed consent: they volunteered to take part, but the true nature of the experiment was not fully explained to them.

This raises the issue of deception in social psychology research. Kelman (1967) distinguishes two reasons for deceiving people: the first is to induce them to take part in an otherwise unpleasant experiment. This is, ethically, a highly dubious practice. The second reason is that in order to study the automatic operation of psychological processes, participants need to be naive regarding the hypotheses, and this often involves some deception concerning the true purpose of the study and the procedures used. The fallout from this debate has been a code of ethics to guide psychologists in conducting research. The principal components of the code are:

- participation must be based on fully informed consent;
- participants must be explicitly informed that they can withdraw, without penalty, at any stage of the study;
- participants must be fully and honestly debriefed at the end of the study.

Modern university ethics committee would be unlikely to approve the impressively brazen deceptions that produced many of social psychology's classic research programmes of the 1950s, 1960s and early 1970s. What is more likely to be endorsed is the use of minor and harmless procedural deceptions enshrined in clever cover stories that are considered essential to preserve the scientific rigour of much experimental social psychology. The main ethical requirements in all modern research involving human participants are also discussed in Chapter 1, and see the American Psychological Association's Code of Ethics (2002) at **http://www.apa.org/ethics/code2002.html**.

Conformity

The formation and influence of norms

Although much social influence is reflected in compliance with direct requests and obedience to authority, social influence can also operate in a less direct manner, through **conformity** to social or group norms. For example, Floyd Allport (1924) observed that people in groups gave

Conformity
Deep-seated, private and enduring change in behaviour and attitudes due to group pressure.

less extreme and more conservative judgements of odours and weights than when they were alone. It seemed as if, in the absence of direct pressure, the group could cause members to converge and thus become more similar to one another.

Muzafer Sherif (1936) explicitly linking this convergence effect to the development of *group norms*. Proceeding from the premise that people need to be certain and confident that what they are doing, thinking or feeling is correct and appropriate, Sherif argued that people use the behaviour of others to establish the range of possible behaviour: we can call this the frame of reference, or relevant *social comparative context*. Average, central or middle positions in such frames of reference are typically perceived to be more correct than fringe positions, thus people tend to adopt them. Sherif believed that this explained the origins of social norms and the concomitant convergence that accentuates consensus within groups.

To test this idea, he conducted his classic studies using autokinesis (see Box 7.2 and Figure 7.4 for details), in which small groups making estimates of physical movement quickly converged over a series of trials on the mean of the group's estimates and remained influenced by this norm even when they later made estimates alone.

The origins, structure, function and effects of norms are discussed later **(see Chapter 8)**. However, it is worth emphasising that normative pressure is one of the most effective ways to change people's behaviour. For example, we noted earlier **(see Chapter 6)** that Kurt Lewin (1947) tried to encourage American housewives to change the eating habits of their families – specifically to eat more offal (beef hearts and kidneys). Three groups of thirteen to seventeen housewives attended an interesting factual lecture that, among other things, stressed how valuable such a change in eating habits would be to the war effort (it was 1943). Another three groups were given information but were also encouraged to talk among themselves and arrive at some kind of consensus (i.e. establish a norm) about buying the food.

A follow-up survey revealed that the norm was far more effective than the abstract information in causing some change in behaviour: only 3 per cent of the information group had changed their behaviour, compared with 32 per cent of the norm group. Subsequent research confirmed that it was the norm not the attendant discussion that was the crucial factor (Bennett, 1955).

Yielding to majority group pressure

Like Sherif, Solomon Asch (1952) believed that conformity reflects a relatively rational process in which people construct a norm from other people's behaviour in order to determine correct and appropriate behaviour for themselves. Clearly, if you are already confident and certain about what is appropriate and correct, then others' behaviour will be largely irrelevant and thus not influential. In Sherif's study, the object of judgement was ambiguous: participants were uncertain, so a norm arose rapidly and was highly effective in guiding behaviour. Asch argued that if the object of judgement was entirely unambiguous (i.e. one would expect no disagreement between judges), then disagreement, or alternative perceptions, would have no effect on behaviour: people would remain entirely independent of group influence.

To test this idea, Asch (1951, 1956) created a classic experimental paradigm. Students, participating in what they thought was a visual discrimination task, seated themselves around a table in groups of seven to nine. They took turns in a fixed order to call out publicly which of three comparison lines was the same length as a standard line (see Figure 7.5). There were eighteen trials. In reality, only one person was a true naive participant, and he answered second to last. The others were experimental confederates instructed to give erroneous responses on twelve focal trials: on six trials they picked a line that was too long and on six a line that was too

---

Frame of reference
Complete range of subjectively conceivable positions that relevant people can occupy in a particular context on some attitudinal or behavioural dimension.

Autokinesis
Optical illusion in which a pinpoint of light shining in complete darkness appears to move about.

Research classic 7.2
Sherif's autokinetic study: the creation of arbitrary norms

Muzafer Sherif (1936) believed that social norms emerge in order to guide behaviour under conditions of uncertainty. To investigate this idea, he took advantage of a perceptual illusion – the autokinetic effect. Autokinesis is an optical illusion where a fixed pinpoint of light in a completely dark room appears to move: the movement is actually caused by eye movement in the absence of a physical frame of reference (i.e. objects). People asked to estimate how much the light moves find the task very difficult and generally feel uncertain about their estimates. Sherif presented the point of light a large number of times (i.e. trials) and had participants, who were unaware that the movement was an illusion, estimate the amount the light moved on each trial. He discovered that they used their own estimates as a frame of reference: over a series of 100 trials they gradually focused on a narrow range of estimates, with different people adopting their own personal range,

or norm (see session 1 in Figure 7.4a, when participants responded alone).

Sherif continued the experiment in further sessions of 100 trials on subsequent days, during which participants in groups of two or three took turns in a random sequence to call out their estimates. Now the participants used each other's estimates as a frame of reference, and quickly converged on a group mean, so that they all gave very similar estimates (see sessions 2–4 in Figure 7.4a).

This norm seems to be internalised. When participants start and then continue as a group (sessions 1–3 in Figure 7.4b), the group norm is what they use when they finally make autokinetic estimates on their own (session 4 in Figure 7.4b).

Note: The results shown in Figure 7.4 are based on two sets of three participants who made 100 judgements on each of four sessions, spread over four different days.

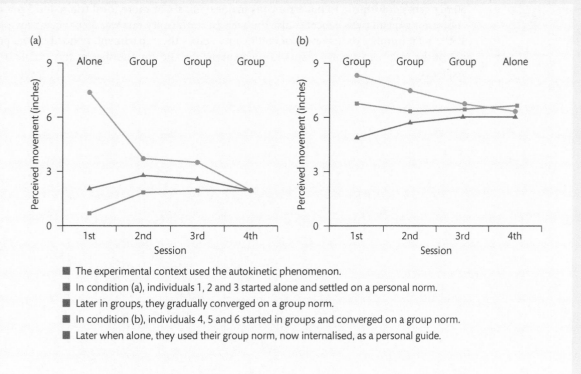

- The experimental context used the autokinetic phenomenon.
- In condition (a), individuals 1, 2 and 3 started alone and settled on a personal norm.
- Later in groups, they gradually converged on a group norm.
- In condition (b), individuals 4, 5 and 6 started in groups and converged on a group norm.
- Later when alone, they used their group norm, now internalised, as a personal guide.

Figure 7.4 Experimental induction of a group norm
Source: Based on data from Sherif (1936)

Conformity and group acceptance
All groups have norms. These women know how to dress for a 'girls' night out'

short. There was a control condition in which participants performed the task privately with no group influence; as less than 1 per cent of the control participants' responses were errors, it can be assumed that the task was unambiguous.

The experimental results were intriguing. There were large individual differences, with about 25 per cent of participants remaining steadfastly independent throughout, about 50 per cent conforming to the erroneous majority on six or more focal trials, and 5 per cent conforming on all twelve focal trials. The average conformity rate was 33 per cent: computed as the total number of instances of conformity across the experiment, divided by the product of the number of participants in the experiment and the number of focal trials in the sequence.

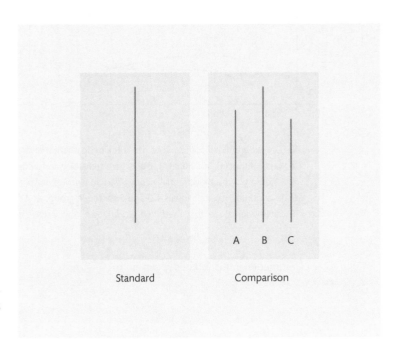

Figure 7.5 Sample lines used in conformity experiment

Participants in Asch's conformity studies had simply to say which one of the three comparison lines was the same length as the standard line

Source: Based on Asch (1951)

After the experiment, Asch asked his participants why they conformed. They all said they had initially experienced uncertainty and self-doubt because of the disagreement between themselves and the group, and that this gradually evolved into self-consciousness, fear of disapproval, and feelings of anxiety and even loneliness. Different reasons were given for yielding. Most participants knew they saw things differently from the group but felt that their perceptions may have been inaccurate and that the group was actually correct. Others did not believe that the group was correct but simply went along with the group in order not to stand out. (Consider how this might apply to Tom's self-doubts in the second focus question.) A small minority reported that they actually saw the lines as the group did. Independents were either entirely confident in the accuracy of their own judgements or were emotionally affected but guided by a belief in individualism or in doing the task as directed (i.e. being accurate and correct).

These subjective accounts should be treated cautiously – perhaps the participants were merely trying to verbally justify their behaviour and engage in self-presentation. For instance an fMRI study by Berns and associates found that those who conformed may actually have experienced changed perception, and that those who did not conform showed brain activity in the amygdale associated with elevated emotions – a cost of nonconformity may be accentuated emotions and anxiety (Berns, Chappelow, Zink, Pagnoni, Martin-Skurski and Richard, 2005).

Nevertheless the subjective accounts suggest, perhaps in line with the fMRI evidence that one reason why people conform, even when the stimulus is completely unambiguous, may be to avoid censure, ridicule and social disapproval. This is a real fear. In another version of his experiment, Asch (1951) had sixteen naive participants confronting one confederate who gave incorrect answers. The participants found the confederate's behaviour ludicrous and openly ridiculed and laughed at him. Even the experimenter found the situation so bizarre that he could not contain his mirth and also ended up laughing at the poor confederate!

Perhaps, then, if participants were not worried about social disapproval, there would be no subjective pressure to conform? To test this idea, Asch conducted another variation of the experiment, in which the incorrect majority called out their judgements publicly but the single naive participant wrote his down privately. Conformity dropped to 12.5 per cent.

Deutsch and Gerard (1955) extended this modification. They wondered whether they could entirely eradicate pressure to conform if: (a) the task was unambiguous, (b) the participant was anonymous and responded privately; (c) the participant was not under any sort of surveillance by the group. Why should you conform to an erroneous majority when there is an obvious, unambiguous and objectively correct answer, and the group has no way of knowing what you are doing?

To test this idea, Morton Deutsch and Harold Gerard confronted a naive participant face-to-face with three confederates, who made unanimously incorrect judgements of lines on focal trials, exactly as in Asch's original experiment. In another condition, the naive participant was anonymous, isolated in a cubicle and allowed to respond privately – no group pressure existed. There was a third condition in which participants responded face-to-face, but with an explicit group goal to be as accurate as possible – group pressure was maximised. Deutsch and Gerard also manipulated subjective uncertainty by having half the participants respond while the stimuli were present (the procedure used by Asch) and half respond after the stimuli had been removed (there would be scope for feeling uncertain).

As predicted, the results showed that decreasing uncertainty and decreasing group pressure (i.e. the motivation and ability of the group to censure lack of conformity) reduced conformity (Figure 7.6). Perhaps the most interesting finding was that people still conformed at a rate of about 23 per cent even when uncertainty was low (stimulus present) and responses were private and anonymous.

The discovery that participants still conformed when isolated in cubicles greatly facilitated the systematic investigation of factors influencing conformity. Richard Crutchfield

Figure 7.6 Conformity as a function of uncertainty and perceived group pressure

- The length of lines was estimated either (a) when they were present (low uncertainty) or (b) after they had been removed (high uncertainty).
- Participants were confronted with the judgements of an incorrect and unanimous majority.
- Influence (percentage of errors) was stronger in the high uncertainty condition.
- Influence was weaker when accuracy was stressed as an important group goal.
- Influence was further weakened when judgements were private and anonymous.

Source: Based on data from Deutsch and Gerard (1955)

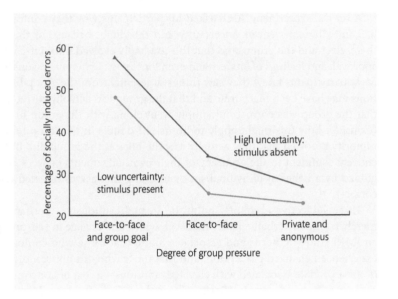

(1955) devised an apparatus in which participants in cubicles believed they were communicating with one another by pressing buttons on a console that illuminated responses, when in reality the cubicles were not interconnected and the experimenter was the source of all communication. In this way, many participants could be run simultaneously and yet all would believe they were being exposed to a unanimous group. The time-consuming, costly and risky practice of using confederates was no longer necessary, and data could now be collected much more quickly under more controlled and varied experimental conditions (Allen, 1965, 1975). Nowadays, one can, of course, use a much more efficient computerised variant of Crutchfield's methodology.

Who conforms? Individual and group characteristics

The existence of significant individual differences in conformity led to a search for personality attributes that predispose some people to conform more than others. Those who conform tend to have low self-esteem, a high need for social support or approval, a need for self-control, low IQ, high anxiety, feelings of self-blame and insecurity in the group, feelings of inferiority, feelings of relatively low status in the group, and a generally authoritarian personality (Costanzo, 1970; Crutchfield, 1955; Elms and Milgram, 1966; Raven and French, 1958; Stang, 1972). However, contradictory findings, and evidence that people who conform in one situation do not conform in another, suggest that situational factors may be more important than personality in conformity (Barocas and Gorlow, 1967; Barron, 1953; McGuire, 1968; Vaughan, 1964).

Alice Eagly drew similar conclusion about gender differences in conformity. Women have been shown to conform slightly more than men in some conformity studies. This can be explained in terms of the tasks used in some of these studies – tasks with which women had less familiarity and expertise. Women were therefore more uncertain and thus more influenced than men (Eagly, 1978, 1983; Eagly and Carli, 1981; **also see Chapters 6 and 9**).

A good example of this was a study by Frank Sistrunk and John McDavid (1971), in which males and females were exposed to group pressure in identifying various stimuli. For some, the stimuli were traditionally masculine items (e.g. identifying a special type of wrench), for some, traditionally feminine items (e.g. identifying types of needlework), and for others the stimuli were neutral (e.g. identifying rock stars). As expected, women conformed more on masculine items, men more on feminine items, and both groups equally on neutral (non sexstereotypical) items – see Figure 7.7. (Is Sarah really a conformist female? See the third focus question.)

Women do, however, tend to conform a little more than men in public interactive settings like that involved in the Asch paradigm. One explanation is that it reflects women's greater concern with maintaining group harmony (Eagly, 1978). However, a later study put the emphasis on men's behaviour; women conformed equally in public and private contexts whereas it was men who were particularly resistant to influence in public settings (Eagly, Wood and Fishbaugh, 1981).

Cultural norms

Do cultural norms affect conformity? Smith, Bond and Kağitçibaşi (2006) surveyed conformity studies that used Asch's paradigm or a variant thereof. They found significant intercultural variation. The level of conformity (i.e. percentage of incorrect responses) ranged from a low of 14 per cent among Belgian students (Doms, 1983) to a high of 58 per cent among Indian teachers in Fiji (Chandra, 1973), with an overall average of 31.2 per cent. Conformity was lower among participants from individualist cultures in North America and north-western Europe (25.3 per cent) than among participants from collectivist or interdependent cultures in Africa, Asia, Oceania and South America (37.1 per cent).

A meta-analysis of studies using the Asch paradigm in seventeen countries (R. Bond and Smith, 1996) confirmed that people who score high on Hofstede's (1980) collectivism scale conform more than people who score low (see also Figure 16.1, which shows summary data for non-Western versus various Western samples). For example, Norwegians, who have a reputation for social unity and responsibility, were more conformist than the French, who value critical judgement, diverse opinions and dissent (Milgram, 1961); and the Bantu of Zimbabwe, who have strong sanctions against nonconformity, were highly conformist (Whittaker and Meade, 1967).

The higher level of conformity in collectivist or interdependent cultures arises because conformity is viewed favourably, as a form of social glue (Markus and Kitayama, 1991). What is

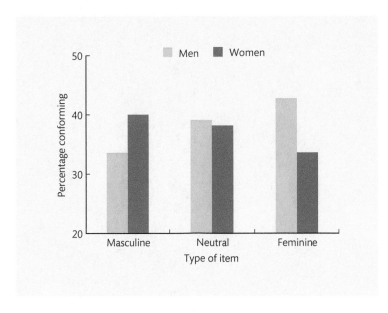

Figure 7.7 Conformity as a function of sex of participant and sex-stereotypicality of task

When a task is male-stereotypical, more women conform
When the task is female-stereotypical, more men conform

Source: Based on data from Sistrunk and McDavid (1971)

perhaps more surprising is that although conformity is lower in individualist Western societies, it is still remarkably high; even when conformity has negative overtones people find it difficult to resist conforming to a group norm.

Situational factors in conformity

The two situational factors in conformity that have been most exhaustively researched are group size and group unanimity (Allen, 1965, 1975).

Group size

Asch (1952) found that as the unanimous group increased from one person to two, to three, and on up to fifteen, the conformity rate increased and then decreased slightly: 3, 13, up to 35 and down to 31 per cent. Although some research reports a linear relationship between size and conformity (e.g. Mann, 1977), the most robust finding is that conformity reaches its full strength with a three- to five-person majority, and additional members have little effect (e.g. Stang, 1976).

Group size may have a different effect depending on the type of judgement being made and the motivation of the individual (Campbell and Fairey, 1989). With matters of taste, where there is no objectively correct answer (e.g. musical preferences), and where you are concerned about 'fitting in', group size will have a relatively linear effect: the larger the majority, the more you will be swayed. When there is a correct response and you are concerned about being correct, then the views of one or two others will usually be sufficient: the views of additional others will be largely redundant.

Finally, David Wilder (1977) observed that size may not refer to the actual number of physically separate people in the group but to the number of seemingly *independent* sources of influence in the group. For instance, a majority of three individuals who are perceived to be independent will be more influential than a majority of, say, five who are perceived to be in collusion and thus represent a single information source. In fact, people may actually find it

Group size and conformity
Could an individual in this throng resist joining in?

difficult to represent more than four or five different pieces of information. Instead, they usually assimilate additional group members into one or other of these initial sources of information – hence the relative lack of effect of group size above three to five members.

Group unanimity

In Asch's original experiment, the erroneous majority was unanimous and the conformity rate was 33 per cent. Subsequent experiments have shown that conformity is significantly reduced if the majority is not unanimous (Allen, 1975). Asch himself found that a correct supporter (i.e. a member of the majority who always gave the correct answer, and thus agreed with and supported the true participant) reduced conformity from 33 to 5.5 per cent.

It seems that support for remaining independent is not the crucial factor in reducing conformity. Rather, any sort of lack of unanimity among the majority seems to be effective. For example, Asch found that a dissenter who was even more wildly incorrect than the majority was equally effective. Vernon Allen and John Levine (1971) conducted an experiment in which participants, who were asked to make visual judgements, were provided with a supporter who had normal vision or a supporter who wore such thick glasses as to raise serious doubts about his ability to see anything at all, let alone judge lines accurately. In the absence of any support, participants conformed 97 per cent of the time. The 'competent' supporter reduced conformity to 36 per cent, but most surprising was the fact that the 'incompetent' supporter reduced conformity as well, to 64 per cent (see Figure 7.8).

Supporters, dissenters and deviates may be effective in reducing conformity because they shatter the unanimity of the majority and thus raise or legitimise the possibility of alternative ways of responding or behaving. For example, Nemeth and Chiles (1988) confronted participants with four confederates who either all correctly identified blue slides as blue, or among whom one consistently called the blue slide 'green'. Participants were then exposed to another group that unanimously called red slides 'orange'. The participants who had previously been exposed to the consistent dissenter were more likely to correctly call the red slides 'red'.

Processes of conformity

Social psychologists have proposed three main processes of social influence to account specifically for conformity (Nail, 1986): informational influence, normative influence, and referent informational influence.

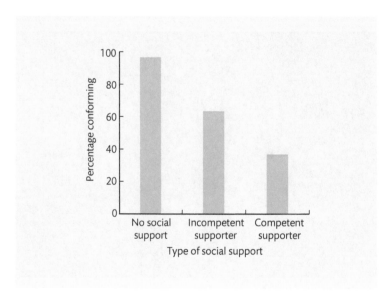

Figure 7.8 Conformity as a function of presence or absence of support, and of competence of supporter

Social support on a line judgement task reduced conformity, even when the supporter was patently unable to make accurate judgements because he was visually impaired

Source: Based on data from Allen and Levine (1971)

Informational and normative influence

The most enduring distinction is between informational influence and normative influence (Deutsch and Gerard, 1955; Kelley, 1952). Informational influence is an influence to accept information from another as *evidence* about reality. We need to feel confident that our perceptions, beliefs and feelings are correct. Informational influence comes into play when we are uncertain, either because stimuli are intrinsically ambiguous or because there is social disagreement. When this happens, we initially make objective tests against reality; otherwise, we make social comparisons, as Festinger and others have pointed out (Festinger, 1950, 1954; Suls and Wheeler, 2000). Effective informational influence causes true cognitive change.

Informational influence was probably partially responsible for the convergence effects in Sherif's (1936) study that we have already discussed. Reality was ambiguous, and participants used other people's estimates as information to remove the ambiguity and resolve subjective uncertainty. In that kind of experimental setting, when participants were told that the apparent movement was in fact an illusion, they did not conform (e.g. Alexander, Zucker and Brody, 1970); presumably, since reality itself was uncertain, their own subjective uncertainty was interpreted as a correct and valid representation of reality, and thus informational influence did not operate. On the other hand, Asch's (1952) stimuli were designed to be unambiguous in order to exclude informational influence. However, Asch did note that conformity increased as the comparison lines were made more similar to one another and the judgement task thus became more difficult. The moral? Informational influence rules in moments of certainty, not times of doubt.

Normative influence is an influence to conform to the positive expectations of others. People have a need for social approval and acceptance, which causes them to 'go along with' the group for instrumental reasons – to cultivate approval and acceptance, avoid censure or disapproval, or to achieve specific goals. Normative influence comes into play when we believe the group has the power and ability to reward or punish us according to what we do. For this to be effective we need to believe we are under surveillance by the group. Effective normative influence creates surface compliance in public settings rather than true enduring cognitive change. There is considerable evidence that people often conform to a majority in public but do not necessarily internalise this as it does not carry over to private settings or endure over time (Nail, 1986).

There is little doubt that normative influence was the principal cause of conformity in the Asch paradigm – the lines being judged were unambiguous (informational influence would

Informational influence
An influence to accept information from another as evidence about reality.

Normative influence
An influence to conform to the positive expectation of others, to gain social approval or to avoid social disapproval.

Normative influence
A peer group exerts a powerful pressure to conform, even when an activity as dangerous as train surfing in Brazil is involved

not be operating), but participants' behaviour was under direct surveillance by the group. We have also seen that privacy, anonymity and lack of surveillance reduce conformity in the Asch paradigm, presumably because normative influence was weakened.

In reflecting on Deutsch and Gerard's (1955) study we can note that, even under conditions in which neither informational nor normative influence would be expected to operate, they found residual conformity at a remarkably high rate of about 23 per cent. Perhaps social influence in groups needs to be explained in a different way.

Referent informational influence

The distinction between informational and normative influence is only one among many different terminologies that have been used in social psychology to distinguish between two types of social influence. It represents what Turner and his colleagues call a dual-process dependency model of social influence (Abrams and Hogg, 1990a; Hogg and Turner, 1987a; Turner, 1991). People are influenced by others because they are dependent on them either for information that removes ambiguity and thus establishes subjective validity, or for reasons of social approval and acceptance.

This dual-process perspective has been challenged on the grounds that as an explanation of conformity it underemphasises the role of group belongingness. After all, an important feature of conformity is that we are influenced because we feel we belong, psychologically, to the group, and therefore the norms of the group are relevant standards for our own behaviour. The dual-process model has drifted away from group norms and group belongingness and focused on *interpersonal* dependency, which could just as well occur between individuals as among group members.

This challenge has come from social identity theory (Tajfel and Turner, 1979; also Abrams and Hogg, 2010; Hogg, 2006; **see Chapter 11**), which proposes a separate social influence process responsible for conformity to group norms, called referent informational influence (Hogg and Turner, 1987a; Turner, 1981b; also Hogg, in press).

When our membership in a group membership becomes psychologically salient several things happen. We feel a sense of belonging, we define ourselves in terms of the group. We also recruit from memory and use information available in the social context to determine the relevant attributes that are based on our group's norms. We can glean information from the way that outgroup members or even unrelated individuals behave. But the most immediate source is the behaviour of fellow ingroup members, particularly those we consider to be generally reliable sources of the information we need. The ingroup norm that fits the context captures and accentuates both similarities among ingroup members and differences between our group and the relevant outgroup – it obeys the metacontrast principle.

The process of *self-categorisation* associated with social identity processes, group belongingness and group behaviour (Turner et al., 1987; **see Chapter 11**) brings us to see ourselves through the lens of our group. We assimilate our thoughts, feelings and behaviour to the group norm and act accordingly. To the extent that members of the group construct a similar group norm, self-categorisation produces intragroup convergence on that norm and increases uniformity within the group – the typical conformity effect.

Referent informational influence differs from normative and informational influence in a number of important ways. People conform because they are group members, not to validate physical reality or to avoid social disapproval. People do not conform to other people but to a norm: other people act as a source of information about the appropriate ingroup norm. Because the norm is an internalised representation, people can conform to it without the surveillance of group members, or for that matter anybody else.

Referent informational influence has direct support from a series of four conformity experiments by Hogg and Turner (1987a). For example, under conditions of private responding (i.e. no normative influence), participants conformed to a non-unanimous majority containing a correct supporter (i.e. no informational influence) only if it was

Social identity theory
Theory of group membership and intergroup relations based on self-categorisation, social comparison and the construction of a shared self-definition in terms of ingroup-defining properties.

Referent informational influence
Pressure to conform to a group norm that defines oneself as a group member.

Metacontrast principle
The prototype of a group is that position within the group that has the largest ratio of 'differences to ingroup positions' to 'differences to outgroup positions'.

the participant's explicit or implicit ingroup (see also Abrams et al., 1990). Other support for referent informational influence comes from research into group polarisation (e.g. Turner, Wetherell and Hogg, 1989; **see Chapter 9**), crowd behaviour (e.g. Reicher, 1984; **see Chapter 11**), and social identity and stereotyping (e.g. Oakes, Haslam and Turner, 1994; **see Chapter 11**).

Minority influence and social change

Our discussion of social influence, particularly conformity, has dealt with how individuals yield to direct or indirect social influence, most often from a numerical majority. Dissenters, deviates or independents have mainly been of interest indirectly, either as a means of investigating the effects of different types of majority or to investigate conformist personality attributes. However, we are all familiar with a very different, and very common, type of influence that can occur in a group: an individual or a numerical minority can sometimes change the views of the majority. Often such influence is based (in the case of individuals) on leadership or (in the case of subgroups) legitimate power (**leadership is discussed in Chapter 9**).

However, minorities are typically at an influence disadvantage relative to majorities. Often, they are less numerous, and in the eyes of the majority, they have less legitimate power and are less worthy of serious consideration. Asch (1952), as we saw above, found that a single deviate (who was a confederate) from a correct majority (true participants) was ridiculed and laughed at. Sometimes, however, a minority that has little or no legitimate power can be influential and ultimately sway the majority to its own viewpoint. For example, in a variant of the single deviate study, Asch (1952) found a quite different response. When a correct majority of eleven true participants was confronted by a deviant/incorrect minority of nine confederates, the majority remained independent (i.e. continued responding correctly) but took the minority's responses far more seriously – no one laughed. Clearly, the minority had some influence over the majority, albeit not enough in this experiment to produce manifest conformity.

History illustrates the power of minorities. Think of it this way: if the only form of social influence was majority influence, then social homogeneity would have been reached tens of thousands of years ago, individuals and groups always being swayed to adopt the views and practices of the growing numerical majority. Minorities, particularly those that are active and organised, introduce innovations that ultimately produce social change: without minority influence, social change would be very difficult to explain.

Minority influence
Social influence processes whereby numerical or power minorities change the attitudes of the majority.

For example, American anti-war rallies during the 1960s had an effect on majority attitudes that hastened withdrawal from Vietnam. Similarly, the suffragettes of the 1920s gradually changed public opinion so that women were granted the vote, and the Campaign for Nuclear Disarmament rallies in Western Europe in the early 1980s gradually shifted public opinion away from the 'benefits' of nuclear proliferation. Most recently the 2011 popular uprisings across North Africa and the Middle East, dubbed the Arab Spring, have to varying degrees changed majority attitudes regarding governance in those countries. An excellent example of an active minority is Greenpeace: the group is numerically small (in terms of 'activist' members) but has important influence on public opinion through the high profile of some of its members and the wide publicity of its views.

The sorts of question that are important here are whether minorities and majorities gain influence via different social practices, and, more fundamentally, whether the underlying psychology is different. There have been several recent overviews of minority influence research and theory (Hogg, 2010; Martin and Hewstone, 2003, 2008, 2010; Martin, Hewstone, Martin and Gardikiotis, 2008), and for an earlier meta-analysis of research findings, see Wood, Lundgren, Ouellette, Busceme and Blackstone (1994).

An active minority with style
Greenpeace activists protest in Madrid in the wake of the 2011 nuclear plant disaster in Fukushima, Japan

Beyond conformity

Social influence research has generally adopted a perspective in which people conform to majorities because they are dependent on them for normative and informational reasons. Moscovici and his colleagues mounted a systematic critique of this perspective (Moscovici, 1976; Moscovici and Faucheux, 1972). They argued that there had been a conformity bias underpinned by a functionalist assumption in the literature on social influence. Nearly all research focused on how individuals or minorities yield to majority influence and conform to the majority, and assumed that social influence satisfies an adaptive requirement of human life, to align with the status quo and thus produce uniformity, perpetuate stability and sustain the status quo. In this sense, social influence *is* conformity. Clearly conformity is an important need for individuals, groups and society. However, innovation and normative *change* are sometimes required to adapt to altered circumstances. Such change is difficult to understand from a conformity perspective, because it requires an understanding of the dynamics of active minorities.

Moscovici and Faucheux (1972) also famously 'turned Asch on his head'. They cleverly suggested that Asch's studies had actually been studies of minority influence, not majority influence. The Asch paradigm appears to pit a lone individual (true participant) against an erroneous majority (confederates) on an unambiguous physical perception task. Clearly a case of majority influence in the absence of subjective uncertainty? Perhaps not.

The certainty with which we hold views lies in the amount of agreement we encounter for those views: ambiguity and uncertainty are not properties of objects 'out there' but of other people's disagreement with us. This point is just as valid for matters of taste (if everyone disagrees with your taste in music, your taste is likely to change) as for matters of physical perception (if everyone disagrees with your perception of length, your perception is likely to change) (Moscovici, 1976, 1985a; Tajfel, 1969; Turner, 1985).

This sense of uncertainty would be particularly acute when an obviously correct perception is challenged. Asch's lines were *not* 'unambiguous'; there was disagreement between confederates and participants over the length of the lines. In reality, Asch's lone participant was a member of a large majority (those people outside the experiment who would call the lines 'correctly': that is, the rest of humanity) confronted by a small minority (the confederates who called the lines 'incorrectly'). Asch's participants were influenced by a minority: participants who remained 'independent' can be considered to be the conformists! 'Independence' in this sense is nicely described by the American writer Henry Thoreau in his famous quote from

Conformity bias
Tendency for social psychology to treat group influence as a one-way process in which individuals or minorities always conform to majorities.

Walden (1854): 'If a man does not keep pace with his companions, perhaps it is because he hears a different drummer.'

In contrast to traditional conformity research, Moscovici (1976, 1985a) believed that there is disagreement and conflict within groups, and that there are three *social influence modalities* that define how people respond to such social conflict:

1 *Conformity* – majority influence in which the majority persuades the minority or deviates to adopt the majority viewpoint.

2 *Normalisation* – mutual compromise leading to convergence.

3 *Innovation* – a minority creates and accentuates conflict in order to persuade the majority to adopt the minority viewpoint.

Behavioural style and the genetic model

Building on this critique, Moscovici (1976) proposed a genetic model of social influence. He called it a 'genetic' model because it focused on the way in which the dynamics of social conflict can generate (are genetic of) social change. He believed that in order to create change active minorities actually go out of their way to create, draw attention to and accentuate conflict. The core premise was that all attempts at influence create conflict based on disagreement between the source and the target of influence. Because people generally do not like conflict, they try to avoid or resolve it. In the case of disagreement with a minority, an easy and common resolution is to simply dismiss, discredit or even pathologise the minority (Papastamou, 1986).

However, it is difficult to dismiss a minority if it 'stands up to' the majority and adopts a behavioural style that conveys uncompromising certainty about and commitment to its position, and a genuine belief that the majority ought to change to adopt its position. Under these circumstances, the majority takes the minority seriously, reconsidering its own beliefs and considering the minority's position as a viable alternative.

The most effective behavioural style a minority can adopt to prevail over the majority is one in which, among other things, the minority promulgates a message that is consistent across time and context, shows *investment* in its position by making significant personal and material sacrifices, and evinces *autonomy* by acting out of principle rather than from ulterior or instrumental motives. Consistency is the most important behavioural style for effective minority influence, as it speaks directly to the existence of an alternative norm and identity rather than merely an alternative opinion. Specifically, it:

• disrupts the majority norm and produces uncertainty and doubt.

• draws attention to the minority as an entity (e.g. Hamilton and Sherman, 1996).

• conveys the clear impression that there is an alternative coherent point of view.

• demonstrates certainty and an unshakeable commitment to this point of view.

• shows that (and how) the only solution to the conflict is espousal of the minority's viewpoint.

From an attribution theory perspective such as Kelley's (1967; **see Chapter 3**), this form of consistent and distinctive behaviour cannot be discounted – it demands to be explained. Furthermore, the behaviour is likely to be internally attributed by an observer to invariant and perhaps essentialist (e.g. Haslam, Rothschild and Ernst, 1998) properties of the minority rather than to transient or situational factors.

All of this makes the minority even more of a force to be reckoned with and a focus of deliberation by the majority. Overall, a minority that is consistent raises uncertainty. It begs the question: if this minority espouses its viewpoint time and time again, is it the obvious and most viable resolution? (Considering these points, might Aleksei and Ivan have a chance against the system in the fourth focus question?)

Moscovici and his colleagues demonstrated the role of consistency in a series of ingenious experiments, referred to as the 'blue–green' studies (Maass and Clark, 1984). In a modified version of the Asch paradigm, Moscovici, Lage and Naffrechoux (1969) had four participants confront two confederates in a colour perception task involving blue slides that varied only in intensity. The confederates were either consistent, always calling the slides 'green', or inconsistent, calling the slides 'green' two-thirds of the time and 'blue' one-third of the time. There was also a control condition with no confederates, just six true participants. Figure 7.9 shows that the consistent minority were more influential than the inconsistent minority (9 per cent versus 2 per cent). We might say that the reported rate of 9 per cent for the consistent minority is not that high when compared with a consistent majority (recall that Asch reported an average conformity rate of 33 per cent). Nevertheless, this simple experiment highlighted the fact that a minority of two could influence a majority of four.

There are two other notable results from an extension of this experiment, in which participants' real colour thresholds were tested privately after the social influence stage: (1) both experimental groups showed a lower threshold for 'green' than the control group – that is, they erred towards seeing ambiguous green–blue slides as 'green'; and (2) this effect was greater among experimental participants who were resistant to the minority – that is, participants who did not publicly call the blue slides 'green'.

Moscovici and Lage (1976) employed the same colour perception task to compare consistent and inconsistent minorities with consistent and inconsistent majorities. There was also a control condition. As before, the only minority to produce conformity was the consistent minority (10 per cent conformity). Although this does not compare well with the rate of conformity to the consistent majority (40 per cent), it is comparable with the rate of conformity to the inconsistent majority (12 per cent). However, the most important finding was that the *only* participants in the entire experiment who actually changed their blue–green thresholds were those in the consistent minority condition. Other studies have shown that the most important aspects of consistency are synchronic consistency (i.e., consensus) among members of the minority (Nemeth, Wachtler and Endicott, 1977) and perceived consistency, not merely objective repetition (Nemeth, Swedlund and Kanki, 1974).

Moscovici's (1976) focus on the importance of behavioural style was extended by Gabriel Mugny (1982) who focused on the strategic use of behavioural styles by real, active minorities struggling to change societal practices. Because minorities are typically powerless, they must negotiate with the majority rather than unilaterally adopt a behavioural style. Mugny

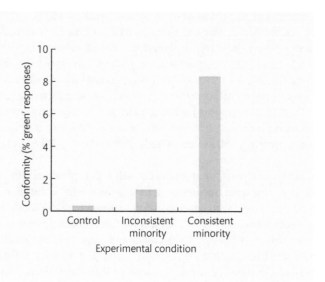

Figure 7.9 Conformity to a minority as a function of minority consistency

Although not as effective as a consistent majority, a consistent two-person minority in a six-person group was more influential than an inconsistent minority; that four people were influenced by two is quite remarkable

Source: Based on data from Moscovici, Lage and Naffrechoux (1969)

distinguished between rigid and flexible negotiating styles, arguing that a rigid minority that refuses to compromise on any issues risks being rejected as dogmatic, and a minority that is too flexible, shifting its ground and compromising, risks being rejected as inconsistent (the classic case of 'flip-flopping'). There is a fine line to tread, but some flexibility is more effective than total rigidity. A minority should continue to be consistent with regard to its core position but should adopt a relatively open-minded and reasonable negotiating style on less core issues (e.g. Mugny and Papastamou, 1981).

Conversion theory

In 1980 Moscovici supplemented his earlier account of social influence based on behavioural style with his conversion theory (Moscovici, 1980, 1985a), and this remains the dominant explanation of minority influence. His earlier approach focused largely on how a minority's behavioural style (in particular, attributions based on the minority's consistent behaviour) could enhance its influence over a majority. Conversion theory is a more cognitive account of how a member of the majority processes the minority's message.

Moscovici argued that majorities and minorities exert influence through different processes:

1 Majority influence produces direct public compliance for reasons of normative or informational dependence. People engage in a *comparison process* in which they concentrate attention on what others say to know how to fit in with them. Majority views are accepted passively without much thought. The outcome is public compliance with majority views with little or no private attitude change.

2 Minority influence produces indirect, often latent, private change in opinion due to the cognitive conflict and restructuring that deviant ideas produce. People engage in a *validation process* in which they carefully examine and cogitate over the validity of their beliefs. The outcome is little or no overt public agreement with the minority, for fear of being viewed as a member of the minority, but a degree of private internal attitude change that may only surface later on. Minorities produce a **conversion effect** as a consequence of active consideration of the minority point of view.

Conversion effect
When minority influence brings about a sudden and dramatic internal and private change in the attitudes of a majority.

Moscovici's dual-process model of influence embodies a distinction that is very similar to that discussed earlier between normative and informational influence (cf. Deutsch and Gerard, 1967), and is related to Petty and Cacioppo's (1986a) distinction between peripheral and central processing, and Chaiken's (Bohner, Moskowitz and Chaiken, 1995) distinction between heuristic and systematic processing (**see Chapter 6**; Eagly and Chaiken, 1993).

Empirical evidence for conversion theory can be organised around three testable hypotheses (Martin and Hewstone, 2003): direction-of-attention, content-of-thinking, differential-influence. There is support for the *direction-of-attention hypothesis* – majority influence causes people to focus on their relationship to the majority (interpersonal focus) whereas minority influence causes people to focus on the minority message itself (message focus) (e.g. Campbell, Tesser and Fairey, 1986). There is also support for the *content-of-thinking hypothesis* – majority influence leads to superficial examination of arguments whereas minority influence leads to detailed evaluation of arguments (e.g. Maass and Clark, 1983; Martin, 1996; Mucchi-Faina, Maass and Volpato, 1991).

The *differential-influence hypothesis,* that majority influence produces more public/direct influence than private/indirect influence whereas minority influence produces the opposite has received most research attention and support (see Wood, Lundgren, Ouellette, Busceme and Blackstone, 1994). For example, the studies described above by Moscovici, Lage and Naffrechoux (1969) and Moscovici and Lage (1976) found, as would be expected from conversion theory, that conversion through minority influence took longer to manifest itself than compliance through majority influence; there was evidence for private change in colour thresholds (i.e., conversion) among participants exposed to a consistent minority, although they did not behave (or had not yet behaved) publicly in line with this change.

Another series of studies, by Anne Maass and Russell Clark (1983, 1986), report three experiments investigating people's public and private reactions to majority and minority influence regarding the issue of gay rights. In one of these experiments Maass and Clark (1983) found that publicly expressed attitudes conformed to the expressed views of the majority (i.e. if the majority was pro-gay, then so were the participants), while privately expressed attitudes shifted towards the position espoused by the minority (see Figure 7.10).

Perhaps the most intriguing support for the *differential-influence hypothesis* comes from a series of fascinating experiments by Moscovici and Personnaz (1980, 1986), who employed the blue–green paradigm described above. Individual participants, judging the colour of obviously blue slides that varied only in intensity, were exposed to a single confederate who always called the blue slides 'green'. They were led to believe that most people (82 per cent) would respond as the confederate did, or that only very few people (18 per cent) would. In this way, the confederate was a source of majority or minority influence. Participants publicly called out the colour of the slide and then (and this is the ingenious twist introduced by Moscovici and Personnaz) the slide was removed and participants wrote down privately the colour of the after-image. Unknown to most people, including the participants, the after-image is always the complementary colour. So, for blue slides the after-image would be yellow, and for green slides it would be purple.

There were three phases to the experiment: an influence phase, where participants were exposed to the confederate, preceded and followed by phases where the confederate was absent and there was thus no influence. The results were remarkable (see Figure 7.11). Majority influence hardly affected the chromatic after-image: it remained yellow, indicating that participants had seen a blue slide. Minority influence, however, shifted the after-image towards purple, indicating that participants had actually 'seen' a green slide! The effect persisted even when the minority confederate was absent.

This controversial finding clearly supports the idea that minority influence produces indirect, latent internal change, while majority influence produces direct, immediate behavioural compliance. Moscovici and Personnaz have been able to replicate it, but others have been less successful. For example, in a direct replication Doms and van Avermaet (1980) found after-image changes after both minority and majority influence, and Sorrentino, King and Leo

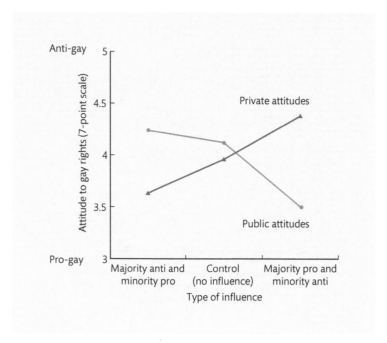

Figure 7.10 Public and private attitude change in response to majority and minority influence

Relative to a no-influence control condition, heterosexual *public* attitudes towards gay rights closely reflected the pro- or anti-gay attitudes of the majority. However, *private* attitudes reflected the pro- or anti-gay attitudes of the minority

Source: Based on data from Maass and Clark (1983)

Conversion
If you and your friends repeatedly and consistently told your friend Pierre that this was the Eiffel Tower, would he eventually believe you?

(1980) found no after-image shift after minority influence, except among participants who were suspicious of the experiment.

To try to resolve the contradictory findings, Robin Martin conducted a series of five careful replications of Moscovici and Personnaz's paradigm (Martin, 1998). His pattern of findings revealed that participants tended to show a degree of after-image shift only if they paid close attention to the blue slides – this occurred among participants who were either suspicious of the experiment or who were exposed to many, rather than a few, slides.

The key point is that circumstances that made people attend more closely to the blue slides caused them actually to see more green in the slides and thus to report an after-image that was

Figure 7.11 Reported colour of chromatic after-image as a result of majority and minority influence

Participants exposed to a majority member who wrongly identified blue slides as green did not change their perception: their after-images did not alter. However, participants exposed to a minority member who called the blue slides green did change their perception: their after-images changed and continued to change even after influence had ceased

Source: Based on data from Moscovici and Personnaz (1980)

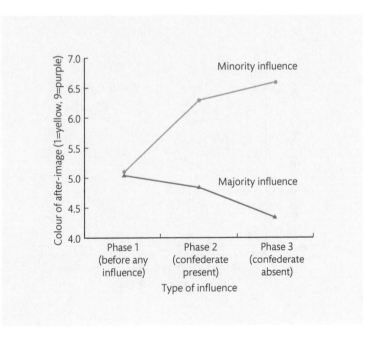

shifted towards the after-image of green. These findings suggest that Moscovici and his colleagues' intriguing after-image findings may not reflect distinct minority/majority influence processes but may be a methodological artefact. This does not mean that conversion theory is wrong, but it does question the status of the blue–green studies as evidence for conversion theory. Martin (1998) comes to the relatively cautious conclusion that the findings may at least partially be an artefact of the amount of attention participants were paying to the slides: the greater the attention, the greater the after-image shift.

Convergent–divergent theory

Charlan Nemeth (1986, 1995) offered a slightly different account of majority/minority differences in influence. Because people expect to share attitudes with the majority, the discovery through majority influence that their attitudes are in fact in disagreement with those of the majority is surprising and stressful. It leads to a self-protective narrowing of focus of attention. This produces convergent thinking that inhibits consideration of alternative views. In contrast, because people do not expect to share attitudes with a minority, the discovery of disagreement associated with minority influence is unsurprising and not stressful and does not narrow focus of attention. It allows divergent thinking that involves consideration of a range of alternative views, even ones not proposed by the minority.

In this way, Nemeth believes that exposure to minority views can stimulate innovation and creativity, generate more and better ideas, and lead to superior decision making in groups. The key difference between Nemeth's (1986) convergent–divergent theory and Moscovici's (1980) conversion theory hinges on the relationship between 'stress' and message processing: for Nemeth, majority-induced stress restricts message processing; for Moscovici, minority-induced stress elaborates message processing.

Convergent–divergent theory is supported by research using relatively straightforward cognitive tasks. Minority influence improves performance relative to majority influence on tasks that benefit from divergent thinking (e.g. Martin and Hewstone, 1999; Nemeth and Wachtler, 1983); majority influence improves performance relative to minority influence on tasks that benefit from convergent thinking (e.g. Peterson and Nemeth, 1996); and minority influence leads to the generation of more creative and novel judgements than does majority influence (e.g. Mucchi-Faina, Maass and Volpato, 1991; Nemeth and Wachtler, 1983).

For example, the Nemeth studies (Nemeth, 1986; Nemeth and Wachtler, 1983) employed Asch-type and blue–green paradigms in which participants exposed to majority or minority influence converged, with little thought, on majority responses; but minorities stimulated divergent, novel, creative thinking, and more active information processing, which increased the probability of correct answers. Mucchi-Faina, Maass and Volpato (1991) used a different paradigm to find that students at the University of Perugia generated more original and creative ideas for promoting the international image of the city of Perugia when they had been exposed to a conventional majority and a creative minority than vice versa, or where the majority and the minority were both original or both conventional.

Research on convergent–divergent theory also shows that minority influence leads people to explore different strategies for problem solving whereas majority influence restricts people to the majority-endorsed strategy (e.g. Butera, Mugny, Legrenzi and Pérez, 1996; Peterson and Nemeth, 1996) and that minority influence encourages issue-relevant thinking whereas majority influence encourages message-relevant thinking (e.g. De Dreu, De Vries, Gordijn and Schuurman, 1999).

Social identity and self-categorisation

We already saw above that the social identity theory of influence in groups, referent informational influence theory (e.g. Abrams and Hogg, 1990a; Hogg and Turner, 1987a; Turner and

Oakes, 1989), views prototypical ingroup members as the most reliable source of information about what is normative for the group – the attitudes and behaviours that define and characterise the group. Through the process of self-categorisation group members perceive themselves and behave in line with the norm.

From this perspective, minorities should be extremely ineffective sources of influence. Groups in society that promulgate minority viewpoints are generally widely stigmatised by the majority as social outgroups, or are 'psychologised' as deviant individuals. Their views are, at best, rejected as irrelevant, but they are often ridiculed and trivialised in an attempt to discredit the minority (e.g. the treatment of gays, environmentalists, intellectuals; **see Chapter 10 for a discussion of discrimination against outgroups**). All this resistance on the part of the majority makes it very difficult for minorities to have effective influence.

So, from a social identity perspective, how can a minority within one's group be influential? According to David and Turner (2001), the problem for ingroup minorities is that the majority group makes intragroup social comparisons that highlight and accentuate the minority's otherness, essentially concretising a majority-versus-minority intergroup contrast within the group.

The key to effective minority influence is for the minority to somehow make the majority shift its level of social comparison to focus on intergroup comparisons with a genuine shared outgroup. This process automatically transcends intragroup divisions and focuses attention on the minority's ingroup credentials. The minority is now viewed as part of the ingroup, and there is indirect attitude change that may not be manifested overtly. For example, a radical faction within Islam will have more influence within Islam if Muslims make intergroup comparisons between Islam and the West than if they dwell on intra-Islam comparisons between majority and minority factions.

Research confirms that minorities do indeed exert more influence if they are perceived by the majority as an ingroup (Maass, Clark and Haberkorn, 1982; Martin, 1988; Mugny and Papastamou, 1982); and studies by David and Turner (1996, 1999) show that ingroup minorities produced more indirect attitude change (i.e., conversion) than did outgroup minorities, and majorities produced surface compliance. However, other research has found that an outgroup minority has just as much indirect influence as an ingroup minority (see review by Pérez and Mugny, 1998) and, according to Martin and Hewstone (2003), more research is needed to confirm that conversion is generated by the process of self-categorisation.

Vested interest and the leniency contract

Overall minorities are more influential if they can avoid being categorised by the majority as a despised outgroup and can be considered by the majority as part of the ingroup. The challenge for a minority is to be able to achieve this at the same time as promulgating an unwaveringly consistent alternative viewpoint that differs from the majority position. How can minorities successfully have it both ways – be thought of as an ingroup *and* hold an unwavering outgroup position?

The trick psychologically is to establish one's legitimate ingroup credentials before drawing undue critical attention to one's distinct minority viewpoint. Crano's context-comparison model of minority influence describes how this may happen (e.g. Crano, 2001; Crano and Alvaro, 1998; Crano and Chen, 1998; Crano and Seyranian, 2009). When a minority's message involves weak or unvested attitudes (i.e. attitudes that are relatively flexible, not fixed or absolute), an ingroup minority can be quite persuasive—the message is distinctive and attracts attention and elaboration, and, by virtue of the message being unvested and the minority a clear ingroup, there is little threat that might invite derogation or rejection of the minority. An outgroup minority is likely to be derogated and not influential.

When the message involves strong or vested (i.e. fixed, inflexible and absolute) attitudes, it is more difficult for the minority to prevail. The message is not only highly distinctive but speaks to core group attributes. The inclination is to reject the message and the minority outright. However, the fact that the minority is actually part of the ingroup makes members reluctant to do so – to derogate people who are, after all, ingroup members. One way out of this dilemma is to establish with the minority what Crano calls a leniency contract. Essentially, the majority assumes that because the minority is an ingroup minority it is unlikely to want to destroy the majority's core attributes, and in turn the majority is lenient towards the minority and its views. This enables the majority to elaborate open-mindedly on the ingroup minority's message, without defensiveness or hostility and without derogating the minority. This leniency towards an ingroup minority leads to indirect attitude change. An outgroup minority does not invite leniency and is therefore likely to be strongly derogated as a threat to core group attitudes.

The logic behind this analysis is that disagreement between people who define themselves as members of the same group is both unexpected and unnerving – it raises subjective uncertainty about themselves and their attributes, and motivates uncertainty reduction (Hogg, 2007b, 2012). Where common ingroup membership is important and 'inescapable', there will be a degree of redefinition of group attributes in line with the minority: that is, the minority has been effective. Where common ingroup membership is unimportant and easily denied, there will be no redefinition of ingroup attributes in line with the minority: that is, the minority will be ineffective.

Attribution and social impact

Many aspects of minority influence suggest an underlying attribution process (Hewstone, 1989; Kelley, 1967; **see also Chapter 3**). Effective minorities are consistent and consensual, distinct from the majority, unmotivated by self-interest or external pressures, and flexible in style. This combination of factors encourages a perception that the minority has chosen its position freely. It is therefore difficult to explain away its position in terms of idiosyncrasies of individuals (although this is, as we saw above, a strategy that is attempted), or in terms of external inducements or threats. Perhaps, then, there is actually some intrinsic merit to its position. This encourages people to take the minority seriously (although again social forces work against this) and at least consider its position; such cognitive work is an important precondition for subsequent attitude change.

Although majorities and minorities can be defined in terms of power, they also of course refer to numbers of people. Although 'minorities' are often both less powerful and less numerous (e.g. West Indians in Britain), they can be less powerful but more numerous (e.g. Tibetans versus Chinese in Tibet). Perhaps not surprisingly, an attempt has been made to explain minority influence purely in terms of social influence consequences of relative numerosity.

Bibb Latané drew on social impact theory to argue that as a source of influence increases in size (number), it has more influence (Latané, 1981; Latané and Wolf, 1981). However, as the cumulative source of influence gets larger, the impact of each additional source is reduced – a single source has enormous impact, the addition of a second source increases impact but not by as much as the first, a third even less, and so on. A good analogy is switching on a single light in a dark room – the impact is huge. A second light improves things, but only a little. If you have ten lights on, the impact of an eleventh is negligible. Evidence does support this idea: the more numerous the source of influence, the more impact it has, with incremental changes due to additional sources decreasing with increasing size (e.g. Mullen, 1983; Tanford and Penrod, 1984).

But how does this account for the fact that minorities can actually have influence? One explanation is that the effect of a large majority on an individual majority member has reached a plateau: additional members or 'bits' of majority influence have relatively little impact. Although a minority viewpoint has relatively little impact, it has not yet attained a plateau: additional members or 'bits' of minority influence have a relatively large impact. In this way,

Attribution
The process of assigning a cause to our own behaviour, and that of others.

Social impact
The effect that other people have on our attitudes and behaviour, usually as a consequence of factors such as group size, and temporal and physical immediacy.

exposure to minority positions can, paradoxically, have greater impact than exposure to majority viewpoints.

Two processes or one?

Although the social impact perspective can account for some quantitative differences between majority and minority influence at the level of overt public behaviour, even Latané and Wolf (1981) concede that it cannot explain the qualitative differences that seem to exist, particularly at the private level of covert cognitive changes. However, these qualitative differences, and particularly the process differences proposed by Moscovici's (1980) conversion theory, remain the focus of some debate, however.

For instance, there is some concern that the postulation of separate processes to explain minority and majority influence has revived the opposition of informational and normative influence (Abrams and Hogg, 1990a; David and Turner, 2001; Turner, 1991). As we saw earlier in this chapter, this opposition has problems in explaining other social influence phenomena. Instead, whether minorities or majorities are influential or not may be a matter of social identity dynamics that determine whether people are able to define themselves as members of the minority (majority) group or not (e.g. Crano and Seyranian, 2009; David and Turner, 2001).

In addition, theoretical analyses by Kruglanski and Mackie (1990) and a meta-analysis by Wood and colleagues (Wood, Lundgren, Ouellette, Busceme and Blackstone, 1994) together suggest that people who are confronted with a minority position, particularly face-to-face with real social minorities and majorities, tend not only to resist an overt appearance of alignment with the minority, but also privately and cognitively to avoid alignment with the minority. This conflicts with Moscovici's dual-process conversion theory.

Summary

- Social influence can produce surface behavioural compliance with requests, obedience of commands, internalised conformity to group norms, and deep-seated attitude change.

- People tend to be more readily influenced by reference groups, because they are psychologically significant for our attitudes and behaviour, than by membership groups, as they are simply groups to which we belong by some external criterion.

- Given the right circumstances, we all have the potential to obey commands blindly, even if the consequences of such obedience include harm to others.

- Obedience is affected by the proximity and legitimacy of authority, by the proximity of the victim, and by the degree of social support for obedience or disobedience.

- Group norms are enormously powerful sources of conformity: we all tend to yield to the majority.

- Conformity can be reduced if the task is unambiguous and we are not under surveillance, although even under these circumstances there is often residual conformity. Lack of unanimity among the majority is particularly effective in reducing conformity.

- People may conform in order to feel sure about the objective validity of their perceptions and opinions, to obtain social approval and avoid social disapproval, or to express or validate their social identity as members of a specific group.

- Active minorities can sometimes influence majorities: this may be the very essence of social change.

- To be effective, minorities should be consistent but not rigid, should be seen to be making personal sacrifices and acting out of principle, and should be perceived as being part of the ingroup.

- Minorities may be effective because, unlike majority influence which is based on 'mindless' compliance, minority influence causes latent cognitive change as a consequence of thought produced by the cognitive challenge posed by the novel minority position.

- Minorities can be more effective if they are treated by the majority group as ingroup minorities rather than outgroup minorities.

Key terms

Agentic state	Dual-process dependency model	Norms
Attribution	Frame of reference	Power
Autokinesis	Informational influence	Reference group
Compliance	Membership group	Referent informational influence
Conformity	Metacontrast principle	Social identity theory
Conformity bias	Minority influence	Social impact
Conversion effect	Normative influence	Social influence

Literature, film and TV

American Beauty and *Revolutionary Road*

Two powerful films by Sam Mendes that explore conformity and independence. Set in American suburbia the 1999 film *American Beauty*, starring Kevin Spacey, is a true classic about suffocating conformity to social roles, and what can happen when people desperately try to break free. *Revolutionary Road* is a 2008 film, starring Leonardo DiCaprio and Kate Winslet, which explores the same theme with a focus on the drudgery and routine of adult life and the lost dreams of youth, and again on the challenge and consequences of change.

Little Miss Sunshine

Hilarious 2006 film, directed by Jonathan Dayton and Valerie Faris. A breathtakingly dysfunctional family sets out in their decrepit VW van to drive from Arizona to Los Angeles for their daughter Olive (Abigail Breslin) to appear in an absolutely grotesque children's beauty pageant. Featuring Toni Collette, Steve Carell, Greg Kinnear and Alan Arkin, this is a film about interpersonal relations and families **(relevant to Chapter 14)** but also about non-conformity and violation of social conventions.

Eichmann in Jerusalem: A report on the banality of evil

1963 book by H. Arendt on the Nuremberg war trials of the Nazis. It shows how these people came across as very ordinary people who were only following orders.

Rebel Without a Cause

1955 film directed by Nicholas Ray, and with James Dean and Natalie Wood. An all-time classic film about non-conformity, counter-conformity and independence. James Dean stands out against social and group roles and expectations, and sets the mould for teenage 'rebellion' in future decades.

Che

2008 two-part biopic of Che Guevara's role in Fidel Castro's toppling of the Cuban Dictator Fulgencia Batista in 1959. The films, directed by Stephen Soderbergh and starring Benicio del Toro as the now legendary Che Guevara, bring to life the nature of social change through revolution.

Made in Dagenham

This feel-good and light-hearted 2010 film directed by Nigel Cole and starring Sally Hawkins dramatises a strike (and surrounding events) by Ford sewing machinists in Dagenham in Britain in 1968. The strike was aimed at securing equal pay for women – and it was successful. The film shows social influence through protest and persuasion rather than violence and revolution.

Guided questions

MyPsychLab

1 Is it true that women conform more than men to group pressure?

2 Why did Stanley Milgram undertake his controversial studies of *obedience to authority*? Watch the video illustrating Milgram's research in Chapter 7 of MyPsychLab at www.mypsychlab.com (watch *Milgram's obedience study*).

3 How does the social context impact on people when they need to state their opinions in public?

4 What are the two major social influence processes associated with conformity?

5 Can a *minority group* really bring about social change by confronting a majority?

Learn more

Baron, R. S., and Kerr, N. (2003). *Group process, group decision, group action* (2nd edn). Buckingham, UK: Open University Press. A general overview of some major topics in the study of group processes; includes discussion of social influence phenomena.

Brown, R. J. (2000). *Group processes* (2nd edn). Oxford, UK: Blackwell. A very readable introduction to group processes, which also places an emphasis on social influence processes within groups, especially conformity, norms and minority influence.

Cialdini, R. B., and Trost, M. R. (1998). Social influence: Social norms, conformity, and compliance. In D. Gilbert, S. T. Fiske, and G. Lindzey (eds), *The handbook of social psychology* (4th edn, Vol. 2, pp. 151–92). New York: McGraw-Hill. A thorough overview of social influence research with a particular emphasis on norms and persuasion.

Fiske, S. T. (2010). Interpersonal stratification: Status, power, and subordination. In S. T. Fiske, D. T. Gilbert, and G. Lindzey (eds), *Handbook of social psychology* (5th edn, Vol. 2, pp. 941-82). New York: Wiley. Detailed and up-to-date overview of research on the psychology of status, which also covers research on power.

Fiske, S. T., and Berdahl, J. (2007). Social power. In A. W. Kruglanski, and E. T. Higgins (eds), *Social psychology: Handbook of basic principles* (2nd edn, pp. 678–92). New York: Guilford Press. A detailed overview of the social psychology of power.

Hogg, M. A. (2010). Influence and leadership. In S. T. Fiske, D. T. Gilbert, and G. Lindzey (eds), *Handbook of social psychology* (5th edn, Vol. 2, pp. 1166–207). New York: Wiley. Up-to-date and detailed coverage of research on social influence processes, with a major section on minority influence.

Martin, R., and Hewstone, M. (2007). Social influence processes of control and change: Conformity, obedience to authority, and innovation. In M. A. Hogg, and J. Cooper (eds), *The SAGE handbook of social psychology: Concise student edition* (pp. 312–32). London: SAGE. An up-to-date and comprehensive review of social influence research, including conformity, obedience and minority influence.

Martin, R., and Hewstone, M. (eds) (2010). *Minority influence and innovation: Antecedents, processes and consequences.* Hove, UK: Psychology Press. An edited book that has contributions on minority influence by most of the leaders in the field of minority influence research.

Moscovici, S., Mugny, G., and Eddy van Avermaet, E. (2008). *Perspectives on minority influence.* Cambridge, UK: Cambridge University Press. An up-to-date overview of research on minority influence by leading scholars of this notably European topic.

Turner, J. C. (1991). *Social influence.* Buckingham, UK: Open University Press. Scholarly discussion of social influence which takes a critical stance from a European perspective and places particular emphasis on social identity, minority influence and the role of group membership and group norms.

Use MyPsychLab to refresh your understanding, assess your progress and go further with interactive summaries, questions, podcasts and much more. To buy access or register your code, visit www.mypsychlab.com.

MyPsychLab

CHAPTER 8
People in groups

Chapter contents

Focus questions

1   Alone in his room, James can reliably play a tricky guitar riff really well –
    precise and fluent. When his friends ask him to play it for them, it all goes
    horribly wrong. Why do you think this happens?

2   You want to make sure that new members of the small organisation you run
    are totally committed to it and its goals. You could make the experience of
    joining smooth, easy and pleasant; or you could make it quite daunting with a
    bewildering array of initiation rites and embarrassing hurdles to clear. Which
    would be more effective, when and why?

3   Would you offer to reward a close family member with money after enjoying
    a meal at their house? Why not? See an amusing account by Dan Ariely of a
    clash between two social norms in Chapter 8 of MyPsychLab at www.
    mypsychlab.com (watch *The cost of social norms* – http://
    sciencestage.com/v/33488/the-cost-of-social-norms.html).

4   Andrea writes very quickly and neatly and is good at taking notes. She works
    for a large corporation and is very ambitious to rise to the top. She finds it
    flattering that her boss assigns her the role of taking notes in important executive meetings. She
    is keen to please and so always agrees – leaving her sitting at the back scribbling away on her
    notepad while others talk and make decisions. Is she wise to agree? Why, or why not?

will use which involves getting you to decide to buy a
car by giving you a very low price

Go to MyPsychLab to explore video and
test your understanding of key topics
addressed in this chapter.

MyPsychLab

Use MyPsychLab to refresh your understanding with interactive summaries, explore topics further with
video and audio clips and assess your progress with quick test and essay questions. To buy access or
register your code, visit www.mypsychlab.com. You will also need a course ID from your instructor.

What is a group?

Group
Two or more people who share a common definition and evaluation of themselves and behave in accordance with such a definition.

Groups occupy much of our day-to-day life. We work in groups, we socialise in groups, we play in groups, and we represent our views and attitudes through groups. Groups also largely determine the people we are and the sorts of lives we live. Selection panels, juries, committees and government bodies influence what we do, where we live and how we live. The groups to which we belong determine what language we speak, what accent we have, what attitudes we hold, what cultural practices we adopt, what education we receive, what level of prosperity we enjoy and ultimately who we are. Even those groups to which we do not belong, either by choice or by exclusion, have a profound impact on our lives. In this tight matrix of group influences, the domain of the autonomous, independent, unique self may indeed be limited.

Groups differ in many different ways (Deaux, Reid, Mizrahi and Ethier, 1995). Some have a large number of members (e.g. a nation, a sex), and others are small (a committee, a family); some are relatively short-lived (a group of friends, a jury), and some endure for thousands of years (an ethnic group, a religion); some are concentrated (a flight crew, a selection committee), others dispersed (academics, computer-mediated communication groups); some are highly structured and organised (an army, an ambulance team), and others are more informally organised (a supporters' club, a community action group); some have highly specific purposes (an assembly line, an environmental protest group), and others are more general (a tribal group, a teenage 'gang'); some are relatively autocratic (an army, a police force), others relatively democratic (a university department, a commune); and so on.

Any social group can thus be described by an array of features that highlight similarities to, and differences from, other groups. These can be very general features, such as membership size (e.g. a religion versus a committee), but they can also be very specific features, such as group practices and beliefs (e.g. Catholics versus Muslims, liberals versus conservatives, Masai versus Kikuyu). This enormous variety of groups could be reduced by limiting the number of significant dimensions to produce a restricted taxonomy of groups. Social psychologists have tended to focus more on group size, group 'atmosphere', task structure and leadership structure than other dimensions.

Categories and group entitativity

Entitativity
The property of a group that makes it seem like a coherent, distinct and unitary entity.

Human groups are quite clearly categories – some people share characteristics and are in the group and people who do not share the characteristics are not in the group. As such, human groups should differ in ways that categories in general differ. One of the key ways in which categories differ is in terms of entitativity (Campbell, 1958). **Entitativity** is the property of a

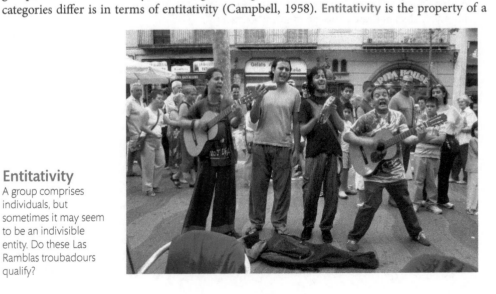

Entitativity
A group comprises individuals, but sometimes it may seem to be an indivisible entity. Do these Las Ramblas troubadours qualify?

group that makes it appear to be a distinct, coherent and bounded entity. High-entitativity groups have clear boundaries, and are internally well-structured and relatively homogeneous; low entitativity groups have fuzzy boundaries and structure and are relatively heterogeneous.

Groups certainly differ in terms of entitativity (Hamilton and Sherman, 1996; Lickel, Hamilton, Wieczorkowska, Lewis and Sherman, 2000). Hamilton and Lickel and colleagues claim there are qualitative differences in the nature of groups as they decrease in entitativity, and that groups can be classified into four different general types with decreasing entitativity: intimacy groups, task groups, social categories, loose associations.

Common-bond and common-identity groups

One classic and important distinction in the social sciences between types of human groups was originally made in 1887 by the sociologist Ferdinand Tönnies (1887/1955) between *Gemeinschaft* (i.e. community) and *Gesellschaft* (i.e. association): that is, social organisation based on close interpersonal bonds and social organisation based on more formalised and impersonal associations. This distinction has resurfaced in contemporary social psychology in a slightly different form that focuses on a general distinction between similarity-based or categorical groups, and interaction-based or dynamic groups (Arrow, McGrath and Berdahl, 2000; Wilder and Simon, 1998).

For example, Steven Prentice and colleagues (Prentice, Miller and Lightdale, 1994) distinguish between *common-bond* groups (groups based upon attachment among members) and *common-identity* groups (groups based on direct attachment to the group). Kai Sassenberg has found that members of common-bond groups operate according to an egocentric principle of maximising their rewards and minimising their costs with respect to their own contributions – in common-bond groups, personal goals are more salient than group goals. In contrast members of common-identity groups operate according to an altruistic principle of maximising the group's rewards and minimising its costs through their own contributions – in common-identity groups, group goals are more salient than personal goals because the group provides an important source of identity (Sassenberg, 2002; Utz and Sassenberg, 2002).

Other research, by Elizabeth Seeley and her colleagues (Seeley, Gardner, Pennington and Gabriel, 2003) has found gender differences in preferences for group type that may have consequences for the longevity of the group. Women were found to be more attached to groups in which they felt close to the other members (common bonds were more important); men rated groups as important when they were attached to individual members and the group as a whole (common identity was more important). If the common bonds in a group disappear, the group may no longer be valuable for women, whereas the common identity of the group would allow men to remain attracted to it. Thus some men's groups may last longer than women's groups because of the greater importance they place on group identity.

Groups and aggregates

Not all collections of people can be considered groups in a psychological sense. For example, people with green eyes, strangers in a dentist's waiting room, people on a beach, children waiting for a bus – are these groups? Perhaps not. More likely these are merely social aggregates, collections of unrelated individuals – not groups at all. The important social psychological question is what distinguishes groups from aggregates; it is by no means an easy question to answer. Social psychologists differ in their views on this issue. These differences are, to some extent, influenced by whether the researcher favours an individualistic or a collectivistic perspective on groups (Abrams and Hogg, 2004; Turner and Oakes, 1989).

Individualists believe that people in groups behave in much the same way as they do in pairs or by themselves, and that group processes are really nothing more than interpersonal processes between a number of people (e.g. Allport, 1924; Latané, 1981). *Collectivists* believe that the behaviour of people in groups is influenced by unique social processes and cognitive representations that can only occur in and emerge from groups (Hogg and Abrams, 1988; McDougall, 1920; Sherif, 1936; Tajfel and Turner, 1979).

Definitions

Although there are almost as many definitions of the social group as there are social psychologists who research social groups, David Johnson and Frank Johnson (1987) have identified seven major emphases. The group is:

1 a collection of individuals who are interacting with one another;
2 a social unit consisting of two or more individuals who perceive themselves as belonging to a group;
3 a collection of individuals who are interdependent;
4 a collection of individuals who join together to achieve a goal;
5 a collection of individuals who are trying to satisfy a need through their joint association;
6 a collection of individuals whose interactions are structured by a set of roles and norms;
7 a collection of individuals who influence each other.

Their definition incorporates all these emphases:

> A group is two or more individuals in face-to-face interaction, each aware of his or her membership in the group, each aware of the others who belong to the group, and each aware of their positive interdependence as they strive to achieve mutual goals.
>
> Johnson and Johnson (1987, p. 8)

You will notice that this definition, and many of the emphases in the previous paragraph, cannot encompass large groups and/or do not distinguish between interpersonal and group relationships. This is a relatively accurate portrayal of much of the classic social psychology of group processes, which is generally restricted, explicitly or implicitly, to small, face-to-face, short-lived, interactive, task-oriented groups. In addition, 'group processes' generally do not mean *group* processes but interpersonal processes between more than two people. However, more recently the study of group processes has been increasingly influenced by perspectives that consider the roles of identity and relations between large-scale social categories (e.g. Brown, 2000; Hogg and Tindale, 2001; Stangor, 2004).

Group effects on individual performance

Mere presence and audience effects: social facilitation

Perhaps the most elementary *social* psychological question concerns the effect of the presence of other people on someone's behaviour. Gordon Allport asked: 'What changes in an individual's normal solitary performance occur when other people are present?' (1954a, p. 46). You are playing a musical instrument, fixing the car, reciting a poem or exercising in the gym, and someone comes to watch; what happens to your performance? Does it improve or deteriorate?

This question intrigued Norman Triplett (1898), credited by some as having conducted the first social psychology experiment, although there has been controversy about this (**see Chapter 1**). From observing that people cycled faster when paced than when alone, and faster when in competition than when paced, Triplett hypothesised that competition between people energised and improved performance on motor tasks. To test this idea, he had young children reeling a continuous loop of line on a 'competition machine'. He confirmed his hypothesis: more children reeled the line more quickly when racing against each other in pairs than when performing alone.

Floyd Allport (1920) termed this phenomenon social facilitation but felt that Triplett confined it too narrowly to the context of competition, and it could be widened to allow for a more general principle: that an improvement in performance could be due to the mere presence of conspecifics (i.e. members of the same species) as coactors (doing the same thing but not interacting) or as a passive audience (passively watching).

Until the late 1930s, there was an enormous amount of research on social facilitation, much of it conducted on an exotic array of animals. For example, we now know that cockroaches run faster, chickens, fish and rats eat more, and pairs of rats copulate more, when being 'watched' by conspecifics or when conspecifics are also running, eating or copulating! However, research has also revealed that social presence can produce quite the opposite effect – social inhibition, or a decrease in task performance.

Contradictory findings such as these, in conjunction with imprecision in defining the degree of social presence (early research focused on coaction, whereas later research focused on passive audience effects), led to the near demise of social facilitation research by about 1940.

Drive theory

In 1965, Robert Zajonc published a classic theoretical statement, called drive theory (see Figure 8.1), which revived social facilitation research and kept it alive for many decades (see Geen, 1989; Guerin, 1986, 1993). Zajonc set himself the task of explaining what determines whether social presence (mainly in the form of a passive audience) facilitates or inhibits performance.

Drive theory argues that because people are relatively unpredictable (you can rarely know with any certainty exactly what they are going to do), there is a clear advantage to the species for people's presence to cause us to be in a state of alertness and readiness. Increased arousal or motivation is thus an instinctive reaction to social presence. Such arousal functions as a 'drive' that energises (i.e. causes us to enact) that behaviour which is our dominant response (i.e. best learnt, most habitual) in that situation. If the dominant response is correct (we feel the task is

Social facilitation
An improvement in the performance of well-learnt/easy tasks and a deterioration in the performance of poorly learnt/difficult tasks in the mere presence of members of the same species.

Mere presence
Refers to an entirely passive and unresponsive audience that is only physically present.

Audience effects
Impact on individual task performance of the presence of others.

Drive theory
Zajonc's theory that the physical presence of members of the same species instinctively causes arousal that motivates performance of habitual behaviour patterns.

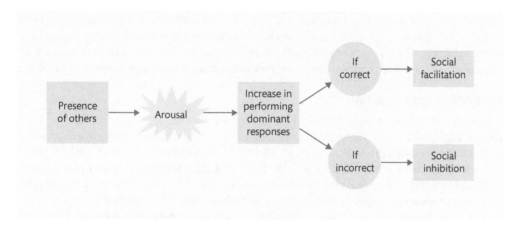

Figure 8.1 Zajonc's drive theory of social facilitation

• The presence of others automatically produces arousal, which 'drives' dominant responses.
• Performance is improved by a 'correct' dominant response, but is impaired by an 'incorrect' dominant response.

Source: Based on Zajonc (1965)

The audience effect
He has been practicing hard at home. What will determine whether he will soar or crash in front of an audience?

easy), then social presence produces an improved performance; if it is incorrect (we feel the task is difficult), then social presence produces an impaired performance.

Let us illustrate this with an example. You are a novice violinist with a small repertoire of pieces to play. There is one piece that, when playing alone, you find extremely easy because it is very well learnt – you almost never make mistakes. If you were to play this piece in front of an audience (say, your friends), drive theory would predict that, because your dominant response is to make no mistakes, your performance would be greatly improved. In contrast, there is another piece that, when playing alone, you find extremely difficult because it is not very well learnt – you almost never get it right. It would be a rash decision indeed to play this in front of an audience – drive theory would predict that, because the dominant response contains all sorts of errors, your performance would be truly awful, much worse than when you play alone.

Evaluation apprehension

Although early research tends on the whole to support drive theory (Geen and Gange, 1977; Guerin and Innes, 1982), some social psychologists have questioned whether mere presence instinctively produces drive. Nickolas Cottrell (1972) proposed an **evaluation apprehension model**, in which he argues that we quickly learn that the social rewards and punishments (e.g. approval and disapproval) we receive are based on others' evaluations of us. Social presence thus produces an acquired arousal (drive) based on evaluation apprehension.

In support of this interpretation, Cottrell, Wack, Sekerak and Rittle (1968) found no social facilitation effect on three well-learnt tasks when the two-person audience was inattentive (i.e. blindfolded) and merely present (i.e. only incidentally present while ostensibly waiting to take part in a different experiment). This audience would be unlikely to produce much evaluation apprehension. However, a non-blindfolded audience that attended carefully to the participant's performance and had expressed an interest in watching would be expected to produce a great deal of evaluation apprehension. Indeed, this audience did produce a social facilitation effect.

Other research is less supportive. For example, Hazel Markus (1978) had male participants undress, dress in unfamiliar clothing (laboratory coat, special shoes), and then in their own clothing again. To minimise apprehension about evaluation by the experimenter, the task was presented as an incidental activity that the experimenter was not really interested in. The task was performed under one of three conditions: (1) alone; (2) in the presence of an incidental audience (low evaluation apprehension) – a confederate who faced away and was engrossed in some other task; (3) in the presence of an attentive audience (high evaluation apprehension) – a confederate who carefully and closely watched the participant dressing and undressing.

The results (see Figure 8.2) supported evaluation apprehension theory on the relatively easy task of dressing in familiar clothing; only an attentive audience decreased the time taken to perform this task. However, on the more difficult task of dressing in unfamiliar clothing, mere presence was sufficient to slow performance down and an attentive audience had no additional effect; this supports drive theory rather than evaluation apprehension.

Bernd Schmitt, Gilovich, Goore and Joseph (1986) conducted a similarly conceived experiment. Participants were given what they thought was an incidental task that involved typing their name into a computer (a simple task), and then entering a code name by typing their name backwards interspersed with ascending digits (a difficult task). These tasks were performed (1) *alone* after the experimenter had left the room; (2) in the *mere presence* of only a confederate who was blindfolded, wore a headset and was allegedly participating in a separate experiment on sensory deprivation; or (3) under the close *observation of the experimenter,* who remained in the room carefully scrutinising the participant's performance.

The results of the study (see Figure 8.3) show that mere presence accelerated performance of the easy task and slowed performance of the difficult task, and that evaluation apprehension had little additional impact. Mere presence appears to be a sufficient cause of, and evaluation apprehension not necessary for, social facilitation effects. (Can you reassure James about his guitar practice problem? See the first focus question.)

Bernard Guerin and Mike Innes (1982) have suggested that social facilitation effects may occur only when people are unable to monitor the audience and are therefore uncertain about the audience's evaluative reactions to their performance. In support of this idea, Guerin (1989) found a social facilitation effect on a simple letter-copying task only among participants who were being watched by a confederate whom they could *not* see. When the confederate could be clearly seen, there was no social facilitation effect.

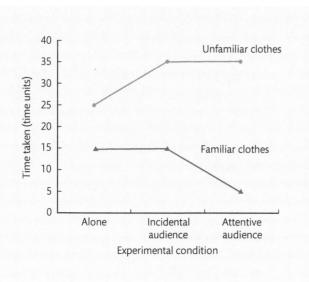

Figure 8.2 Time taken to dress in familiar and unfamiliar clothes as a function of social presence

- Participants dressed in their own clothing (easy task) or in unfamiliar clothing (difficult task).
- They dressed either alone, with an incidental audience present or with an attentive audience present.
- Evaluation apprehension occurred on the easy task: only the attentive audience reduced the time taken to dress up.
- There was a drive effect on the difficult task: both incidental and attentive audiences increased the time taken to dress.

Source: Based on data from Markus (1978)

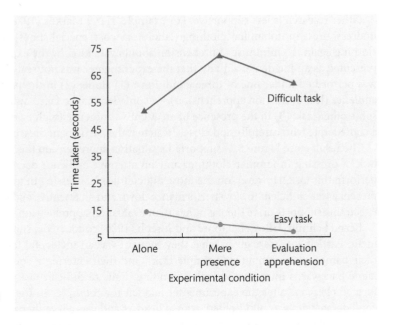

Figure 8.3 Time taken for an easy and a difficult typing task as a function of social presence

- Participants typed their name on a computer (easy task) or typed it backwards interspersed with digits (difficult task), alone, with an incidental audience present or with an attentive audience present.
- There was a drive effect on both the easy and the difficult task.
- The incidental audience improved performance on the easy task and impaired it on the difficult task. The attentive audience had no additional effect.

Source: Based on data from Schmitt, Gilovich, Goore and Joseph (1986)

Distraction-conflict theory

Distraction-conflict theory
The physical presence of members of the same species is distracting and produces conflict between attending to the task and attending to the audience.

According to Glen Sanders (1981, 1983), the presence of others can 'drive us to distraction' (see also Baron, 1986; Sanders, Baron and Moore, 1978). The argument in **distraction-conflict theory** goes as follows. They argue that people are a source of distraction, which produces cognitive conflict between attending to the task and attending to the audience or coactors. While distraction alone impairs task performance, attentional conflict also produces drive that facilitates dominant responses. Together, these processes impair the performance of difficult tasks and, because drive usually overcomes distraction, improve the performance of easy tasks (see Figure 8.4).

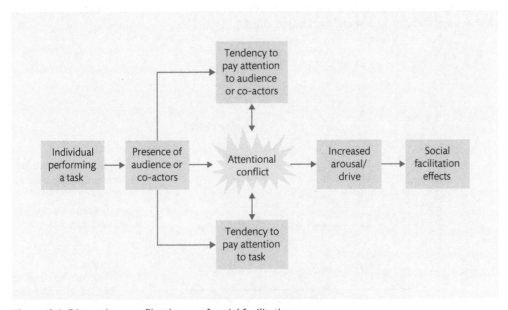

Figure 8.4 Distraction-conflict theory of social facilitation
The presence of an audience creates conflict between attending to the task and attending to the audience: attentional conflict produces drive that has social facilitation effects
Source: Based on Baron and Byrne (1987)

Distraction–conflict theory
Even an audience who cannot see what you are doing can be distracting, and can impair your performance

In support of distraction–conflict theory, Sanders, Baron and Moore (1978) had participants perform an easy and a difficult digit-copying task, alone or coacting with someone performing either the same or a different task. They reasoned that someone performing a different task would not be a relevant source of social comparison, so distraction should be minimal, whereas someone performing the same task would be a relevant source of comparison and therefore highly distracting. As predicted, they found that participants in the distraction condition made more mistakes on the difficult task, and copied more digits correctly on the simple task, than in the other conditions (again, see the first focus question).

Distraction–conflict theory has other strengths. Experiments show that any form of distraction (noise, movement, flashing lights), not only social presence, can produce social facilitation effects. In addition, unlike the evaluation apprehension model, it can accommodate results from studies of social facilitation in animals. It is difficult to accept that cockroaches eat more while other roaches are watching because they are anxious about evaluation; however, even the lowly roach can presumably be distracted.

Distraction–conflict theory also had the edge on evaluation apprehension in an experiment by Groff, Baron and Moore (1983). Whenever a tone sounded, participants had to rate the facial expressions of a person appearing on a TV monitor. At the same time, but as an ostensibly incidental activity, they had to squeeze as firmly as possible a bottle held in the hand (latency and strength of squeeze were measures of arousal/drive). Participants undertook the experiment (1) alone; (2) closely scrutinised by a confederate sitting to one side – this would be highly distracting, as the participant would need to look away from the screen to look at the observer; or (3) closely scrutinised by a confederate who was actually the person on the screen – no attentional conflict. As predicted by distraction–conflict theory, participants squeezed the bottle more strongly in the second condition.

Non-drive explanations of social facilitation

How do we know that 'drive' has a role in social facilitation? Drive is difficult to measure. Physiological measures of arousal such as sweating palms may monitor drive, but the absence of arousal is no guarantee that drive is not operating. Drive is actually psychological concept and could even mean alertness in the context we are discussing. So we should not be surprised that several non-drive explanations of social facilitation have been proposed.

One non-drive explanation of social facilitation is based on *self-awareness theory* (Carver and Scheier, 1981; Duval and Wicklund, 1972; Wicklund, 1975). When people focus their attention on themselves as an object, they make comparisons between their actual self (their actual task performance) and their ideal self (how they would like to perform). Related to this line of reasoning is *self-discrepancy theory* (Higgins, 1987, 1998). **(Both of these theories are described in Chapter 4.)** The discrepancy between actual and ideal self increases motivation and effort to bring actual into line with ideal, so on easy tasks performance improves. On difficult tasks the discrepancy is too great, so people give up trying, and performance deteriorates. Self-awareness can be produced by a range of circumstances, such as looking at oneself in a mirror, but also by the presence of coactors or an audience.

Still focusing on the role of 'self' in social facilitation, Charles Bond (1982) believes that people are concerned with *self-presentation*, to make the best possible impression of themselves to others. As this is achievable on easy tasks, social presence produces an improved performance. On more difficult tasks, people make, or anticipate making, errors: this creates embarrassment, and embarrassment impairs task performance.

Yet another way to explain social facilitation, without invoking self or drive, is in terms of the purely *attentional consequences* of social presence. This analysis is based on the general idea that people narrow the focus of their attention when they experience attentional overload (Easterbrook, 1959). Robert Baron (1986) believes that people have a finite attention capacity, which can be overloaded by the presence of an audience. Attention overload makes people narrow their attention, give priority to attentional demands and focus on a small number of central cues. Difficult tasks are those that require attention to a large number of cues, so attentional narrowing is likely to divert attention from cues that we really ought to attend to: thus social presence impairs performance. Simple tasks are ones that require attention to only a small number of cues, so attentional narrowing actually eliminates distraction caused by attending to extraneous cues and focuses attention on to central cues: thus social presence improves performance.

This general idea has been nicely supported in an experiment by Jean-Marc Monteil and Pascal Huguet (1999). The task was a *Stroop* task, in which participants simply have to name the colour of ink that different words are written in. Some words are neutral or consistent with the colour of ink (e.g. 'red' written in red ink) – this is an easy task with low response latencies (people respond quickly); whereas others clash (e.g. 'red' written in blue) – this is a difficult task with high latencies (people respond slowly). The participants performed the Stroop task alone or in the presence of another person. They found that latencies on the difficult task were significantly lower in the social presence condition. Social presence had narrowed attention on to the colour of ink, so that semantic interference from the word itself was reduced.

Finally, Tony Manstead and Gün Semin (1980) have proposed a similar attention-based model, but with the emphasis placed on automatic versus controlled task performance. They argue that difficult tasks require a great deal of attention because they are highly controlled. An audience distracts vital attention from task performance, which thus suffers. Easy tasks require little attention because they are fairly automatic. An audience causes more attention to be paid to the task, which thus becomes more controlled and better performed.

Social facilitation revisited

Social psychologists have suggested and investigated many different explanations of what initially may have appeared to be a basic and straightforward social phenomenon. Some explanations fare better than others, some have not yet been properly tested, and after more than 100 years of research a number of questions remain unanswered. Nevertheless, the study of audience effects remains an important topic for social psychology, as much of our behaviour occurs in the physical presence of others as an audience. A survey administered by Borden (1980) revealed that people feared speaking in front of an audience more than heights, darkness, loneliness and even death!

However, we should keep in perspective the actual magnitude of impact that mere presence has on behaviour. From a review of 241 social facilitation experiments involving 24,000 participants, using a meta-analysis, Charles Bond and Linda Titus (1983) concluded that mere presence accounted for only a tiny 0.3 to 3.0 per cent of variation in behaviour.

Social presence may have significantly greater impact if we focus on more than *mere* presence. For example, a comprehensive review of the effects of social presence on how much people eat reveals that the nature of one's relationship to those who are socially present has an influence (Herman, Roth and Polivy, 2003). When the others are friends or family and they are also eating, people tend to eat more simply because they spend more time at the table. In the presence of strangers who are eating, people follow the norm set by the others – if others eat more, they do also. In the presence of others who are not eating, people eat less because they are apprehensive about being evaluated negatively for eating too much.

In order to explain additional variation in the way that social facilitation operates, we now move from non-interactive contexts to more interactive contexts and true group processes.

Classification of group tasks

Traditional social facilitation research distinguishes between easy and difficult tasks but restricts itself to tasks that do not of necessity involve processes such as interaction, inter-individual coordination and division of labour. While many tasks fall into this category (e.g. getting dressed, washing the car, cycling), many others do not (e.g. building a house, playing football, running a business). We could expect that social presence will have different effects on task performance, not only as a function of the degree of social presence (passive audience, coactor, interdependent interaction on a group task) but also as a function of the specific task being performed. What is needed is a taxonomy that classifies types of task based on a limited number of psychologically meaningful parameters.

In dealing with the pragmatic question of whether groups generally perform better than individuals, Ivan Steiner (1972, 1976) developed a task taxonomy with three dimensions, based on answering three questions:

Meta-analysis
Statistical procedure that combines data from different studies to measure the overall reliability and strength of specific effects.

Task taxonomy
Group tasks can be classified according to whether a division of labour is possible; whether there is a predetermined standard to be met; and how an individual's inputs can contribute.

1 **Is the task divisible or unitary?**
   - A *divisible* task is one that benefits from a division of labour, where different people perform different subtasks.
   - A *unitary* task cannot sensibly be broken into subtasks. Building a house is a divisible task and pulling a rope a unitary task.

2 **Is it a maximising or an optimising task?**
   - A *maximising* task is an open-ended task that stresses quantity: the objective is to do as much as possible.
   - An *optimising* task is one that has a predetermined standard: the objective is to meet the standard, neither to exceed nor fall short of it. Pulling on a rope would be a maximising task, but maintaining a specified fixed force on the rope would be an optimising task.

3 **How are individual inputs related to the group's product?**
   - An *additive* task is one where the group's product is the sum of all the individual inputs (e.g. a group of people planting trees).
   - A *compensatory* task is one where the group's product is the average of the individuals' inputs (e.g. a group of people estimating the number of bars in Amsterdam).

- A *disjunctive* task is one where the group selects as its adopted product one individual's input (e.g. a group of people proposing different things to do over the weekend will adopt one person's suggestion).

- A *conjunctive* task is one where the group's product is determined by the rate or level of performance of the slowest or least able member (e.g. a group working on an assembly line).

- A *discretionary* task is one where the relationship between individual inputs and the group's product is not directly dictated by task features or social conventions; instead, the group is free to decide on its preferred course of action (e.g. a group that *decides* to shovel snow together).

These parameters allow us to classify tasks. For example, a tug-of-war is unitary, maximising and additive; assembling a car is divisible, optimising and conjunctive; and many group decision-making tasks are divisible, optimising and disjunctive (or compensatory). As to whether groups are better than individuals, Steiner believes that in general the actual group performance is always inferior to the group's potential (based on the potential of its human resources). This shortfall is due mainly to a process loss (e.g. losses due to the coordination of individual members' activities, disproportionate influence on the part of specific powerful group members and various social distractors). However, against this background, Steiner's taxonomy allows us to predict what sort of tasks favour group performance.

For additive tasks, the group's performance is better than the best individual's performance. For compensatory tasks, the group's performance is better than that of most individuals, because the average is most likely to be correct. For disjunctive tasks, the group's performance is equal to or worse than the best individual – the group cannot do better than the best idea proposed. And for conjunctive tasks, the group's performance is equal to the worst individual's performance – unless the task is divisible, in which case a division of labour can redirect the weakest member to an easier task and so improve the group's performance.

Although Steiner emphasised the role of coordination loss in preventing a group performing optimally in terms of the potential of its members, he also raised the possibility of an entirely different, and more fundamentally psychological, type of loss – motivation loss.

Social loafing and social impact

Maximilien Ringelmann (1913), a French professor of agricultural engineering, conducted a number of experiments to investigate the efficiency of various numbers of people, animals and machines performing agricultural tasks (Kravitz and Martin, 1986). In one study, he had young men, alone or in groups of two, three or eight, pull horizontally on a rope attached to a dynamometer (an instrument that measures the amount of force exerted). He found that the force exerted per person decreased as a function of group size: the larger the group, the less hard each person pulled (see Figure 8.5). This is called the Ringelmann effect.

Our previous discussion suggests two possible explanations for this:

1 *Coordination loss* – owing to jostling, distraction and the tendency for people to pull slightly against one another, participants were prevented from attaining their full potential.

2 *Motivation loss* – participants were less motivated; they simply did not try so hard.

An ingenious study by Alan Ingham and his colleagues compared coordination and motivation losses in groups. In one condition real groups of varying size pulled on a rope. The other condition had 'pseudo-groups' with only one true participant and a number of confederates. The confederates were instructed only to pretend to pull on the rope while making realistic grunts to indicate exertion. The true participant was in the first position and so did not know that the confederates behind him were not actually pulling. As Figure 8.6 shows, what transpired was that in pseudo-groups participants reduced their effort. Because there was no

Process loss
Deterioration in group performance in comparison to individual performance due to the whole range of possible interferences among members.

Coordination loss
Deterioration in group performance compared with individual performance, due to problems in coordinating behaviour.

Ringelmann effect
Individual effort on a task diminishes as group size increases.

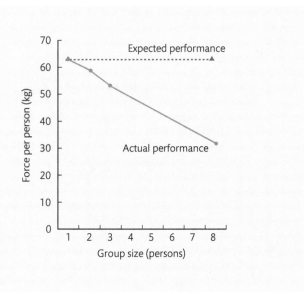

Figure 8.5 The Ringelmann effect: force per person as a function of group size

As the number of people pulling horizontally on a rope increased, each person's exertion was reduced: people pulling in eight-person groups each exerted half the effort of a person pulling alone

Source: Based on data from Ringelmann (1913)

coordination possible, no loss can be attributed to it; the decrease can be attributed only to a loss of *motivation*. In real groups, there was an additional reduction in individual effort that can be attributed to coordination loss (Ingham, Levinger, Graves and Peckham, 1974).

This loss of motivation has been termed **social loafing** by Bibb Latané and his colleagues, who replicated the effect with shouting, cheering and clapping tasks. For instance, they had participants cheer and clap as loudly as possible alone or in groups of two, four or six. The amount of noise produced per person was reduced by 29 per cent in two-person groups, 49 per cent in four-person groups and 60 per cent in six-person groups. For the shouting task, participants shouted alone or in two- or six-person real groups or pseudo-groups (they wore blindfolds and headsets transmitting continuous 'white noise'). As in Ingham and colleagues' experiment, there was a clear reduction in effort for participants in pseudo-groups, with additional coordination loss for participants in real groups (Latané, Williams and Harkins, 1979). See the results in Figure 8.7.

Social loafing
A reduction in individual effort when working on a collective task (one in which our outputs are pooled with those of other group members) compared with working either alone or coactively (our outputs are not pooled).

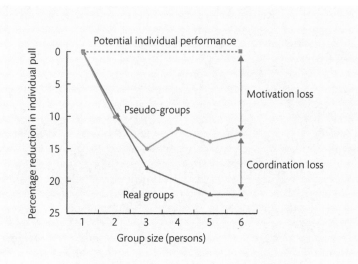

Figure 8.6 Coordination and motivation losses in group rope-pulling

- As group size increased from 1 to 6, there was a decrease in each person's output.
- In pseudo-groups, this is due to reduced effort, i.e. motivation loss.
- In real groups, this is more marked as a result of coordination loss.

Source: Based on data from Ingham, Levinger, Graves and Peckham (1974)

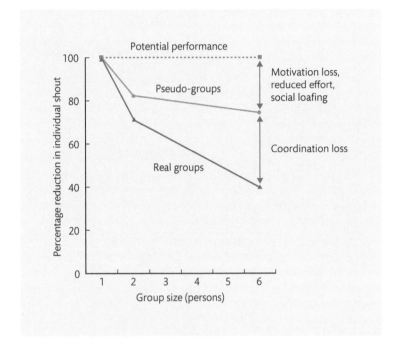

Figure 8.7 Reduction in volume of individual shout in two-person and six-person real and pseudo-groups

- Social loafing: individual students shouted less loudly as group size increased.
- As in Figure 8.6, this demonstrates a loss of motivation in pseudo-groups and an additional loss due to a lack of coordination in real groups.

Source: Latané, Williams and Harkins, 1979 Experiment 2

Social loafing, then, is a tendency for individuals to work less hard (i.e. loaf) on a task when they believe that others are also working on the task. More formally, it refers to 'a reduction in individual effort when working on a collective task (in which one's outputs are pooled with those of other group members) compared to when working either alone or coactively' (Williams, Karau and Bourgeois, 1993, p. 131).

Social loafing
Modern offices can make people feel like clones working on mindless tasks in boring settings - not a great recipe for thrilling personal engagement in hard work

A notable feature of loafing is that as group size increases, the addition of new members to the group has a decreasingly significant incremental impact on effort: the reduction of effort conforms to a negatively accelerating power function (see Figure 8.8). So, for example, the reduction in individual effort as the consequence of a third person joining a two-person group is relatively large, while the impact of an additional member on a twenty-person group is minimal. The range within which group size seems to have a significant impact is about one to eight members.

Social loafing is related to the **free-rider effect** (Frohlich and Oppenheimer, 1970; Kerr, 1983) in research into social dilemmas and public goods **(Chapter 11)**. A free rider is someone who takes advantage of a shared public resource without contributing to its maintenance. For example, a tax evader who uses the road system, visits national parks and benefits from public medical provision is a free rider. The main difference between loafing and free riding is that although loafers reduce effort on coactive tasks, they nevertheless do contribute to the group product (there is a *loss* of motivation); in contrast, free riders exploit the group product while contributing nothing to it (there is a *different* motivation; see Williams, Karau and Bourgeois, 1993).

Social loafing is a pervasive and robust phenomenon. A meta-analytic review by Karau and Williams (1993) of the seventy-eight social loafing studies conducted up to the early 1990s found loafing in 80 per cent of the individual–group comparisons that they made. This is an extraordinarily significant overall effect (see reviews by Harkins and Szymanski, 1987; Williams, Harkins and Karau, 2003; Williams, Karau and Bourgeois, 1993). The general loafing paradigm is one in which individual or coactive performance is compared either with groups performing some sort of additive task (e.g. brainstorming), or with the performance of pseudo-groups, in which people are led to *believe* that they are performing collectively with varying numbers of others but in fact circumstances are arranged so that they are performing individually.

Loafing has been found in the laboratory as well as in the field, and in Western and Asian cultures. The effect has been recorded using physical tasks (e.g. clapping, rope pulling, and swimming), cognitive tasks (e.g. generating ideas), evaluative tasks (e.g. quality ratings of poems) and perceptual tasks (e.g. maze performance). People even loaf when tipping in restaurants! In one study, 20 per cent of people gave tips when seated alone, but only 13 per cent tipped when seated in groups of five or six (Freeman, Walker, Bordon and Latané, 1975).

Free-rider effect
Gaining the benefits of group membership by avoiding costly obligations of membership and by allowing other members to incur those costs.

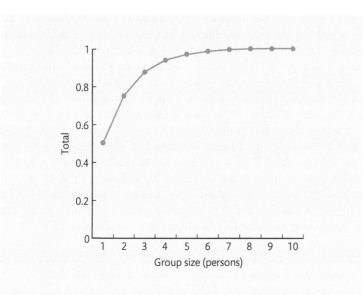

Figure 8.8 Total group output as a negatively accelerating power function of group size

As the group gets larger, each new member has less and less impact on group behaviour: the reduction in effort due to new members gets smaller

In a review of research dealing with social motivation, Russell Geen (1991) concluded that there are three reasons why we loaf when we are in a group:

1 *Output equity* – we believe that others loaf; so to maintain equity (Jackson and Harkins, 1985) and to avoid being a 'sucker' (Kerr and Bruun, 1983).

2 *Evaluation apprehension* – we worry about being evaluated by others; but when we are anonymous and cannot be identified, we hang back and loaf, especially when a task is not engaging (Kerr and Bruun, 1981). However, when we can be identified and therefore evaluated, loafing is reduced (Harkins, 1987; Harkins and Szymanski, 1987).

3 *Matching to standard* – often, we do not have a clear sense of the group's standards or norms, so we hang back and loaf. However, the presence of a clear personal, social or group performance standard should reduce loafing (Goethals and Darley, 1987; Harkins and Szymanski, 1987; Szymanski and Harkins, 1987).

Social impact
The effect that other people have on our attitudes and behaviour, usually as a consequence of factors such as group size, and temporal and physical immediacy.

Group size may have the effect it does due to social impact (Latané, 1981). The experimenter's instructions to clap, shout, brainstorm or whatever (i.e. the social obligation to work as hard as possible) have a social impact on the participants. To the extent that there is one participant and one experimenter, the experimenter's instructions have maximal impact. If there are two participants, the impact on each participant is halved; if three it is one-third, and so on. There is a diffusion of individual responsibility that grows with group size. (**See also how diffusion operates in the context of bystander apathy towards a victim in Chapter 14**).

Loafing is not an inevitable consequence of group performance. Research has identified certain factors, apart from group size, that influence the tendency to loaf (see Geen, 1991; Williams, Karau and Bourgeois, 1993). For example, personal identifiability by the experimenter (Williams, Harkins and Latané, 1981), personal involvement in the task (Brickner, Harkins and Ostrom, 1986), partner effort (Jackson and Harkins, 1985), intergroup comparison (Harkins and Szymanski, 1989) and a highly meaningful task in association with expectation of poor performance by co-workers (Williams and Karau, 1991) have all been shown to reduce loafing.

Social compensation
Increased effort on a collective task to compensate for other group members' actual, perceived or anticipated lack of effort or ability.

In some circumstances, people may even work harder collectively than coactively, in order to compensate for anticipated loafing by others on important tasks or in important groups – there is a social compensation effect. In a study by Stephen Zaccaro (1984), participants each folded pieces of paper to make little tents in two- or four-person groups – the usual loafing effect emerged (see Figure 8.9). However, other participants who believed they were competing against an outgroup, and for whom the attractiveness and social relevance of the task were accentuated, behaved quite differently. The loafing effect was actually reversed: they constructed more tents in the larger group. This was an unusual finding. In contrast to the rather pessimistic view that groups inevitably inhibit individuals from attaining their true potential (Steiner, 1972), Zaccaro's study indicates that group life may, under certain circumstances, cause people to exceed their individual potential, i.e. there may be process gains in groups (Shaw, 1976).

There are other circumstances when people may work harder in groups than when alone (e.g. Guzzo and Dickson, 1996). One is when people place greater value on groups than individuals: that is, they have a collectivist rather than individualist social orientation (Hofstede, 1980). Western and Eastern cultures are significantly different in social orientation (Smith, Bond and Kağitçibaşi, 2006; **see Chapter 16**). So it comes as no surprise, for example, to discover that people can work harder in groups than alone in China (Earley, 1989, 1994) and Japan (Matsui, Kakuyama and Onglatco, 1987). Another circumstance where people may be motivated to work harder in groups is when groups and their members believe and expect that the group will be effective in achieving important goals (Guzzo, Jost, Campbell and Shea, 1993; Sheppard, 1993).

There has also been a revival of interest in the possibility of process gains in groups and in the ability of groups to increase task motivation (Brown, 2000; Kerr and Park, 2001). From their meta-analysis of 78 loafing studies, Karau and Williams (1993) identified task importance

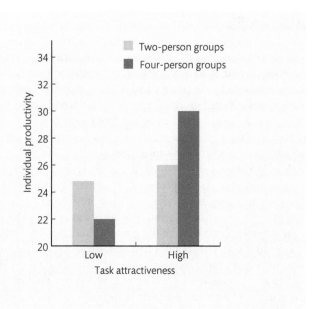

Figure 8.9 Individual effort as a function of task attractiveness and group size

- Social compensation. Participants performing a relatively unattractive paper-folding task loafed.
- Individual productivity was lower in four- than two-person groups.
- For an attractive task, the loafing effect was reversed: individual productivity was higher in four- than two-person groups.

Source: Based on data from Zaccaro (1984)

and the significance of the group to the individual as the two key factors that promote increased effort in groups. These factors may be related. People may be particularly motivated to work hard on tasks that are important precisely because they define membership of a group that is vital to one's self-concept or social identity (see Fielding and Hogg, 2000).

As an example, consider a study by Steve Worchel and his colleagues in which participants made paper chains alone and then as a group (Worchel, Rothgerber, Day, Hart and Butemeyer, 1998). In the group phase of the experiment, participants simply worked in their groups, or they were also in competition against an outgroup. In addition, they either had individual name tags and different-coloured coats, or everyone in the group had identical group name tags and wore identical coloured coats. Worchel and his associates found clear evidence that people worked significantly harder in groups than alone when the group was highly *salient* – group name tags, identical coloured coats and intergroup competition. The productivity increase was five paper chains. In the least salient condition, there was loafing (productivity dropped by four paper chains), and in the intermediate salience conditions there was no significant departure from base rate (productivity changes of 11). Karau and Hart (1998) found a similar process gain in groups that were highly cohesive because they contained people who liked one another.

Generally, research on group performance has assumed that groups perform worse than individuals, and that process and motivation gains are more the exception than the rule. This premise that groups are generally worse than individuals also underpins much classic research on collective behaviours such as crowds (e.g. Zimbardo, 1970; **see Chapter 11**). However, other research emphasises that although people in groups may behave differently to people alone, there is a *change* rather than a deterioration of behaviour (Hogg and Abrams, 1988; Klein, Spears and Reicher, 2007; Reicher, Spears and Postmes, 1995), and that people, in organisational settings, actually like to work in groups and find them satisfying and motivating (Allen and Hecht, 2004).

In his book *The wisdom of crowds,* James Surowiecki (2004) assembled a huge list of instances where the group performs better than the individual. For example, in the TV game show *Who wants to be a millionaire?* – where contestants can call an expert or poll the studio audience to decide which of four answers to the question is correct, Surowiecki found that the expert was correct 65 per cent of the time but the audience (a collection of random people) yielded the right answer 91 per cent of the time.

Group cohesiveness

Cohesiveness
The property of a group that affectively binds people, as group members, to one another and to the group as a whole, giving the group a sense of solidarity and oneness.

One of the most basic properties of a group is its cohesiveness (solidarity, *ésprit de corps*, team spirit, morale) – the way it 'hangs together' as a tightly knit, self-contained entity characterised by uniformity of conduct, attachment to the group, and mutual support between members. The strength of cohesiveness varies between groups, between contexts and across time. Groups with extremely low levels of cohesiveness appear to be hardly groups at all, so the term may also capture the very essence of being a group as opposed to not a group – the psychological process that transforms an aggregate of individuals into a group.

Cohesiveness is thus a descriptive term, used to define a property of the group as a whole. In this respect it is quite closely related to the property of entitativity possessed by categories, which we discussed at the beginning of this chapter. But cohesiveness is also a term that describes the psychological process responsible for an individual's attachment to a group and its members and thus for the overall cohesiveness of the group. Herein lies a potential problem: it makes sense to say that a group is cohesive, but not that an individual is cohesive.

After almost a decade of informal usage, cohesiveness was formally defined by Festinger, Schachter and Back (1950) in a now classic study. They believed that a field of forces, based on the attractiveness of the group and its members and the degree to which the group satisfies individual goals, acts upon the individual. The resultant valence of these forces of attraction produces cohesiveness, which is responsible for group membership continuity and adherence to group standards (see Figure 8.10).

Because concepts such as 'field of forces' are difficult to operationalise, and also because the theory was not precise about exactly how to define cohesiveness operationally (i.e. in terms of specific measures or experimental manipulations), social psychologists almost immediately simplified their conception of cohesiveness. For instance, in their own research into the cohesiveness of student housing projects at the Massachusetts Institute of Technology, Festinger, Schachter and Back simply asked students: 'What three people . . . do you see most of socially?' (1950, p. 37; **see Chapter 14 for further details of this study**).

When we characterise cohesiveness in terms of interpersonal liking we should not be surprised that factors that increase liking (e.g. similarity, cooperation, interpersonal acceptance, shared threat) generally raise cohesiveness. Further, elevated cohesiveness generates conformity to group standards, accentuated similarity, improved intragroup communication and enhanced liking (Cartwright, 1968; Dion, 2000; Hogg, 1992; Lott and Lott, 1965).

Group cohesiveness
Putting it all together, team spirit, total commitment, exhaustion – elation

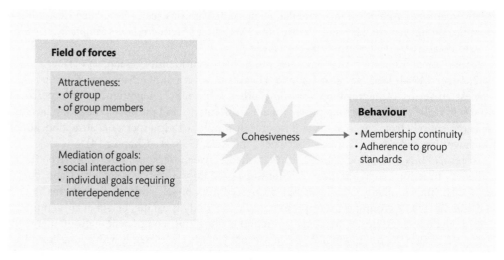

Figure 8.10 Festinger, Schachter and Back's (1950) theory of group cohesiveness

Festinger, Schachter and Back (1950) believed that a field of forces, based on attraction and goal mediation, acts on individual group members to render the group more or less cohesive, and that cohesiveness influences membership continuity and adherence to group norms

Source: Hogg (1992)

It has been suggested (Hogg, 1992, 1993; Turner, 1982, 1984) that this perspective on group cohesiveness represents a much wider *social cohesion* or *interpersonal interdependence* model of the social group (see Figure 8.11), where researchers tend to differ only in which components of the model they emphasise. Because social psychologists have not really resolved the problem of knowing unambiguously how to operationalise cohesiveness (Evans and Jarvis, 1980; Mudrack, 1989), more recent research has tended to be in applied areas (Levine and Moreland,

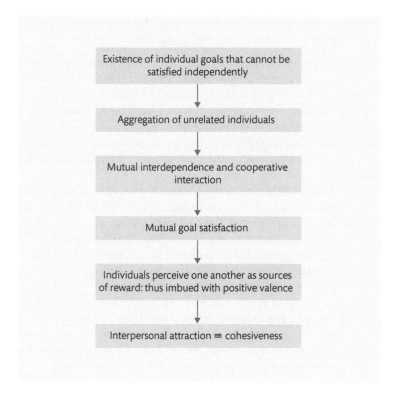

Figure 8.11 General framework of the social cohesion/interpersonal interdependence model

Source: Based on Hogg (1992)

1990). In sports psychology, in particular, some quite rigorous scales have been devised: for example, Widmeyer, Brawley and Carron's (1985) eighteen-item *group environment questionnaire* to measure the cohesiveness of sports teams.

A fundamental question that has been raised by social identity researchers (Hogg, 1992, 1993; Turner, 1984, 1985; **see also Chapter 11**) asks to what extent an analysis of group cohesiveness in terms of aggregation (or some other arithmetic integration) of interpersonal attraction really captures a group process at all. To all intents and purposes, the group has disappeared entirely from the analysis and we are left simply with interpersonal attraction, about which we already know a great deal (Berscheid and Reis, 1998; **see Chapter 14**).

To resolve this issue, Hogg (1993) distinguished between personal attraction (true interpersonal attraction based on close relationships and idiosyncratic preferences) and social attraction (inter-individual liking based on perceptions of self and others in terms not of individuality but of group norms or prototypicality). Strictly speaking, personal attraction has nothing to do with groups, while social attraction is the 'liking' component of group membership. So, for example, you might like Jessica because you are close friends with a long conspiratorial history of intimacy (this is personal attraction) but also like her because you are both members of the same pub darts team (this is social attraction). Of course the converse is that you might dislike Jessica because of a long history of interpersonal animosity (low personal attraction) or dislike her because she throws for a rival pub's darts team (low social attraction).

Social attraction, then, is the liking aspect of group membership. It is one of a constellation of effects (ethnocentrism, conformity, intergroup differentiation, stereotyping, ingroup solidarity) produced by the process of categorising oneself and others as group members and of psychologically identifying with a group, as specified by self-categorisation theory (Turner, Hogg, Oakes, Reicher and Wetherell, 1987; **see Chapter 11**). It is an elegant irony, but also of course true, that you can like someone as a group member but not as an individual, and vice versa (Mullen and Copper, 1994).

This analysis has at least two major advantages over the traditional model:

1. It does not reduce group solidarity and cohesiveness to interpersonal attraction.

2. It is as applicable to small interactive groups (the only valid focus of traditional models) as to large-scale social categories, such as an ethnic group or a nation (people can feel attracted to one another on the basis of common ethnic or national group membership).

This perspective has empirical support. For example, Hogg and Turner (1985) aggregated people with others whom they ostensibly would like or dislike (the fact that the others were people they would like or dislike was irrelevant to the existence of the group), or explicitly categorised them as a group on the basis of the criterion that they would like, or dislike, one another. They found that interpersonal attraction was not automatically associated with greater solidarity (see Figure 8.12). Rather, where interpersonal liking was neither the implicit nor explicit basis for the group (i.e. in the random categorisation condition), group solidarity was unaffected by interpersonal attraction.

In another study, Hogg and Hardie (1991) gave a questionnaire to an Australian football team. Perceptions of team prototypicality and of norms were significantly related to measures of group-based social attraction but were not related to measures of interpersonal attraction. This differential effect was strongest among members who themselves identified most strongly with the team. Similar findings have been obtained from studies of women's netball teams playing in an amateur league (Hogg and Hains, 1996), and of organisational subgroups and quasi-naturalistic discussion groups (Hogg, Cooper-Shaw and Holzworth, 1993).

This broader view of cohesion as linked to group solidarity and social identity may explain why loyalty is so important to group life. For example, in their social glue hypothesis, Mark Van Vugt and Claire Hart (2004) argue that group cooperation can be sustained only if members show ingroup loyalty and willingness to sacrifice self-gain or advantage for the good of the group; thus, disloyalty is reacted to very strongly (also see Levine and Moreland, 2002).

Personal attraction
Liking for someone based on idiosyncratic preferences and interpersonal relationships.

Social attraction
Liking for someone based on common group membership and determined by the person's prototypicality of the group.

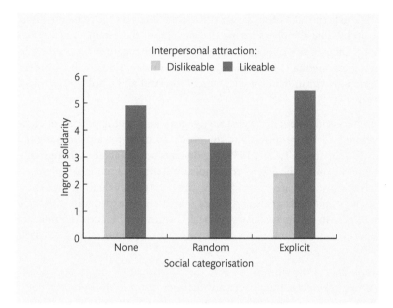

Figure 8.12 Ingroup solidarity as a function of interpersonal attraction and social categorisation

Students who were explicitly categorised as a group on the basis of interpersonal liking or who were merely aggregated showed greater solidarity with likeable groups, while participants who were randomly categorised showed equal solidarity, irrespective of how likeable the group was

Source: Hogg and Turner (1985)

Group socialisation

An obvious feature of many of the groups with which we are familiar is that new members join, old members leave, members are socialised by the group, and the group in turn is imprinted with the contribution of individuals. Groups are dynamic structures that change continuously over time; however, this dynamic aspect of groups is often neglected in social psychology: social psychologists have tended towards a rather static analysis that excludes the passage of time. Many social psychologists feel that this considerably weakens the explanatory power of social psychological theories of group processes and intergroup behaviour (Condor, 1996, 2006; Levine and Moreland, 1994; Tuckman, 1965; Worchel, 1996).

The effects of time are taken more seriously in organisational psychology, where longitudinal analyses are relatively common and quite sophisticated (Wilpert, 1995). For example, Cordery, Mueller and Smith (1991) studied job satisfaction, absenteeism and employee turnover for a twenty-month period in two mineral-processing plants to discover that although autonomous work groups improved work attitudes, they also increased absenteeism and employee turnover.

Focusing on small interactive groups, Bruce Tuckman (1965) described a now famous five-stage developmental sequence that such groups go through:

1 *forming* – an orientation and familiarisation stage;

2 *storming* – a conflict stage, where members know each other well enough to start working through disagreements about goals and practices;

3 *norming* – having survived the storming stage, consensus, cohesion and a sense of common identity and purpose emerge;

4 *performing* – a period in which the group works smoothly as a unit that has shared norms and goals, and good morale and atmosphere;

5 *adjourning* – the group dissolves because it has accomplished its goals, or because members lose interest and motivation and move on.

More recently, Dick Moreland and John Levine (1982, 1984; Levine and Moreland, 1994; Moreland, Levine and Cini, 1993) presented a model of **group socialisation** to describe and

Group socialisation
Dynamic relationship between the group and its members that describes the passage of members through a group in terms of commitment and of changing roles.

explain the passage of individuals through groups over time. They focus on the dynamic inter-relationship of group and individual members across the lifespan of the group. A novel feature of this analysis is that it focuses not only on how individuals change in order to fit into the group but also on how new members can, intentionally or unintentionally, be a potent source of innovation and change within the group (Levine, Moreland and Choi, 2001). Three basic processes are involved:

1 **Evaluation:** Group members and potential members engage in an ongoing process of comparison of the past, present and future rewards of the group with the rewards of potential alternative relationships (Thibaut and Kelley, 1959; **see discussion of social exchange theory in Chapter 14**). Simultaneously, the group as a whole evaluates its individual members in terms of their contribution to the life of the group. This bilateral evaluation process is motivated by the fact that people have goals and needs which create expectations. If such expectations are, or are likely to be, met, social approval is expressed; if they are not met social disapproval is expressed and actions may occur to modify behaviour or to reject individuals or the group.

2 **Commitment:** Evaluation affects the commitment of the individual to the group and the group to the individual in a relatively straightforward manner. Symmetrical positive commitment rests on both the group and the individual agreeing on goals and values, feeling positive ties, being willing to exert effort, and desiring to continue membership. However, at any given time, commitment asymmetry may exist, such that the individual is more committed to the group or the group to the individual. This creates instability because it endows the least committed party with greater power, and it therefore builds pressure towards a more equal level of commitment.

3 **Role transition:** Role transition refers to a sharp change in the type of role a member occupies in a group. Role transitions are superimposed on more continuous variation in commitment over time, and there occurrence is governed by groups' and individuals' criteria for the occurrence of a transition. There are three general types of role: (1) *non-member* – this includes prospective members who have not joined the group and ex-members who have left the group; (2) *quasi-member* – this includes new members who have not attained full member status, and marginal members who have lost that status; and (3) *full member* – people who are closely identified with the group and have all the privileges and responsibilities associated with actual membership.

Role transition
Graduation is a ritualised public ceremony that marks an important role transition in a student's life

Equipped with these processes, Moreland and Levine (1982, 1984) provide a detailed account of the passage of individual members through the group (see Figure 8.13). There are five distinct phases of group socialisation, involving reciprocal evaluation and influence by group and individual, each heralded and/or concluded by a clear role transition (see Box 8.1).

Moreland and his colleagues have conducted research on specific role transitions, particularly those associated with becoming a member (Brinthaupt, Moreland and Levine, 1991; Moreland, 1985; Moreland and Levine, 1989; Pavelchak, Moreland and Levine, 1986). Role transitions are an important aspect of group life. They can be smooth and easy when individual and group are equally committed and share the same criteria about what a transition means and when it occurs, e.g. when a student commences postgraduate studies. Otherwise, conflict can occur over whether a role transition should or did occur, e.g. whether an employee's performance justifies a promotion rather than a bonus. For this reason, transition criteria often become formalised and public, and ritualised rites of passage or initiation rites become a central part of the life of the group. They can be pleasant events marked by celebration and the giving of gifts (e.g. graduation, a wedding), but more often than not they involve a degree of pain, suffering or humiliation (e.g. circumcision, a wake). These rites generally serve three important functions:

Initiation rites
Often painful or embarrassing public procedure to mark group members' movements from one role to another.

- *symbolic* – they allow consensual public recognition of a change in identity;
- *apprenticeship* – some rites help individuals to become accustomed to new roles and normative standards;
- *loyalty elicitation* – pleasant initiations with gifts and special dispensations may elicit gratitude, which should enhance commitment to the group.

In the light of this last function, the prevalence and apparent effectiveness of disagreeable initiation rites is puzzling. Surely people would avoid joining groups with severe initiations,

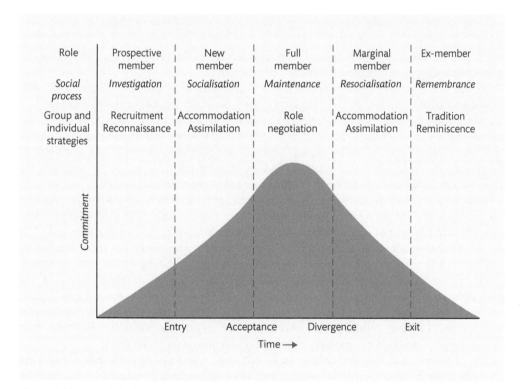

Figure 8.13 A model of the process of group socialisation

Group socialisation. The passage of an individual member through a group is accompanied by variation in commitment and is marked by role discontinuities

Source: Moreland and Levine (1982)

Research highlight 8.1
Phases of group socialisation

Moreland and Levine (1982, 1984; Moreland, Levine and Cini, 1993) distinguished five phases of group socialisation (see Figure 8.13):

1 *Investigation*. The group recruits prospective members, who in turn reconnoitre the group. This can be more formal, involving interviews and questionnaires (e.g. joining an organisation), or less formal (e.g. associating yourself with a student political society). A successful outcome leads to a *role transition*: entry to the group.

2 *Socialisation*. The group assimilates new members, educating them in its ways. In turn, new members try to get the group to accommodate their views. Socialisation can be unstructured and informal, but also quite formal (e.g. an organisation's induction programme). Successful socialisation is marked by *acceptance*.

3 *Maintenance*. Role negotiation takes place between full members. Role dissatisfaction can lead to a role

transition called *divergence*, which can be unexpected and unplanned. It can also be expected – a typical group feature (e.g. university students who diverge by graduating and leaving university).

4 *Resocialisation*. When divergence is expected, resocialisation is unlikely; when it is unexpected, the member is marginalised into a deviant role and tries to become resocialised. If successful, full membership is reinstated – if unsuccessful, the individual leaves. Exit can be marked by elaborate retirement ceremonies (e.g. the ritualistic stripping of insignia in a court martial).

5 *Remembrance*. After the individual leaves the group both parties reminisce. This may be a fond recall of the 'remember when . . . ' type or the more extreme exercise of a totalitarian regime in rewriting history.

Source: Moreland and Levine (1982).

Cognitive dissonance
State of psychological tension, produced by simultaneously having two opposing cognitions. People are motivated to reduce the tension, often by changing or rejecting one of the cognitions. Festinger proposed that we seek harmony in our attitudes, beliefs and behaviours, and try to reduce tension from inconsistency among these elements.

and if unfortunate enough not to be able to do this, then at the very least they should subsequently hate the group and feel no sense of commitment.

We can make sense of this anomaly in terms of cognitive dissonance (Festinger, 1957; **discussed in Chapter 6**). An aversive initiation creates dissonance between the two thoughts: 'I knowingly underwent a painful experience to join this group' and 'Some aspects of this group are not that great' (since group life is usually a mixture of positive and negative aspects). As an initiation is public and cannot be denied, I can reduce dissonance by revising my opinion of the group – downplaying negative aspects and focusing on positive aspects. The outcome for me is a more favourable evaluation of the group and thus greater commitment.

This analysis clearly predicts that the more unpleasant the initiation is, the more positive the subsequent evaluation of the group will be. The Aronson and Mills (1959) experiment **(described in Chapter 6)** is an investigation of this idea. You will recall that Aronson and Mills recruited female students to participate in a group discussion of the psychology of sex. Before joining the group, they listened to and rated a short extract of the discussion – an extremely tedious and stilted discussion of the secondary sexual characteristics of lower animals. It was quite rightly rated as such by control participants, and also by a second group of participants who had gone through a mild initiation where they read aloud five words with vague sexual connotations. However, a third group, who underwent an extreme initiation where they read out loud explicit and obscene passages, rated the discussion as very interesting.

Harold Gerard and Grover Mathewson (1966) were concerned that the effect may have arisen because the severe-initiation participants were either sexually aroused by the obscene passage and/or relieved at discovering that the discussion was not as extreme as the passage. To discount these alternative explanations, they replicated Aronson and Mills's study. Participants, who audited and rated a boring discussion they were about to join, were given mild or severe electric shocks either explicitly as an initiation or under some other pretext

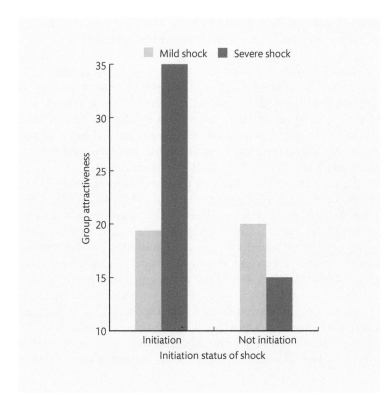

Figure 8.14 Group attractiveness as a function of severity of electric shock and initiation status of the shock

- Cognitive dissonance and the effectiveness of initiation rites.
- Participants about to join a boring group discussion were given a mild or severe electric shock.
- When the shock was billed as an initiation, participants given the severe shock rated the group as more attractive than participants given the mild shock.

Source: Based on data from Gerard and Mathewson (1966)

completely unrelated to the ensuing discussion. As cognitive dissonance theory predicted, the painful experience enhanced evaluation of the group only when it was perceived to be an initiation (see Figure 8.14). (Now answer the second focus question.)

Norms

Many years ago, the sociologist William Graham Sumner (1906) wrote about **norms** as 'folkways' –habitual customs displayed by a group because they had originally been adaptive in meeting basic needs. Later Sherif (1936) described norms as 'customs, traditions, standards, rules, values, fashions, and all other criteria of conduct which are standardized as a consequence of the contact of individuals' (p. 3). Although norms can take the form of explicit rules that are enforced by legislation and sanctions (e.g. societal norms to do with private property, pollution and aggression), most social psychologists agree with Cialdini and Trost (1998) that norms are:

> rules and standards that are understood by members of a group and that guide and/or constrain social behaviour without the force of laws. These norms emerge out of interaction with others; they may or may not be stated explicitly, and any sanctions for deviating from them come from social networks, not the legal system. (p. 152)

Another sociologist, Harold Garfinkel (1967), focused very much on norms as the implicit, unobserved, taken-for-granted background to everyday life. People typically assume a practice is 'natural' or simply 'human nature' until the practice is disrupted by norm violation and people suddenly realise the practice is 'merely' normative. Indeed, Piaget's influential theory of

Norms
Attitudinal and behavioural uniformities that define group membership and differentiate between groups.

cognitive development describes how children only slowly begin to realise that norms are not objective facts, and suggests that even adults find it difficult to come to this realisation (Piaget, 1928, 1955).

Ethnomethodology
Method devised by Garfinkel, involving the violation of hidden norms to reveal their presence.

Garfinkel devised a general methodology, called ethnomethodology, to detect these background norms. One specific method involved the violation of norms in order to attract people's attention to them. For example, Garfinkel had students act at home for fifteen minutes as if they were boarders: that is, be polite, speak formally and only speak when spoken to. Their families reacted with astonishment, bewilderment, shock, embarrassment and anger, backed up with charges of selfishness, nastiness, rudeness and lack of consideration! An implicit norm for familial interaction was revealed, and its violation provoked a strong reaction.

Social identity theorists place a particular emphasis on the group-defining dimension of norms (e.g. Abrams and Hogg, 1990a; Abrams, Wetherell, Cochrane, Hogg and Turner, 1990; Hogg, 2010; Hogg and Smith, 2007; Turner, 1991). Norms are attitudinal and behavioural regularities that map the contours of social groups (small groups or large social categories) such that normative discontinuities mark group boundaries. Norms capture attributes that describe one group and distinguish it from other groups, and because groups define who we are, group norms are also prescriptive, telling us how we should behave as group members. Thus the behaviour of students and lecturers at a university is governed by very different norms: knowing whether someone is a student or a lecturer establishes clear expectations of appropriate normative behaviour. (Reflect on the third focus question: what norms are in conflict?)

As Hogg and Reid (2006) have noted, this perspective on norms transcends the traditional distinction drawn in social psychology between descriptive norms ('is' norms) that describe

Ethnomethodology
Non-normative behaviour (being dressed too casually) draws attention to the implicit norm of being serious when meeting an important client

behavioural regularities, and injunctive norms ('ought' norms) that convey approval or disapproval of the behaviour (e.g., Cialdini, Kallgren and Reno, 1991). Instead, by tying norms to group membership the descriptive and injunctive aspects of norms become tightly integrated.

As an aside, norms and stereotypes are closely related – the terms 'normative behaviour' and 'stereotypical behaviour' mean virtually the same thing. However, research traditions have generally separated the two areas: norms referring to behaviour that is shared in a group, and stereotypes **(see Chapters 2, 10 and 11)** to shared generalisations made by individuals about members of other groups.

Group norms can have a powerful effect on people. For example, Theodore Newcomb (1965) conducted a classic study of norms in the 1930s at a small American college called Bennington. The college had progressive and liberal norms but drew its students from conservative, upper-middle-class families. The 1936 American presidential election allowed Newcomb to conduct a confidential ballot. First-year students strongly favoured the conservative candidate, while third- and fourth-year students had shifted their voting preference towards the liberal and communist/socialist candidates (see Figure 8.15). Presumably, prolonged exposure to liberal norms had produced the change in political preference.

In a better-controlled study by Alberta Siegel and Sidney Siegel (1957), new students at a private American college were randomly assigned to different types of student accommodation – sororities and dormitories. At this particular college, sororities had a conservative ethos and the dormitories had more progressive liberal norms. Siegel and Siegel measured the students' degree of conservatism at the beginning and end of the year. Figure 8.16 clearly shows how exposure to liberal norms reduced conservatism.

Norms serve a function for the individual. They specify a limited range of behaviour that is acceptable in a certain context and thus they reduce uncertainty and facilitate confident choice of the 'correct' course of action. Norms provide a frame of reference within which to locate our own behaviour. You will recall that this idea was explored by Sherif (1936) in his classic experiments dealing with norm formation **(see Box 7.1 in Chapter 7 for details)**. Sherif showed that when people made perceptual judgements alone, they relied on their own

Stereotype
Widely shared and simplified evaluative image of a social group and its members.

Frame of reference
Complete range of subjectively conceivable positions that relevant people can occupy in that context on some attitudinal or behavioural dimension.

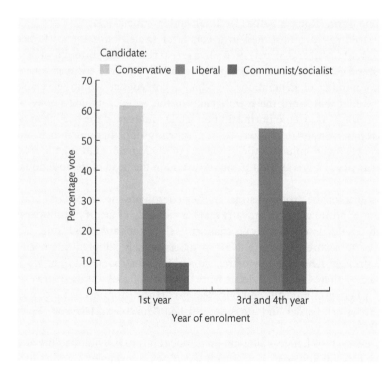

Figure 8.15 Newcomb's 1965 Bennington study: voting preference for 1936 presidential candidates as a function of exposure to liberal norms

First-year students at Bennington college in the USA showed a traditionally conservative voting pattern during the 1936 presidential election, while third- and fourth-year students, who had been exposed for longer to the college's liberal norms, showed a significantly more liberal voting pattern

Source: Based on data from Newcomb (1965)

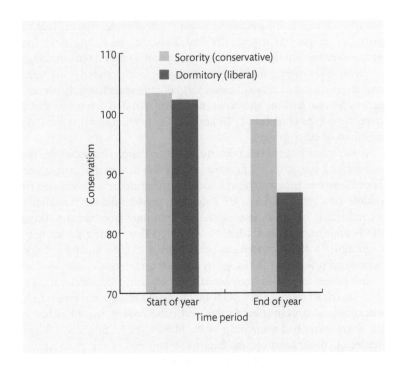

Figure 8.16 Effects of dormitory political norms on students' conservative or liberal voting preferences

Source: Based on data from Siegel and Siegel (1957)

estimates as a frame of reference; however, when they were in a group, they used the group's range of judgements to converge quickly on the group mean.

Sherif believed that people were using other members' estimates as a social frame of reference to guide them: he felt that he had produced a primitive group norm experimentally. The norm was an emergent property of interaction between group members, but once created it acquired a life of its own. Members were later tested alone and still conformed to the norm. In one study people who were retested individually as much as a year later were, quite remarkably, still influenced by the group norm (Rohrer, Baron, Hoffman and Swander, 1954).

This same point was strikingly demonstrated in a couple of related autokinetic studies (Jacobs and Campbell, 1961; MacNeil and Sherif, 1976). In a group comprising three confederates, who gave extreme estimates, and one true participant, a relatively extreme norm emerged. The group went through a number of 'generations', in which a confederate would leave and another true participant would join, until the membership of the group contained none of the original members. The original extreme norm still powerfully influenced the participants' estimates. This is a very elegant demonstration that a norm is a true group phenomenon: it can emerge only from a group, yet it can influence the behaviour of the individual in the physical absence of the group (Turner, 1991). It is as if the group is carried in the head of the individual in the form of a norm.

Norms also serve functions for the group in so far as they coordinate the actions of members towards the fulfilment of group goals. In an early and classic study of factory production norms, Coch and French (1948) describe a group that set itself a standard of 50 units per hour as the minimum level to secure job tenure. New members quickly adopted this norm. Those who did not were strongly sanctioned by ostracism and in some cases had their work sabotaged. Generally speaking, there is good evidence from the study of goal setting in organisational work teams that, where group norms embody clear group goals for performance and production, group members work harder and are more satisfied (Guzzo and Dickson, 1996; Weldon and Weingart, 1993).

Norms are inherently resistant to change – after all, their function is to provide stability and predictability. However, norms initially arise to deal with specific circumstances. They endure as long as those circumstances prevail but ultimately change with changing circumstances.

Norms vary in their 'latitude of acceptable behaviour': some are narrow and restrictive (e.g. military dress codes) and others wider and less restrictive (e.g. dress codes for university lecturers). In general, norms that relate to group loyalty and to central aspects of group life have a latitude of acceptable behaviour that is narrow, while norms relating to more peripheral features of the group are less restrictive. Finally, certain group members are allowed a latitude of acceptable behaviour that is greater than others: higher-status members (e.g. leaders) can get away with more than lower-status members and followers (**this phenomenon is discussed in Chapter 9 when we talk about leadership**).

There is evidence for the patterning and structure of different types of norm from Sherif and Sherif's (1964) pioneering study of adolescent gangs in American cities. Participant observers infiltrated these gangs and studied them over several months. The gangs had given themselves names, had adopted various insignia and had strict codes about how gang members should dress. Dress codes were important, as it was largely through dress that the gangs differentiated themselves from one another. The gangs also had strict norms concerning sexual mores and how to deal with outsiders (e.g. parents, police); however, leaders were allowed some latitude in their adherence to these and other norms.

Norms are the yardstick of group conduct, and it is through norms that groups influence the behaviour of their members. **The exact processes responsible are the subject of much of Chapter 7, which deals with social influence.**

Group structure

Cohesiveness, socialisation and norms refer mainly to uniformities in groups. In very few groups, however, are all members equal, performing identical activities or communicating freely. Differences between members are reflected in roles, status relations and communication networks, as well subgroups, and the central or marginal group membership credentials of specific members. This is what is meant by group structure, and its features may not be easily visible to an outsider.

Group structure
Division of a group into different roles that often differ with respect to status and prestige.

Roles

Roles are much like norms in so far as they describe and prescribe behaviour. However, while norms apply to the group as a whole, roles apply to a subgroup of people within the group. Furthermore, while norms may distinguish between groups, they are generally not intentionally derived to benefit the framework of groups in a society. In contrast, roles are specifically designed to differentiate between people in the group for the greater good of the group as a whole.

Roles are not people but behavioural prescriptions that are assigned to people. They can be informal and implicit (e.g. in groups of friends) or formal and explicit (e.g. in aircraft flight crews). One quite general role differentiation in small groups is between task specialists (the 'ideas' people, who get things done) and socioemotional specialists (the people everyone likes because they address relationships in the group) (e.g. Slater, 1955). Roles may emerge in a group for a number of reasons:

Roles
Patterns of behaviour that distinguish between different activities within the group, and that interrelate to one another for the greater good of the group.

- They represent a division of labour; only in the simplest groups is there no division of labour.
- They furnish clear-cut social expectations within the group and provide information about how members relate to one another.
- They furnish members with a self-definition and a place within the group.

Clearly, roles emerge to facilitate group functioning. However, there is evidence that inflexible role differentiation can sometimes be detrimental to the group. Take a real-life example. Rigid role differentiation (who does what) in pre-flight checks by the flight crew of a passenger airliner caused the crew to fail to engage a de-icing device, with the tragic consequence that the plane crashed shortly after take-off (Gersick and Hackman, 1990).

Roles can sometimes also be associated with larger category memberships (e.g. professional groups) outside the specific task-oriented groups, in which case the task-oriented group can become a context for role conflict that is actually a manifestation of wider intergroup conflict. One example of this is conflict that can occur in a hospital between doctors and nurses (e.g. Oaker and Brown, 1986).

Although we tend to adopt a dramaturgical perspective when we speak of people 'acting' or 'assuming' roles, we are probably only partly correct. We may assume roles much like actors taking different parts, but many people see us only in particular roles and so infer that that is how we really are. Professional actors are easily typecast in exactly the same way – one reason why Paul Greengrass's 2006 film, *United 93*, about the 11 September 2001 terrorist attacks on the United States, is so incredibly powerful is that the actors are not high-profile individuals who have already been typecast. This tendency to attribute roles internally to dispositions of the role player is a likely example of **correspondence bias** (Gawronski, 2004; Gilbert and Malone, 1995; **see Chapter 3**).

One practical implication of this is that you should avoid low-status roles in groups, or you may subsequently find it difficult to escape their legacy. Perhaps the most powerful and well-known social psychological illustration of the power of roles to modify behaviour is Zimbardo's (1971; Banuazizi and Movahedi, 1975) simulated prison experiment (see Box 8.2).

Ultimately, roles can actually influence who we are – our identity and concept of self (see Haslam and Reicher, 2005, 2012). Sociologists have extensively elaborated this idea to explain how social interaction and wider societal expectations about behaviour can create enduring and real identities for people – *role identity theory* (McCall and Simmons, 1978; Stryker and Statham, 1986; see Hogg, Terry and White, 1995).

Correspondence bias
A general attribution bias in which people have an inflated tendency to see behaviour as reflecting (corresponding to) stable underlying personality attributes.

Research classic 8.2
Guards versus prisoners: role behaviour in a simulated prison

Phil Zimbardo was interested in how people adopt and internalise roles to guide behaviour. He was also interested in whether it is the prescription of the role rather than the personality of the role occupant that governs in-role behaviour. In a famous role-playing exercise, twenty-four psychologically stable male Stanford University student volunteers were randomly assigned the roles of prisoners or guards. The prisoners were arrested at their homes and initially processed by the police, then handed over to the guards in a simulated prison constructed in the basement of the Psychology Department at Stanford University.

Zimbardo had planned to observe the role-playing exercise over a period of two weeks. However, he had to stop the study after six days! Although the students were psychologically stable and those assigned to the guard or prisoner roles had no prior dispositional differences, things got completely out of hand. The guards continually harassed, humiliated and intimidated the prisoners, and they used psychological techniques to undermine solidarity and sow the seeds of distrust among them. Some guards increasingly behaved in a brutal and sadistic manner.

The prisoners initially revolted. However, they gradually became passive and docile as they showed symptoms of individual and group disintegration and an acute loss of contact with reality. Some prisoners had to be released from the study because they showed symptoms of severe emotional disturbance (disorganised thinking, uncontrollable crying and screaming); and in one case, a prisoner developed a psychosomatic rash all over his body.

Zimbardo's explanation of what happened in the simulated prison was that the students complied (too well!) with the roles that they thought were expected of them (see Haney, Banks and Zimbardo, 1973). This has been challenged. Steve Reicher and Alex Haslam argue that the participants were confronted by a situation that raised their feelings of uncertainty about themselves and that in order to reduce this uncertainty they internalised the identities available (prisoners or guards), and adopted the appropriate behaviours to define themselves (Reicher and Haslam, 2006; Haslam and Reicher, 2012). The process was one of group identification and conformity to group norms motivated by uncertainty about their self-concept (see Hogg, 2012).

Status

All roles are not equal: some are consensually more valued and respected and thus confer greater **status** on the role occupant. The highest-status role in most groups is the role of leader (**see Chapter 9**). In general, higher-status roles or their occupants tend to have two properties:

1 consensual prestige;

2 a tendency to initiate ideas and activities that are adopted by the group.

For example, from his participant observation study of gangs in an Italian American immigrant community, the sociologist W. F. Whyte (1943) reported that even the relatively inarticulate 'Doc', who described his assumption of leadership of the thirteen-member Norton gang in terms of who he had 'walloped', found that the consensual prestige that such wallopings earned him was insufficient alone to ensure his high-status position. He admitted that his status also derived from the fact that he was the one who always thought of things for the group to do.

Status hierarchies in groups are not fixed: they can vary over time, and also from situation to situation. Take an orchestra: the lead violinist may have the highest-status role at a concert, while the union representative has the highest-status role in negotiations with management. One explanation of why status hierarchies emerge so readily in groups is in terms of social comparison theory (Festinger, 1954; Suls and Miller, 1977) – status hierarchies are the expression and reflection of intragroup social comparisons. Groups furnish a pool of relevant others with whom we can make social comparisons in order to assess the validity of our opinions and abilities.

Certain roles in the group have more power and influence and, because they are therefore more attractive and desirable, have many more 'applicants' than can be accommodated. Fierce social comparisons on behavioural dimensions relevant to these roles inevitably mean that the majority of group members, who are unsuccessful in securing the role, must conclude that they are less able than those who are successful. Thus there arises a shared view that those occupying the attractive role are superior to the rest – consensual prestige and high status. (Do you have any advice for Andrea? See the fourth focus question.)

Status hierarchies often become institutionalised, so that individual members do not engage in ongoing systematic social comparisons. Rather, they simply assume that particular roles or role occupants are of higher status than their own role or themselves. Research into the formation of status hierarchies in newly created groups tends to support this view. Strodtbeck, James and Hawkins (1957) assembled mock juries to consider and render a verdict on transcripts of actual trials. They found that the high-status role of jury foreman almost always went to people who had higher occupational status outside the context of the jury (e.g. teachers or psychologists rather than janitors or mechanics).

One explanation of this phenomenon is proposed by **expectation states theory** (Berger, Fisek, Norman and Zelditch, 1977; Berger, Wagner and Zelditch, 1985; de Gilder and Wilke, 1994; Ridgeway, 2001). Status derives from two distinct sets of characteristics:

1 **Specific status characteristics** are attributes that relate directly to ability on the group task (e.g. being a good athlete in a sports team, a good musician in a band).

2 **Diffuse status characteristics** are attributes that do not relate directly to ability on the group task but are generally positively or negatively valued in society (e.g. being wealthy, having a white-collar occupation, being white).

Diffuse status characteristics generate favourable expectations that are generalised to all sorts of situations, even those that may not have any relevance to what the group does. Group members simply assume that someone who rates highly on diffuse status (e.g. a medical doctor) will be more able than others to promote the group's goals (e.g. analysing trial transcripts in order to render a verdict) and therefore has higher specific status.

Typically, specific status and diffuse status each make their own additive contribution to a person's overall status in a newly formed group. So, if your town was assembling a cast for a musical

Status
Consensual evaluation of the prestige of a role or role occupant in a group, or of the prestige of a group and its members as a whole.

Expectation states theory
Theory of the emergence of roles as a consequence of people's status-based expectations about others' performance.

Specific status characteristics
Information about those abilities of a person that are directly relevant to the group's task.

Diffuse status characteristics
Information about a person's abilities that are only obliquely relevant to the group's task, and derive mainly from large-scale category memberships outside the group.

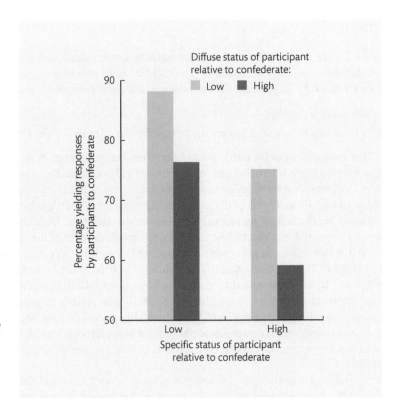

Figure 8.17 Yielding as a function of specific and diffuse status of participants relative to a confederate

Female participants yielded more often to a female confederate's suggestions in a word-construction task if the confederate had higher specific status (had performed well on a similar task) and had higher diffuse status (was older)

Source: Based on data from Knottnerus and Greenstein (1981)

in the local theatre, Brenda may well play a part because of her rich contralto voice (specific status) and Rudolf could be chosen because of his dreamy looks (diffuse status). But star billing will no doubt accrue to Sophie, the soprano – she has been a successful soprano in other productions (specific status); plus, she looks stunning in most costumes (diffuse status). Poor Rudolf can't sing to save his life, so he only has his diffuse status to contribute to his overall status in the group.

David Knottnerus and Theodore Greenstein (1981) investigated the different contributions of specific status and diffuse status in a newly formed group. Female participants worked with a female confederate on two supposedly related tasks. Specific status was manipulated by informing participants that they had performed better or worse than the confederate on the first task – a perceptual task. Diffuse status was manipulated by leading participants to believe that they were either younger or older than the confederate. The second task, a word construction task, allowed measures of yielding to the confederate's suggestions to be used as an index of effective status. The results (see Figure 8.17) showed that participants yielded more if they believed that they were of lower specific or lower diffuse status than the confederate. Other factors shown to contribute to high status in a group include seniority, assertiveness, past task success and high group orientation.

Communication networks

People occupying different roles in a group need to coordinate their actions through communication, although not all roles need to communicate with one another. Thus the structuring of a group with respect to roles entails an internal **communication network** that regulates who can communicate with whom. Although such networks can be informal, we are probably more familiar with the rigidly formalised ones in large organisations and bureaucracies (e.g. a university or government office). What are the effects on group functioning of different types of communication network, and what factors affect the sort of network that evolves?

Communication network
Set of rules governing the possibility or ease of communication between different roles in a group.

Alex Bavelas (1968) suggested that an important factor was the number of communication links to be crossed for one person to communicate with another. For example, if I can communicate with the dean of my faculty directly, there is one link; but if I have to go through the head of department, there are two. In Franz Kafka's (1925) classic novel *The Trial*, the central character 'K' was confronted by a bewildering and ever-increasing number of communication links in order to communicate with senior people in the organisation. Figure 8.18 shows some of the communication networks that have been researched experimentally; those on the left are more highly centralised than those on the right.

For relatively simple tasks, greater centralisation improves group performance (Leavitt, 1951): the hub person is able to receive, integrate and pass on information efficiently while allowing peripheral members to concentrate on their allotted roles. For more complex tasks, a less centralised structure is superior (Shaw, 1964), because the quantity and complexity of information communicated would overwhelm a hub person, who would be unable to integrate, assimilate and pass it on efficiently. Peripheral members would thus experience delays and miscommunication. For complex tasks, there are potentially serious coordination losses (Steiner, 1972; see above) associated with overly centralised communication networks. However, centralisation for complex tasks may pay off in the long run once appropriate procedures have been well established and well learnt.

Another important consideration is the degree of autonomy felt by group members. Because they are dependent on the hub for regulation and flow of information, peripheral members have less power in the group, and they can feel restricted and dependent. According to the Dutch psychologist Mauk Mulder (1959), having more power – being more central and feeling like a 'key person' – leads to a greater sense of autonomy and satisfaction, so peripheral members can become dissatisfied, while hub members, who are often perceived to be group leaders, feel a sense of satisfaction. Centralised communication networks can thus reduce group satisfaction, harmony and solidarity, and instead produce internal conflict. Research on organisations confirms that job satisfaction and organisational commitment are influenced by the amount of control that employees feel they have, and that control is related to communication networks, in particular to employees' perceived participation in decision making (Evans and Fischer, 1992).

In almost all groups, particularly organisational groups, the formal communication network is complemented by an informal communication 'grapevine'. You might be surprised to learn

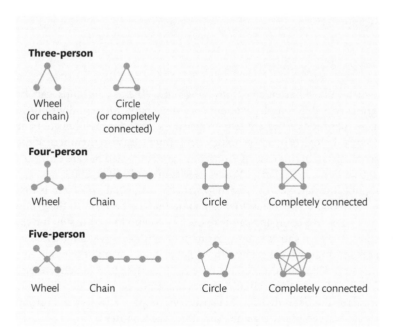

Figure 8.18 Communication networks that have been studied experimentally

The most studied communication networks are those involving three, four or five members (dots represent positions or roles or people, and lines represent communication channels). The networks on the left are highly centralised, and become increasingly less centralised as you move to the right of the figure

Communication networks
A multifaceted activity like making a film requires a division of labour, and a centralised communication network focused on the team leader – something Clint Eastwood knows well

that, contrary to popular opinion and according to a study by Simmonds (1985), 80 per cent of grapevine information is work-related, and 70–90 per cent of that information is accurate.

Finally, the rules for studying communication networks in organisations now need to be rewritten with the explosion of computer-mediated communication (CMC) in the past fifteen years (Hollingshead, 2001). Organisations now have virtual groups and teams that rarely need to meet; they use electronic communication channels instead, and are often highly distributed without a centralised communication hub (Hackman, 2002). One positive effect of CMC is that it can de-emphasise status differences and can thus promote more equal participation among all members (**see Chapter 15**).

Subgroups and crosscutting categories

Almost all groups are structurally differentiated into subgroups. These subgroups can be nested within the larger group (e.g. different departments in a university, different divisions in a company). However, many subgroups represent larger categories that have members outside the larger group (e.g. social psychologists in a psychology department are also members of the larger group of social psychologists). In this case the subgroups are not nested but are crosscutting categories (Crisp and Hewstone, 2007; Crisp, Ensari, Hewstone and Miller, 2003).

Group processes are significantly affected by subgroup structure. The main problem is that subgroups can engage in intergroup competition that can sometimes be harmful to the group as a whole. For example, divisions in a company can take healthy competition one step too far and slip into outright conflict. Research shows that when one company takes over another company and therefore contains within it two subgroups, the original company and the new company, conflict between these two subgroups can be extreme (e.g. Cartwright and Schoenberg, 2006; Terry, Carey and Callan, 2001). In these circumstances it can be very difficult to provide effective leadership that bridges the deep division between subgroups – effective intergroup leadership is called for (Hogg, Van Knippenberg and Rast, 2012; **see Chapter 9**).

When groups contain subgroups that differ ideologically or in their core values and attitudes, a schism can occur in which one group feels that the larger group no longer represents its values and embodies its identity. The smaller group may then decide to split off and try to convert the larger group. This can create extreme conflict that can tear the larger group apart – this often happens in political and religious contexts (Sani and Reicher, 1998, 2000), but can also happen in artistic and scientific contexts. A key factor that transforms ideological disagreement into schism is lack of voice – the probability of schism is greatly amplified if the smaller marginalised group feels its concerns about the majority's ideological and identity slippage is simply not being listened to or heard by the majority (Sani, 2005, 2009).

The problem of subgroup conflict is often most evident, and indeed harmful, when larger groups contain socio-demographic subgroups that have destructive intergroup relations in society as a whole, such as Protestants and Catholics who work together in a Northern Irish business (Hewstone et al., 2005). **See Chapter 11 for a full treatment of intergroup relations, including intergroup relations among crosscutting and nested subgroups.**

Schism
Division of a group into subgroups that differ in their attitudes, values or ideology.

Deviants and marginal members

Many, if not most, groups are also structured in terms of two kinds of member:

1 Those who best embody the group's attributes – core members who are highly prototypical of the group.

2 Those who do not – marginal or non-prototypical members.

Highly prototypical members often have significant influence over the group and may occupy leadership roles – **we discuss them in Chapter 9**. Marginal members are an entirely different story.

Research by José Marques and his colleagues shows that marginal members are often disliked by the group, and treated as 'black sheep' (Marques and Páez, 1994) or deviants. People whose attributes place them on the boundary between ingroup and outgroup are actually disliked more if they are classified as ingroup members than outgroup members – they are treated as deviants or even traitors.

Marques and Abrams and their colleagues have elaborated this idea into a broader theory of subjective group dynamics (Marques, Abrams, Páez and Taboada, 1998; Pinto, Marques, Levine and Abrams, 2010). Non-normative members of a group pose a threat to the integrity of the group's norms and thus identity; and this is particularly threatening if the non-normative member's divergence from the group norm is towards an outgroup (called an 'anti-norm deviant') than away from the outgroup (a 'pro-norm deviant'). Anti-norm deviants are evaluated more negatively than pro-norm deviants. Thus 'black sheep', who are archetypal anti-norm deviants, are particularly harshly evaluated and treated (Marques, Abrams, Páez and Hogg, 2001; Marques, Abrams and Serodio, 2001). Paradoxically, marginal members can therefore serve an important function for groups – groups, particularly their leaders, can engage in a rhetoric of vilification and exclusion of marginal members in order to throw into stark relief what the group is and what the group is not.

Subjective group dynamics
A process where normative deviants who deviate towards an outgroup (anti-norm deviants) are more harshly treated than those who deviate away from the outgroup (pro-norm deviants).

Marginal members may play another important group role – they can be agents of social change within the group. Under the right conditions, marginal members may be uniquely placed to act as critics of group norms, precisely because they are normatively marginal. Research on intergroup criticism by Matthew Hornsey and his colleagues (Hornsey, 2005) shows that groups are more accepting of criticism from ingroup than outgroup members (Hornsey and Imani, 2004; Hornsey, Oppes and Svensson, 2002) and from old-timers than newcomers (Hornsey, Grice, Jetten, Paulsen and Callan, 2007). The rationale for this is that critics can have an uphill struggle to be heard if they are labelled and treated as deviants; and outgroup critics and newcomers can more readily be labelled in this way.

The challenge of gaining voice may be more easily overcome if a number of dissenters unite as a subgroup – we then effectively have a schism (see above), or an active minority within the group. Indeed the analysis of how marginal members, deviants and dissenters may influence the larger group is, in many respects, the analysis of minority influence (**which we discussed fully in Chapter 7**).

Why do people join groups?

This is not an easy question to answer. It depends on how we define a group, and of course 'why' people join groups is not the same thing as 'how' people join groups. We also need to recognise that the groups to which we belong vary in the degree of free choice we had in joining. There is little choice in what sex, ethnic, national or social class groups we 'join': membership is largely designated externally. There is a degree of choice, although possibly less than we might think, in what occupational or political group we join; and there is a great deal of freedom in what clubs, societies and recreational groups we join. Even the most strongly externally designated social-category memberships, such as sex and ethnicity, can permit a degree of choice in what the implications of membership in that group may be (e.g. the group's norms and practices), and this may reflect the same sorts of motives and goals for choosing freely to join less externally designated groups.

Reasons for joining groups

However, we can identify a range of circumstances, motives, goals and purposes that tend to cause, in more or less immediate ways, people to join or form groups (e.g. aggregate, coordinate their actions, declare themselves members of a group). For example, physical proximity can promote group formation. We tend to get to like, or at least learn to put up with, people we are in close proximity with (Tyler and Sears, 1977). This appears to promote group formation: we form groups with those around us. Festinger, Schachter and Back's (1950) classic study of a student housing programme, which we discussed earlier (**see also Chapter 14**), concerned just this – the role of proximity in group formation, group cohesiveness and subsequent adherence to group standards. The recognition of similar interests, attitudes and beliefs can also cause people to become or join a group.

If people share goals that require behavioural interdependence for their achievement, this is another strong and reliable reason for joining groups. This idea lies at the heart of Sherif's (1966) realistic conflict theory of intergroup behaviour (**discussed in Chapter 11**). For example, if we are concerned about degradation of the environment, we are likely ultimately to join an environmental conservation group, because division of labour and interdependent action among like-minded people will achieve a great deal more than the actions of a lone protester. People join groups to get things done that they cannot do on their own.

We can join groups for mutual positive support and the mere pleasure of affiliation: for example, to avoid loneliness (Peplau and Perlman, 1982). We can join groups for self-protection and personal safety: for example, adolescents join gangs (Ahlstrom and Havighurst, 1971) and mountaineers climb in groups for this reason. We can join groups for emotional support in times of stress: for example, support groups for AIDS sufferers and their relatives and friends fulfil this function.

Oscar Lewis's (1969) powerful account of a Catholic wake in Mexico, in his novel *A Death in the Sanchez Family,* describes the way in which people come together in stressful circumstances. Stanley Schachter (1959) has explored the same idea in controlled experimental circumstances. However, a word of qualification is needed. Extreme stress and deprivation (e.g. in concentration camps, or after natural disasters) sometimes produces social disintegration and individual isolation rather than group formation (Middlebrook, 1980). This is probably because the link between stress and affiliation is not mechanical: if affiliation is not the effective solution to the stress, then it may not occur. Thomas Keneally's (1982) account, in his powerful biographical novel *Schindler's Ark,* of atrocities committed by the Nazis against Jews in the Polish city of Kraków, supports this. Despite extreme stress, remarkably little affiliation occurred: affiliation was difficult to sustain and would probably only exacerbate the situation.

Motivations for affiliation and group formation

The question of why people join groups can be reframed in terms of what basic motivations cause people to affiliate (Hogg, Hohman and Rivera, 2008; **see also Chapter 13**). According to Baumeister and Leary (1995), human beings simply have a basic and overwhelming need to belong, and this causes them to affiliate and to join and be members of groups. Furthermore, the sense of belonging and being successfully connected to other human beings, interpersonally or in groups, produces a powerful and highly rewarding sense of self-esteem and self-worth (Leary, Tambor, Terdal and Downs, 1995) – self-esteem acts as a sociometer which provides people with information about how well they are grounded and connected socially (Leary and Baumeister, 2000).

According to **terror management theory** (Greenberg, Pyszczynski and Solomon, 1986; Greenberg, Solomon and Pyszczynski, 1997; Pyszczynski, Greenberg and Solomon, 2004; Solomon, Greenberg and Pyszczynski, 1991; **see Chapter 4**) the most fundamental threat that people face is the inevitability of their own death, and therefore people live their lives in perpetual terror of death. Fear of death is the most powerful motivating factor in human existence. People affiliate and join groups in order to reduce fear of death. Affiliation and group formation are highly effective terror management strategies because they provide symbolic immortality through connection to normative systems that outlive individuals. Thus affiliation and group formation raise self-esteem and make people feel good about themselves – they feel immortal, and positive and excited about life.

Terror management theory
The notion that the most fundamental human motivation is to reduce the terror of the inevitability of death. Self-esteem may be centrally implicated in effective terror management.

One final and important motive for joining a group is to obtain a social identity (Hogg, 2006; Hogg and Abrams, 1988; Tajfel and Turner, 1979). Groups provide us with a consensually recognised and validated definition and evaluation of who we are, how we should behave and how we will be treated by others. According to **uncertainty–identity theory** (Hogg, 2007b, 2012, **see Chapter 11**), one fundamental motivation for joining and identifying with groups is to reduce feelings of uncertainty about who we are, how we should behave, and how others will perceive and interact with us.

Uncertainty–identity theory
To reduce uncertainty and to feel more comfortable about who they are, people choose to identify with groups that are distinctive, clearly defined, and have consensual norms.

Hogg and his colleagues have conducted a number of experiments to show that people who are randomly categorised as members of a group under abstract laboratory conditions (minimal group paradigm; **see Chapter 11**) or as members of more substantial 'real life' groups actually identify with the group, and identify more strongly if (1) they are in a state of self- or self-related uncertainty, and (2) the group has properties that optimise its capacity to reduce self-uncertainty (e.g. it is a highly entitative group). Reflecting back on terror management theory, a number of scholars have suggested that the reason why making people focus on their own death (the mortality salience manipulation used by terror management theorists) is associated with group identification-related phenomena is not so much terror about the process of dying but uncertainty about what happens to oneself after death (Hohman and Hogg, 2011; van den Bos, 2009). Hohman and Hogg (2011) have conducted two experiments that provide some support for this idea that it is self-related existential uncertainty not existential terror that plays the key role in group identification and people's defence of their cultural worldviews.

In addition to uncertainty considerations, because we and others evaluate us in terms of the relative attractiveness, desirability and prestige of the groups to which we belong, we are motivated to join groups that are consensually positively evaluated (e.g. high status). We are motivated to join groups that will furnish a positive social identity (Abrams and Hogg, 1988; Hogg and Abrams, 1990; Long and Spears, 1997; Tajfel and Turner, 1979; **see also Chapter 11**).

Why *not* join groups?

Perhaps the question 'Why do people join groups?' should be stood on its head: 'Why do people not join groups?' Not being a member of a group is a lonely existence, depriving us of social interaction, social and physical protection, the capacity to achieve complex goals, a stable sense of who we are, and confidence in how we should behave (**see Chapter 13**).

Social ostracism
This girl feels the loneliness of exclusion – a loneliness that is amplified when the ostracism is patently intentional

Social ostracism
Exclusion from a group by common consent.

Being excluded from a group, social ostracism, can be particularly painful and have widespread effects (Williams, 2002, 2009). Kip Williams has devised an intriguing and powerful paradigm to study the consequences of being excluded from a group (Williams, Shore and Grahe, 1998; Williams and Sommer, 1997). Three-person groups of students waiting for an experiment begin to throw a ball to one another across the room. After a while, two of the students (actually confederates) exclude the third student (true participant) by not throwing him or her the ball. It is very uncomfortable even to watch the video of this study (imagine how the participant felt!). True participants appear self-conscious and embarrassed, and many try to occupy themselves with other activities such as playing with keys, staring out of the window or meticulously scrutinising their wallets. This paradigm has been very successfully adapted as a web paradigm called cyberostracism (Williams, Cheung and Choi, 2000).

Ostracism has become a significant focus for social psychology research, and we now know a fair bit about the causes and consequences of ostracism. For example:

- Those who ostracise generally underestimate the degree of social pain that it causes (Nordgren, Banas and MacDonald, 2011).
- Being ostracised can induce a lack of feeling of meaningful existence (Zadro, Williams and Richardson, 2004), and can cause aggression (Wesselmann, Butler, Williams and Pickett, 2010; Williams and Warburton, 2003).
- Feelings of ostracism can be easily induced – even by a computer (Zadro, Williams and Richardson, 2004), a hated outgroup such as the Ku Klux Klan (Gonsalkorale and Williams, 2007), and even when being excluded actually pays (e.g. winning money) but being included does not (e.g. losing money; van Beest and Williams, 2006).

Summary

- Although there are many definitions of the group, social psychologists generally agree that at very least a group is a collection of people who define themselves as a group and whose attitudes and behaviour are governed by the norms of the group. Group membership often also entails shared goals, interdependence, mutual influence and face-to-face interaction.

- People tend to perform easy, well-learnt tasks better, and difficult, poorly learnt tasks worse, in the presence of other people than on their own.

- We may be affected in this way for a number of reasons. Social presence may instinctively drive habitual behaviour, we may learn to worry about performance evaluation by others, we may be distracted by others, or others may make us self-conscious or concerned about self-presentation.

- Tasks differ not only in difficulty but also in their structure and objectives. Whether a task benefits from division of labour, and how individual task performances are interrelated, have important implications for the relationship between individual and group performance.

- People tend to put less effort into task performance in groups than when alone, unless the task is involving and interesting, their individual contribution is clearly identifiable, or the group is important to their self-definition, in which case they can sometimes exert more effort in a group than alone.

- Members of cohesive groups tend to feel more favourably inclined towards one another as group members and are more likely to identify with the group and conform to its norms.

- Group membership is a dynamic process in which our sense of commitment varies, we occupy different roles at different times, we endure sharp transitions between roles, and we are socialised by the group in many different ways.

- Groups develop norms in order to regulate the behaviour of members, to define the group and to distinguish the group from other groups.

- Groups are structured internally into different roles that regulate interaction and best serve the collective interest of the group. Roles prescribe behaviour. They also vary in their desirability and thus influence status within the group. Groups are also internally structured in terms of subgroups and central and marginal group members.

- People may join or form groups to get things done that cannot be done alone, to gain a sense of identity and reduce self-uncertainty, to obtain social support or simply for the pleasure of social interaction.

- Being excluded or ostracised by a group is aversive and can lead to extreme reactions.

Key terms

Audience effects
Cognitive dissonance
Cohesiveness
Communication network
Coordination loss
Correspondence bias
Diffuse status characteristics
Distraction–conflict theory
Drive theory
Entitativity
Ethnomethodology
Evaluation apprehension model
Expectation states theory
Frame of reference

Free-rider effect
Group
Group socialisation
Group structure
Initiation rites
Mere presence
Meta-analysis
Norms
Personal attraction
Process loss
Ringelmann effect
Roles
Schism
Social attraction

Social compensation
Social facilitation
Social impact
Social loafing
Social ostracism
Specific status characteristics
Status
Stereotype
Subjective group dynamics
Task taxonomy
Terror management theory
Uncertainty–identity theory

Literature, film and TV

The Damned United

This 2009 biographical sports drama directed by Tom Hooper and starring Michael Sheen, Timothy Spall and Colm Meaney explores the challenges involved in fashioning a cohesive and effective team. Set in the late-60s and early-70s it focuses on the British football teams Derby County and Leeds United – showing how Brian Clough (played by Sheen) over a period of only a few years brings Derby County from near the bottom of the football league to the top of the first division. However, when Clough is appointed in 1974 as manager of Leeds United he fails miserably in the challenge of uniting the team under his leadership. The film is also relevant to our discussion of leadership **(Chapter 9)** and our discussion of intergroup behaviour **(Chapter 11)**. Another biographical sports drama that is relevant is the 2011 film *Moneyball*, starring Brad Pitt and Philip Seymour Hoffman. Set in the world of American baseball it shows how Billy Beane (played by Pitt), the manager of Oakland Athletics, transformed the thoroughly dysfunctional Oakland As into a highly competitive team.

Brassed Off

1996 Mark Herman film with Ewan McGregor. The local Grimley Colliery Brass Band is central to life in a small northern English coal-mining town. The mine is closing down and the conflict between strikers and non-strikers spills over into the band and almost all other aspects of life. A wonderful illustration of the impact of intergroup relations on intragroup dynamics.

Castaway

2000 film directed by Robert Zemeckis, starring Tom Hanks. The film is about the consequences of exclusion, and loneliness. Tom Hanks is abandoned on an island. He uses pictures, and decorates a volleyball to look like a person whom he calls 'Wilson' – Wilson allows him to remain socially connected.

The Full Monty

1997 film directed by Peter Cattaneo. Set in Sheffield, the film is about a group of chronically out-of-work people who decide to become a group of male strippers. This is totally out-of-role behaviour for working-class males in the north of England. The film documents the sorts of reaction they get from their friends, family and the community.

Lost

J. J. Abrams's incredibly popular TV show that follows the survivors of a plane crash who have to work together to survive on an island. This series explores almost all aspects of group dynamics. A small community is formed with the common goal of survival and each character is encouraged to assume a role. Problems always arise when people are unwilling to cooperate for the good of the group.

Fresh Meat

A very successful British sitcom that first aired in 2011. Six students who are freshers at the fictional Manchester Medlock University live in a shared house off-campus – you can probably imagine the endless opportunity for group processes of all sorts. A related British sitcom from the 1980s is *The Young Ones*; a violent punk, a pseudo-intellectual would-be anarchist, a long-suffering hippie, and a smooth-operator all live in one chaotic house.

Guided questions

1 What makes a group a group?

2 How and why does the presence of other people affect an individual's performance?

3 Use your knowledge of *social loafing* to explain why workers are sometimes less productive than expected.

4 *Roles* have an important function in groups – but can role-play be dangerous? Phil Zimbardo sets the scene for his famous guards vs. prisoners experiment in Chapter 8 of MyPsychLab at **www.mypsychlab.com** (watch *The Stanford Prison experiment*).

MyPsychLab   5 Why do people join groups?

Learn more

Baron, R. S., and Kerr, N. (2003).*Group process, group decision, group action* (2nd edn). Buckingham, UK: Open University Press. A general overview of topics in the study of group processes.

Brown, R. J. (2000). *Group processes* (2nd edn). Oxford, UK: Blackwell. A very readable introduction to group processes, which also places an emphasis on social influence processes within groups, especially conformity, norms and minority influence.

Cialdini, R. B., and Trost, M. R. (1998). Social influence: Social norms, conformity, and compliance. In D. Gilbert, S. T. Fiske, and G. Lindzey (eds), *The handbook of social psychology* (4th edn, Vol. 2, pp. 151–92). New York: McGraw-Hill. A thorough overview of social influence research, with an excellent section on norms.

Gruenfeld, D. H., and Tiedens, L. Z. (2010). Organizational preferences and their consequences. In S. T. Fiske, D. T. Gilbert, and G. Lindzey (eds), *Handbook of social psychology* (5th edn, Vol. 2, pp. 1252–87). New York: Wiley. Up-to-date and detailed overview of social psychological theory and research on organisational processes, including group processes in organisations.

Hackman, J. R., and Katz, N. (2010). Group behavior and performance. In S. T. Fiske, D. T. Gilbert, and G. Lindzey (eds), *Handbook of social psychology* (5th edn, Vol. 2, pp. 1208–51). New York: Wiley. Comprehensive, detailed and up-to-date coverage of group behaviour.

Hogg, M. A., and Smith, J. R. (2007). Attitudes in social context: A social identity perspective. *European Review of Social Psychology, 18,* 89–131. A theory-oriented review article that hinges on a discussion of how norms are tied to groups, group membership and social identity.

Hogg, M. A., and Tindale, R. S. (eds) (2001). *Blackwell handbook of social psychology: Group processes.* Oxford, UK: Blackwell. A collection of twenty-six chapters from leading experts covering the entire field of group processes.

Leary, M. R. (2010). Affiliation, acceptance, and belonging: The pursuit of interpersonal connection. In S. T. Fiske, D. T. Gilbert, and G. Lindzey (eds), *Handbook of social psychology* (5th edn, Vol. 2, pp. 864–97). New York: Wiley. This chapter includes detailed discussion of why people might be motivated to affiliate with others and thus form groups.

Levine, J. M. (ed.) (2013). *Group processes.* New York: Psychology Press. Absolutely up-to-date and comprehensive set of chapters by leading scholars on all aspects of group processes.

Levine, J. M., and Hogg, M. A. (eds) (2010). *Encyclopedia of group processes and intergroup relations.* Thousand Oaks, CA: SAGE. A comprehensive and readable compendium of entries on all aspects of the social psychology of groups, written by all the leading scholars in the field.

Levine, J., and Moreland, R. L. (1998). Small groups. In D. Gilbert, S. T. Fiske, and G. Lindzey (eds), *The handbook of social psychology* (4th edn, Vol. 2, pp. 415–69). New York: McGraw-Hill. A comprehensive overview of the field of small groups – the most recent fifth edition of the handbook does not have a chapter dedicated to small interactive groups.

Stangor, C. (2004). *Social groups in action and interaction.* New York: Psychology Press. Comprehensive and accessible coverage of the social psychology of processes within and between groups.

Williams, K. D., Harkins, S. G., and Karau, S. J. (2007). Social performance. In M. A. Hogg, and J. Cooper (eds), *The SAGE handbook of social psychology: Concise student edition* (pp. 291–311). London: SAGE. A comprehensive overview of theory and research focusing on how people's performance is affected by being in a group.

CHAPTER 9
Leadership and decision making

Chapter contents

Focus questions

1   Jane is a fearsome and energetic office manager who bustles around issuing orders. She expects and gets prompt action from her employees when she is around. How hard do you think her employees work when she is out of the office?

2   Your organisation is faced by a crisis that has united you all into a tight and cohesive unit. You need a new boss who is able to be innovative and to have the group's full support. Should you appoint Steve, who has all the leadership skills but comes from outside the organisation? Or should you appoint Martin, who has compliantly worked his way up through the organisation for over ten years? Michael Hogg discusses the nature of intergroup leadership in Chapter 9 of MyPsychLab at www.mypsychlab.com (also watch *Intergroup leadership* – http://www.youtube.com/watch?v=0-QEXmMcAAc).

3   The design group at Acme Aerospace meets to design a rocket for a Mars landing. There are eight of you. Because decisions have to be made quickly and smoothly, your charismatic and powerful group leader has selected members so that you are all very much of one mind. This is a very difficult task and there is a great deal of competitive pressure from other space agencies. Will this arrangement deliver a good design?

Go to MyPsychLab to explore video and test your understanding of key topics addressed in this chapter.

MyPsychLab

Use MyPsychLab to refresh your understanding with interactive summaries, explore topics further with video and audio clips and assess your progress with quick test and essay questions. To buy access or register your code, visit www.mypsychlab.com. You will also need a course ID from your instructor.

Leaders and group decisions

We saw earlier (**Chapter 8**) that groups vary in size, composition, longevity and purpose. They also vary in cohesiveness, have different norms and are internally structured into roles in different ways. However, almost all groups have some form of unequal distribution of power and influence whereby some people lead and others follow. Even in the case of ostensibly egalitarian or leaderless groups, one rarely needs to scratch far beneath the surface to stumble upon a tacit leadership structure (e.g. Counselman, 1991). Although leadership can take a variety of forms (e.g. democratic, autocratic, informal, formal, laissez-faire), it is a fundamental aspect of almost all social groups.

We know (**see end of Chapter 8**) that people can assemble as a group for many different reasons and to perform many different tasks. One of the most common reasons is to make decisions through some form of group discussion. In fact, many of the most important decisions that affect our lives are made by groups, often groups of which we are not members. Indeed, one could argue that most decisions that people make are actually group decisions – not only do we frequently make decisions as a group, but even those decisions that we seem to make on our own are made in reference to what groups of people may think or do.

This chapter continues the discussion of group processes. It focuses on two of the most significant group phenomena – leadership and group decision making.

Leadership

In the many groups to which we may belong – teams, committees, organisations, friendship cliques, clubs – we encounter leaders: people who have the 'good' ideas that everyone else agrees on; people whom everyone follows; people who have the ability to make things happen. Leaders enable groups to function as productive and coordinated wholes. Leadership is so integral to the human condition that it may even serve an evolutionary function for the survival of our species (Van Vugt, Hogan and Kaiser, 2008).

Effective leadership has an enormous impact. For example, one US study showed that highly performing executives added US$25 million more than average performers to the value of their company (Barrick, Day, Lord and Alexander, 1991), and another study showed that effective CEOs (chief executive officers) improved company performance by 14 per cent (Joyce, Nohria and Roberson, 2003). For example, Steve Jobs, the founder and long-time CEO of Apple played an absolutely pivotal role in that company's ascendance – exercising autocratic leadership and extraordinary vision to build Apple into a dominant force in the modern world of computing and electronic communication (Isaacson, 2011). In the sports context, Jacobs and Singell (1993) studied the performance of American baseball teams over a twenty-year period and found that successful teams had managers who exercised superior tactical skills or who were skilled in improving the performance of individual team members.

On a larger canvas, history and political news often comprise stories of the deeds of leaders and tales of leadership struggles – for an enthralling and beautifully written insight into the life of one of the twentieth century's greatest leaders, read Nelson Mandela's (1994) autobiography *The Long Walk to Freedom*. Margaret Thatcher's (1993) autobiography *The Downing Street Years* also makes fascinating reading. There are also (auto)biographies of Richard Branson, Bob Geldof and Bono that provide insight into effective leadership in the business and public spheres.

Biography is frequently about leadership, and most classic accounts of history are mainly accounts of the actions of leaders. Our day-to-day life is pervaded by the impact of leadership – for example, leadership in the political, governmental, corporate, work, educational, scientific and artistic spheres – and we all, to varying degrees, occupy leadership roles ourselves. Not surprisingly, people take a keen interest in leadership and we all have our own views on leaders and leadership.

Incompetent leadership and leadership in the service of evil, in particular, are of great concern to us all (e.g. Kellerman, 2004). Whereas good leaders tend to have the attributes of integrity, decisiveness, competence and vision (Hogan and Kaiser, 2006), extremely bad or dangerous leaders tend to devalue others and be indifferent to their suffering, are intolerant of criticism and suppress dissent, and have a grandiose sense of entitlement (Mayer, 1993). The four most prominent patterns of bad leadership are: failure to build an effective team, poor interpersonal skills to manage the team, insensitivity and lack of care about others, and inability to adjust to being promoted above one's skills or qualifications (Leslie and Van Velsor, 1996).

Dictatorial leaders are particularly harmful because they tend to surround themselves with a ruling elite that they cajole ideologically and through rewards and punishment. This allows them to control the masses by fear and the exercise of raw power rather than by providing leadership (Moghaddam, in press). It is largely the ruling elites, not the masses that play perhaps the key role in creating and toppling dictators. In a similar vein Machiavellian and narcissistic leaders also employ power, which is ultimately a form of bullying and tyranny based on fear (e.g. Haslam and Reicher, 2005), rather than show leadership.

Machiavellian leaders are prepared to do pretty much anything to maintain their status and position of power in the group (they carefully plot and plan and play different individuals and groups off against each other in the group); and narcissistic leaders are consumed with grandiosity, self-importance, envy, arrogance, haughtiness and lack of empathy, as well as a sense of entitlement, feelings of special/unique/high status and fantasies of unlimited success (Baumeister, Smart and Boden, 1996; Rosenthal and Pittinsky, 2006; **also see Chapter 4**).

To understand how leaders lead, what factors influence the person who is likely to be a leader in a particular context and what the social consequences of leadership may be, social psychology has embraced a variety of theoretical perspectives and emphases. However, after the end of the 1970s, social psychology paid diminishing attention to leadership. The 1985 third edition of the *Handbook of social psychology* dedicated a full chapter to leadership (Hollander, 1985), whereas the 1998 fourth edition had no chapter on leadership. Instead, there has been a corresponding frenzy of research on leadership in organisational psychology (e.g. Northouse, 2009; Yukl, 2010) – it is here, in the management and organisational sciences, where most leadership research is to be found. However, leadership is quite definitely a topic that transcends disciplinary boundaries – although organisational leadership is important, so is political/public leadership and team leadership.

Recently, there has been a revival of interest in leadership among social psychologists – for instance, there are two chapters on leadership in Hogg and Tindale's (2001) *Blackwell handbook of social psychology: Group processes* (Chemers, 2001; Lord, Brown and Harvey, 2001), one in Kruglanski and Higgins's (2007) second edition of *Social psychology: A handbook of basic principles* (Hogg, 2007a), one in the fifth edition of the *Handbook of social psychology* (Hogg, 2010), and one in Levine's (2013) edited volume on *Group processes* (Hogg, 2013).

Leadership
Getting group members to achieve the group's goals.

Defining leadership

It is difficult to find a consensual definition of leadership – definitions depend on what aspect of leadership is being investigated, from what disciplinary or theoretical perspective, and for what practical purpose. From a social psychological perspective, Chemers defined leadership as 'a process of social influence through which an individual enlists and mobilises the aid of others in the attainment of a collective goal' (Chemers, 2001, p. 376). Leadership requires there to be an individual, or clique, who influences the behaviour of another individual or group of individuals – where there are leaders there must be followers.

Another way to look at leadership is to ask: what is *not* leadership? If a friend cajoled you to spend the weekend cleaning her flat and you agreed, either because you liked her or because you were afraid of her, it would be influence but not leadership – a classic case of compliance (e.g. Cialdini and Trost, 1998; **see Chapter 6**). Related to this, the exercise of power is generally not considered to be leadership (e.g. Chemers, 2001; Lord, Brown and Harvey, 2001; Raven, 1993), although power may be a consequence of effective leadership (Turner, 2005). If you agreed because you knew that there was a community norm to clean at the weekend, that would be conformity to a norm (e.g. Turner, 1991), not an example of leadership. If, on the other hand, your friend had first convinced you that a community-cleaning norm should be developed, and you subsequently adhered to that norm, then that most definitely would be leadership. Leaders play a critical role in defining collective goals. In this respect, leadership is more typically a group process than an interpersonal process. It is an influence process that plays out more noticeably in group contexts than in interpersonal contexts.

Another question about leadership is: what is 'good' leadership? This question is poorly put; it needs to be unpacked into two different questions relating to effective/ineffective leaders and good/bad leaders. An *effective* leader is someone who is successful in setting new goals and influencing others to achieve them. Here, the evaluation of leadership is largely an objective matter of fact – how much influence did the leader have in setting new goals and were the goals achieved?

In contrast, evaluating whether the leader is good or bad is largely a subjective judgement based on one's preferences, perspectives and goals, and on whether the leader belongs to one's own group or another group. We evaluate leaders in terms of their character (e.g. nice, nasty, charismatic), the ethics and morality of the means they use to influence others and achieve goals (e.g. persuasion, coercion, oppression, democratic decision making), and the nature of the goals that they lead their followers towards (e.g. saving the environment, reducing starvation and disease, producing a commodity, combating oppression, engaging in genocide). Here *good* leaders are those who have attributes we applaud, use means we approve of, and set and achieve goals we value.

Thus, secular Westerners and supporters of al-Qaeda might disagree on whether Osama bin Laden was a *good* leader (they disagree on the value of his goals and the morality of his means) but may agree that he was a relatively *effective* leader (agreeing that he mobilised fundamentalist Muslims around his cause).

Personality traits and individual differences

Great, or notorious, leaders such as Churchill, Gandhi, Hitler, Mandela, Stalin and Thatcher seem to have special and distinctive capabilities that mark them off from the rest of us. Unsurprisingly, we tend to seek an explanation in terms of unique properties of these people (i.e. personality characteristics that predispose certain people to lead) rather than the context or process of leadership. For example, we tend to personify history in terms of the actions of great people: the French occupation of Moscow in 1812 was Napoleon's doing; the 1917 Russian Revolution was 'caused' by Lenin; and the 1980s in Britain were 'the Thatcher years'. Folk wisdom also tends to attribute great leaps forward in science – historian of science Thomas Kuhn (1962) calls *paradigm shifts* – to the independent actions of great people such as Einstein, Freud, Darwin and Copernicus.

Great person theory
Perspective on leadership that attributes effective leadership to innate or acquired individual characteristics.

This preference for a **great person theory** that attributes leadership to personality may be explained in terms of how people construct an understanding of their world. Earlier (**in Chapter 3**) we saw that people have a tendency to attribute others' behaviour to stable underlying traits (e.g. Gawronski, 2004; Gilbert and Malone, 1995; Haslam, Rothschild and Ernst, 1998) and that this is accentuated where the other person is the focus of our attention. Leaders certainly do stand out against the background of the group, and are therefore the focus of our attention, which strengthens the perception of a correspondence between traits and behaviour (e.g. Fiske and Dépret, 1996; Meindl, 1995; Meindl, Ehrlich and Dukerich, 1985).

Social psychologists are little different from people in everyday life. They have, therefore, tried to explain leadership in terms of personality traits that equip some people for effective leadership better than others. The great person theory of leadership has a long and illustrious

Does greatness beckon?
Barack Obama, the first black president of the United States and now in his second term, has been ranked among his country's best ever presidents. Only time will tell

pedigree, going back to Plato and ancient Greece. Although some scholars, for example Francis Galton (1892) in the nineteenth century, have maintained that leaders are born not made, most scholars do not believe that effective leadership is an innate attribute. Instead they believe leadership ability is a constellation of personality attributes acquired very early in life that imbues people with charisma and a predisposition to lead (e.g. Carlyle, 1841; House, 1977).

A prodigious quantity of research has been conducted to identify these correlates of effective leadership. For example, leaders apparently tend to be above average with respect to size, health, physical attractiveness, self-confidence, sociability, need for dominance and, most reliably, intelligence and talkativeness. Intelligence is important probably because leaders are expected to think and respond quickly and have more ready access to information than others, and talkativeness because it attracts attention and makes the person perceptually salient. But we can all identify effective 'leaders' who do not possess these attributes – for example, Gandhi and Napoleon certainly were not large, the Dalai Lama is not 'talkative', and we'll let you generate your own examples of leaders who do not appear to be very intelligent!

Early on Ralph Stogdill reviewed the leadership literature and concluded that leadership is not the 'mere possession of some combination of traits' (Stogdill, 1948, p. 66), and more recently others have exclaimed that the search for a leadership personality is simplistic and futile (e.g. Conger and Kanungo, 1998). In general, correlations among traits, and between traits and effective leadership, are low (Stogdill, 1974, reports an average correlation of 0.30).

Nevertheless, the belief that some people are better leaders than others because they have enduring traits that predispose them to effective leadership persists. This view has re-emerged in a different guise in modern theories of transformational leadership (see below) that emphasise the role of charisma in leadership (e.g. Avolio and Yammarino, 2003; Bass, 1985; Conger and Kanungo, 1998). Rather than focusing on specific traits, this tradition focuses on what are called the Big Five personality dimensions: extraversion/surgency, agreeableness, conscientiousness, emotional stability, and intellect/openness to experience. A definitive meta-analysis of data from 73 studies by Timothy Judge and his associates (Judge, Bono, Ilies and Gerhardt, 2002) found that these attributes have an overall correlation of 0.58 with leadership. The best predictors of effective leadership were being extraverted, open to experience, and conscientious.

Big Five
The five major personality dimensions of extraversion/ surgency, agreeableness, conscientiousness, emotional stability, and intellect/openness to experience.

Situational perspectives

In contrast to personality and individual differences approaches that attribute effective leadership to having particular enduring trait constellations is the view that anyone can lead effectively if the situation is right. The most extreme form of this perspective is to deny any influence at all to the leader. For example, much of Leo Tolstoy's epic novel *War and Peace* is a vehicle for his critique of the great person account of history: 'To elicit the laws of history we must leave aside kings, ministers and generals, and select for study the homogeneous, infinitesimal elements which influence the masses' (Tolstoy, 1869, p. 977). Likewise, Karl Marx's theory of history places explanatory emphasis on the actions of groups, not individuals.

This perspective may be too extreme. For example, Dean Simonton (1980) analysed the outcome of 300 military battles for which there were reliable archival data on the generals and their armies. Although situational factors, such as the size of the army and diversification of command structure, were correlated with casualties inflicted on the enemy, some personal attributes of the leader, to do with experience and previous battle record, were also associated with victory. In other words, although situational factors influenced outcome, so did the attributes of the leader.

From time to time, then, we may find ourselves in situations in which we are leaders. An often-cited illustration of this is the case of Winston Churchill. Although he was considered by many to be argumentative, opinionated and eminently unsuited to government, these were precisely the characteristics needed in a great wartime leader. However, as soon as the Second World War was over he was voted out of government, as these were not considered to be the qualities most needed in a peacetime leader.

Social psychologists have found the same thing under more controlled conditions. For example, in their classic studies of intergroup relations at boys' summer camps in the United States **(see Chapter 11 for details)**, Muzafer Sherif and his colleagues (Sherif, Harvey, White, Hood and Sherif, 1961) divided the boys into groups. When the groups later met in competition, a boy in one group displaced the original leader because of his greater physical prowess and other qualities suggesting he was better equipped to lead the group successfully in a competitive confrontation. In a 1949 study, Carter and Nixon (not the former US presidents!) found the same effect when pairs of school pupils performed three different tasks – an intellectual task, a clerical task and a mechanical assembly task. Those who took the lead in the first two tasks rarely led in the mechanical assembly task.

Overall, leadership reflects task or situational demands and is not purely a property of individual personality, although personal qualities may play a role. Balancing the Churchill example above, leaders can sometimes change to accommodate changed circumstances. When Nelson Mandela was released in 1990 from 26 years of imprisonment, most of it in isolation on Robben Island off Cape Town, the political terrain had altered dramatically. Yet he was able to read the changes and go on to lead the African National Congress to political victory in South Africa in 1994. Effective leadership is a matter of the right combination of personal characteristics and situational requirements.

What leaders do

If effective leadership is an interaction between leader attributes and situational requirements, then we need to know about leader attributes. We have seen that personality may not be as reliable a leadership attribute as one might think. Perhaps what leaders actually do, their actual behaviour, is more reliable? This idea spawned some of social psychology's classic leadership research.

For example, Ronald Lippitt and Ralph White (1943) used after-school activities clubs for young boys as an opportunity to study the effects of different styles of leadership on group atmosphere, morale and effectiveness. The leaders of the clubs were actually confederates of the researchers, and they were trained in each of three distinct leadership styles:

1 **Autocratic leaders** organised the club's activities, gave orders, were aloof and focused exclusively on the task at hand.

2 **Democratic leaders** called for suggestions, discussed plans and behaved like ordinary club members.

3 **Laissez-faire leaders** left the group to its own devices and generally intervened minimally.

Each club was assigned to a particular leadership style. One confederate was the leader for seven weeks and then the confederates were swapped around; this happened twice, so that each confederate adopted each leadership style, but each group was exposed to only one leadership style (although enacted by three different confederates). This clever control allowed Lippitt and White to distinguish leadership behaviour per se from the specific leader who was behaving in that way. In this way they could rule out personality explanations.

Lippitt and White's findings are described in Figure 9.1. Democratic leaders were liked significantly more than autocratic or laissez-faire leaders. They created a friendly, group-centred, task-oriented atmosphere that was associated with relatively high group productivity, which was unaffected by the physical absence or presence of the leader. In contrast, autocratic leaders created an aggressive, dependent and self-oriented group atmosphere, which was associated with high productivity only when the leader was present. (How would you rate bustling Jane in the first focus question?) Laissez-faire leaders created a friendly, group-centred but play-oriented atmosphere that was associated with low productivity, which increased only if the leader was absent. Lippitt and White used these findings to promote their view that democratic leadership was more effective than other leadership behaviour.

Lippitt and White's distinction between autocratic and democratic leadership styles re-emerges in a slightly different guise in later work. From his studies of interaction styles in groups, Robert Bales, a pioneer in the study of small group communication, identified two key

Autocratic leaders
Leaders who use a style based on giving orders to followers.

Democratic leaders
Leaders who use a style based on consultation and obtaining agreement and consent from followers.

Laissez-faire leaders
Leaders who use a style based on disinterest in followers.

An autocratic leader
'I like to do all the talking myself. It saves time and prevents arguments'
(Oscar Wilde)

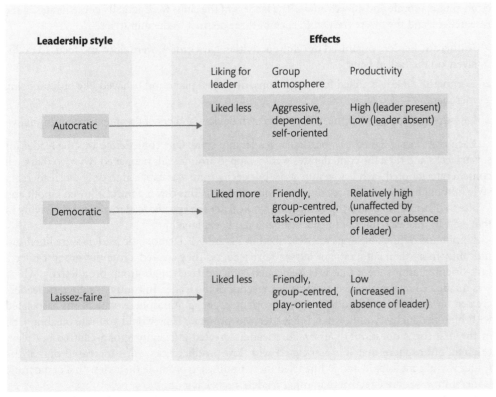

Figure 9.1 Leadership styles and their effects

Autocratic, democratic and laissez-faire leadership styles have different combinations of effects on group atmosphere and productivity, and on liking for the leader

Source: Based on Lippitt and White (1943)

leadership roles – *task specialist* and *socioemotional specialist* (Bales, 1950; Slater, 1955). Task specialists concentrate on reaching solutions, often making suggestions and giving directions; socioemotional specialists are alert to the feelings of other group members. A single person rarely occupies both roles – rather, the roles devolve onto separate individuals, and the person occupying the task-specialist role is more likely to be the dominant leader.

Casual observation of groups and organisations supports this dual-leadership idea. For example, one theme that punctuated election struggles between the Labour Party and the Conservative Party during the 1980s in Britain was to do with what sort of leader the country should have. The Labour leader at the time, Neil Kinnock, was, among other things, heralded as a friendly and approachable leader concerned with people's feelings, and the Conservative leader, Margaret Thatcher, as the hard-headed, task-oriented economic rationalist.

The Ohio State leadership studies constitute a third major leadership programme (e.g. Fleishman, 1973; Stogdill, 1974). In this research a scale for measuring leadership behaviour was devised, the **leader behaviour description questionnaire (LBDQ)** (Shartle, 1951), and a distinction was drawn between *initiating structure* and *consideration*. Leaders high on initiating structure define the group's objectives and organise members' work towards the attainment of these goals: they are task-oriented. Leaders high on consideration are concerned with the welfare of subordinates and seek to promote harmonious relationships in the group: they are relationship-oriented. Unlike Bales (1950), who believed that task-oriented and socioemotional attributes were inversely related, the Ohio State researchers believed their dimensions to be independent – a single person could be high on both initiating structure (task-oriented) and consideration (socioemotional), and such a person would be a particularly effective leader.

Leader behaviour description questionnaire
Scale devised by the Ohio State leadership researchers to measure leadership behaviour and distinguish between 'initiating structure' and 'consideration' dimensions.

Research tends to support this latter view – the most effective leaders are precisely those who score above average on both initiating structure and consideration (Stogdill, 1974). For example, Richard Sorrentino and Nigel Field (1986) conducted detailed observations of twelve problem-solving groups over a five-week period. Those group members who were rated as being high on both the task and socioemotional dimensions of Bales's (1950) system were subsequently elected by groups to be their leaders.

The general distinction between a leadership style that pays more attention to the group task and getting things done, and one that pays attention to relationships among group members, is quite pervasive. For example, as we shall see below, it appears in Fiedler's (1964) influential contingency theory of leadership (see below), and in a slightly different guise in leader–member exchange (LMX) theory's emphasis upon the quality of the leader's relationship with his or her followers (e.g. Graen and Uhl-Bien, 1995).

Furthermore, it is a distinction that may hold across cultures, but with the caveat that what counts as task-oriented or socioemotional leadership behaviour may vary from culture to culture. For example, from their leadership research in Japan, Jyuji Misumi and Mark Peterson (1985) identify a similar distinction – in this case between task performance and group maintenance. They go on to note that whether a behaviour counts as one or the other differs from culture to culture – for example, the leader eating lunch with his or her workmates is associated with high group maintenance in some cultures but not others.

The same conclusion was drawn by Peter Smith and his colleagues (Smith, Misumi, Tayeb, Peterson and Bond, 1989) from research in the United States, Britain, Hong Kong and Japan. They found that performance and maintenance behaviour were universally valued in leaders, but that what counted as each type of behaviour varied from culture to culture. For example, leaders need to assess workers' task performance; in Britain and America, the considerate way to do this is by speaking directly with workers, whereas in East Asia this is viewed as inconsiderate, and the considerate way is to speak with the individual's co-workers.

Having learnt something about what effective leaders do, we now need to turn our attention to what situational factors invite or benefit from which leadership behaviours. How do behaviour and situation interact to produce effective leadership?

Contingency theories

Contingency theories of leadership recognise that the leadership effectiveness of particular leadership behaviours or styles is *contingent* on the properties of the leadership situation – some styles are better suited to some situations or tasks than are others. For example, different behavioural styles are suited to an aircrew in combat, an organisational decision-making group, a ballet company, or a nation in economic crisis.

Contingency theories
Theories of leadership that consider the leadership effectiveness of particular behaviours or behavioural styles to be contingent on the nature of the leadership situation.

Fiedler's contingency theory

The first and best-known contingency theory in social psychology is that of Fred Fiedler (1964). Fiedler, like Bales (1950), distinguished between *task-oriented leaders* who are authoritarian, value group success and derive self-esteem from accomplishing a task rather than being liked by the group; and *relationship-oriented leaders* who are relaxed, friendly, non-directive and sociable, and gain self-esteem from happy and harmonious group relations.

Fiedler measured leadership style in a rather unusual way; with his **least preferred co-worker (LPC) scale** in which respondents rated the person they least preferred as a co-worker on a number of dimensions (e.g. pleasant–unpleasant, boring–interesting, friendly–unfriendly). The resultant LPC scores were used to differentiate between two different leadership styles.

Least-preferred co-worker scale
Fiedler's scale for measuring leadership style in terms of favourability of attitude towards one's least preferred co-worker.

- A high LPC score indicated a *relationship-oriented* leadership style because the respondent felt favourably inclined towards a fellow member even if he or she was not performing well.

- A low LPC score indicated a *task-oriented* leadership style because the respondent was harsh on a poorly performing co-worker.

Least preferred co-worker
A first step in measuring your leadership style is to nominate the person with whom you find it most difficult to work

Fiedler classified situations in terms of three dimensions in descending order of importance:

- the quality of leader–member relations;
- the clarity of the structure of the task; and
- the intrinsic power and authority the leader had by virtue of his or her position as leader.

Good leader–member relations in conjunction with a clear task and substantial position power furnished maximal 'situational control' (making leadership easy), whereas poor leader–member relations, a fuzzy task and low position power furnished minimal 'situational control' (making leadership difficult). Situational control can be classified quite precisely from I 'very high' to VIII 'very low', by dichotomising conditions under each of the three factors as good or bad (high or low) (see Figure 9.2).

Fiedler used the concept of situational control to make leadership effectiveness predictions:

- Task-oriented (low LPC) leaders would be most effective when situational control is low (the group needs a directive leader to focus on getting things done) *and* when it is high (the group is doing just fine, so there is little need to worry about morale and relationships within the group).
- Relationship-oriented (high LPC) leaders are more effective when situational control lies between these extremes.

These predictions are illustrated in Figure 9.3, which also shows a composite of LPC–performance correlations reported by Fiedler (1965) from published studies. The results match the prediction rather well.

Meta-analyses confirm this. Strube and Garcia (1981) conducted a meta-analysis of 178 empirical tests of the theory, and Schriesheim, Tepper and Tetrault (1994) conducted a further meta-analysis of a subset of these studies. Overall, Fiedler's predictions based on contingency theory have generally been supported. However, let's not be too hasty – there is both controversy and criticism (e.g. Peters, Hartke and Pohlmann, 1985):

- Fiedler's view that leadership style is a characteristic of the individual that does not change across time and situations is inconsistent with: (1) contemporary perspectives on personality that views personality as able to vary in these very ways (e.g. Snyder and Cantor, 1998); (2) evidence of relatively low test–retest reliability (correlations ranging from 0.01 to 0.93, with a median of 0.67) for LPC scores (Rice, 1978); and (3) the ease with which Lippitt and White (1943) trained their confederates to adopt different leadership styles in the classic study described earlier.

Situational control
Fiedler's classification of task characteristics in terms of how much control effective task performance requires.

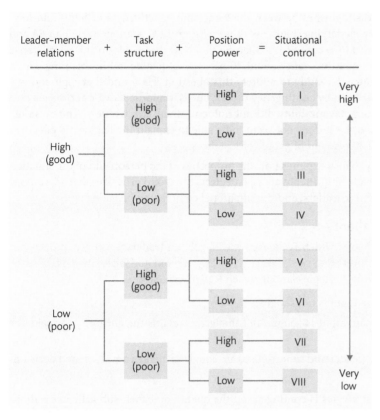

Figure 9.2 Fiedler's eight-category situational control scale as a function of leader–member relations, task structure and position power

- An eight-category scale of situational control (I, very high, to VIII, very low) can be constructed by classifying situations as having good/bad leader–member relations, good/bad task structure, and high/low position power.
- The a priori assumption, that leader–member relations are more important than task structure, which is more important than position power, means that a situation is first classified by leader–member relations, then within that by task structure, and then within that by position power.

Source: Based on Fiedler (1965)

- Fiedler may be wrong to make the a priori assumption that leader–member relations are more important than task structure, which is more important than position power in the assessment of overall situational control. It would not be surprising if the relative order of importance were itself a function of situational factors. Indeed, Ramadhar Singh, and his colleagues (Singh, Bohra and Dalal, 1979) obtained a better fit between predictions and results when the favourability of the eight octants was based on subjective ratings by participants rather than Fiedler's a priori classification.

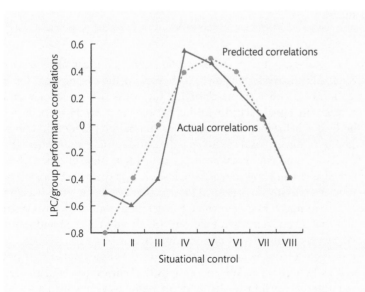

Figure 9.3 Predicted and obtained correlations between LPC scores and group performance as a function of situational control

- When situational control is very high or very low, contingency theory predicts a negative correlation between LPC scores and quality of group performance.
- A group performs poorly for a relationship-oriented leader (high LPC score), but well for a task-oriented leader (low LPC score).
- When control is intermediate a positive correlation is predicted: relationship-oriented leaders are more effective. The obtained correlations came from a series of supportive studies.

Source: Based on data from Fiedler (1965)

- Contingency theory distinguishes between the leadership effectiveness of high- and low-LPC leaders, generally classifying 'highs' as those with an LPC score greater than 64 and 'lows' as those with an LPC score of less than 57. So, how do people in the 57–64 range behave? This is a valid question, since about 20 per cent of people fall in this range. John Kennedy (1982) conducted a study to address this question. He found that high and low scorers behaved as predicted by contingency theory, but that middle scorers performed best of all and that situational favourability did not influence their effectiveness. This certainly limits contingency theory – it does not seem to be able to explain the leadership effectiveness of approximately 20 per cent of people or instances.

- Although contingency theory explores how the properties of the person and of the situation interact to influence leadership effectiveness, it neglects the group processes that are responsible for the rise and fall of leaders, and the situational complexion of leadership.

Normative decision theory

A second contingency theory, which is focused specifically on leadership in group decision-making contexts, is **normative decision theory** (NDT; e.g. Vroom and Jago, 1988). NDT identifies three decision-making strategies among which leaders can choose:

- *autocratic* (subordinate input is not sought);
- *consultative* (subordinate input is sought, but the leader retains the authority to make the final decision); and
- *group decision making* (leader and subordinates are equal partners in a truly shared decision-making process).

The efficacy of these strategies is contingent on the quality of leader–subordinate relations (which influences how committed and supportive subordinates are), and on task clarity and structure (which influences how much the leader needs subordinate input).

In decision-making contexts, autocratic leadership is fast and effective if subordinate commitment and support are high and the task is clear and well structured. When the task is less clear, greater subordinate involvement is needed and therefore consultative leadership is best. When subordinates are not very committed or supportive, group decision making is required to increase participation and commitment. Predictions from NDT are reasonably well supported empirically (e.g. Field and House, 1990) – leaders and managers report better decisions and better subordinate ratings when they follow the prescriptions of the theory. However, there is a tendency for subordinates to prefer fully participative group decision making, even when it is not the most effective strategy.

Path-goal theory

A third contingency theory is **path-goal theory** (House, 1996), although it can also be classified as a transactional leadership theory (see below). PGT rests on the assumption that a leader's main function is to motivate followers by clarifying the paths (i.e. behaviours and actions) that will help them reach their goals. It distinguishes between the two classes of leader behaviour identified by the leader behaviour description questionnaire (LBDQ), described above: *structuring* where the leader directs task-related activities, and *consideration* where the leader addresses followers' personal and emotional needs. Structuring is most effective when followers are unclear about their goals and how to reach them – e.g. the task is new, difficult or ambiguous. When tasks are well understood, structuring is less effective. It can even backfire because it seems like meddling and micro-management. Consideration is most effective when the task is boring or uncomfortable, but not when followers are already engaged and motivated, because being considerate can seem distracting and unnecessary.

Empirical support for path–goal theory is mixed, with tests of the theory suffering from flawed methodology, as well as being incomplete and simplistic (Schriesheim and Neider, 1996). The theory also has an interpersonal focus that underplays the ways in which a leader can motivate an entire work group rather than just individual followers.

Normative decision theory
A contingency theory of leadership that focuses on the effectiveness of different leadership styles in group decision-making contexts.

Path-goal theory
A contingency theory of leadership that can also be classified as a transactional theory – it focuses on how 'structuring' and 'consideration' behaviours motivate followers.

Transactional leadership

Though popular, contingency theories are rather static. They do not capture the dance of leadership – leaders and followers provide support and gratification to one another, which allows leaders to lead and encourages followers to follow (Messick, 2005). This limitation is addressed by theories of **transactional leadership**.

The key assumption here is that leadership is a 'process of exchange that is analogous to contractual relations in economic life [and] contingent on the good faith of the participants' (Downton, 1973, p. 75). Leaders transact with followers to get things done – creating expectations and setting goals, and providing recognition and rewards for task completion (Burns, 1978). Mutual benefits are exchanged (transacted) between leaders and followers against a background of contingent rewards and punishments that shape up cooperation and trust (Bass, 1985). Leader–member transactions may also have an equity dimension (Walster, Walster and Berscheid, 1978; **also see Chapter 14**). Because effective leaders play a greater role in steering groups to their goals than do followers, followers may reinstate equity by rewarding the leader with social approval, praise, prestige, status and power – in other words, with the trappings of effective leadership.

Transactional leadership
Approach to leadership that focuses on the transaction of resources between leader and followers. Also a style of leadership.

Idiosyncrasy credit

A well-known early approach to leadership that focused on leader–follower transactions is Edwin Hollander's (1958) analysis of **idiosyncrasy credit**. Hollander believed that in order to be effective, leaders needed their followers to allow them to be innovative, to be able to experiment with new ideas and new directions – to be idiosyncratic. Drawing on the equity argument, above, Hollander wondered what circumstances would encourage such a transaction between leader and followers – one in which followers would provide their leader with the resources to be able to be idiosyncratic.

Idiosyncrasy credit
Hollander's transactional theory, that followers reward leaders for achieving group goals by allowing them to be relatively idiosyncratic.

He believed that certain behaviours build up idiosyncrasy credit with the group – a resource that the leader can ultimately 'cash in'. A good 'credit rating' can be established by:

- initially conforming closely to established group norms;
- ensuring that the group feels that it has democratically elected you as the leader;
- making sure that you are seen to have the competence to fulfil the group's objectives; and
- being seen to identify with the group, its ideals and its aspirations.

A good credit rating gives the leader legitimacy in the eyes of the followers to exert influence over the group and to deviate from existing norms – in other words, to be idiosyncratic, creative and innovative.

Idiosyncrasy credit
You may take a few liberties, but only once you get to the top

Research provides some support for this analysis. Merei (1949) introduced older children who had shown leadership potential into small groups of younger children in a Hungarian nursery. The most successful leaders were those who initially complied with existing group practices and who only gradually and later introduced minor variations. In another study, Hollander and Julian (1970) found that leaders of decision-making groups who were ostensibly democratically elected enjoyed more support from the group, felt more competent at the task and were more likely to suggest solutions that diverged from those of the group as a whole.

An alternative explanation, not grounded in notions of interpersonal equity and transaction, and idiosyncrasy credit, for why the conditions described above allow a leader to be innovative is based on the social identity theory of leadership (e.g. Hogg and van Knippenberg, 2003; Hogg, van Knippenberg and Rast, 2012b; see below). Here the term *innovation credit* is used instead (Abrams, Randsley de Moura, Marques and Hutchison, 2008; Randsleyde Moura, Abrams, Hutchison and Marques, 2011).

Abrams and colleagues argue that it is actually innovation, not idiosyncrasy, that the group gives the leader leeway to indulge in. Whatever leaders do and however they acquire the mantle of leadership, the key factor that underpins their ability to get group members behind an innovative vision for the group rests on perceptions that the leader is 'one of us' – a *prototypical* and trustworthy group member who identifies with the group and thus will do it no harm (e.g. Platow and van Knippenberg, 2001). If one identifies strongly with the group oneself, then one trusts such a leader (e.g. Yamagishi and Kiyonari, 2000) and is prepared to follow his or her lead largely irrespective of how innovative and counter-normative his or her behaviour may be – whatever he or she does is likely to be in the best interest of the group.

In supporting the notion of innovation credit, Daan van Knippenberg and his colleagues (van Knippenberg, van Knippenberg and Bobbio, 2008) argued that in leading collective innovation and change, prototypical leaders would be more trusted to be 'agents of continuity', guardians of the group identity, than non-prototypical leaders, and thus more effective in motivating followers' willingness to contribute to the change. This is precisely what they found across two scenario experiments focusing on an organisational merger.

Leader-member exchange theory

Leader-member exchange theory
Theory of leadership in which effective leadership rests on the ability of the leader to develop good quality personalised exchange relationships with individual members.

Vertical dyad linkage model
An early form of leader-member exchange (LMX) theory in which a sharp distinction is drawn between dyadic leader-member relations in which the member is treated effectively as ingroup or as outgroup.

Leader–member transactions play a central role in **leader-member exchange (LMX) theory** (e.g. Graen and Uhl-Bien, 1995; Sparrowe and Liden, 1997), which describes how the quality of exchange relationships (i.e. relationships in which resources such as respect and trust, liking are exchanged) between leaders and followers can vary. Originally, LMX theory was called the **vertical dyad linkage (VDL) model** (Danserau, Graen and Haga, 1975). According to VDL researchers, leaders develop dyadic exchange relationships with different specific subordinates. In these dyadic relationships, the subordinate can be treated either as a close and valued 'ingroup' member with the leader or in a more remote manner as an 'outgroup' member who is separate from the leader.

As the VDL model evolved into LMX theory, this dichotomous, ingroup versus outgroup, treatment of leader–member exchange relationships was replaced by a continuum of quality of exchange relationships ranging from ones that are based on mutual trust, respect and obligation (high-quality LMX relationships), to ones that are rather mechanically based on the terms of the formal employment contract between leader and subordinate (low-quality LMX relationships).

In high-quality LMX relationships, subordinates are favoured by the leader and receive many valued resources, which can include material (e.g. money, privileges) as well as psychological (e.g. trust, confidences) benefits. Leader–member exchanges go beyond the formal employment contract, with managers showing influence and support, and giving the subordinate greater autonomy and responsibility. High-quality relationships should motivate subordinates to internalise the group's and the leader's goals. In low-quality LMX relationships, subordinates are disfavoured by the leader and receive fewer valued resources. Leader–member exchanges simply adhere to the terms of the employment contract, with little attempt by the leader to develop or motivate the subordinate. Subordinates will simply comply with the leader's goals, without necessarily internalising them as their own.

LMX theory predicts that effective leadership hinges on the development of high-quality LMX relationships. These relationships enhance subordinates' well-being and work performance, and bind them to the group more tightly through loyalty, gratitude and a sense of inclusion. Because leaders usually have to relate to a large number of subordinates, they cannot develop high-quality LMX relationships with everyone – it is more efficient to select some subordinates in whom to invest a great deal of interpersonal energy, and to treat the others in a less personalised way. The selection process takes time because it goes through a number of stages: *role taking* in which the leader has expectations and tries out different roles on the subordinate, *role making* in which mutual leader–member exchanges (e.g. of information, support) establish the subordinate's role, and *role routinisation* in which the leader–member relationship has become stable, smooth-running and automatic.

Research confirms that differentiated LMX relationships do exist in most organisations; that high-quality LMX relationships are more likely to develop when the leader and the subordinate have similar attitudes, like one another, belong to the same socio-demographic groups and both perform at a high level; and that high-quality LMX relationships are associated with (most studies are correlational, not causal) better-performing and more satisfied workers who are more committed to the organisation and less likely to leave (see Schriesheim, Castro and Cogliser, 1999). The stages of LMX relationship development are consistent with more general models of group development (e.g. Levine and Moreland, 1994; Tuckman, 1965; **see Chapter 8**).

The main limitation of LMX theory is that it focuses on dyadic leader–member relations. There is a problem. As we have noted, leadership is a group process – even if a leader appears to be interacting with one individual, that interaction is framed by and located in the wider context of shared group membership. Followers interact with each other as group members and are influenced by their perceptions of the leader's relations with other group members (e.g. Hogg, Martin and Weeden, 2004; Scandura, 1999).

Let us consider this from the perspective of the social identity theory of leadership (e.g. Hogg and van Knippenberg, 2003; see below). Members who identify strongly with a group might find that differentiated LMX relationships that favour some members over others are too personalised and fragment the group. They would not endorse such leaders. Instead, they might prefer a less personalised leadership style that treated all members relatively equally as group members, and would endorse such leaders more strongly. This hypothesis has been tested and supported in two field surveys of leadership perceptions in organisations in Wales and in India (Hogg, Martin, Epitropaki, Mankad, Svensson and Weeden, 2005).

Transformational leadership

Transactional theories of leadership represent a particular focus on leadership. However, transactional leadership is itself a particular leadership *style* that can be contrasted to other leadership styles. In defining transactional leadership, political scientist James Burns (1978) contrasted it with transformational leadership: transactional leaders appeal to followers' self-interest, whereas transformational leaders inspire followers to adopt a vision that involves more than individual self-interest (Judge and Bono, 2000).

There are three key components of transformational leadership:

1 *individualised consideration* (attention to followers' needs, abilities and aspirations, in order to help raise aspirations, improve abilities and satisfy needs);

2 *intellectual stimulation* (challenging followers' basic thinking, assumptions and practices to help them develop newer and better mind-sets and practices); and

3 *charismatic/inspiring leadership,* which provides the energy, reasoning and sense of urgency that transforms followers (Avolio and Bass, 1987; Bass, 1985).

Transformational leadership theorists were mortified that the charisma/inspiration component inadvertently admitted notorious dictators such as Hitler, Stalin and Pol Pot into the hallowed club of transformational leaders – all were effective leaders in so far as they mobilised

Transformational leadership
Approach to leadership that focuses on the way that leaders transform group goals and actions – mainly through the exercise of charisma. Also a style of leadership based on charisma.

Transformational leadership
A nation yearns for a leader who inspires, who exudes energy and a sense of urgency. How did Gordon Brown rate at 10 Downing Street?

Laissez-faire leadership
A hands-off style of leadership where the leader intervenes minimally in the life of the group.

Multifactor leadership questionnaire
The most popular and widely used scale for measuring transactional and transformational leadership.

groups around their goals. So, a distinction was drawn between good charismatic leaders with socialised charisma that they use in a 'morally uplifting' manner to improve society, and bad charismatic leaders who use personalised charisma to tear down groups and society – the former are transformational, the latter are not (e.g. O'Connor et al., 1995; also see the earlier section of this chapter on defining leadership).

The distinction between transactional and transformational leadership has been joined by a third type of leadership – laissez-faire (non-interfering) leadership, which involves not making choices or taking decisions, and not rewarding others or shaping their behaviour. Avolio (1999) uses laissez-faire leadership as a baseline anchor-point in what he calls his 'full-range leadership model', which has transformational leadership sitting at the apex (Antonakis and House, 2003).

First published by Bass and Avolio in 1990, the multifactor leadership questionnaire (MLQ) was designed to measure transactional and transformational leadership. It is now in its fifth version, and has been used in every conceivable organisation, at every conceivable level, and on almost every continent. It has become the de facto leadership questionnaire of choice of the organisational and management research communities – producing numerous large-scale meta-analyses of findings (e.g. Lowe, Kroeck and Sivasubramaniam, 1996; also see Avolio and Yammarino, 2003).

A contemporary challenge for transformational leadership theory is to fill in the 'black box' of transformation – to specify exactly what happens psychologically in the head of individual followers, which transforms their thoughts and behaviour to conform to the leader's vision. Shamir, House and Arthur (1993) suggest that followers personally identify with the leader and in this way make the leader's vision their own. Dvir, Eden, Avolio and Shamir (2002) suggest that the behaviour of transformational leaders causes followers to identify more strongly with the organisation's core values.

Both these ideas resonate with the social identity theory of leadership (e.g. Hogg and van Knippenberg, 2002; see below). Where group members identify strongly with a group, leaders who are considered central/prototypical group members are able to be innovative in defining a group's goals and practices. Strong identification is associated with internalisation of group norms as one's own beliefs and actions. In this way, leaders can transform groups.

Charisma and charismatic leadership

The notion of charisma is so central to transformational leadership theory that, as we saw above, a distinction was drawn between good and bad charisma in order to distinguish between non-transformational villains (e.g. Hitler) and transformational heroes (e.g. Gandhi).

This distinction is, of course, problematic – one person's transformational leader can be another's war criminal or vice versa (much as one person's freedom fighter is another's terrorist).

Was Osama bin Laden a transformational leader? Your answer may rest more on your political persuasion and ideological leanings than on transformational leadership theory's notion of good versus bad charisma (see the earlier discussion of effective/ineffective versus good/bad dimensions of leadership). How about Rupert Murdoch, founder and CEO of News Corp, and Steve Jobs, founder and CEO of Apple? Both are undoubtedly transformational and charismatic, but did they have 'bad charisma' because they appeared to fail to ensure organisational ethical conduct (in the case of Murdoch and the phone hacking scandal which broke in the media in 2011) or acted narcissistically (in the case of jobs – see Isaacson, 2011)?

There is a more general issue concerning the role of charisma in transformational leadership. Scholars talk of charismatic leadership as a product of (a) the leader's personal charisma and (b) followers' reactions to the leader's charisma in a particular situation – personal charisma alone may not guarantee charismatic leadership (e.g. Bryman, 1992). However, it is difficult to escape the inference that personal charisma is an enduring personality trait – in which case some of the problems of past personality theories of leadership have been reintroduced (Haslam and Platow, 2001; Mowday and Sutton, 1993). Indeed, charismatic/transformational leadership has explicitly been linked to the Big Five personality dimensions of extraversion/surgency, agreeableness and intellect/openness to experience (e.g. Judge, Bono, Ilies and Gerhardt, 2002). Charismatic leadership is also linked to the related construct of visionary leadership (e.g. Conger and Kanungo, 1998) and the view that people differ in terms of how visionary they are as leaders. Visionary leaders are special people who can identify attractive future goals and objectives for a group and mobilise followers to internalise these as their own.

> **Charismatic leadership**
> Leadership style based upon the leader's (perceived) possession of charisma.

There is no doubt that charisma facilitates effective leadership, probably because charismatic people are emotionally expressive, enthusiastic, driven, eloquent, visionary, self-confident and responsive to others (e.g. House, Spangler, and Woycke, 1991; Riggio and Carney, 2003). These attributes allow a person to be influential and persuasive, and therefore able to make others buy their vision for the group and sacrifice personal goals for collective goals. Meindl and Lerner (1983; Meindl, Ehrlich and Dukerich, 1985) talk about visionary leaders heightening followers' sense of shared identity, and how this shared identity produces a collective 'heroic motive' that puts group goals ahead of personal goals.

An alternative perspective on the role of charisma in leadership is that a charismatic personality is constructed for the leader by followers; charisma is a consequence or correlate, not a cause, of effective leadership. For example, Meindl (1995; Meindl, Ehrlich and Dukerich, 1985; also see Shamir, Pillai, Bligh and Uhl-Bien, 2006) talks of the *romance of leadership*; people have a strong tendency to attribute effective leadership to the leader's behaviour and to overlook the leader's shortcomings (e.g. Fiske and Dépret, 1996). The social identity theory of leadership (e.g., Hogg and van Knippenberg, 2003; see below) provides a similar analysis, but with an emphasis on the role of shared identity in charismatic leadership. Social identity processes in groups that members identify strongly with make group prototypical (central) leaders influential, attractive and trustworthy, and allow them to be innovative. Followers attribute these qualities internally to the leader's personality, thus constructing a charismatic leadership personality (Haslam and Platow, 2001; Platow and van Knippenberg, 2001).

Leader perceptions and leadership schemas

Leader categorisation theory

Social cognition (**see Chapter 2**) has framed an approach to leadership that focuses on the schemas we have of leaders and on the causes and consequences of categorising someone as a leader. Called leader categorisation theory (LCT) or implicit leadership theory (e.g. Lord, Brown, Harvey and Hall, 2001; Lord and Brown, 2004; Lord and Hall, 2003), it is assumed that our perceptions of leadership play a key role in decisions we make about selecting and

> **Leader categorisation theory**
> We have a variety of schemas about how different types of leader behave in different leadership situations. When a leader is categorised as a particular type of leader, the schema fills in details about how that leader will behave.

endorsing leaders. This influences leaders' power bases, and thus their ability to influence others and to lead effectively.

People have implicit theories of leadership that shape their perceptions of leaders. In assessing a specific leader, leadership schemas (called 'prototypes' by Lord and his colleagues) based on these implicit theories of leadership are activated, and characteristics of the specific leader are matched against the relevant schema of effective leadership. These schemas of leadership can describe general context-independent properties of effective leaders, or very specific properties of leadership in a very specific situation.

LCT predicts that the better the match is between the leader's characteristics and the perceiver's leadership schema, the more favourable are leadership perceptions. For example, if your leadership schema favours 'intelligent', 'organised' and 'dedicated' as core leadership attributes, you are more likely to endorse a leader the more you perceive that leader actually to be intelligent, organised and dedicated.

LCT focuses on categories and associated schemas of leadership and leaders (e.g. military generals, prime ministers, CEOs), not on schemas of social groups as categories (e.g. a psychology department, a corporation, a sports team). LCT's leader categories are tied to specific tasks and functions that span a variety of different groups: for example, a CEO schema applies similarly to companies such as Apple, Dell, Virgin, Toyota, Starbucks and Google, whereas each company may have very different group norms and prototypes. LCT largely leaves unanswered the question of how schemas of group membership influence leadership, a question which is addressed by the social identity theory of leadership (e.g. Hogg and van Knippenberg, 2003, described below).

Expectation states and status characteristics

Status characteristics theory
Theory of influence in groups that attributes greater influence to those who possess both task-relevant characteristics (specific status characteristics) and characteristics of high-status groups in society (diffuse status characteristics). Also called *expectation states theory*.

Another theory that focuses on leader categorisation processes, but is more sociological and does not go into social cognitive details as extensively as leader categorisation theory, is expectation states theory or **status characteristics theory** (e.g. Berger, Fisek, Norman and Zelditch, 1977; Berger, Wagner and Zelditch, 1985; Ridgeway, 2003). Influence (and thus leadership) within groups is attributed to possession of *specific status characteristics* (characteristics that match what the group actually does) and *diffuse status characteristics* (stereotypical characteristics of high-status groups in society). To be effective, leaders need to have characteristics that equip them for effective task performance (i.e. specific status characteristics) and characteristics that categorise them as members of high-status socio-demographic categories (i.e. diffuse status characteristics). Effective leadership is an additive function of perceived group task competence and perceived societal status.

Social identity and leadership

Leadership is a relationship where some members of a group (usually one member) are able to influence the rest of the group to embrace, as their own, new values, attitudes and goals, and to exert effort on behalf of and in pursuit of those values, attitudes and goals. An effective leader inspires others to adopt values, attitudes and goals that define group membership, and to behave in ways that serve the group as a collective. An effective leader can transform individual action into group action. Thus, leadership has an important identity function. People look to their leaders to express and epitomise their identity, to clarify and focus their identity, to forge and transform their identity, and to consolidate, stabilise and anchor their identity.

Social identity theory of leadership
Development of social identity theory to explain leadership as an identity process in which in salient groups prototypical leaders are more effective than less prototypical leaders.

This identity perspective on leadership (e.g. Haslam, Reicher and Platow, 2011) has been placed centre-stage by the social identity theory of leadership (Hogg, 2001b; Hogg and van Knippenberg, 2003; Hogg, van Knippenberg and Rast, 2012b). As people identify more strongly with a group, they pay closer attention to the group prototype and to what and who is more prototypical of the group: this is because the prototype defines the group and one's identity as a group member. Under these circumstances, prototypical members tend to be more influential than less prototypical members and thus more effective as leaders; and thus prototypical leaders tend to be more effective than non-prototypical leaders as leaders. Although leadership schemas, as discussed by leader categorisation theory (see above), generally do govern leader effectiveness, when a social group becomes a salient and important basis for self-conception and identity, group prototypicality becomes important, perhaps more important than leader schemas.

This idea was first supported in a laboratory experiment by Hains, Hogg and Duck (1997), in which participants were either explicitly categorised or merely aggregated as a group (group membership salience was therefore either high or low). Before participating in an interactive group task, they rated the leadership effectiveness of a randomly appointed leader, who was described as being either a prototypical or non-prototypical group member and as possessing or not possessing characteristics that were consistent with general leadership schemas. As predicted, schema-consistent leaders were generally considered more effective than schema-inconsistent leaders; however, when group membership was salient, group prototypicality became an important influence on perceived leadership effectiveness (see Figure 9.4).

These findings were replicated in a longitudinal field study of Outward Bound groups (Fielding and Hogg, 1997), and in further experiments (e.g. Hogg, Hains and Mason, 1998), and correlational studies (e.g. Platow and Van Knippenberg, 2001). Other studies show that in salient groups, ingroup leaders (i.e. more prototypical leaders) are more effective than outgroup leaders (i.e. less prototypical leaders) (Duck and Fielding, 1999; Van Vugt and De Cremer, 1999).

A number of social identity-related processes (see Abrams and Hogg, 2010; Hogg, 2006, for overview) make prototypical leaders more influential in salient groups:

- Because prototypical members best embody the group's attributes, they are viewed as the source rather than target of conformity processes – they are the ones with whom other members seem to align their behaviour (cf. Turner, 1991).

- Prototypical members are liked as group members (a process of depersonalised social attraction), and, because group members usually agree on the prototype, the group as a whole likes the leader – he or she is popular (Hogg, 1993). This process facilitates influence (we are more likely to comply with requests from people we like – Berscheid and Reis, 1998). It also accentuates the perceived evaluative (status) differential between leader and followers.

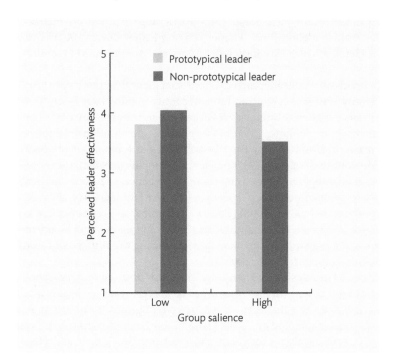

Figure 9.4 Leader effectiveness as a function of group prototypicality of the leader and salience of the group

- When group salience was high, features of the leader that were prototypical for the group became important in determining how effective the leader was perceived as being.
- When group salience was low, being prototypical did not have this impact.

Source: Based on data from Hains, Hogg and Duck (1997)

- Prototypical leaders find the group more central and important to self-definition, and therefore identify more strongly with it. They have significant investment in the group and are more likely to behave in group-serving ways. They closely embody group norms and are more likely to favour the ingroup over outgroups, to treat ingroup members fairly, and to act in ways that promote the ingroup. These actions confirm their prototypicality and membership credentials, and encourage group members to trust them to be acting in the best interest of the group even when it may not appear that they are – prototypical leaders are furnished with legitimacy (Tyler, 1997; Tyler and Lind, 1992; see Platow, Reid and Andrew, 1998). A consequence is that prototypical leaders can be innovative and transformational. Paradoxically, they can diverge from group norms and conform less than leaders who are *not* prototypical (Abrams, Randsley de Moura, Marques and Hutchison, 2008; Randsleyde Moura, Abrams, Hutchison and Marques, 2011).

- Because the prototype is central to group life, information related to the prototype attracts attention. A prototypical leader is the most direct source of prototype information, and so stands out against the background of the group. Members pay close attention to the leader and, as in other areas of social perception and inference, attribute his or her behaviour to invariant or essential properties of the leader's personality – they engage in the **correspondence bias** (Gawronski, 2004; Gilbert and Malone, 1995; **see Chapter 3**). This process can construct a charismatic personality for the leader (the behaviours being attributed include being the source of influence, being able to gain compliance from others, being popular, having higher status, being innovative, and being trusted) which further strengthens his or her position of leadership (Haslam and Platow, 2001).

Correspondence bias
A general attribution bias in which people have an inflated tendency to see behaviour as reflecting (corresponding to) stable underlying personality attributes.

Prototypical leaders succeed in their position by acting as prototype managers – what Reicher and Hopkins have aptly called 'entrepreneurs of identity' (Reicher and Hopkins, 2001, 2003), and Seyranian calls social identity framing (Seyranian, 2012; Seyranian and Bligh, 2008). They communicate in ways that construct, reconstruct or change the group prototype; and this protects or promotes their central position in the group. This process is called *norm talk* (Hogg and Giles, 2012; Hogg and Tindale, 2005; also see Fiol, 2002; Gardner, Paulsen, Gallois, Callan and Monaghan, 2001; Reid and Ng, 2000). A key attribute of an effective leader, therefore, is precisely this visionary and transformational activity that defines or changes: (a) what the group sees itself as being, and (b) the members' identity (Reicher, Haslam and Hopkins, 2005). Leaders who feel they may not be prototypical usually engage in a range of group-oriented acts to strengthen their membership credentials (e.g. Platow and van Knippenberg, 2001). There are many ways in which leaders can engage in norm talk and act as entrepreneurs of identity – see Box 9.1.

There is now substantial evidence that leaders actively construct identity in this way through their communications. Identity entrepreneurship and social identity framing have been shown in studies of Margaret Thatcher and Neil Kinnock's speeches concerning the British miner's strike in 1984–1985 (Reicher and Hopkins, 1996b), the political mobilisation attempts of British Muslims concerning voting or abstaining from British elections (Hopkins et al., 2003), anti-abortion speeches (Hopkins and Reicher, 1997; Reicher and Hopkins, 1996a), the preservation of hunting in the United Kingdom by focusing on the connection of nation and place (Wallwork and Dixon, 2004), Scottish politicians' speeches (Reicher and Hopkins, 2001); US presidents' speeches (Seyranian and Bligh, 2008), Patrice Lumumba's speeches during the Congolese decolonisation from Belgium (Klein and Licata, 2003), and in attempts by prisoners to mobilise both prisoners and guards against management during the BBC prison study experiment (Reicher, Hopkins, Levine and Rath, 2005).

The social identity theory of leadership has empirical support from laboratory experiments and more naturalistic studies and surveys, and it has re-energised leadership research in social and organisational psychology that focuses on the role of group membership and social identity (Ellemers, De Gilder and Haslam, 2004; Haslam, Reicher and Platow, 2011; van Knippenberg and Hogg, 2003; van Knippenberg, van Knippenberg, De Cremer and Hogg,

Real world 9.1
Norm talk and identity entrepreneurship

Five ways in which you as a leader can protect and enhance how group prototypically you are perceived by your followers

1 Talk up your prototypicality and/or talk down aspects of your own behaviour that are non-prototypical.

2 Identify deviants or marginal members to highlight your own prototypicality or to construct a particular prototype for the group that enhances your prototypicality.

3 Secure your own leadership position by vilifying contenders for leadership and casting them as non-prototypical.

4 Identify as relevant comparison outgroups groups that cast the most favourable light on your own prototypicality.

5 Engage in a discourse that raises or lowers salience. If you are highly prototypical then raising salience will provide you with the leadership benefits of high prototypicality; if you are not very prototypical then lowering salience will protect you from the leadership pitfalls of not being very prototypical.

2004; also see Hogg, 2007a). Along with leader categorisation theory (Lord and Brown, 2004; see above), it also connects with a trend in leadership research to attend to the role of followers in leadership – for leaders to lead, followers must follow. One aspect of this trend focuses on what is rather awkwardly dubbed 'followership'; and there is now research that explores how followers can be empowered to create great and effective leaders (e.g. Kelley, 1992; Riggio, Chaleff and Lipman-Blumen, 2008; Shamir, Pillai, Bligh and Uhl-Bien, 2006).

Trust and leadership

Trust plays an important role in leadership (e.g. Dirks and Ferrin, 2002) – we all get very concerned about corporate corruption and untrustworthy business and government leaders (e.g. Kellerman, 2004). If we are to follow our leaders, we need to be able to trust them to be acting in the best interest of us all as a group, rather than in their own self-interest. Leaders also need their followers, as we have seen above, to trust them in order to be able to be innovative and transformational.

Justice and fairness

Leaders need their followers to trust them if they wish to be innovative and transformational. An important basis for trusting one's leaders is the perception that they have acted in a fair and just manner. According to Tom Tyler's **group value model** (Lind and Tyler, 1988) and his **relational model of authority in groups** (Tyler, 1997; Tyler and Lind, 1992), perceptions of fairness and justice are critical to group life. Because leaders make decisions with important consequences for followers (e.g. promotions, performance appraisals, allocation of duties), followers are concerned about how fair the leader is in making these decisions. In judging fairness, followers evaluate a leader in terms of both **distributive justice** and **procedural justice**. Justice and fairness judgements influence reactions to decisions and to the authorities making these decisions, and thus influence leadership effectiveness (De Cremer, 2003; De Cremer and Tyler, 2005).

Procedural justice is particularly important in leadership contexts, probably because fair procedures convey respect for group members. This encourages followers to feel positive about the group, to identify with it and to be cooperative and compliant (Tyler, 2011). As members

Group value model View that procedural justice within groups makes members feel valued, and thus leads to enhanced commitment to and identification with the group.

Relational model of authority in groups Tyler's account of how effective authority in groups rests upon fairness- and justice-based relations between leader and followers.

Distributive justice The fairness of the outcome of a decision.

Procedural justice The fairness of the procedures used to make a decision.

identify more strongly with the group, they care more that the leader is procedurally fair (e.g. Brockner, Chen, Mannix, Leung and Skarlicki, 2000), and care less that the leader is distributively fair. This asymmetry arises because with increasing identification, concern about instrumental outcomes, i.e. incentives and sanctions (distributive justice), is outweighed by concern about relationships within the group (procedural justice) (e.g. Vermunt, van Knippenberg, van Knippenberg and Blaauw, 2001).

Social dilemmas

The fact that justice, particularly procedural justice, facilitates effective leadership because it builds trust and strengthens group identification, raises the possibility that leadership may be a way to resolve social dilemmas. Social dilemmas are essentially a crisis of trust – people behave selfishly because they do not trust others to sacrifice their immediate self-interest for the longer-term greater good of the collective (e.g. Dawes and Messick, 2000; Liebrand, Messick and Wilke, 1992; **see Chapter 11**).

Social dilemmas are notoriously difficult to resolve (Kerr and Park, 2001). However, they are not impossible to resolve if one can address the trust issue. One way to do this is to build mutual trust among people by causing them to identify strongly as a group – people tend to trust ingroup members (e.g. Brewer, 1981; Yamagishi and Kiyonari, 2000) and therefore are more likely to sacrifice self-interest for the greater good (e.g. Brewer and Schneider, 1990; De Cremer and Van Vugt, 1999). Leadership plays a critical role in this process because a leader can transform selfish individual goals into shared group goals by building a sense of common identity, shared fate, interindividual trust and custodianship of the collective good (e.g. De Cremer and van Knippenberg, 2003; Van Vugt and De Cremer, 1999).

Gender gaps, glass ceilings and glass cliffs

Throughout most of the world, men and women both lead and exercise authority in different domains of life. However, in the worlds of work, politics and ideology it is typically men who occupy top leadership positions. If one restricts oneself to liberal democracies like those in western Europe, where more progressive gender attitudes have developed over the past forty years, it is still the case that although women are now relatively well represented in middle management, they are still underrepresented in senior management and 'elite' leadership positions – there is a glass ceiling (Eagly and Karau, 1991; Eagly, Karau and Makhijani, 1995; Eagly, Makhijani and Klonsky, 1992).

Social dilemmas
Situations in which short-term personal gain is at odds with the long-term good of the group.

Glass ceiling
An invisible barrier that prevents women, and minorities, from attaining top leadership positions.

Glass ceiling
Women make it to the top – Facebook's chief operating officer Sheryl Sandberg is a case in point. But they can still encounter more obstacles than men do (watch www.makers.com/sheryl-sandberg)

Are men really better suited than women to leadership? Research suggests not. Although women and men tend to adopt different leadership styles, which implies that different leadership contexts may suit different genders, women are usually rated as just as effective leaders as men – and in general they are perceived to be marginally more transformational and participative, and more praising of followers for good performance (Eagly, Johannesen-Schmidt, Van Engen and Vinkenburg, 2002). If women and men are equally capable of being effective leaders, why is there a gender gap in leadership?

One explanation proposed by Alice Eagly is in terms of role congruity theory (Eagly, 2003; Eagly and Karau, 2002; Heilman, 1983). Role congruity theory argues that because there is greater overlap between general leader schemas and agentic male stereotypes (men are assertive, controlling and dominant) than between leader schemas and communal female stereotypes (women are affectionate, gentle and nurturant), people have more favourable perceptions of male leaders than of female leaders. These leadership perceptions facilitate or impede effective leadership. They place women in a tricky situation position: if they are communal they may not fit the schema of being a leader so well; if they are agentic they run the risk, like Margaret Thatcher, of being dubbed the 'Iron Lady', 'Her Malignancy' or 'Attila the Hen' (Genovese, 1993).

Research provides some support for role congruity theory (Martell, Parker, Emrich and Crawford, 1998; Shore, 1992). One implication of the theory is that the evaluation of male and female leaders will change if the leadership schema changes or if people's gender stereotypes change. For example, research has shown that men leaders are evaluated more favourably than women leaders when the role is defined in more masculine terms, and vice versa when the role is defined in less masculine terms (Eagly, Karau and Makhijani, 1995).

Another obstacle to gender equality in leadership can be understood in terms of the social identity theory of leadership (discussed above). In high-salience groups that members identify with, male or female leaders are seen to be and actually are effective if the group's norms are consistent with the members' gender stereotypes. So, people with traditional gender stereotypes will endorse a male rather than a female leader of a group with instrumental norms (e.g. a trucking company) and a female rather than a male leader of a group with more expressive norms (e.g. a childcare group); but people with less traditional gender stereotypes are less inclined to respond in this way or act in the reverse way (Hogg, Fielding, Johnson, Masser, Russell and Svensson, 2006).

A third obstacle to gender equality in leadership is that women claim authority less effectively than men – men claim and hold many more leadership positions overall than women (Bowles and McGinn, 2005). However, once women or men claim authority they are equally effective. Bowles and McGinn propose four main barriers to women claiming authority. The first is role incongruity, as discussed above. The second is lack of critical management experience. The third is family responsibility, which compromises a woman's ability to find the time commitment required of leadership positions.

A fourth obstacle to gender equality in leadership is lack of motivation – women are not as 'hungry' for leadership as are men. They shy away from self-promotion and take on less visible background roles with informal titles like 'facilitator' or 'coordinator'. Although the link has not been made explicit, one underlying reason for women's alleged reticence to claim authority may be stereotype threat (Inzlicht and Schmader, 2011; Steele and Aronson, 1995; Steele, Spencer and Aronson, 2002; **see Chapter 10**) – women fear that negative stereotypes about women and leadership will be confirmed, and so they feel less motivated to lead. In addition, a woman who promotes herself and claims leadership has to contend with popular stereotypes of women. She runs the risk of being seen as 'pushy', attracting negative reactions from both men and women (Rudman, 1998; Rudman and Glick, 2001). **(We return to the topic of stereotype threat in Chapter 10.)**

Michelle Ryan and her colleagues have recently suggested that women in leadership not only confront a glass ceiling but also a glass cliff (Ryan and Haslam, 2007). Women are more likely than men to be appointed to leadership positions associated with increased risk of failure

Role congruity theory
Mainly applied to the gender gap in leadership – because social stereotypes of women are inconsistent with people's schemas of effective leadership, women are evaluated as poor leaders.

Stereotype threat
Feeling that we will be judged and treated in terms of negative stereotypes of our group, and that we will inadvertently confirm these stereotypes through our behaviour.

Glass cliff
A tendency for women rather than men to be appointed to precarious leadership positions associated with a high probability of failure and criticism.

and criticism because these positions involve the management of groups that are in crisis. As a result, women often confront a glass cliff in which their position as leader is precarious and probably doomed to failure.

Haslam and Ryan (2008) conducted three experiments in which management graduates, high-school students or business leaders selected a leader for a hypothetical organisation whose performance was either improving or declining (i.e. failing). As predicted, a woman was more likely to be selected ahead of an equally qualified man when the organisation's performance was declining rather than improving. Further, participants who made these 'glass cliff appointments' also believed that such positions (a) suited the distinctive leadership abilities that women possess and (b) were good leadership opportunities for women. There is a sting in the tail: the participants also believed that a position in a failing organisation would be particularly stressful for women – because of the 'emotional labour' involved!

Ryan and colleagues report other supportive studies that focus on political leadership (Ryan, Haslam and Kulich, 2010). An archival study of the 2005 UK General Election revealed that, in the Conservative Party, women contested harder-to-win seats than did men. Another study experimentally investigated the selection of a candidate by undergraduates in a British political science class to contest a by-election in a seat that was either safe (held by own party with a large margin) or risky (held by an opposition party with a large margin). Their findings showed that a male candidate was more likely than a woman to be selected to contest a safe seat, but a woman was strongly preferred when the seat was hard to win.

Intergroup leadership

An under-explored aspect of leadership is its intergroup context – leaders not only lead the members of their group, but in different ways they lead their group *against* other groups. The political and military leaders who are often invoked in discussions of leadership are leaders in a truly intergroup context – they lead their political parties, their nations or their armies *against* other political parties, nations or armies.

Leadership rhetoric is often about *us* versus *them,* about defining the ingroup in contrast to specific outgroups or deviant ingroup factions (Reicher, Haslam and Hopkins, 2005; Seyranian, 2012). The nature of intergroup relations can also influence leadership by changing group goals or altering intragroup relations. Earlier, we described how a leadership change in one of Sherif's groups of boys at a summer camp was produced by intergroup competition (Sherif, Harvey, White, Hood and Sherif, 1961). In another study, of simulated bargaining between a union and management, relatively insecure leaders (who were likely to be deposed by their group) actively sought to bargain by competing in order to secure their leadership (Rabbie and Bekkers, 1978). Perhaps this captures the familiar tactic where political leaders pursue an aggressive foreign policy (where they believe they can win) in order to combat unpopularity experienced at home. For example, the 1982 Falklands War between Argentina and Britain, which arose in the context of political unpopularity at home for both governments, certainly boosted Margaret Thatcher's leadership; and the two Gulf Wars of 1991 and 2003 may initially have consolidated leadership for US Presidents Bush senior and Bush junior respectively.

But there is another side to intergroup leadership – the building of a unified group identity, vision and purpose across deep subgroup divisions within the group. Although social identity theory is a theory of intergroup relations (e.g. Tajfel and Turner, 1979), the social identity theory of leadership actually has an intragroup focus – for example, on within-group prototypicality, shared group membership and ingroup trust. The great challenge of effective leadership, however, often is not merely to transcend *differences among individuals,* but to bridge profound *divisions between groups* to build an integrative vision and identity. For example: effective leadership of Iraq must bridge historic differences between Sunnis, Shi'ites and Kurds; effective leadership of the US must bridge a profound gulf between Democrats and Republicans; effective leadership of the EU must bridge vast differences among its 27 member states. 'Leadership', as the term is often used in common parlance, is often better characterised as intergroup leadership (Hogg, 2009; Pittinsky, 2009; Pittinsky and Simon, 2007). (Reflect on focus question 2. Should Steve or Martin take the role of new boss?)

Hogg and his colleagues have recently proposed a model of intergroup leadership (Hogg, van Knippenberg and Rast, 2012a). Effective intergroup leadership faces the daunting task of building social harmony and a common purpose and identity out of conflict among groups. One problem is that intergroup leaders are often viewed as representing one group more than the other; they are outgroup leaders to one subgroup and, thus, suffer compromised effectiveness (Duck and Fielding, 1999, 2003). This problem has been well researched in the context of organisational mergers and acquisitions. Acquisitions often fail precisely because the leader of the acquiring organisation is viewed with suspicion as a member of the former outgroup organisation (e.g., Terry, Carey and Callan, 2001). These problems can be accentuated by ingroup projection – a phenomenon where groups nested within a larger superordinate group overestimate how well their own characteristics are represented in the superordinate group (Wenzel, Mummendey and Waldzus, 2007). In this case, a leader of the superordinate group who belongs to one subgroup will be viewed by the other subgroup as not at all prototypical of the superordinate group.

One interesting wrinkle to this is that lower/minority status subgroups often do not engage in ingroup projection; both subgroups agree that the dominant subgroup's attributes are best represented in the superordinate group (Sindic and Reicher, 2008). In this situation the minority subgroup *will* view a superordinate leader who comes from the majority subgroup as prototypical. However, such a leader will not gain an advantage from this because the minority group feels underrepresented, and therefore is unlikely to identify sufficiently strongly with the superordinate group (Hohman, Hogg and Bligh, 2010).

Hogg and colleagues suggest that effective intergroup leadership rests on the leader's ability to construct an *intergroup relational identity* (Hogg, van Knippenberg and Rast, 2012). Intergroup leaders strive to build a common ingroup identity (Gaertner and Dovidio, 2000; Gaertner, Dovidio, Anastasio, Bachman and Rust, 1993; **see Chapter 11**). However, this needs to be carried out carefully; it can easily backfire when it threatens the subgroup identity of subgroups.

In contrast an intergroup relational identity is a self-definition in terms of one's subgroup membership that incorporates the subgroup's relationship with another subgroup as part of the overarching group's identity – it is an identity that recognises the integrity and valued contribution of subgroup identities and the way that they and the superordinate group are actually defined in terms of collaborative subgroup relations. There are a number of actions that leaders can take to build an intergroup relational identity and thus sponsor effective intergroup performance. These include (a) rhetoric championing the intergroup collaboration as a valued aspect of group identity, (b) intergroup boundary spanning to exemplify the intergroup relationship, and (c) the formation of a boundary-spanning leadership coalition.

In concluding this section, the great challenge of leadership is often not merely to transcend individual differences, but to bridge profound group divisions and build an integrative vision and identity. Most theories and studies of leadership focus on leading individuals within a single group, whereas many if not most leadership contexts involve intergroup relations (Pittinsky and Simon, 2007).

Group decision making

Groups perform many tasks, of which making decisions is one of the most important. The course of our lives is largely determined by decisions made by groups: for example, selection committees, juries, parliaments, committees of examiners and groups of friends. In addition, many of us spend a significant portion of our working lives making decisions in groups.

Social psychologists have long been interested in the social processes involved in group decision making, and in whether groups make better or different decisions than do individuals.

We might think that humans come together to make decisions because groups would make better decisions than individuals – two heads are better than one. However, **as we learnt in Chapter 8**, groups can impair and distort performance in many ways. Another dimension of group decision making comes into play when members of the decision-making group are formally acting as *representatives* of different groups. This is more properly called intergroup decision making and is dealt with later in the text **(see Chapter 11)**.

Rules governing group decisions

A variety of models have been developed to relate the distribution of initial opinions in a decision-making group to the group's final decision (Stasser, Kerr and Davis, 1989; Stasser and Dietz-Uhler, 2001). Some of these are complex computer-simulation models (Hastie, Penrod and Pennington, 1983; Penrod and Hastie, 1980; Stasser, 1988; Stasser and Davis, 1981), while others, although expressed in a formalised mathematical style, are more immediately related to real groups.

One of the best-known models is a set of rules described by James Davis and described as social decisions schemes. The model identifies a small number of explicit or implicit decision-making rules that groups can adopt (Davis, 1973; Stasser, Kerr and Davis, 1989). Knowledge of the initial distribution of individual opinions in the group, and what rule the group is operating under, allows prediction, with a high degree of certainty, of the final group decision. We can apply these rules to institutionalised groups, such as a parliament, but also to informal groups, such as a group of friends deciding which film to go and see (see Box 9.2).

The particular rule that a group adopts can be influenced by the nature of the decision-making task. For *intellective tasks* (those where there is a demonstrably correct solution, such as a mathematical puzzle) groups tend to adopt the truth-wins rule; for *judgemental tasks* (where there is no demonstrably correct solution, such as what colour to paint the living room) the majority-wins rule (Laughlin, 1980; Laughlin and Ellis, 1986).

Decision rules also differ in terms of strictness and the distribution of power among group members:

- *Strictness* refers to the degree of agreement required by the rule – unanimity is extremely strict and majority-wins less strict.

- The *distribution of power* among members refers to how authoritarian the rule is – authoritarian rules concentrate power in one member, while egalitarian rules spread power among all members (Hastie, Penrod and Pennington, 1983).

Social decisions schemes
Explicit or implicit decision-making rules that relate individual opinions to a final group decision.

Social psychology in action 9.2
Social decisions schemes: Ways that a group can reach a decision

James Davis distinguished between several explicit or implicit decision-making rules that groups can adopt:

- *Unanimity* – Discussion is aimed at pressurising deviants to conform.

- *Majority wins* – Discussion confirms the majority position, which is then adopted as the group position.

- *Truth wins* – Discussion reveals the position that can be demonstrated to be correct.

- *Two-thirds majority* – Unless there is a two-thirds majority, the group is unable to reach a decision.

- *First shift* – The group ultimately adopts a decision in line with the direction of the first shift in opinion shown by any member of the group.

Source: Based on Davis (1973); Stasser, Kerr and Davis (1989).

In general, stricter rules have lower power concentration and are thus more egalitarian, with decision-making power more evenly distributed across the group – unanimity is very strict but very low in power concentration, while two-thirds majority is less strict but has greater power concentration (Hastie, Penrod and Pennington, 1983). The type of rule adopted can have an effect, largely as a function of its strictness, not only on the group's decision itself but also on members' preferences, their satisfaction with the group decision, the perception and nature of group discussion, and members' feelings for one another (Miller, 1989). For example, stricter decision rules can make final agreement in the group slower, more exhaustive and difficult to attain, but it can enhance liking for fellow members and satisfaction with the quality of the decision.

Norbert Kerr's social transition scheme model focuses attention on the actual pattern of member positions moved through by a group operating under a particular decision, en route to its final decision (Kerr, 1981; Stasser, Kerr and Davis, 1989). In order to do this, members' opinions are monitored during the process of discussion (Kerr and MacCoun, 1985), either by periodically asking the participants or by having them note any and every change in their opinion. These procedures can be intrusive, so an issue is how much they affect the natural ongoing process of discussion.

One other line of research on group decision making focuses on hidden profiles (Stasser and Titus, 2003). A hidden profile is a situation in which group members have shared information favouring an inferior choice or decision, and unshared private information favouring a superior choice or decision. In this situation groups typically choose an inferior alternative and make an inferior decision. A recent meta-analysis of 65 hidden profiles studies (Lu, Yuan and McLeod, 2012) concluded that groups mentioned more pieces of common information than unique information, and hidden profile groups were eight times less likely to find the correct solution or come to an optimal decision than were groups having full information.

Social transition scheme Method for charting incremental changes in member opinions as a group moves towards a final decision.

Brainstorming

Some decision-making tasks require groups to come up with creative and novel solutions. A common technique is brainstorming (Osborn, 1957). Group members try to generate lots of ideas very quickly and to forget their inhibitions or concerns about quality – they simply say whatever comes to mind, are non-critical, and build on others' ideas when possible. Brainstorming is supposed to facilitate creative thinking and thus make the group more creative. Popular opinion is so convinced that brainstorming works that it is widely used in business and advertising agencies.

Brainstorming Uninhibited generation of as many ideas as possible in a group, in order to enhance group creativity.

Brainstorming
Encouraging an uninhibited outpouring of ideas is a strategy sometimes used to enhance a group's creativity, and it can be fun – but how well does this strategy work?

However, research tells us otherwise. Although brainstorming groups do generate *more* ideas than non-brainstorming groups, the individuals in the group are no more creative than if they had worked alone. In their review, Wolfgang Stroebe and Michael Diehl (1994) concluded that *nominal* groups (i.e. brainstorming groups in which individuals create ideas on their own and do not interact) are twice as creative as groups that actually interact (see also Diehl and Stroebe, 1987; Mullen, Johnson and Salas, 1991).

The inferior performance of brainstorming groups can be attributed to at least four factors (Paulus, Dzindolet, Poletes and Camacho, 1993):

1 *Evaluation apprehension* – despite explicit instructions to encourage the uninhibited generation of as many ideas as possible, members may still be concerned about making a good impression. This introduces self-censorship and a consequent reduction in productivity.

2 *Social loafing and free riding* – there is motivation loss because of the collective nature of the task **(see Chapter 8)**.

3 *Production matching* – because brainstorming is novel, members use average group performance to construct a performance norm to guide their own generation of ideas. This produces regression to the mean.

4 Production blocking – individual creativity and productivity are reduced owing to interference effects from contending with others who are generating ideas at the same time as one is trying to generate one's own ideas.

Stroebe and Diehl (1994) review evidence for these processes and conclude that production blocking is probably the main obstacle to unlocking the creative potential of brainstorming groups. They discuss a number of remedies, of which two have particular promise.

1 *Electronic brainstorming* reduces the extent to which the production of new ideas is blocked by such things as listening to others or waiting for a turn to speak (Hollingshead and McGrath, 1995): groups that brainstorm electronically via computer can produce more ideas than non-electronic groups and more ideas than nominal electronic groups (Dennis and Valacich, 1993; Gallupe, Cooper, Grise and Bastianutti, 1994).

2 *Heterogeneous groups* in which members have diverse types of knowledge about the brainstorming topic may create a particularly stimulating environment that alleviates the effects of production blocking; if production blocking is also reduced by other means, heterogeneous brainstorming groups might outperform heterogeneous nominal groups.

Given convincing evidence that face-to-face brainstorming does not actually improve individual creativity, why do people so firmly believe that it does and continue to use it as a technique for generating new ideas in groups? This paradox may stem from an illusion of group effectivity (Diehl and Stroebe, 1991; Stroebe, Diehl and Abakoumkin, 1992; also see Paulus, Dzindolet, Poletes and Camacho, 1993). We all take part in group discussions from time to time, and so all have some degree of personal experience with generating ideas in groups. The illusion of group effectivity is an experience-based belief that we actually produce more and better ideas in groups than when alone.

This illusion may be generated by at least three processes:

1 Although groups have fewer non-redundant original ideas than the sum of individuals working alone, they produce more ideas than any single member would produce alone. People in groups are exposed to more ideas than when alone. They find it difficult to remember whether the ideas produced were their own or those of other people and so tend to exaggerate their own contribution. They feel that they have been individually more productive and were facilitated by the group when in fact they were less productive. Stroebe, Diehl and Abakoumkin (1992) had participants brainstorm in four-person nominal or real groups and asked them to estimate the percentage of ideas: (1) that they had suggested; (2) that others had suggested but they had also thought of; (3) that others had suggested but they had not

Production blocking
Reduction in individual creativity and productivity in brainstorming groups due to interruptions and turn taking.

Illusion of group effectivity
Experience-based belief that we produce more and better ideas in groups than alone.

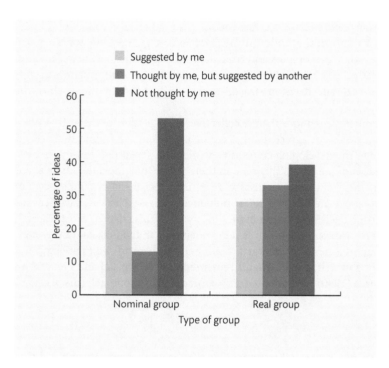

Figure 9.5 Percentage of ideas assigned to self and to others in nominal and real brainstorming groups

Relative to participants in nominal brainstorming groups, participants in real brainstorming groups underestimated the number of ideas they had not thought of and overestimated the number of ideas they had thought of but actually had been suggested by others

Source: Based on data from Stroebe, Diehl and Abakoumkin (1992)

thought of. The results show that participants in real groups overestimate the percentage of ideas that they thought they had but did not suggest, relative to participants in nominal groups (see Figure 9.5).

2 Brainstorming is generally great fun. People enjoy brainstorming in groups more than alone and so feel more satisfied with their performance.

3 People in groups know they call out only some of the ideas they have, because others have already suggested their remaining ideas. Although all members are in the same position, the individual is not privy to others' undisclosed ideas – and so attributes the relatively low overt productivity of others to their own relatively high latent productivity. The group is seen to have enhanced or confirmed their own high level of performance.

Group memory

Another important aspect of group decision making is the ability to recall information. For instance, juries need to recall testimony in order to be able to arrive at a verdict, and personnel selection panels need to recall data that differentiate candidates in order to make an appointment. Group remembering can even be the principal reason for certain groups to come together: for example, groups of old friends often meet mainly to reminisce. On a larger scale, organisations need to acquire, distribute, interpret and store enormous amounts of information. The analysis of exactly how this complex task of *organisational learning* is accomplished is still in its infancy (Wilpert, 1995).

Group remembering

Do groups remember more material and remember material more accurately than individuals? Different people recall different information; so when they come together as a group to share this information the group has effectively remembered more than any one individual (Clark and Stephenson, 1985, 1995). Groups recall more than individuals because members communicate unshared information and because the group recognises true information when it hears it (Lorge and Solomon, 1995). However, the superiority of groups over individuals varies depending on the memory task. On simplistic and artificial tasks (e.g. nonsense words), group superiority is more marked than on complex and realistic tasks (e.g. a story). One explanation is 'process loss' (Steiner, 1976; **see Chapter 8**). In trying to recall complex information, groups fail to adopt appropriate recall and decision strategies, and so do not fully utilise all of the group's human resources.

However, group remembering is more than a collective regurgitation of facts. It is often a constructive process by which an agreed joint account is worked out. Some individuals' memories will contribute to the developing consensus, while others' will not. In this way, the group shapes its own version of the truth. This version then guides individual members about what to store as a true memory and what to discard as an incorrect memory. The process of reaching consensus is subject to the range of social influence processes discussed earlier (**see Chapter 7**), and to the group decision-making biases discussed in this chapter. Most research into group remembering focuses on how much is remembered by individuals and by groups. Recently, however, other approaches have emerged: Clark and Stephenson and their associates have looked at the content and structure of what is remembered (see Box 9.3 and Figure 9.6), and Middleton and Edwards (1990) have adopted a discourse analysis approach (**discussed in Chapter 15**).

Transactive memory

A different perspective on group remembering is that different members remember different things (memory specialisation is distributed), but everyone also needs to remember 'who remembers what' – who to go to for information. Dan Wegner calls this transactive memory, a term suggesting that group members have transacted an agreement (Wegner, 1987, 1995; also see Moreland, Argote and Krishnan, 1996). This idea refers to the way in which individuals in couples and groups can share memory load so that each individual is responsible for remembering only part of what the group needs to know, but all members know who is responsible for each memory domain. Transactive memory is a shared system for encoding, storing and retrieving information. It allows a group to remember significantly more information than if no transactive memory system was present (Hollingshead, 1998).

For example, the psychology departments in our universities need to remember an enormous amount of practical information to do with research, postgraduate supervision, undergraduate teaching, equipment and administrative matters. There is far too much for a single individual to remember. Instead, certain individuals are formally responsible for particular domains (e.g. research), but all of us have a transactive memory that allows us to remember who is responsible for each domain. Transactive memory is also very common in close relationships such as marriage: for example, both partners know that one of them remembers financial matters and the other remembers directions.

Transactive memory is a group-level representation: although it is represented in the mind of the individual, it can emerge only through psychological involvement in a group and otherwise has no value or use. For example, who else beyond her team-mates cares if it is Mary's turn to bring orange juice to the sports team's practice this month? There can be no such thing as individual transactive memory. In this respect, the concept of transactive memory is related to William McDougall's (1920) notion of a group mind (**Chapters 1 and 11**) – a state of mind and mode of cognition found in groups that is qualitatively different from that found in individuals.

Wegner, Erber and Raymond (1991) describe the development of transactive memory. When groups or couples first form the basis of transactive memory is usually social categorisation. People stereotypically assign memory domains to individuals on the basis of their category memberships. For example, members of heterosexual couples might initially develop a transactive memory in which memory is allocated on the basis of sex-role stereotypes (the woman remembers things to do with cooking and believes that information to do with the

Transactive memory
Group members have a shared memory for who within the group remembers what and is the expert on what.

Group mind
McDougall's idea that people adopt a qualitatively different mode of thinking when in a group.

Social psychology in action 9.3
Can two heads remember better than one?

There are differences between individual and group remembering.

Noel Clark and Geoffrey Stephenson and their associates have conducted a series of experiments on group remembering (e.g. Clark, Stephenson and Rutter, 1986; Stephenson, Abrams, Wagner and Wade, 1986; Stephenson, Clark and Wade, 1986). Clark and Stephenson (1989, 1995) give an integrated overview of this research. Generally, students or police officers individually or collectively (in four-person groups) recalled information from a five-minute police interrogation of a woman who had allegedly been raped. The interrogation was real, or it was staged and presented as an audio recording or a visual transcript. The participants had to recall freely the interrogation and answer specific factual questions (cued recall). The way in which they recalled the information was analysed for content to investigate:

- the amount of correct information recalled;
- the number of reconstructive errors made – that is, inclusion of material that was consistent with but did not appear in the original stimulus;
- the number of confusional errors made – that is, inclusion of material that was inconsistent with the original stimulus;
- the number of metastatements made – that is, inclusion of information that attributed motives to characters or went beyond the original stimulus in other ways.

Figure 9.6 (adapted from Clark and Stephenson, 1989) shows that groups recalled significantly more correct information and made fewer metastatements than individuals, but they did not differ in the number of reconstructions or confusional errors.

Source: Based on Clark and Stephenson (1989).

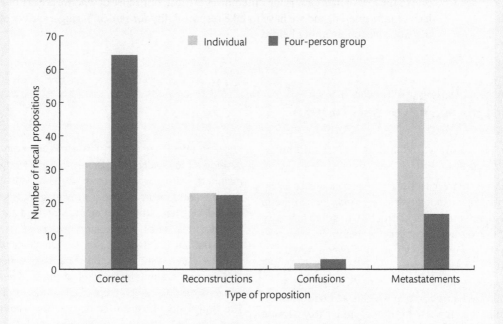

Figure 9.6 Differences between individual and collective remembering
There are qualitative and quantitative differences between individual and collective remembering. Isolated individuals or four-person groups recalled police testimony from the interrogation of an alleged rape victim. In comparison to individuals, groups recalled more information that was correct and made fewer metastatements (statements making motivational inferences and going beyond the information in other related ways)
Source: Based on data from Clark and Stephenson (1989)

car can be obtained from the man, and vice versa). Category-based transactive memory is the default mode. In most cases, however, groups go on to develop more sophisticated memory-assignment systems:

- *Groups can negotiate responsibility for different memory domains* – for instance, couples can decide through discussion who will be responsible for bills, who for groceries, who for cars, and so forth.
- *Groups can assign memory domains on the basis of relative expertise* – for instance, a conference-organising committee might assign responsibility for the social programme to someone who has successfully discharged that duty before.
- *Groups can assign memory domains on the basis of access to information* – for instance, the conference-organising committee might assign responsibility for publicity to someone who has a good graphics package and a list of potential registrants, and who has close contacts with advertising people.

There is a potential pitfall to transactive memory. The uneven distribution of memory within a couple or a group means that when an individual leaves, there is a temporary loss or reduction in group memory (see Box 9.4). This can be very disruptive: for example, if the person in my department responsible for remembering undergraduate teaching matters should suddenly leave, a dire crisis would arise. Groups often recover quickly, as there may be other people (often already with some expertise and access to information) who can immediately shoulder the responsibility. In couples, however, partners are usually irreplaceable. Once one person leaves the couple, perhaps through death or separation, a whole section of group memory vanishes. It is possible that the depression associated with bereavement is, at least in part, due to the loss of memory. Happy memories are lost, our sense of who we are is undermined by lack of information, and we have to take responsibility for remembering a variety of things we did not have to remember before.

Social psychology in action 9.4
The group that learns together stays together

Transactive memory: combating its loss and facilitating its development

Transactive memory means that when an individual leaves a group there is a temporary loss of, or reduction in, group memory, which can be very disruptive for group functioning. Linda Argote and her colleagues performed an experiment in which laboratory groups met over a number of consecutive weeks to produce complex origami objects (Argote, Insko, Yovetich and Romero, 1995). Member turnover did indeed disrupt group learning and performance, and its impact grew worse over time, presumably because more established groups had more established transactive memories. Attempts to reduce the problem by providing newcomers with individual origami training were unsuccessful.

The productivity implications for work groups and organisations are very serious, given that staff turnover is a fact of organisational life and that new members are almost always trained individually. Moreland, Argote and Krishnan (1996) argue that transactive memory systems develop more rapidly and operate more efficiently if group members learn together rather than individually. Thus new members of organisations or work groups should be trained together rather than apart. Moreland and associates report a series of laboratory experiments in which group training is indeed superior to individual training for the development and operation of transactive memory.

A natural example of a pitfall of transactive memory comes from the 2000 Davis Cup tennis tournament. The British doubles team comprised Tim Henman and Greg Rusedski, who had trained together as a smoothly operating team for which Britain had very high hopes. Immediately before the doubles match against the Ecuadorian team, Rusedski had to drop out and was replaced by Arvind Parmar. Henman and Parmar had not teamed up before and so had not developed a transactive memory system. They went down to a wholly unexpected straight-sets defeat by Ecuador.

Group culture

The analysis of group memory in terms of group remembering and transactive memory can be viewed as part of a broader analysis of socially shared cognition and group culture (Tindale, Meisenhelder, Dykema-Engblade and Hogg, 2001). We tend to think of culture as something that exists at the societal level – the customs (routines, rituals, symbols and jargon) that describe large-scale social categories such as ethnic or national groups **(see Chapter 16)**. However, there is no reason to restrict culture to such groups. Moreland, Argote and Krishnan (1996) argue that culture is an instance of group memory and therefore can exist in smaller groups such as organisations, sports teams, work groups and even families. The analysis of group culture is most developed in the study of work groups (Levine and Moreland, 1991): such groups develop detailed knowledge about norms, allies and enemies, cliques, working conditions, motivation to work, performance and performance appraisal, who fits in, and who is good at what.

Groupthink

Groups sometimes employ deficient decision-making procedures that produce poor decisions. The consequences of such decisions can be disastrous. Irving Janis (1972) used an archival method, relying on retrospective accounts and content analysis, to compare a number of American foreign policy decisions that had unfavourable outcomes (e.g. the 1961 Bay of Pigs fiasco, the 1941 defence of Pearl Harbor) with others that had favourable outcomes (e.g. the 1962 Cuban missile crisis). Janis coined the term groupthink to describe the group decision-making process that produced the poor decisions. Groupthink was defined as a mode of thinking in which the desire to reach unanimous agreement overrides the motivation to adopt proper rational decision-making procedures (Janis, 1982; Janis and Mann, 1977).

The antecedents, symptoms and consequences of groupthink are displayed in Figure 9.7. The principal cause of groupthink is excessive group cohesiveness **(see Chapter 8 for discussion of cohesiveness)**, but there are other antecedents that relate to basic structural faults in the group and to the immediate decision-making context. Together, these factors generate a range of symptoms that are associated with defective decision-making procedures: for example, there is inadequate and biased discussion and consideration of objectives and alternative solutions, and a failure to seek the advice of experts outside the group (see the third and fourth focus questions).

Descriptive studies of groupthink (e.g. Hart, 1990; Hensley and Griffin, 1986; Tetlock, 1979) largely support the general model (but see Tetlock, Peterson, McGuire, Chang and Feld, 1992),

Groupthink
A mode of thinking in highly cohesive groups in which the desire to reach unanimous agreement overrides the motivation to adopt proper rational decision-making procedures.

Groupthink
Choosing a new Pope is a high-pressure decision with enormous global consequences - there are 1.3 billion Catholics, almost one fifth of the world's population. The 2013 *papal conclave* was a meeting of 115 like-minded individuals sequestered away for two days in complete isolation in the Sistine Chapel

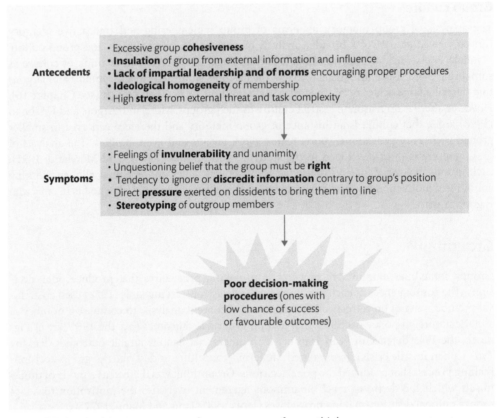

Antecedents
- Excessive group **cohesiveness**
- **Insulation** of group from external information and influence
- **Lack of impartial leadership and of norms** encouraging proper procedures
- **Ideological homogeneity** of membership
- High **stress** from external threat and task complexity

Symptoms
- Feelings of **invulnerability** and unanimity
- Unquestioning belief that the group must be **right**
- Tendency to ignore or **discredit information** contrary to group's position
- Direct **pressure** exerted on dissidents to bring them into line
- **Stereotyping** of outgroup members

Poor decision-making procedures (ones with low chance of success or favourable outcomes)

Figure 9.7 Antecedents, symptoms and consequences of groupthink
Source: Janis and Mann (1977)

whereas experimental studies tend to find mixed or little support for the role of cohesiveness. Experiments establish background conditions for groupthink in four-person laboratory or quasi-naturalistic groups, and then manipulate cohesiveness (usually as friends versus strangers), and either a leadership variable (directiveness or need-for-power) or procedural directions for effective decision making.

Some have found no relationship between cohesiveness and groupthink (Flowers, 1977; Fodor and Smith, 1982), some have found a positive relationship only under certain conditions (Callaway and Esser, 1984; Courtright, 1978; Turner, Pratkanis, Probasco and Leve, 1992), and some a negative relationship (Leana, 1985).

These problems have led people to suggest other ways to approach the explanation of groupthink (Aldag and Fuller, 1993; Hogg, 1993). For example, group cohesiveness may need to be more precisely defined before its relationship to groupthink can be specified (Longley and Pruitt, 1980; McCauley, 1989); at present, it ranges from close friendship to group-based liking. Hogg and Hains (1998) conducted a laboratory study of four-person discussion groups involving 472 participants to find that symptoms of groupthink were associated with cohesiveness, but only where cohesion represented group-based liking, not friendship or interpersonal attraction.

It has also been suggested that groupthink is merely a specific instance of 'risky shift': a group that already tends towards making a risky decision polarises through discussion to an even more risky decision (Myers and Lamm, 1975; see below). Others have suggested that groupthink may not really be a group process at all but just an aggregation of coping responses adopted by individuals to combat excessive stress (Callaway, Marriott and Esser, 1985). Group members are under decision-making stress and thus adopt defensive coping strategies that involve suboptimal decision-making procedures, which are symptomatic of groupthink. This behaviour is mutually reinforced by members of the group and thus produces defective group decisions.

Group polarisation

Folk wisdom has it that groups, committees and organisations are inherently more conservative in their decisions than individuals. Individuals are likely to take risks, while group decision making is a tedious averaging process that errs towards caution. This is consistent with much of what we know about conformity and social influence processes in groups (**see Chapter 7**). Sherif's (1936) autokinetic studies (**discussed in Chapters 7 and 8**) illustrate this averaging process very well.

Imagine, then, the excitement with which social psychologists greeted the results of James Stoner's (1961) unpublished master's thesis (also see Stoner, 1968). Stoner's participants played the role of counsellor/adviser to imaginary people facing choice dilemmas (Kogan and Wallach, 1964), in which a desirable but risky course of action contrasted with a less desirable but more cautious course of action (see Box 9.5). Participants made their own private recommendations and then met in small groups to discuss each dilemma and reach a unanimous group recommendation. Stoner found that groups tended to recommend the risky alternative more than did individuals. Stoner's (1961) finding was quickly replicated by Wallach, Kogan and Bem (1962). This phenomenon has been called **risky shift**, but later research documented group recommendations that were more cautious than those of individuals, causing risky shift to be treated as part of a wider phenomenon of **group polarisation** (Moscovici and Zavalloni, 1969).

Group polarisation (Isenberg, 1986; Myers and Lamm, 1976; Wetherell, 1987) is defined as a tendency for groups to make decisions that are more extreme than the mean of individual members' initial positions, in the direction already favoured by that mean. So, for example, group discussion among a collection of people who already slightly favour capital punishment is likely to produce a group decision that strongly favours capital punishment.

Although forty years of research have produced many different theories to explain polarisation, they can perhaps be simplified to three major perspectives: persuasive arguments, social comparison/cultural values and social identity theory.

Risky shift
Tendency for group discussion to produce group decisions that are more risky than the mean of members' pre-discussion opinions, but only if the pre-discussion mean already favoured risk.

Group polarisation
Tendency for group discussion to produce more extreme group decisions than the mean of members' pre-discussion opinions, in the direction favoured by the mean.

Research classic 9.5
Giving advice on risk-taking

An example of a choice dilemma

Suppose that the participant's task was to advise someone else on a course of action that could vary between two extremes – risky and cautious. The following is an example of such a choice dilemma (Kogan and Wallach, 1964).

> Mr L, a married 30-year-old research physicist, has been given a five-year appointment by a major university laboratory. As he contemplates the next five years, he realises that he might work on a difficult long-term problem which, if a solution can be found, would resolve basic scientific issues in the field and bring him scientific honours. If no solution were found, however, Mr L would have little to show for his five years in the laboratory and this would make it hard for him to get

a good job afterwards. On the other hand, he could, as most of his professional associates are doing, work on a series of short-term problems where solutions would be easier to find but where the problems are of lesser scientific importance.

> Imagine that you (the participant) are advising Mr L. Listed below are several probabilities or odds that a solution would be found to the difficult, long-term problem that Mr L has in mind. Please put a cross beside the *lowest* probability that you would consider acceptable to make it worthwhile for Mr L to work on the more difficult, long-term problem.

The participant then responds on a ten-point scale, indicating the odds that Mr L would solve the long-term problem.

Source: Based on Kogan and Wallach (1964).

Persuasive arguments

Persuasive arguments theory focuses on the persuasive impact of novel arguments in changing people's opinions (Burnstein and Vinokur, 1977; Vinokur and Burnstein, 1974). People tend to rest their opinions on a body of supportive arguments that they express publicly in a group. So people in a group that leans in a particular direction will hear not only familiar arguments they have heard before, but also some novel ones not heard before, but supportive of their own position (Gigone and Hastie, 1993; Larson, Foster-Fishman and Keys, 1994). As a result, their opinions will become more entrenched and extreme, and thus the view of the group as a whole will become polarised.

For example, someone who already favours capital punishment is likely, through discussion with like-minded others, to hear new arguments in favour of capital punishment and come to favour its introduction more strongly. The process of thinking about an issue strengthens our opinions (Tesser, Martin and Mendolia, 1995), as does the public repetition of our own and others' arguments (Brauer, Judd and Gliner, 1995).

Social comparison/cultural values

According to this view, referred to as either social comparison theory or cultural values theory (Jellison and Arkin, 1977; Sanders and Baron, 1977), people seek social approval and try to avoid social censure. Group discussion reveals which views are socially desirable or culturally valued, so group members shift in the direction of the group in order to gain approval and avoid disapproval. For example, favouring capital punishment and finding yourself surrounded by others with similar views might lead you to assume that this is a socially valued attitude – even if it is not. In this example, seeking social approval could lead you to become more extreme in supporting capital punishment. There are two variants of the social comparison perspective:

- *The bandwagon effect* – on learning which attitude pole (i.e extreme position) is socially desirable, people in an interactive discussion may compete to appear to be stronger advocates of that pole. Jean-Paul Codol (1975) called this the *primus inter pares* (first among equals) effect.
- *Pluralistic ignorance* – because people sometimes behave publicly in ways that do not reflect what they actually think, they can be ignorant of what everyone really thinks (Miller and McFarland, 1987; Prentice and Miller, 1993 – **also see Chapters 5 and 6**).

One thing that group discussion can do is to dispel pluralistic ignorance. Where people have relatively extreme attitudes but believe that others are mostly moderate, group discussion can reveal how extreme others' attitudes really are. This liberates people to be true to their underlying beliefs. Polarisation is not so much a shift in attitude as an expression of true attitudes.

Social identity theory

The persuasive arguments and social comparison approaches are supported by some studies but not others (Mackie, 1986; Turner, 1991; Wetherell, 1987). For example, polarisation has been obtained where arguments and persuasion are unlikely to play a role (e.g. perceptual tasks; Baron and Roper, 1976) and where lack of surveillance by the group should minimise the role of social desirability (Goethals and Zanna, 1979; Teger and Pruitt, 1967). In general, it is not possible to argue that one perspective has a clear empirical advantage over the other. Isenberg (1986) has suggested that both are correct (they explain polarisation under different circumstances) and that we should seek to specify the range of applicability of each.

There is a third perspective, promoted by John Turner and his colleagues (Turner, 1985; Turner, Hogg, Oakes, Reicher and Wetherell, 1987; **also see Chapter 11**). Unlike persuasive arguments and social comparison/cultural values theories, social identity theory, specifically its focus on the social categorisation process (self-categorisation theory), treats polarisation as a regular conformity phenomenon (Turner and Oakes, 1989). People in discussion groups actively construct a representation of the group norm from the positions held by group members in relation to those positions assumed to be held by people not in the group, or known to be held by people explicitly in an outgroup.

Because such norms not only minimise variability within the group (i.e. among ingroup members) but also distinguish the ingroup from outgroups, they are not necessarily the mean ingroup position: they can be polarised away from an explicit or implicit outgroup (see Figure 9.8). Self-categorisation, the process responsible for identification with a group, produces conformity to the ingroup norm – and thus, if the norm is polarised, group polarisation. If the norm is not polarised, self-categorisation produces convergence on the mean group position.

Research supports this perspective in (1) confirming how a norm can be polarised (Hogg, Turner and Davidson, 1990); (2) showing that people are more persuaded by ingroup members than outgroup members or individuals; and (3) showing that group polarisation occurs only if an initial group tendency is perceived to represent a norm rather than an aggregate of individual opinions (Mackie, 1986; Mackie and Cooper, 1984; Turner, Wetherell and Hogg, 1989).

A recent experiment by Zlatan Krizan and Robert Baron (2007) suggests some boundary conditions that need to be met for self-categorisation to explain group polarisation – specifically it is in contexts where (a) the ingroup is an important source of social identity, (b) the intergroup distinction is chronically salient, and (c) the group discussion topic is self-relevant or otherwise engaging, that group members' are most affected by the contextual salience of social categories and by their desire to maximise similarity with the ingroup while distancing themselves from the outgroup.

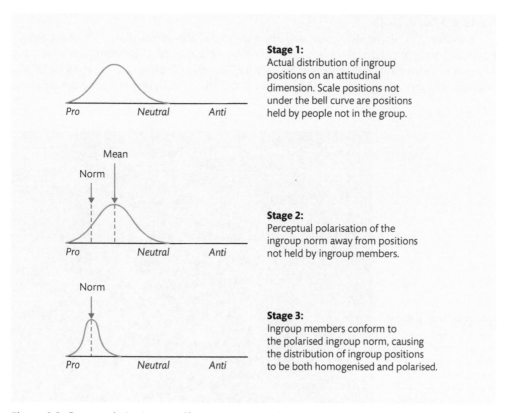

Figure 9.8 Group polarisation as self-categorisation induced conformity to a polarised group

Group polarisation can occur because people categorise themselves in terms of, and conform to, an ingroup defined by a norm that is polarised away from positions not held by ingroup members

Jury verdicts

People are fascinated by juries. Not surprisingly they are the focus of numerous novels and movies – John Grisham's novel *The Runaway Jury* and the 2003 movie adaptation dramatically highlight many of the important social psychological points made below about jury decision making. Returning to reality, the 1995 murder trial of the American sports star O. J. Simpson and the 2004 child 'abuse' trial of Michael Jackson virtually brought the United States to a standstill because people could not miss the exciting televised instalments.

Juries represent one of the most significant decision-making groups, not only because they are brandished as a symbol of all that is democratic, fair and just in a society, but also because of the consequences of their decisions for defendants, victims and the community. A jury consists of lay people and, in criminal law, is charged with making a crucial decision involving someone's innocence or guilt. In this respect, juries are an alternative to judges and are fundamental to the legal system of various countries around the world. They are most often associated with British law, but other countries (e.g. Argentina, Japan, Russia, Spain and Venezuela) have made changes to include input from lay citizens (Hans, 2008). In some cultures a group of lay people symbolise a just society – and when this group is a jury its decision must be seen as fair treatment of all involved.

Jury verdicts can have wide ranging and dramatic consequences outside the trial. A case in point is the 1992 Los Angeles riots, which were sparked by an unexpected 'not guilty' verdict delivered by an all-white jury in the case of the police beating of a black suspect (**see Box 11.1 in Chapter 11**). Juries are also of course groups, and are thus prey to the deficiencies of group decision making discussed in this chapter – which decision schemes should be used, who should lead and why, how are groupthink and group polarisation avoided (Hastie, 1993; Hastie, Penrod and Pennington, 1983; Kerr, Niedermeier and Kaplan, 1999; Tindale, Nadler, Krebel and Davis, 2001).

Characteristics of the defendant and the victim can also affect the jury's deliberations. Physically attractive defendants are more likely to be acquitted (Michelini and Snodgrass, 1980) or to receive a lighter sentence (Stewart, 1980), although biases can be reduced by furnishing sufficient factual evidence (Baumeister and Darley, 1982), by presenting the jury with

Jury decision making
Like all groups, juries may err in reaching an optimal conclusion. An old movie cliché of an emotional appeal may influence the jury, if not the judge

written rather than spoken, face-to-face testimony (Kaplan, 1977; Kaplan and Miller, 1978), or by explicitly directing the jury to consider the evidence alone (Weiten, 1980). Race can also affect the jury. In the United States, for example, blacks are more likely to receive prison sentences (Stewart, 1980). Furthermore, people who murder a white have been more than twice as likely than those who murder a black to receive the death penalty, a sentence determined by the jury in the United States (Henderson and Taylor, 1985).

Brutal crimes often stir up a call for draconian measures. However, the introduction of harsh laws with stiff penalties (e.g. the death penalty) can backfire – it discourages jurors from convicting (Kerr, 1978). Consider the anguish of a jury deliberating on a case in which the defendant has vandalised a car, and where a conviction would carry a mandatory death penalty. Research in the United States has tended to show that whether jurors do or do not support the death penalty has a reliable but small impact on the verdict – one to three verdicts out of one hundred would be affected (Allen, Mabry and McKelton, 1998).

Juries often have to remember and understand enormous amounts of information. Research suggests that there is a recency effect, in which information delivered later in the trial is more heavily weighted in decision making (Horowitz and Bordens, 1990). In addition, inadmissible evidence (evidence that is given by witnesses or interjected by counsel but is subsequently ruled to be inadmissible for procedural reasons by the judge) still has an effect on jury deliberation (Thompson and Fuqua, 1998). Juries also deal with complex evidence, enormous amounts of evidence, and complex laws and legal jargon – all three of which make the jury deliberation process extremely demanding and prey to suboptimal decision making (Heuer and Penrod, 1994).

The jury 'foreman' is important in guiding the jury to its verdict, as he/she occupies the role of leader (see earlier in this chapter). Research suggests that the foreman is most likely to be someone of higher socioeconomic status, someone who has had previous experience as a juror, or someone who simply occupies the seat at the head of the table at the first sitting of the jury (Strodtbeck and Lipinski, 1985). This is of some concern, as diffuse status characteristics (Berger, Fisek, Norman and Zelditch, 1977; Ridgeway, 2001, **discussed in Chapter 8**), are influencing the jury process.

Jurors who are older, less well educated or of lower socioeconomic status are more likely to vote to convict. However, men and women do not differ, except that women are more likely to convict defendants in rape trials (Nemeth, 1981). Jurors who score high on authoritarianism favour conviction when the victim is an authority figure (e.g. a police officer), while jurors who are more egalitarian have the opposite bias of favouring conviction when the defendant is an authority figure (Mitchell, 1979).

With respect to decision schemes, if two-thirds or more of the jurors initially favour one alternative, then that is likely to be the jury's final verdict (Stasser, Kerr and Bray, 1982). Without such a majority, a hung jury is the likely outcome. The two-thirds majority rule is modified by a tendency for jurors to favour acquittal, particularly where evidence is not highly incriminating; under these circumstances, a minority favouring acquittal may prevail (Tindale, Davis, Vollrath, Nagao and Hinsz, 1990).

Jury size itself can matter, according to a meta-analysis by Michael Saks and Mollie Marti (1997). Larger juries, of say twelve rather than six members, are more likely to empanel representatives of minority groups. If a particular minority is 10 per cent of the jury pool, random selection means that a minority member will be included in each twelve-person jury but in only 50 per cent of six-person juries. Furthermore, if minority or dissident viewpoints matter, they have more impact in larger than in smaller juries. If one-sixth of a jury favours acquittal, then in a six-person jury the 'deviate' has no social support, whereas in a twelve-person jury he/she does. Research on conformity and independence, and on minority influence (**see Chapter 7**), suggests that the dissident viewpoint is more likely to prevail in the twelve- than in the six-person jury.

Recency
An order of presentation effect in which later presented information has a disproportionate influence on social cognition.

Summary

- Leadership is a process of influence that does not require coercion – coercion may undermine true leadership and produce mere compliance and obedience.

- Although some broad personality attributes are associated with effective leadership (e.g. extra-version/surgency, intellect/openness to experience, and conscientiousness), personality alone is rarely sufficient.

- Leadership is a group process in which one person transforms other members of the group so that they adopt a vision and are galvanised into pursuing the vision on behalf of the group – leadership is not simply managing a group's activities. Transformational leadership is facilitated by charisma, consideration and inspiring followers.

- Leadership involves transactions between leader and followers – leaders do something for the group and the group in return does something for the leader to allow the leader to lead effectively.

- Leadership has an identity dimension – followers look to their leaders to mould, transform and express who they are, their identity. Being perceived to be 'one of us' can often facilitate leadership.

- Trust plays an important role in leadership – leaders have greater scope to be innovative if the group trusts them.

- Effective and good leadership are not the same thing – effective leaders successfully influence the group to adopt and achieve (new) goals, whereas good leaders pursue goals that we value, use means that we approve of, and have qualities that we applaud.

- There is a general distinction between task-focused (structuring) and person/relationship-focused (consideration) leadership style – their relative effectiveness and the effectiveness of other leadership styles depends on context (e.g. the nature of the group, the nature of the task).

- Leadership effectiveness can be improved if the leaders' attributes and behaviour are perceived to fit general or task-specific schemas that we have of effective leadership, or the norms/prototype of a group membership/identity that we share with the leader.

- Group decisions can sometimes be predicted accurately from the pre-discussion distribution of opinions in the group, and from the decision-making rule that prevails in the group at that time.

- People believe that group brainstorming enhances individual creativity, despite evidence that groups do not do better than non-interactive individuals and that individuals do not perform better in groups than alone. This illusion of group effectivity may be due to distorted perceptions during group brainstorming and the enjoyment that people derive from group brainstorming.

- Groups, particularly established groups that have a transactive memory structure, are often more effective than individuals at remembering information.

- Highly cohesive groups with directive leaders are prone to groupthink – poor decision making based on an overzealous desire to reach consensus.

- Groups that already tend towards an extreme position on a decision-making dimension often make even more extreme decisions than the average of the members' initial positions would suggest.

- Juries are not free from the usual range of group decision-making biases and errors.

Key terms

Autocratic leaders
Big Five
Brainstorming
Charismatic leadership
Contingency theories
Cultural values theory
Democratic leaders
Distributive justice
Glass ceiling
Great person theory
Group mind
Group polarisation
Group value model
Groupthink
Idiosyncrasy credit
Illusion of group effectivity

Laissez-faire leadership
Leader behaviour description
questionnaire
Leader categorisation theory
Leader–member exchange theory
Leadership
Least-preferred co-worker scale
Multifactor leadership questionnaire
Normative decision theory
Path–goal theory
Persuasive arguments theory
Procedural justice
Production blocking
Recency
Relational model of authority in
groups

Risky shift
Role congruity theory
Self-categorisation theory
Situational control
Social comparison (theory)
Social decisions schemes
Social dilemmas
Social identity theory
Social transition scheme
Status characteristics theory
Stereotype threat
Transactional leadership
Transactive memory
Transformational leadership
Vertical dyad linkage model

Literature, film and TV

Triumph of the Will and *Downfall*

A pair of films portraying one of the most evil leaders of the twentieth century in two different ways. *Triumph of the Will* is Leni Reifenstahl's classic 1934 film about Adolf Hitler – a film that largely idolises him as a great leader come to resurrect Germany. The film 'stars' the likes of Adolph Hitler, Hermann Goering and others. **This film is also relevant to Chapter 6 (persuasion).** *Downfall* is a controversial 2004 film by Oliver Hirschbiegel based on a book by the historian Joachim Fest. It portrays Hitler's last days in his bunker beneath Berlin up to his suicide on 30 April 1945. The film is controversial because it portrays Hitler largely as a sad dysfunctional human being rather than a grotesque monster responsible for immeasurable human suffering.

Twelve Angry Men and *The Runaway Jury*

Two films based on books that highlight jury decision making. *Twelve Angry Men* is a classic 1957 film directed by Sidney Lumet and starring Henry Fonda – set entirely in the jury room it is an incredibly powerful portrayal of social influence and decision-making processes within

a jury. *The Runaway Jury* is a 2003 film by Gary Fleder, with John Cusack, Dustin Hoffman and Gene Hackman, that dramatises the way that juries can be unscrupulously manipulated.

Thirteen Days

2000 film by Roger Donaldson. It is about the Cuban missile crisis which lasted for two weeks in October 1962 and was about as close as we got to all-out nuclear war between the West and the Soviet Union. The focus is on Kennedy's decision-making group. Is there group-think or not? Wonderful dramatisation of presidential/ high-level decision making under crisis. **Also relevant to Chapter 11 (intergroup behaviour).**

The Last King of Scotland

This 2006 film by Kevin MacDonald, based on the eponymous novel by Giles Foden, is a complex portrayal of the 1970s Ugandan dictator Idi Amin (played by Forest Whitaker) – an all-powerful and charismatic leader who can be charming interpersonally but will go to any lengths to protect himself from his paranoia about forces trying to undermine him. Amin was responsible for great brutality – 500,000 deaths and the expulsion of all Asians from the country.

Autobiographies

Autobiographies by Margaret Thatcher (*The Downing Street Years*, 1993), Nelson Mandela (*The Long Walk to Freedom*, 1994), Richard Branson (*Richard Branson*, 1998) and Barack Obama (*Dreams from my Father*, 1995), and Walter Isaacson's 2011 biography of *Steve Jobs* – all great leaders but in quite different ways and domains.

Lincoln

2012 Steven Spielberg movie that won a 2013 Golden Globe Award. Daniel Day-Lewis plays Abraham Lincoln in a sombre and serious movie that explores the complexity and challenge of trying to unite a number of disparate groups behind a single noble goal. The film focuses on Lincoln's urgent efforts in 1865, before the Civil War ended, to pass the 13th amendment of the US constitution – to abolish slavery. This is a movie that is very much about leadership, and in particular intergroup leadership.

Guided questions

MyPsychLab

1 What is the *great person* theory of leadership and how effective a theory is it?

2 How is a transformational leader different from a transactional leader?

3 Is it possible for a highly cohesive group to become oblivious to the views and expectations of the wider community? Watch the video in Chapter 9 of MyPsychLab at www.mypsychlab.com for some of the symptoms of *groupthink* that contributed to the Challenger space shuttle launch in 1986 (watch *Groupthink* at http://www.youtube.com/watch?v=qYpbStMyz_I).

4 What factors inhibit the productivity of group brainstorming?

5 Sometimes a group makes a decision that is even more extreme than any of its individual members might have made. How so?

Learn more

Baron, R. S., and Kerr, N. (2003).*Group process, group decision, group action* (2nd edn). Buckingham, UK: Open University Press. A general overview of topics in the study of group processes, with excellent coverage of group decision making.

Brown, R. J. (2000). *Group processes* (2nd edn). Oxford, UK: Blackwell. A very readable introduction to group processes, which takes a European perspective and also covers intergroup relations. It has a section on leadership.

Gilovich, T. D., and Gryphon, D. W. (2010). Judgment and decision making. In S. T. Fiske, D. T. Gilbert, and G. Lindzey (eds), *Handbook of social psychology* (5th edn, Vol. 1, pp. 542–88). New York: Wiley. Although primarily about individual decision making, this detailed and up-to-date chapter is also relevant to group decision making.

Goethals, G. R., and Sorenson, G. (eds) (2004). *Encyclopedia of leadership*. Thousand Oaks, CA: Sage. This is a true monster resource – four volumes, around 2,000 pages, 1.2 million words, 373 short essay-style entries written by 311 scholars including virtually everyone who is anyone in leadership research. All you ever wanted to know about leadership is somewhere in this book.

Gruenfeld, D. H., and Tiedens, L. Z. (2010). Organizational preferences and their consequences. In S. T. Fiske, D. T. Gilbert, and G. Lindzey (eds), *Handbook of social psychology* (5th edn, Vol. 2, pp. 1252–87). New York: Wiley. Up-to-date and detailed overview of social psychological theory and research on organisational processes, including decision making and leadership in organisations.

Hackman, J. R., and Katz, N. (2010). Group behavior and performance. In S. T. Fiske, D. T. Gilbert, and G. Lindzey (eds), *Handbook of social psychology* (5th edn, Vol. 2, pp. 1208–51). New York: Wiley. Comprehensive, detailed and up-to-date coverage of group behaviour.

Hogg, M. A. (2010). Influence and leadership. In S. T. Fiske, D. T. Gilbert, and G. Lindzey (eds), *Handbook of social psychology* (5th edn, Vol. 2, pp. 1166–207). New York: Wiley. Detailed and up-to-date overview of leadership theory and research, which treats leadership as a process of social influence in groups.

Hogg, M. A. (2013). Leadership. In J. M. Levine (ed.), *Group processes* (pp. 241–66). New York: Psychology Press. An up-to-date and comprehensive overview of leadership research, from the perspective of social psychology rather than organisational and management science; although the latter are also covered.

Hollander, E. P. (1985). Leadership and power. In G. Lindzey, and E. Aronson (eds), *Handbook of social psychology* (3rd edn, Vol. 2, pp. 485–537). New York: Random House. A classic review of leadership research in social psychology.

Levine, J. M. (ed.) (2013). *Group processes*. New York: Psychology Press. Absolutely up-to-date and comprehensive set of chapters by leading scholars on all aspects of group processes.

Levine, J. M., and Hogg, M. A. (eds) (2010). *Encyclopedia of group processes and intergroup relations*. Thousand Oaks, CA: SAGE. A comprehensive and readable compendium of entries on all aspects of the social psychology of groups, written by all the leading scholars in the field.

Levine, J., and Moreland, R. L. (1998). Small groups. In D. Gilbert, S. T. Fiske, and G. Lindzey (eds), *The handbook of social psychology* (4th edn, Vol. 2, pp. 415–69). New York: McGraw-Hill. A comprehensive overview of the field of small groups in which most group decision-making research is done – the most recent fifth edition of the handbook does not have a chapter dedicated to small interactive groups.

Stangor, C. (2004). *Social groups in action and interaction*. New York: Psychology Press. Comprehensive and accessible coverage of the social psychology of processes within and between groups.

Tindale, R. S., Kameda, T., and Hinsz, V. B. (2003). Group decision making. In M. A. Hogg, and J. Cooper (eds), *The SAGE handbook of social psychology* (pp. 381–403). London: SAGE. Comprehensive coverage of research on group decision making, with a particular emphasis on the shared nature of group decisions.

Yukl, G. (2010). *Leadership in organizations* (7th edn). Upper Saddle River, NJ: Prentice Hall. Straightforward, comprehensive, completely up-to-date and very readable coverage of leadership from the perspective of organisations, where most leadership research tends to be done.

MyPsychLab

Use MyPsychLab to refresh your understanding, assess your progress and go further with interactive summaries, questions, podcasts and much more. To buy access or register your code, visit www.mypsychlab.com.

CHAPTER 11
Intergroup behaviour

Chapter contents

Focus questions

1. Richard, an old-fashioned conservative, agrees with the newspaper editorial: 'Nurses should stop complaining about their pay. After all, the hospital orderlies, with even lower pay, keep their mouths shut and just get on with their job.' What can you say?

2. Jean and Alison are close schoolfriends. When they go to university they are assigned to different halls of residence that are right next door to one another but that have very different cultures and are in fierce competition with each other. What will happen to their friendship?

3. 'There is no other way. The rainforest has to go. We need the timber now – and if we don't take it, they will.' The news bulletin gets you thinking about the way people abuse scarce resources. Is there a way forward?

4. Have you watched a crowd demonstrating in a TV news item and wondered how it actually started? Is it possible that a fundamental aspect of their belief system has somehow been transformed? See Martin Luther King share his 1963 dream that African Americans might achieve equality in Chapter 11 of MyPsychLab at www.mypsychlab.com (watch *I have a dream* speech; see http://www.youtube.com/watch?v=1UV1fs8IAbg).

5. When football supporters get together in a crowd they seem to regress into some sort of super-beast – emotional, fickle, antisocial and dangerous. You've probably heard this kind of description before, but is it psychologically correct?

will use which involves getting you to decide to buy a car by giving you a very low price

Go to MyPsychLab to explore video and test your understanding of key topics addressed in this chapter.

What is intergroup behaviour?

Conflicts between nations, political confrontations, revolutions, inter-ethnic relations, negotiations between corporations, and competitive team sports are all examples of intergroup behaviour. An initial definition of intergroup behaviour might therefore be 'any behaviour that involves interaction between one or more representatives of two or more separate social groups'. This definition fairly accurately characterises much of the intergroup behaviour that social psychologists study; however, by focusing on face-to-face *interaction*, it might be a little restrictive.

A broader, and perhaps more accurate, definition would be that any perception, cognition or behaviour that is influenced by people's recognition that they and others are members of distinct social groups is intergroup behaviour. This broader definition has an interesting implication: it acknowledges that the real or perceived relations between social groups (e.g. between ethnic groups, between nations) can have far-reaching and pervasive effects on the behaviour of members of those groups – effects that go well beyond situations of face-to-face encounters. This type of definition stems from a particular perspective in social psychology: an intergroup perspective which maintains that a great deal of social behaviour is fundamentally influenced by the social categories to which we belong, and the power and status relations between those categories. A broad perspective such as this on the appropriate type of theory to develop is called a metatheory **(see Chapter 1)**.

In many ways, this chapter on intergroup behaviour brings together under one umbrella the preceding discussions of social influence **(Chapter 7)**, group processes **(Chapters 8 and 9)**, and prejudice and discrimination **(Chapter 10)**. Social influence and group processes are generally treated as occurring within groups, but wherever there is a group to which people belong (i.e. an ingroup), there are other groups to which those people do not belong (outgroups). Thus there is almost always an intergroup, or ingroup–outgroup, context for whatever happens in groups. It is unlikely that processes in groups will be unaffected by relations between groups. As we saw earlier **(in Chapter 10)**, prejudice and discrimination are clear instances of intergroup behaviour (e.g. between different races, between different age groups, between the sexes). One of the recurring themes of this discussion **(see Chapter 10)** is that personality or interpersonal explanations of prejudice and discrimination (e.g. authoritarian personality, dogmatism, frustration–aggression) may have limitations precisely because they do not adequately consider the intergroup aspect of the phenomena.

In dealing with intergroup behaviour, this chapter confronts important questions about the difference between individuals (and interpersonal behaviour) and groups (and intergroup behaviour), and the way in which harmonious intergroup relations can be transformed into conflict, and vice versa. Social psychological theories of intergroup behaviour ought therefore to have immediate relevance to applied contexts: for example, in the explanation of intergroup relations in employment contexts (Hartley and Stephenson, 1992).

Intergroup behaviour
Behaviour among individuals that is regulated by those individuals' awareness of and identification with different social groups.

Metatheory
Set of interrelated concepts and principles concerning which theories or types of theory are appropriate.

Relative deprivation and social unrest

Our earlier discussion **(in Chapter 10)** of the frustration–aggression hypothesis (Dollard, Doob, Miller, Mowrer and Sears, 1939) as an explanation of intergroup prejudice, discrimination and aggression concluded with Leonard Berkowitz's (1962) modification of the original theory. Berkowitz argued that subjective (not objective) frustration is one of an array of aversive events (e.g. heat, cold) that produce an instigation to aggress, and that the actual expression of aggression is strengthened by aggressive associations (e.g. situational cues, past associations).

Berkowitz (1972a) used this analysis to explain collective intergroup aggression – specifically riots. The best-known application is to riots that occurred during long periods of hot weather in the United States: for example, the Watts riots in Los Angeles in August 1965 and the Detroit

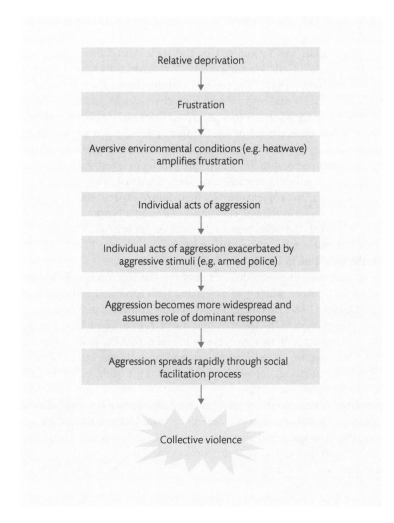

Figure 11.1 A 'long, hot summer' explanation of collective violence

Frustration induced by relative deprivation is expressed as individual aggression due to the presence of aversive and aggressive environmental stimuli, and this becomes collective aggression through a process of social facilitation

Source: Based on Berkowitz (1972a)

riots in August 1967 (see Figure 11.1). Heat can be an 'aversive event' that facilitates individual and collective aggression (e.g. Anderson and Anderson, 1984; Baron and Ransberger, 1978; Carlsmith and Anderson, 1979; **see also Chapter 12**).

Berkowitz (1972a) argues that under conditions of perceived relative deprivation (e.g. blacks in the United States in the late 1960s) people feel frustrated. The heat of a long, hot summer amplifies the frustration (especially in poor, overcrowded neighbourhoods with little air conditioning or cooling vegetation) and increases the prevalence of individual acts of aggression, which are in turn exacerbated by the presence of aggressive stimuli (e.g. armed police). Individual aggression becomes widespread and is transformed into true collective violence by a process of social facilitation (Zajonc, 1965; **see Chapter 8**), whereby the physical presence of other people facilitates dominant behaviour patterns (in this case, aggression).

Relative deprivation

A crucial precondition for intergroup aggression is **relative deprivation** (Walker and Smith, 2002). Deprivation is not an absolute condition but is always relative to other conditions: one person's new-found prosperity may be someone else's terrible deprivation. George Orwell captures this point beautifully in *The Road to Wigan Pier*, his essay on the plight of the British working class in the 1930s: 'Talking once with a miner I asked him when the housing shortage first became acute in his district; he answered, "When we were told about it", meaning that "'til

Relative deprivation
A sense of having less than we feel entitled to.

recently people's standards were so low that they took almost any degree of overcrowding for granted"' (Orwell, 1962, p. 57).

The concept of relative deprivation was introduced by the sociologist Sam Stouffer and his colleagues in their multi-volume, classic wartime study *The American soldier* (Stouffer, Suchman, DeVinney, Star and Williams (1949). The concept was developed more formally in the wider context of intergroup conflict and aggression by another sociologist, James Davis (1959). Relative deprivation refers more generally to a perceived discrepancy between attainments or actualities ('what is') and expectations or entitlements ('what ought to be'). In its simplest form, relative deprivation arises from comparisons between our experiences and our expectations (Gurr, 1970). (Can you respond to Richard in the first focus question?)

In his sociological treatment of political revolutions, James Davies (1969) suggested a J-curve model to represent the way that people construct their future expectations from past and current attainments, and how under certain circumstances attainments may suddenly fall short of rising expectations. When this happens, relative deprivation is particularly acute, with the consequence of collective unrest – revolutions of rising expectations (see Box 11.1). The J-curve gets its name from the solid line in Figure 11.2.

Historical events do seem to fit the J-curve model. For example, the Depression of the early 1930s caused a sudden fall in farm prices, which was associated with increased anti-Semitism in Poland (Keneally, 1982). Davies (1969) himself cites the French and Russian Revolutions, the American Civil War, the rise of Nazism in Germany and the growth of Black Power in the United States in the 1960s. We might add to this the wave of unrest across the globe following the 2008 stock market crash and ensuing recession – the 'occupy' protests, the 2011 UK riots, and the 2011 'Arab Spring' popular uprisings across North Africa and the Middle East, including Tunisia, Egypt, Libya, Yemen, Syria, and Jordan.

In all these cases, a long period (twenty to thirty years) of increasing prosperity was followed by a steep and sudden recession. Systematic tests of predictions from Davies's theory are less encouraging. For example, from a longitudinal survey of American political and social attitudes, Marylee Taylor (1982) found little evidence that people's expectations were constructed from their immediate past experience, or that satisfaction was based on the degree of match between actualities and these expectations.

The British sociologist Gary Runciman (1966) has made an important distinction between two forms of relative deprivation:

1 **egoistic relative deprivation**, which derives from the individual's sense of deprivation relative to other similar individuals; and

2 **fraternalistic relative deprivation**, which derives from comparisons with dissimilar others, or members of other groups.

Studies that include measures of both types of relative deprivation furnish some evidence that they are independent (e.g. Crosby, 1982). Research indicates that it is fraternalistic, specifically intergroup, relative deprivation, not egoistic (i.e. interpersonal) relative deprivation, that is associated with social unrest. Reeve Vanneman and Tom Pettigrew (1972) conducted surveys in large cities in the United States to discover that whites who expressed the most negative attitudes towards blacks were those who felt most strongly that whites as a group were poorly off relative to blacks as a group. The deprivation is clearly fraternalistic and, as whites were in reality *better off* than blacks, illustrates the subjective nature of relative deprivation. Ronald Abeles (1976) found that black militancy in the United States was more closely associated with measures of fraternalistic than egoistic relative deprivation.

There are other studies conducted outside of the United States that support this line of reasoning:

- Serge Guimond and Lise Dubé-Simard (1983) found that militant Francophones in Montreal felt more acute dissatisfaction and frustration when making intergroup salary comparisons between Francophones and Anglophones, rather than egoistic comparisons.

J-curve
A graphical figure that captures the way in which relative deprivation arises when attainments suddenly fall short of rising expectations.

Egoistic relative deprivation
A feeling of personally having less than we feel we are entitled to, relative to our aspirations or to other individuals.

Fraternalistic relative deprivation
Sense that our group has less than it is entitled to, relative to its aspirations or to other groups.

Real world 11.1
Rising expectations and collective protest

The 1992 Los Angeles riots provided a riveting, real-life example of relative deprivation perceived by a large group of people

The Los Angeles riots that erupted on 29 April 1992 resulted in more than 50 dead and 2,300 injured. The proximal cause was the acquittal by an all-white suburban jury of four Los Angeles police officers accused of beating a black motorist, Rodney King. The assault with which the police officers were charged had been captured on video and played on national TV. Against a background of rising unemployment and deepening disadvantage, this acquittal was seen by blacks as a particularly poignant symbol of the low value placed by white America on American blacks.

The flashpoint for the riot was the intersection of Florence and Normandie Avenues in South Central Los Angeles. Initially, there was some stealing of liquor from a local off-licence, breaking of car windows and pelting of police. The police moved in en masse but then withdrew to try to de-escalate the tension. This left the intersection largely in the hands of the rioters, who attacked whites and Hispanics. Reginald Denny, a white truck driver who happened to be driving through, was dragged from his cab and brutally beaten; the incident was watched live on TV by millions and has largely come to symbolise the riots.

South Central Los Angeles was relatively typical of black ghettos in the United States at that time. However, the junction of Florence and Normandie was not in the worst part of the ghetto by any means. It was a relatively well-off black neighbourhood in which the poverty rate dropped during the 1980s from 33 to only 21 per cent. That the initial outbreak of rioting would occur here, rather than in a more impoverished neighbourhood, is consistent with relative deprivation theories of social unrest.

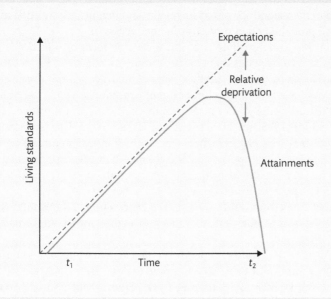

Figure 11.2 The J-curve hypothesis of relative deprivation

Relative deprivation is particularly acute when attainments suffer a sudden setback in the context of expectations which continue to rise

Source: Based on Davies (1969)

- In India, where there had been a rapid decline in the status of Muslims relative to Hindus, Rama Tripathi and Rashmi Srivasta (1981) found that those Muslims who felt most fraternalistically deprived (e.g. in terms of job opportunities, political freedom) expressed the greatest hostility towards Hindus.

- In a study of unemployed Australian workers, Iain Walker and Leon Mann (1987) found that it was principally those who reported most fraternalistic deprivation who were prepared to contemplate militant protest, such as demonstrations, law breaking and destruction of private property. Those who felt egoistically deprived reported symptoms of personal stress (e.g. headaches, indigestion, sleeplessness). This study is particularly revealing in showing how egoistic and fraternalistic deprivation produce different outcomes, and that it is the latter that is associated with social unrest as intergroup or collective protest (see below) or aggression.

Although fraternalistic relative deprivation may be associated with competitive intergroup behaviour or with forms of social protest, there are at least four other factors that need to be considered. First, for fraternalistic relative deprivation to have sufficient subjective impact for people to take action, people may need to identify relatively strongly with their ingroup. This stands to reason – if you do not identify very strongly with your group, the fact that it is relatively deprived is merely academic. In support of this, Sara Kelly and Caroline Breinlinger (1996) found, from a longitudinal study of women activists, that relative deprivation reliably predicted involvement in women's group activities only among women who identified strongly with women as a group. Dominic Abrams (1990) found that Scottish teenagers supported the Scottish National Party more strongly if they felt a sense of fraternalistic relative deprivation relative to the English and they identified strongly with being Scottish.

Second, groups that feel relatively deprived are unlikely to engage in collective action unless such action is considered a practical and feasible way of bringing about social change (see below). A role-playing study by Joanne Martin and her colleagues illustrates this rather nicely (Martin, Brickman and Murray, 1984). They had women workers imagine that they were managers who were slightly to greatly underpaid relative to men of comparable rank in the company. They were also given information that portrayed the women managers as well placed or poorly placed to mobilise resources to change their situation. The results showed that relative deprivation was closely tied to the magnitude of pay inequality, but that protest was tied much more closely to the perceived probability that protest would be successful.

Third, relative deprivation rests on perceptions of injustice. One form of injustice is distributive injustice – feeling that you have less than you are entitled to relative to expectations, other groups and so forth. However, there is another form of injustice – procedural injustice, in which you feel that you have been the victim of unfair procedures. Tom Tyler and his colleagues have explored this distinction between distributive and procedural justice (Tyler and Lind, 1992; Tyler and Smith, 1998; see De Cremer and Tyler, 2005). They suggest that perceived procedural injustice may be a particularly potent motivation for intergroup protest. Procedural justice seems to be especially important within groups – if people experience unfair procedures within a group, they tend to dis-identify and lose commitment to group goals (**see discussion of leadership in Chapter 9**). In intergroup contexts, however, it may be very difficult to untangle unjust procedures from unjust distributions: for example, status differences (distributive injustice) between groups may rest on unfair procedures (procedural injustice) (Brockner and Wiesenfeld, 1996).

Finally, as fraternalistic relative deprivation depends on the particular ingroup–outgroup comparison that is made, it is important to be able to predict whom we compare ourselves with (Martin and Murray, 1983; Walker and Pettigrew, 1984). From social comparison theory (Festinger, 1954; see Suls and Wheeler, 2000), we would expect comparisons to be made with similar others, and some of the work cited above certainly supports this (e.g. Abeles, 1976; Runciman, 1966). For instance, Faye Crosby's (1982) 'paradox of the contented female worker' may arise because women workers compare their salaries and working conditions with those of other women, which narrows the potential for recognising much larger gender-based inequalities in pay and conditions (Major, 1994). However, many intergroup comparisons, particularly those that lead to the most pronounced conflict, are made between markedly different groups (e.g. black and white South Africans). One way to approach this issue is to consider the extent to which groups are involved in real conflict over scarce resources (see below).

Social protest and collective action

Social unrest associated with relative deprivation often represents sustained social protest to achieve social change. However, the study of protest is complex, requiring a sophisticated articulation of constructs from social psychology, sociology and political science (Klandermans, 1997, 2003; Reicher, 1996, 2001; Stürmer and Simon, 2004). As the study of how individual discontents or grievances are transformed into collective action, the study of protest has as its key question: how and why do sympathisers become mobilised as activists or participants?

Bert Klandermans (1997) argues that this involves the relationship between individual attitudes and behaviour (**see Chapter 5**). Sympathisers, by definition, hold sympathetic attitudes towards an issue, yet these attitudes do not automatically translate into behaviour. Participation also resembles a social dilemma (see below). Protest is generally *for* a social good (e.g. equality) or *against* a social ill (e.g. pollution), and as success benefits everyone irrespective of participation, but failure harms participants more, it is tempting to 'free ride' (**see Chapter 8**) – to remain a sympathiser rather than become a participant. Finally, Klandermans notes that protest can only be understood as intergroup behaviour that occurs in what he calls 'multiorganisational fields': that is, protest movements involve the clash of ideas and ideologies between groups, and politicised and strategic articulation with other more or less sympathetic organisations.

Klandermans (1997; for an overview, see Stürmer and Simon, 2004) described four steps in social movement participation:

1 Becoming part of the mobilisation potential. First, you must be a sympathiser. The most important determinants of mobilisation potential are fraternalistic relative deprivation (feeling relatively deprived as a group), an us-versus-them orientation that targets an outgroup as being responsible for your plight, and a belief that social change through collective action is possible.

2 Becoming a target of mobilisation attempts. Being a sympathiser is not enough – you must also be informed about what you can do and what is being done (e.g. sit-ins, demonstrations, lobbying). Media access and informal communication networks are critical here.

3 Developing motivation to participate. Being a sympathiser and knowing what is going on is not sufficient – you must also be motivated to participate. Motivation arises from the value that you place on the outcome of protest and the extent to which you believe that the protest will actually deliver the goods (an expectancy–value analysis; Ajzen and Fishbein, 1980). Motivation is strongest if the collective benefit of the outcome of protest is highly valued (collective motive), if important others value your participation (normative motive), and if valued personal outcomes are anticipated (reward motive). The normative and reward motives are important to prevent sympathisers from free-riding on others' participation. This analysis of motivation is strikingly similar to Ajzen and Fishbein's (1980) theory of reasoned action account of the attitude–behaviour relationship (**see Chapter 5**).

4 Overcoming barriers to participation. Finally, even substantial motivation may not translate into action if there are insurmountable obstacles, such as no transport to the demonstration, or ill health. However, these obstacles are more likely to be overcome if motivation is very high.

Bernd Simon (2003; Stürmer and Simon, 2004) argues that the cost–benefit aspect of Klanderman's model places too much emphasis on individual decision making. Simon proposes a social identity analysis (also see Haslam and Reicher, 2012; Van Zomeren, Leach and Spears, 2012; Van Zomeren, Postmes and Spears, 2008). Drawing on social identity theory (see below for details), Simon argues further that when people identify very strongly with a group they have a tightly shared perception of collective injustice, needs and goals. They also share attitudes and behavioural intentions, trust and like one another, and are collectively influenced by group norms and legitimate group leaders. Furthermore, group motivation eclipses personal motivation – it overcomes the dilemma of social action (Klandermans, 2002). Provided that members believe that protest is an effective way forward, these processes increase the probability of participation in collective protest (Bluic, McGarty, Reynolds and Muntele, 2007).

Realistic conflict

A key feature of intergroup behaviour is ethnocentrism (Brewer and Campbell, 1976; LeVine and Campbell, 1972), described by William Sumner as:

> a view of things in which one's own group is the centre of everything, and all others are scaled and rated with reference to it . . . Each group nourishes its own pride and vanity, boasts itself superior, exalts its own divinities, and looks with contempt on outsiders. Each group thinks its own folkways the only right one . . . Ethnocentrism leads a people to exaggerate and intensify everything in their own folkways which is peculiar and which differentiates them from others.
>
> Sumner (1906, p. 13)

In contrast to other perspectives on prejudice, discrimination and intergroup behaviour that explain the origins of ethnocentrism in terms of individual or interpersonal processes (e.g. frustration–aggression, relative deprivation, authoritarianism, dogmatism), Muzafer Sherif believed that 'we cannot extrapolate from the properties of individuals to the characteristics of group situations' (1962, p. 8) and that the origins of ethnocentrism lie in the nature of intergroup relations. For Sherif:

> *Intergroup relations* refer to relations between two or more groups and their respective members. Whenever individuals belonging to one group interact, collectively or individually, with another group or its *members in terms of their group identifications* we have an instance of intergroup behaviour.
>
> Sherif (1962, p. 5)

Sherif believed that where groups compete over scarce resources, intergroup relations become marked by conflict, and ethnocentrism arises. He tested this idea in a series of famous

Realistic conflict
Sherif showed that intergroup competition led to conflict and then discrimination. This is heightened when groups compete for a goal that only one group can achieve

field experiments conducted in 1949, 1953 and 1954 at summer camps for young boys in the United States (Sherif, 1966). The general procedure involved three phases:

1 *Phase 1*: The boys arrived at the camp, which, unknown to them, was run by the experimenters. They engaged in various camp-wide activities, through which they formed friendships.

2 *Phase 2*: The camp was then divided into two groups that split up friendships. The groups were isolated, with separate living quarters and daily activities, and developed their own norms and status differences. The groups made little reference to each other apart from some embryonic ethnocentrism.

3 *Phase 3*: The groups were brought together to engage in organised intergroup competitions embracing sports contests and other activities. This produced fierce competition and intergroup hostility, which rapidly generalised to situations outside the organised competitions. Ethnocentric attitudes and behaviour were amplified and coupled with intergroup aggression and ingroup solidarity. Almost all intergroup encounters degenerated into intergroup hostility: for example, when the two groups ate together, the meal became an opportunity for the groups to throw food at each other. Intergroup relations deteriorated so dramatically that two of the experiments were hastily concluded at this stage.

In one experiment, however, it was possible to proceed to a fourth stage:

4 *Phase 4*: The two groups were provided with **superordinate goals**, goals they both desired but were unable to achieve on their own. The groups had to work together in cooperation.

As an example of a superordinate goal (also dealt with later in this chapter), the groups were told that the truck delivering a movie that both groups wanted to watch had become bogged down and would need to be pulled out, but that everyone would be needed to help as the truck was very heavy. Sherif had a wonderful sense of symbolism – the rope used cooperatively by the boys to pull the truck was the same rope that had previously been used in an aggressive tug-of-war between the warring groups. Sherif and colleagues found a gradual improvement in intergroup relations as a consequence of the groups engaging in cooperative intergroup interactions in order to achieve superordinate goals.

There are some notable points about these experiments:

- There was a degree of latent ethnocentrism even in the absence of intergroup competition (more of this below).

- Prejudice, discrimination and ethnocentrism arose as a consequence of real intergroup conflict.

- The boys did not have authoritarian or dogmatic personalities.

- The less frustrated group (the winners) was usually the one that expressed the greater intergroup aggression.

- Ingroups formed despite the fact that friends were actually outgroup members (**see Chapter 8**).

- Simple contact between members of opposing groups did not improve intergroup relations (see below).

Realistic conflict theory

To explain his findings, Sherif (1966) proposed a **realistic conflict theory** of intergroup behaviour, in which the nature of the goal relations among individuals and groups determines the nature of interindividual and intergroup relations (see Figure 11.3). He argued that individuals who share goals requiring interdependence for their achievement tend to cooperate and form a group, while individuals who have mutually exclusive goals (i.e. a scarce resource that only one can obtain, such as winning a chess game) engage in interindividual competition, which

Superordinate goals
Goals that both groups desire but that can be achieved only by both groups cooperating.

Realistic conflict theory
Sherif's theory of intergroup conflict that explains intergroup behaviour in terms of the nature of goal relations between groups.

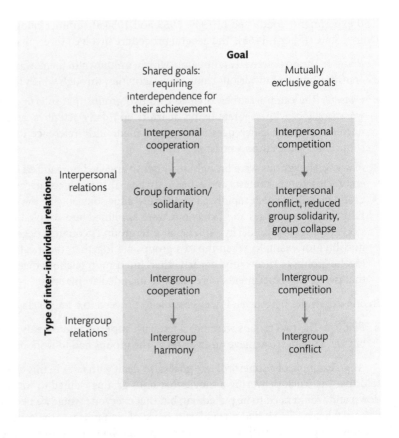

Figure 11.3 Realistic group conflict theory

Goal relations between individuals and groups determine cooperative or competitive interdependence, and thus the nature of interpersonal and intergroup behaviour

Source: Based on Sherif (1966)

prevents group formation or contributes to the collapse of an existing group. At the intergroup level, mutually exclusive goals produce realistic intergroup conflict and ethnocentrism, while shared goals requiring intergroup interdependence for their achievement (i.e. superordinate goals) reduce conflict and encourage intergroup harmony. For a summary of Sherif's range of contributions to social psychology, see Vaughan (2010a).

Sherif's model is generally supported by other naturalistic experiments (Fisher, 1990). For example, Robert Blake and Jane Mouton (1961) employed similar procedures in a series of thirty studies, each run for two weeks, involving more than 1,000 business people on management training programmes in the United States. Phil Zimbardo's simulated prison experiment (Haney, Banks and Zimbardo, 1973; **see Chapter 8**) also illustrates the way in which mutually exclusive intergroup goals produce conflict and hostile intergroup relations. Sherif's studies have been successfully replicated in Lebanon (Diab, 1970) and the former Soviet Union (Andreeva, 1984), but in Britain, Andrew Tyerman and Christopher Spencer (1983) were not so successful. Tyerman and Spencer used an established Scout group as participants and found that the different 'patrols' did not express anywhere near as much hostility as expected. Furthermore, it was easy to increase inter-patrol cooperation even in the absence of a superordinate goal. Tyerman and Spencer attribute this to the fact that a well-established superordinate group already existed.

Realistic conflict theory makes good sense and is generally useful for understanding intergroup conflict, particularly in applied settings. For example, Marilynn Brewer and Donald Campbell (1976) surveyed thirty tribal groups in Africa and found greater derogation of tribal outgroups that lived close by and were thus likely to be direct competitors for scarce resources, such as water and land. (See the third focus question. Jean and Alison have a problem since their 'tribes' live so close to each other). Ronald Fisher (1990, 2005) went a bit further to outline how establishing superordinate goals can be used to help resolve conflict between communities, and even between nations.

Realistic conflict theory suffers from a problem. Because so many variables are operating together in the various studies, how can we know that it is the nature of goal relations that ultimately determines intergroup behaviour? Might the cause actually lie in the cooperative or competitive nature of interaction, or perhaps merely the existence of two separate groups (e.g. Dion, 1979; Turner, 1981b)? These causal agents are confounded – an observation that we pursue later in this chapter.

Cooperation, competition and social dilemmas

Realistic conflict theory focuses attention on the relationship between people's goals, the competitive or cooperative nature of their behaviour and the conflicting or harmonious nature of their relations. We can study these relationships in abstract settings by designing 'games' with different goal relations for two or more people to play. The mathematician John Von Neumann and economist Oskar Morgenstern (1944) introduced a model for analysing situations where people are in conflict over some non-trivial outcome (e.g. money, power). Variously called *decision theory, game theory* or *utility theory,* this initiated a prodigious amount of research in the 1960s and 1970s. **(This topic is also dealt with in the context of interpersonal relations in Chapter 14.)** The highly abstract nature of the research raised questions about its relevance (generalisability) to real-world conflict and led to its decline in the 1980s (Apfelbaum and Lubek, 1976; Nemeth, 1970). Much of this research is concerned with interpersonal conflict; however, much of it also has important implications for intergroup conflict: for example, the prisoner's dilemma, the trucking game and the commons dilemma (e.g. Liebrand, Messick and Wilke, 1992).

The prisoner's dilemma

Introduced by R. D. Luce and Howard Raïffa (1957; Rapoport, 1976), the prisoner's dilemma is the most widely researched game. It is based on an anecdote. Detectives question two obviously guilty suspects separately, with only enough evidence to convict them of a lesser offence. The suspects are separately offered a chance to confess, knowing that if one confesses but the other does not, the confessor will be granted immunity and the confession will be used to convict the other of the more serious offence. If both confess, each will receive a moderate sentence. If neither confesses, each will receive a very light sentence. The dilemma faced by the prisoners can be summarised by a *pay-off matrix* (see Figure 11.4).

Prisoner's dilemma
Two-person game in which both parties are torn between competition and cooperation and, depending on mutual choices, both can win or both can lose.

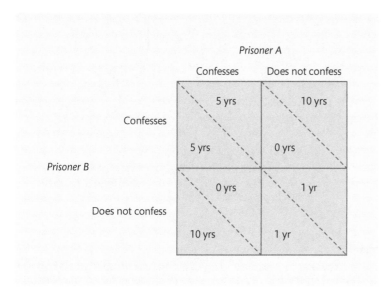

Figure 11.4 The prisoner's dilemma

Each quadrant displays the prison sentence that Prisoner A receives (above the diagonal) and Prisoner B receives (below in diagonal) if both, one or neither confesses

Although mutual non-confession produces the best joint outcome, mutual suspicion and lack of trust almost always encourage both to confess. This finding has been replicated in hundreds of prisoner's dilemma experiments, using a variety of experimental conditions and pay-off matrices (Dawes, 1991). The prisoner's dilemma is described as a 'two-person, mixed motive, non-zero-sum game'. This is quite a mouthful, but it means that two people are involved, they each experience a conflict between being motivated to cooperate and motivated to compete, and the outcome can be that both parties gain or both lose. In contrast, a zero-sum game is one in which one party's gain is always the other's loss – think of a pie: the larger the portion I take, the smaller the portion left for you.

The trucking game

In this game, there are two trucking companies, Acme and Bolt, which transport goods from one place to another (Deutsch and Krauss, 1960). Each company has its own private route, but there is a much faster shared route, which has a major drawback – a one-lane section (see Figure 11.5). Clearly, the mutually beneficial solution is for the two companies to agree to take it in turns to use the one-lane section. Instead, research reveals again and again that participants fight over use of the one-lane section. Typically, both enter and meet head-on in the middle and then waste time arguing until one backs up. Again, mutual mistrust has produced a suboptimal joint outcome.

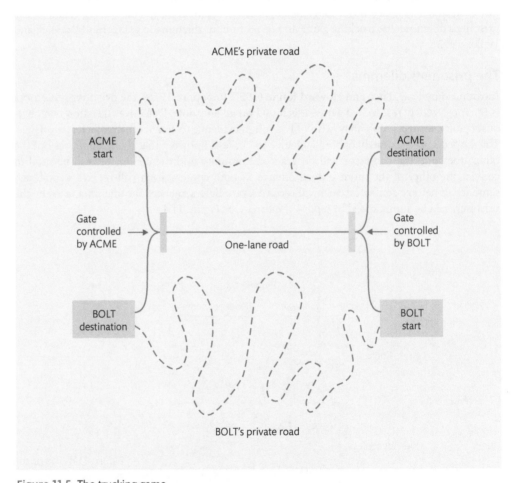

Figure 11.5 The trucking game

Two participants play a game where they work for separate trucking companies that transport goods from one place to another. They can use their own private roads, but there is also a much shorter shared route which has the drawback of having a one-lane section

Source: Deutsch and Krauss (1960)

These games highlight detrimental consequences of lack of trust that have clear real-world analogues. For example, mutual distrust between Iran and Iraq fuelled their terrible conflict in the 1980s over which of them rightfully owned the Shatt-al-Arab waterway. When they laid down their arms in 1988 after horrific atrocities, over a million civilian and military casualties, and the devastation of their economies, the borders remained precisely where they were when the war began eight years earlier.

Game theory rests on a rationalistic characterisation of humankind as *homo œconomicus* – a Western model of human psychological functioning that derives from Western thinking about work and industry (Cartwright, 2011; Stroebe and Frey, 1982; **see also discussion of normative models and behavioural decision theory in Chapter 2**). Possibly due to this perspective, a problem with research based on game theory is that it is relatively asocial. For example, it often overlooks the role of direct communication, although communication in two- and *n*-person prisoner's dilemma games actually reliably reduces conflict and increases cooperation (Liebrand, 1984). Interactants' responses also tend to fulfil a communicative function, such that flexible and responsive partners tend to raise the level of cooperation (Apfelbaum, 1974).

Similarly, subjective perceptions of the game are often overlooked. For example, the allocation or exchange of goods or resources always raises questions of perceived fairness and justice, and it would appear that interactants are more confident of fair solutions, behave more cooperatively and are more satisfied with outcomes if rules of fairness are explicitly invoked (McClintock and van Avermaet, 1982; Mikula, 1980). There is also some evidence that experimental games are spontaneously construed by participants as competitive contexts. When the game is introduced in different terms – for example, as an investigation of human interaction or international conflict resolution – people behave in a more cooperative manner (Abric and Vacherot, 1976; Eiser and Bhavnani, 1974).

The commons dilemma

Many other social dilemmas involve a number of individuals or groups exploiting a limited resource (Foddy, Smithson, Schneider and Hogg, 1999; Kerr and Park, 2001). These are essentially *n*-person prisoner's dilemmas – if everyone cooperates, an optimal solution for all is reached, but if everyone competes then everyone loses. The commons dilemma, or 'tragedy of the commons' (Hardin, 1968), gets its name from the common pasture that English villages

Commons dilemma
Social dilemma in which cooperation by all benefits all, but competition by all harms all.

Commons dilemma
A climatic tragedy in which a failure to cooperate leads to harm for all

used to have. People were free to graze their cattle on this land, and if all used it in moderation, it would replenish itself and continue to benefit them all. However, imagine 100 farmers surrounding a common that could support only 100 cows. If each grazed one cow, the common would be maximally utilised and minimally taxed. However, one farmer might reason that if he or she grazed an additional cow, his or her output would be doubled, minus a very small cost due to overgrazing – a cost borne equally by all 100 farmers. So this farmer adds a second cow. If all 100 farmers reasoned in this way, they would rapidly destroy the common, thus producing the tragedy of the commons.

The commons dilemma is an example of a replenishable resource dilemma – the commons is a renewable resource that will continually support many people provided that all people show restraint in 'harvesting' the resource. Many of the world's most pressing environmental and conservation problems are replenishable resource dilemmas: for example, rain forests and the world's population of ocean fish are renewable resources if harvested appropriately (Clover, 2004) (see the third focus question).

Another type of social dilemma is called a *public goods dilemma*. Public goods are provided for everyone: for example, public health, national parks, the national road network, public radio and TV. Because public goods are available to all, people are tempted to use them without contributing to their maintenance. There is a **free-rider effect** (Kerr, 1983; Kerr and Bruun, 1983; **see also Chapter 8**), in which people self-interestedly exploit a resource without caring for it. For example, if you alone avoid paying your taxes it only minimally impacts the provision of a police force, an ambulance service, or a functioning road system, but if everyone reasoned similarly there would be no emergency services to race to your rescue on the now effectively non-existent road system. Likewise, if I fail to fix my car exhaust or fail to plant trees in my garden, it contributes minimally to noise, atmospheric and visual pollution; if everyone living in my neighbourhood did likewise, then it would become a horrible place to live.

Reflecting on the tragedy of the commons dilemma Garrett Hardin observed:

> Ruin is the destination to which all men rush, each pursuing his own best interest in a society that believes in the freedom of the commons. Freedom in a commons brings ruin to all.
>
> Hardin (1968 p. 162)

Experimental research on social dilemmas finds that when self-interest is pitted against the collective good, the usual outcome is competition and resource destruction (Edney, 1979; Sato, 1987). However, laboratory and field studies also obtain high levels of voluntary social cooperation (Caporael, Dawes, Orbell and van de Kragt, 1989). A series of studies by Brewer and her colleagues (Brewer and Kramer, 1986; Brewer and Schneider, 1990; Kramer and Brewer, 1984, 1986) identifies one condition under which this can occur. When people identify with the common good – in other words, they derive their social identity (see below) from the entire group that has access to the resource – self-interest is subordinate to the common good.

However, the same research indicates that when different *groups*, rather than individuals, have access to a public good, the ensuing intergroup competition ensures ethnocentric actions that are far more destructive than mere self-interest. International competition over limited resources such as rain forests, fish and wetlands tragically accelerates their disappearance.

Resolving social dilemmas

Generally, people find it difficult to escape the trap of a social dilemma. Even appeals to altruistic norms are surprisingly ineffective (Kerr, 1995) – if you know that others are free riding, you certainly do not want to be taken for a sucker (Kerr and Bruun, 1983). Because selfish behaviour is so prevalent in social dilemmas, structural solutions often have to be imposed to cause the dilemma to disappear (Kerr, 1995). Structural solutions include a range of measures such as limiting the number of people accessing the resource (e.g. via permits), limiting the amount of the resource that people can take (e.g. via quotas), handing over management of the resource to an individual (a leader) or a single group, facilitating free communication among those accessing the resource, and shifting the pay-off to favour cooperation over competition.

Free-rider effect
Gaining the benefits of group membership by avoiding costly obligations of membership and by allowing other members to incur those costs.

The problem with structural solutions is that they require an enlightened and powerful authority to implement measures, manage the bureaucracy and police violations. This can be hard to bring about. A case in point is the inability, in the face of global catastrophe, for the world's nations to put a structural solution in place to limit carbon emissions and thus avert climate change. We have had global summit meetings and accords aplenty, hosted by pretty much every major nation on the planet. And yet, some nations still will not sacrifice personal gain for the greater good of humanity – leading, in complete frustration and desperation, to an alliance in 2007 between Richard Branson and Al Gore to provide a 25 million dollar carrot for design initiatives to remove carbon dioxide from the atmosphere.

A structural solution that has been well researched is the appointment of a leader to manage the resource (e.g. De Cremer and Van Vugt, 2002; Rutte and Wilke, 1984; Van Vugt and De Cremer, 1999). Leaders are very effective at resolving social dilemmas under certain circumstances. People with a generally prosocial orientation are relatively open to leadership when their group is faced with a social dilemma, particularly if they identify strongly with the group (De Cremer, 2000; De Cremer and Van Vugt, 1999). Usually, leader charisma is not critical, but it is important that the leader can be viewed as 'one of us', as a representative member of the group (De Cremer, 2002). People with a pro-self orientation are less open to leadership unless they identify strongly with the group and the leader's behaviours and qualities are group serving and representative of the group. Charismatic leaders are particularly good at helping pro-self members behave in prosocial and group-serving ways.

If structural solutions are so difficult, what other options do we have? One factor that seems particularly effective in resolving social dilemmas is group identification (Foddy, Smithson, Schneider and Hogg, 1999; Van Vugt and De Cremer, 1999). Where people identify very strongly with a group that accesses a shared resource, those people act in ways that benefit the group as a whole rather than themselves as separate from the group (e.g. Brewer and Kramer, 1986; Brewer and Schneider, 1990). It is as if a large number of individuals competing for access have been transformed into a single person who carefully tends the resource. Indeed, this is a good analogy. As we see shortly, identification with a group actually does transform people psychologically in this way. Identification seems to facilitate communication that develops conserving norms (e.g. Bouas and Komorita, 1996); it encourages adherence to those norms (e.g. Sattler and Kerr, 1991); it inspires perceptions of distributive and procedural justice (Tyler and Smith, 1998); and it makes people feel that their conserving actions really do have an effect (Kerr, 1995). Indeed, privatisation of a public good can increase selfish non-conserving behaviour precisely because it inhibits these social identity processes (Van Vugt, 1997).

Social identity

Minimal groups

We have seen that realistic conflict theory (Sherif, 1966) traces the origins and form of intergroup behaviour to goal interdependence, and that research tends to confound a number of possible causal agents. Research also suggests that ethnocentric attitudes and competitive intergroup relations are easy to trigger and difficult to suppress. For example, embryonic ethnocentrism was found in phase 2 of Sherif's summer camp studies, when groups had just been formed but there was no realistic conflict between them (see also Blake and Mouton, 1961; Kahn and Ryen, 1972). Other researchers have found that competitive intergroup behaviour spontaneously emerges:

- even when goal relations between groups are not interdependent (Rabbie and Horwitz, 1969);
- under conditions of explicitly non-competitive intergroup relations (Ferguson and Kelley, 1964; Rabbie and Wilkens, 1971);
- under conditions of explicitly cooperative intergroup relations (Rabbie and DeBrey, 1971).

What, then, are the minimal conditions for intergroup behaviour: that is, conditions that are both necessary and sufficient for a collection of individuals to be ethnocentric and to engage in intergroup competition? (Jean and Alison's problem can be approached in the context of the minimal intergroup paradigm. See the second focus question.)

Tajfel and his colleagues devised an intriguing way to answer this question – the minimal group paradigm (Tajfel, Billig, Bundy and Flament, 1971). British schoolboys, participating in what they believed was a study of decision making, were assigned to one of two groups completely randomly, but allegedly on the basis of their expressed preference for paintings by the artists Vassily Kandinsky or Paul Klee. The children knew only which group they themselves were in (Kandinsky group or Klee group), with the identity of outgroup and fellow ingroup members concealed by the use of code numbers. The children then individually distributed money between pairs of recipients identified only by code number and group membership.

This pencil-and-paper task was repeated for a number of different pairs of ingroup and outgroup members, excluding self, on a series of distribution matrices carefully designed to tease out the sort of strategies that were being used. The results showed that against a background of some fairness, the children strongly favoured their own group: they adopted the ingroup favouritism strategy (FAV) described in Box 11.2. This is a rather startling finding, as the groups were indeed minimal. They were created on the basis of a flimsy criterion, had no past history or possible future, the children did not even know the identity of other members of each group, and no self-interest was involved in the money distribution task as self was not a recipient.

Subsequent experiments were even more minimal in character. For example, Billig and Tajfel (1973) explicitly randomly categorised their participants as X- or Y-group members, thereby eliminating any possibility that they might infer that people in the same group were interpersonally similar to one another because they ostensibly preferred the same artist. Turner

Minimal group paradigm
Experimental methodology to investigate the effect of social categorisation alone on behaviour.

Research classic 11.2
The minimal group paradigm

Distribution strategies and sample distribution matrices (participants circled pairs of numbers to indicate how they wished to distribute the points)

A. *Two sample distribution matrices.* Within each matrix, participants circle the column of numbers that represents how they would like to distribute the points (representing real money) in the matrix between ingroup and outgroup members.

1	Ingroup member:	7	8	9	10	11	12	13	14	15	16	17	18	19
	Outgroup member:	1	3	5	7	9	11	13	15	17	19	21	23	25
2	Ingroup member:	18	17	16	15	14	13	12	11	10	9	8	7	6
	Outgroup member:	5	6	7	8	9	10	11	12	13	14	15	16	17

B. *Distribution strategies.* From an analysis of responses on a large number of matrices it is possible to determine the extent to which the participants' distribution of points is influenced by each of the following strategies.

- Fairness — F — Equal distribution of points between groups
- Maximum joint profit — MJP — Maximise total number of points obtained by both recipients together, irrespective of which group receives most
- Maximum ingroup profit — MIP — Maximise number of points for the ingroup
- Maximum difference — MD — Maximise the difference in favour of the ingroup in the number of points awarded
- Favouritism — FAV — Composite employment of MIP and MD

Source: Tajfel (1970); based on Hogg and Abrams (1988).

(1978) abolished the link between points and money. The task was simply to distribute points. Other studies have included, in addition to the points distribution task, measures of attitudinal, affective and conative aspects of ethnocentrism. Another study used actual coins as rewards (Vaughan, Tajfel and Williams, 1981). Children who were either seven or twelve years old simply distributed coins to unidentified ingroup and outgroup members. Marked ingroup bias was reported in both age groups.

The robust finding from hundreds of minimal group experiments conducted with a wide range of participants is that the mere fact of being categorised as a group member seems to produce ethnocentrism and competitive intergroup behaviour (Bourhis, Sachdev and Gagnon, 1994; Diehl, 1990; Tajfel, 1982). Other studies have shown that minimal intergroup categorisation can generate ingroup bias at the implicit level and is thus an effect over which people may have no conscious control (Otten and Wentura, 1999), and that social categorisation can have a very wide range of automatic effects. For example, Jay Van Bavel and William Cunningham (2011) report the intriguing finding that self-categorised Americans living in New York erroneously estimated Mexico (a feared and threatening outgroup) to be geographically closer than Canada (a non-threatening outgroup) – an elegant confirmation of the saying that you should keep your friends close, and your enemies closer!

Social categorisation is necessary, but may not be sufficient for intergroup behaviour. For example, Hogg and his colleagues conducted a number of minimal group experiments to show that if participants are made more certain and confident about how to use the complex and unusual minimal group matrices, categorisation does not produce group identification and intergroup discrimination (e.g. Grieve and Hogg, 1999; see Hogg, 2000c, 2007b, 2012). It seems that one reason why people identify with groups, even minimal groups, is to reduce feelings of uncertainty (see below). Thus categorisation produces identification and discrimination only if people identify with the category, and they identify with the category only if the categorisation is likely to reduce feelings of uncertainty in the situation.

> **Social categorisation**
> Classification of people as members of different social groups.

The minimal group paradigm has not gone unchallenged. For example, there has been a lively debate over the measures, procedures and statistics used (Aschenbrenner and Schaefer, 1980; Bornstein et al., 1983; Branthwaite, Doyle and Lightbown, 1979; Turner, 1980, 1983), and over the extent to which favouritism reflects rational economic self-interest rather than social identity-based intergroup differentiation (Rabbie, Schot and Visser, 1989; Turner and Bourhis, 1996).

Another objection is that the conditions of the experiments create a demand characteristic whereby participants conform to the transparent expectations of the experimenters or simply to general norms of intergroup competitiveness (Gerard and Hoyt, 1974). This interpretation seems unlikely in the light of evidence that discrimination is not associated with awareness of being under surveillance (Grieve and Hogg, 1999) and that discrimination can be reduced when adherence to and awareness of discriminatory norms is increased (Billig, 1973; Tajfel and Billig, 1974). In fact, participants who are not actually categorised but only have the experiment described to them predict significantly less discrimination (i.e. there is no norm of discrimination) than is actually displayed by participants who are categorised (St Claire and Turner, 1982). Also, it can be almost impossible to encourage participants to follow an explicitly cooperative norm in a minimal intergroup situation (Hogg, Turner, Nascimento-Schulze and Spriggs, 1986).

Although it is not a criticism of the minimal group paradigm, Amélie Mummendey and her colleagues have identified a positive–negative asymmetry in the minimal group effect (Mummendey and Otten, 1998; Otten, Mummendey and Blanz, 1996; see also Peeters and Czapinski, 1990). In the usual paradigm, participants give positively valued resources (points); the effect is much weaker or can disappear when they give negatively valued resources (e.g. punishment), or when instead of giving resources they subtract resources.

Finally, the minimal group effect really does reflect what happens in maximal or real-life groups. Groups really do strive to favour themselves over relevant outgroups. For example, Rupert Brown (1978), capitalising on competitive wage negotiations in Britain in the 1970s, found that shop stewards from one department in an aircraft engineering factory sacrificed as much as £2 a week in absolute terms in order to increase their relative advantage over a competing outgroup to £1. Furthermore, studies of nurses revealed that although nurses are supposed to be caring and self-sacrificing, ingroup identification was associated with just as much ingroup favouritism as among other less self-sacrificing groups (Oaker and Brown, 1986; Skevington, 1981; Van Knippenberg and Van Oers, 1984).

Social identity theory

The pivotal role of social categorisation in intergroup behaviour, as demonstrated by minimal group studies, led to the development by Tajfel and Turner of the concept of social identity (Tajfel, 1974; Tajfel and Turner, 1979). This simple idea has developed and evolved over the years to become perhaps the pre-eminent social psychological analysis of group processes, intergroup relations and the collective self – social identity theory. Social identity theory has a number of theoretically compatible and integrated subtheories and emphases – for example, Tajfel and Turner's (1979) original analysis focused on intergroup relations and can be referred to as the *social identity theory of intergroup relations,* and Turner and colleagues' later focus on self-categorisation and group processes as a whole, self-categorisation theory (Turner, Hogg, Oakes, Reicher, and Wetherell, 1987), can be referred to as the *social identity theory of the group* (see Abrams and Hogg, 2001, 2010; Hogg, 2006; Hogg and Abrams, 1988, 2003; Turner, 1999; **see also Chapter 4**). For a summary of Tajfel's range of contributions to social psychology, see Vaughan (2010b).

Social identity and group membership

Two core premises of social identity theory are: (a) society is structured into distinct social groups that stand in power and status relations to one another (e.g. blacks and whites in the United States, Catholics and Protestants in Northern Ireland, Sunnis and Shi'ites in Iraq), and (b) social categories (large groups such as a nation or church, but also intermediate groups such as an organisation, or small groups such as a club) provide members with a social identity – a definition and evaluation of who one is and a description and evaluation of what this entails. Social identities not only *describe* attributes but, very importantly, also *prescribe* what one should think and how one should behave as a member. For example, being a member of the social category 'student' means not only defining and evaluating yourself and being defined and evaluated by others as a student, but also thinking and behaving in characteristically student ways.

Social identity is that part of the self-concept that derives from group membership. It is associated with group and intergroup behaviours, which have some general characteristics: ethnocentrism, ingroup favouritism, intergroup differentiation; conformity to ingroup norms; ingroup solidarity and cohesion; and perception of self, outgroupers and fellow ingroupers in terms of relevant group stereotypes.

Social identity is quite separate from personal identity, which is that part of the self-concept that derives from personality traits and the idiosyncratic personal relationships we have with other people (Turner, 1982). Personal identity is not associated with group and intergroup behaviours – it is associated with interpersonal and individual behaviour. People have a repertoire of as many social and personal identities as they have groups they identify with, or close relationships and idiosyncratic attributes in terms of which they define themselves. However, although we have many discrete social and personal identities, we subjectively experience the self as an integrated whole person with a continuous and unbroken biography – the subjective experience of self as fragmented discontinuous selves would be problematic and associated with various psychopathologies.

Social identity theory distinguishes social from personal identity as a deliberate attempt to avoid explaining group and intergroup processes in terms of personality attributes or interpersonal relations. Social identity theorists believe that many social psychological theories of

Social identity theory
Theory of group membership and intergroup relations based on self-categorisation, social comparison and the construction of a shared self-definition in terms of ingroup-defining properties.

Self-categorisation theory
Turner and associates' theory of how the process of categorising oneself as a group member produces social identity and group and intergroup behaviours.

Social identity
That part of the self-concept that derives from our membership of social groups.

Ethnocentrism
Evaluative preference for all aspects of our own group relative to other groups.

Ingroup favouritism
Behaviour that favours one's own group over other groups.

Intergroup differentiation
Behaviour that emphasises differences between our own group and other groups.

Stereotype
Widely shared and simplified evaluative image of a social group and its members.

group processes and intergroup relations are limited because they explain the phenomena by aggregating effects of personality predispositions or interpersonal relations.

The authoritarian personality theory and the frustration–aggression hypothesis are examples of this latter type of explanation of prejudice and discrimination (Billig, 1976; **see Chapter 10**). To illustrate: if a social psychologist asks why people stick their arms out of car windows to indicate a turn, the question would remain unanswered by an explanation in terms of the biochemistry of muscle action. An explanation in terms of adherence to social norms would be more appropriate (though inappropriate to a biochemist asking the same question). It is the problem of reductionism **(see Chapter 1 for details)** that prompts social identity theorists to distinguish between social and personal identity (Doise, 1986; Israel and Tajfel, 1972; Moscovici, 1972; Taylor and Brown, 1979; Turner and Oakes, 1986).

Social categorisation, prototypes and depersonalisation

Self-categorisation theory (Turner, Hogg, Oakes, Reicher and Wetherell, 1987), the social identity theory of the group, specifies how categorisation is the social cognitive underpinning of social identity phenomena. People cognitively represent social categories/groups as prototypes. A prototype is a fuzzy set of attributes (perceptions, beliefs, attitudes, feelings, behaviours) that describes one group and distinguishes it from relevant other groups. Prototypes obey the meta-contrast principle – they maximise the ratio of intergroup differences to intragroup differences, and in so doing they accentuate group entitativity. Entitativity (Campbell, 1958; Hamilton and Sherman, 1996) is the property of a group that makes it seem like a coherent, distinct and unitary entity **(see Chapter 8)**.

Meta-contrast ensures that group prototypes are not simply the average of ingroup attributes, and that the most prototypical person in a group is therefore not the average group member. Because of their intergroup distinctiveness function, prototypes are typically displaced from the group average in a direction that is further away from the relevant comparison outgroup. Prototypes are thus ideal rather than average types. It is quite conceivable that a group prototype may be so ideal that not a single member actually embodies it.

Prototypes are cognitive representations of groups. As such they are closely related to stereotypes **(see Chapter 2)**. However, from a social identity perspective a prototype is a stereotype only if it is *shared* by group members (Tajfel, 1981a). Finally, prototypes are context dependent. What this means is that the content of a specific prototype changes as a function of the comparison outgroup, the relevant ingroup members present, and the goals of the interactive context. This context dependence can be quite extreme in newly forming groups (a task group), but is probably less extreme in better-established groups (e.g. ethnic groups) that are more firmly anchored in enduring global intergroup stereotypes. Instances of context effects on prototypes can be found in perceptions between national groups (e.g. Rutland and Cinnirella, 2000). Take an example: Nick Hopkins and Christopher Moore (2001) found that Scots perceived themselves to be different from the English, but that this perceptual difference was diminished when they made comparisons between Scots and Germans. Even though the Scots might not like it, they saw their prototype moving a little closer to the English prototype!

Although identities and their associated attributes are influenced by context, they are not *determined* by context. Van Bavel and Cunningham (2010) propose an *iterative reprocessing model* – they cite neuroscience research showing how identity defining attributes stored in memory are activated and modified by contextual cues to meet specific contextual demands, but are not necessarily fundamentally changed in an enduring sense unless a specific context becomes pervasive in one's life.

The process of categorising someone leads to depersonalisation. When we categorise others, we see them through the lens of the relevant ingroup or outgroup prototype – we view them as members of a group, not as unique idiosyncratic individuals. We perceptually accentuate their similarity to (i.e. assimilate them to) the relevant prototype, thus perceiving them stereotypically and ethnocentrically. When we categorise ourselves, exactly the same happens – we

Authoritarian personality
A syndrome of personality characteristics originating in childhood that predispose individuals to be prejudiced.

Frustration–aggression hypothesis
Theory that all frustration leads to aggression, and all aggression comes from frustration. Used to explain prejudice and intergroup aggression.

Reductionism
A phenomenon in terms of the language and concepts of a lower level of analysis, usually with a loss of explanatory power.

Prototype
Cognitive representation of the typical/ideal defining features of a category.

Meta-contrast principle
The prototype of a group is that position within the group that has the largest ratio of 'differences to ingroup positions' to 'differences to outgroup positions'.

Entitativity
The property of a group that makes it seem like a coherent, distinct and unitary entity.

Depersonalisation
The perception and treatment of self and others not as unique individual persons but as prototypical embodiments of a social group.

define, perceive and evaluate ourselves in terms of our ingroup prototype, and behave in line with that prototype. Self-categorisation produces ingroup normative behaviour (conformity to group norms; **see Chapter 7**) and self-stereotyping **(see Chapter 2)**, and is thus the process that causes us to behave like group members. Depersonalisation is not the same thing as dehumanisation – though it can produce dehumanisation **(see Chapter 10)** if the outgroup is deeply hated and is stereotyped in terms that deny its members any respect or human dignity.

Psychological salience

What determines the point at which one social identity or another becomes the psychologically salient basis for social categorisation of self and others? Without an answer to this question, social identity researchers would have a serious scientific problem – they would be unable to predict or manipulate social identity-contingent behaviours.

Penny Oakes and her colleagues have drawn on work by Campbell (1958) and Bruner (1958) to answer this critical question (Oakes, 1987; Oakes, Haslam and Turner, 1994; Oakes and Turner, 1990; **see Chapter 2**). Social categories that are (a) chronically accessible to us (e.g. readily available in our memory), and/or (b) accessible in the situation (e.g. there are obvious situational cues to the category), come into operation as the basis of self-categorisation if they make good sense of the situation (a) by accounting for similarities and differences between people (i.e. they fit the way the situation is structured) and (b) by accounting for why people behave as they do (i.e. they fit the norms that people seem to adhere to). This can be put technically: salience is an interactive function of *chronic accessibility* and *situational accessibility* on the one hand, and *structural fit* and *normative fit* on the other. Van Bavel and Cunningham's (2010) iterative reprocessing model (see above) suggests that this is an iterative process in which attributes in memory are called on and temporarily modified to meet contextual demands and goals.

Positive distinctiveness and self-enhancement

Social identity phenomena are motivated by two underlying processes: self-enhancement and uncertainty reduction. One of the key premises of social identity theory is that groups stand in status and prestige relations to one another – some groups are simply more prestigious and higher status than others, and most people in a given social context know this. Intergroup relations are characterised by a struggle over prestige and status (Tajfel and Turner, 1979; also see Hogg and Abrams, 1988). From a social identity point of view, groups compete to be different from one another in favourable ways because positive intergroup distinctiveness provides group members with a favourable (positive) social identity. Unlike interpersonal comparisons, which generally strive for similarity (e.g. Festinger, 1954; Suls and Wheeler, 2000), intergroup comparisons strive to maximise differences in ways that evaluatively favour the ingroup.

Researchers have found these ideas of positive distinctiveness and positive social identity helpful in understanding a range of phenomena (Ellemers, Spears and Doosje, 1999): for example, delinquency. Nick Emler and his colleagues have suggested that delinquency, particularly among boys, is strategic behaviour designed to establish and manage a favourable reputation among groups of peers (Emler and Hopkins, 1990; Emler and Reicher, 1995). Consistent with this view is the fact that delinquent behaviour is usually a group activity that occurs in public, thus maximising its identity-confirming function (Emler, Ohana and Moscovici, 1987). Furthermore, delinquent behaviour is particularly appealing to children who come from backgrounds that are unlikely to facilitate good academic performance at school: delinquency therefore offers an alternative source of positive identity (it is so attractive that most children toy with it to some extent at one time or another). Reicher and Emler (1985) have suggested that one reason that boys are much more likely than girls to become delinquent is that there is greater pressure on boys to perform well at school and therefore underachievement is more poignantly felt: the motivation to establish an alternative positive social identity is so much stronger.

Positive distinctiveness as a group-level process is believed to map on to a very basic human motivation for self-enhancement (Sedikides and Strube, 1997; **see Chapter 4**). Drawing on this analysis, social identity researchers have suggested that self-esteem is a key motive in social identity contexts. Research (Abrams and Hogg, 1988; Crocker and Luhtanen, 1990; Crocker and Major, 1989; Hogg and Abrams, 1990; Long and Spears, 1997; Rubin and Hewstone, 1998) on self-esteem motivation has shown that:

- intergroup differentiation tends to elevate self-esteem;
- depressed self-esteem does not motivate intergroup differentiation;
- it is collective self-esteem, not personal self-esteem, that is related to group processes;
- people in groups are highly creative and competent at protecting themselves from the low self-esteem consequences of low status group membership.

Uncertainty reduction

Social identity processes are, according to *uncertainty–identity theory,* also motivated by uncertainty reduction (Hogg, 2000c, 2007b, 2012). In life, people are fundamentally motivated to know who they are and how they relate to other people – they need to feel relatively certain about what to think, feel and do, and about what others will think, feel and do. We need to know what to expect from other people in order to make life predictable and allow us to plan effective action.

Group identification is a highly effective way of reducing uncertainty. Identification with a group, through relevant prototypes, immediately and automatically defines our relationships with ingroup and outgroup others and sets out how we and others will act. Experimental research, largely using variants of the minimal group paradigm, has shown that people identify with groups and identify more strongly with groups when they are uncertain (e.g. Grieve and Hogg, 1999).

However, when we feel uncertain about ourselves we prefer to identify with highly entitative groups as they provide a better structured and clearer sense of self (Hogg, Sherman, Dierselhuis, Maitner and Moffitt, 2007; Hogg, Meehan and Farquharson, 2010). In addition, we can perceptually accentuate the entitativity of existing groups we belong to (Sherman, Hogg and Maitner, 2009). This preference for high entitativity groups has an important implication.

When uncertainty is acute, enduring and highly self relevant people may strive to identify with groups that are not merely entitative but extreme. Such groups tend to be normatively homogenous, inward looking, intolerant of dissent, highly ethnocentric, and governed by a powerful, all-embracing, orthodox ideological system. This may explain why extremism, orthodoxy and group intolerance often arise in times of societal uncertainty associated with war, revolution, economic collapse, or natural disaster. It also explains the enduring attraction of religious identities (they provide a distinctive sense of self, a repertoire of customs and rituals, a well-established ideology, a powerful moral compass, and even deal with existential uncertainty), and the tendency for religiosity to drift into religious zealotry (Hogg, Adelman and Blagg, 2010).

Social identity and intergroup relations

Social identity theory was originally founded on an attempt to explain intergroup conflict and social change – this was Tajfel's original social identity theory (Tajfel, 1974; Tajfel and Turner, 1979).

In pursuit of positive social identity, groups and individuals can adopt an array of different behavioural strategies, the choice of which is determined by people's beliefs about the nature of relations between their own and other groups (Ellemers, 1993; Hogg and Abrams, 1988; Tajfel and Turner, 1979; Taylor and McKirnan, 1984) – see Figure 11.6. These beliefs, which may or may not accord with the reality of intergroup relations (they are ideological constructs), hinge first on whether it is possible, as an individual, to 'pass' from a lower-status group and gain

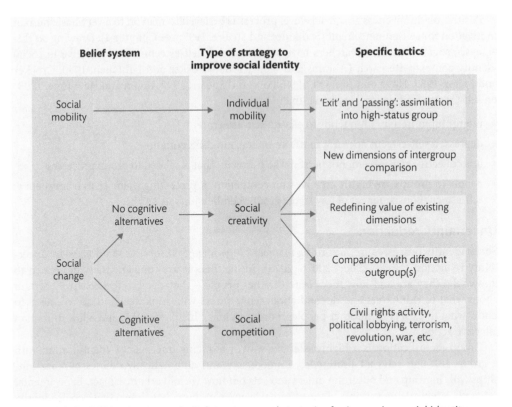

Figure 11.6 Social identity theory: belief structures and strategies for improving social identity

Beliefs about the nature of intergroup relations influence the general strategies and specific tactics that group members can adopt to try to maintain or achieve positive social identity

Social action
Even a peaceful demonstration can challenge the status quo and a state's power base

acceptance in a higher-status group. A social mobility belief system inhibits group action on the part of subordinate groups. Instead, it encourages individuals to dissociate themselves from the group and try to gain acceptance for themselves and their immediate family in the dominant group. The belief in social mobility is enshrined in Western democratic political systems.

Where individuals believe that intergroup boundaries are impermeable to 'passing', a social change belief system exists.

In a social change belief system, positive social identity can be achieved only by forms of group action, and the sort of action taken is influenced by whether the status quo (the existing status and power hierarchy) is perceived to be secure or insecure. Take the case of an insecure system. The traditional Hindu caste system in India has long been secure (Sharma, 1981), but there is recent evidence that this is now challenged on the Indian sub-continent by young people when choosing their mates (Ghimire, Axinn, Yabiku and Thornton, 2006). On the other hand, if the status quo is considered stable, legitimate and thus secure, it is difficult to conceive of an alternative social structure (i.e. no cognitive alternatives exist), let alone a path to real social change. Groups may then tend to adopt social creativity strategies:

- They can engage in intergroup comparisons on novel or unorthodox dimensions that tend to favour the subordinate group. For example, Gerard Lemaine (1966, 1974) had children engage in an intergroup competition to build the best hut, and found that groups that were provided with poor building materials, and thus had no possibility of winning, went on to emphasise how good a garden they had made.

- They can attempt to change the consensual value attached to ingroup characteristics (e.g. the slogan 'Black is beautiful').

- They can compare themselves with other low- or lower-status groups (e.g. 'poor-white racism').

Where social change is associated with recognition that the status quo is illegitimate, unstable and thus insecure, and where cognitive alternatives (i.e. conceivable and attainable alternative social orders) exist, then direct social competition occurs – that is, direct intergroup conflict (e.g. political action, collective protest, revolutions, war). Social movements typically emerge under these circumstances (e.g. Haslam and Reicher, 2012; Klandermans, 1997, 2003; Milgram and Toch, 1969; Tyler and Smith, 1998; see earlier in this chapter).

In a manner closely related to social identity theory, John Jost and his colleagues (Jost and Banaji, 1994; Jost and Hunyadi, 2002; Jost and van der Toorn, 2012; **see Chapter 10**), in their system justification theory, attribute social stasis to an ideology that justifies the status quo. This is an ideology that subordinate group members subscribe to even though it legitimises current status relations and encourages people to protect it and thus maintain their position of disadvantage. It is quite possible that the motivation to do this is uncertainty reduction – better to live in disadvantage but be certain of one's place than to challenge the status quo and face an uncertain future (Hogg, 2007b, 2012).

This macrosocial dimension of social identity theory has been tested successfully in a range of laboratory and naturalistic contexts (Hogg and Abrams, 1988; Ellemers, 1993; see Box 11.3 and Figure 11.7 for a New Zealand study), and has been elaborated and extended in many areas of social psychology (e.g. the study of language and ethnicity; **see Chapter 15**). Social identity theory attributes the general form of intergroup behaviour (e.g. ethnocentrism, stereotyping) to social categorisation related processes, and the specific manifestation (e.g. conflict, harmony) to people's beliefs about the nature of intergroup relations.

Alex Haslam and his colleagues capture this in a study of subtle changes in Australians' stereotypes of Americans that occurred as a consequence of changes in intergroup attitudes caused by the first Gulf War in 1991 (Haslam, Turner, Oakes, McGarty and Hayes, 1992). They discovered that Australians who were making comparisons between Australia, Britain and the United States had a relatively unfavourable stereotype of Americans that deteriorated further during the course of the Gulf conflict, particularly on dimensions reflecting arrogance,

Social mobility belief system
Belief that intergroup boundaries are permeable. Thus, it is possible for someone to pass from a lower-status into a higher-status group to improve social identity.

Social change belief system
Belief that intergroup boundaries are impermeable. Therefore, a lower-status individual can improve social identity only by challenging the legitimacy of the higher-status group's position.

Cognitive alternatives
Belief that the status quo is unstable and illegitimate, and that social competition with the dominant group is the appropriate strategy to improve social identity.

Social creativity
Group-based behavioural strategies that improve social identity but do not directly attack the dominant group's position.

Social competition
Group-based behavioural strategies that improve social identity by directly confronting the dominant group's position in society.

System justification theory
Theory that attributes social stasis to people's adherence to an ideology that justifies and protects the status quo.

Social psychology in action 11.3
Social change: growth of pride in an indigenous people

Maori people are New Zealand's indigenous people and make up about 10 per cent of the population. The remainder of the population is predominantly Pakeha (i.e. European). Graham Vaughan has collected data on ingroup (ethnic) preferences of younger (6–8 years) and older (10–12 years) Maori and Pakeha children from urban and rural backgrounds (Vaughan, 1978a, 1978b). The data were collected at various times during the 1960s, which was a period of considerable social change in New Zealand, and these data are displayed in Figure 11.7. The arrows represent an age trend from younger to older children within each ethnic group at each time and at each location. Choices above 50 per cent represent ingroup preference and those below 50 per cent outgroup preference.

Against an overall reduction in ethnocentrism for older children (presumably a developmental trend), the data show that urban Pakeha preferred their own group but were less ethnocentric than rural Pakeha, and rural Maori showed more marked outgroup preference than urban Maori. The most interesting finding was that, between 1961 and 1971 urban Maori actually changed from making outgroup to making ingroup preferences – a change that reflected the rise in the late 1960s and early 1970s of an assertive Brown (Maori) Power movement modelled on the American Black Power movement of the 1960s.

Intergroup perceptions may be less ethnocentric in the city for a number of reasons, including perhaps inter-ethnic contact. Maori who moved to the city were often cut off from the traditional Polynesian extended family (and from other aspects of Maori culture) and found that they had to compete with Pakeha for work. There was a gradual realignment of ethnic power relations and greater possibility of less unequal-status inter-ethnic contact. Perhaps this contributed to some extent to reduced prejudice on the part of Pakeha and elevated ethnic pride on the part of Maori.

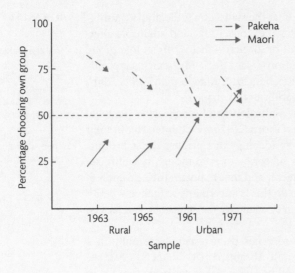

Figure 11.7 Ingroup bias among Maori and Pakeha children as a function of social change (time, nature of intergroup contact)

The direction of the arrows emphasises an age trend from younger to older children in each group. By 1971, older urban Maori were exhibiting more ingroup bias than older urban Pakeha. Between 1961 and 1971 there was a systematic decrease in Pakeha ingroup bias and Maori outgroup bias, which was more pronounced for older than younger children

Source: Vaughan (1978b); in Tajfel (1978)

argumentativeness and traditionalism. The authors argue that the reason why attitudes deteriorated on these particular dimensions rather than others was that these dimensions related directly to the perceived actions of Americans in relation to other nations during the war.

Other aspects

Social identity theory has a number of other important components, most of which are discussed elsewhere in this book. These include the following:

Social change
For this Paralympics athlete victory not only brings glory to her country, but also promotes a positive image of disabled people

- *Referent informational influence* theory (Abrams and Hogg, 1990a; Turner, 1991; Turner and Oakes, 1989), which deals with conformity **(Chapter 7)** and group polarisation **(Chapter 9)**.
- The *social attraction hypothesis,* which deals with cohesion and attraction phenomena in groups (Hogg, 1993, **see Chapter 8**).
- The theory of *subjective group dynamics,* which deals with deviance processes in groups (Marques, Abrams, Páez and Taboada, 1998; Pinto, Marques, Levine and Abrams, 2010; **see Chapter 8**).
- The social identity theory of *leadership* (Hogg and van Knippenberg, 2003; Hogg, van Knippenberg and Rast, in press; **see Chapter 9**).
- The social identity theory of *attitude–behaviour relations* (Terry and Hogg, 1996; Hogg and Smith, 2007; **see Chapter 5**).
- The social identity theory of *deindividuation* phenomena (Klein, Spears and Reicher, 2007; Reicher, Spears and Postmes, 1995; see below).
- *Collective guilt* – where you feel guilty, as a group member, about past transgressions committed by your group (Doosje, Branscombe, Spears and Manstead, 1998).

Social cognition

Although self-categorisation theory has a social cognitive emphasis on the role of cognitive processes and cognitive representations in intergroup behaviour (Farr, 1996), it is a theory that explicitly articulates with a more broadly social analysis (Doise, 1986; **see Chapter 1**). This is because, as we have seen, it is part of the broader social identity theory. Social cognition **(see Chapter 2 for full coverage)**, however, provides a number of other more purely cognitive explanations, which focus on certain cognitive and perceptual effects that have important implications for intergroup behaviour.

Categorisation and relative homogeneity

Accentuation effect
Overestimation of similarities among people within a category and dissimilarities between people from different categories.

The most obvious effect is stereotyping. The categorisation of people (or objects) has been shown to cause an accentuation effect (Tajfel, 1959): the perceptual accentuation of similarities among people in a category and of differences between people from different categories on those dimensions believed to be associated with the categorisation: that is, stereotypical dimensions (Doise, 1978; Eiser and Stroebe, 1972; Tajfel and Wilkes, 1963). There is some evidence that people perceptually homogenise outgroup members more than ingroup members: '*they* all look alike, but *we* are diverse' (Brigham and Malpass, 1985; Quattrone, 1986).

For example, John Brigham and Paul Barkowitz (1978) had black and white college students indicate for 72 photographs of black and white faces how certain they were that they had seen each photograph in a previously presented series of twenty-four photographs (twelve of blacks and twelve of whites). Figure 11.8 shows that participants found it more difficult to recognise outgroup than ingroup faces. This effect is quite robust. It has emerged from other studies comparing 'Anglos' with blacks (Bothwell, Brigham and Malpass, 1989), with Hispanics (Platz and Hosch, 1988) and with Japanese (Chance, 1985), and from studies of student eating clubs (Jones, Wood and Quattrone, 1981), college sororities (Park and Rothbart, 1982) and artificial laboratory groups (Wilder, 1984).

Relative homogeneity effect
Tendency to see outgroup members as all the same, and ingroup members as more differentiated.

The relative homogeneity effect is enhanced on group-defining dimensions (Lee and Ottati, 1993) and when groups are in competition (Judd and Park, 1988) – see Ostrom and Sedikides (1992). The principal explanation for this effect is that, because we are generally more familiar with ingroup than outgroup members, we have more detailed knowledge about the former and thus are better able to differentiate them (Linville, Fischer and Salovey, 1989; Wilder, 1986). Although quite sensible, this may not be the complete story. For example, the outgroup homogeneity effect occurs when participants report no greater familiarity with the ingroup than the outgroup (Jones, Wood and Quattrone, 1981) and when there is equally minimal information about both groups (Wilder, 1984). Walter Stephan (1977) found that children in both segregated and integrated schools (i.e. with lower or higher intergroup familiarity)

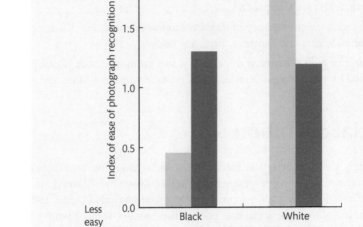

Figure 11.8 Ease of recognition of faces as a function of race of participant and race of person in photograph

Black and white participants had more difficulty identifying faces they had seen before if the faces were of racial outgroup rather than racial ingroup members

Source: Based on data from Brigham and Barkowitz (1978)

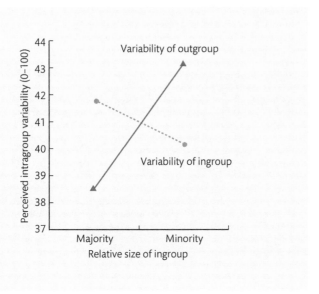

Figure 11.9 Perceived intragroup variability of ingroup and outgroup as a function of relative majority or minority status of ingroup

Majorities rated the outgroup as less variable than the ingroup (the usual relative homogeneity effect). However, minorities did the opposite – they rated the outgroup as more variable than the ingroup

Source: Based on data from Simon and Brown (1987)

actually rated their own group as more homogeneous than two outgroups. If outgroup homogeneity is not inevitable, what factors influence the relative homogeneity effect?

One clue is that, while most research has used majority or equal-sized groups, Stephan's (1977) groups were minority groups (Chicanos and blacks). Also, the relative outgroup homogeneity effect is enhanced when the outgroup is perceived to be relatively small – a minority (Bartsch and Judd, 1993; Mullen and Hu, 1989). To test the idea that relative homogeneity is influenced by the majority–minority status of the ingroup, Bernd Simon and Rupert Brown (1987) conducted a minimal group study. Relative group size was varied, and participants were asked to rate the variability of both ingroup and outgroup and to indicate how much they identified with the ingroup. Figure 11.9 shows that while majorities rated the outgroup as less variable than the ingroup (the usual outgroup homogeneity effect), minorities did the opposite. In addition, this latter ingroup homogeneity effect was accompanied by greater group identification. This is consistent with social identity theory: minorities categorise themselves more strongly as a group and are thus more strongly depersonalised (see above) in their perceptions, attitudes and behaviour.

Memory

Social categorisation is associated with category-based person memory effects (Fiske and Taylor, 1991). For example, Shelley Taylor and her colleagues arranged for participants to listen to taped mixed-sex or mixed-race discussion groups and later attribute various statements to the correct speaker. They rarely attributed the statements to the wrong category, but within categories they were not good at identifying the correct speaker: that is, they made few between-category errors but many within-category errors (Taylor, Fiske, Etcoff and Ruderman, 1978). The category-based memory effect can be quite selective. For example, John Howard and Myron Rothbart (1980) had participants read statements describing ingroup or outgroup members behaving in different ways – some of the behaviour reflected favourably and some unfavourably on the actor. Later, for each behaviour, they had to recall whether it was an ingroup or an outgroup member who performed each behaviour. The participants were equally accurate at recalling whether it was an ingroup or outgroup member who performed the favourable behaviour, but they were more accurate at recalling outgroup than ingroup actors who performed unfavourable behaviour (see Figure 11.10).

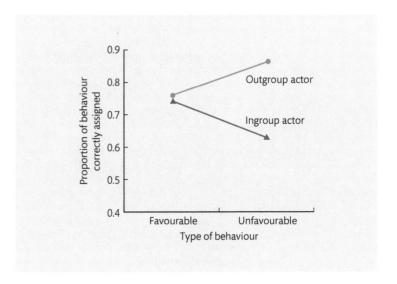

Figure 11.10 Assignment of behaviours to actors as a function of item favourability and ingroup/outgroup status of actor

Participants were equally good at recalling whether it was an ingroup or outgroup member who performed favourable behaviours, but they were better at recalling outgroup than ingroup actors who performed unfavourable behaviours

Source: Based on Howard and Rothbart (1980)

These two experiments illustrate the way in which information about individuals can be represented cognitively and organised as category attributes that reduce individual differences between people in the same category. Furthermore, evaluative biases may influence what information is associated with a particular category.

Distinctive stimuli and illusory correlation

A particularly important influence on what information is associated with which categories is how distinctive the information is. Anything that is out of the ordinary (objects, events and people who are statistically infrequent, rare, unusual, relatively vivid or conspicuous) attracts our attention and we become more cognitively active (Taylor and Fiske, 1978). So, for example, we tend to attend more to a single man in a group of women, a single black in a group of whites, or to a person we understand to be a genius, a homosexual or a movie star. Distinctive individuals can also disproportionately influence the generalised images we construct of groups. There is a tendency to generalise from distinctive individuals to the group as a whole, particularly when we have few prior expectations and/or are unfamiliar with the category (Quattrone and Jones, 1980). For instance, on the basis of meeting one extremely stupid (i.e. distinctive individual) Martian (i.e. unfamiliar group), we are apt to stereotype the group as stupid.

Illusory correlation
Cognitive exaggeration of the degree of co-occurrence of two stimuli or events, or the perception of a co-occurrence where none exists.

Another effect of distinctiveness is that people tend to perceive an illusory correlation, based on *paired distinctiveness* or *associative meaning*, between distinctive events that occur at the same time (Chapman, 1967; **illusory correlation is discussed fully in Chapter 2**). Distinctiveness-based illusory correlation may help to explain stereotyping, particularly negative stereotypes of minority groups (Hamilton 1979; Hamilton and Sherman, 1989; Mullen and Johnson, 1990): negative events are distinctive because they are subjectively less frequent than positive events; and minority groups are distinctive because people have relatively few contacts with them. Illusory correlation based on associative meaning may also be involved in negative stereotyping of minority groups: people have preconceptions that negative attributes go with minority groups (McArthur and Friedman, 1980).

Distinctiveness-based illusory correlation is a robust empirical effect, which is stronger for negative behaviour, under conditions of high memory load (McConnell, Sherman and Hamilton, 1994; Mullen and Johnson, 1990), and when people are aroused (Kim and Baron, 1988). Once an illusory correlation between a group and a negative attribute in one domain (e.g. intellectual) has been established, there is a tendency to generalise the negative impression to other domains (e.g. social; Acorn, Hamilton and Sherman, 1988).

However, the usefulness of an illusory correlation in explaining stereotyping may be limited. It does not consider the emotional and self-conceptual investment that people have in stereotyping, or the material bases of power and status differentials between groups that stereotype one another. As we have seen in this chapter and in Chapter 10, how we construct and use stereotypes is framed by intergroup relations and governed by cognitive, affective and rhetorical motives (Leyens, Yzerbyt and Schadron, 1994; McGarty, Haslam, Turner and Oakes, 1993; Oakes, Haslam and Turner, 1994).

Optimal distinctiveness

Distinctiveness enters into intergroup behaviour in rather a different way in Marilynn Brewer's (1991, 1993) theory of optimal distinctiveness (also see Leonardelli, Pickett and Brewer, 2010). Building on her dual-process model of information processing (Brewer, 1988, 1994; **see Chapter 2**), she argues that the default mode for processing information about others is in terms of their category membership (satisfying a need to recognise similarities among people). However, if one feels ego-involved in the task, or related to or interdependent with the stimulus person, then information processing is based on very specific and personalised information about the stimulus person (this satisfies a need to recognise differences between people). In most contexts, people strive to achieve a satisfactory level of distinctiveness for others and for themselves in order to resolve the tension between the needs for similarity and difference. In intergroup behaviour, this manifests itself as a degree of differentiation between group members, including self, against a background of homogenisation. A related phenomenon was earlier identified by Jean-Pierre Codol (1975), called the *primus inter pares* effect, in which individuals in a group seemed to differentiate themselves from one another in competition to be the most representative or best group member.

From Brewer's perspective, people are driven by conflicting motives for inclusion/sameness (satisfied by group membership) and for distinctiveness/uniqueness (satisfied by individuality), so they try to strike a balance between these two motives in order to achieve optimal distinctiveness. Smaller groups more than satisfy the need for distinctiveness, so people strive for greater inclusiveness, while large groups more than satisfy the need for inclusiveness, so people strive for distinctiveness. One implication of this idea is that people should be more satisfied with membership of mid-size groups than groups that are very large or very small (Hornsey and Jetten, 2004). This idea is usually tested in the laboratory with a restricted range of relative group sizes. To investigate groups that varied enormously in relative size, Dominic Abrams (1994) analysed survey data on political identity from over 4,000 18–21-year-olds in England and Scotland. He found that small parties (Green, Social Democrat, Scottish Nationalist) did indeed provide members with a more solid and distinct identity than did the large parties (Labour, Conservative).

Optimal distinctiveness
People strive to achieve a balance between conflicting motives for inclusiveness and separateness, expressed in groups as a balance between intragroup differentiation and intragroup homogenisation.

Intergroup emotions

People in groups that are important to them can feel strong emotions about outgroups and fellow members of their own groups – indeed, strength of emotion and type of emotion are key features of intergroup relations. Research dealing with this aspect of intergroup relations has until relatively recently been sparse. However, in recent years there has been an upsurge in research on intergroup emotions (Iyer and Leach, 2008). For example, Diane Mackie and Eliot Smith and their associates have proposed intergroup emotions theory (IET) to address emotions in group contexts (Mackie, Devos and Smith, 1999; Mackie and Smith, 2002a; also see Mackie, Maitner and Smith, 2009; Mackie and Smith, 2002b).

IET builds on social identity theory, and on contemporary theories of emotion that argue that individual emotions arise from appraisals of whether a situation is going to harm or benefit oneself personally (e.g. Lazarus, 1991; Parkinson and Manstead, 1992; **see Chapter 2**). IET

Intergroup emotions theory
Theory that, in group contexts, appraisals of personal harm or benefit in a situation operate at the level of social identity and thus produce mainly positive ingroup and negative outgroup emotions.

also argues that, in group contexts, the self is a collective self and so appraisals operate at the level of whether a situation is going to harm or benefit 'us'.

When people identify with a group, associated intergroup emotions come into play. Harm to the ingroup, which often emanates from the actions of outgroups, is appraised as self-harming. This generates negative emotions about the outgroup. Behaviour that promotes the ingroup, often emanating from fellow ingroup members, generates positive emotions about the ingroup and its members. Emotions have an action tendency. Therefore, outgroup emotions may translate into discrimination and ingroup emotions into solidarity and cohesion. From IET it can also be predicted that emotions felt by fellow ingroup members will quickly be felt by self – owing to the common identity bond that exists.

Intergroup emotions may also be affected by people's regulatory focus (Higgins, 1998; **see Chapter 4**), specifically whether group members have a promotion or prevention intergroup focus (Jonas, Sassenberg and Scheepers, 2010). In intergroup contexts, a *promotion focus* strengthens people's positive emotion-related bias and behavioural tendencies towards the ingroup; a *prevention focus* strengthens their negative emotion-related bias and behavioural tendencies against the outgroup (Shah, Brazy and Higgins, 2004).

Other research on intergroup and collective emotions has focused on specific group-based emotions. There have been studies of collective guilt and shame and how these emotions affect people's intentions to perform acts of reparation, specifically public apologies and political action intentions (e.g. Branscombe and Doosje, 2004; Brown, R., Gonzalez, Zagefka, Manzi and Cehajic, 2008; Doosje, Branscombe, Spears and Manstead, 1998, 2006; Iyer, Schmader and Lickel, 2007).

Collective guilt arises if people feel that their group's blameworthy actions are or were under their control and that they are therefore to some extent responsible. Collective shame arises if people feel that their group's actions reflect poorly on the image of the group but that the actions were not under their control and that they largely had no responsibility for the actions. It is collective guilt, not shame that therefore sponsors intergroup behaviours aimed at righting the wrong – such as apologising or making reparation. Collective shame is likely to motivate people to avoid or escape the shame-evoking event or even the ingroup itself if it is seen as the source of the shameful outcome.

Collective behaviour and the crowd

Collective behaviour
The behaviour of people en masse – such as in a crowd, protest or riot.

Collective behaviour usually refers to large numbers of people who are in the same place at the same time, behaving in a uniform manner that is volatile, highly emotional and in violation of social norms (Graumann and Moscovici, 1986; Milgram and Toch, 1969; Moscovici, 1985b). Some social psychologists interpret this to include the study of rumours (**see Chapter 3**), fads and fashions, social movements and cults, and contagions of expression, enthusiasm, anxiety, fear and hostility.

Contagions include some of the most bizarre behaviour imaginable (Klapp, 1972). In the 1630s, tulip mania swept north-western Europe, with people trading small fortunes for a single, ultimately worthless, bulb; in the fifteenth century, there was an epidemic in Europe in which nuns bit each other; in the eighteenth century, there was an epidemic of nuns meowing like cats; between the tenth and the fourteenth centuries in Europe there were frequent episodes of dancing mania, with people continually dancing from town to town until they dropped and even died; and in the mid- and late 1980s, there were epidemics in China of men complaining hysterically about shrinkage of the penis and an overwhelming fear of impending death!

Usually, however, the study of collective behaviour is a more sober business. It is the study of crowd behaviour. The crowd is a vivid social phenomenon both for those who are involved and for those who witness the events first-hand or through literature and the media. Consider the Tiananmen Square protest in 1989, the Los Angeles riots of 1992, Nazi rallies of the 1930s, celebrations at the fall of the Berlin Wall in 1990, political demonstrations in the streets of Tehran in 2009, anti-war demonstrations over Vietnam in the late 1960s and in Iraq in the mid-2000s; and think of rock festivals since the late 1960s, the 2011 protests in Tahrir Square in downtown Cairo, and huge crowds at Queen Elizabeth II's diamond jubilee in London in 2012. Crowd events are nothing if not varied.

Crowd behaviour, in its full manifestation, can be difficult to research in the laboratory, although attempts have been made. For example, John French (1944) locked his participants in a room and then wafted smoke under the door while sounding the fire alarm. Research ethics aside, the study was not successful as an attempt to create panic in the laboratory. One group kicked open the door and knocked over the smoke generator, and members of another group calmly discussed the possibility that their reactions were being observed by the experimenters!

Early theories

One of the earliest theories of collective behaviour was proposed by Gustave LeBon (1896/1908), who lived through a period of profound social turmoil in France. He observed and read accounts of the great revolutionary crowds of the revolution of 1848 and the Paris Commune of 1871 – accounts such as those to be found in Zola's novels *Germinal* and *La Débâcle*, and Hugo's *Les Misérables*. He was appalled by the 'primitive, base and ghastly' behaviour of the crowd, and the way in which people's civilised conscious personality seemed to vanish and be replaced by savage animal instincts. LeBon believed that:

> by the mere fact that he forms part of an organised crowd, a man descends several rungs in the ladder of civilisation. Isolated, he may be a cultivated individual; in a crowd he is a barbarian – that is, a creature acting by instinct.
>
> LeBon (1908, p. 12)

According to LeBon, crowds produce primitive and homogeneous behaviour because (see Figure 11.11):

- members are anonymous and thus lose personal responsibility for their actions;
- ideas and sentiments spread rapidly and unpredictably through a process of contagion;
- unconscious antisocial motives ('ancestral savagery') are released through suggestion (a process akin to hypnosis).

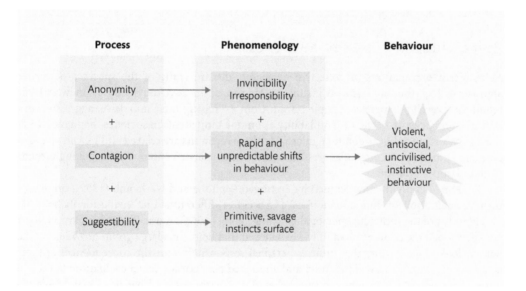

Figure 11.11 LeBon's model of the crowd

Anonymity, contagion and suggestibility operate together to produce antisocial, violent crowd behaviour

Source: Based on Hogg (1992)

LeBon is still important nowadays (see Apfelbaum and McGuire, 1986; Hogg and Abrams, 1988; Reicher, 1987, 1996, 2001), owing mainly to the influence of his perspective, in which crowd behaviour is considered to be pathological/abnormal, on later theories of collective behaviour (e.g. Freud, 1921; McDougall, 1920; Zimbardo, 1970). Freud, for example, argued that the crowd 'unlocks' the unconscious. Society's moral standards maintain civilised behaviour because they are installed in the human psyche as the super-ego. However, in crowds, the super-ego is supplanted by the leader of the crowd, who now acts as the hypnotist controlling unconscious and uncivilised id impulses. Crowd leaders have this effect because of a deep and primitive instinct in all of us to regress, in crowds, to the 'primal horde' – the original brutal human group at the dawn of existence. Civilisation is able to evolve and thrive only to the extent that the leader of the primal horde, the 'primal father', is overthrown. This analysis has been used to explain how the 'Reverend' Jim Jones had such enormous power over his cult followers that more than 900 of them collectively committed suicide at Jonestown in Guyana in 1978 (Ulman and Abse, 1983). (Reflect on the fourth focus question at the beginning of this chapter).

Another important early theorist is William McDougall, who characterised the crowd as:

> excessively emotional, impulsive, violent, fickle, inconsistent, irresolute and extreme in action, displaying only the coarser emotions and the less refined sentiments; extremely suggestible, careless in deliberation, hasty in judgment, incapable of any but the simpler and imperfect forms of reasoning, easily swayed and led, lacking in self-consciousness, devoid of self-respect and of a sense of responsibility, and apt to be carried away by the consciousness of its own force, so that it tends to produce all the manifestations we have learnt to expect of any irresponsible and absolute power.
>
> McDougall (1920, p. 45)

McDougall believed that the most widespread instinctive emotions are the simple primitive ones (e.g. fear, anger), and that these would therefore be the most common and widely shared emotions in any human aggregate. More complex emotions would be rare and less widely shared. Stimuli eliciting the primitive simple emotions would therefore cause a strong consensual reaction, while those eliciting more complex emotions would not. Primary emotions spread and strengthen rapidly in a crowd, as each member's expression of the emotion acts as a further stimulus to others – a snowball effect dubbed 'primitive sympathy'. This effect is not easily modulated, as individuals feel depersonalised and have a lowered sense of personal responsibility.

Deindividuation and self-awareness

More recent explanations of collective behaviour discard some of the specifics of earlier approaches (e.g. the emphasis on instinctive emotions, the psychodynamic framework) but retain the overall perspective. People refrain from exercising their impulsive, aggressive and selfish nature because of their identifiability as unique individuals in societies that have strong norms against 'uncivilised' conduct. In crowds, these restraints are relaxed and we can revert to type and embark on an orgy of aggressive, selfish, antisocial behaviour. The mediating mechanism is deindividuation.

Deindividuation
Process whereby people lose their sense of socialised individual identity and engage in unsocialised, often antisocial, behaviours.

The term 'deindividuation', coined by Festinger, Pepitone and Newcomb (1952), originates in Jung's definition of 'individuation' as 'a process of differentiation, having for its goal the development of the individual personality' (Jung, 1946, p. 561). It was Philip Zimbardo (1970) who developed the concept most fully. He believed that being in a large group provides people with a cloak of anonymity that diffuses personal responsibility for the consequences of their actions. This leads to a loss of identity and a reduced concern for social evaluation: that is, to a state of deindividuation, which causes behaviour to become impulsive, irrational, regressive and disinhibited because it is not under the usual social and personal controls.

Research into deindividuation has tended to focus on the effects of anonymity on behaviour in groups. Festinger, Pepitone and Newcomb (1952) found that participants dressed in grey

Deindividuation
People in uniforms, and in a large group, have a cloak of anonymity

laboratory coats and seated in a poorly lit room for a group discussion of their parents made more negative comments about their parents than did participants in a control condition (see also Cannavale, Scarr and Pepitone, 1970). Similarly, participants dressed in laboratory coats used more obscene language when discussing erotic literature than did more easily identifiable individuals (Singer, Brush and Lublin, 1965).

Zimbardo (1970) conducted a series of experiments in which participants were deindividuated by wearing cloaks and hoods (reminiscent of the Ku Klux Klan). In one such experiment, deindividuated female students gave electric shocks to a female confederate in a paired-associate learning task that were twice the duration of those given by conventionally dressed participants. In another classic study, in which a simulated prison was constructed in the basement of the Psychology Department of Stanford University, Zimbardo (Zimbardo, Haney, Banks and Jaffe, 1982; **see Chapter 8**) found that students who were deindividuated by being dressed as guards were extremely brutal to other students who were deindividuated as prisoners. There is also evidence that people are more willing to lynch someone (Mullen, 1986) or bait a disturbed person to jump from a building if it is dark and if they are in a larger group (Mann, 1981; **see Chapter 12**).

Finally, Ed Diener and his colleagues conducted a clever study that took advantage of Hallowe'en – when the streets were filled with children, disguised and thus anonymous, who were trick-or-treating (Diener, Fraser, Beaman and Kelem, 1976). The researchers observed the behaviour of more than 1,300 children, alone or in groups, who approached 27 focal homes in Seattle where they were warmly invited in and told to 'take *one* of the candies' on a table. Half the children were first asked their names and where they lived, to reduce deindividuation. Groups and deindividuated children were more than twice as likely to take extra candy. The transgression rate varied from 8 per cent of individuated individuals to 80 per cent of deindividuated groups.

Although anonymity often seems to increase aggressive antisocial behaviour (Dipboye, 1977), there are problematic findings. Zimbardo (1970) employed his deindividuation paradigm with Belgian soldiers and found that they gave electric shocks of shorter duration when dressed in cloaks and hoods. Zimbardo suggests that this might be because the soldiers were an intact group (i.e. already deindividuated), and the 'cloak and hood' procedure had the paradoxical effect of reducing deindividuation.

However, other studies reported reduced aggression when a person is anonymous or when a member of a group (Diener, 1976). In one study by Robert Johnson and Leslie Downing (1979), female participants administered shocks to confederate 'learners' in a paired-associate learning task. The women were deindividuated when clothed to resemble either a Ku Klux Klan member or a nurse. The experimenter highlighted the impact of the clothing by explicitly commenting on the resemblance. Half of each group also wore a large badge displaying their name in order to individuate them (i.e. deindividuation was reduced). Deindividuation failed to increase aggression, even among those dressed as Ku Klux Klan members (see Figure 11.12). However, those dressed as nurses were significantly less aggressive than those dressed as Ku Klux Klan members, and deindividuated nurses were the least aggressive of all. These studies tell us two important things:

1 Anonymity does not automatically lead people to be more aggressive and antisocial.
2 Normative expectations surrounding situations of deindividuation may influence behaviour. In the Johnson and Downing study, when women were dressed like a nurse they became more caring.

Regarding this second point, Gustav Jahoda (1982) has noted the similarity between Zimbardo's method of deindividuation (i.e. hood and robe) and the wearing of the *chador* (full-length veil) by women in some Islamic countries. Far from setting free antisocial impulses, the *chador* very precisely specifies one's social obligations.

More recently, Diener has assigned Duval and Wicklund's (1972) notion of objective self-awareness (awareness of oneself as an object of attention) a central role in the deindividuation process:

> A deindividuated person is prevented by situational factors present in a group from becoming self-aware. Deindividuated persons are blocked from awareness of themselves as separate individuals and from monitoring their own behaviour.
>
> Diener (1980, p. 210)

Factors present in crowds reduce self-awareness and create a psychological state of deindividuation that has specific consequences for behaviour (see Figure 11.13). Although these consequences do not inevitably include aggression, they do tend to facilitate the emergence of antisocial behaviour. In support of Diener's model, Steven Prentice-Dunn and Ronald Rogers (1982) found that participants who were prevented from becoming self-aware, by being

Figure 11.12 Administration of electric shocks as a function of deindividuation and type of uniform

- In a paired-associate learning task, women participants dressed in either of two uniforms believed that they gave shocks of various levels to a confederate learner.
- Those dressed as Ku Klux Klan members gave increased levels of shock to the learner, whereas those dressed as nurses gave reduced levels.
- Further, deindividuated participants (i.e. those not wearing large personal name badges) were not more aggressive, and in fact those deindividuated as nurses were the least aggressive of all.

Source: Based on data from Johnson and Downing (1979)

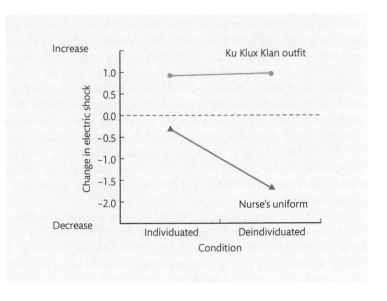

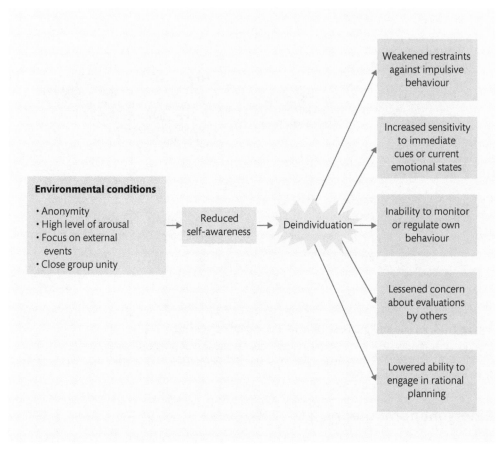

Figure 11.13 Self-awareness and deindividuation

Environmental factors present in crowd situations reduce self-awareness and create a state of deindividuation that produces typical crowd behaviours

Source: Based on Diener (1980)

subjected to loud rock music in a darkened room while working on a collective task, subsequently administered more intense electric shocks to a 'learner' than did participants who had been working individually in a quiet, well-illuminated room under instructions to concentrate on their own thoughts and feelings.

Another perspective on deindividuation distinguishes between public and private self-awareness (Carver and Scheier, 1981; Scheier and Carver, 1981). Reduced attention to one's private self (feelings, thoughts, attitudes and other private aspects of self) is equated with deindividuation, but it does not necessarily produce antisocial behaviour unless the appropriate norms are in place (see Figure 11.14). It is reduced attention to one's public self (how one wishes others to view one's conduct) that causes behaviour to be independent of social norms and thus to become antisocial.

All models of deindividuation, including the latter ones that focus on self-awareness, dwell on *loss* – loss of individuality, loss of identity, loss of awareness and 'loss' of desirable behaviour. Critics have suggested that all this talk about 'loss' may at best seriously restrict the range of collective behaviour we can talk about and at worst provide an inadequate understanding altogether. Instead, we should be focusing on *change* – change of identity, change of awareness and change of behaviour (e.g. Klein, Spears and Reicher, 2007; Postmes and Spears, 1998; Reicher, Spears and Postmes, 1995; also see Haslam and Reicher, 2005, 2012) (see the fifth focus question).

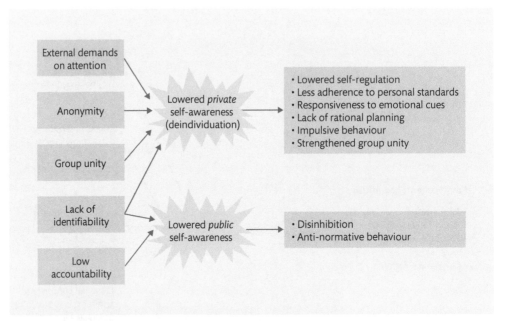

Figure 11.14 Private and public self-awareness and deindividuation

Environmental factors present in crowd situations reduce public and/or private self-awareness, but it is the reduction of public self-awareness that is associated with disinhibited and anti-normative crowd behaviours

Source: Based on Hogg and Abrams (1988)

Emergent norm theory

Emergent norm theory
Collective behaviour is regulated by norms based on distinctive behaviour that arises in the initially normless crowd.

Emergent norm theory takes a very different approach to the explanation of collective behaviour (Turner, 1974; Turner and Killian, 1957). Rather than treating collective behaviour as pathological or instinctual behaviour, it focuses on collective action as norm-governed behaviour, much like any other group behaviour. The sociologist R. H. Turner (not the social psychologist John Turner) believes that what is distinct about the crowd is that it has no formal organisation or tradition of established norms to regulate behaviour, so the problem of explaining crowd behaviour is to explain how a norm emerges from within the crowd (hence, 'emergent norm theory'; see Figure 11.15). People in a crowd find themselves together under circumstances in which there are no clear norms to indicate how to behave. Their attention is attracted by distinctive behaviour (or the behaviour of distinctive individuals). This behaviour implies a norm and consequently there is pressure against non-conformity. Inaction on the part of the majority is interpreted as tacit confirmation of the norm, which consequently amplifies pressures against non-conformity.

By focusing on norms, emergent norm theory acknowledges that members of a crowd may communicate with one another in the elaboration of appropriate norms of action. However, the general nature of crowd behaviour is influenced by the role of distinctive behaviour, which is presumably behaviour that is relatively rare in most people's daily lives: for instance, antisocial behaviour. Two other critical observations have been made. Diener (1980) correctly observes that a norm-regulated crowd would have to be a self-aware crowd (there is no need for people to comply with norms unless they are identifiable and thus individuated and self-aware), yet evidence indicates that self-awareness is very low in crowds. Indeed, an experiment by Leon Mann and his colleagues (Mann, Newton and Innes, 1982) supports Diener's view: irrespective of whether a norm of leniency or aggressiveness had been established by a confederate, participants were more aggressive when anonymous than when identifiable. However, anonymous participants were also more aggressive when the aggressive norm was in place.

The second critical observation comes from Steve Reicher (1982, 1987), who reminds us that crowds rarely come together in a normative vacuum. More often than not, members of a crowd

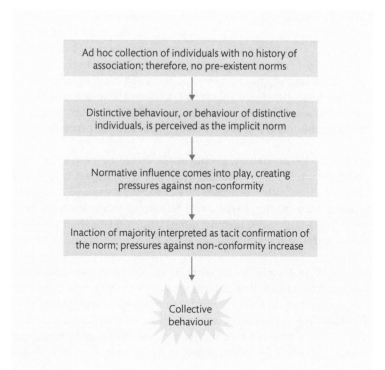

Figure 11.15 Emergent norm theory

In initially normless crowds, distinctive behaviours are the basis for a relevant norm to emerge to regulate behaviour

Source: Based on Turner and Killian (1957)

congregate for a specific purpose and thus bring with them a clear set of shared norms to regulate their behaviour as members of a specific group (e.g. a crowd of people welcoming the Queen, watching the Olympics, demonstrating outside Parliament or protesting on campus). The lack of tradition of established norms that Turner refers to may be more myth than reality. There is a logic to the crowd, Reicher argues, that is not adequately captured by emergent norm theory.

Social identity theory

An important aspect of crowd behaviour that is usually ignored is that it is actually an *inter-group* phenomenon (Reicher and Potter, 1985). Many crowd events involve a direct collective confrontation between, for instance, police and rioters or rival gangs or team supporters, and

Emergent norms theory
Is urban disorder a response to primitive aggressive instincts – or is it an extreme example of normatively regulated goal-oriented action?

even where no direct confrontation occurs, there is symbolic confrontation in that the crowd event symbolises a confrontation between, for instance, the crowd (or the wider group it represents) and the state. For example, Cliff Stott and his colleagues' analysis of riots at football matches shows quite clearly how these events are intergroup confrontations between supporters and police, and that how the rioting supporters behave is impacted quite significantly by how the police behave, and vice versa (Stott and Adang, 2004; Stott, Hutchison and Drury, 2001). Even ostensibly issueless student campus riots are ultimately intergroup confrontations between the rioters and the authorities who are called to quell the disturbance (Ruddell, Thomas and Way, 2005).

A second point is that, far from losing identity, people in the crowd actually assume the identity provided by the crowd: there is a change from idiosyncratic personal identity to shared social identity as a crowd member. These points are made by Reicher (1982, 1987, 1996, 2001), who applies social identity theory (this chapter) to collective behaviour. This analysis has been extended and called the SIDE model, or social identity model of deindividuation phenomena (Klein, Spears and Reicher, 2007; Postmes and Spears, 1998; Reicher, Spears and Postmes, 1995).

Individuals come together, or find themselves together, as members of a specific social group for a specific purpose (e.g. conservationists protesting against environmental destruction). There is a high degree of shared social identity, which promotes social categorisation of self and others in terms of that group membership. It is this wider social identity that provides the limits for crowd behaviour. For example, for certain groups violence may be legitimate (e.g. neo-Nazi groups in Germany), while for others it may not (e.g. supporters at a cricket match).

While these general group norms provide the limits for acceptable crowd behaviour, there are often few norms to indicate how to behave in the specific context of the crowd event. Crowd members look to the identity-consistent behaviour of others, usually core group members, for guidance. Self-categorisation produces conformity to these context-specific norms of conduct. This explains why different groups in a crowd event often behave differently. For example, the police act in one way, while the protesters act in a different way because, despite being exposed to the same environmental stimuli, their behaviour is being controlled by different group memberships.

This analysis seems to be consistent with what actually goes on in a crowd. For example, Robert Fogelson's (1970) analysis of American race riots of the 1960s showed one noteworthy feature: that the violence was not arbitrary and without direction; and Milgram and Toch (1969) report accounts from participants in the Watts riot in which a sense of positive social identity is strongly emphasised. Reicher (1984; Reicher and Potter, 1985) uses his analysis to account for a specific riot, which occurred in the spring of 1980 in the St Paul's district of Bristol (this was a forerunner of subsequent widespread rioting in other cities in Britain during the early 1980s). Three important points that emerged from this analysis were:

1 The violence, burning and looting were not unconstrained: the crowd was 'orderly' and the rioters were selective. Aggression was directed only at symbols of the state – the banks, the police and entrepreneurial merchants in the community.

2 The crowd remained within the bounds of its own community – St Paul's.

3 During and as a consequence of the riot, rioters felt a strong sense of positive social identity as members of the St Paul's community.

All this makes sense when it is recognised that the riot was an anti-government protest on the part of the St Paul's community, an economically disadvantaged area of Bristol with very high unemployment during a time of severe national unemployment. Reicher's general analysis of riots has also been used successfully to explain the spate of urban riots that swept Britain in 2011 (Reicher and Stott, 2011), and the riot that occurred at the 1999 Woodstock music festival marking the 30th anniversary of the original festival (Vider, 2004).

Improving intergroup relations

Different theories of prejudice and intergroup behaviour spawn different emphases in the explanation of prejudice and conflict reduction. From the perspective of personality theories (e.g. authoritarian personality, dogmatism; **see Chapter 10**), prejudice reduction requires changing the personality of the prejudiced person. More precisely, it would involve ensuring that particular parental strategies of child rearing were avoided in order to prevent the creation of bigoted people. From the perspective of frustration–aggression theory **(Chapter 10)** or relative deprivation theory (this chapter), prejudice and intergroup conflict can be minimised by preventing frustration, lowering people's expectations, distracting people from realising that they are frustrated, providing people with harmless (non-social) activities through which to vent their frustration, or ensuring that aggressive associations are minimised among frustrated people.

Minimisation of aggressive cues and increasing non-aggressive cues seem to be important. For example, there is substantial research showing that if weapons are made less available, aggression is reduced. When Jamaica implemented strict gun control and censorship of gun scenes on TV and in films in 1974, robbery and shooting rates dropped dramatically (Diener and Crandall, 1979), and when Washington, DC, introduced handgun control laws there was a similar reduction in violent crime (Loftin, McDowall, Wiersema and Cottey, 1991). The mere sight of a gun, either real or an image, can induce a **weapons effect** (**see Chapter 12**). On the other hand, non-aggressive cues such as infants and laughter can reduce aggression (Berkowitz, 1984; **see also an account in Chapter 12 of how the depiction of violence in the media can increase the incidence of later antisocial acts**).

Weapons effect
The mere presence of a weapon increases the probability that it will be used aggressively.

For realistic conflict theory (this chapter), it is the existence of superordinate goals and cooperation for their achievement that gradually reduces intergroup hostility and conflict. The avoidance of mutually exclusive goals would also help. Finally, from a social identity perspective (this chapter), prejudice and overt conflict will wane to the extent that intergroup stereotypes become less derogatory and polarised, and mutually legitimised non-violent forms of intergroup competition exist.

Propaganda and education

Propaganda messages, such as official exhortations that people should not be prejudiced, are usually formulated with reference to an absolute standard of morality (e.g. humanism). This may be effective for those people who subscribe to the standard of morality that is being invoked. It may also suppress more extreme forms of discrimination because it communicates social disapproval of discrimination.

Since prejudice is at least partly based in ignorance (Stephan and Stephan, 1984), education – particularly the formal education of children – that promotes tolerance of diversity may reduce bigotry (Stephan and Stephan, 2001). This can involve teaching children about the moral implications of discrimination or teaching them facts about different groups. One problem with this strategy is that formal education has only a marginal impact if children are systematically exposed to prejudice outside the classroom (e.g. bigoted parents, chauvinistic advertising and the material consequences of discrimination).

Another educational strategy that may be more effective is to allow children to experience being a victim of prejudice. In 1970 Jane Elliot, an Iowa schoolteacher, made a short movie called *The Eye of the Storm* of a classroom demonstration in which she divided her class of very young children into those with blue and those with brown eyes. For one day the 'brown eyes', and then for one day the 'blue eyes', were assigned inferior status: they were ridiculed, denied privileges, accused of being dull, lazy and sloppy, and made to wear a special collar. It was hoped that the experience of being stigmatised would be unpleasant enough to make the children think twice about being prejudiced against others.

Traditional sex-roles
Stereotypes are difficult to change and perhaps more so in the face of subtle advertising

One problem about prejudice is that it is *mindless,* a knee-jerk reaction to others as stereotypes. Recall from earlier in this chapter that even minimal intergroup categorisation can automatically produce ingroup favouritism (Otten and Wentura, 1999). What would happen if children were taught to be mindful of others, to think about others not as stereotypes but as complex, whole individuals? Would stereotypical reactions be reduced? Langer, Bashner and Chanowitz (1985) explored this idea in the context of how young children think and feel about the handicapped. Children who were trained to be *mindful* of others showed more positive attitudes and behaviour towards other children who were handicapped. Generally, the development of an ability to empathise with others significantly reduces one's capacity to harm those others physically, verbally, or indirectly via decisions and institutions (Miller and Eisenberg, 1988). Empathy is one strand in the development of acting prosocially (**see Chapter 13**).

Intergroup contact

Unfavourable outgroup attitudes are a core feature of prejudice and conflict. Such attitudes are enshrined in widespread social ideologies and are maintained by impoverished access to information that may disconfirm or improve negative attitudes. In most cases, such isolation is reinforced by real social and physical isolation of different groups from one another – the Protestant–Catholic situation in Northern Ireland is a case in point (Hewstone, Cairns, Voci, Paolini, McLernon, Crisp, et al., 2005). In other words, there is simply a chronic lack of intergroup contact, and little opportunity to meet real members of the outgroup. The groups are kept apart by educational, occupational, cultural and material differences, as well as by anxiety about negative consequences of contact for oneself (Stephan and Stephan, 1985).

In their integrated threat model Stephan and Stephan (2000) enumerate four sources of feelings of threat and anxiety that people can experience about and in anticipation of intergroup contact:

1 *realistic threat* – a sense of threat to the very existence of one's group, well-being, political power and so forth;

2 *symbolic threat* – a threat posed by the outgroup to one's values, beliefs, morals and norms;

3 *intergroup anxiety* – a threat to self (e.g. embarrassment, fear of rejection) which is experienced during intergroup interactions; and

4 *negative stereotypes* – fear of intergroup anxiety (not actually experienced intergroup anxiety but imagined or anticipated) based on negative stereotypes of an outgroup.

These feelings of anxiety and threat can cause people to avoid face-to-face intergroup contact and prefer some form of segregated existence. In some cases a more extreme response to perceived intergroup threat may be *collective narcissism* (Golec de Zavala, Cichocka, Eidelson and Jayawickreme, 2009) – in which a group develops a strong sense of ethnocentrism, entitlement, superiority, omnipotence, egocentrism, need for recognition and acknowledgement, coupled with high but unstable self-esteem and a fragile sense of self.

One situation in which contact or anticipated contact always whips up a storm of discontent is immigration. We saw coverage of the 2009 migrant camp near Calais, called 'the jungle', conflict between immigrants and Calabrian locals in Rosarno in southern Italy in early 2010, and the 2011 anti-immigration bomb attack and mass assassination of primarily teenagers in Norway by Anders Breivik. Immigration raises all sorts of fears ranging from competition for employment to erosion of cultural values.

Although the ideas outlined in Box 11.4 make good sense, more than half a century of research on the contact hypothesis yields a complex picture (e.g. Amir, 1976; Cook, 1985; Fox and Giles, 1993; Schofield, 1991), at least partly due to the predominance of uncontrolled field studies and partly because Allport's list of conditions has been extended to become overly specific. Nevertheless, Tom Pettigrew and Linda Tropp (2006) report an authoritative meta-analysis of 515 contact studies conducted between 1949 and 2000 with 713 samples across

Contact hypothesis
The view that bringing members of opposing social groups together will improve intergroup relations and reduce prejudice and discrimination.

Social psychology in action 11.4
Can intergroup contact improve intergroup relations?

One interesting line of research suggests that host nations construe the threat posed by immigration in different ways and thus respond to immigration differently depending on whether they define their national cultural identity in terms of heritage, history, blood ties and ties to the land (e.g. Germany, Italy, France and New Zealand), or in terms of common identity, shared civic values, and the social contract (e.g. Canada, Australasia and the United States) (e.g. Citrin, Green, Muste and Wong, 1997; Esses, Dovidio, Semenya and Jackson, 2005; Esses, Jackson, Dovidio and Hodson, 2005). The former is largely an ethnic national identity that prioritises community and common bonds (*Gemeinschaft*) – immigration is viewed as a cultural threat; the latter is largely a civic national identity that prioritises instrumental association and common identity (*Gesellschaft*) – immigration is viewed as a threat to civil society and access to employment. This distinction closely maps on to Prentice, Miller and Lightdale's (1994) distinction between common bond and common identity groups (discussed in Chapter 8).

Under the right circumstances, however, contact can reduce anxiety and improve intergroup relations (Brown and Hewstone, 2005; Pettigrew, 1998; Pettigrew and Tropp, 2006). This is the contact hypothesis and was first proposed scientifically by Gordon Allport (1954b) in the very year that the United States Supreme Court paved the way for the racial desegregation of the American education system. Here are Allport's conditions for contact:

- It should be prolonged and involve cooperative activity rather than casual and purposeless interaction. It was precisely this sort of contact that improved relations in Sherif's (1966) summer camp studies.

- It should occur within the framework of official and institutional support for integration. Although legislation against discrimination, or for equal opportunities, will not in itself abolish prejudice, it provides a social climate that is conducive to the emergence of more tolerant social practices.

- It should bring together people or groups of equal social status. Unequal status contact is more likely to confirm stereotypes and thus entrench prejudices.

For the role that the Internet can play in intergroup contact, together with a review of the contact hypothesis by the Israeli social psychologists Yair Amichai-Hamburger and Katelyn McKenna (2006), go to **http://jcmc.indiana.edu/vol11/issue3/amichai-hamburger.html**.

38 participating nations that reveals a robust effect – there is good evidence for Allport's core contention that cooperation, shared goals, equal status and the support of local authorities and norms are the most important and beneficial preconditions for intergroup contact to produce positive intergroup attitude change. Certain forms of contact can, paradoxically, reduce stereotype threat – the tendency for people's task behaviour to confirm others' negative stereotypes of one's group (Crisp and Abrams, 2008; **see Chapter 10**).

There are, however, some critical issues concerning precisely how contact may have effects (see overviews by Brewer and Miller, 1996; Brown, 1995, 1996; Hewstone, 1994, 1996; Pettigrew, 1998). These issues include the role of similarity and the process of generalisation of favourable interindividual attitudes to favourable intergroup attitudes.

Similarity

It has long been believed that prejudice is based in ignorance and the perception of irreconcilable intergroup differences (Pettigrew, 1971; Stephan and Stephan, 1984). Contact causes people to recognise that they are in fact a great deal more similar than they had thought and hence to get to like one another (Byrne, 1971; **also see Chapter 13**). There are some problems with this perspective:

- Because groups are often very different, contact is likely to bring to light more profound or more widespread differences, and hence to reduce liking further and produce a deterioration in intergroup attitudes (e.g. Bochner, 1982).

- As groups are actually so different, it may be misleading to promulgate the view that they are similar; this will establish false-positive expectations that are disconfirmed by contact.

- Research indicates that intergroup attitudes are not merely a matter of ignorance or unfamiliarity; rather, they reflect real conflict of interest between groups and are often maintained by the very existence of social categories. New knowledge made available by contact is unlikely to change attitudes.

Generalisation

Contact between representatives of different groups is supposed to improve attitudes towards the group as a whole – not just the specific outgroup members involved in the encounter. Weber and Crocker (1983) suggested three models of how this might happen:

1 *Bookkeeping* – the accumulation of favourable information about an outgroup gradually improves the stereotype. If outgroup information is stored in terms of exemplars, dramatic

The contact hypothesis
Ethnically mixed social occasions, like this street scene, are now common in many countries. When does such close contact between cultures improve intergroup relations?

attitude changes can occur as new exemplars are added or retrieved (Smith and Zárate, 1992).

2 *Conversion* – dramatically counter-stereotypical information about an outgroup causes a sudden change in attitudes.

3 *Subtyping* – stereotype-inconsistent information produces a subtype, so the outgroup stereotype becomes more complex but the superordinate category remains unchanged.

In general, research indicates that contact improves attitudes towards the participants but does not generalise to the group as a whole (Amir, 1976; Cook, 1978). One explanation is that most intergroup contact is actually *interpersonal* contact: that is, contact between individuals as individuals, not group members. There is no good reason why an attitude towards one person should generalise to other people who are not categorically related to that person. For example, if you like Miguel as a friend, and the fact that he happens to be Spanish is irrelevant, then your liking for Miguel will not generalise to anyone else who just happens to be Spanish, or to the category 'Spanish' as a whole.

This raises an interesting paradox: perhaps intergroup contact is more likely to generalise if people's group affiliations are made *more,* not less, salient during contact – the *mutual differentiation model* (Hewstone and Brown, 1986; Johnston and Hewstone, 1990). There is some support for this idea. David Wilder (1984) had participants from rival colleges come into contact over a cooperative task in which the outgroup person, who was either highly typical or highly atypical of that college, behaved in a pleasant or unpleasant manner. Those taking part evaluated the other college as a whole after the contact. Figure 11.16 shows that, relative to a no-contact control, it was only where contact was both pleasant and with a typical outgroup

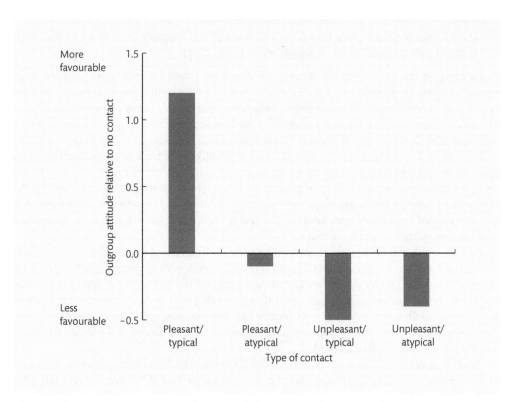

Figure 11.16 Outgroup attitude as a function of pleasantness of contact and outgroup typicality of target

Relative to no contact, attitudes towards a rival college improved only when contact was both pleasant and with a typical member of the other college

Source: Based on data from Wilder (1984)

member that there was generalised improvement of attitude (see also Rothbart and John, 1985; Weber and Crocker, 1983).

Norman Miller and Marilynn Brewer (1984; Miller, Brewer and Edwards, 1985) have a different perspective. They argue that contact that draws attention to people's group affiliations will rapidly degenerate into conflict and thus to a deterioration of generalised attitudes. Instead, they recommend interpersonal encounters that stress socioemotional aspects and avoid group or task-related aspects of the encounter: that is, 'decategorisation' or personalisation. This seems to work (Hamburger, 1994), but as yet the idea has been tested only in abstract experimental settings, where intergroup relations lack the powerful emotions and personal investments associated with 'real' intergroup relations. Where real intergroup conflict exists (e.g. between Catholics and Protestants in Northern Ireland), it may be almost impossible to distract people from their group affiliations.

Stephen Wright and his colleagues have proposed a more promising variant of the interpersonal contact idea, called **the extended contact effect**. They suggest, and provide some evidence, that intergroup attitudes can improve if people witness or have knowledge of rewarding cross-group interpersonal friendships between others – if my friend John has close outgroup friends then maybe the outgroup isn't quite as bad as I thought (Wright, Aron, McLaughlin-Volpe and Ropp (1997). This is able to happen because members of the same group have a common identity that links them and allows them, in the words of Wright, Aron and Tropp (2002), to *include the other in the self* –to develop a degree of intersubjectivity that allows them to experience others as themselves. Davies and her colleagues found in a meta-analysis that cross-group friendships can improve intergroup attitudes. Effective strategies are:

- self-disclosure, which develops intimacy and helps to forge interpersonal emotional bonds;
- longer periods of time spent together; and especially
- acts that engage an outgroup friend, such as doing things together and being mutually supportive (Davies, Tropp, Aron, Pettigrew and Wright, 2011).

Building on the idea of extended contact Richard Crisp and his colleagues have also suggested and provided evidence that *imagined contact* may help improve intergroup attitudes (Crisp and Turner, in press). For example Sofia Stathi and her colleagues report three experiments: participants who imagined a positively toned encounter with a single outgroup member subsequently felt more confident about future interactions with the outgroup in general. They also found that imagining contact was maximally effective at achieving generalisation when group as opposed to individuating information was salient; and when the imagined interaction involved an outgrouper who was typical as opposed to atypical (Stathi, Crisp and Hogg, 2011). Given that prejudice can be sustained by intergroup isolation and therefore many groups simply have limited contact with one another, imagined contact may have significant potential as a tool for improving intergroup attitudes.

Related to the extended contact idea, and perhaps to the role of self-disclosure mentioned above, is the notion that perspective taking plays a role in improving intergroup attitudes. If we are able to take the perspective of another person and experience the world as they do, we are less likely to harbour harmful negative attitudes about that person and perhaps more likely to behave prosocially towards them **(see Chapter 14)**. There is now some evidence that perspective taking can improve intergroup attitudes (Galinsky, 2002; Galinsky and Moskowitz, 2000; Vescio, Sechrist and Paolucci, 2003).

Another process that does not involve drawing attention to the original intergroup context is 'recategorisation'. Sam Gaertner's *common ingroup identity model* (Gaertner and Dovidio, 2000; Gaertner, Dovidio, Anastasio, Bachman and Rust, 1993; Gaertner, Mann, Murrell and Dovidio, 1989; Gaertner, Rust, Dovidio, Bachman and Anastasio, 1996) suggests that if members of opposing groups can be encouraged to recategorise themselves as members of the same group, intergroup attitudes will, by definition, not only improve but actually disappear (see below for some limitations of this process).

Extended contact effect
Knowing about an ingroup member who shares a close relationship with an outgroup member can improve one's own attitudes towards the outgroup.

Contact policy in multicultural contexts

Initially, it might seem that the most non-discriminatory and unprejudiced way to approach inter-ethnic relations is to be 'colour-blind': that is, to ignore group differences completely (Berry, 1984; Schofield, 1986). This is a 'melting-pot' policy, where all groups are ostensibly treated as equal (see also the concept of *assimilation* **discussed in Chapter 16**). There are at least three problems with this approach:

1 It ignores the fact that discrimination has disadvantaged certain groups (e.g. regarding education or health), and that unless positive steps are taken to rectify the problem, the disadvantage will simply persist.

2 It ignores the reality of ethnic/cultural differences (e.g. the Muslim dress code for women).

3 The melting pot is not really a melting pot at all, but rather a 'dissolving' pot, where ethnic minorities are dissolved and assimilated by the dominant social group: minority groups are stripped of their cultural heritage and cease to exist.

The extensive riots in France in November 2005 have been attributed to that country's adoption of cultural monism and ethnic assimilation – an approach that does not formally recognise cultural/ethnic differences within France despite the presence of huge numbers of North African Muslims. This assimilationist policy of being blind to cultural/ethnic/racial differences has, ironically, created ghettos of cultural disadvantage and associated discrimination and prejudice. A quite remarkable side effect of this denial of culture difference is that there are virtually no statistics on cultural/ethnic issues in France.

The alternative to assimilationism is pluralism or multiculturalism (Verkuyten, 2006) – an approach that draws attention to and responds to the reality of cultural diversity in an attempt to improve negative attitudes and redress disadvantage, at the same time as the cultural integrity of different groups is preserved **(see Chapter 16)**. This approach aims to achieve a multicultural society in which intergroup relations between the constituent groups are harmonious. Empirical research suggests that intergroup arrangements that resemble multiculturalism may be quite effective in reducing intergroup conflict (Hornsey and Hogg, 2000a; see below). However, recent events indicate that pluralism may need to be implemented carefully in order for it not to sustain hidden conflicts and nourish separatism. Cases in point are Britain and Australia, two countries that in different ways provide strong political support for pluralism – for example, it was disaffiliated Muslim youths who bombed public transport in London in July 2005, and in Australia there were large anti-Lebanese riots in Sydney in December 2005.

Superordinate goals

In his summer camp studies, Sherif (1966) managed to improve intergroup relations between warring factions by allowing them to cooperate to achieve a number of superordinate goals (shared goals that were unachievable by either group alone). The effectiveness of providing a superordinate goal has been confirmed by other studies (Brown and Abrams, 1986; Ryen and Kahn, 1975; Turner, 1981b; Worchel, 1979). The European Union provides a wonderful natural laboratory to study the effect of a superordinate identity (European) on inter-subgroup relations (between nations within Europe) (e.g. Chryssochoou, 2000; Cinnirella, 1997; Huici et al., 1997). One particularly effective superordinate goal is resistance to a shared threat from a common enemy (Dion, 1979; Wilder and Shapiro, 1984). This is the basis of alliances that can temporarily improve relations between erstwhile opponents (e.g. the existence of the former Soviet Union provided a common foe to unite Western nations for almost forty-five years).

There is an important qualification. Superordinate goals do not reduce intergroup conflict if the groups fail to achieve the goal. For example, Steve Worchel and his colleagues created competitive, cooperative or independent relations between two groups and then provided a superordinate goal that the groups either achieved or failed to achieve. The superordinate goal improved intergroup relations in all cases except where previously competitive groups failed to achieve the goal. In this condition, relations actually deteriorated (Worchel, Andreoli and Folger, 1977).Unsuccessful intergroup cooperation to achieve a superordinate goal appears to worsen intergroup relations only when the failure can be attributed, rightly or wrongly, to the actions of the outgroup (Worchel and Novell, 1980).

Where there is sufficient external justification, and the outgroup is not blamed, there is the more usual improvement in intergroup relations. For example, the 1982 Falklands conflict between Britain and Argentina provided a superordinate goal to reduce factional conflict within Argentina. The cooperative exercise failed (Argentina lost the war), and, because the actions of the junta could easily be blamed, there was renewed factional conflict, which led almost immediately to the junta being overthrown (Latin American Bureau, 1982).

Pluralism and diversity

One of the main problems of intergroup relations is that, in most contexts, groups are actually subgroups wholly nested within larger groups or cross-cut with them (Crisp, Ensari, Hewstone and Miller, 2003; **see Chapter 8**). For example, the psychology department at your university is a group nested with the larger university, whereas the group of social psychologists is a cross-cutting category because its membership stretches across many universities around the world. In these situations it is rare for all subgroups to have an equal representation in the defining features of the overarching identity – more often than not, one group is much better represented, with the consequence that other groups feel subordinate (Mummendey and Wenzel, 1999; Wenzel, Mummendey and Waldzus, 2007). A similar problem exists when one organisation merges with or acquires another organisation – the post-merger entity contains within it both pre-merger entities and usually one pre-merger entity has lower status and poor representation in the post-merger entity (e.g. Terry, Carey and Callan, 2001).

Even where relations among subgroups are reasonably good, another problem, associated with superordinate goals, emerges. Intense or prolonged cooperation to achieve a shared goal can gradually blur intergroup boundaries (Gaertner and Dovidio, 2000; see discussion above of the common ingroup identity model). Although this may seem an ideal solution to intergroup conflict, it can backfire. Even though the groups may have superordinate goals, they may also wish to maintain their individual identities and so resist the perceived threat of becoming a single entity. New conflicts can thus arise to maintain intergroup distinctiveness. This effect has been observed in a chemical plant (Blake, Shepard and Mouton, 1964), an engineering factory (Brown, 1978) and the laboratory (Brown and Wade, 1987; Deschamps and Brown, 1983). It will be interesting to see if the current pressures in Europe for international cooperation in the service of superordinate economic goals (the European Union) increase international conflict on other dimensions in order to maintain national distinctiveness.

Hornsey and Hogg (2000a, 2000b, 2000c) have conducted a programme of research suggesting that a careful balancing of superordinate identity and positive subgroup distinctiveness may provide a promising blueprint for social harmony. This mimics the sociopolitical strategy of multiculturalism or cultural pluralism that is pursued by countries such as Australia and Canada. This arrangement works because by retaining distinct cultural identities there is no threat that would provoke intergroup hostility. At the same time, the existence of a superordinate identity can cause subgroups to see themselves as distinct groups, with complementary roles, all working on the same team towards integrative goals. More broadly, this idea suggests that the answer to intergroup conflict may be to build groups that not only are based on tolerance for diversity but actually celebrate diversity as a defining feature of their social identity (Niedenthal and Beike, 1997; Roccas and Brewer, 2002; Wright, Aron and Tropp, 2002; see also Hogg and Hornsey, 2006).

A final point about goal relations and social harmony picks up on our earlier discussion of zero-sum and non-zero-sum goals. Where two groups see their goal relations as *zero-sum*, they are characterising their relationship as competitive – if they get a lot, we get a little. There is a fixed pie to divide up, and therefore their actions are frustrating our goals. Where two groups see their goal relations as *non-zero-sum,* they are characterising their relationship as cooperative – if they get a lot, we get a lot. The pie can get bigger if we work together, and therefore their actions are helping us to achieve our goals. Goal relations do not have to be accurate perceptions – they are subject to ideology and rhetoric. Take the immigration debates in Britain, France, Germany and virtually any country around the world. One side argues that immigration is bad because immigrants come along and take people's jobs and soak up public money – a zero-sum rhetoric that is associated with xenophobia, prejudice and intolerance towards immigrants. The other side argues that immigration is good because immigrants bring skills, energy and enthusiasm, which create new jobs and additional wealth – a non-zero-sum rhetoric that is associated with internationalism and positive attitudes towards immigrants and immigration.

Communication and negotiation

Groups in conflict can try to improve intergroup relations by communicating directly about the conflict and negotiating to resolve it. This can be done through bargaining, mediation or arbitration. These are very complex procedures that are prey to all sorts of psychological barriers to dispute resolution (e.g. self-esteem, emotion, misattribution; Ross and Ward, 1995; Thompson and Loewenstein, 2003; Thompson, 2009; Thompson, Medvec, Seiden and Kopelman, 2001). One real problem is that it can be difficult for negotiators to take the perspective of the other – a failure that is amplified by the intergroup nature of the negotiation and which makes compromise almost impossible (Carroll, Bazerman and Maury, 1988; Galinsky and Mussweiler, 2001). In addition, many crucial negotiations are between cultures, and thus a host of cross-cultural communication issues can arise to complicate things (e.g. Carnevale and Leung, 2001; Kimmel, 1994; see also R. Bond and Smith, 1996; Smith and Bond, 1998).

Bargaining

Intergroup negotiations are generally between representatives of the opposing groups: for example, trade union and management may try to resolve disputes by direct negotiation between representatives. One of the most significant intergroup negotiations of the twentieth century was the February 1945 meeting in Yalta in the Crimea between Stalin, Churchill and Roosevelt, as representatives of the soon-to-be victorious Allies of the Second World War: the Soviet Union, Britain and the United States. The negotiation of international differences at that meeting has determined the nature of the world to the present day. Social psychological research indicates that when people are bargaining on behalf of social groups to which they belong, they tend to bargain much more fiercely and less compromisingly than if they were simply bargaining for themselves (Benton and Druckman, 1974; Breaugh and Klimoski, 1981). The effect is enhanced when negotiators are aware that they are being observed by their constituents, either directly or through the media (Carnevale, Pruitt and Britton, 1979).

Bargaining
Process of intergroup conflict resolution where representatives reach agreement through direct negotiation.

This 'bullish' strategy of relative intransigence is less likely to secure a satisfactory compromise than a more interpersonal orientation in which both parties make reciprocal concessions (Esser and Komorita, 1975; Komorita and Esser, 1975). Direct negotiation between group representatives is therefore quite likely to reach an impasse, in which neither group feels it can compromise without losing face. A case in point is George Bush senior and Saddam Hussein's media-orchestrated bargaining over the plight of Kuwait in 1990, which seemed mainly to involve Bush threatening to 'kick Saddam's ass' and Hussein threatening to make 'infidel' Americans 'swim in their own blood' – not a good start. More recently, in 2006, the Iranian president Mahmoud Ahmadinejad and the US president George Bush Jr traded insults in which Ahmadinejad accused Bush of being an infidel, and the latter accused the former of being a member of the 'axis of evil' – again, not a promising start.

Ian Morley and his colleagues have explored the interplay of intergroup and interpersonal factors in bargaining (Morley and Stephenson, 1977). They demonstrate that bargaining often follows a sequence of stages. The first stage is an intergroup one, in which representatives act very much in terms of group memberships and assess each group's power and the strength of each group's case. The second stage is more interpersonal, with individuals trying to establish harmonious interpersonal relations with one another in order to be able to solve problems more easily. The final stage is again more intergroup, with negotiators making sure that the final decision is consistent with the historical aims of their own group. Close interpersonal relations, which are encouraged by more informal bargaining procedures and contexts, can facilitate negotiation. However, close interpersonal relations also have a drawback – the group as a whole can become fearful of a 'sell-out' and can resort or return to more confrontational intergroup behaviour, which hinders the negotiation process.

There is a potentially important limitation of much social psychological research on bargaining – the wider intergroup context is often neglected as researchers focus only on the specific bargaining event as a form of social change (Morley, Webb and Stephenson, 1988). In reality, bargaining is often a way to maintain the status quo. Groups in conflict isolate from the wider context of intergroup relations a specific and circumscribed point of disagreement – one that can be solved. The solution of the specific problem then allows broader intergroup issues to remain unchanged.

Mediation

Mediation
Process of intergroup conflict resolution where a neutral third party intervenes in the negotiation process to facilitate a settlement.

To break the deadlock, a third party can be brought in for mediation between the groups (Pruitt, 1981). To be effective, mediators should have power and must be seen by both groups to be impartial (Lim and Carnevale, 1990), and the groups should already be fairly close in their positions (Rubin, 1980). Biased mediators are ineffective because they are not trusted, and weak mediators are ineffective because they exert little pressure on intransigent groups to be reasonable.

Although mediators have no power to impose a settlement, they can help in several important ways:

1 They are able to *reduce the emotional heat* associated with deadlock (Tetlock, 1988).

2 They can help to *reduce misperceptions,* encourage understanding and establish trust.

3 They can propose *novel compromises* that allow both groups to appear to win: that is, to change a zero-sum conflict (one in which one group's gains are precisely the other group's

Mediation
An effective mediator needs to have power and to be seen as impartial. In this respect, a football world cup context is no different from a legal setting

losses; the more one gains, the more the other loses) into a non-zero-sum conflict (where both groups can gain).

4 They can help both parties to make a *graceful retreat,* without losing face, from untenable positions.

5 They can *inhibit unreasonable claims* and behaviour by threatening to expose the group publicly as being unreasonable.

6 They can *reduce intragroup conflict* and thus help a group to clarify its consensual position.

History provides instances of effective mediation. For example, Henry Kissinger's shuttle diplomacy of the mid-1970s, which involved meeting each side separately over a period of two years after the 1973 Arab–Israeli conflict, produced a number of significant agreements between Israel and its Arab neighbours (Pruitt, 1981). In the late 1970s, using a slightly different strategy, Jimmy Carter secluded Egypt's president Anwar Sadat and Israel's prime minister Menachem Begin at Camp David near Washington in the United States. After thirteen days, an agreement was reached that ended a state of war that had existed between Israel and Egypt since 1948.

Arbitration

Many intergroup conflicts are so intractable, the underlying interests so divergent, that mediation is ineffective. The last resort is arbitration, in which the mediator or some other third party is invited to impose a mutually binding settlement. Research shows that arbitration really is the last resort for conflict resolution (McGillicuddy, Welton and Pruitt, 1987). The prospect of arbitration can backfire, because both groups adopt outrageous final positions in the hope that arbitration will produce a more favourable compromise (Pruitt, 1986). A way to combat this is through *final-offer arbitration,* where the third party chooses one of the final offers. This tends to encourage more reasonable final positions.

Arbitration
Process of intergroup conflict resolution in which a neutral third party is invited to impose a mutually binding settlement.

Conciliation

Although direct communication may help to improve intergroup relations, tensions and suspicions often run so high that direct communication is all but impossible. Instead, conflicting groups threaten, coerce or retaliate against one another, and if this behaviour is reciprocated, there is an escalation of the conflict. For example, during the Second World War Germany believed it could move Britain to surrender by bombing its cities, and the Allies believed that they could break Germany's will by bombing *its* cities. Similarly, Japan believed it could dissuade the United States from interfering in its imperial expansion in Asia by bombing Pearl Harbor, and the United States believed it could bring North Vietnam to the negotiating table by sustained bombing of cities and villages.

There are uncountable examples of the terrible consequences of threat, coercion and retaliation. Can this cycle be broken by one side adopting an unconditionally cooperative strategy in the hope that the other side will reciprocate? Laboratory research suggests that this does not work: unilateral unconditional cooperation simply invites retaliation and exploitation (Shure, Meeker and Hansford, 1965).

Charles Osgood (1962) suggested a more effective alternative that involves conciliation (i.e. not retaliation), but with enough strength to discourage exploitation. Called 'graduated and reciprocated initiatives in tension reduction' (with the acronym GRIT), it invokes social psychological principles to do with the norm of reciprocity and the attribution of motives. GRIT involves at least two stages:

Conciliation
Process whereby groups make cooperative gestures to one another in the hope of avoiding an escalation of conflict.

1 One party announces its conciliatory intent (allowing a clear attribution of non-devious motive), clearly specifies a small concession it is about to make (activates reciprocity norm) and invites its opponent to do likewise.

2 The initiator makes the concession exactly as announced and in a publicly verifiable manner. There is now strong pressure on the other group to reciprocate.

Laboratory research provides evidence for the effectiveness of this procedure. For example, a *tit-for-tat* strategy that begins with one cooperative act and proceeds by matching the other party's last response is both conciliatory and strong, and can improve interparty relations (Axelrod and Dion, 1988; Komorita, Parks and Hulbert, 1992). Direct laboratory tests of GRIT by Linskold and his colleagues (e.g. Linskold, 1978; Linskold and Han, 1988) confirm that the announcement of cooperative intent boosts cooperation, repeated conciliatory acts breed trust, and maintenance of power equality protects against exploitation. GRIT-type strategies have been used effectively from time to time in international relations: for example, between the Soviet Union and the United States during the Berlin crisis of the early 1960s, and between Israel and Egypt on a number of occasions.

Summary

- Intergroup behaviour can be defined as any behaviour that is influenced by group members' perceptions of an outgroup.
- Group members may engage in collective protest to the extent that subjectively they feel deprived as a group relative to their aspirations or relative to other groups.
- Competition for scarce resources tends to produce intergroup conflict. Cooperation to achieve a shared goal reduces conflict.
- Social categorisation may be the only necessary precondition for being a group and engaging in intergroup behaviour, provided that people identify with the category.
- Self-categorisation is the process responsible for psychologically identifying with a group and behaving as a group member (e.g. conformity, stereotyping, ethnocentrism, ingroup solidarity). Social comparison and the need for self-esteem motivate groups to compete in different ways (depending on the nature of intergroup relations) for relatively positive social identity.
- Crowd behaviour may not represent a loss of identity and regression to primitive antisocial instincts. Instead, it may be group behaviour that is governed by local contextual norms that are framed by a wider social identity.
- Prejudice, discrimination and intergroup conflict are difficult to reduce. Together, education, propaganda and shared goals may help, and simply bringing groups physically or psychologically into contact with one another can be effective provided a number of conditions are met. Other strategies include bargaining, mediation, arbitration and conciliation.

Key terms

Accentuation effect	Deindividuation	Frustration–aggression hypothesis
Arbitration	Depersonalisation	Illusory correlation
Authoritarian personality	Egoistic relative deprivation	Ingroup favouritism
Bargaining	Emergent norm theory	Intergroup behaviour
Cognitive alternatives	Entitativity	Intergroup differentiation
Collective behaviour	Ethnocentrism	Intergroup emotions theory
Commons dilemma	Extended contact effect	J-curve
Conciliation	Fraternalistic relative deprivation	Mediation
Contact hypothesis	Free-rider effect	Meta-contrast principle

Metatheory
Minimal group paradigm
Optimal distinctiveness
Prisoner's dilemma
Prototype
Realistic conflict theory
Reductionism

Relative deprivation
Relative homogeneity effect
Self-categorisation theory
Social categorisation
Social change belief system
Social competition
Social creativity

Social identity
Social identity theory
Social mobility belief system
Stereotype
Superordinate goals
System justification theory
Weapons effect

Literature, film and TV

Gandhi

1982 classic film by Richard Attenborough, starring Ben Kingsley as Gandhi. A film about social mobilisation, social action and collective protest. It shows how Gandhi was able to mobilise India to oust the British. The film touches on prejudice and group decision making and has wonderfully powerful and diverse examples of crowd scenes.

Germinal

Emile Zola's 1885 novel drawing attention to the misery experienced by poor French people during France's Second Empire. The descriptions of crowd behaviour are incredibly powerful, and were drawn upon by later social scientists, such as Gustave Le Bon, to develop their theories of collective behaviour.

The Road to Wigan Pier

George Orwell's 1937 novel capturing the plight of the English working class. A powerful, and strikingly contemporary, portrayal of relative deprivation.

Gran Torino

Clint Eastwood's 2008 film in which he also stars. Set in contemporary Detroit, Eastwood's character, Walt Kowalski, is a proud and grizzled Korean War veteran whose floridly bigoted attitudes are out of step with changing times. Walt refuses to abandon the neighbourhood he has lived in all his life, despite its changing demographics. The film is about his developing friendship with a Hmong teenage boy and his immigrant family – a poignant, and subtly uplifting, commentary on intergroup friendship and the development of intergroup tolerance and respect.

The Battle for Spain

Antony Beevor's 2006 history of the 1936–1939 Spanish Civil War – supremely scholarly, a bestseller and a real page-turner. A perfect case study for everything discussed in this chapter, it is a powerful account of the multilevel and contradictory complexities of intergroup relations in a global context. There is the ebb and flow of battle between the right-wing Nationalist and the left-wing Republican forces. But this war was also an endless conflict among nations and political factions struggling for power and influence in the early ascendance of Communism and the ominous run-up to the Second World War – Nazis, Fascists, Anarchists, Stalinists, Trotskyites, all play a part, as do the nations of Germany, Italy, France, Britain, Mexico and the Soviet Union.

Guided questions

1 How does the experience of relative deprivation impact on the tendency to aggress?

2 According to Sherif, prejudice arises when intergroup goals are incompatible. What does this mean? Did he offer a solution?

3 What is social identity? Can a person have multiple social identities? Watch *Social identity* in Chapter 11 of MyPsychLab at www.mypsychlab.com (also see http://www.youtube.com/watch?v=USxOoPu5a_g&feature=PlayList&p=CF9BEB353C1ABF85&playnext_from=PL&playnext=1&index=2).

MyPsychLab

4 How are minority group members' beliefs about intergroup relations important in planning for social change?

5 Trying to reduce prejudice by simply providing intergroup contact between people from different groups may not work very well. Why?

Learn more

Abrams, D., and Hogg, M. A. (2010). Social identity and self-categorization. In J. F. Dovidio, M. Hewstone, P. Glick, and V. M. Esses (eds), *The SAGE handbook of prejudice, stereotyping and discrimination* (pp. 179–93). London: SAGE. Up-to-date, detailed and comprehensive coverage of social identity research and theory.

Brewer, M. B. (2003). *Intergroup relations* (2nd edn). Philadelphia, PA: Open University Press. A very readable and complete overview of research on intergroup relations.

Brewer, M. B. (2007). The social psychology of intergroup relations: Social categorization, ingroup bias, and outgroup prejudice. In A. W. Kruglanski, and E. T. Higgins (eds), *Social psychology: Handbook of basic principles* (2nd edn, pp. 785–804). New York: Guilford Press. Comprehensive coverage of research on intergroup behaviour, and prejudice and discrimination.

Brown, R. J., and Gaertner, S. (eds) (2001). *Blackwell handbook of social psychology: Intergroup processes*. Oxford, UK: Blackwell. A collection of twenty-five chapters from leading social psychologists, covering the entire field of intergroup processes.

De Dreu, C. K. W. (2010). Social conflict: The emergence and consequences of struggle and negotiation. In S. T. Fiske, D. T. Gilbert, and G. Lindzey (eds), *Handbook of social psychology* (5th edn, Vol. 2, pp. 983–1023). New York: Wiley. Up-to-date and comprehensive discussion of intergroup conflict and the role of negotiation in resolving such conflicts.

Dovidio, J. F., and Gaertner, S. L. (2010). Intergroup bias. In S. T. Fiske, D. T. Gilbert, and G. Lindzey (eds), *Handbook of social psychology* (5th edn, Vol. 2, pp. 1084–1121). New York: Wiley. Up-to-date and detailed coverage of research on intergroup bias as a feature of intergroup behaviour.

Dovidio, J., Glick. P., Hewstone, M., and Esses, V. (eds) (2010). *Handbook of prejudice, stereotyping and discrimination*. London: SAGE. A collection of chapters by leading researchers on intergroup behaviour in the context of stereotyping and prejudice.

Fiske, S. T. (2010). Interpersonal stratification: Status, power, and subordination. In S. T. Fiske, D. T. Gilbert, and G. Lindzey (eds), *Handbook of social psychology* (5th edn, Vol. 2, pp. 941–82). New York: Wiley. Up-to-date and detailed overview of research on the power and status aspects of intergroup relations.

Hogg, M. A. (2006). Social identity theory. In P. J. Burke (ed.), *Contemporary social psychological theories* (pp. 111–36). Palo Alto, CA: Stanford University Press. Easily readable and still up-to-date overview of contemporary social identity theory.

Hogg, M. A. (2013). Intergroup relations. In J. Delamater, and A. Ward (eds), *Handbook of social psychology* (2nd edn, pp. 533–562). New York: Springer. Very accessible overview and review of social psychology research on intergroup relations, prejudice and discrimination.

Hogg, M. A., and Abrams, D. (1988). *Social identifications: A social psychology of intergroup relations and group processes*. London: Routledge. Detailed coverage of theory and research on group processes and intergroup relations from the perspective of social identity theory – probably still the most comprehensive text-style overview of social identity theory.

Hogg, M. A., and Abrams, D. (eds) (2001). *Intergroup relations: Essential readings*. Philadelphia, PA: Psychology Press. Annotated collection of key publications on intergroup relations. There is an introductory overview chapter and commentary chapters introducing each reading.

Hogg, M. A., and Abrams, D. (2007). Intergroup behavior and social identity. In M. A. Hogg, and J. Cooper (eds), *The SAGE handbook of social psychology: Concise student edition* (pp. 335–60). London: SAGE. A comprehensive overview of research on intergroup relations and social identity processes.

Levine, J. M. (ed.) (2013). *Group processes*. New York: Psychology Press. Absolutely up-to-date and comprehensive set of chapters by leading scholars on all aspects of group and intergroup processes.

Levine, J. M., and Hogg, M. A. (eds) (2010). *Encyclopedia of group processes and intergroup relations.* Thousand Oaks, CA: SAGE. A comprehensive and readable compendium of entries on all aspects of the social psychology of groups, written by all the leading scholars in the field.

Robinson, W. P. (ed.) (1996). *Social groups and identities: Developing the legacy of Henri Tajfel*. Oxford, UK: Butterworth-Heinemann. A collection of chapters from almost everyone who was closely associated with Tajfel's far-reaching insights on intergroup relations; although social identity and self-categorisation theory are well represented, there is also diversity and breadth in these chapters.

Stangor, C. (2004). *Social groups in action and interaction.* New York: Psychology Press. Comprehensive and accessible coverage of the social psychology of processes within and between groups.

Thompson, L. L. (2009). *The mind and heart of the negotiator* (4th edn). Upper Saddle River, NJ: Prentice Hall. The most recent edition of this classic book on the psychology of negotiation.

Yzerbyt, V., and Demoulin, S. (2010). Intergroup relations. In S. T. Fiske, D. T. Gilbert, and G. Lindzey (eds), *Handbook of social psychology* (5th edn, Vol. 2, pp. 1024–83). New York: Wiley. A thorough overview of the field of intergroup relations, in the most recent edition of the classic handbook – a primary source for theory and research.

CHAPTER 14
Attraction and close relationships

Chapter contents

Focus questions

1   Carol finds David more attractive than Paul but bumps into him less often. Who do you think Carol is most likely to get to like and perhaps have a relationship with?

2   Erik and Charles have been chatting over a few drinks when Erik remarks that he is 'profiting' from his latest romantic relationship. Charles doesn't know what to say, but thinks this a callous comment. Can you offer a more benign interpretation?

3   Even when they were dating, Kamesh felt that Aishani was mostly uncomfortable when they were with other people. She also avoided having other members of their families visit them. Now, Aishani does not seem very interested in their new baby. Are these events somehow connected?

4   Can we study love scientifically – or should we pack the statistics away and leave it to the poets? Robert Sternberg discusses his general approach and the main components of his triangular theory of love in Chapter 14 of MyPsychLab at www.mypsychlab.com.

will use which involves getting you to decide to buy a car by giving you a very low price

Go to MyPsychLab to explore video and test your understanding of key topics addressed in this chapter.

MyPsychLab

Use MyPsychLab to refresh your understanding with interactive summaries, explore topics further with video and audio clips and assess your progress with quick test and essay questions. To buy access or register your code, visit www.mypsychlab.com. You will also need a course ID from your instructor.

Liking, loving and affiliating

Collectively we are known as the species *Homo sapiens* – wise, knowing and judicious humans. However, as we have seen throughout this book, the *sapiens* bit is circumscribed – people are also strongly governed by feelings and emotions and by various forms of self-interest all tied tightly to our fundamentally social nature. Not only are our judgements sub-optimal, but we love and help, hate and fight. This chapter deals with the liking and the loving part, and more fundamentally with why we want to be with others. Perhaps there is a term missing from our dictionary: *Homo socius* – humans who can be allies, friends and partners. We start with the process of attraction, then take a step back to explore the reasons why we affiliate with (i.e. choose the company of) and become attached to others, and ask the time-honoured question, 'What is love?' We conclude with how our most intimate relationships can be maintained and what happens when they break down.

Attractive people

We just *know* when we are attracted to someone. We are allured, perhaps charmed, captivated, even enthralled. We want to know and spend time with that person. At one level, attraction is necessary for friendships of any kind to begin, though many first meetings are by chance. At another level, attraction can be the precursor to an intimate relationship. Do you believe in love at first sight?

Perhaps you subscribe to other popular sayings such as: *never judge a book by its cover*, *beauty is only skin deep* and *beauty is in the eye of the beholder*. Unfortunately for some of us, there is evidence that the primary cue in initially determining our evaluation of others is how they look. A meta-analysis of more than one hundred studies by Judith Langlois and her colleagues (Langlois, Kalakanis, Rubenstein, Larson, Hallam and Smoot, 2000) found that these sayings are myths rather than maxims. As a cautionary note, the overall impact of the findings is reduced because some studies focus on just two categories – the attractive and the unattractive. Bearing this in mind, Langlois and colleagues concluded that attractive people are different from those who are unattractive in how they are judged, how they are treated and how they behave. Here are some of the major findings:

> **Meta-analysis**
> Statistical procedure that combines data from different studies to measure the overall reliability and strength of specific effects.

- Attractive children received higher grades from their teachers, showed higher levels of intellectual competence, and were more popular and better adjusted than their unattractive counterparts.

- Attractive adults were more successful in their jobs, liked more, more physically healthy and more sexually experienced than unattractive adults. They had had more dates, held more traditional attitudes, had more self-confidence and self-esteem, and had slightly higher intelligence and mental health.

We can add more to the advantages of having good looks:

- If you are female, babies will gaze longer (Slater, Von der Schulenburg, Brown, Badenoch, Butterworth, Parsons and Samuels, 1998)!

- In computer-simulation studies, attractiveness is associated with some feminisation of facial features, even for male faces (Rhodes, Hickford and Jeffrey, 2000), and with having a slimmer figure (Gardner and Tockerman, 1994).

- An attractive person is a youthful person (Buss and Kenrick, 1998), is judged as more honest (Yarmouk, 2000), and, if a female defendant, gets an easier time from jurors (Sigall and Ostrove, 1975).

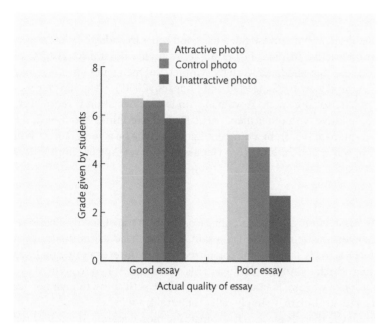

Figure 14.1 Being attractive can lead to better essay grades
Source: Based on data from Landy and Sigall (1974)

We noted above that attractive children receive higher grades than unattractive children. David Landy and Harry Sigall (1974) studied this effect experimentally in university students, asking the question, 'Does beauty signal talent?' Male students graded one or other of two essays of different quality, attached to which was a photograph of the supposed writer, a female student. The same essays were also rated by control participants, but without any photograph. The 'good' and 'poor' essays were paired in turn with either an attractive photograph or a relatively unattractive photograph. The answer to the researchers' question was 'yes' – sad to relate, better grades were given to the attractive female student (see Figure 14.1).

With attractiveness being such an asset, those who spend big on cosmetics and fashion could be making a real investment in their future! Short of this, just a smile can also work wonders Joe Forgas and his colleagues found that students who smile are punished less after a misdemeanour than those who do not (Forgas, O'Connor and Morris, 1983).

Evolution and attraction

Evolutionary theory, which identifies biological factors that trigger aggression, altruism and the emotions (**see Chapters 2**, **12**, **13 and 15**), also may help us understand some aspects of why we are attracted to some people, and how we might go about choosing a long-term partner. In an extreme form, David Buss (2003) used **evolutionary social psychology** to argue that close relationships can only be understood in terms of evolutionary theory. Let us consider what modern research has told us about our natural endowment.

Evolutionary social psychology
An extension of evolutionary psychology that views complex social behaviour as adaptive, helping the individual, kin and the species as a whole to survive.

The role of our genes

In the meta-analysis of studies by Langlois and colleagues cited above, the way that interpersonal attraction develops was related partly to how we select a mate. According to the evolutionary concept of *reproductive fitness*, people guess whether a prospective mate has good genes, using cues such as physical health, youthful appearance, and body and facial symmetry.

Fertility

Steven Gangestad and his colleagues have investigated the 'good genes hypothesis' in the search for traits that women find attractive in men. For example, women who sniffed T-shirts of unknown origin preferred those that had been worn by symmetrical men, but only when they were about to ovulate! (See the review by Gangestad and Simpson, 2000.) A woman's fertility status can affect how she relates to some men. A woman who is near ovulation is more likely to prefer a man who is competitive with other men, particularly if she thinks about having a short-term mate. A long-term mate is seen in a different light – will he be a good father? Will he be financially successful, warm and faithful? (See Gangestad, Garver-Apgar, Simpson and Cousins, 2007.)

Seeing red

Men have their foibles too. One windy day in San Francisco, Teddy is transfixed by Charlotte, an incredibly beautiful woman, whose red dress whooshes over her head as she stands on a grate (*The Woman in Red*, 1984). As it happens, the colour red catches the eye of other males as well as Teddy, according to research by Andrew Elliot and his colleagues. When red is used as a background colour in photos of a woman, it enhances her sexual attractiveness, though not her perceived intelligence. The red-sex link may simply reflect cultural traditions (e.g. red lipstick) or gender stereotypes. But maybe there is more to it – something more visceral. The colour red has been found to be a signal of readiness for mating in a range of animal species (Elliot and Niesta, 2008). The effect of red clothing was studied directly in comparing the evaluations of a woman dressed in either a red shirt or a white shirt. For men, the woman in red was sexually receptive, and in turn this mediated their perception of her as both attractive and sexually desirable (Pazda, Elliot and Greitemeyer, 2012).

The hourglass figure

There is little doubt that men have a strong interest in women's bodies and, consciously or not, respond to the female waist-to-hip ratio (WHR). Typically, men prefer the classic hourglass figure (a ratio of 0.70); the good genes hypothesis suggests this signifies youthfulness, good health and fertility. However, there are cultural and ecological influences: in foraging societies, being thin may mean being ill and so men prefer their women to be heavier (i.e. larger WHRs). In Western societies, where heaviness may indicate ill health, men prefer slimmer women (i.e. smaller WHRs) (Marlowe and Wetsman, 2001). These effects point to the role of social and contextual factors that go beyond genes.

Attractive faces

As well as acknowledging the role of biological explanation, Langlois and colleagues (Langlois, Kalakanis, Rubenstein, Larson, Hallam and Smoot, 2000) also tested the validity of three well-known maxims: *beauty is in the eye of the beholder, never judge a book by its cover* and *beauty is only skin-deep*. These question the assumption that physical beauty is ultimately important in real-life decisions, implying that social factors must play some part in how relationships are formed. For example, socialisation theory emphasises the effects on judgements of beauty of social and cultural norms and of experience; and social expectancy theory argues that social stereotypes (**see Chapter 2**) create their own reality.

How would evolutionary theory deal with the maxim *beauty is in the eye of the beholder*? Is physical attractiveness a matter of personal preference, or of fashion in a particular society and its history, or is it something else – in our genes? As part of her research programme dealing with face perception, Gill Rhodes (2006) has extensively researched the social information that our faces convey, including the cues that make a face attractive. One interesting finding is the 'pulling power' of the averageness effect (see Box 14.1 and Figure 14.2).

Averageness effect
Humans have evolved to prefer average faces to those with unusual or distinctive features.

The search for ideals

There are other characteristics of being attractive that may derive *in part* from our genes. Garth Fletcher (Fletcher, Tither, O'Loughlin, Friesen and Overall, 2004; also see Buss, 2003) studied the ideals (or standards) that college students look for in a partner. In long-term relationships, three 'ideal partner' dimensions appear to guide the preferences of both men and women:

- warmth–trustworthiness – showing care and intimacy;
- vitality–attractiveness – signs of health and reproductive fitness;
- status–resources – being socially prominent and financially sound.

A fair conclusion is that because humans are biological and physical entities, biological and physical characteristics are a major cue to initial attraction and that there is an evolutionary and universal basis for some of this. Let us turn now to a number of social and contextual factors also related to what we find attractive.

Social psychology in action 14.1
Physical appeal – evolutionary or cultural?

What kind of face do we prefer? The preferences of very young children and substantial cross-cultural consistency challenge the notion that standards of beauty are entirely dictated by culture. For example, body and facial symmetry (of right and left halves) in both women and men contributes to standards that most people have in judging beauty. Perhaps surprisingly, facial averageness is another plus.

Gill Rhodes (2006), who has researched extensively how we process information about the human face, asked whether facial beauty depends more on common physical qualities than on striking features. Participants judged caricatures of faces, each of which was systematically varied from average to distinctive. She found that averageness, rather than distinctiveness, was correlated with facial attractiveness (also see Rhodes, Sumich and Byatt, 1999). The averageness effect has also been found in other studies (e.g. Langlois, Roggman and Musselman, 1994).

Rhodes (Rhodes and Tremewan, 1996) suggested an evolutionary basis for this effect: average faces draw the attention of infants to those objects in their environment that most resemble the human face – an average face is like a prototype. Face preferences may be adaptations that guide mate choice. Why would facial averageness (and also facial symmetry) make a person more attractive? One possibility is that these cues make a face seem more familiar and less strange. Another possibility is that both averageness and symmetry are signals of good health and therefore of 'good genes' – cues that we latch on to in searching for a potential mate.

See Figure 14.2 for examples of how averageness has been created by combining sets of real faces into composite faces.

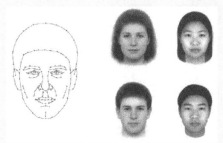

Figure 14.2 What makes a face attractive?
- Landmark points were used to align features across individual photographs.
- Face composites were created by averaging the features of 24 real faces.
- These four faces are composites and are usually rated as more attractive than a real individual face.

Source: Rhodes (2006)

What increases liking?

Suppose that someone has passed your initial 'attraction' test. What other factors encourage you to take the next step? This question has been well researched, to identify several crucial factors that determine how we come to like people even more:

- Proximity – do they live or work close by?
- Familiarity – do we feel that we know them?
- Similarity – are they people who are like us?

Proximity

There is a good chance that you will get to like people who are in reasonable **proximity** to where you live or work – think of this as the neighbourhood factor. In a famous study of a student housing complex, headed by Leon Festinger (who is also associated with the concept of cognitive dissonance, **discussed in Chapter 6**), it emerged that people were more likely to choose as friends those living in the same building and even on the same floor (Festinger, Schachter and Back, 1950). Subtle architectural features that influence social contact, such as the location of a staircase, can also affect the process of making acquaintances and establishing friendships.

Look at the apartment block in Figure 14.3. Of the lower-floor residents, those in apartments 1 and 5 interacted most often with people living on the upper floor. Note that the residents in apartments 1 and 5 are close to the staircases used by upper-floor residents and are therefore more likely to encounter them. Friendships occurred more often between 1 and 6 than between 2 and 7; and likewise between 5 and 10 than between 4 and 9. Although the physical distance between residents within each pair is the same, the interaction rate varied: becoming acquainted depended on the traffic flow.

People who live close by are *accessible*, so that interacting with them requires little effort and the rewards of doing so have little cost. Consider your immediate neighbours: you expect to continue interacting with them and it is better that you are at ease when you do so rather than feeling stressed.

If at the outset you think that you are more likely to interact with John rather than Brian it is probable that you will anticipate (perhaps hope!) that you will like John more (Berscheid, Graziano, Monson and Dermer, 1976). In the first focus question, who will Carol like more, David or Paul?

Proximity
Chatting with neighbours in the street is an important form of social interaction. It increases mutual liking and also promotes cooperation

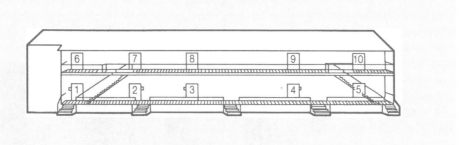

Figure 14.3 Friendship choice, physical proximity and housing design
Source: Based on Festinger, Schachter and Back (1950)

Proximity became a more nuanced psychological concept during the twentieth century. The potentially negative impact of having a 'long-distance lover' is lessened by a phone call, an email, Facebook posting or better still by real-time audio-video contact using, for example, Skype or FaceTime (see the review by Bargh and McKenna, 2004). Can we actually pursue a relationship on the net? (See Box 14.2.)

Familiarity

Proximity generally leads to greater familiarity – a friend is rather like your favourite pair of shoes, something that you feel comfortable about. **Familiarity** can account for why we gradually come to like the faces of strangers if we encounter them more often (Moreland and Beach, 1992). In contrast, when something familiar seems different, people feel uncomfortable. For example, people do not usually like mirror reversals of photos of their own or others' faces (Mita, Dermer and Knight, 1977).

Familiarity
As we become more familiar with a stimulus (even another person), we feel more comfortable with it and we like it more.

Real world 14.2
Meeting on the net

Access to a computer and the Internet allows people to meet, form friendships, fall in love, live together or get married. A cyberspace relationship does not necessarily stop there, and some online friends actually meet.

In cyberspace, traditional variables that you would find interesting about someone else are often missing, such as seeing, hearing and touching them. Even so, cyber-relationships can progress rapidly from knowing little about the other person to being intimate; equally, they can be ended very quickly, literally with the 'click of a button'.

From the outset, Internet-mediated relationships differ markedly from offline relationships. A first meeting via the Internet does not give access to the usual range of physical and spoken linguistic cues that help to form an impression – however, the now prevalent social media posting of photos and videos, and the possibility of using real-time interactive audio-visual media such as FaceTime or Skype, may move online relationship development closer to the offline world.

David Jacobson (1999) investigated impression formation in comparing online expectation with offline experiences: that is, when people who had met online actually met in person. He found significant discrepancies – people had often formed erroneous impressions about characteristics such as talkativeness ('they seemed so quiet in person') and expansiveness ('they seemed so terse online but were very expressive offline'). People online often constructed images based on stereotypes, such as the vocation of the unseen person. One participant reported:

> I had no idea what to expect with Katya. From her descriptions I got the impression she would be overweight, kinda hackerish, but when we met, I found her very attractive. Normal sized, nice hair, not at all the stereotypical programmer.
>
> Jacobson (1999, p. 13)

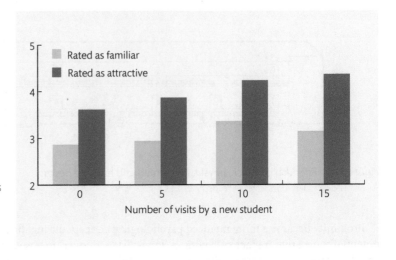

Figure 14.4 Mere exposure and attraction

- This study tested the 'mere exposure' effect in a university class setting.
- Four new women 'students' took part in the class on 0, 5, 10 or 15 occasions.
- At the end of term, students in the class rated slides of the women for several characteristics.
- There was a weak effect for familiarity but a strong and increasing effect across visits for attractiveness.

Source: Based on Moreland and Beach (1992)

Mere exposure effect
Repeated exposure to an object results in greater attraction to that object.

Further, Bob Zajonc (1968) found that familiarity enhances liking just as repeatedly presenting stimuli increases liking for them – the mere exposure effect as used by advertisers to make us feel familiar with new products (**see the effect of repetitive advertising in Chapter 6**). In a classroom setting, Dick Moreland and Scott Beach (1992) found that students rated another new 'student' (actually, collaborating with the investigators) as more attractive the more often they saw her (see Figure 14.4). If you want to be liked, be around!

More recent work by Harry Reis and his colleagues has continued the theme that familiarity leads to attraction (Reis, Maniaci, Eastwick, Caprariello and Finkel (2011), but this has not gone unchallenged. According to Michael Norton and his colleagues, the more we learn about another person, the more we uncover things that make that person dissimilar from ourselves, leading to dislike (Norton, Frost and Ariely, 2007, 2011). Reis and colleagues have argued that there are subtle differences in methods used across the studies in question, ranging from laboratory experiments in which an anonymous other is evaluated on a list of trait adjectives to how real people respond in live interaction. This line of research awaits a more refined model both of: (a) how familiarity increases attraction, and then liking; and (b) when 'familiarity breeds contempt'.

Attitude similarity

There are other important psychological factors that exert some control over attraction. In an early study by Theodore Newcomb (1961), students received rent-free housing in return for filling in questionnaires about their attitudes and values before they arrived. Changes in interpersonal attraction were measured over the course of a semester. Initially, attraction went hand-in-hand with proximity – students liked those who lived close by. Then another factor came into play: having compatible attitudes.

Similarity of attitudes
A powerful and positive determinant of attraction.

Newcomb found that, as the semester progressed, the focus shifted to similarity of attitudes. Students with similar pre-acquaintance attitudes became more attractive. This is logical, because in real life it usually takes some time to discover whether or not a housemate thinks and feels the same way as you do about a variety of social issues.

Donn Byrne and Gerald Clore have conducted extensive research on the connection between sharing attitudes with another person and liking them (e.g. Byrne, 1971; Clore and Byrne, 1974). Attitudes that were markedly similar were an important ingredient in maintaining a relationship. The results were so reliable and consistent that Clore (1976) formulated a 'law of attraction' – attraction towards a person bears a linear relationship to the actual proportion of similar attitudes shared with that person. This law was thought to be applicable to more than just attitudes. Anything that other people do that agrees with your perception of things is rewarding, i.e. reinforcing. The more other people agree, the more they act as reinforcers for you and the more you like them. For example, if you suddenly discover that someone you are going out with likes the same obscure rock band as you, your liking for that person will increase.

Conversely, differences in attitudes and interests can lead to avoidance and dislike (Singh and Ho, 2000). The notion that we should be consistent in our thinking, as stressed in the theory of cognitive dissonance **(see Chapter 4)**, may explain this. An inconsistency, such as recognising that we like something but that someone else does not, is cause for worry. An easy way to resolve this is to not like that person – this re-establishes consistency. Thus we usually choose or preserve the company of similar others – it makes us feel comfortable.

Social matching

There is great scientific, popular, and now commercial interest in match-making where people are paired-up on the basis of having compatible attitudes, but also on sharing demographic characteristics that we discuss further below. But even a seemingly trivial similarity such as one's name can increase attraction. See the study by John Jones et al. (2004) using an **archival research** method in Box 14.3, and Figure 14.5.

Archival research
Non-experimental method involving the assembly of data, or reports of data, collected by others.

Assortative mating

Life is not a lucky dip. People seeking a partner do not usually choose one at random, but try to *match* each other on several features. Peruse the personal columns in your local newspaper, or relevant social media, to see how people describe themselves and what they look for in a potential partner. We bring previously held beliefs to the situation – beliefs about appropriateness such as gender, physique, socioeconomic class and religion. Matching is a form of **assortative mating**. Susan Sprecher (1998) found that in addition to the factors of proximity and familiarity people who are evenly matched in their physical appearance, social background and personality, sociability and interests and leisure activities are more likely to be attracted to one another. There is perhaps some truth in the saying *birds of a feather flock together*.

Assortative mating
A non-random coupling of individuals based on their resemblance to each other on one or more characteristics.

Social psychology in action 14.3
What's in a name? A search in the marriage archives

Marriage records that included the names of brides and grooms were downloaded from the website 'ancestry.com', dating back to the nineteenth century. Several common names were focused on: Smith, Johnson, Williams, Jones and Brown. The researchers predicted that people would seek out others who simply resemble them, and found that people disproportionately married someone whose first or last name resembles their own. It seems that we are egotists at heart. Someone who is similar enough to activate mental associations with 'me' must be a fairly good choice!

In some initial experimental work, the researchers found that people were more attracted to someone with: (a) a random experimental code number (such as a PIN)

resembling their own birth date, (b) a surname containing letters from their own surname, and (c) a number on a sports jersey that had been paired subliminally, on a computer screen, with their own name.

These results prompted them to carry out an *archival study* of marriage among people with matching surnames. They found the most frequent choices of a marriage partner had the same last name. More than 60 per cent of the Smiths married another Smith, more than 50 per cent of the Joneses married another Jones, and more than 40 per cent of the Williamses married another Williams. All of these choices were well beyond chance.

We can note with passing interest that the senior researcher is named John Jones!

Source: Based on Jones, Pelham, Carvallo and Mirenberg (2004, Study 2).

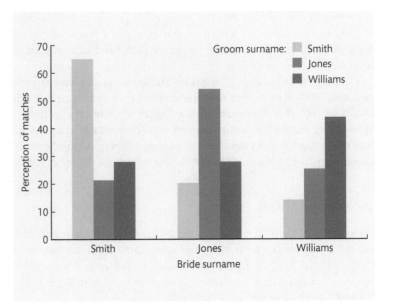

Figure 14.5 'Alias Smith and Jones': name matching and marriage

• A database of surnames was constructed based on early American archival marriage records.
• Commonly occurring names provided large enough samples to find those that were identical prior to marriage.
• Matched surnames – the Smiths, the Joneses and even the Williamses – were well beyond chance.

Source: Based on data from Jones, Pelham, Carvallo and Mirenberg (2004), Study 2

According to Phillip Kavanagh and his colleagues, people rely on the kinds of cues we have discussed to assess potential mates (Kavanagh, Robins and Ellis, 2010). However, there is an ultimate step: they calibrate a level of aspiration by using their personal mating 'sociometer'. A sociometer is a measure of self-esteem based on feeling socially included or excluded by other people. **(We discuss this in relation to the self in Chapter 4.)** This study suggests that people use a form of matching by choosing a mate at a similar level of aspiration to themselves, one that is neither too accepting nor rejecting.

Do cohort studies, conducted across time, support this? Gruber-Baldini and her colleagues carried out such a longitudinal study of married couples over twenty-one years old (Gruber-Baldini, Schaie and Willis, 1995). At the time of first testing, they found similarities in age, education, intellectual aptitude and flexibility of attitudes. An additional finding was that some spouses became even more alike over time in attitude flexibility and word fluency. Thus initial similarity in the phase of assortative mating was enhanced by their experiences

Assortative mating
Similarity of age, ethnicity and culture are some factors that increase interpersonal liking, dating and mating

together. There is also a strong element of reality testing when it comes to looks, since most usually settle on a romantic partner who is similar to their own level of physical attractiveness (Feingold, 1988).

Studies of dating across ethnic or cultural groups reveal a complex interplay of factors involving *similarity of culture* that influence attraction. A study of heterosexual dating preferences among four ethnic groups in the United States (Asian, African, Latino and Euro/white Americans) showed that participants generally preferred partners from their own ethnic group (Liu, Campbell and Condie, 1995). Gaining approval from one's social network was the most powerful predictor of partner preferences, followed by similarity of culture and physical attractiveness.

George Yancey (2007) compared the ethnic choices of white, black, Hispanic and Asian contributors to the Internet site *Yahoo Personals*. Willingness to meet with partners of different race varied: women were less likely than men to date interracially, while Asians were more likely than whites or Hispanics to date blacks. Perhaps unsurprisingly, willingness to date interracially was lower among those who were politically conservative or high in religiosity (the religious right). On the other hand, several demographic factors (age, city size, level of education) had little influence on ethnic dating preferences.

We can reasonably conclude that, while similarity of culture and ethnicity are important determinants of partner choice, interracial studies point to other factors, particularly values, that come into play. In a world where multi-ethnic societies are more prevalent, we clearly need to consider differences between cultures in dating practices and how intimate relationships develop, along with the more obvious factors of proximity and similarity.

Personal characteristics

Personality

Although similarity is an important predictor of attraction, there are other characteristics that people consistently find attractive. In a study of three kinds of relationship (romantic, and same-gender and opposite-gender friendship), Sprecher (1998) confirmed that having similar interests, leisure activities, attitudes, values and social skills were determinants of attraction. However, these factors were less important than other personal characteristics: for example, having a 'desirable personality', warmth and kindness, and reciprocal liking. Proximity and familiarity were also important; in contrast, intelligence, earning potential and competence were relatively unimportant. Catherine Cottrell and her colleagues added another key attribute that topped the list in the profile of an ideal mate – trustworthiness (Cottrell, Neuberg and Li, 2007). Their findings actually generalise to other interdependent relationships as well, such as in work teams and athletic teams. We discuss the importance of *trust* later in this chapter, but can note for now that it takes us beyond attraction when considering how close relationships develop and how they are maintained.

Self-disclosure

A willingness to reveal some aspects of oneself in conversation, or self-disclosure, is an important determinant of long-term intimacy in a relationship. According to the *social penetration* model (Altman and Taylor, 1973), people share more intimate topics with a close friend than with a casual acquaintance or a stranger. People tend to reveal more to people they like and trust. The converse is also true. People tend to prefer people who reveal more about their feelings and thoughts (Collins and Miller, 1994). Disclosing personal information and being sensitive and responsive to our partner's disclosures are central processes, both in developing relationships (Laurenceau, Barrett and Pietromonaco, 1998) and in maintaining them (Cross, Bacon and Morris, 2000).

Self-disclosure
The sharing of intimate information and feelings with another person.

In a study by Jeffrey Vittengl and Craig Holt (2000), students who did not know one another engaged in brief conversations, before and after which they rated their positive and negative affect as well as their willingness to self-disclose. Greater self-disclosure led to an increase in positive affect. Despite this, self-disclosure is not universal; the amount and depth of information shared with another vary according to culture and gender. For example, a meta-analysis of 205 studies of self-disclosure showed that women reveal more about themselves than men (Dindia and Allen, 1992).

With respect to culture, Kurt Lewin (1936) long ago observed differences between Americans and Germans. Americans disclosed more than Germans in initial encounters but did not become as intimate as Germans as their relationships progressed. More recent research focusing on the more profound distinction between individualist and collectivist cultures (America and Germany are both individualistic cultures) finds that people from individualist cultures self-disclose more information than people from collectivist cultures (**see Chapter 16**). When information is shared, individualists give more personal information whereas collectivists share information about group membership (Gudykunst, Matsumoto, Ting-Toomey, Nishida, Kim and Heyman, 1996) (for a review of cultural differences in disclosure, see Goodwin, 1999).

Another reason why self-disclosure is important in relationships may be that trust sustains relationships. In life people try to reduce risk, but they also need and seek out relationships. The problem is that relationships are a risky business in which people make themselves vulnerable to others. People need to build interpersonal trust to manage relationship-based risk (Cvetkovich and Löfstedt, 1999). Self-disclosure plays an important role in reducing risk and building trust – the more that your friend or partner self-discloses, the safer you feel in the relationship and the more you trust him or her. Trust and good relationships go hand-in-hand (Holmes, 2002; Rempel, Ross and Holmes, 2001).

The central role of trust in relationships may cause problems for the development of new relationships and maintenance of established relationships online (Green and Carpenter, 2011). Existing relationships typically benefit from the addition of an online dimension – allowing more ready and frequent communication in an atmosphere of already established mutual trust. However, a rapidly growing number of people use social networking and dating sites as a context in which to meet new people and develop new relationships. It is here the spectres of deception and lowered moral standards loom large. How do you know whether to trust someone, and how much to self-disclose? The paradox here is that the relative anonymity and sense of privacy afforded by online communication also encourages honesty and self-disclosure, both of which are important for trust and relationship development (Caspi and Gorsky, 2006; Christopherson, 2007).

Cultural stereotypes

When collectivist societies are compared with individualistic societies, the former are usually found to:

- nurture a self that is interdependent rather than independent;
- encourage interpersonal relationships that are harmonious rather than competitive.

Big Five
The five major personality dimensions of extraversion/surgency, agreeableness, conscientiousness, emotional stability, and intellect/openness to experience.

These and related issues are discussed in detail in Chapters 4 and 16. Linda Albright et al. (1997) questioned whether a major cross-cultural difference really existed at all. They compared participants from the United States and China, using the same method of data collection in each country. Within-culture data were based on face-to-face interactions, and across-culture data were based on photographs. The results showed that the Big Five personality dimensions (which contain a variety of more specific traits) were used in a consistent way in both countries and both within and across cultures. An attractive person was perceived positively regardless of the ethnicity of the judge or of the target.

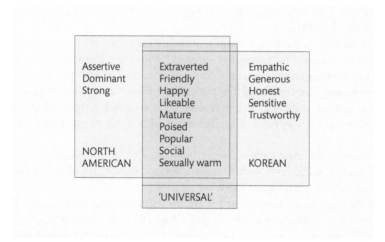

Figure 14.6 Cultural variation and attraction

- Korean participants rated traits for their association with photographs of people who varied in physical beauty.
- Their ratings were compared with previously published American and Canadian data.
- Some traits were 'universal', associated with the three national groups.
- Other traits were specific either to individualistic cultures (North American) or to a collectivist culture (Korean).

Source: Based on Wheeler and Kim (1997)

Although research by Ladd Wheeler and Youngmee Kim (1997) that compared Koreans and North Americans was to an extent supportive of Albright and colleagues' findings, Wheeler and Kim also reported some notable cultural differences (see Figure 14.6). Stereotypes associated with attractiveness include several that are common to both cultures ('universal') and overlap with the Big Five dimensions, but the two cultures did differ to some extent regarding what they considered to represent being physically attractive:

- For North Americans, positive stereotypes include being assertive, dominant and strong – characteristics associated with *individualism*.
- For Koreans, positive stereotypes include being empathic, generous, sensitive, honest and trustworthy – characteristics associated with *collectivism*.

Attraction and rewards

Rarely in psychology does one theory account for a phenomenon in its totality. More often, several theories contribute perspectives that focus on different facets or underlying processes. Theories of attraction are no exception. At the broadest level, theories of attraction can be divided into those that view human nature as a striving to maintain cognitive consistency, and those that view human nature as the pursuit of pleasure and the avoidance of pain – behaviourist or reinforcement approaches. Consistency theories (e.g. balance theory **in Chapter 5**, cognitive dissonance theory **in Chapter 6**) allow a simple proposition. People normally like others who are similar to them – agreement is an affirming experience that generates positive affect. However, if people who like one another disagree, they experience tension, but could then try to modify their attitudes to make them more similar. If relative strangers disagree, an absence of continued interpersonal attraction should not lead to a sense of imbalance or dissonance, and they are unlikely to pursue contact.

We now turn to two approaches based directly on reinforcement, and two other approaches based on a social exchange model of people's behaviour, but also derived from reinforcement principles.

A reinforcement approach

The general idea is simple. People who reward us directly become associated with pleasure and we learn to like them; people who punish us directly become associated with pain and we dislike them. These ideas have a long history in philosophy, literature and general psychology, and they have also been applied in social psychology to help explain interpersonal attraction (Walster, Walster and Berscheid, 1978).

In a variation related to classical or Pavlovian conditioning **(also see Chapter 5)**, Byrne and Clore (1970) proposed a reinforcement–affect model – just as Pavlov's dog learns to associate the sound of a bell with the positive reinforcement of food, so humans can associate another person with other positive or negative aspects of the immediate environment. They proposed that any *background* (and neutral) stimulus that may even be associated accidentally with reward becomes positively valued. However, if it is associated with punishment it becomes negatively valued.

An example of this was an early environmental experiment by Griffitt and Veitch (1971) that showed how simple background features, such as feeling hot or crowded, can diminish our attraction to a stranger (see Box 14.4 and Figure 14.7).

The study of how our feelings can be conditioned is connected to another focus in social psychology, on the automatic activation of attitudes **(see Chapter 5)**. In short, terms such as *affect*, *stimulus value* and *attitude* are related to the fundamental psychological dimensions of *good* versus *bad*, *positive* versus *negative*, and *approach* versus *avoidance* (De Houwer and Hermans, 2001).

Relationships as a social exchange

As we have noted, reinforcement is based on patterns of rewards and punishments. When we look at how economics is applied to studying social behaviour, psychologists talk about social exchange: pay-offs, costs and rewards. Economists, in contrast, focus on how well-established social psychological processes impact people's economic decisions – the field of behavioural economics (Cartwright, 2011).

Is there a relationships marketplace out there, where we humans can satisfy our needs to interact, be intimate, 'love and be loved in return'? While social exchange theory is one of a family of theories based on behaviourism, it is also an approach to studying interpersonal relationships that incorporates *interaction*. Further, it deals directly with close relationships.

Costs and benefits

If two people are to progress in a relationship it will be because they gain from the way that they exchange benefits (i.e. rewards). Social exchange is a model of behaviour introduced by the sociologist George Homans (1961): it accounts for our interpersonal relationships using economic concepts and is wedded to behaviourism. Whether we like someone is determined by the cost–reward ratio: 'What will it cost me to get a positive reward from that person?' Social exchange theory also argues that each participant's outcomes are determined by their *joint* actions.

A relationship is an ongoing everyday activity. We seek to obtain, preserve or exchange things of value with other human beings. We bargain. What are we prepared to give in exchange for what they will give us? Some exchanges are brief and may have shallow meaning, while others are ongoing and long-term and may be extremely complex and important. In all cases, we experience outcomes or payoffs that depend on what others do. Over time, we try to fashion a way of interacting that is rational and mutually beneficial.

Social exchange is a give-and-take relationship between people, and relationships are examples of business transactions. So, is this a dry approach to the study of important relationships? If so, its proponents argue, it is nevertheless valid. Indeed social exchange is a core feature of one of the most significant approaches to leadership – transactional theories of leadership that trace effective leadership to mutually beneficial leader-follower exchanges (e.g. Graen and Uhl-Bien, 1995; Hollander, 1958; **see Chapter 9**).

Broadly speaking, resources exchanged include: goods, information, love, money, services and status (Foa and Foa, 1975). Each can be particular, so that its value depends on who gives the

Reinforcement–affect model
Model of attraction which postulates that we like people who are around when we experience a positive feeling (which itself is reinforcing).

Automatic activation
According to Fazio, attitudes that have a strong evaluative link to situational cues are more likely to automatically come to mind from memory.

Social exchange
People often use a form of everyday economics when they weigh up costs and rewards before deciding what to do.

Behaviourism
An emphasis on explaining observable behaviour in terms of reinforcement schedules.

Cost-reward ratio
Tenet of social exchange theory, according to which liking for another is determined by calculating what it will cost to be reinforced by that person.

Research classic 14.4
Evaluating a stranger when we feel hot and crowded

Imagine that after completing a 24-item attitude scale designed to measure opinions on a variety of social issues, you were later invited to participate by completing a further series of questionnaires along with other students in an investigation of 'judgemental processes under altered environmental conditions'. You were not to know that you were in one of eight different experimental groups. Dressed lightly in cotton shorts and a cotton shirt, you and your group enter an 'environmental chamber', 3 metres long and 2.2 metres wide.

By using eight groups, William Griffitt and Russell Veitch (1971) were able to test three independent variables: (a) *heat*, the ambient temperature, which was either normal at 23°C or hot at 34°C; (b) *population density* which consisted of having either 3–5 group members or 12–16 group members in the chamber at one time; (c) *attitude similarity*. Note that some participants would really have experienced a degree of environmental stress by working on their questionnaires in an environment that was either hot or crowded. As a measure of attitude similarity, each participant also rated an anonymous stranger after they had first inspected the

stranger's responses to the 24-item attitude scale – the same scale that the participants had completed earlier. What they saw was fictitious. The stranger had made similar responses to a proportion of the items – to either 0.25 (low similarity) or 0.75 (high similarity) of them – as those made by that participant.

Finally, the stranger was also rated in order to calculate a measure of attraction based on two questions: how much the stranger would probably be liked, and how desirable would the stranger be as a work partner.

The result for attitude similarity was striking. Not surprisingly, the stranger who was more similar to a participant was considerably more attractive than one who was less similar, confirming the importance of attitude similarity in determining initial attraction, discussed in an earlier section.

The other results show that feeling hot or feeling crowded also affected how attractive a stranger was judged. In the context of classical conditioning, this means that the mere association of a negatively valued background stimulus, in this case two different environmental stressors, can make another person seem less attractive.

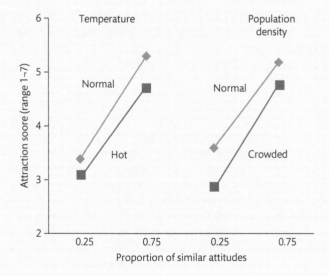

Figure 14.7 Attraction and the reinforcing effects of background features

- Students rated a fictitious stranger as more attractive when they shared a higher proportion of similar attitudes.
- Stressful background factors, such as feeling hot or feeling crowded, reduced the attractiveness of the stranger.

Source: Based on Griffitt and Veitch (1971)

Social exchange
Marriage is not entered into lightly. In long-term relationships, partners carefully weigh up the respective costs and benefits of the relationship

Minimax strategy
In relating to others, we try to minimise the costs and maximise the rewards that accrue.

Profit
This flows from a relationship when the rewards that accrue from continued interaction exceed the costs.

Comparison level
A standard that develops over time, allowing us to judge whether a new relationship is profitable or not.

reward. So a hug (a specific case of 'love') will be more valued if it comes from a special person. Each reward can also be concrete, as money clearly is. There are also costs in a relationship, such as the time it takes to pursue it or the way one's friends may frown on it. Because resources are traded with a partner, we try to use a **minimax strategy** – minimise costs and maximise rewards. Of course, we may not be conscious of doing so and would probably object to the idea that we do!

John Thibaut and Hal Kelley's (1959) *The social psychology of groups* was a major work that underpinned much subsequent research. They argued that we must understand the *structure* of a relationship in order to deal with the behaviour that takes place, as it is this structure that defines the rewards and punishments available. According to the minimax strategy, what follows is that a relationship is unsatisfactory when the costs exceed the rewards. In practice, people exchange resources with one another in the hope that they will earn a **profit**: that is, one in which the rewards exceed the costs. This is a novel way of defining a 'good relationship'. How might you interpret what Erik meant in the second focus question?

Comparison levels

A final and important concept in social exchange theory is the part played by each person's **comparison level** or CL – a standard against which all of one's relationships are judged. People's comparison levels are the product of their past experiences with other parties in similar exchanges. If the result in a present exchange is positive (i.e. a person's profit exceeds their CL), the relationship will be perceived as satisfying and the other person will seem attractive. However, dissatisfaction follows if the final result is negative (i.e. the profit falls below the CL). There is a blessing in this model because it is possible for both people in a relationship to be making a profit and therefore to be gaining satisfaction. The CL concept is helpful in accounting for why some relationships might be acceptable at some times but not at others (see Box 14.5).

Social exchange, equity and justice

Does exchange theory have a future? In sum, the answer is yes. A strong feature of exchange theory is that it accommodates variations in relationships, including:

Real world 14.5
What do you get from a relationship? An exercise in social exchange

An individual's comparison level or CL is an idiosyncratic judgement point, as each person has had unique experiences. Your CL is the average value of all outcomes of relationships with others in your past, and also of outcomes for others that you may have heard about. It can vary across different kinds of relationship, so your CL for your doctor will be different from that for a lover.

Your entry point into a new relationship is seen against a backdrop of the other people you have known (or known about) in that context, together with the profits and losses you have encountered in relating to them. This running average constitutes a baseline for your relationships in that particular sphere. A new encounter could only be judged as satisfactory if it exceeded this baseline.

Take as an example a date that you have had with another person. The outcome is defined as the rewards (having a nice time, developing a potential relationship) minus the costs (how much money it cost you, how difficult or risky it

was to arrange, whether you feel you blew your chance to make a good impression). The actual outcome will be determined by how it compares with other dates you have had in similar circumstances in the past or at present, and perhaps by how successful other people's dates have seemed to you.

To complicate matters a little, your CL can change over time. Although age may not make you any wiser, as you get older you are likely to expect more of some future commitment to another person than when you were younger.

There is an additional concept – the *comparison level for alternatives*. Suppose that you are in an already satisfying relationship but then meet someone new, an enticing stranger. As the saying goes, 'the grass always looks greener on the other side of the fence'. In social exchange language, there is the prospect here of an increase in rewards over costs.

Does all this sound too calculating to you? Be honest, now! Whatever the outcome, the situation has become unstable. Decisions, decisions . . .

- differences between people in how they perceive rewards and costs (you might think that free advice from your partner is rewarding, others might not);

- differences within the person based on varying CLs, both over time and across different contexts (I like companionship, but I prefer to shop for clothes alone).

The theory is frequently used. For example, Caryl Rusbult has shown how *investment* includes the way that rewards, costs and CLs are related to both satisfaction and commitment in a relationship (Rusbult, Martz and Agnew, 1998). It is also a significant perspective in how we understand social justice (explored below) and leadership **(see Chapter 9)**, and in understanding how the breakdown of a relationship often follows a lack of commitment (Le and Agnew, 2003; discussed later). Indeed Western society may actually be founded on a system of social exchange within which we strive for *equity*, or balance, in our relationships with others (Walster, Walster and Berscheid, 1978).

Most people believe that outcomes in an exchange should be fair and just, enshrined in a society's laws and norms: we should comply with the 'rules'. What is thought to be just and fair is a feature of group life **(see the role of leadership in Chapter 9)** and of intergroup relations **(see Chapter 11)**. Equity and equality are not identical concepts. In a work setting, *equality* requires that all people are paid the same, whereas *equity* requires that those who work hardest or do the most important jobs are paid more.

People are happiest in relationships when they believe that the give and take is approximately equal. **Equity theory** was developed in the context of workplace motivation and popularised in social psychology by J. Stacey Adams (1965). It covers two main situations:

1 a mutual exchange of resources (as in marriage);

2 an exchange where limited resources must be distributed (such as a judge awarding compensation for injury).

In both, equity theory predicts that people expect resources to be given out *fairly*, in proportion to their contribution. **(See how a norm of equity has been applied to help understand**

Equity theory
A special case of social exchange theory that defines a relationship as equitable when the ratio of inputs to outcomes are seen to be the same by both partners.

prosocial behaviour in Chapter 13.) If we help others, it is fair to expect them to help us. Equity exists between Jack and Jill when:

$$\frac{\text{Jack's outcomes}}{\text{Jack's inputs}} = \frac{\text{Jill's outcomes}}{\text{Jill's inputs}}$$

First, Jack estimates the ratio between what he has put into his relationship with Jill and what he has been received in return. Next, Jack compares this ratio with the ratio applying to Jill (see Figure 14.8). If these ratios are equal, Jack will feel that each of them is being treated fairly or equitably. Jill, of course, will have her own ideas about what is fair. Perhaps Jack is living in a dream world!

When a relationship is equitable, the participants' outcomes (rewards minus costs) are proportional to their inputs or contributions to the relationship. The underlying concept is **distributive justice** (Homans, 1961). It is an aspect of social justice and refers more generally to practising a norm of fairness in the sharing of goods that each member of a group receives. Equity theory can be applied to many areas of social life, such as exploitative relationships, helping relationships and intimate relationships (Walster, Walster and Berscheid, 1978). The more inequitably people are treated, the more distress they will feel. When we experience continuing inequity, the relationship is likely to end (Adams, 1965), a phenomenon dealt with at the end of this chapter.

Distributive justice (fair allocation of resources) should be distinguished from **procedural justice** (fair procedures – that may or may not result in an equal allocation of resources) – procedural justice seems to be particularly important within groups where members' attachment to the group rests more on being treated fairly (procedural justice) than on equal allocation of resources within the group (De Cremer and Tyler, 2005; Tyler and Smith, 1998; **see Chapter 11**).

Distributive justice
The fairness of the outcome of a decision.

Procedural justice
The fairness of the procedures used to make a decision.

The role of norms

Although Adams (1965) thought that people always prefer an equity norm when allocating resources, this has been questioned (Deutsch, 1975). When resources are shared out according to inputs, we may evaluate our friend's inputs differently from a stranger's. Strangers tend to allocate resources on the basis of *ability*, whereas friends allocate on the basis of both *ability* and *effort* (Lamm and Kayser, 1978). A norm of mutual obligation, rather than equity, to contribute to a common cause may be triggered when a friendship is involved: we expect our friends more so than strangers to pull their weight – perhaps to help us paint our new house!

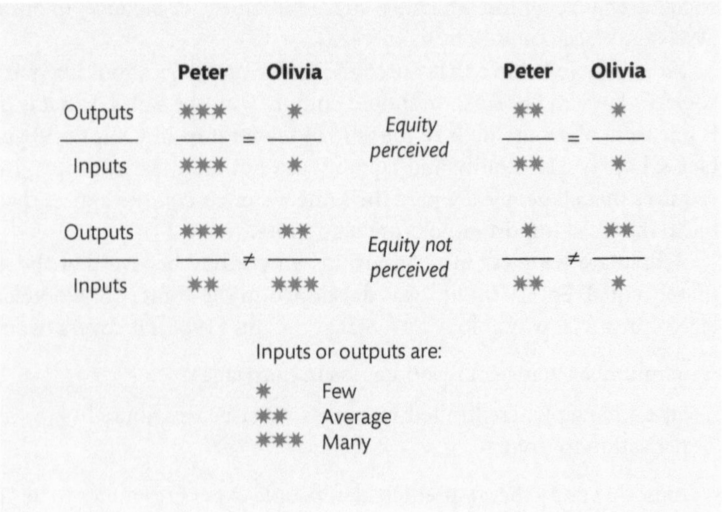

	Peter	**Olivia**			**Peter**	**Olivia**
Outputs	✳✳✳	✳	=	*Equity perceived*	✳✳	✳
Inputs	✳✳✳	✳			✳✳	✳
Outputs	✳✳✳	✳✳	≠	*Equity not perceived*	✳	✳✳
Inputs	✳✳	✳✳✳			✳✳	✳

Inputs or outputs are:

✳   Few
✳✳   Average
✳✳✳   Many

Figure 14.8 Equity theory applied to two equitable and two inequitable relationships
Source: Based on Baron and Byrne (1987)

Gender plays an interesting role: women prefer an equality norm and men an equity norm (Major and Adams, 1983). Such a difference may be based on a sex-stereotyped role in which a woman strives for harmony and peace in interactions by treating people equally. And as noted above **(and in Chapter 11)**, in a group context intragroup procedural justice may be more important than distributive justice or equality.

Attachment

Attachment has become an increasingly central topic in social psychology. Initially focused on the bonding that occurs between infant and caregiver, the study of attachment has expanded to include the different ways that adults make connections with those who are close to them. First, we explore a phenomenon that underpins this topic – affiliation.

Social isolation and the need to affiliate

The **need to affiliate**, to be with others, is powerful and pervasive, and underlies the way in which we form positive and lasting interpersonal relationships (Leary, 2010), and may also play a key role in attachment to groups (Baumeister and Leary, 1995; **see Chapter 8**). There are, of course, times when we wish to be alone, to enjoy our own company; and there are models that deal with people's attempts to regulate their need for privacy (O'Connor and Rosenblood, 1996; Pedersen, 1999). However, the effects of too much social isolation can be dire indeed (Perlman and Peplau, 1998).

Need to affiliate
The urge to form connections and make contact with other people.

There have been many stories of people being isolated for long periods of time, such as prisoners in solitary confinement and shipwreck survivors. However, in situations such as these, isolation is often accompanied by punishment or perhaps lack of food. For this reason, the record of Admiral Byrd is perhaps the most interesting example we have – his isolation was voluntary and planned, with adequate supplies to meet his physical needs. Byrd volunteered to spend six months alone at an Antarctic weather station observing and recording conditions. His only contact was by radio with the main expedition base. At first, he wanted to 'be by myself for a while and to taste peace and quiet and solitude long enough to find out how good they really are' (Byrd, 1938, p. 4). But in the fourth week he wrote of feeling lonely, lost and bewildered. He began to spice up his experience by imagining that he was among familiar people. After nine weeks Byrd became preoccupied with religious questions and, like Monty Python, dwelt on the 'meaning of life'. His thoughts turned to ways of believing that he was not actually by himself: 'The human race, then, is not alone in the universe. Though I am cut off from human beings, I am not alone' (p. 185). After three months, he became severely depressed, apathetic and assailed by hallucinations and bizarre ideas.

The early social psychologist William McDougall (1908) suggested that humans are innately motivated to gather together and to be part of a group, as some animals do that live in herds or colonies. This was a straightforward **instinct** theory. It was roundly criticised by the behaviourist John Watson (1913) who argued that accounting for herding behaviour by calling it a herding instinct was a very weak position. Later biological explanations of social behaviour were much more sophisticated (note what we have covered already regarding evolutionary theory and attraction). Affiliation has been extensively researched, so we have been selective in choosing just two topics. Do people want company when they become anxious? How serious are the consequences of inadequate care-giving for infants?

Instinct
Innate drive or impulse, genetically transmitted.

Isolation and anxiety

In his classic work *The Psychology of Affiliation* (1959), Stanley Schachter described a connection between being isolated and feeling anxious. Being alone can lead people to want to be with others, even with strangers for a short period. Schachter surmised that having company serves

Social comparison (theory)
Comparing our behaviours and opinions with those of others in order to establish the correct or socially approved way of thinking and behaving.

to reduce anxiety, noting that two factors could be involved, either that the other person might serve as a distraction from a worrying situation, or else as a yardstick for the process of social comparison. His results confirmed the latter explanation. James Kulik has studied how social psychological processes can be used to promote recovery from surgery. See Box 14.6 for an example of how social comparison can be used to speed recovery for heart patients.

In summary, the need to affiliate can be affected by temporary states, such as fear. It is not just any person that we want to be with, but someone specific. Schachter's original assertion can be amended to read: 'Misery loves the company of those in the same miserable situation' (Gump and Kulik, 1997). The reduction of anxiety is only one condition that invokes the process of social comparison. In a broader context, we make these comparisons whenever we look to the views of a special group, our friends. How people come to be part of this special group is discussed below.

One situation in which isolation can be particularly painful is when it is intentionally imposed on you by another individual or by an entire group – when you are shunned or ostracised (Williams, 2002, 2009). Earlier **(in Chapter 8)**, we discussed ostracism as something that happens in the context of a group – but of course individuals can ostracise one another in interpersonal relationships with equally dramatic effect. Feeling ostracised, which can even be elicited by something as seemingly trivial as someone averting their gaze, can make one feel ones relationship has been devalued (Wirth, Sacco, Hugenberg and Williams, 2010), cause self-esteem to plummet, and even make people feel that they have no meaningful existence (e.g. Zadro, Williams and Richardson, 2004).

Effects of social deprivation

Additional insights on the nature of affiliation have been provided by the study of the effects of *social deprivation in infancy*. According to the British psychiatrist John Bowlby (1988), the release of two movies had a profound effect on research workers studying children in the 1950s, one by René Spitz, *Grief: A peril in infancy* (1947), and the other by James Robertson, *A two-year-old goes to hospital* (1952). Survival, it transpired, depends on physical needs but also on a quite independent need for care and intimate interaction.

The psychoanalyst René Spitz (1945) reported on babies who had been in an overcrowded institution for two years, left there by mothers unable to look after them. The babies were fed but rarely handled, and were mostly confined to their cots. Compared with other institutionalised children who had been given adequate care, they were less mentally and socially advanced,

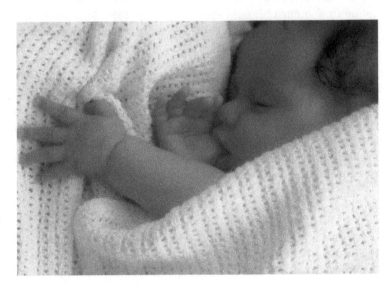

Attachment
Early studies by Harlow and Bowlby showed that babies need nurturing as well as food. Lots of cuddling, warmth and softness works wonders

Research highlight 14.6
Heart to heart: effects of room sharing before surgery

Kulik, Mahler and Moore (1996) recorded the verbal interactions of heart patients, studying the effects of pre-operative room-mate assignments on patterns of affiliation, including how anxious they were before the operation and their speed of recovery afterwards. If social comparison were to play a part in this context then it should reveal itself if the other person is also a cardiac patient. The results indicated that the process of social comparison was at work:

- Patients were significantly more likely to clarify their thoughts, by talking about the surgery and the prospects of recovery afterwards, when their room-mate was a cardiac rather than a non-cardiac patient.

- This effect was strongest when the room-mate had already undergone the operation. When patient A was pre-operative and patient B was post-operative, patient A would be less anxious, as measured by the number of anxiety-reducing drugs and sedatives requested by patients the night before surgery.

- Patients were also more likely to be discharged sooner if assigned to a room-mate who was cardiac rather than non-cardiac, measured by the length of stay following the procedure.

- Patients without room-mates generally had the slowest recoveries.

and their mortality rate was extremely high. Spitz coined the term hospitalism to describe the psychological condition in which he found these children. Hospitalism came to life vividly with heart-wrenching television footage of little children abandoned in Romanian orphanages in the early 1990s. Robertson was a psychiatric social worker and psychoanalyst working at the Tavistock Clinic and Institute in London, and was acknowledged by Bowlby as an inspiration. His remarkable film dealt with the emotional deterioration of a young girl separated from her mother for eight days while in hospital for minor surgery (read about *A Two-year-old Goes to Hospital* at **http://www.robertsonfilms.info/2_year_old.htm**).

Other work of that time by Harry Harlow and his colleagues at the University of Wisconsin dealt with the devastating effects of social isolation on newborn rhesus monkeys (Harlow, 1958; Harlow and Harlow, 1965). (Later, Fraley, Brumbaugh and Marks, 2005, outlined an evolutionary approach to attachment and pair bonding in mammals.) This included deprivation of contact with their mothers. A monkey mother provides more than contact, food, rocking and warmth: she is the first link in the chain of the baby's experience of socialisation. Harlow's investigation was extended to babies that were totally isolated from contact with any living being for up to 12 months. Such long periods of solitary confinement had drastic consequences. The infant monkeys would sometimes huddle in a corner, rock back and forth repetitively, and bite themselves. When later exposed to normal peers, they did not enter into the rough-and-tumble play of the others, and failed to defend themselves from attack. As adults, they were sexually incompetent. In addition, Harlow's early studies pointed to the importance of warmth in contact between a mother and infant, laying the groundwork for attachment (Williams and Bargh, 2008).

Hospitalism
A state of apathy and depression noted among institutionalised infants deprived of close contact with a caregiver.

Attachment styles

Clearly, long-term social deprivation in infants is psychologically traumatic – in particular separation from a long-term caregiver, typically the mother. Bowlby (1969) and his colleagues at the Tavistock Institute in England focused on the attachment behaviour of infants to their mothers, noting that young children keep close to their mothers. Young children send signals to their caregiver by crying and smiling, and maintained proximity by clinging or following, all of which Bowlby attributed to an innate affiliative drive. Compared with affiliation, attachment involves that extra step of a close relationship at a particular point in time with just a few, perhaps one, other person.

Attachment behaviour
The tendency of an infant to maintain close physical proximity with the mother or primary caregiver.

Table 14.1 Characteristics of three attachment styles

Attachment style	Characteristics
Secure	Trust in others; not worried about being abandoned; belief that one is worthy and liked; find it easy to be close to others; comfortable being dependent on others, and vice versa.
Avoidant	Suppression of attachment needs; past attempts to be intimate have been rebuffed; uncomfortable when close to others; find it difficult to trust others or to depend on them; feel nervous when anyone gets close.
Anxious	Concern that others will not reciprocate one's desire for intimacy; feel that a close partner does not really offer love, or may leave; want to merge with someone and this can scare people away.

Source: Based on Hazan and Shaver (1987)

For Bowlby and many other social psychologists, attachment behaviour is not limited to the mother–infant experience but can be observed throughout the life cycle. In Bowlby's words, it accompanies people 'from the cradle to the grave'.

Stable adult relationships 'come from somewhere' (Berscheid, 1994). Research into the genesis of adult attachment in relationships is now clearly linked to the study of human social development in infancy, and Bowlby's work with young children in particular has moved on to include the study of attachment styles in their elders. In accounting for the way that we as adults experience both love and loneliness, Cindy Hazan and Phillip Shaver (1987) defined three attachment styles – *secure*, *avoidant* and *anxious* – that are also found in children (see Table 14.1).

Attachment styles
Descriptions of the nature of people's close relationships, thought to be established in childhood.

Based on their studies of how important the family is to an individual's psychological development, Mary Feeney and Pat Noller (1990) found that attachment styles developed in childhood carry on to influence the way heterosexual romantic relationships are formed in later life. They assessed the levels of attachment, communication patterns and relationship satisfaction of married couples, and found that securely attached individuals (comfortable with closeness and having low anxiety about relationships) were more often paired with similarly secure spouses. On the other hand, people with an avoidant style often report aversive sexual feelings and experiences, and are less satisfied and more stressed from parenting when a baby arrives (Birnbaum, Reis, Mikulincer, Gillath and Orpaz, 2006; Rholes, Simpson and Friedman, 2006), and less close to their children as they grow older (Rholes, Simpson and Blakely, 1995). Now consider the third focus question. What might have happened in Aishani's life before she met Kamesh that could account for her current predicament?

Studies of romantic relationships suggest that Bowlby was right – attachment is a process that is active throughout life rather than simply a feature of infancy, and attachment styles adopted early in life can prevail in later relationships.

Other studies of attachment styles and romantic relationships have found that:

- *Secure* adults found it easier to get close to others and to enjoy affectionate and long-lasting relationships (Brennan and Shaver, 1995).
- *Avoidant* adults were less comfortable being close with others, more hampered by jealousy and less likely to disclose (Brennan and Shaver, 1995); they were more likely to be unfaithful (DeWaal, Lambert, Slotter, Pond, Deckman et al., 2011); and faster than secure adults to generate fight-flight schema when threatened(Ein-Dor, Mikulincer and Shaver, 2011).
- *Anxious* adults fall in love more easily, they experience more emotional highs and lows in their relationships, and were more often unhappy (Brennan and Shaver, 1995); they were also more vigilant to possible threat (Ein-Dor, Mikulincer and Shaver, 2011).

Experimental data from Claudia Brumbaugh and Chris Fraley (2006) show that an attachment style in one romantic relationship is likely to carry over to another relationship. However,

Secure attachment style
Children benefit from contact with compassionate caregivers. They are more likely to be both self-sufficient and trusting of others

people's styles may not be set in concrete. Lee Kirkpatrick and Cindy Hazan's (1994) study carried out over a four-year period has shown that an insecure partner may become less so if a current partner is secure and the relationship engenders trust.

Longitudinal research

Most research into attachment styles has not examined children and therefore is not genuinely developmental. The studies to which we have referred (excluding Kirkpatrick and Hazan's) typically measure the attachment style of adult participants and have no independent estimate of children's attachment style. Even cross-sectional studies of different age groups tested at the one time are not, strictly speaking, developmental. In contrast, Eva Klohnen oversaw a genuine longitudinal programme of research across more than thirty years. Women who had been avoidant or secure in their attachment styles in their 20s still so in their 40s and 50s. Differences in how they related were also maintained across the years. Compared with secure women, avoidant women were more distant from others, less confident, more distrustful, but more self-reliant (Klohnen and Bera, 1998).

Attachment theory has attracted growing attention since the 1980s and has also become fashionable in the popular literature devoted to love, our next topic.

Close relationships

What does a close relationship conjure up for you? Perhaps warm fuzzies, perhaps passion and maybe love. But when you search your memory banks, there can be other worrisome thoughts too – try jealousy for one.

Close relationships are a crucible for a host of strong emotions (Fitness, Fletcher and Overall, 2003). According to the emotion-in-relationships model, relationships pivot on strong, well-established and wide-ranging expectations about a partner's behaviour (Berscheid and Ammazzalorso, 2001). People who can express their emotions are generally valued in close relationships, particularly by others with a secure attachment style (Feeney, 1999). There is, however, a caveat. Julie Fitness (2001) has reported that the elevated tendency to feel *all* emotions in close relationships makes it important for us to manage their expression, particularly negative emotions. If I engage in an orgy of uninhibited expression of all I feel for my partner the relationship may not be long for this world. The way that I show my feelings for my partner needs to be carefully, even strategically, managed.

Emotion-in-relationships model
Close relationships provide a context that elicits strong emotions due to the increased probability of behaviour interrupting interpersonal expectations.

What is love?

We have discussed the general process of interpersonal attraction. We have explored the way we choose acquaintances and friends, the powerful need to affiliate with a range of people, and how we become attached to particular individuals. So now we come to that all-absorbing human interest – love. Can we extend these principles to the important topic of the very special people whom we love – and are liking and loving different? Once a neglected topic of empirical study, love is now a popular focus for research (Dion and Dion, 1996).

Love
A combination of emotions, thoughts and actions which are often powerful, and usually associated with intimate relationships.

People commonly use terms such as passion, romance, companionship, infatuation and sexual attraction, but would have difficulty defining them. Couple this with the way that love is regarded as magical and mysterious – the stuff of poetry and song rather than science – and the difficulty of taking love into the laboratory becomes compounded. Despite this, our knowledge is growing (see the fourth focus question), but not surprisingly, most research on love has used survey and interview methods.

Zick Rubin (1973) distinguished between *liking* and *loving* and developed scales to measure each separately. Take a few examples of some of Rubin's items. Julie thinks Artie is 'unusually well adjusted', 'is one of the most likeable people' she knows, and 'would highly recommend him for a responsible job'. When it comes to Frankie, Julie 'finds it easy to ignore his faults', 'if she could never be with him she would feel miserable', and 'feels very possessive towards him'. Which one does Julie like and which one does she love? Other researchers have added that *liking* involves the desire to interact with a person, *loving* adds the element of trust, and *being in love* implies sexual desire and excitement (Regan and Berscheid, 1999).

Kinds of love

In a study of what kinds of love there might be Beverley Fehr (1994) asked this question: do ordinary people and love researchers *think* of love in the same way? She answered this by analysing the factors underlying several love scales commonly used in psychological research, and also by having ordinary people generate ideas about the kinds of love that they thought best described various close relationships in a number of scenarios. Fehr found both a simple answer and a more complex one:

Love
Romantic love involves intense and occasionally confused emotions. Compassionate love develops slowly from the continuous sharing of intimacy

- There was reasonable agreement across her data sets that there are at least two broad categories of love: (a) companionate love and (b) passionate or romantic love. This result substantiated earlier work by Hatfield and Walster (1981).

- The scales devised by love researchers made relatively clear distinctions between types and sub-types of love, whereas the views of ordinary people were quite fuzzy.

Passionate love is an intensely emotional state and a confusion of feelings: tenderness, sexuality, elation and pain, anxiety and relief, altruism and jealousy. Companionate love, in contrast, is less intense, combining feelings of friendly affection and deep attachment (Hatfield, 1987). A distinction between passionate and companionate love makes good sense. There are many people with whom we are pleased and comforted by sharing time, and yet with whom we are not 'in love'. In general, love can trigger emotions such as sadness, anger, fear and happiness (Shaver, Morgan and Wu, 1996; **see Chapter 15 for a discussion of 'primary' emotions**). Hendrick and Hendrick (1995) also reported some gender differences in the meaning that people give to love: men are more inclined to treat love as a game; whereas women are more friendship-oriented, pragmatic, but also more possessive.

Love and romance

In 1932 the American songwriters Rodgers and Hart asked the question 'Isn't it romantic?' and also tried to tell us what love is. Social psychologists have mostly been more prosaic, sticking to descriptions of acts and thoughts that point to being 'in love'. People report that they think of their lover constantly; they want to spend as much time as possible with, and are often unrealistic about, their lover (Murstein, 1980). Not surprisingly, the lover becomes the focus of the person's life, to the exclusion of other friends (Milardo, Johnson and Huston, 1983). It is a very intense emotion and almost beyond control.

In pursuing the nature of romantic love, we should note that the concepts of love and friendship almost certainly share a common root of becoming acquainted, and are generally triggered by the same factors – proximity, similarity, reciprocal liking and desirable personal characteristics. Our lover is very likely to be a friend, albeit a special one!

Have you ever fallen in love? We speak of 'falling in love' as though it is an accident, something that happens to us rather than a process in which we actively participate. What happens when we fall in this way? Arthur Aron and his colleagues addressed this in a short-term longitudinal study of undergraduate students who completed questionnaires about their love experiences and their concept of self every two weeks for ten weeks (Aron, Paris and Aron, 1995). Those who reported that they fell in love during this period reported positive experiences that were centred on their self-concept. Since somebody now loved them their self-esteem increased. Further, their self-concept had 'expanded' by incorporating aspects of the other person; and they also reported an increase in self-efficacy, e.g. not only making plans but making the plans work.

A widely accepted claim about falling in love is that it is culture-bound: for young people to experience it, a community needs to believe in love and offer it as an option, through fiction and real-life examples. If it is an accident, then at least some people from all cultures should fall in love – but is this the case? Attachment theory has argued that love is both a biological and a social process, and cannot be reduced to a historical or cultural invention (Hazan and Shaver, 1987). Indeed, there is evidence of romantic love, not necessarily linked to marriage which is simply a social contract, in the major literate civilisations of early historic times – Rome, Greece, Egypt and China (Mellen, 1981). For example, although romance was not an essential ingredient in choosing a spouse in Rome, love between a husband and wife could grow (see **http://www.womenintheancientworld.com**).

A biological strand in the nature of heterosexual love underpins a study of sex differences by Ackerman and his colleagues. They blended an evolutionary perspective and a cost/benefit analysis to argue that confessing one's love for the first time is more likely to come from men than from women. Romantic love underpins mate search, but mate retention and kin care require *commitment*: 'Let's get serious' (discussed further below). Sexual access may be a benefit of romantic love but as a partnership it also brings sexual obligation. For a woman, the costs of love can be relatively immediate with prospects of gestation and lactation. Traditionally, the costs for a man are less pressing: a promise of resources down the track – prestige and power ('getting the dream job'); and security which equates to kin care (Ackerman, Griskevicius and Li, 2011).

Labels and illusions

Love as a label

In Elaine Hatfield and William Walster's (1981) three-factor theory of love, romantic love is a product of three interacting variables:

1 a cultural determinant that acknowledges love as a state;

2 an appropriate love object present – in most cultures, the norm is a member of the opposite sex and of similar age;

3 emotional arousal, self-labelled 'love', that is felt when interacting with, or even thinking about, an appropriate love object.

Three-factor theory of love Hatfield and Walster distinguished three components of what we label 'love': a cultural concept of love, an appropriate person to love and emotional arousal.

Label or not, those of us who have been smitten report powerful feelings. Although the idea of labelling arousal may not seem intuitively appealing, it has a basis in research. Our physiological reactions are not always well differentiated across the emotions, such as when we describe ourselves as angry, fearful, joyful or sexually aroused (Fehr and Stern, 1970).

Recall Schachter and Singer's (1962) argument that arousal prompts us to make a causal attribution (**see Chapter 3**) and appraisal theories of emotion that argue that felt emotions are based on our appraisals largely of harm and benefit (e.g. Blascovich, 2008; Lazarus, 1991; **see Chapter 2**). Some cues (e.g. heightened heart rate) suggest that the cause is internal and we then label the experience as an emotion. If we feel aroused following an insult we are likely to label the feeling as anger. However, if we are interacting with an attractive member of appropriate gender depending on our sexual orientation, we will possibly label the arousal as sexual attraction, liking, and even a precursor to love. See Box 14.7 on how even danger, or at least excitement, can act as a precursor to romance!

The three-factor theory stresses that love depends on past learning of the concept of love, the presence of someone to love, and arousal. Even if these components are necessary, they are not sufficient for love to occur. If they were, love could easily be taken into the laboratory. The ingredients would require that John's culture includes a concept of love and that Janet provides arousal by being attractive, or by chasing John around the room, or by paying him a compliment – and hey presto! 'Love'!

Research classic 14.7
Excitement and attraction on a suspension bridge

Donald Dutton and Arthur Aron (1974) conducted a famous experiment on a suspension bridge spanning Capilano canyon in British Columbia. They described the setting in this way:

> The 'experimental' bridge was the Capilano Canyon Suspension Bridge, a five-foot-wide, 450-foot-long, bridge constructed of wooden boards attached to wire cables that ran from one side to the other of the Capilano Canyon. The bridge has many arousal-inducing features such as a tendency to tilt, sway, and wobble, creating the impression that one is about to fall over the side; (b) very low handrails of wire cable which contribute to this impression; and (c) a 230-foot drop to rocks and shallow rapids below the bridge.
>
> Dutton and Aron (1974, pp. 510–511)

The participants were young men who crossed rather gingerly over a high and swaying suspension bridge, one at a time. An attractive young woman approached each one on the pretext of conducting research, asking if they would complete a questionnaire for her. Next, she gave them her name and her phone number in case they wanted to ask more questions later. Many called her. However, very few made the phone call if the interviewer was a man or if the setting was a lower and safer 'control' bridge. Arousal in a perilous situation, it seems, enhances romance!

The phenomenon of accidental arousal enhancing the attractiveness of an already attractive person described is reliable, according to a meta-analysis of thirty-three experimental studies (Foster, Witcher, Campbell and Green, 1998).

We know that sexual arousal itself does not define love, and that lust and love can be distinguished. Think of the anecdote in which a person is called to account for an extramarital affair by a spouse and makes the classic response 'But, dear, it didn't *mean* anything!'

Love and illusions

People bring various ideals or images into a love relationship that can impact on the way it might develop. A person can fall out of love quickly if the partner is not what (or who) they were first thought to be. The initial love was not for the partner but for some *ideal image* that the person had formed of this partner, such as 'the knight in shining armour'. Possible sources for these images are previous lovers, characters from fiction, and childhood love objects such as parents. A physical characteristic similar to one contained by the image can start a chain reaction whereby other characteristics from the image are transferred on to the partner.

It is the images we hold about an ideal partner (discussed further below) that seem best to differentiate love from liking. Some of these images may be based on illusions. One of these is the belief in romantic destiny – *We were meant for each other*. This illusion can be helpful, both in feeling initially satisfied and in maintaining a relationship longer (Knee, 1998). Romance in general is most likely entwined with fantasy and positive illusions (Martz et al., 1998; Murray and Holmes, 1997). A positive illusion may not be a bad thing when it comes to relationships. Probably, the reality is that we need to be in the right relationship with the right person. There is some conviction 'from maintaining a tight, coherent, evaluatively consistent story about one's partner' (Murray, Holmes and Griffin, 2003, p. 290). When a partner falls short of one's ideals, we could highlight virtues and minimise faults. Partner ideals are a feature of the work of Fletcher and his colleagues in maintaining relationships, discussed in a later section.

No greater love

Robert Sternberg (1988) used a psychometric approach in his influential model wherein commitment and intimacy are factors as crucial as passion to some experiences of love. *Passion* is roughly equivalent to sexual attraction; *intimacy* refers to feelings of warmth, closeness and sharing; *commitment* is our resolve to maintain the relationship, even in moments of crisis. These same three dimensions have been confirmed as statistically independent factors (Aron and Westbay, 1996).

While sexual desire and romantic love are linked in experience, Diamond has pointed out that they may have evolved as different biological systems with different goals:

> Desire is governed by the *sexual mating* system, the goal of which is sexual union for the purpose of reproduction. Romantic love, however, is governed by the *attachment* or *pair-bonding* system.
>
> Diamond (2003, p. 174)

It follows that attachment or pair-bonding can be directed towards both other-gender and same-gender partners. Where same-sex sexual attraction fits in this model is not entirely clear.

In Sternberg's model, romance is exceeded by one other experience, consummate love, which includes all three factors. By systematically creating combinations of the presence or absence of each factor, we can distinguish eight cases, ranging in degree of bonding from no love at all to consummate love. Out of this some interesting relationships emerge. Fatuous love is characterised by passion and commitment but no intimacy (e.g. the 'whirlwind Hollywood romance'). The differentiation between varieties of love by Sternberg appears to be robust (Diamond, 2003). Have you experienced some of the relationships in Figure 14.9?

In her recent review, Berscheid noted that research dealing with love, and in particular studies based on psychometric testing, generally do not address the process of change in close relationship love:

> Relationships are temporal in nature. Like rivers, they flow through time and space and change as the properties of the environment in which they are embedded change. The significance of this fact for love and other relationship phenomena is, to paraphrase ancient sage Heraclitus: 'One never steps in the same river twice.'
>
> Berscheid (2010, p. 11)

In the following sections, we include a variety of studies that deal with change, either by tracking a relationship over time or by researching partners who have been together for several years prior to the investigation. This will invite us naturally to ask how a close relationship is maintained and what factors might indicate its impending failure. But first we ask the question: do we marry for love?

Marriage

Love and marriage

Love and romance being the essence of deciding to get married has long been a popular theme in literature. And yet, in Western culture there has been a change in attitude over time, even across a single generation. Simpson and his colleagues compared three time samples (1967, 1976 and 1984) of people who answered this question: 'If a man (woman) had all the qualities you desired, would you marry this person if you were not in love with him (her)?' The answer 'No' was much higher in 1984, but in 1967 women were much more likely to say 'Yes' (Simpson, Campbell and Berscheid, 1986). A later study documented a trend in Western cultures towards long-term relationships outside marriage (Hill and Peplau, 1998). Even so, American data suggest that love is still an accurate predictor of getting married or not, but is not enough to guarantee a happy and stable relationship.

Most research on marriage focus on the Western concept of marriage, and may thus seem culturally myopic. In one sense, it is – because 'marriage', as a social and legal contract, takes different forms in different cultures and groups, and has changed over time. However, almost all love relationships in all cultures and groups have some kind of public contract to identify the relationship.

Consummate love
Sternberg argues that this is the ultimate form of love, involving passion, intimacy and commitment.

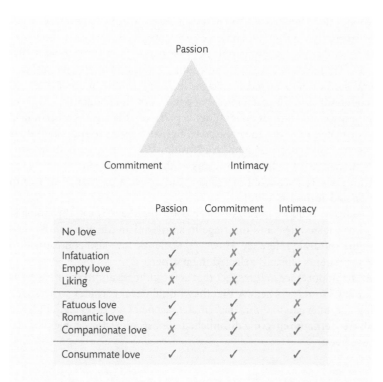

	Passion	Commitment	Intimacy
No love	✗	✗	✗
Infatuation	✓	✗	✗
Empty love	✗	✓	✗
Liking	✗	✗	✓
Fatuous love	✓	✓	✗
Romantic love	✓	✗	✓
Companionate love	✗	✓	✓
Consummate love	✓	✓	✓

Figure 14.9 Sternberg's (1988) triangle of love

- Three factors (passion, commitment and intimacy) are crucial in characterising different experiences of love. When all three are present we can speak of consummate love.
- When only one or two are present we have love in a different way. Two commonly experienced kinds include romantic love and companionate love.

Source: Sternberg (1988).

Arranged marriages

Most cultures have long preferred the careful arrangement of 'suitable' partners for their children. Arranged marriages can be very successful, particularly if we judge them by their duration and social function: having children, caring for aged parents, reinforcing the extended family

Arranged marriages
Marriage serves such an important function for the community that young people may not be able to choose their partner freely

and building a stronger community. They can, and often do, also act as treaties between communities and tribal groups. Historically, this function has been absolutely central (Evans-Pritchard, 1951; Fox, 1971) – it became weaker in post-industrial societies, particularly Western ones, that are organised around nuclear families that have to move around to respond to the job market.

There have been several studies of arranged marriages in India. In one, mutual love was rated lower by arranged couples than by 'love' couples – at first (Gupta and Singh, 1982). Over time, this trend reversed. In a second study, female students preferred the idea of an arranged marriage, provided they consented to it; but they endorsed the 'love marriage' provided their parents consented (Umadevi, Venkataramaiah and Srinivasulu, 1992). In a third study, students who preferred love marriages were liberal in terms of their mate's sociocultural background, whereas those who preferred arranged marriages would seek a partner from within their own kin group (Saroja and Surendra, 1991).

Has the dichotomy of arranged and love marriages been oversimplified? The anthropologist Victor De Munck (1996) investigated love and marriage in a Sri Lankan Muslim community. Arranged marriages were the cultural preference. However, romantic love also contributed to the final decision, even when parents officially selected the partner.

These studies highlight the importance and respect that some cultures afford their elders as legitimate matchmakers. Many Westerners believe that they would never consider an arranged marriage. However, dating and international marriage-match agencies are growing rapidly in popularity in Western culture, perhaps reflecting diminished opportunities for people to meet, particularly those with busy lives.

Same-sex romantic relationships

Same-sex gay and lesbian relationships have been overlooked in research on close relationships. With increasing social acceptance and legal recognition of same-sex relationships that has gathered real momentum in the West since probably the early 1980s this has changed. There is greater recognition that theories of relationships simply cannot assume that close relationships are heterosexual (Peplau and Fingerhut, 2007; also see Herek, 2007), and recognition that the basic social psychology of same-sex relationships will mirror that of heterosexual relationships in most respects but that there may be some differences. However, there is still a long way to go – homosexual acts remain a criminal, sometimes capital, offence in many African, Islamic and Middle Eastern nations.

Even in Western nations same-sex marriages, civil unions, gay adoption and lesbian, gay, bisexual and transgender (LGBT) sexuality have been matters of fierce public debate (Herek, 2011). As mentioned earlier **(in Chapter 10)**, California, probably the most socially progressive state in the US, had legalised same-sex marriage only to have it overturned in 2008 – 52 per cent of Californians voted 'yes' on a ballot proposition actively denying same-sex couples the same legal rights as heterosexuals. The vote, which correlated strongly and predictably with religiosity and sociopolitical ideology, was subsequently overturned in 2012 by the main appeal court in California on the grounds, according to their ruling which was published in the media, that the ballet proposition 'serves no purpose, and has no effect, other than to lessen the status and human dignity of gays and lesbians in California and to officially reclassify their relationships and families as inferior to those of opposite-sex couples'.

Relationships that work (and those that don't)

Maintaining relationships

The literature on relationship maintenance deals mostly with marriage – partly an historical artefact, but also because of the central role still played by traditional heterosexual marriage in child-rearing. However, in view of what we have discussed so far, marriage is only one of a number of love relationships, and in this section we do not draw a distinction between de facto marriage relationships and other long-term intimate relationships.

External influences, such as pressure from in-laws, are other factors beyond love that can perpetuate a marriage relationship; alternatively, a progressive weakening of external obstacles to separation can be linked to an escalating divorce rate (Attridge and Berscheid, 1994). Benjamin Karney and Thomas Bradbury (1995) studied some 200 variables in a longitudinal study of marital satisfaction and stability. Positive outcomes were predicted by groups of positively valued variables (e.g. education, employment and desirable behaviour), whereas negative outcomes were predicted by groups of negatively valued variables (e.g. neuroticism, an unhappy childhood and negative behaviour). However, no factor in isolation was a reliable predictor of satisfaction. Marriage is more than a union of two individuals. Sandra Cotton and her colleagues found that marital satisfaction was related to an overlap between the spousal social networks. For example, wives reported more marital satisfaction when their networks included relatives or friends of their husband; or when members in a wife's network were related to members in the husband's network. Similarly, marital satisfaction was higher among husbands when their networks overlapped with those of their wives (Cotton, Cunningham and Antill, 1993).

Margaret Clark and Nancy Grote (1998) have adopted equity theory's focus on benefits and costs to identify actions that help or hinder a relationship:

- *Benefits* help. They can be intentional (e.g. 'My husband complimented me on my choice of clothing'), or unintentional (e.g. 'I like being in public with my wife because she is attractive').

- *Costs* hinder. They can be intentional (e.g. 'My wife corrected my grammar in front of other people'), or unintentional (e.g. 'My husband kept me awake at night by snoring').

- *Communal behaviour* helps. Sometimes it can be a benefit to one partner but a cost to the other (e.g. 'I listened carefully to something my wife wanted to talk about even though I had no interest in the issue').

Romance novels suggest that 'love endures', whereas TV soap operas and reality shows often focus on relationship break-ups. A longitudinal study spanning ten years of American newlyweds found a steady decline in marital satisfaction among both husbands and wives (Kurdeck, 1999). This decline included two accelerated downturns, one after the first year, 'the honeymoon is over', and the other in the eighth year, 'the seven year itch'! Causes and solutions for distress in longitudinal relationships have been explored by Kieran Sullivan and her colleagues (2010). See Box 14.8.

A relationship that survives is one where partners adapt and change in what they expect of each other. Companionate love can preserve a relationship, based on deep friendship and

Social psychology in action 14.8
Mutual support works in intimate relationships

Kieran Sullivan and her colleagues have studied the longitudinal effects of mutual support among newlyweds, focussing on causes and solutions for *relationship distress*. They recruited 172 couples, aged 18–35 years, who had been married less than six months and observed them in conversations as they solved marital problems they had experienced and discussed ways in which they had given each other personal support. The researchers made contact with the participants 10 times over a 10-year period, the first three times in an observational setting and the remaining times by having each person complete a marital satisfaction questionnaire. During this time 37 couples divorced – a divorce rate of 22 per cent.

Relationship distress occurs when a partner discloses important thoughts or feelings that are not validated or understood by the other; or when either partner acts to invalidate the other. The consequences suggest that one's partner has no understanding, care or compassion.

Source: Sullivan, Pasch, Johnson and Bradbury (2010).

caring, and arising from lives that are shared and the myriad experiences that only time can provide. In this way, we can get a glimpse of how both the Western 'love' marriage and the Eastern arranged marriage could each result in a similar perception of powerful bonding between partners.

The themes summarised in this section tally with Ted Huston's (2009) recent description of the 'behavioural ecology' of marriages that work. His longitudinal studies show that spouses who get on are:

- *domestic partners* – with either traditional or workable and customised gender role patterns;
- *lovers* – since sex is a core element of most marriages;
- *companions and friends* – mostly in genial relationships with shared activities; and are supported by a:
- *social network* – consisting of friends and relatives with whom they visit and socialise.

For better or for worse

When do partners live up to the maxim 'For better or for worse'? Jeff Adams and Warren Jones (1997) pinpointed three factors that contribute to an ongoing relationship:

1 *personal dedication* – positive attraction to a particular partner and relationship;

2 *moral commitment* – a sense of obligation, religious duty or social responsibility, controlled by a person's values and moral principles;

3 *constraint commitment* – factors that make it costly to leave a relationship, such as lack of attractive alternatives, and various social, financial or legal investments in the relationship.

Commitment

Commitment
The desire or intention to continue an interpersonal relationship.

Commitment is a concept we have referred to several times in this chapter. Commitment increases the chance that partners will stay together, and even entertaining the idea of becoming committed is important (Berscheid and Reis, 1998). Wieselquist and her colleagues found a link between commitment and marital satisfaction, acts that promote a relationship, and trust (Wieselquist, Rusbult, Foster and Agnew, 1999).

There is a series of risk factors that predict a relationship break-up, such as negative modes of communication and lack of a social support network. As a counter to a risk approach, Ximena Arriaga and Christopher Agnew (2001) built on Rusbult's concept of investment referred to earlier. Their longitudinal investigation confirmed that a healthy relationship includes high levels of three components: (1) psychological attachment, (2) a long-term orientation, and (3) an intention to persist. These components put a positive slant on the nature of commitment.

Highly committed partners have a greater chance of staying together (Adams and Jones, 1997). The very idea of subjectively committing oneself to a relationship can be more important than the conditions that led to commitment (Berscheid and Reis, 1998). Subjective commitment may be related to our self-construal, the way we think about ourselves (see Chapter 4). In a study by Cross, Bacon and Morris (2000), people who construed themselves as being the sort of people who are interdependent with others were more committed to important relationships than individuals who did not.

Jennifer Wieselquist and her colleagues found that commitment has been linked to marital satisfaction (Wieselquist, Rusbult, Foster and Agnew, 1999), to behaviour that promotes a relationship, and to trust. Promoting a relationship includes 'inspiring' acts, such as being accommodating to one's partner's needs and being willing to make some sacrifices. Wieselquist's model is *cyclical*: inspiring acts bring forth a partner's trust and reciprocal commitment, and subsequent interdependence for both in the relationship. In a similar vein, Dominik Schoebi and his colleagues distinguish between commitment and marital satisfaction as concepts, and though they are empirically related, mutual commitment can add an extra benefit. In an

11-year longitudinal study of married couples they found that when commitment includes an intention to maintain the relationship, separation or divorce is less likely. On the other hand, it takes just one partner to demonstrate a lower level of commitment than the other – a 'weak link' partner – for a slide down the path to probable dissolution to begin (Schoebi, Karney and Bradbury, 2012).

Trust and forgiveness

Trust is a particular case of the way we attribute another's motives (**see Chapter 3**). It can preserve a relationship in the face of adversity (Miller and Rempel, 2004), whereas a lack of trust is associated with an insecure attachment style (Mikulincer, 1998).In a recent study, a feeling of rejection in an insecurely attached partner when coping with a threatening interpersonal situation can be offset when both partners are highly committed (Tran and Simpson, 2009).

Forgiveness also plays a key role in relationship preservation. *To err is human, to forgive divine*: sometimes it pays to turn the other cheek – forgive a partner who has transgressed. It is a benefit with high value (McCullough, Worthington and Rachal, 1997), as is its counterpart, apologising for giving offence (Azar, 1997). Frank Fincham (2000) has characterised forgiveness as an interpersonal construct: *you* forgive *me*. It is a process and not an act, and resonates in histories, religions and values of many cultures. Forgiveness is a solution to estrangement, and a positive alternative to relationship breakdown. Forgiving a partner is also an act that can extend to later prosocial acts (see Karremans, Van Lange and Holland, 2005, **in Chapter 13**).

An ideal partner

Does your partner meet your ideals, how well do you match the expectations of your partner, and are these considerations important to your relationship? These are questions that Garth Fletcher and his colleagues have explored (Fletcher, Simpson, Thomas and Giles, 1999). Our ideal image of a partner has developed over time and usually predates a relationship in the present.

In a study of romantic relationships by Campbell, Simpson, Kashy and Fletcher (2001), people rated their ideal romantic partners on three dimensions: warmth–trustworthiness, vitality–attractiveness and status–resources, the same dimensions proposed by Fletcher as important when selecting a mate (discussed earlier). The results were in accord with the *ideal standards model*: people who think that their current partner closely matches their image of an ideal partner are more satisfied with their relationship.

This model has been extended to include how people maintain and perhaps improve a relationship by trying to regulate or control a partner's behaviour. See how Nickola Overall and her colleagues have expanded this idea in Box 14.9.

Relationship breakdown

George Levinger (1980) points to four factors that herald the end of a relationship, including those of same-sex partners (Schullo and Alperson, 1984):

1 A new life seems to be the only solution.
2 Alternative partners are available (also see Arriaga and Agnew, 2001).
3 There is an expectation that the relationship will fail.
4 There is a lack of commitment to a continuing relationship.

Rusbult and Zembrodt (1983) believe that once deterioration has been identified, it can be responded to in any of four ways. A partner can take a passive stance and show:

- *loyalty*, by waiting for an improvement to occur; or
- *neglect*, by allowing the deterioration to continue.

Alternatively, a partner can take an active stance and show:

- *voice behaviour*, by working at improving the relationship; or
- *exit behaviour*, by choosing to end the relationship.

It is not clear whether the passive or the active approach leads to more pain at the final break-up. Other factors are involved, such as previous levels of attraction, the amount of time and effort invested and the availability of new partners. It can also depend on the person's available social contact, such as support from family and friends. It is often loneliness that adds to the pain and makes life seem unbearable; if this is minimised, recovery from the ending of a relationship can be faster.

Relationship dissolution model
Duck's proposal of the sequence through which most long-term relationships proceed if they finally break down.

Self-regulation
Strategies that we use to match our behaviour to an ideal or 'ought' standard.

Partner regulation
Strategy that encourages a partner to match an ideal standard of behaviour.

Consequences of failure

A break-up is a process, not a single event. Steve Duck (1982, 2007) has offered a detailed **relationship dissolution model** of four phases that partners pass through (see Box 14.10 and Figure 14.10). Each phase culminates in a threshold at which a typical form of action follows.

You may well think, 'This is pretty grim stuff.' It is. Most often, the break-up of long-term relationships and marriages is extremely distressing. Partners who were close have tried hard over a long period to make it work – they have mutually reinforced each other and have had good times along with the bad. In the break-up of marriage, at least one partner has reneged on a contract (Simpson, 1987). The consequences of a family break-up can be serious for children.

Research highlight 14.9
Strategies for sustaining a long-term relationship

According to Nickola Overall and her colleagues, people use a variety of cognitive tactics to maintain their relationships when they judge their partner to be less than ideal. They may weather little storms along the way by:

- enhancing a partner's virtues and downplaying the faults (Murray and Holmes, 1999);
- lowering their expectations to fit more closely with what their partner offers (Fletcher, Simpson and Thomas, 2000);
- adjusting their perceptions so that their partner bears resemblance to their ideal (Murray, Holmes and Griffin, 1996).

Another approach is to work more directly on the partner. You will recall that people use self-regulation when they try to rationalise perceived self-concept discrepancies between how they are and how they want to be **(see Chapter 4)**. Overall, Fletcher and Simpson (2006), have used a similar, but more complex, concept based on the ideal standards model, with its pivotal dimensions of warmth–trustworthiness, vitality–attractiveness and status–resources. This model can throw new light on the way that we can try to improve and sustain a long-term relationship – partner regulation. Begin by comparing what we perceive with what we want relating to our

partner – test the perception against our ideal standards. Regulation kicks in when the reality begins to fall short. Overall et al. give this example: Mary places considerable importance on one of the three dimensions, status/resources; but her partner John has limited potential to be financially secure; Mary encourages John to retrain or look for another job, perhaps a major challenge. But there are brownie points on offer – John's status and resources could come much closer to Mary's ideal and lift the quality of their relationship.

In a longitudinal study extending over one year, Overall, Fletcher, Simpson and Sibley (2009) asked how successful different communication strategies might be in bringing about desired change in a partner. They found that partner regulation is a two-edged sword.

Direct and negative regulation attempts to alter traits or behaviour, e.g. by demanding or nagging, can fail and cause stress in the short-term but actually work in the long term –if a partner is obliging. Subtle and positive regulation attempts, such as being humorous and validating towards a partner, can work in the short term but fail to produce significant relationship change in the long term. 'Sometimes, even in loving, intimate relationships, it may pay to be cruel, or at least candid and honest, in order to be kind' (Overall et al., 2009, p. 638).

Social psychology in action 14.10
Phases in the break-up of a relationship

1 The *intrapsychic phase* starts as a period of brooding with little outward show, perhaps in the hope of putting things right. This can give way to needling the partner and seeking out a third party to be able to express one's concerns.

2 The *dyadic* (i.e. two-person) phase leads to deciding that some action should be taken, short of leaving the partner, which is usually easier said than done. Arguments point to differences in attributing responsibility for what is going wrong. With luck, they may talk their problems through.

3 The *social phase* involves a new element: in saying that the relationship is near an end, the partners may negotiate with friends, both for support for an uncertain future and for reassurance of being right. The social network will probably take sides, pronounce on guilt and blame and, like a court, sanction the dissolution.

4 The final *grave-dressing phase* can involve more than leaving a partner. It may include the division of property, access to children, and working to assure one's reputation. Each partner wants to emerge with a self-image of reliability for a future relationship. The metaphor for the relationship is death: there is its funeral, it is buried and marked by erecting a tablet. This 'grave-dressing' activity seeks a socially acceptable version of the life and death of the relationship.

Source: Based on Duck (1982, 2007).

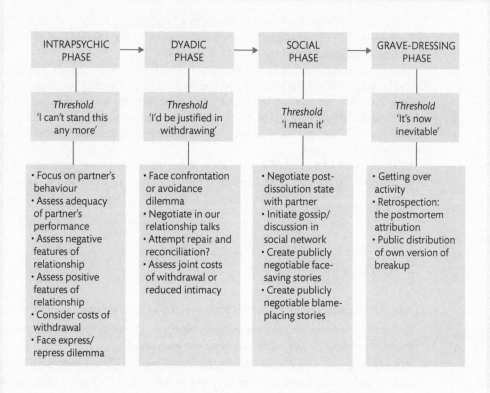

Figure 14.10 When things go wrong: phases in dissolving an intimate relationship
Source: Based on Duck (1982)

Relationship breakdown
'Should I stay or should I go?' According to Duck's model, with an end in sight they will seek support from their respective social networks

Archival research
Non-experimental method involving the assembly of data, or reports of data, collected by others.

Tucker et al. (1997) used **archival research** in a longitudinal study of more than 1,200 people in the period 1921–91, showing that men and women whose parents had divorced were more likely also to experience divorce (Tucker et al., 1997).

Serious domestic conflict also undermines parent–child relationships. Heidi Riggio (2004) studied young adults from families affected by divorce or chronic and high levels of conflict, finding that they more often felt lacking in social support and more anxious in their own relationships. Add divorce to the mixture and the quality of the relationship with the father, though not with the mother, was also diminished, perhaps because interaction with mothers was expected to continue.

In short, most of us probably live in the hope that a long-term intimate relationship will involve loyalty, trust and commitment – forever. There is truth in the adage *Look before you leap*.

Summary

- Attraction is necessary for friendships to form and is a precursor to an intimate relationship.

- Evolutionary social psychology has made strong arguments for the power of human genetic inheritance in accounting for what attracts people to each other.

- Variables that play a significant role in determining why people are attracted towards each other include physical attributes, whether they live or work close by, how familiar they are and how similar they are, especially in terms of attitudes and values.

- Social psychological explanations of attraction include: reinforcement (a person who engenders positive feelings is liked more); social exchange (an interaction is valued if it increases benefits and reduces costs); and the experience of equitable outcomes for both parties in a relationship.

- Affiliation with others is a powerful form of human motivation. Long-term separation from others can have disturbing intellectual and social outcomes, and may lead to irreversible psychological damage in young children.

- Life-cycle studies of affiliation led to research into attachment and attachment styles. The ways that children connect psychologically to their caregiver can have long-term consequences for how they establish relationships in adulthood.

- Love is distinguished from mere liking. It also takes different forms, such as romantic love and companionate love.

- Maintaining a long-term relationship involves partner regulation, using strategies that bring a partner closer to one's expectations or standards.

- The break-up of a long-term relationship can be traced through a series of stages. The relationship dissolution model notes four phases: intrapsychic, dyadic (two-person), social and grave-dressing.

Key terms

Archival research	Distributive justice	Partner regulation
Assortative mating	Emotion-in-relationships model	Procedural justice
Attachment behaviour	Equity theory	Profit
Attachment styles	Evolutionary social psychology	Proximity
Automatic activation	Familiarity	Reinforcement–affect model
Averageness effect	Hospitalism	Relationship dissolution model
Behaviourism	Instinct	Self-disclosure
Big Five	Love	Self-regulation
Commitment	Mere exposure effect	Similarity of attitudes
Comparison level	Meta-analysis	Social comparison (theory)
Consummate love	Minimax strategy	Social exchange
Cost–reward ratio	Need to affiliate	Three-factor theory of love

Literature, film and TV

Dr Tatiana's Sex Advice to All Creation: The Definitive Guide to the Evolutionary Biology of Sex

This 2006 popular science book by an evolutionary biologist, Olivia Judson, is hilarious. Dr Tatiana (Judson) receives letters from a truly bizarre array of creatures about their sex lives and relationships, and responds by explaining the surreal biology of sex to the concerned creatures. Although not directly about people, you will make comparisons, and this will make you examine your assumptions about how 'natural' the nature of human relationships and sexuality really are.

Sex and the City and Friends and Gavin and Stacey

These are classic TV series of a genre that explores, both seriously and with wit and humour, the complexity of friendships and sexual and love relationships. Although these series have finished, they did such an excellent job that we will be seeing re-runs for some time.

When Harry met Sally

1989 film by Rob Reiner, starring Billy Crystal and Meg Ryan. Classic comedy showing how love and attraction can develop over time between very dissimilar people. There are lots of wonderful little vignettes of very long-term relationships and how they first started.

One Day

A very popular 2009 David Nicholls novel that that visits the protagonists (Dexter and Emma) every July 15 for twenty years. It charts the ups and downs of their separate lives and of their relationship from their first meeting as students at Edinburgh University. The theme is similar to When Harry met Sally, but the treatment is more gritty. There is a comic gloss but the book is more about loneliness, the unpredictable cruelty of fate, and the sad gap between youthful aspiration and life's compromises. The novel has been adapted into a 2011 film directed by Lone Sherfig and starring Anne Hathaway and Jim Sturgess.

Scenes from a Marriage

Classic 1973 Swedish film and TV mini-series by Ingmar Bergman, and starring Liv Ullmann. An intense and psychologically demanding film about the pain and the peace that accompanies a lifetime of loving – the film chronicles 10 years of turmoil and love that bind a couple despite infidelity, divorce and subsequent marriages.

Casablanca

Many film critics feel that *Casablanca* is the greatest film ever – a 1942 all-time classic directed by Michael Curtiz, starring Humphrey Bogart (as Rick) and Ingrid Bergman (as Ilsa), and also with Sydney Greenstreet and Peter Lorré. A love affair between Rick and Ilsa is disrupted by the Nazi occupation of Paris – some years later Ilsa shows up in Rick's Café in Casablanca. The film is about love, friendship and close relationships, as well as hatred and jealousy, against the background of war, chaos and other impossible obstacles. Another absolute classic in the same vein is David Lean's 1965 film, *Dr Zhivago* – based on the novel by Boris Pasternak, and starring Omar Sharif and Julie Christie.

The Road

2009 John Hillcoat film based on a Cormac McCarthy novel, and starring Viggo Mortensen. A father and his young son trudge across a brutal and ruined post-apocalyptic world – the only thing that allows them to survive and keeps them sane and human is their relationship.

The Kids are All Right

A highly acclaimed 2010 film directed by Lisa Cholodenko, starring Annette Bening and Julianne Moore as a lesbian couple with two teenage kids. Mark Ruffalo plays the sperm donor who is tracked down by the younger teenager. This is a fabulous, very entertaining and often funny, but deadly serious, portrayal of the normality of non-heterosexual relationships and non-traditional marriage in modern-day society.

The Descendants

An academy award winning 2011 film by Alexander Payne, starring George Clooney. Clooney plays Matt King, a Honolulu-based lawyer, whose world is turned upside down when his wife suffers a boating accident and is thrust into a terminal coma. King has to suddenly get to re-know and rebuild his relationship with his 10-year-old son and 17-year-old daughter, and come to terms with the fact that his wife was having an affair. This is a poignant and sensitive exploration of how a dysfunctional family gradually repairs itself. If you like exuberant Hawaiian shirts, particularly modelled by Clooney, you'll get your fill here!

Love Actually

An absolutely classic 2003 British feel-good movie about . . . love. The cast includes Hugh Grant, Liam Neeson, Colin Firth, Laura Linney, Emma Thompson, Alan Rickman, Kiera Knightley, Bill Nighy, and Rowan Atkinson. Billy Bob Thornton does a fabulous cameo as the assertive US President visiting the new British Prime Minister, played by Grant and transparently modelled on Tony Blair. The movie is all about the ups, downs and obstacles to love, and has too many fabulously memorable scenes to count.

Moonrise Kingdom

A 2012 Wes Anderson romantic comedy starring Bill Murray, Tilda Swinton, Bruce Willis, Edward Norton, and Frances McDormand. Set in 1965 in Rhode Island it focuses on the flowering of a quirky pre-teen romantic relationship between 12-year-old Sam who is at a scout summer camp and 12-year-old Suzy who lives on the island with her weird family. The film is quirky, visually innovative and surreal, and all the characters are eccentric and 'strange'. It is a wonderful portrayal of relationships and love – summer innocence in the context of jaded and tired adult relationships.

Guided questions

1 What does evolutionary social psychology have to say about how humans select a mate?

2 How can a *cost-and-benefits* analysis be applied to predict the future of an intimate relationship?

3 How does a person's attachment *style* develop and can it continue later in life? A student discusses her experience of insecure attachment following years of physical and emotional abuse from her father in Chapter 14 of MyPsychLab at **www.mypsychlab.com** (watch *Attachment style*).

MyPsychLab

4 Is romantic love universal, and is it the only kind of love?

5 What has social psychology told us about why some relationships work?

Learn more

Berscheid, E. (2010). Love in the fourth dimension. *Annual Review of Psychology*, 61, 1–25. An insightful overview of social psychology's sometimes stumbling approach to the nature of love. As its title suggests, this review also deals explicitly with change in the nature of love across time.

Clark, M. S., and Lemay, E. P. Jr (2010). Close relationships. In S. T. Fiske, D. T. Gilbert, and G. Lindzey (eds), *Handbook of social psychology* (5th edn, Vol. 2, pp. 898–940). New York: Wiley. Currently the most up-to-date, detailed and comprehensive coverage of theory and research on close relationships.

Duck, S. (2007). *Human relationships* (4th edn). London: SAGE. Duck is a leading relationship theorist who focuses in this book on people's interactions, acquaintances, friendships and relationships. Students can use the resources provided to apply the concepts in their personal lives.

Fehr, B. (1996). *Friendship processes*. Thousand Oaks, CA: SAGE. An in-depth research-based analysis of friendship in modern society.

Fitness, J., Fletcher, G., and Overall, N. (2007). Interpersonal attraction and intimate relationships. In M. A. Hogg, and J. Cooper (eds), *The SAGE handbook of social psychology: Concise student edition* (pp. 219–40). London: SAGE. Detailed overview of research on close relationships, which includes coverage of emotion in relationships and evolutionary dimensions of relationships.

Goodwin, R. (1999). *Personal relationships across cultures*. London: Routledge. Draws together research from around the world to explore how fundamental differences in cultural values influence how people form and maintain various kinds of relationship.

Leary, M. R. (2010). Affiliation, acceptance, and belonging: The pursuit of interpersonal connection. In S. T. Fiske, D. T. Gilbert, and G. Lindzey (eds), *Handbook of social psychology* (5th edn, Vol. 2, pp. 864–97). New York: Wiley. This chapter includes detailed discussion of why people might be motivated to affiliate with others and thus form groups.

Mikulincer, M., and Goodman, G. S. (eds) (2006). *Dynamics of romantic love: Attachment, caregiving, and sex*. New York: Guilford. Topics such as intimacy, jealousy, self-disclosure, forgiveness and partner violence are examined from the perspective of attachment, caregiving and sex.

Rholes, W. S., and Simpson, J. A. (2004). *Adult attachment: Theory, research, and clinical implications*. New York: Guilford. Attachment theory is considered from physiological, emotional, cognitive and behavioural perspectives.

Rose, H., and Rose, S. (eds) (2000). *Alas, poor Darwin: Arguments against evolutionary psychology*. London: Vintage. Scholars from a variety of biological, philosophical and social science backgrounds raise major concerns about the adequacy of genetic and evolutionary accounts of social behaviour, including partner selection.

Shaver, P. R., and Mikulincer, M. (2007). Attachment theory and research: Core concepts, basic principles, conceptual bridges. In A. W. Kruglanski, and E. T. Higgins (eds), *Social psychology: Handbook of basic principles* (2nd edn, pp. 650–77). New York: Guilford Press. A comprehensive coverage of research and theory on human attachment and affiliation.

MyPsychLab

Use MyPsychLab to refresh your understanding, assess your progress and go further with interactive summaries, questions, podcasts and much more. To buy access or register your code, visit **www.mypsychlab.com**.

Section II

Chapter 1
What is developmental psychology?

Learning Outcomes

After reading this chapter, with further recommended reading, you should be able to:

1. Understand the history of developmental psychology;

2. Critically evaluate both the early and modern theories of developmental psychology;

3. Critically evaluate the role of developmental psychology in understanding and describing the nature of development in the child.

Introduction

When parents look proudly down at their new-born infant, many thoughts will cross their minds. What do we do now? How do we look after our baby? How will we know if we are doing this right? But once the parents settle into caring for their baby, it is likely that they will start to wonder what will this child be like and even who will this child be when he or she grows up? Developmental psychology is the branch of psychology that tries to understand how a child grows and develops and how the role of the family and schooling can impact on this. It looks at how our behaviour, our thinking patterns, our emotions and our personalities begin and change from birth to adulthood. Developmental psychologists are interested in all aspects of our behavioural and psychological development. We are interested in the *social* development of a child: from trying to understand the complexity of the relationship between a new-born infant and parent to the role of play in developing long-lasting friendships. We are interested in the *cognitive* development of the child: the development of language; understanding numbers; and developing an appreciation for art and poetry. We are interested too in *emotional* development and the way we make decisions and the role of parents and friends in developing our sense of morality and teenage decision-making: careers, friendships, sexuality and risk taking. Developmental psychology ties together social, emotional and cognitive development through the study of the growing child. It is a wide-reaching branch of psychology and for that reason is, in our point of view, one of the most rewarding to study.

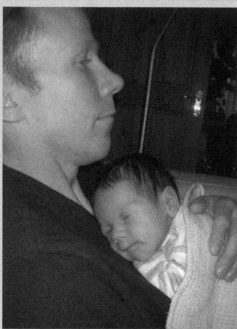

Parent holding a newborn.
Source: Lam

This chapter will introduce you to both the traditional theorists and modern developmental psychologists. To help you understand the theories that are presented in this book we will first discuss the key philosophical debates of developmental psychology and see how they have influenced the thinking of modern psychologists.

The debates of developmental psychology

Nature vs nurture

Give me a dozen healthy infants, well-formed, and my own specified world to bring them up in and I'll guarantee to take any one at random and train him to become any type of specialist I might select–doctor, lawyer, artist– regardless of his talents, penchants, tendencies, abilities, vocations and race of his ancestors

(J.B. Watson, 1930, p. 104)

One of the key debates in developmental psychology is that of nature versus nurture. The basic tenet of this debate is centred around whether the child is born with capacities and abilities that develop naturally over time regardless of up-bringing or whether the child needs social interaction and society in order to shape them. The question of whether we are born as social, functioning beings or whether our mind and behaviour are shaped by our interactions has long been the question of philosophers and psychologists alike.

In early literary history, little evidence remains of any research conducted into the experience of childhood as a specific period of human development. Children were believed to arrive as pre-formed mini-adults and, beyond measuring physical maturation, little thought was given to anything else. Historian Aries (1960) researched the view of childhood through the limited texts and paintings surviving from the Mediaeval period and, based on the evidence presented there, supposed that early scientists, artists and thinkers represented children as mini-adults. Mediaeval portraiture of children often gives them an adult face on a small, not particularly childish, body and shows the child dressed in a miniature version of adult clothes. Texts and stories of the time reveal that children were present in all the adult places including working in the fields and accompanying adults

in bars and taverns. Although the evidence is limited from this period in time, there does seem to be evidence that some children were taking a place in the adult world from the age of six or seven years and all children by the age of twelve years (Shahar, 1990).

The period of Enlightenment (the late 1600s to early 1800s) brought forward great thinkers and scientists who challenged this way of thinking, and key figures such as Locke and Rousseau were enormously influential in changing our understanding of the process of learning and acquiring knowledge. Locke's writings in particular helped lay the foundations of our modern education system and set the tone of our judicial system. In order to begin to understand the complexities of the nature vs nurture debate, let us first take a look at the key principles of these philosophers in turn and see how they have shaped our way of thinking in the new millennium.

John Locke (1632–1704)

The writings of the British philosopher John Locke described the influence of society on a person and were instrumental in the development of law and government in European society. His essay *Concerning Human Understanding* (1690) is key to the nature vs nurture debate and to understanding the principles of developmental psychology. Locke was an empiricist (someone who relies on observation and experimentation to determine the truth about something) and wrote of the *tabula rasa* – the soft or blank tablet of the mind. By applying this concept to the child, this meant that the child is born essentially as a 'blank canvas' and only through social interaction does the child learn to speak, learn emotions and morals, learn to exist within a society that ultimately has been created for the safe keeping of its inhabitants. Is this concept, however, rather simplistic when considering the development of a child? Compare Locke's philosophy with that of Rousseau.

Jean-Jacques Rousseau (1712–1778)

The philosopher Rousseau was keenly influenced by John Locke and closely studied his texts on the humanisation and understanding of society. Rousseau agreed with Locke that social norms and values were a strong factor in creating a person through experiences and contact with others. However, where Rousseau and Locke differed was in their vision of the new-born infant. Locke believed the

Definitions

Nature: the role of genetics in forming our behaviour, our personality or any other part of ourselves.
Nurture: the role of family, society, education and other social factors in forming our behaviour, our personality or any other part of ourselves.

Rousseau's 'noble savage'?

Source: Alamy Images/AfriPics.com

infant to be a 'clean slate' to be manipulated into a form acceptable to society; whereas Locke saw value and integrity in the spirit of society, Rousseau saw life from a different perspective and coined the term the 'noble savage' to describe the innocent, good child who becomes corrupted by society and all that is wrong within it. For Rousseau, society was an insincere and crooked place that was harmful to children who by sheer luck of birth he considered were almost angelic in nature.

STOP AND THINK

What do these early philosophers and theorists have to contribute to our understanding of the child in modern society?

To understand the application of early philosophers to our perception of early childhood, we need to evaluate the contribution each had to the changing role of children in society. We have John Locke, a philosopher who believed in the scientific methods of observation and systematic experimentation in finding truth and knowledge. Locke declared that the infant is born with a mind resembling the *tabula rasa* and believed that society tames, creates and nurtures the infant. Finally, we have Rousseau declaring that the infant is corrupted by the sins and deviances of a ruthless society. Consequently, we have in place the seeds of the nature vs nurture debate. Are we born with our capabilities, knowledge, morals and values or does society shape, cultivate and support our infant into a full

member of humanity? To attempt to answer this question in more recent society, we will look at one of the findings of the Minnesota Twin Study; a large-scale study of over 8000 twins that was begun in the early 1980s.

In 1981, Thomas Bouchard as a researcher connected with The Minnesota Twin Study began a study comparing the experiences of genetically identical twins raised by different parents. Theoretically, if Locke or Rousseau are correct, then twins should show considerable differences throughout their life-span if they have been raised in different environments. Yet the outcome of The Minnesota Twin Study provided evidence of slightly different outcomes for the twins but mostly of considerable similarities in the temperaments, educational and career choices and even relationship patterns in the separated twins. Bouchard argued that this study provided evidence for the importance of genetics in determining, and his paper published later (Bouchard *et al.*, 1990) confirmed his initial findings. This report of long-term findings on the 100 sets of twins who had been raised by different parents showed a consistent effect. Essentially, there was no significant difference in twins raised apart and twins raised together on measures of personality and temperament, occupational and leisure-time interests and social attitudes. Bouchard's conclusion was criticised for relying too heavily on the assumption that genetics were responsible for the twins' similarities in temperament, career paths and relationship choices (Joseph, 2001). Joseph argued that the twins who took part in the study were motivated by a sense of sameness and similarity and that this bias influenced the reporting by the twins of their childhood experiences and life outcomes. However, Bouchard did not disagree on this point and argued in the 1990 paper that the very nature of the twins' temperament could influence the environment they were raised in. For instance, Bouchard noted that twins who were considered fairly calm and easy-going as children would be more likely to report experiencing a calm and easy-going childhood regardless of whether they were raised together or apart.

What, therefore, does this tell us about the argument of nature *versus* nurture? Bouchard's work appears to demonstrate that the two cannot be meaningfully separated and distinguished in research of this kind. Perhaps the nature vs nurture debate is an academic one that has little application in real-life settings. How can we truly distinguish our very own nature if it is defined by genetics, by our social environment, our upbringing and our responsiveness to events happening around us?

The 21st century debate: nature vs nurture – is there another way?

In the 21st century, most psychologists have decided that neither the nature debate nor the nurture debate on its own is likely to be fully accountable for the physical, emotional and cognitive development of the child. Although some theorists may cling more tightly to either side of the nature vs nurture debate, most will concede that it is likely that there is an interaction between the two that can be identified as a point on a *continuum*. Take for example the figure below. Figure 1.1 represents the connection between the influence of *nature* and the influence of *nurture* on an aspect of behaviour:

Figure 1.1. The nature-nurture continuum.

If the behaviour is 'walking', then we might represent the prominence of *nature* over *nurture* by marking the connecting line with an 'X' nearer the *nature* end of the continuum (Fig. 1.2). Learning to walk requires a certain amount of physical development, but the propensity to walk present at birth combined with parental encouragement to walk is more significant in encouraging a child to walk than parental encouragement alone. Thus at the point of learning to walk, the influence of the *natural* skills a child is born with and develops is more influential than the simple *nurturing* of the parents.

Compare this to a more complex example of a child learning to socialise with other children and engage in play with them on his first day at pre-school. If we follow Locke's philosophy that the child is born as a *tabula rasa* then the child will need to learn how to play with other children. In this instance, the influence of nature vs

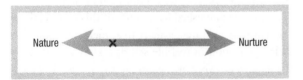

Figure 1.2. The nature–nurture continuum: *nature* is the dominant force.

Figure 1.3. The nature–nurture continuum: *nurture* is the dominant force.

nurture in the child's social development might be represented on the graph by a point Y (Fig. 1.3).

Although this is a simplistic way of looking at the current nature vs nurture debate, it does reveal the complexity of the issues at hand. When considering the role of nature or nurture in developmental psychology, we need to consider many factors: the age of the child; the biological stage or physical development; the behaviour under investigation; the social situation and the cognitive powers present or needed in order to achieve the phenomenon under investigation. Thus our young boy who is standing apart from the game on his first day at pre-school can be considered in this way: is he old enough to play with the other children? Is he strong enough or tall enough to take part in the game? What is the game and could he take part? Does he know the children playing the game? Can he understand the rules of the game? In answering these questions, you will be able to come to a conclusion on the reason why the little boy is not taking part in the game. Is it more to do with nature (not old enough, strong enough or tall enough) or is it more to do with nurture (does not know the rules of the game, is unsure how to take part, is lacking in confidence).

The importance of early experiences

How important are your early childhood experiences in shaping the person you are in adulthood? Much of developmental psychology deals with what we can and cannot do at different times in our lives. Consider some of the questions raised in the field of developmental psychology that investigate the importance of early experiences (Ainsworth *et al.*, 1978). What will our adult love relationships be like if we had a close relationship to our mothers as children? How would our adult relationships be different if we had been raised without a mother, perhaps we had been raised in institutional care? How important is that early relationship between a mother and her child in shaping who we are as adults? Equally as importantly, can the effects of that early relationship be changed once we reach adulthood?

One of the key factors in the argument of the importance of early experiences is whether we continue to develop socially, emotionally and cognitively into adulthood or whether we are essentially fully formed during early childhood. Although the study of developmental psychology focuses on childhood as the most important time of development, there is also a growing recognition of the nature of adulthood as a period of continuing change and development. Jean Piaget (1952) for instance created a theory of cognitive development that covered the period from birth to around the late teenage years; yet Erikson, who was highly influenced by Piaget's work, argued that our psychosocial development extended from birth right through to late adulthood. Both theorists, however, believed that in early infancy the child learns key skills that provide the building blocks for later life. As those foundation skills such as forming an attachment to a carer, learning to make sounds or grasping wooden blocks are acquired, so the child, teen and then adult can steadily build on these skills and form complex attachments to friends and lovers, learn one or more languages and build play or even real houses.

Thus, early experiences in developmental psychology are important in moulding who we are as children and in helping us to understand who we are as adults. It is also important to know how critical the experiences of the early years are. Developmental psychology tries to answer the question: is the child who is shaped by his early experiences a child who will continue to grow emotionally and psychologically through the teenage years and into adulthood or are we fully formed and our personalities unchangeable by the time we go to school?

STOP AND THINK

- Are you a product of your early experiences or are you continuing to change and grow as an adult?
- What are the implications of your answer when trying to understand what type of parent you are/will be?
- Can you change who you are?

Stage theories of development

Much of what you read in developmental psychology talks about stage theories – the acquisition of skills via a series of stages. All the key developmental theorists describe a series of age-related phases which all have the same key features. First, at a defined age, the child enters into a 'developmental stage'. At this point, the child cannot do the task that is described in that stage. Over a prescribed period of time, the child learns to complete that task and will then leave that developmental stage in readiness to enter the next.

Take as an example, children at play (see Chapter 9, Attachment and Early Social Experiences). Developmental psychologist Mildred Parten described a theory of play that suggested that at age two, children engage in something called *parallel play*. This is when children play beside each other but not with each other. They might use the same toys, but the children do not interact with each other and are not working together to achieve a goal. Compare this to *cooperative play* when children engage in formal games that she saw in children aged 3 years and over. Here children play together rather than side-by-side and the games have rules and boundaries. They may involve role-playing social roles (such as playing 'mummies and daddies' or 'doctor and patient') and can develop into quite complex games. This type of play is more complex than parallel play as it involves effective communication and cooperation rarely seen before the child is three years of age. So, the type of play shown by a child is determined by other aspects of their psychological development. The degree of language skill (so that they can convey the meaning of the game to each other), memory (so that they can remember who is who in the game and what the purpose of the game is) and an understanding of what other people

Definitions

Attachment: a strong enduring affectionate bond an infant shares with a significant individual, usually the mother, who knows and responds well to the infant's needs.

Stage theories: theories based on the idea that we progress through a pattern of distinct stages over time. These stages are defined by the acquisition or presence of abilities and we generally pass through them in a specified order and during a specified age range.

Role play is an important part of a child's development

Source: Pearson Education Ltd./Jules Selmes

do (so that 'mummies' and 'daddies' are doing the 'right things' and everyone knows who is who in the game).

There is plenty of evidence supporting stage theories in child development. With play, you have a case where certain play styles are more prominent at certain ages because of the needs for other cognitive skills to be sufficiently developed. Without the ability to communicate and remember complex game patterns, the child will be unable to engage in that game. However, if you were to observe children at play you would see that in fact more than one style of play is taking place in a school playground. Some younger children will be playing complex games more suited to their older counterparts and some older children will be playing very simple games, better suited to the younger children.

Does this mean then that the different play styles do *not* follow a stage theory? Take the experience of the only child in the family and compare his play style to that of a child with many siblings. Children with older siblings often display play styles more advanced than their peers because the older siblings have taught them these more complex games. Stage theories generally do not account for the impact older siblings may have for instance on a child's play style or even their language development. Stage theories too are often seen as inflexible and unidirectional. Piaget's theory of cognitive development (Piaget, 1932) (see Chapter 2, Theoretical Perspectives), for instance, suggests that children progress in a linear fashion through increasingly complex stages of cognitive skills. Within each stage there are many phases which describe in detail our progression through each stage. Each phase is characterised by the acquisition of an ability – physical or mental – and only through successful completion of this phase can there be progression to the next. Piaget does not appear to make allowance for

the developing child to return to a stage, or even to miss a stage out and jump to the next. Thus there is a certain rigidity to Piaget's theory that does not reflect the individual experience of a child. However, for many psychologists, stage theories have endured as useful and often remarkably robust tools for understanding the child's social, psychological and behavioural development.

Continuous vs discontinuous development

Some developmental psychologists see children's development as a continuous process of change where the child becomes steadily more skilled at what they are doing, whilst others see children's development as a discontinuous process of change, where the child becomes skilled in a series of leaps and bounds separated by periods of calm and little change.

The stage theorists tend to hold the view that development is a discontinuous process of change. Piaget and other theorists saw children of different ages as being qualitatively different, that is that there is a significant, remarkable difference in how the older children think and appear to make sense of the world. Piaget noted that younger children were not able to complete certain tasks that an older child could, and would, with ease. Piaget demonstrated this with the Conservation of Liquid task (see Chapter 7, The Development of Mathematical Thinking). An experimenter has two identically shaped flasks of coloured water. She pours one into a tall, thin flask and asks the child, which has the most water in it. The four year old will reply that the taller, thinner flask contains more water. The six year old will reply (correctly) that both flasks contain the same amount of water. Although both children see the water being poured from identical short flasks, only the six year old knows that, even though the one flask looks taller, it still contains the same amount of water.

> **Definitions**
>
> Continuous development: change that occurs at a steady pace, perhaps showing a constant, consistent improvement or growth.
>
> Discontinuous development: change that occurs in what appear to be great bursts of achievement following a period of steady consolidation of perhaps knowledge or skill.

Which flask has more liquid in it?

STOP AND THINK

How does Piaget's Conservation of Liquid task
provide support for discontinuous development in
a child?

Piaget's work has been extremely influential and, in
particular, the Conservation of Liquid task is still carried
out to test children's level of thinking. However, recent research has shown that most of child development appears
to follow a continuous process of change. The work of
modern developmental psychologists such as Dr Linda
Smith at the Indiana University Cognitive Development
Laboratory has revealed that most development occurs
methodically, skill by skill and may develop faster in one
skill than in another, resulting in asynchronous staging
(Fischer and Bidell, 2006).

So, which way of addressing child development is
correct? Should we be striving to find clearly defined
stages in behaviour that we can tie to age ranges in our
theories or should we be looking at behaviour as a learning process that progresses sometimes quickly sometimes slowly through childhood? The chapters in this
book will help you to make up your mind. For some behaviours and skills, the stage theories work very well in
helping us to understand that particular aspect of child
development. For other skills, however, the stage theories do not work so well and we will consider the role of
other development theories in understanding a child's
behaviour. To help you evaluate the contribution a theory makes to our understanding of child development,
we have produced a 'checklist' of six criteria that you
should consider. Remember, a theory is never true or
false, but can be considered to provide either a 'good' or
a 'poor' contribution to our understanding of human
behaviour.

Difinition

Asynchronous development: the situation that
arises when a child is performing at a more
advanced stage in one developmental skill and a less
advanced stage in a second developmental skill, for
example, the child may be performing well in Piaget's
Conservation of Liquids task but less well in
Kohlberg's Heinz dilemma task (see Chapter 13,
Adolescence) measuring moral development
(Kohlberg, 1976).

How good is your theory?

1. Is the theory specific to a particular behaviour or is it
   more generally applicable?

   For example, a researcher wants to know whether a
   child knows right from wrong. Consider the theories
   that you might want to apply to answering this question. You could start with Piaget's theory of cognitive
   development. How might you use Piaget's theory to
   support your argument? Is Piaget's theory a general
   theory of cognitive development or a specific theory
   of moral decision-making? Would Kohlberg's theory
   of moral development be more appropriate?

2. Is the theory appropriate for use?

   Find the original source of the theory – usually a
   paper has been written and presented in a peer-
   reviewed, academic journal. Is there evidence of a
   strong consideration of the rationale for the theory?
   Does it seem to have a strong evidence base? Have
   the theorists given sufficient thought to the strengths
   and weaknesses of other people's theories when
   developing their own?

3. Is the theory useful? Can it be tested?

   There should be enough detail in the theory that you
   could set up a study that would allow you to test the
   application of the theory on a group of participants
   of your choice.

4. Is the theory valid?

   Does the theory make predictions? If so, can you
   work out how you might obtain the outcomes it

predicts? If you were to conduct your study following the theory, would you get the same findings as the authors? Conversely, if you conduct your study and your findings are not the same as the authors, can you argue that the theory is then false?

5. Is the theory 'parsimonious'?

   Is the theory overly complicated or does it represent the simplest (parsimonious) explanation of the behaviour or concept? If a theory comes together with a certain element of elegance, it may generally be the case that the theory has touched on the key or fundamental elements underpinning the concept and therefore has considerable 'goodness of fit'. If the theory feels complex and unwieldy, then you may want to see if it is 'missing the point' and would benefit from a reconsideration or restructuring of the key elements.

6. Does the theory fit alongside other psychological theories?

   Theories, like people, should not exist solely in isolation. A strong theory should be connected to other theories relating to behaviour, development or other psychological principle and you should be able to demonstrate this connection. For instance, Kohlberg's theory of moral development is strongly influenced by Piaget's theory of cognitive development and Erikson's theory of psychosocial development.

What is 'normal' development?

The final debate we are going to consider in this chapter concerns why we are interested in what 'normal' development is and how we can use this information as psychologists. Let us return to the stage theories of child development as an example. As we have briefly discussed, some behaviours fall neatly into stage theories and other behaviours do not. What we have not discussed yet is the *value* of a stage theory in describing child development. If our child develops behaviours and skills that align to a particular stage in a theory, do we say that our child is developing 'normally'? Perhaps, more importantly, if our child does *not* develop behaviours and skills in accordance to a particular stage in a theory, do we say that out child is developing 'abnormally'?

Later in the book you will encounter many examples of child development that may reflect either 'abnormal' development or 'individual differences' in development. We will look at whether it is possible to make a judgement on whether the child is unable to accomplish the task or whether the child will in time mature in his capabilities and 'catch up' with the other children in his class. Mathematicians and psychologists have spent a lot of time creating measurement tools to see whether the child is developing normally or not. For instance, for decades now scientists have been using and modifying scales for measuring intelligence (such as the Intelligence Quotient scale) in a bid to find out what level of cognitive skills are present in most of the population at different years of age. By defining what tasks most children can do, at say age 7 years, researchers can say what is 'normally' achieved by children of age 7 years. The researchers can then also say, therefore, that a child with level of cognitive skill above the 'norm' is achieving beyond her years and that a child with a level of cognitive skill below the 'norm' is not achieving well for her years. If used appropriately, knowing this information can help teachers provide higher level work to the high performing child and more support and help to the lower performing child.

RECOMMENDED READING

For a critical review of modern developmental psychology:

Burman, E. (2000). *Deconstructing Developmental Psychology*. London: Routledge.

RECOMMENDED WEBSITES

The developmental section of the British Psychological Society has news and events relating to developmental psychology:

www.bps.org.uk/dps

The European Society for Developmental Psychology also has news and events relating to developmental psychology and useful resources:

www.esdp.info

 Watch an interview with Jean Piaget in which he talks about his cognitive developmental theory. Further resources can be found at www.pearsoned.co.uk/gillibrand

Chapter 2
Theoretical perspectives

Learning Outcomes

After reading this chapter, with further recommended reading, you should be able to:

1. Critically discuss what makes a theory;

2. Evaluate the key theoretical perspectives in developmental psychology;

3. Understand the philosophical perspectives underlying key developmental psychology theories;

4. Critically evaluate the use and application of theories and perspectives in understanding real-life examples of human behaviour from a developmental perspective.

How do we know what is the 'right' way to raise a child?

Any trip into the parenting and family section of a bookshop will reveal shelves upon shelves of books telling parents what to expect during pregnancy, what to expect following the birth, how to raise a child and how to get the best from your child. New parents often receive well-meant advice from doctors, other mothers and their own families on looking after their baby: how to get him to sleep, how much should she be eating and how often, should you let them cry or respond to their every need. Later on, parents are often given more advice – 'read to your child every night, he should know his numbers and letters before going to school' or 'you should let your child play – there's plenty of time for her to learn to read when she goes to school'. Every week there seem to be stories in the newspapers and magazines about this or that innovation in child-rearing and tips for raising a 'happy' child. It is not surprising parents often talk about being overwhelmed with information on raising their child and feeling confused about doing what is 'right'.

- Do you think you can learn to be a parent or is parenting a natural skill that comes with having a child?
- Can psychology help us to be better parents or do the day-to-day realities of parenting make it difficult to make time to change the way we do things?

Introduction

Developmental psychologists and scientists have spent decades trying to find the answer to all of these difficult questions. Some have made their careers observing children grow and learn and have created developmental *stage* theories that describe what is 'normal' to achieve at certain ages. Some of the researchers describe the abilities that the child seems to be born with, some look at the role society has in teaching a child abilities and skills whilst others take a combined approach and integrate what we seem to be born with and how society shapes our development over time. In this chapter, we will discuss the role of these theorists in shaping our understanding of human development. We will look in detail at the theories devised by key researchers in the field of developmental psychology and seek to understand how to relate these theories to our real-life experiences of growing up. We will then conclude this chapter by discussing the role of these theories in understanding how we develop as children and adults and how as psychologists we might apply these theories to investigating patterns of behaviour. Throughout this chapter, we will illustrate the main points with examples of application of theory in the real world. There will also be a few quick questions along the way to ensure that you have understood the material. This chapter will help form the foundation of your study of developmental psychology so when you are reading the other chapters, do return to this one if you need reminding of the detail of the different approaches.

What is a theory?

A theory is a statement that we use to understand the world about us. We can use theories to understand why fire heats water, why people vote for particular politicians and how children learn language. A good theory begins by *describing* or *defining* the focus of the theory. In psychology, this is invariably a behaviour that we are interested in. So a theory seeking to understand the way a child learns language must first define what language is. Defining the behaviour at the focus of the theory is very important. Without a good description of the behaviour, we are unable to develop a good theory. Next a theory must seek to *explain* the behaviour. Why does the child learn language in the way they do? Is it due to a biological facility in the brain or is it due to the mother talking to the child, an impact of the social environment? You will see that some theorists prefer the biological argument in understanding behaviour and some theorists prefer the social environment argument in understanding behaviour. Other theorists prefer a combination of biology and environment in understanding human behaviour. As you study psychology, you will form an idea of which theoretical angle you align to. Often it depends on the aspect of human behaviour you study, for example, the bond between a mother and child has both biological aspects and social influences. Memory, on the other hand, has more predominantly biological influences whilst the formation of adult relationships has more predominantly social influences. The choice of which theory or theoretical perspective you prefer should always be the result of a critical appraisal of the strengths and weaknesses of the theory in describing and explaining the behaviour. This appraisal process is normally centred around the ability of the theory to *predict* behaviour. Does a social learning theory explain the development of language in children raised in isolation? Does a biological theory of learning explain the ability to write poetry? Theories are useful tools for structuring our understanding of human behaviour, but take note, theories are not necessarily exact statements – they tend to be useful for understanding a situation *most* of the time but, particularly when we are trying to understand *human* behaviour, there always seem to be situations when the theory does not quite fit. This does not mean that the theory has no value or use, but it often means that the human behaviour is more complex than initially thought. Many psychological theories are constantly under review – look at a selection of journals in your library to see evidence of this review process and the often lively debate surrounding it.

STOP AND THINK

Why do we want psychological theories to not only describe behaviour but to have a predictive quality too?

Theoretical perspectives

Stage vs continuous theories

The majority of theories of child development can be conceptualised as being either stage theories or theories of continuous change.

Stage theories

Stage theories tend to map out the development of competency in a pattern of behaviour that has been devised from the observation of behaviour and the calculation of what most children can do and at what age. An example of a stage theory is Piaget's *cognitive development theory* (Piaget, 1962). In this theory, Piaget describes in detail what a child should be able to do at three months of age, six months, twelve months and so on. Piaget's theory evolved from observing children of all ages at play and in other interactions with each other and with their environment. He

Definitions

Theory: a statement that we use to understand the world about us with three important component parts: it defines, explains and predicts behaviour.
Stage theories: theories based on the idea that we progress through a pattern of distinct stages over time. These stages are defined by the acquisition or presence of abilities and we generally pass through them in a specified order and during a specified age range.

was interested in developing a statement of what was 'normal' behaviour in a child and how you could use this information to assess possible developmental delay.

There are a number of stage theories in developmental psychology, but all stage theories have a number of common elements. First, the stages are precisely defined and describe very specific abilities. They may describe the ability of a child to say the letter 'b' or they may describe the young person's ability to consider the outcome of a hypothetical question but, either way, both theories will clearly define the skill being acquired. Second, the theories assume that the child enters the stage unable to accomplish the task, develops competency over a period of time and then usually is considered to have completed that stage when they demonstrate an easy familiarity with that skill or task. Third, there is an assumption that every stage will be completed in the order presented in the theory. There is no jumping ahead to a stage much later in the theory and there is no omission of a stage. Finally, there is a strong belief that every child will progress through the stages within the age ranges described in the theory.

The strengths of stage theories in developmental psychology lie in the ability to describe in detail the development of a behaviour according to age-specific 'norms'. From the psychological perspective, it is useful to know that a child is developing 'normally' but it is perhaps more useful to know when a child is *not* developing in line with other children. From the educational perspective, it is also useful to know when children are ready to learn about mathematics for instance and when to introduce the study of poetry. However, there are weaknesses with stage theories. For instance, consider the implications that might arise if a child does not fit into the precise age ranges for acquiring a certain behaviour, say language, and thus does not appear to be developing 'normally'? Is the child in need of further support to help her develop language at the same rate as other children, or will she just take a little bit longer? Stage theories present quite rigid, precise statements of what is 'normal' development but do not take into account the individual's rate of development. Stage theories conceptualise development as a linear, hierarchical process, but the reality is often less well-defined. A child with older siblings may show advanced skills in play because he has learned advanced games from his older brothers. Another child may take longer to learn the basics of mathematics but gets there in the end.

Theories that take a less rigid view of development take a more continuous approach to development.

Reading together helps build the bond between father and son.

Source: Pearson Education Ltd./Lisa Payne Photography

The continuous or lifespan perspective

The continuous perspective has at its core four assumptions: development is life-long, is multidimensional, is *plastic* and can ebb and flow across the lifespan, and can be affected by many elements, predictable and unpredictable. This perspective is gaining in popularity as it explains well the individual differences in experiences throughout life and how these experiences affect our individual course through childhood and right into late adulthood.

The continuous perspective believes that development is life-long and does not stop as we reach adulthood. Thus, our emotional development begins with the formation of simple attachments driven by our need for food, warmth and security, through the formation of childhood friendships to the building of long-term emotionally rewarding relationships in adulthood. This perspective sees development as occurring in many dimensions and directions – development can occur along physical, emotional and cognitive dimensions; some development is progressive – acquire more functions, some development is regressive – stop studying languages in order to focus more on behavioural sciences. Often there is a combination of the two, for example, moral development. As we get older, our decision-making becomes more complex, integrating knowledge, experience and more advanced philosophical skills and we reduce our reliance on simple, *reductionist* philosophies in everyday problem-solving activities.

In the continuous perspective, development is highly plastic – there may be 'bulges' of accelerated development or 'slim' periods of slow or steady development. For instance, language development in a child starts slowly in the early years and then word acquisition and grammar competence 'explode' in the pre-school years with the child learning thousands of words before the age of six years. Exponents of continuous development believe that development is affected by many elements or influences. Age-related influences can be seen in the age at start of school, learning to drive, being able to vote or age at retirement. All these time-points create a specific social cohort, e.g. school peer group, car drivers, voters or pensioners, all of whom usually have a certain status attributed to them. These cohorts may be used as population identifiers for government purposes such as distributing school attainment tests, public policy on road tax or pension provision, or could be used for marketing purposes such as cartoon character detailing on school lunch boxes, advertising campaigns for particular brands of cars or in developing promotional material for life insurance products. This perspective also takes into account cohort effects of 'history-graded influences'. Thus, those people born in the 1930s have had the similar experience of childhood and early adulthood being influenced by the Second World War and periods of food rationing. Their 'make-do' philosophy is very different to that of people born in the 1980s – a period of financial growth and technological advancement. These people are more likely to have a 'use it and throw it away' philosophy and may find it difficult to empathise with the older generation's belief that things once broken can be repaired and re-used.

In the continuous perspective, development can also be affected by what may be called 'non-normative' influences. These are influences that occur to an individual or small group of individuals that perhaps cannot be predicted or their effect be pre-determined. An example of this might be the experience of a visit to a place of particular historical interest that triggers a life-long interest in studying history, or becoming a home-carer looking after a poorly elderly parent or child with severe disabilities. None of these events could perhaps be predicted in the person's developmental life path but are important and have a significant impact on the direction in which that person's life experiences head. As we get older, these non-normative influences become much more important in steering our developmental path and age-related effects become much less influential.

The continuous approach also suggests that many of these influences work in conjunction with each other, for example, look at the position of puberty in our physical development. The timing of onset of puberty can be determined by a combination of three factors: biological triggers; quality of diet and level of fitness; and environmental stressors. Those with a good, healthy diet living in a low-stress environment and taking plenty of exercise are more likely to experience slightly later onset of puberty than those living in a high-stress environment with a high-fat diet and low levels of exercise (Graber *et al.*, 1994).

Definition

Continuous perspective: development is a continuous, life-long experience which does not follow specific steps and stages but early experiences are built upon and skills expanded continuously.

STOP AND THINK

What are the strengths and weaknesses in adopting a stage theory approach to child development? Support your argument with reference to a particular aspect of development, for example, language.

Psychoanalytical perspective of development

The key assumptions of the psychoanalytic perspective are:

- There are three levels of consciousness: the conscious, the pre-conscious and the unconscious.
- The unconscious mind is key to understanding human behaviour.
- The unconscious mind houses our instinctual drives which strive to maximise our ability to survive.

- The core of our personality is determined by the age of five or six years and will not change after this age, even in adulthood.

Sigmund Freud (1856–1939) psychoanalytic theory of development

Key aspects of Freud's psychoanalytic theory stem from his work with patients with psychological disorders like anxiety and depression that manifested in physical problems such as partial paralysis or sudden blindness, what Freud called 'hysterical' disorders. Freud thought that as these disorders did not seem to have physical origins, then they must have origins in our 'psyche' or our mind. The mind therefore had to be investigated if he was to understand why these patients were experiencing such devastating physical problems.

Take for example our decision to study psychology. Why have you chosen to do this? Is it to study in more detail something, human behaviour perhaps, that fascinates you? Are you studying psychology in order to get the foundation education needed to go into a therapeutic

LIFESPAN

Word retrieval across the lifespan

A study by Kave *et al.* (2010) asked 1145 participants to name 48 black-and-white drawings of simple items such as a hat. Each participant had as much time as they needed to remember the word for each item and, if the word given was too general a term for the item (for example, the participant named the item "hat"), the participant was prompted for the more specific name for the item (for example, the participant named the item "hat"), the participant was prompted for the more specific name for the item (for example, "top-hat"). If the name of the item could not be recalled, the researchers provided a cue either of the item's use (for example, you might wear this on your head) or of the first letter sound of the word (for example, this word begins with the sound 't'). Participants varied in age from 5 years to 86 years. There were roughly 50%

female participants up to age 50 years and then the percentage of female participants rose to around 65% in the over-75s.

The researchers found that word recall was approximately 35% accurate in the five to six year olds, rising steadily to 48% in the 40–60 year olds, then returned to approximately 35% in the 75–80+ year old participants. The researchers conclude that word recall therefore improves into middle age and then declines into older age.

- Think about the findings of this research.
- Why is it that word recall increases from age 5 years to age 35 years?
- Why do we then see a steady performance in word recall during middle adulthood?
- What are the implications for the decrease in word recall as we get older?

profession? Whatever your reason, according to Freud, you will all be doing it for the fundamental motivation of encouraging pleasure, e.g. following your passion for studying human behaviour, or it could be the motivation of avoiding pain, e.g. going into the workplace into a profession or career you have little interest in.

Freud's theory of psychosexual development (Freud, 1949) expanded on the nature of the pleasure/pain motivation in developing each of our personalities. Freud argued that our personality is composed of three parts: the id, the ego and the superego. The id effectively reflects our basic biological impulses. The id controls our sexual needs, our food and drink needs, our warmth and comfort needs. The ego describes our conscious decision-making part of us. It develops in the first few years to life to manage and deliver the needs of the id. The third part of the personality, the superego, reflects the social norms of the community the child is growing up in. This part of the personality naturally becomes more sophisticated as the child ages and is exposed to more rules and regulations.

Definitions

Id: our biological impulses.
Ego: our conscious decision-making process.
Superego: our sense of morality and social norms.

The job of the ego becomes much harder the older the child is and the more aware they are of the social norms regulating their behaviour. Its role is to satisfy the id (the biological urges) whilst satisfying the needs of the superego (the social regulations of behaviour). When the ego is successful at balancing the needs of both the id and the superego, the person feels content. However, when the ego is unable to balance the needs of the id and superego, Freud argues that the person feels anxious. It is these feelings of anxiety that Freud explored with his patients. Freud felt that high levels of anxiety were causing his patients to have physical manifestations of problems for which there were no other apparent causes. Freud described a number of ways in which people try to cope with anxiety as defence mechanisms. If you were unable to cope with the anxiety of unresolved libido, then you would experience psychological tensions – anxiety, depression and other mental illness – whether that anxiety stemmed from events recently or events a long time in your past childhood. What type of mental illness you experienced could be linked to the age at when you experienced the anxiety induced by an unsuccessfully acting ego and the defence mechanisms or manner in which you tried, also unsuccessfully, to cope.

Definition

Defence mechanisms: coping styles used during moments of anxiety brought on by unresolved libidinous urges.

Freud described a number of key stages in a person's life that corresponded with different demands of the pleasure/pain motivation, the libido. Freud believed from talking to his patients that the main driving force behind the libido was not satisfying the survival needs of hunger, thirst and warmth, but of sexual satisfaction. Thus, his theory is called the *theory of psychosexual development* (see Table 2.1 for a brief description of the stages).

Table 2.1. Freud's stages of psychosexual development.

Stage	Approximate age	Focus of libido	Developmental task associated with this stage
Oral	0–12 months	Mouth	Feeding: moving from breast and other forms of milk on to solid foods.
Anal	12–36 months	Anus	Toilet training: moving from passing urine and faeces without control to manipulating the need to go to the toilet and using a potty rather than a diaper or nappy.
Phallic	36 months–6 years	Genitals	Gender: gender awareness, genital stimulation and resolving anxiety by identifying with same-sex parent.
Latent	6–12 years	No focus	This is a period of calm and resolution of the previous stages. No dramatic development occurs.
Genital	12 years onwards	Genitals	Sexuality: becoming sexually aware of self and others, sexual stimulation and formation of intimate relationships.

Source: adapted from Boyd & Bee (2006).

Freud's theory of psychosexual development gave him a framework for understanding the sources of his patients' anxiety. The patient who presented as obese and found herself feeling socially ostracised because of it he described as having unresolved issues at the *oral* stage of development. Her id wanted food and experienced pleasure with eating. The superego was constructed of the social norm possibly based in the religious ideal of slim body shape and the rejection of overeating as the sin of gluttony. Her ego could not resolve the conflict between her hunger and pleasure from eating and her religious beliefs of moderation and thus she experienced a high level of anxiety. The patient who found himself unable to settle into relationships and experience sexual intimacy with his wife had unresolved conflict at the phallic stage. He had not been able to identify well with his father as a child and had not developed a stable sexual identity for himself and others. His id wanted sexual satisfaction at any cost and his superego required sexual behaviour within the realms of marriage. His ego struggled to moderate his sexual libido and he therefore experienced anxiety within his relationship and sought satisfaction outside the marriage.

Freud's interest in the causes of his patients anxiety developed into an interest in the coping strategies his patients used to alleviate the anxiety. Rather than resolving the sources of the emotional upset, all his patients used what Freud called *defence mechanisms* to 'cover up' their feelings. Some patients used *denial* and behaved as if the problem did not exist. Others used *repression* and pushed the memory away to the back of their minds or *rationalised* their behaviour to justify their feelings. Other defence mechanisms reported were *projecting* the beliefs of yourself onto others or *displacing* emotions onto someone else instead of the person the anger or anxiety was provoked by, and some patients even *regressed* their behaviour to a younger age (such as sucking their thumb when an adult in the face of adversity).

Critique

Freud's writing on the theory of the conscious and unconscious mind initiated discussion and research into understanding the motivations for behaviour and the causes of emotional upset in people. Other theorists discredited him for his lack of academic rigour in constructing and presenting his theories and many people believe his theory to be lacking in empirical evidence. However, it is important to know Freud's work as many other more critically

acclaimed developmental theories arose from his work, and his notion of age-related stages of development forming a hierarchical model of behavioural achievement is evident in many developmental scientists' work.

Erik H. Erikson (1902–1994) psycho-social theory of development

Erik Erikson was born in Germany during a period of intense social and economical change. As a young adult, he was heavily influenced by the work of Sigmund Freud and studied psychoanalytic theory alongside Sigmund's daughter, Anna, in Vienna, Austria. The events of the Second World War forced Erikson and his wife to relocate to America where he wrote his seminal text *Childhood and Society* (Erikson, 1950). This book contained his detailed observations on the psychological changes we experience in the period from infancy to late adulthood, changes he described as the *eight ages of man*.

Erikson, like Freud, saw child development as following a specific pathway through a series of stages that reflect our ability to achieve a certain task. Table 2.2 demonstrates how similar Freud and Erikson's theories are. Erikson believed that we each of us follow the same pathway through these stages. The route is linear and uni-directional: we do not double-back on ourselves, miss any of the stages or skip ahead. Erikson's proposed stages of child development map neatly onto Freud's theory of psychoanalytic development and expand on it into adulthood and old age.

Each of Erikson's stages is described as a *crisis* (Erikson, 1968) between our biological or psychological needs and the experiences we have with others and our social world. This crisis is fought in a similar way to the way that Freud describes in the role of the *ego*. We have 'wants' that need fulfilling, but we need to acknowledge the role of our environment and the people around us in setting parameters for our desires. The end of each stage is marked by a state of *resolution*. The child learns to balance their own needs with those of the people around them. For some children there is a satisfactory resolution of their needs and they come out of a stage with what Erikson described as certain positive personal characteristics. For other children, there is an unsatisfactory resolution of a stage and they may display difficulties in moving onto the next stage and 'problematic' personal characteristics. Erikson wrote that each stage has its own unique personal characteristic associated with it and

Table 2.2. Comparison of the age-related stage theories of Freud and Erikson.

Freud	Age of child	Erikson	Personal characteristic
Oral stage	Infancy to 12 months	Trust vs mistrust	*Hope*
Anal stage	12 months to 3 years	Autonomy vs shame	*Will*
Phallic stage	3 to 6 years	Initiative vs guilt	*Purpose*
Latency stage	6 years to puberty	Industry vs inferiority	*Competence*
Genital stage	Adolescence	Identity vs role confusion	*Fidelity*
	Young adulthood	Intimacy vs isolation	*Love*
	Middle adulthood	Generativity vs stagnation	*Care*
	Older adulthood	Ego integrity vs despair	*Wisdom*

Source: adapted from Crain (2005).

that it is possible that problems reported in adulthood may relate to difficulties experienced at a particular developmental stage in childhood.

Erikson's eight stage theory of development (Erikson, 1950)

Trust vs mistrust – infancy to 12 months

In the very earliest stage of life, Erikson proposed that we must learn to trust both ourselves and the people around us. We are born with basic needs such as hunger and warmth and need to have these satisfied. If we receive regular care and attention then we learn to trust that others will care for us and will fulfil our need for food or blankets. Erikson did not write that any particular style of parenting (whether it was child-centred or not) was any better for the child, just that there needed to be consistency and predictability to the care. Without predictability, Erikson argues, the child cannot learn to trust that the parent will be there when needed and thus develop a sense of contentment and safety. The baby must also learn to trust himself. During breastfeeding, the baby has to learn that sucking too hard or too softly will affect the rate at which milk is released. When the baby grows teeth, he has to learn to feed without hurting the mother. Babies who have learned to trust themselves and their parents to provide adequate care will often be calm and comfortable in the presence of others and show low levels of upset when the parent leaves the room. In contrast, babies who have not found predictability in their parents' care and have not built up a level of trust are more likely to show distressed behaviour and to become very upset when the mother leaves the room.

This is not to say, however, that the child should not learn some mistrust. Erikson argued that it is important that the baby learns that others (and possibly himself) are not always trustworthy. Without knowing *mistrust*, our baby cannot regulate his feelings of trust or he would become vulnerable to others and not wary of the dangers society can hide. The optimum outcome then for this stage of development is to experience high levels of trust tempered by awareness of mistrust. A child that succeeds in achieving this state will then, according to Erikson, develop a core personal characteristic he labelled *hope*. Hope that the world is generally a good and safe place to be and that all obstacles can be overcome. With a strong feeling of hope, the infant is now ready to progress into the next stage of development: the crisis between autonomy and shame.

Autonomy vs shame – twelve months to three years

During this stage of development, the infant learns to control her actions. Freud described this stage as the anal stage when the child experiences pleasure at defecation. During this stage the child learn to control when she needs to use the toilet and progresses from using nappies to a potty and then a full toilet. Erikson agreed with Freud that the child's development is dominated by toilet-training at this age but developed the notion of learning control further. It is typical for children at this age to use the word 'no' more than the word 'yes' for instance. Erikson argues that the child is developing the notion of self-control over objects and events in her world and by saying 'no' the child is developing a sense of *autonomy*.

Autonomy can be seen in other behaviours of a child. The child may grab a toy from a sibling and not give it back under pressure from their brother or their parent. They may demand to be held by a parent or to be let down seemingly at random. As the child's expression of need for control increases, however, so the parent starts to set parameters of what they consider acceptable behaviour. Parents start to use phrases such as 'be a good boy for Mummy' or 'be a nice girl for Granny now' to encourage the display of socially acceptable behaviour. Through this process, Erikson suggests that the child learns to feel *shame* and doubt about some of the ways in which they want to act and develops sensitivity to the needs of behaving in accordance with the rules of society or their social *norms*.

Again, the child is engaged in a crisis. This time the crisis is to develop independence and autonomy from their parents and to engage in behaviours they enjoy whilst at the same time doing so within a pattern of social norms and avoiding the feelings of shame. Resolving this crisis successfully will develop the core personal characteristic of *will*. Erikson purported that the development of will at this stage will result in an adult who in a social context is able to both restrain himself from making poor choices but who also is independently able to make decisions that satisfy himself.

Initiative vs guilt – three to six years

Children of early school age start to introduce an element of competitiveness in their activities. They want to know who is the tallest, who can run the fastest and who is their 'best' friend. Children at this stage often talk in hierarchies, for example, 'I'm the tallest, Sally is shorter than me and John is the shortest', and make games of building the highest tower from blocks and bricks. This stage demonstrates the child's need for *initiative*, Erikson writes, in that their play becomes goal-oriented and more spirited. Their play can swiftly get out of hand, however, and anyone who has ever looked after a four or five year old will know that this can happen. For instance, what starts as a simple game of jumping off a step to the ground can soon escalate to the child wanting to jump off a higher then a higher step until they start to put themselves in danger of falling and hurting themselves.

This desire to go higher and higher drives the child to accomplish more and more, but at some point the adult or carer will aim to put a stop to it, often mindful of the safety of the child. Curbing the activity, for whatever reason, then provides the child with their third crisis,

Erikson argues, that of *guilt*. By controlling the degree to which the child can show initiative, the parent is introducing more parameters to the child's behaviour. Telling the child 'Mummy wants you to stop that or you will hurt yourself' means that the child has to weigh up their desire to continue jumping from a high step with the guilt of upsetting their mother and even hurting themselves. Erikson believed that limiting activity at this stage of life really has a negative effect on the child and he felt that, after the age of six years, the child will have lost all his natural drive and energy and become a more staid, less inventive person. Later, Erikson wrote that this stage might in fact not be all bad. With the right balance of parenting and instruction, Erikson conceded that the energies of initiative could be focused into activities that are more appropriate and that children of this age could be encouraged to find artistic or sporting outlets that allowed them to develop the personal characteristic *purpose*.

Industry vs inferiority – six years to puberty

So far, our child has gained to a greater or lesser degree the personal characteristics of hope, will and purpose. Our child has developed a sense of trust, is gaining in autonomy and is learning to display initiative within prescribed boundaries. The next stage of development Freud called the *latent* stage and he described it as a period of time when little of any consequence happened, but that the child consolidated developments in the previous years in readiness for the next stage, preparing for adulthood. Erikson, however, saw this stage quite differently. He saw the pre-pubertal years as being of increasing *industry*. In many cultures, these years are ones of learning, whether this occurs within the family unit or within a structured schooling system, the child is taught necessary skills in preparation for independent adult living.

The crisis at this stage comes from the interactions with the tutor of those skills. How many of us remember the shame of being criticised for our lack of achievement in a task at school or the pleasure of receiving a commendation? Teachers use verbal praise, sticky coloured stars and league tables to reward their pupils and to encourage them in their work, but the downside of schooling can be felt when you do not receive that praise and are ridiculed for your poor performance in sport or art, writing or mathematics. These feelings of *inferiority* last a long time. We can probably all recall failing at a task or feeling embarrassed and still perhaps now do not follow pursuits that we were discouraged from at such an early age. However, with the right encouragement Erikson argues that we can all succeed at our talents and by achieving the right balance between our industry and our feelings of inferiority, we develop a sense of *competence*, our fourth personal characteristic.

Identity vs role confusion – adolescence

Erikson described this stage as a period of intense energy and drive. Freud has described this period as being one of striving for sexual identity, but Erikson went further than that in his theory. Erikson saw the focus of energy in adolescence as being directed at all aspects of life. He saw teenagers becoming upset and confused at all the new demands on them. Teenagers are keen to establish a more permanent sense of *identity* that is more complex than ever before at a time when even their very physical shape is changing on what can seem like a weekly basis.

Teenagers, Erikson argued, have to deal with creating an identity based on a new physical self, a new sexual self and a self that is concerned with other, more worldly worries such as religious belief and political persuasion. The teenager changes at such a rate that the only way she can cope with this sudden loss of the old self is to try and identify with others. This drive towards identification takes the teenager to different styles of music, clothes and activities in their need to feel like they belong, somewhere.

For many, the pursuit of identity continues through adulthood, but nowhere is it as painful or acute as in the teenage years. As more social, educational and other options open up to teenagers so some may feel ill-equipped to deal with this wide choice and, rather than embrace the opportunities, they withdraw and settle into a state of impasse. This crisis of *role-confusion* means that the young person may not be able to assimilate these choices into his identity and instead may feel as if he has fallen off the track or that life is passing him by. Many teenagers take 'time out' from their studies and spend a period of time travelling, trying different jobs or even in a complete state of inertia until they are ready to cope with the adult world ahead of them.

As the young person works towards developing her sense of identity and reducing the amount of role-confusion she feels, the teenager is building on her ability to make long-term goals and developing the ability to make decisions with far-reaching consequences.

Without this newfound skill, she will not develop the personal characteristic of *fidelity*, the ability to pursue a goal to its conclusion and will find it difficult to make long-term commitments in adulthood.

Intimacy vs isolation – young adulthood

Where teenagers take the self-centred approach and strive for a sense of identity based on who they are, what they like and what they believe in, young adults change the focus of that drive for identity by searching for intimacy with another. Erikson believed that the teenager is too caught up in finding out about himself to engage in true intimacy with another person. Only in adulthood when the sense of self is robust and your identity firmly held can you start to develop a relationship that encourages intimacy whilst also allowing for both your and the other person's strengths and weaknesses.

Erikson believed that the adult who has a poorly-defined identity and has not yet been able to settle their role confusion is unlikely to form a satisfactory intimate relationship. Erikson keenly advocated the delay of marriage until both partners had developed full identities, for without them he saw that the marriages often failed as the man and woman grew emotionally in different directions. Erikson's proposition that you cannot be comfortable with another person until you are comfortable with yourself it seems has become the foundation stone of many marriage and relationship counsellors and probably for good reason. True intimacy in adulthood means accepting each other's strengths and faults and sharing many aspects of your lives. If you are uncomfortable with yourself, you are unlikely to be able to really accept your partner's perceived failings.

The crisis facing young adults at this time is that of *isolation*, of being alone and without experiencing an intimate relationship with another. It is perhaps this fear of being alone that drives many young people into relationships that they are not ready for or able to succeed with. However, with time many adults do maintain successfully, intimate relationships that are emotionally and sexually rewarding and they experience the personal characteristic *love*.

Generativity vs stagnation – middle adulthood

Erikson described the purpose of middle adulthood to be focused on care and nurturing, particularly of children. He proposed that success at this stage involved the giving of yourself and your priorities to the raising of children. It is not simply enough, he argued, to have children in order to be *generative*; the children you have must be nurtured and you must sacrifice some of your own needs in order to satisfy theirs. Without giving to others, Erikson believed that an adult becomes *stagnant* and self-absorbed.

Although Erikson's theory was child-focused at this stage, he did write that childless couples and other adults without children did not necessarily have to become stagnant. *Generativity* could come through working with others or caring for others and through roles such as teacher, nurse or priest, but the essential element for Erikson is that these roles require you to change the focus of your efforts away from yourself to the care of others. Without the experience of nurturing and encouraging others, you are left unable to develop fully your potential personal characteristic of *care*.

Ego integrity vs despair – older adulthood

Once the children have left home and are happily settled on their own life path Erikson wrote that the older adult begins a journey of reflection on their past and a reconciliation of the past on the present and future. As we get older, we begin to make comparisons between what is now and what was before. It is common to hear members of the older generation passing comment on how 'things aren't like they used to be' and 'life's changed'. Erikson believed that adults who can look back on their lives with happiness and contentment are more likely to see the future more positively and to feel satisfied. If the older adult feels that they have achieved what they wanted to and have been able to satisfy their needs, they are more likely to have *ego integrity* and to accept that their life has panned out the way it was intended.

Adults who are not able to do this are more likely to experience *despair* and disappointment and to fear getting older. Such adults may become aggressive and dispassionate. They may complain about all changes and about the failings of people around them. This is likely to reflect the disappointment they feel in themselves for not having had what they perceive as a satisfactory and fulfilling life. The internal struggle of coming to terms with what has been and that perhaps there is little time left for them to make amends is often forgotten in our perception of the older adult. We are quick to note physical and possibly mental

This child will likely benefit from growing up in a large, diverse family.

Source: Pearson Education Ltd./Gareth Boden

deterioration, but we rarely make the effort to understand the role of reflection on the past and its integration into the present. With successful reflection and the development of strong ego integrity, the older adult is rewarded with the personal characteristic *wisdom*, the personal reflection on the meaning and value of life, but it can be difficult to achieve if all you feel is despair.

Critique

Erikson's theory depends highly on the resolution of your personal sense of identity as the main thrust of human development. Compared to many other theorists, Erikson's theory is unique in describing development beyond the years of childhood and right through into older adulthood. Its strengths lie in the consideration of the full lifespan in personal development and does not assume we are 'complete' or unchangeable after the adolescent years. Erikson's theory allows us scope to evolve complexity in our identity as we age and to keep assimilating new experiences. The weaknesses of Erikson's theory stem from his stage-theory approach to identity formation. In using Freud's psychoanalytic theory as a foundation for his own theory, he is very clear which personality characteristics we attain at different ages. However, consider the individual differences in development and thus the implications of this approach in understanding your own personal development. Is it possible to be so strictly adherent to the stage-theory approach when we are talking about personality development?

STOP AND THINK

- Think about Erikson and Freud.
- How closely is Erikson's psychosocial theory of development related to Freud's psychoanalytic theory of development?
- What distinguishes them both from each other?

Biological perspectives of development

The key assumptions underlying the biological perspective are:

- Psychologists should study observable and measurable behaviour only.
- All behaviours are learned, we are not born with any set of behaviours.
- Mental process cannot be observed or measured and therefore cannot be studied scientifically.
- The adult personality can change but only as a result of exposure to different experiences.

Arnold Gesell (1880–1961) Gesell's maturational theory

The biological perspective on development suggests that all physical and psychological changes occur because they are biologically and genetically pre-ordained to do so. Thus, we are born with a developmental 'clock' inside that will determine at what age we will sit, walk, talk and make decisions. We cannot rush our child into walking before they are physically able or into talking before they are biologically ready. The role of *nature* is dominant in this perspective and the first proponent of this perspective was Arnold Gesell.

Gesell (1933) believed that a child is the product of his environment but also that a child's development is genetically determined. His theory describes child development as a series of stages that are defined by our biological make-up. Thus, we will learn to sit when our bodies are physically strong enough and we will stand when we are physically able to. Gesell saw that children followed the same pattern of achievements – we learn to sit, then stand, walk and then run, but that children learn these skills at different rates. Gesell believed that the reason for this was our individual genetic make-up. Gesell also believed that, since our individual rate of development is pre-determined by our genetics, we cannot force advancement ahead of schedule. There is therefore no point in trying to teach a child to walk before he is physically able to do so.

Gesell's work was extremely influential in child-rearing books written during the 1940s. He believed that children were born with an internal body clock developed over millions of years of evolution which determines what is best for that child. Gesell pioneered the debate that parents should respond to the needs of the child as they arise and not force the child into following the schedule of the household. This meant that new parents were to feed the baby when they baby wanted to be fed, let the baby sleep when it wanted to sleep and play when the baby wanted to play. By responding to the baby's demands Gesell argued that the parents would

Konrad Lorenz with
single file of geese
Source: Science Photo
Library Ltd.

learn more about the individuality of their child and be more sensitive to her needs in childhood.

You might think that full on-demand parenting might lead to very spoiled children, and if pursued through childhood it almost certainly would. What Gesell argued was that on-demand parenting was only necessary in the early months and as the child grew physically so its concern with immediate satisfaction lessened. When the baby is new-born, it does not have the ability to wait for feeding and will cry until food is presented. As the baby grows older so his needs become less intense and the baby learns to cope with a delay in gratification. As the child gains in language proficiency he will understand when the parent says 'later' or 'in a minute' and will wait contentedly for longer periods before food is produced.

Critique

Gesell's work produced a number of 'norms' – behaviours that children *should* be carrying out at quite specific ages. For this he has often been critisised. Given that his theory seeks to explain the individual differences in children's maturational processes, it seems odd that he would report child development as a series of norms. However, there has been (and still is) a large body of researchers who acknowledge his theory and some (Bell and Ainsworth, 1972, in particular) have found evidence that on-demand parenting, particularly in the early months, results in satisfied, content infants and toddlers.

Konrad Lorenz (1903–1989) modern ethology

Lorenz was trained primarily as a medical doctor but was fascinated also by the study of human behaviour or ethology. Lorenz was highly influenced by Darwin's writing on the evolution of species and thought you could see evolution not only in a person's biology but also in a person's behaviour. Lorenz was particularly interested in what we call innate behaviour – those abilities we appear to be born with and do not have to learn. He was keen to understand behaviour in its natural environment and was therefore an ethologist.

Ethologists believe that many behaviour patterns we see in animals and humans are *instinctive* and serve a number of functions. One such instinct might be a specific behaviour pattern in response to a threat or stressor. An example of this could be a duck quacking loudly and

---

Definitions

Ethology: the study of behaviour in its natural setting. Ethologists do not conduct experiments on behaviour in unnaturalistic settings, they prefer to observe and catalogue behaviour as it occurs naturally and without intervention from the researcher.
Innate behaviour: behaviour that appears instinctive, is natural and not learned, behaviour or abilities that we are born with.

CUTTING EDGE

Biological influences on intellectual ability

In the England and Wales, Standard Assessment Tests are distributed in school to children at the age of 7 years, 11 years and 14 years. These tests examine each child's ability in a range of subjects including reading, writing and mathematics and indicate how well each child is performing in school. Scores are compared to a mean of 100 points with a standard deviation of 15 points. Thus, achieving a score between 85 and 115 points suggests that the child is performing well at school. Below 85 and the child might need further support in school and beyond 115 the child could be considered particularly able.

The use of norms to calibrate performance on these tests suggests that most children will achieve an average grade, but could we improve a child's performance? There are many websites available with example test sheets to use with a child to help him prepare for the tests. Schools devote a large amount of time to studying the subjects covered by these tests and also use practice test sheets in the hope that each pupil will perform as well as can be expected on the day of the formal test. However, what if performance on these tests can be attributed not only to practice and schooling, but also to biological factors?

A study by Dr Mark Brosnan at the University of Bath, UK suggests that performance on these tests could be predicted by the chemical environment of the womb during pregnancy (Brosnan, 2008). In Brosnan's study of 75 children he found a clear link between the child's performance in these tests and the ratio of finger length between the first and third fingers. Children with longer third fingers (and therefore a smaller ratio between the length of the first and third fingers) were more likely to do well in test of literacy and mathematics. Research has shown that if the chemical environment of the womb is high in testosterone, then the child will be born with a longer third finger. Thus, the research team concluded that greater exposure to testosterone in the womb predicts better performance in reading, writing and mathematics. When seeing if this effect was different for boys or girls, the research found that mathematical performance is most influenced for boys. Interestingly, exposure to low levels of testosterone in the womb was more likely to predict high levels of literacy in girls.

So what can we take from the findings of this study? Intellectual development and performance is affected by the level of exposure to testosterone in the womb. Is there any point in studying to improve performance in these tests? Well, the brief answer is yes. This research is important in helping us to understand the individual differences in attainment in all our children, but the research is still in its early stages. Until we fully understand the biological influences on our intellectual ability we will continue to set goals for educational performance and encourage our children to study hard.

drawing her ducklings close to her when a cat or fox is nearby. In humans this could be the start of an aggressive response in a man when his children are threatened or a mother pulling her children near when a large dog bounds over during a picnic. Instincts are considered *species-specific* by ethologists and, although many patterns of behaviour seem similar across the animal kingdom, each species will have a unique signal (display of a puffed throat in a toad, a verbal call in a human) that can be understood only by its members. Importantly, instincts have a particular *motivation* or drive (for example reproduction or communication) and all have *survival value.*

Lorenz is particularly well known for his study of imprinting (Lorenz, 1952). Ethologists have found that anything remotely like the intended trigger can act in its

Definition

Imprinting: a process in which newborns of most species will recognise and seek proximity with the first object they encounter (usually the primary caregiver) following the activation of a trigger during a critical period after birth.

place. The trigger could be the presence of another animal to trigger bonding and the development of a nurturing relationship between adult and offspring. In cases of orphaned offspring, often another adult animal will successfully take on the role of parent and the infant animal will bond with that adult and follow it. When raising geese, Lorenz found that when he was the first face the goslings saw, they appeared to imprint him as 'mother' and followed him about wherever he went. The goslings' instinct was to follow the 'mother' in single file and to ignore other geese, responding only to their 'mother'. In this situation, Lorenz's face had been the trigger for this instinctive behaviour and he had been imprinted by the goslings into the role of 'mother'. Lorenz proposed a critical period when imprinting would occur, after which no imprinting and therefore no bond would happen. This idea was taken by the researcher, John Bowlby, to address the situation with humans.

STOP AND THINK

- How do the theories of Gesell and Lorenz help us to understand human behaviour?
- What is the value in understanding about the biological nature of development?

John Bowlby (1907–1990) attachment theory

John Bowlby (Bowlby 1953, 1969) was influenced highly by the work of Konrad Lorenz and suggested that humans also have an innate ability to imprint a carer soon after birth. Previously it had been believed that babies would form a bond or an attachment to any adult who

Definitions

Critical period: the time period that was thought to be critical for the formation and development of any attachment relationship, hypothesised to be six months to three years, beyond which it is seen as highly difficult for such a bond to be formed.
Attachment: a strong enduring affectionate bond an infant shares with a significant individual, usually the mother, who knows and responds well to the infant's needs.

satisfied their needs – for food or warmth. However, Bowlby suggested that there was more to it than that. He believed that infants have a biological pre-disposition to attach to their mother not just for practical reasons but also for emotional reasons. Bowlby's work has been very influential in the treatment of mothers and children following birth and encouraged midwives and hospital staff to put the baby in the mother's arms immediately in order for bonding to begin as soon as possible. Chapter 9, Attachment and Early Social Experiences gives a full discussion of attachment theory, but here is an overview of the key points of the theory.

Bowlby and Lorenz believed very much in the idea of a *critical period* for imprinting or forming a bond with a parent or carer. Whilst Lorenz believed that the moments immediately after birth were the most important, Bowlby thought that in humans the critical period for healthy emotional growth required a strong sense of a bond or attachment to a parent or carer that extended well into the toddler years, from 6 months to 3 years of age. Bowlby came to this conclusion after working as a psychiatrist with children who had been raised in orphanages during and after the Second World War. These children were orphaned from their parents and cared for by a raft of nurses and orphanage staff who took on no particular responsibility for any one child. These children had lost any feeling of a strong emotional bond to a single person and as a result, Bowlby concluded, displayed distressing, highly volatile behaviour.

Bowlby wrote that the existence of a strong, emotional bond was essential in producing emotionally stable, happy children (Bowlby, 1953). Without this bond, perhaps through experiencing death of a parent, long periods of hospitalisation or long periods of time spent in nursery care, the child would experience *maternal deprivation* and the child would be damaged forever. Bowlby, as with many developmental theorists, proposed a stage theory of attachment: the formation of a bond between a child and its mother.

The first stage in his attachment theory is called the *pre-attachment* stage. From birth to 2 months of age, Bowlby says that the infant is socially responsive to anyone and shows no preference for one person over another. If the person provides food and warmth, the baby is happy. It is only in the second stage, the *early attachment* stage, that the baby learns to discriminate his mother from the other adults around him. By the time the baby is seven months old, she will turn towards her mother's voice, smile more at her face and be more easily comforted when crying. It is not until the baby is eight months old or more that Bowlby believed the baby forms a real and strong attachment to her mother. In this stage, the *attachment* stage, babies show a much stronger preference for their mothers and will now cry when the mother leaves the room. This separation anxiety can be seen quite clearly in infants when the parent walks away after dropping the child at day-care. It takes a while for the child to learn that the mother will return for them and, until that happens, the child will often show signs of visible distress on parting.

During the attachment stage, infants will also show signs of wariness around people they do not know. This stranger anxiety, like separation anxiety, is perfectly normal and can also be seen quite frequently in common interactions. Think about a time perhaps when you met a family friend in the street and you were introduced to her young child. The child probably suddenly became shy, hid partially behind his mother and held onto her clothes for comfort. In these situations it can seem to take a lot of coaxing from the mother for the child to step out and say hello! Later, when the child is a little older at about 2–3 years of age, the child becomes aware that the attachment can work in two directions. The *partnership* stage is the last stage in Bowlby's theory of attachment and describes a process whereby the child learns that other people have needs too. Children's play activity at this stage is much more likely to involve working together to build a bridge or a sandcastle and, with encouragement, children of this age will share their pencils and crayons. In this way, they discover that relationships are not simply about seeing another person as a source of everything you need, but that you can help others and experience enjoyment when there is 'give and take' on both sides.

Definitions

Separation anxiety: the anxiety a child experiences when separated from the mother or primary carer.
Stranger anxiety: the wariness or fear of the infant when encountering those who are unfamiliar, often characterised by the seeking of proximity to the caregiver.

Critique

There are criticisms of Bowlby's work. First, there seems to be no evidence for the imprinting of a parent's face in the hours immediately after birth. However, as Bowlby suggests in his theory, this is not a problem as he believes that attachments form over a much longer period of time. Does the attachment have to happen only with the mother? Well, in practice, no. Many children are raised by fathers, grandparents and nannies and many of these children form stable attachments to these carers. What does seem to be important to the emotional welfare of the child is that the carer provides a steady and dependable presence in the child's early months and years, regardless of who they are. Second, he believed that without a stable attachment figure (usually the mother) in the first three years of life, the child would be irreparably damaged emotionally. This, however, does not seem to be the case. Parents who use child-care facilities when the mother and father both work still form strong attachments to their children, even though the child spends fairly long periods of time with other carers. The current belief is that if the time you spend with your child is well spent, then the child will be able to adjust to child-care comfortably. What is time 'well spent' however? Some people advocate intense periods of child-centred activity in order to 'make up' for the absence of both parents during the day. Other researchers advocate the maintenance of a stable and predictable structure to family life so that the child feels safe and secure at home. What is known, however, is that what really affects the child's ability to settle into day-care and separation from her parents is the *quality* of the day-care. With a regular pace to the day, a wide range of activities and staff who take a personal interest in the children, the child is much more likely to thrive (for example, De Schipper *et al.,* 2004).

Bowlby's work on attachment has dominated research into early child development and is highly influential in modern child-care practice and the provision of care facilities. Bowlby's stage theory of attachment has support from Mary Ainsworth (Ainsworth *et al.,* 1978) who saw evidence of children passing through these stages in a wide range of cultures and social contexts. It therefore has universal appeal to people working with children across the board for its ability to clarify how our early experiences can have a quite considerable impact on our development across the lifespan.

Mary D.S. Ainsworth (1913–1999) patterns of attachment

The work of Mary Ainsworth followed on naturally from that of her peers in developmental research. Ainsworth sought to find a way to measure the emotional state of a child and to illustrate the effects of parenting on child behaviour. Ainsworth began her research observing parent and child interactions in Africa and noted similarities with what she had seen in Europe. This caused her to think that there could be patterns to this behaviour that are common across all cultures. What particularly interested her was observing what behaviour the child displayed when the parent left the room and what behaviour was displayed when the parent returned. This observation of parent–child interaction grew into a formal study of parent and child separation and reunification called the *Strange Situation study* (Ainsworth *et al.*, 1978).

The Strange Situation study

This is a seven-phase study designed to reflect the naturalistic observations Ainsworth had made of parent–child daily interaction. Usually it is conducted in a comfortable room in a research centre where the psychologist can watch events happen through a two-way mirror or via a camera onto a screen in a room next door. In the Strange Situation study, the parent and child are introduced into a plain room and asked to play together for three minutes (phase 1). A stranger (usually a research assistant) then enters the room, sits down for one minute, talks to the parent for one minute and then plays with the child for one minute (phase 2). The parent then leaves, the stranger then plays with the child up to three minutes and sits back on the chair (phase 3). In phase 4, the parent then returns and the stranger leaves. The parent then settles the child down and sits with them for three minutes. After this, the parent leaves the room and the child is left alone for up to three minutes (phase 5). The stranger then comes into the room and tries to settle the child (phase 6). Finally, the parent returns and the stranger leaves. The parent settles the child down and sits with them (phase 7). The whole process takes around 20 minutes but can be shorter if the child becomes distressed at any time and a phase is then cut short.

How can this study tell us anything about the attachment behaviour of the child? Ainsworth hypothesised that if the child is secure and content within the relationship, then in phases 1, 2 and 4, the child will use the parent as base to explore the room and the toys within it. When the mother is absent (phases 3, 5 and 6) the child should become distressed – but not too much; in this case, the mother would return before the three minutes are up. What Ainsworth was really interested in was the behaviour of the child when the parent returned after the period of absence (in phases 4 and 7). She observed many instances of this Strange Situation study and as a result compiled four main categories of the parent–child attachment relationship according to the way in which the child behaved when the parent returned (see Chapter 9, Attachment and Early Social Experiences for a full description of them).

Attachment types

- *Type A form of attachment, **avoidant** attached*: If the infant shows few or no signs of missing the parent and actively ignores and avoids her upon reunion, the infant is said to show **insecure-avoidant attachment**.
- *Type B form of attachment, **secure** attached*: Some children showed signs of missing the mother when she left and when she returned, the child made efforts to reunite with the mother. Satisfied that the mother was back to stay, the child returned to playing with the toys. Mary Ainsworth called this behaviour a sign of **secure attachment**.
- *Type C form of attachment, **ambivalent** attached*: If the infant becomes distressed when the mother leaves but cannot be settled by the parent on reunion, the infant is said to show **insecure-ambivalent attachment**.
- *Type D form of attachment, **disorganised** attached*: These infants were considered unclassifiable as they seemed to show reunion behaviours that could not be included in the other categories.

Critique

Why would these different attachment types come about? Is our attachment style pre-determined at birth? If this were so, then within the family both biological and adopted children would display very different attachment behaviours with their mother. However, studies have shown this not to be the case. A study by Dozier *et al.* (2001) found that the attachment behaviours of the adopted children were very similar to those of the biological children, demonstrating that the nurturing environment the children were raised in was more important in determining attachment behaviour than any biological factors. Why is this? Ainsworth proposed the *maternal sensitivity hypothesis*.

The maternal sensitivity hypothesis states that the more in-tune the mother is with her infant's emotional state, the more likely the child is to grow up with a secure attachment. So if a mother is responsive to her child and encourages him to play when he wants to play and sleep when he wants to sleep, that child will grow up feeling a strong, stable and nurturing relationship with his mother. If the mother is discordant with her infant and is unable to understand her child's moods, then that mother is less likely to build a satisfying relationship with her child and the child is more likely to grow up showing an *avoidant* or *disorganised* style of attachment.

STOP AND THINK

How might understanding Ainsworth's description of attachment behaviour help you to improve the experience of a young child attending school for the first time?

NATURE–NURTURE

Attachment

It can be difficult finding the research tool to identify whether something like the ability to form relationships is present from birth or is something we learn in the years following. After all, we may be able to assess the type of up-bringing someone has and whether they have experienced good or bad relationships and even make changes to their environment to improve their experiences, but what we cannot do is make any kind of assessment based on their genetic make-up. We cannot investigate what biological factors there are in attachment or even locate some kind of genetic marker for defining someone who is 'good at making friends' or someone who is 'bad at making friends'. Any kind of research we conduct into attachment has to effectively ignore the biological aspects of this behaviour.

However, there is a research method that allows us to *control* for the biological aspects of behaviour and to determine whether the social environment someone is raised in is *wholly* responsible for their attachment behaviour or whether biology does have a part to play. This research method is called a 'twin study'. Twins are useful to study in that if they are identical twins (in that they appear identical in looks and build) then they are monozygotic twins (twins from the same maternal egg) and therefore share the same genetic code. Thus, any differences seen between twin siblings could be argued to be a result of environmental factors, not biological ones.

A study by Fearon *et al.* (2006) investigated attachment behaviours in 136 pairs of twin infants from either Leiden (the Netherlands) or London (the UK).

When the infants were 9–10 months old the mothers were assessed for their ability to respond to the twin's emotional and physical needs and given a score of *maternal sensitivity*. At 12 months, the mothers and children were assessed for attachment behaviours. Research had suggested that the reason different children within a family could display different attachment behaviours was that the mother showed a different level of sensitivity to each child's needs because the children were different genetically and thus in personality and temperament. If this was the case, then the mothers of the infant twins should have shown similar sensitivity to their needs regardless of which child they interacted with.

The results of the study showed that when there were differences in maternal sensitivity to each of their twin infants, this finding could not be explained genetically. When the mother showed equal sensitivity to each child, the attachment rating between her and her children was the same for each child. When there were differences in the attachment rating between her and each of her children, it appeared that this was affected by how the child saw the mother interacting with the other twin. The researchers conclude that attachment *is* affected by the environment the child is raised in and, even with twin children, the mother may be more sensitive to the needs of one over the other and this discrepancy will result in a difference in attachment experience for both children. Thus, biological differences in children are not what accounts for differences in attachment with their mothers – it is the nurturing environment that impacts the most.

Learning perspectives on development

So far we have discussed two perspectives on development. The psychoanalytic theories of Freud and Erikson take the view that developmental change comes from the balancing actions of our *psyche* on our emotional needs and social requirements, whilst the works of Gesell, Bowlby and Ainsworth have proposed that it is our pre-determined biological 'clock' that lays the foundation for our developmental changes. Both these perspectives address *internal* motivations for change. There are other perspectives, however, that address *external* motivations for our development.

The key assumptions of the learning perspectives on development are similar to the assumptions of the behaviourist perspective and are:

- Behaviour change results from our interactions with the world about us.
- Anyone can be trained to do anything.
- With the right system of reward, a behaviour can be encouraged and with the right system of punishment, a behaviour can be inhibited.
- The strong focus on the manipulation of behaviour in these perspectives puts them in the *learning* or *behaviourist* category of theories of developmental change.

Ivan Pavlov (1849–1936) classical conditioning

Pavlov coined the term classical conditioning to describe the process of learning an association between two stimuli. He discovered that you can teach an animal to learn that two previously unconnected stimuli – a bell and food – can become connected and produce the same response, saliva. Pavlov was conducting an unrelated study with dogs in his laboratory when he became interested in the response the dogs made at mealtimes. He

noticed first that when you present a dog with food, the dog produces saliva in response. However, what was more interesting to Pavlov was the reaction the dogs made when the researchers were bringing the food to the dogs. Pavlov noticed that when the technician who normally fed them walked up to the dogs, the dogs started making saliva whether or not the technician had food in his hands. The dogs had associated the technician with the food and had therefore learned to associate two previously unconnected stimuli. Figure 2.1 shows the process of classical conditioning experienced by the dogs.

How, though, does an understanding of the process of classical conditioning help us to understand human behaviour? Consider the way you felt when you went to university. Did you feel uncomfortable in the new and often noisy environment? Did you take photos of your family and friends or your favourite teddy bear with you to keep in your bedroom? Did looking at these photos or bear help you to feel secure? The theory of classical conditioning suggests that as infants we associated warmth, comfort and security with a mother who held us and soothed us, or who tucked us up in bed with our teddy bear when we were tired or frightened by the dark. The associations we learned as children hold strong for us as adults when we seek comfort in looking at photographs of family members or feel strong emotions when we find our old teddy bear hidden away in a forgotten box.

Critique

Pavlov's theory of classical conditioning presents us with a model for understanding how we make emotional associations between a number of stimuli, but it is a limited theory in its application in developmental psychology. It was the slightly later work of B.F. Skinner which took this theory further and demonstrated how these associations can be manipulated by external events and forces.

B.F. Skinner (1904–1990) operant conditioning

B.F. Skinner (1957) wrote that behaviours can be encouraged or inhibited by the effective use of reward or punishment. The reward can be anything that *reinforces* the repetition of a behaviour. This *reinforcement* of behaviour can be achieved by positive means or negative means. A *positive reinforcer* could be giving someone a

> **Definition**
>
> Classical conditioning: describes the process of learning an association between two stimuli.

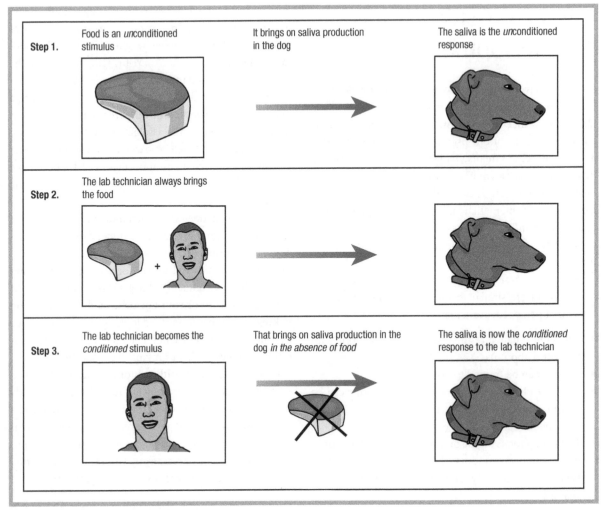

Figure 2.1. The process of classical conditioning.

CASE STUDY

Little Albert

In 1920, researcher John Watson conducted an emotional conditioning experiment based on the principles of classical conditioning as described by Pavlov. Watson introduced a nine month old child called 'Albert' (not his real name) to a white rat, which the child enjoyed playing with. After a while, Watson started making loud sounds behind Albert's head whenever he played with the rat, scaring Albert. Eventually, whenever Watson presented Albert with the rat to play with, Albert would show signs of fear even in the absence of the loud noise. It appeared that Albert had been conditioned to feel fear when he saw the white rat.

- Why did Albert feel fear when he saw the white rat?
- Describe the process of conditioning that might explain his newly developed fear.
- What are the ethical implications of a study like this?
- What might be the long-term implications for Albert?

smile, verbal encouragement or pat on the back, as long as it is something which makes the person experience pleasure. A *negative reinforcer* is something that takes away discomfort or displeasure such as using a painkiller to take away the pain of a headache or using a cold cloth to soothe a bump or graze of the knee. As the end-result of these actions is a reduction in pain and discomfort, we learn to use a painkiller or cold cloth when we experience a headache or bumped knee through the use of negative reinforcement. A *punishment* is something that follows a behaviour and causes it to stop. A punishment can be many things but often takes the position of the removal of a reward. A mother may stop smiling or playing with her child and remove the reinforcement of attention that the child has previously been getting for her behaviour. A father might remove the favourite toy from the child until the unwanted behaviour stops. Effective punishment can cease an unwanted behaviour such as crying, pinching or having a temper tantrum quite quickly.

We can observe parents using operant conditioning techniques with their children – often perhaps unwittingly – as they coax and cajole their infants into complying with a request. Parents might use positive reinforcement to encourage the child to climb or jump, saying 'See, I knew you could do it!' or perhaps to eat their vegetables 'What a good girl you are for eating those carrots'. Parents use positive reinforcement a lot with their children in all sorts of situations, but they also use negative reinforcement with them. Do you remember these phrases: "If you eat your greens, you can have ice-cream for dessert!" or perhaps 'You can play outside when you've finished tidying your room'? Operant conditioning can be a very effective method of manipulating behaviour in children and the messages can stay with us for a long time and into adulthood. How often have you thought during school 'I can't go out until I've finished my revision'? Where did you pick up that life lesson, at home?

Some of the techniques of operant conditioning can be used to *shape* more complex behaviour over a period of time. When we are learning to write, we first need to learn our letters. Our parents and teachers will use reinforcement to encourage the accurate drawing of all the

letters of the alphabet. Later on, we learn to spell our names and again, our parents and teachers give us praise when we have written our names correctly. As we progress through school we develop our abilities in writing and begin to construct sentences and then stories, all the while receiving feedback on our performance. With the correct use of reinforcement, even the child with the worst spelling or the messiest handwriting will gain confidence. Rewarding the steady progression from holding a pen to writing a poem reinforces the child at each step and shapes their acquisition of a complex skill.

Sometimes, however, we all get the technique wrong. Take the example of a child who wants attention and calls out to his father repeatedly. Initially the father, who is engaged in conversation, wants to reduce this kind of behaviour from the child and ignores his requests. After a while, however, the father gives in and turns to the child and replies. The father's intention has been to inhibit the child's repeated calling of his name to get attention and thinks that by not responding immediately, the child will learn to wait for a response. However, as a method of operant conditioning, this is the wrong way to go about it. What the father has now done is teach the child that he will respond on the child's tenth or so request for attention. He has positively reinforced the child's tenth attempt to get attention and not, as he supposed, inhibited his behaviour. If he persists in this method of response to the child, the child will simply learn that if he keeps calling out to his father, he will eventually respond.

The father in this situation could have used an alternative method of behaviour change, that of *extinction*. The extinction of a behaviour results from repeated non-reinforcement. In this example the father might have chosen to distract the child from the repeated name-calling and instead asked him to wait a moment until he was able to respond to the child. By doing this, the father might have been able to eliminate the repetitive behaviour and taught the child a lesson in waiting a short while for attention whilst his father is talking on the telephone.

Critique

Operant conditioning is a technique that can be replicated very well in a laboratory setting but, in the real world, the use of reinforcement and punishment in moderating a child's behaviour can be sporadic at best. Very often behaviours that might be tackled regularly at home might go unrewarded or unpunished when at a friend's house and the use of *partial reinforcement* is

---

Definition

Operant conditioning: the process that describes how behaviours can be encouraged or inhibited by the effective use of reward or punishment.

much more common. Under these conditions, behaviours are modified much more slowly than under laboratory conditions, and it will be near impossible to actually extinguish in full some unwanted behaviours. The father in our example above is actually engaged in a form of partial reinforcement of his son's repetitive behaviour and he will now find it difficult to stop it fully.

Albert Bandura (1925–) social-learning theory

Bandura believed that very few of us were raised under the near-perfect conditions of reinforcement and punishment that operant conditioning requires and that many of us experienced moments of partial reinforcement during childhood. In fact, Bandura extended his theory beyond partial reinforcement and suggested that we learn to moderate our behaviour by observing social norms. His *social learning theory* (Bandura and Walters, 1963) proposes that we learn from seeing someone else's behaviour reinforced or punished.

One of Bandura's key studies was that concerning the use of the *Bobo Doll*, an inflatable doll painted to look like a clown 'Bobo'. Bandura asked one of his research associates to go up to 'Bobo' and shout at it, punch it and kick it to the ground. Bandura video-taped the researcher and the doll and then showed it to some pre-school children. He then gave the children a Bobo doll to play with and watched their behaviour. Bandura noted that the children's play was much more aggressive than it had been previously and involved much more shouting and physical contact with the doll. The children had observed the researcher's violent behaviour towards the doll and had copied it.

Bandura argued that children learned a lot of behaviour from the imitation of others, whether the behaviour was playful or aggressive. His theory has been extremely influential in forming the basis of arguments on topics ranging from the causes of street violence to gender role identity and the choice of toys in boys and girls. As a theory it has perhaps been treated too simplistically and possibly given rather too much weight in 'proving' the causes of behaviour. Certainly many of us have observed people behaving in an aggressive way but do not behave aggressively ourselves for instance. When we look into the detail of Bandura's theory, however, we see that he does not believe that imitation of behaviour happens necessarily or automatically. Bandura proposes that a behaviour will only be imitated when four conditions are satisfied: what

In these images the child is copying the actions of the adult researcher and hitting the toy.

Source: Professor Albert Bandura/Stanford University

aspect of the behaviour the child focuses on; how much of the behaviour the child is able to remember; whether the child is physically capable of carrying out the behaviour; and finally, whether the child is actually motivated to carry out the behaviour. If the child does not *want* to act aggressively towards the clown doll then even if she can remember what the researcher did, how the researcher did it and she is strong enough to copy the aggressive behaviour, then the child will probably *not* act aggressively under these circumstances. In this situation, the child has learnt self-efficacy – the ability to choose how to behave in the circumstances according to her own expectations, her understanding of social norms and her belief in the appropriateness of aggressive behaviour.

Critique

Social learning theory is popular with developmental psychologists as it encompasses the role of parents in setting social norms for behaviour and in providing examples of behaviour for the child to copy whilst also putting the responsibility for behaviour in the hands of the child. However, in practice, Bandura's studies revealed that imitation of behaviour only occurred in approximately 10% of the research participants. This small effect can be explained by

---

Definition

Self-efficacy: a person's belief about how effectively he or she can control herself, her thoughts or behaviours, particularly when intended to fulfil a personal goal.

In the earlier months of the preoperational thought stage, the child learns something called object permanence. In the later part of the first year of life we have proposed that the child will use schemas to locate a toy hidden under a cloth. The assumption Piaget makes is that the child will only attempt to lift the cloth to reach the toy if she believes that the toy is under the cloth. In the early months of development, placing a toy under a cloth will result in the child losing all interest in the toy. If she cannot see the toy, the suggestion is that she believes the toy is no longer there. Later, the child develops a sense of object permanence. Now the child knows that even though the toy is covered by a cloth, it has not disappeared and lifting the cloth will reveal the toy.

This mother and baby are playing 'peek-a-boo'. The child is 'hiding' from his mother by covering his eyes with his hands.
Source: Corbis/Jim Craigmyle

Phase 6 The beginning of mental representation (18 months to 2 years)

Now that they know that the object remains even when hidden out of view, children in phase 6 start to form mental images of routes to getting what they want and will climb out of and onto anything to reach it. All kinds of mental representations develop at this point and children begin to put words together and to make decisions without needing to have tangible examples put in front of them. They decide what they want to eat, what they want to do and how they want to do it. The child is becoming stronger and more physically active and will run further and climb higher in order to attain his goal.

Stage 2 Preoperational thought (age two to seven years)

The next stage of cognitive development Piaget describes for young children is that of *preoperational thought*. This stage describes the child's burgeoning abilities in imaginative play and the use of symbols. By the age of two years children often engage in *symbolic* play: play that represents real life. They may play 'mummies and daddies' with a toy doll: feeding the doll with a miniature bottle and pushing it around in a toy pushchair for example, or they may play 'doctors and nurses' and pretend to fix problems in their dolls or other children such as a bumped head or a scraped knee. Symbolic play is an important part of development and reflects the child's ability to observe and copy what is happening in the world around her. Other symbols that children use as they progress in the preoperational thought stage are letters and words and children show an enormous capacity for learning new words in these years of development.

Children in the preoperational thought stage of development are egocentric, they understand the world

> **Definitions**
> Object permanence: the understanding that objects exist even when they have disappeared from view.
> Egocentric: understanding the world only from your own perspective and finding it difficult to understand the point of view of another person.

from their own perspective and find it difficult to understand the point of view of another person. Piaget demonstrated this egocentrism with his now famous 'three mountains' study (Piaget and Inhelder, 1956). Piaget and Inhelder constructed a three-dimensional model of three differently sized and shaped mountains (see Fig. 2.2), placed a doll on one side of the model and stood the child on the other side. The researchers then asked the child to describe the scene that the doll could see and to select from a series of pictures the doll's view of the mountains. The four and five year old children described their own view of the mountains when describing the doll's view as the children were not able to mentally construct the doll's perspective of the model.

Another feature of this stage in development is the child's inability at first to complete conservation tasks (Piaget, 1981). Conservation is understanding the principle that the shape or appearance of something can change without there being a change in quantity. For example, if you were to put two short tumblers of water next to each other and ask the child if they were equal, the child would confirm this. However, if you poured the contents from one of the tumblers into a thinner, taller glass and asked the same question, the pre-school child would say that no, there was more water in the taller glass. Similarly, if you had taken two equal balls of plasticine dough and rolled one into a long thin shape, the pre-school child would again assert that the longer, thinner shape contained more dough than did the round ball of dough.

Definition

Conservation: the principle that the shape or appearance of something can change without there being a change in quantity.

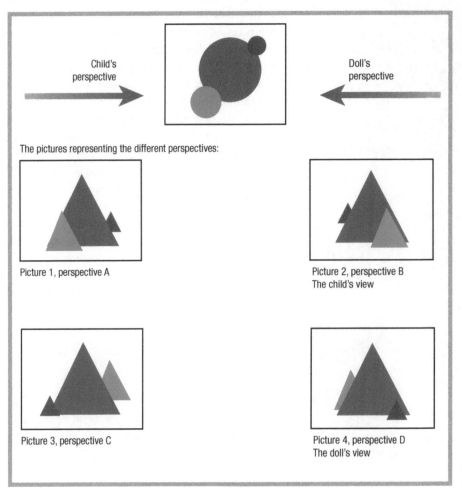

Figure 2.2. The 'three mountains' study.

Children frequently make the mistake of thinking that the taller or longer item has more content and do not acquire the ability to make the mental transformation of mass or volume until around the age of seven years.

During the preoperative stage of thinking, the child progresses her cognitive abilities remarkably quickly. In these five years of development the child will learn to use symbols in play and language, he will learn about the different perspective of other people and understand the principles of mass and volume conservation. At around the age of seven years, the child will move into the stage of concrete operational thought and start to lose her egocentric way of thinking, begin to look at problems from another person's perspective and use this information in making decisions.

Stage 3 Concrete operational thought (age seven to eleven years)

At around the age of 7 years, the child enters into the stage Piaget called *concrete operational thought*. This stage is dominated by learning to use logic to solve real, actual problems. There are many types of logical thinking that the child will learn (see Table 2.3). For instance, the child will learn to sort objects into a hierarchical order based on their size or shape, for instance from smallest to largest. Ask children of this age to line up in order of size and they will quickly places themselves in order of the shortest child up to the tallest child, a process called *seriation*.

Other abilities include learning to name and sort objects into categories based on similar characteristics. This ability to categorise objects is known as *classification* and allows the child to make certain assumptions about objects based on their membership to a particular category. For instance, if you know that all mammals are warm blooded, then if you read in school about an animal you have not encountered that is a mammal, then you can assume that the animal is warm blooded.

Children at this stage are able to begin to use complex mathematical skills. They have used symbols to reflect numbers already in class, but by the age of 8 or 9 years are able to complete mathematical equations. Thus the child will be able to do simple additions such as $5 + 5 = 10$, but will also be able to reverse the sum and do subtractions such as $10 - 5 = 5$. This ability to understand that numbers can be changed and then returned to their original state is known as *reversibility* and is more than being able to simply do the sums but reflects an understanding of the mathematical flexibility of numbers.

Stage 4 Formal operations (age 11 to adulthood)

Piaget's final stage of development, the formal operations stage, signifies a move from being able to consider the *concrete* (or real, physically present) concepts in problem solving, to being able to consider *abstract* concepts. These abstract concepts could be the use of letters to solve algebraic mathematical equations or could be the discovery of the meaning behind the words of poetry or song lyrics. From the age of 11 years the young person begins to comprehend a world where sometimes what is said does not match what is meant in a conversation, a poem or a song and, most importantly, why someone would mislead you in this way. Piaget described the key skills emerging during this stage as logical thought and deductive reasoning, abstract thought and systematic problem solving.

Logical thought and deductive reasoning

Prior to this stage, children have developed the ability to categorise and classify information and to do simple mathematics. Now, in the formal operations stage, the young person learns that you can use letters to represent missing numbers and use your knowledge of reversibility to work out which number the letter represents. Learning the skills of algebra is not possible until the child

Table 2.3. Summary of the main abilities learnt during the concrete operations stage of development.

Piaget's logical task	Child is able to convert this . . .	To this . . .
Seriation	A A ᴀ ᴀ A A	ᴀ ᴀ A A A A
Classification	ABBBAABABA	(AAAAA) (BBBBB)
Reversibility	$5 + 5 = 10$	Therefore, $10 - 5 = 5$

enters into this stage as it requires him to use *deductive logic*. Deductive logic is the ability to use a general principle to determine a specific outcome. This type of thinking involves the manipulation of hypothetical situations – an ability not seen until now.

Abstract thought

The ability to think about abstract concepts emerges during the formal operational stage. Previously the child was able to consider solving problems only in terms of their experiences. The child had to learn to take the perspective of another person. Now, however, the young person is able to consider possible outcomes and consequences of actions for which they have no life experience. Take for instance a class discussion on the value of volunteering at a home for adults with various forms of dementia. Although possibly none of the class have direct experience of this type of work, each student will be able to consider hypothetically the need for this type of home facility, the care needs of the older adults and the value to him or herself of gaining work experience in this type of environment. The young person initially will find this type of discussion difficult when asked to consider the perspectives of everybody involved, for instance, the different needs of the adult with dementia, his wife and close family, the carer and the needs of the wider society. Often she will over-emphasise the impact on herself when considering this hypothetical question and focus on her personal development needs. However, with time and practice she will be able to make decisions that have long-term consequences not just for herself but for others and society as a whole. Developing this type of thinking is important for long-term planning such as making decisions on what course to study to prepare you for a future career and it is not something that happens overnight. Many young people entering university, for instance, have no real idea of what career path they desire, but still understand the importance of higher study in creating career choices.

Systematic problem solving

For children in the earlier stages of development, problem solving was often a matter of trial-and-error rather than the use of any structured strategies. During the formal operational stage, however, the young person develops the ability to systematically solve a problem in a logical and methodical manner. Piaget gave young people the 'pendulum problem' to see what strategies they used to solve it. The young people were given different lengths of cord and different weights and were asked what affected the rate of swing of a pendulum. Children in the concrete operations stage of development tend to approach this task quite randomly and change two or more features of the pendulum in trying to answer the question. Young people in the formal operations stage of development, however, approach this task systematically, testing each variable in turn: dropping the pendulum from a greater height, changing the length of the string (correct answer) and changing the weight of the pendulum itself.

STOP AND THINK

Use Piaget's theory of cognitive development to decide at what age a child should be able to study poetry effectively in school.

Critique

Piaget's theory of cognitive development is highly thought of and used frequently in understanding children's development both in the field of educational policy and in psychology. However, there are a few criticisms of his theory. First, research has shown that the stages are not as age-related as previously thought. Children develop at their own pace and do not necessarily achieve proficiency in each stage at exactly the age Piaget describes. However, it is agreed that children do progress through the stages in just the order that Piaget has written.

Another criticism is directed at Piaget's belief that we all engage in the formal operations stage of development and acquire proficiency in hypothetical deduction, logic and systematic problem solving, and the ability to understand the abstract nature of life. However, research has shown that not everyone acquires these skills and, certainly, not everyone uses these skills in everyday life. Some adults will often fall back on concrete principles when considering matters of political or ethical importance and rarely show competence in highly abstract thinking. Others may never have understood the principles of algebra at school and find the use of mathematical symbols difficult.

Further criticism has been directed at Piaget's theory for under-estimating the abilities of children. Piaget asserts that children in the preoperational stage of development are unable to consider another person's perspective (in the 'three mountains' task for instance). However, children in this stage will often tailor their language and behaviour to the appropriate level for a young sibling when necessary and must therefore be demonstrating an awareness of the limitations in the ability of that younger brother or sister. This appears to be evidence counter to Piaget's theory of cognitive development – certainly in the ability to empathise with another. However, even with these criticisms, Piaget's theory is still considered highly useful in understanding the cognitive development in children and is still used as the foundation stone of research by developmental psychologists.

Integrative perspectives in developmental psychology

There are other theories and perspectives of developmental psychology that are gaining in popularity as psychologists and other human and behavioural scientists search for theories that integrate the biological, physiological effects of development with social and environmental factors. Some researchers use a combination of approaches to help understand very specific behaviours. For example, a psychologist wanting to understand why a young boy set fire to a car might want to call upon many theories to create an holistic view of the influential factors in the onset of that act. The psychologist might invoke the use of social learning theories (does the child come from a dysfunctional family?); cognitive theories (is the child unable to understand consequences of that action?); environmental factor theories (does the child come from poverty or a home physical environment that is unpleasant?); and biological development theories (is the child experiencing strength and conflict from early onset puberty?). Using perspectives from all these theories will provide a full picture of the young boy sat in front of her and help her to target therapeutic intervention.

A key researcher supporting an integrative approach in developmental psychology is the Russian, Lev Vygotsky (1896–1934). Vygotsky was heavily influenced by the works of Gesell, Freud, Pavlov and Piaget and his theory combines the two approaches: the biological nature or 'natural line' of development with the 'social–historical' influences from family, friends and society generally (Vygotsky, 1962). He unfortunately died at a young age and he did not have time to develop his theory in detail but, following the release of his writings after the end of the Cold War in Europe, we have some insight into what he proposed.

Vygotsky's *sociocultural theory* of development (Vygotsky, 1978) suggests that we develop as children as a result of our biological drive to do so, but also as a result of our social interactions. Without contact with other people, Vygotsky believed we would not progress beyond very primitive patterns of thinking. Vygotsky introduced a concept called *scaffolding* that describes how adults and older children try to advance the child's abilities – by correcting his language use or encouraging him with his homework. Vygotsky believed that we each advance by working in the *zone of proximal development*. When we find a task difficult to do but with help from a parent or older sibling for example, we find we are able to complete it, then we are said to be in the zone of proximal development. According to Vygotsky, we do not develop as children or adults without the help of others, whether we are learning our alphabet or learning to drive. Without guidance and support from our social community, we can only develop our skills and abilities so far.

Urie Bronfenbrenner (1917–2005) bioecological theory

Urie Bronfenbrenner's bioecological theory expands on the influences of other people and the social environment in shaping our development. Bronfenbrenner's theory describes social influence as a series of concentric circles with the person at the centre (see Fig. 2.3). Bronfenbrenner's theory was initially described as an ecological theory (1979, 1986) based on its reliance on socialisation as a powerful factor in the young child's development, but in his paper in 2000, Bronfenbrenner reworked his theory to take into account the influence a child's biology has on her development and his theory is now called the bioecological model of human development (Bronfenbrenner and Evans, 2000).

Bronfenbrenner sees the child at the centre of his model existing within a microsystem of daily activities and interactions. The child is an active part of these activities and interactions; for example, if the child is hungry, he will cry and cause other people around him to

> **Definition**
>
> Microsystem: the activities and interactions immediately surrounding a person.

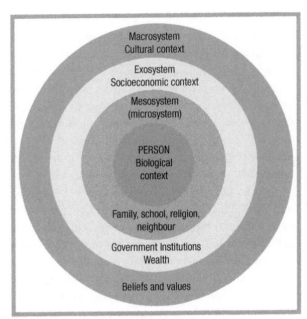

Figure 2.3. Bronfenbrenner's bioecological theory of the social influences on our development.

(*Source*: adapted from Boyd and Bee, 2006)

come to him and bring him food. The parents too may come to him and smile, tickle him or present toys to him, encouraging the child to smile back and engage in the games. The relationships are therefore bidirectional – the child and the parents are both active in these daily interactions. The microsystem can also be affected by the nature of the child and the quality of the parents' relationship. A placid, smiling child will likely elicit calm, smiling reactions from the parents whereas an active, distracted or fussy child might elicit quite different behaviour from his parents. Similarly, if the parents are content and supportive in their relationship, their ability to respond to the child is enhanced and both the child and the parents experience a positive interaction. However, if the parents are in conflict and are unable to provide consistent parenting, the child may experience hostile parenting and develop a hostile perspective himself (Hetherington and Stanley-Hagen, 2002).

Bronfenbrenner saw connections between each of the elements of the microsystem which he called the mesosystem. If the child's microsystem consisted of parents, a neighbour and children attending the same pre-school, then the child was not only influenced by each of these people separately, but was influenced by how all these people worked together. For example, one day the neighbour might help out and pick up the child from the pre-school and notice that she is being bullied by another child. The neighbour then tells the parents who then work together with the pre-school to get the bullying stopped. The mesosystem, the connections between elements of the microsystem, has therefore affected the child's development by working to bring about change in the child's experience of pre-school.

As the child gets older, so Bronfenbrenner's exosystem becomes more important in the child's development. The exosystem consists of a formal structure of school governors, the board of directors in the workplace, health services and community welfare systems (Boyd and Bee, 2006). For example, the child is not directly aware of or knowingly affected by their local health authority's policy on early years parenting classes, say, but he will benefit indirectly by having parents who, early on in his life-time, have access to parenting resources and other coping strategies to help them foster a strong, supportive home environment. The exosystem can also include the wider family unit and circles of friends. The child raised in a large welcoming extended family, for instance, has access to cousins, aunts and uncles, grandparents and possibly great-grandparents all of whom will be important people throughout the child's life.

Finally, Bronfenbrenner's macrosystem describes the cultural values, norms, laws, customs and other social influences that will guide the child's development. A child raised in a culture that values children and supports the parents with child-care facilities and flexible working hours will experience a more positive socialisation process and her parents too will feel more valued and supported in raising their child.

Bronfenbrenner's bioecological theory of development does not just apply to the experiences of the child but is a flexible, dynamic theory that accounts for the experiences of all of us right up to old age. The quality of our social care and welfare systems has an impact on us whatever our age, and the ability to adopt flexible working patterns is just as important as we head towards

Definitions

Mesosystem: the connections between elements of the microsystem.

Exosystem: the social settings that do not immediately impact on a person, but surround them and are important to their welfare.

Macrosystem: the cultural values, laws, customs and resources available to a person.

retirement as it is when we have a young family in tow. Bronfenbrenner's theory integrates our biology with our social upbringing and does not see one as being more important than the other. Importantly, Bronfenbrenner described us all as being both products and producers of our environments, as dynamic drivers of our personal development and influencers of social change (Bronfenbrenner, 1986).

SUMMARY

We began our introduction to the theoretical perspectives of developmental psychology by providing you with four learning objectives. Now you have completed this chapter, let us return to them in turn. First, in order to be able to critically discuss what makes a theory, we need to know what the three main factors are that comprise a theory: define, explain, predict. Do all the theories presented here do this to your satisfaction? Are the behaviours at the focus of each theory well described and defined? Do the theories explain the changes in development sufficiently? Do any of the theories have predictive value, or some sort of discriminative value? Can you use the theory to discriminate between children who are developing in line with their peers and those children who are not? Can you predict adult relationship behaviour from an understanding of their social development as a child and the attachment formed with their mother or primary carer? The next factor that needs to be considered when evaluating a theory is whether the theory describes development occurring as a process of continuous change or whether it happens in distinct stages. For instance, does language development happen in successive, age-specific incremental stages or is it a more fluid process that each child works through in their own time?

The second learning objective, evaluate the key theoretical perspectives in developmental psychology, requires you to be able to first list the four main theoretical perspectives in developmental psychology, then describe the key assumptions underlying these perspectives. Take for example, the biological perspective. What are the key assumptions underlying this perspective? Psychologists should study observable and measurable behaviour only; all behaviours are learned, we are not born with any set of behaviours; mental process cannot be observed or measured and therefore cannot be studied scientifically; and the adult personality can change,

but only as a result of exposure of different experiences. What did you learn about the works of Gesell, Lorenz, Bowlby and Ainsworth that supported these assumptions? What did you learn that went counter to these assumptions? Consider comparing the biological perspective to the social learning perspective, what are the strengths and weaknesses of each approach? How do they compare with each other?

The third learning objective requires you to understand the philosophical perspectives underlying key developmental psychology theories. This builds on the second learning objective. So, think about these questions. Which theories take the biological perspective? Which theories take the social learning perspective? Which theories take the psychoanalytic perspective? What theory takes the cognitive-developmental perspective? Knowing the underling perspective to each of the theories will help you to understand the application of these theories to real-life situations and help you in your essays when you are asked to compare and contrast different the different theorists.

Finally, the last learning objective requires you to critically evaluate the use and application of theories and perspectives in understanding real-life examples of human behaviour from a developmental perspective. The boxed features are each aimed at helping you to understand the application of theories to real-world psychology. How do each of the features help us to decide how much of development is biologically driven (or 'nature') and how much of development is learned (or 'nurture')?

To conclude this chapter, the theories and perspectives we have learned about here all help us to describe and explain human development. Some of the theories, such as Bowlby's theory of attachment, are quite specific and focus on the development of one particular behaviour. These theories can be called *micro-theories* in that they are focused tightly on understanding very specific elements of behaviour. Others are more general, such as Piaget's cognitive development theory and Erkison's theory of psychosocial development, and focus on our development across the life-span. These theories can be called *grand-theories* in that they seek to explain human behaviour in all or many aspects of life such as personality development, memory and decision-making, social development and play behaviour. When you are reading the remainder of this book,

consider whether the behaviour could be understood within the context of a grand-theory of development or within the context of a micro-theory of development. We will refer to these theories throughout the book, so look for evidence of these theories being applied in practice and, if you are not sure of the theory or cannot remember it in detail, come back to this chapter when you need to.

REVIEW QUESTIONS

1 What makes a good theory?
2 How do stage theories differ from continuous or lifespan perspective theories?
3 How have the works of Rousseau and Locke influenced our understanding of child development?

4 What contribution have Lorenz and Pavlov made to our understanding of human development?
5 What contribution do the integrative theorists make to our understanding of child development?

RECOMMENDED READING

Further reading on the critical evaluation of Piaget and other developmental theorists can be found in the excellent book:

Crain, W. (2005). *Theories of Development: Concepts and Applications (5th Ed.).* Englewood Cliffs, NJ: Pearson Prentice Hall.

Further reading on the 'nature vs nurture' debate in developmental psychology can be found in:

Ceci, S. & Williams, W. (Eds). (2000). *The Nature-Nurture Debate: The Essential Readings.* New York: Blackwell.

Further reading on Bronfenbrenner's bioecological theory of development can be found in:

Bronfenbrenner, U. & Evans, G. (2000). Developmental science in the 21st Century: Emerging questions, theoretical models, research designs and empirical findings. *Social Development, 9,* 115–125.

RECOMMENDED WEBSITES

The Jean Piaget Society:
http://www.piaget.org/aboutPiaget.html

The Erikson Institute:
http://www.erikson.edu/

The Anna Freud Centre:
http://www.annafreud.org/

The Bronfenbrenner Life Course Centre:
http://www.blcc.cornell.edu/

 Watch a short video defining attachment between child and caregiver. Further resources can be found at www.pearsoned.co.uk/gillibrand

Chapter 3
Research methods

Learning Outcomes

After reading this chapter, with further recommended reading, you should be able to:

1. Understand how theoretical paradigms apply to children in a research setting;

2. Understand the range of research methods available for the study of child development;

3. Critically evaluate what the ethical issues are of conducting research with children;

4. Critically evaluate what the practical issues are of conducting research with children;

5. Critically evaluate the research methods of studies reporting research with children.

On the 3rd of March 2009, researchers at the University of Bristol issued a press-release reporting that young children who watched television for more that two hours every day doubled their risk of developing asthma. These findings were based on a study they had been conducting on more than 3,000 children, tracked from birth to 11.5 years of age. So how did the researchers set up their study and come to these conclusions? This chapter is designed to help you understand how we research children and how we, as developmental psychologists, can work rigorously and ethically in our pursuit of knowledge.

Introduction

If we think back to Chapter 2, Theoretical Perspectives, you will remember that we discussed a number of quite varied theories of human development. We looked at Gesell's maturational theory with a biological underpinning that explained our psychological development occurring alongside our physical development. We reviewed Freud's theory of the psychosexual development of the child. Erikson's theory looked at the psychosocial development of the child whilst Piaget looked at understanding the cognitive development of the child. All these theories, although quite different in their theoretical perspective, together helped us to understand the wider picture of the personal and psychological development of the child. Whilst all these theories have a strong philosophical base, they also have a strong experimental or research base. That is, these theories are all the result of research studies of children in various settings. Some, like Jean Piaget, conducted hours of research observing children in their natural environment, at play, looking for patterns of behaviour, which he noted down meticulously. Others, like Mary Ainsworth, set out to test her ideas, based on her observations of mother and child behaviour, in a laboratory setting where she could control what events occurred and, again, record her findings in great detail.

Without such painstaking record keeping by Piaget and Ainsworth, as well as all the other researchers of the twentieth century, we would not have the great understanding of children that we currently have. Through reading the detailed papers of studies conducted by key developmental psychologists, education specialists and family therapists, we are able to understand the key issues in researching children and to make use of their recommendations for best practice. Research in developmental psychology generally fits into a number of themes: understanding children's social development (e.g. attachment and bonding behaviour, play and relationship behaviour); understanding their cognitive development (e.g. the development of skills such as language, memory, empathy); or understanding children with differences (e.g. children who are very high achievers, children with developmental delay, children with other learning difficulties). In order to make sense of these theories and studies, we need to understand how research is conducted on children and why the study of children presents quite different challenges to the study of adults.

What is research?

The term research refers to the series of activities we carry out when we want to find out the answer to a question or a problem. Sometimes the questions are set for us by our teachers and work colleagues, sometimes the questions come from reading and reflect our interest in a topic and sometimes the questions come when we see something happen and want to know why it occurred. Although on occasion we may think we intuitively know the answers to the questions, using appropriate research methods to solve the question or the problem can allow us to state the answer with a certain amount of certainty.

Research can therefore be carried out for many reasons. It can be *exploratory* and seek to understand something that we know little about. It can be *speculative* and try to work out what might be the long-term implications of changing, say, a policy on health care, education or funding. It can be *descriptive* and aim to show patterns and connections in behaviour. It can be *explanatory* and show why those patterns and connections exist. Research can also be *predictive* and be used to develop and test a model that aims to predict what circumstances result in a certain behaviour or other outcome, and research can be *evaluative* and seek to measure the impact of a change in say policy, illness medication or educational technique (Leary, 2008).

The importance of understanding theoretical paradigms

When thinking about conducting research in developmental psychology, we need to consider first your position in a key research paradigm, positivism vs constructivism. Do you think that it is possible to know and measure a child, for them to be investigated in a structured, scientific way that tests hypotheses and factual statements (a positivist approach)? Or do you think that children are part of the social fabric of life, dynamic and interactive?

Can children only be understood in the context of being active members of relationships which are both proactive and responsive (a constructivist approach, Grieg *et al.,* 2007)?

According to the positivist assumption, research with children can be carried out in the same way as research in the fields of chemistry, geology or plant biology. Children are biological beings that fit into the fundamental laws of science and can therefore be tested in exactly the same way. A researcher can set a hypothetical question and then test it to see if the statement is true or false. Positivist researchers thus use experimental hypotheses in their research and design studies to test the truth of them. For example, a positivist might set the hypothesis that children who are good at mathematics are poor at learning a second language. The researcher will then measure a number of children's ability in maths and in a second language and run statistical analysis to determine if the hypothesis is true. The researcher can control the test conditions of the children, make sure that the study is carried out systematically and test enough children to confidently state that his research findings indicate that the statement is true.

The difficulty with this approach is that the researcher, although controlling the test conditions, cannot control for any other external factors known as

Definitions

Research: 1. a. the systematic investigation into and study of materials, sources, etc., in order to establish facts and reach new conclusions. b. an endeavour to discover new or collate old facts, etc. by the scientific study of a subject or by a course of critical investigation. (Oxford Dictionaries, 2008)

Positivism: (concept) a system recognising only that which can be scientifically verified or logically proved, and therefore rejecting metaphysics and theism. (Oxford Dictionaries, 2008)

Constructivism: constructivism is a philosophy of learning founded on the premise that, by reflecting on our experiences, we construct our own understanding of the world we live in (Piaget, 1967).

confound variables. For instance, one example of a confound variable happens as soon as the research takes place, both the researcher and the child know that they are in an artificial situation that has been created for a purpose. The child and researcher may have quite different ideas on what that purpose is, but it is likely that both will change their natural behaviour as a result, affecting the validity of the study. Confound variables can be found in the interpretation of both the process and outcome of the research study. In everyday life, each of us individually interprets the meaning of the words, actions and gestures of others, and it is no different in the research setting. As a researcher, we think we know what message we are putting across when we describe the aims of the research to the child and we think we are making accurate interpretations of the data we collect. However, what we often fail to consider is the context of that language and behaviour. For us as researchers, we are accustomed to using language in a particular way, are familiar with research techniques and we have an expectation of the findings of the study. The child, however, does not have those influences, and may indeed see things quite differently. Take, for example, research conducted by Herbert P. Ginsberg (1997). Ginsberg asked a child to 'count the toys out loud'. The child patiently named all the toys in front of her. When he asked instead 'How many toys are there?', the child accurately counted all the toys. Ginsberg concludes that by not asking the right question, he would have thought that this child could not add, but in fact she could, she had simply misunderstood the question (Ginsberg, p. 11). This also illustrates a further confound variable which is the ability of the child to understand what is required of him or her in the research setting. A researcher who has decided to investigate, say, children of seven years of age needs to be aware that the development of language, empathy, other cognitive and even motor ability varies from child to child and what might be understood by one child may not be understood by the next. The positivist researcher may have to develop research methods that will test effectively children of all abilities and to devise a measure that is suitable not just for a range of age groups but also for the range of abilities within those age groups.

The constructivist approach sees children very differently. Constructivists see children and their parents and carers, teachers and peers as working in a dynamic way. Children and the people around them interact by talking, playing, crying and caring and construct the meaning of these events from the context where they occur. The constructivist approach sees children and the people around them as a network of relationships where all players are important. The context of the interaction is very important to the constructivist approach, as it is the context (history, time, culture) that gives meaning to the behaviour. Constructivist researchers try to understand as much about the behaviour as they possibly can by investigating smaller groups of people in detail, trying to enter the world of the child to see what his or her perspective is, who the important people are and where behavioural influences come from. Constructivist researchers do not try to generalise their findings on a small group to the population as a whole and, from this methodological perspective, their findings can be limited in their application. However, the constructivist argument supports the notion that findings from such detailed, individualist research have a great deal of validity when the whole social, cultural and historic context of the child is understood as, without this, the researcher's ability to describe and interpret the behaviour is highly restricted (Hatch, 1995).

Therefore, depending on your perspective, you may see children as readily testable and measurable, participants that you can conduct your research *on* (positivist) or you may see children as people you can learn from, that need to be understood in context, participants that you can conduct your research *with* (constructivist). To understand the importance of understanding, questioning and debating the positivist–constructivist research paradigm, think about the implications for your research method. To put it simply, if your theoretical perspective is positivist, then you are more likely to find using quantitative methodologies appropriate to answer your research question whilst, if your theoretical perspective is constructionist, then you are more likely to find the use of qualitative methodologies more appropriate in answering your research question.

Definition

Confound variables: extraneous factors in a research study that are not specifically measured or manipulated and that may affect the results of that study.

Methods in developmental psychology research

The research methods used in developmental psychology research have evolved to take into account the particular difficulties of investigating behaviour and other phenomena in infants and young children. A questionnaire might be a suitable tool to use with the adult population to measure, for example, voting behaviour, choice of washing powder or even emotional states. However, when dealing with young children, developmental psychologists need to consider other factors such as reading ability, comprehension and linguistic capability. A four year old child, for instance, may not be able to read the questions, or write an answer, but if asked the questions by the researcher, it is possible that the child will be able to reply verbally. Developmental psychologists employ a number of research methods to aid them in answering their research questions, but the most commonly used are observations, case studies, questionnaires and experimental methods. All of these methods are used by psychologists and other behavioural scientists but, for developmental psychologists in particular, the methods are often refined for use with very young participants. Whichever method is used, it tends to fall into one of two categories: either it is a longitudinal or cross-sectional study design or it involves quantitative or qualitative research. These reflect the ideology behind the research question and, often, the researcher himself.

Cross-sectional and longitudinal research designs

As part of the process of designing your research method, you need to consider how much time you have to complete the research. For much of your research carried out as part of your degree studies, you will only have a very short period of time to complete your work. In the first year of study, you may find you have less than an hour to collect your data, whilst in your final year you may find yourself able to devote perhaps a longer period of, say, three to four months. Evidently, the type of method you choose to collect data in these circumstances is dependent on the time available. However, in larger-scale research projects, the method design can be directed more easily

by the needs of the research question. Take for example the following research questions:

> What is the average score in a maths test given to seven year old children?
> Does maths score at age seven years predict ability in maths at age sixteen years?

To answer the first research question, you will need to design a research project that measures every seven year old child's ability in mathematics. One way of doing this would be to go into all the schools in the region, hand out the same maths test to all the seven year old children there and collect in their scores. When you have retrieved all the scores, you can then work out what the average score in the maths test is for this age group and confidently report your findings. The research design you have used here is a cross-sectional research design.

Cross-sectional research design

The cross-sectional research design allows researchers to collect data that describe the current situation, in our example, mathematical ability. Data collected in this way can reveal the lowest and highest score, the most common score (the modal score), the mid-point score (the median score) and the average score (the mean score). All of these

---

Definitions

Cross-sectional research design: a method of collecting data that administers a test or series of tests to a participant or group of participants on one occasion only.

Mean: a statistical term which refers to the numerical average of a set of numbers. To calculate the mean, add all of the numbers in the set and divide by the number of items in the set.

Median: the mid-point in the range of scores that the participants received on a measure. If we place our participants' maths scores in ascending order (5, 5, 5, 7, 8) we can see that the score at the mid-point in the range from 5 to 8 is the third 5 and the median score is therefore 5.

Mode: the most frequently obtained score that the participants received on a measure. In our example, the most frequently obtained score is 5 (5, 5, 5, 7, 8) and the modal score is therefore 5.

scores are useful indicators of performance and are frequently used to create statements of norms of behaviour and ability. In this example, the research design will allow you to calculate the norm or average maths ability in seven year olds and to show what the range of ability in seven year olds might be. This information could then be used by educators to identify children who are particularly able in maths who might be encouraged to study more difficult problems and children who are struggling with maths and who might need more help.

The cross-sectional research design is therefore, a useful way of conducting research, but it does, however, have its weaknesses. This research method only allows us to calculate mathematical ability in children aged seven years at one point in time. It does not allow us to calculate whether maths scores in children aged seven years have changed over time and it does not tell us whether maths ability at age seven years predicts maths ability (or any other type of ability) at a later age. The research design has only allowed us to see a 'snapshot' of mathematical ability. Like a photograph, the research can only provide us with information on one form of ability in one age group of children at one point in time. Thus, the researcher is limited in what she can infer from her findings.

Longitudinal research design

The longitudinal research method, however, allows the researcher to measure change over time and to find evidence of strong associations or predictors of this change.

The second research question (does maths score at age seven years predict ability in maths at age sixteen years) requires a longitudinal research design. To answer this question, you need to start in the same way as before and hand out a standard maths test to all the seven year old children in a region and collect in all their scores. At this point, however, the method of data collection changes. You must then return to the same children when they are sixteen years old and collect their scores in another standard maths test. By comparing the children's scores when they are sixteen years of age to when they were seven years of age, you will be able to see if

> **Definition**
>
> Longitudinal research method: a method of collecting data that administers a test or series of tests to the same participant or group of participants on a number of occasions.

there is any connection between the two and indeed, if maths ability at age seven years predicts maths ability at age sixteen years. By administering the same test to the same participants at two different points in time, this research question can be answered quite effectively.

The longitudinal research design is an extremely useful tool for measuring change over time. It does though, like the cross-sectional research design, have its limitations. Longitudinal research relies on testing the same participants on at least two time points using the same test of measurement. It can be carried out over a couple of days or, as in this example, over a number of years. If the research is to be carried out over a couple of days, it is usually achieved with only a minimal number of participants failing to return for the second data collection. However, if the research is carried out over a number of years, quite often a fairly large number of participants are not present for the second data collection point. In our example, nine years pass between data collection point one (children aged seven years) and point two (children aged sixteen years). During this time, some families may move away from the area and the children change school or some children may not be present due to illness or other changed circumstance. Thus, your participant group at the end of the study might be fewer in number than at the beginning making it difficult to see patterns and connections in the data.

A second weakness of this method that particularly applies in developmental psychology research is that of developmental change in ability. If you were to give the sixteen year old children the same maths test as you gave the seven year old children, then we might predict that after nine years of cognitive development and education in mathematics, all the sixteen year old children will obtain near maximum scores in the test and render the findings of the study void. With a nine-year age gap, therefore, you will need to select a standard test of maths ability that is appropriate for sixteen year olds. However, complications in forming conclusions can arise by changing the test of maths ability. This test will now in all likelihood test ability in more complicated problem-solving skills and more sophisticated analytical techniques such as algebra and geometry as well as arithmetic. Many people will struggle to attain these complex cognitive skills even though they may be quite proficient in more simple arithmetic. The researcher is in danger then of not measuring a developing ability in maths but a different cognitive process altogether. By introducing the different test, you have now altered a fundamental part of your research study and will have to consider this in your report as you now have a factor that limits your ability to state with confidence whether maths ability at age seven years predicts maths ability at age sixteen years.

Quantitative methods

Quantitative methods can be described as methods that use numbers to describe and define concepts (Neuman, 2007). A typical quantitative method would use a survey or questionnaire to collect numerically coded data.

Quantitative methods have the advantage of being quick and easy to carry out. This also means that quantitative methods can often be a fairly inexpensive way of collecting large quantities of data. Another advantage of quantitative methods is that the data collected can often be analysed mathematically and statistically to provide information on norms and variation within the studied population.

Commonly used quantitative methods

Questionnaires and surveys

A questionnaire or survey is a quick way of collecting a lot of information. It comprises simply a list of questions that could be derived from the background literature search you have carried out or which may come from a measure that has been through a process of validation and publication. Questionnaires usually require answers to be collected in a structured format. Thus you can collect yes/no answers, answers on a scale of 1 to 5, answers that fall into categories and answers on a continuous scale. Inventories are a little different from questionnaires in that they do not measure opinions but are composed of questions measuring aptitude and ability.

Definitions

Quantitative methods: use a systematic approach for collecting data that has or is assigned a numerical value.
Pilot study: a small-scale, preliminary run of a study that aims to test for example, the appropriateness of the measurement tools, methods used and then the quality of the data collected. A pilot study is usually conducted to refine the full-scale run of a study.

You can, if you choose, create your own scientific method in order to create a good quality measurement tool. A good discussion of how to develop a questionnaire can be found in Chapter 11 of Breakwell *et al.* (2006), but briefly, first, you need to formulate a good research question and identify precisely what information you want to get from the measure. Then the individual questions or items need to be written based on a comprehensive background literature search and/or from personal and professional experience. The questions should then be reviewed by other experts in the field and rank ordered for how well they relate to the research question. The researcher then selects the questions or items with the highest ranks and tests the measure on a few people. Only by analysing the results of this pilot study can the researcher know how effective the measure is in collecting the information needed to answer the research question. When the researcher is satisfied, he or she can then start testing the questionnaire or inventory on a larger population. It can take a long time to produce a good-quality questionnaire or inventory, and many of the 'standard' measures currently used by psychologists have undergone modifications and revisions to become the version that we use today.

Inventories in developmental psychology

An example of an inventory used in developmental psychology is the MacArthur–Bates Communicative Development Inventories (CDI). The MacArthur–Bates CDI forms are parent-based forms for assessing a child's language and communication abilities. There are versions for infants aged 8–16 months, toddlers aged 16–30 months and children aged 30–37 months. The CDI form for infants measures their ability to understand words and gestures, whilst the CDI forms for toddlers and children measures their ability to say as well as understand words and short sentences. There are then two further versions of each of these inventories, the long version and the short version. The long version can take up to 40 minutes to complete and provides a comprehensive view of the child's language and communication abilities whilst the short version takes much less time but can still provide a good indication of language and communication ability. The parent simply works through the form marking which words and gestures the child understands and, for the older ones, speaks, then the inventories are scored by a qualified professional. The short form is a one-page document where the parents marks how many of the 89 words (infant version) or 100 words (child and toddler version) and a few phrases that the child understands and/or says. The short version is particularly useful as an alternative to the long version in cases when a quick assessment of the child is needed or the parent has low literacy skills. The CDI is an excellent way of collecting data on language vocabulary, comprehension and sentence construction in young children. It allows the parents to have some input in the assessment of their child, but there can then be reporting bias. A parent may mark a word as 'spoken' when the child repeats a word they have heard but without any understanding of its meaning. However, these tools have proven extremely useful in developmental psychology, and many versions now exist in both the English and the Spanish language. Published norms for the different age groups are widely available for comparison purposes.

Quantitative measures have to follow a strict process of development to ensure the validity of their use (see further reading recommendations) but, when complete, these tools can provide a wealth of information to the researcher. There are, however, factors that need to be considered when collecting quantitative data in research and limitations on the interpretation the researcher can give to his or her findings. Quantitative methods provide numerical data on behaviour but rarely provide a satisfying answer to why the behaviour occurs. The methods are good for listing opinions, beliefs and knowledge but are unlikely to help you truly understand why a person thinks they way they do or how events in their past have affected the person they are now. Thus, quantitative methods are useful for providing an overview of behaviour but are unable to reveal the personal, in-depth experience of your participants.

Reading and comprehension tests are common in schools.
Source: Pearson Education Ltd./Jules Selmes

STOP AND THINK

This is just a short list of the limitations associated with quantitative methods. Can you think of others that particularly relate to working with children?

Experimental methods

Experimental methods in psychology refer to a manipulation of behaviour, usually in a laboratory setting but also recently in more naturalistic settings. Just like in science classes at school where you set up an experiment to assess the effect of adding one chemical to another, in psychology, an experiment can be set up to assess the effect of adding or changing a variable on certain types of behaviour.

Examples of experimental methods are measuring recall of a list of words under conditions of silence or noise, measuring mathematical performance under conditions of high or low stress and measuring young babies' responses to their mother's and other faces. All of these experiments involve the manipulation of a variable (silence or noise, high or low stress, mother's or other's face) on a type of behaviour – memory, maths ability and face recognition. The environment in which these experiments occur can be anything from a laboratory at the university, to a schoolroom or comfortable living room. There are pros and cons of course of using a laboratory setting over a naturalistic setting for your experiment. Considering the validity of the setting, you need to consider the value of each against the quality of the data you will be able to collect. For instance, using a natural or near-natural setting to observe and measure change in behaviour increases the likelihood of finding accuracy in the results and improves the ecological validity of the experiment. However, using a sound-proofed laboratory setting can help distinguish for instance the effect of the variable being manipulated (silence vs noise) from the effect of confounding variables (e.g. background noise).

Definition

Experimental methods: the manipulation of events to see if change in one variable effects change in another variable.

NATURE–NURTURE

A born musician?

A paper by Ericsson *et al.* (2005) proposed that the key to becoming a specialist in a field of study, such as music, was not natural talent but, more mundanely, down to repeated hours of structured practice. The authors cite studies of 1993 and 1996, respectively, that demonstrated that expert violinists based at the Music Academy in Berlin had spent more time than other, even excellent, violinists in practice by the age of entry to the academy at 18 years (Ericsson *et al.*, 1993). Using a survey methodology to record the number of hours each person had put in to practising, the authors concluded that by the age of 20, the very best musicians at the academy had put in more than 10 000 hours of practice compared with the 5000–7500 hours of practice that the less accomplished violinists had completed and the average of 2000 hours of an amateur musician (Krampe and Ericsson, 1996).

However, Ruthsatz *et al.* (2008) challenge this pure nurture perspective. They believe that confound variables relating to other aspects of musical ability were not being tested by the methods of Ericsson *et al.*

Ruthsatz *et al.* used a survey technique to count the number of practice hours but supplemented it by using questionnaires and inventories to measure the effects of some of their proposed confound variables (intelligence and other musical skills) on acquiring expertise. Their study of 178 high school band members and 83 classical music students found that, although practice hours had a significant effect on developing expertise in musical ability, only those students with high general intelligence and a good aptitude for music became what might be considered accomplished musicians. The authors therefore conclude that, even with unlimited practice hours, few if any of us have the innate abilities that will make us expert musicians. Thus, by looking at studies using one methodology, a survey of practice hours, papers by Ericsson *et al.* (1993) and Krampe and Ericsson (1996) were only able to tell part of the story. However, by supplementing their approach with measures of other abilities, Ruthsatz *et al.* were able to build a much bigger picture of how musical ability is influenced and the researchers were able to take into account the confound variables present (but not measured) in the Ericsson papers.

Interpretation and use of the data

The research methods we have described here will all elicit numerical data that need to be interpreted. Most if not all published standardised measures come with instructions for coding and scoring the child's results and present a range of outcome scores that fall within the 'normal' range for children of different ages. For example, if we were to administer the MacArthur–Bates scale to a 24 month old child and record a score of 200 words, then looking at the accompanying notes for the scale, we can see that the MacArthur–Bates scale tells us that a score of between 150 and 300 words is 'normal', fewer than 150 words is 'low' and over 300 words is 'high' for a 24 month old (Fenson *et al.*, 1994). Therefore, the score we have for our child falls into the 'normal' ability for language. However, what use is that knowledge? Perhaps

when you consider that our child's result falls into the 'normal' range for language, we can suggest that this information is only moderately useful. However, if the score we had collected placed the child in the 'low' range for language, what then? The researcher has to always remember that she has a responsibility for the data that she has collected and the interpretation she subsequently makes. Is the data being collected for the purpose of measuring language ability across a number of 24 month old children within a pre-school facility, or is the data being collected for a diagnostic purpose, perhaps to begin the process of identifying children with language difficulties? Either way, the researcher needs to be confident of how the data was collected from the child, in what setting, what the data collected and how the data was recorded. Only when these concerns are addressed can the researcher state that the score is an accurate

The Avon Longitudinal Study of Parents and Children (ALSPAC)

The Avon Longitudinal Study of Parents and Children (ALSPAC) is a long-term health research project that recruited more than 14 000 mothers during pregnancy from the Bristol and Bath area of England in 1991 and 1992. The purpose of the study is to measure the physical and psychological health of the children through to adulthood and beyond and the study has so far provided a vast amount of information on these families. Some of the published key findings are listed here:

- Women who take the contraceptive pill for a long time get pregnant more quickly than the average when they stop taking it.
- Babies of mothers who smoke cannabis tend to be smaller at birth.
- Laying babies to sleep on their backs has no harmful effects and can reduce the risk of cot death.

- Eating oily fish when pregnant improves the child's eyesight.
- Eating fish in pregnancy improves a child's IQ and communication skills.
- Peanut allergy may be linked to the use of certain nappy rash and eczema creams.
- Children brought up in very hygienic homes are more likely to develop asthma.
- Use of air fresheners and aerosols is associated with more diarrhoea and earache in babies, and more headaches and depression in mothers.
- The discovery of a gene associated with a tendency to be overweight.
- Just 15 minutes of moderate or vigorous exercise a day cuts the risk of obesity by 50%.
- Less than 3% of 11 year olds do the 60 minutes of exercise a day recommended by the Government.

(*Source*: http://www.bristol.ac.uk/alspac/, accessed September, 2010)

reflection of the ability of the child. If the data is being used as part of a diagnostic process, then the researcher needs to consider how to use this data, keeping in mind the best interests of the child and the implications for the child, his family and his schooling.

In the Lifespan box, we describe an important longitudinal study of children and young people conducted in the south-west region of England. The researchers are using a wide range of methods to collect information on their participants: postal questionnaires, biological samples taken in a clinic and interviews conducted at home to name a few. They have involved ethical committees in every decision and plan of research they have made as there are important issues to consider when engaging in research of this nature. Here are some of the issues for you to think about relating to the methods employed in this study. First, the use of questionnaires completed by both the parent and child, to assess a variety of psychological and behavioural factors such as eating behaviour and feelings of

anxiety and depression. Using questionnaires in this way can have limitations as there is a reliance on the parent and child to fully understand the nature of the questions so that they can fill them in accurately. Also, if the parent completes the questionnaire for the child, then the parent will likely interpret the questions for the child, interpret their answers given and/or interpret the behaviour under investigation for the researcher, thus reducing the validity of the measure.

Second, the research medical team collect blood, urine and other samples in the clinic setting. This method follows standard medical procedure and provides objective data. The interviews are carried out by a number of trained researchers in the family home. The interviewers follow a standard interview template, but the advantage of this method is that the interviewers can check that the participant has fully understood the question and encourage them to give a full answer. The limitations of this approach are the privacy restrictions on carrying out research asking children and teens about possibly risky behaviours in earshot of their parents.

A further consideration of this study is that, to date, the parents gave consent for data to be collected from the children. Now that they are aged 18 years, the young people are being asked to consent to the study for themselves. It is important to question this approach to gaining consent. First, it is unlikely that when they were young the children were able to comprehend the needs and demands of the research and could not be said to provide informed consent for the study – indeed, as they were recruited during pregnancy, they were unable to consent at all initially. As the children grew older, they could give verbal assent to the measures being taken, but there is an issue of coercion to be addressed – would the children really be able to refuse to take part in the study if their parents were taking them to the clinic? Power relationships are strong for children as they look to adults for their care, for guidance, for reward and for punishment (Piaget, 1962). Now the children are adults, what pressures will they feel to continue with this study? If you had been part of a study for 18 years, would you feel a personal obligation to continue as a participant even if you did not want to? All of these questions are important to consider when planning any research involving children and young people.

STOP AND THINK

The ALSPAC group publishes their findings on a regular basis both in academic journals and in published press releases. What are the implications of releasing the results of a study when the study itself is still ongoing?

Definitions

Qualitative methods: methods that describe and define concepts, *without* the use of numbers and are usually conducted with smaller participant numbers.
Observation study: the researcher views behaviour in either a laboratory or natural setting and records events that take place. The researcher generally tries not to influence events unless this is a necessary feature of the study design.

Qualitative methods

Qualitative methods can be described as methods that describe and define concepts, *without* the use of numbers. A typical qualitative method involves observing behaviour or, more commonly, talking to individuals or groups to discover their personal experiences.

Neither quantitative nor qualitative methods exists in isolation. The researcher will decide which method will most effectively answer the research question. In our example of measuring communication ability in children with the MacArthur–Bates CDI forms, quantitative methods were appropriate as the researcher wanted to obtain numerical scores of linguistic ability and to compare the scores with published norms. If the researcher wanted to discover why, for instance, one child did not fit the pattern in the data it may be appropriate to use a qualitative methodology. To understand the unique experience of that child, the researcher might consider talking to the child, his parents and schoolteacher. By adopting a qualitative approach, the researcher can seek to understand the personal experiences of the child and parents without making any prior assumptions as to why that child was different to his peers in language and communication ability from the same environment. The researcher can also discover particular circumstances that led to the child having a lower score and carefully assemble the data into a coherent 'story' of that unique case.

Commonly used qualitative methods

Observations

Using an observation study essentially involves watching a person or group of people in a particular situation. The researcher can use observation to *develop* a strong research question or the researcher can use observation to *answer* their research question.

A good example of the use of observation in developmental psychology comes from the work of Mary Ainsworth and Sylvia Bell in 1970. Researchers Schaffer and Emerson had reported in 1964 that some babies seemed to be more sociable than others, that they displayed differences in attachment, with some liking to be cuddled more than others. The babies demonstrated this preference at a very early age, leading Schaffer and Emerson to conclude that this was an example of innate (natural or instinctive) differences in children.

This research is carefully taking notes while watching mother and daughter at play.

Source: Alamy Images/Photofusion Picture Library

Noting that the babies were unable to explain their differences in sociability, Ainsworth devised an observational study to detect the individual differences in attachment behaviours of children called the 'Strange Situation' study.

The 'Strange Situation' study is described in detail in Chapter 9, Attachment and Early Social Experiences however, the basic details are this. The observation occurs in a laboratory setting, usually a room with a one-way mirror that is set up to resemble a family living room. The observer views a series of behaviours involving the mother, the child and a 'stranger' (another researcher). Each event lasts for three minutes and follows a set format:

1. Parent and infant alone.
2. Stranger joins parent and infant.
3. Parent leaves infant and stranger alone.
4. Parent returns and stranger leaves.
5. Parent leaves; infant left completely alone.
6. Stranger returns.
7. Parent returns and stranger leaves.

Throughout these events, the observer records the infant's separation anxiety, stranger anxiety and behaviour when reunited with the parent. Ainsworth and Bell's observations of 100 children and parents allowed them to develop a classification of attachment according to the behaviour of the child during these 'strange' situations.

The observation research method is an excellent way of collecting descriptive information and is considered to have good research validity. It can be a difficult method to master, however, and it is time-consuming. One of the key problems with carrying out an observation is maintaining an objective viewpoint as it is easy to become involved in the events you are observing and to frame your observations within your own social and cultural norms, not necessarily those of the person observed. Yet, if carried out well, the information collected can provide the researcher with a solid base from which to begin developing a theory or model of behaviour (Breakwell *et al.*, 2006).

Interviews

There are two main types of interview used in psychology, the structured and the open interview. The structured interview is useful for collecting opinions and preferences or data that require the respondent to answer every question from a pre-planned list. The data collected are useful for market analysis purposes and usually respond well to quantitative as well as qualitative analysis. Whilst the structured interview ensures that all respondents answer all the same questions, the open interview allows the interviewer and respondent the flexibility to explore the answers given and the issues raised within them. Neither the interviewer nor the participant is required necessarily to answer a set of questions and the flow of the interview depends on the answers given. It takes time to train to become fully competent in hosting an open interview, but the quality of data collected is usually vastly superior to that of the structured interview. Some researchers employ a combination of methods in their interviews, using a closed format to obtain data on participant age, sex and other factual characteristics and then invoking a more open format when asking about opinions and beliefs or descriptions of events and so on. In this way, the researcher attempts some standardisation of the process of the interview and can collate enough information to group the participants according to common features. The researcher can, if she chooses, then consider the

Definition

Interview: the interview is conducted by the researcher following either a strict list of questions (a closed or structured interview) or an open format that evolves from the answers the respondent gives (an open interview).

individual participant's experiences alongside those of other similar respondents.

Lawrence Kohlberg (1963) used interviews in his famous paper on moral development (see Chapter 13, Adolescence for a full discussion of his theory). Kohlberg was a researcher highly influenced by the works of Jean Piaget on the stages of cognitive development in children. Kohlberg believed that as part of our cognitive development we also show a development in our ability to think morally or ethically about real and hypothetical dilemmas. In order to test this, Kohlberg set up interviews with a number of children, young people and adults. Each interviewee was presented with a series of hypothetical situations and asked to describe whether he thought the person in the situation had acted rightly and to explain why he thought this. Kohlberg was not so much interested in whether the interviewee thought the person had acted rightly or wrongly, but he was more interested in the reasoning behind the decision made. In using an interview method, Kohlberg could address many of the limitations of a self-complete questionnaire type of study. It would have taken less time and fewer resources to distribute questionnaires with copies of the dilemmas asking participants to make decisions and explain their reasoning. However, one limitation of the questionnaire method used in this way is that people completing them often miss out questions (usually by mistake) or do not give full answers to the questions. You also have to assume that each of your participants has interpreted the dilemmas and subsequent questions in the way you intended. You can rarely go back to a participant after reading their completed questionnaire and ask them, 'did you mean to say this or did you misread the question?'

Kohlberg, however, could discuss each hypothetical situation with each participant and make sure that every participant had understood the dilemma posed and the nature of the moral question. He could also ensure that the participants did not reply simply 'yes' or 'no' to the questions, but gave detailed answers, rationalising their interpretation of each dilemma posed. If the participant said something that Kohlberg did not fully comprehend, he could ask the participant to expand, to clarify and to confirm their response. The interview method allowed Kohlberg to collect a vast amount of good-quality data that he subsequently categorised into three main types of moral decision-making and thus began his theory of moral development.

Case studies

The case study approach to research might be employed in a number of situations but invariably because the researcher notes something unique or interesting about a person or situation that warrants further investigation. The researcher may have collected data from a number of participants and, on analysing those data, found that one of the participants is unusual in some way. Perhaps that person had a significant emotional response to the study or had a particularly interesting story to tell. In which case, the researcher may decide to approach that participant to carry out a detailed investigation, or case study.

Case studies can provide a wealth of information if carried out accurately. The researcher may use this method to report the effectiveness of a particular counselling technique or teaching method that brought about significant behavioural change in the participant. The detail that can be elicited from devoting time to a case study can reveal information that might expand or elucidate a theory or process that has previously been poorly understood. However, the downside of the case study approach is that it simply reveals the experiences of the person under investigation. It is difficult to extrapolate the research findings to make sense of behaviour in a large population when the research has only investigated one person. Case study researchers would argue that this is not the point of the approach and that a carefully planned and executed case study can add to the understanding of a phenomenon but it is not designed to explain the experience of the masses (Neuman, 2007).

An example of case study work comes from some of the most influential work on child–mother attachment and the effects of periods of brief separation carried out in London in the 1960s and early 1970s by researchers James and Joyce Robertson (Robertson and Robertson, 1989). Highly regarded by both John Bowlby and Mary Ainsworth, the Robertsons are probably best known for their work revolutionising the way that children are cared for in hospitals. In their book titled *Separation and the Very Young*, the Robertsons describe their efforts to

Definition

Case study: the detailed investigation of the experience of one person or of a small group of people.

understand the psychological effects on a child of being separated from his mother. Prior to their work, parents were actively discouraged from visiting their children in hospital as it was felt to be upsetting for the child and detrimental to their recovery. The Robertsons conducted a series of studies observing and filming children aged from 17 months to two years and five months experiencing separation ranging from 10 to 27 days. The experience of each child is presented as a case study and arguably the most famous of these is the study of John.

John was placed in a residential nursery for nine days at the age of 17 months whilst his mother stayed in hospital for the birth of his brother. During this time, James Robertson filmed John's experiences and Joyce watched him carefully noting down his behaviour, temperament and mood. Over the course of the nine days, John's behaviour changes and he shows distress, eventually rejecting his mother when she returns to collect him. At no point does Joyce Robertson deliberately interact with John, leaving his care to the nurses. A couple of times, John does try to make contact with Joyce, but during those episodes, she busies herself with other activities and sometimes looks away.

The value of the case study approach here is the detailed information the Robertsons were able to collect on John's experiences. The filming allows the objective observer to discuss the interpretations offered by the Robertsons and the careful use of filming allows you to see the changes in John during his time in the nursery. He was only filmed for four minutes each day due to the expense of filming at the time of the study, but the visual impact of the brief clips is a powerful illustration of Joyce Robertson's written observations. The case study approach allows us to focus completely on John's experiences and to interpret them in relation to the sequence of events for John. Therefore, we can see evidence of his strong, secure attachment to his mother prior to her entering hospital. We then follow him after he enters the care facility, day-by-day as he finds himself in an unusual, frightening situation, surrounded by noisy, boisterous children without his mother offering him safety and support. Finally, we are able to monitor the reunion with his mother and observe how he rejects her and finds no comfort in her presence. Without this and the other case studies conducted by the Robertsons, we would not be able to see the short- and long-term effects of brief separation on children or to seek ways of improving their experiences. The case study approach provides a wealth of information on a person's experiences, perhaps following them as they prepare and experience a major event and then observing the psychological processes involved. However, the limitations of the case study approach prevent generalisations of experience to the wider population. Information gleaned from a case study can help you interpret another's behaviour and experiences, but cannot be used to predict their response or to completely inform your interpretation.

When to bring the study to a close?

As with adults, qualitative research in the form of observations, interviews and case studies with children needs to be carried out carefully. Observations, for example, need to be prepared for well in advance so that any cameras required can be maximally placed to collect as much data as possible. The participants, adults and children, need to be aware of the purpose of the study and give their consent for the observation to take place. The researchers need to have developed and tested a schema for coding what takes place and how to make sense of it. When children are involved, the researcher needs to pay close attention to what she is observing. All researchers need to consider whether the child is becoming tired or distressed, whether the child needs to take a break for some reason, and whether the child's experiences are wholly necessary for the research. The Stanford Prison Study in the Case Study box describes an experimental situation that got out of control, even with a number of researchers observing the events and recording them. It took an outsider to step in and bring the study to a stop. The participants in the Stanford Prison Study were all adults and were able to voice their concerns about how the study was progressing, but were unable to convince the researchers to cut short the experiment. We can see from this study that it takes a great deal of researcher sensitivity to note signs of distress in their participants, and a great deal of objectivity to position the needs of the participant above the demands of the study and bring it to a close. When conducting research with children it is even more important to develop a sensitivity to your participants; the very young infants will not be able to tell you that they want the study to stop – you will have to look for signs of tiredness or distress and guidance from the parent when deciding whether to continue the study or not. At all times, the needs of the children come first, the needs of the study come second.

CASE STUDY

The Stanford Prison Experiment

Researchers recruited 24 male college students to take part in what was intended to be a two-week study of the psychology of prison behaviour. The students were randomly allocated to either the 'prisoner' group or the 'prison warden' group.

The 'prisoners' were arrested at home and hand-cuffed by real police officers. The prisoners were then taken to a police station, warned of their rights, finger-printed and taken to a holding cell. The 'prison wardens' were given uniforms, mirrored sunglasses and had a truncheon each. The wardens were given the instruction to 'do whatever they thought was necessary to maintain law and order in the prison and to command the respect of the prisoners' and so the study began.

The prisoners were spoken to not by name but as the inmate number printed on their clothes. They were woken at 2:30 am for a roll-call, made to do lots of press-ups for minor infringements and given plain, basic meals. Over a period of five days the behaviour of the wardens steadily became more controlling and aggressive. On the sixth day Christina Maslach, a recent Stanford Ph.D. graduate walked into the researchers observation suite, was horrified by what she saw and demanded an immediate stop to the study.

During the study, friends and family of the prisoners, a Catholic priest and a number of professional psychologists had all visited the prison and seen what was going on, yet none of them requested that the study be stopped. Maslach was the only person who protested on moral and ethical grounds (Blass, 2000, p. 18).

- How could you introduce measures in your own study that will protect your participants?
- How would you monitor the effectiveness of these measures in discontinuing a study that is causing your participants distress or harm?

(*Source*: http://www.prisonexp.org/)

Working with children

When working with children, it is particularly important to consider how, where and when the research is going to take place. How will the data be collected? Will the parent or researcher rather than the child complete the measures or observations? Where do you want to collect the data? Do you want to go into the family home or into the school classroom? When do you want to collect the data? Is it important if the data is collected during the day, in the evening, during the week or at the weekend? Before data collection can commence, the researcher needs to have a good understanding of the development capacity of the child. She needs to consider whether the child can understand the questions or tasks she wants to use. She also needs to consider if she wants to speak with the child directly, or does she want to speak about the child with a parent or teacher? According to Grieg *et al.* (2007), depending on the age of the child, the types of questions that can be understood will vary. Very young children can usually understand questions such as 'Who? What? Where?'. If the child cannot verbally identify, he can usually point to people or objects in response to these questions. Early school-age children can usually answer more complex questions such as 'Why? When? How?'. Until children enter schooling, they often refer to time in relation to activities and events. Morning, for instance means 'after breakfast', afternoon could be 'after lunch' and evening is characterised by bath time and bed. Young children's lives are structured around meals and activities and it is not until they learn about clocks and how that relates to time that they can offer a more precise indication of when something occurred. More complex questions relating to memory and recall need to be handled carefully in children. Memory in children is affected (just as in adults) by the social and emotional context of the event. As a researcher, you can help facilitate detailed recall of events by encouraging the child to re-enact the events with toys or through drawing. However, long-term memory in young children can be difficult to elicit. The ability of young children to remember events that happened a long time ago is limited and accuracy can be poor.

When thinking about where the research will take place, we need to consider the many contexts of children's lives and how those contexts will affect the types of responses we might achieve. For instance, children may spend their early years in and around the family home, visiting relatives, playing in the park and attending kindergarten. The mealtimes, play and learning opportunities in each of these places are quite different and if the researcher is interested in one particular aspect of the child's development, then only one or two of the locations will be appropriate for the study. To appreciate the complexity of choosing the right methodology when researching with children, take, for example, a researcher interested in measuring language ability in a child, what research method could he use? Take for instance a measure of vocabulary to answer the question of how many different words a child might use in a day. One way of measuring this could be to ask the parent to record each night what words a child has used that day and when. This method is highly dependent on the parent being in the unlikely position of remembering every word the child has used throughout the day and also of being present every time the child speaks. Language use is highly context-dependent so you might want to make the task easier by asking the parent to think about what they did with the child during the day and what words the child used during those activities. Of course then, you may not get a full record of the child's vocabulary as the parent may not write down other words spoken outside of the activities. An alternative method could be to ask the parent to take five minutes at regular points during the day to write down every different word the child has spoken up to that point. However, if the telephone rings, the child falls over or something else distracts the parent during this process, then it is likely that you will not get a full record of the child's vocabulary using this technique either.

Research of this nature is extremely difficult and, rather than depend on the parent to collect the data, you may prefer to carry out the data collection yourself. In this case, do you go into the family home, the classroom or simply follow the child around all day recording their word use? Following and observing a child for a full day might seem like a very time-intensive approach, but think of the alternatives. If you arrive at the house in the morning whilst everyone is having breakfast, it is highly likely that the conversation around the table will revolve around food, getting dressed for school, checking school bags, arranging pick-up after school and the parents discussing their plans for the day. Thus, the vocabulary you will be able to collect will relate to words on these quite specific topics. Likewise, if you drop into a classroom to collect data and the conversation is about Tudor kings and queens, then the vocabulary you will collect will relate to another very specific topic. In order to gain an idea of the range of vocabulary a child has, you will therefore need to assess them in a wide number of contexts, which will take time and probably more resources than you have available. Researchers have therefore been working on developing measures that allow for a comprehensive assessment of vocabulary in a child that can be completed by the parent or teacher or even, at a later age, by the child him or herself. These measures, for example, the MacArthur–Bates CDI that we discussed earlier, have become invaluable in research studies with children. However, although it may appear that a quantitative measure is the solution to this research problem, quantitative research methods are not necessarily a quick fix for all qualitative problems, as you will see in examples of research presented throughout this book.

Addressing the subject of norms and typicality

Much research in developmental psychology is aimed in one of two directions: measuring and describing 'normal' or 'typical' behaviour or investigating 'unique' or 'individual' behaviour. Choosing the appropriate method to answer research questions of this nature is vital and, simply speaking, quantitative methods are useful for identifying norms and typical behaviour whilst qualitative methods are useful mostly for investigating unique and individual behaviour. The danger in describing typical behaviour patterns in children lies with the wide range of variance in each child's abilities. As children develop, so some forge ahead and acquire some skills such as language ahead of others whilst others are slower to develop language but faster at developing, say, their sensory-motor skills. Although developmental psychologists can collect data that describe the 'normal' age at which, say, two-word utterances are used by most children, it is important to recognise that these norms are actually statistical average points in the data and not to get too caught up in seeing these points as deadlines for skills acquisition. For example, if a child is not yet using two-word phrases at the age of 18 months when her sister was happily using them at that age, it is crucial that rather than worrying that the child has not reached that developmental milestone, the developmental psychologist should reassure the parent that each child develops at a different pace and that her daughter will probably catch up by the time she is two years of age.

However, with such variation in individual development, it becomes difficult for the developmental psychologist to identify areas where the child is not developing at a typical pace and where the child is therefore unique in his or her abilities. For some children who show particular ability at school, they might be considered atypical by teachers, parents and psychologists alike and be encouraged to follow an advanced stream in education separate to their peers. However, this action might isolate the child from children his own age and he may experience difficulties making friends and building relationships. Other children, on the other hand, may find certain aspects of school particularly difficult and be considered for separate schooling with extra support. For these children too, they might experience isolation and problems forming friendships. Chapter 16, Atypical Development, discusses these issues in more detail and, in particular, the difficulties that parents, teachers and psychologists face when making these types of decisions. When you are reading this chapter and others throughout this book, consider the implications of theories that state age norms of ability for children whether they might be in the school classroom or in the family home and reflect on what this knowledge can mean for parents, teachers and developmental psychologists.

Cohort effects

A cohort is a group of people who have something collectively in common. This could be the same year of birth, the same year of entry to school or people who have all passed their driving test. On a larger scale, a cohort might be defined as people who were children during the Second World War, children who were born in the 'Swinging Sixties' or people who are now all retired from work. Researchers from the many fields of social and behavioural studies all make use of cohorts in defining their activities. For example, a company that is trying to sell a new alcoholic drink will identify the target cohort drinkers for advertising and use that information to develop their marketing campaign. In another example, a government agency for health awareness that wants to reduce deaths from lung cancer will identify a target cohort of people who smoke and direct their promotional campaign at these people in order to encourage them to quit smoking and reduce their chances of getting lung cancer. In developmental psychology, just as in those other examples, researchers define their research target population by the use of cohorts in order to obtain the most relevant findings. Although we present many theories and principles of developmental psychology according to chronological age, age in itself is not necessarily a cohort. Take for instance the first year of formal schooling. In the UK, that classroom will have children whose ages range from four to five years of age yet, in most of Europe, compulsory schooling does not begin until the age of six years (Sharp, 2002). Thus if we are to conduct a study that requires children to be in their first year of formal education, we cannot choose our children based simply on their age but on whether or not they are actually in school and what year of school they are in.

Cohort groups have the advantage of being identified by factors that are perhaps more descriptive of the similarities of the group members (for example, children of refugee parents) rather than mere demographic data such as born in the year 1971, the risk of course being that too much emphasis is placed on the supposed similarities of the cohort without an understanding of the differences between members. Yes, the children in the example of refugee parents have all been born to parents for whom the country is not their natural home, but the experiences of children whose parents have fled war-torn nations might be very different to the experiences of children whose parents fled due to a change of political leadership. However, cohort effects are an extremely useful way of identifying similarities in a target research group and can be much more meaningful than group membership by any other means such as random or convenience selection methods (Neuman, 2007).

> **Definition**
>
> Cohort: a cohort is a group of people who are defined by having something collectively in common.

A cohort of World War survivors.

Source: Pearson Education Ltd./MindStudio

A cohort of teenagers born into the technological age.

Source: Getty Images/Olivier Morin/AFP

Ethical working practice

Ethical working practice in developmental psychology is usually regulated not just by the university where the researcher is resident, but also (and for practitioners and researchers not resident in a university) by the regulatory body of the profession. In the EU, these professional bodies are members of the European Federation of

Psychologists Associations (the EFPA). In the UK the professional body is the British Psychological Society, in Iceland it is the Icelandic Psychological Association, in Luxembourg it is the Société Luxembourgeoise de Psychologie, in France it is the Fédération Française des Psychologues et de Psychologie and so on. A full list of the members of the EFPA according to member nation of the EU is available at http://www.efpa.eu/members. When you have located the relevant professional body for your country of registration, you can follow the links to the specific details of ethical practice that you need to observe. In the meantime, common threads of ethical working practice for psychologists registered all over the world are discussed here in relation to working with children in particular.

Consent and assent

An important part of research is to make sure that your participants are aware of your project and that they choose to take part in the full knowledge of what they will be asked to do. This is known as informed consent: the participants know what the study is about and what type of activity they will be involved in and agree to take part, usually signing a form confirming this. With children under the age of 16 years, you have to not only get permission from the children but also from their parents to approach them for your study and, if you are conducting the study in a school, from the teachers and head teacher. In the UK, children under the age of 16 years are considered one of the vulnerable groups for research purposes (another is people with learning difficulties) and cannot truly give informed consent until they have attained adult status, so a written or verbal statement of agreement from them

to taking part in the study is known as *assent*, whilst the agreement of the adult teachers and parents to the children taking part in the study constitutes informed *consent*.

Power relationships, demand characteristics and coercion

One of the concerns with research is that of the power relationship that can exist between researcher and participant. We discussed the issue of the impact of the research on the behaviour of your participants earlier in the chapter and, in particular, we discussed the idea of demand characteristics in your participants. This is where the participant feels under pressure to act in a certain way either as a result of simply taking part in the research, or because they feel pressure to act in a way that they think will please the researcher. The researcher therefore needs to be aware of the impact they may have on the behaviour of the participant and to work hard to provide a suitable atmosphere for the research that will encourage an honest reaction from the participant. Related to this concept is the notion of coercion. Offering a financial reward or some other benefit for completing a study may convince a participant to continue with a study that is making them feel uncomfortable rather than legitimately asking to withdraw from the study. Researchers commonly offer to pay travel and other expenses to their participants rather than a fee for completing the work, and it is vital that the researcher makes the participant (especially a child) aware that they can withdraw from the study at any time. It is good practice to provide breaks in the study so that the participant can be offered the opportunity to discontinue the research project. No participant should feel that they have been forced either to take part in the study or to continue with the study beyond a point where they feel uncomfortable.

Deception and debriefing participants

Occasionally you may want to introduce a factor into your research project that you do not want your participants to know about in advance. For example, you may think that if the participant knows everything about your study, then the knowledge she has will change her behaviour. So in order to counteract this, you may want

Definitions

Informed consent: agreeing to take part in a study whilst knowing as far as possible the details of the study methodology including all possible risks and benefits of taking part.

Demand characteristics: when a participant anticipates what the researcher wants from them and changes their behaviour to conform to that perceived desirable performance.

to introduce an element of deception into your study. If the participants have to know all the details of the study in advance in order to give informed consent, then how do you do this and still follow ethical working practices?

The rules of research state 'deception is acceptable only if the researcher can show that it has a clear, specific methodological purpose, and . . . should use it only to the minimum degree necessary' (Neuman, 2007). Researchers using deception must obtain informed consent (describing the fundamental details of the research study) from their participants, make use of deception safely and always debrief the participants afterwards to explain the use of the deception and the purposes for which it was used (Neuman, 2007). It is important to think through how you might use deception in your study and, in particular, how child participants might be affected by it. If you are in any doubt as to its purpose, it is usually best to redesign your study and remove the deception completely.

STOP AND THINK

- Think of a study design that would use deception in order to get the result you want.
- How could you now redesign the study so that you still answer your research question effectively but in a way that is agreeable to your university ethics committee?

Protection from physical harm and psychological harm – distress, upset, guilt, loss of self-esteem

The fundamental principle underlying all these considerations is the safety of you and your participants. All universities require a statement of ethical working practice to be submitted for consideration for all research projects whether the researcher is an undergraduate student, a lecturer planning a practical workshop session for her students or a researcher involved in a large-scale

Definition

Deception: the deliberate act of creating false knowledge in your participants for the purpose of influencing the outcomes of the research study.

project. It may seem like an arduous and probably slightly dull part of the research process, but it will help you to consider all the ways in which you can protect everyone involved in the study.

Care must be taken to prevent both physical and psychological harm. Physical harm may come from the use of apparatus in your study, but also from furniture in the study area. Researchers working with young children need to be aware also of sharp objects and keeping an eye on young children who may put things in their mouths. It is the researcher's responsibility to ensure that the study is conducted in a safe environment and to stop any study when harm occurs or the researcher sees a potentially harmful situation arise (Neuman, 2007).

Part of ethical working practice is to consider whether psychological harm could occur to your participants in any way as a result of carrying out your research study. Take some of the examples of studies we have considered in this chapter and think about how they could possibly cause psychological distress to the participants. The Stanford Prison Study illustrates the importance of the researcher taking the responsibility for maintaining control and even stopping the study when faced with risk of distress to the participant. This study shows how even a team of experts can be drawn into fascinating details of a study yet remain unaware of the broader impact of its workings on the participants. When you are working with children and infants, it is imperative that the children are not placed under any undue amounts of stress and that if the child or the parent request the study be stopped, then it must be stopped.

Another case in point showing the importance of protecting children and young people from the effects of psychological harm is the Robertsons' observations of children experiencing brief separation. Although it now seems common-sense to stay with a child during hospital treatment, it is largely due to the Robertsons challenging the practice of keeping parents away that we are now encouraged to do so. However, when watching the films and reading the reports on the experiences of the child John in particular, it feels that the children experienced a significant amount of emotional distress during the studies. Could the distress have been avoided? As a research study, the Robertsons were merely observing the experience of a child put into care whilst his mother was in hospital. They did not ask his parents to put him into care or ask them to have little contact with him and they did not therefore manipulate John into the situation he found himself in.

Were they therefore responsible for his emotional distress? As far as the parents were concerned, they were doing the best they could for John. His father worked and could not take the time off to care for him whilst his mother was in hospital. He visited John everyday and played with him, could he have done more? The care facility provided meals and toys as well as a bed to sleep in and nurses to care for the children. They were unable to give John the one-to-one attention he had been accustomed to at home as they had a number of children to look after but, again, they were doing the best they could. It is important to remember when looking at studies such as this conducted 50 years ago and more, that everyone was working within their understanding of best practice at the time. It is because of studies like these that we now have a better understanding of childhood and the importance of strong attachments to a child's wellbeing. It is also because of studies like these that we are able to work more ethically, both as researchers and carers, with children and young people.

A current example of working with children and young people, the Avon Longitudinal Study of Parents and Children (ALSPAC), shows how far we have come as researchers in understanding good working and ethical practice. This study is producing a vast amount of data on the biological, social and psychological experiences of children and young people and, through its longitudinal study design, is looking for connections between early and late experiences and between the effects of nature and nurture. The researchers have a rare and exciting opportunity to carry out a truly long-term study on a wide range of participants, collecting samples as they go and employing a range of experts to interpret the findings. The difficulty with a study this large, however, is making sure that you are constantly working within changing ethical guidelines. As our understanding of ethical practice deepens, so changes have been made to the way we work with children and young people. At first, when the study began, parents were responsible for giving consent for their child to take part in research. Now we make sure that we not only ask the permission of parents (and teachers if we are collecting data in a school setting) to work with children, but we ask permission of the children too. Currently it is considered that young children are unable to give fully informed consent to a study. This is because our understanding of the way that cognitive development occurs during childhood prevents the child from understanding the main concepts of consent such as

the right to withdraw at any time or the subsequent use and publication of the data collected. It is also important to consider that the child is unlikely to be able to make an informed decision to take part in research as it is unlikely that they will fully understand what the research is about and what it is you want them to do. However, that does not mean that we do not ask the child if they assent to taking part in the research. We ask the parent (and teacher) to decide whether their child can be approached to take part in the study and the parent signs an agreement of fully informed consent. Then, when the study is about to begin, we ask the child if they would like to carry out the study, telling them they can stop the study at any time. It remains, however, the responsibility of the researcher to ensure that the child is safe, not experiencing distress and to bring the study to a close if required.

Participant confidentiality

Finally, when conducting research in an ethical manner, it is necessary to consider the issue of participant confidentiality, i.e. how to maintain the privacy of the participant and the confidentiality of data you collected so that readers cannot identify any participants or their individual responses in the research report. It can be difficult to do this if you also want to publicly thank the school, say, for taking part in the study or perhaps your participant group comes from a fairly rare cohort. However, by keeping individual's names and personal details out of the report write up and by taking considerable care in storing your data, you can minimise the risk that people might be identified as participants in your study (Neuman, 2007).

STOP AND THINK

- What do you think of the research findings presented in the Cutting Edge entry on page 67?
- What methodology would you use to explore the reasons why the teenagers are engaged in risky online behaviours? Critically evaluate your choice of method.

Definition

Participant confidentiality: the treatment of any data collected on a participant to prevent the identification of the participant.

CUTTING EDGE

The EU Kids Online Project

The EU Kids Online project is using the internet as a research tool for investigating how children and young people use the internet. The research project was set up in 2006 and aimed to collect data over three years from people in 21 countries across the European Union. The site http://eukidsonline.net provides a searchable database of European research on children's experiences of using the internet and provides some examples of best practice, FAQs and other resources of interest to researchers. Participating countries are:

Austria	Ireland
Belgium	Italy
Bulgaria	Norway
Cyprus	Poland
Czech Republic	Portugal
Denmark	Slovenia
Estonia	Spain
France	Sweden
Germany	the Netherlands
Greece	the United Kingdom
Iceland	

The research uses a survey method to measure the experiences of children and young people across Europe, to draw conclusions about the safe use of the internet by children and the cultural context of using the internet and to make recommendations to policy makers and parents alike. The most recent publication from this study reveals that the more parents use the internet, the more children will do so. Teenagers are quickest to take up advancements in digital media, but most parents are able to understand the internet sufficiently to guide appropriate use. The researchers also state that children use the internet as an educational resource but also for fun and games. Boys think they are better at using the internet and certainly use it for longer than girls, and use of the internet increases with age for both sexes. Approximately 15–20% of the teenagers questioned were engaging in risky online behaviours such as giving out personal information, seeing pornography and violent content or receiving unwanted bullying, harassing or sexual comments (Hasebrink *et al.* 2008).

SUMMARY

Our discussion of different methods should help you decide which is most appropriate for answering your research question and allow you to produce a good critical evaluation of the limitations each method has. You should now be aware that each method has its strengths and can be applied effectively in the right situation. However, you should also now be able to consider the weaknesses of each method and how this can limit the interpretation of your findings.

This chapter has also introduced you to the notion of good working practice and some of the key ethical issues of conducting research in devel-

opmental psychology. It is important to remain sensitive to the particular needs of children and young people in research settings and to check carefully that your study is designed to care for and protect your participants.

This chapter serves to introduce you to the key issues in research design when applied in the field of developmental psychology but does not profess to be a full review of research methods. There are many excellent books available that focus purely on research methods in psychology and a few are recommended in the further reading section at the end of this chapter.

REVIEW QUESTIONS

1 In the Nature–nurture box, the studies presented discussed the nature of musical ability. What are the practical implications of the research findings?
2 In the Lifespan box, the ALSPAC study was briefly described. What type of research methodology does this study represent? What are the strengths and weaknesses of this methodology. List three of each.
3 The Stanford Prison study was described in a Case Study box. What have we learnt as researchers from the conduct of this study? Answer with reference to:
a. Informed consent
b. Good working practice
c. Ethical considerations
4 In the Cutting Edge box, we listed an example of an internet-based study. What are the limitations to conducting research in this way? List at least three.

RECOMMENDED READING

For a clearly presented, informative book on all aspects of research planning and design:

Leedy, P. & Ormrod, J. (2004). *Practical Research Planning and Design: International Edition (8th Ed.).* London: Pearson Education.

Offering a good resource for new researchers that will guide you through designing your own research project:

Cresswell, J.W. (2008). *Research Design: Qualitative, Quantitative and Mixed Methods Approaches* (3rd Ed.). Thousand Oaks, CA: Sage.

A good resource for learning about the all the methods of research included in this chapter, especially questionnaire design:

Breakwell, G.M., Hammond, S., Fife-Schaw, C. & Smith, J.A. (2006). *Research Methods in Psychology* (3rd Ed.). London: Sage.

An excellent investment resource that will take you through all the analytic processes step by step:

Keppell, G. & Wickens, T.D. (2007). *Design and Analysis: A Researcher's Handbook* (5th Ed.). Englewood Cliffs, NJ: Pearson Prentice Hall.

An excellent resource on how to conduct research with children's needs in mind:

Grieg, A., Taylor, J. & MacKay, T. (2007). *Doing Research With Children* (2nd Ed.). London: Sage.

RECOMMENDED WEBSITES

For a good resource of materials describing the scientific method and worksheets to help you design your own project:

http://www.scientificmethod.com/

For a good starting point to research academic materials. The scholar version of Google currently scans peer-reviewed and published papers and books etc., only:

http://scholar.google.com

A good resource to help you locate the webpage of your national professional body and the ethical and practical guidelines of working as a psychologist:

http://www.efpa.eu/members

Full details of the Avon Longitudinal Study of Parents and Children:

http://www.bristol.ac.uk/alspac/

Watch a video discussing research methods and approaches. Further resources can be found at www.pearsoned.co.uk/gillibrand

Chapter 4
Prenatal development and infancy

Di Catherwood

Learning Outcomes

After reading this chapter, with further recommended reading, you should be able to:

1. Describe the process of human development from zygote through to birth and infancy, particularly in relation to the development of the brain;

2. Discuss the close interaction between genes and environmental factors in prenatal development and infancy;

3. Describe and evaluate the different research methods which are used to explore prenatal abilities and behavioural capacities *in utero* and in infancy;

4. Critically discuss the evidence surrounding infants' sensory-perceptual capacities (vision, audition, touch, taste and smell);

5. Evaluate classic and contemporary evidence, theory and debates about infant cognition (attention, learning and memory, basic knowledge, categorisation, reasoning and problem solving).

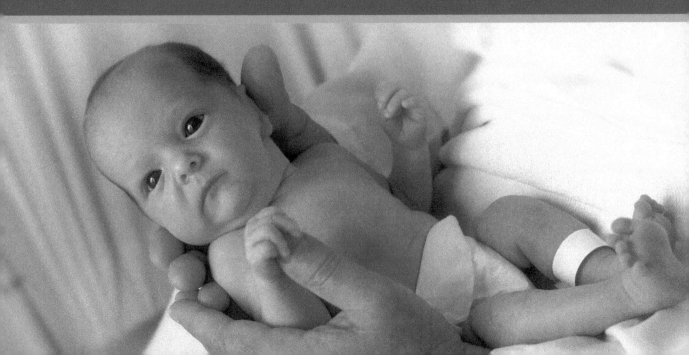

No 'blooming, buzzing, confusion': babies separate cats and dogs!

Recent work has used electroencephalography (EEG) equipment (Quinn *et al.* 2006) to record the brain waves of infants watching pictures of cats and dogs. This has shown that after seeing many examples of cats, the six-month-old brain will show essentially a 'bored' pattern of response when shown another new cat, but will revert to an interested pattern when shown a dog.

In contrast to older views, this suggests that infants do not have a chaotic, jumbled or fleeting experience of the world. Instead it suggests that infants as young as three months see cats and dogs as different in kind. The well-quoted 'blooming, buzzing confusion' proposed by James in 1890 is not an accurate portrayal of the infant's impression of the world. Even if not fully mature, perception and cognition are orderly and structured at birth and provide the basis for subsequent understanding and learning.

- What might be the implications for our interactions with infants, if their perception is orderly and structured from birth?
- How might we alter the way that we engage with them?
- Do you have any personal experience with infants that would support the findings from this research?

Introduction

This chapter will chart the remarkable development of the human infant from the humble beginnings of a single cell. This event-filled journey provides a basic roadmap for the rest of the human lifespan so it is critical to understand these early beginnings. For other texts which focus specifically on infant development, see Recommended Reading at the end of this chapter. This period of life was once considered to be limited to 'sensorimotor' experience (Piaget, 1952, 1958) with no true cognitive activity and only fractured and fragmentary impressions of the world (James, 1890). This portrayal under-estimates infant capacities, and decades of more recent research confirm that infant experience is richer and more coherent than previously proposed (Bremner and Fogel, 2001; Johnson *et al.*, 2002; Slater and Lewis, 2002; Keil, 2006). This chapter will focus on this updated portrayal of infant capacities.

Other chapters in this book will also cover topics and material that overlap with this to some extent: for example, Chapter 7 The Development of Mathematical Thinking will provide further discussion of knowledge in infancy and its relationship to the development of scientific and mathematical thinking in children and Chapter 2 Theoretical Perspectives will provide a broader background to the debate on early cognitive competence. The theme of the interaction between nature and nurture in human development is explored throughout this book and so it is useful to begin by considering how these forces work together from the very moment of conception to shape infant development.

How to grow a baby: the roles of nature and nurture in early development

Human development at all ages depends on the close interaction of two powerful sets of forces: nature (the processes controlled by our genes) and nurture (input from the environment and experience). These forces guide and direct development over the human lifespan. One of the oldest debates in psychology is about the relative contribution of nature and nurture to human development, but contemporary research with humans and other animals makes it clear that these factors are so closely intertwined in shaping human growth and capacities that it is almost nonsensical to ask which is more important. To find out more about recent developments in how nature and nurture interact in development, see Recommended Reading. Before considering how this close relationship operates, it is useful to firstly describe how nature and nurture can each influence early human development.

How does the environment affect early development?

Environmental factors affecting early development are the physical, cognitive, linguistic, social and emotional stimuli that impact on the child. The physical environment can include nutritional factors affecting physical growth or sensory stimulation affecting the development of perceptual and cognitive abilities. The child's cultural–social–interpersonal environment also provides experiences influencing many aspects of early development (Bronfenbrenner and Morris, 1998). The environment can have a lasting impression on the child's capacities via memory and learning, leaving a residue in the brain circuitry (see Prenatal abilities and behaviours). In prenatal life, the maternal environment is the conduit for the external world to impact on the developing child. Maternal diet or habits can influence the child's physical growth (see Risks to prenatal development) and sensory input can permeate the uterine environment and stimulate the growing sensory organs and systems, possibly even providing content for earliest memories and learning (see Prenatal abilities and

behaviours). Maternal emotional state can also provide environmental shaping of the child's development *in utero*. For example maternal stress gives rise to cortisol, a hormone that is released into the mother's bloodstream reaching the infant and possibly affecting subsequent brain and emotional development (Mennes *et al.*, 2009). Such environmental factors, however, invariably work in close relationship with the child's genetic endowment in a two-way dialogue that allows genes to modify the effects of environmental experience and allows experience to directly influence the activity of genes (Diamond, 2009a).

How do genes affect early development?

To find out more about human genetics generally, see Recommended Reading. Genes are strings of biochemical material called DNA (deoxyribonucleic acid) found in all body and brain cells. They influence the way in which all body and brain cells grow and function. Like beads on a necklace, genes are arranged on strands called chromosomes that are found inside each cell, so that one gene is one segment of the chromosome (see Fig. 4.1). Each gene has its own DNA pattern, with this providing the biochemical plan for building and copying the cell in the correct way like the blueprints or designs for building a house.

In all human cells there are 23 pairs of chromosomes and there are collectively tens of thousands of genes along all of these chromosomes. Genes are passed from parent to infant and each human cell generally has two versions (alleles) of each gene. This is because chromosomes come in pairs (one from each parent) and so we have two versions of each gene. These alleles may be the same or different, with any difference resulting either in a mixture or with one dominating the other (such as happens with dark hair genes over fair hair genes).

All cells have the same set of genes, but only certain ones need to be turned on for any particular cell and then only at the correct time. For example, you wouldn't want to have a brain cell gene switched on in the cells

Definition

DNA (deoxyribonucleic acid): strings of biochemical material that provide the code for genes.

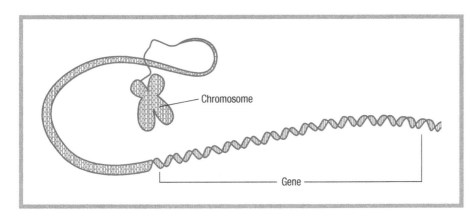

Figure 4.1. Illustration of a 'gene' as one section of a chromosome.

(*Source*: http://ghr.nlm.nih.gov/handbook/illustrations/geneinchromosome)

that make up your feet! Nor would you want the genes controlling the hormones of puberty to turn on in infancy. To make sure that the correct genes are active in the correct cells at the correct time, there are 'operator' or 'boss' genes that control where and when the 'builder' or 'worker' genes do their job.

The timetable and direction of prenatal growth of brain and body is controlled by switching on and off the correct genes at the appropriate time in this way. The Human Genome Project (http://www.yourgenome.org/hgp) has indicated that 40% of our genes are specialised for brain growth and function (Pennington, 2002). For example, prenatal brain development is known to be affected by a gene called *PAX-6* (Mo and Zecevic, 2008). For more information about the ways in which genes control the early development of brain structures and regions, see Recommended Reading.

Does this mean that our brains are simply the product of our genes then? There is certainly a growing list of psychological functions considered to be influenced by genes, including both cognitive processes and emotional tendencies in regard to stress, anxiety, depression or happiness (Caspi and Moffitt, 2006; Ramus, 2006; Hariri and Forbes, 2007). Even the ways we cope with attachments and loss are associated with particular genes (Caspers *et al.*, 2009).

Nonetheless, most human capacities or characteristics are unlikely to be due to simple links to one gene or another. Most psychological functions are likely to involve many genes (polygenic) and complex genetic–environment interactions. It is important to stress the difference between genotype (the basic genetic blueprint) and phenotype (the expression of the gene in actual development). Phenotype may differ from genotype because of the influence of environment that can modify, add to or even inhibit the action of genes.

How do genes and environment interact in early development?

Nature and nurture are clearly both required in development and interact with each other in direct and indirect ways. A classic example of this mutual relationship comes from cases of phenylketonuria (PKU) in which a faulty gene impairs the ability to process protein, with devastating effects on the development of the brain (Diamond *et al.*, 1997). The condition can be contained by restricting the dietary intake of protein – a clear instance of interaction between nature and nurture. Such interactions can take different forms, however. It may not be that genes contribute X% and the environment contributes Y% to development. There may be an actual interface between experience and genes so they can directly impinge on each other's activity or effects.

On the one hand, nurture (experience) can turn nature (genes) on or off. The direct activation or conversely deactivation of genes by environmental factors (called 'epigenetic' effects) has been shown in many animal studies. Many genes are inactive and are only switched on by particular environmental triggers. For example, research with laboratory rats or rhesus monkeys (Meaney, 2001; Weaver *et al.*, 2004) has confirmed that maternal stress or styles of care directly affect the expression (switching on or off) of genetic factors linked to the response to stress in the offspring, with this being further modifiable by additional experiences over the lifespan. There is even a suggestion that maternal stress prior to the conception of offspring can alter genes in the maternal ova, with this altered genome passed on to any offspring (Diamond, 2009a). Epigenetic interactions of this type are yet to be explored in human development, but there is evidence which suggests such effects. For example, adolescents who have a short version of the

5-HTTLPR gene linked to the neurotransmitter serotonin (5HT) are prone to develop antisocial behaviour – but not if they have supportive parenting (Brody *et al.*, 2009), indicating that the parental environment may influence this gene expression.

On the other hand, there is growing evidence for human development of the converse: that genes can alter the effects of environment (Ramus, 2006). Individuals with different versions (alleles) of the same gene may react differently to the same experiences. In other words, genes can limit or filter the effects of experience. For example, people with a particular version of the *5-HTT* gene involved in making the serotonin neurotransmitter are more likely to develop depression after stressful life events than those with a different allele of this gene (Caspi and Mofitt, 2006). Likewise, abused children are more likely to develop antisocial personality traits if they have a particular version or allele of a neurotransmitter (*MOAO*) gene than if they have a different allele (Caspi and Mofitt, 2006).

The relationship between genes and environment is thus a very intimate one. This is apparent in regard to the development of attachment in early life (see Nature–nurture box).

Nature and nurture are thus knitted together in an almost seamless way to direct the course and pattern of early development, with this mutual relationship taking a range of possible forms (Karmiloff-Smith, 1999; Ramus, 2006; Pennington *et al.*, 2008). Genes and environment may interact directly as in the epigenetic processes described above or more indirectly. For example, children with genes involved in musical skills may seek out or be offered music experiences which reinforce these tendencies. To find out more about human genetics, see Recommended Reading. In any case, the dividing line between the effects of genes and those of environment may well be undetectable since both forces are so closely intertwined in shaping human development. We can now explore the way in which this close link between nature and nurture builds a human being in prenatal life and infancy.

STOP AND THINK

Reflection

Choose some aspect of your own development. How do you think this has been influenced by your genetic endowment from your parents and/or your early childhood experiences?

NATURE–NURTURE

How genes and parenting influence early attachment patterns

New evidence on the close dialogue between nature and nurture comes from research into how genes and parenting interact in producing patterns of infant attachment. It is well-established that early parenting style or environments directly affect attachment patterns in children (see Chapter 9 for details). Nevertheless, there is also evidence of genetic factors in this regard as well. In particular, shortened alleles (versions) of genes linked to the neurotransmitters dopamine and serotonin (namely the *DRD4* and *5-HTTLPR* genes, respectively) are associated with

disorganised or dysfunctional attachment in children and unresolved attachment in adults (Gervai *et al.*, 2007; Caspers *et al.*, 2009), possibly indicating the role of these neurotransmitters in aspects of emotion in attachment. Further research, however, shows how both parenting environment and genes work hand-in-hand to shape the final form of children's development. Inconsistent or disrupted maternal behaviour may only have an impact on children's attachment if they have the short version or allele of the *DRD4* gene (Gervai *et al.*, 2007). Nature and nurture work very closely together to produce the patterns of early attachment.

Prenatal physical development

The 40-week journey from a single cell zygote to the complex structures and systems that comprise the new-born human involves many steps and processes under the influence of both genetic and environmental forces. There are three main phases in prenatal life: the germinal period (0–2 weeks), the embryonic period (3–8 weeks) and the foetal period (9–40 weeks) (see Fig. 4.2). The main features of physical development in these periods are summarised in Table 4.1 below. Another mapping of prenatal life is by trimesters: (0–3 months, 4–6 months and 7–9 months). You can read in more detail about landmark events and features of the physical aspects of prenatal development elsewhere (Moore *et al.*, 2000; Moore and Persaud, 2003) (see Recommended Reading or see http://www.visembryo.com/baby/index.html for a graphic representation of weekly stages of prenatal growth).

Definition

Zygote: the single cell formed from the union of sperm and ovum.

Prenatal development of the brain

Before considering how the brain develops *in utero*, it is useful to describe some of the main brain features and structures.

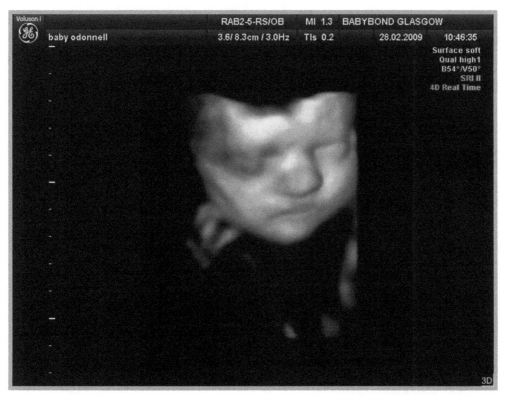

Figure 4.2. Baby Harriet at 28 weeks gestation.

Source: O'Donnell

Table 4.1. Major physical developments during the prenatal period.

Prenatal phase	Weeks gestation	Key features at beginning of phase	Key features at end of phase	Main developments during phase
Germinal period	0–2 weeks	Single-cell zygote	Ball of 60–70 cells called a blastocyst	Creation of embryonic disc inside the blastocyst, which will form the human being, whilst an outer shell protects it.
Embyonic period	3–8 weeks	About 2 mm long	About 2.5 cm long, weighing about 4 g. Looks human. Eyes are open. Shows reflexive response to touch	Heart begins to beat. Not yet a viable organism outside the uterus. Development of neural tube which will eventually form brain and spinal cord. Neuron production begins and neurons migrate to correct parts of body and brain. Development of buds for arms, legs, fingers and toes.
Foetal period (see Fig. 4.2)	9 weeks onwards	7.5 cm long, weighing 20 g in third month	Average length 50 cm, weighing 3.2 kg	Body and nervous system begin to operate in an organised way, 'breathing', swallowing and urinating. Frequent movements of limbs. Sex can be determined. May survive premature birth from 21–22 weeks. By week 24 most brain neurons are formed. Massive growth.

A quick tour of the brain: some important brain features and landmarks

The human brain consists of billions of tiny cells called neurons that transmit signals to one another in organised networks. They have a typical shape that helps them communicate with each other, looking a lot like tiny trees, comprising a head or cell-body, with branches called dendrites, a tail or trunk called the axon and root-like extensions called terminals. When stimulated, neurons propel a tiny charge or impulse (the 'action potential') from the head to the terminals. This impulse passes from one neuron to another across tiny gaps called synapses, with each neuron potentially having thousands of such connections. Chemicals called neurotransmitters (e.g. serotonin or dopamine) are needed in most cases to help pass the message over the synapse. These connections allow complex networks of neural activity that underlie the functions of the brain and nervous system (see Pinel, 2008; Purves *et al.*, 2008).

The older hindbrain regions are responsible for basic survival functions, states of alertness and well-learned movements, and the midbrain for rapid response to sensory signals. The forebrain has internal structures such as the hippocampus for working memory and aspects of emotional processing and a thin wrinkled outer layer, the cortex, for most higher-level perceptual, cognitive and emotional analysis and for complex aspects of memory and learning. These areas of the brain are illustrated in Fig. 4.3b. The cortex is described in four lobes corresponding to the skull bones, as illustrated in Fig. 4.3a – frontal, parietal, occipital and temporal – and to some degree, there is specialisation of functions in different regions of the cortex (e.g. primary visual processing occurs in the

Definitions

Dendrites: the branches or extensions at the top of neurons that allow contact with other neurons and so form neural networks.
Synapses: the gap between neurons across which the neural signal is passed.

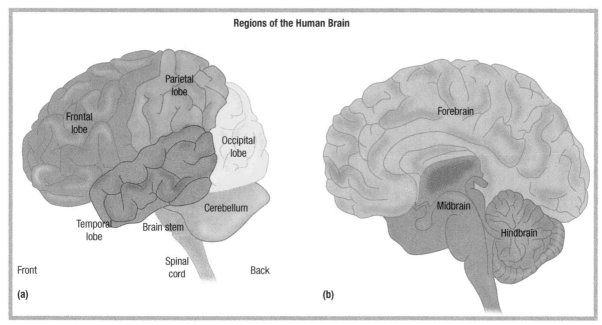

Figure 4.3. Basic regions of the human brain.

occipital cortex) (see Pinel, 2008 or Purves *et al.*, 2008 for more details).

Stages of prenatal brain development

The brain develops very early *in utero* in stages (Huttenlocher, 1990; Johnson *et al.*, 2002; Nowakowski and Hayes, 2002; Strachan and Read, 2003; Rosenzweig *et al.*, 2005). The basic pattern and timetable is under genetic control: about 40% of the structural or worker genes in the human genome are exclusively involved in brain growth and maintenance while the other 60% are also involved to some degree as well (Pennington, 2002; Ramus, 2006), but prenatal environment can also impact on this early development of the brain.

During the embryonic period, the embryonic disc develops into a three-layered sandwich of cells comprising an outer layer called the ectoderm, a middle layer called the mesoderm and an inner layer called the endoderm. The ectoderm will eventually form the skin, hair and nervous system. By day 15, a small group of cells begins to grow rapidly at one end of the ectoderm, creating a primitive basis for the head and brain.

By weeks three to four, the development of the nervous system begins in earnest. By day 18, chemical signals are sent to the ectoderm from the layer below causing the growth of a thick 'neural plate'. The cells in this plate continue to multiply rapidly, although at uneven rates so that by about day 20, the plate has a groove all along its midline with folds of tissue either side (like a river bed with canyon walls) (see Fig. 4.4).

By the start of week four (about day 22), these folds arch over the groove, wrapping around to form a hose-shaped structure, the neural tube, the precursor to the brain and spinal cord. This folding starts at the middle of the groove, moving towards each end in a 'zipping' manner until the tube is sealed except at the ends. The tube opening at the anterior (head) end now closes, followed by that at the tail end. In about 1 in 1000 births

> **Definition**
>
> Neural tube: hose-shaped structure forming the basis of the brain and spinal cord in the embryo.

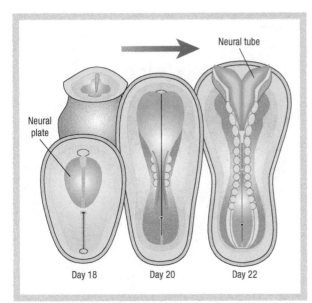

Figure 4.4. Development of the neural tube.

(*Source:* http://www.sciencemuseum.org.uk/on-line/lifecycle/11.asp)

(Bukatko and Daehler, 2004), the neural tube fails to close – either at the head end resulting in 'anencephaly' (a severe impairment of brain development usually fatal after birth) or at the tail end producing 'spina bifida' which can result in paralysis.

By about three and a half weeks, there is a defined swelling at the top end of the tube and by week four, this shows three clear divisions corresponding to the future forebrain, midbrain and hindbrain. The entire nervous system becomes a clearer structure as the neural tube separates from the surface ectoderm. Many different genes control this process: for example, forebrain development involves genes from the E_{mx} family.

After the closure of the tube in week four, neural development proceeds frantically in several phases which can overlap in different brain areas. The first phase is neurogenesis, the rapid and teeming production of neurons within the neural tube. Neurons cannot copy themselves but are made from other cells in the neural tube that rapidly divide to form more cells which are in turn changed under genetic control into neurons. Neurogenesis begins in weeks 3 to 4 and is especially active up to week 16, with hundreds of thousands of neurons being made each minute and most of the brain neurons formed by about week 24. This frantic proliferation of neurons is reflected in the corresponding growth in the size of the infant brain, with the head enlarging to one-half of the body size by week eight. Neuron production generally ceases at birth, although some new neurons

may be made in the adult brain (possibly in the hippocampus, the part of the brain important in making new memories) (Erikson *et al.*, 1998). Most brain development in the final months of prenatal life (and after birth) consists of the growth of connections (synapses) between neurons and of the myelin tissue that coats the neural membrane (see below), leading to a tenfold increase in brain weight from 20 weeks to birth.

The second important phase is neuronal migration in which the neurons move to different locations in the emerging brain and nervous system. Some only go short distances but others have to travel far. By a pushing or pulling process under the control of genetic and biochemical factors, they move along fine filaments sometimes swinging like monkeys from one filament to another (Feng and Walsh, 2001; Hatten, 2002) (see Fig. 4.5 and for 'movies' of migrating neuronal cells, see: http://hatten-server.rockefeller.edu/HattenLab/movies.html). Migration begins in earnest after the final sealing of the ends of the neural tube. This exodus of neurons establishes different neural groups or populations that will eventually contribute to different structures and systems in the brain and nervous system. If this migration is disrupted for any reason (genetic or environmental), then there may be impairment of subsequent brain function. Numerous disorders such as dyslexia and autism have been linked to the impairment of neuronal migration in the prenatal brain (Watts, 2008) (see Chapter 16, Atypical Development for more on autism).

The third phase – neuronal differentiation – begins when genes further modify the newly-arrived cells to make them specialised for their future roles in the brain regions and systems.

During the process of embryonic cell differentiation, two other 'phases' also occur at the same time. One of these is synaptogenesis: the development of potential connections or synapses amongst the emerging neurons due to the growth of extensions or branches at the top of the neuron called dendrites and at the bottom called

Definitions

Neurogenesis: the production of neurons in the embryo.

Neuronal migration: the movement of neurons to appropriate locations in the brain and body.

Synaptogenesis: rapid growth of dendrites to form neural connections or synapses.

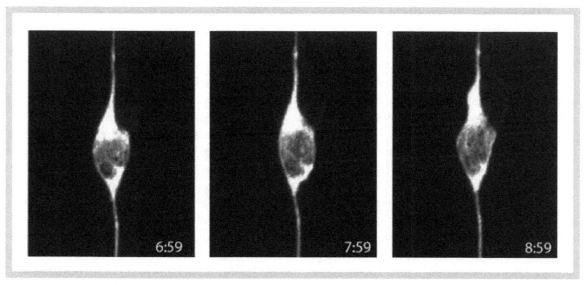

Figure 4.5. Images of a migrating neuronal cell.

(*Source:* Courtesy of The Hatten Laboratory at Rockefeller University

terminals. There is also the beginning of myelinisation or myelination – the coating of the axons in fatty insulating material to improve their efficiency, although this process increases markedly after birth with use of the brain (see The postnatal development of the brain).

In the prenatal brain there is considerable over-supply of synapses. This leads to the final phase or aspect of neural development involving 'pruning' of connections and rivalry amongst neurons for target neurons. Success in this regard may be due to good availability of connections or even to repeated stimulation of the 'lucky' neural pathways from environmental factors such as sensory input (see next section). This whole process of synapse-building and pruning does not only occur *in utero*, but will also continue vigorously after birth (and to some extent across the lifespan) in response to input from new learning and experience (see The postnatal development of the brain).

The basic brain structures are in place early in the foetal period by weeks nine to ten, with the main aspect of development thereafter being the growth in brain mass. During the last few months of prenatal life, the cerebral cortex of the brain shows increasing folding due to neuron production and growth of synapses and myelin. Not all regions of the brain develop at the same pace and, even within the cortex, there are different timetables for

different regions with these discrepancies continuing after birth (see The postnatal development of the brain). As a result of this rapid development of the brain and nervous system, even the embryo soon displays basic behaviours and responses reflecting organised neural activity.

STOP AND THINK

Reflection

The development of the brain *in utero* is an amazing achievement under the control of genes, biochemical factors and even environmental factors. Imagine the whole sequence as a movie, from start to finish. Could you draw and label rough diagrams for yourself about each step of the way?

Prenatal abilities and behaviours

One of the most fundamental human capacities is the ability to sense and respond to a stimulus external to the body. Imagine how isolated you would be without your senses to connect you to the world or how frustrating it would be not to be able to react to some stimulus. But what is it like for the developing foetus? Is there any sign that the foetus can 'sense' and react to the world? Indeed there is: the rapid development of the brain and nervous system supports the early emergence of sensory

Definition

Myelinisation: the growth of fatty insulating coating along axon of the neuron.

capacities and behavioural responses and even within the cloistered world of the uterus, these basic abilities are exercised and refined as the infant develops.

By the end of the embryonic period, there is already the capacity to react to external stimulation, initially with simple 'reflex' responses (not engaging the brain), but increasingly with responses under brain control. The five main sensory systems of vision, touch, audition, taste and smell all begin to develop in the embryo. All such channels involve bodily receptors (eyes, ears, etc.), as well as specialised neural pathways and brain regions. For example, processing in the visual system begins with the components of the eye (lens, retina, etc.), continues along the optic tracts to the brain and involves further processing in the visual cortex and other subsequent brain areas. These systems operate to some extent and provide channels for perceiving even in foetal life (Hepper, 1996). Moreover, as the brain develops across the foetal period there is an increasing ability to retain this sensory information, which shows the capacity for memory and learning (Hepper and Leader, 1996).

Foetal touch, taste and smell

The earliest sensory channel to develop is that of touch. During intrauterine diagnostic procedures, it has been established that by eight or nine weeks, the foetus moves its head if touched in the mouth region and by 12 weeks will grasp at anything touching the fingers (Fifer et al., 2001). Taste and smell are also functional early in the foetal phase as shown by ultrasound images of the reaction of the baby to substances introduced into the uterine environment (although it is somewhat difficult to distinguish between these senses in the watery world of the foetus since substances can enter both nose and mouth). The foetus is more likely to swallow a sweet substance in the amniotic fluid than an unpleasant one, suggesting innate preferences for sweet flavours (Liley, 1972; Hepper, 1992) and, of more concern, is likely to increase swallowing if alcohol is in the amniotic fluid (Molina et al., 1995).

Foetal hearing?

The auditory system is also functional to some extent by about 20 weeks even though the ear and auditory brain regions are not yet mature. The foetus will respond to loud sounds with movements, perhaps showing a 'startle reflex' (Zimmer, et al., 1993). By 22 weeks, the foetus will show a more sophisticated reaction by orienting or attending to sounds as evident by movement and a decline in heart rate. Furthermore, if the tone or sound is repeatedly presented, the foetus will eventually show 'habituation' or a decline in responsiveness, evidence of simple learning (Leader et al., 1982). The foetus is capable of simple associative learning in regard to the pairing of a sound with a touch stimulus (Hepper and Leader, 1996), but is also able to learn and remember complex sound patterns from the external world. Many natural sounds penetrate the uterine environment, and the foetus can not only hear them but also learns about or remembers them. In particular, newborns show preferential response to the maternal voice (DeCasper and Fifer, 1980) and even to theme tunes from television shows watched by the mother during pregnancy (Hepper, 1988), indicating perception and learning of these sounds during foetal life. There is even remarkable evidence of newborn preference for the sound patterns of nursery rhymes (DeCasper et al., 1994) or Dr Seuss stories presented during pregnancy (DeCasper and Spence, 1986). More recently there has even been more direct evidence of foetal learning in that foetuses of eight to nine months familiarised to either their mother or a female stranger reading a passage showed a reaction when the opposite voice was then used (Kisilevsky et al., 2009). Some of this research, and its role in helping us to understand the development of memory from infancy, is explored further in Chapter 6 Memory and Intelligence.

Foetal vision

The least developed of the sensory channels in prenatal life is vision. The murky light of the uterine world is not optimal for vision, so it is probably just as well that the visual system does not operate fully, or else it may become attuned to poor lighting levels and become ill-equipped to deal with the more intense light outside the uterus. Nonetheless by about the fourth month, although the retina is still immature, the main parts of the eyes have developed and the next month sees the specialisation of cells along the visual pathways for colour and spatial detail. A foetus of six months will try to shield its eyes with its hands if a bright light is introduced into the mother's abdomen in diagnostic procedures (Nilsson and Hamberger, 1990) and by the seventh month, the visual region of the brain (the visual cortex) has developed its basic structure with the capacity for analysing the main features of the visual world, as shown by studies of post-mortem tissue (Huttenlocher, 1990).

It is thus clear that basic abilities for sensing, perceiving, remembering and learning operate in foetal life and that the life-long task of the brain to detect, process and retain information from the external world begins even before birth.

Risks to prenatal development: environmental teratogens and genetic errors

Regrettably, not all prenatal development runs smoothly according to the plan outlined so far. It is estimated that about 3% of newborns have some congenital malformation – that is, a problem present at birth (Kalter, 2003). These are due to either noxious or damaging environmental factors known as teratogens, such as maternal disease or environmental pollutants), or to failures in genetic processes. About 10% of congenital problems are due to environmental teratogens and 15–25% involve genetic problems (with the causes of the rest being undetermined) (Kalter, 2003; Reece and Hobbins, 2006).

Environmental teratogens

The embryonic period is the most vulnerable to the effects of teratogens as this is the time in which all the basic organs and structures including the nervous system and brain are being formed (see above), and so teratogens at this time can be particularly destructive. In contrast, there is little effect in the germinal period. The effects in the foetal period are less severe than in the embryonic period, but nonetheless the sensory organs (especially the eyes) and the central nervous system are still susceptible right across the foetal period up until birth (Moore and Persaud, 2003).

Most teratogens involve either maternal conditions or behaviour (nutritional insufficiency, stress, ingestion of alcohol, smoking, caffeine intake, etc.) or derive from wider environmental factors (such as radiation) (Kalter, 2003; Brent and Fawcett, 2007).

Malnutrition

One of the most common teratogens is maternal malnutrition. There are many nutrients that are essential to healthy prenatal development, although lack of folic acid (vitamin B9) seems especially serious as it is essential for producing the genetic material (DNA) used in the formation of new cells including neurons and blood cells. Lack of folic acid is a key factor in neural tube defects for example (Brent and Fawcett, 2007).

Maternal drug use

Legal drugs can be of equal or greater concern than illegal drugs in regard to effects on the developing child. Even the caffeine in a few cups of coffee a day may have harmful effects such as poor growth and high excitability in the infant (Scheutze and Zeskind, 1997), and some of the most disabling effects have come from the use of prescribed medications, such as the 1960s sedative thalidomide that produced major deformations of the limbs in the developing embryo (Moore and Persaud, 2003). The most commonly available legal drugs are of course alcohol and nicotine, and both of these can have profound effects on the developing brain and body (see Case Study box).

The evidence on the effects of illegal drugs such as cocaine is not as clear-cut because their use may be linked to other risk factors such as poverty and use of other drugs which also have an impact on the developing child. However, maternal use of illegal drugs such as heroin or cocaine is generally considered to lead to low birth weight and disruption of 'state' in the infant, such as poor sleeping patterns, under- or over-excitability (Friedman and Polifka, 1998).

Maternal disease

Maternal disease is also another risk factor in prenatal development. There are a number of teratogenic viruses. Rubella is especially destructive in the first few months of prenatal life when it can cause damage to the developing

> **Definition**
>
> Teratogen: an environmental hazard to prenatal development.

CASE STUDY

Baby has a drink and a smoke

In May 2007, the Department of Health in the UK issued new guidelines for women, advising that they should avoid alcohol altogether during pregnancy. This is because of the risks which alcohol poses to the developing foetus. Alcohol readily crosses the placenta and affects the infant, impacting on the differentiation and migration of neurons in the developing brain. As noted in Prenatal abilities and behaviour, the foetus will swallow more of the amniotic fluid if alcohol is present (Molina *et al.*, 1995).

Even one drink a day may lead to Foetal Alcohol Syndrome (FAS) which is estimated to affect three to four out of every 1000 babies born in the USA (Streissguth *et al.*, 1994; Carr and Coustan, 2006).

FAS is associated with brain and facial abnormalities, poor growth and cognitive and learning impairments in childhood. Also of concern is the fact that either passive or active smoking of tobacco with its nicotine and many other noxious substances is harmful to the developing child, due to the restriction of blood supply and nutrients that leads to low birth weight (Dejin-Carlsson *et al.*, 1998).

- Have you read or heard any recent press reports about alcohol or drug use in pregnancy?
- How do they compare with the research reported here?
- What advice might you give a pregnant woman concerned about the effects of alcohol on her unborn baby?

---

eyes and ears, heart and brain, resulting in visual and auditory impairments and heart and brain abnormalities (Moore and Persaud, 2003; Reece and Hobbins, 2006).

Maternal psychological state

It is not only maternal physical state that can affect prenatal development. Maternal psychological or emotional state also appears to have an impact. Maternal stress or anxiety produces high levels of cortisol linked to growth problems and postnatal cognitive problems (Bergman *et al.*, 2007). For example, extreme maternal anxiety in pregnancy is linked to brain activity reflecting poor cognitive control in the offspring in adolescence (Mennes *et al.*, 2009). It is difficult, however, to be certain that it is prenatal stress alone that is the causal factor in such studies. A stressed pregnant woman may continue to be stressed after the child is born, thereby affecting the child in this way beyond the prenatal period. Nonetheless, animal research has confirmed that maternal stress can affect prenatal development in two direct ways: either via the effects of maternal stress hormones on the developing brain circuitry of the offspring (Nathanielsz, 1999) or by actually influencing the activity of genes in the embryo or foetus (Gluckman *et al.*, 2007) (see How to grow a baby).

Environmental toxins

Pollutants and toxins in the natural environment may also impact on the prenatal infant although the evidence in this regard is sometimes controversial (Kalter, 2003). One of the confirmed cases of environmental teratogens occurred in Minimata in Japan in the 1950s when industrial mercury waste was released into the food chain and water supply, causing prenatal brain damage that resulted in physical and cognitive impairments (Clarkson, *et al.*, 2003).

There are many environmental teratogens but, as noted above, a greater percentage of problems in prenatal development are due to the effects of faulty genetic processes.

Genetic factors that impair prenatal development

As explained in How to grow a baby, genes influence prenatal cell growth and development, but there can be errors in this process. For example, a mutation in the *Sonic Hedgehog* gene that controls the left–right organisation of the neural pathways can lead to the development of a single eye in the centre of the face (Gilbert, 2000). One of the most common genetic errors, however, leads to the condition known as Down Syndrome or Trisomy 21 (Tocci, 2000). This occurs for about one in every 800 births, with risk increasing markedly with maternal age or most likely the age of the maternal ova which are formed in infancy (the risk rising from 1 in 1900 at 20 years to 1 in 30 at 45 years: Halliday *et al.*, 1995). Most cases are due to the failure of the twenty-first pair of chromosomes to separate properly during cell replication (usually in the copying of the ovum) so that the new cells have three chromosomes for this twenty-first pair instead of the usual two. This causes abnormalities in both body and brain, with impairments in cognition, speech and motor capacities, though less severe forms from only a partial failure of chromosomal separation are associated with less marked impairments.

Although this list of potential hazards seems daunting, by and large most new-borns are not affected by them and make the journey from zygote to neonate intact.

STOP AND THINK

Reflection

Think about the factors that can penetrate the uterine world.

■ Which can have beneficial effects on the development of a baby's brain?

■ Which can have detrimental effects?

Birth

The social and cultural practices surrounding labour and birth vary considerably. For example, the presence of the father is welcomed in some societies but forbidden in others (Read, 1968). Nonetheless, in physical terms, the birth process is universal, following clear phases or stages as described below.

Why does birth begin?

After about 38 weeks or 266 days, the foetus is ready to arrive in the world. Birth is initiated by chemical communication between mother and baby. The foetus sends hormonal signals causing the uterus to contract and also produces 'stress' hormones such as adrenaline that enhance labour contractions and help the infant prepare for birth by clearing the lungs and improving alertness (Emory *et al.*, 1988; Hepper, 2002). The mother then begins labour which averages about 12+ hours for a first baby and half that for subsequent babies (Niswander and Evans, 1996).

Stages of labour

Labour proceeds in three stages. Stage 1 (eight + hours) involves rhythmic uterine contractions increasing in strength and frequency and causing the dilation of the cervix (the narrow opening of the uterus into the birth canal). In Stage 2 (about one to two hours) the baby's head enters the cervical opening and the mother pushes the baby out into the world. In the final stage (about five minutes) the placenta is expelled.

Complications

There can be complications with labour, and protracted deliveries can lead to possible brain damage in the infant due to anoxia – the loss of oxygen – but nonetheless most infants whose mothers have had good care arrive intact without problems.

The importance of birth weight for gestational age

As noted in Table 4.1 earlier, the 'average' neonate weighs about 3.2 kg (7 lbs) and is 50 cm (20″) long, with boys slightly heavier and longer than girls on average. Birth weight is a key factor in postnatal survival since low birth weight may be associated with immaturity in the lungs

Definition

Placenta: the organ which connects to the wall of the mother's uterus, and which connects to the foetus by the umbilical cord. It allows for the uptake of nutrients by the foetus, and for the elimination of waste.

and other organs. An optimal weight-range is about 3–5 kg (6.6–11 lbs) (Rees *et al.*, 1996), although 2.5 kg (5.5 lbs) is within normal range and rare birth weights of 9 kg (20 lbs) have been recorded (Smolak, 1986). The survival chances of babies with birth weight lower than 2.5 kg have improved markedly and even babies weighing as little as 700–800 g may have a good chance of survival with intensive support (Macdonald, 2002). However, low birth weight can occur if infants are pre-term (three or more weeks prematurely) or small-for-gestational-age (SGA) – or both. Babies who are pre-term, but within the expected weight range for their gestational age, are more likely to survive and make better developmental progress after birth than SGA infants (McCormick *et al.*, 1993; Macdonald, 2002).

Is the new baby in good shape?

To ensure that the infant has arrived in good order, physical condition and state may be assessed by a number of means (Lipkin, 2005) such as one minute and five minutes ratings against the Apgar Scale estimating aspects of the infant's condition (see Table 4.2, taken from Apgar, 1953). An overall score of seven or better reflects good condition, but scores of four to six indicate that the baby may require breathing support, and three or below, that the baby is in urgent need of assistance.

> **Definition**
>
> Apgar scale: a rating scale for the condition of the new-born.

STOP AND THINK

Reflection

- Is there someone you know who has had a baby?
- If (*and only if*) they are happy to talk about it, ask them to tell you about the experience.

The neonate: basic states, movements and reflexes

No blooming or buzzing confusion?

The neonate arrives with a functional brain and nervous system allowing a coherent experience of and response to the world. Indeed for about 30 minutes after birth most infants show a period of 'quiet alertness' when they appear to scan the world into which they have arrived (Klaus *et al.*, 1995). Decades of research (Bremner and Fogel, 2001; Slater and Lewis, 2002) have overturned Piaget's view that the new-born has only disjointed and momentary impressions, limited to representing the world in terms of actions upon it, rather than by its features and properties. William James' similar opinion (1890) that the neonate exists in a 'blooming, buzzing confusion' has also been shown to be inaccurate. Contrary to these perspectives, more recent research confirms that the neonate is

Table 4.2. Features used in Apgar Scale Scoring (a total score out of 10 is derived by adding the ratings for each of the five features).

Breathing	Skin colour	Heart rate	Reflexes	Muscle tone	Rating scale:
None	Grey/blue	None	None	None	0
Shallow and irregular	Grey extremities/body appropriate colour for ethnicity	< 100 bpm	Slow or moderate	Weak or moderate	1
Regular with crying	Appropriate colour for ethnicity	100–140 bpm	Clear and strong	Flexed limbs, strong movements	2

capable of organised sensation, perception, attention, memory and learning and displays not only simple reflexes but also voluntary responses relying on complex brain functions. This is not to say that the neonate is fully developed in these terms, but rather that the basic mechanisms for registering and reacting to the world are in place and operate in a coordinated manner to provide a springboard for further development.

Neonatal states of arousal

One of the key signs that the neonatal nervous system is operational is that after an initial state of quiet attentiveness following birth, new-borns show six different states of arousal or alertness (Wolff, 1966): deep and light sleep, drowsiness, quiet alertness, alert activity (awake but restless) and, finally, crying (often to signal discomfort such as hunger). Sleep in young babies is not controlled by the brain 'sleep hormone' melatonin and so is not tied to cycles of light and dark. Although it may not seem the case to new parents, new-borns do, however, sleep about 16–18 hours a day, though in shorter intervals and with more REM (rapid eye movement) sleep than for adults (Louis *et al.*, 1997).

Neonatal movement and reflexes

Neonates have relatively poor control of body movement, but can move their heads and kick their feet when lying on their stomachs, and studies of the trajectories of neonatal arm movements indicate that they have some visual control of arm movements (Von Hofsten, 1982). They also show many reflex reactions which are an indicator of the maturity of the nervous system, as is their eventual disappearance in the first year of life. A few reflexes continue across the lifespan (e.g. eye blink reflex), but most should vanish in the first year of life as higher brain centres take control of movement. The Moro Reflex is a good example: neonates will react to a sudden stimulus by a startle response, throwing their head and limbs back and then retracting them. This is a healthy sign that the nervous system is functioning well at birth, but it should disappear by about 4–6 months (Hepper, 2002). Infants are able to moderate reflex movements to some extent, such as adjusting the sucking reflex relative to the flow of breast milk (Craig and Lee, 1999), with this reflecting more deliberate control of action that will increasingly develop after birth (see Motor abilities in infancy).

STOP AND THINK

Reflection

The human neonate is relatively helpless in terms of movement control. What do you think the effects of this might be for the overall development of a child?

The postnatal development of the brain

The new-born brain is relatively mature in some ways, but undeveloped in others. Many basic aspects of brain development are under genetic control. For example, the structure of the cortex in many areas seems to be 'inherited' via genes (Ramus, 2006), but there is also considerable room for change and plasticity.

Many of the brain systems for sensation and perception of the world are functioning well at birth, as is the basic ability to learn and store information in memory. Nonetheless, these basic competencies undergo refinement in the months after birth and some aspects of the brain require many months or even years to reach full function. The neonatal brain is therefore sufficiently developed to allow the infant to perceive and learn about the world, but also sufficiently pliant to allow adaptation to the context for development.

The neonatal brain resembles the adult brain apart from being only about 25% of its weight (Thatcher *et al.*, 1996), but the main structures and all of the 100 billion neurons are present, having been produced in foetal life (see Prenatal physical development). However, the neonatal brain differs from that of the adult in two main ways, as discussed in the next two sections.

Connecting and pruning the brain after birth

One difference is that the new-born brain only has about one sixth of the connections or synapses of the adult brain, but then, in the months after birth, the synaptogenesis that began in prenatal life (see Prenatal physical development) increases in earnest. There is now a massive increase in the number and length of dendrites and terminal branches, leading to such a rapid increase in number of synapses that by about 12 months of age, the infant brain has twice as many as the adult brain (Huttenlocher, 1990). It is as if the brain has generated maximum material to ensure that its messages are transmitted. This over-production is eventually corrected or refined as neurons compete with each other for favoured pathways and connections, leading to severe pruning of the connections. Only the most used connections survive this trimming process (Eisenberg, 1999).

Synaptogenesis and pruning do not occur uniformly across brain areas and are linked to the usage of the brain region. The earliest regions to show these processes are the brain areas for sensory processing. For example, there is rapid synaptognesis in the visual cortex after birth, peaking at about eight months, before falling to adult levels by the end of childhood (Huttenlocher, 1990). In contrast, synaptogenesis occurs later in the language areas (Thatcher, 1991). The frontal lobes are the last of all to develop in this way, showing a high level of synaptic growth throughout childhood, with a peak in synaptic density around two years and pruning ongoing across childhood (Johnson, 2001). Chapter 14, Developmental Psychology and Education, explores some recent research which points to other periods of over-production and rapid synaptic pruning in adolescence, and the implications of these for education.

Coating the neurons: myelinisation

The usage of the brain is also reflected in increased myelinisation (the coating of neurons in fatty myelin), which begins in prenatal life (see Prenatal physical development) but expands rapidly after birth, not slowing until adolescence. It occurs first of all in the spinal cord, then the hindbrain, midbrain and forebrain, enabling the increasingly efficient use of these regions. In the cortex, it occurs firstly in the sensory areas (Huttenlocher, 1990) and appears in brain areas for controlling the arms and trunk at about one month of age and later for areas controlling the legs, fingers and hands (Tanner, 1990). Myelinisation of the frontal lobes begins in infancy but continues throughout childhood to adult life (Nelson, 2002a).

Lateralisation: how the left and right brain grows after birth

The neonatal brain also shows some lateralisation of brain function (differences in function across the two halves or hemispheres) that continues to develop after birth. For example, in anticipation of later hemisphere differences in adults, there is a left hemisphere bias in new-born speech perception (Davidson, 1994) and some movement control (Grattan et al., 1992) and, by 12 months or so, most infants show a right-hand preference reflecting control by the left hemisphere (Hinojosa et al., 2003). By four months, there is also left hemisphere bias for positive emotions such as happiness in 4 month olds (Hane et al., 2008) and for the categorical perception of orientation in 5 month olds (Franklin et al., 2010). The right hemisphere shows early dominance for processing the relational aspects of facial patterns (de Schonen and Mathivet, 1990; Catherwood et al., 2003), colour categorisation (Franklin et al., 2008) and negative emotional arousal such as fear or sadness (Hane et al., 2008).

Although basic left–right organisation of the brain may be in place early in infancy, there is nonetheless still considerable plasticity. One big change comes with the onset of language, mainly handled by the left hemisphere. This can have effects on other functions. For example, in infants the right hemisphere is especially sensitive to the main differences between hues or colours but, as colour naming abilities develop, the left hemisphere becomes more dominant in this regard (Franklin et al., 2008). While lateralisation develops over childhood, so does communication between the two hemispheres. The latter occurs with the myelinisation of the corpus callosum, the nerve fibres connecting the hemispheres, with this process starting by 12 months of age, increasing between 3 and 6 years of age and slowing in adolescence (Giedd et al., 1999).

Mapping activity in the infant brain: developmental neuroscience

A most promising future direction for studying the infant brain and its abilities is that provided by research approaches in developmental neuroscience (studying brain regions and systems) and developmental cognitive neuroscience (studying the brain during different states and activities related to perceptual–cognitive processing).

To find out how our understanding of the brain and cognitive development has been informed by neuroscience research, see Recommended Reading. These approaches use brain mapping and imaging technology such as EEG (electro-encephalography). Patterns of EEG activity in the resting brain undergo development in the first 12 months, becoming adult-like during that time (Chugani, *et al.*, 1987; Szücs, 2005), and studies with infants around 7–8 months have found infant EEG patterns to be indicative of infant cognition (e.g., Szücs, 2005; Orekhova *et al.*, 2006; Csibra and Johnson, 2007) (see Cognitive abilities in infancy for more details on this).

EEG is being increasingly used to map infant brain activity during different states and cognitive tasks. In infants, as for adults, brain activity in the form of 'waves' from the scalp can be detected by EEG technology and 'dense-array' sensor-nets have made it easier to apply this technique to young infants.

A very recent EEG approach is to search for bursts of activity in particular frequencies in the EEG waves that have been linked to different types of cognitive processing. EEG frequencies are conventionally grouped in bands related to how frequently the waves occur (like fast or slow ripples on a pond), with these bands denoted by Greek letters: δ (delta: very slow: 0–4 Hz or cycles per second), θ (theta: 4–8 Hz), α (alpha: 8–12 Hz), β (beta: 12–20 Hz), γ (gamma: fastest of all: 30+ Hz) (Purves *et al.*, 2008).

In adults, for example, the brain shows theta waves when holding items in working memory, beta activity when processing information from the environment and alpha activity when awake but in relaxed mode (as with eyes closed). The superfast gamma may arise when there is a need to synchronise processing across different brain regions – for example, when different visual features of an object such as colour and shape need to be bound together. There is growing evidence of similar types of EEG activity in the infant brain (Szücs, 2005; Orekhova *et al.*, 2006; Csibra and Johnson, 2007; de Haan, 2008) (see Infant vision and Cognitive abilities in infancy for more detail).

Nature and nurture in postnatal brain development

Nature and nurture work in harmony in early brain development. Although the basic processes in growth of synapses are under genetic control (Li *et al.*, 2000), paradoxically this growth also reflects the plasticity and adaptability

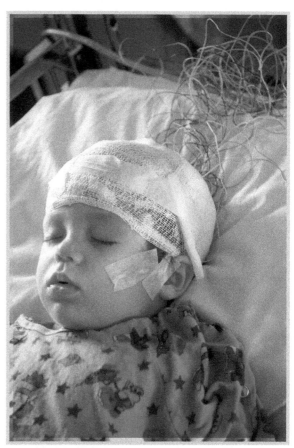

Child undergoing EEG testing

Source: Getty Images/Stephen Simpson

of the human brain to learning and experience. Input to the brain from learning and experience directly affects synapse growth. New brain pathways and patterns are built to encode new memories and learning, not just in infancy but right across the lifespan. Synaptogenesis is the perfect example of genes and experience working together to create human capacities. As studies with other animals show, even innate brain capacities can be either strengthened or weakened by early experiences. For example, rats raised in enriched environments (with lots of toys, handling and stimulation) show richer development of the visual cortex (Rosenzweig, 1984), while monkeys and cats raised under restricted visual conditions suffer impairments in innate visual abilities (Held and Hein, 1963; Sugita, 2004).

Definition

EEG (electroencephalogram): record of brain activity recorded by means of electrodes placed around the scalp.

For humans, studies of institutionalised infants have shown that highly impoverished early environments can have a deleterious effect on natural perceptual–cognitive ability while moderate stimulation can enhance it (White and Held, 1966). Early musical training increases the cortical area devoted to musical processing (Pantev *et al.*, 2003) and early blindness can lead to the expansion of auditory cortical areas to nearby brain regions to enhance the processing of sounds (Rauschecker and Henning, 2000).

Critical periods for brain plasticity?

The brain is thus adaptable in infancy, but there are also limitations or 'critical periods' for major changes in brain organisation. In general, the brain is less plastic in later childhood and adulthood (Banich, 2004). Earlier maturing areas such as the visual cortex may be more plastic and resilient to early damage since they can 'poach' or borrow brain power from nearby regions. This comes at a cost, though. The 'crowding hypothesis' (Teuber and Rudel, 1962) suggests that later-maturing functions such as language or movement control may be affected as a result (since their intended brain territory has already been used). Hence late-maturing functions like language are more vulnerable to damage in early life.

The infant brain has many basic systems and structures already in place by birth and shows rapid development with increasing brain usage, but to what extent do these support useful functions and operations? One key source of information on this issue is research into the infant ability to sense and perceive the world. We will consider this in the next section.

STOP AND THINK

Reflection

How do we know that the infant brain is 'turned on' at birth or in the early months of life?

Infant vision

Sensation involves activity in special body receptors (such as the tiny rods and cones lining the retina of the eye) and in special channels in the nervous system that enable us to detect stimulation from the environment (light, sound waves, etc.). Perception is the additional processing in these neural pathways and brain regions providing a more complete or coherent impression of the nature of the stimulus. The five main sensory–perceptual systems: visual, auditory (hearing), tactile–haptic (touch), olfactory (smell) and gustatory (taste), operate from birth (or before). Decades of research (Bremner and Fogel, 2001; Slater and Lewis, 2002) have overturned earlier views (Piaget, 1952, 1958; James, 1890) and confirmed that, while perception undergoes development and refinement after birth, even in neonates it is operational and largely 'coherent', providing structure to the flux of stimulation arriving from the outside world. As for adults, different sensations are processed as separate from each other, but sensations can also be bound together into unified wholes where necessary. For example, for adults, the colour blue can be distinguished from green but can also be linked to a round shape as in a blue balloon. Young infants appear to have similar capacities.

What visual equipment do new-borns have?

Visual sensation and perception relies on the response of the nervous system to light emitted or reflected from objects. The main components of the visual system include: the eyeball(s) for collecting light; a lens for focusing the light by 'accommodation' (bulging for close things, flattening for far objects); the retina lining the inner eyeball with neural pathways from the retina to the brain and; the visual (occipital) cortex (with ordered groups of neurons for analysis of the visual signals). These are illustrated in Figure 4.6.

New-borns have this basic visual kit, although some components are still immature for the first year, with some lingering development across childhood (Hainline, 1998). In particular, the cones are not in their final place in the fovea and the lens may not readily focus at a range of distances. It was once considered that the infant lens was fixed to focus at about 20 cm, however, even new-borns can focus on objects 75 cm away (Hainline, 1998) but may not do so, often under- or over-accommodating. The lens and brain need to cooperate for correct focusing, and it takes a few months of practice before this fine-tuning works smoothly.

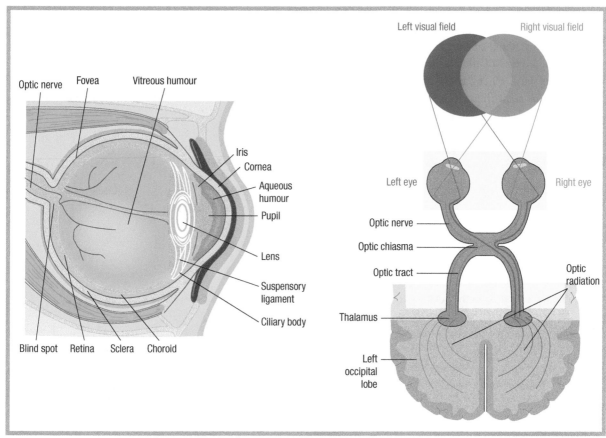

Figure 4.6. The eye and visual pathways.

(*Source*: http://webschoolsolutions.com/patts/systems/eye.htm#fields)

How strong is infant vision?

The power of this infant visual system to see fine detail (visual acuity) has been assessed. Adult visual acuity is usually tested by reading a Snellen chart with rows of letters of diminishing size. You will have seen this kind of chart if you have ever had your eyes tested. The limit of acuity is the line of the letters that cannot be clearly read (e.g., where 'P' is read as 'R'). An estimate of 20/20 vision means seeing as well as the 'average' person at 20 feet (or 6/6 in metres). If vision is weaker than the average then the number on the right side will be bigger than 20. For example, 20/600 vision means seeing at 20 feet what the average observer sees at 600 feet (so you would have weak vision).

Infant acuity obviously cannot be measured with Snellen charts, but it can be measured in a similar way with the preferential looking method (Fantz, 1964; Dobson and Teller, 1978; Atkinson, 2000) based on the idea that babies (like adults) prefer to look at something rather than nothing. The baby is observed while being shown a black-and-white striped pattern on one side and a blank display on the other. If the baby prefers to look towards the stripes then he must be able to see them. At first, patterns with thick stripes are shown and then progressively finer ones – like the rows of Snellen letters. Eventually the baby won't show a clear preference for the pattern, with this taken as the limit of the baby's acuity – just as the lowest readable line of the Snellen chart is for adults. A more sensitive test uses VEPs (visually evoked potentials) or EEG measures of brain activity that arise

Definition

Preferential looking method: a procedure for testing infant perceptual and cognitive skills by observing infant viewing preferences to two or more items.

as the baby views striped patterns. From both preferential looking and VEP methods, the estimate of new-born visual acuity is about 20/600. Newborns can certainly see important aspects of their world, including the main features of faces 50 cm away (Atkinson and Braddick, 1981). Visual acuity improves rapidly to about 20/60 by 6 months and adult levels (20/20) by about 9 months, though precise estimates vary with different methods (Atkinson, 2000; Gwiazda and Birch, 2001). Small improvements continue across childhood but 10–12 month olds see about as well as adults.

Do infants see a 'coherent' world?

So infants can 'see', but do they do so in a coherent or sensible way? That is, do they distinguish one thing from another or is everything a chaotic jumble? And if so, when does the shift from chaos to coherence occur? This question has been answered by preferential looking, habituation-recovery or familiarisation procedures (see Research Methods box).

Definitions

Habituation-recovery: a procedure for testing infant perceptual and cognitive skills by repeatedly presenting an item until the infant's interest drops to some criterion or set level, then presenting a novel item to see if the infant shows refreshed interest and so can distinguish it from the familiar one.
Familiarisation: a procedure for testing infant perceptual and cognitive skills by presenting an item for a set number of times or trials and then comparing infant interest in the familiar item with interest in a novel one.

Do young babies see shape in a coherent way?

New-borns who are habituated to one shape show recovery to a different shape – for example, neonates habituated to a square showed recovery to a rectangle and vice

RESEARCH METHODS

Windows on the infant brain and mind

Several procedures developed since the 1970s have been especially powerful as tools for appraising infant abilities, and in later chapters you will come across examples of research which has used these methods. For example, in preferential looking tasks, infants are presented with different stimuli simultaneously and observed to see which ones they look at longest (Fantz, 1964; Adams and Courage, 1998).

Habituation-recovery methods (Slater *et al.*, 1983) involve repeatedly showing an infant some item until some preset criterion is reached (for example, until the baby is looking 50% of the time compared to the amount that they were looking during the initial trial or baseline) and then measuring the baby's fixation to a 'novel' item. If infants can perceive the change to this

novel stimulus, they may show 'recovery' of interest, looking longer at the novel item than on the previous trials of the old item. If they can't see any difference, they won't show refreshed interest. An alternative method, called the familiarisation approach (Catherwood *et al.*, 1996), is usually faster to complete since the first item is presented for a set time or for a set number of trials determined by the experimenter in advance, instead of being determined by the infant's level of fixation on the trials. The 'test' phase in these methods involves presenting the old and new items either together or one after the other (with the order random or balanced out to avoid order or carryover effects). These approaches have been used in many studies to confirm that neonates and older infants see basic visual features such as shape and colour in an ordered way.

versa (Slater *et al.*, 1983). New-borns also show visual preference for certain shapes indicating that they can discriminate them. They have a particular bias for facial shape (Dannemiller and Stephens, 1988; Leo and Simion, 2009) and, after only four hours of exposure to the mother, show preferential fixation for their mother's face (Field *et al.*, 1984). Importantly for socio-emotional development, they can also distinguish between basic emotional expressions such as happiness or sadness at about two days old (Field *et al.*, 1983).

This evidence suggests that the ability to see shapes in a structured way depends either on innate mechanisms in the visual system or rather on mechanisms that can be fine-tuned with minimal experience after birth (Morton and Johnson, 1991). Animal research has confirmed, however, that even innate mechanisms can be undone by postnatal environments that are poor in visual stimulation (see The postnatal development of the brain for further details).

When can babies see colours?

The research on new-born colour vision and perception has been somewhat more contentious. Nonetheless, the current view based on studies using both preferential looking and habituation procedures (see Research Methods box) is that neonates have at least some functional colour vision. New-borns appear to perceive greenish, yellowish or reddish hues (middle to long wavelength light) as long as the items are sufficiently big, but may not perceive bluish (short wavelength) hues well (Adams and Courage, 2002). This ability matures by about three months of age, albeit with weaker sensitivity than in adults (Hainline, 1998; Teller, 1998; Adams and Courage, 2002; Bornstein, 2006).

Infants also seem to see colour in terms of the same basic hue groups as adults do (broadly corresponding to the labels: blue, green, yellow and red). This is shown by the fact that 3–4 month old infants habituated to one hue (e.g. a blue) show more recovery of interest to hues from different categories (e.g. green) than a new hue from the same category (i.e. another blue) (Franklin and Davies, 2004; Bornstein, 2006). This ability may be in evidence for younger babies if the hues are clearly different and the items within the infant's acuity limits (Teller and Bornstein, 1987; Hainline, 1998).

Do infants see in 3-D or do they see a flat world?

Another key aspect of visual perception is that we use cues to see the world in depth or 3-D (e.g., nearby objects and patterns look bigger than those far away). Habituation and preferential looking studies have shown that infants start to perceive the world in depth by about 3 months with this developing rapidly over the first year (Sen *et al.*, 2001; Slater and Lewis, 2002; Brown and Miracle, 2003).

A classic method to test infant depth perception involves an illusory depth apparatus (the 'visual cliff' (Gibson and Walk, 1960; Adolph, 2000)). The apparatus involves a table with a transparent surface or top. The illusion of depth (a 'visual cliff') is provided by attaching a patterned checked material to the under-surface of one half of the tabletop and using the same patterned material on the floor under the other half. The difference in pattern size on the shallow and deep sides provides a strong illusory impression of depth (the 'cliff'). Babies old enough to crawl (around 7 months) who are placed on the 'shallow' side will stop at the cliff in distress. On the other hand, 2 month olds may show a decline in heart rate if placed on the cliff side, suggesting they are processing the depth cue but in an interested rather than fearful way (Campos *et al.*, 1978).

Do infants see 'constant' objects?

More complex aspects of visual perception have also been confirmed in infants. Infants perceive that the same object can appear different from different angles or distances – that is, they have both size constancy and shape constancy, respectively. Piaget would not have credited new-borns with these abilities (Piaget, 1952, 1958), but neonates showed size constancy in a study that habituated them to a small cube-shaped item then showed this old shape in comparison with a new larger copy (Slater *et al.*, 1990). The new larger shape was shown further away than the old smaller shape, so that the two shapes were the same size on the infant's retina. The infants still showed more interest in the new shape, however, indicating that they could distinguish between actual changes in size as opposed to apparent changes in size. In a similar habituation procedure, neonates also showed evidence of shape constancy (Slater and Morison, 1985).

This ability to see 'constant' objects suggests that infants do appreciate the wholeness of objects. This is at odds with the proposal from Piaget (1952, 1958) that in the first 12 months or so infants perceive only fragmentary and disjointed impressions of objects not combined into wholes (infants would think they had many mothers according to this view of their abilities). Infants also seem to see objects as 'wholes' in other ways too.

Babies 'join up' the parts of an object

Objects consist of many features such as colour, texture and size, and these need to be 'bound' together to form a whole impression of the object. Evidence from habituation and familiarisation studies confirms that young infants do bind together such features into a 'whole' object, given sufficient time (Catherwood et al., 1996). Recent research using EEG data shows brain activity in 8 month olds suggestive of this binding together of object features (Csibra and Johnson, 2007).

This 'whole' view of objects also involves joining up information from different senses. Even in the early months, infants act as if they 'expect' visual and auditory aspects of the same object to link up. For example, babies of 3 months will show a distress or indifference reaction if there is a mismatch between vision (lip movements) and sound (the voice of adult speakers) (Broerse et al., 1983). This resembles adult discomfort at watching asynchronised films and soundtracks. Likewise 4 month olds prefer to look at synchronised puppet displays (i.e. puppets jumping in rhythm with a sound) than asynchronised ones (Spelke, 1979). Such studies are consistent with infant expectations of a coordinated sensory world.

STOP AND THINK

Reflection

Why do psychologists no longer think that the infant sees a disordered jumble of visual impressions?

Infant audition

The auditory system is more developed physically than the visual system at birth, and coherent auditory perception may emerge even before birth (see Prenatal abilities

and behaviours). The contemporary view is therefore that neonates can distinguish between sounds (pitch and loudness) as well as being able to perceive similarities and patterns among sounds, but that auditory sensitivity (Trehub et al., 1991) improves over childhood. Much of auditory development in childhood in fact consists of the loss of neonatal auditory capacities, in regard to the shaping of sensitivity to speech and musical patterns of the surrounding environment.

How do we know that the infant auditory channels are working?

Infant audition can be tested for basic operation at birth using Evoked Otoacoustic Emissions (EOAE) in which a tiny microphone in the infant ear picks up 'feedback' if hearing is functional (Chabert et al., 2006). A simpler method is to observe whether the baby orients towards a sound. Neonates will turn their eyes and head towards sounds if they are presented for long enough and are pleasant or interesting (e.g., voices or rattles).

More complex auditory capacities are often measured with the 'high-amplitude' (HAS) or 'non-nutritive' sucking procedure (Eimas, 1975; Nazzi, et al., 1998). Babies are given a dummy or pacifier linked to equipment that controls the production of some sound such as music. The sound will turn on when the baby's sucking increases to a certain rate (amplitude). If the baby can and wants to hear the sound, she will keep sucking at this elevated rate, but if the baby habituates to the sound then the sucking rate will decline. At this point, another sound is played to the baby. If the sucking rate returns to the high level, then the baby has perceived that sound as different from the old one. The non-nutritive dummy method can be used to assess infants' responses to visual as well as auditory displays, and is discussed further in Chapter 6, Memory and Intelligence.

Definition

HAS (high-amplitude sucking) method: a procedure for testing infant auditory skills (especially in regard to speech and music) in which infants suck on a dummy or pacifier to maintain a sound if interested.

As discussed in Prenatal abilities and behaviours, the auditory system is functional to some degree by the fifth month after conception so that even the foetus can 'hear' through the medium of the amniotic fluid. EEG methods show that new-borns detect changes in the pitch, loudness and duration of a sound stream (Sambeth *et al.*, 2009). Infants in general are less sensitive than adults so sounds need to be louder, but this is less so for high-frequency sounds. Sensitivity to these actually declines before adolescence, and adults are less sensitive than infants to higher-pitch sounds (Trehub *et al.*, 1991).

Do babies hear sound patterns or is it all just noise for them?

The new-born hears sounds, but is this coherent perception? Do babies hear organised sound patterns as in speech or music? Research using observation of infant preferences and HAS methods suggests that they do. Babies show preferential orientation to speech and music (Kuhl and Rivera-Gaxiola, 2008) and, as described in Prenatal abilities and behaviours, even the foetus seems capable of some processing of these sounds, as evident from new-born preference for the mother's voice (DeCasper and Fifer, 1980), her favourite TV theme tunes (Hepper, 1996), her native language (Mehler *et al.*, 1988) and Dr Seuss stories heard while *in utero* (DeCasper and Spence, 1986). So the new-born arrives with a bias to speech and music, and the research described next indicates that this reflects coherent perception.

Infants show better ability than adults to detect the basic speech sounds

Brain imaging (Kuhl and Rivera-Gaxiola, 2008) and the HAS method have confirmed that young infants are highly responsive to the language environment around them. Neonates arrive with a strong natural ability to detect speech patterns. In fact, studies using the HAS method (Eimas *et al.*, 1971; Ramus, 2002) have shown that very young infants can discriminate or perceive the basic sounds (phonemes) from a wider range of languages than adults can.

This remarkable ability is, however, lost by 12–18 months as the native language environment takes over

and the ability to hear non-native speech sound differences is reduced. For example, in the first six or so months of life, Japanese babies can hear the difference between 'l' and 'r', but by 12 months they – like Japanese adults – cannot detect this difference (Jusczyk *et al.*, 1998). Similarly, babies in English-speaking families can distinguish Hindi and North American Indian (Salish) language sounds at 6–8 months, but not at 12 months (Werker and Tees, 1984).

Kuhl and Rivera-Gaxiola (2008) describe this trend as an example of how experience (nurture) can in fact both strengthen and curtail natural abilities (nature). This shaping begins early, with recent evidence (Mampe *et al.*, 2009) that even new-born crying has an intonation pattern (rising or falling) shaped by the native language. The development of speech sound perception and its role in language is explored more fully in Chapter 5, Language Development.

Babies can also detect musical patterns

A similar pattern of development occurs for the perception of musical sounds. Even neonates perceive basic features of music such as rhythm in a coherent way (Winkler *et al.*, 2009). Older infants of 8 months can recognise changes in pitch for a single note in six-note melodies (Trehub *et al.*, 1985). Even more remarkably 4–6 month olds can distinguish typical and atypical versions of musical pieces by Mozart (Trainor and Heinmiller, 1998), while 7 month olds can distinguish between two Mozart sonatas after a few weeks of exposure and can still do so two weeks later (Saffran *et al.*, 2000). Infants also have a better ability to detect musical patterns in foreign music than adults do (Hannon and Trehub, 2005). Music perception is thus another example of how natural abilities can be curtailed by the prevailing environment (see Lifespan box).

STOP AND THINK

Reflection

Given what you've read about infants' auditory abilities, when do you think might be the best time to learn another language?

The musical brain

As the research discussed in Infant audition shows, infants show an early capacity to detect musical patterns and are better at this than adults for a wider range of musical forms, apparently because the brain becomes accustomed to the dominant musical forms of the culture in which the child is raised. This research highlights the general issue of brain plasticity. The infant abilities suggest innate programmes or processes that allow the detection of musical patterns, but the curtailment of this early ability by the dominant musical culture also shows the plasticity of the brain.

This could be seen as a case of negative plasticity – of restriction of early abilities – but research into musical training also reveals positive plasticity across the lifespan. Brain reactions change with musical training in childhood. For example, Shahin *et al.* (2008) found that 4–5 year olds who had piano training showed higher rates of gamma-band EEG activity in response to piano tones than untrained children. Adults showed a similar response to tones from instruments on which they had been trained.

The gamma activity suggests that musical training can directly influence how well the brain binds musical sounds together. The effects of training though are not limited to childhood: even short-term training of adults in aspects of musical perception has been shown to produce changes in brain response (Pantev *et al.*, 2003; Trainor *et al.*, 2003). Such research into the response to music thus shows how the human brain arrives with natural abilities that can nevertheless be shaped and moulded at least to some degree by experiences across the lifespan.

Infant touch, taste and smell abilities

Vision and hearing are key perceptual abilities, but neonates also rely heavily on the other sensory–perceptual channels to engage with and learn about their world.

Using touch to learn about objects

Basic aspects of touch perception operate early since the embryo and foetus and neonate show clear reflex reactions to touch (see Prenatal abilities and behaviours). However, new-borns also use touch in a 'haptic' way – that is: using touch to get 'information' about the world, for example, by altering their sucking or mouthing responses to dummies with different textures (Hernandez-Rief *et al.*, 2000). The pathways for painful touch also seem to develop in the foetus around 25 weeks, and the neonate responds to medical procedures such as circumcision with distress (Jorgensen,

1999). More complex haptic perception has been examined by habituation or familiarisation methods. Babies allowed to explore a stimulus through touch alone (either in the dark or with a bib covering their hands) will subsequently show more manipulation for a novel item that varies from the familiar one in texture, shape, rigidity and so on (Streri and Spelke, 1988; Catherwood 1993). Such evidence confirms that touch can be used by infants to acquire knowledge or information about important properties of objects.

How babies can use taste and smell to 'know' the world

Taste and smell (gustatory and olfactory perception, respectively) are perhaps most closely related to early survival and so mature early. Taste sensitivity actually weakens with age. Neonates react as if they perceive the four basic tastes of sweet, sour, salty and bitter as shown by their facial expressions, sucking rate and swallowing when solutions are placed in their mouths. They prefer sweet tastes and dislike bitter, sour and strong salty tastes (Rosenstein and Oster, 1988; Harris, 1997), but taste is affected by subsequent learning, and taste preferences can and do change with age and experience.

Smell (olfactory) perception is also well-developed in new-borns and may help them to identify the familiar or safe things and people in their world. The sensitivity of early olfaction was shown in research in which breast milk from the baby's mother was presented to the baby on a pad and another mother's milk on another pad. By 4–6 days of age, babies orient to, and so are able to identify, their own mothers' milk (MacFarlane, 1975; Cernoch and Porter, 1985). New-borns also show positive facial expression towards odours considered pleasant by adults (banana, vanilla, strawberry) and negative expressions to odours considered unpleasant or noxious (fish or rotting eggs) (Crook, 1987). Taste and smell perception clearly operate at a sensitive level in new-borns giving them an important basis for coherent experience of one very important aspect of the world, namely food.

STOP AND THINK

Reflection

Consider how babies make maximum use of the senses other than vision to learn about the properties of objects. Do you think these are as important for them as visual learning? Why/why not?

Motor abilities in infancy

Although new-borns arrive with good sensory–perceptual abilities, their movement (motor) capacities are much weaker. Control over body posture, gross limb movements and fine movements of hands and fingers takes considerably longer to develop. New-borns have many reflex movements and some basic abilities for acting on and reacting to the world (see The neonate: basic states, movements and reflexes), but after birth, motor control develops in both *cephalo–caudal* (head-to-toe) and *proximo–distal* (midline to extremities) directions with each new skill building on the previous one and contributing to the next.

This kind of control is essential for effective action on and reaction to the environment, but presents a considerable developmental challenge. Mastery of body and hand movement involves both higher and lower brain centres that communicate via the spinal cord with the muscles of the body (Purves *et al.*, 2008). Effective initiation and control of action and movement therefore requires coordination across many brain regions, and it takes considerable time in infancy and early childhood to achieve this efficiency.

The development of gross-motor and fine-motor control depends on innate routines for action that mature in conjunction with stimulation from the environment. It is also closely tied to the infant's perceptual, cognitive and communicative abilities and motivational states (Thelen and Smith, 1994; Goldfield and Wolff, 2002; Diamond, 2009b; Gallese *et al.*, 2009). For example, infants may grasp at desired objects or point to an object to draw attention to it.

Typical patterns of gross-motor development are shown in Table 4.3, but there are wide individual variations in the timing and even the sequence of these achievements (Goldfield and Wolff, 2002; Bukatko and Daehler, 2004; Bayley, 2005):

Fine motor development also reflects the integration of both innate programmes and feedback from experience and learning. The primary focus for fine-motor development is the growth of control over the hands and fingers especially in the act of reaching for and grasping objects. This skill is critical to infant exploration of the properties of objects, an essential basis for all knowledge and understanding about the physical world.

Visual control of reaching seems to be present at birth (Van der Meer *et al.*, 1996) as neonates show 'pre-reaching' – poorly coordinated swiping at objects that

Table 4.3. Major developments in gross motor abilities in infancy.

Approximate age	Gross motor developments
1–4 months	Reflex movements, lifts head when prone on stomach, sits with support
5–9 months	Sits without support
5–10 months	Pulls self to standing position
5–11 months	Crawls
10–17 months	Stands then walks alone
18–30 months	Runs, jumps, etc.

they can see. This quickly improves, though, so that by about 5 months infants can accurately reach for an object even in the dark (McCarty and Ashmead, 1999). In general, however, reaching improves as it becomes increasingly under visual control. Accurate visual guidance of reaching with adjustments to the size and shape of objects develops between 4 and 6 months (McCarty and Ashmead, 1999; Newman *et al.* 2001).

It takes time for hand movements to become efficient. Even the 22 week old foetus may exercise a degree of control over their hand movements (Zoia *et al.*, 2002), but neonatal hand control is generally poor (Von Hofsten, 1984). Initially infants may hold objects in a clumsy '*ulnar*' grip, that rigidly holds the object between fingers and palm. By about 9 or 10 months, infants are using a more mature '*pincer*' grip with coordination of thumb and fingers, and by 12 months children are so adept at this that they can pick up all manner of debris from carpets or floors!

STOP AND THINK

Reflection

How do you think infants' changing motor abilities allow for increasing learning about and exploration of the world as they get older?

Cognitive abilities in infancy: general models and approaches

The word cognition refers to thinking or brain processes which go beyond sensory–perceptual encoding, and allow for further analysis of information. Depending on the model of cognition, there are differing views as to how cognitive development occurs. In Chapter 2, Theoretical Perspectives we learned about Piaget's influential theory of cognitive development, in which cognition is defined as 'operations on mental structures'. The child's action on and exploration of the world leads to the assimilation of new information into older structures and the accommodation or revision of older structures in light of new information. According to Piaget, cognitive development moves through four stages with the

period of infancy being the sensorimotor stage, and true cognitive function or formal operations are not attained until adolescence. One of the main criticisms of this model, however, is that the mental operations described do not sufficiently resemble actual brain processes nor the way that cognition typically operates even in adults.

To find out more about current debates in infant cognition, see Recommended Reading. Most current views of cognitive development (e.g., Karmiloff-Smith, 1999; De Haan and Johnson, 2003; Keil, 2006; Nelson *et al.*, 2006) are based on contemporary models of cognitive processing that relate more closely to actual brain functions and systems. These models draw on information-processing, neural network and neuroscience approaches which describe cognition in terms of the brain processes for handling information, with this involving the activity of many groups or networks of neurons often distributed across many regions and pathways in the brain (Rummelhart *et al.*, 1986; Atkinson and Shiffrin, 1968; Baddeley, 2003; Purves *et al.*, 2008). Even for adults, contemporary models of cognition acknowledge that we have a tendency to rely on past knowledge (or even biases) rather than abstract logical streams of thought (Tversky and Kahneman, 1973), and that there are important influences of emotional and unconscious processing on cognition (Libet *et al.*, 1979; Le Doux, 1999).

In such contemporary models, cognition is defined in terms of basic processes such as attention, working memory, long-term memory and categorisation which are more readily linked to patterns of brain activity than the 'operations' described by Piaget. Some of these processes are discussed in more detail in Chapter 6, Memory and Intelligence. Higher-order cognition (thinking, reasoning, problem solving) uses these basic processes to combine information within or across the neural networks of the brain. A thought is not a static well-defined 'structure', but rather involves dynamic, shifting webs of brain activity, with groups of neurons working in concert like the sections

Definitions

Assimilation: within Piagetian theory, this is the process of taking new information into existing knowledge structures.
Accommodation: within Piagetian theory, this is the revision of older knowledge structures to take account of new information.

of a large orchestra, representing sensory–perceptual information, as well as more abstract–symbolic content (e.g. words) and even motor or emotional responses.

These contemporary views differ considerably from those of Piaget. From this current frame of reference, infants are seen as capable at least of basic cognitive function and are not limited to the essentially 'pre-cognitive' existence defined in Piaget's sensorimotor period. This view of infant cognition is being confirmed by studies using neuroscience methods reflecting infant brain activity during cognitive tasks (see Cutting Edge box). Moreover, the gap between adult and child thinking may not be as wide as proposed by Piaget. For example, neuroimaging evidence suggests that there are child-like tendencies in adult thinking (such as judging quantity by appearance), and that adults then have to inhibit these initial reactions (Daurignac *et al.*, 2006; Leroux *et al.*, 2009), which suggests a continuity between child and adult cognition.

Contemporary views of cognition (e.g., Karmiloff-Smith, 1999; Keil, 2006; Spelke, 2000; Slater and Lewis, 2002; Onishi and Bailargeon, 2005; Rose *et al.*, 2005;

Goswami, 2006) in general propose that infants display basic cognitive abilities, although the use of these improves over childhood, due to:

- the acquisition of a more extensive and interconnected knowledge base which provides more efficient attention and memory, and;
- more efficient control of cognitive processes, or metacognition, due to developing frontal lobe capacity for inhibiting irrelevant responses and promoting better attention, awareness and organization of knowledge (Johnson, 2001).

Definitions

Metacognition: a person's knowledge or awareness of their own cognition. Sometimes referred to as 'knowledge about knowledge' or 'cognition about cognition'.
Object permanence: the understanding that objects exist even when they have disappeared from view.

CUTTING EDGE

Using EEG to explore the infant 'mind'

Contemporary neuroscience evidence using EEG arrays shows infant brain activity consistent with cognition far beyond the sensorimotor abilities which Piaget associated with infants. For example, there are changes in theta activity during correct eye movements to the location of a hidden object (Bell, 2002), and changes in alpha activity during anticipation of the appearance of an adult in a peek-a-boo game (Orekhova *et al.*, 2001). There is an increase in gamma activity during the viewing of illusory figures, or in object permanence tasks or when there is a mismatch between current information and that sustained in working memory (Kaufman *et al.*, 2003a; Csibra and Johnson, 2007).

Kaufman *et al.* (2003a) showed 6 month old infants videos of a toy train moving into a tunnel and then either staying inside or passing out of the tunnel. The tunnel was then lifted. If the train should still have been inside

the tunnel but was not, there was a burst of gamma activity in the infant EEG record. This activity did not occur if the train was where it should have been. Such activity is strongly suggestive that the infants held a representation of the train in memory, despite it being hidden in the tunnel, and the researchers suggest that there was consequently brain activity to resolve the mismatch between this mental expectation and the disappearance of the train. This was taken as evidence of expectation of object permanence in the infants.

All of this evidence is counter to Piaget's traditional views about infants' cognitive limitations, and suggests that infants have brain activity even in the absence of a currently visible stimulus. Moreover, in denial of the infant confusion posed by James and Piaget, 8 month olds show distinctly different EEG patterns to ordered as opposed to random visual stimulation (Van der Meer *et al.*, 2008), which suggests an ability to distinguish a chaotic world from an ordered one.

There is ongoing debate about the continuity of cognitive function from childhood to adulthood, with some views suggesting that infant and adult thinking is fundamentally and qualitatively different in character (e.g., Haith, 1998; Mandler, 2003) and others proposing a more continuous developmental pathway (e.g., Keil, 2006, 2008). Nevertheless, there is at least widespread consensus that infant cognitive capacities far exceed those proposed by Piaget or James. Piaget's under-estimation of the cognitive capacity of infants and children and the implications of this for education, are discussed in Chapter 14, Developmental Psychology and Education.

STOP AND THINK

Reflection

■ Given the material in this last section, how do you think that infants 'think'?

■ Do you think that there is genuine cognitive activity in the infant brain before language develops?

Infant attention

Attention is the selective processing of some stimulus or event and is essential for acquiring information about the world. It can be covert attention or overt attention (apparent in behavioural reactions such as eye movements) and measured by physiological responses such as decline in heart rate (a sign of attention). It can involve sudden orienting to a stimulus or a more sustained focus, with these two aspects calling on different brain systems.

The attentive new-born?

New-borns show basic attentional responses adapted to the requirements of the situation. These can be defensive

Definitions

Covert attention: the act of mentally focusing on one of several possible stimuli.
Overt attention: the act of directing the senses towards a particular stimulus.

reactions to threatening stimuli (e.g., increased heart rate) or an orienting reaction (visual fixation, decline in heart rate) to non-threatening stimuli such as a coloured pattern (Sokolov, 1963; Finlay and Ivinskis, 1984). More sustained attention is also shown by new-borns through their preferential or prolonged fixation to particular stimuli, especially human faces (Slater and Johnson, 1999; Slater and Lewis, 2002). Even just after the rigours of birth, neonates will turn their heads and fixate on visual stimuli like moving facial patterns (Morton and Johnson, 1991) or orient towards sounds (Morrongiello *et al.*, 1994). New-borns therefore show a clear capacity for selectively orienting and attending, which is an essential tool for all cognitive activity.

What attracts the attention of babies?

Preferential looking or habituation or familiarisation studies show that many sensory features can elicit sustained attention in infants. For example, infants prefer coloured stimuli to those in greyscale (Bornstein, 2006), they prefer red and blue and purple to greens and yellows (Zemach *et al.*, 2007) and facial patterns to most other patterns (Pascalis and Slater, 2003). In general, older infants have more efficient attention than younger babies (Rose *et al.*, 2004). Indeed, babies showing unusually longer attention time than others in the same age group may actually have poorer information processing skills and show lower cognitive competence in later childhood (Colombo, 2001; Rose *et al.*, 2004). Nonetheless, attention at all ages is affected by factors such as knowledge, interests and emotional state. For example, one study showed that older infants looked longer than younger babies at items from the *Sesame Street* TV programme, possibly reflecting the personal experience of the former group (Valkenburg and Vroone, 2004; Courage *et al.*, 2006).

Different aspects of attention may develop at different rates

There may be also different rates of development for different aspects of attention (Ruff and Rothbart, 1996; Colombo, 2001; Johnson 2002; Bartgis *et al.*, 2008). Rapid orienting may develop sooner due to the earlier development of the posterior (rear) attentional systems of the brain (in the parietal cortex and brainstem: see Fig. 4.3) (Posner and Rothbart, 1981; Johnson, 2002). In contrast, sustained attention requires the involvement of more anterior (frontal) regions of the brain, which are especially important in the ability to resist distraction, and these take longer to mature (see The postnatal development of the brain).

Infant learning and memory

Memory and learning are different views of the same phenomena. Memory is the set of processes for storing information in the networks of the brain and for later being able to retrieve or reactivate that stored information by either recognition (if the item is present again) or by recall (if the item is not actually present and must be located in long-term memory). As the result of memory, we 'learn' or show enduring and obvious changes in our behaviour, capacities and responses. Most models (e.g., Baddeley, 2003) propose different phases of memory: *sensory memory* (brief persistence of sensory impressions), *working memory* (the temporary maintenance of information in an active state) and *long-term memory* (enduring biochemical and structural changes in brain connections or synapses). Contemporary accounts propose that these aspects of memory may work in parallel (at the same time) or that working memory is simply the currently active part of long-term memory (Cowan, 1999). The development of memory across childhood is discussed in Chapter 6, Memory and Intelligence.

One of the classic demonstrations of infant recognition ability was that by Friedman (1972) who habituated newborns to chequerboard patterns and then showed them a novel chequerboard pattern. The infants showed recovery of visual interest to the novel pattern but not the familiar one, only feasible if they had in fact detected the familiarity of the old one. Many more recent studies using habituation and familiarisation methods have confirmed recognition memory even in neonates (e.g., Slater *et al.*, 1983) for all manner of sensory information (auditory, tactile, etc.). It would thus seem that recognition memory develops early and, indeed, children's recognition memory can match that of adults (Siegler, 1996).

Infant recall of absent items

As noted above, memory may involve either recognition of an item that is present or recall of one that is absent. It is more challenging to study recall in infants. Tasks requiring memory for a hidden object (see Basic knowledge and understanding in infancy) show that 6–12 month olds look at the location of hidden items (Ahmed and Ruffman, 1998) or show associated EEG brain activity (Bauer, 2007; Csibra and Johnson, 2007) suggesting recall of the items. In more natural surroundings, 2 year olds can easily find a hidden toy after delays of an hour (Deloache and Brown, 1983). Delayed imitation may also reflect elementary recall ability, and infants can imitate the movements of others possibly even at birth (Meltzoff and Moore, 1977).

The mobile conjugate reinforcement paradigm (Rovee-Collier and Cuevas, 2009) has also offered evidence on infant recall. Using this method, one end of a ribbon is attached to a baby's ankle and the other end to a mobile. The baby soon learns to kick to make the mobile move, but if the mobile is changed to a new one, the baby does not kick, suggesting recall of the old absent mobile. There is also evidence of more active recall capacity in older infants who have been trained to perform a lever-pulling action that operates a toy train. For example, 6 month olds show recall of the action after delays of 2 weeks and 12 month olds after delays of 2 months (Rovee-Collier and Boller, 1995). This research is discussed further in Chapter 6, Memory and Intelligence.

Is infant memory the same as that of adults?

Memory and learning clearly operate from birth, but there is disagreement about the exact nature of this early memory. In general, however, it is considered that by about 6 months, infant memory resembles the explicit declarative memory of adults (Rose *et al.*, 2004) with both using similar brain structures. In particular, the hippocampus (see Fig. 4.7) is essential in explicit memory and in the transfer of information from working memory to long-term store (Purves *et al.*, 2008), and this appears to develop early in infancy (even before the visual cortex) (Nelson, 2002b). However, parts of the hippocampus and its connections to the prefrontal cortex of the brain important in consolidating new memories may not reach functional maturity until 20–24 months

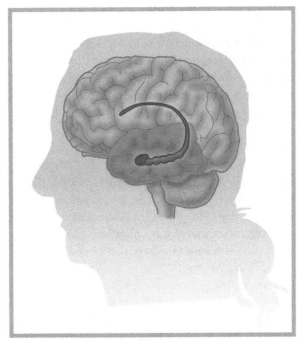

Figure 4.7. The hippocampus is a brain structure important in consolidating memories and a focus for debate about infant memory.

of age (Bauer, 2007). Hence, there is ongoing debate about whether infant memory in the first six or so months of life is in fact 'explicit'.

One view is that early memory is implicit and procedural, with explicit memory developing at 6–12 months, especially with the increasing involvement of the prefrontal cortex (Nelson, 2002b). However, recent evidence using a brain-imaging method called *near-infra-red spectroscopy* does not fit with this view, since it showed activity in the prefrontal cortex of 3 month olds in response to novel stimuli during memory tasks (Nakano *et al.*, 2009).

Moreover, the implicit-to-explicit account of memory development is at odds with infant performance in the conjugate reinforcement paradigms (Rovee-Collier and Cuevas, 2009). Infant memory and learning in such contexts is often rapid and does not reflect the extensive trials often required for procedural learning. For example, adult cats require over 1300 trials to learn a limb-flexion movement while 3 month old human infants can learn to kick to a mobile in minutes. Rather than infant learning being seen to develop from implicit to explicit

knowledge then, infants may simply display the type of memory and learning most adaptive for the circumstances (Rovee-Collier and Cuevas, 2009).

In any case, whatever the exact nature of early infant memory and learning, it is clear that from birth, memory operates well enough to allow infants to learn and build up a storehouse of knowledge about the world.

STOP AND THINK

Reflection

Try to design a simple study to see whether infants can recognise a colourful toy after a delay of a few minutes.

Basic knowledge and understanding in infancy

Cognition is not only defined in terms of these basic processes that we have been discussing, but also in terms of its content or knowledge. Initial knowledge or understanding about the properties of people, other animals, objects, places and events arises in the first instance from the sensory–perceptual channels. There is ongoing debate about whether such early knowledge is innate or acquired and whether it is used in an aware manner by infants (Haith, 1998; Karmiloff-Smith, 1999; Rovee-Collier and Cuevas, 2009; Spelke, 2000), but it clearly provides the foundation for subsequent and more complex networks of understanding.

Object permanence?

One fundamental aspect of knowledge and understanding that was a focus in Piaget's work, and which we discussed in Chapter 2, Theoretical Perspectives is whether infants have an understanding of object permanence, that is, that objects continue to exist independently from our perception of them. This is a more complex concept than the other aspects of object identity discussed in infant vision, and may be harder to develop simply because the world offers contradictory information.

Objects can disappear from view in many ways. They can go behind or inside other objects or can be projected out of visual range altogether. They may or may not reappear and if they do reappear, they may be either intact or in an altered form. For example, while a train speeding behind a mountain will (hopefully) reappear in the same form on the other side, does a sweet that is swallowed and so vanishes from view continue to exist as such? It certainly won't reappear in the same form!

Piaget's conclusion was that for children younger than 18 months, objects are linked to actions and so for these infants they do not exist permanently or independently of such actions. This conclusion was founded on infant performance in tasks requiring searching for a hidden toy. Infants of 8–12 months may search for a toy at one location (A), but when the object is then moved to at a new location (B), the infants may still return to search to the first hiding place. This is therefore known as the A not B error.

More recent studies have used approaches which don't rely on infants having to search for objects. In particular, infant responses to impossible events have been assessed. In one example (Baillargeon and De Vos, 1991) infants observed two carrots moving behind a wall, or behind a screen with a window opening. One of the carrots was short and so not visible at the window, while the other one was tall and so should have been visible, but it wasn't. This was therefore an 'impossible' event, violating the idea of object permanence. Infants of 3½ months showed more visual interest in this impossible event than the former. In another example, 2–3 month olds showed more interest when a container that had covered a moving toy duck was subsequently lifted to reveal the duck was absent (Baillargeon, 2004). The conclusion from such studies is that infants' responses reflect their expectations about object permanence. Some studies using this approach have had more mixed results (Cashon and Cohen, 2000), and there is continuing debate about whether object permanence is innate knowledge (Karmiloff-Smith, 1999).

Nevertheless, recent evidence from EEG studies has provided a fresh perspective with compelling indication of expectations about object permanence in young infants. Even 6 month old infants show high-frequency (gamma) brain activity while observing locations of hidden objects or when confronted with the unexpected disappearance of objects (Csibra et al., 2000; Csibra and Johnson, 2007), and this gamma activity in adults is linked to maintaining an item in working memory (Tallon-Baudry et al., 1998).

In general, studies requiring infants to search for hidden objects are less likely to confirm the early development of understanding of object permanence. The ability to search requires the coordination of motor skills, memory and attention systems that may not be easily achieved in infancy. For example, 6–12 month olds will look at the correct location in the A not B task even while reaching to the wrong location (Ahmed and Ruffman, 1998), and infants may have difficulty preventing themselves from reaching to a previously rewarded location (Diamond et al., 1994). So infants may well have more understanding about object permanence than they can reveal in search tasks.

Categorisation in infancy

A central aspect of knowledge development in infancy (and indeed over the life-span) is categorisation, which allows for the grouping or organisation of items based on similarity, and concepts, which are the defining representations on which categories are based. For example, instead of knowing about their own dog Pluto and their neighbour's dog Saturn, infants evolve a concept about dogs in general. Dogs are items that bark, have tails, have fur, etc. Infants also evolve a category associated with that concept (e.g., including poodles, collies, boxers, etc.). This process enables them to classify new dogs in that category, but to exclude other animals such as cats (see Chapter 5, Language Development). This process is a powerful cognitive tool, enabling the efficient organisation of knowledge. In fact the tendency to categorise is so potent that infants, like adults, will even classify fabricated objects (Younger and Cohen, 1986; Gauthier et al., 1998). Categorisation is also important within the development of maths skills, which is explored in Chapter 7, The Development of Mathematical Thinking.

Definitions

Categorisation: the grouping or organisation of items based on their similarity.
Concepts: mental representations upon which categories are based.

All categories are based on similarities, but this can involve different levels of obvious similarity ranging from superordinate or global categories where there is low similarity amongst items (e.g. 'living things' or 'animals') to subordinate categories where there are high-similarity items (e.g. 'poodles'). Somewhere in between these extremes are basic categories with moderate similarity in item appearance (e.g. 'dogs'). Some items will be better examples of a category than others. For example, a robin is a better example of the category 'bird' than a penguin is (Rosch, 1978). The best example and/or a prototype (an abstraction of main properties of the examples) may be stored in memory. When new items are experienced, any overlap with these leads to inclusion in the category and any dissimilarity to exclusion.

Do infants detect categories?

A number of different research methods confirm that categorisation does occur in infancy (Quinn, 2002). A common method is to habituate or familiarise infants to items from the same category (e.g., different pictures of dogs) and then present two new items: one from the familiar category (e.g. a new dog) and one from a new category (e.g. a cat). Greater fixation to the new category item is evidence that infants can distinguish the two categories as different. This method has indicated that infants as young as 3–4 months detect basic categories such as the four hues (Franklin and Davies, 2004; Bornstein, 2006) and natural-kind categories such as cats and dogs (Quinn and Eimas, 1996). Recently, brain activity in 6 month olds has also been measured using EEG to confirm that these categories are processed distinctly by infants (Quinn *et al.*, 2006).

Other behavioural methods involve observing older infants playing with toys from different categories. 'Sequential touching' of items from the same category indicates that the category similarities have been detected (Rakison and Butterworth, 1998). For example, 9–10 month olds showed more serial touching of bird items after they had played with or touched a series of toy planes and vice versa, suggesting that the categories were guiding responses (Mandler and McDonough, 1993).

Infants also show responses consistent with subordinate categorisation such as *Tabby Cat* (Quinn, 2004) and, at the other extreme, of broad superordinate categories. For example, in contrast to Piagetian proposals (1952; 1958), 3–4 month olds categorise 'animate' things as different from 'inanimate', especially if these have clearly different features such as legs versus wheels (Quinn, 2002). Indeed, infants show quite subtle understanding about animacy (Keil, 2008) (see Going Further box on next page).

Issues about infant categorisation

There are, however, three debates about infant categorisation. The first is about whether basic categories develop before superordinate ones or vice versa (Quinn and Johnson, 2000; Mandler, 2003; Keil, 2006, 2008; Quinn, 2008). As noted above, many basic categories do appear early, but some broader categories may precede them. For example, in one study, 2 month olds seemed to learn the category of 'mammal' more readily than that of 'cat' (Quinn and Johnson, 2000). It may be that infants will use whatever level is fit-for-purpose, and even adults may be flexible and use different categorical levels depending on their needs. For example, a hungry adult may seek any food (superordinate), but a well-fed person may want caviar (subordinate). Such flexibility has also been shown in infant cognition. For example, infants attend to the colour or shape of two-dimensional objects, but attend to the location of three-dimensional objects they can pick up (Kaufman *et al.* 2003b).

The second debate is about whether infant categories are the same as adult categories. One view is that for infants, even superordinate categories are more perceptually based than those of adults (Rakison, 2000). An alternative view is that infant categories are too general, and require further enrichment to achieve maturity (Mandler, 2003). In contrast to these views is the proposal that although early categories may not have the full semantic richness of adult categories, they are basically similar with continuity between early categories and later ones (Carey, 2002; Keil, 2006, 2008). This debate is ongoing in developmental psychology.

The third debate is about whether categories need language. A traditional view, called the Whorfian Hypothesis, is that language is needed for categorisation. Clearly this is not the case, as shown by the research with very young infants cited above but, nonetheless, language helps to enrich and refine categories. Older infants are more likely to show categorical responses to items with a common name (Graham and Kilbreath, 2007) and language links up with pre-language categories. For example, the basic hue categories emerge prior to language development (see Infant vision), but with the development of colour naming, hue categorisation moves from the right

STOP AND THINK

Going further

Piaget proposed that the concept of animacy did not develop until after infancy, but this study shows that 14 month olds can respond in terms of object features essential in a concept of animacy. In one experiment Newman *et al.* (2008) familiarised children to computer-animations showing two moving 'cats in hats' – a cat with a blue stomach and blue hat and one with a red stomach and red hat. The stomach was a fixed feature but the hats were shown to be removable. The cat in the blue hat moved back and forwards while the other one jumped up and down. This is shown in Fig. 4.8.

In two test events, the infants were then shown two new cats whose stomach and hat colour now did not match to the previous displays (i.e. blue hat–red stomach or red hat–blue stomach). In one test trial, the cat's motion was the one previously linked to the hat colour while in the other test trial, the motion was the one previously linked to the stomach colour (see Fig. 4.8). The toddlers showed more interest when the stomach colour and motion did not match up than when the hat colour and motion did not match. This suggests that the toddlers were rating the cat's body feature as more important in regard to the cat's motion than the external feature of hat colour and so were more interested when this association between internal features and movement was violated than if the link between external features and motion was changed. A second experiment confirmed that 14 month olds only responded this way when an object's motion was self-generated. In other words, 14 month olds especially tied the internal features of an object to motion only when the object was able to move under its own power.

This pattern of response could reflect the foundations of an animacy concept – that internal characteristics are linked to animate identity and the ability to move. While this may not reflect a mature concept of animacy, it nonetheless suggests a level of inference about animate objects that goes beyond the approach proposed for young children in Piagetian theory.

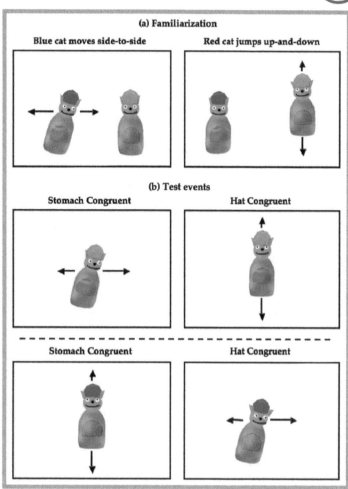

Figure 4.8. Newman *et al.*'s study of 14 month olds, reasoning about object identify.

(*Source*: Newman et al., 2008, p. 423)

Although there is ongoing discussion about the precise nature of early categorical abilities, it is clear that infants can and do respond categorically, and that this is a powerful tool for building knowledge and understanding, especially when it integrates later with language.

Definition

Animacy: the concept of animacy refers to an understanding of the difference between living (animate) and non-living (inanimate) things.

to left hemisphere of the brain, which reflects the left hemisphere's verbal enrichment of these basic concepts (Franklin *et al.*, 2008). In addition, there is evidence that more sophisticated categorisation abilities may be linked to vocabulary growth in older infants, and this is explored further in Chapter 5, Language Development.

Reasoning and problem solving in infancy

So far we have considered how attention, memory and categorisation develop in infancy. All of these work together to support the most complex cognitive activities of the human brain – reasoning and problem solving – the processes involved in combining information from the external world or from memory to produce a solution to a problem. There is ongoing debate (e.g., Haith, 1998; Keil, 2006; Kagan, 2008; Quinn, 2008) about whether infant problem solving is essentially similar or different to that of adults. Piaget proposed that there is a qualitative difference in the ways in which children and adults reason, with adults using formal operations in accordance with the principles of logical deduction, but is this a fair standard against which to judge children's reasoning?

How do adults reason?

Adult reasoning can in fact take two quite different forms. Deductive reasoning is consistent with logic, and provides a certain or definite conclusion. Inductive reasoning uses knowledge or information beyond that which is given and provides less certain conclusions.

Adults are of course capable of reasoning deductively, but may fail to do so, even on Piagetian tasks (Merriwether and Liben, 1997). In fact adults often sidestep logical deduction altogether and rely on 'fuzzier' or knowledge-based reasoning. For example, they may solve a problem by analogical reasoning based on its similarity to a previous

> **Definition**
>
> Analogical reasoning: a method of problem solving which makes use of the similarity of a new problem to some previously solved problem.

problem, or use mental shortcuts called 'heuristics', such as drawing conclusions based on how readily they come to mind (Tversky and Kahneman, 1973). Deductive and fuzzy approaches use different brain regions, with the right hemisphere more active in deduction and the left hemisphere in knowledge-based reasoning (Parsons and Osherson, 2001), so even the adult brain can use different pathways to reason and solve problems.

Adults are also said to use more abstract information while children rely on perceptual properties such as size or shape (Piaget, 1952, 1958) but, as mentioned earlier, neuroimaging research shows that adults firstly respond in terms of appearances in Piagetian-type tasks, and that these reactions then have to be inhibited (Daurignac *et al.*, 2006; Leroux *et al.*, 2009). It may be therefore that there is closer overlap between child and adult thinking than might be predicted. The yardstick for comparing child to adult reasoning might need to include knowledge-based or heuristic approaches as well as the deductive processes identified in Piagetian theory.

So do infants 'reason' or 'solve problems'?

Using the 'fuzzier' view of adult reasoning, infants can be said to 'reason' within the bounds of their motor and sensory abilities and their knowledge of the world. Young infants are certainly capable of inductive processing to develop new knowledge and information, as shown in the evidence on infant categorisation and concept-formation (see Categorisation in infancy). These are relatively passive modes of processing that arise out of sensory-perceptual channels, but there is evidence of more active problem-solving. For example, infants of 14 months adopt different strategies to achieve the goal of feeding themselves with a spoon presented in awkward orientations (McCarty *et al.*, 1999).

There is also evidence that infants, like adults, are able to solve problems and reason by using prior knowledge in an analogical way. For example 10 and 12 month olds were tested in a task in which they had to retrieve a toy from behind a barrier and then repeat this with different toys and barriers (Chen *et al.*, 1997). They showed increasing efficiency with each retrieval, reflecting an analogical-type approach to the problem. Another study (Holyoak *et al.*, 1984) showed that children as young as 2 years could use analogy to solve a problem with more abstract information. After being told stories such as that of a genie who retrieved a precious jar without leaving his lamp by using a magic staff, the children solved problems in an analogous way. They had to reach some sweets without moving from their chair and did so by using items like the staff used by the genie.

Are young children limited, then, to inductive or heuristic approaches to problems? In one study of reasoning, 2 year olds were able to correctly respond to logical problems such as '*All sheep ride bicycles. Bill is a sheep. Does Bill ride a bicycle?*', so long as they were encouraged to imagine the contexts. This is despite the fact that the problems involved hypothetical information which was counterfactual to real life (Richards and Sanderson, 1999). The correct answer here, by the way, is that Bill does ride a bike!

The debate continues about whether infants are explicitly aware and in control of their reasoning. However, the range of evidence suggests that within the limits of their physical and motor development, and of their knowledge, attention and working memory, infants certainly exhibit behaviours and responses consistent with elementary reasoning and problem-solving abilities.

STOP AND THINK

Reflection

- Can you think of a routine problem that an infant might solve in everyday life?
- What cognitive processes might be used by the infant to solve this problem?

SUMMARY

The remarkable body of research described in this chapter highlights major routes and landmarks along the pathway from zygote to birth and through infancy, the significance of the prenatal period in understanding development, the interaction of nature and nurture and the ways in which early research and theory have under-estimated infants' abilities to learn and know about the world. Many of the topics explored here will be developed in later chapters within the book.

Development begins from the moment of conception. We have learned that the brain begins to develop very early in the embryonic period and that this development continues through infancy. The developmental pathway can be affected by genetic factors and environmental factors in the prenatal period as well as in infancy, and so to understand the psychology of a child we have to understand what happens *in utero* as well as what happens after birth.

Much of the research which this chapter has considered indicates the interweaving of nature and nurture in early development. Genetic and environmental factors interact to affect development in the prenatal period, and this interaction continues after birth. The infant is born with certain basic capacities for learning about the world, but the brain is still highly plastic in infancy and experiences

can turn genes on or off and vice versa, genes can limit or influence the impact of experiences. There is an ongoing dialogue over the human lifespan between our innate abilities and our environmental experience, and the Nature–Nurture boxes which you will find in every chapter of this book highlight this interaction.

Researchers have had to be extremely inventive in coming up with methods that will allow for the study of prenatal and infant development. In this chapter, we have explored some of the classic and the cutting edge methods which have all contributed to the body of knowledge that we have about this period of development. These include contemporary methods such as EEG (electroencephalography), VEP (visually evoked potentials) and EOAE (evoked otoacoustic emissions), as well as methods like preferential looking, habituation-recovery, familiarisation, high amplitude sucking and the visual cliff. Some of these methods will be explored in other chapters throughout the book.

The new-born arrives with many basic capacities for sensing, perceiving and knowing the world using vision, audition, touch, taste and smell. The evidence we have considered in this chapter certainly does not suggest that infants experience the chaotic, transient and 'non-cognitive' universe which was proposed by James and Piaget. In fact, it seems as though infants have a richer and more coherent early experience of the world than these authors ever proposed.

Piaget believed that the world of an infant was limited to sensory and perceptual experience. The research and theory considered in this chapter contrasts with this view. We have seen that infants' abilities include attention, learning and memory, basic knowledge about the world, categorisation, reasoning and problem solving. The evidence we have explored therefore suggests that infants are capable of cognition and the analysis of information beyond the stage of mere sensory-perceptual encoding.

REVIEW QUESTIONS

1. Discuss how genes and environment work together to influence infant development, making reference to recent research with humans and other animals.
2. Describe the key features of the physical development of the brain in prenatal life and in the first year after birth.
3. Critically evaluate Piaget's and James' view of early infant perception in the light of some recent evidence on infant visual abilities.
4. Describe one of the methods used to study infant memory.
5. Do infants have explicit and aware cognitive capacities? Justify your answer with reference to recent research on infant categorisation and problem-solving abilities.

RECOMMENDED READING

For a more general overview of infant development, see:

Bremner, G. & Fogel, A. (2001). *Blackwell Handbook of Infant Development*. Oxford: Blackwell.

Slater, A. & Lewis, M. (2002). *Introduction to Infant Development*. Oxford: Oxford University Press.

For more information on the brain and cognitive development from a neuroscience perspective, see:

De Haan, M. & Johnson, M.H. (2003). *The Cognitive Neuroscience of Development*. Hove: Psychology Press.

Luciana, M. (2007). Special issue: developmental cognitive neuroscience. *Developmental Review, 27*, 277–282.

Nelson, C.A. & Luciana, M. (2001). *Handbook of Developmental Cognitive Neuroscience*. Cambridge, MA: MIT Press.

Nelson, C.A., de Haan, M. & Thomas, K.M. (2006). *Neuroscience and Cognitive Development: The Role of Experience and the Developing Brain*. New York: Wiley.

For more information about physical development during the prenatal period, see:

Moore, K.L. & Persaud, T.V.N. (2003). *The Developing Human: Clinically Oriented Embryology*. Philadelphia, PA: Saunders.

Moore, K. L. Persaud, T. V. N. & Shiota, K. (2000). *Colour Atlas of Clinical Embryology*. Philadelphia, PA: Saunders.

Tanner, J.M. (1990). *Foetus into Man: Physical Growth from Conception to Maturity* (2nd Ed.). Cambridge, MA: Harvard University Press.

For more information about human genetics, see:

Strachan, T. & Read, A. (2003). *Human Molecular Genetics*. New York: Wiley.

For more information about the interaction between nature and nurture, see:

Diamond, A. (2009). The interplay of biology and the environment broadly defined. *Developmental Psychology*, 45, 1–8.

For more information on current debates about infant cognition, see:

Haith, M.M. (1998). Who put the cog in infant cognition? Is rich interpretation too costly? *Infant Behavior & Development*, 21, 167–179.

Keil, F. (2006). Cognitive science and cognitive development. In W. Damon & R. Lerner (Series Eds) & D. Kuhn & R.S. Siegler (Vol. Eds), *Handbook of Child Psychology: Vol. 2: Cognition, Perception, and Language (6th Ed.)* (609–635). New York: Wiley.

For more information on the relationship between genes, brain development and cognition, see:

Johnson, M.H., Munakata, Y. & Gilmore, R.O. (2002). *Brain Development and Cognition: a Reader*. Oxford: Blackwell.

Ramus, F. (2006). Genes, brain, and cognition: a roadmap for the cognitive scientist. *Cognition, 101*, 247–269.

RECOMMENDED WEBSITES

For a detailed account of prenatal growth, click on the circular chart at:

http://www.visembryo.com/baby/index.html

For ongoing updates on the Human Genome Project:

http://www.ornl.gov/sci/techresources/ Human_Genome/home.shtml

http://www.genome.gov

http://ghr.nlm.nih.gov/handbook

To see 'movies' of neuronal cells migrating, go to:

http://hatten-server.rockefeller.edu/HattenLab/ overview.html

Watch a video discussing sensory development of a newborn baby. Further resources can be found at www.pearsoned.co.uk/gillibrand

Chapter 5
Language development

Talk to your baby

In 2003 the National Literacy Trust (NLT), a UK organisation, launched a campaign called 'Talk to Your Baby', aimed at encouraging parents and caregivers to talk more to children from birth to 3 years. It came about as a result of a joint NLT/National Association of Head Teachers survey carried out in 2001 which revealed that 75% of head teachers were concerned about a significant decline in the level of children's language when they enter school or nursery.

Part of the NLT's campaign is aimed at increasing the number of buggies available on the market which have the child's seat facing the person who is pushing rather than facing forwards. In October 2008, Suzanne Zeedyk, a psychologist at the University of Dundee in the UK, presented the initial findings of collaborative research carried out with the NLT into the effects of baby buggies on parent–infant interactions (http://www.literacytrust.org.uk/talk_to_your_baby/resources/642_talk_to_your_baby_ 2008_conference_report-communication_the_childs_perspective).

- What might be responsible for a decline in children's language?
- Do we talk less to our children than we used to and, if so, why might that be?
- Can talking to babies before they can talk themselves really facilitate language development?
- Could something as seemingly simple as a pusher-facing baby buggy really have a significant effect on a child's language development?

A full report of Suzanne Zeedyk's findings can be downloaded from http://www. literacytrust.org.uk/assets/0000/2531/Buggy_research.pdf

Introduction

Language is a system of symbols which we use to communicate with one another. It consists of sounds, which can be combined in various ways to make words, and those words each carry their own meanings. There are grammatical rules which govern how those words may be combined in order to construct sentences correctly, and social rules which govern how language is used appropriately in different situations. The foundations of this complex system of communication are laid well before a child even utters his first words. This chapter will explore the process of developing language beginning in the pre-verbal stage and following children's progress through childhood to the point where they can use language very effectively to communicate and engage in social interactions.

What is language?

Language is a system of communication, although not all communication occurs through language. We will see later in this chapter that, before they are able to understand or produce words, infants can communicate quite effectively with us. Language is a symbolic system. That is, each word (and sometimes even parts of words) means something, stands for something or refers to something else. So long as we all share a common understanding of what words refer to then we can communicate. The precise word that we choose to represent something is to a certain extent unimportant. Take, for example, the word 'bed'. This is the word which we use in the English language to refer to objects like the one in the photograph.

However, if we were speaking German we would use the word 'bett'. If we were speaking French we would say 'lit' and if we were using British Sign Language then we would make the sign pictured on the right. The relationship between the object and the word which we use to refer to it is, therefore, not a necessary one – there is no intrinsic reason why another word could not be used. From now on, we could all use the word 'kofu' to refer to objects like that in the photo. So long as everyone did it, and we all understood what we were referring to, kofu would serve just as adequate a symbol for such objects, as the word 'bed'.

The individual words themselves, though, are only the building blocks of language. There are rules which

British Sign Language for 'bed'.

Source: Education Photos/John Walmsley

children must learn about how those words can be combined, and these serve as the cement which holds the words together. There are also rules about how words can be altered to make, for example, different tenses or to create plurals. Again, these rules differ between different languages. What is amazing about language is that, although there are only a finite number of words and rules available to us, there are a potentially infinite number of ways in which those words may be combined. Young infants use words to communicate only their basic needs but, by adulthood, we can talk about abstract ideas and concepts meaningfully. As children begin to develop language they start by naming and describing objects. Eventually, though, they will be able to discuss how they feel and what they like, and will not rely upon the immediate environment for communication. Developing language enables us to talk about the past and the future. Language is therefore incredibly creative and productive.

An object which may be referred to using many different words.

Source: Pearson Education Ltd./Comstock Images

What communication is there before verbal communication?

We have referred to the fact that language is a system of communication, but that not all communication occurs through language. In this section, we will consider some of the ways in which early communication occurs even before spoken language.

Infants are social and emotional beings, and are able to send emotional messages from the time that they are born. Using facial expressions and early vocalisations such as crying, screaming, smiling or laughing, we can interpret an infant's emotional state. In fact, some researchers suggest that there is a universal repertoire of facial expressions that infants are born with so that regardless of culture they are able to communicate their basic emotions and their primary physiological needs (Izard, 1994). Crying has received particular attention from researchers as a key way in which infants communicate. However, there has been controversy in the research literature about the exact purpose and function of a baby's cry. The next stop and think box explores some of the arguments which have arisen from recent research exploring infants' crying, an interesting and controversial topic in understanding language development.

There are disagreements about whether crying should be viewed as an attempt to communicate some physiological need, a way to manipulate parents and caregivers or a way for an infant to simply signal that she is healthy and strong. In Chapter 9 Attachment and Early Social Experiences we discuss the development of a healthy mother–infant bond. The work of John Bowlby (1969, 1982) in the field of attachment suggested that crying had an important function for infants since most mothers will return to an infant if she begins to cry, and thus crying can restore the infant's proximity to her mother. This is important since the infant is more likely to remain fed and warm, but also because proximity to the mother is important for the development of that infant's social and emotional wellbeing. Bowlby believed that crying may have developed as part of infants' behavioural repertoire through the process of human evolution. Remaining close to her mother will have made the early human infant less vulnerable to predators and thus will have served an important function in evolutionary terms in ensuring the continuation of the species.

Lummaa *et al.* (1998) suggest that excessive crying on the part of an infant is a manipulative signal and would have us believe that on some level there is an intent to 'send' a message. Research by Lorberbaum *et al.* (2002) suggests that when infants cry, their mothers are 'receiving' information. They used functional magnetic resonance imaging (fMRI) to examine the brain activity of first-time mothers whilst listening to infant crying, and

compared this to their brain activity during a control condition where they listened to white noise and to a third condition where they heard nothing. Some previous research by the neurologist Paul MacLean (see Recommended websites) had suggested that a part of the brain called the thalamocingulate division would be important in mother–infant attachment behaviour (MacLean, 1990). If there are particular parts of the brain which are involved in maternal behaviour then clearly it is important to investigate which parts these are in order to better understand normal mothering and also potentially to understand what might underpin some instances of abnormal, neglectful or abusive mothering. The fMRI study showed that parts of the brain within the thalamocingulate division were indeed more active when mothers heard infants' crying than in the control conditions. Overall the results were consistent with other research which has identified areas of the brain involved in maternal behaviour with non-human mammals.

Interviews with the mothers in that research also asked them to report their emotional reactions to the different stimuli which they had heard, and the results of these interviews showed that hearing infants' crying resulted in the mothers experiencing significantly more sadness, and significantly more 'urges to help' than the control conditions. This evidence using fMRI techniques and interviews indicates that merely by crying, infants elicit a consistent response in particular parts of mothers' brains and an accompanying desire on the part of the mothers to behave in a certain way (to help). It could therefore be argued that complex pre-verbal communication is occurring. This research shows how infants' crying can have a very real physiological effect on mothers, and supports the very early view of Bowlby that crying may have a survival function by ensuring that an infant remains in close proximity to its mother.

Should we really consider these early emotional expressions to be communication, though? Are infants and mothers really sending and receiving messages (see the next photo)? What is generally agreed is that in the very

> **Definition**
>
> Thalamocingulate division: part of the human brain suggested within Paul Maclean's 'Triune Brain' theory (that we have three brains, each developed from the preceding ones through evolution) as important in family-related behaviour.

Mother–infant smiling. What is being communicated?

Source: O'Donnell

earliest days of life these kinds of emotional expressions do not occur as deliberate attempts on the part of the infant to communicate something to someone. At first they are merely reactions to physiological states. For example, new mothers may mistake an attack of wind for their baby's first smile! It is not until around 6 weeks of age that smiling begins to occur in response to something in the child's external world (Emde *et al.*, 1976). By 12 months of age it seems as though infants are able to use smiling as a much more complex device, to communicate their positive feelings about an object to a social partner. For example, Venezia *et al.* (2004) observed a group of normally developing infants of between 8 and 12 months in situations where they had both an object and a social partner to attend to. The amount that these infants smiled in these situations did not increase during the four months that they were studied, but the amount that they smiled and then immediately made eye contact with their social partner did increase significantly and suggests that, even at 12 months of age, infants have already made some important progress in using facial expressions deliberately to communicate.

Definitions

Infanticide: intentionally causing the death of an infant.
Colic: a condition where babies cry for long periods of time (most commonly in the first three months of life) without obvious reason, but possibly due to trapped wind or infant temperament.
Shaken baby syndrome: a type of child abuse which occurs when a baby is vigorously shaken; it can result in neurological damage and may be fatal.

STOP AND THINK

Going further

In 2004 the journal *Behavioural and Brain Sciences* published an article by Joseph Soltis (a researcher in vocal communication). This suggested that infant crying is a behaviour which has evolved in human babies as a way of ensuring their survival (Soltis, 2004), but for slightly different reasons to Bowlby. Using evidence from research with a variety of different species of animals, Soltis argued that crying is a sign of physical strength and health. After discussing cross-cultural evidence from communities where there are instances of infanticide, and from research with a variety of non-human species, Soltis suggests that a crying infant is less likely to be killed by its family. This is because by crying he advertises himself as a healthy and viable specimen. If for some reason parents cannot support all of their offspring, then they will be more likely to spare the healthiest whilst weak or injured offspring will be killed or allowed to die. Crying is therefore a way of signalling physical vigour. This suggests some sort of communicative function given that the infant's caregiver responds to the crying and acts a certain way as a result of it.

In a response to Soltis' article, Barr (2004) suggests an alternative account of crying, and argues that during the first three months crying is a behavioural state, in the same way as an infant may be described as being 'awake' or 'asleep'. Barr agrees that caregivers may respond to the crying in particular ways, but that this result of the crying 'signal' is secondary only and not a primary function of crying.

Another important point to note about crying is that, in spite of the positive effects it may have in terms of ensuring an infant's survival or psychological health, there may be some negative effects, particularly when the amount of crying an infant does is perceived to be excessive or abnormally high. In such cases, the infant's crying may lead to abuse or neglect. Infants suffering from colic engage in prolonged bouts of crying. Yet instead of eliciting positive maternal behaviour, Hagen (2002) found that the opposite was true. He surveyed 129 mothers of babies between 3 and 32 weeks of age and found that the more the infants cried the less positive emotions the mothers experienced towards the infant. Even more worrying is that some anecdotal reports from perpetrators of shaken baby syndrome (see Recommended Reading) suggest that in some cases an infant's crying may be an important trigger for this kind of child abuse. Research published in the medical journal *The Lancet* supports this, by showing that 5.6% of parents reported having smothered, slapped or shaken their baby at least once because of its crying (Reijneveld *et al.*, 2004).

- Should we view crying as an important part of infants' early communication, or as a normal behavioural state like waking or sleeping?
- Is the communicative function of crying merely a side effect of evolutionary processes, or does it still have an important function in developing the mother–infant bond and ensuring healthy psychological development?
- Or does crying do more harm than good?

The four components of language

Language is made up of four main component parts. These four components are: phonology; semantics; syntax; and pragmatics. We will now consider each of these in turn in order to get a better understanding of this complex system, and how the different parts of it develop.

What is phonology?

When we talk about phonology, we are talking about the sound system of a language. Different languages contain different sounds, and if you have ever learned another language then you will know that just mastering the speech sounds you need to be able to pronounce certain words can be a big challenge. In fact, there are significant phonological differences even just between different dialects of the English language. The Scottish word 'loch' contains the phoneme /ch/ which does not feature in other English speakers' repertoire of sounds, and which they may therefore struggle to pronounce. In contrast, that same phoneme is a key part of the phonology of the German language, and Scottish students may find mastering the sounds necessary to pronounce German words easier than their traditional-English-speaking counterparts. Phonology also determines which sounds can precede or follow other sounds in a given language. For example, in English /s/ can be followed by /t/ as in the words 'star' or 'fast'. However the sound /z/ cannot be followed by /x/, nor /p/ by /q/.

It is important to note that it is not just the ability to produce the speech sounds of a language which is important in understanding children's phonological development, but also the ability to recognise and to tell the difference, or discriminate between different phonemes within a language. For example, in spoken English the /k/ sound in the word 'cat' actually sounds different to the /k/ sound when it appears in the spoken word 'ski'. However, if we get speakers of English to listen to different instances of the /k/ sound (say, by different speakers or taken from different words), they are unable to tell the difference between them. This means that these different instances of the speech sound /k/ all form one category of sound within spoken English. English speakers do not discriminate between different instances within the category of speech sound /k/. In contrast, speakers of Arabic can readily discriminate between different instances of the /k/ sound, because in Arabic these constitute different phonemes. Later in this chapter we will see how the ability to produce the sounds of a language develops, as well as the ability to perceive the sounds of language.

What are semantics?

Semantics refers to the part of language to do with the meanings of words, and also of sentences. As children learn language, they develop a vocabulary of words to which they attach certain meanings (not always correctly

Definitions

Phonology: the sound system of a particular language.
Semantics: the part of language concerned with the meanings of words and parts of words.
Syntax: the part of language concerned with the rules which govern how words can be combined to make sentences.
Pragmatics: the part of language concerned with its use in social contexts.
Phoneme: the smallest units of sound in a language.
Discriminate: in speech-sound perception, to be able to tell the difference between speech sounds of a language.
Category: a set of sounds or words perceived as belonging to the same group (e.g. all instances of the sound /s/ or all words relating to female humans).

at first, as we will see later on). As children's vocabularies grow they are able to organise the words they know into groups of words which are semantically related. The words 'cat' and 'kitten' have a lot in common in terms of their meanings and the animal to which they refer. They are therefore semantically related, but have key semantic differences in terms of the age of the animals to which they refer. Nevertheless, recognising that there are commonalities in their meanings is important in language development.

Even sentences which are grammatically correct may not be semantically accurate, if they do not make sense. For example, the sentence 'The carrot sang to the boy' is constructed correctly from a grammatical point of view, but it contradicts our semantic knowledge that the word 'carrot' denotes a vegetable which cannot sing.

What is syntax?

Syntax refers to the way in which words can be acceptably combined to create sentences or phrases in a given language. The sentence 'I am going to the shop' is syntactically correct in English, but combining the same words in a different way to say, 'I am to the shop going' is syntactically incorrect. Nevertheless, we may still be able to infer the meaning of what someone is trying to say from a sentence which is syntactically incorrect. The character Yoda in the *Star Wars* movies constructed sentences in this way and yet we are still able to follow what he is trying to say!

What are pragmatics?

Pragmatics refers to the social part of language and determines how language can be used appropriately in different contexts, and how meanings can be conveyed which go beyond the words themselves. For example, the convention of taking turns during conversations is part of the pragmatic system, and this begins to develop even before children have developed any spoken language, as

A cat or a kitten?
Source: O'Donnell

we will see later in the chapter. Telling jokes, or using language deliberately to make people laugh is part of this system as well, as is the ability to modify the way we use language depending upon who we are talking to.

STOP AND THINK

Reflection

- Have you ever heard anyone refer to things children say as 'refreshingly honest'?

- Young children often say things which we, as adults, may be thinking, but would not dream of saying out loud. Can you think of occasions where you have not said something, perhaps because of concern for causing embarrassment or insulting someone?

- How do you think a child learns the 'rules' concerning these aspects of language?

Consider the way that you might talk to a group of close friends when you are on a night out, and compare it to the way you might talk to your lecturer or to your grandparents? What are the differences between these different ways in which you use language? Knowledge and understanding of social contexts and of the effects of using language in different ways allows us to modify and adapt what we say and how we say it, to different situations.

Definition

Semantically related: words which have something in common in terms of their meaning.

How do infants' early social interactions prepare them for later language?

Turn-taking in feeding

Earlier in the chapter, we mentioned the importance of turn-taking for successful conversations to occur. This is a social aspect of language and researchers have found evidence that early social interactions which infants have with their caregivers may be important in preparing them for turn-taking in formal conversations later on. When they are feeding, infants fall into a rhythmic pattern which includes bursts of sucking separated by pauses. It seems as though these pauses are unique to human babies, as they have not been found in other mammals' feeding patterns (Wolff, 1968). The purpose and function of these pauses is not clear, as there does not seem to be any logical reason for them to occur. Infants are perfectly able to suck continuously without needing to take a break in between. They can suck and breathe at the same time and, although their bouts of sucking may get shorter over the course of a feed, the pauses stay at roughly the same length (Kaye and Brazelton, 1971). This is curious and has led researchers to investigate what happens during these pauses in order to try to explain what purpose they might serve.

It seems as though the infant's mother matches her own cycles of activity and rest with the infant's burst–pause sequences, by remaining passive whist the infant is sucking, and then inserting dialogue or 'jiggling' the baby during the pauses (Kaye, 1977; Kaye and Wells, 1980). This mirrors the conventional patterns of language which occur during conversational exchanges in later life. These cycles of resting and feeding may therefore play a part in the development of reciprocal turn-taking as part of the development of the pragmatic system.

Interestingly, some research has compared these kinds of rhythmic exchanges between infants and their mothers, in babies who were born prematurely and those who were born after a full-term pregnancy (Lester *et al.*, 1985). This research showed that these kinds of mother–infant interactions are less well synchronised in premature babies than in babies born at full-term. Other research has reported that children born prematurely show some delays in language development (e.g. Friedman and Sigman, 1981). Lester *et al.* (1985) suggest that this lack of synchrony in the earliest interactions between infants and their mothers may be at least partly responsible for these delays in language development seen in children who were born prematurely. If this is the case then it shows how important these early social interactions can be for later language development. These sorts of cycles and rhythms of social interaction also occur in contexts other than feeding, as the next section shows.

Cycles of attention

In other interactions between infants and their caregivers, there is evidence of the same kinds of rhythms as discussed in the previous section. For example, studies of mother–infant gazing show that babies will engage in cycles of attention and looking away. In adult communication, meeting someone's gaze is interpreted as an invitation to engage socially, and this seems to be mirrored in these infant interactions, where babies are able to indicate their willingness to engage socially by attending visually to their mother or other caregiver. They can control the amount of interaction that takes place by then looking away. Interactions between babies and their caregivers are very stimulating for babies and too much attention can lead to over-stimulation and upset. Babies can use these cycles of attention and looking away to regulate their level of excitement. Nonetheless, caregivers also need to be sensitive to the baby's state. Understanding the need to lower the level of stimulation when a baby looks away is an important part of the parent's role in an interaction, as persisting in trying to engage a baby who is not receptive to interaction can have adverse effects and lead to upset. Chapter 9, Attachment and Early Social Experiences, explores the development of an infant's bond with her mother or primary caregiver. It is interesting to note that parental sensitivity to infants may play an important part in the development of a child's attachment style (for more information about attachment styles in general, see Recommended Reading), and this sensitivity to an infant's cycles of attention regulation in pre-verbal interactions may indicate a parent's sensitivity to the infant.

For both parties, engaging in this kind of social interaction provides a positive shared experience. We will see later in this chapter how learning theorists' accounts of language development would conceptualise the importance of this kind of positive reinforcement for language development. But equally, if the interaction produces negative effects for the infant it may lower the likelihood of the infant engaging in this kind of interaction again. Thus, these early social interactions pave the way for later communicative exchanges and language.

Infant-directed speech

In the literature you may see this referred to as mother–child speech, parentese, baby talk, motherese or infant-directed speech. What we are talking about here is the kind of speech that is heard when adults talk to infants. This kind of speech has a number of distinct characteristics which make it quite different from normal adult-to-adult speech. It is generally of a higher pitch. It also tends to use a greater range of pitch, from high to low, which sounds exaggerated. This kind of speech is often slower, and words are articulated much more clearly. It is also simpler, using less complex words as well as less complex clauses and phrases. There is also more repetition than is usually heard in adult-to-adult speech.

Adults seem to make use of this kind of speech, almost without realising it, in their interactions with infants. There is evidence from research which shows that infant-directed speech exists in many different languages, even sign language (for more information on this, see Recommended Reading). Acquiring the speech sounds (phonology) of a language may be facilitated by the use of infant-directed speech, which exposes babies to their language in an exaggerated and simplified form, and this may therefore prepare them for its more complex forms later on. Having said this, it is important to note that exposure to infant-directed speech is not something which is necessary in order for language development to occur, as studies of different cultures have shown us that in some communities this special way of interacting with infants does not happen, and yet children in those communities develop in approximately the same ways and at the same rates as children who are exposed to infant-directed speech.

In one Mayan society, parents have been observed not to use infant-directed speech at all and yet children seem to acquire language quite normally (Pye, 1986). In Papua New Guinea, the Kaluli tribe treat children as though they do not have any understanding and so parents do not really address children verbally at all until later in life (Schiefflin and Ochs, 1983). Again, these children still go on to acquire language normally. So in spite of these examples of cultures where children's earliest exposures to the phonology, syntax and semantics of their language are not especially simplified, such children are nevertheless able to develop language normally, suggesting that whilst infant-directed speech may facilitate the development of language, it is not strictly necessary for development, as a component of a child's early exposure to language.

Theories of development

Having established what language is, what its component parts are, and how some of the foundations of language may be laid in infants' earliest social interactions, we will now explore some of the theoretical perspectives which try to explain how language develops. Before reading on, stop and think about your own beliefs regarding language.

STOP AND THINK

Reflection

- How significant is language as a feature of what makes humans different from other animals?

- Is there something 'special' or 'different' about language, or is it just one of many abilities that we have? What makes you think so?

- What do you think would happen to a child's language development if they had no contact with other people? What makes you think so?

Learning theory accounts

Learning theorists argue that language is just another kind of behaviour which we learn, albeit a verbal behaviour. If we accept this account then it implies that there are no in-born language abilities. This contrasts with Nativist accounts of language, which we will discuss in the next section, and which suggest that there are some abilities or aptitudes which infants are born with which allow for the development of language.

STOP AND THINK

Reflection

Consider some of the research we have already discussed in this chapter about children's earliest communicative encounters. Would these fit with the view that children are not born with any specific language abilities?

Learning theorists point out that from the time they are born, children are surrounded with language. We talk to babies all the time, even though we know that they cannot respond or even understand us. For example, Rheingold and Adams (1980) collected samples of speech which was directed to new-born infants by staff in a hospital neonatal nursery over a period of two months. Ten two-hour samples of speech were collected and analysed in terms of their grammatical characteristics, topic and whether they expressed warm regard or instructions. The researchers found that the speech which was directed to these infants was extensive, grammatically well-formed and occurred from the day the infants were born. This suggests that infants have ample opportunities to learn language quickly after birth without us needing to believe in the existence of abilities that are present within the child from birth.

The discussion in the previous section about the use of motherese is another way in which exposure to language after birth could arguably provide opportunities for infants to be exposed to their native language and thus learn it from an early age. Perhaps infants imitate the sounds of language to which they have been exposed, and learn the words and the grammatical rules by copying what they have heard. Social learning theorists emphasise how important parental approval and positive regard is in the process of language development, by influencing which sounds, words and sentences are repeated in future and thus shaping a child's

language development. Consider this example taken from an observation of a mother as she holds her 7 month old infant on her knee:

Baby Ivor: *Baba ba ba na na*
Mum: *(smiles) What are you saying baby?*
Ivor: *Ba ba ba na*
Mum: *Yes, I know (kisses baby on the nose)*
Ivor: *Ba ba ba da*
Mum: *(eyes wide, big smile) What did you say? What did you say?*
Ivor: *Ba ba ba da*
Mum: *Da! Did you say Da! Clever boy! What a clever boy! (touches nose to nose)*
Ivor: *Bababa da*
Mum: *Da! Yes baby! Yes! Dada! What a clever boy!*
Ivor: *Da da da da (jiggles)*
Mum: *Dada! (excited voice) That's a clever boy! You love your dada? Yes, you love your dada! Where's your dada? Where is he?*
Ivor: *Da da da da (big smile)*
Mum: *Dada! That's my clever boy! (three kisses) Dada! What a beautiful boy!*

It is likely that Ivor's vocalisation of the 'da' sound was produced as part of his expressive experimentation with speech sounds, along with 'ba' and 'na' sounds which were also produced in the early part of the exchange above. But clearly Mum picks up on the 'da' sound and repeats that particular sound to Ivor rather than the others. She also responds much more positively and enthusiastically to his production of the 'da' sound and by the end of this exchange we can see that Ivor is making that sound to the exclusion of others which were present at the beginning. Ivor therefore received a great deal of positive reinforcement from his mother for producing the 'da' sound, making it much more likely that this sound would be produced again. It is unlikely that Ivor actually intended to say 'Dada' (meaning Dad), but the likelihood of Ivor now saying 'Dada' in the future is increased.

Definition

Shaping: a process by which children's utterances move closer to correct speech as the result of positive reinforcement which leads to a series of successive approximations.

In this way, social learning theorists suggest that language is learned through a process of gradually shaping sounds into word-like sounds, which will eventually become words associated with specific meanings. So do we really need to believe in any in-born language abilities to be able to explain how the process of language develops? Well, some people suggest that learning in infancy is not enough to account for all of the aspects of language development, as we will see in the next section.

The Nativist account

Noam Chomsky (see Recommended Websites) is a leading linguist who has suggested that humans are born with something called a language acquisition device (LAD). Chomsky does not believe that learning in infancy can account for all of the different aspects of language development. In particular, the suggestion that children can develop an understanding of the complex rules of grammar or syntax of a language through simple learning by imitation and reinforcement is unlikely. If you listen to adults talking, it is rare that they speak in fully-formed grammatically correct sentences, making it improbable that children would be able to learn the rules which govern language in this way. Figure 5.1 gives an excerpt from a transcript of a conversation between two colleagues at work and illustrates the fact that adult language does not always involve grammatically correct sentences. Adult conversation is quite messy, with lots of hesitation and unnecessary or superfluous words. Exposed to this kind of language, it is difficult to imagine how infants could make sense of what they heard to such an extent that they could work out what was correct and incorrect syntax. Perhaps infant-directed speech helps with this, by exposing babies to exaggeratedly simplified speech which cuts out the unnecessary aspects of adult speech. Yet we have already considered evidence from other cultures which shows that even when the different kind of infant-directed speech does not feature in a

> A: So it's just like (1) I don't know (.) you know the thing is (1) um (1) it's like there's no appreciation of what they have to
> B: I know (.) I know how you feel (.) I feel the
> A: I know (1) and so I think we have to (.) like
> B: We do (.) say something about it
> A: Yeh because otherwise it's just gonna keep on and (.) there's never gonna be
> B: I know (.) it'll just be the same again
> A: And it's not even just about him (.) it's a general
> B: I know (.) like principle
> A: Yeh the principle or something (.) I don't know
> Key: (.) = short pause; (1) = 1 second pause

Figure 5.1. Excerpt from transcript of a conversation between colleagues.

society's interactions with infants, they develop language in approximately the same ways, so even the use of motherese cannot account for the learning of syntax.

Chomsky has also pointed out the predictability of the way in which language develops, and the fact that regardless of country, culture or which specific language is to be learned, children reach certain developmental language milestones at roughly the same points in development. In fact, there are numerous websites which parents can visit which contain information on the speech and language abilities which typically developing children are expected to reach at different ages (see Recommended Websites). This lends further weight to the argument that learning from environmental influences and behaviour cannot be solely responsible for language development. If it were then we would expect to see far more variation in language development as a result of variations in the learning environment.

Studies of the kinds of mistakes which children make in their attempts to master language suggest that instead of learning syntax directly from speech, a LAD which they are born with enables children to pick up on the regularities which do exist in everyday speech. On the basis of these regularities, the LAD comes up with mini-theories about the rules which govern speech. For example, children may say 'mouses' instead of mice, and yet it is very unlikely that they would have learned to say

> **Definition**
>
> Language acquisition device: a hypothetical cognitive structure predisposed towards the acquisition of language and sensitive to rule-based regularities in everyday speech, therefore allowing for the development of grammar and syntax.

'mouses' as the result of hearing it said by other adults. An adult would not make this error in the construction of this plural noun, and so learning theories of language cannot account for these kinds of mistakes in children's development. But if there is a LAD which has generated a mini-theory (based on lots of instances of pluralised nouns in the English language) that you make a plural by adding an /s/, then it is possible to understand how this error (of saying 'mouses') might have come about. It is only after more exposure to language that children's mini-theories will be modified, as they come across instances of plurals which contradict their existing theory. Eventually they will arrive at a more sophisticated understanding of the rules which govern the pluralisation of nouns, which incorporates some of the exceptions too. We will be looking at some other kinds of errors that children make in their developing language later in this chapter, because they can offer us useful insights into the way in which language is acquired, the mini-theories which children have about language at different stages of development and the way in which they come to appreciate the relationship between words and their referents.

A LAD, if there is such a thing, would have to have some sort of biological basis, but it is not entirely clear what this might be. It is possible that the LAD might represent a particular part of the brain, and there is certainly evidence that there are particular parts of the brain which are involved in language. It is widely understood that in adults the left hemisphere of the brain is important for language, and in 1987 a review of the literature about lateralisation of brain functioning confirmed that this is also the case for children from birth (Hahn, 1987). Evidence from patients who have suffered brain injuries has helped us to understand which parts of the left hemisphere may be implicated in language.

Pierre Paul Broca, a French neurosurgeon and pathologist, was the first to identify a specific part of the left hemisphere which is involved in language. In 1961 Broca conducted an examination of a patient with a specific language impairment following that patient's death, and found lesions in a particular part of the posterior of his left hemisphere which has come to be known as 'Broca's area'. This part of the brain is important for the production of speech (and is sometimes referred to as the speech centre). Individuals whose speech and language is affected by damage to this area are often referred to as suffering from Broca's aphasia, which means that they have problems with expressive language, their sentences will be short and their speech very broken and sometimes distorted (for more information, including classic and contemporary papers about Broca's area, see Recommended Reading). Broca's area is connected by a pathway of nerves to another part of the brain implicated in language, called Wernicke's area. The location of these two areas of the brain is illustrated in Fig. 5.2.

Wernicke's area is most important for the comprehension of language, and is named after the German psychiatrist and neurologist Carl Wernicke who first described the symptoms associated with damage to the area, in 1908. Individuals with damage to this area are able to produce speech which has the same kind of sound and rhythm as normal speech, but which does not have any real meaning, and they have difficulty in understanding language. Such symptoms are known as Wernicke's aphasia.

It is thought that Wernicke's area is important for language development. Damage to the area means that children will be unable to make sense of the language that they are exposed to, thus seriously impairing its development. Figure 5.2 illustrates the connection between

Definition

Lateralisation: the principle that some specific psychological functions are located in one or the other side of the brain's two cortical hemispheres.

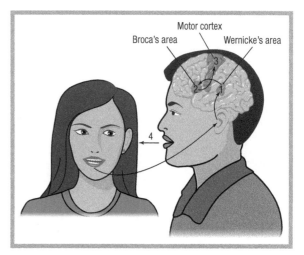

Figure 5.2. Broca's area and Wernicke's area are both important for language.

Broca's and Wernicke's areas, and their involvement in language, from comprehension to production.

Contemporary research into these biological bases for language have lent support to the critical period hypothesis, through studies of children who have suffered traumatic brain injuries. Adults who develop language impairments following these kinds of injuries are likely to be permanently impaired, and some research with children suffering head injuries has also found long-lasting effects on language for at least some children. For example, Jordan and Murdoch (1993) studied 11 children over a period of 18 months following head injuries, assessing various different aspects of their language abilities, and found that few of them recovered to what would be considered 'normal' levels on all of the measures after 18 months. However, the youngest child in that study was 7 years old at the time of their injury. Another longitudinal study, this time of an infant who was 17 months and 10 days old when she suffered a head trauma suggests that despite an initial decline in her language ability immediately following the injury, six months after her injury there were no longer any significant impairments on any of the measures of language that were used (Trudeau *et al.*, 2000). This kind of evidence supports the idea that there may be a period in the early part of a child's life where parts of the brain develop specifically for language but that, if there is damage to those parts of the brain, there can be some compensation and other parts of the brain may be recruited for language. This ability of brains to recover their functioning is referred to as plasticity. In the 1960s, Eric Lenneberg suggested that the critical period for children's language learning was between 18 months of age and the onset of puberty (Lenneberg, 1967). This original suggestion was based on the fact that language develops quickly during the

early years of a child's life, and Lenneberg believed that there was a biological basis for this, in that language develops due to the development of the brain as children mature. The fact that more contemporary research has shown that brain damage in children over the age of 5 typically leads to at least some long-term effects on language, though, suggests that the critical period for language development has passed by this time, and that the opportunity for the brain to recover its functioning in this area is lost.

Overall, the ideas which Chomsky put forward about a possible LAD and the research from neuroscience regarding the importance of certain parts of the brain for language do suggest that external input and learning alone cannot account for how language is acquired and develops. Yet it is clear from the evidence regarding learning and the social world that environmental influences do affect how language develops too. Alternative accounts of language have evolved which emphasise the interaction between in-born abilities with a biological basis and input from the environment. These 'interactionist' accounts suggest that language can be understood best as an interaction between these two factors, and they are explored in the next section.

Interactionist accounts

Some interactionist accounts of language development make us think about the interaction between the development of language and the development of cognition and thinking abilities in general. For example, if we consider Piaget's theory of cognitive development (explored in Chapter 2, Theoretical Perspectives) then we recall that he believed in a progression through stages of development for children. Each stage means that a child is able to think and interact with the world in a particular way, which is fundamentally different to the way in which they thought about and interacted with the world in the previous stage. Early on in the present chapter, we discussed the fact that language is a symbolic system, where words represent things in the world. Language development can therefore be seen as part of a child's broader representational development, as they move into Piaget's later stages of development (see Chapter 2), where language and thinking are no longer dependent upon the immediate environment. Acquiring language allows us to think and talk about objects, people or events which

---

Definitions

Critical period hypothesis: the suggestion that there is a specific period of time in the early part of a child's life (suggestions about when this begins and ends vary), during which language learning should occur in order to develop normally.

Plasticity: the ability of the brain to reorganise neural pathways either to recover lost functioning due to damage, or in response to learning from new experiences.

are not present in our environment. Eventually, more sophisticated language allows us to talk and think about abstract concepts like justice or truth, which have no concrete referents in the external world. An 18 month old infant has not yet reached the stage of cognitive development where thinking about such abstract concepts is possible. At this age, infants' thinking is focused on basic concepts like 'mummy' or 'food', 'hot' or 'sad' – these are things that they know about, and their language reflects the level of development of their knowledge and thinking. As children encounter new concepts, they will learn new words to associate with those concepts and then they will be able to talk about and think about the new concepts. Learning a new word which does not fit with any existing concepts will mean that a new concept is constructed (Kuczaj, 1982).

One of the Stop and Think boxes earlier in this chapter asked you to think about how important language really is, and whether you think it is much different to some of the other abilities we develop. In this particular theoretical framework, we can see that language is presented as part of the process of cognitive development, which means that we should not regard it as a special or significantly different aspect of development.

Other interactionist accounts emphasise the fact that children do not develop language in isolation, and allow us to consider how input from the external world works with innate abilities that a child brings into the world.

Looking at some of the cases of children who have developed without input from the external world can help to illustrate this.

In 1992, an American journalist called Russ Rymer published a book called 'Genie: A Scientific Tragedy', one of many such books which tells the true and harrowing story of a young girl who was discovered aged 13 years of age, locked away in her parents' home in California, USA. She had spent her entire childhood strapped to a chair and was kept almost completely isolated during this time. Her father subjected her to physical beatings if she made any sounds, and when she was rescued, as well as having various physical problems, she could not speak. For many years after she was found, Genie was surrounded by therapists of many kinds, and although she did eventually learn some basic words and word combinations, she did not develop normal language abilities and in particular she did not acquire an understanding of grammar or syntax. Sadly there have been other instances of children who for various reasons have lived the early parts of their lives without being exposed to language. Such cases lend weight to the critical period hypothesis discussed previously, which suggests that language needs to develop within the first few years of life if a typical developmental pattern is to be established (see Recommended Websites for a link to a site devoted to cases of these kinds of children).

RESEARCH METHODS

Single case study research in language development

The study of Genie following her rescue is an example of single case study research. Unlike other large-scale research methods, single case studies do not necessarily allow us to generalise to an entire population. So the fact that Genie's language was affected in certain ways by her deprivation does not allow us to conclude that any child subject to the same circumstances would develop in the same way. However, case studies like this do allow us to carry out in-depth studies of naturally occurring phenomena which would simply not be

possible to manipulate artificially for the purposes of an experiment.

Obviously we could not remove infants from their families and keep them in conditions similar to those which Genie experienced, merely for the purposes of studying the effects on their development. But when cases like these occur, tragic though they are, they provide an opportunity for psychologists to learn something. What is crucial, though, is that the welfare of the child is always paramount, and that the researchers' interests are always secondary to the need to provide the best possible support and care for the child.

In these ways then, interactionist approaches to understanding and explaining how and why language develops allow us to think about how abilities which are specific to language may interact with other cognitive abilities, and also how they may interact with input from the social world. Having explored these three major theoretical explanations for language development, the next part of this chapter will focus on the four component parts of language (phonology, semantics, syntax, pragmatics), and will describe what developments occur in those four domains across childhood, so that we can start to build up a picture of what language looks like (or, more accurately, *sounds* like), at different stages of development.

Phonological development

The development of speech-sound perception

In order to use language, we need to be able to understand the spoken words that we hear, as well as to be able to produce words ourselves. Hearing and understanding spoken words requires auditory perceptual abilities, and this section explores some of what we know about how the ability to perceive speech sounds develops in children. For adults to effectively use language, it is important to be able to discriminate (to hear the difference) between different categories of speech sound, and there is little point in us being able to discriminate between different sounds *within* a category of speech sound. As discussed earlier, in Arabic, it is important to be able to discriminate between the different categories of /k/ sound, because these constitute different phonemes in Arabic. However, when speaking English there is little advantage in being able to discriminate within the single category of /k/ sound, since these are perceived by English speakers as belonging to the same category of phoneme.

In a piece of groundbreaking research published in the esteemed journal *Science* in 1971, four psychologists presented convincing evidence that children are able to make these kinds of discriminations between categories of speech sounds, yet not within categories of speech sound, at a surprisingly early age (Eimas *et al.*, 1971). Using a habituation technique and a non-nutritive

dummy, infants from English-speaking families aged just 1 and 4 months of age were exposed to the phonemes /p/ and /b/. By measuring changes in the infants' rates of sucking these psychologists were able to establish that even at 1 month of age infants could tell the difference between /p/ and /b/ and would respond to them as different sounds, but that they did not discriminate within the categories of /p/ and /b/. For infants' speech sound perception to so closely mirror that of adults' was very surprising, given that at such a young age these infants will have had only a very limited exposure to spoken language. This evidence suggests that from early in the very first year of life, children can already make important distinctions between the sounds which, in their native language, constitute different phonemes. This evidence of infants' early abilities to discriminate between different phonemes has been shown to extend beyond the languages to which an infant has been exposed. Streeter (1976) found that Kenyan infants aged around 2 months were able to discriminate between phonemes which are not distinct in their own native language. This may indicate that the ability to perceive differences in speech-sounds is in-born, rather than learned as a result of exposure to language. The Nature–Nurture box considers what the implications of these sorts of findings might be for the different theories of language development considered earlier, and how the conclusions which we draw might be affected by other research.

In terms of the continued development of speech-sound perception, it is interesting that despite the very good abilities which young infants have to discriminate between different phonemes as mentioned above, their abilities have actually been shown to diminish as they get older, as discussed in Chapter 4, Prenatal Development and Infancy. This is an interesting phenomenon as we tend to assume that, as a general rule, children get better at things as they get older. In the area of speech-sound perception, though, they get worse as they get older. Can you think of why this might be the case? Consider Chomsky's ideas about the existence of a language acquisition device. If all humans are born with one of these then it must be capable of facilitating the development of whichever language a child is exposed to, since we can assume that the LAD would not know in advance which language to prepare for. Yet it then needs to be able to respond specifically to whichever language the child needs to learn. Perhaps, then, the LAD comes equipped with generic capacities to respond to all possible languages, but as it begins to

NATURE–NURTURE

Is speech-sound perception innate?

Let's consider what the significance of this evidence from Eimas *et al.* (1971) might be to our understanding of how children develop language. Earlier on in this chapter we considered different theoretical approaches to the understanding of language development, and one of the key questions was about whether children are born with innate language abilities, innate predispositions towards language acquisition, or whether learning is more responsible for language development. What do you think this key piece of research suggests in terms of language development? Could it be that infants of just 1 month old have already learned which speech sounds belong to one category and which represent different categories, as a result of their limited experience with spoken language? This seems unlikely to explain the results, and the original authors suggested that the evidence supported a view that some aspects of language development are 'part of the biological makeup of the organism' (p. 306) and that children are therefore born with innate language abilities. Some more recent research suggests that it is unlikely to be this straightforward either, though.

Patricia Kuhl, a Professor of Speech and Hearing Sciences, did several pieces of research in the 1970s and 1980s which suggest that animals such as chinchillas and macaques are able to make the same kinds of categorical discriminations between human speech sounds as infant children and adult humans can (see Recommended Reading). It is difficult to see why these kinds of animals would also have a built-in capacity for perceiving human speech sounds. What

seems more likely is that humans (and other animals) are born with some innate mechanism for making sense of sounds generally, but that this is not exclusively for the purposes of developing language. This mechanism is likely to be sensitive to auditory information generally, and for human infants would then provide the basis for the categorisation of speech sounds specifically.

The particular language to which an infant is exposed in infancy would then allow for the development of categorical discrimination between the sounds of that language, suggesting an interaction between children's in-born abilities and learning from the world around them. This suggestion is supported by the fact that infants' ability to discriminate between phonemes is one of the few areas of development where children get worse as they get older! Infants at 6 months of age are able to discriminate more phonemes than they can at 12 months. This seems to reflect the effects of environmental input on infants' initial auditory processing abilities, which leads to a gradual specialisation that enables the discrimination of phonemes from the child's native language, and a decrement in the ability to discriminate phonemes from other languages.

These pieces of research therefore lead us towards an understanding of the development of language which does not stem from innate language abilities per se, but from innate mechanisms or abilities to process certain types of information. Development occurs as the result of the interaction between those mechanisms and the particular information which infants are then exposed to.

specialise in a particular language it develops an expertise in hearing and responding to the sounds of that language at the expense of others. In some groundbreaking research in the 1980s, an American child psychologist Janet Werker investigated exactly this possibility and was able to show that the decline in infants' abilities to perceive differences between different categories of speech-sounds in languages

other than their own occurs between 6 and 12 months of age (Werker, 1989). This seems to be one area of children's development, then, where their abilities are actually considerably better than those of adults, and reminds us that understanding children's development is more complicated than just following improvements in their abilities over time.

The development of speech-sound production

Having looked at some of what we know about children's developing abilities to perceive speech-sounds, we will now explore the pattern of development which characterises children's speech-sound production. Following a Piagetian approach to development in this area, initial research identified a series of stages through which children's vocalisations progress, and which seem to be remarkably similar across children despite differences in language, culture and context (see, for example Oller, 1980; Stark, 1980; 1981). Table 5.1 presents an overview of the main stages (adapted from Stark, 1981). Physical maturation in the child's vocal system was thought to underpin the development of vocalisation through these stages, as infants then explore their developing abilities in interaction with others. We will see a little later that more recent research places greater significance on the influence of social interaction on the development of speech-sound production than previously.

Infants' earliest vocalisations include burping, crying, coughing and sneezing, all of which are produced in response to physiological or emotional states. An infant may be able to communicate some physiological need to us through crying, and in the first 2 months of life these vocalisations are referred to as 'reflexive' and are not viewed as language proper. Earlier in this chapter, we explored what kinds of communication can occur before verbal communication, and we discussed the significance of crying in particular. The amount of crying which infants do seems to decrease after the second month of life, and it is then that more speech-like vocalisations occur. Cooing and laughing characterise a

great deal of the vocalisations of infants between 2 and 4 months of age. The third stage is characterised by what is referred to as babbling or vocal play and features between 4 and 6 months. During this stage, infants have begun to master some of the physical movements and manipulations which are required to make sounds (such as moving their lips and tongue and making their vocal chords vibrate) and they begin to play, explore and experiment. This is the vocal equivalent of exploring a new object which they have begun to be able to grasp – to see what it does, how it feels and what they can do with it. The next stage, canonical babbling, features sounds and combinations of sounds which actually sound like words (such as mama or dada, as seen in the example of Baby Ivor's exchange with his mother earlier in the chapter), though it is unlikely that infants are attaching any meaning to the word-like sounds that they produce during this stage. Next comes more complex babbling which is often referred to in the literature as modulated babbling, and which features between 10 and 15 months. During this stage, infants begin to play and explore the patterns of intonation, stress, pitch and tone which characterise more adult speech. This is the final stage before proper articulation and the use of referential words occurs at between 12 and 15 months. These stages are summarised in Table 5.1.

Definition

Referential words: common nouns used to denote real objects.

Table 5.1. Stages of infant vocalisation.

Stage	Main features	Approximate age range
I: Reflexive vocalisation	Crying, burping, coughing, sneezing	0–6/8 weeks
II: Interactive sound making	Cooing, laughing	6–19 weeks
III: Vocal play	Deliberate exploration of sounds	18–30/35 weeks
IV: Canonical babbling	Sounds and sound-combinations which begin to sound like words	35 weeks–1 year
V: Complex/modulated babbling	Interactive use of babbling; exploration of stress, intonation etc.	10–15 months
VI: Referential words	First words used to refer to things	12–15 months

Source: adapted from Stark (1981).

Semantic development

The growth of vocabulary in infancy

Once a child produces her first referential words, her vocabulary begins gradually to grow. This process is fairly slow for the first three or four months, adding just a few new words to her vocabulary each month. Once her vocabulary has reached between 50 and 100 words, however, the process of vocabulary growth accelerates rapidly. This is commonly referred to in the literature as the vocabulary spurt. Different authors disagree as to the exact rate at which a child's vocabulary grows during this spurt period, but some have reported cases where a child's vocabulary growth has increased from learning less than 10 new words one week, to learning as many as 40–70 new words the next week (e.g. Dromi, 1987; Mervis *et al.*, 1992). The vocabulary spurt often occurs at around 18 months of age, but the exact point varies between children, and some children may not display a spurt at all (see, for example, Ganger and Brent, 2004).

There is a subtle but important distinction to be made between the size of a child's vocabulary and the rate of their vocabulary growth. Think about a Porsche Carerra driving down the M1 motorway. As it joins the motorway at junction 26 the Porsche is doing 57 miles per hour (mph), and by the time it reaches junction 27 it is doing 70 miles per hour. This tells us the absolute speed at which the Porsche was travelling at these two points, but it doesn't tell us about the Porsche's rate of acceleration between those two points. A Ford Fiesta could also join the M1 at junction 26 doing 57 mph, and have reached 70 mph by junction 27, but we would imagine that the Porsche's rate of acceleration would have been greater than the Fiesta's, and that this would be due to differences in the engine capacity of the two cars. The spurt which is seen in children's vocabulary growth is evidence to many psychologists that there is suddenly a different 'engine' powering the process of word acquisition – that there has been some fundamental change in children's language abilities which allows for a much faster rate of vocabulary growth. In other words, it is suggested that some kind of underlying cognitive developments may be responsible for the spurt. This possibility is explored in the next section.

Cognitive development and semantic development

One suggestion as to what fundamental cognitive change might underlie the dramatic increase in vocabulary growth seen in the second year of a child's life is that they experience what is known as the naming insight. The majority of infants' first words are nouns which refer to objects or people. The naming insight theory suggests that at first infants associate words with particular objects, activities, people or routines in their lives, but they do not yet realise that in fact every thing has a name, and conversely that every name refers to some thing (Reznick and Goldfield, 1992). Once they experience this realisation, their interest in naming things and their ability to learn new names for things, increases. This may be why the vocabulary spurt often coincides with children beginning to ask the question 'What's that?' as they start to realise that everything that they encounter has a name.

Another feature of this period of development is the development of semantic relations – grouping words together according to their common membership of some kind of group or category. The development of early categorisation in infancy is discussed in Chapter 4, Prenatal Development and Infancy, and its role in mathematical thinking is explored in Chapter 7, The Development of Mathematical Thinking. Alison Gopnik and Andrew Meltzoff are both eminent developmental psychologists who have carried out some research into the role of categorisation in children's language development. In one study, infants between 15 and 21 months of age were observed playing with different sets of objects (Gopnik and Meltzoff, 1987). Each set of eight objects consisted of four objects of one type (for example, four plastic boxes) and four objects of another type (for example, four balls). The infants' behaviour as they played with and

Definitions

Vocabulary spurt: a point in language development where the rate of acquisition of new words is thought to accelerate rapidly.

Naming insight: the realisation that all things have names, leading to a fundamental change in the way children think about the world.

manipulated these objects was observed, with the researchers paying particular attention to whether the infants exhibited any of three different levels of grouping behaviour: (1) single category grouping – this is when a child systematically displaces four objects of one type and groups them together. The other type of object does not need to have been manipulated in order for single-category grouping to be said to have occurred; (2) serial touching of both object types – this is when a child touches the four objects of one type one after the other, and then touches the four objects of the other type one after the other; (3) two category grouping – this is when a child moves all eight objects from their original locations and systematically sorts them into two distinct groups. This was the highest level of categorisation to be observed. They observed each infant on these categorisation tasks at three-weekly intervals until he or she had passed all of the tasks. In addition to the infants' categorisation, the researchers were also interested in their vocabulary development, and noted when each infant's vocabulary spurt occurred.

They found quite a lot of variation in the ages at which individual infants each began to produce the three levels of categorisation behaviour, but the mean age at which level three categorisation was observed was 17.24 months. They also found a great deal of individual variation in the age at which the vocabulary spurt occurred, but the mean age at which it happened was 18.33 months. What was particularly interesting, though, was that these researchers found a strong correlation between the age of the vocabulary spurt and the age of the development of level three categorisation. None of the infants in this study had a vocabulary spurt before they were able to make level three categorisations. This makes it seem as though the development of this understanding of semantic relations or category membership is a necessary prerequisite to the spurt in vocabulary which is seen in children at around this point in their development. None of the infants in this study had a vocabulary spurt before they reached level three categorisation, and the mean amount of time which elapsed between this kind of categorisation and the vocabulary spurt was 33 days, which again suggests that the two are closely linked developmentally. Think again about the different theories of language development which were considered earlier in this chapter. This kind of evidence seems to lend support to the interactionist accounts of language development which emphasise the interrelationships between the development of language and the development of other more general cognitive abilities.

The Cutting Edge box which follows explores an interesting, and somewhat controversial topic in contemporary language development – that of baby signing. The underlying symbolic nature of language means that, for hearing-impaired children and adults, signing can be used as a form of communication, and this has been extended to pre-verbal infants on the assumption that whilst they may not yet be able to use words, symbols of a visual form can be learned.

Learning the meanings of words

After the vocabulary spurt, children's vocabularies continue to grow, so that by the time they reach 6 years of age some estimates suggest that their vocabularies may be as large as 14000 words. Initially, the words which infants produce are primarily common nouns and action verbs, but they also include sound effects such as animal noises (for example, 'moo') and people words (for example, 'Daddy'). Common nouns include animals, vehicles, toys and food, such as 'dog' or 'ball'. Action verbs include words such as 'go' and 'give'. One cross-cultural study of English-speaking infants, Mandarin-speaking infants and Cantonese-speaking infants found that there were a lot of cross-cultural commonalities in the first words which are produced, and that six of the top 20 first words produced by infants are shared across all three of these languages (Tardif et al., 2008). These were 'Daddy', 'Mommy', 'Bye', 'Hi', 'UhOh' and; 'WoofWoof'. These are the kinds of words which reflect objects or people which are immediately present in infants' environments, or which reflect infants' routines. This is consistent with theories of development such as Piaget's (explored in Chapter 2, Theoretical Perspectives) which suggest that at this stage infants' cognitive development reflects a reliance upon the immediate environment. Their language development here allows them to interact with their environment and is limited to that with which they have had direct experience.

Learning a new word is not as easy as you might think, though. Imagine you are walking down the street with a young child in a buggy, and the child points across the road and asks, 'What's that?'. As you look across the

CUTTING EDGE

The debate surrounding baby signing

In recent years, there has been an explosion of movements advocating the use of sign language with babies, all of which tell us that there are a variety of benefits which sign language can bring in terms of an infant's development, from assisting in the development of spoken language to increasing a child's intelligence. Yet at present there is not a large body of research evidence upon which to base all of these assertions. As a result, it has sparked debate amongst contemporary psychologists, and a recent issue of the British Psychological Society's own publication *The Psychologist* ran an article on the subject as its cover story (Doherty-Sneddon, 2008).

The arguments in favour of baby signing suggest that it may be a way of supporting the development of language in the period before speech emerges, because manual communication is easier at that age than vocalisation. Babies develop broad motor control fairly early in development when compared to the more complex and fine motor control which is required to allow for the manipulation of vocal chords, lips, mouth, tongue and other associated manipulations which are necessary for articulation.

The underlying structure of both kinds of language as symbolic systems means that objects or actions can be referred to using any symbol, whether it is a word or a sign. Chimpanzees and other non-human primates have been taught to use sign language based on this argument in the past as well. Yet many of the systems of sign language which have been produced for parents to use with their children come from interpreters of sign language for the deaf, and psychologists are questioning whether findings from work with deaf children can simply be extended to hearing children. One system which has been designed by psychologists is called Baby Signs ® Inc. (see Recommended Websites). Linda Acredolo and Susan Goodwyn based this system on the kinds of gestures which are made naturally by children as they move from pre-verbal communication to early vocalisations, and also on signs used in American Sign Language.

A review of 17 research reports about baby signing failed to conclude that early exposure to sign language is beneficial to children's development, primarily because there were methodological weaknesses in the research which was done (Johnston *et al.*, 2005). Some of the results are also contradictory and difficult to interpret. For example, in a study carried out by the psychologists behind Baby Signs ® Inc. the development of a first group of infants whose parents received training in sign language at 10 months of age was compared with the development of a second group whose parents received training to encourage verbal language and with a third group whose parents received no training (e.g. Acredolo and Goodwyn, 2000). The results are somewhat contradictory in that whilst children in the first group showed higher receptive language scores relative to the third group when they were tested at 19 and 24 months, at 15, 30 and 36 months there were no significant differences between the groups. Children in the first group also had higher expressive language scores relative to the third group at 15 and 24 months, yet there were no differences at 19, 30 or 36 months. This suggests that any advances which sign language brings to language development is variable and only evident at certain points in development, but also that by 36 months there is no advantage to signing.

In terms of the scientific evidence, then, it is clear that more evidence is needed before we can draw any conclusions about the extent to which baby signing may be a useful tool in facilitating the development of language. Yet as an emerging field of study this is a new and interesting area which is likely to be a focus for developmental psychology in the years to come.

street you see a man walking a dog, and you reply, 'Doggy'. The first thing to consider here is whether your assumption about what the child was pointing to is correct. Perhaps the child was pointing at a bus stop or a tree! What effect is this exchange going to have on the child's word-learning, do you think? How will we know whether the child has successfully learned a word or not? What would 'count' as successful word learning? When dealing with common nouns like 'dog', 'daddy', 'apple' or 'train', we want children eventually to arrive at an understanding of the appropriate object or category of objects, to which the referential word applies. For example, we want this child to use the word 'doggy' to refer to all dogs, but not to cats or cows. We would not want them to use the word 'doggy' to refer to bus stops or trees! But when children do use words incorrectly, it provides us with an insight into how their learning of that word has occurred. The next section explores what kinds of errors commonly occur in children's word learning, and what these can tell us about the process of learning words.

Using children's errors to understand referential word learning

There are four common types of errors which children make in their learning of referential words. These are underextension, overextension, overlap and mismatch.

Underextension

Underextension is when a child uses a word to refer to only a sub-group of the category of objects to which that word applies. For example, in the case of the situation described above, underextension would occur if the child subsequently uses the word 'doggy' to refer to that particular dog, each time he encounters it on the street, but does not apply it to any other dog that he comes across. This might seem odd, but let's think about what else could have happened in the example above. Imagine once again that you are walking this child in his buggy and he points across the road and says, 'What's that?'. As you look across the road, you see your neighbour walking his dog, Buster. You respond, 'Buster'. In actual fact, Buster is just one exemplar of the broader category of dogs. Saying 'Buster' is correct, but saying 'Doggy' is also correct. How is the child supposed to understand

the difference between these two possible responses, and recognise that the two words 'Buster' and 'Doggy' should be applied to a different range of objects? Clearly the process of learning a word and what it refers to is not as simple as it seems.

When children underextend their use of a word, then, we know that in the process of learning the word they have mistakenly associated it with only a sub-group of the category of objects to which it actually refers.

Overextension

Overextension is almost the opposite of underextension, and occurs when a child uses a word to refer to the whole category of objects to which it refers, but more besides! Again, let's think about the example above, and assume that you have responded, 'Doggy' when the child points across the road. Some time later, you pass another dog on the street, and the child shouts, 'Doggy!'. But later still, you pass a cat and the child shouts, 'Doggy!'. And when the child sees a goat on television the following day he shouts, 'Doggy!'. These are examples of overextension.

Think back to when the child initially pointed across the road and said, 'What's that?'. Your interpretation of the question was, 'What's the name for that particular kind of animal?', and so you answered, 'Doggy'. It is possible, though, that to the child, the question 'What's that?' meant 'What's the name for hairy things with four legs?' and so your answer 'Doggy' is now the word that the child applies to refer to all instances of hairy things with four legs. The difficulty for us in interpreting the child's question 'What's that?' is that this simple two-word question could potentially mean many different things. This is something that we will explore more fully in the next section on the development of syntax. But when children overextend a word, we know that in the process of learning that word they have mistakenly associated it with more than just the category of objects to which it refers.

Overlap

Overlap can be thought of as a cross between underextension and overextension. Let's use a different example this time. Imagine you are with a young child at home and the child points to the mug of coffee you are holding and says, 'What's that?'. You reply, 'Coffee'. The child then correctly says, 'Coffee' whenever she sees someone with a mug of coffee, but not when she sees someone with coffee in a cup or in a Styrofoam container. However, the child also says, 'Coffee' whenever she sees someone with a mug of tea. In this way the child is correctly using the word 'coffee' to refer to some appropriate referents, but not all appropriate referents (this is underextension) whilst also using the word to refer to some inappropriate referents as well (this is overextension). This tells us that in learning the meaning of the word 'coffee' this child has correctly associated it, but with only a sub-set of the category to which it refers, whilst simultaneously incorrectly associating it with referents from other categories as well.

Mismatch

Mismatch occurs when there are no correct associations between a word and its category of referents. For example, in the example above when the child pointed and said, 'What's that?', you answered, 'Coffee'. Let's imagine, though, that the child was not pointing at your coffee mug at all, and was instead pointing at the window behind you. If the child subsequently used the word 'coffee' to refer to windows, then this would be an example of mismatch.

When we think of examples like these, it is surprisingly easy to see how these kinds of errors could occur in the process of children's learning of referential word meanings. It is clear that children may initially simply associate words with specific instances of categories of objects, like when the child used the word 'doggy' to refer only to one particular dog that he encountered regularly on the street. To arrive at a more sophisticated understanding that the single word 'doggy' should be used to refer to an entire category of a particular type of animal, children need to be able to group words together and to recognise that some words refer to whole sets of related objects. This means that upon encountering any new dog that they have never seen before, they will nevertheless be able to correctly name it, and this allows their language to move beyond the world which is immediately surrounding them. This is why the kinds of conceptual insights which children achieve with things like the naming insight or an understanding of semantic relations, as discussed above, mean that children's language development can move beyond their immediate environment, and this is reflected in a more sophisticated understanding of language and words. Learning that words can be

related to one another in groups provides a framework within which children can organise their words.

We also need to bear in mind that children may infer the meaning of new words from the language which surrounds them in everyday life, and not just from situations where they have directly asked for the meaning of an object. This leaves even more room for potential errors in word learning, but research has also shown that the more speech which surrounds a child, the better their vocabularies, so we should probably not worry too much about the possibilities which exist for errors, and view these as a normative part of the development of language.

For example, Huttenlocher *et al.* (1991) studied 22 children from the age of 14 months to 26 months. They observed the children in their daily activities with their mothers and took measures of the children's vocabularies as well as the amount of exposure to their parent's speech which each child had. The results of this study showed that the amount of exposure to their parent's speech was very important in explaining differences in vocabulary growth which were observed between different children. Think back to the 'Illustrative example' at the beginning of this chapter. If it is the case that children's vocabulary development is better if they have more exposure to speech then this might be an argument in favour of the rear-facing buggies which have been proposed.

Syntactic development

Single word utterances

Once infants have produced their first words, we have seen that their vocabularies then continue to grow. However, there comes a point where language development moves beyond just the accumulation of single words to the production of phrases where words are combined, and also to the application of rules to individual words. In this section, we will explore the development of the rules of grammar, which govern how words can be changed within a language and how they may be combined.

The period before children start to combine words is known as the one-word period. However, there is evidence to suggest that even in this period, children are condensing more complex meanings into their single words, which go beyond just naming objects or labelling things. When words condense more complex meanings in this way they are known as holophrases. This is a difficult issue, because ultimately it is difficult to know whether children intend to convey more complex meanings with their single-word utterances. Imagine though, that a child is sitting in his high chair with his favourite toy, which then drops on to the floor. He points down at it on the ground and shouts, 'Teddy! Teddy!' Is this a simple case of his naming and labelling his toy, or is it possible that he is actually trying to convey something like, 'I've dropped my teddy!' or 'I want my teddy back!' The problem with these possible interpretations of a single-word utterance is where we draw the line. For example, could it be that the child is actually trying to convey 'My favourite teddy has fallen on the floor and I can't reach it. Could someone pick it up and give it back to me?' Something this complex seems unlikely. However, if we are prepared to attribute some more complex meanings to holophrases then we need to beware of the dangers of over-estimating the complexity of what they are likely to mean. In other words, in doing so we are attributing children with an understanding of language (comprehension) which far exceeds their ability to themselves produce language (production). Having said this, it is generally accepted that production does lag behind comprehension, at least during the second year of life, and some psycholinguists suggest that children may comprehend between five and ten times as many words as they actually produce (Benedict, 1979).

Combining two words

Children begin to put words together in combinations from about 18 months of age. Slobin (1972) reported that children are able to convey an immense amount of meaning with just two words, through the use of accompanying gestures and by their tone. For example, two words allow a child to indicate possession by saying 'My candy', or to attribute features to something by saying,

> **Definitions**
>
> Holophrase: a single word which expresses some more complex idea.
> Telegraphic speech: speech consisting of phrases of a small number of words (usually nouns, verbs and adjectives) combined to make sense, but without complex grammatical forms.

for example, 'Big car'. Children can convey information about location, by saying 'Book there' or can attribute someone with an action, like 'Mama walk'. The phrase 'Hit you' conveys a direct action of theirs to someone else, whilst saying 'Give papa' conveys an indirect action towards someone else. They can also ask simple questions, like 'Where ball?' and reveal an understanding of negation, through phrases such as 'Not wolf'.

These sorts of two-word phrases were observed by Slobin (1972) in children from a variety of countries whose first languages included English, Samoan, Russian and Finnish, and the similarity of this process of development between children speaking a variety of languages lends support to those theories which argue that there is some sort of universal form underlying the development of language generally. Such two-word phrases carry a significant amount of meaning because the words which are combined tend to be nouns, verbs and adjectives. Words like 'in', 'on', 'the' or 'and' are not generally featured in these two-word combinations, but despite their omission children are able to communicate very effectively. For this reason, such speech is often called telegraphic speech because of its similarity to old-fashioned telegrams, where unnecessary words are omitted yet a great deal of meaning is retained.

Combining three and four words

After the end of the second year, children begin to put three and four words in combination. Their word combinations are still condensed and telegraphic in nature, and are not yet grammatically correct. However, it is interesting that despite this their speech contains evidence that they already understand some of the rules which govern their language. Earlier in this chapter we saw that some of the mistakes which children make in their use of referential words are useful in helping us to understand the process of acquiring new words. In terms of syntactical development, once again the errors which children make provide us with insights into the process of learning the rules of language. For example, in this stage of development we would not be surprised to hear a child say 'sheeps' or 'mouses' as the plural forms for these animals. To us this may seem like an amusing and insignificant mistake, but actually it tells us that the child has learned a rule – namely that adding /-s/ to the end of a noun makes it into a plural. The child has not yet learned that in English there are exceptions to this rule which need to be learned separately, but her error tells us that she is already making progress in the learning of the rules which govern the English language. Jean Berko Gleason, a well-known psycholinguist, carried out a classic study in this area in 1958, where she developed a test commonly known as the Wug Test, which allows for an understanding of how children develop their rules of word formation.

In the Wug Test, children are shown a picture of a single creature with a fictional name. Next, they are shown more of these creatures and asked what they are. The child is therefore forced to produce a plural version of a noun which they could never have heard before since it is fictional, and their answers allow for an insight into how they understand the rules which govern, for example, the construction of plurals. Figure 5.3 shows an example of a stimulus used in Berko's (1958) original study. The results showed that the majority of children correctly produced the word 'wugs' as the plural form of the fictional word 'wug'.

Similar errors are made in verb construction, and particularly in the creation of the past tense. For example, you might hear a child say 'I runned' or 'we swimmed'. Again, this reveals an understanding that adding /-ed/ to the end of a verb makes it into the past tense, although the child once more has not yet learned that there are exceptions to this rule where verbs are constructed differently.

STOP AND THINK

Going further

Think about how these kinds of errors relate to different theories of language development considered earlier.

- Could such errors could be the result of simple learning or imitation?
- Does it seem likely that something like a LAD could account for these kinds of rule-based errors?
- What other cognitive developments do you think a child would need to have undergone before reaching this level of language ability?

Figure 5.3. Example of stimulus from Berko's (1958) Wug test.

(*Source*: http://childes.psy.cmu.edu/topics/wugs/01wug.jpg)

A later development in syntax comes when children begin to re-order their sentences to construct questions. For example, a younger child may say, 'Mummy eating?' as a question, by raising his pitch at the end of the phrase. By 3 or 4 years this may have developed to something like 'What Mummy is eating?' which represents a syntactical development with the inclusion of 'what' at the beginning of the phrase to denote a question. However, this child has still yet to learn that the auxiliary verb needs to be 'inverted' and exchanged with the subject of the sentence so that it is transformed from 'mummy is eating' to 'is mummy eating' when forming a question. By the time children move into their early school years, their use of irregular verbs and grammatical rules in general will have increased dramatically, so that they are now competent language users capable of constructing complex utterances which convey complex ideas and meanings.

The development of pragmatics

The pragmatic system is that part of language concerned with its appropriate use in social situations, our ability to extract and to convey meaning which goes beyond just syntax and semantics (for more information on pragmatics, see Recommended Reading). As this develops, children become more sensitive to the needs of other people in conversations, and show a greater awareness of, for example, what other people know and do not know. This may be linked to developments in other areas of cognition, such as theory of mind (see Chapter 8, Theory of Mind) and in Piagetian theory the development of non-egocentric thought. One clear example of this is when children begin to show an awareness of the difference between 'a' and 'the' in their conversations with others. Let's imagine you were having a conversation with your friend. They say, 'I was sitting at the bus stop last night, and the man just started laughing.' Your immediate response might be to ask, 'What man?' Since

your friend had not introduced a man into the story previously, you could not have known that there was even a man there, and so it feels as though there is a step missing in the chronology of the tale. Yet this use of 'the man' or 'the dog' is common in younger children's speech, and seems to be the result of their assumption that other people know what they know. In Piaget's theory of development this may be due to egocentrism, and reflects a younger child's lack of awareness that other people have thoughts, ideas and perspectives which are different from their own. Once children develop this awareness, they seem to recognise the need to introduce 'a man' into a story before then referring to 'the man' and this represents a significant improvement in the success of their conversations. Even so, some 5 year olds still

LIFESPAN

Pragmatics and working memory

Some researchers have discussed the importance of working memory to understanding the pragmatic aspects of language, and have found that adults with damage to their brains' right hemispheres have problems with their pragmatic skills because of difficulties with their working memory capacities (e.g. Tomkins *et al.*, 1994; Stemmer and Joanette, 1998). Pragmatics involve awareness and understanding of the particular context in which we find ourselves, in order to infer some of the meaning of conversations. Inferring that someone is joking or being sarcastic, for example, requires that we integrate several varied aspects of the context in which we find ourselves. It is thought that this places complex demands on working memory, and that this therefore affects the pragmatic aspects of language.

Previous research has shown that people with dyslexia also have a reduced working memory capacity (e.g. Baddeley, 1998), and several studies have found lower pragmatic competence in adults with dyslexia. For example, Griffiths (2007) compared groups of dyslexic and non-dyslexic adults' on four tests from the Right Hemisphere Language Battery (Bryan, 1995) which assess pragmatic competence, as well as on a self-report

pragmatic competence questionnaire and on the Dyslexia Adult Screening Test (DAST). Participants ranged in age from 18 to 45 years and had to show their understanding of metaphorical (as opposed to literal) information, inferential storylines (where they had to extract information from stories which had not been made explicit) and joke punch lines (where they had to choose the correct one from four possibilities). All of these are examples of pragmatic understanding.

Griffiths found that the dyslexic group consistently misunderstood aspects of pragmatics more often than the non-dyslexic group. She also found that there was a correlation between increasing pragmatic impairment and performance on the part of the DAST which tests working memory: the poorer the working memory, the greater the pragmatic impairment. The study of pragmatics therefore clearly demonstrates the ways in which language and cognition interact across the lifespan.

Definition

Dyslexia: a learning difficulty which affects a person's ability to read despite otherwise normal levels of intelligence.

do not consistently use 'a' before 'the'. It is therefore an important part of the development of pragmatics, and another example of the ways in which language and cognition may interact.

The ability to repair faulty communications or to put right misunderstandings is a part of the pragmatic system which has been observed in children as young as 33 months. When there is a breakdown in communication, a sensitivity to the amount of information needed to put things right provides an important indicator of the maturity of the child's pragmatic system. For example, imagine you approach a woman on the street to ask for directions. You say, 'Where is the nearest tube station?'. If she replies, 'What?', how would you respond? It is likely that you would interpret her response as indicating that she has generally failed to understand you at all, and that you would therefore repeat the whole of your question. On the other hand, if she responded by saying, 'Where is the nearest what?', you would interpret this as indicating that she had simply failed to understand a part of what you had said, and that you would therefore repeat just that part, by saying, 'Tube station'. Your mature pragmatic system therefore enables you to appreciate the difference between general or more specific queries for information, and to modify your provision of additional information based on those differences. In one study of how this sensitivity to conversational queries develops, researchers used a talking toy robot who responded to children's utterances with either general or specific queries (e.g. 'What?' or 'Baby's eating what?') (Ferrier

et al., 2000). The researchers found that at 27 months of age, children were more likely to respond to both of these types of queries with complete repetitions of their previous utterances, whilst at 33 months of age, children would respond to general queries with complete repetitions, and would give only the necessary partial information in response to specific queries. This illustrates an important development in children's pragmatics within the third year of life.

Earlier in this chapter, we discussed the ways in which early social interactions assist with the later development of children's language, and in this context we explored how children may be prepared for turn-taking in conversations through some of their earliest interactions with their caregivers. Turn-taking is an important part of pragmatics, since conversations are generally quite well-organised interactions, and research has shown that normal adult conversation contains very few noticeable overlaps or interruptions (see, for example, Levinson, 1983). Understanding the rules which govern turn-taking in conversation is important for successful conversations. For example, knowing when in a conversation it is possible and appropriate for there to be a change in speaker, how to go about taking your turn in a conversation and knowing what to do to correct mistakes in the turn-taking sequence, all enable there to be fairly trouble-free transitions between speakers (Sacks *et al.*, 1974). Infants' early interactions lay the groundwork for later social interactions, including conversations, and as such are an important part of the development of the social side of language.

CASE STUDY

Early Pragmatics in everyday life

Louise is 4½ years old and enjoying a day at home with her Mum. Mum's friend, Alison, pops round and the three of them decide to take a walk to the park. Whilst pushing Louise on the swings, Mum and Alison carry on a conversation. After a few minutes, Louise asks to get off the swing and then says, 'Mummy, I want to talk to you.' She motions for Mum to bend down and then whispers in her ear, 'When you are talking to Alison I think you have forgotten about me.'

- Why did Louise whisper instead of talking out loud?
- What does this tell us about her understanding and awareness of other people?
- What could we say about the development of Louise's pragmatic system on the basis of this example?
- How might this link to other aspects of Louise's cognitive development that you have read about elsewhere in the book?

Earlier on in this chapter we discussed the lateralisation of brain function in relation to language. One interesting point to note here is that in fact not all language abilities are located in the left hemisphere. When it comes to pragmatics and the social side of language, the right hemisphere is involved. The fact that both 'sides' of the brain are involved in language emphasises just what a complex human function it is.

SUMMARY

At the beginning of this chapter, we set out to discover what language is and what elements it comprises. We have seen that language is more than just speech and grammar. It is a logical yet creative symbolic system, and its development is a complicated business, dependent upon developments in four component parts: phonology, semantics, syntax and pragmatics.

The foundations of language are laid in infants' earliest social interactions in the pre-verbal stage, and these may pave the way for later developments. Early exposure to language assists with the specialisation of infants' phonological awareness so that they can discriminate between categories of sounds in their native language. The special kind of speech which adults direct towards infants may also help with developing language by exposing children to it in a simplified and more accessible form. Infants may get some preparation for the social side of language through patterns of turn-taking which are established during feeding or activities which involve joint attention.

The abilities of infants in the first months of life force us to consider what language abilities or capacities children enter the world with, and how much of language is learned. Some of the mistakes which children make during the process of learning language may suggest the existence of an innate mechanism which allows for the acquisition of language generally, but which depends upon input from the external world to fuel the acquisition process. The language which children are exposed to from infancy affects the development of language in various ways, but there is also evidence that developments in cognition and thinking more generally may underpin the development of language.

Before children can begin to learn words, they must be able to recognise and produce the speech sounds of their language. The learning of referential words is a complicated process, with lots of room for errors. It may be facilitated by more general cognitive developments which allow for a dramatic acceleration in vocabulary growth in the second year of life, and other cognitive developments may be necessary before children can learn and understand words which relate to abstract concepts. Even once children have learned lots of words, there is still work to be done in learning how to combine those words in grammatically correct ways. Children progress through combinations of two, three and four words, using condensed and telegraphic forms of speech, before eventually being able to produce fully-formed grammatically correct sentences. The rules of grammar may be acquired through some innate language acquisition device which is sensitive to the regularities in the adult language which children are exposed to, and some of the mistakes which children make as they move towards a full grasp of the rules of syntax can provide us with useful insights into the process that they go through. How to use language appropriately in different social contexts and how to interpret and communicate meanings which go beyond the mere semantics of the words themselves is another important aspect of the development of language. Speech and grammar alone cannot ensure successful communication, but the development of pragmatics enables children to be confident and competent users of language in the social world.

REVIEW QUESTIONS

1 Discuss what the possible benefits to children's language development might be, of backward-facing prams and buggies.

2 In what ways might infant-directed speech or 'motherese' facilitate children's language development?

3 Compare and contrast Nativist with learning theory explanations of language development. Which do you think is most convincing, and why?

4 Discuss some of the ways in which cognitive development and the development of language may interact.

RECOMMENDED READING

To read more about Patricia Kuhl's work on the perception of speech sounds by non-human animals, see:

Kuhl, P.K. (1988). Auditory perception and the evolution of speech, *Human Evolution, 3*, 19–43.

Kuhl, P.K. and Miller, J.D. (1975). Speech perception by the chinchilla: voiced-voiceless distinction in alveolar plosive consonants. *Science, 190*, 69–72.

Kuhl, P.K. and Padden, D.M. (1982). Enhanced discriminability at the phonetic boundary for the voicing feature in macaques. *Perception and Psychophysics, 32*, 542–550.

Kuhl, P.K. and Padden, D.M. (1983). Enhanced discriminability at the phonetic boundaries for the place feature in macaques. *Journal of the Acoustical Society of America, 73*, 1003–1010.

For more information about infant-directed speech or 'motherese' in different languages and cultures, see:

Lieven, E.V.M. (1994). Crosslinguistic and crosscultural aspects of language addressed to children. In C. Gallaway & Brian J. Richards (Eds). *Input and Interaction in Language Acquisition* (56–73). Cambridge: Cambridge University Press.

For more information about Broca's Area, see:

Grodzinsky, Y. and Amunts, K. (Eds) (2006). *Broca's Region*. Oxford: Oxford University Press.

For more information about the development of pragmatics, see:

Ninio, A. and Snow, C.E. (1996). *Pragmatic Development*. Boulder, CO: Westview Press.

RECOMMENDED WEBSITES

To find out more about Paul MacLean's triune brain theory, see:

http://www.kheper.net/topics/intelligence/MacLean.htm

To find out more about the ideas of linguist Noam Chomsky, see:

http://www.chomsky.info/

To find out more about the developmental milestones which typically developing children are expected to reach at different ages, see:

http://www.childdevelopmentinfo.com/development/language_development.shtml

To find out more about cases of children who have grown up in social isolation, like Genie, see:

http://www.feralchildren.com/en/index.php

To find out more about Baby Signs ® Inc, see:

https://www.babysigns.com/index.cfm?fuseaction=aboutus.main

 Watch a short video discussing and exploring language development. Further resources can be found at www.pearsoned.co.uk/gillibrand

Chapter 6
Memory and intelligence

Learning Outcomes

After reading this chapter, with further recommended reading, you should be able to:

1. Explain what memory is, what processes it consists of and what different types of memories children have;

2. Describe research into memory abilities in infancy, explain how memory develops through childhood, and what might be responsible for different instances of children's forgetting;

3. Discuss the difficulties which are associated with traditional approaches to intelligence testing in children;

4. Compare and contrast some different conceptualisations of intelligence;

5. Discuss some of the ways in which memory and intelligence develop and change across the adult lifespan.

The pub quiz

Karen, Raymond and Paul have formed a team called 'The Fourth Floor' and are taking part in a pub quiz. The quizmaster asks questions about subjects such as music, sport, history, entertainment, geography, the human body, animals and food. For example, which composer's eighth symphony is also known as the 'Unfinished Symphony'? Which country hosted the World Cup Soccer Finals in 1930? All three members of 'The Fourth Floor' have university undergraduate degrees, and between them they also have several masters and even a doctoral degree. Yet they struggle to answer many of the questions!

- What explanations could there be for their difficulties?
- Do these well-educated individuals lack intelligence?
- Perhaps they simply cannot remember the answers?
- Would winning this quiz make you the most intelligent person in the pub?
- Does remembering the details of every World Cup final make you intelligent?

Introduction

Cognitive psychologists study the way in which we process information from the world around us. To understand cognitive development, we need to study the development of memory and intelligence as these are important parts of cognition. Our memory can be thought of as a database within which knowledge and information is stored. Prior to storage, information has to be processed. This can be thought of as similar to identifying what the content of a particular piece of data is and what it means, and deciding how it should be entered into the database. Then we have to be able to get information back out of the database when it is required. This will depend on how efficient our original entering and recording of the data was, how good a system of cross-referencing we have and how easily we can track down a particular source of data when we want it. Intelligence is a general term used to describe how efficiently we are able to process information and includes, for example, how quickly we can solve problems or respond to a new situation and how fast we can get information out of storage when required. Memory and intelligence are therefore closely linked to one another, and this chapter will explore how each of them develops.

What is memory?

Memory is an important part of our cognitive processes, as mentioned above. It has been said that our individual identities are made up of the sum total of all of our experiences. If this is true then who would we be if we could not remember any of those experiences? Piaget's theories of cognitive development referred to previously in Chapter 2, Theoretical Perspectives continue to dominate developmental psychology. He suggests that for infants, the primary focus is on the world which is immediately present to them, and that previously stored information does not influence their behaviour until late infancy or early childhood. In the first part of this chapter, we will explore what more contemporary research has revealed about the memory abilities of infants. By adulthood, we have a sophisticated memory system which stores all sorts of knowledge and information of many different types (see Table 6.1). For example, our memories may contain factual information, such as the date of the Battle of Trafalgar or how many players make up a football team. This kind of stored knowledge is called semantic memory. Our memories also contain knowledge about ourselves, our past experiences and lives and things which have happened to us. This is known as autobiographical memory.

Some of the memories we have are explicit, in that we can talk about them and declare what we remember. We also have implicit memories, such as procedural memories for skills and abilities, like riding a bike or driving a car. Our memories also contain scripts for procedures or events – for example, what happens at a dinner party or a university lecture. All of these memories make up who we are and what we know and will be discussed in the first part of this chapter, which provides an introduction to the processes involved in memory, explores research on the memory abilities of children from infancy onwards, and discusses how these processes develop through childhood.

Memory is not just one thing, and it is more useful to think of memory as a system made up of several different component processes (see Fig. 6.1). At its most basic level, our memory system consists of three major component processes. Information is taken in from the world

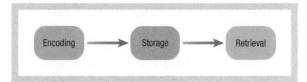

Figure 6.1 The three stages of memory.

STOP AND THINK

Reflection

- What is your earliest memory? How old were you then?
- Are you sure that you really remember this, or do you really just remember what other people have told you about this? Is there any way that we could tell the difference?
- Do you think you have any memories prior to that which could be accessed?

Definitions

Semantic memory: long-term memory for facts, concepts and meanings.
Autobiographical memory: an individual's personal memory for their life experiences and events and for information about themselves.
Procedural memory: implicit, unconscious long-term memory for skills or how to do things.
Scripts: mental representations which we have of certain types of events, which include our general expectations of such events based on prior experience.

Table 6.1 Key features of some of the main types of memories.

Type of memory	Explicit or implicit?	Main features	Example
Episodic	Explicit	Memory for events or episodes	Remembering what you had for breakfast this morning
Semantic	Explicit	Memory for knowledge and facts	Remembering the date of the great fire of London
Procedural	Implicit	Memory for skills or procedures	Sitting down at a computer and remembering how to type
Autobiographical	Explicit	Memory for our own life experiences, our interpretations of those experiences and personal facts about ourselves	Remembering the events of your wedding day, how you felt and what it meant to you; also being able to answer 'yes' to the question, 'Are you married?'

CASE STUDY

Early memory in everyday life

Baby Ella is 5 months old. Her mum and dad have gone out for the evening, leaving Ella in the care of Marie, a family friend who has agreed to babysit. Ella sleeps for most of the evening. When she wakes up crying, she is easily comforted by Marie, despite the fact that the two of them have met only six or seven times in Ella's short life. Marie feeds Ella a bottle and then they play together and watch television until Ella's parents return home. As her mum enters the living room, Ella catches sight of her and immediately her face breaks into a smile. Dad enters the room behind mum, and when Ella sees him her smile broadens. She gurgles and begins to kick her legs and, as Dad lifts her from the babysitter's arms, Ella lets out a squeal.

- **What does all of this mean?**
- **Does baby Ella really recognise her mother and father?**
- **At what age would she first have been able to do this?**
- **What kinds of knowledge and information about her parents does Ella really have stored in her memory?**

around us, and this process is the part of memory known as encoding. That information then needs to be kept, which is the process known as storage. Initially, information enters our short-term memory store, but may eventually pass on to our long-term memory store. Finally, we need to be able to bring that information back out of storage when it is required, and that process is known as retrieval.

Not only are there these three processes involved in memory, but there are several different types of information which our memory systems deal with, as we have mentioned already. Imagine bumping into someone in the street that you recognise. You may remember their name, as well as other information about them such as where you know them from, what they do for a living or what colour their hair was the last time you saw them. Whether you were aware of it or not prior to bumping into them, if all those things came to mind when you met them, then all of that information about that person must have been encoded and stored in your memory.

In contrast, each time we get into a car and drive off, we are accessing a different type of memory again. When driving, we do not search our memories for knowledge and information about cars, gears and motion. Imagine what a complex process driving would be if we did! Instead we access procedural memories – implicit memories which we have for actions or procedures which we have learned at some point, but which have now become automatic and can be carried out without information needing to be consciously retrieved. Our memories also store episodic memories for events or occurrences which have happened in the past. Remembering your tenth birthday party or your first day at school would be examples of episodic memories. So our memory systems enable the encoding, storage and retrieval of very different types of information, all of which are vital for our functioning in the human world. Yet memory is like an iceberg, in that the parts which we can easily retrieve are often only a very small proportion of what there actually is. Much of it is hidden from view or not easily accessible, and the problem may be in trying to get to it.

Definitions

Encoding: the first stage of information processing in memory, where information is taken in via the senses.
Storage: the second stage of information processing in memory, by which information is retained for short or long periods of time.
Retrieval: the third stage of information processing in memory, by which information is brought back out of storage and recalled.
Episodic memory: memory for specific events or occurrences, including details of time, place and emotions associated with it.

When we forget something, that forgetting may be due to a failure in any one of the three major parts of our memory system mentioned already, and it is not always obvious which one of the three is responsible for the failure. If we are unable to recall the name of the person we bumped into in the street, is it because their name was never successfully encoded in the first place? Or could it be that the information was encoded, but that there has been a failure in its storage? Or alternatively, could it be that the information was encoded and has been stored, but that we are experiencing problems in retrieval and are unable to get it out of storage? Difficulties in separating out these three parts of memory can make it tricky to study how children's memory develops too. With children who are not yet able to talk, this is even more difficult. The lack of language ability in infants and young children means that researchers have had to develop novel and innovative ways of studying memory that do not rely upon the ability to communicate verbally. We will explore all of these issues in the development of memory within the first part of this chapter.

Memory in children

What can infants remember?

In the 1950s and 1960s, Robert Fantz, a psychologist studying both chimpanzees and infants, came up with a research technique which would enable infant memory to be studied systematically for the first time. Fantz noticed that when presented with pairs of stimuli, chimps spend different amounts of time looking at each member of the pair (Fantz, 1956). Secondly, he noticed that infants' preferences for different stimuli change over periods of time, so that eventually familiar stimuli are given less attention and new or unfamiliar stimuli are given more attention (Fantz, 1964). These influential observations by Fantz provided a method of judging whether infants remember things which they have seen before, even before those infants are able to talk. This pioneering work on visual recognition memory led to the development of the visual paired comparison (VPC) task which has paved the way for a wealth of infant memory research subsequently. The Research Methods box explains this particular task in more detail.

Using techniques such as these, it has been possible to gain some insights into the memory abilities of even newborn infants. Joseph Fagan, a colleague of Fantz, first used the VPC task and presented infants of between 3 and 6 months of age with a target visual stimulus (a black and white pattern) (Fagan, 1970). He then tested the infants' recognition memory by presenting a pair of stimuli, including the original target, and measuring how long the infants looked at each one. Because they looked longer at the novel stimulus, Fagan inferred that infants recognised the target as familiar and that they therefore have a recognition memory for it. You may want to refer back to Chapter 4, Prenatal Development and Infancy to remind yourself of other research methods which have been used by developmental psychologists to study infants.

Other research has since suggested that this kind of recognition memory exists in infants even younger than 3–6 months. It has also been shown to extend to senses other than just vision, as explored in Chapter 4. For example, DeCasper and Fifer (1980) carried out an important piece of research using the non-nutritive dummies discussed in the Research Methods box with infants who were no more than 3 days old. The dummies were linked to recordings of both the infant's own mother and another infant's mother. Depending on how fast they sucked the infant could control whose voice they heard. Each infant in this study had had less than 12 hours contact with their mother since birth (they spent most of their time in a nursery and were cared for primarily by staff), yet they still showed a clear preference for their own mother's voice, and would modify their rate of sucking in order to hear her rather than another mother. This suggests that these infants at just 3 days old already recognised their mother's voice and could distinguish it from another voice. This would not have been possible if the infants did not have some stored memory for their mother's voice.

Definitions

Stimulus (plural stimuli): anything which elicits or evokes a response, such as a sound, a picture, a taste or a smell.

Visual recognition memory: memory for a visual stimulus which has been seen before. This type of memory can be assessed from very early in life and so is often used in infant memory research.

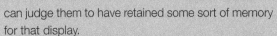

RESEARCH METHODS

Exploring infant visual recognition memory

Visual recognition memory can be assessed by placing an infant in front of a single visual display. In recent research, such displays are usually on computer screens, and so the amount of time which the infant spends looking at the display can be carefully controlled (see the photo below for an example).

In visual paired comparison (VPC) tasks, after the infant has viewed a display there is a delay, and they are then presented with two displays at the same time, one of which is the familiar one, and of which is new. The time which the infant spends looking at each of these two displays can be measured. Since Fantz and others' pioneering work has shown that infants have a preference for, and look longer at, novel or unfamiliar stimuli, it is possible to infer whether an infant perceives one of the displays to be familiar. If so, then we

Infant viewing a visual display.

Source: Alamy Images/Picture Partners

can judge them to have retained some sort of memory for that display.

It is important to recognise that this research method assesses recognition memory. Responses to a stimulus which has been seen before allow us to judge that the child recognises it and we can infer that they have a memory of it. It is an appropriate method to use with pre-verbal infants because it does not rely upon their ability to tell us what they remember. In contrast, asking a child to tell us as many words as they can remember from a previously presented list would be an example of free recall. Here the onus is on the child to retrieve as many items as they can from memory without being provided with any additional cues as to what may or may not have been on the original list. Sometimes participants in memory research will fail to remember things using recall, but using a recognition technique they will be able to correctly identify more items.

Another technique which assists psychologists in research with infants is the use of a specially designed non-nutritive dummy which infants can suck. Non-nutritive sucking is sucking which occurs without any milk being given. The rates at which infants suck can be carefully measured. For example, Wolff (1968) found that 4 day old infants' baseline suck-rate was 2.13 sucks per second. Researchers have found that suck rates decline when infants become familiar with a stimulus. Their suck-rate can therefore be measured to assess whether they perceive something to be familiar or unfamiliar. It is also possible to link the dummy to visual or auditory displays in such a way that infants can themselves control what they see or hear, by varying their suck-rate.

The authors of that study suggested that it could have been exposure to their mothers' voices whilst in the womb which led to these findings. As discussed in Chapter 4, many researchers have shown that to understand the development of infant memory, we have to go back even further, to the prenatal period. For example, DeCasper and Spence (1986) asked pregnant women to read a particular piece of text aloud twice a

day during the last six weeks of their pregnancy. When their infants were 2 or 3 days old, a non-nutritive dummy was linked to audio recordings of the piece which had been read to them, as well as to an unfamiliar piece. The infants could control which one they heard by adjusting their suck-rate. It was found that infants would alter their suck-rate to hear the familiar piece of text, and that this was the case regardless of whose voice was on the recording reading the text. In other words, it did not matter whether their mother was the one reading the piece or not, they would alter their suck-rate to hear the familiar one. They were not just showing a preference for a familiar voice, but had encoded complex verbal information prior to their birth. The fact that the study took place two or three days after birth tells us that these infants had the capacity for memory storage for at least that long, as well as encoding and retrieval capabilities.

In addition to auditory and visual memories, some research suggests that infant memory extends to touch and feel (e.g. Catherwood, 1993) as well as to smell (Cernoch and Porter, 1985). All of this shows that infants have the ability encode information even before birth, that they can store information for at least a couple of days even just after birth and that they can access that stored information sufficiently to be able to recognise familiar stimuli straight from birth.

The exact nature of the memories which infants have is not known, and neither is it clear whether an infant is aware at a conscious level of having viewed a particular display or having heard a particular piece of prose being read before. In studies of adult memory, a distinction is made between explicit memories and implicit memories. Explicit memories are those which we can consciously and deliberately recollect, such as our date of birth or the offside rule. Implicit memories are those which we know must be stored because our behaviour reveals them, but which we are not necessarily conscious of recalling. For example, I know that I know how to swim, because I do it every time I get into the water, but when swimming I do not have to think about the actions necessary to get to the other side of the pool – it just happens. Because their language abilities have not developed enough for them to be able to articulate what they can and what they cannot remember, it is very difficult for us to make judgements about the exact nature of very young children's memories, and how they compare with the kinds of memories that we have as adults.

How does memory develop with age?

The section above suggests that even very young infants have some memory abilities, and this section explores what it is within the memory systems of children that changes over time, and what gives rise to improvement in memory abilities from childhood to adulthood. To better understand this process of development, we need to look once again at the different processes which make up memory – encoding, storage and retrieval – and examine whether children get better at taking information in as they get older, whether they get better at retaining it, whether they get better at retrieving it or whether improvements in all of these areas of memory occur.

Developments in encoding

Encoding and retrieval are closely linked and so, as we discuss one, we will inevitably discuss the other. This is because we can only really assess how things are encoded into memory by looking at how they are subsequently retrieved from memory. One aspect of encoding which may improve memory as children get older is the speed at which it happens. Using visual recognition memory techniques, such as the VPC task explored earlier in this chapter, research has shown that younger infants need longer periods of time for initial encoding to occur before they will show the kinds of preferences for novel stimuli we discussed previously, thus demonstrating memory for the previously viewed stimulus. For example, Morgan and Hayne (2006) showed children visual displays with two identical stimuli. Children therefore became familiar with that stimulus during this familiarisation phase. In the subsequent test phase of the experiment, the familiar stimulus and a novel stimulus were presented and the researchers measured how long they spent looking at the novel stimulus. Two groups of children took part – one group of one year olds and a second group of four year olds. The length of the familiarisation phase was either 5 seconds, 10 seconds or 30 seconds, and their memories for the stimuli were tested either immediately, after a delay of 24 hours or after one week. The results showed that when tested immediately, encoding occurred for the older children with a familiarisation phase of just five seconds. In contrast, the younger infants required 10 seconds of familiarisation in order to encode information. This suggests that older children take shorter times to successfully encode information.

In addition, as we have mentioned above, encoding and retrieval are very closely linked. One way in which this has been demonstrated is through research which shows that the amount of time available for initial encoding affects the length of time for which information will be retained and then successfully retrieved. Morgan and Hayne's (2006) work showed that not only did older children require shorter encoding times overall, but that for all children, the longer the encoding time, the longer the time for which information will be retained. The one year olds in their study showed retention times of 24 hours with the longest (30 second) familiarisation phase, but not with the familiarisation phase of 10 seconds. These kinds of changes in encoding and retention with age have been demonstrated by other research studies as well (e.g. Hayne, 2004; Rose *et al.*, 2004).

From a wealth of research on adult memory, we also know that not all of the information which our senses are exposed to will be encoded at all. Imagine that you spend the evening in a restaurant with friends. Upon leaving the restaurant, one of your friends comments on how much he liked the tablecloth. You realise that you cannot even recall what colour the tablecloth was. You would certainly have seen it, so the information about the tablecloth must have filtered through your visual system, but it has been encoded in such a way that it is not available to you later for conscious recall (although the next Stop and Think box touches upon one method by which this could be addressed). In this way, the nature of the initial encoding affects how easily that information is available for recall. The world around us contains far too much information for us to be able to take all of it in, and so attention allows us to focus on certain things, to the exclusion of others. This means that we make judgements, consciously or unconsciously, about what is most important in a given situation. At the restaurant, if you focused on the conversation and the food, then other information about the decor may simply not have been attended to. It is possible, then, that children get better at focusing their attention on what is important as they get older, leading to more efficient encoding. Perhaps this explains some aspects of the development of memory.

To be able to focus on what is important, children need to have learned what kinds of things are important in given situations. Without this knowledge they will be none the wiser as to what is important and what is unimportant (see Recommended Reading for advice on where to look for a thorough review of the development of selective attention). Making links between new information and information already stored in memory may also lead to better encoding of that new information, making it more likely that it will be recalled at a later date. If we think of the storage part of memory as a system within which information is stored, then we can

begin to see how this might work. Paperwork is not just dumped randomly into a filing cabinet, but is filed away in different drawers or within different hanging files based on a system of organisation. New papers are filed away alongside other, related papers, and this means that information on a particular topic can be more easily retrieved when needed than if the drawers just contained piles and piles of unorganised paperwork. It also means that other related information can be accessed alongside the 'target' information when that is retrieved. There might also be overlaps or relationships between information stored in different parts of the system which necessitate a system of cross-referencing.

As children get older, they accumulate knowledge and information which means that new information can be linked with existing information as it is encoded. Perhaps it is this accumulation of knowledge which improves memory through childhood then, by allowing information to be organised more efficiently as it is encoded and, as a more complex system of cross-referencing develops, there are more possible routes through which a target piece of information can be reached. Some specific ways in which prior learning may affect memory through encoding are explored later in this chapter (see The influence of prior knowledge and expectations). When prior knowledge or information affects the encoding of new information as it comes in, this is known as top-down processing.

STOP AND THINK

Reflection

- What are your views on hypnosis?
- Could this be a way of accessing information which has been encoded on some level, but is not available for conscious recall?
- What do you think might be the potential problems with such methods?

Definitions

Attention: the part of our cognitive processes which controls ability to focus efficiently on specific things and ignore others.

Top-down processing: when the processing of information coming in via the senses is heavily influenced by prior knowledge.

STOP AND THINK

Going further

Repeating something over and over again (rehearsal) is an encoding strategy which may increase the likelihood of it being remembered later. Why might this be the case? As mentioned earlier, the three-stage model of memory as represented in Fig. 6.1 is a simple view of that system. In cognitive psychology, the 'storage' part of memory is thought to comprise several separate but interrelated sub-systems. In particular, there is a distinction between short-term, or working, memory and long-term memory. Alan Baddeley (1986; Baddeley and Hitch, 1974; Baddeley, 1992), a leading researcher in the field of memory, suggests that working memory mediates between encoding and long-term storage, and consists of a 'central executive' (which controls the activities of working memory and allocates processing resources accordingly), as well as two 'slave' systems, one dealing with verbal information and the other with non-verbal information. New information can be maintained and manipulated within working memory for a relatively short period of time, and may then pass to the long-term store. Verbal information, in particular, requires rehearsal in order for it to be maintained in working memory, otherwise it decays quite rapidly. Working memory can also maintain information which has been re-acquired from long-term storage when it is needed for some additional processing.

The way in which working memory operates is of interest within cognitive psychology generally, but in developmental psychology research has begun to explore the development of working memory in children (the implications of developments in working memory capacity for learning and teaching are explored in Chapter 14, Developmental Psychology and Education). Simpson and Riggs (2005) tested children on a modified version of a game called the 'day–night task' (Gerstadt *et al.*, 1994) which requires children to respond 'day' to a picture of the moon and stars and to respond 'night' to a picture of the sun. This requires two things of the child. First they need to inhibit their usual response of 'day' or 'night' to the appropriate picture and respond instead the opposite way around but, second, they need to maintain information about the rules of the game within working memory whilst they complete the task. In general, children's performance improves on this task between three-and-a-half and five years of age. Could this be due to developments in working memory during this period? In a comparison task, the researchers tried to remove the 'inhibitory' demands of the task so that children had to respond 'night' to one abstract picture and 'day' to another abstract picture. In this case children still had to maintain the rules of the game in working memory, but since there was nothing intrinsic to the abstract pictures which would require the inhibition of an 'opposite' response, there should be no inhibitory demands on the children. The results suggested that the improved performance on the day–night task with children between three-and-a-half and five years is actually associated with improvements in inhibitory control rather than in working memory.

One way in which working memory does seem implicated in memory improvements more generally, though, is through children's use of memory strategies like rehearsal. These kinds of strategies allow for information to be manipulated in some way prior to storage, and can increase the likelihood of retention and therefore subsequent retrieval. Have you ever tried to remember a phone number when you do not immediately have a pen and paper to hand? How would you go about this? Do you have any other 'tricks' which you like to use as aids to your memory?

Children's use of strategies increases as they get older, and the complexity of the strategies used also seems to increase. The next section of this chapter looks at some of these developments.

Rehearsal is just one of a whole variety of memory tricks or mnemonics, which as adults we use regularly, and which may also contribute to improvements in memory abilities across childhood. Mnemonic devices are important strategies which act as memory aids, and so it may be that improvements in children's memory

Definitions

Rehearsal: the repetition of information in a deliberate attempt to aid memory.
Mnemonics: memory aids which are used to assist with the learning or memorisation of information.

are the result of their increased use of such encoding strategies. Rehearsal is a fairly simple strategy, but there are much more complex strategies which can be used as well.

For example, as a child, did you learn a rhyme or a song to help you remember how many days are in each month of the year? If so, then you encoded that information more elaborately than if all you had learned were mere numbers and months. More elaborate encoding means taking information (in this case months and numbers) and expanding it into a more meaningful format (in this case a rhyme or a song). You are more likely to be able to recall the information at a later date if it has been elaborately encoded than if you had just tried to rote learn it.

One good example of how elaborate encoding can assist children's recall is that of paired-associate tasks. Paired-associate tasks are used to test children's ability to recall pairs of items – usually pairs of words. Children are encouraged to learn the word-pairs by linking them together, often using visual imagery. So if the pair of words was 'kite–tiger' then the child might imagine a tiger standing on its hind legs in a park, flying a kite. After learning the words by linking each pair together in this way, children are prompted with one of the pair, and then have to remember what its partner was. If prompted with the word 'tiger' the correct response would be 'kite'. The prompt word should generate the image of the tiger flying a kite which the child had previously created, and help them to correctly recall the word which they are trying to remember. In this way, elaborating the information being encoded can improve recall. Very early research suggests that using this kind of imagery technique can improve children's recall between the ages of about 6 and 12 (e.g. Levin, 1976), but that at the younger end of this age range children only really benefit if they are given additional instructions to help them use the strategy (e.g. Varley et al., 1974; Bender and Levin, 1976). In other words younger children cannot spontaneously elaborate information during the encoding process without more concrete help.

Simpler memory strategies like rehearsal are spontaneously used by children as young as 10 years of age (e.g. Beuhring and Kee, 1987), but as they get older children

seem to rely less and less on such simple strategies, and instead use more complex strategies like elaboration and association (Pressley, 1982). Younger children do not make use of these more complex strategies themselves unless they are prompted or trained to do so. The use of memory strategies and the increasing complexity of those strategies may therefore lead to improvements in memory as children get older.

Some recent research suggests that memory development may be closely linked to developments in other areas of cognition, such as theory of mind (ToM) (e.g. Perner and Ruffman, 1995; Naito, 2003). Theory of mind is the ability to attribute mental states (such as desires, beliefs or intentions) to others, and to understand that other people have mental states which differ from our own. This ability develops in children between around three and four years of age, and is discussed in full in Chapter 8, Theory of Mind. Perner et al. (2007) conducted some research which explored the relationship between ToM and memory development. Children of between three-and-a-half and six-and-a-half years of age had the opportunity to form episodic memories under one of two conditions. In one condition, children placed 12 picture cards into a box after looking at each picture for several seconds. This group therefore had the opportunity to directly experience the pictures themselves. In the second condition, children placed 12 picture cards into a box, but were blindfolded throughout and so did not have the opportunity to directly experience the pictures themselves. This second group were then shown a video presentation of what the 12 pictures had been. All of the children were subsequently tested on their ability to recall what pictures they had put into the box, and their ToM was also assessed. The results showed an interaction between ToM and direct experience of the events. In other words, as children's ToM scores increased, so their recall of pictures which they had directly experienced improved as compared to those which had not been experienced. On the basis of this research, the researchers suggest that recall of events which children have directly experienced is associated with the development of ToM. Fully understanding memory development then, seems to require us to look at its relationship to other areas of cognition as well.

STOP AND THINK

Going further

The involvement of working memory and the use of strategies has been studied in relation to other areas of children's cognitive development, such as the development of mathematical or arithmetical skills (see Chapter 7, The Development of Mathematical Thinking). For example, Imbo and Vandierendock (2007) tested 10 to 12 year old children using something called the 'dual task' method, where children are required to solve arithmetic problems (the primary task) whilst a secondary task (responding by hitting a button on a computer keyboard to indicate whether an audible tone they hear is high or low) occupies their working memories. The results showed that children used mathematical strategies less efficiently when their working memories were loaded with the secondary task. However, the negative impact of this working memory load gets less as children get older. The authors suggest that as children get older they get better at selecting appropriate strategies, and more efficient at using those strategies, so that the impact of having their working memories loaded with another task declines. This shows how fundamental memory is to other areas of cognition and development. To find out more about the development of mathematical abilities and memory see Recommended Reading.

LIFESPAN

Memory strategy use in adulthood

The development of strategy use seems to be something which improves children's memory as they get older, but does it continue to improve memory across the lifespan, into adulthood and old age? There are many myths and assumptions which we all have about memory across the lifespan, particularly in relation to older adults. We seem to accept the idea that becoming forgetful is simply a feature of getting older, but is this really the case? In fact, most of the research suggests that when adults are cognitively healthy (in other words, when they do not have any degenerative conditions such as Alzheimer's) their memories remain good and they can continue to improve their performance by using memory strategies, right up until they are in their 80s (e.g. Kramer and Willis, 2003).

When compared to younger adults, older adults seem to have less potential for improvement through strategy use, but nonetheless there is no reason to suppose that older adults experience poorer memory performance as a matter of course, nor is there reason to suppose that we will not be able to continue to improve our memories by using strategies or other techniques as we get older. However, the psychological studies on which we base these conclusions tend to have been carried out with one or other of these three key groups at a time: children, younger adults or older adults. By looking at the results from many different studies, we can make rough judgements about the relative memory abilities of the three groups as compared to one another. However, we cannot make direct comparisons between all three groups using exactly the same tasks under the same conditions. One area where psychological research on memory development is lacking then is in direct comparative research between different age groups across the lifespan.

One study which addresses this gap studied children's and adults' memory for words which they learned using a modified version of a memory technique known as the 'Method of Loci' (Brehmer et al., 2007). This is a mnemonic which works by linking targets visually with images of locations. You could try this out yourself. Make a list of six words to be learned, and then visualise the journey that you make from home to class each day. Pick six locations along the route, and mentally place one of the words at each location. Repeat the journey in your head until you are confident you have paired the words with their locations. Now do something else for an hour and after that time try to recall the six words by making the journey again in your mind.

Four groups of participants took part in the study altogether – one group of younger children (mean age 9.6 years), one group of older children (mean age 11.9 years), one group of younger adults (mean age 22.5 years) and one group of older adults (mean age 66.9 years). Using the modified Method of Loci, during the encoding phase of the study, target words were shown to participants paired with visual images of a particular location. During the test phase, participants were shown images of the locations, which served as cues to help them to remember the target words.

Before the study, each participant's baseline memory performance was measured to see how well they could remember lists of words without the use of any particular strategy. Then participants were introduced to the memory strategy over multiple sessions, and each participant received individual practice and training sessions over a period of time to try and maximise their memory ability.

The results of the study showed that younger adults had the highest level of baseline memory ability of all of the four groups, suggesting that this may be the period of our lives when our memory abilities have reached their natural optimum level. All four groups showed an improvement in memory after instruction in using the mnemonic technique, although again it was the group of younger adults who benefitted most from this. Older adults seemed to be most at a disadvantage over the other groups in the extent to which they improved following the extended period of practice and training.

This study supports the view that baseline memory ability improves through childhood, peaks in younger adulthood and then declines in older adulthood. However, it also shows that even older adults have the potential to improve their memory by using specific strategies, although repeated practice and training in such strategies will have less of an effect on older adults than it will with younger adults or children. Bear in mind, too, that the 'older adults' in this study were between 65 and 78 years of age, and so these kinds of decrements in performance really are occurring only very late in the human lifespan.

Developments in storage

One of the areas in which children's memories are limited is the length of time for which information can be stored. In this section, we consider how improvements in storage affect the development of memory in childhood.

In terms of long-term memory storage, most of the research with infants which uses the visual recognition memory techniques discussed earlier in this chapter allows us to judge that infants recognise previously viewed stimuli a few seconds or minutes later. For example, Rose (1981) found that infants aged just six months could recognise previously viewed stimuli after delays of 5 seconds and 20 seconds. A delay of two to three minutes was problematic for the six month olds, but not for infants of nine months. This suggests that in the first six months, long-term storage is limited. However, some research has shown that even young infants can remember things for much longer periods than that and, during their first year, there is evidence of an improvement in the length of time for which infants can retain information.

For example, early research by Fagan (1973) reveals that at four or five months of age, infants show recognition memory for images which were viewed up to two weeks previously. Some studies have shown that by 18 months of age, infants can retain information for as long as 13 weeks (Hartshorn *et al.*, 1998).

These experimental studies of children's memories tell us about what infants can remember of carefully controlled visual stimuli in laboratory settings. Such stimuli are viewed for short periods of time, during which the infant has the opportunity to become familiar with them. This is a different situation to when infants appear

Definition

Mean: a statistical term which refers to the numerical average of a set of numbers. To calculate the mean, add all of the numbers in the set and divide by the number of items in the set.

to recognise their parents, with whom they have had long periods of exposure on a regular basis since birth. Think back to the example of baby Ella at the beginning of this chapter. Anecdotal reports of children like Ella's responses to their parents also suggest that infants have the ability to encode, store and remember. Within cognitive psychology generally, the study of face recognition has become an important field of investigation, exploring this very specific aspect of human memory. Within developmental psychology, the study of face recognition in infancy and early childhood is also now an established field of enquiry (see Recommended Reading).

There is an interesting phenomenon in the study of memory development which seems to contradict this general improvement in long-term retention, though, and this is referred to as infantile amnesia. Right at the beginning of this chapter, you were asked to Stop and Think about what your earliest memory is. The memory we have for our own lives, things which have happened to us, places we have seen and things we have done, is called autobiographical memory. For most of us, the first three years of our lives are simply not available for conscious recall, despite the memory abilities which infants and young children have been shown to have. So our autobiographical memories have a significant gap in them. Think back to the example of baby Ella at just five months of age. Despite her obvious recognition of her mother and father at that age, and the novelty of being left with a babysitter for the evening, as an adult Ella is unlikely to have any memories of that evening, or of anything else which happened to her during those first three years of her life. Much has been written about this phenomenon and the extent to which it can be explained by the research to date about developments in children's memory (see Recommended Reading), but it is still not clear whether infantile amnesia is a problem with the encoding, storage or with the retrieval of information. One theory put forward by several authors concerns the importance of language for recall. Perhaps in the pre-verbal stage of their lives, the absence of language somehow cre-

ates problems for children's long-term storage of information. Maybe language is necessary for long-term storage, in order to make abstract representations more concrete and meaningful. Alternatively, perhaps once language is acquired, memories which were stored during the pre-verbal stage somehow become inaccessible. This could be another example of the relationship between memory development and developments in other areas of cognition, a possibility which we discussed earlier in relation to theory of mind. There may also be links to the development of identity which is discussed in Chapter 11, Development of Self-concept and Gender Identity as some researchers suggest that a sense of self may be necessary before autobiographical memory can truly begin (Howe and Courage, 1997). In any case, this is an area of children's memory development which is still very much open to investigation, and perhaps new technologies being used in psychological research may help to shed some more light on the issue in the decades to come (see Cutting Edge box).

Interestingly, in 2006 the BBC's Radio 4 broadcast a series of programmes called The Memory Experiment, which invited listeners to submit details of their own memories, including their earliest memory. The information has been collected and analysed in conjunction with Martin Conway, a cognitive psychologist. He reported that around 10 000 recorded memories had been received by March 2007, and this has therefore become the biggest collection of memories anywhere (Conway, 2007). Analysis of the memories supports previous research about infantile amnesia, in that when we attempt to recall things from the early part of our lives, the average age of people's earliest memories is three-and-a-half years. So, whilst there seem to be general improvements in infants' ability to store information for longer and longer periods of time during infancy, there is very little in the way of any long-term retention of that information into adulthood. Either that, or the way in which that information is encoded during infancy makes it inaccessible in adulthood and therefore not retrievable.

Developments in retrieval

In this section, we explore the age-related improvements in retrieval which may assist with memory development in childhood. Encoding and retrieval are closely linked processes, and memory research in general supports this.

Tulving's (1983) encoding specificity principle states that retrieval will be better in the presence of cues which were also present at the time of encoding. Cues may be any other stimuli which were present at the time of encoding, from the particular colour or precise shape of the stimuli which were encoded, to the context in which encoding occurred – like the room in which it took place or the music which was playing at the time. This has been found to be particularly true of infants. So for young infants, retrieval will only occur if the cues at the time of retrieval are practically identical to those which were present at encoding. Slight variations in the cues which are present can reduce memory performance to almost nothing. One study found that just changing the appearance of an infant's playpen from a striped pattern to a squares pattern can affect the infant's memory (Borovsky and Rovee-Collier, 1990). What might this mean for infants who move house? What advice would you give a parent considering repainting their child's nursery? As children get older, though, their retrieval system becomes more flexible and they can recall information despite variations in the retrieval context and even despite variations in the stimuli presented.

There is also evidence that if certain reminders are given prior to an attempt at retrieval, these can help with the retrieval of memories which would previously have been assumed to be forgotten. In a key study, Rovee-Collier *et al.* (1980) used a technique known as the mobile conjugate reinforcement paradigm (mentioned in Chapter 4), to demonstrate that reminders could serve as important aids to retrieval by infants as young as three months. Using this technique, an infant is placed in a cot with a mobile suspended above it. The mobile is attached to the infant's leg with a ribbon, and by kicking their legs the infant can make the mobile move. Infants quickly learn that they can make the mobile move, and after training they will start to kick as soon as they are placed in the cot. However, they are quick to forget this, and after a gap of just two weeks from the end of their training, when placed back in the crib with their legs attached to the mobile, infants do not seem to remember what they had previously learned. What this study found, though, was that if an infant was given a reminder of the task the day before testing by simply being shown the mobile, then the following day their recall was much better. This suggests that the infants had not forgotten what they had learned after all. It was still stored in their memory somewhere, but they needed a reminder in order to be able to retrieve the information.

Subsequent research has shown that as children get older reminders can still be effective, even given longer gaps since the original encoding took place and also that the interval between the reminder and a subsequent successful retrieval gets shorter as children get older. Following a reminder, it takes younger children longer to successfully retrieve the memory, whilst older children can retrieve the memory more rapidly (e.g. Boller *et al.*, 1990). As children get older, the reminder itself can be shorter and yet still be effective. Hsu and Rovee-Collier (2006) found that a two-minute reminder could reactivate the memory of 15 month old infants, whilst a 10-second reminder was sufficient to reactivate the memories of 18 month olds. All of this suggests that retrieval improves with age. Getting access to memories which seem to have been forgotten is possible, and children's retrieval systems seem to get more flexible as they get older.

The influence of prior knowledge and expectations

As children get older, they accumulate knowledge and information about the world. This results in children having quite well-formed expectations as to how the world works. For example, by the time baby Ella reaches five years of age she will have attended the birthday parties of many of her friends, and will have developed a set of expectations, or a script, for birthday parties. Based on the numerous parties she has attended, the specific details of which will have varied from party to party, Ella has developed a very generalised script for what should happen at a birthday party. Ella's script includes the knowledge or expectation that she should take a present and a card along for the child whose birthday it is. She

---

Definitions

Encoding specificity principle: a principle which states that memory is improved when contextual information present at the time of encoding is also available at the time of retrieval.

Cues: stimuli which assist with the retrieval of information from memory by providing a hint or by helping to recreate something of the original encoding environment.

Neuroimaging in memory development research

Recently, psychological research has begun to make use of advances in technology which allow us to study which parts of the brain are activated under certain conditions, by showing images of which parts of the brain 'light up' when we are engaged in certain mental tasks. These are known as neuroimaging techniques, and one such technique which has recently been applied to the study of children's memory is fMRI (functional magnetic resonance imaging).

Chiu *et al*. (2006) were particularly interested in the encoding of episodic memories by children. They studied which parts of the brain were involved when children attempted to encode episodic memories, and compared these to the parts of the brain which are involved when adults encode episodic memories. Using fMRI, the authors were able to identify which parts of the brain were active when children attempted to encode information. Two tasks were carried out by the children – one where they had to generate a verb from a noun that they had heard, and a second where they listened to short stories. During a subsequent test phase, they assessed children's recognition memory for the information presented (that is, whether the children recognised stimuli as having been presented previously or not). By analysing which information was successfully remembered by children, and examining which parts of the brain had been active during the encoding of that information, the authors were able to conclude which parts of the brain had been involved in the successful encoding of episodic memories in children of different ages, and how this compares to the activity of adults' brains during such encoding.

Definition

Neuroimaging: techniques which provide images of the structure and/or functioning of the brain.

In adults, the prefrontal cortex and the medial temporal lobe (MTL) have been shown to be associated with encoding episodic memories. The researchers in this study found that with children, the left prefrontal cortex was involved in the verb generation condition, but the MTL was not. For the story comprehension condition, activation of the left posterior MTL was found to be involved in encoding episodic memories, but the left anterior MTL and the prefrontal cortex were only involved in encoding for older children (10 years plus).

More traditional research methods tell us about what children can or cannot do in terms of the memory-related performance and behaviour which we observe. This cutting edge technique allows a new dimension to be added to our understanding of how children's memory develops, by indicating which parts of the brain are involved. By comparing children's brain activity to that of adults, and by examining the brain activity of children of different ages, we can start to build up a picture of the neurological changes which take place during development.

Such techniques have their limitations, however. The photo below is a scanner. Children are required to lie on a moveable table which slides in and out of a large, cylindrical tube. Whilst this occurs, they are instructed to carry out whichever mental tasks or activities are required. In the study we are discussing here,

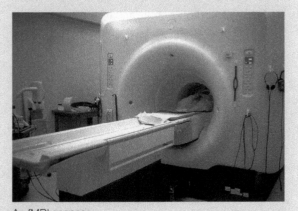

An fMRI scanner.

Source: Alamy Images/Tina Manley

the task required children to simply listen to auditory stimuli which they heard through headphones. However, it is important to note that the scanner itself makes a considerable amount of noise, not all of which will be eliminated by headphones. In addition, someone undergoing an fMRI scan has to lie as still as they possibly can. Even adults find this uncomfortable and difficult. This makes fMRI scanning virtually impossible to use with very young children, and the whole experience is likely to feel very strange for children of any age.

It is worth thinking about how demanding even a short scanning session like this is likely to be for a child. Nonetheless, as advances in such neuroimaging technologies continue, more 'user-friendly' versions may appear. Already there are variations of the traditional scanners available (for example, open MRI machines) which are open on all sides and therefore feel less threatening. In the future, perhaps, researchers will be able to make more use of these, particularly for research with young children.

also expects that there will be party games. Her script includes the expectation that certain types of food will be served, including jelly and ice-cream for pudding, and that at some point there will be a cake, with candles, which the 'birthday boy' or 'birthday girl' will blow out, whilst the guests all sing 'Happy Birthday!'. Ella's script also includes the expectation that there will be 'goody bags' for all of the guests to take home with them, and that a slice of birthday cake will be included in each bag.

Children as young as three years of age have general scripts for everyday events such as going to the supermarket (e.g. Nelson and Gruendel, 1981). When asked what happens during an everyday event like that, children give general accounts which are organised according to the order in which things occur. 'You buy things and then you go home' is one such account which is simple but structured and general. This account is not referring to a spe-

cific instance of going to the supermarket yesterday, but reveals that the child has a more generalised understanding of what happens every time one goes to the supermarket. The fact that children tend to use the impersonal pronoun "you" in these accounts, rather than the personal pronoun "I", further supports the assumption that their understanding of a trip to the supermarket goes beyond any specific instance of that event.

Each party Ella attends will lead to the encoding of lots of new information specific to that particular party, for example, what colour the goody bags were, or which particular party games were played. These details vary from event to event, but Ella's script for birthday parties means that all of that information can simply be slotted in to the appropriate part of the script, to fill in the blanks. The script serves almost like a box within which there are various compartments for organising specific information. New information is placed into the appropriate compartment within the box, and can be stored and subsequently accessed if required, in a much more structured way than if there were no script. As children get older, then, the development of scripts is one way in which prior knowledge and expectations may help with the encoding, storage and subsequent retrieval of information. For more information on scripts see Recommended Reading.

What is responsible for 'forgetting'?

It is clear from the previous section that all three parts of memory develop across childhood, and that when a child is unable to recall something, it is often difficult to

Eating cake will be a feature of children's experiences of birthday parties from early in life

Source: O'Donnell

separate out the role of the three different memory processes in forgetting. It could be that information was never encoded successfully in the first place. It could be that it has been lost from storage. Or it could be that the information is stored, but the child is unable to retrieve it. In addition, the mystery of infantile amnesia shows us that it is possible for large chunks of information to have been forgotten, and yet for us to have only a limited understanding of why this might be the case. However, there are certain instances of forgetting or incorrect remembering which are worthy of some special consideration – post-traumatic amnesia and false memories. Post-traumatic amnesia is when memories are forgotten or repressed following some traumatic event, and so it occurs when real memories appear to be lost. False memories occur when children report something which did not actually happen.

Post-traumatic amnesia

Repression is a feature of human memory which some psychologists believe allows memories for difficult, troubling or traumatic events to be hidden from our conscious minds, sometimes for decades, before emerging from the unconscious and making themselves known to us consciously. The very idea that human memory is capable of repression forms the basis for psychoanalysis; however, it is a hotly contested issue (e.g. Holmes, 1990). Loftus (1993) published a groundbreaking review of the evidence for how real such repressed memories are, in the light of increased numbers of alleged cases of childhood sexual abuse which were being reported by people many years after the abuse was said to have occurred. Loftus concluded that memory is incredibly malleable, and that in fact it is possible for our minds to create entirely false memories for traumatic events which in fact never took place. Nonetheless, as Loftus pointed out, that does not mean that all memories for traumatic events are false, and nor does it help us to distinguish between real repressed memories and false memories.

Definition

Repression: a psychological defence mechanism which allows uncomfortable memories to be stored in the unconscious mind.

Childhood sexual abuse is one of the most difficult and sensitive issues in the study of children's memory for traumatic events, and some research has focused specifically on the forgetting of child sexual abuse (e.g. Ghetti et al., 2006). However, the study of post-traumatic amnesia has also included cases of repressed memories for other events, including witnessing a murder. The evidence suggests that there is no good reason to suppose that at least some of the reported cases of repression and subsequent recovery of traumatic memories are not genuine. For example, Ghetti et al. (2006) interviewed adults who were known to have been victims of child abuse as children, and found that 15% of those adults reported having experienced a complete forgetting of the abuse at some point in their lives. Even now we cannot be sure which memory processes are involved in repressing these memories. However, there is certainly enough evidence to suggest that something different is happening when traumatic childhood memories are repressed, as compared to the forgetting of ordinary memories, and that this may involve specific mental processes which affect our memories in order to defend us against the possible negative effects of traumatic events (see Brewin [2007] for a comprehensive review of the empirical research in this area). Nevertheless, many psychologists are uncomfortable with accepting the notion of repressed memories because there seems to be no rigorous, scientific way to validate their authenticity. In fact, one psychologist has remarked, 'Warning. The concept of repression has not been validated with experimental research and its use may be hazardous to the accurate interpretation of clinical behaviour' (Holmes, 1990, p. 97).

False memories

A false memory occurs when someone recalls something which did not actually occur, or recalls the details of it incorrectly. False memories represent a different kind of failure of memory to those referred to in the previous section. However, false memories and recovered memories pose similar questions for psychologists. When someone tells us that they remember something happening, how can we possibly know whether their recall is accurate or not? Children's memories appear to be particularly susceptible to false memories. They will often tell far-fetched and fantastic stories about things they have seen or done, with amazing conviction and detail. Imagine, for example, a five year old boy on the journey

STOP AND THINK

Going further

Within the study of memory in mainstream cognitive psychology, 'fuzzy trace theory' (FTT) offers a framework for understanding how information is processed and stored (Brainerd and Reyna, 1990). When applied to the area of false memories in both adults and children, it offers one possible explanation of how and why these might occur. FTT suggests that two types of memory traces are represented or stored – gist traces and verbatim traces. Roughly speaking, verbatim traces are representations of the specific details of target information, whilst gist traces are representations of more general meanings or things associated with the target. Think of someone you have recently met. You might have specific memories of their name and what they were wearing or what they looked like, but you might also have memories for how you feel about them, places you associate them with, knowledge of how you met or things you have in common. Verbatim traces are internal representations of your actual experience with that person, and could therefore be shared by anyone else who was also there at the time; Gist traces are the representations which you have added to your memory, through your understanding of the person and what that encounter meant to you.

Memories can be accessed through either gist or verbatim traces, depending upon the retrieval cues, and the processing of both verbatim and gist information generally improves with age (Bjorklund and Jacobs,

1985; Brainerd and Reyna, 2001). Younger children are more suggestible when it comes to accepting gist-consistent false information. Imagine a young child who was wearing a blue dress the day before, but to whom we say 'That was a lovely red dress you were wearing yesterday'. Our statement is gist-consistent (in that the child was indeed wearing a dress the day before) and that child is more likely than an older child to falsely remember wearing a red dress when tested subsequently on recall or recognition. This general pattern of younger children being more susceptible to false information has been observed in many studies (see Bruck and Ceci 1997 for a review).

Interestingly, FTT suggests that the increase in gist processing as children get older may actually make older children and adults more susceptible than younger children to certain types of false memories (Brainerd and Reyna, 2004). When presented with a list of words which overlap in meaning (gist) or are semantically related (see Chapter 5, Language Development), adults and older children will be more likely to incorrectly remember a semantically related word which was not on the list (Brainerd *et al.*, 2002).

- Can you recall an instance where you or someone else incorrectly remembered something?
- Think about some of the issues we have covered in this chapter to do with encoding, storage and retrieval. What do you think might have been responsible for your false memory?

home from nursery with his dad, explaining clearly the details of the trip he made to the moon that afternoon! Whilst we might generally find such tall tales charming and entertaining, what should we do if a child tells us something which we find disturbing? Can we ever know whether a child's stories are fact or fiction?

There is an important distinction to be made between the deliberate reporting of false memories by children, and the incorrect reporting of false memories. If a child reports false information knowing that it is false, then this constitutes lying, deceit or sometimes storytelling. However, what is of interest in the study of memory development are instances of children reporting information which is false, but which they believe to be true.

Suggestibility is the term which is used to refer to how likely a child is to report false memories. A child

may be suggestible because of cognitive and/or social factors (Ceci and Bruck, 1993; Reyna *et al.*, 2002). Cognitive factors relate to the memory system itself – in other words, the processes of encoding, storage and retrieval. Social factors require us to look at the context in which the child's report is made, in order to understand their false memories. For example, we know that children are suggestible to reporting false memories if they are asked leading questions. Let's consider a child who has been on a day trip to a farm, where they saw pigs, cows and sheep. Asking the question, 'What colour was the gorilla?' itself

Definition

Suggestibility: how susceptible someone is to ideas or information presented by others.

suggests that there was in fact a gorilla, even though there wasn't! This kind of question is difficult for a child to respond to adequately, and is likely to lead them to respond with a colour. To even understand the question, the child needs to imagine a gorilla at the farm, and merely by doing so they have incorporated a gorilla into their memory of day at the farm, making them more susceptible to falsely reporting that they saw a gorilla at the farm when they are asked about it later.

Scripts, which we discussed earlier in the chapter, may also affect children's suggestibility, because a child's expectations of an event may influence their recall of the reality of that event. Let's think again about Ella's script for birthday parties. Part of her script includes the expectation that at parties there is jelly and ice-cream for pudding. After attending yet another party, her mum asks what she had for pudding, to which Ella responds, 'Jelly and ice-cream'. In fact she had Angel Delight! This incorrect report is not due to any deliberate attempt on Ella's part to mislead her mother, but simply because her recall of an event is highly influenced by her prior knowledge and expectations of birthday parties. In this way, a script can impose itself upon children's memories in a top-down way, and can influence the information which is recalled. For much more information about false memories, see Recommended Reading.

Cognitive interviews

In recent years, the incidence of children giving evidence in court has increased. Video-recorded or video-linked evidence from children has become admissible (e.g. Home Office and Department of Health, 1992), and the age at which children are permitted to give evidence is getting lower. In Scotland, there is no legal minimum age at which a child may be considered capable of giving evidence. All of this brings other important reasons to research the nature of false memories. Judges and juries need to know what the likelihood is of a child being able to give an accurate account of things which have happened to them, or which they have witnessed, and those interviewing children for such purposes need to know how to go about this in such a way that it maximises the chances of children providing accurate accounts. For this reason, a technique is used called the cognitive interview (CI) which is described in full by Milne and Bull (1999) (see also Recommended Reading). There are four key elements to the cognitive interview. Firstly, the interview

should entail context reinstatement. In other words, instead of the child being encouraged to simply recall a small amount of 'target' information, the interviewer should assist the child to mentally reconstruct the physical and personal context which surrounded the event. Where did it take place? What was the weather like? What else could you see? What noises were there? How were you feeling? Where had you been previously? What were you planning for that day? Secondly, the child should be encouraged to recall everything. In other words, no attempts should be made to filter out information which is perceived to be irrelevant. The child should be encouraged to recall as much detail as possible. The reason for these first two elements of the CI links back to the discussion of encoding specificity earlier in this chapter. The principle of encoding specificity states that information is more likely to be successfully retrieved if the specific context in which in was encoded can be replicated. By getting children to remember as much as they can about the circumstances surrounding the 'target' information in a CI, it is hoped that the original encoding context can be re-created, and that this will help with accurate recall.

The third key element of a CI is that the child should be encouraged to change their perspective. In other words, the interviewer should try to facilitate the child recalling what events or things would have looked like, or sounded like, from the perspective of someone else who was involved in the situation, or from a different position in the situation. In much research into these interview techniques, psychologists have had to make use of events or situations which children have been routinely involved in, such as eye tests or doctors' examinations, and then interview children about these events. So a child could be asked to think about what the receptionist would have seen from her seat, or what something would have looked like from the opposite side of the room to that on which the child was sitting herself. Fourthly, the CI attempts to get the child to remember things in a different order to the chronological order in which they

---

Definition

Cognitive interview: a technique developed specifically for interviewing witnesses in legal situations, using principles of memory from cognitive psychology, to maximise the amount of information which is accurately recalled.

actually happened. These third and fourth elements of the CI are included in order to vary the way in which information is retrieved. Retrieval can be thought of as the process of following a route which eventually leads to a memory. Most memories have several such routes which we could follow in order to gain access to them. For example, FTT suggests that memories can be accessed through verbatim and gist information, as discussed earlier in the chapter. This is known as varied retrieval. Some routes are faster, some are slower, some are more accessible than others whilst some are very difficult to follow. By attempting to access a memory via alternative routes, recall is less likely to rely upon a child's prior knowledge or expectations of the situation (such as scripts, which were discussed earlier).

Milne and Bull (2002) provide an overview of these four components of the CI, and report the results of a study which they conducted to determine whether any one of these four on their own improves recall more than the others. Three groups of participants (adults, eight/nine year olds and five/six year olds) took part in the research, and were interviewed after viewing a video of an accident. The participants were allocated to groups, each of which was interviewed according to just one of the four elements of the CI. A fifth group were interviewed using a combination of the 'report everything' and 'context reinstatement' components, and a sixth (control) group were simply asked to 'Try again'. The results showed that each of the four components of the CI were of equal benefit to participants' recall, and that there were no age-related differences in the extent to which recall improved using each of the four components.

To find out the truth about what Ella really had for pudding at the birthday party using the CI technique, an interviewer might try asking her to recall the meal from the perspective of one of the other children at the party, or from the point of view of the 'birthday boy's' mum. This should allow access to the memory of what was eaten via a route which is free from Ella's own general knowledge and expectations about what one eats at a party. By reconstructing an event from someone else's point of view, or in a different order to that which actually took place, a child should be able to recall without the influence of additional information which is imposed onto their memory of the event, and it is hoped that their recall will be closer to the event as it actually occurred.

Memory is a key part of a child's cognitive processes, and memory tasks often feature in tests of intelligence.

If we think back to the case study of Baby Ella at the beginning of the chapter, we might consider her to be an intelligent baby, due to the fact that she showed some recognition of her parents at such a young age but, as she gets older, how might Ella's intelligence be tested more formally? How might our expectations of her as an intelligent child change as she grows up? What would she have to do to impress us and convince us of her intelligence at the age of five, for example? The rest of this chapter considers the nature of intelligence and intelligence testing, in order to understand the development of intelligence.

What is intelligence?

When we talk about someone being intelligent, or make judgements about one person being more or less intelligent compared to another, what is it that we are actually talking about? This is a contentious issue, and not all psychologists agree with one another about what constitutes intelligence. We will explore some of these different perspectives in the rest of this chapter. Generally speaking, intelligence is thought to be made up of the cognitive processes of memory, problem solving and thinking. How intelligent a person is is an indicator of how well they process information, solve problems and adapt or learn from experience. The developments in memory which have been explored in the first part of this chapter are therefore a part of the development of intelligence.

STOP AND THINK

Reflection

Which of the following four men would you consider to be the most intelligent? Rank them in order from the one you would consider to be the most intelligent, to the least intelligent:

Bill Gates

Gandhi

Stephen Hawking

William Shakespeare

- What is it about each of them which led you to rank them as you did?
- What does this tell you about your own personal ideas regarding the nature of intelligence?

Intelligence in children

What makes for an intelligent child? How intelligence is defined, and the importance of this for education and schooling, are discussed in Chapter 14, Developmental Psychology and Education. Should we be looking for the same kinds of behaviours or abilities that we have considered in the men above, just on a smaller scale? Or does intelligence in children manifest itself in different ways? In adults, as we have considered above, intelligence is generally judged on the basis of things like what they say, their ability to answer different questions or solve problems and the way they express themselves and interact with others. One particular challenge for developmental psychologists studying intelligence in children is that their language abilities may be limited or even absent, depending upon their age. Children's answers to questions might be affected by their language development rather than a reflection of their intelligence. In the remainder of this chapter, we will consider various issues relating to the study of intelligence in children, including how intelligence testing has been approached, how it has been conceptualised and how nature and nurture interact in its development.

Approaches to intelligence testing

When thinking about testing intelligence, what most frequently comes to mind is the notion of IQ, which stands for 'intelligence quotient'. A person's IQ is calculated by assessing their mental age, dividing it by their chronological age (their age in years) and multiplying by 100. The very notion that there is such a thing as mental age originated from the French psychologist Alfred Binet in the early 1900s, and his work with children. Binet was asked by the French government to come up with a way of identifying children who would not benefit from education within a standard school setting. Binet thought that a mentally retarded child would perform at the level of a younger child, and so he tested a number of normally developing

> **Definition**
>
> IQ: abbreviation for intelligence quotient – a score obtained from an individual's performance on tests designed to measure intelligence.

children aged between 3 and 11 years on a variety of different tasks, to establish what would constitute normal performance for children of different ages. Subsequently, any child could be tested and their results compared to these norms, and a judgement then made about their mental age. The use of intelligence tests in education is discussed further in Chapter 14.

> **STOP AND THINK**
>
> ### Reflection
>
> - What makes an intelligent baby? Think back to what you have read about infancy in Chapter 4, Prenatal Development and Infancy, about language in Chapter 5, Language Development, and about memory in the earlier part of this chapter. Think about your own children or talk to someone who has children. Did they consider their babies to be particularly 'bright'? What did they base their judgements on?
> - How reliable are these kinds of parental reports?
> - How else might we explore whether one baby was more intelligent than another?
> - What kinds of behaviours would you look for if you wanted to investigate intelligence in babies?

William Stern then took the idea of mental age and came up with the specific formula for calculating IQ explained above. If a child performs at the appropriate level for their age (for example, if a six year old child performs at the level of a six year old) then their IQ should be 100 (because $6/6 \times 100 = 100$). A child performing above the normal standards for their age would therefore have an IQ of above 100, and a child with an IQ of below 100 would be considered to be below average for their age.

Over the years, substantial revisions to Binet's intelligence test have been carried out, to incorporate some of the ideas about IQ, but also to enable an individual child's performance on the different tests to be broken down into four separate areas. These revisions were done at Stanford University in the US and, because of this, the test is now known as the Stanford–Binet. The four areas in which we can now assess a child's performance are quantitative (numerical) reasoning, abstract/visual reasoning, verbal reasoning and short-term memory.

Interpreting IQ

Consider the case of two children, both of whom have been identified by their teachers as particularly able in class. Both children have been IQ tested, and both have IQs of 125, calculated as follows:

James: Mental age = 5
            Chronological age = 4
            IQ 5/4 × 100 = 125

Inanya: Mental age = 10
            Chronological age = 8
            IQ 10/8 × 100 = 125

The fact that both children have the same IQ might lead you to believe that they both have the same level of general intellectual ability. In fact these two children's IQs reveal some important individual differences. James' mental age is one year greater than would be expected according to his chronological age, whilst Inanya's mental age is two years greater than her chronological age. Thus, their level of intellectual superiority is quite different.

In addition, whilst their overall IQ may be the same, when broken down into the four subscales defined by the Stanford–Binet test, we may discover very different patterns of ability in these two children. James may score very highly on verbal and abstract reasoning, and less well on memory and numerical reasoning. Inanya's score may reflect the opposite pattern. Taken in isolation, a child's IQ may not provide us with enough information to give a clear insight into the nature of their intelligence, but the more contemporary revisions to Binet's tests can provide useful information, not just about a child's intelligence relative to other children, but about their own intellectual strengths and weaknesses.

- How would you explain the differences between these two children's level of intellectual ability to someone who didn't know them?
- What do you think might be the benefits of using IQ as a measure of children's intelligence?
- What are its limitations?

One criticism which has been levelled at traditional tests of IQ is that from the normative data we know that mental age plateaus in our mid-teens. This means that there comes a point in development where the mental age part of the calculation will not increase much more. Yet our chronological age continues to increase across the lifespan. It has been argued that this puts adults at a disadvantage when calculating IQ and suggests that such tests ought to be used only with children. To address this, there are intelligence tests which have been devised specifically for use with adults, such as the Wechsler Adult Intelligence Scales.

One intelligence or many?

So far, although it is clear that there is some disagreement about what intelligence is and how it ought to be measured, there is still an assumption that when we talk about intelligence, we are talking about just one thing. Is it more useful to think of there being different types of intelligences? Consider your assessments of the different intelligences of the four famous men previously. Some standard IQ tests do have several sub-tests embedded within them. For example, the Stanford–Binet test includes sub-tests for verbal ability and for numerical reasoning as we have already discussed. Instead of looking at these as constituent parts of one general intelligence (sometimes referred to as 'G'), maybe it would be more helpful to think of these as two completely separate intelligences. Gardner (1993) suggested exactly that, and in fact he argued that there are eight different types of intelligence.

Definition

G: an abbreviated way of referring to general intelligence, the common factor believed by some to underpin performance on all intelligence tests.

The eight types of intelligence which Gardner proposed are: (1) verbal; (2) mathematical; (3) spatial; (4) bodily-kinaesthetic; (5) musical; (6) interpersonal; (7) intrapersonal; (8) naturalist. There is certainly an appeal to thinking about children's intelligence in this kind of way. Instead of labelling a child as having either a high or a low level of intelligence, this approach allows us to consider each child's unique set of strengths and weaknesses. To be labelled as having below average intelligence as a child carries a considerable stigma and the effects of that may lead to a lowering of a child's self-esteem or motivation to succeed. In contrast, using a multiple intelligences approach removes the dangers inherent in this kind of labelling and allows each child to be considered as simply different.

Another school of thought suggests that other theories of intelligence fail to recognise the importance of children's emotional intelligence. Emotional intelligence includes children's ability to interpret the emotions of others and the ability to manage their own emotions. Goleman (1995) suggests that emotional intelligence is a far better predictor of someone's actual competence in the real world than more traditional tests of IQ.

However, critics of these multiple intelligence theories ask where we should draw the line in identifying different types of intelligence. For example, if musical ability is to be considered a specific type of intelligence, then why not also writing ability? Should we be adding poetic intelligence to the list? There is an argument that things like musical and artistic abilities should be considered under the banner of creativity, not intelligence, and creativity is explored in the next section. More important is the question of whether the belief that there is only one type of intelligence and only one way of measuring it is actually helpful to understanding children and their development. Using traditional IQ tests allow us to compare children to one another, and to the levels of ability which would normally be expected from a child of their age, and can potentially assist with the identification of children who may require additional support for their learning or development. However, they do not allow us to acknowledge that different children may have different strengths and weaknesses in terms of their abilities. More and more, there seems to be an acknowledgement that there is more than one way in which a child can be intelligent.

Intelligence versus creativity?

The word 'creativity' refers to the ability to think about something in an original or unique way or in a way which differs to how the majority of other people would think about it. Sternberg (1985) developed another theory of multiple intelligences, but one which included just three types as opposed to Gardner's eight types. Referred to as the 'triarchic' theory of intelligence, it includes (1) analytical intelligence; (2) creative intelligence and; (3) practical intelligence. Children who are creatively intelligent might not perform well on standard tests of IQ but they are quick to come up with solutions to novel questions or problems, or to come up with novel solutions to standard questions. Analytically intelligent children are those who would score highly on traditional IQ tests and would do well on standard maths or verbal problems. Practically intelligent children are good at many of the kinds of things which are not taught at school. Such children might be 'streetwise' and have a good understanding of people, or be good with their hands. Viewed in this way, children who score highly on standard tests of intelligence may not be at all creative, yet creativity is often associated with high intelligence or even genius (see also Gifted children).

STOP AND THINK

Reflection

- Consider some of the great artists or musicians throughout history. Would you consider them to be unintelligent because of the nature of their particular abilities?

- Think again about Bill Gates, Ghandi, Stephen Hawking and Shakespeare, who featured earlier in this chapter. Which one did you consider to be most intelligent, and why? Which one would you judge to be most creative?

Culture fair intelligence testing

Another criticism which has been levelled at traditional intelligence tests is that success on them is dependent

Definition

Creativity: the ability to think in new or different ways or to come up with original ideas, concepts or solutions.

upon a child having prior knowledge and experience with a particular culture. Success on traditional tests often relies upon knowledge of the language in which they were constructed – usually English – because the questions require verbal responses. Western cultural norms and expectations also dominate traditional tests, which means that children from different cultures may interpret a particular question differently and lead to them giving a response which lowers their score on the test, but which is in no way due to their lack of intelligence. In fact, it is interesting that within educational psychology there is a particular phenomenon called divergent thinking which is often seen in gifted or able children (see Gifted children) and is a particular feature of creativity, as explored in the previous section. Thinking about something in a way which differs from the way everyone else thinks about it could actually be an indication of high intelligence. Yet using traditional tests of intelligence, able children as well as non-white children and non-English-speaking children may be at a disadvantage. For that reason, culture fair intelligence tests have been developed.

> **Definition**
>
> Divergent thinking: the type of thinking which is usually the product of creativity and is therefore original.

Cattell's (1940) Culture Fair Intelligence Test (CCFIT) is one example of such a test. It relies mainly on non-verbal test items and uses things like mazes, classification tasks and mirror-images as alternative ways of assessing intelligence which do not depend upon language and culture. For example, after viewing a series of abstract geometric forms, you might have to then select from a set of five other abstract geometric forms the one which completes the progressive series.

> ## STOP AND THINK
>
> ### Reflection
>
> - Can any test can be truly culture fair?
> - The CCIFT is a timed test, so children must attempt to complete the various tasks as quickly as they can within the permitted time. Is the ability to work as quickly as possible really valued equally in all cultures?
> - Is it really a marker of intelligence at all?

Gifted children

Having considered several different approaches to understanding and testing intelligence, this section considers the case of children who, for one reason or another, stand out from the rest in terms of their high level of intelligence or ability. Such children are referred to as gifted, talented or able children. The precise definition of giftedness varies depending upon where you look, but traditionally a child will be considered to be gifted if their IQ is measured at 130 or more. Gifted children may also have a special talent for something, or a particular area in which they excel.

It is important to consider what is responsible for giftedness. Do gifted children have better memories, for example? Or does creativity, which has been discussed earlier in this chapter, have a role to play in explaining giftedness? One study found that mathematically gifted children did not differ from their non-gifted peers in terms of memory ability, but that the conceptual structures they were using were equivalent to those of children about a year older than them (Okamoto *et al.*, 2006). These gifted children were thinking about maths in a way which was fundamentally different to their peers. This can be viewed as the kind of divergent thinking referred to earlier in the chapter, and indicates that creativity, or the ability to think about things in novel ways, may be what is important in understanding giftedness in children.

In early 2008, the digital television channel E4 launched a new series called *Big Brother: Celebrity Hijack,* where 12 young people who each had an exceptional level of ability in a particular field moved into a house together for just over three weeks. These included: Victor, a circus performer; John, a politician; Amy, an artist; and Calista, a singer–songwriter. It is interesting to consider how each of these young people would fare on a 'traditional' test of IQ. Could creativity be an alternative way to think about their exceptional talents? Or would the theory of multiple intelligences be the best way to account for the abilities each of them has?

Interactions between heredity and environment in development

The information in the nature-nurture box allows us to make some judgements about the relative effects of genetic material which children inherit from their parents

NATURE–NURTURE

'Twin' research in the study of intelligence

The issue of how children are affected by the interaction of 'nature' and 'nurture' is a recurring theme in developmental psychology, and nowhere is it a more important or interesting area of investigation than in the study of intelligence. Having explored the question of what intelligence is and how it is measured, this box considers what is responsible for the level of a child's intelligence. Putting aside the questions we have considered about the extent to which various tests are effective measures of intelligence, we now turn to the question of what factors influence or affect intelligence.

Ask yourself: How intelligent am I? Where do I get this intelligence from? Do you think that you have inherited your intelligence from one or both of your parents? How similar or different do you think your intelligence is to that of your siblings?

As has been apparent throughout this book, it is difficult to disentangle the influences of heredity in development from the influences of the environment. Research which has been carried out in an attempt to disentangle these two factors has often made use of twins. This is because identical twins share exactly the same genetics. If intelligence is strongly influenced by genetics then identical twins would be expected to have very similar levels of intelligence. In contrast, non-identical twins share only about half their genetic material. If intelligence is strongly influenced by genetics then non-identical twins would be expected to have less similar levels of intelligence when compared to identical twins.

As well as the influence of genetics, twins (identical and non-identical) will have a certain amount of their environmental influences in common, through being raised in similar environments. Non-identical twins will also have had some unique experiences which differentiate them from their twin. For these reasons, studies of the intelligence of twins who were separated at birth and raised in different environments altogether have been important. If there are large differences between the intelligence of identical twins who were raised separately, then this would suggest that intelligence is strongly influenced by the environment. If, on the other hand, such twins' intelligence remains similar despite their separate upbringings, then the influence of the environment is likely to be weak.

The results of a variety of studies over the years indicate that the influence of genetics is quite strong. Plomin and DeFries (1980) took the results from lots of such studies, combined them, and then analysed them all together, a technique known as a meta-analysis. The results of this meta-analysis showed that pairs of identical twins who were brought up together had IQ scores which were most closely related to one another. Identical twins that were brought up separately showed the next most closely related IQs. Non-identical twins brought up together were next, and then came ordinary siblings brought up together. After them came ordinary siblings that had been brought up separately, and finally came adopted siblings who were brought up together but were not genetically related to each other.

The results from ordinary siblings add another dimension to this kind of research because they share approximately half of the same genetics, which is the same proportion as non-identical twins. But crucially, ordinary siblings will have had more unique environmental experiences than non-identical twins so, whilst the influence of genetics will be approximately the same for these two groups, there will be more variation due to environmental factors.

These results allow us to begin the process of disentangling the relative effects of genetics and the environment, but it is quite clear that both factors do influence intelligence. The fact that identical twins' IQs are more closely related than non-identical twins, regardless of whether those identical twins have been brought up separately or together, shows us that the genetics which we inherit from our parents have a large effect upon our intelligence. Yet the fact that there is still a relationship, albeit a much weaker one, between the IQs of adopted siblings that have no genetic material in common at all shows that the environment does have some effect on intelligence.

Definition

Meta-analysis: a method of statistical analysis which combines the results of many studies to identify an overall effect or change, often in an attempt to overcome problems of small sample sizes in research.

and the environment that they grow up in on intelligence. Yet one interesting finding to emerge is that the effects of heredity and the environment do not necessarily remain the same across the whole of childhood, nor across the whole of a person's lifespan.

As children get older, they accumulate life experiences. By the time they reach adulthood they will not only have had more experiences, but they are likely to have gained a considerable amount of independence. We would probably expect that as twins get older, the number of experiences which each of them have had which are unique to them as individuals and not shared with their twin, will also be greater. Intuitively, we might expect that young children's intelligence will be strongly affected by genetics, in the absence of a great deal of environmental experience. Older children and adults' intelligence might then be expected to be more influenced by experience and less by genetics. In fact, the opposite pattern seems to be true (e.g. McClearn et al., 1997) in that the older we get, the more influenced by genetics our intelligence is. Maybe you can think of some possible explanations for this? One suggestion from those working in this field is that as we get older we are more able to live the kind of life and have the kinds of experiences that our genetic inheritance was always pushing us towards. For example, whilst genetically we might be driven towards experiencing rural living, the influence and control which our parents have over us as children means that we nevertheless spend our childhood living in a city. As we get older, we have more control over our own lives and can follow the direction in which our genetics are pushing us. This means that the older we get, the more our environments are actually the product of the genetics we have inherited (see Recommended Reading). It is almost certainly true that the older we get the more environmental influences we will have had, but if those environmental influences are themselves the product of our genetics then this could explain the greater influence which genetics seem to have as we get older. Some longitudinal research conducted in Scotland supports this, and is discussed below.

The Scottish mental surveys

On Wednesday 1 June 1932 almost every child attending school in Scotland who had been born in 1921 took the same test of mental ability. The same thing happened in 1947, when every child attending school who had been born in 1936 was tested. In 1932, a total of 87 498 children were tested and in 1947 70 805 children were tested. The Scottish Mental Surveys are described in more detail by Deary et al. (2004). The test used was called the Moray House Test, and for each child their performance on the test generated a single score out of a total possible score of 76. The test included questions assessing various aspects of intelligence, including following directions, opposites, word classifications, analogies, reasoning, proverbs, arithmetic, spatial abilities and practical issues. In 1947, data was also obtained for each child tested about their school, its size and location and the number of teachers it had. In addition, specific details including each child's position in their family, date of birth, gender, the size of their family and their attendance at school were obtained.

Deary et al. (2004) report on follow-up data which they obtained between 1999 and 2001, from a sub-set of those individuals who, as children, had participated in the 1932 survey. Participants in this follow-up research were tested using the original Moray House Test, but also using an array of other cognitive tests (including a sub-scale of the Wechsler Memory Scale, the National Adult Reading Test and a test of verbal fluency) as well as the hospital anxiety-depression scale and various physical tests. Many other articles have published findings from follow-up studies of other sub-sets of individuals who participated in the original surveys (e.g. Deary et al., 2000, 2003).

The results from the 2004 study show that there is a great deal of stability in measurements of intelligence, in that an individual's intelligence as measured at the age of 11 would be similar to that at the age of 80. When compared to follow-up data obtained from a sub-set of the 1947 survey, the results also showed that general intelligence (G) plays a greater role in intelligence as we get older.

SUMMARY

Within this chapter we have explored two aspects of cognition – memory and intelligence. Memory is a system, made up of three major component parts – encoding, storage and retrieval. Encoding is the process by which information is taken in from the world around us; storage concerns the way that information is then kept; and retrieval is the process of getting information back out of storage when required. There are different types of memories which children may have. From the earliest days of life, they demonstrate recognition memory for visual and auditory stimuli. As they get older, children demonstrate that they have semantic memories for factual information, and develop autobiographical memories about themselves and their lives. They have implicit memories for skills like riding a bike, and they have scripts for procedures or events.

Researchers face difficulties in trying to study infant memory, because they cannot tell us what memories they have or what the nature of those memories is. Techniques which enable us to make some judgements about memory abilities in infancy include the visual paired comparison task, the mobile conjugate reinforcement paradigm and the use of non-nutritive dummies. At just a few days old, infants can encode information, store it for at least a couple of days and retrieve it. Younger infants take longer to encode information than older infants, and during their first year the length of time for which infants can store information increases. All three parts of the memory system develop through childhood, so that the general improvements we see as children get older are likely to be due to a combination of the improvements which take place in all three areas. The development of working memory and the use of memory strategies may also help with encoding and subsequent retrieval. Encoding and retrieval are closely linked, and the way in which something is initially encoded can affect how it is subsequently retrieved. Overall, as children get older they have more tools at their disposal to help with encoding, and forgetting may occur if encoding is not successful.

Children can generally maintain information in memory for longer periods as they get older. However, this is contradicted somewhat by the infantile amnesia phenomenon, which affects autobiographical memory. This type of forgetting is still not fully understood, but theories suggest that the lack of language in the first years of life may create storage or retrieval difficulties for children, or that true autobiographical memory cannot develop prior to a child's sense of self.

Older children are less sensitive than younger children to differences between the encoding context and the retrieval context. Forgetting may occur in younger children if there are not enough retrieval cues to allow access to the memory. In addition, reminders are more effective with older children even with long gaps since the original encoding, and those reminders can be shorter and still have the desired effect.

The fact that sometimes our memories can be hidden from our conscious mind suggests that additional memory processes may exist to protect us against the potentially damaging psychological effects of a negative event. However, when these kinds of repressed memories subsequently come to light, it can be difficult to validate them and establish whether they are accurate or not. This is because we know that sometimes people recall things which did not actually happen, and children are particularly susceptible to this. Leading questions can cause false information to be incorporated into a child's memory, and prior knowledge and expectations may influence their recall of reality. Cognitive interviews put the knowledge and understanding which we have of children's memory systems to use in order to maximise the amount of accurate information which a child is able to recall.

Traditional tests of intelligence measure IQ, assess a child's mental age as compared to their chronological age and suggest that general intelligence (G) is one thing. Tests of IQ measure a child's overall intelligence using sub-tests of (for example) verbal ability and numerical ability, but have been criticised for being culture-specific, asking questions which assume a certain way of looking at the world, and asking questions in such a way that children from minority backgrounds may understand and respond to them differently. IQ tests have also been criticised for their assumption that children's responses to a variety of different questions are indicative of one underlying level of general intelligence. Traditional IQ tests may disadvantage children who take novel or creative approaches to solving problems. Creativity and divergent thinking are often associated with highly intelligent or gifted children, yet this type of thinking may lead to lower scores on traditional tests of IQ.

Alternative perspectives suggest that tests of verbal and numerical ability should be considered to be measuring fundamentally different types of intelligence. However, critics ask where we should draw the line in associating particular abilities with different intelligences. More recently, theories have been developed which suggest that emotional intelligence should be considered another kind of intelligence. Supporters of multiple intelligences point out that this way of thinking allows us to acknowledge individual differences which exist between children in terms of their strengths and weaknesses, instead of labelling children as above or below some normal level of intelligence.

Despite developmental psychology's focus on childhood, we have seen that in both of these areas of cognition there are changes through adulthood as well. Research suggests that we reach the peak of our memory abilities in young adulthood, at which point it appears to plateau and then declines in older adulthood. For adults who remain physically healthy, a general deterioration in memory may be due to loss of ability in any of the three sub-systems. However, recent research seems to point to encoding as the part of memory where a decline in ability is particularly apparent, because older adults appear less able to benefit from the use of memory strategies.

Mental age increases through childhood and then plateaus in the mid-teenage years, whilst chronological age continues to increase right through the lifespan. When calculating IQ, adults will therefore be at a disadvantage as they get older. This has led to the development of intelligence tests specifically for adults. Twin studies have led researchers to believe that whilst our genetic inheritance is largely responsible for intelligence, the influence of the environment is still important. So intelligence comes about as the result of interaction between these two factors.

REVIEW QUESTIONS

1 Compare and contrast three different types of memories which children may have.
2 Explain the encoding specificity principle, and describe the changes in encoding specificity in children's development.
3 Describe one method designed to research infant memory.
4 In what ways might top-down processing affect children's memory?
5 What is a cognitive interview? Explain the rationale for its different components.
6 How many different intelligences do you think there are, and why?
7 What are the pros and cons of using traditional IQ tests to measure intelligence?

RECOMMENDED READING

For a comprehensive review of the research on infant memory development specifically, see:

Hayne, H. (2004). Infant memory development: Implications for childhood amnesia. *Developmental Review*, *24*, 33–73.

This paper also contains a useful review of comparisons between adult memory research and infant memory research, which may help to answer these questions.

To read other research about the development of children's mathematical abilities and the role of working memory, see:

Barrouillet, P. & Lepine, R. (2005). Working memory and children's use of retrieval to solve addition problems. *Journal of Experimental Child Psychology*, 91, 183–204.

For a thorough examination of the development of children's ability to selectively attend, see:

Miller, P.H. (1990). The development of strategies of selective attention. In D.F. Bjorklund (Ed.), *Children's Strategies: Contemporary Views of Cognitive Development* (157–184). Hillsdale, NJ: Erlbaum.

For more information on the field of face recognition in children, see:

Pascalis, O. & Slater, A. (Eds) (2003). *The Development of Face Processing in Infancy and Early Childhood: Current Perspectives*. New York: Nova Science.

For a consideration of memory research and how it helps us to understand the phenomenon of infantile amnesia, see:

Hayne, H. (2004). Infant memory development: Implications for childhood amnesia. *Developmental Review*, 24, 33–73.

For an overview of the foundations of research into the role of scripts in the development of memory, see:

Nelson, K. & Gruendel, J. (1986). Children's scripts. In K. Nelson (Ed.), *Event Knowledge, Structure and Function in Development* (231–247). Hillsdale, NJ: Erlbaum.

For further reading about false memories, see:

Brainerd, C.J. & Reyna, V.F. (2005). *The Science of False Memories*. Oxford: Oxford University Press.

For a detailed exploration of the development of cognitive interviewing as a technique for improving the witness testimony of children, see:

Fisher, R.P. & Geiselman, R.E. (1992). *Memory Enhancing Techniques for Investigative Interviewing: The Cognitive Interview*. Springfield, IL: Charles C. Thomas.

Geiselman, R.E. & Fisher, R.P. (1997). Ten years of cognitive interviewing. In D.G. Payne & F.G. Conrad (Eds), *Intersections in Basic and Applied Memory Research* (291–310). Mahwah, NJ: Erlbaum.

For a consideration of the influences of heredity and the environment on cognition right across the lifespan, see:

McGue, M., Bouchard, T.J., Iacono, W.G. & Lykken, D. T. (1993). Behavioural genetics and cognitive ability: A lifespan perspective. In R. Plomin & G.E. McClearn (Eds), *Nature, Nurture and Psychology* (59–76). Washington: APA.

RECOMMENDED WEBSITES

Human memory: test yourself:
http://human-factors.arc.nasa.gov/cognition/tutorials/ModelOf/index.html

Cognitive Interviewing: A 'How-To' Guide:
http://appliedresearch.cancer.gov/areas/cognitive/interview.pdf

Mnemonics: fun with words:
http://www.fun-with-words.com/mnemonics.html

The mystery of infant memories:
http://www.brainconnection.positscience.com/topics/?main=fa/infantile-amnesia

fMRI:
http://www.radiologyinfo.org/en/info.cfm?pg=fmribrain&bhcp=1

Take An IQ Test Online:
http://www.iqtest.com/

National Association for Able Children in Education:
http://www.nace.co.uk/

Watch a short video about short-term/working memory capacity. Further resources can be found at www.pearsoned.co.uk/gillibrand

Chapter 8
Theory of mind

Learning Outcomes

After reading this chapter, with further recommended reading, you should be able to:

1. Describe and define what theory of mind is;

2. Critically evaluate the developmental nature of theory of mind;

3. Critically evaluate methods of measuring false-beliefs;

4. Critically evaluate theories underpinning the development and existence of theory of mind;

5. Critically evaluate the research investigating theory of mind in children with autism.

What do we mean by theory of mind?

Mary finished putting her groceries into a bag. "That will be £27.63," said the till assistant. Mary looked in her handbag, shuffled her gloves and keys and looked thoughtful. Then she put her hand into each of her coat pockets, first the right, then the left and sighed.

What did Mary need? What did she believe was in her handbag? Why did she sigh? The ability to understand this scenario and to provide answers to these questions is an example of a concept called by some 'folk psychology' and by others 'theory of mind'. Both describe a process that connects our cognitive development with our social development, for without it we are unable to understand the meaning of other people's emotions or the focus of other people's attention. As we grow in cognitive competence, so we develop the ability to identify the goals, intentions, desires and beliefs of other people.

- Do you ever feel that you have misread a situation or perhaps you know of someone who commonly seems to misread situations?
- Sometimes these mistakes are simply due to a lapse of concentration: we are busy talking on the telephone whilst partly listening to a conversation being held in the same room. But what if you frequently misread situations? Does this have a meaningful effect on your ability to socialise?

Introduction

The scenario described above demonstrates that we are able to infer a person's beliefs, desires and intentions from observing their behaviour. In order to do this, we must each hold a substantial amount of information about our minds and the minds of others, and this is the basic principle of something called 'folk psychology'.

Folk psychology constitutes a large part of psychology, but the main discussion within cognitive science has been how folk psychology allows us to predict and explain behaviour. Being able to predict another person's behaviour has important consequences for us all in everyday life. We try to understand why our work colleagues behave as they do, why our infants cry and why we find ourselves sometimes proven wrong when we think we know where we left something but cannot find it! This ability to predict and make sense of events intrigued the cognitive psychologists in the late 1940s onwards as a challenge to the purely behaviourist perspective that denounced all involvement of the mind in our behavioural responses to events. The influence of the psychoanalytical perspective of introspection providing us with knowledge of the mind had also begun to lose favour, and psychologists were looking for another way to explain our ability to infer desires and beliefs and, in turn, to predict another ▶

> **Definition**
>
> Folk psychology: the information that ordinary people have about the mind and how it works. It is usually based in a common set of traditions and customs that are used to explain people's emotions and behaviour.

▶ person's behaviour. Research into this part of folk psychology has attempted to theorise how we are able to understand and make judgements about other people's behaviour, and it is often conceptualised under the heading of a *theory of mind*. This chapter is designed to help you understand how theory of mind develops in a child, what it means to us and how as developmental psychologists we go about measuring this complex principle.

What is theory of mind?

The term 'theory of mind' was first coined by Premack and Woodruff in 1978, and describes the ability to figure out what a person might believe to be the case in any given situation and, from that, to describe what that person might then do. Think of our example of Mary at the shop. You might infer that she *believes* that her purse is in her bag to pay for her shopping, but her behaviour reveals that she has forgotten her purse. If asked, you might then *predict* that Mary will ask for her shopping to be put aside until she can return with her purse. This ability to predict others' behaviour by inferring a person's motivation is an important social skill and one that uses sophisticated cognitive skills. Premack and Woodruff state that, in order to understand the mental states of others, we must first be able to understand our own mental state. Although the definition of theory of mind describes a wide range of cognitive abilities, these researchers state that most importantly, in order to be able to predict and even explain the behaviour of others, we must be able to make judgements based on two core cognitive skills. First, we must be able to judge what that other person seems to want or desire and second, we must be able to judge what that other person believes to be true. Research demonstrates that this ability to 'mind-read' follows a developmental pathway that maps neatly onto both our cognitive development and our social development, but first let's consider how theory of mind displays itself in the developing child.

The development of empathy and other 'mind-reading' skills

How, then, do we develop the ability to know what another person feels or desires? Take the following scenario. A father takes his son to the park. They walk past a pool of water and the father sees some ducks swimming. He looks at his son and says, 'Look, ducks!' As he does this,

he looks away from his child and towards the ducks. His son follows his gaze towards the ducks, spots them and says excitedly, 'Ducks! Ducks!' At around the age of eight months, when an adult looks away from the child and towards something else, the child will turn his head and look there too. At around 12 months, if the adult points at something of interest to the child, then the child will point at it too. Baron-Cohen (1995) describes these behaviours as first, gaze-following and second, proto-declarative pointing as evidence that the child is learning to coordinate his own mental state (e.g. attention to the object being looked at or pointed at) with that of another person's mental state. Gaze-following in the child shows that the child is aware that the adult is looking at something of interest. Proto-declarative pointing in the child then shows that the child confirms that he knows the adult is pointing at something of interest. These subtle behaviours Baron-Cohen argues are the first early signs and the building blocks of 'mind-reading'.

The next step in 'mind-reading' is to understand that what a person knows about a situation depends partly on what a person sees of a situation. At about age 36–48 months, the child begins to grasp the concept that what another person knows about an event of interest is based in what that person has seen of the event of interest. For example, if the child observes the adult *see* a toy being put away in a box, the child understands that the adult *knows* that the toy is in the box. This principle that

---

Definitions

Theory of mind: being able to infer the full range of mental states (beliefs, desires, intentions, imagination, emotions, etc.) that cause action (Baron-Cohen, 2001).

Gaze following: the ability to follow where another person is looking and to look in the same direction.

Proto-declarative pointing: the ability to point at the same object of interest as another person.

'seeing leads to knowing' is again an important part of a child's cognitive and social development. By learning this key principle, the child is able to make a judgement of what another person may know based on what that person has seen happen.

At around the same time as developing these mind-reading skills, the child begins to show 'meta-representational' or 'pretend' play. Leslie (1994) proposes that children learn to separate what is the truth of a situation from what a person may believe about a situation. For example, if you give a small child a banana, Leslie reports, then that child may play with that banana and pretend it is perhaps a telephone, or a car, a pistol or anything else that comes to that child's mind. Being able to separate out what is true (it is a banana) from what you can believe (it is a telephone, car or pistol) demonstrates that the child is engaging in the skill of meta-representation. Most children demonstrate this skill by the age of 48 months and the research appears to show that the use of meta-representation or 'pretend' play therefore illustrates a child's developing ability to understand that a thought can be based in fantasy and not based necessarily in reality.

All of these abilities – gaze-following, proto-declarative pointing at items of interest, learning that 'seeing leads to

knowing' and using cognitive meta-representations in pretend play – together complete a complex picture of the child's early cognitive development. The gaze-following demonstrates the child's ability to follow the attention of another person. The proto-declarative pointing reveals that the child understands the focal point of the other person, in our example the ducks. The concept of 'seeing leads to knowing' helps the child figure out how another person knows what he knows, whilst pretend play reveals that the child understands that objects can represent other things like the banana representing a telephone, car or pistol. Combining these skills together, you can see that the child is beginning to learn the skills necessary for

> **Definitions**
>
> Seeing leads to knowing: the principle that a person's belief/knowledge about a situation depends partly on what they have seen.
> Meta-representation: (1) The ability to separate reality from fantasy, for instance, during pretend play (Leslie, 1987). (2) Additionally, knowing the difference between what might be represented in a photograph or painting of an object and what the reality of that object might be (Perner, 1991).

This young boy is showing proto-declarative pointing – he is pointing at the same object as his father.

Source: Corbis/Patrick Kociniak/Design Pics

effective social awareness and social interaction. This is demonstrated neatly when observing the behaviour of young children who encounter someone showing emotional upset or distress.

From an early age (around two years), children appear to show an awareness of other people's feelings. If another child or an adult shows sadness or upset, a toddler may go up to them and give them a hug or even say 'there there' and offer comfort. In a paper by Cole *et al.* (1992), the authors discuss this awareness of emotional upset in two year olds responding to two events: breaking a doll and spilling a drink. In the study, Cole *et al.* found that the toddlers would try and fix the problem when it occurred, either by trying to put the doll back together or by trying to mop up the spilt drink. The toddlers' responses were described as 'tension and frustration' at the break or mishap and 'concerned reparation' in trying to repair the damage. The toddlers' response also appeared to reflect the emotional response of their mothers to the mishaps. For instance, the response of the children was different if they had mothers who reported experiencing depression and anxiety. These children were more likely to respond to the incidents in a subdued way, mimicking the response of the mother, when compared to children of mothers not reporting depression and anxiety. The toddlers appeared to be responding to the physical expression of their mother's response and the authors argue that as such this demonstrated that the children had learned empathy.

STOP AND THINK

What other psychological theories might help to explain the subdued reaction of the child of the depressed mother to the breakage?

However, empathy is a complicated notion that describes our ability to understand that how a person feels on the 'inside' (our private self) can be expressed by how the person behaves on the 'outside' (our public self). Were the children of depressed mothers being empathic

Definition

Empathy: the ability to identify with the emotions of others and to read the physical expression of emotions in others.

or were they simply copying the response of the mother? For example, children learn that a person who is smiling on the 'outside' is feeling happy on the 'inside'. The ability to read feelings by the physical expression of them is important if the child is going to be able to empathise with others and have successful social interactions (Baron-Cohen, 1995). The findings of the Cole *et al.* study show that the children of mothers who report depression and who show sadness and disinterest on their faces pick up on this when the toy breaks and react accordingly. Also at this age, children begin to show what we call 'pro-social' behaviours, or behaviours that encourage and support social interaction. For instance, the two year old begins to share her toys and snacks with other people and helps other people out. Children of this age understand that when another child is crying that child is upset and will often react to reduce this feeling of upset by giving them a hug, a toy or a biscuit. The child also at this age starts to develop an understanding of deception and will enjoy hiding objects from sight whilst professing no idea of where the objects are! All of these behaviours reflect the ability to understand the minds of others and are a sign that the child is developing a theory of mind.

Beliefs and desires

The child is developing at this time a sense of the 'private self' and the 'public self'. The 'private self' denotes how we feel 'inside' and the 'public self' denotes how we display our notion of 'self' to others. By learning the distinction between a person having a 'private self' and a person having a 'public self', the child is gaining an important understanding of the adult world. It is a complicated cognitive skill for the child to understand that a person may act happy on the outside but that inside they might be unhappy, although the child will eventually learn to distinguish this. However, initially the child is starting to learn that if another person is acting happy on the outside, they are also happy on the inside. This ability to read feelings by the physical expression of them is important if the child is going to be able to empathise with others. The ability of children to empathise with others is discussed in Simon Baron-Cohen's work on the theory of mind (1995).

An example of theory of mind in action would be this. Show a child a picture of an event, say a girl on a bicycle, a boy on the pavement crying. If you ask the child what is happening, they might say that the girl is riding the bicycle and the boy is crying because he wants a go and she will not let him on it. Alternatively, the child might say that the boy is crying because it is his bike and she has taken it from him. In order to explain the picture, the child has to describe and understand another person's emotions, desires and intentions from this simple vignette. Thus, the child has learnt to deduce a mental state from a visual image which allows them to explain why the behaviour occurs. This is an important ability to acquire. If we were not able to infer a series of events based on key amounts of information, we would not be able to 'read' a social situation. Consequently, if we 'read' a social situation incorrectly, we might find ourselves displaying inappropriate behaviour. By behaving inappropriately in a situation we might be putting ourselves at risk – physically or, more likely, socially. None of us want to feel uncomfortable at a party because we were unable to 'read' the situational cues and see that the party was no longer 'fancy dress'!

This boy is demonstrating empathy as he seeks to console his friend.

Source: Getty Images/Dorling Kindersley

Between the age of 12 and 24 months, the child develops important social skills that correspond to the desire stage of theory of mind. The desire stage suggests that we understand that people have internal states or emotions that correspond to desire. This allows us to predict what people want from understanding their internal state or public display of emotions. For example, a child might say that the boy was crying because he was *upset* at not being able to ride the bicycle. A child who has developed the ability to predict desires from a person's behaviour would be able to understand that the boy was crying because he had the desire to ride the bicycle and for some reason could not. The next step in understanding other people's desires is to also understand that people will act to satisfy their desires. So, in our example the child might continue discussing the story and propose that the boy's crying might attract the girl's attention. If she sees that he is upset because she is riding the bicycle, she may pass it over to him, for him to ride. Thus, from this simple vignette, a child with well-developed desire stage of theory of mind can deduce from the scenario that by crying, the boy has communicated that he is not happy that the girl is riding the bicycle, that he wants to ride the bicycle (otherwise he would not be upset) and his act of crying has brought about the response he wants, for the girl to hand over the bicycle and let him ride it.

By the age of three years, the typically developing child has developed a much more sophisticated level of social interaction. The child's language skills are improving rapidly and their vocabulary is increasing by an average of 10–20 words a week. The child is engaging in cooperative play and has started to allocate a hierarchy to their friendships. Children of this age start to have 'best' friends – a status that may change from day to day. This hierarchy is an important part of childhood as it demonstrates the child is able to allocate greater importance to certain people and lesser importance to others. The child's ability to sympathise with other children's feelings expands to an ability to *empathise* with other children. The child can understand what the other child is thinking and act accordingly. An important part of this

Definition

Desire stage of theory of mind: the ability to detect in someone a strong feeling of wanting to have something or wishing for something to happen.

learning is that the child is also beginning to understand deception. The child might, for instance, be able to keep a birthday party a secret from a younger sibling, knowing that part of the act of surprise is that the recipient does not know that the event is about to happen.

The child's ability to empathise and to predict how another person might act is known as the belief-desire stage of theory of mind. In this stage, the child understands that a person has both *beliefs* as well as desires. Thus using our example above, the boy might have a desire to ride the bicycle and may also have the belief that he is allowed to ride the bicycle. If the beliefs match the desires then the subsequent action will have the goal of resolving those desires. For example, the boy will go to the bicycle, pick it up and ride it. However, what children of this age are also beginning to understand is that someone may have a desire for something but have a conflicting belief. In our example, the boy might have the desire to ride the bicycle but has the belief that he is *not* allowed to ride it, perhaps as he is too small or too young to do so. As a result, the child learning that the boy might have a conflicting belief might interpret the vignette as the boy, although upset because he wants to ride the bicycle, does not do so as he knows he is not allowed to ride the bicycle. Children at age three are beginning to understand that you might not act on your desire if it goes against your beliefs. However, they do not understand yet that the beliefs may be false. In our example, the child interprets the picture as the boy not riding the bicycle because he believes he is not allowed to. However, it may be that he is not allowed to ride the bicycle on the road because it is deemed dangerous, yet he is allowed to ride the bicycle in the relatively safe garden. The child cannot make the judgement yet that the boy's belief might be false.

> **Definitions**
> Belief-desire stage of theory of mind: the ability to make a mental representation of the world.
> Representational stage of theory of mind: the ability to know that someone may believe something is true even when it is not and understand that the mistake happens because they are relying on incorrect or false knowledge.
> False-belief: the wrongly-held belief that something is true.

In Chapter 11 (Development of Self Concept and Gender Identity) we learnt that at age four years the child engages in associative play and as a result starts to encounter conflict in his peer relationships. Associative play does not need cooperation between children. As long as there are sufficient play materials, the children will happily work alongside each other. At age four, the child is considered to be at the representational stage of theory of mind. The child has learnt that beliefs may be false and that someone might misrepresent a situation because of these false beliefs. There are many examples of tasks that can be used to test whether children have a fully developed sense that people act according to their beliefs, even if these beliefs are false.

False-beliefs in theory of mind

Daniel C. Dennett proposed in his essay on the philosophies of the mind that the only way to test the ability to impute mental states is to test the understanding of false-belief (1978). This theory was tested by Wimmer and Perner (1983) who constructed a test of the child's understanding of false-beliefs called the *Maxi and the chocolate* task. In this task, the child is talked through the following scenario: Maxi has some chocolate. Maxi puts the chocolate in a cupboard and goes out to play. Maxi's mother then moves the chocolate to the refrigerator. Maxi comes in from playing and wants his chocolate. The researcher then asks the child: 'Where does Maxi look for his chocolate?' The researchers found that a child of three years of age is likely to answer 'refrigerator' whereas a child of four years of age is likely to answer 'cupboard'. The authors suggest that the three year olds have not yet understood that Maxi's belief about where the chocolate is to be found is different to where the chocolate really is. Maxi has a false-belief about the location of the chocolate, one that the older children only are able to recognise. However, some researchers have criticised the Maxi and the chocolate story for being overly complicated for children of three years of age, reporting instead that the younger children may have simply been confused by the story length rather than being unable to comprehend the perspective of Maxi.

So to address this limitation, Baron-Cohen *et al.* (1985) proposed a simplified story to test a child's recognition of false beliefs. The Sally-Anne task requires the researcher to show a child a card (Fig. 8.1) and to talk her through the following scenario.

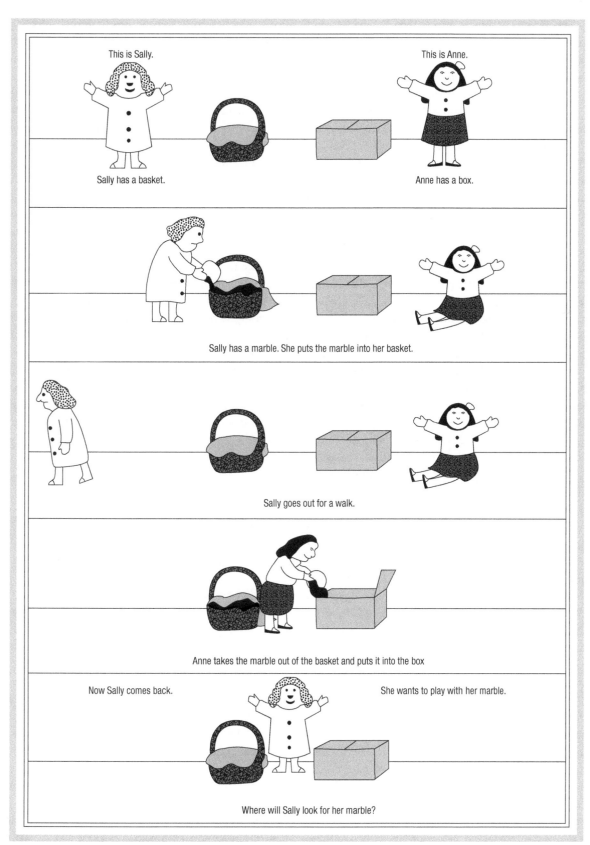

Figure 8.1. The Sally-Anne task.

(*Source*: Frith, U. (1989) *Autism: Explaining the Enigma:* Oxford: Blackwell Ltd)

The researcher points to each of the figures and names them 'Anne' and 'Sally' and explains the scene. To paraphrase the card, Sally puts her marble in the basket and leaves the room. Anne moves the marble to the box. Sally returns to get her marble and the researcher asks the child a number of questions. First the researcher asks the child where Sally will look for her marble. This question tests the child's ability to understand Sally's *belief* about the marble, the correct answer being 'in the basket'. The researcher then asks the child where the marble actually is. This question tests the child's understanding of *reality*, the correct answer being 'in the box'. Finally, the researcher asks the child where the marble was in the beginning. This is a *memory* question that tests the child's ability to recall events and the correct answer is 'in the basket'. These are all critical skills, skills that Baron-Cohen (1995) calls 'mind-reading', that the child needs to learn in order to function well in a social environment. The authors in the 1985 study found that all 27 of the children (age range 3.5 years to 5.9 years) were able to answer the reality and memory questions accurately and that only 23 were able to answer correctly the belief question. The children who could not answer the question correctly were all under the age of four years. Baron-Cohen *et al.* suggest that this shows that the children understood the task, but that the children under the age of four years were unable to recognise or identify with the false-belief part of the test.

Other studies have produced similar results. A study by Perner *et al.* (1987) shows this in what is called the 'Smarties task'. In this test, the researcher shows a tube of Smarties (coloured chocolate buttons) to a four year old and asks them what is in the tube. The four year olds always reply, 'Smarties.' The researcher then opens the tube and shows the child that what is in the tube are actually pencils. The researcher asks the child what they think the other child would say when asked what is in the tube. Again, there appears to be a distinct difference in what children of different ages will say. The four year old will generally answer, 'Smarties'. The four year old knows that pencils are in the tube but appears to understand that another child does not know this and will assume the tube contains sweets. It appears that the four year old child understands the nature of false beliefs. However, when the researcher asks a three year old child what is in the tube, the three year old will invariably say, 'pencils'. The implication here is that the three year old does not understand the nature of false beliefs. Studies like this appear to show the developmental nature of understanding the perspective of others' beliefs, desires and behaviour in young children. However, the findings of studies like these are not without criticism.

Siegal and Beattie (1991) argue that the reason the three year old children fail on this task is because the children make a mistake in understanding the question "Where will Sally look for her marble?" The authors argue that with this standard question, approximately 35% of the children answer correctly. However, if the question is changed to "Where will Sally look *first* for her marble?", the children perform better and just over 70% are able to answer this question correctly. Does changing the question in this way mean the children are now able to better understand the story or is the question now simply easier to answer? Surian and Leslie (1999) first replicated a false-belief task then adapted it to investigate this point with a group of three year olds. Surian and Leslie chose a slightly different story based on Leslie and Thaiss (1992) story of a boy Billy, a ball and three items of furniture: a bed, a dressing-table and a toy-box. The children were told that Billy puts his ball on the dressing-table. Billy leaves the room and his mother enters, picks up the ball and puts it away in the toy-box. The researchers then asked the children a series of questions.

Know question:	'Does Billy know where the ball is?'
Think question:	'Where does Billy think the ball is?'
Memory question:	'Where did Billy put the ball in the beginning?'
Reality question:	'Where is the ball now?'
Look-first question:	'When he comes back, where is the *first* place Billy will look for his ball?'

(*Source:* taken from Surian and Leslie, 1999, p. 148)

This series of questions was designed to test how much the child understands of the story as well as how able the child is to understand the perspective of the boy Billy. Surian and Leslie found that the three year olds were more likely to answer the look-first question accurately than the think question, suggesting that the method of asking is important in gauging whether or not the child has developed the ability to detect false beliefs. The authors propose that by being able to answer the look-first question more accurately than the think question, the children demonstrate that they have some burgeoning understanding of the concept behind the false-belief task without yet having a full understanding of it. Perhaps, too, there is more to these tasks than that of understanding beliefs? The task itself describes a hypothetical event and therefore requires the child to consider what an imaginary child might do in an imaginary situation. Possibly the child needs to develop the appropriate cognitive skills necessary to mentally consider this supposed event and that this cognitive ability may develop *after* the ability to know about beliefs in a real-life situation. The argument in this case suggests that performance on the false belief tasks might have more to do with a child's developing cognitive skills than their capacity for mind-reading.

Wellman *et al.* (2001) conducted a meta-analysis on a wide range of papers published on the theory and measurement of false belief. The meta-analysis sought to find patterns of consistency in 178 studies reporting on the false-belief task and found that, even when accounting for age, country of origin and the type of task described (the Sally-Anne task, Maxi and the chocolate task, Billy and the ball, etc.), there is a clear pattern in the development of understanding the conceptual nature of false-beliefs in young children. The data showed that there is a true change in the understanding of false-beliefs that is unrelated to the limited ability to process such complex information in the very young. The authors report that manipulation of the style in which the questions were asked (such as by Surian and Leslie) improved the performance of children of all ages and not just of the younger children. They conclude that none these studies actually provides evidence of early development of competence: that older children were simply better at the false-belief tasks than younger children. The analysis also showed that prior to developing the understanding of false-beliefs, the children performed at 'chance' levels of accuracy, i.e. their responses were 50/50 right or wrong. Thus the children could not be considered to be making false-belief mistakes on these tasks,

Definition

Meta-analysis: a method of statistical analysis which combines the results of many studies to identify an overall effect or change, often in an attempt to overcome problems of small sample size in research.

rather that they fail to understand the concept of false-belief altogether and understand human behaviour in other, different ways.

It is important to note, that performance on false-belief tasks does not in itself indicate a child's development of theory of mind: however, false-belief tasks do illustrate an important part of a person's early cognitive development. Theory of mind continues to develop in young to middle childhood at the same time as the child's social behaviour becomes more complex. By the time the child reaches the age of six years, there is a sharp increase in the amount of time they spend with their peers. The number of friends a child has increases in number and their peer interactions start to occur in a number of different situations, for example in their own home, in a friend's home and at school. A developing theory of mind helps to facilitate the child's ability to understand the emotional and practical implications of these friendships. For instance, the child's friendships begin to be based on shared interests and their play style is coordinated and involves rules and role-play. Without theory of mind, the child would not be able to infer a child's interests from their choice of toy or game, or to pick up the subtle rules of play.

Theory of mind researchers explain this development in play by describing the children's stage of theory of mind as *second-order states*. This means that the children understand that people may want to evoke an emotion in another person and that we might say or do something to make someone feel good or bad. For example, children understanding second-order states will be able to make sense of this scenario: Fred wants Bill to think he has a present waiting for him at home. The child will understand that Fred has a desire to make Bill believe he is being rewarded. Alternatively, if presented with the scenario: Susan tells Mary that no-one wants to play with her, the child will understand that Susan has a desire to make Mary believe she is unpopular. Children of this age also develop an understanding that people sometimes say things that mean the opposite of what they want to convey and they begin to understand sarcasm. Children of age six will understand when for instance the following story is told to them. 'Fred won the lottery, passed all his exams and got lots of presents. Fred said, "I had a really bad day".' Until the child understands that people sometimes say the opposite of what they mean, they will not be able to make sense of Fred's statement at all.

How does theory of mind fit into a developmental perspective?

As our discussion of theories shows, certain cognitive abilities have to be in place before the child is able to empathise with the viewpoint, the beliefs and behaviours of another. The Wellman *et al.* paper presented the results of a meta-analysis of 178 studies showing that there is definitely a trend in developing theory of mind in young children. Wellman argued that fewer than 20% of children aged two years and six months could complete the false belief task compared with 50% of children aged three years and eight months and with 75% of children aged four years and eight months. Thus theory of mind fits into a similar trajectory of development as other cognitive abilities, such as language and reasoning. Although small changes to the methods used in the false-belief tasks improved performance slightly, change was only seen in those children on the 'cusp' of acquiring theory of mind, i.e. changing the wording of the task helped those children who had a partially developed sense of theory of mind. However, even with changes to the wording of the task, none of the children aged three years and under showed anything other than chance rates of performance when given repeated testing.

Theory of mind and the development of language

The false-belief tasks described by Baron-Cohen *et al.* (the Sally Anne task), Wimmer and Perner (Maxi and the chocolate) and Perner *et al.* (the Smarties task) all rely on the child understanding what the experimenter is asking him to do. All of these studies revealed that there was a developmental aspect to theory of mind but, as Siegal and Beattie suggest, perhaps the studies actually measured development in language competence instead. Siegal and Beattie's study changed the wording in the Sally Anne task to ask 'Where will Sally look *first* for her marble?' and recorded a significant improvement in the accuracy of the children's responses. Similarly, the Surian and Leslie study asked the children a number of questions leading up to the 'look *first*' question and, again,

noted an improvement in the children's performance. All of these studies connect the child's linguistic ability with their theory of mind status, but what if language is a separate cognitive ability to theory of mind? Writers DeVilliers and DeVilliers (in *Children's reasoning and mind* edited by Mitchell and Riggs, 2000, pp. 191–228) propose just this, that perhaps those children who perform less well on the false-belief tasks do so because they do not understand fully what is being asked of them?

There is certainly evidence that children who are more linguistically competent perform better on false-belief tasks and that language training can improve performance on these tasks. Hale and Tager-Flusberg (2003) worked with 60 children between the age of three and five years who had previously made mistakes on the false-belief tasks. Over a period of two weeks, the children were told false-belief stories using phrases such as '_ said he hugged _ but actually he hugged _. Who did _ hug?' For each incorrect answer, the children were corrected and the scenario played out again with emphasis on where the children had made their mistake. The children were tested on standard false-belief-type tasks between three and five days after completing the training. Hale and Tager-Flusberg found that the children's performance on these tasks significantly improved from an initial accuracy of approximately 10–20% to a final accuracy of approximately 70%. This suggests that by helping the children understand the language used, their performance in false-belief tasks improved and therefore their understanding of theory of mind.

As the child's language abilities become more complex, so then it appears does their understanding of theory of mind. What happens, however, if the child does not hear or speak? A study by Meristo *et al.* in 2007 compared the development of theory of mind in deaf children from Italy learning Italian sign language to hearing children. The deaf children in this study had either been taught sign language from birth (native signers) or were introduced to it at school (late signers). All the native signers had at least one deaf parent who used sign language whilst the late signers had parents who could hear and who were not proficient in sign language. The findings of the study showed that deaf children who had been introduced to sign language from birth had theory of mind skills comparable to the hearing children, whilst those children who were late signers had a much poorer score on the false belief tasks.

CUTTING EDGE

Development of theory of mind in children

A paper by researchers at the Radboud University of Nijmegen, the Netherlands, has found evidence that a person's ability in theory of mind tasks at age five years appears to predict their ability later on in life. The authors followed 77 children aged 5 years old for 3 years and found that their theory of mind relating to understanding false-beliefs and emotions continued to develop over the 3 years. The children were given a series of theory of mind related tasks to complete as well as measures assessing language development.

Ketelaars *et al.* (2010) found that increased ability in the false-belief tasks was correlated with the child's ability to understand complex emotions and that both these theory of mind-related abilities developed alongside the child's linguistic capabilities, thus supporting the theory that language and theory of mind are closely connected in child development. This important study is one of few longitudinal designs that attempts to plot theory of mind development in children and it will be interesting to follow this study mapping theory for mind development in children right into adulthood to support the lifespan theory of development proposed by Pardini and Nichelli (2009).

STOP AND THINK

Why do children classed as native signers show better performance on false-belief tasks than children who are late signers?

In further research connecting language development to theory of mind, Peskin and Ardino (2003) report that children start keeping secrets at about the age of four years and those children able to keep secrets perform better at the false belief tasks. At this age, too, children begin to show the ability to detect another person's perspective. Astington (1994) proposed that four year olds can understand that their interpretation of a picture and someone else's interpretation of a picture can be two very different things. In a study of child delinquency, researchers found that children of four years of age begin to lie and not tell the truth, which is another expression of the ability to understand that a person's behaviour is related to their interpretation of events (Stouthamer-Loeber, 1986). All of these cognitive developments relate very much to the child's ability to use language. Thus all the measures of the false belief task are reliant on the child's linguistic skills, and a child with poorly developing language may not be able to vocalise their thoughts and beliefs.

Clements and Perner (1994) set out to investigate just this: whether theory of mind was present in young children unable to express their beliefs verbally. Their argument was that theory of mind might still be present in the younger children, but present as an implicit (not-conscious) concept rather than as an explicit (conscious) concept. As the child learns syntax and semantics in language, so these researchers argue that the child is able to understand another person's beliefs and behaviour. Without the ability to construct meaning from language, the child is unable to make sense of the behaviours of others. Yet, what if the child was able to understand behaviour before she developed the ability to understand language? Clements and Perner set up a study to test whether theory of mind is implicitly present in children and whether this is reflected in their vocal responses. The children were shown a scenario where a doll placed a toy

Definitions

Implicit: implicit knowledge comes from an understanding of what is meant or suggested even when it has not been directly stated.
Explicit: explicit knowledge is that which has been stated clearly and in detail and where there is no room for misunderstanding, confusion or doubt.

in a box on the left-hand side, the doll left the room and whilst absent, the toy was moved to a box on the right-hand side. The children were then asked where the doll would look for the toy and their answers were recorded. When the doll returned, the child's visual gaze was measured. When the researchers asked the children, 'where will the doll look?', they recorded whether the children looked at the box on the left or looked at the box on the right. The researchers proposed that where a child looked during this task indicated where the child implicitly believed the doll would look. Where the child said the doll would look indicated where the child explicitly believed the doll would look. The results of their study show that children under the age of two years and 11 months looked at neither the box on the left nor the box on the right. However, children of approximately three years and seven months looked to the box on the left (the correct answer in the false-belief task), yet only 23% of them spoke the correct answer. The researchers suggested therefore that these younger children knew where the doll would look (showing an implicit understanding of the task) but were unable to explicitly represent the doll's behaviour.

This study by Clements and Perner suggests that these younger children were able to understand the demands of the task and that the incorrect answers given in previous studies actually reflect the immature language abilities of the child rather than an inability to complete the task. By modifying the task to include measurements of eye-gaze, Clements and Perner introduce a refinement to the experiment that detects more sensitively the child's abilities. Since this study was published, many other researchers have attempted to refine the design of their studies to improve the sensitivity of their experiment. In particular, a key paper published by Onishi and Baillargeon in 2005 has shed light on the ability of infants to understand false-beliefs from the age of 15 months. Onishi and Baillargeon used a simple yet sophisticated design involving a yellow box, a green box and a plastic slice of watermelon. The infants were sat in front of a small stage, the two boxes were placed side by side with their openings (covered with a fine fringe) facing each other. The slice of watermelon was placed between the two boxes and behind these objects were doors that were opened and closed during the experiment (see Fig. 8.2, taken from Onishi and Baillergeon, 2005).

First, the infants were shown two scenes that familiarised them with the nature of the event. First, the infants saw the stage set with the two boxes and piece of watermelon. An actor opened the doors behind the boxes, played with the toy watermelon and then placed it in the green box on the right. The scene ends with the

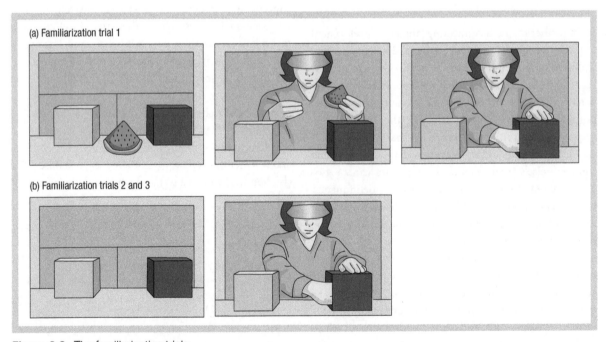

Figure 8.2. The familiarisation trials.

(*Source*: Onishi and Baillergeon, 2005)

actor keeping her hand in the green box and a curtain falls in front of the stage. The second scene opens to show the yellow box and the green box, the actor opens the doors behind the boxes and reaches inside the green box (as if to take the watermelon out). The scene ends with her hand in the green box and a curtain again falls in front of the stage. These trials help the infant become accustomed to the objects and scenarios being played out in front of them.

Next, the researchers created a number of conditions to test whether the infants could detect false-belief in the actor (see Fig. 8.3). The first two conditions create true beliefs in the actor. In condition A the doors open and the actor looks at the boxes and watches the yellow box move towards the green box and return to its original position. The actor in this condition has the true belief that the watermelon is in the green box. In condition B the doors open and the actor looks at the boxes and watches the watermelon move from the green box to the yellow box. The actor in this condition has the true belief that the watermelon is now in the yellow box. The third and fourth conditions create false beliefs in the actor. In condition C the doors remain closed and the actor does not see the watermelon move from the green box to the yellow box. The actor now has the false-belief that the watermelon is in the green box when it is in fact in the yellow box. In condition D the doors open and the actor watches the watermelon move from the green box to the yellow box. The doors close and the watermelon returns to the green box. The actor now has the false-belief that the watermelon is in the yellow box when in fact it has returned to the green box. After each of these conditions the curtain falls signalling an end to the scenario. The curtain rises and the infants see the actor open the doors behind the boxes and reach for the toy.

Onishi and Baillergeon argue that if an infant expects the actor to reach for the watermelon on the basis of her belief about its location, rather than where the infant knows the watermelon to be, then the infant should look for measurably longer when the actor looks elsewhere and confounds the infant's expectations. So for instance, in condition D the actor believes the watermelon is in the yellow box, but the infant knows the watermelon has returned to the green box. When the actor returns to search for the watermelon, if the infant understands the actor's perspective, she will expect the actor to look in the yellow box. If the actor looks in the yellow box, he has confirmed the infant's expectations and the infant's gaze

will be relatively short. If the actor looks in the green box, then he surprises the infant and she will spend longer gazing at the green box. What the researchers found was that the infant's behaviour confirmed their hypotheses, and they argue that these 15 month old infants were displaying representational theory of mind.

Critics of this research, however, have pointed out that these and other authors have over-stated the contribution of their work in discovering young infants' understanding of false-beliefs. Perner and Ruffman (2005), for instance, believe that the infant's long attention to the task does not reflect an ability to attribute beliefs to the actor but that the infant simply notices that something unusual is happening. However, Buttelmann *et al.* (2009) propose that a solution to the limitations of Onishi and Baillergeon and others' studies is to adopt a testing situation whereby the child is an active part of what is going on.

Buttelmann *et al.* recognise that from the age of about 12 months, most children begin to help other people with tasks and problems (Warneken and Tomasello, 2006). Therefore, Buttelmann *et al.* argue, if the child goes to help another child or adult who is trying to complete a task, then that child must be able to understand what the focus of that task is and therefore be able to make a judgement on what the other person intends to happen. This, the authors say, suggests that these children are demonstrating theory of mind rather than simply noticing something unusual going on. In order to test their ideas, Buttelmann *et al.* set children aged both 16 months and 18 months a false-belief task that involved helping behaviour. Each child watched whilst an adult placed a ball in a basket and left the room. An experimenter then moved the ball from the basket into a box. When the adult returned to the room, he went to the basket to retrieve his ball. When he could not find it, the adult set about looking for the ball. As they expected, most of the children behaved in accordance with the nature of the false-belief task and helped the adult find the ball in the box. There was a developmental aspect to the successful completion of the task: the 18 month old children were much more likely to successfully interpret the actor's perspective on the task, but a substantial number of the 16 month old children managed the task too. Thus, by introducing a behavioural aspect to the false-belief task, any bias based on language abilities is eliminated and arguments suggesting that the gaze-following studies simply measure the child's interest in something

Belief-induction trial

(a) TB-green condition

(b) TB-yellow condition

(c) FB-green condition

(d) FB-yellow condition

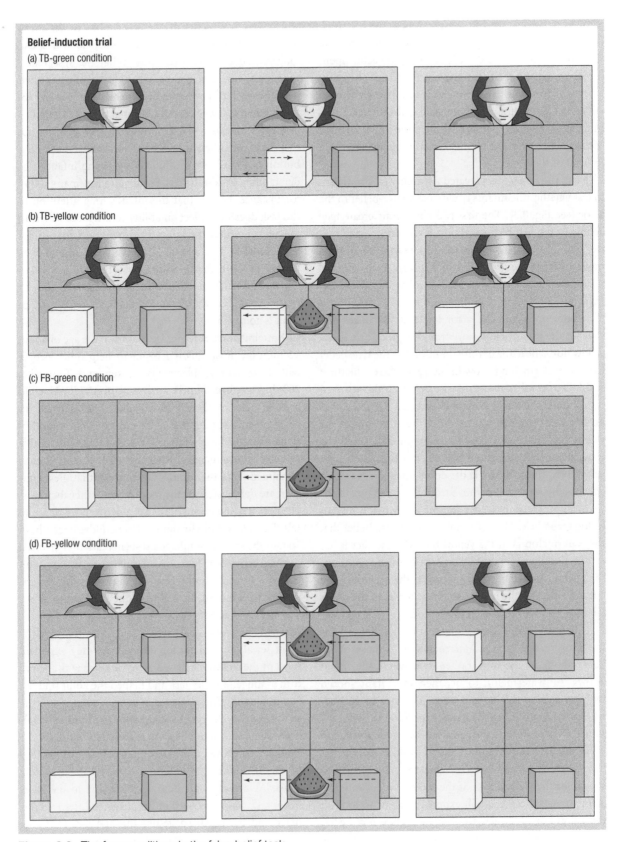

Figure 8.3. The four conditions in the false-belief task.

(*Source*: Onishi and Baillergeon, 2005)

RESEARCH METHODS

Theory of mind–research path

The papers discussed in this section are each proposing varied methods for identifying whether or not young children have theory of mind and can understand the nature of false-beliefs. Following the papers in a chronological fashion, we can see that each set of authors has reflected on the limitations of the previous paper and then sought to address these either through slight changes to wording and/or the situation described or with more significant changes to the design and process of each experiment. If we take the Maxi and the Chocolate task described by Wimmer and Perner (1983) we can see that the results of the paper led the authors to believe that theory of mind was not present in three year old children. However, criticisms of the paper suggested that the story of where the chocolate *is* and where Maxie might *believe* the chocolate is was considered by many as too complex for young children to understand. Furthermore, criticisms of the task were also directed at the length of the story with critics suggesting that the story was too long for three year olds to understand. So in response to these criticisms, Baron-Cohen *et al.* (1985) proposed a shorter, simpler story (the Sally-Anne task). However, even with this change to method they were unable to detect significant evidence of theory of mind in the under-threes.

Reviewing these papers and considering the cognitive development of the child, Siegal and Beattie (1991) noted that by simply changing the question asked of the children from 'Where will Sally look for her marble?' to 'Where will Sally look *first* for her marble?' accurate performance on this false-belief task improved from around 35% to over 70% in three year olds. Thus, considering the developmental stage of a child when devising an experimental technique can be crucial when you are devising the questions you might ask of her. The researchers did not stop there, however, and continued to refine and revise their methodologies in an attempt to develop a measure sensitive enough to detect the development of theory of mind in children too young to have the language ability to express their beliefs. With each paper that was published, there was evidence that the researchers were reflecting on each other's successes and failures and each new paper pushed the boundary of our knowledge further. Thus, by reviewing previous research evidence, revising theory in the light of new evidence and devising new hypotheses, these developmental psychologists have designed new experiments to test those hypotheses. The process described here should help you to understand how developmental psychologists are continually reflecting and revising their methods in an attempt to refine their understanding of human development.

happening in front of them can be rejected. We can conclude then that a child's ability to understand and interpret others' behaviour in the context of beliefs, desires, intentions and goals can be measured using false-belief tasks and, to date, appears to be present from a very early age.

STOP AND THINK

What might be the implications for the older adult whose ability to gauge emotional states is weakening?

Theories explaining theory of mind

There are two dominant theories behind research into theory of mind: the 'theory-theory' (often abbreviated to TT in texts) and the 'simulation theory' (often abbreviated to ST in texts).

'Theory-theory' or representational account of theory of mind

The theory-theory or representational account of theory of mind suggests that a child cannot have a full understanding

LIFESPAN

Theory of mind through adulthood

The focus so far in this chapter has been on looking at how early in life a child begins to show evidence of theory of mind but, as we get older, does our ability to infer a person's beliefs, desires and motivations change? A study conducted by Pardini and Nichelli published in 2009 used a version of the 'Reading the Mind in the Eyes Test' (Baron-Cohen et al., 2001). In this test, participants see only the eye region of the face of a person who is enacting an emotional state. The participant then has to choose from four words which emotion is being represented. The three 'incorrect' words relate to emotions that when expressed might have similar facial characteristics but mean the direct opposite of the target emotional state. The advantage of this method is that it does not rely on participants' working memory abilities yet is sophisticated enough to pick up on more subtle messages than the false-belief tasks directed at young children.

Pardini and Nichelli put this test to 120 people equally split into four age groups – 20–25 years old,

45–55 years old, 55–65 years old and 70–75 years old. All participants in the groups were matched for gender and education level and reported good vision. The results showed that the mean number of correct recognitions of the emotional states were 26.79, 25.3, 23.5 and 21.6, respectively, indicating that the ability to recognise emotional state declined with advancing age (ANOVA test revealed the significance of these findings: $f(3,116) = 24.5$, $p < 0.001$). The authors conducted further analysis and propose that the significant point at which a person's ability to deduce another's emotional state weakens is around the age of 55 years. Therefore, this study illustrates that as we get older, so our ability to infer a person's state of mind becomes less accurate. Further research is needed to understand why this happens, but at present the literature suggests that there is age-related decline on a number of cognitive skills that could be explained by subtle changes in the frontal lobes of the brain (McPherson et al., 2002), and theory of mind could be one of those abilities that is affected in this way.

of the nature of false-beliefs until he can make a cognitive decision using meta-representation. Earlier in the chapter we defined meta-representation as 1) the ability to separate reality from fantasy, for instance, during pretend play (Leslie, 1987) and 2) additionally, knowing the difference between what might be represented in a photograph or painting of an object and what the reality of that object might be (Perner, 1991). Leslie points out that children start to engage in pretend play at around the age of 18 months – at a time when the child is learning the true words for objects. At a time when the child is also learning to categorise items (for example, fruit, animals, people, furniture), pretend play should theoretically be very confusing for the child. If she is still learning that the word for a curved yellow fruit is 'banana', then to play with it and pretend it is a 'telephone' should be beyond the young child's cognitive grasp. Yet children enjoy this type of pretend play and it does not appear to have any

effect on their ability to learn that the yellow fruit is called 'banana' or that the real telephone is not a yellow fruit.

The reason Leslie offers to explain this apparent discrepancy is that young children develop two types of representations during pretend play: the first, the primary representation, is 'banana' for the curved yellow fruit and the second, the secondary representation, is 'pretend-telephone' for the game of playing on the telephone. These secondary representations are what Leslie calls meta-representations and demonstrate the child's ability to fantasise in her own game. Leslie also noted that meta-representations are not solely present in the child's own fantasy game, but that the same child will successfully join another child's fantasy game, thus demonstrating that the child is aware of the meta-representation of the banana in the second child's pretend play of, say, 'cops and robbers', 'cars' or

This boy is having fun using a meta-representation of the box, which is now a bus.

Source: Getty Images/Blend Images LLC

any other game that might be being played at that moment. This, Leslie argues, is evidence that the child is able to mind-read and is therefore developing a theory of mind.

Perner (1991) however, disagrees with Leslie's representational account and argues that the child is not showing a meta-representation of the banana as a telephone, but is in fact simply acting out talking on the telephone using the banana as a prop. If children were truly capable of using meta-representation, Perner argues, then they would not routinely fail the basic false-belief tasks such as the Sally-Anne task or the Maxi and the Chocolate task. However, since Perner's paper was published in 1991, much research has been carried out that shows that the reason children were failing these tasks was not because of a deficit in meta-representation skills but in the way the tasks were presented to the children. Taking the examples of research presented earlier in this chapter, the Onishi and Baillergeon paper in 2005 demonstrated that children as young as 16–18 months showed differences in their gaze patterns that correlated with the nature of the false-belief task, and the paper by Surian and Leslie in 1999 found that rewording the question helped the children understand what was being asked of them and their performance on the false-belief tasks improved dramatically. Thus there appears to be evidence of some ability to form meta-representations in young, pre-verbal children as evidenced in their pretend play and some ability to complete a false-belief task.

'Simulation theory' of theory of mind

The simulation theory or simulation account of theory of mind proposes that we are biologically designed to understand beliefs, desires and motivations in the minds of others and that we initially do so by using our own mind as a model or template for understanding the minds of others (Apperly, 2008). By thinking that the mind of another person is similar to your own mind, you can then make predictions of that person's behaviour based on how you think you would behave under the circumstances. Thus, researchers who follow the simulation theory of theory of mind suggest that we do not need to learn other people's mental states and make judgements about them as is proposed in the theory-theory but, instead, use what Meltzoff called a 'like me' comparison (Meltzoff, 1995). Simulation-theorists suggest that we are born with the ability to make the self–other comparison and indeed there is some biological evidence that supports this. Present in the brain are neurons called mirroring neurons that appear to be activated by either performing an intentional action or by observing an intentional action. Simulation theory argues that these mirroring neurons are what enables this 'like-me' appraisal to take place. For example, we see a behaviour take place, the mirroring neurons process the action and we experience empathy or resonance (Schulkin, 2000).

Both theories are well argued in the literature and many researchers believe that both theories have something to contribute to our understanding of theory of mind. Failure to understand another person's perspective and failure to predict another person's behaviour can both be explained by either theory-theory or simulation-theory accounts. Theory-theory would explain these failures as not being able to fully understand the other person's beliefs and making a false meta-representation of those beliefs will lead to making a false prediction of that person's behaviour. Simulation-theory would explain these failures as making a 'like-me' mistake and expecting the other person to behave 'like-me' when the person is not 'like-me' at all (Nichols and Stich, 2003). Research methods have so far failed to demonstrate the dominance of either theory-theory or simulation-theory in understanding theory of mind, so it seems likely that a hybrid approach to theory-theory and simulation-theory might be more influential in the future.

Debates about the origin of theory of mind

Is there an over-reliance on false-belief tasks to explain theory of mind?

As we have seen, Siegal and Beattie in 1991 argue that children, rather than not having theory of mind, instead misunderstand the questions and therefore the nature of the task. This argument was supported by Freeman *et al.* (1991) who found that young children were unable to articulate the false-belief held by the actor in a false-belief task. These arguments point to communications skills and theory of mind being tightly interconnected and lead us to the conclusion that theory of mind does not or cannot develop until the child reaches a certain level of cognitive maturity. However, Perner's counter-argument proposes that theory of mind may be present in the child before the child is able to complete these tasks and, therefore, that false-belief tasks are not suitable for picking up theory of mind in the very young. Perner noted that children engage in pretend play and use deception or lies at an early age, the key defining principle of theory of mind is that a person can understand another person's *belief* and this he states does not fully occur until the age of four years. Therefore, Perner argues, we can see evidence of theory of mind in young children unable to put into words the false-belief held by the actor in the false-belief tasks.

Gopnik *et al.* (1994) also present the argument that pretend play, deception and lying in young children indicate a pre-theory of mind. The authors propose a four-stage model of development of theory of mind whereby first, children aged 30 months and under have a basic level of understanding of other people's motivations

NATURE–NURTURE

Is theory of mind innate?

In a paper titled 'Origins of individual differences in theory of mind: from nature to nurture?' Hughes *et al.* (2006). investigated the contribution of genetic and environmental influences on individual differences in development of theory of mind in the first large-scale population-based study of twins born in England and Wales in 1994 and 1995. As part of a larger study called the Environmental Risk (E-Risk) Longitudinal Twin Study, 1104 five year old monozygotic (MZ) or dizygotic (DZ) same-sex twins were selected for home visits, one-third of whom were born to young mothers (aged under 20 years at child's birth) and two-thirds of whom were born to mothers aged 20–48 years. The children were given four false-belief tasks to complete similar to the smarties and pencils study, the Sally-Anne task and the Maxi and the chocolate task.

Of the twins 56% were monozygotic (sharing the same genetic make-up) and 44% were dizygotic (sharing only half the same genetic make-up): 49% of the twin pairs were male. The results of the study show that the verbal abilities of each twin per pair showed no significant difference but there was a small but significant difference on the theory of mind tasks with girls performing slightly better than boys. Statistical analysis of the effects of genetics and environment on the twin pairs' performance on theory of mind tasks showed that there was no significant difference in performance based on whether you were an MZ twin or a DZ twin. Further analysis revealed that only about 7% of the variation in children's ability to complete the false-beliefs tasks could be accounted for by whether you shared your full genetic make-up or only half your genetic make-up with your twin. When family socio-economic status was taken into account, the authors found that they could account for 48% of the children's performance on false-belief tasks. Child's verbal ability was significantly related to socioeconomic status (SES) (a greater vocabulary was seen in children from families with higher SES) and accounted for about 50% of the impact of SES on performance on false-beliefs tasks. The authors conclude that the individual differences shown in each child's development of theory of mind can in the main be accounted for not by genetic factors but by environmental factors. This study found that approximately 48% of performance in the false-belief tasks was accounted for by family SES but the authors acknowledge that there still remains 45% of variance accounted for by other environmental factors.

based on their own needs (hence the child engaging in pretend play–but for his own satisfaction rather than based out of an understanding of the beliefs and motives of others). Gopnik *et al.* describe how by 30 months the child is able to understand that another person might see things differently and might have different desires to him. Nevertheless, it is not until the age of three years that the child starts to make formal connections between the other person's perspective and desires and starts to form a more complex understanding of other people's motivations. When the child is four years old, however, the authors state that the child is able to make the association between other people's perspective and, in the case of the false-belief tasks, their misrepresentation of events and predict what behaviour might ensue. Thus, Gopnik's study reveals that although the younger children may display evidence of a basic understanding of other people's motivations (and therefore aspects of a burgeoning theory of mind), the dramatic shift in performance accuracy on the false-belief tasks at age four years reflects the child's state of change in cognitive development, and a concurrent dramatic improvement in the complexity of understanding theory of mind. Therefore, although criticisms are levelled at researchers who use false-belief tasks to ascertain a child's theory of mind capability, Gopnik's work demonstrates that a limited theory of mind might be detectable in the very young child through their use of pretend play, lying and deception.

Theory of mind and children with autism

Autism Spectrum Conditions (ASC) occur in 1% of the population, are strongly heritable, and result from atypical neurodevelopment. Classic autism and Asperger Syndrome (AS) share difficulties in social functioning, communication and coping with change, alongside unusually narrow interests. IQ is average or above in AS with average or even precocious age of language onset. Many areas within the 'social brain' are atypical in ASC. ASC has a profile of impaired empathy alongside strong 'systemising'. Hence, ASC involves disability (when empathy is required) and talent (when strong systemising would be advantageous). Psychological interventions that target empathy by harnessing systemising may help.

(Baron-Cohen, 2008)

People with autism spectrum condition (abbreviated to 'autism' from hereon in) have difficulty in understanding the mind of others – that is other peoples' perception of events, their beliefs and their motivations. People with autism also find it difficult to see the context of events and are said to have poor central coherence (Happe, 1994). For example, a person with central coherence will be able to put together images such as balloons on the front door with the birthday cake on the table and the presents next to it into the context of a home hosting a birthday party. A person with autism may find this difficult and not make the connection between the balloons, the cake and the presents to form a representation of a birthday party. However, what the person with autism does have in this and other situations is the ability to note the detail of each of those items and may be able to tell precisely the location of the balloons, how many, what is written on each, what colour they are, what colour the thread is tying them to the front door and how many knots are tied on each thread! The other key cognitive characteristic of people with autism relates to executive function, that is control of actions. People with autism often show difficulties with their executive function, for example in displaying repetitive behaviours or in focusing attentively on one thing to the detriment of everything else happening around them. For example, you may see a person with autism compulsively arranging their books by order of size or repeatedly drawing an action figure. The person with autism may sway from side to side or hop continuously for an excessive period of time or when they are talking to you. For more information on autism spectrum disorders, see Recommended Reading.

Beliefs and mental states

There is a great deal of evidence relating autism to deficits in cognitive skills including theory of mind in the literature. First, children with autism fail to make the distinction between what is mental (held in the mind) and

> **Definition**
>
> Central coherence: the ability to put together information in context to form a whole picture (Frith, 1989).

Lining up your toys is a common behaviour seen in children with autism.

what is physical. For example, a study conducted by Wellman and Estes (1986) found that typically developing children can distinguish the two quite easily at the age of three to four years. Wellman and Estes told children a story of two characters, one thinking about a dog (a mental experience) and one holding a dog (a physical experience). The authors then asked the children, 'which character can stroke the dog?' The typically developing children aged three to four years could make this judgement quite easily, but when this study was replicated with children with autism, it was found that they frequently made mistakes in this task, despite having a mental age equivalent to the children in the other study (Baron-Cohen, 1989). Wellman and Estes also found that typically developing children knew what the brain was 'for'. The children could describe its mental functions such as thinking, dreaming, wanting but would also describe its physical function of making you move and so on. Yet when the children with autism were asked this question they knew about the physical activity-related functions of the brain but would say nothing of its mental functions (Baron-Cohen, 1989). Other studies have

shown that children with autism find it difficult to distinguish between appearance of an object and the reality of an object. For instance, a child with autism presented with a pen in the shape of a dinosaur will either decide it is a pen or a dinosaur but, unlike the typically developing child, does not seem to appreciate the nature of the 'dinosaur pen' as a concept.

The child with autism also finds the false-belief tasks difficult. In their paper investigating whether children with autism have a theory of mind, Baron-Cohen et al. gave the Sally-Anne task to children with autism and compared their performance with that of typically-developing children and children with Down's Syndrome (1985). Their results showed that 23 out of 27 typically-developing 4 year olds and 12 out of the 14 children with Down's Syndrome passed the false-belief tasks. Compare that with only four of the 20 children with autism passing the belief question on this task. All of the 16 children who failed the task pointed deliberately at where Anne knew the marble *was* rather than where Sally would *believe* the marble was on returning to the room. The authors suggest that the children's performance on the false-belief task demonstrated an inability to represent mental states. They argue that children with autism are therefore unable to deduce the beliefs of others and thus predict the behaviour of other people.

Why these children with autism cannot represent mental states might stem from their apparent inability to make the connection that a person knows what she knows because of what she sees. This concept of 'seeing leads to knowing' is present in typically-developing three year olds but is infrequently seen in children with autism. A paper published by Leslie and Frith (1988) showed this with a story of two characters, one who looked in a box and the other who merely touched the box. The children were then asked 'which character knows what's in the box?' The typically-developing children knew that it was the character who had looked in the box. The children with autism performed at chance levels of accuracy on this task and showed no preference for the character who had looked inside the box. Thus there appeared to be no indication that the children with autism understood that knowledge comes from seeing, a precursor skill to being able to understand the concept behind the Sally-Anne task: that a person may believe a situation to be true but be proven wrong when that situation is changed without them seeing it happen.

STOP AND THINK

How might you explain why a child with autism finds it difficult to make friends?

Deception

Deception is essentially a skill that you need in order to change somebody else's mind. In order to be able to deceive someone, you need to understand that 'seeing leads to knowing' and that what a person knows can be proven wrong when the situation is manipulated without their knowledge (as demonstrated in the false-belief tasks). Deception also

Definition

Deception: trying to make someone else believe that something is true when in fact it is false (Baron-Cohen, 2001).

carries an element of motivation. Why else would you seek to deceive someone if you did not believe that by doing so you would benefit from the act? If, for example, there is no material or emotional gain following the deception or avoidance of punishment or emotional disappointment, what reason is there to deliberately create a false-belief?

Deception appears in typically-developing children around four years of age and, although not sophisticated, the child's attempts to cover up his actions by pointing to his infant sister or denying eating all the sweets when he is surrounded by the wrappers, these attempts at deception do illustrate the complexity of his developing theory of mind. However, the child with autism appears to find deception a difficult concept to pull off effectively. A paper by Baron-Cohen in 1992 described a 'penny hiding game' where the child is asked to hide a penny in one hand and not tell the experimenter which hand it is in when asked. The typically developing four year old child is fairly proficient at this game yet the child with autism finds this game very difficult, often revealing the position of the penny before the experimenter asks its location.

CASE STUDY

Gary McKinnon – autism and the position of personal responsibility

In March 2002, Gary McKinnon was arrested by British police for breaking into American military computer systems. In a BBC interview in 2005 he said: 'I found out that the US military use Windows and having realised this, I assumed it would probably be an easy hack if they hadn't secured it properly.' In a later interview, he claimed that he was convinced that American government intelligence agencies had access to 'crashed extra-terrestrial technology which could . . . save us in the form of a free, clean pollution-free energy'. However, the American authorities did not accept his claim and pursued his extradition for trial on the basis of hacking into computers 'with the intention of intimidating the US government' claiming that many government files were accessed, altered and even deleted by Gary McKinnon.

In August 2008, Gary McKinnon was diagnosed with Asperger's Syndrome, a form of the Autism Spectrum Disorder. People with Asperger's Syndrome share many of the same features of autism but show

normal or above average IQ and show regular development in language skills (Autism Research Centre). As with autism, Asperger's Syndrome has as one of its characteristics difficulties in social interaction and people with Asperger's Syndrome find it difficult to establish the consequences of their actions. Thus since his diagnosis, lawyers and other professionals have been working to prevent Gary McKinnon's extradition order to be tried in the US, arguing that he was not fully cognisant of the implications of breaking into the computer system and was not therefore wilfully engaged in breaking the law. Specialists have also advised that a person with Asperger's Syndrome would be unlikely to do well in a prison environment. Since the diagnosis, McKinnon's team of lawyers have been applying for his case to be heard in the UK and for lesser charges to be put against him reflecting this.

- What do you think the decision should be in these circumstances?
- Should Gary McKinnon be extradited to the US to answer charges?

SUMMARY

This chapter has introduced you to the psychological concept of theory of mind. Theory of mind is very much a cognitive skill that appears to follow a developmental pathway starting in very early infancy and progressing through to late adulthood. Research shows that using false-belief tasks can help us to understand the developmental nature of theory of mind and that skills learned in early childhood continue with us into our adult lives. Although the ability to understand a person's mental states such as their beliefs, desires, intentions and emotions is substantially a cognitive one, the implications for a person's social development are considerable. Without being able to make sense of someone's behaviour, their motivations and decision-making, we perform poorly in social situations and may make mistakes in predicting what an outcome could be. Researchers working with children with autism have found considerable differences in performance between these children and typically developing children. Children with autism find it difficult to understand the perspective of others and routinely fail the false-belief tasks. The large amount of evidence collected by researchers using false-belief tasks has revealed the complexity of cognitive deficit underlying autism spectrum disorder and has provided key information that underlies support and intervention programmes for these children. However, how a person learns theory of mind is still debated, and the implications for understanding the difficulties children with autism have become apparent. The theory-theory or representational account of theory of mind requires the child to have the cognitive ability to use meta-representations; to separate reality from fantasy. This is something that the child with autism and poor theory of mind is commonly unable to do, and theory-theory seemingly accounts for this. However, simulation theory can also account for the difficulties a child with autism experiences on the false-belief tasks. Simulation theory requires the child to be able to perform a 'like-me' comparison in order to predict behaviour and perhaps the child with autism can carry out the 'like-me' comparison but finds no-one behaves 'like-me' and is therefore unable to make appropriate judgements of that person's beliefs and desires. These and other debates continue in theory of mind research. To find out more, follow up the Recommended Reading.

REVIEW QUESTIONS

1 What are the key features of theory of mind?
2 How does theory-theory account for theory of mind and how does it differ from simulation theory?
3 Why is the false-belief task used to test for the presence or otherwise of theory of mind in the young child?
4 Why does the ability to recognise emotional states weaken as we get older? What are the implications of this for the older adult?
5 How can the use of false-belief tasks help us to understand the difficulties children with autism have in social interaction?

FURTHER READING

For further information on the theory-theory vs simulation-theory debate:

Schulkin, J. (2000). Theory of mind and mirroring neurons. *Trends in Cognitive Sciences*, *4*, (7), 252–254.

Goldman, A. & Gallese, V. (2000). Reply to Schulkin. *Trends in Cognitive Sciences*, *4*, (7), 255.

For further information on autism and theory of mind:

Baron-Cohen, S. (2001). Theory of mind and autism: A review. *Special Issue of the International Review of Mental Retardation*, *23* (169).

Baron-Cohen, S. (2008). *Autism and Asperger Syndrome: the facts*. Oxford: Oxford University Press.

Baron-Cohen, S. (2009). Autism: the Empathizing-Systemising (E-S) Theory. *Annals of the New York Academy of Sciences*, *1156*, 68–80.

RECOMMENDED WEBSITES

The false-belief task in action:

http://www.open2.net/healtheducation/family_childdevelopment/development/theoryofmind.html

This page has lots of information on the Environmental Risk (E-Risk) Longitudinal Twin Study.

http://www.scopic.ac.uk/StudiesERisk.html

 Watch a video focused on false-belief tasks and theory of mind at different ages. Further resources can be found at www.pearsoned.co.uk/gillibrand

Chapter 9
Attachment and early social experiences

Learning Outcomes

After reading this chapter, with further recommended reading, you should be able to:

1. Evaluate the importance of a parent or consistent primary caregiver to a child's early development characterised by the concept of attachment;

2. Describe attachment theory in terms of its key features which underpin the emotional ties between the child and her primary caregiver;

3. Describe and evaluate the key procedure and assessment tools that have been used to measure attachment behaviours and relationships;

4. Apply all of the above in discussing the possible impact of changes in child-rearing practices, including paternal care and day care, on development;

5. Describe research documenting the implications of attachment relationships for later childhood and adulthood.

Description of two toddlers

Daisy, 13 months old

Daisy and her mummy have entered the room . . . Mummy settles Daisy down on the floor in front of her . . . Daisy looks cautious and, although clearly curious about the objects in front of her, she barely touches them until mummy enthusiastically encourages her to play . . . Daisy frequently turns round to look at mummy, to which she responds with a smile and encourages Daisy to continue to play. She gets up to reach mummy once for a 'cuddle' . . . When the female stranger comes in the room, Daisy stares at her and then clings on to mummy as she sits down next to mummy . . . When mummy gets up and goes for the door, Daisy toddles over to follow her and then gives out a loud cry as mummy closes the door behind her . . . Daisy continues to wail and whimper as the stranger tries to comfort her and engage her to play . . . Mummy returns and promptly picks up Daisy and holds her in her arms . . . she eventually quietens down and mummy is once again encouraging her to play. . . .

Chloe, 18 months old

Chloe and mummy have just entered the room. Chloe spots the toys straight away and approaches them before mummy settles herself down on the chair . . . She touches each and every object before she starts playing with the biggest with apparent interest, and mummy quietly watches. Though facing mummy, Chloe does not appear to make any eye contact with her during play . . . The stranger arrives; Chloe says 'Ah' and smiles at her as she goes to sit by mummy, and Chloe 'gives' her one of the other toys . . . When mummy gets up to leave the room, Chloe watches her throughout, but does not get up to follow nor make any sound, before she starts playing again, this time ignoring the stranger . . . When the door opens again and mummy comes in, Chloe looks at her for a few seconds before settling back to play again. . . .

The above are snippets of descriptions of two infants' interactions with their mothers, in the first half of a highly established procedure (which you will come to learn about later in this chapter) that is used to assess the kind of emotional bonds a child shares with her significant caregiver.

- What are the major differences between the behaviour of Daisy and Chloe?
- Are there any differences between the behaviour of their mothers too?
- What do you think are the reasons for such differences?
- Do you believe that their behaviour in sessions like these reflects some things about the relationship the girls have with their mothers?

▶

▶ # Introduction

This chapter will overview and evaluate the first ever relationship we experience in our lives, that is the relationship between a child and her earliest primary caregiver, typically the mother. Whereas the importance of this early relationship to children's development is hardly ever doubted, over the years the substantial amount of work in this area has still not totally addressed certain questions, from the exact origins of this one-to-one relationship to its longer-term implications. Must it be our mothers that we bond with? How do we know we have bonded strongly 'enough' with a person? What about children in out-of-home care or those who are cared for by several caregivers? Even as adults, the closeness of our relationships with our parents varies a great deal, as much as that of the relationship between us and other people. Some question whether this closeness goes back a long way to our childhood concerning the quantity or quality of time that we spent with our mothers. If so, are some of us doomed in our current and future relationships if we have missed out on a 'good start' in the form of a warm loving relationship with our mothers? Clearly, this topic has theoretical, personal and practical significance; it may make some of us want to reminisce about our own childhood and upbringing, and those who are parents to reflect on our child-rearing, or to re-evaluate the quality of the places or people providing day care for our children. Not giving 'right' answers to these questions, this chapter will nevertheless investigate some possibilities by looking at the work of influential figures in the past as well as later research that dissects and evaluates this important relationship in our early childhood.

What is attachment?

STOP AND THINK

Reflection

- Try to jog your memory to as far back as you can remember in your childhood.
- Who was the person that you spent the most time with at home?
- Who was the person that knew you best, that you felt most 'safe and secure' with?
- Was it the same person for both questions?

With increasing competence in their physical, perceptual and cognitive faculties (see Section II of this book for such development in infancy), by the latter half of the first year of life most infants can recognise the familiar people they encounter and interact with the most. It is almost invariably the case that these are the people who also know the infant better than other people in that they understand her needs and behaviours well, since they respond to these needs regularly, usually in the role of parents.

As surmised in the introduction, attachment is often referred to as an affectionate bond or emotional tie, where such a tie is often strong and enduring, that we have with significant people in our lives. Attachment, in developmental psychology, is normally understood as the first such tie an infant has with her primary caregiver, typically the mother, for it is often (though not always) the case that after the birth the mother goes on to look after the infant. Numerous psychologists have explored the nature of this important relationship for over half a century, but nowadays many still look to the starting points articulated by the forefather of what is regarded as one of the landmark theories in developmental psychology. That is, the attachment theory of John Bowlby. Below we will take a close look at Bowlby's influential theory.

Definition

Attachment: a strong enduring affectionate bond an infant shares with a significant individual, usually the mother, who knows and responds well to the infant's needs.

The strong affectionate bond between mother and child is often plain to see.

Source: Pearson Education Ltd./Lisa Payne Photography

Bowlby's early attachment theory

As a practising British child psychiatrist in the 1950s, John Bowlby (1907–90) drew his original ideas from various disciplines, most notably the psychoanalytic school of thought (see Chapter 2, Theoretical Perspectives for premises of psychoanalysis), but also evolution and ethology (see later in this chapter), as well as his own observations and his clinical work with those he regarded as having inadequate attachment (see Maternal deprivation hypothesis).

According to Bowlby (1958), our tendency to form and develop strong enduring affectionate bonds with certain individuals is an evolved biological 'given', in that it has critical survival and adaptation values. Because the attachment figure tends to be, or is to start with at least, the mother or someone responsible for the feeding and day-to-day care of the baby, this relationship acts to source and maintain nurturance as well as protection and security from this figure. This bond hence caters for far beyond the physiological needs of a child (like food), but also for the psychological needs, such as comfort or the sense of a 'safe base' for the child. The latter is

required as the human young (and many other animals) also have an opposing (to attachment) tendency to explore the world around them, taking the infant momentarily away from the safe base. A return to this available base is paramount when, during his exploration, the child feels threatened or distressed by an object, event, setting or experience (such as meeting a new person or animal, entering a new place or feeling illness or discomfort). To this end, this relationship will reflect certain recognisable characteristics that function to establish and maintain closeness between the mother and her child. We will first explore these characteristics one by one before structuring the key ones within the development of attachment.

Monotropism. The first step towards any attachment is the ability for the infant to discriminate between her parents and other individuals. There is evidence that babies recognise their mothers' voice by birth, and by sight and smell at just a few days old (see Chapter 4, Prenatal Development and Infancy). Further to this, Bowlby argued that eventually most infants will become more attached to the primary caregiver, and prolonged separation from or unavailability of her would have enduring serious and deleterious consequences for the child (see Maternal deprivation hypothesis below).

Proximity-seeking. Bowlby first conceptualised early attachment as a goal-driven system with the goal of maintaining optimum proximity with the primary caregiver on the part of the child. The child should display a concomitant set of behaviours that draw the caregiver's attention, and who will then get close to him. The exact starting point and behaviours will depend on the age and cognitive and physical development of the child, but these include recognition of the caregiver, distinguishing her from other people, representations of objects, including the mother, in their absence (Piaget, 1954; see Chapter 4), and the ability to vocalise and mobilise oneself. A new baby not long after birth may only be able to cry

Definitions

Monotropism: the idea that any child only forms a strong attachment to one person.
Proximity-seeking: a set of typical behaviours displayed by children to draw the attention of the primary caregiver towards themselves or reach her when separated, with the goal of restoring proximity.

Once mobile, an infant can take more active steps to restore proximity to mother.

Source: O'Donnell

Smiling to draw attention and seek proximity.

Source: Lam

for attention or at most make eye contact as he feels discomfort, but later he will be able to smile or even reach out or cling to mother, and later still he can call out or follow her as a toddler. In any case, this mechanism is such that separation from the caregiver should activate this behavioural system to restore proximity.

Separation protest. His work with infants led Bowlby to notice not only the sorts of behaviours that they displayed when they were with their caregivers but, even more importantly, those behaviours that they displayed during the departure of or separation from the caregiver. By the time an infant has started to use his mother as a secure base from which to explore, in the second half of the first year, he also starts to show some recognisable signs of 'protest' as he gets parted from her. Even a stay-at-home mother will have moments where she has to attend to other business, such as answering the

telephone or door, turning the cooker off in the kitchen or checking on another child. On many occasions the infant will cry and may reach out in an attempt to prevent her departure as a form of protest and may continue such behaviour in her absence.

Stranger anxiety. At around the same period the child shows clear regular signs of anxiety on separation

Definitions

Separation protest: a set of typical behaviours displayed by the infant to register a form of protest against their caregiver's departure.

Stranger anxiety: the wariness or fear of the infant when encountering those who are unfamiliar, often characterised by the seeking of proximity to the caregiver.

CASE STUDY

Attachment behaviours in real-life settings

Imagine yourself at a party in a friend's house. The friend has also invited many other guests, some of whom have brought along their children. You have been playing with a sociable little boy of about eighteen months to two years for a short while in the conservatory, among other children. His mother returns with a

few other women – you don't know her or the others – but you can tell immediately with some certainty that she is the mother, just from the expression and behaviour that the woman and child display.

- What kind of 'expression' and 'behaviour' would you expect of the child?
- What kind of 'expression' and 'behaviour' would you expect of the mother?

from mother, after being able to differentiate her from other people, behaviours pertaining to wariness or fear (anxiety) of such unfamiliar people (strangers) also emerge. The child may wince, but will often want to cling on or stay close to mother as if to obtain her protection from these unfamiliar human objects.

Critical period. Attachment as characterised by the above features is seen to have time boundaries for its formation. Based on his work with older children having gone without this goal-driven relationship earlier on, Bowlby specified the period in which attachment ought to be strived for and achieved as being between six months and three years of age. If good parenting is not attempted until after age two and a half years, it was argued that it is immensely difficult for an attachment to be formed (also see the next sections).

Judging from the features and criteria of the above characteristics, you may find some of them reasonable or predictable whilst others seem slightly inflexible or unrealistic. Whilst we will evaluate Bowlby's principles later, it should be noted that his original theory was refined several times (Bowlby, 1953, 1969, 1973, 1980). On establishing his initial theory, more work was given to charting the age-related stages at which the features of attachment emerge, as attachment 'phases', described in the following.

The attachment phases

Since, as noted above, some attachment behaviours are related to physical (mobility) and cognitive (object recognition and representation) development, Bowlby proposed that attachment develops in stages (see Table 9.1 for ages and key characteristics).

Due to the lack of differentiation between familiar and unfamiliar faces in the earliest two months, the baby is said to be in a phase with little or no recognition of mother. Even at the next phase, those prerequisites for attachment are merely being set up as the infant begins to recognise his mother or primary caregiver, but

Definition

Critical period: the time period that was thought to be critical for the formation and development of any attachment relationship, hypothesised to be six months to three years, beyond which it is seen as highly difficult for such a bond to be formed.

Table 9.1. Bowlby's attachment phases by approximate ages.

Phase	Approx. age	Key characteristics of child
Pre-attachment	0–2 months	Shows little differentiation in responses to mother and other people, familiar or unfamiliar
Early attachment	2–7 months	Begins to recognise mother, gradually more likely to be comforted by her
Separation protest	7–9 months–2 years	Seeks to maintain proximity with mother, wary of strangers and protests when separated
Goal-corrected	2–3 years & upwards	Has more abstract representations of attachment, (trust, affection, approval), begins to understand mother's needs, with increased independence

the lack of object representation (including of mother) at this age (Piaget, 1954) means that separation protest is not yet evident, even if he is comforted more easily by this familiar figure.

Behaviours towards separation and clearer signs of proximity-seeking, as well as stranger anxiety, will emerge from the second half of the first year in the third phase, and such behaviours will be more apparent as the child enters into the second year of his life. However, as the child grows further still, with even greater physical mobility, thus exploration, and cognitive skills (such as developing language and more complex thoughts), attachment transcends into a more abstract idea. This final so-called 'goal-corrected' phase signifies the more confident independent toddler, who can now better understand his mother's needs and motives apart from her availability (that she can be absent, but will return and respond). This milestone of an 'internal' representation will be explored more thoroughly later, in terms of its implications for future relationships (see Internal working model). For now, it is important to bear in mind that there is not a one-to-one mapping of behaviour to phase. Infants vary in the frequency or intensity of their attachment behaviour even though the goal is the same.

Maternal deprivation hypothesis

Apart from the features of 'normal' attachment, the other essential part of Bowlby's theory had stemmed from his work as a child psychiatrist, with those who suffered the consequences of severe parental neglect or long-term separation from parental figures. Such prolonged bouts of disruption to the attachment to a mother figure are known as maternal deprivation which can be a result of such things as illness of either the mother or the child, abandonment by or bereavement of the key parent during the critical period, or even being orphaned. The notion that there are a host of profound negative outcomes, widely documented at the time, that deprivation can lead to, according to Bowlby (1953), has come to be known as the maternal deprivation hypothesis.

Bowlby drew on both his clinical work and research by others on institutionalised children. For instance, well before his theory came into being, Bowlby's retrospective study (see Chapter 2) in the 1940s documented how delinquent adolescents recalled their early experiences. He wrote that many such young males shared a history of a lack of consistent parenting figures; some were in serial foster care, others in impersonal institutions for most of their childhoods, whilst many were periodically in transit between foster care and institutions throughout childhood. Their common outcomes and early experiences led Bowlby (1944) to his early conclusions about the ill effects that a lack of attachment relationships can bring.

At around the same period, the American psychiatrist, William Goldfarb (1947) followed up 30 children who had been given up by their mothers before 9 months of age. Whilst half of them went to foster homes, the other half were first placed at an institution until they were fostered at about three-and-a-half years old, then remained in foster care. Goldfarb carried out a batch of tests on these children between the ages of 10 and 14, including intelligence, reading and arithmetic, and also took observations and notes on the children and their caregivers and teachers. He found that those who had spent their first few years in institutions performed worse than those in continual foster care, and were reported as being more fearful and restless and less popular with their peers, and being more needy with adults.

Since Goldfarb evaluated the quality of foster care that the two groups had received to be comparable, like Bowlby, he attributed the formerly institutionalised children's delayed or maladaptive development to institutionalisation. From this, Bowlby (1951) further concluded that, even if an infant who has undergone deprivation in the first half-year can be salvaged with prompt and proper care, delayed attempts to form attachment beyond the age of two-and-a-half years will likely be futile.

Such reports of profound negative outcomes and stunted development led to early formulations of the maternal deprivation hypothesis. As Bowlby (1953) was invited by the World Health Organisation to comment on the issues of homeless children, he asserted that the vital ingredient for healthy development of any child is a continuous, warm and intimate relationship with her mother (or a suitable mothering figure). After further years of work, he went on to articulate that there is no other childhood variable more influential on the child's later personality than her experience of a loving parent figure within her family on which her expectations about future relationships will be based (Bowlby, 1973).

Bowlby's work with young children who had to be separated from their family due to hospitalisation was given much support by the husband-and-wife team of social workers, James and Joyce Robertson (1989), who made a vivid series of films illustrating the children's responses beyond separation protest. The children were shown to go through a stage of being inconsolable before eventually becoming indifferent and unresponsive towards the parents upon reunion. Support for Bowlby's work did not stop here. As the next section shows, features of attachment behaviours and maternal deprivation also seem to hold for many non-human beings.

Definition

Maternal deprivation hypothesis: the notion that later serious deleterious outcomes will result from the lack of a consistent attachment figure in early childhood.

STOP AND THINK

Going further

- What are the problems with drawing the conclusion that a lack of early attachment leads to later negative outcomes from the kind of research Bowlby and others did?

- Despite these problems, why do you think his theory was so popular?

Animal research

Much of the information on the attachment relationship from studying non-humans is founded on a relatively modern branch of zoology called ethology. With close links to evolution, ethology is the study of natural animal behaviour primarily concerned with survival and adaptation, through a combination of outside fieldwork and laboratory settings. One of the most influential figures to inform us about attachment was Konrad Lorenz (1903–89), winner of the Nobel Prize in Physiology and Medicine in 1973.

A keen researcher of animal behaviour, Lorenz carefully observed and replicated the invariable process of imprinting, first in the newborns of several species of birds. He found that, upon hatching from the eggs, the babies will follow the first thing that they see, usually the mother, for the next few days. Lorenz discovered that if it was a human that they saw, in this case himself, they would follow him in that early period. The young offspring in this case were said to have been 'imprinted' on their surrogate human parent. In fact, the first 'thing' on which the newborns will imprint themselves does not even have to be a living creature; animals will imprint on objects like a ball, a box or even a light (Ridley, 1995). Whatever the imprinted target, the infants will recognise it by its sight, sound, smell, movement, or some other distinctive features that characterise it.

The other key aspect of imprinting that Lorenz discovered was its irreversibility. That is, once an animal has imprinted itself on a certain target, it remains attached to him/her/it, and will not 're-imprint' on another. Lorenz also found this to be the case with other species that require a relatively extensive period of parental care including mammals such as sheep. The animal would recognise the first person that handfed it and rejoin that person when he/she appeared even after the animal had been weaned.

Drawing from the predictable pattern of imprinting behaviour across the different species, Lorenz concluded

Definition

Imprinting: a process in which the newborns of most species will recognise and seek proximity with the first object that they encounter (usually the primary caregiver) following the activation of a trigger during a critical period after birth.

that imprinting is an adaptive process as it enables the new offspring to soon recognise and attach themselves to, under normal circumstances, the 'right' individual, that is the mother who will provide for and protect their young from a hostile world which is critical for their survival.

Bowlby could draw support for his theory from the above work on several counts in terms of the observed behaviours themselves, as well as the principles that Lorenz deduced from them. The imprinting behaviours, pertaining to proximity-seeking, are similar to those of human infants with the purpose of getting and staying close to the primary caregiver, who is normally the first person with whom the infant spends his early days for survival needs. The irreversibility of imprinting further offered Bowlby the impetus to propose the critical period applicable for humans introduced by Lorenz (1966) for animals. Although of course the exact timeframe will differ across species, the idea that there is a limited window of opportunity in which bonding can be forged through continuous care from the same caregiver (monotropic), and that any delayed attempt will most likely fail, is similar between humans and their animal counterparts. In addition, comparable evidence of the deleterious impact on the infant's social and emotional development upon the failure to bond in this period is available from more animal research in another setting, as we will read below.

STOP AND THINK

Going further

- How convinced are you by the apparent parallels between imprinting behaviours in animals and attachment behaviours in humans?
- Can you think of any species that does not go through the imprinting process?

Another notable set of research that supported Bowlby's theory came from Harry Harlow, who conducted experiments on rhesus monkeys in the controlled laboratory setting in the 1950s. Harlow (1958) separated otherwise healthy monkeys from their mothers at birth and placed them in isolated cages. At first, Harlow noticed that, like Lorenz's imprinted animals, if the monkeys obtained regular attention from a human surrogate mother who not only provided food but also warmth and comfort, they had a better chance of survival even when compared with monkeys that were cared for by their biological mothers in captivity.

Later on, the more famous experiments (Harlow and Zimmerman, 1959) involving other objects as the surrogate mother yielded findings that were even more revealing about the nature of the attachment relationship. In their isolated cages, monkeys were given a mesh wire surrogate mother that held a milk bottle, and a terry cloth one that did not provide food. What Harlow discovered was that, although the monkeys used the wire model as the source of food, they went to the softer cloth model as a source of comfort, like a 'mothering' figure. They would go straight to it and held on tightly when they were frightened, and its presence in a new room appeared to reduce their anxiety level as if they were using this cloth surrogate as a 'secure' base from which to explore the unfamiliar environment. Essentially, feeding times aside, whenever the cloth model was available, the infant showed a preference for it as she regularly clung on to it. In fact the monkeys actually made increasing use of this softer figure as they grew bigger. While these behaviours are strongly reminiscent of humans' behaviours during the mid-attachment phases, the findings also provide evidence that attachment, whether in humans or non-humans, is much more than just about the bare essentials of nourishment. As Bowlby argued, it offers a safe base from which the infant explores the world and to which she can return when distressed or threatened.

Although the monkeys appeared to be able to make reasonably good progress with a cloth 'mother' as a source of comfort, once they grew into adolescence and ventured outside the confines of the cages, it was obvious that the lack of any 'real' attachment figure had caused untold psychological damage to the youngsters (Harlow and Harlow, 1969). They were usually withdrawn, and when put in the company of same-age peers who had not been separated from their mothers, they became fearful and might even attack the others. If the separated monkeys were not reunited with their birth mothers by the age of three months, such ill effects appeared to be irreversible, as if they had missed that critical window of opportunity for bonding. Furthermore, as adolescents, few of these monkeys were able to mate successfully, and even if they did, the females were very unlikely to provide adequate care for their own offspring, as if they were perpetuating a cycle of absent parenting.

The profound and enduring negative consequences of animals reared apart from their mothers offer powerful support for Bowlby's maternal deprivation hypothesis. Like the delinquent boys that Bowlby interviewed, or the older children that Goldfarb assessed for delayed cognitive, social and emotional development, Harlow's monkeys displayed what would be expected as the 'animal-equivalent' of serious damage. Still, how much can we extrapolate from such findings with animals to ourselves? Is a lack of or inadequate attachment totally irredeemable? With the benefit of later studies and more

NATURE–NURTURE

Is attachment innate?

The fact that not just humans, but various animals also display behaviours that reflect the mother–child bond functional for the survival and development of the child has led many to believe that the attachment relationship is an innate one – as Bowlby put it, a predisposition based on our evolved needs to bond with the one who takes care of us.

If attachment is innate, we should expect it to be universal. Just how universal are attachment behaviours? Much cross-cultural research has shown that in most cultures infants do have a tendency to form close

relationships with a consistent set of people, if not one unique individual; but there are exceptions as well as cultural variations in *how* parents relate to infants (Flanagan, 1999; or see Attachment and childcare). Even animal attachment behaviours are subject to a combination of conditions in their contact setting such as the length of continuous exposure to the attachment figure and its distinctiveness (Cairns and Cairns, 2008). Therefore, even if we may say that the tendency per se to bond with others is innate, not every characteristic of attachment, particularly by how we have defined them so far, will apply to every living being.

critical analysis, next we will evaluate the premises of Bowlby's original theory before we move on to cover the more recent areas of interest in attachment.

Critique of Bowlby's theory

Bowlby's theory gained a lot of momentum in the first few decades that followed its initial inception in that it did not just influence the academic perspective on children's early social experiences, but also public perception of childhood and child-rearing and social policy on associated issues such as childcare provision and parenting education. However, although studies available at the time such as those we have just read could support Bowlby's arguments well, later extensive empirical work and the social trends that followed meant that those relatively deterministic principles of his original theory were viewed in a less favourable light, and some were revised by Bowlby himself.

Firstly, the maternal deprivation hypothesis received a great deal of criticism with newer waves of findings and more caution in interpreting earlier research. In the case of animals, Suomi and Harlow (1972) found that the appalling effects of isolation on monkeys were reversible under certain conditions. An 'intervention' which introduced the company of normal (not isolated) younger monkeys, who tended to 'cuddle' the older deprived peers, was reported to soon have a comforting effect. After a few weeks, the deprived monkeys started exploring their environment and even playing with the others, and six months on their behaviours were comparable to that of normal peers of the same age. Evidence challenging the inflexibility of attachment timing led ethologists as well as Bowlby to replace the concept of 'critical period' by the more appropriate sensitive period where affectionate bonds are more readily forged than other times in life.

In humans, early evidence, such as that of Goldfarb's study, on the effects of early separation has also been called into question. One cannot be sure that the children's negative outcomes were due to separation from the mother per se, instead of some of the other negative factors linked to institutionalisation, such as the quality of the institutions themselves. Indeed, places like orphanages at the time were often renounced for their unstimulating environment with a high turnover of staff, who were discouraged from forming relationships with the infants.

Since Goldfarb's work, more research with children who had been institutionalised was published, most notably several studies by Barbara Tizard, the renowned British educationalist. Tizard followed up children who had been taken into institutional care by or within the sensitive period that were later fostered, adopted or returned to their birth mothers. In most cases, the children's cognitive and linguistic development was on par with non-institutionalised children from four-and-a-half years through to late adolescence (Tizard and Rees, 1975; Tizard and Hodges, 1978) and many had settled well into family life, with affectionate relationships resembling attachment ties (Tizard, 1977; Hodges and Tizard, 1989). Still, the children had in common certain social or emotional issues; some were reportedly unpopular with peers or even antisocial and aggressive or seen by adults as attention-seeking and over-friendly with strangers. However, it should be noted that, although the conditions of the institutions were a marked improvement on the orphanages in Goldfarb's study, there was a large amount of shared care that saw a constant change of staff per child. On the other hand, a few studies in the 1990s of children in severely overcrowded, squalid Romanian orphanages by Chisholm (Chisholm *et al.*, 1995; Chisholm, 1998) showed that, despite such conditions and their late adoption (up to five-and-a-half years), the children were still able to form affectionate bonds with their family, if the strength of such bonds was less than what it might have been if formed earlier.

In a Romanian orphanage of the 1980s.
Source: Rex Features/Steve Back/Daily Mail

Definition

Sensitive period: revised from critical period, the timeframe that is most conducive to forming strong attachment compared to other times in the child's life.

Apart from overruling the notion of a critical period in favour of a more flexible sensitive period and discrediting the maternal deprivation hypothesis, such evidence also questions basic premises such as monotropism or stranger anxiety in this period. The fact that, after deprived conditions or inconsistent care provision, human and non-human young can still go on to have functional family lives or relationships indicates that it may not be as damaging as previously thought for infants not to bond with just one person. Also, reviews as early as the 1960s and 1970s already revealed that, by 18 months, fewer than one-fifth of children had just one primary caregiver, and in one-third of cases the strongest bond was with someone other than the mother (Schaffer and Emerson, 1964; Gallimore and Weisner, 1977). In addition, far from being wary of new people, between one and two years old infants are perfectly able to form new relationships with others. Bowlby (1973) himself came to emphasise that, as long as ongoing and reliable care is given, attachment relationships are not limited to the birth mother, and that a variety of figures, particularly the father, complement the mothering figure well (read about fathering later – How important is father?). These insights are significant in view of the social and economic shifts in the last few decades, at least in Western societies, that saw many mothers return to employment after childbirth.

STOP AND THINK

Reflection

- Before and around school ages, were you only looked after by your mother?
- If not, who else took care of you when your mother was not there?
- How close did you feel towards that person/those people that also looked after you?

Hence the popularity of Bowlby's original theory has to be put into the context of its time, in the 1940s and 1950s, during and immediately after the Second World War. The events at the time had invariably disrupted the prior way of life of a great number of families, propelling women into the workforce to fill the gap left by men who went to war. Until then, in a typical family the mother was the key, if not sole, caregiver as the man worked as the breadwinner. As the war ended, many longed for a return to the 'traditional' nuclear family, coinciding with a need

for work by the returning men. These social and economic pressures might have, if by accident rather than by design, added more public appeal to a theory that could be taken to promote the mother's role back in the home whilst giving way to more jobs for the male population.

Finally, devastating as the effects of maternal deprivation may be, as we have read, since Bowlby's era, with the decline in institutionalisation and a rise in the number of working mothers and day childcare provision, research has 'moved on' from focusing on the effects of maternal deprivation. Nevertheless, Bowlby's essential ideas on the attachment experience and its functional significance are still very highly regarded to this day. As the next sections of the chapter unfold, rather than *whether* an attachment relationship has been formed, many psychologists in the last few decades have studied how strong or 'secure' a child's attachments are and the implications of these.

Measuring attachment

Although the severity and irreversibility of maternal deprivation have been contested since Bowlby's days, the 'essence' of his theory concerning the infant's experience of using the primary caregiver(s) as a safe base or a source of security is well established and can be easily understood by many, academics and laypeople alike. Still, assuming that most children do have an attachment figure(s), we can imagine that their experiences of this supposed early and intimate bond with that figure may differ somewhat, depending on the characteristics of that figure, the child, or perhaps the dynamics of their relationship. One concept that has received a great deal of attention is the degree or pattern of 'security' this relationship begets, with researchers also endeavouring to systematically study individual (and group) differences in this relationship.

Security of attachment

The influential concept that different children may obtain different senses of security from the attachment relationship owes itself to the work of Mary Ainsworth, who had been a student of Bowlby in the 1950s. She was particularly interested in attachment behaviours in action, and how they translate into the later internalised 'goal-corrected' mechanism, which Bowlby proposed, that purportedly influences future outcomes and relationships. She went to observe attachment behaviours among the Ganda people in Uganda in 1954, and then later compared them to American samples from Baltimore (Ainsworth, 1963, 1967). She noticed certain differences in the intensity of separation protest and stranger anxiety (stronger in Ganda children), but both groups showed the typical behaviours through the attachment phases, despite communal childcare among the Ganda. On the other hand, she noticed considerable variations *within* each sample in terms of the infants' frequency and intensity of such behaviours. This prompted her to look closely at the nature of the attachment relationship, by how readily the infant is able to use the caregiver as a secure base, or attachment security, which should be reflected by their observed behaviour. Influenced by Bowlby's theory and drawing on her own observations, this readiness was considered to be most apparent in the critical events of separation from and, in particular, reunion with the caregiver. It is from this starting point that Ainsworth devised the now very widely used standard experimental procedure, and its associated scheme of classification, for measuring and categorising children's attachment security.

The Strange Situation

Ainsworth's procedure, known as the Strange Situation experiment, is based on a series of timed episodes that take place in an unfamiliar, but comfortable, controlled laboratory setting, while being observed unobtrusively by a (or a set of) researcher(s) (see the Research Methods box). The seven episodes involved the mother (or primary caregiver) and child being together with and without the addition of a stranger, the departure of the mother in the presence and absence of the stranger, and the return of the mother in the presence of the stranger. This procedure was designed for infants in the second year of their life as it was thought that the moderate stresses inherent in such a 'strange' situation would activate the relatively clear attachment behaviours in that phase (particularly the reunions after the mother's departures), thus reflecting the security of the infant's attachment to this primary caregiver. By gauging and charting the frequency and intensity of such critical behaviours, Ainsworth and her colleagues (e.g., Ainsworth and Bell, 1974; Ainsworth *et al.*, 1978) highlighted the ways in which individual children differed in their

attachment security with their caregiver(s), giving rise to the 'types' of attachment relationship they might have formed with this person.

Types of attachment

By the Strange Situation, Ainsworth identified a few patterns in which infants display signs of their differing ability and willingness to use their mother or primary caregiver as a safe base to derive a sense of security. Such patterns reveal what are commonly referred to as attachment types. The types, and their labels and behavioural descriptions, are found in Table 9.2. Ideally, if an infant has a secure attachment to the caregiver as a safe base, the procedure will see him initially pausing his exploration to draw himself closer to the mother or primary caregiver upon the stranger's entry (stranger anxiety). In particular, the departure of mother should at least cease his exploration and may well trigger him to cry and seek her (separation protest). However, her subsequent return should bring enough comfort to him to halt his distress and then restore his exploration. It can also be expected that the second separation and reunion will bring these behaviours to a greater intensity. Indeed, this general set of behaviours has been observed in roughly two-thirds of children from samples in most Western countries (e.g., van Ijzendoorn and Kroonenberg, 1988) who are seen as 'securely attached' infants (Type B).

Definitions

Attachment security: the readiness of an infant to use the primary caregiver to derive a sense of security that can be reflected in her pattern of attachment behaviours.
Strange Situation: a seven-part staged procedure employed to observe the behaviours and interactions between a child and the primary caregiver in a controlled laboratory setting, from which the type of attachment security between the dyad can be deduced.
Attachment types: patterns of behaviour observed in the Strange Situation denoting differing security of attachment to the primary caregiver as a safe base to explore.

RESEARCH METHODS

The Strange Situation experiment

The classic Strange Situation procedure consists of seven staged episodes, each with a set time limit of three minutes. The child is observed in interaction with either or both his mother and a stranger, as well as in solitary. The physical location is that of a room behind a one-way mirror (for the researcher to observe the participants unobtrusively) containing chairs and a rug or carpet laid with toys and objects for the child to explore.

The procedure goes as follows:

1   Mother and child enter and settle in the room (three minutes).
2   Stranger enters the room and interacts with mother (three minutes).
3   Mother leaves the room – child alone with stranger (three minutes or less if child shows excessive stress).
4   Mother re-enters the room. Stranger leaves – mother and child alone in room (three minutes).
5   Mother leaves the room – child alone in room (three minutes or shorter if child shows excessive stress).
6   Stranger enters room (three minutes or shorter if child shows excessive stress).
7   Mother re-enters room (stranger leaves) and remains (three minutes).

In summary, a series of entries, departures and re-unions and one solitary moment are featured. Of the most interest to researchers are the child's behaviours at reunions (stages 4 and 7). It is mainly based on these behaviours that the categorisation into the attachment 'types' denoting differing attachment security is evaluated.

- What are the main advantages of this procedure?
- What are the potential problems of this procedure?

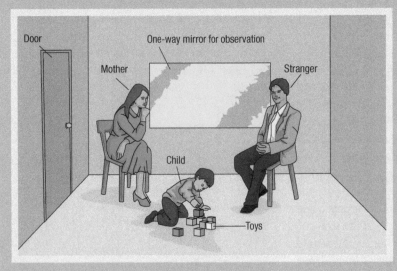

The physical setting of the Strange Situation experiment.

(*Source*: Grahame Hill, 2001. http://books.google .co.uk/ books?id=-rYkNmp4EPcC)

On the other hand, a substantial minority of children display less readiness to use their mother or primary caregiver as a safe base and are labelled as one of the 'insecure' types depending on the behaviours observed. For Type A, 'insecure-avoidant' infants, they appear indifferent to the caregiver's departure (and there may be even signs of the lack of distinction between the caregiver and stranger beforehand) and will ignore or even avoid contact with the caregiver upon her return. The Type C, 'insecure-resistant' (or 'insecure-ambivalent') infants are the opposite to Type A in that they seem extremely distressed by the caregiver's departure, so that not only will they resist the stranger's effort to comfort them, they are 'ambivalent' in their approach to the

Table 9.2. The four attachment types and key behaviours of the child towards mother during the Strange Situation experiment.

Type	Name	Key behaviours in Strange Situation
A	Insecure-avoidant	Lack/avoidance of contact with mother, treating her and stranger in a similar way; not upset by her departure and ignoring her or even turning away upon her return
B	Securely attached	Moderate amount of proximity-seeking to mother, upset by her departures followed by positive greetings during reunions
C	Insecure-resistant/ambivalent	Great distress at mother's departure, resisting comfort by stranger, but difficulty in being comforted upon reunion with a mixture of proximity-seeking, resistance or anger
D	Insecure-disorganised	Lack of a consistent behavioural pattern; apprehension about approaching mother; confusion about separation and reunion

caregiver on her return, seeking contact while rejecting her in anger. In this vein, Type A and Type C are considered to reflect the child's respective lesser willingness and ability to use the mother or primary caregiver as a source of security, and each accounts for between 10 and 20% of Western samples (van Ijzendoorn and Kroonenberg, 1988).

Later on, some researchers interested in atypical development (Main and Solomon, 1990) identified an additional 'insecure' type called 'insecure-disorganised' in that the infant appears to have no consistent patterns of behaviours or responses in the Strange Situation procedure. These children are generally apprehensive about approaching the caregiver; they may seek some proximity and then back away, as if to avoid her with fear, among other odd, incoherent behaviours. Overall they seem to be totally 'out of their depth' about the situation and uncertain about how to make use of the caregiver in that situation. It is said that these infants' behaviours are due to some experience of having been frightened by the caregiver or having seen the caregiver being frightened. Indeed this pattern of disorganisation is much more prevalent in infants from families with parental dysfunction or pathology such as bereavement or separation and divorce (Main and Hesse, 1990), or depression, maltreatment, neglect or abuse (Lyons-Ruth *et al.*, 1991, 1999; see The mother for more details).

It would appear that the relatively simple procedure of the Strange Situation allows us to distinguish, by observing their behaviour, between children with differing security of attachment to their caregivers and even to identify possible family discord or pathology. Still, how far can we really rely on this procedure and its classification system?

STOP AND THINK

Going further

Think back to the opening examples of two toddlers at the start of this chapter.

- Now that we have learnt about the classifications associated with the Strange Situation, how would you categorise each of the toddlers from their behaviours as described?
- Can you identify any problems with categorising these cases in this way?

Critique of the Strange Situation

Before launching into criticisms, it is worth first pointing out the significant practical value of the Strange Situation research procedure. Entering new spaces, encountering new people and being temporarily separated from the key caregiver(s) are events that many children in the first years of life and most cultures do go through, if some more so than others. Thus the procedure is not too far removed from infants' experiences at the stage of development, even though it is confined to the artificiality of a laboratory. With its utility and uncomplicated set-up, both the procedure and its associated classification system have been almost universally adopted to describe variations in attachment.

It is also important to identify that the attachment type a child has with a caregiver signifies the property of the *relationship* between the child and that caregiver, instead of something which is solely about the general propensity inherent in the child to bond. Thus, it is highly

Table 9.3. Percentage of main attachment types in children across eight countries.

Country	No. of studies available	Attachment type (%)		
		Secure	Avoidant	Resistant
UK	1	75	22	3
Sweden	1	75	22	4
Japan	2	68	5	27
Holland	4	67	26	6
USA	18	65	21	14
Israel	2	64	7	29
Germany	3	57	35	8
China	1	50	25	25
Average		65	21	14

Source: Van Ijzendoorn and Kroonenberg (1988).

plausible that a child could exhibit different attachment behaviours with different people according to the kind and quality of relationship he has with each of them. As we will explore in the next section, children do seem to interact and relate rather differently to mother, father and other family and non-family caregivers and vice versa. Differences in interactions and communication will invariably lead to differences in relationships, and this is not only the case for attachment relationships, but also for other forms of relationships (such as those with peers; see Chapter 12, Peer Interactions and Relationships).

The Strange Situation was designed in such a way that the child is exposed to an increasing amount of stress, on entering an unfamiliar environment, through the entry of a stranger and absence of the caregiver, to getting left alone in the unfamiliar room. As already suggested in the earlier section of the chapter, most children in the second year of life are often exposed to adults other than the primary caregiver who takes care of them. It is likely that the impact of some of the episodes is not as stressful as once thought and, by that token, classification just by the infant's responses to these events may not reflect his 'real' degree of attachment to the primary caregiver. For example, a child already used to being cared for by his father, grandparents or in a nursery may, due to his regular experience, not be unsettled by the stranger nor upset by his mother leaving. Even if the mother is still the 'primary' caregiver, and mother and child share a relatively strong relationship, his behaviour may have him labelled as 'insecure' due to his lack of distress shown upon her departure and his lack of need to be comforted by her

when she returns. This is particularly the case when much of the classification is based on the limited subset of behaviours during reunions.

Not only may the Strange Situation be inappropriate for use with children used to non-maternal care, whose deviations from the majority may be a reflection of relative independence rather than insecure attachment, such variations from the 'secure' type may in fact be a facet of cultural norms that are encouraged in some societies.

Table 9.3 lists the average percentages of children placed in each of the three major attachment types from research in eight countries across Europe, America and Asia in the 1980s soon after Ainsworth's classification types were established. A very striking feature is the contrast in proportions of 'secure' children between countries, although this category was still the commonest *within* each country. Both the UK and Sweden had the most secure children whilst only half of the Chinese sample was in that category, slightly behind Germany (although one ought to be concerned with generalising from a single study in three of these four countries). What also stands out are the contrasting figures for the insecure categories; Japan and Israel, though with high proportions of secure children, had also relatively high proportions of resistant ones versus very low proportions of avoidant ones.

It is unlikely that infants of some ethnic groups have a 'naturally' higher tendency to attach securely (or insecurely) to the primary caregiver than those of other groups, since any pattern of highs or lows is not unique to one part of the world. Instead, it is quite likely that certain attachment behaviours are interpreted and valued differently, thus promoted to differing degrees, in different cultures. Then differences in parental attitudes and childcare practices may be translated into different styles of interactions in the Strange Situation setting. For instance, one possible explanation for the relatively high rate of 'avoidant' attachment in Germany is that the traditional culture prefers and encourages independence in children near the second year (Grossman, 1985). In sharp contrast, in Japan infants are rarely left alone, even for short periods, particularly in the first year. In fact the infant at this stage is seen as a 'mono' (object), which means extension, of the mother rather than a separate being (Goodman, 2000; p. 165). The mother carries him around in the day and sleeps with him at night. The Strange Situation is likely to bring great distress to him, and so he will be less easily comforted after separation from the mother (Takahashi, 1990). Thus, although child-rearing methods do evolve over time, especially in the East as more women become work-oriented, cultural specificities in parental values do exist to challenge the validity of the Strange Situation procedure (Grossman *et al.*, 1986; Nakagawa *et al.*, 1992).

Ultimately, many shortcomings of the Strange Situation and attachment types are due to the fact that they are entirely 'behaviour-based', in that only overt behaviours and expressions 'count' towards the classification. This is because the procedure was designed for a narrow age band where infants are still in the pre-linguistic stage (see Clarke-Stewart *et al.*, 2001, for a fuller review). As we have learnt (in Bowlby's 'goal-corrected' phase) that the older child is supposed to 'represent' the attachment relationship internally as she matures, with greater understanding of others and more cognitive competences, one question is whether she will remain in the same attachment type. This concerns the stability of attachment security and its bearing on the future (Goldberg, 2000), which will be explored later on in the chapter. Associated with this are the variables which influence attachment relationships in the meantime, and such variables inevitably involve the people the child regularly engages with and the kind(s) of care that she receives. These will be covered in the following section.

Attachment and childcare

Notwithstanding the caveats and limitations of the key measurement of attachment, it suffices to say that different patterns of this relationship do exist, and since attachment usually starts from home, such differences have their likely origins in the environment of the child's family. The mother is the obvious starting point; as variously mentioned so far, most children still have their birth mother as the primary caregiver. However, it has become more and more common for the father or other family relations to take on at least part of the responsibility of childcare. Additionally, more and more formal and informal 'out-of-home' childcare arrangements such as childminding services and day nurseries have become established all over the West (as well as in many non-Western countries) in the last few decades for children as young as a few weeks old. What are the implications of such 'alternatives' on attachment security? This section will begin by considering how some characteristics of the mother may affect her relationship with the child, before venturing into a discussion of whether and how paternal and out-of-home day childcare may have a bearing on the child's attachment security.

The mother

Despite the alternative childcare available, it is still taken for granted that the mother as primary caregiver is the best 'scenario' for both mother and child. Indeed, in most cases the child does feel closest to his mother even if he is also looked after by other adults. So, what aspects of mother are the key ingredients for such closeness?

According to Bowlby's work, but also from further research, it is suggested that it is not so much about her physical availability, but that the mother's *emotional* availability or 'responsiveness' is essential for establishing that 'secure' bond with her own child. Bowlby termed this maternal sensitivity, which is the emotional sensitivity on the part of the mother (or mother substitute) to recognise the infant's cues and respond to them promptly, appropriately and consistently. A 'sensitive' mother is one who is able and willing to watch out for her child, so that she can attend and cater to him when he tries to engage her or in his times of needs. For instance, when he cries, she picks him up, when he smiles,

Definition

Maternal sensitivity: the emotional sensitivity of the mother to recognise her child's cues and to respond to them promptly, appropriately and consistently.

she smiles back, and when he babbles, she often talks to him in a high-pitched voice (see the section on Infant-directed speech in Chapter 5, Language Development). That a mother is supposedly constantly contingent to her own baby's signals has obvious implications (for working mothers, especially); an absent mother cannot be sensitive (or 'enough') for she is just not available to 'be there' to meet her baby's needs at all times.

Ainsworth followed Bowlby's argument while developing the idea of attachment security, adding that a secure attachment is founded on such sensitivity of the parent during the first year of life. There does seem to be overall support for a link between sensitive parenting and attachment security. By observing parent–child interactions in other settings and the child's behaviours in the Strange Situation, research has shown that warm, attentive or positive parenting, usually also characterised by harmony and apparent mutual enjoyment, is associated more with the 'secure' type attachment, and this is regardless of culture, socioeconomic status and whether the attachment figure is the biological mother or an adoptive parent (e.g., de Wolff and van Ijzendoorn, 1997; Posada et al., 2002, 2004; van Ijzendoorn et al., 2004). Children of mothers who may at times act in a negative or rejecting manner while at others over-stimulate them tend to show the 'insecure-avoidant' type attachment, and children who receive unreliable or inconsistent care (sometimes unresponsive and sometimes overbearing) are likely to be 'insecure-resistant' (e.g., Ainsworth et al., 1978; Isabella, 1993, 1995).

There is further evidence that inadequate care is associated with the 'disorganised' type of attachment. Earlier, we already touched on the links between this and adverse family conditions. Depression in a parent or parents suffering from bereavement has been seen to lead the parent to inadvertently display contradictory, unpleasant or even threatening behaviours, such as looking frightened or frightening, handling the infant roughly or even using the infant as a source of comfort for their conditions (Lyons-Ruth et al., 1999; Schuengel et al., 1999). In turn, the infant is likely to express more negative emotions when interacting with her mother and to develop other problems, such as with feeding (Rahman et al., 2004), all of which will interfere with the development of a secure attachment.

More worryingly, the disorganised type of attachment is also over-represented by children who have been maltreated through neglect or even abuse (Barnett et al.,

1999). In the extreme cases, the caregiver not only fails to provide basic security and protection, but may even do the opposite by causing emotional or physical hurt to the child (see Cutting Edge box). In many such cases, the attachment disorder in the child will persist and even influence her interactions and relationships with other people (such as peers) later on. Importantly, abused children are far more likely, compared with those who have never been abused, to become abusive parents, passing on the pathological relationship through the generations (Cichetti and Barnett, 1991; Barnett et al., 1999; and see Attachment in later childhood and adolescence).

The potential consequences of maternal pathology on children's attachment seem to be as daunting, if not more so, than those of deprivation that we read earlier. Still, it is important to stress that the association between maternal sensitivity and attachment security is not a perfect one; a minority of formerly maltreated children do manage to form secure attachments with caregivers and good relationships with others, and some form attachment to parents who lack sensitivity, if in an incoherent manner (Barnett et al., 1999). Then not all such children are condemned to a life of attachment disorders; sensitivity may be a key ingredient, but is not the only one necessary for secure attachments.

In addition, not only are there variations in maternal sensitivity, there is also a lot of variation in how maternal 'sensitivity' is viewed and expressed, particularly cross-culturally. We have broached this concept in a relatively 'Eurocentric' manner, based on the observable moment-by-moment responsiveness of the mother. Earlier we read about the close physical contact between mother and baby in Japan. Such contingent interactions and overt closeness may not be the norm in other cultures, where parents respond to their children's needs in other ways, such as guiding their actions (Carlson and Harwood, 2003). Hence, it is worth remaining open-minded about what 'counts' as sensitivity; some may say warmth, others stimulation, or simply general attentiveness.

The nature and criteria of maternal sensitivity have great implications for mothers who may have a need to consider returning to work, and are under pressure due to the apparent need for constant availability by their young. Thus far, this kind of sensitivity has been presented as if it almost comes 'naturally' from the biological mother but, in reality, there is some gap between the aspiration to become a sensitive mother and the actual experience of being one which may feature routine

CUTTING EDGE

Responses to the Baby P case

In November 2008, a news story stunned and outraged the public in the UK and beyond. The case of 'Baby P', a toddler who died at the age of 17 months after a horrific series of injuries was inflicted on him in his home, was one that angered and puzzled many. It was reported that Baby P regularly received a catalogue of neglect, physical attacks and emotional turmoil for no less than eight months. The reports said that Baby P endured at least 50 injuries including a broken back and ribs, and was losing weight in the last few months of his life. Separated from his father when Baby P was two months old, his mother (and grandmother at one time) had been arrested twice for assault and neglect. His mother, her partner (who moved into her house a few months after Baby P's father left) and a male lodger were sentenced for causing and allowing Baby P's death.

Some of the disbelief expressed by the public was based on the fact that, although the physical attacks on Baby P were caused by his mother's partner, his mother was at least complicit in such acts, because she 'stood by' when the violent abuse took place and made no attempt to prevent further abuse. She was also responsible for Baby P's maltreatment through neglect and starvation. Additionally, she actively attempted to hide evidence of physical abuse and made up cover stories about Baby P's injuries to social workers, who visited their home more than 60 times due to concerns raised by the childminder, family members, health professionals and neighbours.

Another reason for the public outcry was the young age of Baby P. A similar case, that of Victoria Climbie, of severe child abuse which ended in her death had emerged four years earlier; but Victoria was eight years old, and the perpetrators were her aunt and her aunt's partner. The wilful maltreatment or abuse of an infant by his own mother is beyond the imagination of most people, in particular parents of young children. Many public online forums were filled with comments that labelled the killers of Baby P as 'evil', 'sick' or words to that effect, and some called for more to be done by the Social Services towards 'at risk' children, apart from an investigation into and improvements of the Services itself (which many believed had 'failed' Baby P).

Amidst the public shock and outrage and media frenzy of blame and shame, some psychologists (e.g., NHS clinical psychologist, Jenny Taylor) responded controversially with a reminder that those adults who fail so dramatically in their parenting are often far from being 'evil', but were once children themselves who were not properly cared for or protected in their own childhood. It was also argued that, even in the face of maltreatment, removing children from their parents might not improve their chances due to the traumatising effects of frequent changes of carers within our overburdened care systems. Others have remarked that Baby P's case was 'just one of thousands of children who are vulnerable and who live with parents in need of support and greater supervision' (Boynton and Anderson, 2009, p. 8).

- What is your response to this case?
- Do you agree with the psychologists' idea that Baby P's mother is likely to have been abused as a child herself? What about giving support to such parents?
- To what extent do you think the way we were treated by our parents can influence the way we will treat our own children?

Sources: Boynton and Anderson (2009); Taylor (2008).

boredom or even occasional depressive episodes rather than mutual fulfilment (Boulton, 1983). On the other hand, it has been shown that it is possible to 'train' such sensitivity (van den Boom, 1994). Participating in short parenting sessions for interacting with their babies identified as having an irritable temperament seemed to help economically disadvantaged mothers to become more responsive, and their infants were more likely to be securely attached one year later compared with those of mothers who did not go through training.

More recently, research has explored other characteristics of the mother that may promote secure attachment.

The British psychologist Elizabeth Meins (Meins *et al.*, 2001, 2002), first introduced the concept of mind-mindedness as the ability of a parent to look at her child as an individual with her own thoughts and feelings (similar to theory of mind; see Chapter 8, Theory of Mind). Meins argues that, instead of treating her infant as a vulnerable dependant with needs, the mother's ability and willingness to treat her as a person 'with a mind' reflected by engagement with her using talk about mental states will help her achieve secure attachment by enabling her to see other people's needs and motives (building up a 'representation' of others as in the last attachment phase). Her work found that, from as young as six months old, mothers who made more verbal references to their infants' psychological states in their interactions were more likely to have their infants assessed with a secure attachment at one year old. In fact, mind-mindedness predicts later attachment security better than maternal sensitivity.

The idea that it is not about constant contingent responsiveness, which also may be acquired, but that 'good mothering' may be more about the *quality* of interactions, is a welcome one for many in that it lessens the obligation of mothers to remain at home and gives more scope for non-maternal care. In fact, Bowlby (1969) himself did not believe in a mother attending to all her baby's discomfort or distress at every turn, but suggested that part of the process is to allow waiting with moderate stress to learn tolerance and independence. As covered before, Bowlby also advocated the complementary role of the father, and it is to this other key figure in modern-day parenting that we turn our attention next.

How important is father?

After a period in which the role of the father was 'sidelined' since Bowlby's theory first emerged, by the 1990s

research that included fathers as attachment figures was burgeoning. Some of the work has compared infant attachment to the father with that to the mother or the parents' engagement with their infant. The pattern of findings can be summarised as indicating some similarity in attachment security, but suggests differences in the *quality* of attachment or engagement between the two parenting figures. That is, in a two-parent family, although a child with a secure attachment to her mother is likely to also show secure attachment to her father (signalling matching characteristics between the parents), parenting factors such as sensitivity, warmth or availability which have been identified as predicting maternal attachment often do not predict paternal attachment (e.g., Grossman *et al.*, 2002; Caldera, 2004; Brown *et al.*, 2007).

STOP AND THINK

Reflection

If your primary caregiver was your mother:

- Did your father (at least sometimes) look after you by himself?
- What things did you enjoy doing with your father the most?
- Was there any difference between your relationships with your mother and father?

The more recent research seems to confirm the idea that the amount of involvement aside, fathers play a different role to mothers in that they typically have a smaller part in the practical and emotional aspects of caregiving (such as feeding and soothing the baby). Fathers spend more time in play with their infants, particularly sons, with more physical activities and stimulation (see Lamb, 1997). Mothers tend to engage in more 'traditional' games (such as peekaboo) with affectionate interplay between herself and the infant. These differences may go to explain why, in general, infants prefer to turn to mother rather than father in times of discomfort or distress (Lamb, 1987).

Is fathers' playful engagement a factor contributing to paternal attachment? It is likely. Some have called this

Definition

Mind-mindedness: the ability of a parent to see and treat her child as an individual with his own thoughts and feelings, through her interactions with him using talk to refer to mental states.

Fathers spend more time in play with their infants.

Source: O'Donnell

play sensitivity, which includes adapting play to the infant's ability, letting her take the initiative and responding to her facial expressions (Grossman *et al.*, 2002). Such sensitivity is argued to convey warmth and confidence to the child, and predicts attachment much better than conventional sensitivity up to the age of 16. At the same time, this image of father as 'playmate' has been diversified to include more practical tasks, with more mothers returning to employment, but it is promising that other research has found that greater involvement in sensitive care giving by fathers can predict secure attachment (Cox *et al.*, 1992; van Ijzendoorn and deWolff, 1997). Even though they tend to show less affection in such tasks, they are just as capable as mothers in performing them, and so researchers are calling for a closer look at the multiple dimensions of fathering quality (Brown *et al.*, 2007).

There is still a much richer literature on maternal attachment compared to that on paternal attachment, and so more work is required to tap into this relationship, with the greater sharing of parenthood today. Change in childcare patterns also concerns other possible caregivers,

Definition

Play sensitivity: responsiveness to the infant during play through cooperation and motivation by accepting her initiative, adapting play to her cognitive capability and responding to her emotional expressions.

such as nursery workers and childminders, and the impact of such change has been debated even more as we will discover below.

Impact of day care

The concerns about the impact of day care on attachment have, again, originated from Bowlby's theorisation. His work on the deleterious effects of permanent placement in institutions in support of the maternal deprivation hypothesis led some to consider the possibility that placing children in non-parental care at all, particularly before the age of three years (the end of the sensitive period), might have adverse effects on their attachment relationships. This has provoked a great deal of debate as the need for many mothers to return to work often means at least the occasional use of childminding or day care services, unless fathers or other family members are available to provide care during her working hours.

The early findings, in the 1970s by the now internationally respected researcher in child development, Jay Belsky, were at first reassuring. It was concluded that there was no reason to suspect day care would disrupt the child's attachment to his mother and that children of working mothers still preferred their mothers to any other caregiver (Belsky and Steinberg, 1978). However, based on further reviews of the research, he amended his statements accordingly (Belsky, 1988, 1992). He noticed that children who were in out-of-home care for more than 20 hours per week by the end of the first year were more likely to show insecure (usually avoidant) attachment to their mothers compared to children who had more maternal care.

Although Belsky was more inclined to attribute the day care children's attachment insecurity to their regular experience of separation from their mother, leading them to doubt her responsiveness or availability, the results may be interpreted in other ways. Earlier we analysed the Strange Situation and associated attachment types, and identified that events in the procedure that are supposed to cause anxiety and trigger attachment behaviours are perhaps not that distressing to some. In the case of children who are used to multiple caregivers, their responses may be viewed as reflecting independence rather than avoidance of mother (Clarke-Stewart *et al.*, 2001). This seems plausible as later evidence showed that children in different forms of non-maternal care (relatives, childminders and nursery) had similar behaviours during reunion with their mothers, and those in nursery were also more likely to show some desirable social traits such as empathy and sharing, if also less of others such as affection (Melhuish *et al.*, 1990).

Methodological issues aside, it is also not possible to be sure that the patterns of attachment were in fact caused by being in day care as such, rather than the conditions of the particular care provisions. This is similar to attributing the negative outcomes of children who had been in orphanages with appalling conditions to being institutionalised, rather than to the conditions of the institutions. This is worth considering as overall more of Belsky's day care samples than not, as comparable to most American children, still showed secure attachment to their mothers (Clarke-Stewart, 1988).

It is thus important to consider the kinds of childcare available (of which parents often use a combination), and the variables that denote quality of care such as the ratio of children to caregivers, experience of caregivers, the structure of day-to-day routines and the physical setting. There seems to be much variation and, unsurprisingly, with a sub-standard environment or higher staff–children ratio, day care workers find it more difficult to interact positively with individual children (Melhuish *et al.*, 1990).

On the other hand, associations between high-quality day care and attachment security have been found, even when the day care is full-time (Love *et al.*, 2003). Children in such centres show more secure attachment than those cared for by childminders, family or friends. Furthermore, state-funded quality day care can even ameliorate the effects of poverty and related disadvantages (such as poor parental education) by promoting, from early on, competences in children that their families do not have the resources to do (Lamb, 1998). However, the availability and affordability of such day care varies, both between and within countries, and poorer families are more likely to 'settle for' poorer quality care. Frequent and long periods spent in such care coupled with insensitive mothering due to poverty and stress makes a likely combination for insecure attachment.

It can be said that alternative care arrangements give relief to mothers that need to return to work, but the quality of care, and the family circumstances under which care is taken, must be taken into account. As we will explore in the next section, children form expectations about others and relationships from care experiences at home and beyond, which can in turn have implications for their development in the long term.

A good amount of high-quality day care can be beneficial to children's development.
Source: Pearson Education Ltd./Studio 8

Attachment beyond infancy

In the more recent strands of research, attachment theory has been given longer term and potential lifespan implications, especially for social and emotional development. In the last section, we learnt that maternal characteristics, including their experience of abuse, can have a bearing on their child's attachment to them and future parenting capacity. 'Cross-generational' factors such as this give an idea of both continued and discontinued patterns of relationship development within families. These patterns are said to be based on the 'notion' of the child in each generation about her relationships with the caregivers, and how she carries forward this notion as she grows and forms new relationships with other people in her life. Below, we will first investigate the nature of this 'notion' of relationships, before moving on to complete the chapter by looking at research that has assessed its influence on the child's later development.

Internal working model

We have already learnt (in the attachment phases) that a key milestone of attachment development is that the child depends less and less on the actual physical proximity of a constantly present caregiver, but more and more on the notion that she is 'available'. We have emphasised the child's understanding of a responsive parent or a consistent and good-quality childcare routine. The central function of this notion is that the child learns about how to 'relate'. Through these early relationships she has with the closest people to her, she builds up expectations about herself, others and the relationships between them which make up what Bowlby (1969, 1973) originally called the child's internal working model (IWM).

Note that in assuming that the child is able to 'internally' represent relationships in his mind, the IWM part of attachment goes beyond the behavioural and emotional elements, and signifies a 'cognitive' side to attachment. Such a cognitive structure, or model, contains past interactions with the attachment figure(s) and incorporates new ones as the infant is engaged with them more and more, and these will guide his later interactions with these figures and other people. This is why their characteristics (such as sensitivity) matter, since these get associated with his experiences as part of the model, which informs his further actions using the expectations formed from the experiences.

Accordingly, the different attachment types can be represented by different IWMs (Ainworth *et al.*, 1978). For a securely attached child, his IWM of his caregiver(s) will be one of warmth and attentiveness or of someone who is often available. He expects her to return to him after separation which helps him become accepting of others and relationships and see himself as someone worthy of love. The IWMs of the caregiver of insecurely attached children will be either one of more coldness, or even rejection (avoidant type), which leads the child to display little or no distress at separation and expect little from the reunion; or one of inconsistency and unpredictability (resistant type), leading the child initially into excessive distress, but possibly anger over time, towards the caregiver. Such children are said to have a less worthy sense of self and have more difficulty building close relationships due to their pessimistic outlook on others or their preoccupation with their relationships as a result of their experiences.

For the cases of insecure-disorganised children, their experiences of disturbed or distorted caregiving mean that they are unable to organise a coherent set of actions

towards or expectations about their caregiver, thus the lack of a coherent IWM. This means they lack the usual know-how for approaching or interacting with others to form new relationships, even if they still have the motivation to do so.

Obviously, to actually see whether the features and functions of these hypothetical cognitive models 'work' as they are prescribed, we need to review the evidence about the later development of children classified with different attachment types, and thus with different IWMs. We touched on some support for the cycle of dysfunctional interactions and relationships in insecure-disorganised children through neglect or abuse previously. Next we will examine the wider evidence base that includes the major attachment types.

STOP AND THINK

Going further

Refer back to the opening examples once again, and the likely attachment types you gave them earlier at another Stop-and-think.

- What kind of an IWM do you think each of these toddlers has?
- How do you imagine they may relate to other people a year later and then in school?

Attachment in later childhood and adolescence

The IWM purportedly relays children's past experiences to guide present interactions. In theory, it will equip a secure child with confidence and self-worth to develop closer relationships with family and build friendships with peers. An insecure child will lack these desirable social and emotional traits (or even carry their reverse) for developing healthy relationships. There is empirical support for both ideas, with some of the early research being carried out by Mary Main, who derived the insecure-disorganised attachment type.

A keen follower of Ainsworth's ideas, Main and her teams (e.g. Main *et al.*, 1985; Main and Cassidy, 1988) devised variants of the Strange Situation for measuring quality of relationships in pre-school children. She found that children who had been securely attached at 12 months went on to show more emotional coherence

Definition

Internal working model: the mental representation about oneself, others and their relationships on which one's expectations about future relationships are based.

and openness, while insecurely attached toddlers were more likely to give irrational or negative answers or stay very quiet, in an interview discussing imagined parent–child interactions and relationships at six years. Main also reported that secure children were more likely to see themselves as lovable, and liked by peers, but insecure children had lower expectations of relationships as well as actually engaging less in social activities. Their behaviour during reunion with parents at that age was reminiscent of that at 12 months (such as greeting then ignoring the parents or being clingy but whiny). There were also age-appropriate signs of hostility or fear in insecure-disorganised children towards their parents, indicating maladjusted relationships.

Later research has also more or less confirmed the above pattern while using more measures of social and emotional developmental outcomes. For instance, Alan Sroufe, who specifically assessed peer relationships (e.g., Elicker et al., 1992; Shulman et al., 1994; Carlson, et al., 2003), found that from pre-school through school, children who had been securely attached as infants showed greater skills in and enthusiasm for social play, had more close friendships, and were rated by teachers as higher in self-esteem, social competence and emotional maturity (such as showing more pro-social behaviour and empathy).

There is even evidence that attachment security can predict social adjustment into adolescence (Sroufe et al., 1993; Ostoja et al., 1995; Carlson et al., 2004). Adolescents securely attached to their parents during infancy and adolescence (assessed by interviews) have higher self-esteem, school attainments and social skills, and more friendships than those with insecure attachments. In particular, the insecure-avoidant adolescents have less social support and are more likely to have earlier sexual experiences and riskier sexual practices. With the extra complications of biological changes during puberty, along with the ongoing cognitive and social changes, adolescence marks a critical period in which a 'balance' between consolidating relationships with the family and norms within the society, whilst exploring and experimenting with more independence and autonomy, can be difficult without the positive, but authoritative, support by parents (Baumrind, 1991; and see Chapter 13, Adolescence).

It seems that attachment security in infancy can predict development well into the future, but there are, of course, exceptions (e.g. Schneider et al., 2001; Stams et al., 2002). Insecure infants do not always end up 'worse off' than their secure counterparts (except for disorganised infants, but then there are still some who

develop normally as covered earlier). Part of the inconsistency can be due to the stability of attachment – that is, whether children continue with the same attachment type. Infants do tend to do so in the short term as assessed by the Strange Situation. In the longer term, with the complication of different measures, and longer lapses between measurements, more children do change attachment patterns (Thompson, 2000). This is because key factors such as childcare arrangements (e.g. mothers working more as children get older) and family environment (e.g. separation, divorce) can change. It is also possible that a change in circumstances may lead to a change in attachment security as well as to other developmental outcomes. For example, parental separation can lead to the child feeling less attached to the estranged parent, and its stress can cause him to have less positive peer interactions. Hence, although long-term secure attachment cemented by continuity of good-quality caregiving may facilitate healthy development, this does not always mean that the security of attachment that started in infancy determines the development.

Adulthood and intergenerational cycles

Because attachment security, if stable along with parenting and family stability, can predict later childhood outcomes quite well, researchers have also explored how well it predicts other outcomes in adulthood. In fact, for Bowlby, the earliest representations (as IWMs) of attachment are most likely to remain stable since, drawing from psychoanalysis, he believed that these models exist outside of our consciousness and influence us through the lifespan. If that is the case, one would expect that the IWMs representing different attachment types in infancy or childhood will be associated with different attachment types in adulthood. Once again, it is Mary Main who devised a method that measures attachment quality in adults for this purpose.

Main and her co-workers (Main et al., 1985; Main and Goldwyn, 1994) developed a semi-structured interview schedule, called the Adult Attachment Interview (AAI) to measure how much an adult is able to integrate memories of her earliest relationships with her primary caregivers into her present state of mind concerning relationships. In this respect, this is a retrospective way of tapping into former attachment security with the aim of mapping on to present relationship quality, thus charting cross-generational patterns of attachment.

Table 9.4. Adult attachment types and their matching infant attachment types.

Type	Characteristics	Matching
Dismissive	Dismisses the significance of (or denies or claims to forget the existence of) early experiences. Recalls events with little detail and emotion. Acknowledges the importance of relationships in past and present.	Insecure-avoidant
Autonomous	Talks frankly and in detail about both positive and negative experiences. Shows insights into others' motives and feelings.	Secure
Preoccupied	Remembers experiences in a lengthy, unstructured way, often with repetitions. Talks emotionally about events as if overwhelmed.	Insecure-resistant
Unresolved	Failed to organise mental life after a traumatic past.	Disorganised

Main maintained that it is not so much about 'what' the person remembers about the past, but 'how' she does in terms of emotional openness and the coherence between former and present experiences.

Again, influenced by Ainsworth's ideas of attachment types, Main's classification of adult attachment contains three major categories plus an additional one that denotes an inability to form attachments in the person's past. Table 9.4 lists such adult attachment types, along with the infant attachment types with which each is hypothesised to be linked.

According to Main, if the adult has positive memories of her past relationships at home, she will talk more openly about the relationships and will be more likely to build a secure attachment with her own child. If her childhood relationships were difficult so that she 'blocks' them out (dismissive) or is still emotionally burdened by them (preoccupied), then she is more likely to have an insecure attachment with her own child because she cannot draw on positive experiences to build on. Indeed it was found that 75% of securely attached infants had mothers assessed as 'autonomous' (Main and Goldwyn, 1994), and there is even evidence for three-generational continuity (Benoit and Parker, 1994). This indicates that the representation that the parent has of her attachment with her own parents will affect the way she interacts with her child, who will in turn form the corresponding type of attachment, which will go on to affect the way that her child interacts with her future children, within an inter-generational cycle.

Indeed, differences in parenting behaviours and perceptions of people's own children have been associated with differences in the parent's adult attachment model or history of attachments (van Ijzendoorn, 1995; Steele *et al.*, 2003; Pesonen *et al.*, 2004). Mothers who are assessed as securely attached are more sensitive towards their children whilst those who have a history of insecure attachment are more likely to view their children negatively. In addition, the relationship that insecure parents form with their children, itself likely to be insecure, can have consequences for other relationships the children will form as future adults such as romantic relationships (see the Lifespan box).

Longitudinal studies that follow up infants who had been assessed by Ainsworth's Strange Situation for their adult attachment years later lend further support to Main's ideas. Some research has shown direct mapping

Representations of attachment relationships may be maintained across generations.

Source: Pearson Education Ltd./Medio Images

Definition

Adult Attachment Interview: a semi-structured interview method for probing into an adult's early childhood relationship experiences with attachment figures and assessing the extent to which she integrates such experiences into her current relationships.

LIFESPAN

Parental insecure attachment and adult children's romantic relationships

In their 2008 article, marriage and family therapists in Slovenia, Tomaz and Katarina Erzar, argue that parents' insecure attachment can result in channelling their children unconsciously into helping them with their former attachment issues. In doing so, the child may come to learn that his relationship security depends on this way of being in the relationship. This insecure pattern of bonding in childhood will continue, argued the authors, to manifest itself in the child's later adult relationships, such as romantic relationships. Drawing from Bowlby's writings, based on their experiences with their insecure parents, these children may take on 'exaggerated' care for others or hide their relationship needs in other ways, which go against the development of intimate adult relationships as they require mutual acceptance. This transition is problematic as the children require new ways of regulating their affect associated with their experiences with their parents. The parents are also said to feel as if they are being abandoned and betrayed when their children leave home or commit to romantic relationships.

On that note, the authors presented extracts from a therapy session with a couple that have experienced this kind of family relationship. By probing into their past and present affect, the article illustrates the potential consequences that parents' insecure attachment can have on their child's self-perception and relationships. The empathic conversation about their childhood wounds also elicited some mutual understanding and acceptance between the couple, forming part of the intervention to help break the intergenerational cycle of insecure attachment.

Source: Erzar and Erzar (2008).

from infant to adult attachment types, particularly when family circumstances remain stable, but changes were also detected (Hamilton, 1994). Changes might be due to the predictiveness of infant attachment types, the reliability of the AAI or life events. The latter reveals that changes in family circumstances such as separation, divorce, illness and bereavement in the intervening years between assessments can exert a very significant impact on adult attachment (Zimmerman, 2000). It can be said that, apart from early secure attachment, a stable home-life is also a key contributor to secure relationships in the future. Such patterns also call for more research with parents of their own perspective and history, not just as caregivers, to examine the effects of parenting representations (Mayseless, 2006).

Gathering the evidence thus far, the longer term impact of the earliest attachment relationship a child has with her parents is not yet conclusive, but this relationship is quite clearly at least relevant to the one that resembles it the most, the relationship that the child will go on to form with her own children in the future.

SUMMARY

This chapter has introduced us to the earliest social experiences that a child has in her life. From Bowlby's original theory through to intergenerational cycles of attachment security, and from the Strange Situation and AAI, we have explored the nature and origins of a highly important part of development and its implications for theoretical, personal and practical issues.

We have evaluated Bowlby's original theory and the importance placed upon the relationship with the primary caregiver to early development, considering the maternal deprivation hypothesis and animal research as well. We have also looked at more recent research which helps us to understand how other caregivers and consistent parenting allow for the development of attachment. Whether the characteristics of attachment relationships are a nature 'given' or are nurtured by our conditions, we humans, like most animals, are social creatures and, as such, have a tendency to bond with and relate to others. Exactly how this bonding is done, and the effects that the lack of bonding has, can vary across human cultures and animal species.

We have explored the key features of the attachment relationship, including monotropism, proximity seeking, separation protest, stranger anxiety and the critical or sensitive period for its formation. We have also looked at the phases of attachment which children go through at different ages in the development of attachment.

We have critically considered the Strange Situation procedure, how it works and what it is supposed to reveal about a child, as well as considering some of its potential shortcomings, alternative accounts of its usefulness and other explanations as to what it might reveal about a child's relationships.

We have looked at the reality of modern society in order to consider how optimum relationships can be achieved within its demands and constraints. Fathering, working mothers and shared care are all prevalent phenomena and whether they mean compromised attachment relationships is unclear. As such, more support might be offered to families to optimise their relationships with children.

We have discussed a great deal of research which suggests that a child's early attachment experiences can have long-term psychological impacts which may be positive and negative. We have also seen various ways in which the long-term negative effects of disturbances in early attachments can be minimised. The current and future direction of research in this field is to examine the combination of factors that lead to optimum attachment relationships and to minimise the ill effects of deprivation or disturbed attachment relationships.

REVIEW QUESTIONS

1 Outline and evaluate Bowlby's attachment theory in relation to its implications for non-maternal and out-of-home childcare provisions with research evidence.

2 Describe and critically evaluate the Strange Situation procedure.

3 What is an internal working model? How does it relate to attachment relationships and predict future relationships?

4 What are the deleterious effects of maternal deprivation? Are such effects entirely inevitable once the mothering figure has been absent in an infant's life?

5 Are Bowlby's original proposals for attachment applicable for contemporary family life in Western society?

RECOMMENDED READING

For a detailed evaluation of the Strange Situation procedure:

Clarke-Stewart, K.A., Goosens, F.A. & Allhusen, V.D. (2001). Measuring infant mother attachment: Is the Strange Situation enough? *Social Development*, *10*, 143–169.

For looking at attachment (as well as imprinting and deprivation) in the wider context of socialisation and emotional development cross-culturally:

Flanagan, C. (1999). *Early Socialisation: Sociability and Attachment*. London: Routledge.

For predictors of attachment and later development:

Goldberg, S. (2000). *Attachment and Development*. London: Arnold.

For workings of the internal working model to parenting and attachment:

Mayseless, O. (2006). *Parenting Representations: Theory, Research and Clinical Implications*. New York: Cambridge University Press.

For a succinct evaluation of the stability of attachment and it as a predictor:

Thompson, R.A. (2000). The legacy of early attachments. *Child Development*, *71*, 145–52.

RECOMMENDED WEBSITES

The 'Attachment Theory Website' (ATWS) with regularly updated information on books, chapters, presentations, manuscripts and journal articles on attachment:
www.richardatkins.co.uk/atws

The website of a charity specialised in supporting parents and professionals who work in parenting education, with details on online, printed and multimedia resources:
www.parenting.org.uk

For some facts and figures and publications about day care:
www.daycaretrust.org.uk

Watch a demonstration video of stranger anxiety. Further resources can be found at www.pearsoned.co.uk/gillibrand

Chapter 11
Development of self-concept and gender identity

Learning Outcomes

After reading this chapter, with further recommended reading, you should be able to:

1. Recognise and define the different components of self-concept;

2. Critically evaluate the development of these different components and the influences on their development in children;

3. Critically describe children's understanding of their own and others' gender groups at different ages;

4. Outline the principles of the key theories that have been proposed to explain the development of gender identity.

5. Critically review the associated research that has been conducted for support of such theories.

Self awareness

'I'm five years old . . . I'm a boy, and . . . I have brown hair, brown eyes . . . I'm fast! I like to eat sweeties, and . . . draw and . . . play . . . I like to play, like all the time!' (5 year old boy, in response to 'who are you?'; student's coursework fieldnotes).

'[I'd play with her cos] she's like me, we're both girls, we're like . . . the same . . . ' (7 year old white English girl in a London state primary school).

- How has the five year old boy described himself?
- Has he talked about his personal psychological characteristics?
- Why do you think this is?
- Look at what the seven year old girl has said about her friend. Why is it important that her friend is a girl?

Introduction

The examples above are a couple of typical responses from children of their gender or age of how they think of themselves or how they would describe themselves to others. As we shall see later in the chapter, personal features (or 'attributes') such as those the five year old boy used in the form of age, gender, appearance and likes and dislikes tend to be some of the most prominent 'self-descriptions' by children at this age. Similarly, the clear (and perhaps very conscious) awareness of the seven year old girl of her own sex together with a clear preference for peers of her gender group is very common among both boys and girls at that age. Although adults' responses might well be worded very differently, if we were asked to describe ourselves in any way we liked, invariably we would draw on some of these attributes and qualities which children as young as three years of age would use to describe themselves. All of these are part and parcel of our senses of self and identity. In this chapter we will first explore the definitions of self-concept and social identity before moving on to examine how they develop over the stages of childhood and the perspectives and theories that explain this development.

What are self-concept and social identity?

We have already had a glimpse of the 'ingredients' that make up a sense of self from the points of view of a five year old and a seven year old. It has also been hinted that some of our 'grown-up' views may not be all that different. Let's spend a few moments on the questions in the exercise 'Who am I?' to explore this a little more.

STOP AND THINK

Consider the opening examples of children's answers to the question, 'Who am I?' What answer would you give now, as an adult, to the question, 'Who am I?'

It is quite likely that you would have thought about at least one of these items in your 'who am I' search: name, age, gender, birthplace and/or nationality, occupation, religion, mother/father (if you have children). For some of us, it may be the case that one (or more) of the items on this list also makes us 'proud' (such as our job or being a parent). For others, an item or two may distinguish us as the same as (or different from) other people we know (such as our birthplace or nationality). For some of us still, we might have preferred to use other features, abilities or interests, such as our dress sense and cooking, sporting or musical skills or tastes, to mark out ourselves. Whatever they are on our 'who am I' list, and whether they are judged positively or negatively by ourselves or others, or in fact whether or not they can be observed by others, it is these characteristics, roles and ideas that we have built up or hold about ourselves that make up this jigsaw known as our self-concept.

Notice how some of these attributes, such as gender, age or nationality, are readily adopted by society as a whole to categorise individuals into groups. Such groupings are often seen to share common characteristics, either external or internal, which we use to describe ourselves and others (as we have done in the exercise). However, we do not just describe each other, we also develop feelings towards our own as well as other groups (such as a sense of belonging and preference as we have seen in the case of

the seven year old girl in the opening example). Moreover, sometimes, whether consciously or subconsciously, we even make assumptions and evaluations of each other based on such membership or think and behave in ways seen as typical of members in our own group. Our sense of social identity concerns all of these thinking (cognitive), feeling (affective) and behavioural components (Tajfel, 1978). The latter part of the chapter will look at these issues closely that concern the ever-important gender categories.

It is clear that our self-concepts and social identities are a highly important aspect of our lives. As we have explored in the exercise and examples above, for many of us, those ingredients which build up our self-concepts and social identities serve as a kind of framework for thinking about our social world, structuring social experiences and guiding social conduct and interpersonal interactions and relationships. Thus what we perceive of ourselves is highly central to our personality and behaviour. And we will see shortly, the self-concept develops very early in life and is influenced by a variety of factors, both cognitive and social, which makes it all the more important for us to try to understand its development.

Theories in the development of the self-concept

An influential theorist in self-concepts, Maccoby (1980), once pointed out that a sense of self develops by 'degrees', in a gradual and cumulative manner As every one of us develops ideas about who we are, those ideas are continually reviewed and revised through childhood

Definitions

Self-concept: ideas we have about ourselves, including our physical and mental qualities, emotional and behavioural attributes.
Social identity: a sense of identity derived from our membership of social groups, including categorising ourselves as members, feelings of belonging, and behaviour consistent with what is expected of group members.

in the light of our cognitive development and social experiences. For example, any fast-growing toddler will become more and more aware of her own behaviour as well as *others'* responses to and maybe their perception and evaluations of it. All these inputs, as we will see later, are likely to play a role in shaping her later more competent, realistic and reflective concept of herself as she grows.

Children's self-concepts through the years

Before delving into the stages of development of children's self-concepts, and factors that influence this development, it is a good idea to examine what kinds of attributes and qualities children actually have about themselves at different ages. The opening examples in this chapter have given us some of the commonest kinds of descriptions children and adolescents give in response to their being asked questions that include 'Who am I?'. This open-ended question has been indeed one of the most popular, if simple, means of obtaining children's self-descriptions.

Susan Harter, a prominent researcher in the 1980s, reviewed the studies in which children were asked about themselves at differing ages that involved, among others, the 'Who am I?' question. What she noticed is an apparent developmental pattern in which children at different ages predominantly use different kinds of attributes and qualities to describe themselves. For the youngest children (aged five years or younger), observations based on their physical or external characteristics (such as appearance or activities) feature the most in their self-descriptions. For older children, there is often a shift towards more 'internal' descriptions, with characteristics such as relationships with others or their inner feelings, beliefs and attitudes. For instance, in Rosenberg's (1979) study of 8 to 18 year-olds in Baltimore, when asked about what kind of person they would like to become, 36% of the eight year olds' answers were to do with interpersonal traits (e.g. 'shy', 'friendly') versus 69% of the 14–16 year olds. The oldest (up to 18 years) group also made far more use of the inner qualities that were only available to themselves and referred more to self-control (e.g., 'I don't show my feelings') when concerned with such emotions, motivations, wishes and secrets. Some of the most

Table 11.1. Children's self-descriptions at different ages.

Age	Self-descriptions	Examples
5 years or under	Physical features or facts, overt preference or possessions	'I've red hair.' 'A girl' 'I like milk.' 'I've a bike.'
5–9 years	More character references and gradually interpersonal traits	'I'm happy.' 'I'm brave.' 'Sometimes I'm shy.'
Beyond 10 years	Increasing qualifiers for above by considering private self-knowledge	'I try not to be selfish but I find it hard sometimes.'

popular features of self-descriptions at different ages are summarised in Table 11.1.

Of course, there may be a big difference between how children, particularly older children, describe themselves to a stranger, such as a researcher, and how they really think and feel about themselves (and in the sections below and later in this chapter, studies that have used methods other than self-reporting will be reviewed). Also, as children get older, their increasingly complex language will enable them to express themselves more thoroughly. Nevertheless, such research gives us a 'taste' of the increasing level of complexity of the developing child's self-concept. Indeed, the development of our self-concept as unique individuals, at least in Western cultures, is seen as a lengthy and complex journey, which goes through at least several stages throughout childhood, and likely even more over our lifetime (Maccoby, 1980). So, where, or at what age, is the starting point of this journey? And how does this self-understanding become more complex over time?

The emerging sense of self: early self-awareness

An awareness of the self, or the establishment or realisation that we simply 'exist' as our own individual entity, is the very first constituent that emerges during the course of the development of self-concept. It has been argued that in early infancy children do not have this basic awareness of the self; that is, they do not perceive themselves as distinct beings, as separate from other beings, with their own unique appearance, properties or agency (that they can have an effect on other objects or beings in their physical and social world, that they can 'make

RESEARCH METHODS

Early sense of self

Developed initially for research with apes, Lewis and Brooks-Gunn (1978, 1979) experimented using a technique with young children by asking some mothers to unobtrusively apply a spot of rouge to their children's nose. Later the children's reactions to their self-image were monitored when they were placed in front of a mirror, with the assumption that if they were able to recognise that the image was of themselves (thus possessing a sense of self), they would reach for the spot on their nose on which the rouge had been applied. This response was rarely observed before the age of 15 months, even though at one year old, children were amused at what they saw in the mirror – without any interest shown in the spot of rouge – as if looking at another child whose nose had been painted on! It was not until the second half of the second year that children showed signs that they knew definitely the spot was of interest as it was on their *own* nose.

There are other techniques of assessing self-awareness that rely more on verbal indicators, such as asking children to name or describe photographs of themselves (Bullock and Lutkenhaus, 1990) and examining their use of relevant terms like 'I' and 'me'

(Bates, 1990). Still, these studies have found that, like the rouge test, in general self-awareness (the recognition that the self exists as a separate and distinct individual with its own attributes) as the essential first stepping stone in the development of self-concept, is achieved by the end of the second year (see Fig. 11.1).

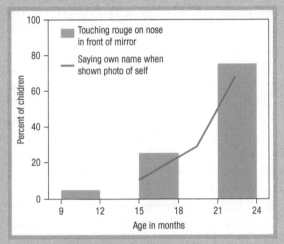

Figure 11.1. Self-recognition by the rouge test and self-naming from 9 to 24 months.

(Source: Lewis and Brooks-Gunn, 1978)

things happen'). Such self-awareness can be illustrated using a simple visual recognition technique commonly known as the 'rouge test' (see Research Methods box).

The subjective or existential self

We have just seen how the earliest awareness of the self, the recognition that we exist as a separate and unique entity

Definition

Self-awareness: the first step in the development of self-concept; the recognition that we are distinct from others with physical and mental properties of our own.

has been studied in infancy. This early self-recognition has in fact long been labelled as the 'self-as-subject', or the self 'I', by the pioneering American psychologist and philosopher, William James (1892). This initial feature of the self as a 'subject' of experience is usually thought of in terms of its distinction from, or as a precursor to, the later feature of the self as an 'object' of knowledge (we will explore this concept in the next section). James further articulated four conditions or elements for this existential self that refers to an awareness of: (1) our own agency in life events; (2) the uniqueness of our own experience as distinct from other people; (3) the continuity of our identity; (4) our own awareness, implying an element of self-reflexivity (that we are able to reflect on our awareness of the self).

Lewis (1990, 1991), of the rouge test, calls this aspect of the self the 'subjective self' or 'existential self' and argues that this self endures over time and space, in line with James's original four elements. Even though, as we have seen in Lewis's studies, the child does not reach an elaborate understanding of the self until the second year of life, Lewis places the starting points of early existential understanding in the first few months of life. These early and basic starting points are rooted in numerous everyday interactions the infant encounters with the objects and people in their world. During such encounters, the infant learns that his actions can affect objects or people around him (their agency), that he is able to 'make' things happen, control objects and 'cause' others to respond. These can be very simple interactions such as an infant's attempts to move or manipulate a toy or, as he smiles, his mother smiles back or, when he cries, she coos and comforts. This is particularly true in the early months when parents spend a lot of time imitating the infant's behaviours, expressions and vocalisations (Melzoff, 1990). It is through these experiences that the infant begins to separate the self from everything else (such as her parents or objects around her) and learn that this separate existence (as 'I') continues over time and across contexts.

The objective or categorical self

It is not enough to understand ourselves as separate from, and having agency on, other physical and human objects. As cited earlier, James's configuration of the self consists of another key feature that he called the 'self-as-object', or the self as the 'me'. This is more commonly known as the 'objective self' or the 'categorical self' (Lewis, 1990). This aspect of the self concerns the emerging process of defining the self in relation to the kinds of attributes and qualities that are commonly used to describe groupings of people, such as size, gender, ethnicity and relationship to others (as we have explored briefly in the beginning of the chapter with the concept of social identity and will do so again later for gender identity). By this point of development, usually beyond two years of age, children have achieved self-awareness, or the existential or subjective self, they begin to be able to place themselves within, or to become aware that they can be seen by others in relation to, a great array of social categories (like gender and race) that human societies tend to use to define the individuals living among them.

The exact process of how, and the degree to which children make use of, human social categories to define

themselves and each other will be detailed in the second part of this chapter (understanding of gender categories: children's gender identities). Here, it is important to simply note the key distinction between the categorical 'me' and the existential 'I'. The categorical self does not refer to basic properties such as agency, but emphasises our 'roles' as commonly seen in the wider social world, and their associated attributes in relation to other members in society (such as being a girl versus being a boy, being a child versus being a grown-up).

The looking-glass self

It has been pointed out that a child's emerging self-awareness as the existential self and later understanding of their roles as the objective self are influenced by social factors, in particular the child's understanding of their relationships with other people and of other people's perception of themselves. Cooley and Mead were two of the key theorists who first conceptualised this close relationship between an individual child's understanding and others' understanding of the self formally (Cooley, 1902; Mead, 1934). This idea, termed the 'looking-glass self', refers to the way others hold up a 'social mirror' in which we may see ourselves as we are 'reflected' by them and, from there, we build up our senses of the self from the views we come to understand that others may have of us.

Within this view, the importance of social interactions is emphasised as the tool through which the self and the social world are inextricably linked. Through repeated social exchanges such as games and play, most of which involve the use of language, children gradually

> **Definitions**
> **Subjective or Existential self:** the recognition of the self that is unique and distinct from others, endures over time and space, and has an element of self-reflexivity.
> **Objective or Categorical self:** the recognition of the self as the person seen by others and defined by the attributes and qualities used to define groups of people.
> **The looking-glass self:** the sense of self we develop as we respond to interactions with others and see how others react to us. We see ourselves reflected in other people's behaviour towards us.

Infant looking at himself in the mirror and reaching towards reflected image.
Source: Lam

come to adopt the perspectives that others have of them, and with such knowledge they also become more able to reflect on themselves. According to Cooley and Mead, a child cannot develop a sense of self without interactions with others, to realise how others view the world and the people within it, including the child him- or herself.

Until this point, in spite of the acknowledgement of social factors, the construct of self-concept *itself* has been covered as if the 'goal' of this development is the gradual achievement of a sense of an individual, unique and autonomous self, if also a very reflective self. Even though this may make sense to a lot of people, the concept of a separate, almost individualistic, self is by no means a universal experience or desire, but a rather 'Western' cultural view little understood in other parts of the world. The cross-cultural research by Tobin and his colleagues in 1998 described in the Cross-cultural Research box illustrates how other cultures can actually have a very different view about the self and its relationship with others and society at large.

Self-esteem

Apart from the common attributes and social roles and categories we use to describe ourselves, we also have a more reflective and evaluative feature of our self-concept. Remember how in the first exercise of the chapter we

reflected on the things about ourselves that make us feel proud? Suffice to say there will also be things for which we do not feel very proud about ourselves. Children do often reflect on and evaluate themselves, and such evaluations form an important part of their self-concept, or their self-esteem.

Children's self-evaluations also go through stages of development, similar to the other features of the self-concept. For instance, younger children tend to have more general or 'global' self-evaluations, such as how happy they are about themselves or how much they like the way they are. Entering early adolescence, their evaluations become increasingly differentiated with separate judgments about their physical appearance, peer acceptance and academic and athletic performance and so forth. Susan Harter, mentioned before with her work on children's self-descriptions, has distinguished five areas in which to assess children's self-evaluation: (1) scholastic competence, how competent the child considers

Definition

Self-esteem: the evaluative and reflective features of our self-concept that can vary from high to low and draw in part from others' evaluations of ourselves.

NATURE-NURTURE

Behavioural expectations across cultures

From their cross-cultural comparative research based in pre-schools in Japan, China and the United States, Tobin *et al.* (1988) reported their study which examined how teachers viewed the videotaped behaviour of a child who attended a Japanese pre-school. What was found are various startling differences between the interpretations of the same behaviours of the same child by teachers of the different nationalities. For instance, the American teachers were more likely to describe the child as 'intellectually gifted', if 'easily bored', but the Japanese teachers would comment on his lack of social skills or his 'inability to be dependent'.

It is important to note that in Japan, like several other Asian nations, it is popularly upheld that, apart

from the education of children, one of the main roles of pre-schools is the promotion of a sense of collective identity, through which empathy, obedience and cooperativeness, widely seen as desirable traits for effective learning, can be nurtured. Hence, the downplaying of individual differences and highlighting of group similarities among children, reflected in a homogeneous and harmonious classroom experience, is perceived by many educators as beneficial to children and the 'norm'. This focus on the normative grouping as the principle source from which children derive their educational experience as well as learn social behaviour and identity contrasts with more 'Western' educational practices which, whether deliberately or inadvertently, may allow for more independence and autonomy in the child's development of a self-identity.

Source: Tobin *et al.* (1998).

herself to be at school; (2) athletic competence, the child's self-assessment of her competence in sporting activities; (3) social acceptance, the child's self-assessment of popularity among her peers; (4) physical appearance, how good- or bad-looking the child thinks of herself; (5) behavioural conduct, how acceptable the child thinks her behaviour is to others (Harter, 1987, 1990).

Harter also considers that our self-esteem functions as the discrepancy between two internal assessments of ourselves, our *ideal* self and our *real* self, that is, what we would like ourselves to be or think we ought to be versus what we think we really are. When there is little difference between the two, discrepancy is low, and self-esteem is generally high. When the discrepancy is high, self-esteem will be lower. The latter suggests that the child sees himself as failing to 'live up' to their ideals or standards. Obviously, such standards are not the same for everybody. A child who sees athletic competence as more important than academic competence and who does not do that well in his school work but is reasonably sporty will not suffer much from a low self-esteem compared with another child who achieves similar standards as the first child but values academic competence more highly.

Nevertheless, developmentally, from junior school ages onwards, children show increasing consistency in their self-esteem, and these judgements become increasingly more realistic, with an overall fall in self-esteem levels compared to earlier childhood as they are more and more aware of their positive as well as negative attributes (see also the Lifespan box for continuity of self-esteem into adulthood). Social influences are the likely explanation; children's self-judgements become increasingly closely matched with the evaluations from others (such as those of teachers; Marsh, *et al.*, 1998). The evaluations of others thus may be seen to function like elements of the looking-glass self where others provide a reference point from which we reflect on ourselves and build up aspects of our self-concept. Here such influences bear more specifically on the evaluative aspects of the self.

Summing up: self-concept development

As we have seen above, the child's self-concept, including self-esteem, is a highly significant part of her development. This development seems to emerge from quite rudimentary senses and gradually evolve into more complex

LIFESPAN

Is self-esteem a stable psychological factor or does it change as we get older?

A paper published by Orth *et al.* (2010) reports findings from the Americans' Changing Lives study which followed 3617 individuals (aged 25–104 years) for 16 years. The Changing Lives study collected data on, among other things, self-esteem, and analysis showed an interesting effect. Self-esteem increased fairly steadily during young and middle adulthood, reaching a peak at 60 years of age, then appeared to decline during older adulthood. When the authors investigated the data more closely, they found that women generally had lower self-esteem than did the men in young adulthood but, by old age, that difference

had disappeared. There also appeared to be an effect of race with self-esteem in people describing themselves as 'black' seeing a more dramatic fall in self-esteem in late adulthood than did the people describing themselves as 'white'. Education too played a part with more educated people reporting higher self-esteem than less educated people although, for both groups, the lifespan arcs in self-esteem were the same (Orth *et al.*, 2010).

- Why do you think is there a sharp fall in self-esteem around the age of 60 years for all the participants in this research study?
- Why should self-esteem be lower in women, individuals describing themselves as black and less educated people?

understandings that are influenced by a multitude of factors, and the above has only touched on a few, most notably the social actors around the child such as her parents, peers or teachers. All these qualities, roles and evaluations taken on by the child also tend to become increasingly consistent with those expected by social groups and social institutions over time. In the next part of the chapter, we will indeed draw our attention to such relationships between the child's sense of self and one of the most pervasive systems of social groupings or categories, gender.

Understanding of gender categories: children's gender identity

We have seen how children gradually develop a sense of self across different ages. As the self-concept becomes more stable, children categorise and evaluate themselves as well as others along a wide range of social category systems, such as age, gender and race. As we have explored in the early part of the chapter, social categories are those groups in society that are seen to share common attributes,

and social identities refer to the way we think and feel about, and behave towards, our own and others' social groups. Social identity develops very early in life. Indeed, Lewis and Brooks-Gunn (1979), whose work (the rouge test) we looked at earlier, argue that gender is among the earliest social categories learned and that knowledge about these are concurrently developed in relation to the child himself and other individuals. First, we will explore the child's basic understanding of gender in this section.

Development of gender identity

How do children understand that they are a boy or a girl? And when and how do they realise that they will grow up to be a man or a woman? How do they identify (or even endorse) those behaviours, attitudes and expectations considered appropriate for their own gender in their society? These are some of the questions we will address below.

Gender identity, like self-concept, has different levels and aspects, which develop gradually in stages. Children appear able to differentiate people by gender very early. By 9 to 12 months, they respond differently to photographs of male and female faces (e.g. Brooks-Gunn and Lewis, 1981; Fagot and Leinbach, 1993) and to male and female strangers in person (Smith and Sloboda, 1986). Soon after, from about 12–18 months, they acquire some verbal labels for these categories ('mummy', 'daddy'). However, at two years, many children still do not know how to answer if asked directly whether they are a boy or a girl. This is helped if they are shown stereotypical pictures of boys and girls and asked which one(s) are them (Thompson, 1975). However, by three years of age, most children can correctly label themselves by their gender (Weinraub *et al.*, 1984).

Kohlberg's Cognitive developmental theory (1966, discussed fully later in this chapter) describes gender identity development as a three-step process that results from the child's attempt to understand sex role behaviour. The three steps are: gender labelling (the child is aware of their own sex but believes it can change); gender stability (the child is aware that their sex is stable over time, i.e. if I am a boy now then I will still be a boy in a year's time); and gender consistency (the child is aware that their sex remains the same, regardless of time or circumstance, i.e. even if I dress as a girl, I am still a boy).

The correct labelling of oneself and others by gender is only the first step towards an understanding of gender identity, and it can be seen that at the age of three children are very much reliant upon external physical characteristics in the 'here and now' as they identify each other. When children of this age are faced with 'deeper' questions about their gender, such as 'When you were a baby, were you a little girl or little boy?' or 'When you grow up, will you be a mummy or daddy?', many are very confused. This aspect of gender identity, known as gender stability, refers to the understanding that our gender group membership is a permanent part of ourselves that remains the same through time. This is usually achieved by about four years of age (Slaby and Frey, 1975).

However, at this age, the recognition of gender relies upon stereotypical features. This can be illustrated by an experimental procedure where, for example, the picture of a stereotypical looking boy (with short hair and shorts) is presented, and only the stereotypical elements (hair and clothing) are switched into those stereotypical of a girl (see Fig. 11.2). Although the transformation is performed in front of them, many pre-schoolers are confused, or say that the boy in the picture is a girl after the switch (Emmerich *et al.*, 1977; Gouze and Nadelman, 1980).

Non-pictorial methods, such as hypothetical questioning (e.g. 'Can you be a girl if you really want to be?', 'If a boy lets his hair grow very long, is he still a boy?')

Definitions

Gender labelling: correct identification of 'male' or 'female' of oneself and others.
Gender stability: the understanding that gender group membership is normally stable and permanent over time.

This is Tom.
Is Tom a boy/girl?

Tom grows his hair.
He puts a dress on.

Is Tom a boy/girl?

Figure 11.2. An example of the experimental transformation used for testing gender constancy in children.

can also be used. When children recognise that gender stays the same despite changes in appearance, gender constancy is achieved, and this tends to occur after five years old. It seems odd that children who understand the permanency of gender can be 'fooled' by superficial changes, even though research of children in Western and Eastern cultures has confirmed this trend (Munroe *et al.*, 1984). This may be because gender constancy requires knowledge of biological sex differences as it is achieved earlier if children understand the genital differences between the sexes (Bem, 1989).

The fulfilment of all of gender labelling, stability and constancy, though a major milestone in the young child's development, is only a basic part of gender identity. A larger part is learning about what is associated with 'being' a boy or a girl, what being a member of one's own gender is supposed to mean in various social contexts. In fact, around the time of gender labelling, about two-and-a-half years (Kuhn *et al.*, 1978), children have already begun building up basic ideas about the activities, abilities or preferences and, later, attitudes and expectations that are appropriate for, or typical of, their own and the other gender. These may surround adult daily activities, such as cooking and cleaning is for women, repairing the house and car for men, or activities familiar to children, such as playing with dolls for girls versus playing with trains for boys. Gender stereotypes also include beliefs about more subtle tendencies such as 'girls cry and give kisses' and 'boys fight and don't cuddle'. Gender stereotyping also increases rapidly with age; before middle childhood (by the age of five), children already associate different occupations and crude personality traits (such as 'strong', 'soft-hearted', 'cruel' and 'gentle') with men and women, and by age eight to nine years, their stereotypes are already very similar to those of adults (e.g. Best *et al.*, 1977; Martin, 1993; Serbin *et al.*, 1993).

Perhaps it is not surprising that children's stereotypes mimic those of adults. After all, in many societies, adults

Definitions

Gender constancy: the understanding that gender group membership is unchanged despite changes in appearance.
Gender stereotypes: beliefs about what is appropriate for or typical of one's own or the other gender group.

have clearly divided gender roles and stereotypes (most childcare is still done by women and men take on heavier manual work, for instance) – children's beliefs may simply reflect practical reality. However, gender roles have, at least in post-industrial societies, been changing a great deal whilst children's beliefs have not always caught on but seem to in fact exaggerate common stereotypes. Apart from that, what is startling is that stereotyped behaviours are shown in children earlier than stereotyped beliefs are expressed, as the following reviews.

Children's preference for gender-stereotyped toys and games is apparent by about 18–24 months, before the ability to reliably label gender categories, and this continues well into middle childhood (O'Brien, 1992). By the age of three, before gender stability, children have begun to show a preference for peers of their own gender for play and friendship and actually interact more with them. By the time they are in school, their peer groups are almost exclusively of their own gender, and this continues well into adolescence (Maccoby, 1988, 1990). Boys also tend to prefer to play outdoors in less structured large-group activities (such as team games and play-fighting) whereas girls prefer to socialise in pairs or smaller groups or engage in more structured 'traditional' games (such as skipping and hopscotch).

STOP AND THINK

- How typical do you rate yourself as a member of your gender group? Alternatively, how masculine or feminine do you see yourself?
- Did you see yourself as a 'boyish' (or 'girlish') child? What criteria did you use?
- Do you think children nowadays think and behave in more or less gender-stereotyped ways compared with when you were a child yourself?

However, it is important to look at the above evidence with caution. Much of the research involved observations of behaviours or interactions in the home, classrooms or playgrounds and required researchers' categorisation and interpretations, and thus a level of bias may have drawn from these inputs. Furthermore, some of the differences observed are often quite small and many studies of infants under two years of age do not find many consistent behavioural differences between boys and girls (see reviews by Maccoby, 1998, 2000). Still, the division between boys and girls in social interactions and same-sex preference in friendships are such prevalent phenomena that we cannot deny that gender exerts a strong force on children's identity and relationships.

Taken together, gender is a system of social categories that permeate children's lives from very early on. Even before they learn the gender labels or grasp the idea of its permanency, stereotyped behaviours and thinking are already apparent. Then, what may explain this pervasive phenomenon? There are myriad arguments that are centred upon either the 'nature' or 'nurture' side of the debate, whilst others focus on the role played by the child. We will explore some of the major theories in the next sections.

Biological explanations for gender identity

It is of little surprise that many researchers have located biological factors as being at least in part responsible for gender differences. Men and women are clearly different in terms of their genetic make-up and physiology, and some such inherent differences may underpin the psychological differences observed between boys and girls.

The basic genetic difference (the male has an XY pair and the female an XX pair of chromosomes) means differential sex hormone production before birth and later in adolescence (the male with more testosterone and female more oestrogen). This leads to differential bodily and physical attributes including the male's larger average size, relatively greater physical strength and lung capacity and, arguably, more aggressive instincts. According to most biological accounts, gender differences social role patterns have taken shape through the course of evolution as an outcome of human adaptation to their environment with men and women being equipped with such physical characteristics and instinctual tendencies. For instance, the gender division of hunters and gatherers is a result of the male's size and strength being better suited for the demands of the former, and the female's childbearing and breast-feeding ability making her a 'natural' caregiver and homemaker. Gender differences in psychological functioning are however less clear and probably over-stated (Hyde, 2005). Whilst there appears to be an effect of social influences on development of aspects of self-esteem (women generally score higher on behavioural conduct and moral–ethical self-esteem, Gentile *et al.*, 2009), other studies seem to demonstrate the importance of biological influences, for instance, that men are better at mental rotation tasks and women are better at

verbal tasks (Hausmann *et al.*, 2009). However, performance in mental rotation tasks can be improved with priming and practice (Ortner and Sieverding, 2008), suggesting that social opportunity to engage in 'masculine' tasks is a more important factor than biological sex.

Parental investment theory

Some theorists and researchers, namely the sociobiologists, have taken up the above ideas further to explain the contemporary behaviours, relationship patterns and even status disparity between the sexes. The logic of their reasoning, termed the parental investment theory (Wilson, 1972, 1978; Archer, 1992; Kendrick, 1994), is set around the specifics of male–female reproduction, which is seen as the primary goal of human survival – to pass on one's own genes. Reproduction is less 'costly' for the male as he does not need to carry the unborn offspring or give birth. However, he does not have the important advantage of the female in being certain that any offspring born to her will possess her genes – unless he remains with his mate to preclude her from mating with other males. Thus a 'trade' is struck whereby the sexes each assess and offer the other the relevant attributes; he needs to assess her reproductive capacity and offer a level of commitment towards providing for and protecting their offspring, which she takes time to assess for his suitability as a reproductive partner.

Sociobiologists argue that the reproductive trade-off has led to the different ideas about what is attractive in males and females. For instance, greater emphasis is placed upon youthfulness and physical attractiveness for the female whereas traits such as ambition and competitiveness associated with the pursuit of conquest and territory and resource guarding are more valued for the male (Buss, 1987). It is debatable whether women really take greater care in their appearance than men do in modern societies

> **Definition**
>
> Parental investment theory: a theory used to explain gender differences on the basis of biological sex differences. The theory states that reproduction has different implications for males and females and that men and women therefore look for different traits in each other, which through the course of evolution have been adapted as the modern-day observed gender role, behaviour and status differences.

(if we consider phenomena such as the 'metrosexual' male) but, as we have read earlier, research shows that boys do engage in more activities that command dominance and competitiveness compared with girls. However, whether these behaviours have their origins in biological differences evolved through a *very* long history of environmental changes is rather more difficult to ascertain.

Biological evidence

In order to ensure that the biologically given sex differences underpin children's psychological and behavioural outcomes, some signs of their impact should be shown before the child experiences socialisation, to pinpoint that it is inherent biology that is responsible for gender differences. This requires research in early infancy and makes evidence difficult to obtain, at least in humans, as we know from earlier in the chapter and previous chapters that from very early on the infant is already very receptive and responsive to the social world around them. Some evidence has come from research on animals that manipulates the sex hormone levels of offspring through the mothers. Scientists have administered doses of testosterone to pregnant monkeys prenatally and observed their female offspring. They found that the offspring displayed more 'rough-and-tumble' play and aggression towards each other compared with female offspring who had not received testosterone (Young, 1964).

Short of doing the same on human participants for obvious ethical reasons, a small number of studies on children who have received abnormal amounts of sex hormones due to their mothers' conditions or accidents and errors in the medical sciences have shed light on the question. The earliest cases were reported by Money and Ehrhardt (1972) who examined girls with congenital adrenal hyperplasia, a

---

Definition

Congenital adrenal hyperplasia: congenital adrenal hyperplasia can affect both boys and girls. People with congenital adrenal hyperplasia lack an enzyme needed by the adrenal gland to make the hormones cortisol and aldosterone. Without these hormones, the body produces more androgen, a type of male sex hormone. This causes male characteristics to appear early (or inappropriately). About 1 in 10 000–18 000 children are born with congenital adrenal hyperplasia (MedLine Plus, 2010).

---

condition resulting from exposure to excessive levels of androgen (a male sex hormone) before birth as a treatment given to mothers prone to miscarriages. The girls were born with male genitalia that were corrected surgically and were raised as girls. Follow-ups showed that they saw themselves as more 'tomboyish' and played less with other girls compared with a matched sample who had not received treatment. We must bear in mind, however, that the knowledge of their daughters' history might have affected the parents' attitudes and behaviour, although in these cases it would be unlikely that they encouraged the masculine behaviour rather than the opposite.

Money and Ehrhardt (1972) further reported a high-profile case that, many years later, was to become one of the most controversial in the medical and psychological professions and beyond. This case is summarised in the Case Study box with discussion points.

The true story of the twins makes a compelling case for the part biology plays in developing gender identity. It would appear that no matter what interventions are put in place, we simply cannot stop the effects of the biological sex that we are born with. However, similar to the study of girls who were exposed to excess hormones before birth, the parents knew the biological sex of the twin, who was already in his second year when he underwent reconstructive surgery, whilst hormonal and psychological treatment continued through to his adolescence (indeed his unease about the visits to medical and psychological professionals was documented in media coverage). These events could have raised the child's doubts about his assigned gender and his parents' behaviours towards him. Finally, even when findings converge with prescriptions of the biological accounts, published cases such as this are rare.

In general, evidence of the direct effects of hormonal manipulation and biological dysfunction on gender identity is difficult to obtain, even though some reviewers have noted that, in normally developing individuals, male sex hormones have the strongest effects on play, aggression (Collaer and Hines, 1995) and sexual orientation (Patterson, 1995). But is gender identity all about play, aggressive instincts and sex? Many of the limitations of the biological accounts, and in particular the parental investment theory, concern their narrow scope centred on dominance and sexual behaviours. Much focus is placed on male physical strength and 'innate' aggressiveness to explain dominance when, even among animals, dominance can be strategic and learned, and is not always associated with strength and aggressiveness (Sayer, 1982). Even if biological instincts are directly responsible

CASE STUDY

Gender realignment

Documented in a few televised programmes is the case of identical twin boys, studied initially by Money and Ehrhardt (1972). Born as a normal male, at 7 months of age one of the twins had his penis destroyed during a spoiled routine circumcision. It was not until nearly a year later (before which the child continued to be treated as a boy), that the confused and upset parents were referred to Money, who advised for the boy to undergo a radical surgical reconstruction, followed by years of hormonal therapy, to become a girl. The surgery went ahead when the boy was 17 months old and the case was soon hailed as a 'success' story of nurture overcoming nature to shape a child's gender identity when Money's early follow-ups showed a well-adjusted child with feminine characteristics, if energetic and a little tomboyish. In fact, this was the first case ever conducted on a developmentally normal child – Money had pioneered the procedure originally on hermaphrodites (individuals born with both female and male sexual organs) – leading doctors around the world to perform many more sex reassignments on infants with injured or abnormal genitalia.

The reality was somewhat more complicated. Decades later, when the child was a grown-up, and decided to cast aside his anonymity to the media, the story of a truly harrowing childhood was recounted. He felt awkward around girls, was not interested in girls' activities but in running, fighting and climbing, and was later on teased by his peers for his masculine mannerisms. A follow-up study (Diamond, 1982) of his teens was one of isolation and depression, with a great deal of uncertainty about his gender. But it was not until the disturbed 14 year old became suicidal that his parents revealed the truth at the advice of a local psychiatrist, and he soon embarked on the painful journey of reverting back to his biological sex. As an adult man, he married, adopted children, and cooperated again, with other scientists, to participate in further follow-ups (Diamond and Signmundson, 1997) and various media coverage. However, depression plagued his adolescence and adulthood (although that could be attributed to other problems, such as marital and financial difficulties and a history of clinical depression in the family that also affected his mother and twin brother). In 2004, at the age of 38, he took his own life.

- Do you think the twin's troubled gender identity was a result of biology entirely?
- What other factors might have influenced his gender development?

for such behaviours, as we reviewed earlier, gender *identity* is much more than just behaviour. It includes complex cognitive and affective processes, that is our thinking and feeling components, such as identifying ourselves with others of our own gender, forming stereotypes and expectations based on such memberships, all of which vary across societies and can change over time.

Social learning theories of gender identity

We have seen the effects as well as limitations of biological sex on gender identity. We have identified that, as different societies hold different conceptions of gender-appropriate thinking and behaviour, which can change over time, it is plausible that the social environment plays a part in forming children's gender identity. Almost an antithesis to biological accounts, one other early approach, social learning theories (Bandura, 1969, 1977; Mischel, 1966, 1970), proposes that children are 'shaped' into gender roles by the behaviour of adults and other children. Children are recipients of social information about what is appropriate for their own gender in their own culture.

Definition

Social learning theories: an approach that explains gender identity development in terms of the child's accumulating learning experience from their social environment, in particular, through modelling others' behaviour and being rewarded for adopting approved mannerisms.

By this token, gender identity is acquired (rather than pre-programmed by genes) as a product of accumulating learning experiences, and the socialising 'agents' are the key players in the child's life – adults, peers and the media. Learning operates through two complementary processes called reinforcement and modelling. For reinforcement, the child is rewarded for behaving in gender-role-appropriate ways and punished for behaving in gender-role-inappropriate ways, according to gender roles in their culture. So-called 'rewards' and 'punishment' often do not come in a tangible or overt manner (treats or reprimands). The socialising agents' attention or engagement, or the lack of or withdrawal from them, already serve effectively as rewards or punishment (such as parents offering their children toys seen as appropriate for their gender, or being more encouraging when they engage with these toys, and less so when the children pick up toys seen as appropriate for the opposite sex).

The agents themselves often also demonstrate gender-role-appropriate behaviours, serving as 'models' for how to perform such behaviours as well as the consequences of conforming to the gender norms in that culture. There are many everyday examples of gender-role demonstrations (such as fathers and mothers taking on different chores in the home, commercial advisements showing the popularity of children who engage with gender-stereotyped toys). The agents' actions and responses, whether conscious or unconscious, as we will see, likely lead to gender-role learning in the child.

Adults as socialising agents

STOP AND THINK

Think back to your childhood: the daily routines that your parents engaged in (work, household duties and pastimes) and their interactions with you (caring roles and play). Then talk to or observe some parents about their daily activities.

- How much of those are gender-typical behaviours?
- Do the fathers and mothers take part in such behaviours to different extents?
- Has the pattern changed over the years?

Since its inception in the 1970s, the social learning approach to gender development has attracted a great deal of research, with the early period focusing on the behaviour or attitudes of adults towards children. For example, parents were observed to reward gender-stereotyped behaviour and activities on infants of as young as 18 months,

Copying dad's behaviour is part of the gender-learning process.

Source: Corbis/Gary Salter

NATURE–NURTURE

The Baby X experiments

A series of studies since the 1970s, collectively known as the 'Baby X' experiments, illustrated clear differences in the reactions towards and expectations of the same baby by adults due to dress code or labelling along gender lines. Take the classic study by Will *et al.* (1976). The same baby girl was either dressed in blue and called 'Adam', or dressed in pink and called 'Beth', when presented to adult participants who were unaware of the purpose of the study. The adults were observed interacting with the baby, including their choice of toys (doll, train or 'gender-neutral' fish) to give to the baby. The results showed that the adults interacted differently with the baby depending on the colour of clothes and the name given ('Beth' was given the doll more often and received more smiles from the adults). Other Baby X studies vary in detail such as the choice of toys, the baby being presented

in person or via a video link or the evaluations adults had to make and so on, while retaining the same basic design. These studies still found similar patterns as that by Will *et al.* Both men and women were more likely to refer to the baby as 'big' and 'strong' when labelled as a boy, and 'small' and 'soft' when labelled as a girl (Rubin *et al.*, 1974). They also encouraged the boy with more vigorous play and exploration and treated the girl more gently and helped her more (Condry and Condry, 1976).

- Why do you think the adults responded to the baby differently when they thought they knew if the baby was a girl or a boy?
- Why do we hold such strong gender schemas for such young children?
- Do you see any advantages to treating girls and boys differently from birth?
- What might be the disadvantages?

such as encouraging girls more for touching and cuddling than boys (Lewis, 1975), giving more encouragement to children for picking up gender-appropriate toys or engaging them for more gender-role-appropriate style of play or activities (e.g. Fagot, 1978; Caldera *et al.*, 1989; Fagot and Hagan, 1991).

On the other hand, reviews of Baby X studies (see the Nature-Nurture box) and similar research (Stern and Karraker, 1989; Golombok and Fivush, 1994; Maccoby, 2000; Golombok and Hines, 2002) noted that some findings varied according to the kind of measures used. Adults had less stereotyped responses if they were asked to evaluate the child's personality traits (e.g. how friendly or playful s/he was) compared with when they actually interacted with the child. This implies that it is the adults' *behaviour* that bears out their existing gender stereotypes more, whereas their views (of the child) will be based more on the child's characteristics as they observed them.

Children do not only receive reinforcements through the behaviour and reactions of adults who hold gender-typed ideas. Even without such direct inputs, adults act as models of gender-typed behaviours which children

can observe and imitate. Studying children and their mothers, Fagot *et al.* (1992) found that those with mothers who endorse more traditional gender roles tend to gender-label objects earlier than those with mothers of more egalitarian views. Reviewing a large body of work, it is noted that it is the daily activity contexts (e.g. who is the one doing which chores in the home) that account for much of the modelling observed (Leaper, 2000).

However, from either reinforced or observed behaviour, what is taken on board by the child, and whether it gets translated into gender-typed behaviour, is far less clear-cut. More recent reviews suggest that boys and girls have very similar experiences, if slightly more gender-typed reinforcement by fathers (Lytton and Romney, 1991). This, in practice, is far from favouring social learning theories, as the majority of caregivers and educators are women. Theoretically speaking, if the strength of children's gender identity was dependent upon the rewards from and their observation of available adult agents, then many young children would acquire a feminine identity. Clearly, more is at work to foster gender development, and we will turn to these other agents next.

Peers as socialising agents

By middle childhood (around age five and upwards), at least half of the child's waking hours will be spent in the social institution that is school where most of the socialising agents are other children. All these agents bring with them their existing gender views as well as sharing (if at times challenging) such views, and constructing and reproducing more. In fact, by three to four years of age, children already recognise the gender-appropriateness of play and activities and criticise their peers for what they see as gender-inappropriate behaviour. The stereotypes that are recreated (e.g., 'daddies don't cook', 'mummies don't drive cars') can in fact be even more rigid than those of adults (Fagot, 1977). As we read earlier, both boys and girls like to play and associate more with those of their own gender. It is unsurprising that peers are such a dominant force in children's lives.

In one study that compared directly the behaviours of mothers, fathers and peers towards three to five year olds' gender-appropriate or inappropriate play, Langlois and Downs (1980) found that peers had the strongest responses. Children were first instructed to play with highly gender-stereotyped toys for either boys or girls. Once the child was settled into play, the parent or peer was invited into the room to observe and interact with the child. Mothers displayed little differentiation in their responses towards their children, but fathers were rather more responsive about gender-appropriateness; they were positive towards the children in gender-appropriate play but were overtly hostile (with disparaging remarks or ridicule), in particular when their sons engaged in cross-gender behaviours. Still, the peers' reactions towards gender-inappropriate play were the strongest of all, again most negative when boys were playing with girls' toys.

Reviewing Baby X research, Stern and Karraker (1989) noted that, when children are asked to play with Baby X, they are more strongly influenced by the information about the baby's alleged sex than are adults. They suggest that it is because children are themselves still learning about their own gender and adopt more extreme attitudes. Still, recent reviews of other studies (Maccoby, 2000; Golombok and Hines, 2002) have found relatively few consistent differences in the responses towards boys and girls, or towards gender-appropriate versus inappropriate play and behaviour. Also, similar to adult reinforcement and modelling, whether or not peer responses translate into later more gender-stereotyped behaviour in children is more difficult to study.

A few researchers have tried to explore the real effects of agents by asking adults or rewarding children to actively promote certain activities (such as cooperative play) and then measuring the children's behaviour at some later point. For example, Fagot (1985) found that girls were influenced by teachers and other girls but not so by boys, but boys were only influenced by other boys, and not by teachers or girls, preferring noisy, rough-and-tumble play. Perhaps cooperative activities involve more 'feminine' behaviour (such as being quiet and sharing) to which girls are already more receptive than boys. In that case, children's selective attention to different socialisation *content* (rather than socialising agents per se) should be studied. This is what we will do next.

The media

STOP AND THINK

When you next watch television with commercials, make notes of the behaviour and communication of the actors. How much of this can be called gender-stereotyped?

Since the postwar years, the mass media, in particular television, has been a very prominent feature in children's lives in industrialised countries. Children spend more time watching television than they do in school or interacting with their families and friends (Buckingham, 2003). Where the content of media is concerned, it is strongly stereotyped. Despite societal shifts and political trends in that adult broadcasters and actors of the sexes are now more equal in status, it is still the case that, in series and commercials, even in children's during prime-time, many themes and roles are highly 'gendered', with some being more 'action-packed' or fantasy-based and others more sedentary or 'real-life' that might influence the viewing patterns of different children.

A study by Huston and colleagues found that, although the average time spent on watching television showed no gender differences, *what* boys and girls watched were vastly different from each other. Where boys' interests are more uniform and 'action-oriented', girls' are more diverse and 'people-oriented' (Huston *et al.*, 1999). Later, Livingstone and Bovill (2001), in a large-scale European study, surveyed children's favourite shows between the ages of 6 and 16 and found distinct developmental patterns of interests between boys and girls (Table 11.2).

Table 11.2. Results by Livingstone and Bovill (2001).

Favourite TV shows by age and gender: A European study

	Boys	Girls
6–7 years	Cartoons	Cartoons
9–10 years	Cartoons	Soap operas
12–13 years	TV series, sports	Soap operas
15–16 years	Sports	TV series

The sexes are largely interested in cartoons until nine to ten years, when girls' interests turn to soaps, and this continued to 12–13 years, before turning to other series. On the other hand, boys are equally likely to tune in to series or sports programs at 12–13 years, before sports become dominant for the oldest group.

More recently, electronic media such as computer games and the internet offer a highly attractive, or even addictive, source of entertainment (Larson, 2001). Research in children's engagement with these newer media is relatively recent and findings are thus less conclusive. Still, a study by Roberts and associates showed a consistent pattern where between the ages of 8 and 18 years boys spend three times as much time as girls do on video games (Roberts *et al.*, 2004). If we consider the style and content themes of popular video games such as Super Mario, Call of Duty and Football Manager 2010 (all within the top 10 best-sellers on Amazon at time of writing), often highly masculine and action-oriented, the findings are perhaps not overly surprising. However, other games in the list are Lego Harry Potter, Just Dance and Dance on Broadway, so perhaps the gaming industry is becoming wise to the needs of girl players.

These findings are informative to the extent that they show children are selectively attending to media content that contains material appropriate for their own group. Yet an obvious and critical issue remains – the nature of the relationship between TV viewing or game-playing and gender identity. Early studies already established a very tenuous relationship between the two (see Durkin, 1985). Durkin noted that TV in the 1970s and 1980s portrayed women quite negatively, rarely in a starring role and often fulfilling gender-stereotyped behaviour. It could be that already stereotyped children simply prefer to engage with such material as they find confirmation of their own views, so they are simply responding to their existing preferences and tendencies. However, since *selective* attention

and modelling are happening, children should have some *cognition* (or awareness) of their own gender to guide them *which* behaviour to take on board, and it is some such processes we will explore in the next approach.

Cognitive theories of gender identity

We have just considered the possibility that, in order for children to acquire a sense of gender identity, they ought to have some knowledge or awareness (cognition) of their own gender to steer them towards those agents of their own group. Indeed, the pioneer of the earliest cognitive theory of gender identity, Lawrence Kohlberg (1966), argued that, 'our approach to the problems of sexual development starts directly with neither biology nor culture, but with cognition' (p. 82).

Drawing heavily on Piaget's school of thought (see Chapter 3, Research Methods), Kohlberg (1966, 1969) saw gender development, like other cognitive developments, as a constructive process; an active child is guided by reason, or logic, when dealing with gender-role knowledge. But where does this knowledge come from? And 'how much' knowledge is required for developing gender identity? According to Kohlberg, gender knowledge comes from children's interactions with the world around them, a process that he calls 'self-socialisation' (Maccoby and Jacklin, 1974). As for how much knowledge, we can find some suggestions in Kohlberg's (1969) own cognitive-developmental theory. Interestingly, Kohlberg's theory also linked a child's cognitive capacity with the capacity for moral reasoning. These ideas and their role in managing behaviour in schools, are explored in Chapter 15, Understanding Bullying.

Cognitive-developmental theory

Matching closely with Piaget's (1953) stage-theory of intellectual development, Kohlberg expounded that the

> **Definition**
>
> Cognitive-developmental theory: a theory, derived by Kohlberg, that explains gender identity development by the child's developing cognitive skills in three stages, which underpin critical milestones in understanding about gender as gender labelling, gender stability and gender constancy.

Table 11.3. Stages in Kohlberg's (1969) cognitive-developmental theory.

Stage/age	Gender feature	Cognitive feature
Stage 1 2½–3½ years	Gender labelling Slow recognition of gender labels Treat labels as personal terms	Egocentrism
Stage 2 3½–4½ years	Gender stability Gradually aware of gender durability Dependent on physical cues	Poor conservation skills
Stage 3 4½–7 years	Gender constancy Understand gender is constant across time and contexts	Conservation skills achieved

self-socialisation of gender identity develops gradually through three stages from early through middle childhood. In fact the key milestones of such stages are those that we have earlier covered as gender labelling, stability and constancy, each stage featured by a key (or rather a lack of) cognitive skill (see Table 11.3). For instance, in stage 2 the lack of conservation means that children are prone to being confused by physical transformation (as illustrated by the counter and liquid experiments in Chapter 3) including the transformation for testing gender constancy.

Unlike either the biological accounts or social learning theories that see the child's gender development as being imbued by the effects of her genes or socialising agents, this theory hinges on the assumption that the child's own role in seeking gender-role information driven by her cognitive awareness and skills. Stage 3 skills are pivotal in Kohlberg's model, because this is when the child is equipped with the fullest essential knowledge about her own gender, that it is a differentiating, permanent and immutable part of her identity (gender labelling, stability and constancy all achieved).

Research evidence supporting Kohlberg's theory therefore has come mostly from studies that found a close relationship between the achievement of gender constancy and children's gender-appropriate or stereotyped behaviour or attitudes. For instance, Slaby and Frey (1975) examined pre-school children's level of gender constancy and attention towards same-gender models. They found that boys with a higher level of performance on gender constancy paid more attention to male models than female ones compared with those with a lower level of constancy. Similarly, Ruble *et al.* (1981) investigated the relationship between gender constancy and effects of commercials featuring gender-stereotyped toys. They found that gender constancy influenced children's responsiveness to the commercials such that those who achieved constancy were more likely to play with the toys and judge that they were appropriate for their own gender compared with those who were not gender-constant.

Although such studies make a strong case for the importance of gender constancy, later research (e.g. Fagot, 1985; Carter and Levy, 1988) revealed that, although gender constancy *helped* children seek gender-appropriate behaviour, it is not always *needed*. Indeed, as we reviewed earlier, gender-stereotyped tendencies (such as same-sex peer preference) are clearly apparent in pre-school – that is, well before gender constancy can be expected to happen. Perhaps a lesser understanding of gender is already sufficient. The next cognitive approach is one that takes this critical point into account.

Gender schema theories

Gender schema theorists do not dispute Kohlberg's point regarding the child's active role, but this relatively recent approach differs from his theory in that its focus

> **Definition**
>
> Gender schema: a system of beliefs about the attributes and behaviours associated with gender that help the child to form evaluations of, and to make assumptions about, each other and social objects and situations based on gender group memberships.

departs from gender constancy to, simply, gender labelling. According to the theorists (Bem, 1981; Martin and Halverson, 1981, 1983, 1987), once children can label social (gender) groups and, crucially, know to which group they belong (that they are a boy or a girl), they will increasingly search their social environment for information about behaviour and values consistent with their own gender (to be like others in their own group) that build up or enrich their (gender) schema. A schema is a system of beliefs (including stereotypes) about those characteristics associated with social groups. They provide a set of thinking structures that help the child form evaluations of or make assumptions about each other, social objects and situations based on group membership.

Therefore, simply knowing one's own gender (gender labelling) alone is sufficient to construct gender schemas, and further development of gender identity builds on this knowledge. However, it is important to bear in mind that in the beginning, the young child's schemas are very basic, based on a simple 'in/outgroup' division and the most typical characteristics for each sex. Then the child learns more first about the ingroup, including a grasp of deeper, less superficial characteristics which help build up part of his self-concept (more coherent sophisticated sense of self that we read earlier) before he begins to pay attention to the outgroup (see Martin and Halverson, 1981, 1987).

To demonstrate the workings of the schemas, an example using toy choice is used (see Fig. 11.3). The child perceiver first identifies an item as gender-appropriate (or inappropriate) or his/her own liking of a new toy. Then with the key knowledge of own gender, the child will attend to it/prefer it more if it is deemed appropriate to the ingroup or attribute that others of ingroup will prefer it.

The first mapping shows that, for a common, stereotyped toy like a car, the child knows that this item is

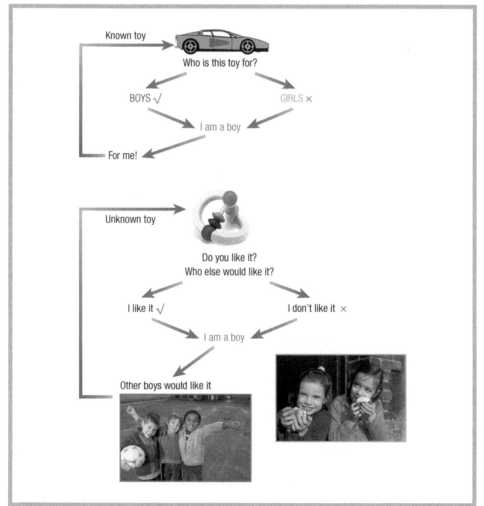

Figure 11.3. The workings of gender schemas for known and novel toys.

(*Sources*: (a) Martin and Halverson, 1987; (b) Martin *et al.*, 1995)

usually designed 'for boys', hence the awareness of his own gender group leads him to decide that playing with the item is 'for him' (Martin and Halverson, 1981). A similar cognitive operation that relies on the child's awareness of his own gender can also apply to thinking about a new, non-stereotyped toy (in the second mapping). Obviously, the child's own liking of a new toy will depend on how attractive it is to him. But when he has to predict how much other boys and girls will like the toy, he may base his predictions on his own liking *in combination with the gender group membership* of himself and other children. Here, when the perceiver is a boy and he likes the toy, he will infer that since he likes it, other boys will like it as much as he does (and girls not so much) – even though the toy itself is new and non-stereotyped. The child is effectively generalising his own preference *selectively* to the others of his gender ingroup about gender-neutral objects.

Research on gender schemas

The pattern of thinking illustrated above is indeed what Martin *et al.* (1995) found in their work using a range of attractive and unattractive new toys with children as young as four years of age. They asked children how much they liked these toys and how much other boys or girls would like them. Children predicted that same-sex others would like the toys as they themselves did even though the toys themselves were highly novel and non-stereotyped to the children. One may argue that perhaps by asking children whether other 'boys' and 'girls' would like something, children will be led to think along gender divisions. However, later research (Lam and Leman, 2003) found that the above thinking pattern still holds when photographs of boys and girls were shown, avoiding the use of gender labels of 'boys' and 'girls'.

Gender schemas also influence gender-segregated play and playmate choice (e.g. Fagot, 1985; Martin *et al.*, 1999) and recall of gender-stereotyped information (e.g. Ruble and Stangor, 1986; Carter and Levy, 1988; Liben and Signorella, 1993). The general pattern is that children process faster or remember better material that is consistent with their gender schema (beliefs about what is gender-appropriate) and less of those inconsistent with it (e.g. stories or descriptions about boys and girls that are stereotypical in character or behaviour). Furthermore, children perform better at tasks labelled as being for their own gender (Davies, 1986). This is of considerable practical implications in that children do not only actively organise their thinking and behaviours

around what is expected of their ingroup, they are more motivated towards doing well in newly gender-typed tasks (simply because these are said to be 'for' their own gender) than others.

A great strength of the schema theories to gender identity is that they can account for the rigidity with which long-standing gender stereotypes are held by children. This is because the theories denote that, once children are aware of their own gender group membership and start building up the gender schema, they will also attend to and take on board more of that information which confirms such beliefs (and attune less to that which deviates from them), and these will enrich the schema further. This way, the child should also be more mindful about the gender-appropriateness *already learned* about the attributes displayed or behaviours performed by any model, rather than the gender per se of the model – that is what the social learning approach falls short in explaining. These features fit particularly well with the basic assumption of a cognitive approach that sees the child as playing an active role in constructing her own gender knowledge. However, this construction is nevertheless susceptible to stereotypes in the environment and will in turn shape their values and behaviours and inform their future decisions.

Despite the above, there are at least several major limitations with this recent and popular approach to explaining our gender identity. The first limitation concerns the cognitive branch of theories in general. Although it is ideal, and empowering even, to conceptualise children as 'active' in developing their own gender identity, the idea of 'self-socialisation' is at best vague. Information such as 'cars are for boys' is taken for granted as common gender stereotypes in the social environment to be 'picked up' by children. This leaves a 'black box' of unknowns like *how* children pick up this kind of information; the approach concentrates on what happens within the child's cognition assuming the child already holds this information. We therefore know very little about *what* the child's schemas actually contain (what beliefs and stereotypes), even though we know quite well *how* schemas 'work' (as we have seen in the earlier illustrations).

However, it is well established (in Chapter 3) that cognitive development occurs within and depends on the social context (cf. Vygotsky, 1978), which is particularly important for developing social identities including gender identity (Lloyd and Duveen, 1992). Furthermore, if general cognitive abilities (such as labelling and conservation) determine gender-typed thinking and behaviour, we would expect similar stereotypes between boys and girls (unless they have different cognitive levels). However, this is not the case; as we have read earlier, boys tend to be more stereotyped than girls.

Finally, newer infancy research poses difficulties for the basic premise of schema theories in that, by 18 months, infants already attend more to gender-appropriate toys (Campbell *et al.*, 2000). Although we should exercise caution when interpreting observational data of pre-verbal infants, the findings are intriguing in that at this age infants cannot reliably identify each other by gender let alone assign gender to novel toys. Unless stereotyped toys have attributes 'intrinsically' interesting to boys and girls differently, other (cognitive or non-cognitive) factors ought to be revisited.

A combined approach: Social cognitive theory

Kay Bussey and Albert Bandura (1999) propose a combined social cognitive theory of gender development that draws on both social learning theory and cognitive theories of gender development. Social cognitive theory describes a three-factor model of personal factors, environmental factors and behaviour patterns influencing gender development. Bussey and Bandura suggest that we learn our gender through three routes: tuition, enactive experience and modelling. Gender tuition occurs when, for instance, a mother teaches her daughter how to bottle feed a baby or when a father teaches his son the rules of football or the different types of cars on the road. Enactive experience describes the reaction of others to a child's behaviour and facilitates gender development by reinforcing gender-stereotyped behaviour and disapproving of non gender-stereotyped behaviours. Most commonly experienced, say Bussey and Bandura, is gender modelling where children learn about gender through observing other people. As with Bandura's social learning theory describing the influences affecting aggression in young children, so his social cognitive theory of gender development describes four factors influencing the learning potential of observed behaviour. Bussey and Bandura argue that observation of behaviour alone is not enough for the child to model it. For observations to have any effect on learning, four key cognitive processes must be activated: attention, memory, production and motivation. Therefore, children must notice that the information is related to gender and must be able to store this information in their memory. Next, the child must practice (produce) the behaviour they have learned and be rewarded for it (motivation).

With these four processes successfully in place, the girl's observation of her aunt making the tea whilst her uncle watches football with her brother becomes a gender learning experience for her – reinforced when she offers to help her aunt or when her uncle suggests she help out whilst he and her brother catch up on the game.

Social cognitive theory is a complex model describing gender development in children that provides a framework for understanding the complicated interactive nature of personal factors, environmental factors and biological patterns of behaviour. According to the theory, children monitor their behaviour and their emotional reaction to that behaviour – does the girl matching her behaviour to her aunt's feel a sense of pride or a sense of shame in helping to make the tea whilst her brother watches the football? If the girl feels pride, she will add this experience to her developing sense of self-efficacy in attaining this gender-desirable role. This self-efficacy will then be reinforced and developed through further exposure to situations where she can practice (making the tea), through social modelling (seeing her mother and friends making the tea) and through social persuasion (seeing other fathers persuading women to make the tea whilst they watch sport on TV).

Gender identity development: synthesis and transaction

STOP AND THINK

- Of the three approaches above that have been proposed to explain gender identity development, which one do you find the most convincing?
- Why is that?

From what we have read of the major theoretical approaches, none alone can give a complete explanation for the complex and multidimensional jigsaw that is the development of gender identity. It seems that there are biological forces in place that are irrepressible, where some of the instincts and tendencies based on such forces we

Definition

Self-efficacy: a person's belief about how effectively he or she can control herself, her thoughts or behaviours, particularly when intended to fulfil a personal goal.

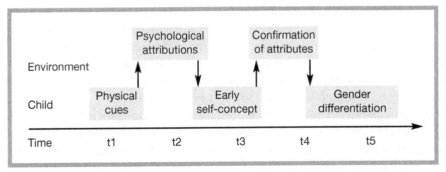

Figure 11.4. A transactional model of gender identity development.

(*Source*: adapted from Richardson, 1994)

just cannot seem to change. At the same time, it is clear that, from day one, the social forces are already at work. These operate through the way in which the child's life is structured by those closest to them. Their responses to and expectations of the child based on his or her gender can be both overtly and covertly conveyed while, at the same time, they themselves provide ready examples of gender-appropriate behaviours. At the same time, the child is not a passive recipient 'imbued' by the actions of their genes or people around them. Children actively seek and make sense of information about the gender groups available in their social environment and, from there, build up and refine a system of thinking that will guide further discovery. This is helped by the understanding of crucial concepts, such as the knowledge of to which group they belong. None of these processes works in isolation. Figure 11.4 offers a model of 'transaction', between the factors and processes inherent in the child and those found in the environment with which the child interacts.

Transaction here refers to the continual interactions between forces derived from the child's own characteristics (be they the in-born biological sex or later self-concept constructed by the child) and the environment in which he or she is placed (which contains socialising agents). One crucial point is that each stage of development itself will lead to further interactions. Following the diagram, it is not so much that there are physical differences between the sexes from birth (that influence some behavioural tendencies) but the psychological attributions made by socialising agents in the child's immediate environment based on seeing such physical cues. These attributions influence the way adults and peers behave towards the child, who is also actively making sense of their behaviour, to build up an early sense of self. The child, meanwhile, continues to seek information about gender groups and may find confirmation for the gender-relevant attributes from the environment through the agents again. This may lead the child to differentiate further between the gender groups in terms of these attributes.

Although itself logical and plausible, the validity of transaction models like this is difficult to attest empirically, since it involves several interactions all happening at the same time. It is also difficult to apply the model to explain gender development on an individual basis, especially in cases where a child has an 'atypical' identity. The Cutting Edge box features one such case. What could possibly explain this kind of phenomena?

It is noteworthy that unlike the twins earlier here is a case that concerns a boy who was born with the usual sets of male chromosomes, hormones and genitalia. It is then difficult to use biological explanations, unless there are unknown biological forces at work. The author raises the questions of how much hormones 'shape the brain' to be male or female and whether this development can be 'interrupted'. This opens up the possibilities of other kinds of inputs on gender identity. The parents apparently do not see the boy's gender identity as a 'problem' and lead a 'normal' life. Can this be seen as their 'condoning' gender-inappropriate behaviour, contrary to what we read earlier about social learning theories where adults actively reinforce gender-appropriateness? However, since we read that their son's feminine tendencies started by the age of two, should the parents have intervened by actively 'shaping' him into a boy and referring him to professionals earlier? There are no simple answers to such questions, or indeed a 'right' solution to such cases, but what they do highlight, as the author argues, is the complex of biopsychological processes that form our gender development.

Summing up: gender identity development

Undoubtedly, gender provides one of the most, if not the most, pervasive systems of classification in societies that permeates most aspects of adults' and children's lives. Since infancy children already recognise the basic male–female distinctions, and from there, a more sophisticated

CUTTING EDGE

Gender identity disorder (abridged from original article)

Mistakes in God's Factory

Two years ago, a twelve-year-old German boy became the world's youngest person to start hormone treatments for a sex change.

Kim P. is 14 years old. She's had enough of psychiatrists who ask weird questions. She's had enough of doctors who reject her case because this fashion-conscious girl – previously called 'Tim' in her patient file – unsettles them.

She was born as a boy. Her body, chromosomes and hormones were all undoubtedly masculine. But she felt otherwise. For Kim it was clear from the beginning that, as she says, 'I wound up in the wrong body'.

At the age of two, Tim tried on his older sister's clothes, played with Barbies and said, 'I'm a girl'. Her parents thought it was a phase, but at the age of four Tim was still bawling after every haircut. At last he ran into his room with a pair of scissors and hollered that he wanted to 'cut off my thing!' and it was clear to his parents that the problem was serious. From then on, at home, Tim went by 'Kim'. By age eight there was nothing boyish about her. She played typical girl games with other girls, went to their birthday parties and even dressed up for the ballet. Her teachers praised her exemplary social skills. When she was teased in the schoolyard and called names like 'tranny' or 'queer', she walked away.

'We always saw Kim as a girl, but not as a problem,' says the father. 'In fact, our life was surprisingly normal.' Normal until Kim was twelve, and experienced the first signs of puberty. She was overcome by panic when her voice began to drop. She had no interest in becoming one of those brawny creatures with gigantic hands and deep voices who dressed like women but looked unfeminine. Only hormones could prevent Kim from turning into Tim again, and time was of the essence.

'Hormone treatment! Gender adjustment! How could you possibly do this to the child?' the family's pediatrician barked at the father – in Kim's presence.

Then came the sessions at the state psychiatric hospital, where Kim would sit in green rooms with high ceilings, playing with experimental blocks, while her parents answered endless questionaires.

Kim's is a classic case, according to Bernd Meyenburg. Gender identity disorders are not rare among children, and they often appear as soon as a child starts to speak. The problem goes away in about a quarter of these children. In about 2 to 10% of the cases, though, early gender identity disorders lead to transsexualism.

'From a purely medical standpoint we are dealing with the mutilation of a biologically healthy body,' says Meyenburg. But in Kim's case, says Meyenburg, 'it would have been a crime to let her grow up as a man. There are very few people in whom it's so obvious.'

Meyenburg has been studying transsexuality since the 1970s. In those days, orthodox psychiatry believed that adverse social circumstances – namely the parents – were to blame when someone felt out of place in his or her biological gender.

Even Meyenburg was long convinced that severe emotional trauma in childhood caused transsexualism. 'On the other hand,' he says, 'depression isn't exactly rare in mothers. Wouldn't that mean there should be far more transsexuals?' Meyenburg points out another inconsistency: 'There are cases in which you could poke around in the parents' relationship as long as you wish and still find nothing.'

Gender development in human beings is a complex of bio-psychological processes, and when something goes wrong, not everyone understands. The medical community in particular tends to impose order. Developmental psychologists long believed that children were born emotionally neutral, and that a person's perceived gender affiliation was the result of social influence. Experts still think a lot of gender-specific behaviour is learned, but they also believe some of it is pre-wired in the womb. The extent to which androgen or estrogen shapes the brain to be male or female is debatable; the age at which gender identity is established is unknown. Whether the development of an identity can be interrupted during early childhood isn't clear.

▶ 'Nowadays we believe that it's both,' says Meyenburg – 'environment and biology.'

'From an emotional standpoint, Kim comes across as a healthy, happy and balanced child,' Meyenburg wrote in his report. She had never behaved like a boy, not even for a short period of time. 'There is no doubt that her wish is irreversible, because it has been evident since very early childhood.'

In the past, Meyenburg was strictly opposed to hormone treatment before a child came of age. He began to question the wisdom of his own rules when one of his patients resisted his advice and ordered hormones over the Internet. She went abroad at 17 and had a sex change operation for a few thousand euros. Meyenburg was angry at the time. Today this woman, a law student, is one of his happiest patients.

Now Meyenburg allows his young patients to enter hormone treatment early, before puberty complicates a sex change. 'They simply suffer less,' he says.

Kim is already much closer to realising her dream. The first letter of her name has been changed in her record, and her school now treats her as a girl. Thanks to the hormones, her breasts are developing, like those of other girls in her class. She's allowed to use the girls' locker room during gym class.

One thing hasn't completely changed for Kim, though – heckling in the schoolyard. But now her best friend sticks up for her. Kim says she feels good about herself in spite of the taunts. 'My girlfriends see me as a completely normal person,' she says.

'It's out of the question for me,' says Kim, who still wants to get rid of the parts of her body that remind her that she was born as Tim. By law, in Germany, she'll have to wait until she's 18 to take the next step. Meanwhile, she resorts to wearing tight pants.

'I just happen to be a girl,' says Kim. She keeps a piggybank in her bedroom filled with change she has been saving for the operation – since the age of five. Once it's over, her new life will start. 'In Paris,' she says, 'where no one knows me.'

Source: Spiegel online magazine, January 26, 2007 (translated from the German)

- **What do you think is the explanation for Kim's gender identity?**
- **Do you agree with Bernd Meyenburg's assessment and decision to conduct hormone treatment (and later a sex change) on Kim?**
- **Do you think Kim will ever think of himself as a boy?**

understanding about gender group memberships develops. Gender identity is a multidimentional construct in that it encompasses all of cognitive, affective and behavioural components, and none of the purely biologically, socially or cognitively oriented approaches alone can explain the this spectrum of developments. An inclusive approach in the form of transactions between the innate, individual and environmental elements offers the most reasonable account. It is, however, difficult to obtain empirical evidence for the simultaneous transactions, and many atypical cases of gender identity development remain unresolved.

SUMMARY

This chapter has covered the development of children's self-concept and, related to this, their gender identity. First, we read that the self-concept develops by degrees, from an infant's rudimentary awareness of their own existence as separate from that of others, to a more evaluative and reflective sense of the self as the child recognises how they may be perceived by others. Accordingly, through the ages, children's self-descriptions develop from ones about the more physical, observable and measurable features to ones derived from interpersonal relationships and inner qualities. Notably, this gradual development is likely influenced by the social interactions in which the child engages with those around them. Over time, their perceptions and evaluations become increasingly consistent with what is expected by others.

The chapter then looked at the part of a child's self-concept that is derived from gender group membership. We read that, by the second year in life, infants respond differently to male and female stimuli and, soon after, they learn the gender labels to identify others and themselves, although such is based on superficial features – even when children learn that gender is a permanent part of the self. It is not until children grasp that gender remains constant despite outward changes in middle childhood that they have a fuller understanding of their membership. Still, gender encompasses other aspects, particularly the knowledge of stereotypes and gender-appropriate behaviour.

Three major theoretical approaches were put forward to explain the development of gender identity. The biological accounts propose that the different role, status and behavioural patterns between the sexes originate from biological differences evolved over time as humans adapted to environmental demands. In contrast, social learning theorists argue that children acquire gendered behaviour and values by modelling on and reinforcement by parents, peers and the media. Cognitive theories concentrate on the child's role in seeking and processing gender material from the environment and, in doing so, constructing their own gender identity. Each approach has its merits and empirical support; especially strong are the medical cases for the biological accounts, experiments showing different responses by adults or peers to the same child labelled differently or gender-appropriate and

inappropriate behaviour for social learning, and studies showing the effects of schemas on gendered behaviour and recall for schema theories. Each approach also has its drawbacks such as the narrow list of behaviours explained by biological factors, the issue of selective attention or modelling for social learning theories and newer research of pre-labelling infants' differential responses to stereotyped toys. A transaction model was suggested which integrates the approaches, though the assessment of its validity requires further extensive research.

It is indeed the case that there is still plenty of 'unknowns' to be discovered about children's development of self-concept and gender identity. Questions remain such as what in the social environment is 'most' significant in facilitating the development of self-concepts and gender identities – parents, peers, school or the media? What makes male–female distinctions so 'intrinsically' salient to begin with? How do we integrate the different biological, environmental and individual-child factors and processes to explain cases of atypical gender identity development? A great deal of work has set up much of the crucial foundational knowledge and explicated the workings of each branch of factors and processes. The direction for future ventures in the area is to find out how these branches operate in conjunction with each other.

REVIEW QUESTIONS

1 What are the major milestones towards the child's establishment of a self-concept? What abilities does each of them require and reflect?

2 'A child's gender identity is neither biologically determined, acquired through their social environment nor constructed by the child him- or herself.' Evaluate the validity of this statement.

3 How important is self-esteem to our overall self-concept and what may influence its development?

4 What are the key factors that determine a child's sense of gender identity? Are some stronger than others?

5 Compare and contrast two major theoretical approaches that have been used to explain the development of gender identity.

RECOMMENDED READING

For further reading on self-identity development:

To understand the development of the looking-glass self, read:

Tice, D.M. & Wallace, H.M. (2005). The reflected self: creating yourself as (you think) others see you. In M.R. Leary & J.P. Tangney (Eds), *Handbook of Self and Identity* (91–105). New York: Guilford Press.

To understand more on the development of self throughout childhood and adolescence, read:

Harten, S. (2005). The development of self-representations during childhood and adolescence. In M.R. Leary & J.P. Tangney (Eds) *Handbook of Self and Identity* (610–642). New York: Guilford Press.

For an in-depth discussion on self and identity development:

Fischer, K.W. & Harter, S. (2001). *The Construction of the Self: a Developmental Perspective*. New York: Guildford Press.

For further reading on gender development:

For a classic text covering a range of issues on gender development:

Golombok, S. & Fivush, R. (1994). *Gender Development*. Cambridge: Cambridge University Press.

Maccoby, E.E. (1998). *The Two Sexes: Growing up Apart, Coming Together*. Cambridge, MA: Belknap Press.

Updated in:

Maccoby, E.E. (2000). Perspectives on gender development. *International Journal of Behavioral Development*, *24*, 398–406.

For a more cutting edge perspective on gender development:

Blakemore, J.E.O., Berenbaum, S.A. & Liben, L.S. (2009). *Gender Development*. Hove: Psychology Press.

RECOMMENDED WEBSITES

The Max Planck Institute for Human Development has a number of research centres devoted to understanding our development of the self and self-concept:

http://www.mpib-berlin.mpg.de/index.en.htm

The SELF Research Centre (the Self-concept Enhancement and Learning Facilitation Group) based at Oxford University encompasses 450 members from 45 countries across six continents and a network of satellite centres producing research on enhancing positive self-concept:

http://www.self.ox.ac.uk/index.htm

For further information in issues relating to gender identity and research:

http://www.gires.org.uk/

 Watch a video demonstrating infant self-awareness using a mirror task. Further resources can be found at www.pearsoned.co.uk/gillibrand

Chapter 12
Peer interactions and relationships

Learning Outcomes

After reading this chapter, with further recommended reading, you should be able to:

1. Describe the nature of the peer group at different ages and appreciate the potential importance of this social structure to a child's development;

2. Critically evaluate the significance of peer interactions, in particular play, for a child's social and cognitive development;

3. Understand the issues surrounding social status in peer groups including acceptance, rejection and neglect, the factors that influence social status, and its consequences;

4. Critically evaluate the key functions of friendship for children, the factors that influence its formation and development, and its longer-term implications;

5. Compare and evaluate the research studies and related methods that have been used to study the above developments and how they may impact on findings.

Interaction in the playground

The following is an (abridged) extract of a skipping game observed in a junior school, in June 1970, by Iona Opie, author of the book *The People in the Playground*:

> . . . the boss (of the game – often the one who thought of playing it) was a girl called Mandy, and the five other skippers looked to her for instructions. She decided that they should play 'Down in the kitchen, Doin' a bit of stitchin', *In* comes a burglar, And knocks you *Out*.' Mandy jumped into the rope first. She was certainly a good skipper. The routine went smoothly for several changes, a new skipper coming into the rope at '*In*' and leaving it at '*Out*'. Then someone less skilful came in, stumbled, and had to take an end. Being a less skilful turner, as well, she dropped the rope. There was a restless rearrangement of the group and murmurs of 'Mandy, shall I?' They had a few more turns at this game, then Mandy said they would play a different one. They started skipping through the rope in a continuous line, Building Up Bricks, doing one skip, each, then two, then three, and so on. The clumsy 'ender' dropped the rope again. It is not customary to dismiss a player from a game. Mandy had to choose whether to let her continue as an incompetent turner or let her become a skipper again and even more certainly interrupt the flow of the game. She darted forward like a dervish. 'Stop dropping the rope!' she said, picking up the end and thrusting it into the girl's hand. 'We got to three.'. . .

> 'It isn't always easy to join in a game,' an 11 year old girl explained to me. 'People are a bit fussy about who plays with them.' I asked a group of younger girls, 'What do you do if you want to join in a game and they won't let you?' 'You go and play the same game on your own somewhere else,' was the prompt response; and she meant 'with your own set of friends'. A solitary child trying to attach herself to a game is an unusual occurrence, and that child is likely to be an oddity of some kind. 'We usually play with our own friends,' they said. 'We usually play in a four, and that is usually enough for a game. If we need any more we go and ask some more people, people we know.' There is a centre ring of friends, and an outer ring who can be co-opted. The four friends come out to play as a group, and are thus insulated against any social problems. They have no need to wheedle or bludgeon their way into other groups or games. 'What if there's a new game that you've never seen before, and you want to learn it?' I asked. 'We watch, and if they say we can't join in we just watch, and soon they tell us to go away.'

Think about when you were learning games in the school playground.

- Did you find it easy to join in or did you find it difficult?
- Was it easier to join in if one of your friends was already playing that game?

(Opie, 1993, pp. 5–6) ▶

▶ # Introduction

The opening example taken from the vivid descriptions in Iona Opie's book epitomises some of the key concepts and raises some important questions that will be addressed in this chapter. So far in this part of the book, we have covered the earliest social interactions and relationships the child will establish with her family members, and the factors which can influence this first social development. As the child grows older, the environments that she enters into and learns from expand to outside of the home, and the number and types of people within the environments also grow. These people include adults other than the child's parents and caregivers, but importantly as she continues her journey of socialisation and associated learning in more formalised settings, such as that of the nursery and then full-time school, social interactions and relationships involving what will be her 'peer groups' will take on the centre-stage in her day-to-day life.

This chapter overviews, examines and evaluates the kinds of interactions that children engage in with their peers and the relationships that they develop with these other children through the course of their development. We will first take a look at the nature of children's peer groups from a young age to later in childhood, and the kinds of things that they do in such groups, in particular the key theme of play, from which children are seen to learn a lot about themselves and others and which sets up a stage for other aspects of development including language and cognition. Next, the chapter will go further to explore the more enduring relationships that children form with their peers throughout development, including the most significant issues, such as a child's 'place' or social status within a peer group, the functions of friendship and the factors that influence the course and consequences of these relationships.

The peer group and peer interactions

Children's peer groups have offered the basis for studying development for a long while. But what is a peer group and how do we define a peer? Generally speaking, a peer is another child of the same or similar age to a child, often within a year or so of the child's own age, and the peer group refers to the people other than the children's family members (Salmon, 1992). In this sense, the children's siblings are not 'peers', although quite often they are close enough in age and of course a key social influence in a child's life (Dunn and Kendrick, 1982).

Definition

Peer group: the other children or young people with whom a child or young person engages that are of a similar age and not a family member.

Even though children interacting and playing with each other may look rather natural to us casual observers, it actually requires social skills and understanding that are not demanded (or demanded as much) by interactions with older, more competent people such as the parents and other adults. The unequal adult–child combination (also known as 'vertical relationships'; see Hartup, 1989) functions with the adult being the provider of security and protection, enabling the child to gain knowledge and skills – as seen in the attachment relationship (Chapter 9, Attachment and Early Social Experiences). Such provision and support is not found in the peer group (also known as 'horizontal relationships') as the children are similar in age and social powers, but each of them may have different needs, desires and wishes. This means that peer groups tend to be more difficult to sustain, because their interactions require a greater level of reciprocity, and each child will learn skills in the other's company, such as sharing and cooperation as well as conflict resolution and moderating competitions, if the peer group is to continue relatively harmoniously without hostility. Hence the way that children socialise within such groups is distinct from parental socialisation and, once a peer group is formed, children within it may develop their own norms, ideas and identities. In fact, the influence of the peer group on development has been argued to be of utmost importance, over and above that of parental socialisation, by some of the most renowned psychologists, whether they are proponents from the 'nature' (such as Steven Pinker, 2002) or 'nurture' (Judith Harris, 1998) side of the debate (see later).

Children's peer groups and interactions through the years

> ### STOP AND THINK
>
> You may find this question easier if you have had experiences with young children, or you may ask someone who has young children:
>
> How young are children when they start to 'engage' one another – take an interest or even attract another's attention in order to initiate interactions or to actually play?

Infancy

Even though, when we think about the 'peer group', many of us tend to create a picture of friendship groups in school (the opening example is one such illustration), in reality very young infants already seem to take an interest in peers of their own age by the end of the first year in life. As early as six months of age, two babies when faced with each other may stare and make noises at and even reach for the other, to explore the other's body, hair or clothing, and such behaviours become more evident towards the end of this first year (Hay *et al.*, 1983). However, it needs to be said that, although this might reflect how babies can be 'interested' in one another, infants this young still prefer to explore and interact with objects and will display this interest in human others often only when no toy objects are around. It is not until well into the second year that infants are seen in more frequent and elaborate interactions, in which longer sequences of initiating and responding behaviours ensue. Still, toddlers usually play with toys alongside each other (see next subsection) rather than in a coordinated way involving mutual imitation or continuous reciprocation, which is observed closer to age two, but even then their interactions often end up in conflict (Hay and Ross, 1982). This is possibly due to the stage of development where neither party has acquired the social skills to accommodate each other's differences for long.

Even young infants are already interested in their peers, but this interest is transient and they are more interested in objects at this stage.

Source: Lam

Early childhood/pre-school ages

Apart from the rapidly increasing physical mobility and social understanding, from two to three years old, many children in the west at least will go to day nurseries or play groups; thus, their opportunities to 'practise' social interactions with same-age others also increase. There is evidence that, between two and five years of age, children can play with increasing reciprocation and cooperation with each other. One of the first people to document this systematically was Mildred Parten (1932), who observed children in nurseries as part of her doctorate studies. She found that, while the younger two to three year olds appeared more solitary as they engaged in more 'parallel' activity alongside each other, rather than in so-called 'associative' or 'cooperative' activities *with* each other (also see Play), the latter of which started to appear more and more often as children got older. Parten also defined several other categories, and the progression of children decreasing in alone-time without interacting with their peers towards increased social participation with them along this set of categories was later taken as the 'benchmark' that reflects children's development of social skills (see Table 12.1).

Over the years, however, research has suggested that the emphasis on activity with others as a yardstick for more 'advanced' social skills is over-simplistic and that both older and younger children engage most commonly in parallel activities. In fact, by parallel play initially while being an onlooker of others' interactions, children can gradually bring themselves closer to the joint activities and eventually proceed to join in as they have acquired the appropriate entry skills (Fantuzzo *et al.*, 1998; Rubin *et al.*, 1998).

Therefore, during the pre-school years children show an increase in tendency to participate in joint activities and with that the size of the peer group starts to increase. However, they still spend a great deal of time in parallel activities, but this appears to be able to serve the function of allowing children to learn about and easing them into a peer group's etiquette and activity if it is first coupled with observing the peers.

Middle childhood/school ages

While peer interactions seem to change in a notable, but gradual, way through early childhood, by the end of first year in school children already have a very strong tendency for 'belonging' to a peer group. This may be because, by this time, children spend most of their day in school in a broad range of contexts, with free play periods where interactions with peers are less closely followed, and even less structured and maintained by adults, compared with the earlier years in preschool.

The dynamics of the peer groups also evolve rapidly in the sense that there is an emerging structure (often involving leadership and followers, with the example at the beginning of the chapter illustrating this), as the size of the grouping continues to grow and the activities and interactions within it become more complex. As mentioned above, peers within the group come with different backgrounds, interests, wishes and so on. The increase in exposure and exchanges will increase children's awareness of differing perspectives and 'over time' interactions will further develop their ability to interpret and understand others' perspectives and motives and refine the social rules to accommodate others' roles and intentions (Denham *et al.*, 2004; and see Chapter 8, Theory of Mind).

At the same time, with the increasing freedom children enjoy for associating with only others they prefer, some 'chasm' quickly and clearly becomes apparent as, in particular, boys and girls usually go separate ways in developing their peer groups with distinct structure and nature of interactions. In fact, by junior school years (age seven years), boys are already far more likely to be observed to play in larger groups at team sports such as football, while girls form more close-knit smaller units or 'cliques' that engage in more organised or 'traditional' activities, such as skipping, as we observed in the opening

Table 12.1. Parten's (1932) categories of play behaviour in preschool.

Category	Description
Unoccupied	Child not being involved in any activity
Onlooker	Child watching others but not joining in
Solitary	Child playing alone away from others
Parallel	Child playing alongside others with the same objects or in a similar activity as others without interacting with others
Associative	Child interacting with others while participating in the same activity
Cooperative	Child interacting with others in well-coordinated complementary ways that may involve sharing with and supporting each other

Source: Parten (1932)

example (see also Lloyd and Duveen, 1992). As explored in the previous chapter, by school ages, peers provide some of the strongest socialising agents (often stronger than parents) of gender behaviours and stereotypes as they readily recognise the gender-appropriateness of activities and may even criticise each other for what is commonly seen as gender-inappropriate behaviours. Not surprisingly then, over time in school, children are more and more likely to associate with same-sex others in the increasingly gender-stereotypical activities, with boys being more competitive while girls strive for more collaboration and agreeableness generally (Leaper, 1991).

Adolescence

With a longer part of the weekday spent on the school grounds, and even more freedom than ever before allowed to socialise with peers after school and often also in the weekend, adolescence is the time when the peer group exerts arguably the greatest influence on the teenager (examined in more detail in Chapter 13, Adolescence). Indeed, by mid-adolescence (13–14 years), teenagers spend more time with peers than with any other set of social agents.

Through the journey from infancy to adolescence, the peer group evolves in obvious ways, and the key nature and functions of interactions within it transforms progressively. It goes from the kind of exchanges that parents will have a key part in orchestrating in the early years, as they arrange visits to others' homes and nurseries, towards greater and greater autonomy on the part of the children as their social skills, choices and experiences expand and adults' supervision and guidance decline. This is not to say that family does not matter; there is evidence that the family is the primary reference point where advice for education, career and finance is concerned, and the peer group is sought for 'social' issues such as appearance and relationships (Sebald, 1989). Nevertheless, it can be said that the peer group has the key function of helping to bring the young from being dependent on the family to a more independent person.

Play

So far, we have identified the key features of children's interactions with peers over the course of development and some of the major functions that such groups and interactions serve. Some of the questions that remain still concern the 'what', and the 'how'. While children

engage with each other, exactly what 'kinds of things' do they do? How do they actually acquire or develop the skills, which we have just read that they acquire through doing such things? We all know that the commonest activity in schoolchildren do with each other outside of class is play. Here we take a closer look at play in the context of social interactions.

> ## STOP AND THINK
>
> You may draw on your own experiences or observations of children for this exercise.
>
> - What do you understand as 'play'? Do you still 'play'?
> - If you do, how is your kind of play different from those you engaged in as a child?
> - Why do you think they are different? Are there similarities too?

However you have answered the questions in the last Stop-and-think box, one key theme that you may well have brought up concerning 'play' is that it is an activity that you *enjoy*. Researcher Jane Howard has spent a lot of time researching play behaviour in young children and has adopted a novel approach in defining its usefulness within an educational framework. She reported that what a child defined as play was no more complex than the belief that play was time away from the teacher (Howard *et al.*, 2006)! Howard's work has also revealed that when learning is fun, more is learned by the child. This could be due to increased motivation of children within a fun environment. For instance, when children learn from play, it is different from many forms of learning, as they absorb information, knowledge or skills at least from something that they feel motivated to do (Göncü and Gaskins, 2007). This is one of many reasons why there has been such a push towards learning through play at least in nurseries and even in early years' school settings in the past few decades, so as to offer a 'natural' way through which children can learn.

As a dominant part of the interactions with peers, the complexity of peer play increases with age as well as the kinds of development that comes with it. Saying that, it is plausible that even early play with a peer group is helpful for a child to acquire or practise social skills and cognitive understanding. In order to sustain play, a child will have to sometimes subdue his own agenda in the interest of the

NATURE–NURTURE

Is the tendency to form peer groups innate or learned?

To consider this question, we will evaluate the perspectives of two influential psychologists, Steven Pinker (1954–) and Judith Harris (1938–), who have taken on a similar position in that they put forward the notion that the bulk of socialisation that is of main influence comes from peers and that the influence of family is less important. However, they come from slightly different angles; Pinker's theory is based on evolutionary principles that all human potentials or tendencies are innate and Harris's work is built around social psychology's group theories that children become socialised, while still acknowledging the role of evolution in driving group socialisation.

Most well-known for his book *The Blank Slate* in 2002, among others, Pinker's most controversial view is that of child-rearing. The key reason is his claims first that the effect of genes is more powerful than that of the environment and second that children are more influenced by their peers than their parents. In his book, he goes as far to assert that genes determine the fact that we have cultures and social groups that we form. Even though such groups 'themselves' are not genetic, they are inherited for as long as we have been a species as they are essential for our existence, and we build our experiences on those groups. Similarly Harris, in her best-selling but controversial landmark book in 1998, *The Nurture Assumption*, argues that parents do not influence the long-term future of their children as much as once thought. In fact, she argues that parents, apart from passing on their genes, which explain about half of the variations between people, have less impact on children than other aspects of their environment, most notably the peers.

She draws on what she terms 'group socialisation theory', the idea that children's peers with other groups that they may become involved in are the key factors in addition to genes that shape personality and behaviour. It is through this 'groupness' that children become socialised – they get ideas about how to behave by identifying with a group and taking on its attitudes, behaviours, speech and dresscode. Both Pinker and Harris also look to research with the children of immigrants, among others, to provide clues that they are more like their peers rather than their parents.

We read in Chapter 9, Attachment, that cross-cultural research has shown that since infancy children have a tendency to form relationships with a consistent set of people. Comparative studies (with animal species) have also shown that many traits in humans for interpersonal communication and cooperation can be found in our close animal cousins such as chimpanzees (gesturing directions and sharing of information) to assist others towards their goals (Warneke and Tomasello, 2009). However, there are idiosyncrasies unique to humans that are not found in most other species (like sharing resources). We may also review rare cases like that of Genie (Chapter 2, Theoretical Perspectives) where very basic social skills may be 'taught' through intensive training after a child's prolonged social isolation and emotional deprivation through formative years, but full functional recovery cannot be achieved.

It is important therefore not to be drawn into the extreme and dualistic 'nature *versus* nurture' concepts that can plague our understanding of human interaction. It is fair to say that we are likely equipped with a basic need to relate to others but, for the more meaningful interactions, we require social skills that will take time to fine-tune.

joint activity, and that requires an awareness of the peer's agenda, and the ability to regulate one's own behaviours and emotions (Gottman, 1986). As we read in earlier chapters (Chapter 8, Theory of Mind, and Chapter 10, Childhood Temperament and Behavioural Development) the prerequisite skills emerge during early childhood and play offers an arena to refine them. However, as we have learnt in the last section, children up to age five spend much of their time in solitary activities. We ought therefore to identify the kinds of play that are 'social' and 'non-social' and

Play, at any ages, is usually seen as an activity that the participants enjoy.

Source: Pearson Education Ltd./Jules Selmes

what kinds of learning can be included with them. As Parten (1932) labelled six categories of social interactions, later researchers have assembled these further, along children's ages, into a few categories of play (see Table 12.2).

Although solitary play involving functional activities and construction remains proportionally higher in frequency through the preschool years, there is a noticeable rise in the amount of time spent on the more complicated form of social play, namely make-believe play. We will first look closely at this form of play and its related, but simpler, form of play, symbolic play, which emerges earlier in childhood, their major characteristics and the skills that they reflect in the sections below. We will also look at what has often been overlooked as a simpler 'physical' form of play, 'rough-and-tumble' play, to

Table 12.2. Categories of play.

Play / age group	Description	Examples
Functional (first 2 years)	Simple, physical activities with or without toy objects	Running, bouncing a ball, jumping over something
Symbolic (2 to 6 years)	Representing absent objects/ events with available ones or own body	Pretending to eat from an an empty dish or hand
Make-believe/ sociodramatic (2–6 years)	Acting out roles or pretend games involving real social roles or made-up imaginary ones	Playing house/ school or 'real-life' (e.g., hospital) or fictional scenarios
Constructive (3–6 years)	Creating or building a tangible object or representation of one	Using building blocks, drawing, making jigsaws
Games with rules (6 years up)	Structured games with publicly accepted rules	Football, other ball games, skipping, hopscotch

(*Source:* adapted from Piaget, 1951; Smilansky, 1968; Rubin *et al.*, 1983, 1998)

Definitions

Make-believe play: also known as sociodramatic or role-play, play that involves two or more children acting out social roles, whether real-life or fictional ones, in pretend games and usually requires negotiation and reciprocation with each other with agreed rules in the shared imaginary scenario.

Symbolic play: also known as fantasy or pretend play, play that involves 'symbolic' representation, where the child pretends that an absent object is present and acts out the relevant behaviours involving that object.

Rough-and-tumble play: also known as 'play-fighting', play that involves physical activity, often without objects, such as wrestling, tumbling, kicking and chasing and is commonest during middle childhood among boys.

examine its main features. Soon after, we will examine the learning and development that such play may foster, including language, cognitive and social skills, emotional development and group-order adjustment.

Symbolic play

The earliest systematic description and interpretation of children's early play, perhaps unsurprisingly, came from Piaget. Piaget (1951) observed and labelled three main stages of play in a sequence (with certain overlapping) where the simplest stage of play involving basic functional activities (in Table 12.2) was called 'sensorimotor play'. The next stage, which starts from around 15 months and continues to six years, was called 'symbolic play', also known as 'fantasy' or 'pretend' play. This form of play, as the term suggests, marks the beginnings when the child can 'symbolically' represent something, be it an object or an event, which is absent in their immediate setting. An example of this is a child pretending to drink from an empty cup, where there is no liquid inside, making the requisite slurping sound. These behaviours like gesturing and imitation suggest that the child has 'symbolic' understanding, that she knows that the (usually key) object (liquid) is not there, but she is simply mimicking the relevant act, one of the key milestones in her cognitive development. As children become more skilled, they may start to mimic a series of representational behaviours, such as pretending to 'pour the tea' apart from drinking. These will not only involve a broader behavioural repertoire, and thus more representations, but quite likely also the use of language as children narrate more and more complicated series of acts. This will be particularly the case when such play begins to involve more than one child, paving the scenes for more elaborate 'make-believe' play.

Make-believe play

Also known as role- or sociodramatic play (Smilansky, 1968), 'make-believe' play reflects an extended version of the development of representations in children's cognitive skills. Emerging often shortly after the simpler forms of symbolic play at two to three years and becoming more complex with the inclusion of peers, such play marks the key advances from earlier solo pretences. Until the end of the second year, the child's pretences are relatively inflexible in terms of the nature of the acts they

represent and the choice of objects they use. For instance, most 18 month olds can only mimic real actions that adults perform (such as drinking and serving tea) and use objects that are actually used for the actions (cups), and cannot act out imaginary events or substitute with other objects (such as using a hand to mimic the shape of a cup). The use of less realistic objects as the ones they represent in imaginary situations emerges from age two (Striano *et al.*, 2001).

Furthermore, the involvement of peers in this form of 'social' play means that the child is a co-participant in acts that include not only himself, but others. This may not begin with a 'real' peer at first, but she may 'serve tea' to a doll or act out a scene between two dolls before she plays out the scene with another child. Through acting, she realises the different perspectives between the co-participants in the interactions. The benefits of involving peers do not stop here; having more children means having more ideas and roles. Often only one act or one set of acts can be thought and played out at one time by one child. With more children, the series of acts that are imagined can be combined as each child takes on a different role and builds on another's storylines, often spontaneously. This requires the skills of reciprocating the other's efforts and often negotiating a plan of pretence (who plays what) with pre-assigned rules. In particular, when the child is involved with another with more sophisticated skills, she needs to 'raise the level' of pretence where the play becomes richer, more diverse and sustained (Bornstein, 2006). Such games depart from 'real' roles into fantasy with age and exposure to inputs by sources like comics and TV (see the Case Study box). The fact that children are aware that such play is 'make-believe' reflects their understanding of the distinction between the imaginary and reality (Rakoczy *et al.*, 2004).

Rough-and-tumble play

So far in this section, we have focused on the kinds of play that involve more cognitive and social skills (such as language, imagination and negotiation) rather than physical skills, and are 'higher up' on the play chart (Table 12.2) as more advanced or 'mature' forms of play. However, just as many children continue to engage in solitary rather than joint activities, much play in fact involves the more gross physical activity without objects, particularly in the vastness of the school grounds. One

CASE STUDY

Lost Babies

This example describes how two six year old girls role-play at being two 'lost babies'.

Laura: We're the two lost babies, yeah

Aalliyah: Yeah we're the two lost babies . . .

Laura: Pretend we saw a boat

Aalliyah: No this is the boat, yeah. (*moving onto a low stool*) Now get behind. (*Both shuffle the 'boat' around the 'water' amid some argument about which way it should go*)

Laura: Pretend we were in a fight. (*play-fighting in boat*) Then something terrible happens.

Aalliyah: What?

Laura: Happens to the water and then I couldn't swim . . . (*both children fall out of the 'boat'. Laura moves Aalliyah face down on the 'water'*) Pretend you couldn't swim. Here's your help. (*throws a jumper over Aalliyah*)

Aalliyah: Get it off of me.

Laura: Pretend I'm the horrible one, yeah, and she's the good one . . . No you're still stuck in the water (*begins to cover Aalliyah with newspaper*)

Aalliyah: No more paper on me, your mum's gonna . . .

Laura: One more. Then you came out. You messed up all the papers.

(*Source:* The Open University, 2003)

- What does this example of play show us?
- Can we use play to understand the experiences of children who perhaps might not be able to tell us what has happened to them?

The girls' play demonstrates imagination and spontaneity as they improvise both their script and props, and it is unlikely that they have experienced the situation they enact: being lost at sea and drowning. This shows how make-believe play offers the contexts for sharing and making sense of experiences that are fantasy rather than real-life.

---

oft-overlooked activity is 'rough-and-tumble' play (Pellegrini and Smith, 1998) or 'play-fighting'. This form of play, more common among boys and commonest during school ages (10% vs 4% during pre-school and adolescence; Pellegrini, 2006), involves wrestling, chasing, kicking, tumbling or rolling on the ground, thus resembling real fighting. It does, however, differ from real fighting in that afterwards children continue playful interaction rather than going their own way as they do after real fighting. Still, it is often misunderstood by well-meaning teachers, who break up the participants, or clamp down on it altogether on school grounds as they believe that such activity can lead to aggressive behaviours. Very occasionally this does happen, but often for a reason – either that one participant misinterprets another's acts (when a play-fighting advance is seen with hostile intent), or when one breaks some understood or agreed 'rule' or expectation of a game – both of which are more likely elicited by certain children

than others (see Peer groups and social status). In fact, the understanding of such rules in this form of play is argued to serve certain social functions among the peer group, as we will examine below.

Play, learning and development

We have seen the critical characteristics that involve peer interactions in a few major forms of play and the skills that they reflect which children realise as they play. A further potentially controversial question of interest not only to child psychologists, but also educators and policy makers for education, is: do children learn and develop skills from play? This is a difficult question because it is almost impossible to 'prove' that play actually 'causes' learning or development to take place rather than requiring and reflecting the child's existing skills repertoire. At the same time, there are certain clear relationships between a child's advances in play and achievements in numerous domains of development, and evidence of children lacking or lagging behind in some skills if they are deprived of certain forms of play.

Perhaps because of their complex representational nature, the bulk of research has examined the impact of symbolic and make-believe play. For instance, it has been noted that the gestures and sounds that are used for symbolic play appear at about the same time as children's first vocabulary and those who are skilled enough to link up a chain of acts (pouring and drinking tea) are also the first to link up words within their speech (Bates *et al.*, 1987). Although it is plausible that the children already know the words before they use them to narrate their play, it is still possible that certain words that children hear will be learned (or learned more quickly) if they can 'connect' with what they can see, do, think or feel. Language delay also typically goes hand-in-hand with delays in play that involves imitation and symbolic functions (Bates *et al.*, 1987). Similarly, it has been observed (Smilansky, 1968) that immigrant and disadvantaged pre-schoolers who did not engage in sociodramatic play lag behind in both language and cognitive skills. However, it is worth noting that the delays may be due to their general under-stimulation rather than the lack of certain play only.

As the various forms and levels of pretend play emerge and develop at around the same age (four to five years) as those of theory of mind (see Chapter 8), it has been said that such play promotes the child's understanding of others' perspectives. In elaborate sociodramatic play in particular, where playmates take complementary and reciprocal roles, with an agreed set of rules and symbolic meanings beyond everyday life (such as action heroes from movies), the need to hone their coordination and negotiation is even greater to sustain that shared fantasy world. There is evidence of a link between the skills in such play and theory of mind abilities (Taylor and Carlson, 1997), if such correlational work should be treated with caution (see Chapter 3, Research Methods). There has been experimental work, where children are 'trained' in complex pretend play (Dockett, 1998), and the children not only perform more pretend activities and excel in make-believe skills, they also show substantial improvements in theory of mind tasks compared to those who have not gone through training. Such studies are hard to come by and sample sizes often relatively small, but they do offer evidence that elements from the play can help develop social and cognitive skills over time.

Apart from its cognitive functions, Piaget (1951) went a step further regarding the usefulness of make-believe play. He noticed how some young children used their representational skills to revisit events or situations that were anxiety-provoking (such as a visit to the dentist). In so doing, the child is said to be more in control the second time and to come to terms with the experience better. In fact, long before then, others (such as Freud, 1920) already explored how the inner world of a child's psyche could be revealed through play. Some observed how children re-enact difficult or troubling situations through pretend play as a vehicle to express and control their feelings. Still, it is difficult to ascertain the impact of such play without due empirical evidence even though its potential therapeutic value and emotional significance are noteworthy.

Besides rehearsing and consolidating representational skills, which is Piaget's position on play, Vygotsky (1933/1978) actually regarded make-believe play itself as a zone of proximal development (ZPD; Chapter 2) – a vital tool for extending cognitive and social skills. He saw such play contexts as liberating the child from situational constraints to explore novel ways of thinking, behaving and relating that would not be used in other activities which do not require imagination or rely on external stimuli. Meanwhile, with assigned roles and rules, such play demands that they suppress their impulses to comply with such expectations, particularly as the child needs to think or plan with peers before or during play in such contexts. Studies have shown that make-believe can enhance performance on cognitive tasks including attention (Ruff and Capozzoli, 2003), self-regulation (Elias and Berk, 2002) or emotional understanding (Lindsey and Colwell, 2003), among others. Children who display more sociodramatic play are seen as more socially competent, with their interactions lasting longer and attracting more additional peers to the group, compared to social play that does not include pretend elements (Creasey *et al.*, 1998).

STOP AND THINK

Revisit the case study of six year old Alliyah and Laura playing at 'lost babies'. Now, imagine them building a jigsaw puzzle together. Can you think of what kind of skills they show in 'lost babies' that are not needed for playing the puzzle? And vice versa?

Less research has examined the functions of physical play such as rough-and-tumble play, perhaps because its 'obvious' benefits in physical development such as strengthening muscles and increasing fitness are taken for granted. At the same time, the play-fighting behaviour and interactions are very similar to those on show in the young of many mammal species, suggesting that this form of play can serve a social function from an evolutionary perspective (see Pellegrini, 2006).

It has been argued that rough-and-tumble play sets the path for establishing a 'dominance hierarchy' (Pellegrini and Smith, 1998), which is a stable 'pecking order' that denotes each member's position in conflict settings. The more dominant members are able to win over others in conflict and have an advantage over them with access to resources. Thus, rough-and-tumble play may be seen as a way for children to test and realise their own and others' strength and establish their positions with respect to this kind of dominance. In regular scuffles or arguments between children, there is often a consistent pattern of winners and losers that remains relatively stable through middle childhood, and during adolescence play-fighting is often used (especially by boys) to challenge each other and attempt a rise in status on a 'safe' situation (without getting harmed in a 'real' fight). Interestingly, not only does rough-and-tumble play not lead to aggression, it can lead to continued affiliation (through further games) as it usually involves friends. Boys who play-fight tend to be popular (see Peer groups and social status) and have a wider variety of strategies for solving social problems (reviewed by Pellegrini, 2006). Perhaps rough-and-tumble play affords the opportunities to practise initiating and maintaining more interactions with peers.

Play, as a dominant and dynamic form of peer interactions, is multifaceted and multifunctional. Although the jury is out as to whether play 'causes' specific learning and development, it is clear that it is demanding on social and cognitive skills and can serve as a platform towards further interactions. It is noteworthy that, whether play is physical and vigorous or sedentary and symbolic, children have to engage themselves and each other as active participants in the process to sustain the shared activity. With advances in modern technology, particularly the electronic kinds, some of such active agency may not be as much in demand and it is worth pondering on the impact that it may have on the interactive learning we have just come across (see Cutting Edge box).

Peer groups and social status

At this point, we have read that the nature of the peer group and its interactions evolves with age, and evaluated some of the most influential forms of play along with their likely functions in learning and skills development. Meanwhile, many researchers have noticed individual differences between children in their 'readiness' for this kind of social interaction, that some children seem to be 'better' than others at interacting with their peers or be more easily accepted into a peer group than others. In the same vein, some children find it particularly hard to join peer groups, or even get 'rejected' by others in such groups. Some children seem to 'hang in the balance' in that they are not strictly rejected, but nor are they welcome by their peers at all. These phenomena are what are often referred to as children's peer social status. This is a way to look at the extent to which different children are accepted and liked (or rejected and disliked) by their peers. It is important to point out that, unlike friendship (which we will cover later), this kind of acceptance, liking or popularity by peers, does not involve a mutual reciprocal relationship between two children, but only the peer group's perspective of a child and not the child's perspective of the group. Even a widely rejected child may still have a friend or two, if popular children are likely to have more friends since they are well liked by a much bigger pool of peers with whom they can make friends.

Over the years, psychologists have investigated 'what makes' some children more or less accepted and liked than others. Research has investigated whether it is something to do with the accepted or rejected child herself or whether it is more to do with the peer group. Such

Definitions

Dominance hierarchy: a relatively stable ordering of different status members by their ability to win in conflict that signifies different access to resources accordingly, established by challenges through rough-and-tumble play.
Social status: the extent of acceptance or likeability of individual children by the peer group, different from friendship as the group's general view of the individual.

CUTTING EDGE

Does gaming damage or 'teach' children about interactions?

A recent government poll (Williams, 4 January 2010, in *The Guardian*) reports that one in six children under the age of seven have 'difficulty talking', a problem that worried families may blame on their children's on-screen gaming experiences.

Tom Chatfield (a web designer/developer and regular contributor to *Guardian Technology*) suggests that we tried to understand the '21st century generation' who inherit it and learnt the dynamics of gaming life, which can be a place that is not so much about 'escaping the commitments and interactions that make friendships "real" as it is about a sophisticated set of satisfactions with their own increasingly urgent reality and challenges' (Chatfield, 2010).

Chatfield cites and describes a list of computer games involving virtual worlds some of which offer users a chatroom where they can 'interact' with each other within virtual graphical locations, which they themselves had created and could 'have and do anything you liked'. Others involve players 'banding together' to earn greater rewards through accumulative 'achievement' points – only attainable by hundreds of hours of effort – while also lifting their individual score

in the global rankings which is seen as an 'awesome' engine for 'engaging a networked community'. Indeed LAN (Local Area Network) parties are becoming quite common, with the largest hosted in 2007 at DreamHack in Jönköping, Sweden with 10 445 connected computers. Thus computing games can actually be very creative and very sociable.

- Have you played any computer game of the descriptions above?
- Do you agree or disagree with Chatfield's analysis and comments? How strongly?
- How do 'virtual' interactions differ from 'real' ones when children play such games?

As the author comments, virtual interactions cannot replace real ones, but some elements of gameplay may be comparable to those in 'real life', such as how to collaborate and negotiate towards a shared goal. However, one key missing element is the true identity of the player. Within these LAN parties, a strong sense of identity appears to be asserted with each player generating an avatar that they become known by which, although not true, can have benefits as it conceals social categories such as gender, ethnicity or attractiveness, which can affect peer status (see the next sections).

It is argued that some elements of interactive computer game-play may be comparable to those in real life.

Source: Pearson Education Ltd./Photodisc/Ryan McVay

work is obviously important, as a child's peer status could affect how she feels; no one wants to be rejected! And, of course, with very few peers accepting them, or even some actively rejecting them, some children may 'forego' the opportunities for peer interactions and play, like those we read earlier, which can then in turn affect their learning and development. In the following we will review research that has identified these different types of children, their characteristics that may make them accepted, rejected or neglected and the consequences that peer status can lead to.

There have been different methods for measuring children's social status over the years. Some of these involve directly asking members in a peer group to nominate others within the group who they favour the most, or want to associate with the most. Similarly, they can also be asked to nominate those that they least like or want least to associate with (e.g. each pupil in a class may be asked to name a few classmates by a researcher saying, 'Who in this class would you like to sit with/play with the most?' and 'Who in this class would you not like to sit/play with?'). Then those that receive the most nominations of 'most liked' and 'least liked' would be the most accepted and rejected, respectively (and those that receive few of either can be seen as the neglected children). Alternatively, children may be asked to evaluate each other within the peer group, by giving a rating on a Likert scale (from 1, most dislike, to 5, most like), for instance. Then each child will have a popularity/acceptance score.

Children may also be directly observed, say, in a school playground, over a set period of time, to see who interacts with whom, and how often, which gives an idea of how 'sought after' each child is by other children. The most 'popular' children would be those who are approached or engaged by the greatest number of other children, the 'rejected' children may approach their peers but are usually avoided by them, and the neglected ones are those that neither approach nor 'get approached' by other (see the Research methods box for sociometry).

Peer acceptance

Accepted children are those who are generally most liked and chosen as a 'playmate' by their peers. Not surprisingly, attraction can be 'skin-deep' and physical appearance can make a child more popular; both attractive and physically larger children (Dion and Berscheid, 1974) and adolescents (Boyatzis *et al.*, 1998) tend to fall

into this category. Still, other characteristics that can be helped (by children) contribute more to social status. Many accepted or popular children are academically and socially competent, in that they are able to communicate with others in a friendly, warm and sensitive way, and are generally more positive, cooperative and supportive compared with other types of children (Cillessen and Bellmore, 2004). In conflicts, such children excel at negotiation and compromise (Rose and Asher, 1999), and in joining in activities, they are adept at adjusting their behaviour to 'fit in' (Rubin *et al.*, 1998; Cillessen and Bellmore, 2004). Perhaps this is due to their better emotional understanding (Underwood, 1997) and perspective-taking skills (Fitzgerald and White, 2003).

More occasionally, and usually in later childhood or adolescence, children are identified as popular *due to* their belligerent or 'antisocial' behaviour being associated with being 'cool'. In particular, among boys, they tend to have good athletic skills, but will deliberately challenge authority or get into trouble and fights, which can enhance their status further, especially among a youth culture that values aggressive behaviour (Stormshak *et al.*, 1999). Among girls, such 'antisocial popularity' tends to decline with age as they become increasingly socially aggressive and controlling where peers start to question and resent their manipulative tactics and reject them (Cillessen and Mayeux, 2004).

Peer rejection

Rejected children are the most concerning group since rejection is related to poor developmental outcomes (see later); hence this phenomenon has received more research. These are children who are least liked or even disliked the most or are least likely to be picked as playmates. Such unpopularity most likely comes from a child's aggressive, disruptive or uncooperative behaviour. They lack social skills in that they may fail to take turns and interrupt play, for instance. It may be

Definitions

Accepted children: children who are popular, accepted or well liked by the majority of other children in the peer group.
Rejected children: children who are unpopular, avoided as a playmate or least liked or disliked by others in the peer group.

RESEARCH METHODS

Sociometry

How accepted each child within the peer group is can be identified as an 'index' of that child's relative standing, and this way of charting their social status is known as sociometry, or sociometric techniques. The data obtained can then be used to plot a 'sociogram', which illustrates the pattern of overall interactions between children in the wider peer group, apart from individual children's 'sociometric status'. One of the early researchers to do this kind of charting of peer group statuses was Anne Clark with her colleagues in the 1960s (Clark *et al.*, 1969). Figure 12.1 shows their sociogram based on the observations of free play in a US nursery. Each small circle (girl) or triangle (boy) represents a child in the group. The lines between them indicate the proportions of time these relevant children play together. The large circles indicate the number of playmates each child has.

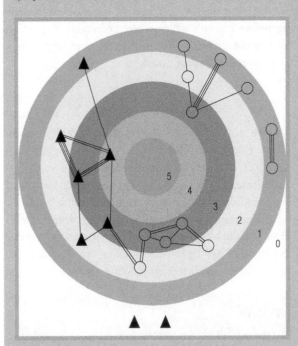

Figure 12.1. Sociogram of peer social status in a nursery.

(Source: Clark *et al.,* 1969)

One of the first features that 'stands out' immediately from the sociogram is the two boys that are isolated (outside of the concentric circles). The rest of the group are socially linked in some way; in particular, the other boys are part of a loose 'network' around a 'triad' of boys closely associated together. In contrast, the girls are relatively segregated as a larger gender group, though they have their own 'cliques' in the form of dyads and smaller groups. Finally, it is clear that the children do not interact across gender much at all; there is only one boy–girl connection in the peer group. This is in line with other research in both nursery and school interactions (as we read earlier).

- Do you think the sociometric technique is a good way to measure peer social status?
- Are there differences between the different ways of collecting data about social status: peer nominations, peer ratings and direct observations?
- Which way do you think is the most accurate? Which one is the most consistent?

As with using the different relevant data collection methods in other research topics, both reliability and validity (see Chapter 3, Research Methods) depends in part on the informants that give or chart the data, here the children and the researchers. Whereas the self-reporting methods (peer nominations and ratings) depend on the perspectives, memory and honesty of children who supply the data, direct observations of children depend on the skills and interpretations of the researchers that observe and document the children's interactions.

Definition

Sociometry: a technique that charts the relative standing of children within their peer group where data of their popularity/acceptance can be collected by self-reporting of peer preferences or observations of their interactions with each other.

because many have poor control of their emotional expressions (Eisenberg *et al.*, 1995). There is some evidence that such children also have poorer perspective-taking skills (Crick *et al.*, 2002). This has been manifest in how boys may misinterpret their peers' innocent and playful behaviours as having hostile intent – for example, in the case of play-fighting, as we read earlier – and respond in kind with aggression. Thus, unlike the 'antisocial' kind of aggression that older popular children display that enhances their peer status, these aggressive and rejected children tend to be more antagonistic against their peers and get into conflicts that elicit these peers' hostility, which in turn confirm their own expectation that other people are hostile to them (Dodge *et al.*, 1990).

In contrast, rejection or unpopularity of some children may also arise from the characteristics opposite to those of aggression. These children are seen as 'withdrawn' in that they are passive, timid even, or socially awkward. They may suffer from social anxiety, so much so that they fear the challenge of approaching their peers as they hold negative expectations about how others will treat them and worry about being rejected which itself then becomes a self-fulfilling prophecy (Ladd and Burgess, 1999). In fact, rejected and withdrawn children are often aware that they are disliked (Harrist *et al.*, 1997), but many rejected and aggressive children assume that others like them (Zakriski and Coie, 1996).

Although it is the case that many rejected children lack some social skills that are needed to interact effectively with peers, it is important to note that rejection may not always be a *result* of the child's lacking such skills. Sometimes children may react strongly to rejection by already formed and popular 'cliques' that exclude others, and in doing so exhibit what is labelled as maladjusted behaviour. These children may not lack social skills and be rejected in other situations.

Peer neglect

There are certain children that are neither strongly liked nor strongly disliked, unlike either of the categories of children above. Not particularly aggressive or shy, many neglected children are nevertheless socially inept and unassertive, and tend to play by themselves or on the fringes of larger peer groups. Surprisingly, despite their rarer interactions with others, many neglected children do not report feeling unhappy and lonely, nor are they

that bothered about being neglected or ignored by their peers (McElhaney *et al.*, 2008). It is possible that their peer status is simply a function of their personality; they prefer to be by themselves.

Many neglected children are in fact as 'well adjusted' as their peers, and may even share some of the characteristics with their 'accepted' counterparts. Some such children are skilled enough to join in with peer activities if they so wish (Harrist *et al.*, 1997; Ladd and Burgess, 1999). As such their 'neglect' status may be just temporary as it is possible for them to raise their level of acceptance over time (Rubin *et al.*, 1998). By this token, we then may start to question how it is 'exactly' that children come to be classified into their social status categories, and how accurate, fair and consistent such classification is (see the Research Methods box).

Consequences of social status

Now we have identified a few major categories of children, according to their status with their peers and how they come to be categorised as such, it is worth noting that once a child has been associated with a given status, such an association tends to remain as the child is known by his 'reputation', even if the child's behaviour changes (Rubin *et al.*, 1998). That can be particularly 'hard-going' for a child who is known to be rejected, to try to be accepted even if he improves his social skills. This is because, once that bad reputation is attached, his behaviour tends to be interpreted accordingly whether or not it fits with this reputation.

It is also important to note that not all children fall into the popular, rejected or neglected categories; many are none of these. For instance, children may be 'average' in that they are measured as having average popularity/acceptance or peer ratings and they arouse no strong feelings in others. Furthermore, there is a minority of so-called 'controversial' children who are most liked by some peers *as well as* most disliked by others (Coie *et al.*, 1983). As noted earlier, certain children do show some status 'mobility', particularly many neglected children

> **Definition**
>
> Neglected children: children who are neither accepted nor rejected, or not strongly liked or disliked, by their peer group

whose status is unstable. As they are at least not totally without social interaction, neglected, average and even controversial children do not seem to be particularly disadvantaged by their status, as many manage to make some friends (see Children's friendships in the next section). However, although neglected children can do quite as well in school as popular children (Wentzel and Asher, 1995), they are more prone to loneliness and depression (Cillessen et al., 1992), and may blame their teachers for not dealing with their social dilemma (Galanaki, 2004). The link between depression and peer neglect may be explained by brain-imaging research showing that social neglect and physical pain stimulate the same part of the brain (Eisenberger, 2003).

Not surprisingly, the most accepted or popular children, perhaps due to their friendly and outgoing dispositions, tend to show the highest levels of sociability and cognitive ability and the lowest of aggressiveness and withdrawal, compared with other status groups in later years. They also tend to enjoy greater academic success and are better adjusted in adult life (Bagwell et al., 1998). However, this may have more to do with their characteristics that have led them to become popular rather than being a direct benefit resulting from their social status. Also, the reasons for their popularity are important within the peer context. As covered earlier, some older peer cultures value 'antisocial' inappropriate behaviour such as challenging authority. Obviously, such behaviours and the popularity that comes with it go against positive school adjustments (Allen et al., 2005).

As mentioned previously, it is the rejected children that are most problematic; they form the group that suffers the greatest disadvantages, as they are most likely to experience a lack of regular social contact. For the rejected and aggressive children, they spend more time arguing and fighting rather than in social play or conversation, and even if they do that is often in smaller groups and with younger or other rejected children. As they are often unaware that they are disliked or even over-estimate their popularity, this can make them increasingly unpopular over time (Hughes et al., 1997). By adolescence, these children often do poorly in school (Wentzel and Asher, 1995) and are at greater risk of so-called 'externalising problems' which are the negative 'acting out' behaviours including interpersonal violence and delinquency. They are more likely to drop out from school due to adjustment difficulties, including playing truants or becoming bullies, and are also at risk of associating with antisocial gangs (Cairns et al., 1988).

Without intervention, and excluded from 'normal' peer interactions, rejected and aggressive children could continue to miss out on the opportunities presented by these exchanges to learn to handle competitions and conflicts and create cooperation. Indeed there is evidence that such individuals are at risk of longer-term rejection and troubled relationships (Rubin et al., 1998). Excess aggressiveness in fact is one of the few definite aspects of earlier functioning that predicts future emotional disturbances and behavioural problems (see Chapter 10). However, it should be noted that problematic peer interactions in early childhood can themselves be a 'sign' of deeper maladjustments that are reflected in later disturbances, rather than rejection which itself may have resulted from such maladjustments.

At the same time, the rejected but withdrawn children have a rather different set of developmental outcomes. These children may have tried to gain acceptance by their peers and failed, then eventually give up and become even more withdrawn and feel extremely lonely. This can happen as early as in nursery and, as their feelings of loneliness rise, while self-esteem lowers, their school achievement suffers and many may avoid school (Buhs and Ladd, 2001). Such are seen as 'internalising' problems as social anxiety and depression. Since they distrust others, most have few or no friends (see Friendship), who tend to be also withdrawn children lacking in social skills and confidence (Rubin et al., 2006).

Both types of rejected children are at risk for peer harassment, but they would take on the opposite roles due to their disposition. The aggressive children tend to act as bullies (see Chapter 15, Understanding Bullying), as they behave with hostility and read hostile intent into others' behaviour. Withdrawn children are particularly likely to be picked on as victims due to their insecure, fearful and submissive demeanour (Sandstrom and Cillessen, 2003).

We have seen how different children can have different propensities to interact effectively with peers partly due to their existing characteristics, but also the nature of the peer context. As such, they fall into several types of peer social status, which come with different developmental outcomes and even likelihood towards longer-term adjustment issues (the main traits of key status groups and their possible outcomes are summarised in

Neglected children may prefer to be alone or join in play if they wish.

Source: Bubbles Photolibrary/ Loisjoy Thurston

Table 12.3). These findings are important for a variety of interventions that are aimed to improve peer interactions and psychological adjustments of those at-risk children (rejected children in particular), such as through coaching positive social skills and emotional understanding or reinforcing friendly interaction and cooperation (DeRosier, 2007). As part of the pathway towards better adjustments, but itself also a positive outcome, children

Table 12.3. Characteristics and outcomes of accepted, rejected and neglected children.

Status type	Characteristics	Outcomes
Accepted	Physically attractive Warm and friendly character Interact positively and cooperatively Good at negotiation and compromise Adjust behaviour to join in play Good perspective-taking skills	High sociability Good cognitive skills Low aggressiveness Little social withdrawal Academic success Better adjusted as adults
Rejected aggressive	Aggressive, disruptive or uncooperative Poor control of emotions Lack etiquette for joining in play Poor perspective-taking skills Antagonistic and hostile/read hostile intent Unaware that they are disliked	Poor school performance At risk of school dropout, violence and delinquency Longer-term behavioural/ emotional maladjustments and troubled relationships
Rejected withdrawn	Passive, timid or socially awkward Hold negative expectations of others Do not approach/hesitate to join peers Aware that they are disliked	Low self-esteem Poor school achievement and school avoidance Social anxiety/depression
Neglected	Socially inept and unassertive Play alone or on the fringes of large groups May not be unhappy/prefer to be alone May join in peer group and raise acceptance	Not always disadvantaged Can make some friends More prone to loneliness May trigger depression

strike promising relationships with one another, or 'make friends'. In the following final section of this chapter, we will look at friendship as a special relationship between peers, its nature through development, the factors which influence it and its functions and implications.

Children's friendships

The vast majority of children, as we have read, in one form of another engage in meaningful interactions with their peers, and some peers are more sought after than others. However, just being preferred the most by many other children is not the same as being a 'friend' to those children. Friendship usually refers to a *mutual* association between two (or more) children, that is both/all parties involved in the companionship want to be with the other(s) and are more positive and cooperative towards each other than other peers. Epstein (1989) distinguished three bases for selection of friends by children. The first basis is simple physical proximity: children are more likely to choose friends from the children they meet in the home, in their street and in their pre-school

Definition

Friendship: a mutual reciprocal relationship between two or more people where both or all parties involved want to spend more time with the other(s) than other peers.

or class at school. The second basis of friendship is sharing characteristics like age and sex. Boys are more likely to make friends with other boys of the same age and girls are more likely to make friends with other girls of the same age. Once a child has selected other children as friends based on these characteristics, Epstein argues that the friendships are more likely to continue if the children share similar interests and attitudes. Within this special kind of relationship where the children choose to spend more time with each other than other peers, sensitivity, trust and closeness tend to build up over time. Meanwhile, friends can also have more disagreement with each other than they do with other people, probably because we have more opportunities to disagree with those we spend more time with. However, with trust and understanding and other complex psychological elements involved in friendships, it is expected that disagreements can be resolved by more negotiation or compromise to find a mutually acceptable solution. Disagreements with those who are not friends are less likely to be resolved with such an outcome.

Over the next subsections we will look closely at children's friendships across the age groups to review their differences in quality before we look into other factors that influence the development of friendships between different children. Finally, we will evaluate the research that investigates the functions of children's friendships and the developmental outcomes and long-term implications of these friendships.

Friendships through the years

Just as there are qualitative differences in peer interactions over the age groups in terms of complexity, there are differences in friendship quality too, not surprisingly as friendships evolve from such interactions. We will first look at the different ages children see each other as 'friends' and the features of their friendships. Then we will evaluate a stage model that has been used to explain such changes.

Early childhood/preschool ages

Although there is evidence that toddlers show play preferences for some peers over others (Howes, 1983, 1987), it is difficult to ascertain that they consciously view these peers as 'friends'. Also, although we have already mentioned complex ideas like 'trust' and 'closeness', ask pre-schoolers to tell us who their friends are, and why those are their friends, their responses tend to be much simpler, such as 'they play with me' (Selman, 1980). This will in part have something to do with their limited vocabulary, but it is indeed true that, as we read earlier in the chapter, at such tender ages children spend most of their time playing. At this stage, children regard friendships casually, as something that can start easily and 'concretely', such as by seeing each other regularly even in passing, or sharing toys a lot, and thus such friendships will also end abruptly, such as when one party refuses to share or cannot play with the other.

Still, the stability of friendships increases even during this period; almost 20% of three year olds spend more of their time with one other child and this rises to over half at four years (Hinde *et al.*, 1985). Compared to other associations, such pairs also show extended interaction, mutual liking, more reciprocity and support and less negative behaviour towards one another (Maguire and Dunn, 1997), Moreover, as we saw in Clark *et al.*'s (1969) study, in nursery children already largely segregate themselves by gender, forming regular associations only with those of their own sex.

Middle childhood/school ages

Through the school years, many interactions are still dominated by the shared activities within the school and those afforded by the family outside of school, though the contexts in which such interactions take place widen compared to pre-school. Thus although friendship in earlier school ages (around six to eight years) is still based on common activities and physical proximity (Bigelow and La Gaipa, 1980), eventually a 'friend' is more than just a regular playmate, but someone that shares beliefs, rules, expectations about sanctions and so on. The progression reflects children's distinction of friendship from acquaintances or more casual relationships, and a cognitive shift from a focus on the 'physical' to the more 'psychological' (see Chapter 2, Theoretical Perspectives). This is when the 'deeper' elements of closeness and trust start to emerge, and children as friends recognise each other's personal qualities, needs and wants where each party is expected to support the

other in times of need. For instance, it has been found that if children view that a child should help a friend when the friend is being teased by other peers even if it might risk the child being teased by others also, they are more likely to have more friends than those who think that the child should not help her friend in this scenario to avoid lowering her own status (Rose and Asher, 2004). Indeed, any violation of trust, including not helping a friend when help is needed and breaking a promise, is seen as a serious breach of friendship

Behaviourally, children who claim to be friends with each other do tend to talk more with each other, and are more tactile and affectionate, as well as supportive and cooperative towards each other than when they are with other children (Hartup, 2006). Because of these features, school-aged children's friendships are more selective than pre-schoolers' and they do claim fewer if closer friends than preschoolers, particularly among girls, who value closeness and exclusivity more than boys.

Adolescence

By the time children are 11–12 years old, they begin to value closeness or intimacy in friendship where they can share more of their 'inner feelings', such as secrets, with their friends and are also more knowledgeable and understanding about one another's feelings. In turn, they expect a friend to be loyal, faithful, trustworthy and supportive (Hartup, 2006). The individuals involved work harder on compromise and negotiation towards maintaining their exclusiveness. As a result, friendships between adolescents tend to be more stable and enduring than those of younger children; only about 20% of friendships formed before the age of 11–12 years last as long as a year, versus 40% of the friendships formed three years later by the same individuals (Cairns and Cairns, 1994). As the adolescent's focus is more on 'quality' rather than 'quantity' of her friendship, the degree of selectivity becomes even higher where the number of 'best friendships' declines (from four to six in middle childhood to just one or two in adolescence), particularly among girls (Hartup and Stevens, 1999).

Meanwhile, compared to younger children adolescents are also more 'realistic' about the durability of friendship; they acknowledge that their friends cannot fulfil all their needs and that friendships can change over time, that friends can become closer or less close as people or circumstances change. For example, a girl who changes her status by getting a boyfriend will spend less time with her female friends and this can lead to their ending the friendships if those friends have not yet got boyfriends. Some adolescents may also mature faster or achieve higher academically or athletically than their friends and if such achievement domains are important to them, such differences in status can mark the beginning of an end in some friendships (Akers *et al.*, 1998). However, at these ages, adolescents also surmise that good-quality friendships can adapt to changes and last long.

Stages in children's conception of friendships

Looking at the features identified above of children's friendships at different ages, from a developmental perspective it would appear that children's ideas of what friendships are 'about' go through a sequence of stages that reflect certain changes in their socio-cognitive understanding. The well-regarded American psychologist Robert Selman (1980) clearly advocates this school of thought. He observed the age-related transformations in how children construe and interpret friendships and related these to general development of social cognition. To do so, he interviewed many children and told

Mary and Sally have been friends since they were five years old. A new girl, Rosie, starts in their class. Mary doesn't like Rosie much because she thinks Rosie is a show-off. One day Rosie invites Mary to go with her to the park, and this places Mary in a dilemma because she has already promised Sally that she will go to her house on that day. What will Mary do?

Selman's stories and questions probe into the kind of friendship (e.g., how much trust and understanding) between the protagonists, and a comparison between striking new friendships (Mary and Rosie) and keeping old ones (Mary and Sally).

Figure 12.2. An example of a friendship dilemma by Selman (1980) (names and some features of story changed).

them stories, which were centred around a friendship 'dilemma'. He asked them some questions about the relationships between the characters in the story, and how the dilemma should best be resolved (an example is given in Fig. 12.2).

From his analysis of the responses provided by 3 to 15 year old children, Selman claimed to find evidence for four main stages in the development of their conceptions of friendship corresponding to their perspective-taking skills. These stages are listed in Table 12.4.

Table 12.4. Selman's (1980) stages of friendship definition.

Stage	Age (years)	Description
Momentary physical playmate	3–5	Define friends in terms of shared activities and geographical associations; friends are children they play with, live nearby or go to same school; refer to friends in here-and-now; no reference to personal characteristics/psychological attributes
One-way assistance	6–8	Friend is someone who helps you or does things that please you; need to become aware of each other's likes/dislikes; no reciprocal nature yet
Fairweather cooperation	9–12	Key feature reciprocal understanding; evelutate friends' action/know friends can judge them and adapt or take account of each other's preferences. Disagreement/conflicts still end friendship
Mutual concern	11–15	Can take perspective of other people; friendship as a bond built over time and made strong/stable by mutual support, concern and understanding; compatible interests, values and personalities; fiercely protected; can withstand minor conflicts

STOP AND THINK

- Do you agree with Selman's stages of friendship?
- Do you think some children may be capable of a more or less sophisticated notion of friendship at those ages?

It is clear that Selman sees children's understanding of friendships as a linear progression from their focus on the physical characteristics of friends (such as where they live, what they do) to the psychological attributes (from likes/dislikes to values). This is likened to general development in social and cognitive abilities (like Piaget's theory; see Chapter 2) where the child's focus turns from the external to the internal, and he can increasingly take another person's perspective.

While Selman's stages make sense and are supported by his and others' data, other researchers that have explored children's associations in other ways have found that young children's meanings of friendships can be broader and deeper than what is in Selman's descriptions. For example, the sociologist William Corsaro spent several months in a nursery to make extensive 'natural' observations of children's activities. He paid particular attention to how these children talked with one another when they referred to the word 'friend' (Corsaro, 1985). He identified six categories from such talk where the most frequently invoked were when children used being 'friends' as a gateway to join in play and when they played they mentioned that they were 'friends'. While these do fit with the activity-based description appropriate for the age group in Selman's model, the other four categories, less frequently observed, showed children using friendship in abstract ways: to mark 'sides' in competitions (friends versus non-friends), to exclude others from joint activities (only friends play), to express concern for others (when a friend is absent) and to use 'best friends' as a measure of their care and mutual concern for each other and their feelings (see the example in Fig. 12.3).

From the example, their talk can be seen to show implicitly a more advanced level of understanding about friends even though both children are under age four years. One child felt the need to justify being away from her friend and the other had felt the need to know. Such mutual concern is expected only from the last stages in Selman's model. Corsaro did say that the children involved had a closer relationship than most others (and this is the only example in this category). Nevertheless, the intricacies of interactions show that it is useful to consider the context in which friendship is made sense of by children, some of who may develop understanding beyond their years.

Jenny and Betty, not quite four years old, are climbing into a large wooden box. Betty has just returned to play with Jenny after having been with another girl for most of the morning.

Betty to Jenny:	I do like you, Jenny. I do.
Jenny to Betty:	I know it.
Betty to Jenny:	Yeah. But I just ran away from you. You know why?
Jenny to Betty:	Why?
Betty to Jenny:	Because I –
Jenny to Betty:	You wanted to play with Linda?
Betty to Jenny:	Yeah.
Jenny to Betty:	I ranned away with you. Wasn't that funny?
Betty to Jenny:	Yes.
Jenny to Betty:	Cause I wanted to know what happened.
Betty to Jenny:	I know you wanted – all the time you wanna know because you're my best friend.
Jenny to Betty:	Right.

Figure 12.3. An extract of 3 year olds' talk about friendship.

(*Source:* Corsaro, 1985, p. 166.)

Factors influencing children's friendships

We have seen how the quality of children's friendship changes over the course of development; with age, most friendships tend to become more intimate, reciprocal and enduring, even though some children may strive to achieve these features in their friendships a little younger. Apart from age, there are other factors that can influence the nature of friendship, in that children involved in certain friendship groups may do different things from those in other groups, or children from similar backgrounds and who share some other characteristics may become friends more easily or stay friends for longer. We will look at some of these factors in the following.

Personality and preferences

As the saying goes 'birds of a feather flock together', and this certainly seems to be true for the formation of friendships. We tend to choose others like ourselves to become friends as we have the same frame of reference and thus are more likely to share each other's points of view. Children are no different and their friends also resemble themselves in personality, social status, academic achievement, pro-social behaviour and interpersonal judgements (Haselager et al., 1998). This is particularly important for adolescents as they value even more mutual affirmation and cooperation. Their friends tend to be similar to themselves in identity status (see Chapter 13, Adolescence), academic orientation, political beliefs, attitudes to drugs and law-breaking behaviour (Akers et al., 1998). Occasionally, a change in circumstances such as entering a new school or neighbourhood can mean exploring friendships with those with alternative views. Also, in early adolescence, some may forgo similarity in favour of a popular peer. However, once similarities in personality and preference are identified, children tend to spend more time together, thus becoming even more alike in their attitudes, values, behaviour and achievements (Berndt and Keefe, 1995).

Gender group and identity

As we have explored earlier in this chapter and in Chapter 11, Development of Self-Concept and Gender

Identity, by school ages children already show preferences for same-sex playmates and this tendency increases into adolescence. The friendships that they build on, and get reinforced by, segregated interactions unsurprisingly are also single-sex (Lloyd and Duveen, 1992), and there are qualitative differences in gender friendships. As boys' interactions are often activity-based and competitive (like team sports), their friendship groups are larger and more inclusive but focus on competition or dominance over school or sport achievements, and conflict is quite common. In contrast, girls' friendship groups tend to be smaller, and more exclusive and intensive as they share more emotional closeness and support by talking about their feelings (Maccoby, 2002). Such differences are linked to gender identity and role expectations (see Chapter 11); more 'masculine' boys are less likely to have intimate friendships, and there is recent evidence that emotional management is linked to having fewer friends among boys (Dunsmore et al., 2008). However, girls have more friends if they can better manage to control their emotions which is critical for self-disclosure and agreeability.

Still, it is important to emphasise that there are overall commonalities between boys' and girls' friendships; both value collaboration and cooperation among friends. Also, although boys' friendships differ in the style of communication and exchanges, it does not mean that intimacy is less important to them. Boys' friendships have been likened to 'contradictions of masculine identities' (Frosh et al., 2002). As toughness and masculinity are inextricably linked, there is a discrepancy between their need for emotional closeness and difficulty in discussing it with male friends.

Friendship and technology

Earlier we examined the contentious issues surrounding computer game-play and children's ability to communicate and interact with each other. Since the massive increase in computer use and access to the internet and other interactive technologies in the 1990s, children all over the industrialised world and beyond have been utilising these means to also make and develop friendships. The forms of this medium include email, instant messaging, chatrooms, blogs, social networking sites (such as MySpace and Facebook) and of course texts and calls with personal mobile phones. In the early days, the medium was particularly popular with boys, who often started collaborative simulation games, like the ones we looked at, before moving on to visiting chatrooms, and studies suggest that such game co-playing experiences promote the development of the masculine identity in teenage boys (Sanford and Madill, 2006).

These days, children use computers in much the same ways as they use other environments. Through online 'spaces', they explore issues that they may or may not discuss in 'real life', including sexuality, peer and parental relationships and conflicts and even personal issues such as drug-taking and eating disorders, particularly among teenagers. Perhaps because of the 'non-face-to-face' contexts of communication, they may feel less inhibited and 'open up' more. Indeed there is some evidence that instant messaging, teenagers' preferred form of 'virtual' interactions, increases the feelings of intimacy and well-being between existing friends (Valkenburg and Peter, 2007).

Interestingly, the division of gender roles is still very apparent in this context as it is in real life (with girls interacting in more verbal and boys in more graphical role-play). However, when a cross-sex pair interacts, the boy adopts a more feminine interacting style (Calvert *et al.*, 2003). This may be due to the anonymity that 'frees' boys from the need to behave in a stereotypical way.

Although the anonymous and relatively unmonitored virtual environments of the internet may seem to offer more freedom and discretion to children who conduct their friendships in this medium, there are also certain hazards from online exchanges that adults are particularly concerned about. The internet is not only used for keeping in touch, but some friendships are started this way, particularly in chatrooms, forums and networking sites. Some such friendships, often between the sexes, are then taken 'offline' where the friends meet face-to-face. Parents may be rightly concerned about such meetings as, with anonymity, online identities can be assumed and manipulated, and some online 'friends' may have disingenuous motives other than making friends, including impostors who are adults befriending children in such websites.

The frequently uncensored processes of 'e-communication' can also mean that children are more likely to encounter (sexual or racial) harassment, abuse or bullying in this medium (Tynes *et al.*, 2004). Indeed such non-face-to-face threats can be even more easily conveyed through the use of mobile phones that offer children and young people even more 'parent-free' and literally

'mobile' interactions. The prevalence, nature and co. quences of the negative impact from such electron. forms of communication on children's relationships will be unveiled later in the book (see Chapter 15, Understanding Bullying for cyberbullying). At the same time, it is worth keeping in mind that although things may 'go wrong' between friends through the electronic medium, these are but a set of 'tools' children use to conduct usually existing friendships.

STOP AND THINK

Imagine your friend sends you an email or a text that makes you very unhappy or tells you some unwelcome news (say, they heard a mutual friend speak badly of you).

Do you think that you would be unhappier or less unhappy if this was communicated to you in person? Why?

Functions and implications of children's friendships

Now that we have learnt about the nature of friendship over development and how children make and keep friends, and what may facilitate or hinder the processes, this final section focuses on the functional question of what children's friendships are 'for' and what may be the implications of their having or not having good friendships. Intuitively it may seem obvious that having friends is better than having no friends; no one wants to be friendless or lonely! The crux of the matter is: how 'useful' exactly is having friends (especially when we have reviewed some of the potentially dubious or negative aspects of some kinds of friendship)? What is even more difficult is to show that any positive or negative outcome is *due to* having or not having friends. Here, we evaluate some of the social, cognitive and longer-term psychological developments in which children's friendships are argued to at least play a part.

Self-concept

As we covered in depth in Chapter 11, one achievement of development is to establish a sense of self, 'who we are'.

...es how we think about the world, ...xperiences and guides our social ... relationships. The objective self ...ves in relation to others – it is ...in the context of social relationships, first with parents and then more and more with peers. We have also read that what others think about and how they behave towards a child matters since early childhood, and increases in importance through to adolescence. This is a reason why being accepted, especially by those that we do care about or whose opinions we value – our friends – is important as this gives us a positive sense of self. With friends, the child also explores the social role and identity she has (e.g., leader or follower, boy or girl), and over time the norms of appearance, attitudes and behaviour will become absorbed into the child's self-concept.

'Belonging' is particularly significant for the adolescent's psychological wellbeing as in how others judge you, as peer group pressure (see Chapter 13) has never been more salient than it is in adolescence. As commitment to crowds and cliques wanes towards later adolescence, and before mixed-sex friendships begin, friends become even more sensitive to each other's personalities and strengths and weaknesses, a process that explores both themselves and others well and supports self-development, identity and perspective-taking (Savin-Williams and Berndt, 1990).

Problem-solving, learning and cognitive development

Children may not just play and chat with their friends; they may also interact in more formal capacities, such as working on a class-based task or other intellectual problems. There has been a great collection of evidence that collaboration with peers, particularly those that are friendly with them, can advance children's cognitive as well as social development (see Chapter 14, Development Psychology and Education). Without any adult instructions, two otherwise 'ignorant' (unknowing of the solution) children confronted with a problem, whether in a perceptual, number or moral decision task among others, often reach the solution eventually when neither has been able to achieve it alone. It is argued that, starting from each with a partial and incomplete perspective, the children exchange their ideas through active discussion until the new approach combining their individual ideas arrives; learning is promoted this way as a

joint discovery for greater cognitive development (Howe, 1993; Howe and Mercer, 2007). There is even evidence that friends – compared with non-friends – perform more effectively in such tasks (Fonzi et al., 1997). This is likely because they tend to propose more ideas than non-friends, and are better at sharing, negotiating and making compromises during potential conflicts, particularly between stable friendships that last through the school year as they display more sensitivity towards each other.

Psychological and school adjustments and future relationships

Apart from the obvious benefits shown for social and cognitive development, there are also more latent advantages from having friends. As friends are supposed to offer support, sensitivity and concern for one another, they should serve as a 'buffer' against stressful events such as family difficulties or maladaptive behaviours such as delinquency. Indeed evidence shows that friendships can promote psychological wellbeing by reducing the needs for antisocial acts, and adolescents who are under family stress but have close friends are comparable in wellbeing to those who are not under such stress (Gauze et al., 1996).

Having close friends in school is also conducive to better academic adjustment as school becomes a place where children enjoy interacting with others and they view school life in a more positive light (Berndt and Keefe, 1995). This is plausible; as we read earlier, children with poor peer acceptance (which likely leads to the shortage of friends) are at risk of school avoidance and dropout. There is also the argument that closer friendships lay the groundwork for later romantic relationships. It may be that emotional discussions first to same-sex friends prepares the adolescent for a similar disclosure to a romantic partner; indeed, we have also read that sexuality and relationships are common topics between friends.

There is even suggestion that the lack of friendships in childhood can lead to later psychopathology, such as being involved in juvenile or adult crime and needing psychiatric help. However, research is often correlational and cannot show any causal effect (Parker and Asher, 1987). There have been a handful of longitudinal studies (see the Lifespan box) that show such trends, but the results are still far from conclusive.

LIFESPAN

Stable childhood friendships – lifelong implications?

Research team, Catherine Bagwell, Andrew Newcomb and William Bukowski, followed up a small sample of 60 23 year old adults, in mid-Western USA, who had participated in one of their earlier studies some 13 years ago, aged 10 years. Thirty (fifteen males, fifteen females) adults had reported having a stable, mutual 'best friend' (who had also chosen them as best friend) at the earlier study, and this reciprocal friendship lasted over at least a month. As adults, the participants completed a questionnaire which asked them about how they had fared in school and their jobs, and their family interactions, social life, aspirations and participation in activities, and to report any mental health difficulties or criminal records. Standardised scales were also used to measure their perceptions of self-worth, self-reported work competence, friendships and romantic relationships and psychopathological symptoms. Furthermore, they were invited to be interviewed about the quality of friendship they had reported 13 years ago – as childhood friends, what they did together and features of the friendship including negative ones – which were rated according to the intensity and intimacy. The participants also gave details about their current same-sex best friend, who was invited to complete a questionnaire about the participants themselves.

The analyses revealed a clear association between the quality of childhood friendship and positive relationship with the family. Childhood friendship status (whether or not they had a best friend) strongly predicted feelings of positive self-esteem in adulthood. Not having had a best friend as children was associated with the presence of depressive symptoms in adulthood. However, interestingly, those having had a good-quality friendship in childhood did not rate themselves as being more competent in their friendships and romantic relationships in adulthood compared to those who had not had a best friend as children. The quality of childhood friendship did not correlate with the quality of adult friendship, as reported by the participants' current best friend, and self-reported level of social competence in the current best friendship.

- What would the researchers be able to establish about the links between childhood friendships and later outcomes in adulthood?
- What were they not able to show from the study?

As the researchers themselves warned, though there are statistical associations between some of the measures made when the children were 10 and those when they were 23, these are not causal links. It could be that some features about the children's personality that attracted peers to them at age 10 continued to have an impact on adult peers years later. Then the lack of childhood friends could just be one earlier 'marker' for an underlying difficulty that might later precipitate further maladjustments, or that might aggravate such a difficulty into more severe problems. However, the strengths of this study lie in its robust longitudinal methodology that has illuminated a link that can now be investigated further.

Source: Bagwell *et al.* (1998)

SUMMARY

The phenomenon of peer socialisation marks the child's transition from having the nuclear family as his primary influences to a wider social world where others with characteristics more different from his own become his key influences. Since infancy, the child seems to already have a natural curiosity and basic need to engage his peers, although the skills required to enact more meaningful interactions will take some time to hone. These skills, such as perspective-taking, turn-taking, sharing and negotiation, will grow with age as the size and structure of the child's peer group and its nature of interactions become larger or more complex.

As a key theme of peer interactions, play is also argued as natural and central to the child's day-to-day life, and as an activity useful for learning and development. As with other types of social interactions, the complexity of play also increases with age, from solitary and largely physical forms to the more collaborative and symbolic ones that incorporate pretend elements, objects, rules and reciprocation between two or more children. Although it is impossible to establish a causal link, play is nevertheless at least involved in enhancing language and other cognitive skills (such as theory of mind), promoting emotional understanding and leading to further social interactions with others. Even physical (non-symbolic) forms of play, such as rough-and-tumble between boys, can serve to establish and maintain an orderly hierarchy within a safe environment, leading possibly to other friendly interactions.

At the same time, there are individual differences in children's effectiveness for peer interactions. Partly due to their personal characteristics and partly to the peer context in which they find themselves, some children are more accepted by others and some are more likely to be rejected whereas some are not strongly preferred or disliked by their peer group. These phenomena may result from children's social skills (sociability and aggression, for instance), preference (whether they want to be alone) and expectations (whether they expect to be accepted or rejected by others). Still, children's peer social status is associated with a host of positive and negative consequences, such as school achievement and psychological

disturbances. Understanding such relationships helps with interventions aimed to improve interactions and adjustments of at-risk children.

As children engage more and more over time with peers that they prefer, some forms of friendships evolve. Just as the complexity of peer interaction itself increases with age, so does the complexity of children's friendship. Older children tend to have more intimacy, sensitivity and mutual concern and understanding, and their friendship groups are smaller and more stable, than younger children. Similarities in personality, a common social group and identity (most notably gender) and technology may act to facilitate the formation and progress of friendship, although at times such may hinder these processes through stereotyped expectations and misunderstanding.

Children's experiences with their peer groups and friends do have implications for several areas of their development; at least self-concept and identity, collaborative learning and social and cognitive skills, and quite possibly longer-term psychological adjustments (such as general wellbeing, school success and even psychopathology). These developmental outcomes are likely implicated through the child's continuing relationships that she builds and develops with others, even though the precise cause and effect cannot yet be ascertained.

The onus for researchers is in detecting the processes within peer socialisation that lead to the developmental, particularly long-term, consequences of both positive and negative kinds, and identifying effective methods that can maximise the potential for positive change and minimise the ill effects of any negative starting points, so that children can mutually benefit from each other in their peer group.

REVIEW QUESTIONS

1 What are the key features of children's interactions with peers at different ages through development and what are the key functions they serve?

2 How do children 'play' at different ages? What may they learn from it?

3 How do children become popular, rejected, or neglected by their peers?

4 How can the ways we study children's interactions and relationships affect the outcomes we obtain from such research?

5 How do children make 'friends' at different ages? Do friendships in childhood have any significant impact on other developments or later life experiences?

RECOMMENDED READING

For a very wide variety of 'close-up' observations of children's peer interactions:

Opie, I. (1993). *The People in the Playground*. Oxford: Oxford University Press.

For theories, arguments and evidence for importance of peers over other influence:

Harris, J.R. (1998). *The Nurture Assumption: Why Children Turn Out the Way They Do*. New York: Free Press.

For an evolutionary perspective on the origins of peer cultures and interactions:

Pinker, S. (2002). *The Blank Slate: The Modern Denial of Human Nature*. London: Allen Lane.

For different perspectives on play:

Göncü, A. & Gaskins, S. (2007). *Play and Development: Evolutionary, Sociocultural and Functional Perspectives*. Hove: Psychology Press.

For various perspectives on the importance of and functions of children's friendships:

Hartup, W.W. (2006). Relationships in early and middle childhood. In A.L. Vangelisti & D. Perlman (Eds), *Cambridge Handbook of Personal Relationships* (171–190). New York: Cambridge University Press.

RECOMMENDED WEBSITES

For a report on peer interactions and classroom learning (The Primary Review) by Christine Howe and Neil Mercer, Cambridge University, produced in 2007:

http://www.primaryreview.org.uk/Downloads/Int_Reps/4.Children_development-learning/Primary_Review_2-1b_briefing_Social_development_learning_071214.pdf

For information on children's play, including theory, research, policy and practice, the Children's Play Information Service (CPIS), part of the National Children's Bureau:

http://www.ncb.org.uk/cpis/home.aspx

For discussions on online gaming and virtual interactions and relationships:

http://www.guardian.co.uk/technology/2010/jan/10/playing-in-the-virtual-world

For a snapshot on the benefits and hazards of friendships (NYU Child Study Center):

http://www.aboutourkids.org/articles/do_kids_need_friends

For a suggestion of the problems children without friends/experiencing rejection face:

http://www.nncc.org/Guidance/dc26_wo.friends1.html

Watch a video examining friendship in childhood across different cultures. Further resources can be found at www.pearsoned.co.uk/gillibrand

Chapter 14
Developmental psychology and education

Malcolm Hughes

Learning Outcomes

After reading this chapter, with further recommended reading, you should be able to:

1. Recount and evaluate the extent to which the main theories of developmental psychology and theories of learning have been applied in children's centres, schools, colleges and universities;

2. Assess the likely effectiveness of applying differing perspectives of educational theorists and practitioners in relation to key themes of teaching and learning;

3. Critically analyse the value to educational systems and pedagogy of adopting developmentally appropriate approaches;

4. Construct an argument about what to do for learners with special needs which is rooted in a thoroughgoing knowledge of psychosocial development.

Edward – written by Elizabeth, his class teacher

Background: Edward is a non-identical seven year old twin brother. Both boys, Edward and Richard, were taken into care soon after birth as their mother was a drug addict. The boys lived with foster parents until they were two-and-a-half. They now live with their maternal grandmother who they call 'Mum'. Both grandmother and her boyfriend are alcoholics. The grandmother's boyfriend sleeps in the same room as the boys. The boys are fiercely competitive and argue most of the time. They are very physical with each other and Edward has been known to self-harm. The boys have got persistently worse at home so grandmother is struggling more and more. They have set fire to furniture including a cot containing a baby.

School behaviour: In September 2009, the boys were placed in my class which lasted two-and-a-half weeks before they had to be separated. They were physically and mentally abusive to each other and Edward would be the same with other children in the class. At first the class was a very tense and scared group of people, adults and children alike, as the boys could fly off the handle at a moment's notice.

At break times Edward regularly falls out with other children and is rude and abusive to children and staff. Sometimes the headteacher is called four or five times a day to remove Edward. He is then brought back not long after in a terrible mood which makes him impossible to manage.

Recently a behaviour therapist observed Edward for an hour and claimed that he was 'angelic', that the school were doing a fantastic job and that there was nothing she need do. She also advised that Edward remain in the same class next year which would mean that his brother would go into the class above him.

Cognitive development: Edward is the brighter of the twins. This is most apparent in maths and topic work. He can enjoy PE, PSHE and French but, as he cannot co-operate with other children, he misses a lot of these sessions or simply does not join in. It has been calculated that he is in the 92nd percentile for non-verbal communication which the therapist said was his strength and should be exploited, but she did not tell me how or why. He is very good at mental arithmetic and enjoys his numeracy lessons.

My feelings: This has been a very difficult year in which I have felt a range of emotions: guilt that I am not actually helping Edward and feeling that I am letting down my class; despair at being left to deal with Edward by myself; relief when he is away and then in turn shame that I feel that way. Most days I just feel like a failure.

- How do you feel about Edward, Richard and Elizabeth, based on these notes?
- What action would you take next as the headteacher in this school?
- What advice would you offer Elizabeth?

▶

▶ Introduction

The story presented in the opening example is true and the words are written 'from the heart'. Both Edward and his brother pose significant challenges to their teachers which can be traced back to problems during their psychological development. These circumstances – where a relatively young but highly committed and inspirational teacher feels she is a failure, is letting down her class and feels ashamed – reflect a dilemma in education. To what extent can what learners experience in schools and colleges – the educational provision – be varied to suit their psychological development? This chapter explores to what extent developmental psychology is and can be applied not only to relatively extreme cases such as Edward and his brother but to the way education generally is organised and delivered.

Behaviour in school is the result of many factors, internal and external to the child and to the school itself.
Source: iStockphoto

There are three main sections. Firstly, we explore the ways in which understanding education requires an understanding of children's personal, social and cultural influences. Secondly, we review the main theories of human development and learning, and develop arguments about how these theories have been both shaped and applied by teachers and developmental psychologists in a range of educational settings. Thirdly, we explore areas of educational provision – what we refer to as 'themes of developmentally appropriate provision' – that together orchestrate the educational experiences of our children, young people and adult learners.

As you have read in Nature–nurture boxes throughout this book, children's development is affected in profound and complex ways by the circumstances – the culture – in which they grow up, and the case of Edward is no exception to this. Why does Edward behave as he does? What aspects of Edward's upbringing to date have had the strongest influence on Edward's development? How do different aspects of children's experiences relate to each other? Who is more influential: parents, teachers or peers? To try to answer such questions we can turn to a model developed by Urie Bronfenbrenner, discussed previously in Chapter 2, Theoretical Perspectives. Bronfenbrenner was a renowned psychologist and a co-founder of the Head Start programme for challenging and disadvantaged preschool children. He mapped the many interacting social contexts that affect development in his bio-ecological model of development (Bronfenbrenner, 1989; Bronfenbrenner and Evans, 2000). However, the *bio* aspect of the model recognises that people bring their biological selves to the developmental process. The small child sitting in the middle of Fig. 14.1 represents this very important idea. Remember from the example that Edward behaves differently to his brother despite many genetic factors being similar (but not identical) and both boys sharing many defining experiences. The *ecological* part of the model recognises that the social contexts in which we develop are ecosystems because they are in constant interaction and influence each other. Bronfenbrenner's model depicts the different cultural systems which 'surround' and influence a young child like Edward.

You can see that every child develops within a microsystem of his immediate relationships and activities which make up the child's own 'little world'. As discussed in Chapter 2, relationships within this world are reciprocal and interactive – they flow in both directions. The child's behaviour affects the parents and the parents' influences the child. Microsystems exist and interact within a mesosystem, which is the set of interactions and relationships among all the elements of the microsystem – the family members interacting with each other or with the teacher. These are slightly more distant from the child because they do not involve him directly, but nevertheless they influence his life. Again, all these relationships are reciprocal.

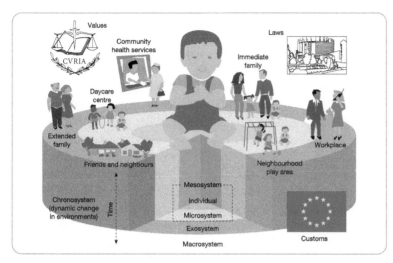

Figure 14.1. Urie Bronfenbrenner's biological model of human development

Source: Berk, L.E. (2006). *Child development* (7th ed.). Boston: Allyn & Bacon. Copyright © 2006 Pearson Education, Inc. Reproduced with permission.

The mesosystem of interacting microsystems also interact with the exosystem, the layer which includes all the social settings that affect the child, even though the child is not a direct member of the system. For example, the teachers' relations with school managers; parents' jobs and social pursuits; the community's resources for health, employment or recreation; or the family's religious affiliation. The macrosystem is the larger society – its values, laws, conventions, and traditions, all of which influence the conditions and experiences of the child's life. These systems help us to think about the many dynamic forces that interact to create the context for children's development.

We asked earlier 'Who is more influential, teachers or friends?' Well, according to Bronfenbrenner's model, teachers are part of the child's mesosystem and friends are part of the microsystem. Therefore friends are closer to the child than teachers and certainly closer than local employers or national politicians. Perhaps one of the problems with Bronfenbrenner's model is that it is not explicit about how different ecologies (interactions of people within their environment) impact at different times during a lifespan. As discussed in Chapter 2, the exosystem will become more important in a child's life as she gets older. Put simply, earlier in life, homes and families will be more influential and so, when thinking about why Edward behaves as he does, this is an important idea to consider.

Study of Bronfenbrenner's bio-ecological model suggests that genetic, biological and social determinants are important factors in understanding why Edward behaves as he does. For example, as the children have been taken into care very soon after birth and Grandmother is an alcoholic, we might assume that there are some family problems that span generations; perhaps a genetic disposition. There could have been drug abuse and/or malnutrition during pregnancy affecting the boys' heath and development

(see Chapter 4, Prenatal Development and Infancy). There will almost certainly be an attachment problem (see Chapter 9, Attachment and Early Social Experiences) as the children were separated from their mother as babies and their foster family at the age of two. There may also be socioeconomic problems, possibly violence or other traumatic experiences, and probably a lack of parenting capacity in the grandmother. All of this makes it clear that Edward's education is a problem which the teacher cannot solve alone, particularly as the problems are generated in life outside school. The boys need to be assessed thoroughly by a specialist in developmental and educational psychology.

What the example of Edward does demonstrate is that cognitive development, learning and academic achievement are not distinct from the socio-cultural factors that have a profound impact on our lives. Edward is described as bright by his teachers and so far there is no significant difference in language and reading, memory and intelligence, mathematical thinking or general academic attainment between Edward and the normal expectations for his age (see Chapter 6, Memory and Intelligence). So what aspects of his development have been most affected by bio-ecological factors? In Edward's case it is probably his temperament and emotional development; his self-concept and identity; his ability to engage in comfortable social interactions; and his capacity to make and maintain supportive relationships. In the longer term, impoverished and warped development in these areas will have an adverse impact on the academic achievement of learners if they continue to find engagement with teachers and peers so difficult. It is also true that Edward is having a significant impact on his classmates and teachers, but what else is affecting the experiences and development of the children in Elizabeth's class and in all the other classrooms of our schools, colleges and universities?

From your past reading – perhaps of Chapter 2 in particular – you should have a good idea of what theoretical frameworks might underpin the application of developmental psychology to classrooms. These are the sort of understandings that would inform a specialist in developmental and educational psychology who was asked to assess Edward and to suggest care and teaching programmes that might help him. A number of names may already have sprung to mind – Piaget, Vygotsky, Bruner, Bowlby – and we have already discussed Bronfenbrenner. All of these influential scientists have contributed to our understanding of the application of developmental psychology in educational settings, and so it is to the application of developmental theory in classrooms that we turn next.

STOP AND THINK

Reflection

Review the example of Edward at the start of the chapter.

- Why is Edward behaving as he is? Review the summaries of Chapter 9, Attachment and Early Social Experiences, and Chapter 10, Childhood Temperament and Behavioural Development. They will provide the language for you to frame a response.

- Why might the behaviour therapist have considered Edward to be 'angelic' given the accounts of the class teacher and other staff?

The application of developmental theory in classrooms

As we discussed in Chapter 1, What is Developmental Psychology, developmental psychology is concerned with helping to understand the various processes that determine our psychological make-up during important phases of human growth. Continuous processes such as maturation, growth and enhanced capacity mould the way we change and develop throughout our lives. However, as discussed in Chapter 2, Theoretical Perspectives, development is also commonly presented by psychologists in periods of time or stages. Many theoretical frameworks (for example Jean Piaget's four stages of cognitive development from Chapter 2) give an impression of distinctly

separate stages closely linked to chronological age, and describe a very precise ordering of change (Piaget, 1972). Piaget's stage model is the most commonly applied set of theories in early years settings and schools in Europe, Australasia and in North America. The Nature–nurture box which follows highlights Piaget's contribution to education policy and practice, and shows how even Bronfenbrenner's bio-ecological model has been informed by earlier developmental scientists such as Piaget.

The separation and precise ordering which define stage theories is one of the criticisms of developmental theories, although the idea of different stages does provide a structure for the different phases of schooling and what is taught in each phase. For example, there may be an attempt to have developmental stages correspond with the key stages prescribed in a national curriculum for schools, or with age phases represented in school age groupings (there is more explanation of this later). For example, compulsory schooling in Sweden and Denmark begins at the age of seven. In Norway, 'primary' schooling is normally 6 to 13 years, 6 to 12 in Belgium and 5 to 11/12 in England and Wales (Woolfolk et al., 2008). Why are there differences in the stages of schooling across broadly similar cultures? How are developmental stages applied to schooling provision in the UK or in your country?

STOP AND THINK

Going further

It is argued by some commentators that Piaget gave greater attention to early and mid-childhood and showed insufficient interest in adolescence and emerging adulthood.

- Do you agree?
- Why do you think Piaget might have done this?

To find out what might characterise cognitive maturation through adolescence, see Recommended Reading. Also review your study of Chapter 13, Adolescence.

- In what ways do you think the education of adolescents should differ from that of younger children?
- Why do you think so?
- What would you change about secondary schooling to make it more appealing or relevant to adolescents?

Justify your answers by referring to theories and research you have read about.

developed his work to such an extent that these later ideas became known as neo-Piagetian theory.

Neo-Piagetian theory

Neo-Piagetian theory (e.g. Case, 1992, 1998) builds on the stages and changes in Piaget's cognitive development theory. The influential and highly thought of psychologist Professor Robbie Case (1945–2000) believed that changes within each stage resulted from changes in increased mental capacity. For example, the Piagetian conservation of number task (see Chapter 7) requires more than one cognitive strategy to be successful. In this task children are shown an array of counters or buttons in a line bunched up together or spread out. Their task is to recognise that the number remains the same regardless of changes in their arrangement. Young children fail because they are unable to hold different pieces of information in their short-term memory at the same time. Older primary-aged children hold information from previous experiences that allows them to go on to more complex tasks. Case's theory and its underpinning empirical research was a major advance in developmental psychology, integrating important aspects of the Piagetian stage theory and cognitive information-processing theory to capitalise on the strengths of each, and particularly to draw out from this incorporation implications for teaching methods used at different phases of schooling. According to Case, cognitive structures in infancy are sufficient for immediate responses to sensory-motor information – that is, what we see, hear and feel. In early childhood, cognition relates to creating internal representations of information; and in later childhood, transformations of those representations through experience (Case, 1985). Let's unpick this last complex and important idea.

Case believes that changes in development result from changes to information-processing capacity in working memory (see Chapter 6, Memory and Intelligence) or what he calls *m space*. Growth in capacity, he argues, is linked to how well children can use their limited memory capacity. This involves four processes:

- *Stage 1 Encoding:* maturation of the brain enables increased speed of processing of working memory over time. The brain makes sense of what it 'sees' much faster. If six sweets are placed in a line in groups of two, and young children (at Piaget's pre-operational stage) are asked, 'How many sweets are there?', they will count them one by one. Older children with their increased capacity will arrive at the answer faster and with fewer steps (recognising an array of six). Younger children cannot 'see' or make sense of the whole picture as yet.

- *Stage 2 Strategies:* these free up mental capacity. Case sees merit in the strategies used by children that Piaget referred to. Such strategies include how learners try to understand something new by fitting it into what they already know (assimilation). When this strategy becomes more expert and automatic – this leads to more 'cognitive room' to change existing schemes to respond to a new situation (accommodation). (This links to Point 2 in the 'top ten' list previously.)

- *Stage 3 Automatisation:* the automisation of knowledge leads to central conceptual structures. This allows more complex thinking which also frees up information-processing capacity and allows more advanced thinking. When ideas are fully formed, children can 'move up a level'. Pre-school children understand stories in one dimension (e.g. what the story line is); by the primary years several sub-plots can be understood and combined into a main plot. By

Definitions

Neo-Piagetian theory: a recent interpretation of Piaget's theory in an information-processing framework that places greater emphasis on cognitive processes than maturation.

Information-processing theory: the likening of human cognition to the working structures of a computer, with input, processing, memory, output, etc. that helps us 'conceptualise' what is happening in the brain.

Assimilation: within Piagetian theory, this is the process of taking new information into existing knowledge structures.

Accommodation: within Piagetian theory, this is the revision of older knowledge structures to take account of new information.

Central conceptual structure: a well-formed mental scheme of a concept like 'horse' that can be generally applied to all horses and requires little more assimilation until we experience a zebra for the first time.

adolescence children can handle multiple and overlapping storylines due to development in the conceptual structures in the higher, more forward parts of the brain.

- *Stage 4 Generalisation:* this involves moving from being quite task-specific to more general. Here children learn to apply what they know to other contexts, but this takes time. Take our example of conservation to illustrate this. A child pours liquid from one container to another and demonstrates understanding of the 'height' and 'width' of the liquid and begins to create understanding of how liquid is conserved. Once automatic, a central conceptual structure of conservation is formed that enables that general concept to be applied to other similar situations, not just liquid and containers.

Collaborating with his research students, many of whom were experienced schoolteachers, Case developed innovative teaching schemes and lesson designs, especially in mathematics. These support successful learning by students, and exemplify and advance important principles of learning, like those put forward earlier in the 'top ten' of ways Piaget's work has influenced education and, later on in this chapter, how to conceive of developmentally appropriate learning and assessment tasks. Neo-Piagetian theory is still developing, but has already shown applications to explaining dyslexia and reading difficulties (Snowling, 2000), and studies on academic skills using this approach have proved very valuable, for example in the teaching of mathematics (Askew *et al.*, 1997).

Critics of neo-Piagetian theory (like critics of Piaget's own theories) assert that the theory avoids the biological underpinnings of how the brain functions and places little emphasis on the social or cultural influences of cognition – such as those suggested in Bronfenbrenner's bio-ecological theory. However, information-processing theories offer applications to many educational settings. For example, firstly the emphasis which information-processing theories place on memory helps to explain how younger learners' limited memory causes difficulties with many reading and problem-solving tasks; secondly, teachers can encourage learners to actively engage with their learning (remember points 1 and 2 from Piaget 'top ten' list) by teaching pupils cognitive strategies to kick-start various cognitive processes. For instance:

- 'self-questioning' ('What do I already know about this topic?', 'How have I solved problems like this before?')

- 'thinking aloud' while performing a task ('OK so far', 'This isn't making sense', 'I need to change strategies')
- writing down 'self-questions' and 'thinking aloud' statements
- making graphic representations (e.g. concept maps, flow charts, semantic webs) of one's thoughts and knowledge.

STOP AND THINK

Reflection

- What examples from your own learning can you think of where you have been taught or have used cognitive strategies such as self-questioning and thinking aloud – sometimes referred to as meta-cognitive strategies?
- Are you using any at the moment as you work your way through this chapter?
- Does writing things down help? Why/why not?

These are just a few examples of strategies to encourage cognitive development when viewing the development of our capacity as information processors. We have acknowledged and celebrated the contribution made by Jean Piaget and of neo-Piagetian theorists such as Robbie Case to our understanding of cognitive development, and demonstrated to some extent the application of their theories to schools and schooling. However, it is now timely to compare and contrast the application of Piaget's research and theories with that of another hugely influential scientist, the Russian psychologist Lev Vygotsky.

Vygotsky's social-constructivist theory

Lev Vygotsky's social-constructivist approach (first described in this text in Chapter 2) offered a major alternative to Piaget in the period between 1920 and 1930, although his work did not appear in English and therefore gain wider recognition until the 1960s. Where Piaget took the view of child as an 'experimental scientist', Vygotsky likened the child to an apprentice, where cognitive development and capacity is promoted through interaction with those who already possess cognitive capacity, knowledge and skills (Vygotsky, 1978). It is

Group work is often used in university teaching, and in socio-cultural theory is key to development and learning.

Source: Pearson Education Ltd./Robert Harding/Bananastock

through our social interactions with parents and teachers that we develop our intellectual capabilities. Development and learning occur from processes first on a social plane (i.e. between people) and then second on a psychological one (i.e. individually).

It is not just parents or other 'significant' adults who can support learning in Vygotsky's theory. Supporting learners to competency also involves knowledgeable or skilful peers helping less advanced ones. This takes place in contemporary classrooms and playgrounds when learners work together, perhaps on a collaborative task in a process called cooperative learning. Most primary classrooms have furniture arranged in table groups to positively promote children's interaction with each other. If you spent ten minutes observing well-structured and organised group work, you would (hopefully!) see and hear children at any of these tables helping each other, learning from one another in pursuit of a common goal and without the direction of a teacher. This is a broader idea than Vygotsky's original view where there is a single child and another more expert child/adult. In cooperative learning, groups of children with varying degrees of

expertise have been found to stimulate learning in each other (Forman and McPhail, 1993; Doymus, 2008). Other research, while supportive of this, also indicates that cooperative learning is more effective when children have been trained in cooperative procedures (Gillies, 2000) and the teacher has prior experience of working with children in this way (Oortwijn *et al.*, 2008).

Implications of Vygotsky's theory for teaching and learning

There are important implications of Vygotsky's work for education. One key factor is the important role of the teacher in structuring learning. In the UK as long ago as 1992, Robin Alexander, Jim Rose and Chris Woodhead (known then as the 'Three Wise Men' of UK educational policy) criticised child-centred education (widely associated with the theories of Jean Piaget) and the notion of fixed stages development, which they believed led to lowered expectations, inhibited teachers' interventions and confined the role of the teacher to 'facilitator'. They stated;

> More recent studies demonstrate what children, given effective teaching, can achieve. . . . [The more recent studies] place proper emphasis on the teacher as teacher rather than facilitator. Such insights are, in our view, critical to the raising of standards in primary classrooms. (Alexander et al., 1992, p. 14)

Definition

Cooperative learning. working in small groups, acting together to meet a learning goal or goals.

Lev Vygotsky stressed intellectual development rather than structuring learning to match a stage of cognitive development. The activities selected in school are very important to challenge and extend learning, and should include meaningful and stimulating classroom activities pitched to be within each child's individual ability to cope – what has become known as 'personalised learning'. In particular, Vygotsky believed that teaching children at all stages should reflect many opportunities for pretend play for language development. This is seen as good practice in the early years, but much less so later on. In the same way as we selected our 'top ten' ways in which the work of Piaget is reflected in schools we now present a 'top ten' of the ways we believe Vygotsky's work has influenced education:

1. Teachers use language across the curriculum and in all phases of education to develop higher mental functions (Wegerif *et al.*, 2004).
2. Pupils are encouraged to talk out loud when engaged in problem-solving exercises.
3. Pupils develop their own cognitive capacity at their own pace, but this process requires access to rich and stimulating environments (O'Toole, 2008).
4. Teachers and practitioners watch for states of developmental readiness (McBryde *et al.*, 2004).
5. Children advance their learning by pretend play. There are bountiful opportunities for young children to do this (Swindells and Stagnitti, 2006).
6. It is the defining skill of a teacher to decide what kind of support is necessary, when to give the support and how much support is necessary for an individual – what has become known as 'personalised learning' (Courcier, 2007).
7. Packaging or 'chunking' learning is a very common practice in many learning contexts – skilled teachers break down a task and adjust the methods of presentation (Allen, 2008).
8. Teachers design collaborative tasks to encourage co-operative learning. Most European primary classrooms have furniture arranged in table groups to positively promote children's interaction with each other (Veenman *et al.*, 2000).
9. Teachers train learners in cooperative and reciprocal procedures so that learning is more effective (Wong *et al.*, 2003).
10. High-quality teaching is as important as providing discovery learning opportunities in promoting a learner's development. Given effective teaching, all learners can achieve (Dunphy, 2009).

The Vygotsky 'top ten' summarises the effect of how many writers and researchers, including those cited in both the Piaget and the Vygotsky lists, believe developmental psychology has been applied in many schools and colleges. To summarise, Piaget, the neo-Piagetian theorists, such as Robbie Case, and Lev Vygotsky represent the clearest links between developmental psychology and its application in educational settings. However, there is a complex and very important link and distinction between theories of developmental psychology and learning theories or how pupils learn best. Before considering how best to apply developmental psychology, let's try and tease out the distinction between these two in order to establish the important focus on developmental psychology.

Moving from developmental theory to learning theory

Theories that have their roots in developmental psychology (Piaget, Vygotsky and others) are based upon the 'clinical observation' of behaviour which demonstrates individual capacity or lack of capacity in developed or developing cognitive processes. An example of this can be found in the Cutting Edge box. Clinical observation allows for the development of theories which can describe, analyse and predict the behaviour of individuals as they move through stages of development. These theories (as we have already seen in our examples of Piaget, Case and Vygotsky) inform curricular provision, the content and the structure of formal schooling, the layout of the classroom and therefore the development of approaches to teaching and learning for groups of pupils as well as individuals.

Learning theories arise in part from the application of developmental psychology to educational settings, and also from the observation and analysis of teaching and learning behaviours. These theories have a particular focus (not unsurprisingly) on how learners learn best, how teachers can become better teachers and include the principles adopted during initial teacher training and the continuing professional development of teachers. Learning theories explain how learning happens and then promote strategies to improve the quality of learning experiences. How the brain works and how it develops during key developmental stages such as adolescence (Chapter 13) are important matters of concern for those engaged in applying developmental psychology to education.

CUTTING EDGE

Brain Development in Adolescence

There has been a recent surge of research on neurological development in adolescence (Chapter 13) that sheds new light on cognitive development during these years (Giedd, 2008). Research technologies, especially fMRI (functional magnetic resonance imaging) and PET scans (positron emission tomography) give us a much better understanding of how the brain develops, because these new technologies show how different parts of the brain work when performing a cognitive task (e.g. memorising, making decisions), by focusing on the connections or synapses between the neurons – the cells of the nervous system including the brain.

For years we have known about the over-production of these synaptic connections during prenatal development and through the first 18 months of life (see Chapter 4), but now it turns out that a new period of over-production also occurs in early adolescence (Giedd, 2008). Over-production peaks at about age 12 or so, but obviously that is not when we reach our cognitive peak. After 12, there follows a huge amount of synaptic pruning, in which the number of synapses is whittled down considerably. Interestingly, recent research using fMRI methods shows that synaptic pruning is more rapid among adolescents with high intelligence (Shaw *et al.*, 2006). Why might this be? Well, synaptic pruning allows the brain to work more efficiently, as brain pathways become slicker.

Another recent surprise for researchers has been in the growth of the cerebellum – a structure in the lower brain. This is perhaps the most surprising recent finding because the cerebellum is part of the lower brain and was thought to be involved only in basic functions such as major movement. Now, however, it turns out that the cerebellum is important for many higher functions as well, such as musicianship, mathematical problem solving, making decisions and appreciating humour (Strauch, 2003). In fact, the cerebellum is the last structure of the brain to stop growing, not completing its phase of over-production and pruning until the mid-20s. So what can we conclude about brain development in adolescence and emerging adulthood on the basis of this new research?

1. The brain grows and changes a lot more than we had understood in the past.
2. The neurological changes increase cognitive abilities substantially.
3. Although adolescents are more advanced in their thinking than children, their cognitive development is not yet mature.
4. Synaptic pruning that makes thinking faster and more efficient also makes thinking more rigid and less flexible so, for example, it becomes harder to learn a new language.
5. After adolescence, it is easier for people to make balanced judgements about complicated issues because they have a well-pruned set of connections in the brain that are quicker and slicker.

The Cutting Edge box begs the question of how this new information can and should be applied in educational contexts. The second part of this chapter should help provide an answer by considering what is meant by 'developmentally appropriate provision' in education – a fundamental idea in the application of developmental psychology – that can be considered as the match between the educational experience of the learner (the status of their cognitive development, perhaps the neurological surge or the speed of synaptic pruning) and the learner's ability to make the most of the experience. We will explore what we term the 'five themes of developmentally

Definition

Developmentally appropriate provision: when the educational experiences of learners are matched with the learners' ability to make the most of the experience.

appropriate provision'. These are developmentally appropriate curricula; developmentally appropriate teaching; developmentally appropriate activities; developmentally appropriate behaviour management; and developmentally appropriate schools.

Five themes of 'developmentally appropriate provision'

Developmentally appropriate curricula

The curriculum is what is taught in schools, colleges and universities organised by age group (usually into academic years) and by subject. There is also something called 'the hidden curriculum': the values, attitudes and insights which are not overtly taught, but may be modelled and demonstrated by teachers and managers in institutions. The curriculum is usually organised into schemes of work informed by over-riding aims and detailed lists of learning objectives. Many examples of curricula are organised in spiral forms, so that pupils will come across similar subject content year on year, but with more complex or difficult ideas introduced. Further structure is usually given to curricula by grouping them into stages linked to school phases.

Since the 1980s, a statutory National Curriculum for schools in England has been developed. Many other countries have developed national curricula and the next Stop and Think box asks you to explore comparable arrangements in your own country or another country. The National Curriculum in England sets out the stages and core subjects that children will be taught during their time at school. Children aged 5 to 16 in 'maintained' or state schools must be taught the National Curriculum. The National Curriculum is organised into blocks of years called 'key stages'. There are four key stages as well as an Early Years Foundation Stage (EYFS). The EYFS covers education for children before they reach five (compulsory school age). For each National Curriculum subject, there is a programme of study. The programmes of study describe the subject knowledge, skills and understanding which pupils are expected to develop during each key stage.

STOP AND THINK

Going further

Review the structure of the National Curriculum for Schools in England at **http://curriculum.qcda. gov.uk/**

Use the internet to search for another country's national curriculum. Try to identify some similarities and differences between the two. To what causes would you ascribe any differences?

For example, the programmes of study for science were written by teams of subject experts and were based on research into progression in conceptual understanding within the science levels, by Liverpool University's Centre for Research in Primary Science and Technology, in partnership with Kings College London. So it could be argued that for some of the children, some of the time there is a good match between the state of individual cognitive development and the curriculum. However, it is recognised that for some children, the mismatch between programmes of study and cognitive development is so great that some or all of the programmes should be disapplied from a pupil. Disapplication is permitted, for individual pupils for a temporary period, through a statement of special educational need, or to allow for curriculum development or experimentation (DfES, 2006).

Why does disapplication occur? Most of the time disapplication happens because a pupil is finding it very difficult to make the same progress as other pupils – there is a developmental gulf opening up. It may seem unlikely that that gulf can be bridged; it may be that attempts to do so are counterproductive, or that lack of development in a particular area has a damaging effect on other subject areas. Probably the biggest problem that older pupils have, and one of the greatest causes of disapplication, is

Definition

Disapplied: the term used to indicate that a pupil or group of pupils need no longer be taught part or all of a programme study.

poor reading skills (Mumtaz and Humphreys, 2001; Duff et al., 2008; Ricketts *et. al.*, 2008).

A pupil's access to the curriculum depends to a large extent upon their ability to fluently and effortlessly read the many texts that are presented in the course of a timetable week. Cognitive capacity that is consumed with the difficulties of decoding and making sense of sometimes complex technical texts, leaves 'no room' for information processing, problem solving and the other higher order cognitive capacities of analysis, argument, synthesis, etc. There are all sorts of reasons why some pupils fall behind with their reading development. Some are environmental and some may be related to brain structure or phonological development. These are summed up as the cognitive capacity to learn (Molfese *et al.*, 2003), and are how a number of experts describe 'intelligence' (see Chapter 6, Memory and Intelligence). One good example of this was a study by psychologist Mark Eckert and colleagues of 39 11 year old children. The team found that temporal lobe asymmetry, hand preference, family history of reading disability and socioeconomic status explained over half of the variance in phonological and verbal performance (Eckert *et al.*, 2001).

One effect of the environment is the ability of parents, teachers and others to observe a child's readiness to read. Reading readiness is a term that in 1970s Britain informed the practice of schools and teachers, but oddly and, to begin with, in a negative way. It was suggested to teachers (and at this author's own training college in Cheltenham, England) that there was no point in pushing children to learn to read until they were ready, and the work of Piaget was the primary source of justification for this. Education lecturers made a connection between Piaget's Stage 3, concrete operations (age 7 to 11 years) and children's more effortless acquiring of reading skills. Trainee teachers were taught that it was simply a pointless waste of time to give formal phonological training before many children were ready.

However, approaches to reading readiness have changed in the last 40 years. Teachers were and are encouraged to look for signs that individual children are ready for formal instruction, usually phonological approaches with the development of 'phonemic' awareness being a consequence rather than a precursor of reading (Seymour *et al.*, 2003). What are the signs of readiness to learn to read, then? Table 14.1 is an example of the kind of checklist that trainee teachers of Early Years and the Foundation Stage are encouraged to use. It will help you identify this aspect of developmentally appropriate curricula.

A six year old reads to her 10 month old baby sister. Is there any point? At what age is it useful to start reading to children?

Source: O'Donnell

Table 14.1. Tick list of some signs of reading readiness.

Some signs of reading readiness – that formal reading instruction as part of the curriculum is developmentally appropriate. Observe some children over time at ages 3, 4 and 5. How many signs of reading readiness can you record?

A child..............	Observed
displays a greater interest in books and takes pleasure in looking at them, though it may appear that they're looking primarily at the pictures	
acts as if a reader	
grips books the correct way up	
turns pages at the correct times	
discusses what is happening and will relate their own experiences, e.g. television programmes and advertisements	
understands that the reader is focusing on the print and that the print is transmitting a message	
conjectures on what is read and the meaning of the pictures	
enjoys stories being read again and again, and 'joins in' regularly	
determines meaning from context by saying things like, 'I am scared of cats too'	
can recognise their own name, brands (e.g. the McDonald's 'M') and other public signs	
asks, 'What does that say?'	
identifies and imitates sounds of letters including by identifying, 'Train starts with "t" – the same as my name!'	

In this section, we have discussed how the Programmes of Study making up the National Curriculum in England are formally structured to take account of a cognitive developmental sequence that owes much to the theories of stage development put forward by Jean Piaget. We looked at how some children have aspects of the curriculum disapplied to them when a developmental gulf opens up that cannot be bridged. We looked at the teaching of reading in terms of structuring the curriculum to take account of reading readiness, and what some of the signs of reading readiness might be. There's clearly an overlap here with ideas of 'developmentally appropriate teaching' and it is to that idea that we next turn.

STOP AND THINK

Reflection

- What do you think might be the outcomes of trying to teach children to read too early, before they show the signs of reading readiness?
- Think back to when you learned to read. When did you start and how did you learn? You may have to ask somebody in the family if you learned at a very early age!

Developmentally appropriate teaching

If curriculum is about what is taught then this section on developmentally appropriate teaching is about how it is taught. Teaching methods vary widely within and between formal subject areas. Effective developmentally appropriate teaching in physical education will be very different to mathematics. Even within mathematics, how effective teachers of mathematics design their teaching will vary – from enabling pupils to gain automatic recall of number bonds ($50 + 70 = 120$ is like $5 + 7 = 12$) and multiplication facts ($9 \times 7 = 63$) to the very different set of knowledge and understanding required in using the properties of common regular polygons to solve problems. There are obviously different ways of teaching different subjects, but what are the most common types of teaching?

In this section we are going to describe three broad types of teaching which are founded on the questioning technique used by the teachers – directive exposition, non-directive discovery and interactive connection building. The kinds of questions teachers ask is a good way to recognise what is going on, how the teacher relates to the learners and the type of learning that might be taking place. Before exploring the types of teaching that are found in classrooms, it is worth thinking about how we know what kinds of teaching are happening. Much of the empirical evidence that underpins and is cited in this chapter comes from the systematic observation of classrooms. In the Research Methods box information and discussion is provided about an observational methodology that is now often used in classrooms – the video camera.

RESEARCH METHODS

Observation using classroom video

In Chapter 3, Research Methods, we discussed various research methods, including observation. The use of video cameras has enabled observational studies to capture more extensively the behaviours in a particular setting, and has also allowed observations to be viewed by other people, leading to greater reliability and validity in the coding and interpretation of observations. In addition, Heath and Hindmarsh (1997) consider that 'it is not possible to recover the details of talk through field observation alone, . . . it's unlikely that one could grasp little more than passing sense of what happened' (p. 107). They feel that 'traditional' ethnography fails to attend to the situated and interactional nature of practice and action (Heath and Hindmarsh, 1997, p. 104).

The video camera is therefore a good tool with which to access detailed classroom behaviour, and detailed and repeated observation of video data provides 'a methodological orientation from which to view "naturally occurring" activities and events' (Heath and Hindmarsh, 1997, p. 110). In addition, the potential for confusion or misunderstanding is still rife if audio alone is used to augment written notes, since the complexity of kinaesthetics and body language would be missed. Despite all of these positive aspects of using video, its most common criticism is the unnatural effects it can have on the classroom research subjects.

In one study which used this method, a school was approached for permission for a classroom-based research project on how teachers used questioning when teaching using the school's interactive digital whiteboards (IWBs). The school was well-equipped with digital display technologies linked to the internet available in all classrooms. The study asked the children and their teacher to engage in a collaborative task with a video camera; 'telling a story' of how teachers asked questions when using the interactive whiteboard over the period of a week (Hughes and Longman, 2006).

The locations chosen for the camera were often limited, whether due to the position of power sockets or to teachers' preferences. The typical positioning of the camera created problems for the researchers in using some of the data. For example, pupils/teachers often chose to use a corner or side position not normally taken by a teacher or by pupils. In some sense, the camera became a visitor in the classroom and was not accepted as part of the teaching and learning. Because of this constraint, the camera's viewpoint meant that in some lighting conditions the images and text on the IWB were not discernible. Teachers and pupils chose positions that attempted a panopticon of the whole classroom. 'so we could see everything that was happening . . .'. The position of a small boom microphone on the camera meant a good deal of background classroom noise was picked up and so often masked the question and answer interactions.

Classrooms are difficult places to capture good-quality video data and, with hindsight, the teachers and children reported that they would do things very differently. Despite these difficulties, the children were able to capture something of what kinds of questions their teachers asked during a school week, but the experiences which the researchers had reveal some of the pitfalls and limitations of this method of data collection.

Directive exposition

'Chalk and talk' instruction (now often done through PowerPoint presentation) occurs using a programme of experiences that are structured to provide small amounts of learning about things, and demonstrations or modelling of the desired outcomes, which can be recorded, assessed, reinforced and outcomes rewarded. Progress is driven by the structure of the lesson or part of lesson. Responses to closed questions are limited to one or two words. For example, 'Name the five largest castles in Wales' is a closed question with a correct set of responses. The answers can be found quickly, recovering the answers from memory, using a reference book or database

Traditional lectures do not lend themselves to much more than passive listening and recording of information.

Source: iStockphoto

of castles containing a field relevant to the area within the walls (or some similar dimension). Pupils can show their ability to memorise, to search text or to interrogate a database, but not much else.

Learning is passive, concerned with the limbic processing of information and is associated with the psychology of behaviourism (see Chapter 2, Theoretical Perspectives). Teaching does not take account of preferred learning styles, nor the learner's intuitive engagement with the learning process. This view of the teacher and teaching style broadly corresponds with the 'Teacher as Sage – the Sage-on-the-Stage' (Stinson and Milter, 1996) and the Nuremberg Funnel model of delivering or transferring the curriculum.

Non-directive discovery

Discovery instruction is when teachers provide a range of experiences that are unstructured, but are informed by programmes of study considered appropriate for a non-linear and integrated curriculum. Progress is driven by the interests of the learners, and teachers will pursue a range of ideas concurrently and in partnership with pupils. The emphasis is on personal discovery and personal construction. Responses to open questions are unlimited. For example, 'What can you find out about castles?' is a very open question that gives enormous scope for pupils to gather huge amounts of information. ICT can make that gathering exercise very fast and can also produce large quantities of beautifully presented 'work'. However, it is very unlikely that the information gathered will be processed in a way that will provoke and allow learning to take place. Little notice is taken of cognitive processes.

Teachers negotiate the starting point in which knowledge and concepts of a particular subject are the learning intentions of the session, and provide vivid and powerful means to these ends. This approach provides for a common starting experience for pupils, and so can emphasise a social dimension to the learning. Learning is active, but constrained within the limitations of the pupils' perceptions of what is possible or known. Teachers provide opportunities and support for any curiosity shown to discover 'What would happen if . . . ?' The learner has the ability to explore in a content-free environment, but this does not necessarily allow for the learner to stray beyond the confines of current knowledge. Learning defaults to conceptual connections that are most obvious within the chosen context. This style of relationship broadly corresponds with 'Teachers as Guide – the Guide-by-the-Side' (Stinson and Milter, 1996).

Interactive connection building

Using this method, teachers provide a 'programme' of experiences that are structured to provide wide-ranging opportunities for learning about things, and demonstrations or modelling of an approach to learning that draws out the connections between prior learning and new learning, and between different subject areas, which can be celebrated, assessed, reinforced and outcomes rewarded. Progress is inspired by the teacher who cannot only 'talk the talk', but can also 'walk the walk' – argue for the methods she uses and her approach to problem solving.

Responses to structured questions are focused and offer opportunities for argument. These are questions requiring learners to engage in one or more of the cognitive processes: criticism, synthesis, transformation, experiment, creation, incorporation, categorising, discarding, refining, sequencing, explaining and connecting. Teachers set out to engage the pupil in their own learning and to structure the experience. For example we might ask the question 'Why do spiral stairs in castle towers often ascend in an anti-clockwise direction?' (There are some interesting theories around about this.) Teachers can then plan to use vivid materials and media to make the learning focus on making causal connections between observed phenomena. The emphasis on cognitive process provides the best opportunity out of the three approaches for developmentally appropriate teaching.

to be very helpful. However, this depends upon a high level of cognitive activity perhaps best kept for older teenagers and emergent adult learners (Sutherland *et al.*, 2002).

- *Reporting*: this is one of the most cognitively demanding activities (requiring analysis, synthesis and interpretation) although sometimes delivery of the report can be little more than reading all the tiny text on a PowerPoint presentation (Harden, 2008).

So, which of these activities are appropriate at different stages of development or phases of schooling, or should we plan for all learners to engage in a wide variety of activities? Is baby Jack Davies exploring an object ('Is it a hat, is it a sandwich?') fundamentally the same activity as a 13 year old absorbed in the pendulum experiment used by Piaget? Is discussion an appropriate activity for five year olds, or are we mixing that up with playing at having a tea party in a 'Wendy House' (a very important activity, as Vygotsky lay great store by the importance of pretend play to advance learning)? What kind of learning is happening when pupils watch teachers modelling activities? Let's look to the teaching of science to explore some of these questions.

STOP AND THINK

Reflection

Can young children discuss things? In the last few years a movement has grown in the UK for teaching philosophy to children of five and six (check out the news reports archive on your favourite daily paper website). One example question for five year olds is 'Why does the music sing so nicely?' Try answering that one with a group of your friends.

Activities in the teaching of science

Some would argue (Dori and Herscovitz, 2005; Pedrosa de Jesus and Coelho Moreira, 2009) that no other school subject promises so much active learning in conceptually complex contexts than science. What could be more enjoyable than imploding old oil cans by sucking out the air, or exploding rising gas bubbles and creating carbon rings on the school lab ceiling? Who has not looked in awe at the construction of a honeycomb or with fascination at the goings on in a glass-sided ants nest? Consider the pleasure in discovering the method of making

Science teaching has the potential to be exciting and interactive.

Source: iStockphoto

hydrogen sulphide (H_2S). What about the sense of achievement in raising the heaviest weight by just a simple pull of a rope going through the right configuration of pulleys?

Compare all of this with the reaction of one 14 year old called Tom. 'Why do we have to do writing in every subject? Today we did writing in PE and home ec. and all we've done in science this year is copy writing from the board and drawing diagrams in our books. It's so boring and I can't wait to give it up.' (Author's unpublished journal note). Tom is not alone. When students can choose subjects they wish to study, the dropout rate for sciences is worrying (George, 2006). What is the problem here? Look at Table 14.2. There is a representative checklist of some of the cognitive activities that are most relevant to the learning of science knowledge, skills and principles by the key scientific activities of investigation and experiment. Take a moment or two now to note down in the second column how often, in your experience, science lessons contained

Table 14.2. Cognitive activities in science.

Alphabetical order	Estimate of incidence in science lessons	Level of increasing cognitive complexity
Analysis		
Application		
Communication		
Conceptualisation		
Conjecture		
Memorisation		
Observation		
Organisation		
Pattern seeking		
Practice		
Recall		
Recording		
Refinement		
Replication		
Schema forming		

Source: Christine Chin, David Brown. Student-generated questions: a meaningful aspect of learning in science. *International Journal of Science Education*, Volume 24, Number 5 (2002), pp. 521–549.

opportunities to develop each of these cognitive activities. Then use the final column to rank each activity by level of increasing cognitive complexity.

There is no right or wrong set of answers – you may not know what some of the cognitive activities are. However, it is likely that you estimated observation and recording to be amongst the most frequently occurring, but also as two of the least complex activities. What would that tell us? There is evidence to suggest that science lessons in the main do not provide for cognitively appropriate learning activities (Osborne *et al.*, 2003) – learners may be too busy observing and recording – and there is little progression in the activities required particularly for those considered less able (Hallam and Ireson, 2005).

Of course, whilst there may be an argument that says guided discovery through the social construction of knowing 'what, how and why' should underpin all stages of learning in science, there are clearly some processes that cannot and should not be formalised at too early a stage. These include conjecture, analysis (including pattern seeking) and formal, multilevel pre-test/post-test experimentation. However, effective teachers of science engage children in a variety of learning activities and

part of the art of the teachers is to devise tasks that provide for cognitive development and progression without taking learners beyond their ability to cope. Psychologists can suggest developmentally appropriate learning activities in science and in other subject areas and there is a good deal of professional and academic literature (Edelson, 2001; BouJaoude, 2002; Psillos, 2004; Zohar, 2006; Lavonen *et al.*, 2006) which provides developmental frameworks for the selection of learning activities.

Psychologists also get heavily involved in developing and carrying out assessment activities on learners, particularly those learners that do not conform to the expected norms of cognitive development and learning. Assessing children's attainment and potential is an important application of developmental psychology in education and so it is to assessment that we next turn.

Developmentally appropriate assessment activities

All learning activities can, to a greater or lesser extent, be 'used' by teachers to assess how well a pupil is doing in achieving the learning that is envisaged, when designing and programming the activities. Assessment is an important strand of pedagogy – the science of teaching and learning – and there are three main phases of assessment: Initial assessment, Formative assessment and Summative assessment.

Initial assessment

Distinguished educational psychologist Dr David Ausubel wrote:

> If I had to reduce all of educational psychology to just one principle, I would say this: The most important single factor influencing learning is what the learner already knows. Ascertain this and teach him accordingly.
> (Ausubel *et al.*, 1978, p. 163)

It makes good sense for teachers to discover as much as possible about the developmental stage of a pupil before designing a programme of learning activities to take account of where she has got to. However, in school settings things are seldom so individual or personal. Broad assumptions are made that most children will have reached a certain stage of cognitive and emotional/moral development and that initial assessments are screening exercises to identify those who may fall outside of the expected norms and for whom special arrangements need to be made. Where individual differences from expected norms are identified as being acute (for example an 18 month difference at the age of 7, so the child may be displaying behaviours expected of a typical child of five-and-a-half), this may trigger a set of diagnostic assessments, normally delivered by a developmental specialist such as an educational psychologist who would then help teaching professionals to design a personal education plan including appropriate interventions. This may trigger part or parts of a national curriculum being disapplied from the child.

Assessment at the start of schooling or of a phase of schooling is common in European schools (Devís-Devís. 1997; Bakker, 1999; Huber and Grdel, 2006; Pasztor, 2008), in many of the other developed countries (Crooks, 2002; Moni *et al.*, 2002; Bierman *et al.*, 2008) and in the developing world (Liddell and Rae, 2001; Chae, 2003). What are sometimes called baseline assessments are used for making international comparisons (Tymms *et al.*, 2004; Hasseltgreen 2005). In England, initial assessments are associated with the start of the Foundation Stage and Key Stage 1, and these are carried out by teacher observation of pupils engaged in a range of learning activities. Such assessments are concerned with process and what

the child can do rather than assessing the worth of outcomes like a page of completed calculations or a written story. Observations are linked with developmental targets called 'Stepping Stones' associated with the Six Areas of Learning and Development (see http://www.education.gov.uk/ for more information).

Remember, many of these kinds of assessments are by observation of what the child can do in a variety of play and activity situations. Learning and development are closely linked at these early stages, but later on teachers tend to rely on what other teachers report about the successful progress of individual pupils through the programmes of study, drawing on the Levels of Attainment set forth in the National Curriculum for each subject. Written tests of what pupils can remember and do (the outcomes) become more common during the later primary years, and some of those tests provide summative and normative (see below) information which can be used as an initial assessment for a new phase of schooling. It is typical for pupils to enter secondary school armed with a set of level grades and that after some time and a test or two, usually in mathematics, pupils are then grouped by ability for some, or all, of the curriculum.

Formative assessment

Formative assessment is the ongoing evaluation of how pupils are doing whilst engaged in learning activities of one kind or another. The judgements made by teachers help to formulate what will be the next set of ideas covered and what are the most appropriate activities through which to engage pupils in the programme of study. An important skill for teachers is to use opportunities where a pupil finds an activity difficult or admits that he doesn't understand, by adapting the activity to diagnose what the problem may be. What follows is an example of the kind of diagnostic conversation that can take place:

T: How can you work out the number of squares in this array if there are 7 rows and 9 columns?
P: I don't know, is it 16?
T: That's interesting. How did you get 16?
P: I just added the 7 and 9?
T: OK let's look at this array of 2 rows and 3 columns?
P: That's easy, it's 6 squares
T: How did you get that?
P: I just looked at it.
T: Go on, anything else you can tell me?

P: Well there are 2 lots of 3, which makes 6
T: What kind of sum is 2 lots of 3 to make 6?
P: I don't know . . .

What is the teacher's diagnosis of the difficulty faced by the pupil? This youngster's schema for multiplication doesn't include the concept of 'lots of' to spark the retrieval of multiplication facts, irrespective of how automatic those facts are. As is very familiar to many teachers, this pupil doesn't know what sum to do because there's an important bit 'missing' from his multiplication schema and the schema needs to be refined.

Formal diagnostic assessments are also carried out by educational psychologists and special educational needs teachers (sometimes referred to as SENCOs) who 'identify' there is a problem by using normative tests, such as tests of intelligence (see Chapter 6). These compare an individual pupil's results on an individual test with many thousands of other children of (usually) the same age, to place them within a statistical framework. Remember from our opening example about Edward: 'It has been calculated that [Edward] is in the 92nd percentile for non-verbal communication which the therapist said was his strength and should be exploited, but she did not tell me how.'

Once a general problem has been identified by an Educational Psychologist or a SENCO, she may follow this up with a series of criteria-based tests where the performance of pupils is compared with statements (criteria) of what a pupil can or cannot understand in order to complete the elements of the test. By looking at the profile of criteria unsuccessfully met, an expert can diagnose the likely causes of under-performance and support the design of an intervention to remediate the difficulties. These processes are some of the most important applications of developmental psychology and theories of learning to education, and are worthy of additional study by following the references to assessment in the Recommended Reading at the end of the chapter.

Summative assessment

At the end of a topic (a defined part of a programme of study), a term, year or phase, summative assessment can take place. The content of an assessment summarises the substance of the programme of study – the expected learning outcomes – and provides information about how well an individual pupil has acquired and developed the understandings, skills and knowledge met during the topic, term, year or phase. Almost all these kinds of assessments are written tests, with full marks for complete and correct answers or no mistakes made. As pupils get older, the empha-

Source: iStockphoto

sis of school assessment moves away from what pupils can do and how they do it to what pupils can remember, or remember how or what to do. Straightforward scores are often generated which can be compared with other pupils and groups of pupils, with standards required by an accrediting body or with targets set by national organisations.

Examples of summative tests are the End of Key Stage Tests in England for pupils aged 7, 11 and 14 (now under considerable threat in their present form), the General Certificates of Secondary Education at age 16 (the end of compulsory schooling in Britain) and 'Finals' – examinations held at the end of three or four year undergraduate degree programmes at many British and European universities. These examinations mark and sometimes allow access to the next phase of education, or permit entrance to professions and membership of professional bodies.

All of this begs a question. How developmentally appropriate are different forms and types of assessment at any stage of schooling? A typical pattern in English schools and colleges is for children at three to six to be individually assessed by observation, children at 7 to 13 to be assessed by a combination of formative, diagnostic (in the best classrooms) and short written tests focused on recent learning experiences, and pupils/students aged 14–21 to be assessed on formal presentations, longer written examinations or the making of artefacts completed over a longer period of time. The Lifespan Box compares the typical pattern of assessment practice in English schools with the defining age-related psycho-social theories of psychologist Erik Erikson (described in Chapters 2 and 13, Adolescence). Remember that Erikson emphasised the emergence of the self, the search for identity, the individual's relationships with others and the role of culture throughout life (Erikson, 1963). Furthermore, Erikson suggests that children and adults at every age face a conflict between a potential positive outcome, such as learning to trust other people, and an unhealthy

LIFESPAN

Comparison of the age-related stage theories of Erikson with forms and outcomes of assessments

Infancy to 12 months – trust vs mistrust

Assessments are made by medical practitioners, developmental experts and 'knowing' parents of 'milestones of development' during the sensorimotor stage: e.g. weight gain; perceptual cognition through physical reactions to light, sound and orientation; grasp reflex to deliberate use of opposing grasp. Baby record and baby book records are shared between parents (who often 'own' the record) and practitioners (Woods, 2006).

12 months to 3 years – autonomy vs shame

Parents, carers and educational practitioners maintain a reassuring, confident attitude, informally noting achievements in basic motor and cognitive skills. Assessments are by observation of attempts to master new skills. Care is taken not to highlight unsuccessful attempts as children may begin to feel shame; they may learn to doubt their abilities to manage the world on their own terms. Remember, Erikson believes that children who experience too much doubt at this stage will lack confidence in their own abilities throughout life (McGregor and Elliot, 2005).

3 to 6 years – initiative vs guilt

Observations by early years practitioners and teachers are compared to early years developmental stages in defined areas of learning and development. Profile is maintained in school and nursery and shared with parents. There are no formal comparisons with others and assessments are formative, criteria-referenced and diagnostic. The key idea is that pupils look for positive feedback and encouragement to engage with assessment tasks without any sense of failure. To make sure each pupil has a chance to experience success, practitioners assess in small steps and avoid competitive situations altogether. Assessment is tolerant of mistakes, especially when children are attempting to do something on their own (Kochanska et al., 2002).

7 years to puberty – industry vs inferiority

Children confront an increased focus on outcomes, grades and performance as well as more academic, social and athletic competition on all fronts. Children move from preoperational to concrete-operational thinking, so accept grades as concrete reflections of the actuality of their performance and poor comparative grades are a cause for feelings of inferiority. To encourage industry and avoid feelings of inferiority, pupils are encouraged to set their own achievable goals for the outcomes of assessments and to record their own progress. Teachers regularly praise and reward pupils for making the most progress rather than being the best (Corpus and Lepper, 2007).

Adolescence – identity vs role confusion and young adulthood – intimacy vs isolation

Not all adolescents will move to formal thinking, and formal thinking may seldom be required at college and university. This means that students can still be successful by using pre-formal or perhaps concrete operational thinking to satisfy their examiners. A resilient sense of identity is based upon successful and meaningful attachments (Chapter 9, Attachment and Early Social Experiences). Adolescents (and those in emerging adulthood) need a lot of realistic feedback about their work and advice on how to improve, from those with whom they have formed robust attachments. When adolescents and young adults perform poorly, teachers and counsellors make sure they understand the consequences for themselves. Most importantly, because learners are 'trying on' roles (Morgan and Stevens, 2008), all those working with young people keep the roles separate from the person by realistically feeding back on performance without criticising the student (Currie et al., 2006).

Middle adulthood – generativity vs stagnation

There are no developmentally appropriate adaptations to the process of assessment for this stage. However, engagement with new learning and new ideas is essential to avoid stagnation, and assessment regimes encourage rather than hinder fresh engagement. Career change or resumption may require new engagement with formal or statutory assessment arrangements, and these might prove to be more difficult hurdles for those in middle adulthood (Langer, 2003).

Older adulthood – ego integrity vs despair

It is unlikely that many people will be subject to formal assessment practice at this stage, as learning activity is not usually subject to that kind of scrutiny, but there are examples where older people take up or continue learning activities in the arts, languages, painting and singing in choirs that can sometimes include a competitive aspect (Heuser, 2005). Those with ego integrity will often 'meet with triumph and disaster, yet treat these two imposters just the same.' (Rudyard Kipling: *If*)

alternative like becoming wary and apprehensive. What effect may the form of assessment used have upon a person's self-image and view of society?

Are the methods of assessment used in schools and colleges developmentally appropriate, based on your reading of the Lifespan box? Why/why not? There is an obvious link between development, learning and assessment practice during infanthood and the early years of schooling, and up to puberty many teachers hold to the idea that achievement is more important than attainment. However, formal and statutory testing arrangements in England, and formerly in other parts of the United Kingdom, have reinforced in children's and parents' minds the idea that by the age of 11 or so the die is cast and, for policy makers, any personal inferiority felt by some pupils is an unfortunate consequence of celebrating the attainment of other pupils and schools (Abbas, 2007; Tomlinson, 2008).

During adolescence, a youngster may become informally established as a class clown, a victim, a bully, sporty, brainy, lazy or 'cool'; sometimes reinforced by

Definitions

Achievement: personal accomplishment of skills, knowledge and understanding in comparison to an individual's former achievement. A measure of personal progress.

Attainment: personal accomplishment of skills, knowledge and understanding in comparison to typical accomplishments. Comparisons are made with examination requirements or the attainments of others.

formal reporting arrangements which include summative comments about attainment. However, there is a danger that most formal assessment is relatively impersonal (McLaughlin and Simpson, 2007) and summative because of large group sizes and students experiencing many different teachers during the school week (Williams and Gersch, 2004). Even at college or university, assessment regimes are dominated by individual extended writing tasks and examination 'finals' (Smith and Miller, 2005). Perhaps these shortcomings flow from the scale and characteristics of classrooms and schools in many parts of the developed world. Large classes and many different teachers can contribute to problems with managing learning and assessment activities, so let's take a look at a major concern for teachers at all phases of schooling: behaviour management.

Developmentally appropriate behaviour management

Let's begin with a true story: William (age 26) had just taken up a deputy headship at a village primary school. His previous post had been in a secondary school in a local town where he was Head of Maths. It was his first lunchtime and he was on the 'deputy head prowl' to seek out the ne'er-do-wells and other assorted miscreants that can make the lunch hour a challenging time for school staff. In the entrance hall was a particularly attractive display of windmills made by some older children in the school as part of a science topic on gears and pulleys. The sails of many of the windmills rotated beautifully when a handle at the back or the side was turned. Also in the entrance hall was a little lad from the Reception class (four to five years) who was having a fine old time turn-ing the handles and looking inside to see how it worked. 'What the blazes do you think you are doing young man?' William bellowed in his best Head-of-Maths-now-Deputy-Head voice. A terrified face spun around, a lov-ingly constructed windmill crashed to the floor and the little lad scarpered only to be found 10 minutes later hid-ing under the temporary classroom at the back of the school, still crying and inconsolable.

Was this appropriate behaviour management? Was this an act of behaviour management at all? Did the little chap need managing? What should William have done? Many years later when William told this story to a group of mature trainee teachers, one of them argued that the only behaviour here that needed managing was the teacher's, and that the outcomes of the behaviour were a broken windmill, a broken-hearted youngster, a broken relationship and an inauspicious start to a career as a pri-mary school teacher. The 'windmill incident' – the more embarrassing for William as time goes by – begs the important question of what behaviours need managing in schools and how this is best done?

To secure robust moral and social development, behav-iours and activities need to be managed and the way in which they are best managed depends upon the stage of development. Behaviours that need managing are those concerning both conduct and performance. Conduct is-sues relate to the way individuals and groups act and react towards others within the school or college community, and the buildings and resources that are the capital of the institution. These issues pertain to moral questions and decisions about what is right and wrong, and to acceptable or unacceptable social behaviour. We can draw on the theo-retical ideas of Jean Piaget, Lawrence Kohlberg and Erik Erikson to help us understand the behaviour management needs of children at different stages in their development. Clearly, disruptive, damaging or violent behaviour in schools is viewed as unacceptable behaviour and is subject to a range of sanctions that are usually well rehearsed and understood (Shreeve *et al.*, 2002; Goodman, 2006), but there is a good deal of disagreement about what sanctions are appropriate and how unacceptable behaviour should be dealt with (Goodman, 2006).

Performance relates to the behaviour of individuals and how effectively they are engaging with the learning activities provided by the school in order to make their expected academic progress. Absorbed engagement with developmentally appropriate learning activities is con-sidered successful activity provoked by intrinsic incen-tives or rewards (pleasant feelings and an improvement to self-image), or extrinsic incentives or rewards. Lack of engagement with learning activities can be deemed un-successful activity and so the intrinsic incentives are not satisfied and the extrinsic rewards are withheld. Success-ful performance behaviour is often rewarded and/or has its own rewards; unsuccessful performance behaviour is usually acknowledged then new targets set to take a 'first step to success' (Seeley *et al.*, 2009). Of course social competence and successful learning are associated, par-ticularly for children with special educational needs (Wight and Chapparo, 2008).

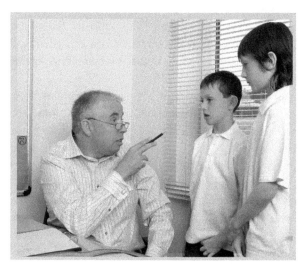

How best to manage bad classroom behaviour is the subject of much debate.

Source: iStockphoto

STOP AND THINK

Going further

Analyse and discuss with some fellow students the implications of the two statements: 'Clearly, disruptive, damaging or violent behaviour in schools is viewed as unacceptable behaviour and is subject to a range of sanctions that are usually well rehearsed and understood' and 'successful performance behaviour is often rewarded and/or has its own rewards; unsuccessful performance behaviour is usually acknowledged then new targets set to take a "first step to success"'.

This difference between conduct and performance is important in knowing how teachers and others should attempt to apply developmentally appropriate behaviour management. The little boy exploring the windmills was not engaged in bad behaviour, but was probably engaged in successful learning behaviour provoked by curiosity. This was successful behaviour 'rewarded' by being shouted at by a young teacher with a regrettable lack of confidence and understanding. Playing with the windmills was not bad behaviour and no sanction or punishment should have applied at all. He was getting his own reward by satisfying his curiosity and William could have further rewarded him by praising him and answering some of his questions – giving the little chap some 'teacher-time' would have been reward enough.

The first four stages of psychologist Lawrence Kohlberg's 'Six Stages of Moral Development' apply here and included in Table 14.3 is information about the application of developmental principles to classroom and school behaviour management practices in relation to each of the stages. Kohlberg allied a child's cognitive capacity (explored in Chapter 11, Development of Self-concept and Gender Identity) with the capacity for moral reasoning, and was more concerned with reasoning than children's understanding of right and wrong (Kohlberg, 1969). His research and theory about moral reasoning are explored fully in Chapter 13.

STOP AND THINK

Reflection

- Is there anything here that helps us to understand how best to deal with and help Edward (the subject of the opening example in this chapter)? It may be worth flicking back and re-reading the sections dealing with his behaviour and engagement with learning tasks.

- Do Kohlberg's stages and the commentary provided in Table 14.3 apply to Edward at all (remember he is eight) and will they ever apply? For example, can Edward empathise?

- When do children develop the ability to empathise and how does this happen (you may want to check back to Chapter 8, Theory of Mind).

Table 14.3 seeks to highlight ways that teachers and counsellors work with children and young people which take account of many of the themes of development that have been presented in Section III of this book (Chapters 9–13). In an ideal world, there would not be any need for teachers to reprimand children, or for

schools to use sanctions to modify the behaviour of the students, but sadly this is not the case. Indeed, some commentators report that schools and colleges are increasingly challenged by the behaviour of some of their pupils and students (Tyler and Jones, 2002; Leach, 2003; Derrington, 2005; Potts, 2006). One of the explanations for this trend (there is no more recent contradictory evidence) is that large secondary schools are finding it increasingly difficult to offer developmentally appropriate experiences for their students (Newman, 2008). Our final section will now consider what is meant by developmentally appropriate schooling and schools. In the UK we seldom talk about developmentally appropriate provision, but in some northern European countries, creating developmentally appropriate schools is a national and political aspiration (Wetz, 2009). Denmark is one such country whose current provision makes a marked contrast with that of many other European countries including the UK.

Developmentally appropriate schools

Learning from the Danish educational system

In search of developmentally appropriate schools, the author travelled to Denmark and spent a week visiting local schools, lecturing, questioning and having discussions in a teachers' training college in Skarup. The following account looks at the way that the Danish authorities have attempted to engage with the national aspiration for developmentally appropriate schools and includes a comparative commentary on equivalent UK provision drawing on ideas that have emerged in this chapter.

An important review of schooling in Denmark arose out of a national 'conversation' in the early 1990s. The review's findings were enacted in an education act (the Folkeskole Act of 1994) which gives emphasis to a national shared responsibility for the education and wellbeing of its young people. In England, the link between education and children's wellbeing was one adopted in 2002 in response to the tragic case of Victoria Climbie enshrined in the Every Child Matters programme (see **http://www.dcsf.gov.uk/everychildmatters/**). So far, Every Child Matters seems to have had little effect upon the structure of schooling and schools or on policy about the nature of

Table 14.3. Kohlberg's six stages of moral development and developmentally appropriate behaviour management in relation to conduct.

Level 1: Pre-conventional morality – to age 10		
Stage and title	Kohlberg's description	How effective teachers manage behaviour
Stage 1: Punishment-avoidance and obedience	Children will make moral decisions purely on the basis of self-interest. They will disobey rules if they think they can do so without getting caught.	Set clear rules about what is not acceptable behaviour (Woods, 2008). Children at this stage generally submit to authority so a reprimand will generally be accepted and all that is needed (Infantino and Little, 2005). Children obey rules to avoid being punished and expect their own and others' unacceptable behaviour to be punished (Beaman and Wheldhall, 2000).
Stage 2: Exchange of favours	Children recognise that others have needs, but prioritise their needs over those of others.	Teachers can agree with children a range of rewards and sanctions that would apply in certain circumstances (Shreeve *et al.*, 2002). Children now seek rewards for their actions because they believe they should behave well for their own gains (Osler, 2000). Children also attempt to engage in negotiation, so a school age child might be heard to say, 'I will be good if I can watch the TV programme afterwards' (Shreeve *et al.*, 2002). Amongst other aspects of practice, effective teachers hold hard to the idea that good behaviour is the expected norm and will challenge unacceptable behaviour (Swinson and Cording, 2002; Olive and Liu, 2005; Duncan-Andrade, 2007).
Level 2: Conventional morality		
Stage 3: Good boy/good girl	Young people make decisions on the basis of what will please others and are very concerned to keep friends.	Teachers emphasise the effect of bad behaviour on others including themselves. Being reprimanded includes being faced with the effects and outcomes of behaviour, and sanctions include removal from the social setting in which the behaviour took place for the benefit of all (Marzano and Marzano, 2003). This is where the 'cool-off space' is important and the giving of options to emphasise that consequences are fully understood (Levin and Nolan 2000; Elias and Schwab, 2006).
Stage 4: Law and order	Young people look to society as a whole for guidelines about moral decisions. They think of rules as absolute, inflexible and unchangeable.	What is considered unacceptable in the school or college is congruent with, and is understood by students in similar terms to, laws and sanctions found in wider society (Apel *et al.*, 2009). Therefore, violent, abusive or racist activity is considered the same in school as out of school. Unlawful acts such as the selling of drugs or stealing are dealt with by involving community support officers and the police service (Casella, 2002; Lyle and Hendley, 2007). Challenging behaviour is sometimes related to poor mental health and schools are often seen as the optimum setting to deliver inter-agency interventions (Spratt *et al.*, 2006).
Level 3: Post-conventional morality		
Stage 5 Social contract	Recognises that rules are social constructions – agreements that can be changed or ignored when necessary.	Does not readily apply in school and college settings.
Stage 6 Universal ethical principle	Adheres to a small number of universal abstract principles that transcend specific rules. Answers only to the inner conscience.	Does not readily apply in school and college settings.

schooling in England (Hudson, 2006; Payne, 2007; George and Clay, 2008).

The Folkeskole Act endorsed and required the design of a 12-year inclusive school experience for all children, with a commitment to a curriculum built on ideas of social relevance in a variety of schools which should be part of and be accountable to the local community. Grouping children by ability was made unlawful. All schools are well resourced and have status. In the UK (and elsewhere) schools are labelled 'good schools' and 'failing schools'. Different levels of resourcing are provided in private and state schools, and between areas where parents and local organisations (e.g. churches and businesses) contribute to school funds in formal and informal ways (Walford, 2001; Gillard, 2008). In impoverished underperforming schools, rolls (the headcount of pupils attending) fall as parents try to move their children into good schools (Gorard et al., 2002) or move house to a different area to 'win' places at good schools during the transition from primary to secondary schooling (Leech and Campos, 2003).

In Denmark, there are no transition difficulties, as primary and secondary provision is integrated into one Folkeskole (people's school) for all children aged from 6 to 16, with no more than 500 students in a school. In practice this means a two-form entry throughout (that is, there are two classes of each age group). There are nine years of compulsory education with an optional additional year at age 16; children are divided into groups by age, but not by ability; and progression from one year to the next is automatic.

Most UK primary schools are one- or two-form entry, but after transition pupils enter secondary school of typically 1000 pupils or more. Indeed there are a growing number of super-sized schools of pupil rolls between 1500 and 3000 (Power and Prasad, 2003; Spielhofer et al., 2004; Gillard, 2008). The contrast between primary and secondary schooling is stark and transfer can be a significant ordeal for children (Selman, 2003), many of whom make negative progression in educational attainment and social development (Sainsbury et al., 1998; Capel et al., 2004).

Teaching practice throughout Danish schools is based on group work and learning together which leads to ways of working required for the completion of a significant final-year project. Assessment is continuous and formative, and teachers are required not to give their students marks until they are 14 years of age. School status is not linked to public or statutory examination results, but to school ambience, the wellbeing of pupils, the quality of attachment relationships between teachers and pupils and the quality of learning experiences.

Much teaching practice at UK secondary schools and elsewhere in Europe is didactic (Veugelers and Vedder, 2003; Meyer, 2007) and 'skewed' by teaching to the statutory tests and public examinations taken in Britain at 16 and 18 years (Greatorex and Malacova, 2006). Assessments are generally summative and form the basis for reports to parents which include attainment grades and examination marks with positions relative to other pupils of the same age (Power and Clark, 2000).

In Denmark, the class group remains the same throughout so that students have continuity both with their subject teachers (who have a four-year training programme in child development and are expected to teach three or four subjects) and their class group. The key person for all students is the *Klasslaerer* (class teacher or tutor) who stays with the group all the way, providing a consistent attachment for pupils (and families) through school to young adulthood. In the UK, the class teacher or form tutor usually changes every year in both primary and secondary schools. Although the primary school class teacher will teach his class for almost the whole curriculum, at secondary school the form tutor may not teach her form for any subject (Osborn, 2001; Lodge, 2002; Marland, 2002; Reid, 2006) and it is not out of the ordinary for teenagers to be taught by 11 or 12 different teachers in a week and for a teacher to teach 400 different pupils in a week (Wetz, 2009).

The foregoing comparative descriptions demonstrate that the Danish folkeskoles represent developmentally appropriate schools, capable of delivering developmentally appropriate teaching and learning experiences and appropriate programmes of study. These schools in Denmark contrast sharply with current provision in secondary schooling in the UK and other parts of Europe where the application of developmental psychology to education is far less obvious. There are now increasingly urgent and powerful calls for this matter to be addressed by policy makers in the rest of Europe, and for the development of small 'different' secondary schools, particularly in areas of social and economic deprivation (Tasker, 2008; Rainey & Murova, 2004; Papatheodorou, 2002).

STOP AND THINK

Going further

Responses to the case study – Edward

The same case study notes from the beginning of the chapter were sent to a number of professionals working within the children's workforce who were asked for their response, including any ideas about what could be done. We have provided just a taste of their responses here:

'He would be placed in a school for children with special needs, where pupils learn to know other pupils with different kinds of problems and learn to deal with other pupils' problems as well as with their own.'

(Lisbeth Jonsson, School Teacher,
`Sotenäs Kompetenscentrum, Kungshamn, Sweden).

'This should not be a personal challenge for an individual teacher which results in a sense of failure but one where properly supported and resourced teaching teams address children's diagnosed learning and emotional needs in a carefully structured programme.'

(James Wetz, Secondary School Headteacher,
Visiting Fellow Bristol University).

'Try to arrange things so they have the maximum contact with areas of the curriculum that they enjoy, without skewing things too far away from the statutory obligations. If they are "statemented", I think they can be taught with less regard for the National Curriculum.'

(Michael Nicholson, Senior Lecturer in Education,
University of the West of England).

'Conversations with Edward should be focused on solutions rather than analysing what has gone wrong – not productive. When children mimic inappropriate behaviours it is usually an indication that boundaries are not secure or clear for them.'

(Marie Walker, Lead Behaviour Support Teacher,
Gloucestershire & Forest Pupil Referral Service).

During this chapter you have reflected on Edward's experience of school and considered whether there are ways in which the application of developmental psychology can shed some light on what troubles him, and what practically can be done to help him. How do these professionals' responses compare to your own judgements? Can you recognise the developmental or educational theories which underpin the different responses above?

Think about the ideas of developmentally appropriate provision, and the learning and developmental theories we have explored. What binds all of this together? What are the connections you can make between theory and practice; between developmental psychology and educational provision; between principles in action and reacting to personal and profound need? We learn by making these kinds of connections. What are the connections between this chapter the following, Chapters 15, 16 and 17 on bullying, ADHD and atypical development?

SUMMARY

The chapter contains an analysis and evaluation of the extent to which the main theories of developmental psychology and learning have been applied in schools, colleges and universities and has provided an assessment of the likely effectiveness of applying differing perspectives of educational theorists in relation to key themes of teaching and learning. Specifically, consideration was given to Urie Bronfenbrenner's mapping of the many interacting social contexts that affect development in his bio-ecological model of development, e.g. those which influence Edward. The model does not show how socio-cultural influences change over time. However, Jean Piaget framed one of the most influential age-related stage models of cognitive development. His stage model, which is the most commonly applied set of theories in early years settings and schools, forms part of the 'nature versus nurture' debate. Critics complain that Piaget ignored young children's inborn cognitive architecture and that what happens to us is what really matters.

Robbie Case's information-processing theory argues that the development of working memory is a key cognitive development for learning but, like Piaget's theory, it is criticised for giving too little emphasis to social and cultural influences. However, Lev Vygotsky emphasised the social construction of knowledge through interaction with more knowledgeable others. Ideas of the importance of the teachers, language development and cooperative learning provided the basis for a top ten of applications of Vygotsky's ideas. Critics claim that Vygotsky gave too little emphasis to the cognitive functioning of the brain and the Cutting Edge box provided information about recent attempts to understand what is happening in the brain at various important stages of learning.

The second part of the chapter builds on ideas of how educational systems and pedagogy can be enhanced by adopting developmentally appropriate approaches. Five themes of 'developmentally appropriate provision' were explored. These included curricula; teaching; learning and assessment activities; behaviour management; and the structure, size and organisation of schools. Observations of current practice evidenced in the research literature were used to show how effective teaching can be enhanced when principles of developmental psychology (e.g. information processing models which encourage teachers to provide timely and high-quality formative assessment feedback) can enhance provision and determine high-quality learning experiences for all age groups.

The example of Edward and his brother Richard was used to construct an argument about what to do for learners with special needs which is rooted in a thorough-going knowledge of psycho-social development. Respondents and others who have commented, many at length, about the opening example of this chapter are unanimous in this respect: the case study represents a problem that the teacher cannot solve alone, particularly as the problems are generated in life outside school. The boys need to be assessed thoroughly by a specialist in developmental and educational psychology. There can be no better definition or summary of the need for the application of developmental psychology in education.

REVIEW QUESTIONS

1 Outline two of the main developmental theories that have impacted on classroom practice in Britain during the last 40 years. Which has been most influential, and why?

2 What is meant by developmentally appropriate provision in schools and colleges? Give examples from your own experience and from your wider reading, and critically evaluate its effectiveness.

3 Discuss some of the ways in which cognitive development and learning theories are connected.

4 Which learning theory can best inform the practice of teaching and support developmentally appropriate learning activities? Justify your answer with reference to educational practice that you have experienced, and from your wider reading.

5 Are assessment practices at your own institution developmentally appropriate? Justify your answer with reference to theory, research and educational practice.

6 Describe the experience of learners attending schools which reflects the principles of developmentally appropriate provision. Compare and contrast the experience of learners at such schools with that of learners at other schools.

RECOMMENDED READING

To find out what might characterise cognitive maturation through adolescence, see:

Luna, B., Garver, K.E., Urban T.A., Lazar, N.A. & Sweeney, J.A. (2004). Maturation of cognitive processes from late childhood to adulthood. *Child Development*, *75* (5), 1357–1372.

For a full description and explanation of learning and teaching concepts, read Chapter 8 in:

Woolfolk, A., Hughes, M. & Walkup, V. (2008). *Psychology in Education*. Harlow: Pearson.

An important presentation of Robbie Case's research and theorising on these topics and one to browse on your next trip to the library is:

Case, R. & Okamoto, Y. (1996). *The Role of Central Conceptual Structures in the Development of Children's Thought.* Chicago, IL: University of Chicago Press.

One of the most useful sources for conceptualising how cognitive processes can inform teaching, learning and assessment and which, as the title suggests, is a most useful revision of work by educational psychologist Benjamin Bloom, is:

Anderson, L.W., Krathwohl, D.R., Airasian, P.W., Cruikshank, K.A., Mayer, R.E., Pintrich, P.R., Raths, J. & Wittrock, M.C. (Eds) (2001). *A Taxonomy for Learning, Teaching and Assessing – a Revision of Bloom's Taxonomy of Educational Objectives.* Boston, MA: Allyn & Bacon.

RECOMMENDED WEBSITES

For a comprehensive summary of over 50 theories of learning, see the website of educational psychologist, Dr Greg Kearsley:

http://tip.psychology.org/theories.html If you disagree with his 'take' on any of the theories or find the website useful, why not email him at: **gkearsley@sprynet.com.**

For helpful advice on the application of developmental psychology in classroom management, explore the behaviour4learning website for which the home page claims: 'The site provides access to the research & evidence base informing teacher education. All materials are quality assured through a rigorous process of academic scrutiny and monitoring undertaken by a team of expert teacher educators':

http://www.behaviour4learning.ac.uk/

Watch the video (or search for 'Teaching with Bayley' – a series of videos by psychologist John Bayley) on how the application of developmental and behavioural psychology in challenging situations can prove to be very successful:

http://www.teachers.tv/videos/attention-seekers

Reference is made in this chapter to the Every Child Matters agenda. What is 'Every Child Matters' and where did it come from? What is the envisioned impact in educational and social service contexts? Explore the HM Government web site at:

http://www.dcsf.gov.uk/everychildmatters/

One of the most important roles in applying developmental psychology in education is that of the 'Educational Psychologist'. 'Ed Psychs' are responsible for understanding children's learning, emotional and behavioural difficulties, for testing and diagnosis, developing learning plans and for designing interventions. Find out more about the role at:

http://www.educational-psychologist.co.uk/ roleofep.htm

or read:

Kelly, Bo, Woolfson, L. & Boyle, J. (2008). *Frameworks for Practice in Educational Psychology: A Textbook for Trainees and Practitioners.* London: Jessica Kingsley.

 Watch a school years video exploring education-oriented cognition. Further resources can be found at www.pearsoned.co.uk/gillibrand

Chapter 15
Understanding bullying
Elizabeth Nixon and Suzanne Guerin

Learning Outcomes

After reading this chapter, with further recommended reading, you should be able to:

1. Explain the issues in defining and investigating 'bullying' and reflect on different definitions of the behaviour;

2. Describe prevalence rates of bullying, gender-related trends in prevalence rates and the nature of involvement in bullying;

3. Discuss the development of bullying behaviour across early and middle childhood, and adolescence;

4. Identify the key features associated with cyberbullying and understand the distinctions between traditional forms of bullying and cyberbullying;

5. Critically evaluate key theoretical perspectives on bullying;

6. Compare the different types of interventions that have been developed to address the issue of bullying, and reflect on issues relating to their effectiveness.

Bullying in the press

'Many children too afraid to report bullying' The Hastings & St Leonard Observer 6 February 2009

'Third of youngsters victims of cyberspace bullying' The Scotsman 3 March 2009

'Bullies turn to hi-tech torment' The Dominion Post (Wellington, New Zealand) 16 March 2009

'Teachers need help with bullies' Sunday Times (South Africa) 29 March 2009

These newspaper headlines all appeared in the press within two months of each other in early 2009. Bullying is often discussed in the media, and stories range from reports of research studies or policy changes to stories of individual young people and their experiences of dealing with the challenges of bullying. As we can see from the headlines, the issues being considered here range from supporting teachers to considering more recent phenomena such as cyberbullying. It is interesting that within one month in 2009 the views of over 5500 young people in the UK were reported in the national and local press. The articles from the UK reported the findings of two different surveys completed by young people: one gathered the views of over 2000 11–18 year olds, while the other was completed by over 3500 young people between the ages of 10 and 16 years. But what type of messages do these reports give us about bullying?

The article in the *Hastings & St Leonard Observer* reports quite positive messages, saying that the large majority of young people enjoy going to school and feel safe there. The positive messages continue with the statement that three-quarters of the young people felt that bullying was taken seriously by the school staff. However, in contrast to these positive messages, the newspaper reports that almost one in three young people have been bullied in the last year. More problematic, perhaps, is the finding that one in four of those bullied had not told anyone – the message at the heart of the headline.

Interestingly, the article from the *Scotsman* focuses on the more recent phenomenon of cyberbullying. Given the explosion of media interest in young people's use of the internet, it is topical to consider this 'new' form of bullying. The newspaper piece reports that a third of young people had experienced cyberbullying but contrasts this with the finding that one in seven teachers describe being cyberbullied by pupils. This brief piece highlights this particular form of bullying and, given the interest in this behaviour, we will return to the topic of cyberbullying later in this chapter.

- Were you, or anyone you know, bullied as a child?
- Was it ever reported?
- Was it resolved?
- What advice might you give today to a child who is being bullied?

▶

▶ Introduction

Bullying is an important social issue that affects the lives of countless children and young people around the world. It is sometimes said that the exploitation of the weak by the strong is a long-standing feature of how nature works (Rigby, 2002a). Some even argue that bullying can be understood as an expression of an evolutionary drive to socially dominate others in order to acquire additional resources or improve one's social standing (Hawley, 1999). Notwithstanding these ideas about the possible evolutionary basis of bullying behaviours, being the victim or target of bullying is a grim daily reality that undermines children's healthy development. There appears to be a reliable relationship between being the victims of bullying and impaired physical and mental health – these children tend to be unhappy, lonely and have low self-esteem, and display various forms of psychological distress, including anxiety, depression and high levels of social dysfunction (Rigby, 2001). The negative effects of bullying are not restricted to victims, however. Children who bully others also suffer from poor psychological adjustment, higher levels of behaviour problems and more criminal convictions later in life (Whitney and Smith, 1993; Kumpulainen and Räsänen, 2000).

There is little doubt that there is heightened awareness nowadays about bullying in the media, among parents, educators and policy makers, although this may not necessarily reflect radical shifts in the prevalence of bullying. The first systematic research on the topic of school bullying was the pioneering work of Dan Olweus in Sweden and Norway in the early 1970s. Since that time, there has been a proliferation of research into the issue, some of which we will look at in this chapter. What has become clear is that bullying is a complex social process that can have extremely damaging consequences for both bullies and their victims. In this chapter, we consider how the problem of bullying is conceptualised and understood, and examine what can be done to reduce the scale of the problem.

What is bullying?

In conducting research on any topic it is important to have a clear definition of the target behaviour(s). This is essential both to focus the research and to ensure that the potential for learning is maximised. In this section, we will consider the question: what is bullying? Different definitions of bullying and how they have evolved over time will be considered. In addition, we will explore the small body of research that has examined what bullying means to children and young people.

In the UK, the Department for Children, Schools and Families defined bullying as 'behaviour by an individual or group, usually repeated over time, that intentionally

> **Definition**
> Bullying: an interaction which is intended to and does cause harm to a person who is seen as being less powerful than the perpetrator.

hurts another individual or group either physically or emotionally' (DCSF, 2007, p. 7). This is an important definition as it forms the basis for the UK Government's policy position on bullying in school. However, when we look at the different definitions of bullying that have been presented in research and policy documents, it is clear that the definition of bullying has changed significantly over the course of the last 20 years of research.

Early attempts at defining bullying

One area of change relates to the perpetrators of bullying behaviour, with early formulations focusing more on the group's rather than the individual's activities. For example, Lagerspetz et al. (1982) stressed the collective or group nature of bullying behaviours while Erling Roland's (1989) definition included behaviours that were carried out by individuals or groups. Interestingly Roland's formulation was one of the first to stress the power imbalance between bullies and victims, describing the victim of bullying as 'an individual who is not able to defend himself' (p. 21). David Lane (1989) also reported on changes in the types of behaviours that are cited in definitions, highlighting the move from more concrete behaviours such as physical and verbal aggression to more psychological forms such as exclusion.

A comprehensive summary of the criteria common to most definitions of bullying was provided by David Farrington, a forensic psychologist, whose research has explored the full range of human aggressive behaviour, from bullying to serious criminality. He defined bullying as:

> physical, verbal, or psychological attack or intimidation that is intended to cause fear, distress, or harm to the victim; an imbalance of power, with the more powerful child oppressing the less powerful one; absence of provocation by the victim; and repeated incidents between the same children over a prolonged period
>
> (Farrington, 1993, p. 384)

This definition summarises what are generally accepted to be the key elements of bullying behaviour and the influence of these criteria can be clearly seen in the definition applied by the Department of Children, Schools and Families mentioned above.

STOP AND THINK

Reflection

Take a few minutes and think about this definition of bullying. Does it reflect your own views of what bullying is? Imagine yourself in a school playground trying to establish whether or not an incident between two children constitutes bullying.

- What questions do you need to ask?
- Whose views are important to obtain?
- What might influence your ability to determine the true nature of the incident?

While there is general agreement among researchers about the definition of bullying, when we look at research which has asked children, young people and adults for their definitions of bullying, a more complicated picture emerges. As children and young people are the perpetrators, victims and witnesses of school bullying, it is important to consider how they conceptualise the behaviour. A number of studies have specifically explored these definitions and have shown that children and young people have quite well-developed definitions of bullying (Arora, 1996).

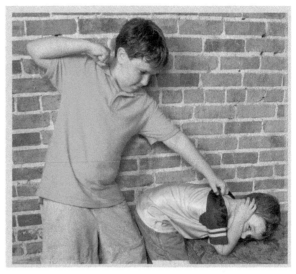

Traditionally bullying may be conceptualised as direct and physical.

Source: iStockphoto

Children and young people's definitions

One of the patterns that has emerged clearly from the research looking at children and young people's definitions of bullying is the range of behaviours that are incorporated. This is a key area of agreement between children's and researchers' definitions. One of the most important studies in this area was led by Peter Smith, and was coordinated across 14 countries (Smith *et al.* 2002). This study used cartoons of different behaviours to explore the views of over 1200 children and young people aged 8 and 14 years. The data showed that children distinguished between physical, verbal and psychological forms of bullying, and distinguished these from other behaviours. This study also highlighted age differences, which we will return to below.

However, just as there are areas of agreement, this is not consistent across all of the criteria highlighted by David Farrington above. Interestingly, studies where children are asked about their views using more open-ended methods such as interviews and focus groups (group-based interviews) often produce different results. One of the first interview studies of children's and young people's definitions of bullying was conducted by Kirsten Madsen (1996), who looked at groups of children and adults aged 5 to 6 years, 9 to 10 years, 15–16 years, and 18–29 years. All the groups were interviewed about their perceptions and definitions of bullying. Madsen found that children and young people rarely mentioned repetition (3%), intention (5%) or provocation (7.5%) as defining features of bullying. Another study, which involved interviews with 168 Irish 11 and 12 year olds, also supported these findings (Guerin and Hennessy, 2002).

Developmental changes in definitions

In addition to looking at children's definitions of bullying, a number of recent studies have considered developmental patterns in definitions from childhood to adulthood. Smith and Levan (1995) found that six year olds were not able to distinguish between fighting and bullying, and Smith *et al.*'s (2002) 14-country study found that eight year olds were able to contrast aggressive and non-aggressive scenarios, but were not able to distinguish among the different forms of bullying. Claire Monks and Peter Smith (2006) later showed that four to eight year olds differentiated between aggressive and non-aggressive acts while adolescents and adults had a more sophisticated understanding of bullying, considering imbalance of power and repetition of behaviour in their definitions. Other research comparing children's, parents', teachers' and researchers' views supports the argument that differences exist between adult and child definitions, particularly around the nature of bullying as intentional (Smorti *et al.*, 2003; Naylor *et al.*, 2006). Thus, it is important to take on board the child's view, given the extent to which teachers (and indeed other adults) may not be aware of the level of bullying in a school.

The implications of a lack of consensus in definition

Given that there are areas of both agreement and disagreement between the individuals who are the victims, perpetrators and witnesses of bullying, and the experts whose work informs practice in tackling the behaviour, it is important to ask: what are the implications of disagreement? The most important implication relates to the way in which we tackle bullying. We discuss interventions later in this chapter, but it is fair to say that approaches where adults and children work together with a common understanding of what bullying is may have greater potential to succeed than approaches involving either

group's perspective alone. If the two groups differ in their views of the behaviour that is supposed to be targeted, they may find themselves working at cross-purposes. As it is adults who act to implement interventions in schools, we must be careful that we do not address only those behaviours that fit with adult definitions.

While we began this section by stressing the importance of having a clear definition of target behaviours for the purpose of research (and indeed practice), it seems that this is not something that exists in bullying research. Throughout this book, you have come across other areas of research where developmental psychologists have different conceptualisations of certain constructs (think back to Chapter 6, Memory and Intelligence for example, where different ideas about intelligence are discussed; or Chapter 10, Childhood Temperament and Behavioural Development where different ideas about temperament are considered). However, it could be that it is more important to recognise the views of different groups, than to attempt to decide who is right! This issue is further complicated by historical changes in definitions of bullying. We touched on this earlier but now turn to an example of how our understanding of bullying

Cyberbullying is a relatively new form of bullying.
Source: iStockphoto

CUTTING EDGE

Bullying in cyberworld

Despite the significant amount of research conducted on the nature of bullying, our awareness of the constellation of behaviours that make up this concept continues to develop. One of the most recent forms of the behaviour to be considered is cyberbullying.

While cyberbullying research is still (relatively) in its infancy, a number of definitions have been proposed. For example, Kowalski *et al.* (2008) define it as 'bullying through email, instant messaging, in a chat room, on a website or gaming site, or through digital messages or images sent to a cellular phone' (p. 1), while Peter Smith and colleagues describe this subset of behaviour as 'an aggressive, intentional act, carried out by a group or individual, using electronic forms of contact, repeatedly and over time against a victim who cannot easily defend him or herself' (2008a, p. 376). Looking at these two definitions, we can see that while the first focuses more on the distinct behaviours that might be classified under this term, the second definition draws more on the criteria discussed in general definitions, i.e. repetition, intention and an imbalance of power.

A recent paper by Vanderbosch and Van Cleemput (2008) at the University of Antwerp reports the findings of a study that explored the views of a large sample of Belgian adolescents. Focus groups were used to explore the young people's views of cyberbullying. Many aspects of this group's definition were comparable to existing views, including intentionality and repeated occurrence. However, in one of the key findings they highlighted that the term cyberbullying is aligned more with internet-based behaviours, rather than the broader forms of electronic media-based interactions described by Kowalski and colleagues above. Despite this finding, the term cyberbullying is generally taken to refer to the broad range of electronic media-based behaviours, and it is this definition that will be applied in this chapter.

What are the implications of this new form of bullying? We know that peer victimisation is a precursor of children's loneliness and school avoidance (Kochenderfer and Ladd, 1996). However, skipping school may no longer make things easier for victims of bullying.

Children with mobile phones or computers at home may now be subjected to electronic forms of bullying like harassing or threatening emails or text messages, defamatory websites and online polls in which individuals post mean or insulting comments about them. Unlike traditional bullying that usually takes place during circumscribed periods of time (e.g. on the way to and from school or during school), these electronic forms of bullying can transcend school grounds and the school day and can potentially happen anytime and anywhere. As this is a relatively new issue for research, many of the studies are focused upon establishing prevalence rates of cyberbullying and relations between involvement in cyberbullying and more traditional forms of bullying. Even less research examines the impact of cyberbullying on victims.

The phenomenon of cyberbullying has been labelled an emerging public health problem with devastating – even fatal – effects for some victims. One example is the case of Ryan Halligan from Vermont in the USA, reported by Kowalski and colleagues (2008). Ryan died by suicide at 13 years of age following persistent bullying and humiliation by peers at school, which continued online. Towards the end of the school year, it was rumoured in instant messaging conversations and at school that Ryan was gay. Following his death, Ryan's father discovered that he had been cyberbullied in regard to these rumours. His father also discovered that Ryan had befriended one of the popular girls from school online, as a means to quash the 'gay' rumour. When Ryan approached the girl in person after the summer holidays, he discovered that she had joked about liking him and had circulated their private online conversations to her friends in order to humiliate him. Two weeks before his death just weeks into the new school year, Ryan wrote an instant

Definition

Traditional bullying: forms of bullying behaviour that involve physical, verbal or psychological attacks without the use of electronic media.

message stating: 'Tonight is the night, I think I'm going to do it,' to which his 'friend' replied: 'It's about f** time.' As technologies become increasingly prevalent in the lives of children and young people, we will undoubtedly hear and read more tragic stories such as these. Following Ryan's death, Vermont enacted a Bullying Prevention Policy Law in May 2004 and later adopted a Suicide Prevention Law which provides measures to assist teachers and others to recognise and respond to depression and suicide risks among teens. Ryan's case has also been cited by legislators in other US states proposing legislation to curb cyberbullying (Halligan, 2009).

It is likely that the effects of cyberbullying are similar to those of traditional bullying. In one of the few studies on the effects of cyberbullying, Ybarra and Mitchell (2004) found that youths who are both online bullies and victims are most likely to reveal serious psychosocial challenges, including problem behaviour, substance use, depressive symptoms and low school commitment.

Online bully/victims (those who bully others online and are online victims themselves) were six times more likely to report emotional distress as a result of being the target of internet harassment, compared to those who are online victims only.

Some researchers believe that the long-term effects of cyberbullying are as bad if not worse than those that accompany traditional bullying because it is much more difficult to escape from cyberbullying – a child who is electronically bullied must cease to communicate electronically in order to escape from the bullying. This may have other implications for the child such as becoming disconnected from his social network. Further, the public nature of cyberbullying increases the impact of the bullying – victims of cyberbullying can be potentially humiliated and denigrated in the view of thousands of individuals (Kowalski *et al.*, 2008). However, much more research is needed to further understand the long-term impact of cyber bullying on victims.

continues to change, as a new form of bullying – known as cyberbullying – has emerged.

Involvement in bullying

A great number of studies have been conducted to explore how commonly bullying occurs (its prevalence) and the nature of children's involvement in bullying. These studies have generally presented participants with a definition of bullying and asked them to report their involvement based on that definition. However, as we have seen in the previous section, this may be problematic if bullying means something different to children than it does to adults or researchers. It is important to bear in mind that the majority of studies using researchers' definitions may not represent the extent and nature of bullying as it is experienced and perceived by children themselves.

Who is involved in bullying?

When we think about the people involved in bullying, what type of people do we think about? Many people might hold the stereotypes of the quiet, shy and academically orientated victim and the popular, physically developed and perhaps less academically orientated bully. However, looking at what we know about the types of children who are involved in these behaviours the reality is more complex. Later in this chapter, we will consider the way in which children can be involved in bullying both directly and indirectly (as part of the group process); however, for now let us consider the characteristics of the groups most directly involved in the behaviour: bullies, victims and bully/victims.

Definitions

Cyberbullying: forms of bullying behaviour that use electronic media such as the internet, mobile phones, etc.

Bully/victims: children and young people who engage in bullying others and are bullied themselves.

Table 15.1. Key characteristics of different groups involved in bullying as identified by research.

Group	Personal characteristics	Family characteristics
Victims	Lower self-esteem than children not involved (O'Moore and Kirkham, 2001)	For females – poor communication (Rigby, 1994) More cohesion than bullies (Stevens *et al.*, 2002)
Bullies	Lower self-esteem than children not involved, but higher than victims (O'Moore and Kirkham, 2001) Feel more helpless than non-bullies (Barboza *et al.*, 2009)	Families show less cohesion (Bowers *et al.*, 1992) Low levels of emotional support (Rigby, 1994) More perceived family conflict (Stevens *et al.*, 2002)
Bully/Victims	Lower self-esteem than bullies and victims (O'Moore and Kirkham, 2001)	Similar levels of perceived family conflict to bullies (Stevens *et al.*, 2002)

Children and young people who bully others are generally referred to as bullies or perpetrators, while those who are bullied or victimised are generally referred to as victims. The term bully/victim is used to refer to individuals who are involved both as bullies and victims. There has been a large body of literature on the characteristics of these groups, and studies have considered both personal characteristics (e.g. self-esteem), and family characteristics. Table 15.1 highlights just some of the patterns that have been identified.

One of the key challenges in this area is the extent to which findings from individual research studies might contradict each other. In discussing patterns of self-esteem among children involved in bullying, Mona O'Moore (O'Moore and Kirkham, 2001) highlights some of the different patterns identified in research. However, reviewing the findings it appears that the most consistent pattern is that all of those involved in bullying have lower levels of self-esteem than those not involved in bullying while, within the participant group, bully/victims seem to show the lowest levels of self-esteem.

In relation to features of the family, the general pattern is that the families of bullies and bully/victims appear to show more conflict and less cohesion then families of victims and children not involved in bullying. However, a study by Stevens *et al.* (2002) highlighted an interesting pattern. While ratings of family functioning by children showed differences across the groups as highlighted in the table above, ratings given by parents showed no differences.

So how do we draw a clear conclusion from this literature? On a simplistic level, there is evidence to suggest that children and young people who are involved in bullying show different patterns of personal and family functioning when compared to non-involved children and to each other. However, on a more intricate level, there is a need to consider whether there are causal relationships in these patterns. It is unclear whether participation in or exposure to bullying behaviour is caused by these factors, whether these factors are themselves the result of bullying or whether some common third factor is the cause. As many students know, establishing causation in human behaviour research is a major challenge (see Chapter 3, Research Methods).

Interestingly, very few studies have attempted to reflect on this issue from a qualitative perspective. While some qualitative studies ask children about their views of bullying generally, very few have asked children about their own experience of being involved. It is understandable that the challenges of doing this ethically might prevent a researcher from pursuing this topic. However, two studies have looked at children's experiences in this way. Gamliel *et al.* (2003) report a study of six young American students, one of whom was identified as a bully. In contrast, Mishna (2004) focuses on the views of victims only, but did also explore parents' and teachers' views. There is no doubt that there are additional insights to be gained from talking to children about their experiences of being bullied and their own reasons for participating in bullying. However, this continues to be a gap in the existing literature.

NATURE–NURTURE

Are some children biologically predisposed to become bullies?

Could the kind of qualities associated with bullying others be at least to some degree biologically inherited? What can behavioural genetics – the study of nature and nurture – tell us about the origins of bullying? In an early study by O'Connor et al. (1980) conducted in the US, mothers of 54 pairs of identical twins (who share 100% of their genes) and mothers of 33 pairs of non-identical twins (who share 50% of their genes) rated their eight year old children on their tendency to bully others. The identical twin correlation (0.72) was substantially higher than the fraternal twin correlation (0.42). As we have seen previously, if genetic influence is important for a trait, identical twins will be more similar than fraternal twins. Therefore, this difference was interpreted as a sign of a genetic influence upon the predisposition to bully others.

Behaviour geneticists have been concerned for some time now about the heritability of aggressive behaviours, a central quality related to bullying. One impressive report was based on data from British and Swedish studies involving over 1500 twin pairs. This study found that identical twin correlations (ranging from 0.68–0.82) were greater than non-identical twin correlations (ranging from 0.41–0.44) for aggressive symptoms, again suggesting that a tendency towards aggressive behaviour is highly heritable (Eley et al., 1999). Yet there is still a long way to go to understand how genetics influence aggressive behaviour and to identify the particular biological pathways involved. It may be that particular aspects of temperament (such as self-regulation), which have a strong genetic base, may render the individual more likely to respond aggressively in social situations and that gene-controlled neurotransmitters, such as serotonin, have a role to play in this relationship.

Of course, at the heart of the nature–nurture debate and understanding genetic influence is the study of environmental influences. Beyond genetic influence, the roles of the family environment and parenting have been investigated with respect to involvement in bullying.

In his book *Friends and Enemies: Peer Relations in Childhood*, Barry Schneider (2000) reviewed a number of studies examining the relationship between parenting behaviour and childhood aggression and peer acceptance. These studies consistently showed that parenting characterised by high levels of restrictiveness and harsh discipline (authoritarian parenting) was associated with aggressive behaviour in children. Of course, just because we have observed a relationship does not mean that we can assume that harsh parenting gives rise to aggressive behaviour. It is possible that the aggressive behaviour is a cause rather than an effect of punitive parenting.

One useful study adopted a prospective (forward-looking) approach to mapping early family experiences onto later involvement in bullying. Schwartz et al. (1997) studied the early family experiences of a group of 198 5 year old boys. Four to five years later, aggressive behaviour and peer victimisation were assessed in school. Sixteen boys were identified as aggressive victims, 21 as non-aggressive victims, 33 as non-victimised aggressors and 128 as normative boys. Analysis of the early family experiences of the aggressive boys (both victimised and non-victimised groups) revealed some interesting patterns. Compared to the other groups, boys who emerged as aggressive victims were found to have had pre-school histories of experience with harsh, disorganised and potentially abusive home environments. Mother–child interactions were characterised by hostility and overly punitive and restrictive parenting. These children were also exposed to higher levels of marital conflict. In contrast, these experiences did not characterise the home experiences of non-victimised aggressors. However, the home environments of these children did incorporate exposure to aggressive and conflictual role models.

These authors concluded that observation of violence among adults may dispose a child towards aggressive behaviour, but only the experience of violence disposes a child towards the combination of peer victimisation and aggressive behaviour. This prospective study enables us to infer with greater confidence that harsh parenting is a likely contributory factor to children's aggressive behaviour. However, it is still possible that a third variable (such as biological vulnerabilities) leads to both particular family experiences and maladaptive social behaviour. Thus, it seems that bullying is a complex phenomenon that must be understood as a product of the characteristics of the individual bully and their family characteristics, as well as the broader social settings in which bullying incidents take place.

STOP AND THINK

Going further

Try to design and plan out an imaginary research project which would explore bullying from a qualitative perspective, interviewing bullies, victims and bully/victims.

- Using your knowledge of ethics in research (refer back to Chapter 3 if necessary) what ethical issues might you encounter and how could you overcome them?

- Consider your obligations to protect all of your participants; to obtain informed consent from children/parents/teachers; to maintain the anonymity and confidentiality of your participants. What are the challenges? How might you resolve them?

How prevalent is traditional bullying?

Since the late 1980s, studies of the extent and nature of bullying have been carried out in a range of countries. However, reviewing the prevalence of the behaviour reported in these studies highlights the challenge of representing the patterns of involvement across groups of victims, bullies and bully/victims. In order to consider these patterns, we will consider prevalence for each of these three groups separately.

Prevalence of victimisation

The percentage of children bullied by others reported within nine studies has been summarised in Table 15.2.

As we can see from the table, these surveys across a range of countries have yielded considerable variations in the prevalence of victimisation. It is difficult to know whether these differences are real or reflect methodological or classification differences. The definitions for bullying vary across the studies, as do the time frames used and the age of the participants. Some studies report specifically how frequently bullying occurred (for example, at least once a week), others use less clearly defined time frames, such as 'regularly', 'frequently' or 'occasionally'. Other studies record whether children have ever been bullied, while some studies refer to the last school term or school year only. Thus, prevalence rates are not directly comparable across the studies. A general trend, however, is that many studies report greater involvement at less frequent levels with a lower proportion of children being bullied on a more frequent basis.

The most comprehensive cross-national study of bullying along with other health behaviours was the Health Behaviour of School-aged Children (HBSC) study of 162 000 children aged 11–15 years reported by Currie *et al.* (2004). This study found that 11% of children across 34 countries were bullied at least twice a month during the previous months. Rates of being bullied for 13 year old girls ranged from 4.2% in Malta and Sweden to 34% in Lithuania. Rates of being bullied for boys ranged from 5.9% in Sweden to 38.6% for boys in Lithuania. We can have greater confidence in the comparability of these rates, given that a standard questionnaire was administered across the different samples.

STOP AND THINK

Going further

Consider the high level of variation evident in the studies presented above and the possible explanations posed.

- Can you think of other possible reasons for these national differences?

- Are there factors within a social or cultural group that may increase or decrease the reported incidence of bullying?

Table 15.2. Details of prevalence of being bullied in different countries from different published reports.

			Sample size	Prevalence of being bullied	
				Infrequently/at all	Regularly
Olweus (1993a)	Norway	7–16 years	130 000	Not reported	9% once a week or more
Whitney and Smith (1993)	England	8–11 years	2623	27% sometimes or more	10% once a week or more
		11–16 years	4135	10% sometimes or more	4% once a week or more
O'Moore *et al.* (1997)	Ireland	8–12 years	9599	18.7% once or twice 8.4% sometimes	1.9% once a week 2.4% several times a week
		12–18 years	10 843	11.6% once or twice 3.2% sometimes (all referring to during last term)	0.8% once a week 1.5% several times a week (all referring to during last term)
Rigby (1997)	Australia	9–18 years	5396	35% sometimes or more often	12.8% at least once a week
Tomas de Almeida (1999)	Portugal	6–9 years	2746	Not reported	21.9% more than twice
		10–11 years	3270	Not reported (all referring to during last term)	21.6% more than twice
Borg (1999)	Malta	9–14 years	6282	41.5% 'once or twice' and 'sometimes'	19% about 'once a week' and 'several times'
Wolke *et al.* (2001)	England	6–8 years	2377	Not reported	24.5% at least once a week 34.7% four or more times in past six months
	Germany	8 years	1538	Not reported	8% at least once a week 21% four or more times in past six months
Currie *et al.* (2004)	34 countries	11–15 years	16 2000	34% at least once during the previous couple of months	11% at least two to three times a month
East Sussex County Council (2008)	England	10–14 years	3863	30.8% in the past year	6% bullied 'a lot'

Prevalence of bullying others

In examining the rates of perpetration of bullying, similar issues emerge in comparing findings across studies. The findings relating to perpetrators of bullying from the nine studies previously mentioned are reported in Table 15.3.

As with figures for reported involvement as a victim of bullying, there is significant variation in figures here, ranging from less than 1% to over 30%. Recognising the methodological variation in these studies, it is again useful to reflect on the multinational Health Behaviour of School-aged Children (HBSC) study (Currie *et al.*, 2004).

This study found that 9%, 12% and 13% of 11, 13 and 15 year olds, respectively, reported frequently perpetrating bullying against another. There was considerable variability across the countries: Germany, Lithuania and Austria were among the countries with the highest rates, while Wales, Scotland and Ireland were among the countries with the lowest rates.

Prevalence of bully/victims

One form of involvement in bullying which is important to consider is that of the bully/victim – as mentioned

Table 15.3. Details of prevalence of bullying others in different countries from different published reports.

Authors	Country	Age range	Sample size	Prevalence of bullying others	
				Infrequently/at all	Regularly
Olweus (1993a)	Norway	7–16 years	130 000	Not reported	7% once a week or more
Whitney and Smith (1993)	England	8–11 years	2623	12% sometimes or more	4% once a week or more
		11–16 years	4135	6% sometimes or more	1% once a week or more
O'Moore et al. (1997)	Ireland	8–12 years	9599	19.7% once or twice 5% sometimes	0.7% once a week 0.7% several times a week
		12–18 years	10 843	12.8% once or twice 2.7% sometimes (all referring to during last term)	0.35% once a week 0.8% several times a week (all referring to during last term)
Rigby (1997)	Australia	9–18 years	5396	23.9% sometimes or more often	4% at least once a week
Tomas de Almeida (1999)	Portugal	6–9 years	2746	Not reported	19.6% more than twice
		10–11 years	3270	Not reported	15.4% more than twice (all referring to during last term)
Borg (1999)	Malta	9–14 years	6282	34.7% 'once or twice' and 'sometimes'	14.2% about 'once a week' and 'several times'
Wolke et al. (2001)	England	6–8 years	2377	Reported as never/seldom so not included	14% four or more times in past six months 2.4% at least once a week
	Germany	8 years	1538	Reported as never/seldom so not included	17.1% four or more times in past six months 4.8% at least once a week
Currie et al. (2004)	34 countries	11–15 years	162 000	35% at least once during the previous couple of months	11% at least two to three times a month
East Sussex County Council (2008)	England	10–14 years	3863	11% in the past year	2% bullied 'a lot'

earlier, these are the children who both bully others and are bullied by others. There are two important reasons for including the category of bully/victim in research in bullying. The first is that failing to identify the number of bully/victims might mean that the involvement in bullying is over-estimated, as bully/victims are included in the figures for both bullies and victims. The second important reason is that, as discussed earlier in the section on characteristics, this group potentially differs from bullies, victims and uninvolved pupils in their experiences, background and later life adjustment. While these children share characteristics of both bullies and victims,

bully/victims are not a simple average or composite of the bully and victim groups (Bowers et al., 1992). Though fewer in number than 'pure victims', these children appear to be at a higher risk for maladjustment across many domains of functioning (Schwartz et al., 2001). Table 15.4 summarises some of the studies that have reported the prevalence of this group.

This table highlights one of the main difficulties with understanding the prevalence of this type of involvement in bullying – that there is a high degree of inconsistency in reporting on the category of bully/victim. It is only more recently that this group seems to have been given

Table 15.4. Details of prevalence of bully/victims in different countries from different published reports.

Authors	Country	Age range	Sample size	Prevalence of being a bully/victim
Olweus (1993a)	Norway	7–16 years	130 000	1.9%
Whitney and Smith (1993)	England	8–11 years	2623	Not reported
		11–16 years	4135	
O'Moore et al. (1997)	Ireland	8–12 years	9599	14.1%
		12–18 years	10 843	
Rigby (1997)	Australia	9–18 years	5396	Not reported
Tomas de Almeida (1999)	Portugal	6–9 years	2746	Not reported
		10–11 years	3270	
Borg (1999)	Malta	9–14 years	6282	Not reported
Wolke et al. (2001)	England	6–8 years	2377	12%
	Germany	8 years	1538	13%
Currie et al. (2004)	34 countries	11–15 years	162 000	24% reported fighting or bullying and victimisation
East Sussex County Council (2008)	England	10–14 years	3863	Not reported

attention. Schwartz et al. (2001) suggested that 4–8% of children are identified as bully/victims, although some studies report higher rates than this.

How prevalent is cyberbullying?

Given the focus of this chapter in part on the relatively new issue of cyberbullying, it is important to consider the prevalence of this particular form of bullying. As a relatively recent phenomenon, it was rarely included as a distinct option in many of the studies reported above. Over the past number of years, however, a growing body of research is focusing specifically on this behaviour.

Based on a survey of a small sample of 84 teens in the US, Raskauskas and Stolz (2007) found that 49% of their participants had been victims of cyberbullying and 21% had cyberbullied another, at least once or twice over the previous school year. In another survey, conducted on a larger sample of 533 11–16 year olds in England, Smith et al. (2008a) found that a substantially lower proportion of young people than reported in the US study – 14.1% – had been cyberbullied over the previous school year. Bullying via instant messaging (9.9%) and picture phones (9.5%) was most common, followed by text message bullying (6.6%). Smith et al. (2008a) reported that 11.1% of London youth had cyberbullied another over the previous school year, again a substantially lower rate than

reported by Raskauskas and Stolz (2007). Both studies found that most cyberbullies were also traditional bullies and many cybervictims had also been victimised by traditional forms of bullying. These studies suggest that traditional victims and bullies are likely to retain their roles across the context of the physical and the cyberworld.

Based on these studies, what can we conclude about the prevalence of cyberbullying? Very little really, as both studies arrived at very different rates! What might account for the different rates of cyberbullying found across both studies? Do the differences relate to the samples included in the studies or variations in the survey methods used? Or perhaps the divergent findings reflect 'true' differences between American and British youths' experiences of cyberbullying?

In fact, both studies used a similar methodology in that participants were required to complete questionnaires. Raskauskas and Stolz (2007) asked students to consider the nature of bullying incidents (through text messages, picture phone or website) within the current school year and the frequency of those incidents (ranging from zero incidents to 16 or more). Smith et al. (2008a) presented participants with a series of questions on cyberbullying including whether they had been cyberbullied and, if so, through which medium and how long ago this had happened (last week or month, this term, last school year, over a year ago and never). So, although using similar methodologies, the response categories in both studies were not directly comparable. Furthermore, the sample in the US study was a small convenience sample recruited from two youth development events held at their school. Bias may exist in the sample because of the characteristics of young people who attend such events. In contrast, in the larger English study, participants were recruited from their classes in a range of secondary schools and it is likely that a broader range of participants were accessed than in the US study. Thus, methodological characteristics need to be considered when 'weighing up' the prevalence rates presented. We could also consider whether there is any further research to draw upon.

Based on a survey of 3767 middle school students (11–14 year olds) in the US, Kowalski and Limber (2007) found similar rates of cyberbullying to those reported by Smith *et al.* (2008a) – 11% of their participants had been victims of cyberbullying, 4% had cyberbullied another and 7% had both bullied another and been victimised electronically, at least once in the preceding months. Interestingly, almost half of the bully victims in this study did not know the identity of the perpetrator of the bullying. Thus it seems that the two studies based on larger samples yielded relatively similar prevalence rates of between 11 and 14%. These convergent findings make us feel more confident in what we know about the prevalence of cyberbullying.

Having considered definitions and prevalence of bullying, we now turn our attention to examining how involvement in bullying is associated with factors such as gender and age.

Gender patterns in involvement in bullying

Both boys and girls are frequently involved in bullying. There have been numerous reports that boys are more likely than girls to engage in bullying behaviour (Olweus, 1993a; Whitney and Smith, 1993). In the HBSC study, boys reported bullying more than girls. The difference was particularly evident in relation to frequent bullying with three-quarters of countries showing higher rates of bullying others for boys than girls. Some studies have found that boys are victims of bullying more than girls

(Olweus, 1993a), while others have found no consistent gender differences. For example, in the HBSC study (Currie *et al.*, 2004), some countries had higher rates of victimisation among boys while other countries had higher rates among girls, making it difficult to identify a clear pattern.

There does, however, appear to be a clear pattern in terms of the types of bullying in which boys and girls engage, with boys more likely to be physically bullied by other boys (rarely girls), and girls more likely to be victimised through indirect bullying (by both boys and girls). Indirect bullying is distinct from physical and verbal bullying in that the actions may not be observed by the victim at the time, but nonetheless have intentional and negative consequences for the victim. Examples of indirect bullying include behaviours such as exclusion from a group, spreading rumours about somebody or turning people against someone. Kaukiainen and colleagues have defined indirect bullying as: 'a noxious behaviour in which the target person is attacked not physically or directly through verbal intimidation but in a more circuitous way through social manipulation' (1999, p. 83). Crick and Grotepeter (1995) later applied the term 'relational aggression' to a similar construct, which they described as 'harming others through purposeful manipulation and damage of peer relationship' (p. 711). A number of studies have demonstrated that girls are subject to this indirect or relational bullying more frequently than boys are, and this difference is particularly apparent during early and middle childhood (Crick *et al.*, 2002). In an interesting qualitative study conducted by Owens *et al.* (2000), focus groups with 54 teenage girls found that girls engage in indirect bullying to eliminate boredom, to seek attention, to ensure that they are a member of the 'in group', because of jealousy and to get revenge.

Definitions

Indirect bullying: forms of bullying that may not be observed by the victim at the time, but nonetheless have intentional and negative consequences for the victim, e.g. spreading rumours.
Relational bullying: forms of bullying whereby the bully manipulates children in the social setting of the victim, with the intention of causing harm or distress.

Girls are more likely than boys to be the victims of indirect or relational bullying.
Source: Fotolia

Gender patterns in cyberbullying

Are boys or girls more likely to be victims and perpetrators of cyberbullying? It seems that cyberbullying may also be an effective means for girls to achieve the kinds of goals highlighted above in the Owens *et al.* study, so we might expect girls to engage in cyberbullying more frequently than boys. The research does seem to indicate that this is the case: both Kowalski and Limber (2007) and Peter Smith *et al.* (2008a) found that girls outnumber boys in terms of the overall frequency with which cyberbullying occurs (both perpetration and victimisation). However, we must be cautious in drawing this conclusion, as some contradictory evidence has also been found – data from the Fight Crime Invest in Kids Surveys (2006) reported that gender differences in experiencing cyberbullying only emerged at later ages. For pre-teen children, no gender differences were apparent; among the teen group, however, a significant difference emerged with girls almost twice as likely as boys to report being the victim of cyberbullying in the past year.

Developmental patterns in involvement with bullying

When thinking about child development it is important to recognise that behaviours develop and change over time, and in considering bullying this is no less important. Looking back to the tables summarising prevalence patterns, it appears that there is evidence of patterns across age, with lower rates of participation apparent for older groups. So at what ages are children most likely to be involved in bullying? Research begins looking at bullying from early childhood within pre-school and kindergarten settings, although the number of studies of bullying with this age group is small relative to the number of studies on school-aged children. Nevertheless, it is useful to explore some of the research conducted with different age groups.

Bullying among pre-school children

One of the first things you will notice when reviewing studies with young children is a tendency to use aggression rather than bullying as a behavioural label. Claire Monks *et al.* (2004) suggest that while many of the behaviours considered among this age group may be considered as bullying, it is difficult to determine the presence of an imbalance of power between the bully or aggressor and the victim, a factor that is central to most definitions of bullying. In addition, studying bullying during this early childhood period is difficult. Self-report measures – the most commonly used method of obtaining data on bullying – are difficult to administer to younger children. Therefore, studying bullying among younger age groups (three to seven years) demands more time-consuming and labour-intensive methods, such as direct observation and individual interviews.

Nevertheless, there is evidence that pre-school children can be perpetrators and victims of behaviours that would be called bullying among older children. For example, high rates of physical aggression have been seen particularly among pre-school boys. Typically, these episodes centre on contested toys or objects, and such incidents are referred to as instrumental aggression. Into the pre-school period and early childhood period, physical aggression declines and verbal aggression increases as children develop better means of communication with each other and the ability to internally regulate their emotional states (Underwood, 2002). Relational kinds of aggression (e.g. not letting others join a game) are evident among girls and less commonly among boys during early childhood (Crick *et al.*, 1997). Of course, aggression and bullying are distinct concepts and attempts to distinguish these concepts within the research with

Instrumental aggression in pre-schoolers.
Source: iStockphoto

younger children are rare (Rigby, 2002a). However, there is clear evidence that early experiences of aggression, particularly physical aggression, are associated with later experiences (Barker *et al.*, 2008) and, because of this, it is important to consider the studies of pre-school behaviour as part of the developmental continuum of bullying in children.

Bullying in middle childhood

Given the difficulties associated with studies of bullying in pre-schoolers, it is unsurprising that much of the research has been conducted with older children. The result is that the patterns of behaviour in this age group have been carefully examined. Over the course of middle childhood (7 to 12 years), it seems that the incidence of reported victimisation declines with age. In one review of studies, Peter Smith *et al.* (1999a) cited figures from several large-scale studies previously mentioned to note that a steady decline in bullying is evident for both boys and girls over this developmental stage (Olweus, 1993a; Whitney and Smith, 1993, O'Moore *et al.*, 1997; Rigby, 1997). This may be the result of children developing better social skills, which help them to interact more effectively with their peers. However, Smith *et al.* argued that bullying may be perceived differently by younger and older children – so results for groups that vary in age may not be directly comparable. Among perpetrators of bullying, however, there is little evidence of a change in the tendency to bully others – this seems to remain stable across middle childhood (Hanish and Guerra, 2004).

Bullying in Adolescence

Looking finally to adolescence, the pattern of declining rates of victimisation appears to continue. In one study based in the US, Tonya Nansel *et al.* (2001) found that 24% of 6th graders (age 11–12) had been bullied often compared with 16% of 8th graders (age 13–14) and 9% of 10th graders (age 15–16). However, there may be an exception to this continued decline: Rigby (1997) documented a temporary rise in reported bullying that coincided with the transition to secondary school. This may be an example of how the social context in which children of a particular age find themselves is crucially important and may even take precedence over developmental factors. However, an interesting explanation for this pattern has been proposed by Anthony Pelligrini. He argues that aggression can serve a purpose during the transition between different school levels. Pelligrini and Bertini (2001) discuss the way in which adolescents, particularly males, may use aggression to establish dominance within the group during this transition and suggest that this highlights the possible evolutionary function of bullying and aggression. We should, however, be cautious in how we interpret these perceived declines in bullying from early childhood to adolescence. It is possible that older children are simply less likely to report being the victim of bullying, for fear of being perceived as weak or vulnerable.

Developmental patterns in cyberbullying

To date, little research has considered developmental patterns in cyberbullying. Here we might expect factors to do with the social environment to play an important role – one must have access to electronic communication tools in order to be a perpetrator or victim of cyberbullying. Kowalski and Limber (2007) found that children aged six to eight years were less likely than children aged 9–11 years to have been cyberbullied, a trend that is somewhat at odds with that observed with more traditional forms of bullying. This may be because older children have more unsupervised access to the internet and mobile phones. This study also found that 8th graders (13–14 year olds) cyberbullied others more frequently than 6th and 7th graders (11–13 years). Much more research is needed to explore these patterns.

Considering the issues discussed in this section, it appears that bullying behaviours have their foundations in early childhood aggression and, from a peak in the school years, rates of victimisation appear to decrease over time. In comparison, rates of perpetration of bullying show less radical reductions over time. From an applied perspective, there is a clear need to consider the implications of these developmental patterns of bullying behaviour. Recognising related behaviours among pre-schoolers may help prevent later problems, while recognising the potential function of these behaviours in adolescence may help educators to understand bullying among this group. It is also worth considering how bullying is a lifespan phenomenon that extends well beyond childhood and adolescence into adulthood. This is explored further in the Lifespan box.

STOP AND THINK

Going further

This section has considered the influence of factors such as age and gender on involvement in bullying. However, there are other factors that might be influential. For example, we might consider whether involvement in bullying depends on whether children are in a racial/ethnic majority or minority group. One study conducted in England found that children of non-white ethnic origin experienced more racist name-calling than other children of the same age and gender (Boulton, 1995). It is hard to establish that it is the racial difference between the target and bully that has given rise to the bullying. A child of a different racial group may be bullied for reasons other than their racial origin (Rigby, 2002b).

For what other reasons might these children be susceptible to being the target of bullying?

Bullying as a group process

So far, we have been very much focused upon bullying as an individual-oriented phenomenon – research has been concentrated mainly on bullies and victims and, more recently, there has been an increased focus upon bully/victims. However, bullying is a social process, usually taking place within a group context. While many children report negative attitudes towards bullying, it is important to know how these children actually behave in bullying situations (Sutton and Smith, 1999). For example, do they join in? Do they actively encourage the bully (perhaps by shouting or cheering)? Do they passively accept the bullying (perhaps by being present but doing nothing about it or by being amused by the situation)? Do they stick up for the victims or tell somebody about it? Do they tackle the bully anyway?

Christine Salmivalli *et al.* (1996) wanted to address these questions and so developed the Participant Role Questionnaire (PRQ) in which each child assesses each classmate's as well as her own typical behaviour in bullying situations. Six roles were identified in bullying, which are outlined in Table 15.5.

The PRQ also enables bully/victims to be identified, as the secondary roles of the victimised children can also be analysed. A small number of studies have utilised the PRQ to study the prevalence of these roles. In the UK,

LIFESPAN

Bullying in the workplace

Bullying is most commonly associated with childhood and the teenage years, and this is reflected in the research which has primarily focused upon school contexts. However, bullying is not restricted to schooldays but can extend beyond adolescence into adulthood. As Smith (1997) points out, bullying can potentially occur whenever groups of people meet together. Research on bullying in adulthood has gained momentum in recent years and has focused on contexts such as the workplace and prisons. Here we will discuss bullying in the workplace, which is increasingly recognised as a serious issue.

In the workplace, bullying takes on complex, subtle and indirect forms. Rayner and Hoel (1997) describe several different types of workplace bullying including: threats to professional and personal status (such as humiliating, accusing someone of lack of effort, belittling opinion, name-calling, insulting), isolation (such as preventing access to opportunities, withholding important information), overwork (such as giving unrealistic deadlines or an impossible workload) and destabilisation (such as removing responsibility, assigning meaningless tasks, failing to give credit when it is due and setting someone up to fail). Behaviours such as intimidation, public humiliation and unwanted physical contact can undermine the integrity and confidence of employees, increase absenteeism and reduce efficiency, with substantial costs to the victims, as well as to the organisation as a whole (Cowie *et al.*, 2002).

Factors to do with the organisational climate can also contribute to bullying in the workplace. Vartia (1996) found that organisational features such as inadequate opportunities to influence matters concerning oneself at work, lack of reciprocal conversations about the tasks and goals of the work unit, poor mechanisms to exchange information among employees and a strained and competitive atmosphere promote bullying. Organisations are now recognising the need for policies and procedures to protect their employees from bullying and harassment, as well as the need to create an organisational culture that does not facilitate bullying.

However, while organisational factors are no doubt important, the role of individuals must also be considered. There may be some continuity in the extent to which individuals are victimised in childhood and then go on to be victimised in adulthood. The same may be true for those who bully others. Very little research, however, has considered this issue. In one study, Smith *et al.* (2003) sought to examine whether being a victim of bullying at school would increase the likelihood of being a victim of bullying in the workplace. Over 5000 adults in various work settings completed an anonymous questionnaire on their school experiences in relation to bullying and their conditions and relationships at work. The study found that individuals who had been either a victim or a bully/victim at school were more likely to have been bullied at work in the last five years, compared with those who had not been a victim or a bully/victim at school. The authors concluded that being victimised at school increases one's risk of being victimised later in life in the workplace. One limitation of this study is that it is a retrospective study, meaning that it relied upon people's reports of their bullying experiences at school, rather than assessing their experiences at that time and then following them up later when they were adults. An additional issue relates to the ability to establish a causal link between early and later experiences, which is a challenge for all research in developmental psychology.

The conclusion arising from this study – that there is consistency in patterns of victimisation across different life stages (from childhood to adulthood) and across different contexts (from school to the workplace) – highlights the need to provide support and skills to those at risk of victimisation at a young age, in order to prevent continuity of victimisation experiences.

Table 15.5. Participant roles with descriptions and examples of items from the PRQ.

Participant role	Description	Examples of items on questionnaire
Bully	Active, initiative-taking, 'ring-leader' bullying behaviours	Starts bullying; makes others join in the bullying
Assistant to bully	Following the bully, assisting him or her	Joins in the bullying; assists the bully
Reinforcer to bully	Providing bully with feedback that encourages him or her	Comes around to watch the situation; laughs
Defending victim	Takes sides with the victim	Says to the victim, 'Never mind'; tries to make others stop bullying
Staying outside	Withdrawing, not reacting to bullying	Is not usually present (in bullying situations); does not even know about the bullying
Victim	Target of systematic harassment	

Source: Salmivalli (2001).

Sutton and Smith (1999) found the following prevalence rates: victims 18.1%, bullies 14.0%, assistants 7.3%, reinforcers 5.7%, defenders 27.5% and outsiders 11.9% of the sample. However, in this study, children (7 to 10 years) were only asked to rate classmates of the same sex. Findings from studies such as this illustrate that victimisation (being the victim of bullying) is not something that goes on exclusively between the bully and the victim. Most children in the class are affected in some way. Salmivalli (2001) has also reported that these roles also tend to be relatively stable and the most stable of all roles is that of the victim. Much work remains to be done in further understanding the group processes involved in

Bullying is a group process, in which children other than just bully and victim play a role.

Source: iStockphoto

bullying. The participant role approach could have important implications for intervention programmes such as targeting the whole group and seeking to change various participant roles.

Theoretical perspectives on bullying

So far in this chapter, we have drawn on research studies to inform our discussion of bullying. However, psychological theories can also make an important contribution to our understanding of the issue. Theories can form an important basis for anti-bullying prevention and intervention programmes. For example, if we believe that bullies lack particular social skills or empathy for others, interventions may be targeted at teaching children these skills. Alternatively, if we consider that bullying is a group process in which the bully's actions are reinforced by peer onlookers, interventions may target observers and peers who fail to intervene in bullying incidents. Different theories can be used to explain why some children bully others and why others are bullied. Some of these theories are drawn from work on aggression in children and have been applied to bullying; others have been developed specifically to explain bullying. While it is not possible to consider all of these, we will look at four in detail now. The theories are summarised in Table 15.6, with attention drawn to their origins and their focus.

Table 15.6. Main features of four key theories of bullying.

Theory	Key references	Origins	Focus
Social information processing theory	Crick and Dodge (1994)	Social cognition, aggressive behaviour	The bully's cognitive processing
Bullying and theory of mind	Sutton *et al.* (1999a, b)	Bullying	The bully's social intelligence
Attribution theory	Graham and Juvonen (2001)	Social cognition	The victim's cognitive processing
Disinhibition	Suler (2004)	Online behaviour	Cyberbullying

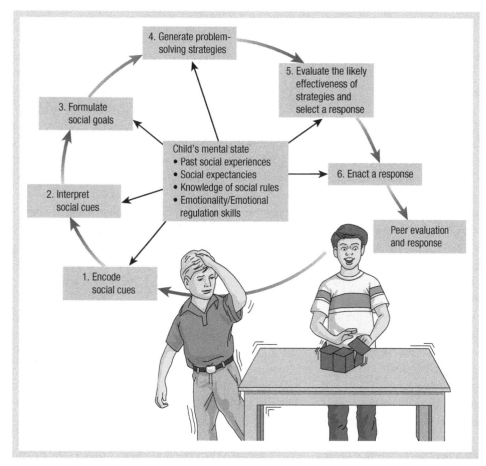

Figure 15.1.
Representation of Crick and Dodge's model.

(*Source*: Shaffer and Kipp, 2010)

Social-information processing model

One of the most influential perspectives on childhood aggression has been the social-information processing model of children's social adjustment proposed by Crick and Dodge (1994). This six-step model illustrated in Fig. 15.1 proposes that in their social interactions, children proceed through five stages in 'reading' different social situations before they respond in the sixth and final step of the model. This model was initially developed to understand the broad range of aggressive behaviours exhibited by children and young people. However,

> **Definition**
>
> Social-information processing: the way in which people make sense of information relating to social interactions and social contexts.

it has clear potential to be applied to the study of bullying behaviour.

For example, imagine you are a nine year old child who is playing a game alone at a table. A peer walks by, knocks into the table and the game falls to the floor. In Stages 1 and 2 of the model, *encoding and interpretation of cues* take place. First, you select and attend to information (cues) about the social situation and then you interpret the cues to make sense of the social situation. In Stage 1, the social cues you choose to attend to might be influenced by your ability to gather information from the setting. The interpretation of these cues in Stage 2 might involve making assumptions about why particular events have occurred or the intention of the peer. For example, what happened? Why did this situation happen (causal attribution)? Did the peer mean to bump into the table or was it accidental (intent attribution)? What was the peer's reaction to the event? Other encoding that might take place at this stage includes attending to internal cues, such as emotional arousal. In Stage 3 of the model, *clarification of goals* occurs, in which you formulate a goal or desired outcome for the situation. Do you want help picking up the game? Do you want the peer to apologise? Do you want to move onto a new game? Do you want to 'get even' with the provocateur?

In Stage 4, it is hypothesised that children *access possible responses* to the situation from their memory store and in Stage 5, *decide upon a response*. You might think about a range of possible responses to this situation or remember how you behaved in the past in response to similar experiences. Did a particular response in the past lead to a favourable or unfavourable outcome? In deciding what you do, you evaluate the likely outcomes of various responses (outcome expectations). You might ask yourself what will happen if I hit the provocateur, or ignore him/her? Your moral values (e.g. beliefs that hitting somebody is a bad thing to do) may influence the response that you decide upon. In Stage 6 of the model, the chosen *response is enacted*.

Crick and Dodge hypothesised that children who bully or are aggressive towards peers display patterns of social-information processing that are distinct from those of non-aggressive peers. One of the most widely studied components of their model is how children interpret social cues to infer the motives of others (intent attributions, Stage 2 of the model) – for example, determining whether a peer acted with benign or hostile intent. Crick and Dodge argue that physically aggressive children tend to display a hostile attributional bias when interpreting social cues. That is, they tend to attribute malicious intent to peer provocateurs even when such intent is not actually present. Crick *et al.* (2002) presented hypothetical vignettes to groups of aggressive and non-aggressive children aged 9 to 12 years. Each vignette described a provocation situation in which the intent of the behaviour of the provocateur is ambiguous. Children were asked to state whether the provocateur's behaviour was intentional (hostile) or benign (accidental). Results from the study found that sub-groups of aggressive children did process social information in distinctive ways from non-aggressive children. Children who were rated as being high on physical aggression exhibited more hostile attributions or explanations than did children rated as low on physical aggression. This study supports claims made by Crick and Dodge's social-information processing theory which suggests that physically aggressive children display a hostile attributional bias when interpreting social cues.

In considering this theoretical approach, it is important to see that research suggesting that aggressive children exhibit social-information processing deficits has rarely focused on the bully per se. As discussed previously in the chapter, although bullies are aggressive by nature, they are more than that – they are aggressive people who seek to take advantage of less powerful people in situations in which they can be dominant (Rigby, 2002a). In addition, it is important to remember that children come to social situations with a set of biologically predisposed capabilities (such as a tendency to be impulsive) and a database of memories of previous experiences, which also influence how they process social information and how they typically behave.

The second theoretical position, proposed by Sutton *et al.* (1999a), takes issue with the deficit view of Crick and Dodge and instead argues that bullies are skilled manipulators and better mind-readers than others.

Definition

Hostile attribution bias: the tendency for some people to attribute hostile intention to the actions of others in non-hostile situations.

Bullying and theory of mind

As we have seen, bullying is an antisocial and aggressive act but one that is often conducted in a social way and within a social setting. Sutton *et al.* (1999a, b) suggest that, in order to truly understand bullying, we need to take account of the context in which bullying occurs, the roles which different children assume within this context and the skills that may be of use to a bully. It seems plausible that a variety of mind-reading skills (involved in theory of mind, see Chapter 8, Theory of Mind) are in operation when children bully others. As noted earlier in the chapter, bullying usually occurs in the presence of peers, who may take on one of a variety of roles (assistant to or reinforcer of the bully, defender of the victim, or uninvolved). Being an effective bully may involve firstly grasping and then manipulating the internal mental states – beliefs, thoughts and feelings – of all those involved. Thus, bullies may be at an advantage if they possess superior theory of mind skills to those of their victims and followers.

In order to test this, 193 children aged 7 to 10 years were presented with a version of the Participant Role Scale (Salmivalli *et al.*, 1996) to ascertain the nature of their involvement in bullying. Children were classified as a bully, assistant to a bully, reinforcer, defender, outsider or victim. For those children who were identified in the bully role, teachers completed a questionnaire to assess the type of bullying (physical, verbal or indirect bullying). All children were then read 11 short stories in order to assess their understanding of mental states or emotions. Here is an example of one such story, which tapped into mental states:

> During the war, the Red army captured a member of the Blue army. They want him to tell them where his army's tanks are; they know they are either by the sea or in the mountains. They know that the prisoner will not want to tell them, he will want to save his army, and so he will certainly lie to them. They know that the prisoner will not want to tell them. The prisoner is very brave and very clever, he will not let them find his tanks. The tanks are really in the mountains. Now when the Red side asks him where his tanks are, he says: 'They are in the mountains.'
>
> (Happé, 1994, p. 150)

The children were then asked a series of questions such as: is it true what the prisoner said? Where will the army look for his tanks and why did the prisoner say what he said? Responses to the questions were scored from 0 (fail), to 1 (pass but without reference to a mental state) to 2 (pass including reference to a mental state or belief). For example, a child scored as 2 might respond in the following way: 'They will look by the sea because they think that the prisoner is lying to them.'

The findings from this study revealed that bullies had higher social cognition scores than any other group. Furthermore, it was the children who bullied others verbally, rather than indirectly or physically, that scored highest on the theory of mind stories. It may be that theory of mind skills are particularly adaptive in order to tease somebody effectively and know what names or taunts will be most hurtful. However, one could also argue that theory of mind is important even in physical bullying, as the bully will still have to choose an effective time and method, avoid detection, maximise the victim's vulnerability and minimise chances of being hurt themselves.

So what can be concluded from this research? Do bullies have superior theory of mind skills? The results of the study do shed some doubt on the claims made by the social skills deficit model of aggression that bullies have poor social skills. Instead, Sutton *et al.*'s findings lend support to the idea that bullies may not be socially inadequate in the way Crick and Dodge described. However, much more research is needed to explore the relation between specific theory of mind skills and bullying. For example, bullies with good theory of mind skills may still show deficits in particular areas, for example, in their beliefs involving moral emotions, such as guilt, shame and sympathy. Do bullies understand these emotions but not share them with others? Bullies may show a good awareness of others' emotional states but still demonstrate an unwillingness to feel empathy towards others. If this is the case, intervention strategies which aim to enhance the mind-reading skills of bullies may be misguided, if bullies already have these skills but do not have empathic capacities.

Definitions

Theory of mind: being able to infer the full range of mental states (beliefs, desires, intentions, imagination, emotions, etc.) that cause action (Baron-Cohen, 2001).

Empathy: the ability to identify with the emotions of others and to read the physical expression of emotions in others.

Understanding victimisation using attribution theory

The theories above focus on the actions, skills and intentions of the bully; however, they have little to say about the experiences and actions of the victims of bullying. In some ways, this reflects the common belief that bullying is the result of actions on the part of the bully. While it is not appropriate to suggest that victims should be blamed for being bullied, it is important to remember that bullying is a social behaviour that is the result of the dynamic interaction of the bully and the victim. It is important to consider what the role of the victim may be in this interaction.

There are many possible roles that have been considered in the literature on bullying. Looking at bullying from a behaviourist perspective, it could be that the reaction of the victim reinforces the bully. On one hand, we might expect that displays of distress reinforce the bully whose aim is to hurt or upset the victim. On the other hand, researchers in Canada have argued that displays of anger on the part of the victim might provoke the bully further (Mahady-Wilton *et al.*, 2000). In addition, researchers have identified different types of victims, with different roles in the interaction. For example Stephenson and Smith (1989) proposed a particular type of victim – the provocative victim – whose behaviour in some way provoked the attention and indeed the anger of the bully. These examples highlight the complexity of the bully–victim dynamic and the need to reflect on the victim in this dynamic.

One theoretical approach that has been applied to victims of bullying is attribution theory. This explores the way in which a person explains or attributes cause to behaviours. We have already seen in the social-information processing theory how bullies tend to make hostile attributions. Extending this general theory, Graham and Juvonen (2001) have applied the framework to victims of bullying. They consider how victims of bullying explain the cause of their victimisation. They describe causes in terms of their locus (i.e. do they see the cause as being something inside them or outside them), stability (i.e. does the cause change over time) and controllability (i.e. can the cause be controlled). They link the idea of the locus of attributions to self-esteem, suggesting that attributing the cause of bullying to something that is external to them (e.g. a lack of supervision by teachers) is less damaging to an individual's self-esteem than attributing

the cause to something that is internal (e.g. because you are short). In this way, the authors frame these attributions as differing in terms of the level of self-blame attributed, and suggest that the cause which the victim assigns to the behaviour could increase or decrease the potential harm caused by the bullying.

Graham and Juvonen have conducted research on attributions of bullying. In studying young people's responses to statements regarding reasons for bullying, they identified four patterns or themes. These have been summarised in Table 15.7, along with an overview of the characteristics of this attribution type and examples cited. They have found that victims of bullying are more likely to attribute bullying to each of these causes, but that the type most associated with adjustment difficulties such as anxiety is characterological self-blame, which locates the cause within the person (thus reducing self-esteem), is uncontrollable (thus not manageable or resolvable) and stable over time (so unlikely to improve).

Considering the possible implications of this theory for understanding bullying, Graham and Juvonen discuss the extent to which young people could be supported to change the way in which they attribute the causes of their victimisation and thereby improve their ability to cope with victimisation. They also argue for the use of this approach to change the attributions of peers and therefore make them more likely to support the victim. This approach is interesting in the context of the current popularity of cognitive behavioural therapy

Table 15.7. Attribution types in bullying.

Attribution type	Characteristics	Examples
Characterological self-blame	Internal Uncontrollability Stable over time	'If I were a cooler kid, this wouldn't happen to me'
Behavioural self-blame	Internal Personal control Can change over time	'I shouldn't have been there'
Threat from others	External	'These . . . kids pick on everyone'
Passivity	Not reported	'I would feel helpless'

(*Source*: after Graham and Juvonen, 2001, examples taken from p. 55)

(CBT) as a mental health intervention. CBT focuses on changing the way in which an individual thinks and behaves in relation to challenges. There is scope to explore the application of therapeutic models that support changing attribution styles in victims of bullying.

Understanding cyberbullying: disinhibition in online behaviour

The theories presented in this section can help us to understand cyberbullying at least to some extent. However, as we have seen, cyberbullying is distinct from traditional bullying in a number of important ways. To date, no specific theory of cyberbullying has been proposed and researchers have tended to draw upon theories explaining online behaviour more generally to understand electronic bullying.

One important difference between traditional 'schoolyard' bullying and cyberbullying relates to the anonymity afforded to the cyberbully. In one survey of over 3000 teenagers, half of the electronic victims reported not knowing the identity of the perpetrator (Kowalski and Limber, 2007). In another study, based on 1211 completed questionnaires, almost 40% of secondary school pupils and one-third of primary school pupils who were victims of cyberbullying reported not knowing the identity of the bully (Dehue *et al.*, 2008). Anonymity in online interactions gives rise to what is known as the phenomenon of disinhibition. According to Suler (2004), when people have the opportunity to separate their online actions from their in-person identity, they may feel less vulnerable about acting out and behaving in ways than they might not otherwise be willing to do if their identities were known. In effect, people dissociate themselves from their online persona and can avert responsibility for their online behaviour. As Kowalski *et al.* (2008) state: 'with electronic communication, [people] can hide behind an assumed identity and wreak havoc' (p. 64).

A second feature of online communication relates to invisibility, which also contributes to disinhibition.

Definition

Disinhibition: the tendency to behave in ways other than one might normally, showing a lack of restraint or regard for social norms.

Given that interaction occurs via technology and not through face-to-face interaction, neither perpetrator nor victim is visible to the other. Bullies cannot see the emotional reaction of their victims (or of bystanders) and so the opportunity for their behaviours to be inhibited by the emotional responses of others is missing. As Kowalski and others suggest, it is as if some bullies fail to remember that they are actually communicating with another person. It is likely that this disinhibition effect contributes, at least in part, to the phenomenon of cyberbullying, but the relation between disinhibition and cyberbullying remains to be empirically tested.

Where to from here in theorising bullying?

It is clear that the first two theories discussed are a world apart in their predictions about the social–cognitive processes of those who bully others. One theory predicts that bullies have deficient social–cognitive skills that manifest themselves in hostile attributional biases, which give rise to an increased likelihood of aggressive behaviour in response to ambiguous social situations. In contrast, the other theory predicts that bullies are good perspective takers who can skilfully manipulate social situations.

Crick and Dodge (1999) argue that even if bullies are good mind-readers, other cognitive processes are operating which contribute to their engagement in negative behaviours. Sutton and his colleagues go further to state that perhaps bullies may perceive and interpret social cues very accurately (the first two stages of Crick and Dodge's model), but their process of response selection (Stages 4–5) may be driven by distinct goals (Stage 3) reflecting different values and beliefs. Bullies may attach more value to the rewarding outcomes of aggression and less value to the negative outcomes associated with aggression.

Deviant values and beliefs may well be influenced by the child's peer network or broader cultural context. The norms inherent within a peer or school culture may be as important as hostile attributions in predicting hostile responses among children. Taking this perspective demands that we pay attention to everybody's role in bullying, and do not focus exclusively on the bully. For example, what about the social–cognitive skills of those who defend the victims or remain uninvolved? What skills prevent these children from becoming bullies or victims? Could their skills be used to promote prosocial behaviour among other children or provide positive social support to those involved in bullying?

Neither of these theories addresses the social skills of children and young people involved in cyberbullying. Theories of online behaviour provide some insights, but their contribution to understanding what goes on in the minds of those who bully others is limited. Finding answers to questions such as these could have important implications for how anti-bullying interventions are designed, and it is to this that we will turn our attention in the next section.

STOP AND THINK

Going further

- Based on your reading of the different theories of bullying, and about the nature of cyberbullying as opposed to traditional bullying, would you argue that cyberbullies are thugs or thinkers?
- What other explanations of behaviour might help us to understand this relatively new form of bullying?

Tackling bullying: methods of intervention and prevention

Within the context of applied psychology, the goal of research is to apply knowledge and inform practice. In the same way, the drive to understand bullying was fuelled by the need to develop ways to address the problem in schools. Before the surge of interest in bullying in the 1990s, there were few resources available to help school principals and teachers with this. As with research in the area, it was in Scandinavia, in particular in Norway, where new interventions for use in schools first developed. In 1983, the Norwegian government funded a nationwide campaign in all of its 3500 schools (Smith and Sharp, 1994). Since then, education authorities in more countries have moved to provide resources for dealing with bullying in schools. In the UK, the Department of Children, Schools and Families' document *Safe to Learn* (DCSF, 2007) states that anti-bullying strategies should: prevent or minimise bullying behaviours, respond to

bullying in 'a reasonable, proportionate and consistent way' (p. 87), ensure that victims of bullying are supported and ensure that disciplinary sanctions are applied to those who perpetrate bullying.

Two main approaches to intervention and prevention are described and discussed in the literature, and a significant body of research has considered the impact of these approaches. Firstly, educational approaches tend to focus on the education of class groups, whole schools, and other groups about what bullying is and its effects on those involved. An example of this approach is the internationally-known Olweus Prevention Programme (www.olweus.org). These programmes generally focus on education and prevention in the school setting. Secondly, the participant approach focuses on direct intervention with those individuals and groups that are actively involved in bullying. One example of this approach is the The No-Blame Approach (Maines and Robinson, 1998). In addition to these approaches, in recent years a third approach that seeks to address bullying in more creative ways such as through utilising peer counselling or peer support has emerged (Cowie and Wallace, 2000). The decision to implement one approach over another will often rest with the school and/or the Local Education Authority. Each of these approaches will now be discussed.

The educational approach

The main aim of this approach is to educate people about what bullying is, its effects and what to do about it. The educational approach can be used in a number of different ways, depending on who is to be educated. A classroom intervention focuses on the pupils within a classroom and may be implemented by the class teacher. On a wider level, a school-based intervention may involve educating the staff in the school, as well as the pupils. In addition, a school-based intervention will generally include the parents.

Definitions

Intervention: acting to stop a behaviour from continuing.
Prevention: acting to reduce the likelihood that a behaviour may occur.

An educational curriculum is often used as part of the educational approach. Cowie and Sharp (1994) described two objectives of educational curricula, namely raising awareness about bullying and challenging pupils' attitudes. A number of methods and resources are available for use as part of a classroom curriculum. Examples include quality circles, drama, videos, role-playing and literature. Quality circles refer to structured group meetings aimed at devising practical solutions to the problem of bullying. Through the quality circle process, pupils learn about the nature of bullying, formulate solutions and evaluate the advantages and disadvantages of putting a solution into practice (Cowie and Sharp, 1994).

The educational approach is used in a number of anti-bullying interventions. Olweus (1993a) included aspects of curriculum-based education at the class level in his intervention. This programme also included conference days and parent–teacher meetings to educate parents about bullying. The Sheffield project in England (Whitney et al. 1994) also used aspects of education in tackling bullying. Whitney et al. (1994) reported that schools were given the option of including aspects of classroom curricula, for example literature and video-based discussion, in their intervention.

There are also a number of 'Anti-bullying Packs' available to schools, which work as educational resources. One of the most widely used packs in the UK was the *Don't Suffer in Silence* pack published in 2000 by the Department for Education and Employment (DFEE, 2000). This pack was updated in 2002 and included information for pupils, parents and teachers on what bullying is and what to do about it. In 2007, the Department of Children, Schools and Families (DCSF) published the latest resource pack on bullying, *Safe to Learn* (DCSF, 2007).

A core feature of the educational approach is a comprehensive school policy on bullying. Whitney et al. (1994) described a school policy document as an 'essential framework within which other interventions could operate successfully and maintain continuity' (p. 21). Schools in Britain and Ireland are required to have anti-bullying policies, and a recent paper by Peter Smith et al. (2008b) conducted a review of these policies in over 140 schools in one English county. This review involved identifying a set of key criteria for policies and assessing the extent of their inclusion in the schools' documentation. Criteria included: defining what constitutes bullying, specifying procedures for reporting and responding to bullying incidents, evaluating the school policy and outlining prevention strategies. Smith et al. found that, on average, 40% of the criteria were evident in schools' anti-bullying policies. In addition, they reported that few policies considered cyberbullying specifically. This highlights a continuing need for schools to review and update the policy documents that guide and govern responses to bullying.

There are many benefits to the educational approach in addressing the problem of bullying. From a practical perspective, an educational curriculum can be included as part of the school's day-to-day curriculum, which may result in a long-running intervention, rather than one of limited duration. Also, this approach goes beyond those involved directly in the behaviour and can be extended to the whole school community. The inclusion of parents and the wider community might mean that there is a greater degree of consistency in the messages that young people receive about bullying. Indeed the DCSF 'recommends wide consultation with the whole school community on all aspects of the anti-bullying policy' (2007, p. 8). Finally, the implementation of an educational intervention may require less financial investment than some of the other approaches which will be considered later. There is a growing range of resources available for schools to use as part of an educational curriculum and there may be less need for specialised training for those involved in the implementation of these methods, unlike aspects of the participant approach which is considered next.

Conversely, there are some issues to be aware of with this broad approach. Firstly, if the programme is being delivered by a number of groups both inside and outside the school it will require consistency in the delivery. Also, such an intervention, if it is to be included as part of the wider school curriculum, will have to be evaluated and updated on a regular basis in order to ensure its effectiveness. It is interesting to note that procedures for evaluating school anti-bullying policies were evident in only one-third of the schools included in Smith et al.'s review (2008b).

The participant approach

This approach to tackling bullying differs from the educational approach in that it generally focuses directly on those involved in bullying, either as individuals or groups. The methods by which this approach can be implemented range from those of a disciplinary perspective, as seen in the use of sanctions, to more therapeutic approaches, as described below. However, the common theme is that the school is called on to deal with the individuals directly involved in bullying – that is, both the bullies and the victims.

One of the most common methods of dealing with these individuals is through the use of discipline, including talking with the bully to raise their awareness of their behaviour and its effects, conveying disapproval for their actions and administering appropriate sanctions. The Olweus programme (1993a) includes serious talks with both the victim and the bully, which may subsequently involve meeting with their respective parents. Methods have also been developed which focus on providing skills to those involved in bullying (both bullies and victims) to help them respond in difficult situations. Smith *et al.* (1994) described the use of interventions such as conflict resolution, peer counselling and assertiveness training. A major advantage is that these methods provide pupils with the skills to deal with the problem, recognising the reality that, as an amount of bullying will probably always remain hidden, pupils must be equipped to deal with it.

There are also a number of more 'therapeutic' individual programmes that are becoming more common. The best examples of these are Pikas's (1989) 'Method of Shared Concern' and Maines and Robinson's (1998) 'No Blame Approach'. The Method of Shared Concern is a method of therapeutically intervening in bullying, which involves individual interviews with each of the people involved (bullies and victims), followed by a group meeting with the bullies. These meetings are organised and facilitated by a therapist (who is possibly either a counsellor or educational psychologist) and focused on developing a shared concern among the group for the victim. Pikas argued that one of the benefits of interviewing the victim was that it assists the therapist in identifying whether the pupil is a classic or a provocative victim (discussed previously in the section on understanding victimisation). This allows the therapist to adjust his interactions with the various individuals involved. The end stage of this process is a meeting between the bullies and the victims; however, the therapist decides when this is appropriate.

The No Blame Approach is a method of tackling bullying first outlined by Maines and Robinson (1991), and then published as a resource pack (Maines and Robinson,

1992). Similar to the Pikas method, this approach tackles bullying by working to create a supportive group of students around the victim and, as the title states, no blame for the behaviour is attributed. The group's behaviour is seen as a problem that must be solved and the group is given the responsibility for solving it. This approach differs from the Method of Shared Concern in that while the victim is interviewed to gain insight into the effects of the bullying, she is not included in the problem-solving process. As with the Shared Concern Method, the process works through a series of group discussions with those involved in bullying the victim. During these discussions, the group is presented with the victim's perspective and asked if there are ways they could help. Again, follow-up meetings are used to reinforce positive decisions.

It is clear that there are a wide variety of methods available for use as part of the participant approach, ranging from didactic discipline-based methods to more inclusive methods. One of the benefits of participant approaches is that they target those involved in bullying directly. However, the challenge for these methods is that those involved must be identified. This is a challenge since, as we saw in the example at the beginning of the chapter, two-thirds of young people do not report bullying. From the point of view of the implementation of such methods, there is also a question around who is responsible for facilitating the various methods. Pikas described a therapist facilitating the group. The training necessary to introduce these methods into schools may mean that schools are hesitant to introduce them and that they would only be used in serious cases where the individuals come into contact with an educational psychologist.

These methods have been used as part of interventions that also include elements of the educational approach. This was the case with the Sheffield project (Whitney *et al.*, 1994) where the Method of Shared Concern and peer counselling were both offered as options to schools involved in the study. Peer counselling or peer support is the next and final method of intervention to be considered in this chapter.

Definition

Peer support: a method by which children and young people are trained to act as supports for others who are experiencing difficulties such as bullying.

CASE STUDY

The No Blame Approach

Young (1998) gave a brief report of an evaluation of a modified version of the No Blame Approach, referred to as The Support Group Approach. She reported on 51 cases where this approach was used with primary school children. All cases had been referred through a Special Educational Needs Support Service over the course of a two-year period and were described as serious cases of bullying. These cases were selected from 80 in total as being suitable for the intervention. She reports that one case was not completed but that for the remaining 50 cases the success rate (based on the ending of the bullying, or the victim no longer needing support) was 100%. She goes on to report that 80% of cases had 'immediate success' (p. 36), defined as situations where the child, the support group and the parents (where they were involved)

reported that the bullying had stopped from the time the group had been established. The remaining cases had either delayed success (taking approximately five weeks) or limited success (the bullying reduced to a tolerable level).

Young is very positive about this approach as an anti-bullying intervention, and considers it a form of brief therapy. However, the point should be made that this evaluation used observational methods rather than a controlled assessment of outcome, and further empirical study may improve researchers' knowledge of the effectiveness of approaches such as this one.

- **Can you think of any ways in which researchers could establish the success or otherwise of an intervention like this one?**
- **What challenges might they face in assessing how well it has worked?**

Peer support

As highlighted in the example at the beginning of the chapter, one of the most significant challenges affecting our ability to prevent or intervene in bullying is the significant number of children and young people who do not report the behaviour to an adult. Within this context, and recognising that bullying takes place in the presence of other children and young people but generally away from adults, Sonia Sharp (1996) argues that peers should be directly involved in prevention and intervention. Across the approaches already considered, children and young people have been actively involved in anti-bullying work to different extents; however, peer support (or peer counselling as it is also known) represents an approach that maximises the involvement of peers in addressing bullying.

One of the main figures in the development of peer support programmes is Professor Helen Cowie, Director of the UK Observatory for Non-Violence (www.ukobservatory.com). She states that 'Peer support

interventions recognize that pupils themselves have the potential to assume a helpful role in tackling a problem' (Cowie, 2000, p. 87). Cowie goes on to describe the mechanisms for peer support, whereby adults support young people in the development of listening skills and empathy, which they in turn use to support their class-mates. A very useful textbook by Cowie and Wallace (2000) provides detailed guidance on the development and implementation of peer support programmes.

Similar to some of the more participatory approaches above, and in contrast to the educational approach, there has been limited large-scale evaluation of peer support programmes. Peter Smith (2004) argues that despite evidence of benefits in terms of the general school climate and more specifically for the pupils who work as supports, there is little evidence of a systematic positive effect on victims of bullying. While peer support may be seen to actively involve young people, there is no doubt that the demands of training and supporting the peer supporters represents a challenge for even the most committed schools.

STOP AND THINK

- How influential can children and young people be in tackling bullying themselves?
- What are the key elements for supporting them to do this effectively and safely?
- Can you see any negative effects of peer support?
- What might teachers and parents think of a peer support programme?

How successful have school-based interventions been?

Given the range of options available to schools wanting to tackle bullying, it is important to think about the effectiveness of these interventions. As mentioned earlier, one of the most widely known prevention and intervention programmes for bullying in school is the Olweus Prevention Programme (www.olweus.org). This programme was first described in detail as the basis for Dan Olweus's book *Bullying at School: What We Know and What We Can Do About It* (Olweus, 1993a). The programme functions across three levels: the classroom, the wider school and at the level of individual children involved in bullying as both bullies and/or victims. Central to the effectiveness of the programme at the school level is the provision of training for teachers and engagement with parents. A set of school rules is also identified and clearly communicated at all levels. These rules are then implemented consistently at the classroom level, alongside classroom discussions which are designed to promote awareness and improve knowledge. Finally, the programme specifies intervention methods for children directly involved in bullying, through meetings with staff and parents in which the bullying problem is discussed and steps/outcomes agreed.

Olweus (1994) reported the findings of an early large-scale evaluation of the effects of the intervention programme, which is generally referred to as the Bergen Study after the location in which the study was completed. Levels of bullying in participating schools were assessed before the intervention, and at a one- and two-year interval following the intervention. The results suggested that the intervention was a success with involvement in bullying falling by approximately 50%.

However, few studies have been able to replicate such a dramatic impact on involvement. The Sheffield Study in the UK (Whitney *et al.*, 1994) reported changes after intervention of about 12–15% in the numbers of children bullying others and being bullied.

Also of importance are the studies that have found an increase in bullying behaviour after intervention. Examples of studies showing an increase in involvement include one reported by Debra Pepler and colleagues, which evaluated a school-based intervention in Canada (1994) and another by Earling Roland (1989), who reported the results of a study that implemented Olweus' intervention in another part of Scandinavia.

A recent paper by Merrell *et al.* (2008) conducted a meta-analysis – a statistical review of the body of literature on a particular effect – of school-based anti-bullying interventions. Overall 16 studies were included, including the Olweus Programme and variations on this approach. Together, the studies had over 15 000 participants and focused on a range of self-report and teacher-report outcomes. These outcomes included variables ranging from reports of participation in bullying, to witnessing bullying, to positive attitudes regarding bullying. Merrell and colleagues found that the effects included both positive and negative effects (which is in line with the individual studies reported above), but that the majority of studies did not report strong effects on bullying behaviour. They conclude that 'Although antibullying interventions appear to be useful in increasing awareness, knowledge, and self-perceived competency in dealing with bullying, it should not be expected that these interventions will dramatically influence the incidence of actual bullying and victimization behaviours' (Merrell *et al.*, 2008, p. 41). The findings of this meta-analysis highlight the level of inconsistency in the research literature whereby the significant changes reported following Olweus's original intervention have not been widely replicated – a finding that undermines to some extent the evidence for this programme.

The challenge of tackling cyberbullying

The review of school policies on bullying described earlier highlighted a lack of consideration of cyberbullying as a specific form of bullying behaviour. While it could be argued that this is a reflection of this sub-type's relatively

RESEARCH METHODS

Issues in researching bullying

As a rule, the findings of psychological research are only as reliable and valid as the research methods used to conduct the research. As a result, it is important to consider the way in which methodological issues might impact on our understanding of bullying.

If we consider the research that has been discussed in this chapter, it is clear that researchers working on the topic of bullying have drawn on a wide range of research methods from qualitative interviews to experimental evaluations. A number of the studies assessing the prevalence of bullying in school have used large-scale anonymous surveys, while more exploratory studies have tended to used qualitative methods. Each method comes with its benefits and limitations. Ahmad and Smith (1990) compared various survey methods, including anonymous and non-anonymous surveys. They observed lower rates of involvement when pupils had to write their names on the surveys and concluded that anonymous questionnaires were most suitable when examining involvement in bullying. It may be that people are more likely to report either victimisation or perpetration if they know that they cannot be later identified. With respect to qualitative methods, these can be very effective in exploring group and individual perspectives on bullying, as we have seen in the research on children's definitions of bullying. These qualitative methods strive to elicit participants' perspectives in a manner which is not biased by the researchers' preconceived views. For other research purposes, however, such as the assessment of large-scale involvement in bullying, we do have to consider the practicality of using interviews and focus groups which can be expensive and time-consuming.

Aside from the relative merits of different methods of data collection, there are broader challenges in conducting research in this area. One of the most practical

challenges is the fact that bullying is a behaviour that generally occurs if not in secret, then away from adults. The secrecy that surrounds bullying raises concerns about the validity of self-reported involvement and peer report, both of which have been used in research. However, it is generally believed that young people's reports are more accurate than adult reports. Ahmad and Smith (1990) reported that peer nominations showed better agreement with self-report questionnaires than teacher nominations did, suggesting that we should try to elicit reports from the individuals involved rather than relying upon teacher- or parent-report. Another challenge relates to the variations in definitions of bullying discussed earlier. If people have different understandings about what constitutes bullying, then valid and reliable assessment of the nature and extent of bullying becomes difficult. In addition, it is challenging to design and deliver an appropriate intervention if individuals have distinct perspectives on the nature of the problem.

Finally, thinking about future research on the topic of bullying, there is a huge need for longitudinal designs to be used. As we have seen, bullying is not just a problem that impacts upon children and young people. The behaviour extends across the life course, as discussed in the Lifespan box. Limited psychological research has utilised longitudinal designs to identify precursors to being a bully or a victim, or to understand the potential long-term negative consequences of bullying for both bullies and victims. One such longitudinal study conducted by Olweus (1993b) found that former victims of bullying at school had lower self-esteem and tended to be more depressed than non-victimised peers at age 23. Thus, we know that the negative effects of bullying have the potential to continue into adulthood. Much more longitudinal research is needed to trace the developmental pathways of both bullies and victims across the lifespan.

recent emergence, it is also important to reflect on the additional challenges that cyberbullying incorporates. A paper by Australian researcher Marilyn Campbell (2005) reflects on some of the challenges of preventing and

directly intervening in this area. These challenges include the need to raise awareness about these new forms of bullying behaviour among children and adults and adults' lack of familiarity with the electronic media used in cyberbullying and the implications of this for their ability to supervise children and young people.

However, one of the key issues Campbell highlights is the lack of clarity around who is responsible for tackling cyberbullying. While many schools target traditional forms of bullying because they occur in the school environment and on the school grounds, these physical boundaries do not exist for cyberbullying. Campbell stresses the fact that this issue is further complicated by debates regarding the responsibility of phone and internet-service providers for intervening in these behaviours.

Putting aside the magnitude of these challenges, a basic limitation is the lack of research specifically on cyberbullying as a unique behaviour. While cyberbullying shares many features with the more traditional forms of bullying, it is important that we systematically explore the impact of different approaches to intervention on this increasingly common behaviour.

SUMMARY

In this chapter, we have explored the topic of bullying. Six learning outcomes were identified and, in this concluding section, we will revisit and consider each learning outcome in turn. Firstly, in attempting to define bullying's target behaviours, delineating the specific behaviours that constitute bullying has not been easy. However, most researchers generally accept that bullying involves repeated physical, verbal or psychological attack in the absence of provocation, which is intended to cause harm or distress to the victim. There is also assumed to be an imbalance of power between the bully and victim. However, a more complex picture emerges when children and young people are asked for their perspectives on what constitutes bullying, and adult and child definitions do not appear to be directly comparable. Eliciting children's and young people's conceptualisations of bullying is important since bullying most commonly occurs out of the sight of adults, and it is children and young people who perpetrate, witness and are the victims of bullying. Unlike adult definitions, elements such as repetition and intention are not central to young people's definitions. Such divergences in perspectives can have important implications for how we research bullying and how we design and evaluate effective prevention and intervention programmes. Moreover, with the emergence of new forms of bullying via electronic media, there is a need to refine and update how we conceptualise bullying.

Secondly, findings arising from a range of studies on the prevalence of bullying indicate that it is a very common experience that affects many children's lives. Prevalence estimates for victimisation range from 4% to almost 50%, while rates for perpetration vary from 1% to 21%. However, there is also considerable inconsistency in prevalence rates across the studies, reflecting variation in the methods used within research, differences in how bullying is understood by children of different ages or perhaps different cultural patterns. Some clear gender patterns are also evident, particularly with regard to the types of bullying behaviour boys and girls engage in. In looking at prevalence rates, we have seen a tendency to focus upon the involvement of bullies and victims and, more recently, there has been a renewed focus upon the bully/victim. A number of researchers have reminded us that bullying is a social and group-oriented phenomenon, so we should not ignore the fact that most children in a group are affected in some way by bullying. Six roles in bullying have been identified, and further understanding of these participant roles in bullying is needed, so that their implications for intervention can be considered.

Thirdly, we have considered developmental changes in bullying. Even very young children engage in aggressive behaviour. During the pre-school period and early childhood, physical aggression declines and verbal aggression increases. Relational kinds of aggression are also evident during this stage, particularly among girls. A steady decline in victimisation is evident from 7 to 12 years, and this continues into the period of adolescence. Among perpetrators of bullying, these behaviours appear to remain relatively stable across childhood and adolescence. However, we should be cautious in how we interpret the decline in victimisation throughout middle and later childhood and into adolescence – older children may be less likely to admit to being victimised for fear of being perceived as vulnerable. Little research to date has considered developmental patterns in relation to cyberbullying.

Fourthly, in relation to cyberbullying, we have considered its distinctions from traditional forms of bullying. The prevalence of cyberbullying varies somewhat from study to study, but reliable estimates suggest that between 11% and 14% of young people had been victims, with some research suggesting that girls may be more likely than boys to become involved in it. Little research has documented developmental patterns in cyberbullying, although there are suggestions that it becomes more prevalent in the teenage years, possibly relating to older children having increased access to mobile phones and computers. Thus, cyberbullying may be distinct from other forms of bullying in terms of the gender and developmental patterns associated with it. Other important differences include the visibility of the bullying, where bullying via social networking sites may be observed by unlimited numbers of people, and the fact that cyberbullying via the internet or mobile phone could potentially happen at any time or in any place, in contrast to other forms of bullying which tend to occur during circumscribed periods of time. Few studies have assessed the psychological impact of being the victim of cyberbullying, although some commentators suggest that due to its relentless and public nature, the impact could be even greater than that experienced by victims of more traditional forms of bullying.

Fifthly, we have considered theoretical perspectives on bullying. Crick and Dodge's social-information processing model argues that children who are aggressive display a hostile attributional bias which increases the likelihood that a child will react to an ambiguous social situation with aggression. In stark contrast, Sutton and colleagues suggest that bullies are skilled manipulators who display competent theory of mind skills. Research based on the theories lends some support to both perspectives, and there has been debate in the literature about which is correct. In addition, the application of attribution theory to understanding how both bullies and victims explain the causes of bullying allows us to compare the different perspectives of those involved in the behaviour and to understand how bullying may differentially impact upon individuals. Critically reflecting upon the merits of these divergent perspectives could have important implications for how we address the problem of bullying. To date, no theory of cyberbullying has been proposed, although theories of online behaviour have been utilised to understand cyberbullying. Specifically, anonymity often inherent in online interactions gives rise to disinhibition where people are less likely to act in socially acceptable ways than they would if their identity was known. However, there has been little research to explore the role that disinhibition plays in cyberbullying.

Finally, the sixth learning outcome was concerned with interventions, and two broad approaches were described: educational approaches and participant approaches. A third approach – peer support or peer counselling – involves children directly in anti-bullying programmes. Each approach comes with advantages and disadvantages and, to date, there has been limited large-scale evaluation of many of the programmes. One exception is the Olweus Programme which has been subject to a number of evaluations and seems to bring about a modest impact on rates of bullying. It is important to reflect upon the efficacy and potential for success of the various approaches along with considerations of the challenges and potential pitfalls of implementation.

REVIEW QUESTIONS

1 Based on the different perspectives on defining bullying, what are the key elements of the behaviour?
2 What are the key distinctions between bullies, victims and bully/victims?
3 How do variables such as gender and age affect involvement in bullying?
4 Compare and contrast the different theoretical positions that have been used to explain bullying.
5 What are the strengths and limitations of existing methods of preventing bullying in a school setting?
6 What are the additional challenges associated with understanding and addressing the problem of cyberbullying?

RECOMMENDED READING

For more on international trends in bullying, see:

Smith, P.K., Morita, Y., Junger-Tas, J., Olweus, D., Catalano, R. & Slee, P. (1999). *The Nature of School Bullying: A Cross-national Perspective*. London: Routledge.

For more on cyberbullying, see:

Kowalski, R.M., Limber, S.P. & Agatston, P.W. (2008). *Cyber Bullying*. Malden, MA: Blackwell.

For more on intervention and prevention, see:

Smith, P., Pepler, D. & Rigby, K. (2004). *Bullying in Schools: How Successful Can Interventions Be?* Cambridge: Cambridge University Press.

For more on peer support, see:

Cowie, H. & Wallace, P. (2000). *Peer Support in Action: From Bystanding to Standing By*. London: Sage.

For more on bullying as a group process, see:

Salmivalli, C., Lagerspetz, K., Bjorkqvist, K., Österman, K., & Kaukiainen, A. (1996). Bullying as a group process: Participant roles and their relations to social status within the group. *Aggressive Behaviour, 22*, 1–15.

For more on theories of bullying, see articles by:

Sutton, J., Smith, P.K. & Swettenham, J. (1999) and Crick & Dodge (1999) in *Social Development, Volume 8*, 117–127.

RECOMMENDED WEBSITES

The website for the UK Department for Education; use the search function to find policy documents and resources on bullying; you can also follow the links to www.teachernet.gov.uk, which has additional information for teachers:

http://www.education.gov.uk

The website for a major UK-based charity with a commitment to reducing bullying and other forms of abuse – it contains information and resources for young people, parents and professionals:

http://www.kidscape.org.uk

The website for the UK Observatory for the Promotion of Non-Violence, a national initiative which targets behaviours such as aggression and bullying, with the aim of promoting wellbeing:

http://www.ukobservatory.com

Website containing information on the Olweus Bullying Prevention Programme:

http://www.olweus.org/public/index.page

 Watch a semi-structured interview with a single child talking about what bullying means to her. Further resources can be found at www.pearsoned.co.uk/gillibrand

Chapter 16
Atypical development
Shabnam Khan and Emma Rowley

Learning Outcomes

After reading this chapter, with further recommended reading, you should be able to:

1. Describe some of the key developmental difficulties and disorders associated with childhood, their prevalence and causes;

2. Compare and contrast the different approaches to developmental assessment, critically evaluate their strengths and weaknesses and consider their predictive value for later development;

3. Show an awareness of the issues surrounding clinical diagnosis of a child's difficulties, and the positive and negative impact this may have on the child and family;

4. Understand the ways in which disorders of development can impact upon the child's emotional health, and consider the risk and protective factors associated with positive and negative outcomes;

5. Examine the research evidence to support different approaches to intervention.

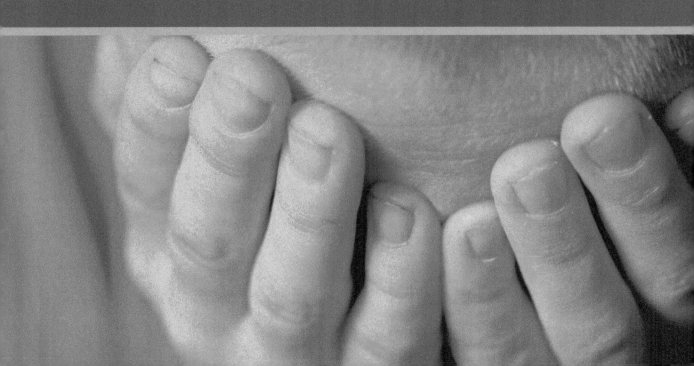

Daniel

Daniel is a three year old boy who lives with his mother, Linda, and his eighteen month old sister. Over the past few months, Linda has become increasingly concerned about Daniel's development: He has been slow to talk and uses only two words 'car' and 'drink'. His younger sister has already overtaken him with her language, and is much better at getting what she wants, pointing and bringing things to her mother when she needs help. With Daniel, it is much more of a guessing game. Linda has to work hard just to get him to look at her, and he often just seems to ignore her when she calls him or tries to play with him. It can be very frustrating.

At playgroup, although he looks just like any other three year old, Daniel stands out from the other children because of his behaviour. Every day he heads to the same corner, where he will sit, placing toy cars in a long line and peering at them closely. He doesn't play with the other children or join them for 'circle time', and cries when someone disturbs his play. He finds it hard to share or follow instructions, and needs a lot of support to join in with group activities.

- What could be the cause of Daniel's difficulties and what do they mean for his development?
- Will he be able to catch up and develop the skills he needs to learn and communicate?
- What will help him to do this?

Introduction

Child development is a complex and dynamic process, involving the interaction of a multitude of different genetic, neurological, emotional, behavioural and environmental factors. This chapter is designed to help you understand some of the ways in which a child's development can progress along an 'atypical' route and how, as developmental psychologists, we can use our assessment skills to identify and support children who may be experiencing developmental difficulties, within the context of the wider family, school and social system.

As the scenario above suggests, a child's progress through the different stages of development can be far from straightforward. As children grow and develop, they must each face their own individual challenges, building up a vast array of skills over time to become healthy, happy, fully functioning members of society.

Whilst most children will go on to achieve the expected developmental milestones, many others, just like Daniel in the example above, may face an uphill struggle from birth, experiencing significant difficulty in some or all areas of their development. So far in this book, we have looked in detail at some of the key areas of development, and the processes through which healthy, typically-developing children acquire different skills, from learning and memory in infancy to the development of sophisticated 'theory of mind' understanding and formation of social relationships in childhood. ▶

▶ But what happens when children do not show this same pattern of skill acquisition? What if they are born with difficulties which mean that they will not develop at the same rate or in the same way as other children of their age? This chapter aims to introduce you to some of the important ways in which a child's development can follow an 'atypical' path, highlighting key areas of developmental disorder and disability in childhood, their causes and prevalence. Among the disabilities included are:

- developmental delay and disorder;
- learning disability;
- specific learning difficulties (e.g. dyslexia, dyspraxia);
- pervasive developmental disorders (e.g. autism spectrum disorder);
- genetic disorders (e.g. Down's sydrome, Turner's syndrome).

Next, we shall look at how we, as developmental psychologists, can apply our assessment and intervention skills within different settings, to help understand the nature of a child's difficulties, and effectively support their ongoing development by using specific interventions such as behavioural, educational and therapeutic strategies. Finally, we shall look at the impact of childhood disorder and disability on the growing child's emotional and mental health, and consider the wide-ranging impact of a child's disability on parents, siblings and the wider family system.

What is atypical development?

In the pre-school years, children typically develop a large number of skills in a relatively short period of time, from their first attempts at communication, e.g. crying and smiling, through to symbolic play, all the way to taking their first tentative steps. Whilst it is widely acknowledged that children tend to develop at their own pace, the range of skills they show largely follows a typical and predictable trajectory, with the acquisition of one skill providing a stepping stone to the next. This sequence of skills and abilities (often referred to as developmental milestones) provides a framework for our understanding of child development, allowing us to gauge the child's level of functioning from the behaviour, skills and abilities they demonstrate. Development that deviates significantly from this developmental sequence is considered 'atypical', and may be an early indication of possible difficulties in childhood.

Table 16.1 shows some of the typical developmental milestones from birth to five years, in the key areas of development. As Table 16.1 suggests, individual differences between children will mean that there is typically some variation (usually several months) in the age at which the different physical, cognitive, social and emotional milestones are reached. In the same way, the rate of development between different areas of skill varies considerably: some children may show early advances in one area, such as motor ability, while others may race ahead with language, their first words appearing much earlier than expected. Children who show early progress in one area do not necessarily show a similar rate of development across other areas. In fact, it is not uncommon to see a slowing down in the development of some skills during a burst of development in another; with the child using all of his biological and psychological resources to develop one skill at a time. Children with special needs often move through the different developmental stages in unusual and very uneven ways. For example, they may sit or walk at the usual age but show delay in their language skills. Parents, health visitors and other caregivers have the critical role of observing and charting the child's early development, keeping records of skill attainment and behaviour, which may later help to identify specific areas of need or difficulty. In the case of unusual or atypical development, this is often the first step in the identification and assessment process, assisting clinicians and child development specialists in determining the specific needs and/or possible developmental diagnosis relevant to the individual child.

Table 16.1. Developmental milestones chart.

Area of development	Milestone	Age range in typically developing children
Gross motor skills (physical movement)	Holds head steady in sitting position	1–4 months
	Sits independently	5–9 months
	Stands alone	9–16 months
	Walks alone	9–17 months
Fine motor skills and eye hand coordination	Follows object with eyes	1–3 months
	Reaches out and grasps object	2–6 months
	Passes objects from hand to hand	4–8 months
	Builds a tower of two wooden blocks	10–19 months
	Copies a circle	24–40 months
Communication skills	Babbles 'dada', 'mama'	5–14 months
	Responds to familiar words	5–14 months
	First words spoken with meaning	10–23 months
	Shows need using gesture	11–19 months
	Uses two word phrases	15–32 months
Personal and self-help skills	Feeds self with biscuit	4–10 months
	Drinks from cup	9–17 months
	Dry by day	14–36 months
	Bowel control	16–48 months
Social interaction	Smiles when talked to	1–2 months
	Plays peek-a-boo games	3–6 months
	Distinguishes between familiar adults	6–9 months
	Shows anxiety at separation	9–12 months
	Watches other children and copies play	24–36 months
Cognitive skills	Shows anticipation for expected events	0–3 months
	Imitates others' facial expressions	3–6 months
	Understands object permanence	6–9 months
	Basic trial and error and problem solving	6–9 months
	Understands cause-and-effect	12–18 months

Source: adapted from Cunningham, 1988, *Down's Syndrome – An Introduction for Parents.* Souvenir Press Ltd. Human Horizon Series

Understanding the process of child development

The developmental milestones provide a helpful guide for parents and professionals alike, and can act as an important indicator of later developmental problems. However, as we learnt in Chapter 9, Attachment and Early Social Experiences, progression through the different stages of development is not simply a matter of genetics or predetermined physical maturation. As well as being influenced by the child's genetic and neurological characteristics, it is also dependent upon the dynamic interactions between biological and environmental influences (see Fig. 16.1, Sheridan, 2008).

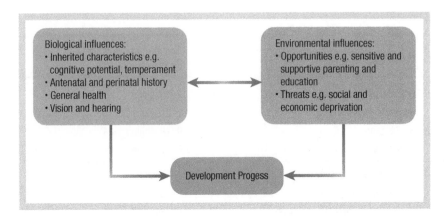

Figure 16.1. Influences on development.

(*Source:* taken from Sheridan, M., 2008, *From Birth to Five Years*: Routledge)

These interactions between biology and environment result in a high level of variability in children's developmental outcomes. For example, a child growing up in a country in which war, conflict and food shortage are an everyday reality may show a vastly different developmental profile from a child who lives in a safe, stable and economically secure part of the world. In the same way, a child experiencing abuse, neglect or growing up with parents with mental health difficulties may experience many more developmental challenges than the child who has a healthy, secure parental attachment relationship and grows up in a supportive environment. As we shall see in this chapter, in order to really understand a child's developmental difficulties, we must consider both the sequences of development as well as the context within which this development takes place (see Fig. 16.1).

Source: Photolibrary/BSIP Medical

STOP AND THINK

Revisit the case study of Daniel at the beginning of this chapter.

■ Using Fig. 16.1, can you identify any biological or environmental factors which may be impacting upon his developmental progress?

■ What else would you need to find out to explore the different influences on his development more fully?

Child development in context

Throughout this chapter, we will be looking at the way in which biological and genetic influences, as well as illness and disease, can impact upon a child's development. However, as we have learnt, of equal importance are the environmental influences of the child's past learning experiences, her immediate social and psychological environment (e.g. parents, siblings, schoolteachers and relatives) and the wider cultural, political, religious and social surroundings in which they grow and develop. Today, developmental psychologists have a much wider appreciation of the significance of environmental factors in shaping the child's development, and much research has been carried out to determine the extent to which these factors play a causal role in childhood difficulties (see Rutter *et al.*'s study from 2001 examining the effects of institutional deprivation on later childhood development).

One of the pioneers in this field, Urie Bronfenbrenner, highlights the role of environment or 'nurture' in shaping a child's development. His 'Ecological systems theory' (Bronfenbrenner, 1989) defines a series of five sociocultural systems or 'layers' ranging from family and school interactions to the beliefs, values and traditions of the child's culture and wider social system, which interact with each other to help shape the child's development. In this way, changes or difficulties in one layer will cause a ripple-effect, causing changes throughout the other layers or systems. Bronfenbrenner's theory has recently been renamed 'bio-ecological systems theory', to emphasise the role of the child's own biology – arguably one of the most fundamental environmental influences fueling later development (see Chapter 2, Theoretical Perspectives, for a full discussion of this theory).

Culture and developmental 'norms'

So far in this chapter, we have discussed a model of child development which is well-established within Europe and large parts of the Western world, in particular, the 'milestone approach', which maps neatly onto a Western model of healthcare and education, with its specific, culturally-bound physical, cognitive and social targets. However, research suggests that different cultural expectations and child-rearing practices can strongly influence the rate and expression of children's development.

Consider, for example, the stage at which children are encouraged by their parents or caregivers to feed themselves. In the Western world, adults encourage their infants early on to learn self-feeding, even if learning to self-feed means making a mess. By contrast, in non-Western cultures, the adult's primary purpose in feeding the infant is to ensure that they have eaten an adequate meal with the minimum amount of waste or mess. As such, they may continue to spoon-feed their child for a much longer period than is considered the 'norm' in Europe. Similarly, babies in the West tend to spend much longer periods of time by themselves – sleeping in separate rooms, and amusing themselves in playpens. As a result, they learn to use verbal communication to get the attention of adults, e.g. calling out to the parent or caregiver out of necessity, whereas babies from non-Western cultures, who spend much of their time in close physical contact with their parents, learn to use non-verbal communication such as hand gestures or changes in muscle tone or posture to get their needs met. Figure 16.2 summarises some of the research findings highlighting the variation in child development across cultures.

Developmental Milestones across Cultures

- Motor precocity of African infants who sit, crawl and walk at least two months earlier than Caucasian infants (Ainsworth, 1977; Geber and Dean, 1957; Capute *et al.*, 1985)
- Delayed self-feeding and cutlery skills in African and South Asian children compared to US norms (Gokiert *et al.*, 2007)
- Advanced attainment of pencil skills in Japanese children compared to British norms (Saida and Miyashita, 1979)
- Earlier, reverse-style rolling skills in infants born in Hong Kong compared to Caucasian infants (Nelson *et al.*, 2004)

Figure 16.2. Cultural differences in child development.

As developmental psychologists, a curiosity and awareness of the differences that exist across cultures in terms of child-rearing, social, cultural and religious practices is vital in understanding the individual child. Whilst comprehensive assessment of the effects of culture on children's wellbeing may not always be possible, careful consideration of issues of cultural identity and acknowledgement of the importance of culture in the child's behaviour and development may enable us to develop a more complete picture of the child, incorporating this information into an holistic formulation of his individual strengths and difficulties.

STOP AND THINK

Consider your own early development, or that of siblings or relatives. You may want to discuss with someone who knew you as you were growing up.

- What family, cultural or religious beliefs helped influence your parents/caregivers' ideas about child development?
- What impact did these ideas and beliefs have on your early experience and learning?

Holding all of these important contextual factors in mind, how might we identify when children are showing signs of atypical development? What might such an assessment look like, and who might be involved? What kinds of developmental problems do we see in children, and how can we offer support to enable them to lead a happy and fulfilling life? These are just some of the questions which we shall explore throughout the rest of this chapter.

Assessment

For the child with atypical development, this is only the first step: once differences in development have been identified, a journey begins in which parents and caregivers generally seek to understand what might be causing their child's difficulties. Although the process can vary enormously, parents, just like the parents of David in the case example above, often express their concerns to a health professional, who may refer the child for assessment. But what is assessment, and how can it be used to identify areas of difficulty? What are the approaches which clinicians use to better understand a child's developmental trajectory?

Definition

Assessment: assessment is the process of collecting information on children, typically through observations, tests, clinician/teacher rating scales, etc., in order to make inferences about their development, typically within a school or clinical context.

What is assessment?

General developmental assessment can take a variety of forms, and typically involve the gathering of information from a range of different sources such as parents, teachers, specialist health visitors and other health professionals, as well as the use of a range of different assessment methods, from history-taking and structured parent questionnaires to cognitive assessments and play-based observations. This holistic approach to information gathering ensures that there is as much information as possible available about the child's functioning and behaviour in all different areas of their life. This thorough and often time-consuming process necessarily draws upon the skills of a range of different health professionals, including paediatricians, clinical psychologists, speech and language therapists, occupational therapists and physiotherapists, who may work jointly or in parallel to carry out assessments' and bring together information crucial to the assessment process. By using different forms of assessment, we can begin to develop an understanding of the child's skills and abilities over a range of important developmental domains, from physical growth and development of motor skills like walking, running and jumping, to cognition (thinking and learning), communication and social development.

Why assess?

Psychological assessment is a complex, detailed, in-depth process. Broadly speaking, psychological assessments are

---

CASE STUDY

Extract from a Health Visitor's referral letter to the community child development team

Dear Colleagues,
Re: David Thomas, Dob: 12/09/2008

Thank you for seeing this lovely three year old boy who was brought to my clinic today by his parents. David has left-sided hearing loss and experiences recurrent ear infections. His speech is showing signs of significant delay, and his speech sounds for familiar objects are often

unclear. Since he started nursery, his parents have noticed that David is behind his peers in a number of key areas, including his play skills, which they describe as rather 'babyish'. He is also reluctant to finger-feed, and still insists on parents spoonfeeding him at each mealtime. He is not yet potty trained, and mum tells me that he doesn't yet appear aware of when he may have a full nappy.

Parents are naturally quite concerned, and wonder whether David may have more global difficulties with his development. I wonder if you could offer the family an assessment in your clinic.

used to (Standards for Education and Training in Psychological Assessment, 2006):

- provide a diagnosis for a treatment plan,
- assess a particular area of functioning or disability, such as for school settings, to enable more appropriate support and intervention to be provided,
- assess treatment outcomes,
- help courts decide issues such as child custody or competency to stand trial,
- help assess job applicants or employees,
- provide career development counselling or training.

In the case of child development assessments, the purpose is to understand the trajectory of development that a child is following in order to diagnose a disability and to inform future interventions.

Ethical dilemmas in the assessment and diagnosis of young children . . . to diagnose is to label – pros and cons of 'diagnosis'

Assessment of young children, when it is done in an appropriate way, can be an extremely useful way of providing information to caregivers, parents, teachers and clinicians about the child's skills, abilities and areas of difficulty. Within a clinical context, assessment can be used to help identify and, where appropriate, diagnose specific disorders of development. Opinion varies widely as to the value and possible negative implications of giving young children a diagnostic label. Nevertheless, Western models of health care are based on diagnoses. But, how helpful it is to the client? Do clinicians do more harm than good by using labels?

Benefits to diagnosis include guiding appropriate treatment and making the process of assessment more efficient (Jellinek and McDermott, 2004), ensuring that diagnostic labels are based on scientifically sound evidence (APA, 1994) and facilitating effective clinical practice by using treatments that work (Roth *et al.*, 1996). The APA (1995) has argued that diagnosis aids communication across health disciplines within the context of multidisciplinary teams. Pilgrim (2001) also states that having a diagnosis might be helpful for a client because the fact that the disorder is easily researchable can be useful, for example, when requesting additional support, such as from the education system. It is possibly for these

reasons that only diagnostic methods of describing problems are accepted for insurance claims and in courts of law (Butler, 1998).

On the other hand, diagnoses can be problematic. For example, diagnostic categories can often overlap and, on their own, do not provide clinicians with a clear indication of a client's disorder (e.g. Johnstone, 2006), nor do they always capture the rare or complex symptoms of the disorder (Butler, 1998). In addition, diagnosis, as defined by the *Diagnostic and Statistics Manual* (DSM), is consistently found to have low reliability and validity (Aboraya *et al.*, 2006). Jellinek and McDermott (2004) stated that clients' context needs to be known otherwise the problem will not be understood. For example, a child's defiant behaviour can be indicative of a number of issues: to hide a learning difficulty, to gain attention from parents, to be accepted into a peer group or even in response to a stressful situation at home. As Boyle (2001) stated, without a context or further details about the problem's causes, a treatment plan is difficult to develop and is not likely to produce positive outcomes.

Finally, one of the most damaging problems with diagnosis is the social stigma that it can create. Social labels and categories given to groups of similarly perceived people assume certain characteristics and traits. These assumptions lead to expectations of an individual and can lead to stereotypes and prejudice (Devine, 1989). While stereotypes may contain a kernel of truth (Jones, 1997), individual differences must still be considered before category assumptions are applied.

Assessment methods

Now that we have understood what assessment is and why it is useful to clinicians, the following section introduces you to some of the common assessment methods that a psychologist (or paediatrician) might use as part of a generalised assessment of functioning within a child development context. These include:

- play-based assessment and observation;
- standardised cognitive assessment;
- developmental history-taking.

Play-based assessment and observation

As earlier chapters suggest, play is one of the most fundamental ways in which a child can learn about herself and the world around her. It is through play that the child can practise, elaborate on and perfect skills before they become necessary for survival in adulthood (Rubin, 1982). In this way, play represents an important tool for learning and developing personal resources for life.

Play provides a naturalistic opportunity for the child to test out and develop their sensory and motor skills (Piaget, 1962), social abilities (Rubin *et al.*, 1989) and language (Caplan and Caplan, 1973). It is also a natural means of expression for most children, and it allows children to experience a wide range of emotions and situations. By observing how children play and what they play with, it is possible to gain a rich understanding of a child's developmental level, as well as providing important information about their cultural and social context. As such, clinical assessments may utilise formal and informal play-based assessment observations alongside other types of assessment to inform children's developmental profiles.

Bronfenbrenner argued that 'much of contemporary developmental psychology is the science of the strange behaviour of children in strange situations with strange adults for the briefest possible periods of time'. Accordingly, he considered that only 'experiments created as real are real in their consequences' and stressed that research should begin to focus on how children develop in settings representative of their actual world (i.e. in 'ecologically valid' settings). For instance, instead of studying children only in the laboratory, we should study them in their homes, schools and playgrounds (Bronfenbrenner, 2004).

Today, developmental psychologists continue to believe that, in order to be able to observe a child in a way that would indicate his true skills, we must seek to make the assessment process as relaxed, naturalistic and appealing to children as possible. By using play, children are able to have the freedom to express themselves, focusing on a range of items and activities which are of interest to them, and with which they are happy to engage for a period of time. Assessments of play involve observations of how a child plays alone, with peers and with adults in free play or in specific games, as well as how they use communication, problem solving and imaginative skills to enhance their play. Table 16.2 highlights the types of toys that can be used in a play assessment and what types of skills a child can demonstrate.

The main areas of interest for professionals (and no doubt, parents) assessing a child's level of development are their cognitive, social and communication skills.

Play and cognitive skills

Cognitive aspects of play are varied and wide, and they can provide information about a child's thinking and learning ability. How children engage and persevere with age-appropriate tasks provides valuable information about their cognitive abilities.

'Pure' problem-solving tasks such as completing inset puzzles of different shapes, sizes and colours, sorting shapes, matching colours, exploring items with the purpose of operating them (such as searching for an on–off button) indicate a good learning ability in a child. Cognitive skills can also be applied to situations, such as considering how children go about adapting their environment to achieve a goal, like using a chair to get a toy from a high shelf.

Drawing indicates an ability to replicate what they see or imagine in an abstract form. A child's drawing skills move from scribbles to lines and circles, to drawing other shapes to form people and objects. Children who find these tasks difficult and are unable to develop them over time may have a cognitive difficulty (Smith, 2009).

An ability to generalise thinking is also a cognitive strength (Kaufman, 1994). Does the child enjoy play

How children play with age-appropriate toys can give you an insight into their cognitive abilities.

Source: Pearson Education Ltd./Lisa Payne Photography

Table 16.2. **Examples of how toys and activities can be used to assess a child's development.**

Toy/activity	Assessment/questions	Domain of skill displayed
Cause and effect toy (toys with buttons that result in immediate results, e.g. flashing lights or a sound)	Operates it? How?	Cognitive, motor
	Asks for help if stuck?	Communication
	Shows emotion on his face?	Social
	Involves others, directly (calls them over) or indirectly (looks at them)?	Communication, social
	Attention level?	Cognitive
	Move on to something else?	Social, communication, cognitive
	Verbal or non-verbal?	Communication
Drawing	Pencil grip?	Motor
	Type of drawing?	Cognitive
	Attention level?	Cognitive, behaviour
	Shows drawings to others?	Social
	Brings others into activity?	Social
	Sharing drawing tools?	Social
Puzzles, problem-solving tasks, e.g. threading, colour-matching	Communicates needs?	Communication
	Able to complete?	Cognitive
	If the task cannot be done?	Communication, social, cognitive, behaviour
Physical play	Emotional expression?	Social, communication, behaviour
	Shares his enjoyment with others?	Social
	Able to regulate emotion after being aroused?	Social, behaviour
	Ability to transition to another task?	Social
	Movement and coordination?	Motor
Home corner, dolls, cars	Initiates play?	Social, cognitive
	Follows someone else's lead?	Social
	Builds on a story brought in by someone else?	Social, cognitive
	Tolerates intrusion from others?	Social
	Repetitive?	Behaviour
	Verbal or non-verbal?	Communication
Building blocks	Can replicate structures?	Cognitive
	Can stack?	Cognitive
	Shares blocks?	Social, behaviour
	Communication style?	Communication

items that have more than one purpose, such as blocks? Such toys allow functional play to occur in a range of different ways, allowing indications of flexibility in thinking and the ability to utilise objects variously but appropriately. For example, blocks can be used to build a house in doll play, to form a bridge in train play, to raise something off the ground or even to weigh something down.

Definition

Functional play: the use of objects in play for the purposes for which they were intended and making objects do what they are made to do, e.g. pushing a car on a surface or pressing the buttons on a mechanical toy.

However, the relationship between play and cognition is complex and difficult to isolate (Dunn and Herwig, 1992) because factors such as attention, social skills, language development, motor skills and anxiety can interfere with the level at which a child appears to engage with a toy. For example, if a child has a poor attention span and does not complete a colour-matching puzzle, this might suggest that she is unable to colour match, or if a child is not able to form a tripod grip with her hands and fingers to hold a pencil, it is also unlikely that she will be able to draw. In other words, the simple completion, or non-completion as the case may be, of play activities may not necessarily indicate the child's true cognitive ability.

Play and social interaction

By observing children's play behaviours, professionals can also identify those who may struggle with social interaction. One typical function of play is to make up social rules that are likely to govern interactions with others, as well as understanding better the meanings behind social interaction (Hughes, 1999). How these social rules and elements of understanding develop can be broken down into the building blocks of basic interaction.

Basic social interactions that a child would exhibit from as early as three months include using eye contact, a variety of facial expressions (e.g. smiling, getting upset), sharing enjoyment with others' (e.g. taking a picture home to mummy, shouting 'come look' to friends), attending to what others are doing (e.g. responding to someone else saying 'wow, that's amazing', using others' facial expressions to know where to direct attention) and sharing or taking turns in play (e.g. waiting turns in a board games or tolerating sharing a box of Lego pieces). The mere presence of these behaviours may not be suggestive of developmental problems in and of themselves, as they can be found to some extent in all children; however, their quality, frequency, timing and duration can be indicators of the child's social skills development. For example, even children with social interaction difficulties (such as autism) can display eye contact in response to highly motivating situations; however, eye contact may typically be reduced and/or absent at other times when it is most expected, e.g. when a child is greeted or called by their parent.

The absence or only fleeting display of appropriate social skills at times when this would be expected is noteworthy in young children, and suggests that the child may struggle with expressing themselves and interacting appropriately with others. Whilst other important contextual and emotional factors (e.g. early life trauma, insecure attachment, passive personality) may also contribute to difficulties with social interaction, children who consistently struggle to use or learn the social interaction skills described above are likely to find it much harder to form friendships and relationships with others.

Play and communication

It is commonly accepted that certain aspects of play are strongly linked to children's communication ability. When children play, they are also involved in the communicative function of sharing objects with others and developing ideas upon which to expand their play. They are also expressing their needs, verbally and non-verbally, and responding to questions asked of them. Hence, play is closely associated with language use and communication (McCune-Nicolich and Bruskin, 1982). In particular, the level of language development can be an informal predictor of a child's level of abstract play. Therefore if a child's communication skills are limited, it is likely that their play will also be limited in terms of its pretend, symbolic, relational and imaginative features.

It may also be unlikely that a child will engage in appropriate social communication, that is the ability children develop to use language regularly to appropriately meet their needs via someone else. For example, a child who wants a toy from a high shelf but does not understand the benefits of communicating to others would perhaps attempt to get the toy from the shelf themselves rather than ask for help. Or, alternatively, they might use others as an inanimate tool (e.g. by standing on them) to achieve a goal. Whilst the relationship between communication and 'use of others' is mediated by other factors, such as attachment style and personality traits, features of play can be helpful indicators of a child's communication skills.

Thus, the way children play can be useful in understanding the developmental abilities and difficulties in a naturalistic way. However, there are some criticisms of using play to assess children's skills. We have already identified that personality, attachment style, attention span and anxiety factors can confound play assessment data. In addition, it must be remembered that our understanding of play is based on Western child-rearing practices. Thus, an assumption is made that the child is familiar with the toy, understands its purpose and function and that this form of play is positively construed by parents.

It is possible that in large parts of the world, children do not have access to the Western toys used in such play assessments. As such, it would not be a fair assessment of a child's development if these same toys and activities were used to assess a child who had recently moved to the country from another part of the world. In this instance, it would be perfectly understandable if the child were to show uncertainty as to the function of a 'jack-in-the-box', perhaps become alarmed and upset by the 'popping-up' of the figure at the end of the play routine. Such play with toys may not be a 'practised skill' for this child because it is not considered a worthwhile activity by his parents. Caution must therefore be paid in interpreting the play skills of children from different cultures, particularly if playing with toys in this way is not usually encouraged or understood. Finally, Russ (2004) states that play-based approaches need to be better supported by empirical studies. This is particularly important for European models of healthcare and education, which strive to offer the very best evidence-based, scientifically driven assessment and support for children with developmental difficulties.

STOP AND THINK

Think about the children you know.

- What does their play say about their level of cognitive and social development?
- Is their play affected by other factors, such as culture, anxiety or poor attention?
- Are their play skills different in different places, such as home and nursery? If so, in what ways?
- Could attachment style account for this difference in any way?

Standardised assessment

As we have seen, direct observation of young children at play can be one of the most valuable ways to gather information about key aspects of their cognitive, language, social, emotional and physical (or motor) development. This is because it enables us to gain a 'fly-on-the-wall' view of the child's development, communication and behaviour in a relaxed and familiar context, doing what comes most naturally to them – playing. With such an effective and naturalistic approach to assessments, it is

easy to see why so many clinicians value observation of the child's play above other, more structured forms of assessment.

However, whilst play assessment is undeniably a vital part of the assessment process, it does not give us any way of accurately measuring the child's skills in an exact (quantitative) way over time, or systematically and reliably comparing their abilities to those of other children of a similar age. Providing this information can be helpful not only in monitoring an individual child's progress over time, but also in knowing what kinds of support, and at what level, a child may need within their school or nursery setting, according to their profile of strengths and difficulties.

Standardised assessment tools can provide a useful way of looking in greater detail at the different areas of a child's development. Complementing more informal parent report and observational methods, they offer a uniform way of comparing an individual child's level of functioning to that of a large sample of other children of the same age. The results of such assessments allow clinicians and parents to see more clearly whether there are specific areas of the child's development which fall below the expected or typical range (often referred to as the 'developmental norm'), and whether their specific profile of strengths and difficulties fits with a particular clinical diagnosis. Moreover, administration of the same test at key points in the child's developmental trajectory can give valuable information about progress and/or possible loss of skill in the major developmental domains, as well as allowing us to predict the child's level of functioning in later childhood.

Child development specialists use a wide range of different standardised measures, some of which aim to measure functioning in one specific area of development (for example, language and communication), whilst others offer a comprehensive profile of the child's strengths and difficulties in all five key developmental domains (cognition, language, social–emotional, motor and adaptive behaviour). An assessment tool widely used across much of Europe and the US is the Bayley Scales of Infant Development (Bayley-III, Bayley, 1969, 1993). This measure, which includes a core battery of five scales, can be used to assess children from as young as one month of age (although more typically children aged from one to three years). The Bayley uses a combination of interactive (mainly non-verbal) play-based tasks and parent questionnaires, designed to measure specific strengths

A standardised developmental assessment uses interactive, play-based tasks to identify specific strengths and difficulties in children from as young as one year old.

Source: Pearson Education Ltd./Jules Selmes

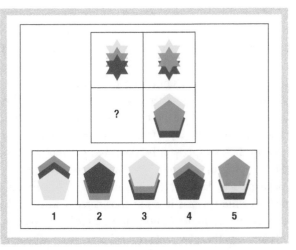

Figure 16.3a. Picture concepts (a non-verbal measure of fluid reasoning, perceptual organisation, and categorisation). From each row of objects, the child selects objects that go together based on an underlying concept.

and competencies, as well as identifying any areas of difficulty. It also provides a valid and reliable measure of a child's abilities, in addition to giving comparison data for children with high-incidence clinical diagnoses.

One of the key areas of the developmental assessment often undertaken by a developmental psychologist is cognitive assessment (the Stanford–Binet Intelligence Test and Wechsler Intelligence Scales are the most widely used measures in the world). This specialised form of testing is used to gain a more detailed understanding of the child's cognitive or intellectual ability so as to identify specific areas of strength and difficulty, to help understand fluctuations in concentration and attention levels and identify specific learning difficulties (e.g. dyslexia), or more global impairment, often referred to as a learning disability. The test itself usually comprises a number of different tasks and activities (see photo above and Figs. 16.3a and 16.3b), which are administered by the clinician during one or more individual sessions with the child. Sub-tests are designed to measure abilities such as verbal and non-verbal fluid reasoning, receptive and expressive vocabulary, working memory and processing speed.

The sum of the child's performance on key tasks allows an overall intelligence quotient (IQ score) to be calculated. As with other standardised assessments, this overall score can be usefully compared to the test's own same-age sample norms, to give an indication of whether the child's thinking and learning skills are at the level expected for their age (or within the 'normal range').

Figure 16.3b. Matrix reasoning (a measure of fluid reasoning). The child is presented with a partially filled grid and asked to select the item that properly completes the matrix.

Definition

Intelligence quotient (IQ): devised by the German psychologist William Stern (1912), the intelligence quotient or IQ is a score derived from one of several different standardised tests designed to measure ability over a range of different cognitive tasks.

IQ and the normal distribution curve

IQ scores in the general population are known to follow a normative distribution, which can be represented graphically as a bell-shaped curve (see Fig. 16.4). As the graph shows, in a typical population, the largest percentage of scores fall within the 'average' range (between 85 and 115), whilst a much smaller number score moderately below (70–85; indicative of 'mild to moderate learning disability') or moderately above (115–130) the average range. Very high (above 130) and very low (below 70) scores are rare. Children gaining an IQ score of 70 or below are likely to have significant learning disability.

IQ is often expressed in 'percentiles'(or 'centiles' as they are sometimes called). Different from the percentage scores used to indicate the number of tasks the child completed correctly, the percentile rank of a score highlights the percentage of scores within the same age range which are the same or lower than the child's actual score. For example, a child with an overall IQ score of 100 has a percentile rank of 50. This means that the child has scored the same or higher than 50% of the children within her age range. By contrast, a child with an IQ score of 80 has a percentile rank of only 9, meaning that only 9% of children within her age range would score the same or lower (i.e. the majority of children tested would gain an IQ score above 80).

Unfortunately, there has been much criticism of the use of cognitive assessment or 'IQ testing' in the past. Historically, such assessments may have been carried out in order to make ruthless decisions about who might be eligible for limited resources and, in some cases, to exclude those with a lower score from being able to access particular educational and employment opportunities. Whilst most health and education professionals would agree that these practices are no longer employed within a modern healthcare system, valid concerns still remain about the usefulness of intelligence tests in accurately capturing a child's everyday functioning. Critics argue that formats of many intelligence tests do not capture the complexity and immediacy of real-life situations, thus limiting their ability to predict non-test or non-academic intellectual abilities.

Best practice dictates that, just as with any other assessment, cognitive testing should not be used in isolation as a measure of a child's skills and abilities. Rather, it should form part of a comprehensive package of assessment which examines the child's full range of abilities across different settings, taking into consideration important individual, familial and contextual factors.

Developmental history assessment

As well as using play-based and standardised assessments to get a sense of the current abilities of a child, it is crucial to the assessment process that the history of

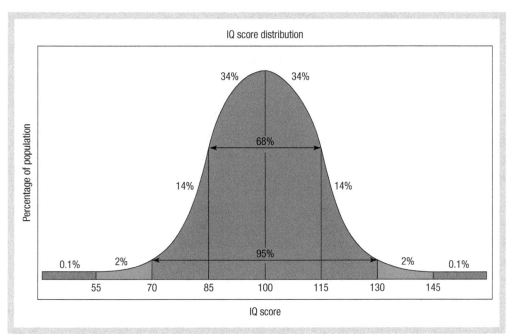

Figure 16.4. IQ scores across the general population.

the child's development is also considered and understood alongside the child's presentation at the time of investigation.

Developmental history-taking is an assessment that typically asks parents or main caregivers to describe their child's behaviours, skills and abilities throughout the child's life from pregnancy through to their current age. A clinician will ask the informant a series of in-depth and specific questions relating to their child, eliciting information about the age at which the behaviour was shown, the quality of the behaviour and, if applicable, the frequency of its occurrence.

The clinician initially asks the parents for details about the child's early development using questions that are guided by the developmental milestones. These questions also focus on the child's current strengths and difficulties as a way to understand the carer's concerns and the child's current abilities. Clinicians also try to assess the child's abilities at around the ages of five to seven (even if the child is older at the time of assessment), because a child would usually have developed a wide range of skills and behaviours by this age and the pattern of skills acquisition is clearer. In addition, the developmental profile at this age is somewhat predictive of future progress, so the details can be used to advise about prognosis (Bolton, 2001). This is also the age range at which children generally enter the education system in most countries within Europe, so it can act as a convenient anchor point for the parents' recall.

Interviewing parents or other informants about a child's early developmental history can be difficult and should be approached with two issues in mind. The first is that the ability for most parents to remember what their child did, at what age, for how long and to what extent can be challenging, particularly if they have other children or if the period of time was busy for them. Forewarning parents that they will be asked questions about their child's development to date can be useful to encourage them to think about their child's past and prepare for the interview.

As indicated above, asking questions about specific events such as birthdays, moving home or the birth of a sibling can help parents to anchor their memories and to describe their child at those times. The second issue is that the professional should elicit from parents descriptive statements rather than evaluative ones about their child's development. This is aimed at distinguishing the parents' perceptions, which can be biased by anxiety and meaning, from more objective descriptions of what their child was like.

STOP AND THINK

As you might imagine from the example questions above, clinicians ask for in-depth, detailed and sometimes circumstantial, and therefore personal, information about and around a child's life to date.

- How do you think a parent might feel about such questions?
- How might a clinician make the developmental history-taking session less stressful on the parents?

Assessments by other health professionals

Far from being the preserve of psychologists and paediatricians, comprehensive assessment of a child's development necessarily involves a wide range of health professionals, who may work together, or alongside, the multidisciplinary team to help develop a more complete understanding of the child's strengths and difficulties.

Given the wide range of factors to consider during a developmental assessment, it is common for colleagues from speech and language therapy, occupational therapy, physiotherapy and community nursing, as well as nursery and school staff, to all play a role in bringing together important information about the child's functioning. Like psychologists, allied health professionals use a range of different assessment techniques, observations and standardised measures to explore the child's skills and abilities. Whilst an exhaustive description of these assessments is beyond the scope of this chapter, the following section aims to summarise some of the ways in which the important contribution of these professionals is delivered.

Specialist health visitor

A specialist health visitor is a qualified nurse and health visitor with additional experience, knowledge and skills in the area of childhood disability. He works closely with the child and family within their own community, playing an important role in the early screening and detection of developmental difficulties. From the moment a difficulty is identified, the specialist health visitor works to link the child and family with the appropriate specialist services, supporting them through the process of assessment and diagnosis, offering advice and encouraging parents to take an active role in the child's care and decision-making process.

Specialist health visitors work collaboratively with colleagues from health, education and social care agencies to coordinate and facilitate a multi-agency package of care and support for the child and wider family system. They may also act as the named key-worker for the family, ensuring that the child's current needs are met and future needs anticipated.

Speech and language therapy

Speech and language therapists (sometimes referred to as speech and language pathologists) are a vital component of any child development team. As we learnt earlier, speech and language difficulties are some of the most common issues affecting young children, accounting for a large number of referrals to child health services. Alongside detailed medical history-taking, speech and language therapists are intrinsically involved in the assessment of these difficulties, carrying out a range of assessments from informal games and observation to structured speech and language evaluation using standardised measures. The speech and language therapist can provide important information about structural difficulties affecting language production (for example, in children suffering from cleft palate or other muscular abnormalities), difficulties of word production, expressive language and understanding, and those difficulties which may be part of a wider syndrome or disorder, such as those seen within the autism spectrum.

In addition to direct assessment, speech and language therapists (who, in the UK, tend to carry out much of their work in schools), often provide a vital link between health and education services. As well as observing the child's use of language and communication in the familiar environment of the classroom, their role allows them to gain valuable insight into the nature and quality of the child's interactions and social initiations with their same-age peers. Moreover, the speech therapist is often able to take advantage of the class teacher or teaching assistant's impartial knowledge of the child to complete information-gathering or diagnostic questionnaires, to further complement the assessment process.

Occupational therapy

Occupational therapists work with young children from birth onwards, treating both physical and developmental disorders through purposeful activities that improve and develop important functional skills needed for everyday independence, e.g. feeding, brushing teeth and hair and dressing. They may work with children with physical delay or disability where there are concerns regarding the development of fine and gross motor, visual–motor, oral–motor, self-care and motor planning skills, often where children have a limited sensory experience or lack normal motor control. In addition, they can provide specialist therapeutic input around sensory integration techniques which, some research suggests, can be particularly helpful in managing irregular levels of sensory stimulation with children with autism and other developmental disabilities (Schaaf and Miller, 2005).

Whilst occupational therapists do not tend to play as central a role in the developmental assessment of young children, the information they provide can usefully contribute to a detailed profile of the child's strengths and abilities. Their use of standardised assessment tools, parent interviews and clinical observations provides a rich source of information that can be used to assess the child's performance across a number of important developmental domains. Following assessment, occupational therapists may work together with clinical psychologists to help develop children's adaptive skills, particularly where a behavioural approach to skill acquisition may be useful.

Psychiatry

Psychiatrists, like their paediatric colleagues, commonly play an important role in the neuropsychological and developmental assessment of children presenting with developmental difficulties. Whilst they may carry out many of the same tasks as a paediatrician, their specialist knowledge of mental health difficulties means that they are ideally placed to carry out assessments where there is a question of psychiatric morbidity, such as psychosis, differential diagnosis or identification and diagnosis of complex neurological disorders such as epilepsy and Tourette's syndrome. Child and adolescent psychiatrists play an integral role in the prescribing and monitoring of medications to help control some of the serious symptoms of a number of developmental disorders.

Disorders of development

The identification of developmental difficulties as early as possible is key to the wellbeing of the child and her family. The previous section described how crucial it is to involve parents, education workers and health professionals in the assessment and measurement of developmental problems, and how different methods and approaches can be used to understand the child's developmental presentation.

As can be imagined, such a multifaceted assessment, across time and in different settings, can generate a lot of observational data. Given that there is no clear way to diagnose observed developmental behaviours, how this information is pulled together lies in the skill of the clinicians involved in the care of the child. But, what disorders can children have? And what does it mean to be 'diagnosed' with a disorder?

This next sections will describe the following diagnoses:

- developmental delays, disorders and learning disabilities;
- specific learning difficulties (e.g. dyslexia, dyspraxia);
- pervasive developmental disorders;
- speech and language disorder;
- genetic disorders (e.g. Down's syndrome, Turner's syndrome);
- physical impairments (e.g. blindness, hearing impairment, cerebral palsy).

Developmental delay and disorder, and learning disability

Like Sandra in the Case Study below, many parents become aware of their child's developmental abilities when they see other children performing tasks that their child is apparently not yet able to do or only recently completed. We already know that for each developmental milestone and ability, there is a range of age in which we might see skills develop. However, when a child does not meet expected developmental milestones and there is no specific diagnosis or apparent explanation, a number of questions can be raised about the child's developmental trajectory: is it evidence of a delay in development whereby the milestone will indeed be met given more time? Is it a sign of a disordered development suggesting an inconsistent developmental pathway? Or are we looking at a global delay that may be indicative of a learning disability? The next sections will tease apart the differences between delayed, disordered and disabled developments.

Developmental delay

A child who has a developmental delay exhibits slower-than-expected rate of attainment of developmental milestones, although progress still occurs in the anticipated sequence within each developmental domain. In other words, a child's speech and language, fine and gross motor skills, personal and social skills or a combination thereof develop slower than expected. While children are known to develop at different rates (e.g. it is considered that walking typically starts in a spread of ages between eight months and 15 months), sometimes children can display abnormal delays in development.

CASE STUDY

Parental perspectives on atypical development

I had my only child, Molly, two and a half years ago. I was not an experienced mother and before Molly, I did not feel particularly inclined towards babies or children. My knowledge about children was somewhat limited. Molly was born at full term with a normal delivery. However, she was a restless and difficult-to-soothe child. But, to me, that's what children are like. It was not until I saw Molly with other children that I realised that something was not quite right. Children her age were speaking words clearly, not just babbling on occasion. They were sharing toys and playing with dolls, not casting them around the room or looking for a TV remote to chew on. I overheard another mother saying her child's quite good at kicking a ball. Molly only learnt to walk a few months ago! When the nursery key-worker said that Molly was less able than the other children her age, that's when I panicked. Molly's now got a general developmental assessment appointment tomorrow with a paediatrician. How could I have been so unaware of her difficulties?

Sandra, mother to Molly, 2 years 6 months old

Developmental disorder

A child who has a disordered developmental profile has gaps or 'scatter' in their attainment of developmental milestones. Progress occurs in a non-sequential pattern within the developmental domain in question. Sometimes this is referred to as a 'deviant' pattern of development. Adding to the confusion is the fact that a child with developmental disorder often has developmental delay as well, i.e. not only have developments occurred in a non-standard order, but the developments that have occurred are also above the age range in which we would expect to see that skill first displayed.

A child with a disordered developmental pattern may first come to the attention of care providers when parents notice that a younger sibling has surpassed an older one in some areas. Yet, at the same time, the older child has successfully achieved some age-appropriate skills. This pattern offers evidence of gaps or scatter in the older child's skills. Sometimes a child's inability to perform certain tasks, while successfully completing others, is misinterpreted as non-compliance. As a result, the child may be at risk for punishment for not doing something that they actually cannot do or do not understand. Identifying disorder in a child's developmental pattern is particularly important for the early identification of developmental language disorders and autistic spectrum disorders, and for distinguishing these conditions from others such as a learning disability.

Global developmental disability and learning disability

A learning disability is an overall problem with receiving, processing, analysing and storing information. People with a learning disability (LD) find it harder than others to learn, understand and communicate. People at the milder end of the LD spectrum can gain an education, work and enter meaningful relationships. These experiences are more difficult for people with profound and multiple learning disabilities, who might need full-time help with every aspect of their lives including eating, drinking, washing, dressing and toileting.

It is possible that a child with a global developmental delay who does not receive support is then considered to have a learning disability at a later age. Typically, global delay that has not been 'caught up' by approximately nine years of age is considered a learning disability.

There are approximately 1.5m people with mild to profound LD in the UK (Department of Health, 2007). Two to three children in every 100 will have an LD, and those with IQ scores of 55 or less will generally have a physiological reason for their disability (Tervo, 2003). The US Department of Education (2001) states that 5% of all children in public schools have a LD. In Germany, the majority of children with LD attend one of the three 'special schools' in the system and statistics suggest that 5% of children attend a special school (Pixa-Kettner, 2005). According to Holland (2002), there are 80 000 children with LD in Denmark.

Aetiology

Developmental delays and disorders have a number of possible causes. They may be due to the neurological formation of the child's brain whilst in gestation, a premature birth, genetic and heredity disorders or infections. Sometimes, if a child is using their mental resources to learn a particular skill, e.g. speaking, they may avoid learning other skills in the meantime, e.g. walking. Speech and language delays may also be secondary issues reflecting other primary problems, such as audiological function, larynx, throat, mouth or nose difficulties, limited experience of communicating from parents or other adults and learning problems.

Those children with more severe developmental problems are likely to be chromosomal and genetic-based, such as Down's syndrome and fragile X syndrome, or other abnormalities with the structure or development of the brain or spinal cord such as cerebral palsy or spina bifida. Other causes can include prematurity, infections (e.g. congenital rubella or meningitis) and metabolic diseases (e.g. hypothyroidism). Whilst various tests can be done to identify the underlying cause, the cause typically remains undetermined.

Diagnostic assessment

In order to ensure a thorough and accurate assessment of a child's developmental abilities, it is imperative that the

> **Definition**
>
> Learning disability: 'a condition of arrested or incomplete development of the mind, which is especially characterised by impairment of skills manifested during the developmental period, which contribute to the overall level of intelligence, i.e. cognitive, language, motor and social abilities . . . Adaptive behaviour is always impaired' (ICD-10)

NATURE–NURTURE

A multidimensional approach to developmental disorders

Pioneering work by Karmiloff-Smith and colleagues (Karmiloff-Smith, 1998; Paterson et al., 1999) on infants and children with Williams syndrome reveals the complexity of the nature–nurture debate in developmental psychology. Williams syndrome is a rare genetic disorder caused by an abnormality in chromosomes that presents quite differently from person to person. People with Williams syndrome have a range of cognitive delay and physical impairments such as lack of coordination, muscle weakness and sometimes heart and kidney damage.

Research suggests that the differences in the individual experience of Williams syndrome supports neither the purely nature perspective nor the purely nurture perspective. Karmiloff-Smith argues that conditions like Williams syndrome point therefore to an interaction between the biological (genetic) impairment, but also to

how the physical impairment can affect the environment of the child and result in certain behaviours such as impulsivity and hyperactivity. The study of Williams syndrome has therefore encouraged a multidimensional approach, including both nature and nurture perspectives in understanding the condition and how best to support individuals living with the syndrome.

- How might a cognitive impairment affect the social environment of a child?
- Can other developmental disorders be understood within a multidimensional approach?
- How might this approach translate into a programme of support for the child with a developmental disorder?
- For example, how would you combine knowledge gained from understanding both the nature and the nurture perspective in developmental disorders?

sources of information for the assessment are varied and widely drawn. Without such a comprehensive and careful assessment, it is unlikely that an accurate diagnosis will be made, owing to the subtleties in how a child's abilities present. This in turn will have an impact on the support made available to the child.

The diagnostic assessment of developmental problems uses a range of methods to elicit information about the child (see Table 16.3). These include parent interviews, formal testing of development, informal observations of the child in naturalistic environments such as home and

school, questionnaire-derived measures and physical examinations including blood tests. Observing the child across time and in different environments is key to understanding how the environment may have an affect on the child's functioning, thus providing valuable information about the child's 'true' abilities.

Specific learning difficulties

People can also have specific learning difficulties that can make learning more difficult. It does not mean that these individuals have a global learning problem; indeed, these

Table 16.3. Assessment tools and approaches for assessing a child's development.

Standardised assessments	Non-standardised assessments	Interviews	Questionnaires	Physical examinations
• Wechsler cognitive assessments • Griffiths Mental Development Scales	• Play-based assessments • Home-based assessments • School observations	• Developmental history • School teachers	• Bayley Scales of Infant Development • Vinelands Adaptive Behaviour Scales	• Blood tests • Height • Weight • Head circumference • Reflex response • Gait/posture

Life course outcomes for siblings of adults with learning disabilities or mental illness

A study by Taylor *et al.* (2008) investigated the impact of having a sibling with either a learning disability or a mental illness on the psychological wellbeing of adults following them in a longitudinal study from 18 years to 64 years of age. This paper is reported as part of the larger Wisconsin Longitudinal Study. The authors studied 268 adults who had siblings with mild intellectual disability and 83 adults who had siblings with mental illness and compared them with the experiences of adults with siblings without intellectual disability or mental illness.

The data reveals that adults with a sibling with intellectual disability were more likely to live nearby the sibling and to have more regular contact with the family compared with the adults without siblings with intellectual disabilities. The adults with siblings with mental illness, however, reported higher levels of psychological distress and poorer psychological wellbeing. These findings were more significant for adults whose sibling with the mental illness was male.

- Consider the findings of this study. Why are the adults with a sibling with intellectual disabilities more likely to live nearby that sibling and to have more frequent contact with the family?
- Why is this not the case for adults with a sibling with mental illness?
- Why do the adults with a sibling with mental illness report a more significant effect on their psychological wellbeing in adult life?

specific difficulties can co-exist alongside the full range of cognitive abilities. Often, learning difficulties are grouped by their related school–area skill set or cognitive weakness. If a child is in school, it will probably be apparent if she is struggling with reading, writing, or maths, and so narrowing down the type of difficulty may well be easier. However, the more subtle forms of these difficulties may not be detected until later in a person's academic career. Table 16.4 outlines some of the more common specific learning problems that people can experience.

Pervasive developmental disorders: autistic spectrum disorder

Autistic spectrum disorders (ASD; abbreviated to 'autism' from hereon in) have gained much attention from academics and media alike, as well as the general public. After all, people with autism can be portrayed in a fascinating way, such as the girl who cannot speak, but can calculate sums instantaneously, or how memory

Table 16.4. Common types of specific learning difficulties.

Diagnostic term	Learning difficulty	Learning problem
Dyslexia	Difficulty processing language	Problems reading, writing, spelling, speaking
Dyscalculia	Difficulty with maths	Problems doing maths problems, understanding time, using money
Dysgraphia	Difficulty with writing	Problems with handwriting, spelling, organising ideas
Dyspraxia (sensory integration disorder)	Difficulty with fine motor skills	Problems with hand–eye coordination, balance, manual dexterity
Auditory processing disorder	Difficulty hearing differences between sounds	Problems with reading, comprehension, language
Visual processing disorder	Difficulty interpreting visual information	Problems with reading, maths, maps, charts, symbols, pictures

CASE STUDY

A referral to a Child Development centre from a Paediatrician

Jack is a 26 month old boy who I have been seeing under my general developmental clinic. He has not progressed beyond babbling yet and is not compensating for his lack of verbal communication skills with non-verbal skills, such as consistent eye contact, expressive facial affect and gesture. He seems to prefer doing things on his own terms. Mother reports that she does not always know whether he understands what is being asked of him or whether he is simply ignoring her because he can get quite fixated on spinning the wheels of his car or watching TV. Mother is therefore struggling to get him to do things he needs to do, such as getting ready to go out or going to bed, which typically results in tantrums.

I have spoken to Mother about my concerns regarding Jack's social communication skills and I would be grateful if you could see this little boy for further assessment in your clinic.

about trains can be so impressive in a boy who struggles with school work. We only need to mention *Rain Man* to conjure a popular culture picture of disorder and brilliance existing in one being. However, how people present with autism and the recent interest in autism is not always so positive or heart-warming. Indeed, many parents of young children in Europe will have heard of the reports linking the measles, mumps and rubella (MMR) inoculations with autism (and bowel disorders), as well as reports stating that the prevalence of the disorder is increasing (e.g. Wakefield *et al.*, 1998; Fombonne, 2001). But, what is autism and is there really an epidemic of it? This next section will describe what is meant by autism and its associated behaviours, as well as describe the current understandings of the causes and the specific assessment tools that contribute to identifying the disorder.

Autism is a life-long neurodevelopmental condition that affects how a person communicates with, and relates to, those around them. The three main areas of difficulty which people with autism share are sometimes known as the 'triad of impairments' (see Fig. 16.5):

- difficulty with communication;
- difficulty with social interaction;
- difficulty with imagination and flexibility of thinking.

Criteria for the diagnosis of autism are set out in the ICD-10 (*International Classification of Diseases*, 10th revision) and the Diagnostic and fourth version of the *Statistical Manual of Mental Disorders* (DSM-IV) and are based on behavioural characteristics and patterns of behaviours (see Table 16.5).

Prevalence rates of autism vary considerably due to definitions and assessment approaches. Towards the end of the last century, in Europe and the US prevalence rates for autism have ranged between 5 to 72 cases per 10 000 children (Sponheim and Skjeldal, 1998; Kadesjo *et al.*, 1999). More recently, estimates of autism are between 25 and 60 cases per 10 000 children (Baird *et al.*, 2006; Center for Disease Control, 2007), with autism rates hovering between the 10 and 20 cases per 10 000 children (Newschaffer *et al.*, 2007). Recent research suggests that around 1 in 100 people in the UK have autism (UCL paper – SNAP study). It is thought to affect four times as many males than females, although the reason for this is unknown.

While some feel that clinical signs can be seen in children as young as 6 to 12 months (Volkmar and Charmarska, 2008), children are more reliably diagnosed at age three, although language development might interfere with diagnosis (e.g. when it is unclear as to whether language delay causes poor social interaction or whether social interaction would be problematic anyway).

Severity of autism symptoms can be affected by a range of additional factors, for example, intellectual disabilities, attention deficit hyperactivity disorder or anxiety-based disorders, such as obsessive–compulsive disorder (OCD). Thus, it is not uncommon to see

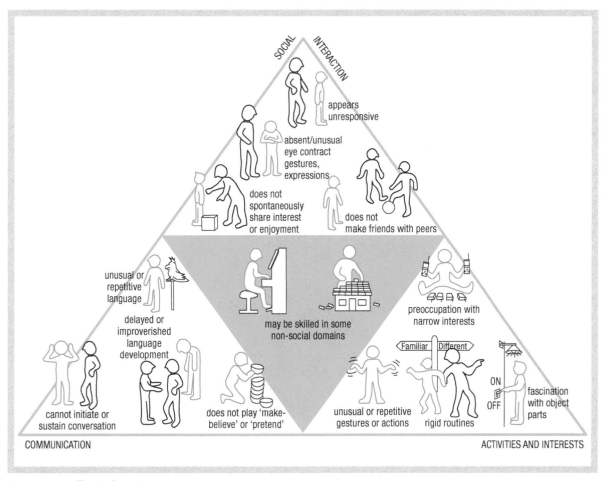

Figure 16.5. Triad of impairment.

(*Source:* The Open University website)

Table 16.5. Typical symptoms of autism in children.

Communication	Social interaction	Flexibility of thoughts
• Impairment in language development, especially comprehension, e.g. no babbling or gestures before 12 months, no single words by 18 months, no spontaneous 2-word phrases by 24 months, • Non-verbal communication, including gestures, facial expressions and social smiling, limited in range and frequency: – unusual use of language – poor response to name • Regression of verbal and social skills	• Self-directed and wanting things to be on their own agenda/'in her own world' • Lack of interest in other children/odd approach to others • Limitation in, or lack of imitation of, actions (for example, clapping during nursery rhymes) • Lack of showing toys or other objects to others • Limited recognition or responsiveness to others' emotions • Limited variety of imaginative play or pretence, especially social imagination (i.e. not being able to build on play directed by others) • Failure to initiate or sustain simple play with others • Inappropriate responses to adults (e.g. getting too close or not acknowledging them)	• Motor mannerisms, e.g. flapping hands when excited • Repetitive play/preferring sameness • Inability to cope with change • Biting, hitting, or aggression to peers; oppositional to adults • Hyper- or hypo-sensitive to the body's sensory receptors • Compulsive behaviours, e.g. turning light switches on and off, regardless of scolding

Table 16.6. Co-morbidities with autism.

Area of difficulty	Frequency of co-morbid symptoms %
Developmental	
• Intellectual disability	40–80
• Language problems	50–63
• Attention, concentration, impulsivity, hyperactivity	59
• Motor delays	9–19
Psychiatric	
• Anxiety	43–84
• Depression	2–30
• Obsessive–compulsive disorders	37
• Tics, Tourettes	8–10
• Oppositional defiant behaviours	7
• General behaviour problems	3
Sensory	
• Tactile	80–90
• Auditory	5–47
Neurological	
• Seizures, epilepsy	5–49
Sleep	
• Sleep disruption	52–73
Gastrointestinal	
• Food selectivity difficulties	30–90
• Gastro-oesophageal reflux, constipation	8–59

Source: adapted from Levy *et al.* (2009).

children with autism experience co-morbid problems (see Table 16.6).

The autism 'spectrum'

As with any disorder, the characteristics of autism can vary widely from person to person. Autism is conceptualised to describe a group of disorders that typically include the disorders autism, Asperger syndrome and atypical autism. The word 'spectrum' is used because the characteristics of the condition exist on a continuum of skills that vary considerably between individuals. As such, it is not possible to categorise people squarely into one diagnosis or another, or to say that someone is 'more autistic' than someone else. It might be helpful to think about autism being a cluster of dimensions that can be grouped together in a multitude of different combinations to provide a picture that fits one of the three main autism descriptions. The ICD and DSM diagnostic manuals are continually altering their definitions for autism and its sub-categories, and attempting to categorise what is essentially a dimensional disorder is inevitably problematic. The reliability of sub-groups varies across studies, and their long-term relevance is uncertain (Szatmari, 2000). Although the term 'autistic spectrum disorder' does not appear in either diagnostic manual, professionals find that this term is much more easily understood by parents and professionals than the manuals' term of 'pervasive developmental disorders' (PDD). The two terms, ASD and PDD, are now used almost synonymously.

To complicate the picture further, those with autism may, though not necessarily, have a learning disability. Those who have Asperger syndrome tend to have average, or above average, cognitive function, but still have difficulty relating to other people and making sense of the world. It is likely that those with more severe and persevering autism symptoms will have a learning disability as well. Therefore, people with autism can present in different ways where some are able to function in the world, supporting themselves, whereas others will need a lifetime of specialist support and professional input on a daily basis.

CUTTING EDGE

Sensory needs of children with autism and the proposed DSM-V revisions

In addition to the triad of impairments described above, children with autism can have difficulties with their sensory system (sight, smell, touch, taste, sound, balance and spatial awareness of their body), resulting in a hypersensitivity or a hyposensitivity to sensory input. For example, some children might cover their ears at the smallest sounds or others may be overly active as a way to stimulate their physical senses. Sometimes, sensory interests can be stress-busting for children with autism and can act as a calming or coping strategy when anxious. When children are unable to understand or explain their needs, as is typical with many children with autism, the sensory needs can become so overwhelming that the need interferes with the child's functioning or increases their anxiety levels which affects their behaviours. Therefore, it is

important for parents and those working with children with autism to understand the impact of the environment on a child's senses as a way to understand better any challenging behaviours displayed.

The diagnostic manuals used in the US and Western Europe, the *Diagnostic and Statistics Manual* (DSM) and *International Classifications of Disease* (ICD), respectively, do not in their latest versions, DSM-IV and ICD-10, address aspects of sensory needs in children with autism. The triad of impairment is described as in this chapter and is thus devoid of the impact sensory needs have on children with autism. However, the DSM-IV is currently being revised into the DSM-V (due out in 2013) and the 'flexibility in thinking' domain of the triad has been expanded to explicitly include 'unusual sensory behaviour'.

Given the frequency and severity of some children's sensory interests and the effect this can have on children's behaviours, as observed by clinicians and parents, this proposed change to the DSM manual is welcome.

Children with atypical autism display difficulties from two domains of the triad of impairments. Children with atypical autism may have difficulties in the communication and social interaction domains of functioning, but not so clearly so in the imagination or behaviours category of impairment. In other words, a child diagnosed under this sub-category of spectrum will have social communication problems, but much less overt difficulties in the rigid behaviours, special interests and imaginative domains.

While there are similarities with autism, children with Asperger syndrome have fewer problems with speaking and have an average, or above average, intelligence. They do not usually have the accompanying learning disabilities sometimes associated with autism, but they may have specific learning difficulties. These may include dyslexia and dyspraxia or other conditions such as attention deficit hyperactivity disorder (ADHD) and epilepsy. Children with Asperger syndrome will not have had a language difficulty prior to the age of three (often cited as the basic marker of difference between a high-functioning child with autism) and they are most typically diagnosed

within the first few years of starting school because of the marked difficulties in social interaction and imagination or behaviours. With the right support and encouragement, people with Asperger syndrome can lead full and independent lives.

Aetiology

Although autism is behaviourally defined, it is widely accepted that autism has a biological basis sometimes as a result of a range of problems, such as tuberous sclerosis to rubella *in utero* and postnatal infection like encephalitis (Baird *et al.*, 2003). Despite these clear organic associations, a specific medical cause is found in only a minority of people with autism (6–10% depending on the study), and more often in those with pronounced learning problems (e.g. Fombonne, 1999). Genes are thought to play a key role. For example, twin studies have shown that in monozygotic twins the chance of concordance for autism is 60%, with a greater concordance for some social impairment, compared with a much lower rate in dizygotic twins (Szatmari, 2003). The rate of autistic spectrum disorders in individual siblings is 2–6%, a marked increase above population rates. Autism has been associated with many cytogenetic abnormalities, especially on chromosome 15, and is also found in Fragile X syndrome (Veenstra-Vander-weele and Cook, 2003).

Autism is also agreed to be a neurobiological disorder, despite results from structural brain scans not showing consistency of diagnostic markers. However, functional imaging has shown abnormalities of face processing (the area of the fusiform nucleus) in several studies (Baird *et al.*, 2003). Neuroanatomists will talk about the brains of people with autism forming at different rates from conception (e.g. Arndt *et al.*, 2005) which results in faster then slower growths in certain parts of the brain to some cognitive functions typical in autism (Geschwind, 2009). Cognitive theorists, on the other hand, talk about 'mind blindness' (Baron-Cohen *et al.*, 1985) in terms of limited understanding of own or others' thoughts and feelings, 'executive functioning' problems with respect to deficits in working memory, inhibition and planning (Kenworthy *et al.*, 2008) and 'central coherence' weaknesses which explains difficulties seeing the full picture (Happé and Frith, 2006).

Possibly due to a combination of more compelling research linking autism to organic causes and the 1994 outcry that the MMR vaccine is linked to autism, public anxiety has resulted in a dramatic fall in immunisation rates (NHS immunisation statistics, 2001). The epidemiological evidence is unconvincing (e.g. Fombonne and Cook, 2003), and the UK's Department of Health and Royal College of Paediatrics and Child Health have endorsed the safety of the MMR vaccine. Even so, parents of children with autism continue to express the view that the medical profession does not take their concerns about possible causes of autism seriously. Unfortunately, many professionals and business-minded people across the globe have tried to market 'miracle cures' for autism behaviours, such as secretin. These approaches have received wide publicity, but scientific methods, including double-blind trials, have not confirmed a curative effect.

Diagnostic assessment

The aim of assessment is to confirm a diagnosis, assess strengths and difficulties in the child and associated developmental and mental health impairments (co-morbidities), as well as assess for wider impacting factors, such as family needs. However, what makes autism different is the great variation in presentation, the wide range of skills and deficits and the high rate of associated behavioural, mental health and often subtle learning problems. It is for these reasons that the UK's National Austism Plan for Children (2006) recommends a range of professionals to be involved in the autism assessments of children. Diagnosis of autism can be a lengthy and emotional journey for all involved. Assessment includes a full developmental history and, later, a more specialised multidisciplinary diagnostic autism assessment would typically be conducted. The assessment would address the core domains of autism – social interaction, communication and behaviour – as well as looking at the individual child's overall cognitive ability, adaptive or self-help skills, motor development and sensory sensitivity. Such assessments can be completed by a range of different child health specialists, including paediatricians, psychologists, speech and language therapists, occupational therapists, educational and social work colleagues.

Professionals utilise a range of different methods and tools in order to assess the child for autism. Questionnaires are a useful way to gain qualitative data about the frequency and severity of symptoms. Parent interviews include the Autism Diagnostic Interview – Revised (ADIR) and Developmental, Dimensional and Diagnostic Interview (3di). Observational measures, such as the semi-structured, standardised Autism Diagnostic Observation Schedule (ADOS), look at social behaviours, communication abilities and repetitive behaviours using the medium of play. The ADOS and ADI-R are based on DSM criteria and, as such, are typically used in research settings, as well as clinical settings, although the ADI-R is a lengthy and therefore less favourable clinical tool. These methods have arguably improved the accuracy and reliability of diagnoses.

STOP AND THINK

'Everyone is on the autism spectrum somewhere.'

- Do you believe this?
- When you read the table of autism behaviours, could you relate any of them to yourself or to people you know?

Rett syndrome

Rett syndrome is a rare pervasive neurodevelopmental disorder which affects significantly more females than males, making it the most common genetic cause of severe disability in females. A large proportion of people with Rett syndrome have a mutation, or fault, on the *MECP2* gene on the X chromosome. While it is a genetic (though not hereditary) disorder and so present at birth, it is not usually detected until children are one year old because of the major developmental regression. Children will lose skills they have developed, and this regression can be accompanied by distress and anxiety, for both children and parents. People with Rett syndrome have severe and multiple disabilities, physical and learning, and become totally reliant on others for support throughout their lives.

For people with Rett syndrome, there are significant communication and mobility issues. Most will not speak and only 50% will walk in adulthood. Co-morbid physical health problems include epilepsy, chronic spinal curvature and breathing and feeding difficulties. However, due to improved treatment and care, people with Rett syndrome are living into their 50s and beyond (Retts Syndrome Association UK, 2010).

Childhood disintegrative disorder

Childhood disintegrative disorder (CDD), also known as Heller's syndrome and disintegrative psychosis, is also a rare pervasive neurodevelopmental disorder that affects the domains of communication, social interaction and motor skills. To date, there is no known cause for CDD.

Like Rett syndrome, CDD is characterised by the regression of functioning. However, onset is usually late at three years old and in some cases almost six years old (Fombonne, 2009). Therefore, until the age of three, children will demonstrate age-appropriate levels of functioning in the expressive communication, receptive understanding, social skills, motor skills, play skills, self-care and toileting domains. CDD is likely if the acquired skills are then lost in at least two of these seven areas of functioning. In addition, children with CDD exhibit difficulties in at least two of the autism triad of impairment domains.

Genetic disorders

Genetic and chromosomal disorders are illnesses or developmental abnormalities arising as a result of *in utero* deviations or mutations in the child's genetic material,

or where a large part of the genetic code has been disrupted. Whilst some mutations in a gene may cause few or no problems, other changes can cause serious illnesses such as sickle cell anaemia and cystic fibrosis. It is, as yet, unclear how most genetic abnormalities occur. Some appear to arise spontaneously, whilst others are probably a result of exposure to toxic substances, such as radiation. When parents are close relatives, the child faces an increased risk of having a genetic disorder, as there is a higher likelihood that both parents have the same abnormal genes. Having two such genes can lead to serious diseases or degenerative conditions, such as Tay-Sachs disease.

Chromosomal abnormalities can affect any of the 23 pairs of chromosomes (each of which is made up of around 4000 genes), including the sex chromosomes. Chromosomal abnormalities include having extra chromosomes (addition or duplication), missing chromosomes (deletion) or parts of one chromosome wrongly positioned on another. Some chromosomal abnormalities are so severe that they cause the death of the embryo or foetus before birth. Other abnormalities can cause physical deformities and difficulties, as well as some developmental disorders such as Down's syndrome (Trisomy 21) and fragile-X syndrome.

Table 16.7 summarises some of the most common chromosomal and genetic disorders in children, their incidence, signs and symptoms.

Speech and language disorder

In Chapter 5, Language Development, we learnt about the importance of early parent–infant interaction in promoting the young child's development of language. In fact, it is difficult to under-estimate the crucial role that speech, language and communication play in enabling children to develop and lead fulfilling lives, access education and develop meaningful social relationships with others. Children acquire language and communication skills through naturalistic interactions with their world (Rossetti, 2001). Language acquisition is a robust biological attribute; however, as with other important areas of development, it is dependent on the powerful role of the environment and the availability of plentiful opportunities for the young child to interact with the world around him. Interference with a child's ability to interact normally can result in development, and communication

Table 16.7. Genetic developmental disorders.

Genetic disorder	Incidence	How is it diagnosed?	Physical features	Developmental difficulties
Down's syndrome (also known as Trisomy 21) Children with Down's syndrome inherit an extra copy of chromosome 21 from either the mother or father	The most common single cause of birth defects, affecting approximately one in every 660 infants of both sexes	• *In utero*, via amniocentesis • Following birth, diagnosis can be made based on distinctive physical features and blood test	Microcephaly (small head), flat facial profile, hypotonia (low muscle tone), small mouth and protruding tongue and upward slanted eyes. 40–50% of children present with heart problems, and a significant number also have some degree of vision and hearing loss.	All children with Down's syndrome experience a degree of learning disability, from mild delay to severe global difficulties. Delayed developmental milestones, including motor, functional and language skills.
Prader–Willi syndrome Genetic deletions (missing genetic material) on chromosome 15	Affects one in every 12 000–15 000 infants of both sexes	• Genetic testing (usually prompted by parental concerns about their child's feeding and motor development in the early years)	Hypotonia with a poor suck reflex, hypogonadism (immature development of sexual organs), obesity (caused by excessive eating and preoccupation with food).	Children with Prader–Willi syndrome experience global developmental delay, developing into mild or moderate learning disability in later childhood. Behavioural difficulties and temper tantrums, particularly around food, due to excessive desire to eat.
Klinefelter syndrome A syndrome arising as a result of an extra X chromosome in most cells (XXY)	Affects one in 500–1000 males	• Genetic testing (often only detected in later childhood, when child's testes and other sexual characteristics fail to develop and mature)	Few observable features, but immature testicular development. In later childhood and adolescence, boys show immature sexual development, including sparse body and facial hair, breast development and poor muscle development.	Boys with Klinefelter's syndrome often present with speech and language disorders, short attention span, specific learning difficulties and poor self-expression and communication skills.
Angelman syndrome Gene mutations on chromosome 15	Affects one in 15 000 infants	• Genetic testing (often only detected between 2 and 5 years, when characteristic behaviours and facial features become more evident)	Children with AS may have a small head, wide mouth, protruding tongue, sometimes associated with a prominent chin. AS is often associated with seizures and unusual bouts of laughter.	Children with AS typically show developmental delay leading to severe learning disability, as well as language and communication difficulties.

Neurofibromatosis Gene mutation on chromosome 17 (NF1 – 90% of cases) or 22 (NF2)	Affects one in 2500–4000 children, with the more severe form occurring in one in 40 000–50 000 births	• Concern often raised following identification of dermal neurofibromas • Diagnosis confirmed by blood test	Benign and malignant tumours of the central nervous system, 'café au lait' spots on the skin, dermal neurofibromas (showing as lumps under skin), brown spots on iris, occasional short stature and mild macrocephaly (large head size).	40–60% of children have some degree of learning difficulty (such as dyslexia) or generalised learning disability. Difficulties with concentration, co-ordination (affecting fine and gross motor skills), memory, visuo-motor and visuo-spatial skills, organisation and processing. Occasional language and social difficulties.
Turner syndrome Second X chromosome is absent or abnormal	A relatively common syndrome, affecting one in 2500 girls	• Concern often raised due to noticeable physical characteristics • Diagnosis confirmed by genetic testing	Girls with Turner syndrome are typically of short stature, with a webbed neck, wide-spaced under-developed breasts and puffy hands and feet. Abnormalities of the eyes and bones. Amenorrhea.	Although girls with Turner syndrome generally have cognitive ability within the normal range, they show a relative weakness in visuo-spatial processing. For example, non-verbal reasoning and memory skills tend to be weaker than verbal reasoning and memory. Difficulties with peer relationships due to immaturity, shyness and social anxiety.
Williams syndrome Microdeletion of chromosome 7 at the elastin gene focus	Affects one in 20 000 infants	• A blood test (called the FISH technique) can detect whether the elastin gene is missing	Facial features include prominent cheeks, upturned nose, wide mouth, irregular teeth. Children may have a heart problem, typically supravalvular aortic stenosis; peripheral pulmonary artery stenosis or both. These heart murmurs are often present at birth. Some children develop hypercalcaemia, usually within the first two years of life. This may cause failure to thrive, feeding problems, irritability, vomiting, constipation and kidney problems.	Williams syndrome is associated with global developmental delay, leading to moderate to severe learning disability. Children may initially show delayed language development, although this becomes a relative strength in later childhood. Children are impulsive and disinhibited, with a chatty, outgoing personality. Despite this, they can have difficulties forming same-age friendships. They also show difficulties with visuo-spatial integration.

Table 16.8. Environmental factors that impact on speech and language delay.

Factor	Studies
Economically deprived backgound (lower socioeconomic status)	Horwitz *et al.*, 2003
	Locke *et al.*, 2001
	Toppelberg and Shapiro, 2000
	Maas, 2000
	Beitchman *et al.*, 1996
Low parental education	Horwitz *et al.*, 2003
Amount of maternal talk (number of words and length of utterances); quantity and sophistication of parent's vocabulary	Horwitz *et al.*, 2003
	Toppelberg and Shapiro, 2000
	Hart and Risley, 1995
	Snow, 1994
Poverty	Horwitz *et al.*, 2003
	Locke *et al.*, 2001
	Beitchman *et al.*, 1996
High levels of parental stress	Horwitz *et al.*, 2003
Reading and discussing children's stories and quality of dinnertime conversations	Beals *et al.*, 1994
Adolescent mother	Rossetti, 2001
Parent with four or more pre-school aged children	Rossetti, 2001
Physical or social isolation and/or lack of adequate social support	Rossetti, 2001
	Beitchman *et al.*, 1996
Lack of stable residence, or dangerous living conditions	Rossetti, 2001
	Beitchman *et al.*, 1996
Parent or primary caregiver with severe or chronic illness, acute mental illness, history of loss and/or abuse, with drug or alcohol dependence	Rossetti, 2001
Parental concern	Horwitz *et al.*, 2003
	Rossetti 2001
Birth order	Horwitz *et al.*, 2003
	Rossetti 2001

delay (Rossetti, 2001). Table 16.8 collects together some of the research demonstrating the factors that can interfere with normal environmental interaction, thus increasing the risk of speech and language delay.

There is wide individual variation in the age and rate at which young children acquire language, although the majority of children are typically producing their first words at around 10 to 12 months. In their study, Fenson *et al.* (1993) report that, at the age of 16 months, 80% of children understand between 78 and 303 words. Between the ages of two and three, parents often witness an 'explosion' in their child's speech, with a rapid increase in vocabulary and an ability to combine three or more words into sentences and, by the age of five, most typically developing children have learned 90% of the grammar they will need throughout life.

Unfortunately, according to research, delayed speech and language development is the most common symptom of developmental disability in children under the age of three, affecting one in every ten children in the UK (Lee *et al.*, 2004), and accounting for a considerable proportion of referrals to child health services. Children who do not develop age-appropriate language skills are often described as having a speech and language delay or disorder. Such difficulties can be classified according to the specific area of impairment (see below), although commonly children with language problems present with several different overlapping areas of difficulty:

- receptive language (understanding and formulating spoken language);
- expressive language (processing and producing speech sounds);
- speech (articulation);
- dysfluency (hesitating or stumbling over words);
- using and understanding all aspects of language appropriately in different social contexts.

Understanding and formulating spoken language

Some children may not be able to understand the words being spoken to them and/or the grammatical rules of sentence construction (Bishop and Adams, 1992). These difficulties with understanding can have serious and wide-ranging implications when children reach school age, as they prevent children from accessing vital classroom learning opportunitites (for example through class discussion or pair-work). They also make it hard to remember information given verbally, meaning that these children struggle to follow more than one instruction at a time and may need to have verbal instructions supplemented with a visual prompt (such as a photograph or picture) in order to better understand. Aside from the implications for learning, there are less obvious social consequences for this group, as they not only find it difficult to join their peers in conversation but may also fail to detect the subtle but important nuances of their peer-group's speech, leaving them at risk of low self-esteem, social isolation and bullying (see Jerome *et al.*, 2002).

Processing and producing speech sounds

Children with speech and language difficulties may not be able to effectively process the speech sounds that make up words. This means they cannot identify which sounds come at the beginning of words or break up

words into their component parts (Carroll and Snowling, 2004). These skills are essential for children starting primary school, as this is the age at which they learn to read and to spell (tasks which involve the linking of sounds to letters and breaking up words to make them easier to read). Research shows that children who struggle to process speech sounds are at risk of literacy difficulties (Stackhouse and Wells, 1997; Goswami and Bryant, 2007).

An inability to produce speech sounds appropriately can have a significant impact upon a child's ability to make herself understood. As such, children with these problems may experience extreme frustration and difficulty in making their needs known, sharing information about themselves, answering questions and joining in with conversations with peers.

Using and understanding all aspects of language appropriately in different social contexts

Difficulties with pragmatic language – the ability to understand and use language in a social context – can cause significant problems with social interaction. Children may have difficulty knowing when and how to use their language in different social situations (Bishop *et al.*, 2000), or knowing the differences in how to speak to adults or peers. They may not understand jokes or sarcasm, or may struggle with metaphorical language, taking

---

Definitions

Dysfluency: an abnormal degree of hesitation or stumbling over words, making speech difficult to understand. Stammering (or stuttering) is the most common form of dysfluency. The speech of people who are dysfluent may be hard to understand; it may seem jerky or disjointed and it does not flow easily from one word to the next.

Pragmatic language: pragmatics is a sub-field of linguistics devoted to the study of how context contributes to meaning. Specifically, it examines how the transmission of meaning depends not only on the linguistic knowledge (grammar and words used) of the speaker and listener, but also on the context of the utterance, knowledge about the subject matter, etc., all of which help to attribute meaning to language.

well-known phrases literally (Leinonen and Letts, 1997). Consider, for example, the double meaning of popular phrases 'It's raining cats and dogs' or 'He threw the rule book out the window', both of which might mean very different things to a child (or adult) who does not have a social understanding of language. Such misunderstandings can cause children to respond in unusual and unpredictable ways to what might have appeared to be a perfectly normal comment, putting them at risk of social exclusion or appearing misbehaved to parents and teachers.

Aetiology

There are a wide range of different aetiological factors associated with speech and language problems in children. Some difficulties may be secondary to other causal factors, such as hearing impairment, motor disorder and acquired disorders resulting from neurological damage (e.g. strokes), whereas others occur in the context of a more complex developmental syndrome, such as autism, cerebral palsy or general learning disability.

A language disorder is said to be 'primary' when there appears to be no other underlying reason or recognised clinical syndrome to explain the child's difficulties. Primary problems or 'specific language impairment' can be characterised as those affecting the structural aspects of language (lexical knowledge, syntax and phonology), and those affecting mainly pragmatics and abstract understanding or 'higher-order functions'. The profiles of children with specific language impairment are dynamic over time, such that children with a particular pattern of difficulties may make improvements in some areas and not others, giving a different profile from year to year. In some cases, problems resolve naturally over time; however, for others, specialist intervention from child development services may be required.

Diagnostic assessment

Assessment of young children presenting with speech and language difficulties, as with any detailed developmental assessment, should be multidimensional, including a full developmental history, family history and hearing test, to rule out hearing impairment as a causal factor. As we discussed earlier, given the wide range of underlying factors which may contribute to developmental speech and language difficulties, a broad assessment, encompassing communication, both verbal and non-verbal, play and imagination, cognitive skills, attention and concentration, motor skills, emotional regulation and behaviour, is vital in ruling out alternative

The Bus Story Test is a fun assessment used by speech and language therapists to assess the age level of consecutive speech in children from 3 to 8 years. Children are told a story about a bus, which is read out to them alongside a series of twelve pictures. They must then retell the story in their own words.

Their speech is assessed for information content, sentence length and grammatical usage, and an age-equivalent language score calculated.

The Bus Story Test (Renfrew, 1991).

explanations for the child's difficulties, such as selective mutism or autism. In addition, formal assessment of global language function by a speech and language therapist (for example, using the Bus story test for pre-school children, Renfrew, 1991 – see above) can give an indication of overall language competence, whilst being a good prognostic indicator of long-term language functioning (Bishop and Edmundson, 1987).

Developmental speech and language difficulties are common, with an estimated prevalence of 3.8% (Shriberg et al., 1999). Fortunately, recent research suggests that, of those that are diagnosed, the majority of speech problems abate, whilst those that are more persistent often respond well to specialist intervention (Law et al., 2004). However, children with these kinds of difficulties are at a major disadvantage compared to their peers once they begin primary school, since they must learn within an environment where the medium for learning (which, in most education systems within Europe, is spoken language) is their biggest obstacle. The massive impact which speech and language disorder can have on a child's life and future development means that early recognition, understanding and multidisciplinary intervention are key to ensuring that the child is able to reach his full potential.

Therapy and intervention

The process of assessment and diagnosis of a child's developmental difficulties can be a difficult and emotionally overwhelming time for the whole family. Unlike in traditional medicine, there is rarely one prescribed treatment or approach which will make the child's symptoms improve or restore areas of skill that appear to have been lost or damaged. Rather, it is the role of the child health professional to help the child and family to understand and adjust to the child's diagnosis, whilst establishing a package of care aimed at supporting the child's specific developmental needs in the most appropriate way.

In the first instance, intervention may often be concerned with helping the parents and family of the child to understand the difficulties and/or diagnosis which has been given as well as setting aside time and space to think about what changes may need to be made to everyday life in order to accommodate a new way of doing things (for example, relying on picture communication rather than speech), or to make room for specialist equipment to support the child's physical needs. Parents may also be concerned about behaviours their child shows which are difficult to understand, or impact upon the everyday activities of the family, such as over-activity, hitting or pushing other children or limited awareness of danger. Still others may seek medical intervention for their child's condition, particularly if there are particular medications which have been shown to stabilise or improve their child's symptoms, e.g. epilepsy medication.

Given the wide range of difficulties which may arise within the context of a child's developmental difficulties, support and intervention, just like assessment, must be multifaceted, involving a range of professionals, according to the needs of the individual child and family. Within this system of professionals, there is a defined and important role for psychologists to play: offering therapy and support to identify and manage emotional responses to diagnosis, support around expectations of the child in terms of skill attainment and future progress, interventions for challenging behaviours, assessing for co-morbid mental health concerns in the child or family and supporting the wider system around the child, including linking in with other professionals and systems, such as school.

The next section of this chapter will look at some of the ways in which developmental psychologists can offer support and intervention to the families of children with developmental difficulties. We shall focus on the following interventions:

- psychoeducation;
- psychopharmacotherapy;
- parent training and support;
- behavioural intervention;
- recognising the mental health needs of the child;
- supporting the wider system.

Psychoeducation

A key role for the child clinical psychologist in supporting families is in providing information and psychoeducation around the child's specific needs. Psychoeducation, as the name suggests, involves helping the child, family and wider social system (such as school staff) to understand the child's diagnosis and its associated symptoms and difficulties. This can take various forms, from individual discussion and guidance, provision of relevant child- or parent-friendly literature and electronic resources to psychoeducation groups for parents, aimed at providing information as well as an opportunity to share and seek support from other parents.

Psychoeducation is not only beneficial at the time of a child's diagnosis. It continues to play an important role throughout early childhood and beyond. Parents may seek support in thinking about ways to manage important developmental milestones (e.g. toilet training, feeding and establishing a sleep routine) and behavioural difficulties (e.g. hitting siblings, tantrums and over-activity) in the context of their child's developmental difficulties.

Psychopharmacotherapy

As we know from the earlier parts of this chapter, development problems typically require multidisciplinary assessment and input into fully understanding the different aspects of the child's difficulties. Part of this multidisciplinary input is to also consider how multidisciplinary teams support the behavioural symptoms children with developmental problems can have. One type of treatment offered by medically-trained colleagues is medication and its use is largely, though not exclusively, for the management of challenging behaviours.

Challenging behavioural problems, such as tantrums, aggression and self-injurious behaviours, in children with autism have been known to be reduced with risperidone, an antipsychotic drug (McCracken et al., 2002). Methylphenidate, branded as Ritalin, which is similar to amphetamines, can be prescribed to help reduce ADHD symptoms. Melatonin, a naturally occurring hormone that induces sleep, can be artificially altered with pharmaceuticals for children who have difficulties sleeping.

However, the role of medication in the treatment of child development problems is controversial. Johnstone (2006) states that there is no known biological cause for behaviour problems in child developmental problems, and thus it is unfounded and irresponsible, given the side effects and unknown longer term outcomes, to use medication as a first-choice treatment option. Side effects can often be difficult for children and their families to manage and their impact should not be under-estimated (e.g. Hollander *et al.*, 2006). Examples of common side effects include confusion, suicidal thoughts, depression or withdrawal, as well as restlessness, irritability, sleeping problems, loss of appetite, weight loss, stomach ache, headache, rapid or irregular heartbeat, elevated blood pressure, and sometimes muscle twitches of the face and other parts of the body, which could lead to Tourette's syndrome, and possibly the suppression of growth. In addition, scientific trials to validate the effectiveness and safe use of drugs in developmental problems are poor (e.g. Esch and Carr, 2005; Broadstock *et al.*, 2007).

More recently, medical and psychological research on behaviour management tends to agree that a combination of psychological interventions, such as parent training alongside medication can result in better behavioural outcomes for children with developmental problems (Aman *et al.*, 2009).

Parent training and support

Parent training approaches have become increasingly popular in recent years, and many different systems – such as Incredible Years Webster-Stratton (2006); Bavolek's Nurturing programme (Bavolek, 2010); 'Strengthening families, strengthening communities' (Steele *et al.*, 2000) – have been developed over the years for parents to manage their child's behaviours. Overall, behavioural parent training programmes have been found to be very effective in reducing a range of children's behavioural symptoms (e.g. Barlow and Parsons, 2006). Techniques need to be clear and consistent, and include:

- praising positive behaviours parents wish to see more of;
- ignoring completely unhelpful behaviours parents wish to see less of (unless the child is doing something unsafe);
- rewards that motivate the child to behaviour positively;
- setting appropriate boundaries;
- outlining the consequences, such as time-out, for the child's unhelpful behaviours.

Although many of the ideas and techniques taught in behavioural parent training appear uncomplicated, many parents need careful teaching and support to learn and use them appropriately in the different situation that they find themselves in with their child. Therefore, help from a professional may be required to help parents develop their understanding of the principles of the approaches, as well as their child's idiosyncrasies.

With children with developmental problems, some of the techniques may be unrealistic and therefore unfair because of their difficulties and so the implementation of techniques used would need to be adapted to fit more appropriately around the child's difficulties. For example, a child with a learning disability may require longer time to respond to commands (e.g. 'Come here, please') or to learn that praise is given to positive behaviours. A child with autism may not be able to retain spoken information and so a visual reminder of the request may be more effective. Using time-out techniques for five minutes may be too long for a child with an ADHD diagnosis and so a shorter time-out period may be just as effective.

In addition to offering parents direct behavioural approaches for their child's behaviours, emotional support should be offered to parents. Parents typically find themselves experiencing a range of different emotions regarding their child's diagnosis and associated difficulties (Barnett *et al.*, 2006). Some of those feelings might be sadness for the loss of the child they were expecting, or uncertainty about what the future might hold for their child and their family. The grief response of and adjustment to a child's new and life-long diagnosis is a hugely emotional journey that can require professional understanding and support.

Behavioural intervention

Behavioural problems are common in children with disabilities (Rutter, 1970), representing a large proportion of referrals to specialist child mental health services. Research shows that, whilst the same behaviours that present in all children and young people may also present in children with developmental difficulties, certain patterns of behaviour are seen much more frequently in children with additional learning or developmental difficulties (WHO, 1992).

Behavioural intervention can play a key role in the management of a wide range of common childhood difficulties, from over-activity and challenging behaviour to sleeping, feeding and toileting problems. Its flexibility and adaptability is well suited to the field of developmental disability, allowing the therapist to tailor interventions to the child's developmental level as well as train parents in the day-to-day management of their child's behaviour.

RESEARCH METHODS

Evidence-based practice vs practice-based evidence

Evidence-based practice (EBP) is the scientific approach to delivering rigorous research. The key role is to provide *efficacious* evidence with respect to the psychotherapies. From this evidence, guidelines are produced and therapists are required to practice accordingly. Examples of methods of EBP are clinical case descriptions, observational studies, process–outcome links, non-randomised outcome studies and randomised controlled trials (RCTs). Practice-based evidence (PBE) is the generation of relevant research for clinical practitioners in routine clinical settings to enhance treatment quality. The key role of evidence here is to better the effectivity of interventions in clinical settings. From this evidence, therapists improve their practice and services become more efficient. Examples of methods of PBE are clinical opinion, single case studies, sessional data, client feedback and practice research networks (PRNs).

There are many strengths to EBP. For one, findings will be generalisable across groups of similar cases, such that if cognitive behaviour therapy works well in RCT settings for those with, say, anxiety disorder, it is likely that this will always be the case. Clinicians can then utilise this therapy on clients on the basis that it is a 'tested' tactic for anxiety relief. EBP gives practitioners the confidence to know that what they are applying to their patients has been shown to be helpful, which is necessary in the current political and financial climates (Bower, 2003). EBP can also be used to protect professionals in legal matters by validating their use or alluding to incompetent clinical practice (Parry et al., 2003).

On the other hand, EBP fails and PBE gains ground when considering the true complexities of or subtle changes in psychological and cultural processes that underlie the mental distress of the individual. Parry (2000) states that EBP outcomes are based on diagnostically homogeneous samples which are not representative of real-life clients. One of the biggest successes of PBE has been the development of the PRN. According to Margison et al. (2000), PRNs can be defined by a large number of clinicians who collaborate to collect and report data as a method to help practising clinicians meet EBP and PBE agendas. PRNs adopt a naturalistic approach by gathering data from routine clinical settings rather than from RCTs; the clinicians use the same measures and tools in order to generate large datasets to allow comparisons between client populations, treatment, clinicians and services. Ultimately, the PRN will allow consensual setting of standards and benchmarking of outcomes to enhance delivery and services. In the UK, networks have already been set up in York, Leeds and London.

In sum, it seems that EBP is only going to be as good as the methodology it is based on. The limitations of the EBP approach are such that evidence supporting safe and effective therapy is driven from the practice-side in. On the other hand, PBE is only as good as the clinicians' training in practice *and* research. While the emphasis is on the applicability of evidence to clinical practice, PBE also has the scope to include more empirical components of evidence through its use of PRNs. Therefore, the PBE approach in psychotherapy per se is not sufficient without the rigour of a scientific approach, but such an inclusion makes this approach more appropriate for the needs of psychotherapy theory and practice.

Grounded in learning theory, interventions are built on the premise that most human behaviour is learned through the interaction between the child and her environment. In this way, behaviours which are reinforced (for example by social praise or tangible reward) tend to be repeated by the child and, conversely, those which are not reinforced become less frequent. Behavioural work with children thus focuses upon teaching and increasing specifically targeted positive behaviours, whilst reducing or eliminating those which are inappropriate or less adaptive.

As with any intervention, the implementation of a successful behavioural plan depends upon detailed and carefully conducted assessment, with the aim of understanding where, when and how often the target behaviour occurs, what it looks like and what the direct consequences might be, as well as identifying any factors that seem to influence the behaviour. This is sometimes called a functional analysis or behavioural ABC (antecedent, behaviour, consequence) assessment.

In many cases, an assessment can identify specific learning tasks that may help to reduce a particular behaviour, where this is linked to some deficit in a skill. For example, a non-verbal child with autism may express his frustration at not being able to communicate his needs through aggressive or disruptive behaviour. Identifying and working to help the child acquire alternative skills (in this case teaching the child more adaptive ways to communicate, e.g. via Makaton or PECS; see below), which are then rewarded, will encourage him to use alternative forms of communication in order to get his needs met.

As well as identifying gaps in the child's learning skills, a functional assessment may bring to light ways in which parents are unwittingly reinforcing and perpetuating problem behaviour, for example, the parents who get their daughter dressed for school every day to avoid her early morning tantrums, or the mother who allows her son to come in the living room and watch television when he can't sleep. Once these reinforcing patterns have been identified, the clinical psychologist can work with the child and family to think about alternative strategies to manage the behaviour, emphasising the importance of rewarding and encouraging appropriate behaviour, whilst ignoring or minimising that which is inappropriate or undesirable.

Behavioural interventions, like any other approach, must be tailored to the child's own developmental level.

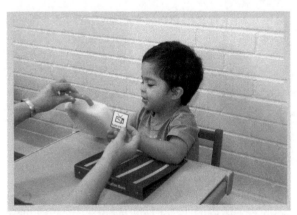

PECS (Picture Exchange Communication System) A system through which pictures and symbols are exchanged in place of spoken language, to aid communication in children with autism and other developmental disorders.

Source: Pearson Education Ltd./Jules Selmes

Targets should include a series of developmentally-appropriate steps towards the desired behaviour, with an emphasis on rewarding and reinforcing each small milestone reached. Sometimes, the use of a concrete visual cue, such as a sticker reward chart or 'token economy' system, can help to involve the child in reaching her goal behaviour, whilst providing an easy way of monitoring progress (see Fig. 16.6).

Given their central role, parents are ideally placed to carry out much of the behavioural work with their child with a developmental disability. Behavioural parent training, a common form of behavioural intervention, rests on the assumption that, if parents can be trained to use specific behavioural skills in managing their child within the home on a day-to-day basis, then they can effect significant changes in their child's behaviour. A number of different behavioural parent training courses have been built upon this fundamental premise, including the popular 'Incredible Years' parent training programme (Webster-Stratton, 2006).

STOP AND THINK

Thinking about the principles of learning theory, consider a change you would like to implement in your own life (e.g. eating more healthily/going to the gym).

■ What are the reinforcing factors that will help motivate you to change your existing behaviour?

■ What are the barriers to this change?

Recognising the mental health needs of the child

Like all children, those with a developmental disorder or learning disability may be faced with emotional challenges at key developmental stages. In fact, studies suggest that some emotional (or internalising) problems of childhood, such as fear, worry and shyness, are so common that they could be described as normal. Whilst for many, such symptoms may improve over time with little need for outside help, the additional challenges faced by children and adolescents with developmental disabilities mean that they are at greater risk of developing more severe and enduring mental health difficulties, for which specialist intervention may be appropriate.

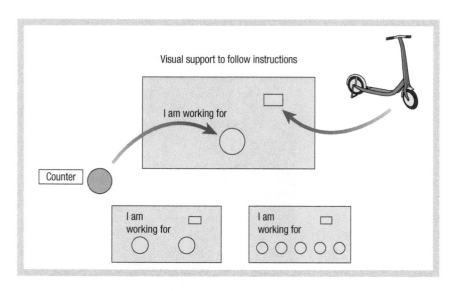

Visual support to follow instructions

I am working for

Counter

I am working for

I am working for

Figure 16.6. Visual support using behavioural techniques to encourage the child.

Research findings suggest that as many as one-third of children and young people with a learning disability experience mental health problems, compared with only 8% of children in the general population. In fact, a study by Corbett (1979) showed that, of a sample of children with severe learning disability, as many as 47% had some form of psychiatric disorder. Amongst those most at risk are children with an autism spectrum disorder and those with hyperkinesis (ADHD). Such findings are of great concern, given the evidence that mental health problems can contribute to poorer wellbeing, social inclusion and life opportunities of children (Quilgars *et al.*, 2005). For children with a developmental disorder, these effects can be far-reaching, having a particularly negative impact on the wellbeing of the wider family, and especially the mother (Baker *et al.*, 2003; Hatton and Emerson, 2003).

Worryingly, emotional and mental health difficulties presenting in children with additional difficulties may often be overlooked by parents and the wider professional system. Diagnostic overshadowing, in which psychiatric symptoms may be wrongly attributed to a primary diagnosis of learning disability or developmental delay, is a common phenomenon, occurring even amongst the most experienced clinicians. Moreover, it may be much more difficult for parents and other caregivers to detect these symptoms in children who struggle to communicate verbally, and who already face a number of other additional challenges. Consequently, these children often have to wait some time before a mental health difficulty is recognised, placing them at risk of developing more severe symptoms and increased social withdrawal.

As professional awareness has increased, so too have we seen a rise in the number of specialist services offering emotional support and intervention to children with disabilities and their families. Often based within multidisciplinary teams, clinicians may work with the child or young person to address issues of poor self-esteem and self-image relating to their disability. Similarly, they may spend time exploring issues of identity and self-acceptance with children who have an awareness of themselves as 'different' from those in their peer group at school. Where children are experiencing distress as a result of their difficulties with social interaction and anxiety, the clinician's role may include teaching important new social skills, or helping them with relaxation techniques to take control of the physical and emotional symptoms of stress and anxiety.

For many children with developmental difficulties, language and social interaction ability can prove to be a significant barrier to communication. Therapists often use creative approaches to engage with these children at the appropriate developmental level, using drawing, play, photographs and pictures. Moreover, they may spend time working with the family, school and wider system, to support them and increase their awareness of the child's concerns and difficulties, enabling them to put in place small changes to support the child's emotional needs, e.g. a 'circle of friends' to promote friendships and peer acceptance in a child experiencing feelings of loneliness and social isolation at school.

The wider systems

From assessment right through to intervention, working with children with developmental difficulties necessitates collaborative team working. Health care, education, mental health and medical professionals as well as parents/carers are all involved in the process. In some cases, social service involvement may be necessary in the case of child protection issues, and respite options may also be important in helping the families cope with their children's needs. The management and support around children with developmental problems can be vast and complex.

Given the different agencies that can be involved in the identification of a child with developmental difficulties, it is also important to think about who has raised the problem and what they are hoping to gain from such a thorough clinical assessment. Whose problem is it? In thinking about this question, it is imperative to hold the child and family in the centre of any debate to help guide how best to manage the referral, what the added value is of undertaking such an assessment for the child/family and where intervention should be placed.

Another important consideration when working with children's developmental problems is considering the needs of the families, especially fathers and siblings. Being a parent is a challenge even without having a child with special needs. When a family first learn about the child's disability, it is not uncommon for parents to re-evaluate some of the hopes and expectations they had for their child. How to manage this news alongside continuing to grow as a family and value each member and ensure that he has an equal share of family time becomes the focus. Fathers and siblings are typically marginalised members of the family due to their roles, but research suggests that the impact on these family members of living with a child or sibling who is developing atypically can be negative. For example, fathers can be excluded from key decisions about the child's care, and managing the emotional impact of having a child with such needs can be difficult to express,

Sharing your experiences with other parents can bring much needed emotional support when caring for a child with developmental difficulties.
Source: Getty Images

particularly if there are cultural or gender role factors preventing this (see Lamb, 2004). Siblings often have less time to spend with their parents and their choices can sometimes be limited due to the disability, resulting in expression of emotions that might be unhelpful to them (Deisinger, 2008). Considering the wider professional and family aspects is important in providing effective therapy to children with developmental needs.

SUMMARY

This chapter has introduced us to the complex, multifaceted and often emotional process that child development professionals have to manage when posed questions like 'Why isn't my child talking yet?', 'Why does my child not play with other children?' and 'Did I do something wrong to cause my child's disability?'

The assessment of children's developmental pathways can be difficult, particularly in the absence of any scientific confirmation. Clinicians have to work in a multidisciplinary team to bring together observations from their expertise, over time and across different settings, to consensually agree about the developmental needs of the child, accurately and sensitively. Often through the assessment alone, professionals also learn a large amount of information about the family which helps inform the contextual aspects in which the developmental assessment is taking place.

However, as the chapter outlines, the needs of the child and her family do not stop with a diagnosis. A clinician's role is also very much so about the development of a package of care that provides appropriate interventions to support the child and her family through what can be a distressing and challenging time. Often, offering support around current difficulties can give families something concrete and real to focus on, while also helping minimise natural fears about the present problems and future concerns for their child.

Finally, there are two key messages from health professionals for families with a child being assessed for atypical development problems. The first is that, like all children that are ever born, their child will make progress for the rest of their lives. It may not be as quickly as we might like, nor might it be to the same extent. Nonetheless, input from services and parents can facilitate this learning and, while it may be different, progress is a given.

The other message is that, aside from the atypical development difficulties, every child has his or her own personality, interests, likes and dislikes. Atypical development does not affect these characteristics and it does not necessarily stop a child from being happy. To remind parents that their child will feel and also give them huge amounts of pleasure is to state a fact – it is also a message of joy in times of upset and understandable worry.

REVIEW QUESTIONS

1. Discuss the different biological, social and cultural factors which influence the way in which a child develops. How might these factors interact with each other to contribute to developmental difficulties?
2. What advantages does a play-based form of assessment have over more structured assessments in helping us to understand a child's strengths and difficulties?
3. How can behavioural learning theory help us to understand and develop strategies to support positive behaviour in children with developmental difficulties?
4. In what way does the 'triad of impairments' help inform our thinking about the key strengths and deficits present in children with an autism spectrum disorder?

RECOMMENDED READING

For an evaluation of the evidence for many widely used child and adolescent mental health treatments:

Fonagy, P., Target, M., Cottrell, D., Phillips, J. & Kurtz, Z. (2005). *What Works for Whom? A Critical Review of Treatments for Children and Adolescents*. New York: Guilford.

For an overview of the practice of early childhood intervention:

Shonkoff, J.P. & Meisels, S.J. (Eds) (2000). *Handbook of Early Childhood Intervention*. Cambridge: Cambridge University Press.

RECOMMENDED WEBSITES

The National Autistic Society is an established UK-based autism charity with information and advice for families and professionals:

http://www.autism.org.uk

Contact a Family provides support, advice and information for families with disabled children:

http://www.cafamily.org.uk

Mencap provides advice and support for young people and adults with learning disabilities:

http://www.mencap.org.uk

SIBS provides advice and support to children and young people who have a sibling with a disability, and for parents:

http://www.sibs.org.uk

 Watch a video exploring what Autism is, including expert advice and footage of children with an ASD diagnosis. Further resources can be found at www.pearsoned.co.uk/gillibrand

Glossary

Accepted children: children who are popular, accepted or well liked by the majority of other children in the peer group.

Accommodation: within Piagetian theory, this is the revision of older knowledge structures to take account of new information.

Achievement: personal accomplishment of skills, knowledge and understanding in comparison to an individual's former achievement. A measure of personal progress.

Additive composition: the property of numbers that allows any to be defined as the sum of two other numbers.

Additive relations: relations between quantities defined within a part–whole schema.

Adolescent egocentrism: the young person's preoccupation with himself, likened to being on a permanent social stage where he or she is the focus of attention.

Adult Attachment Interview: a semi-structured interview method for probing into an adult's early childhood relationship experiences with attachment figures and assessing the extent to which she integrates such experiences into her current relationships.

Algebra: a domain of mathematics that involves representing quantities and relations by letters, rather than numbers, and operating on these in ways that respect the properties of the operations and the relations.

Analogical reasoning: a method of problem solving which makes use of the similarity of a new problem to some previously solved problem.

Animacy: the concept of animacy refers to an understanding of the difference between living (animate) and non-living (inanimate) things.

Apgar scale: a rating scale for the condition of the new-born.

Assessment: assessment is the process of collecting information on children, typically through observations, tests, clinician/teacher rating scales, etc., in order to make inferences about their development, typically within a school or clinical context.

Assimilation: within Piagetian theory, this is the process of taking new information into existing knowledge structures.

Asynchronous development: the situation that arises when a child is performing at a more advanced stage in one developmental skill and a less advanced stage in a second developmental skill, for example, the child may be performing well in Piaget's Conservation of Liquids task but less well in Kohlberg's Heinz dilemma task (see Chapter 13, Adolescence) measuring moral development (Kohlberg, 1976).

Attachment security: the readiness of an infant to use the primary caregiver to derive a sense of security that can be reflected in her pattern of attachment behaviours.

Attachment types: patterns of behaviour observed in the Strange Situation denoting differing security of attachment to the primary caregiver as a safe base to explore.

Attachment: a strong enduring affectionate bond an infant shares with a significant individual, usually the mother, who knows and responds well to the infant's needs.

Attainment: personal accomplishment of skills, knowledge and understanding in comparison to typical accomplishments. Comparisons are made with examination requirements or the attainments of others.

Attention: the part of our cognitive processes which controls ability to focus efficiently on specific things and ignore others.

Autobiographical memory: an individual's personal memory for their life experiences and events and for information about themselves.

Behavioural inhibition: a concept Kagan has defined to characterise young children's behaviour in unfamiliar settings, mostly by independent observations, into two qualitatively distinct types: Belief-desire stage of theory of mind: the ability to make a mental representation of the world.

Bully/victims: children and young people who engage in bullying others and are bullied themselves.

Bullying: an interaction which is intended to and does cause harm to a person who is seen as being less powerful than the perpetrator.

Cardinal numbers: numbers used in counting, to denote how many items are in a set.

Cardinality: the property of being represented by a cardinal number.

Case study: the detailed investigation of the experience of one person or of a small group of people.

Categorisation: the grouping or organisation of items based on their similarity.

Category: a set of sounds or words perceived as belonging to the same group (e.g. all instances of the sound /s/ or all words relating to female humans).

Central coherence: the ability to put together information in context to form a whole picture (Frith, 1989).

Central conceptual structure: a well-formed mental scheme of a concept like 'horse' that can be generally applied to all horses and requires little more assimilation until we experience a zebra for the first time.

Classical conditioning: describes the process of learning an association between two stimuli.

Cognitive dysregulation: The term used to describe the set of deficits in higher order cognitive processes such as planning and working memory that individuals with ADHD exhibit.

Cognitive interview: a technique developed specifically for interviewing witnesses in legal situations, using principles of memory from cognitive psychology, to maximise the amount of information which is accurately recalled.

Cognitive-developmental theory: a theory, derived by Kohlberg, that explains gender identity development by the child's developing cognitive skills in three stages, which underpin critical milestones in understanding about gender as gender labelling, gender stability and gender constancy.

Cohort: a cohort is a group of people who are defined by having something collectively in common.

Colic: a condition where babies cry for long periods of time (most commonly in the first three months of life) without obvious reason, but possibly due to trapped wind or infant temperament.

Common fractions: notations for rational numbers that use the form a/b, in which b can have any value.

Concepts: mental representations upon which categories are based.

Confound variables: extraneous factors in a research study that are not specifically measured or manipulated and that may affect the results of that study.

Congenital adrenal hyperplasia: congenital adrenal hyperplasia can affect both boys and girls. People with congenital adrenal hyperplasia lack an enzyme needed by the adrenal gland to make the hormones cortisol and aldosterone. Without these hormones, the body produces more androgen, a type of male sex hormone. This causes male characteristics to appear early (or inappropriately). About 1 in 10 000–18 000 children are born with congenital adrenal hyperplasia (MedLine Plus, 2010).

Conservation: the principle that the shape or appearance of something can change without there being a change in quantity.

Constructivism: constructivism is a philosophy of learning founded on the premise that, by reflecting on our experiences, we construct our own understanding of the world we live in (Piaget, 1967).

Context-dependence: related sets of behaviour or expressions depending on settings.

Continuity: related ranges of behaviour appropriate to age.

Continuous development: change that occurs at a steady pace, perhaps showing a constant, consistent improvement or growth.

Continuous perspective: development is a continuous, life-long experience which does not follow specific steps and stages but early experiences are built upon and skills expanded continuously.

Continuous quantities: quantities to which one must apply a unit of measurement in order to determine their magnitude, such as length, mass, time, etc.

Cooperative learning: working in small groups, acting together to meet a learning goal or goals.

Counting all: term used to describe behaviour in addition tasks whereby children join sets and start counting from one, e.g. when adding seven and five tokens, they count all the items in the first set starting from one and then continue counting as they point to the items in the second set.

Counting on: term used to describe behaviour in addition tasks whereby children start counting from the number after the value of one set, e.g. when adding seven and five tokens, they point to an item in the second set and start to count from 8.

Co-variation or isomorphism of measures problems: multiplicative reasoning problems in which there is a fixed ratio between two quantities or two measures. For example, there is usually a fixed ratio between the number of sweets you buy and the price you pay.

Covert attention: the act of mentally focusing on one of several possible stimuli.

Creativity: the ability to think in new or different ways or to come up with original ideas, concepts or solutions.

Critical period hypothesis: the suggestion that there is a specific period of time in the early part of a child's life (suggestions about when this begins and ends vary), during which language learning should occur in order to develop normally.

Critical period: the time period that was thought to be critical for the formation and development of any attachment relationship, hypothesised to be six months to three years, beyond which it is seen as highly difficult for such a bond to be formed.

Cross-sectional research design: a method of collecting data that administers a test or series of tests to a participant or group of participants on one occasion only.

Cues: stimuli which assist with the retrieval of information from memory by providing a hint or by helping to recreate something of the original encoding environment.

Cyberbullying: forms of bullying behaviour that use electronic media such as the internet, mobile phones, etc.

Decades: values in a numeration system with a base 10 that include one or more groups of 10 units. In English, twenty, thirty, forty, etc. up to ninety are the number labels for decades.

Deception: (in Research Methods) the deliberate act of creating false knowledge in your participants for the purpose of influencing the outcomes of the research study.

Deception: trying to make someone else believe that something is true when in fact it is false (Baron-Cohen, 2001).

Decimal fractions: fractions in which the denominator is a power of 10. Decimal fractions can be expressed as a/b, but they can also have a different notation. 8/10 can also be expressed as 0.8.

Defence mechanisms: coping styles used during moments of anxiety brought on by unresolved libidinous urges.

Demand characteristics: when a participant anticipates what the researcher wants from them and changes their behaviour to conform to that perceived desirable performance.

Dendrites: the branches or extensions at the top of neurons that allow contact with other neurons and so form neural networks.

Denominator: in the common notation of fractions (a/b), the denominator is b, which can also be conceived as the divisor in the division represented by the a/b notation.

Depression: a common mental disorder that presents with depressed mood, loss of interest or pleasure, feelings of guilt or low self-worth, disturbed sleep or appetite, low energy, and poor concentration (World Health Organisation).

Desire stage of theory of mind: the ability to detect in someone a strong feeling of wanting to have something or wishing for something to happen.

Developmentally appropriate provision: when the educational experiences of learners are matched with the learners' ability to make the most of the experience.

Disapplied: the term used to indicate that a pupil or group of pupils need no longer be taught part or all of a programme study.

Discontinuous development: change that occurs in what appear to be great bursts of achievement following a period of steady consolidation of perhaps knowledge or skill.

Discrete quantities: quantities which can be counted using natural numbers –1, 2, 3, etc.

Discriminate: in speech-sound perception, to be able to tell the difference between speech sounds of a language.

Disinhibition: the tendency to behave in ways other than one might normally, showing a lack of restraint or regard for social norms.

Divergent thinking: the type of thinking which is usually the product of creativity and is therefore original.

Dividend: in division, the quantity that is being divided.

Divisor: in division, the quantity by which another quantity (the dividend) is to be divided.

DNA (deoxyribonucleic acid): strings of biochemical material that provide the code for genes.

Dominance hierarchy: a relatively stable ordering of different status members by their ability to win in conflict that signifies different access to resources accordingly, established by challenges through rough-and-tumble play.

Dopamine: a neurotransmitter that occurs in a wide variety of animals, including both vertebrates and invertebrates.

DSM IV criteria for ADHD: current classification for combined type ADHD (DSM IV; APA, 1994) requires a minimum of six out of nine symptoms of inattention and a minimum of six out of nine symptoms of hyperactivity/impulsivity to be present in the child. Symptoms of inattention include daydreaming, distractibility and disorganisation; symptoms of hyperactivity include restlessness and fidgeting, while symptoms of impulsivity include impatience and not being able to stop yourself from acting. In addition there must be some impairment from symptoms in two or more settings (e.g. home and school) and clear evidence of significant impairment in social, school or work functioning.

Dyscalculia: impaired number comprehension, number production or calculation. When attributed to brain damage, it is known as acquired dyscalculia. With no evidence of brain damage, and a discrepancy between number abilities and general intelligence, it is known as developmental dyscalculia.

Dysfluency: an abnormal degree of hesitation or stumbling over words, making speech difficult to understand. Stammering (or stuttering) is the most common form of dysfluency. The speech of people who are dysfluent may be hard to understand; it may seem jerky or disjointed and it does not flow easily from one word to the next.

Dyslexia: a learning difficulty which affects a person's ability to read despite otherwise normal levels of intelligence.

Early emergence: in infancy, product of biology and/or environment since birth.

EEG: (electroencephalogram): record of brain activity recorded by means of electrodes placed around the scalp.

Effortful control: a concept Rothbart identified to characterise how people voluntarily suppress certain responses in order to substitute with other, usually more appropriate ones as a process which is likely mediated by the brain system of frontal lobes known to be involved in resolving conflicting tendencies between different parts of the brain.

Ego: our conscious decision-making process.

Egocentric: understanding the world only from your own perspective and finding it difficult to understand the point of view of another person.

Empathy: the ability to identify with the emotions of others and to read the physical expression of emotion in others.

Encoding specificity principle: a principle which states that memory is improved when contextual information present at the time of encoding is also available at the time of retrieval.

Encoding: the first stage of information processing in memory, where information is taken in via the senses.

Episodic memory: memory for specific events or occurrences, including details of time, place and emotions associated with it.

Ethology: the study of behaviour in its natural setting. Ethologists do not conduct experiments on behaviour in unnaturalistic settings, they prefer to observe and catalogue behaviour as it occurs naturally and without intervention from the researcher.

Exosystem: the social settings that do not immediately impact on a person, but surround them and are important to their welfare.

Experimental methods: the manipulation of events to see if change in one variable effects change in another variable.

Explicit: explicit knowledge is that which has been stated clearly and in detail and where there is no room for misunderstanding, confusion or doubt.

Factor analysis: a statistical method that reduces large numbers of questionnaire items down to a smaller number of clusters or underlying factors.

False-belief: the wrongly-held belief that something is true.

Familiarisation: a procedure for testing infant perceptual and cognitive skills by presenting an item for a set number of times or trials and then comparing infant interest in the familiar item with interest in a novel one.

Folk psychology: the information that ordinary people have about the mind and how it works. It is usually based in a common set of traditions and customs that are used to explain people's emotions and behaviour.

Friendship: a mutual reciprocal relationship between two or more people where both or all parties involved want to spend more time with the other(s) than other peers.

Functional play: the use of objects in play for the purposes for which they were intended and making objects do what they are made to do, e.g. pushing a car on a surface or pressing the buttons on a mechanical toy.

G: an abbreviated way of referring to general intelligence, the common factor believed by some to underpin performance on all intelligence tests.

Gaze following: the ability to follow where another person is looking and to look in the same direction.

Gender constancy: the understanding that gender group membership is unchanged despite changes in appearance.

Gender labelling: correct identification of 'male' or 'female' of oneself and others.

Gender schema: a system of beliefs about the attributes and behaviours associated with gender that help the child to form evaluations of, and to make assumptions about, each other and social objects and situations based on gender group memberships.

Gender stability: the understanding that gender group membership is normally stable and permanent over time.

Gender stereotypes: beliefs about what is appropriate for or typical of one's own or the other gender group.

Goodness-of-fit: this concept defines how both genetic components as the innate part of temperament and environmental forces will combine and interact to over time to produce positive (through good 'fit') or negative (through bad 'fit') developmental outcomes.

Habituation-recovery: a procedure for testing infant perceptual and cognitive skills by repeatedly presenting an item until the infant's interest drops to some criterion or set level, then presenting a novel item to see if the infant shows refreshed interest and so can distinguish it from the familiar one.

HAS (high-amplitude sucking) method: a procedure for testing infant auditory skills (especially in regard to speech and music) in which infants suck on a dummy or pacifier to maintain a sound if interested.

Heterogeneous developmental disorder: a condition that might have many different causes that affects the normal development of the child.

Holophrase: a single word which expresses some more complex idea.

Hostile attribution bias: the tendency for some people to attribute hostile intention to the actions of others in non-hostile situations.

Hyperactive: a descriptive term that is frequently applied to children who have low levels of attention to a task, can behave impulsively and without consideration of the consequences and/or who may be unable to sit quietly with other children.

Hypothesis: a proposed explanation for why or how two events might be related to each other.

Id: our biological impulses.

Identity vs role-diffusion stage of development: Erikson's description of the pursuit of a coherent sense of self during the teenage years. Role-diffusion can occur when the teenager is unable to put together aspects of himself (see Chapter 2).

Implicit: implicit knowledge comes from an understanding of what is meant or suggested even when it has not been directly stated.

Imprinting: a process in which newborns of most species will recognise and seek proximity with the first object they encounter (usually the primary caregiver) following the activation of a trigger during a critical period after birth.

Indirect bullying: forms of bullying that may not be observed by the victim at the time, but nonetheless have intentional and negative consequences for the victim, e.g. spreading rumours.

Induction: a type of reasoning where a factual conclusion is reached on the basis of empirical evidence, but need not necessarily be true.

Infanticide: intentionally causing the death of an infant.

Infantile amnesia: a phenomenon whereby memories from the first three or four years of life are relatively scarce.

Information-processing theory: the likening of human cognition to the working structures of a computer, with input, processing, memory, output, etc. that helps us 'conceptualise' what is happening in the brain.

Informed consent: agreeing to take part in a study whilst knowing as far as possible the details of the study methodology including all possible risks and benefits of taking part.

Inhibited: tendency to be timid, cautious or restrained and withdraw from novelty

Innate behaviour: behaviour that appears instinctive, is natural and not learned, behaviour or abilities that we are born with.

Intelligence quotient (IQ): devised by the German psychologist William Stern (1912), the intelligence quotient or IQ is a score derived from one of several different standardised tests designed to measure ability over a range of different cognitive tasks.

Internal working model: the mental representation about oneself, others and their relationships on which one's expectations about future relationships are based.

Intervention: acting to stop a behaviour from continuing.

Interview: the interview is conducted by the researcher following either a strict list of questions (a closed or structured interview) or an open format that evolves from the answers the respondent gives (an open interview).

IQ: abbreviation for intelligence quotient – a score obtained from an individual's performance on tests designed to measure intelligence.

Language acquisition device: a hypothetical cognitive structure predisposed towards the acquisition of language and sensitive to rule-based regularities in everyday speech, therefore allowing for the development of grammar and syntax.

Lateralisation: the principle that some specific psychological functions are located in one or the other side of the brain's two cortical hemispheres.

Learning disability: "a condition of arrested or incomplete development of the mind, which is especially characterised by impairment of skills manifested during the developmental period, which contribute to the overall level of intelligence, i.e. cognitive, language, motor and social abilities . . . Adaptive behaviour is always impaired" (ICD-10)

Longitudinal research method: A method of collecting data that administers a test or series of tests to the same participant or group of participants on a number of occasions.

Macrosystem: the cultural values, laws, customs and resources available to a person.

Make-believe play: also known as sociodramatic or role-play, play that involves two or more children acting out social roles, whether real-life or fictional ones, in pretend games and usually requires negotiation and reciprocation with each other with agreed rules in the shared imaginary scenario.

Maternal deprivation hypothesis: the notion that later serious deleterious outcomes will result from the lack of a consistent attachment figure in early childhood.

Maternal sensitivity: the emotional sensitivity of the mother to recognise her child's cues and to respond to them promptly, appropriately and consistently.

Maturation: change over time which is naturally occurring and genetically programmed.

Mean: a statistical term which refers to the numerical average of a set of numbers. To calculate the mean, add all of the numbers in the set and divide by the number of items in the set.

Median: the mid-point in the range of scores that the participants received on a measure. If we place our participants' maths scores in ascending order (5, 5, 5, 7, 8) we can see that the score at the mid-point in the range from 5 to 8 is the third 5 and the median score is therefore 5.

Menarche: a woman's first menstrual period.

Mesosystem: the connections between elements of the microsystem.

Meta-analysis: a method of statistical analysis which combines the results of many studies to identify an overall effect or change, often in an attempt to overcome problems of small sample sizes in research.

Metacognition: a person's knowledge or awareness of their own cognition. Sometimes referred to as 'knowledge about knowledge' or 'cognition about cognition'.

Meta-representation: (1) The ability to separate reality from fantasy, for instance, during pretend play (Leslie, 1987). (2) Additionally, knowing the difference between what might be represented in a photograph or painting of an object and what the reality of that object might be (Perner, 1991).

Microsystem: the activities and interactions immediately surrounding a person.

Mind-mindedness: the ability of a parent to see and treat her child as an individual with his own thoughts and feelings, through her interactions with him using talk to refer to mental states.

Mnemonics: memory aids which are used to assist with the learning or memorisation of information.

Mode: the most frequently obtained score that the participants received on a measure. In our example, the most frequently obtained score is 5 (5, 5, 5, 7, 8) and the modal score is therefore 5.

Molecular genetics: molecular genetics is the field of biology that studies the structure and function of genes at a molecular level. It focuses on how genes are transferred from generation to generation.

Monotropism: the idea that any child only forms a strong attachment to one person.

Myelinisation: the growth of fatty insulating coating along axon of the neuron.

Naming insight: the realisation that all things have names, leading to a fundamental change in the way children think about the world.

Natural numbers: the set of counting numbers. Does not include negative numbers, but some people include zero as a natural number. The cardinality of a finite set will be a natural number.

Nature: the role of genetics in forming our behaviour, our personality or any other part of ourselves.

Neglected children: children who are neither accepted nor rejected, or not strongly liked or disliked, by their peer group

Neo-Piagetian theory: a recent interpretation of Piaget's theory in an information-processing framework that places greater emphasis on cognitive processes than maturation.

Neural tube: hose-shaped structure forming the basis of the brain and spinal cord in the embryo.

Neurogenesis: the production of neurons in the embryo.

Neuroimaging: techniques which provide images of the structure and/or functioning of the brain.

Neuronal migration: the movement of neurons to appropriate locations in the brain and body.

Norepinephrine: a neurotransmitter that influences parts of the brain where attention and responding actions are controlled. It underlies the fight-or-flight response and directly increases heart rate, triggering the release of glucose from energy stores and increasing blood flow to skeletal muscle.

Numerator: in the common notation of fractions (a/b), the numerator is a, which can also be conceived as the dividend in the division represented by the a/b notation.

Numerical calculation: the arithmetic operations that children carry out to find the answer to a problem.

Nurture: the role of family, society, education and other social factors in forming our behaviour, our personality or any other part of ourselves.

Object permanence: the understanding that objects exist even when they have disappeared from view.

Objective or Categorical self: the recognition of the self as the person seen by others and defined by the attributes and qualities used to define groups of people.

Observation study: the researcher views behaviour in either a laboratory or natural setting and records events that take place. The researcher generally tries not to influence events unless this is a necessary feature of the study design.

Operant conditioning: the process that describes how behaviours can be encouraged or inhibited by the effective use of reward or punishment.

Ordinality: in set theory, this is the use of numbers to measure the position of a number in an ordered set.

Overt attention: the act of directing the senses towards a particular stimulus.

Parental investment theory: a theory used to explain gender differences on the basis of biological sex differences. The theory states that reproduction has different implications for males and females and that men and women therefore look for different traits in each other, which through the course of evolution, have been adapted as the modern-day observed gender role, behaviour and status differences.

Participant confidentiality: the treatment of any data collected on a participant to prevent the identification of the participant.

Partitioning: the process of dividing a whole into parts.

Peer group: the other children or young people with whom a child or young person engages that are of a similar age and not a family member.

Peer preference: choosing friends who have similar interests to our own and who have a similar set of beliefs or outlook on life

Peer pressure: when the friendship group convinces the young person to say or do something that they would not ordinarily say or do in order to gain positive regard or acceptance.

Peer support: a method by which children and young people are trained to act as supports for others who are experiencing difficulties such as bullying.

Phoneme: the smallest units of sound in a language.

Phonology: the sound system of a particular language.

Pilot study: a small-scale, preliminary run of a study that aims to test for example, the appropriateness of the measurement tools, methods used and then the quality of the data collected. A pilot study is usually conducted to refine the full-scale run of a study.

Placenta: the organ which connects to the wall of the mother's uterus, and which connects to the foetus by the umbilical cord. It allows for the uptake of nutrients by the foetus, and for the elimination of waste.

Plasticity: the ability of the brain to reorganise neural pathways either to recover lost functioning due to damage, or in response to learning from new experiences.

Play sensitivity: responsiveness to the infant during play through cooperation and motivation by accepting

her initiative, adapting play to her cognitive capability and responding to her emotional expressions.

Positivism: (concept). a system recognising only that which can be scientifically verified or logically proved, and therefore rejecting metaphysics and theism. (Oxford Dictionaries, 2008)

Positivism: (in research methods). a. the systematic investigation into and study of materials, sources, etc., in order to establish facts and reach new conclusions. b. an endeavour to discover new or collate old facts, etc. by the scientific study of a subject or by a course of critical investigation. (Oxford Dictionaries, 2008)

Pragmatic language: pragmatics is a sub-field of linguistics devoted to the study of how context contributes to meaning. Specifically, it examines how the transmission of meaning depends not only on the linguistic knowledge (grammar and words used) of the speaker and listener, but also on the context of the utterance, knowledge about the subject matter, etc., all of which help to attribute meaning to language.

Pragmatics: the part of language concerned with its use in social contexts.

Preferential looking method: a procedure for testing infant perceptual and cognitive skills by observing infant viewing preferences to two or more items.

Prevention: acting to reduce the likelihood that a behaviour may occur.

Procedural memory: implicit, unconscious long-term memory for skills or how to do things.

Product of measures problems: multiplicative reasoning problems that involve three variables, where the third one is the product of the first two.

Propositional thought: the ability to consider a hypothetical concept without having to actually see the events happening in order to come to a conclusion.

Proto-declarative pointing: the ability to point at the same object of interest as another person.

Prototype: a person or a thing that serves as an example of a type.

Proximity-seeking: a set of typical behaviours displayed by children to draw the attention of the primary caregiver towards themselves or reach her when separated, with the goal of restoring proximity.

Psychiatric co-morbidity: the experience of two psychological conditions at the same time; for example, anxiety and depression or ADHD and conduct disorder.

Psycho-stimulant medication: psycho-stimulant medications, used for their ability to balance chemicals in the brain that prohibit the child from maintaining attention and controlling impulses, may be used to reduce the major characteristics of ADHD.

Puberty: the period of physical maturation from a child into an adult.

Qualitative methods: methods that describe and define concepts, without the use of numbers and are usually conducted with smaller participant numbers.

Quantitative methods: use a systematic approach for collecting data that has or is assigned a numerical value.

Quantity: a property of magnitude or multitude used to express how much or how many of something there is.

Quotient: in division, the number of times by which the dividend is divisible by the divisor.

Ratio: expresses the magnitude of one quantity relative to another.

Rational numbers: numbers which can be expressed as a simple fraction.

Referential words: common nouns used to denote real objects.

Rehearsal: the repetition of information in a deliberate attempt to aid memory.

Rejected children: children who are unpopular, avoided as a playmate or least liked or disliked by others in the peer group.

Relational bullying: forms of bullying whereby the bully manipulates children in the social setting of the victim, with the intention of causing harm or distress.

Relational calculation: the operations of thought that children must carry out in order to handle the relations between quantities in the problem.

Relations: the positions, associations, connections, or status of one person, thing or quantity with regard to another or others; relational statements have an implied converse, so that (for example) if A is greater than B, then B must be less than A.

Representational stage of theory of mind: the ability to know that someone may believe something is true even when it is not and understand that the mistake happens because they are relying on incorrect or false knowledge.

Repression: a psychological defence mechanism which allows uncomfortable memories to be stored in the unconscious mind.

Retrieval: the third stage of information processing in memory, by which information is brought back out of storage and recalled.

Rough-and-tumble play: also known as 'play-fighting', play that involves physical activity, often without objects, such as wrestling, tumbling, kicking and chasing and is commonest during middle childhood among boys.

Schemes of action: representations of actions that can be applied to a variety of objects leading to predictable outcomes independent of the objects.

Scripts: mental representations which we have of certain types of events, which include our general expectations of such events based on prior experience.

Seeing leads to knowing: the principle that a person's belief/knowledge about a situation depends partly on what they have seen.

Self-awareness: the first step in the development of self-concept; the recognition that we are distinct from others with physical and mental properties of our own.

Self-concept: ideas we have about ourselves, including our physical and mental qualities, emotional and behavioural attributes.

Self-efficacy: a person's belief about how effectively he or she can control herself, her thoughts or behaviours, particularly when intended to fulfil a personal goal.

Self-esteem: the evaluative and reflective features of our self-concept that can vary from high to low and draw in part from others' evaluations of ourselves.

Semantic memory: long-term memory for facts, concepts and meanings.

Semantically related: words which have something in common in terms of their meaning.

Semantics: the part of language concerned with the meanings of words and parts of words.

Sensitive period: revised from critical period, the timeframe that is most conducive to forming strong attachment compared to other times in the child's life.

Separation anxiety: the anxiety a child experiences when separated from the mother or primary carer.

Separation protest: a set of typical behaviours displayed by the infant to register a form of protest against their caregiver's departure.

Shaken baby syndrome: a type of child abuse which occurs when a baby is vigorously shaken; it can result in neurological damage and may be fatal.

Shaping: a process by which children's utterances move closer to correct speech as the result of positive reinforcement which leads to a series of successive approximations.

Social identity: a sense of identity derived from our membership of social groups, including categorising ourselves as members, feelings of belonging, and behaviour consistent with what is expected of group members.

Social learning theories: an approach that explains gender identity development in terms of the child's accumulating learning experience from their social environment, in particular, through modelling others' behaviour and being rewarded for adopting approved mannerisms.

Social status: the extent of acceptance or likeability of individual children by the peer group, different from friendship as the group's general view of the individual.

Social-information processing: the way in which people make sense of information relating to social interactions and social contexts.

Sociometry: a technique that charts the relative standing of children within their peer group where data of their popularity/acceptance can be collected by self-reporting of peer preferences or observations of their interactions with each other.

Stability: similar level relative to other same-age peers.

Stage theories: theories based on the idea that we progress through a pattern of distinct stages over time. These stages are defined by the acquisition or presence of abilities and we generally pass through them in a specified order and during a specified age range.

Stimulus (plural stimuli): anything which elicits or evokes a response, such as a sound, a picture, a taste or a smell.

Storage: the second stage of information processing in memory, by which information is retained for short or long periods of time.

Storm and stress: described by G.S. Hall as the emotional and physical volatility of adolescence.

Strange Situation: a seven-part staged procedure employed to observe the behaviours and interactions between a child and the primary caregiver in a controlled laboratory setting, from which the type of attachment security between the dyad can be deduced.

Stranger anxiety: the wariness or fear of the infant when encountering those who are unfamiliar, often characterised by the seeking of proximity to the caregiver.

Subjective or Existential self: the recognition of the self that is unique and distinct from others, endures over time and space, and has an element of self-reflexivity.

Suggestibility: how susceptible someone is to ideas or information presented by others.

Superego: our sense of morality and social norms.

Symbolic play: also known as fantasy or pretend play, play that involves 'symbolic' representation, where the child pretends that an absent object is present and acts out the relevant behaviours involving that object.

Synapses: the gap between neurons across which the neural signal is passed.

Synaptic pruning: the elimination of excess synapses.

Synaptogenesis: rapid growth of dendrites to form neural connections or synapses.

Syntax: the part of language concerned with the rules which govern how words can be combined to make sentences.

Telegraphic speech: speech consisting of phrases of a small number of words (usually nouns, verbs and adjectives) combined to make sense, but without complex grammatical forms.

Temperament: a general underlying set of tendencies to behave in a particular way. It should show:

Teratogen: an environmental hazard to prenatal development.

Thalamocingulate division: part of the human brain suggested within Paul Maclean's 'Triune Brain' theory (that we have three brains, each developed from the preceding ones through evolution) as important in family-related behaviour.

The looking-glass self: the sense of self we develop as we respond to interactions with others and see how others react to us. We see ourselves reflected in other people's behaviour towards us.

Theorems in action: propositions held to be true which are only implicitly known to the person who holds them.

Theory of mind: being able to infer the full range of mental states (beliefs, desires, intentions, imagination, emotions, etc.) that cause action (Baron-Cohen, 2001).

Theory: a statement that we use to understand the world about us with three important component parts: it defines, explains and predicts behaviour.

Tool for thinking: a culturally developed system of signs that allows the user to represent something and operate on the representations in order to reach a conclusion about the represented reality.

Top-down processing: when the processing of information coming in via the senses is heavily influenced by prior knowledge.

Traditional bullying: forms of bullying behaviour that involve physical, verbal or psychological attacks without the use of electronic media.

Transformations: changes in the number of a set resulting from an event (e.g. an increase in the number of marbles you have due to winning a game). May also refer to changes of position (e.g. if you walked 2 km away from a house, your position changes).

Transitivity: a property of relations where new logical conclusions about one relation can be reached on the basis of premises about two other relations. For example, if A 5 B and B 5 C, then A 5 C.

Uninhibited: outgoing, spontaneous and approach novelty in the same settings.

Variables: has different meanings in different contexts. Here it is understood as quantities that we can measure through counting or using conventional measuring tools.

Visual recognition memory: memory for a visual stimulus which has been seen before. This type of memory can be assessed from very early in life and so is often used in infant memory research.

Vocabulary spurt: a point in language development where the rate of acquisition of new words is thought to accelerate rapidly.

Whole numbers: also referred to as directed numbers. The natural numbers together with the negatives of the non-zero natural numbers (21, 22, 23, . . .).

Working memory: Working memory (WM) is the part of memory that is critical to conscious thought because it permits internal representation of information (e.g. rules) to guide decision-making and overt behaviour (responses) during an activity so that behaviour is not dominated by the immediate sensory cues in the environment (for a review see Baddeley, 1986).

Zygote: the single cell formed from the union of sperm and ovum.

References

Abbas, T. (2007). British South Asians and pathways into selective schooling: Social class, culture and ethnicity. *British Educational Research Journal*, 33 (1), 75–90.

Abitz, M. Nielsen, R.D., Jones, E.G., Laursen, H., Graem, N. & Pakkenberg, B. (2007). *Excess of neurons in the human newborn mediodorsal thalamus compared with that of the adult. Cerebral Cortex*, 17 (11), 2573–2578.

Aboraya, A., Rankin, E., France, C., El-Missiry, A. & John, C. (2006). The reliability of psychiatric diagnosis revisited: The clinician's guide to improve the reliability of psychiatric diagnosis. *Psychiatry*, 3 (1), 41–50.

Abraham, C., Sheeran, P., Spears R. & Abrams, D. (1992). Health beliefs and promotion of HIV-preventive intentions among teenagers – a Scottish perspective. *Health Psychology*, 11 (6), 363–370.

Acredolo, L. P. & Goodwyn, S. W. (2000). *The long-term impact of symbolic gesturing during infancy on IQ at age 8*. International Conference on Infant Studies, 16–19 July, Brighton, UK.

Adams, R. J. & Courage, M. C. (1998). Human newborn colour vision: Measurements with chromatic stimuli varying in excitation purity. *Journal of Experimental Child Psychology*, 68, 22–34.

Adams, R. J. & Courage, M. L. (2002). A psychophysical test of the early maturation of infants' mid- and longwavelength retinal cones. *Infant Behaviour & Development*, 25, 247–254.

Adamson, L., Hartman S.G. & Lyxell, B. (1999). Adolescent identity – a qualitative approach: Self-concept, existential questions and adult contacts. *Scandinavian Journal of Psychology*, 40 (1), 21–31.

Adolph, K. E. (2000). Specificity of learning: Why infants fall over a veritable cliff. *Psychological Science*, 11, 290–295.

Ahmad, Y. S. & Smith, P. K. (1990). Behavioural measures review No. 1: Bullying in schools. *Newsletter of the ACPP*, 12, 26–27.

Ahmed, A. & Ruffman, T. (1998). Why do infants make A not B errors in a search task, yet show memory for the location of hidden objects in a nonsearch task? *Developmental Psychology*, 34, 441–453.

Ainsworth, M. (1963). The development of infant-mother interaction among the Ganda. In B. M. Foss (Ed.), *Determinants of Infant Behavior*, Vol. 2 (67–104). London: Methuen.

Ainsworth, M. (1967). *Infancy in Uganda: Infant Care and the Growth of Love*. Baltimore, MD: Johns Hopkins University Press.

Ainsworth, M. D. S. (1977). Infant development and motherinfant interaction among Ganda and American families. In P. H. Leiderman, S. R. Tulkin & A. Rosenfeld (Eds), *Culture and Infancy* (49–68). New York: Academic Press.

Ainsworth, M. & Bell, S. M. (1974). Mother-infant interactions and the development of competence. In K. Connolly & J. Bruner (Eds), *The Growth of Competence* (97–118). London: Academic Press.

Ainsworth, M.D.S., Blehar, M.C., Waters. E. & Wall, S. (1978). *Patterns of Attachment: A Psychological Study of the Strange Situation*. Hillsdale, NJ: Erlbaum.

Akers, J., Jones, R. & Coyl, D. (1998). Adolescent friendship pairs: Similarities in identity status development, behaviors, attitudes, and interests. *Journal of Adolescent Research*, 13, 178–201.

Alexander, R., Rose, J. & Woodhead, C. (1992). *Curriculum Organization and Classroom Practice in Primary Schools: A Discussion Paper*. London: DES.

Allen, C., Porter, M., McFarland, F., Marsh, P. & McElhaney, K. (2005). The two faces of adolescents' success with peers: Adolescent popularity social adaptation, and deviant behavior. *Child Development*, 76, 747–760.

Allen, P. (2008). Managing knowledge in technical demonstration plans: A template. *Knowledge Management Research & Practice*, 6 (3), 245–253.

Aluja-Fabregat, A. (2000). Personality and curiosity about TV and films violence in adolescents. *Personality and Individual Differences*, 29 (2), 379–392.

Aman, M. G., McDougle, C. J., Scahill, L., Handen, B., Arnold, L. E., Johnson, C., Stigler, K. A., Bearss, K., Butter, E., Swiezy, N.B., Sukhodolsky, D. D., Ramadan, Y., Pozdol, S. L., Nikolov, R., Lecavalier, L., Kohn, A. E., Koenig, K., Hollway, J. A., Korzekwa, P., Gavaletz, A., Mulick, J. A., Hall, K. L., Dziura, J., Ritz, L., Trollinger, S., Yu, S., Vitiello, B. & Wagner, A. (2009). Medication and parent training in children with pervasive developmental disorders and serious behavior problems: Results from a randomized clinical trial. *Journal of the American Academy of Child and Adolescent Psychiatry*, 48 (12),1143–1154.

American Psychiatric Association (1994). *Diagnostic and Statistical Manual of Mental Disorders* (4th Ed.). Washington, DC: APA.

American Psychiatric Association (1995). *Diagnostic and Statistical Manual of Mental Disorders*, Fourth Edition–Primary Care Version (DSM-IV®–PC). Washington DC: APA.

Anastopoulos, A. D., Shelton, T. L., DuPaul, G. J. & Guevremont, D. C. (1993). Parent training for attentiondeficit hyperactivity disorder: Its impact on parent functioning. *Journal of Abnormal Child Psychology*, 21, 581–596.

Apel, R., Pogarsky, G. & Bates, L. (2009). The sanction-sperceptions link in a model of school-based deterrence. *Journal of Quantitative Criminology*, 25 (2), 201–226.

Apgar, V. (1953). A proposal for a new method of evaluation in the newborn infant. *Current Research in Anaesthesia and Analgesia*, 32, 260–267.

Apperly, I.A. (2008). Beyond simulation-theory and theory-theory: why social cognitive neuroscience should use its own concepts to study theory of mind. *Cognition*, 107 (1), 266–283.

Archer, J. (1992). Childhood gender roles: Social context and organisation. In H. McGurk (Ed.), Childhood Social Development: *Contemporary Perspectives* (31–61). Hillsdale, NJ: Erlbaum.

Aries, P. (1960). *L'Enfant et la vie familiale sous l'Ancien Régime*. Paris: Plon Translated into English by Robert Baldick as *Centuries of Childhood. A Social History of Family Life*. New York, US.

Arndt, T. L., Stodgell, C. J. & Rodier, P. M. (2005). The teratology of autism. *International Journal of Developmental Neuroscience*, 23 (2), 189–199.

Arnett, J.J. (1999). Adolescent storm and stress, reconsidered. *American Psychologist*, 54 (5), 317–326.

Aronen, E.T. & Kurkela, S.A. (1998). The predictors of competence in an adolescent sample - A 15-year followup study. *Nordic Journal of Psychiatry*, 52 (3), 203–212.

Arora, C. M. J. (1996). Defining bullying: Towards a clearer general understanding and more effective intervention strategies. *School Psychology International*, 17, 317–329.

Askew, M., Brown, M., Rhodes V., Wiliam D., & Johnson D. (1997). *Effective Teachers of Numeracy in Primary Schools: Teachers' beliefs, practices and pupils' learning*. British Educational Research Association Conference, 10–14 September.

Astington, J. (1994). *The Child's Discovery of the Mind*. Cambridge, MA: Harvard University Press.

Atkinson, J. (2000). *The Developing Visual Brain*. Oxford: Oxford University Press.

Atkinson, J. & Braddick, O. (1981). Acuity, contrast sensitivity and accommodation in infancy. In R. N. Aslin, J. R. Alberts & M. R. Petersen (Eds), *Development of Perception: Psychobiological Perspectives: Vol. 2: The Visual System* (245–277). New York: Academic Press.

Atkinson, R. C. & Shiffrin, R. M. (1968). Human memory: A proposed system and its central processes. In K. W. Spence & J. T. Spence (Eds), *The Psychology of Learning and Motivation. Advances in Research and Theory (Vol. 2)*. (742–775). New York: Academic Press.

Ausubel, D., Novak, J. & Hanesian, H. (1978). *Educational Psychology: A Cognitive View*. New York: Holt, Rinehart and Winston.

Baddeley, A. D. (1986). *Working Memory*. Oxford: Claredon.

Baddeley, A. D. (1992). Working memory. *Science*, 255, 556–559.

Baddeley, A. D. (1998). *Working Memory*. Oxford: Oxford University Press.

Baddeley, A. (2003). Working memory: looking back and looking forward. *Nature Reviews Neuroscience*, 4, 829–839.

Baddeley, A. D. & Hitch, G. (1974). Working memory. In G. H. Bower (Ed.), *The Psychology of Learning and Motivation* (Vol. 8, 47–90). San Diego, CA: Academic Press.

Bagwell, C., Newcomb, A. & Bukowski, W. (1998). Preadolescent friendship and peer rejection as predictors of adult adjustment. *Child Development*, 69, 140–153.

Baillargeon, R. (2004). Infants' reasoning about hidden objects: Evidence for event-general and event-specific expectation. *Developmental Science*, 7, 391–424.

Baillargeon, R. & DeVos, J. (1991). Object permanence in young infants: Further evidence. *Child Development*, 62, 1227–1246.

Baird, G., Simonoff, E., Pickles, A. *et al.* (2006). Prevalance of disorders on the autism spectrum in a population cohort of children in South Thames: The Special Needs and Autism Project (SNAP). *Lancet*, 368, 210–215.

Baird, G. E., Cass, H. & Slonims, V. (2003). Diagnosis of autism. *British Medical Journal*, 327, 488–493.

Baker, B. L., McIntyre, L. L., Blacher, J., Crnic, K., Edelbrock, C. & Low, C. (2003). Pre-school children with and without developmental delay: Behavioural problems and parenting stress over time. *Journal of Intellectual Disability Research*, 471, 217–230.

Bakker, A., van Kesteren, P.J.M., Gooren, L.J.G. & Bezemer, P.D. (2007). The prevalence of transsexualism in the Netherlands. *Acta Psychiatrica Scandinavica*, 87 (4), 237–238.

Bakker, S. (1999). Educational assessment in the Russian Federation. *Assessment in Education: Principles, Policy & Practice*, 6 (2), 291–303.

Baldry, A.C. & Winkel, F.W. (2003). Direct and vicarious victimization at school and at home as risk factors for suicidal cognition among Italian adolescents. *Journal of Adolescence*, 26 (6), 703–716.

Bandura, A. (1969). Social learning theory of identificatory processes. In D. A. Goslin (Ed.), *Handbook of Socialization Theory and Research* (213–262). Chicago, IL: Rand McNally.

Bandura, A. (1977). *Social Learning Theory*. Englewood Cliffs, NJ: Prentice Hall.

Bandura, A. & Walters, R.H. (1963). *Social Learning and Personality Development*. New York: Holt, Rinehart & Winston.

Banerjee T.D., Middleton, F. & Faraone, S.V. (2007). Environmental risk factors for attention-deficit hyperactivity disorder. *Acta Pædiatric*, 9, 1269–1274.

Banich, M. T. (2004). *Cognitive Neuroscience and Neuropsychology*. Boston, MA: Houghton Mifflin.

Barboza G.E., Schiamberg L.B., Oehmke J., Korzeniewski S.J., Post L.A. & Heraux C.G. (2009). Individual characteristics and the multiple contexts of adolescent bullying: An ecological perspective. *Journal of Youth and Adolescence*, 38, 101–121.

Barker, E.D., Boivin, M., Brendgen, M., Fontaine, N., Arseneault, L., Vitaro, F., Bissonnette, C. & Tremblay, R.E. (2008). Predictive validity and early predictors of peer-victimization trajectories in preschool. *Archives of General Psychiatry*, 65, 1185–1192.

Barkley, R. A., Fischer, M., Smallish, L. & Fletcher, K. (2002). The persistence of attention-deficit/hyperactivity disorder into young adulthood as a function of reporting source and definition of disorder. *Journal of Abnormal Psychology*, 111 (2), 279–289.

Barlow, J. & Parsons, J. (2006). Group-based parent-training programme for improving emotional and behavioural adjustment in 0-3 year old children (Cochrane Review). In *The Cochrane Library*, Issue 2. Oxford: Update Software.

Barnett, D., Clements, M., Kaplan-Estrin, M., McCaskill, J. W., Hill Hunt, K., Butler, C. M., Schram, J. L. & Janisse, H.C. (2006). Maternal resolution of child diagnosis: Stability and relations with child attachment across the toddler to preschooler transition. *Journal of Family Psychology*, 20 (1), 100–107.

Barnett, D., Ganiban, J. & Cicchetti, D. (1999). Maltreatment, negative expressivity, and the development of Type D attachments from 12 to 24 months of age. In J. E. Vondra & D. Barnett (Eds), Atypical Attachment in Infancy and Early Childhood Among Children at Developmental Risk. *Monographs of the Society for the Research in Child Development*, 64 (3), Serial No. 258, 97–118.

Barnow, S., Lucht, M. & Freyberger, H.J. (2005). Correlates of aggressive and delinquent conduct problems in adolescence. *Aggressive Behavior*, 31 (1), 24–39.

Baron-Cohen, S. (1989). Are autistic children behaviourists? An examination of their mental-physical and appearance-reality distinctions. *Journal of Autism and Developmental Disorders*, 19, 579–600.

Baron-Cohen, S. (1992). Out of sight or out of mind: Another look at deception in autism. *Journal of Child Psychology and Psychiatry*, 33, 1141–1155.

Baron-Cohen, S. (1995). *Mindblindness: an Essay on Autism and Theory of Mind*. Cambridge, MA: MIT Press/Bradford Books.

Baron-Cohen, S. (2001). Theory of mind and autism: A review. Special Issue of the *International Review of Mental Retardation,* 23, (169).

Baron-Cohen, S. (2008). 100 words: Autism. *British Journal of Psychiatry*, 193, 321.

Baron-Cohen, S, Leslie, A.M. & Frith, U, (1985) Does the autistic child have a 'theory of mind'? *Cognition*, 21, 37–46.

Baron-Cohen, S., Wheelwright S., Hill J., Raste Y. & Plumb, I. (2001). The "Reading the Mind in the Eyes" Test revised version: A study with normal adults, and adults with Asperger syndrome or high-functioning autism. *Journal of Child Psychology and Psychiatry*, 42, 241–251.

Barr, R. G. (2004). Early infant crying as a behavioural state rather than a signal. *Behavioural and Brain Sciences*, 27 (4), 460.

Barry, T. D., Lyman, R. D. & Klinger, L. G. (2002). Academic underachievement and attention-deficit/hyperactivity disorder: The negative impact of symptom severity on school performance. *Journal of School Psychology*, 40, 259–283.

Bartgis, J. P., Thomas, D. G., Lefler, E. K. & Hartung, C. M. (2008). The development of attention and response inhibition in early childhood. *Infant and Child Development*, 17, 491–502.

Basow, S.A. & Rubin, L.R. (1999). Gender influences on adolescent development. In N.G. Johnson & M.C. Roberts (Eds), *Beyond Appearance: A New Look at Adolescent Girls* (25–52). Washington, DC: APA.

Bateman, B., Warner, J. O., Hutchinson, E., Dean, T., Rowlandson, P., Gant, C., Grundy, J., Fitzgerald, C. & Stevenson, J. (2004). The effects of a double blind, placebo controlled, artificial food colourings and benzoate preservative challenge on hyperactivity in a general population sample of preschool children. *Archives of Diseases in Childhood*, 89, 506–511.

Bates, E. (1990). Language about me and you: Pronominal reference and the emerging concept of self. In E. Cicchetti & M. Beeghly (Eds), *Self in Transition: Infancy to Childhood* (165–183). Chicago, IL: University of Chicago Press.

Bates, E., O'Connell, B. & Shore, C. (1987). Language and communication in infancy. In J. D. Osofsky (Ed.), *Handbook of Infant Development* (2nd Ed.) (149–203). New York: Wiley.

Bates, J. E. (1989). Concepts and measures of temperament. In G. A. Kohnstamm, J. E. Bates & M. K. Rothbart (Eds), *Temperament in Childhood* (3–26). Chichester: Wiley.

Bauer, P. J. (2007). Recall in infancy: a neurodevelopmental account. *Current Directions in Psychological Science*, 16, 142–146.

Baumrind, D. (1991). Parenting styles and adolescent development. In R. M. Lerner, A. C. Petersen & J. Brooks-Gunn (Eds), *Encyclopedia of Adolescence, Vol. 2* (746–758). New York: Garland.

Bavolek, S. J. (2010). The art and science of raising healthy children. Retrieved November 6 from http://www.nurturingparenting.com/research_validation/articles_for_professionals.php.

Bayley, N. (1969). *Bayley Scales of Infant Development*. New York: Psychological Corp.

Bayley, N. (1993). *Bayley Scales of Infant Development* (2nd Ed.). San Antonio, TX: Psychological Corp.

Bayley, N. (2005). *Bayley Scales of Infant Development* (3rd Ed.). Oxford: Harcourt Assessment.

Beaman, R. & Wheldall, K. (2000). Teachers' use of approval and disapproval in the classroom. *Educational Psychology*, 20 (4), 431–446.

Beals, D. E., De Temple, J. M., Dickinson, D. K. (1994). Talking and listening that support early literacy development of children from low-income families. In D. K. Dickinson (Ed.), *Bridges to Literacy: Children, Families and Schools* (19–40). Cambridge, MA: Blackwell.

Becker, J. (1993). Young children's numerical use of number words: Counting in many-to-one situations. *Developmental Psychology*, 19, 458–465.

Beitchman, J., Wilson, B., Brownlie, E. B., Walters, H., Lancee, W. (1996). Long term consistency in speech/language profiles: 1. Developmental and academic outcomes. *Journal of American Academy of Child and Adolescent Psychiatry*, 35 (6), 804–814.

Bell, M. A. (2002). Power changes in infant EEG frequency bands during a spatial working memory task. *Psychophysiology*, 39, 450–458.

Bell, S.M. & Ainsworth, M.D. (1972). Infant crying and maternal responsiveness. *Child Development*, 43 (4), 1171–1190.

Belsky, J. (1988). The "effects" of infant day care reconsidered. *Early Child Research Quarterly*, 3, 235–272.

Belsky, J. (1992). Consequences of child care for children's development. A deconstructionist view. In A. Booth (Ed.), *Child Care in the 1990s: Trends and Consequences* (83–94). Hillsdale, NJ: Erlbaum.

Belsky, J. & Steinberg, L. D. (1978). The effects of day care: A critical review. *Child Development*, 49, 929–949.

Belsky, P., Steinberg, L. & Draper, P. (1991). Childhood experience, interpersonal development, and reproductive strategy: An evolutionary theory of socialization. *Child Development*, 62, 647–670.

Bem, S. L. (1981). Gender schema theory: A cognitive account of sex-typing. *Psychological Review*, 88, 354–364.

Bem, S. L. (1989). Genital knowledge and gender constancy in preschool children. *Child Development*, 60, 649–662.

Bender, B. G. & Levin, J. R. (1976). Motor activity, anticipated motor activity, and young children's associative learning. *Child Development*, 47, 560–562.

Benoit, D. & Parker, K. C. H. (1994). Stability and transmission of attachment among three generations. *Child Development*, 65, 1444–1456.

Bem, S. (1981). Gender schema theory: a cognitive account of sex typing. *Psychological Review*, 88 (4), 354–364.

Benedict, H. (1979). Early lexical development: Comprehension and production. *Journal of Child Language*, 6, 183–200.

Bergman, K., Sarkar, P., O'Connor, T. G., Modi, N., Glover, V. (2007). Maternal stress during pregnancy predicts cognitive ability and fearfulness in infancy. *Journal of the American Academy of Child & Adolescent Psychiatry*, 46, 1454–1463.

Berko, J. (1958). The child's learning of English morphology. *Word*, 4, 150–177.

Bermejo, V., Morales, S. & deOsuna, J. G. (2004). Supporting children's development of cardinality understanding. *Learning and Instruction*, 14, 381–398.

Berndt, T. J. & Keefe, K. (1995). Friends' influence on adolescents' adjustment to school. *Child Development*, 66, 1312–1329.

Best, D. L., Williams, J. E., Cloud, J. M., Davis, S. W., Robertson, L. S., Edwards, J. R., Giles, H. & Fowles, J. (1977). Development of sex-trait stereotypes among young children in the United States, England, and Ireland. *Child Development*, 48, 1375–1384.

Beuhring, T. & Kee, D. W. (1987). Developmental relationships among metamemory, elaborative strategy use and associative memory. *Journal of Experimental Child Psychology*, 44, 377–400.

Biederman, J. (2005). Attention–deficit/hyperactivity disorder: A selective overview. *Biological Psychiatry*, 57, 1215–1220.

Bierman, K. L., Domitrovich, C. E., Nix, R. L., Gest, S. D., Welsh, J. A., Greenberg, M. T., Blair, C., Nelson, K. E. & Gill, S. (2008). Promoting academic and social-emotional school readiness: The Head Start REDI Program. *Child Development*, 79 (6), 1802–1817.

Bigelow, B. J. & La Gaipa, J. J. (1980). The development of friendship values and choice. In H. C. Foot, A. J. Chapman & J. R. Smith (Eds), *Friendship and Social Relations in Children* (15–44). Chichester: Wiley.

Bishop, D. V. and Adams, C. (1992). Comprehension problems in children with specific language impairment: Literal and inferential meaning. *Journal of Speech and Hearing Research*, 35 (1), 119–129.

Bishop, D. V. Chan, J., Adams, C., Hartley, J. & Weir, F. (2000). Conversational responsiveness in specific language impairment: Evidence of disproportionate pragmatic difficulties in a subset of children. *Development and Psychopathology*, 12 (2), 177–199.

Bishop, D. V. M., & Edmundson, A. (1987). Specific language impairment as a maturational lag: Evidence from longitudinal data on language and motor development. *Developmental Medicine and Child Neurology*, 29, 442–459.

Bjorklund, D. F. & Jacobs, J. W. (1985). Associative and categorical processes in children's memory: The role of automaticity in the development of free recall. *Journal of Experimental Child Psychology*, 39, 599–617.

Blakemore, S.J. & Choudhury, S. (2006). Development of the adolescent brain: Implications for executive function and social cognition. *Journal of Child Psychology and Psychiatry*, 47 (3), 296–312.

Blass, T. (2000). *Obedience to Authority: Current Perspectives on the Milgram Paradigm*. New York: Psychology Press.

Bogaert, A.F. (2008). Menarche and father absence in a national probability sample. *Journal of Biosocial Science*, 40 (4), 623–636.

Boller, K., Rovee-Collier, C., Borovsky, D., O'Connor, J. & Shyi, G. (1990). Developmental nature of changes in the time-dependent nature of memory retrieval. *Developmental Psychology*, 26 (5), 770–779.

Bolton, P. (2001). Developmental assessment. *Advances in Psychiatric Treatment*, 7, 32–40.

Bor, W., Sanders, M. R. & Markie-Dadds, C. (2002). The effect of the Triple-P Positive Parenting Programme on pre-school children with co-occurring disruptive behaviours and attention/hyperactive difficulties. *Journal of Abnormal Child Psychology*, 30, 571–587.

Borg, M.G. (1999). The extent and nature of bullying among primary and secondary schoolchildren. *Educational Research*, 41, 137–153.

Bornstein, M. H. (2006). Hue categorization and colour naming: Physics to sensation to perception. In N. J. Pitchford & C. P. Biggam (Eds), *Progress in Colour Studies. Volume 2: Psychological Aspects* (35–68). Amsterdam: John Benjamin.

Bornstein, M. H. (2006). Social relationships in early symbolic play. In A. Göncü. & S. Gaskins. (Eds). *Play and Development: Evolutionary, Sociocultural and Functional Perspectives* (101–129). London: Erlbaum.

Borovsky, D. & Rovee-Collier, C. (1990). Contextual constraints on memory retrieval at six months. *Child Development*, 61, 1569–1583.

Botvinick, M. M., Braver, T. S., Barch, D. M., Carter, C. S. & Cohen, J. D. (2001). Conflict monitoring and cognitive control. *Psychological Review*, 108, 624–652.

Bouchard, T.J. Jr, Lykken, D.T., McGue, M., Segal, N.L. & Tellegen, A. (1990). Sources of human psychological differences: the Minnesota Study of Twins Reared Apart. *Science*, 250 (4978), 223–228.

BouJaoude, S. (2002). Balance of scientific literacy themes in science curricula: The case of Lebanon. *International Journal of Science Education*, 24 (2), 139–156.

Boulton, M. G. (1983). *On Being a Mother: A Study of Women with Preschool Children*. London: Tavistock.

Boulton, M.J. (1995). Patterns of bully/victim problem in mixed race groups of children. *Social Development*, 4, 277–293.

Bower, P. (2003). Efficacy in evidence-based practice. *Journal of Clinical Psychology and Psychotherapy*, 10, 328–336.

Bowers, L., Smith, P.K. & Binney, V. (1992). Cohesion and power in the families of children involved in bully/victim problems at school. *Journal of Family Therapy*, 14 (4), 371–387.

Bowlby, J. (1944). Forty-four juvenile thieves: Their characters and home life. *International Journal of Psychoanalysis*, 25, 1–57; 207–228.

Bowlby, J. (1951). *Maternal Care and Mental Health: Report to the World Health Organization*. New York: Shocken Books.

Bowlby, J. (1953). *Child Care and the Growth of Love*. Harmondsworth: Penguin.

Bowlby, J. (1958). The nature of the child's tie to his mother. *International Journal of Psychoanalysis*, 39, 350–373.

Bowlby, J. (1969). Attachment and Loss: Attachment. New York: Basic Books.

Bowlby, J. (1969; 1982). *Attachment and Loss. Volume 1: Attachment* (2nd Ed.). New York: Basic Books.

Bowlby, J. (1973). *Attachment and Loss: Separation*. New York: Basic Books.

Bowlby, J. (1980). *Attachment and Loss: Loss, Sadness and Depression*. New York: Basic Books.

Boyatzis, C., Baloff, P. & Durieux, C. (1998). Effects of perceived attractiveness and academic success on early adolescent peer popularity. *Journal of Genetic Psychology*, 158, 337–344.

Boyd, D. & Bee, H. (2006). *Lifespan Development* (4th Ed.). Boston, MA: Allyn & Bacon.

Boyle, M. (2001). *Abandoning diagnosis and (cautiously) adopting formulation*. British Psychological Society Centenary Conference, 28–31 March, Glasgow.

Boynton, P. & Anderson, I. (2009). Baby P – what is our response?, *The Psychologist*, 22, 2, 8–9.

Brainerd, C. J. & Reyna, V. F. (1990). Gist is the gist: Fuzzy-trace theory and the new intuitionism. *Developmental Review*, 10, 3–47.

Brainerd, C. J. & Reyna, V. F. (2001). Fuzzy-trace theory: Dual processes in memory, reasoning and cognitive neuroscience. *Advances in Child Development and Behavior*, 28, 41–100.

Brainerd, C. J. & Reyna, V. F. (2004). Fuzzy-trace theory and memory development. *Developmental Review*, 24 (4), 396–439.

Brainerd, C. J., Reyna, V. F. & Forrest, T. J. (2002). Are young children susceptible to the false-memory illusion? *Child Development*, 73, 1363–1377.

Breakwell, G.M., Hammond, S., Fife-Schaw, C. & Smith, J.A. (2006). *Research Methods in Psychology* (3rd Ed.). London: Sage.

Brehmer, Y., Li, S.C., Muller, V., von Oertzen, T. & Lindenberger, U. (2007). Memory plasticity across the lifespan: Uncovering children's latent potential. *Developmental Psychology*, 32 (2), 465–478.

Bremner, G. & Fogel, A. (2001). *Blackwell Handbook of Infant Development*. Oxford: Blackwell.

Brent, R. L. & Fawcett, L. B. (2007). Developmental toxicology, drugs and foetal teratogenesis. In E. A. Reece & J. C. Hobbins (Eds), *Clinical Obstetrics: the Foetus and Mother* (215–235). Oxford: Blackwell.

Brewin, C. R. (2007). Autobiographical memory for trauma: Update on four controversies. *Memory*, 15 (3), 227–248.

Broadstock, M., Doughty, C. & Eggleston, M. (2007). Systematic review of the effectiveness of pharmacological treatments for adolescents and adults with autism spectrum disorder. *Autism*, 11 (4), 335–348.

Brody, G. H., Beach, S. R. H., Philibert, R. A., Chen, Y. F., Lei, M. K., Murray, V. M. & Brown, A.C. (2009). Parenting moderates a genetic vulnerability factor in longitudinal increases in youths' substance use. *Journal of Consulting and Clinical Psychology*, 77, 1–11.

Broerse, J., Peltola, C. & Crassini, B. (1983). Infants' reactions to perceptual paradox during mother-infant interactions. *Developmental Psychology*, 19, 310–316.

Bronfenbrenner, U. (1979). Beyond the deficit model in child and family policy. *Teachers College Record*, 81 (1), 95–104.

Bronfenbrenner, U. (1986). Ecology of the family as a context for human development: research perspectives. *Developmental Psychology*, 22 (6), 723–742.

Bronfenbrenner, U. (1989). Ecological systems theory. In R. Vasta (Ed.), *Annals of Child Development* (vol. 6, 187–249). Boston, MA: JAI Press, Inc.

Bronfenbrenner, U. (2004). *Making Human Beings Human: Biological Perspectives on Human Development*.

Bronfenbrenner, U. & Evans, G. (2000). Developmental science in the 21st Century: Emerging questions, theoretical models, research designs and empirical findings. *Social Development*, 9, 115–125.

Bronfenbrenner, U. & Morris, P. A. (1998). The ecology of developmental processes. In R. M. Lerner (Ed.) *Handbook of Child Psychology, Vol., 1, Theoretical Models of Human Development* (535–584). New York: Wiley.

Brookes, K., Xu, X., Chen, W., Zhou, K., Neale, B., Lowe, N., Aneey, R., Franke, B., Gill, M., Ebstein, R., Buitelaar, J., Sham, P., Campbell, D., Knight, J., Andreou, P., Altink, M., Arnold, R., Boer, F., Buschgens, C., Butler, L., Christiansen, H., Feldman, L., Fleischman, K., Fliers, E., Howe-Forbes, R., Goldfarb, A., Heise, A., Gabriels, I., Korn-Lubetzki, I., Marco, R., Medad, S., Minderaa, R., Mulas, F., Muller, U., Mulligan, A., Rabin, K., Rommelse, N., Sethna, V., Sorohan, J., Uebel, H., Psychogiou, L., Weeks, A., Barrett, R., Craig, I., Banaschezski, T., Sonuga-Barke, E., Eisenberg, J., Kuntsi, J., Manor, I., McGuffin, P., Miranda, A., Oades, R. D., Plomin, R., Roeyers, H., Rothenberger, A., Sergeant, J., Steinhausen, H.C., Taylor, E., Thompson, M., Faraone, S. V., Asherson, P. & Johansson, L. (2006). The analysis of 51 genes in DSM-IV combined type attention deficit hyperactivity disorder: association signals in DRD4, DAT1 and 16 other genes. *Molecular Psychiatry*, 11, 934–953.

Brooks-Gunn, J. (1988a). Antecedents and consequences of variations in girls' maturational timing. *Journal of Adolescent Health Care*, 9, 365–373.

Brooks-Gunn, J. (1988b). The impact of puberty and sexual activity upon the health and education of adolescent girls and boys. *Peabody Journal of Education*, 64, 88–113.

Brooks-Gunn, J. & Lewis, M. (1981). Infant social perception: Responses to pictures of parents and strangers. *Developmental Psychology*, 17, 647–649.

Brosnan, Mark J. (2008). *Digit ratio as an indicator of numeracy relative to literacy in 7-year-old British schoolchildren*.

Brousseau, G., Brousseau, N. & Warfield, V. (2007). Rationals and decimals as required in the school curriculum Part 2: From rationals to decimals. *Journal of Mathematical Behavior*, 26, 281–300.

Brown, A. M. & Miracle, J. A. (2003). Early binocular vision in human infants: Limitations on the generality of the superposition hypothesis. *Vision Research*, 43, 1563–1574.

Brown, G., McBride, B., Shin, N. & Bost, K. (2007). Parenting predictors of father-child attachment security: Interactive effects of father involvement and fathering quality. *Fathering*, 5, 197–219.

Brown, M. (1981). Number operations. In K. Hart (Ed.), *Children's Understanding of Mathematics*: 11–16 (23–47). Windsor: NFER-Nelson.

Bruck, M. & Ceci, S. J. (1997). The nature of applied and basic research on children's suggestibility. In N. Stein, P. A. Ornstein, B. Tversky & C. J. Brainerd (Eds), *Memory for Everyday and Emotional Events* (83–111). Hillsdale, NJ: Erlbaum.

Brutsaert, H. (2006). Gender-role identity and perceived peer group acceptance among early adolescents in Belgian mixed and single-sex schools. *Gender and Education*, 18 (6), 635–649.

Bryan, K. L. (1995). *The Right Hemisphere Language Battery* (2nd Ed.). Kibworth: Far Communications.

Bryant, P., Morgado, L. & Nunes, T. (1992). Children's understanding of multiplication. Paper presented at the Conference on Psychology of Mathematics Education, Tokyo, Japan, in Nunes, T., Bryant, P. (1996). *Children Doing Mathematics*. Oxford: Blackwell.

Bryant, P., Nunes, T., Evans, D., Campos, T. & Bell, D. (2008). *The number line as a teaching tool*. American Educational Research Association Annual Meeting. New York, 24–28 March.

Buckingham, D. (2003). Multimedia childhoods. In M. J. Kehily & J. Swann (Eds), *Children's Cultural Worlds* (183–228). Milton Keynes: The Open University/Chichester: Wiley.

Buhs, E. S. & Ladd, G. W. (2001). Peer rejection as antecedent of young children's school adjustment: An examination of mediating processes. *Developmental Psychology*, 37, 550–560.

Bullock, M. & Lutkenhaus, P. (1990). Who am I? Selfunderstanding in toddlers. *Merrill-Palmer Quarterly*, 36, 217–238.

Busch, B., Biederman, J., Cohen, L. G., Sayer, J. M., Monuteaux, M. C., Mick, E., Zallen, B. & Faraone, S. V. (2002). Correlates of ADHD among children in pediatric and psychiatric clinics. *Psychiatric Services*, 53, 1103–1111.

Buss, D. M. (1987). Selection, evocation, and manipulation. *Journal of Personality and Social Psychology*, 53, 1214–1221.

Bussey, K. & Bandura, A. (1999). Social cognitive theory of gender development and differentiation. *Psychological Review*, 106, 676–713.

Bukatko, D. & Daehler, M. W. (2004). *Child Development: A Thematic Approach*. New York: Houghton Mifflin.

Buss, A. H. & Plomin, R. (1984). *Temperament: Early Developing Personality Traits*. Hillsdale, NJ: Erlbaum.

Butler, G. (1998). Clinical formulation. In A.S. Bellock & M. Hersen (Eds), *Comprehensive Clinical Psychology* (1–23). Oxford: Pergamon.

Buttelmann, D., Carpenter, M. & Tomasello, M. (2009). Eighteen-month-old infants show false-belief understanding in an active helping paradigm. *Cognition*, 112, 337–342.

Cairns, R. B. & Cairns, B. D. (1994). *Lifelines and Risks: Pathways of Youth in Our Time*. Cambridge: Cambridge University Press.

Cairns, R. B. Cairns, B. D., Neckerman, H. J., Gest, S. D. & Gariépy, J. L. (1988). Social networks and aggressive behavior: Peer acceptance or peer rejection? *Developmental Psychology*, 24, 815–823.

Cairns, R. B. & Cairns, B. D. (2008). Aggression and attachment: The folly of separatism. In A. C. Bohart & D. J. Stipek (Eds), *Constructive and Destructive Behavior: Implications for Family, School, and Society* (3rd Ed.) (21–48). New York: APA.

Caldera, Y. (2004). Paternal involvement and infant-father attachment: A Q-set study. *Fathering*, 2, 191–210.

Caldera, Y. M., Huston, A. C. & O'Brien, M. (1989). Social interactions and play patterns of parents and toddlers with feminine, masculine, and neutral toys. *Child Development*, 60, 70–76.

Calkins, S. D., Fox, N. A. & Marshall, T. R. (1996). Behavioral and physiological antecedents of inhibited and uninhibited behavior. *Child Development*, 67, 523–540.

Calkins, S., Dedmon, S., Gill, K., Lomax, L. & Johnson, L. (2002). Frustration in infancy: Implications for emotion regulation, physiological processes, and temperament. *Infancy*, 3, 175–197.

Calvert, S., Mahler, B., Zehnder, S., Jenkins, A. & Lee, M. (2003). Gender differences in preadolescent children's online interactions: Symbolic modes of self-presentation and self-expression. *Applied Developmental Psychology*, 24, 627–644.

Campbell, A., Shirley, L., Heywood, C. & Crook, C. (2000). Infants' visual preference for sex-congruent babies, children, toys and activities: A longitudinal study. *British Journal of Developmental Psychology*, 18, 479–498.

Campbell M.A. (2005). Cyber-bullying: an old problem in a new guise? *Australian Journal of Guidance and Counselling*, 15, 68–76.

Campos, J. J., Hiatt, S., Ramsay, D., Henderson, C. & Svejda, M. (1978). The emergence of fear on the visual cliff. In M. Lewis & L. Rosenblaum (Eds), *The Origins of Affect* (149–182). New York: Plenum.

Capel, S., Zwozdiak-Myers, P. & Lawrence, J. (2004). Exchange of information about physical education to support the transition of pupils from primary and secondary school. *Educational Research*, 46 (3), 283–300.

Caplan, F., & Caplan, T. (1973). The Power of Play. New York: Doubleday.

Capute, A. J., Shapiro, B. K., Palmer, F. B., Ross, A. & Wachel, R. C. (1985). Normal gross motor development: The influences of race, sex and socioeconomic status. *Development Medicine & Child Neurology*, 27, 635–643.

Carey, S. (2002). The origin of concepts: continuing the conversation. In N. L. Stein, P. J. Bauer & M. Rabinowitz (Eds), *Representation, Memory and Development: Essays in Honour of Jean Mandler* (43–52). Mahwah, NJ: Erlbaum.

Carey, S. (2004). Bootstrapping and the origin of concepts. *Daedalus*, 133 (1), 59–69.

Carey, S., Diamond, R. & Woods, B. (1980). The development of face recognition – a maturational component. *Developmental Psychology*, 16, 257–269.

Carey, W. B. with Jablow, M. M. (2005). *Understanding your Child's Temperament*. New York: Macmillan, Simon & Schuster.

Carlson, V. J. & Harwood, R. L. (2003). Attachment, culture, and the caregiving system: The cultural patterning of everyday experiences among Anglo and Puerto Rican motherinfant pairs. *Infant Mental Health Journal*, 24, 53–73.

Carlson, E., Sampson, M. & Sroufe, A. (2003). Implications of attachment theory and research for developmental-behavioral pediatrics. *Journal of Developmental and Behavioral Pediatrics*, 24, 364–379.

Carlson, E., Sroufe, A. & Egeland, B. (2004). The construction of experience: A longitudinal study of representation and behavior. Child Development, 75, 66–83.

Carpenter, T. P., Ansell, E., Franke, M. L., Fennema, E. & Weisbeck, L. (1993). Models of problem solving: A study of kindergarten children's problem-solving processes. *Journal for Research in Mathematics Education*, 24, 428–441.

Carpenter, T. P., Hiebert, J. & Moser, J. M. (1981). Problem structure and first grade children's initial solution processes for simple addition and subtraction problems. *Journal for Research in Mathematics Education*, 12, 27–39.

Carpenter, T. P. & Moser, J. M. (1982). The development of addition and subtraction problem solving. In T. P. Carpenter, J. M. Moser & T. A. Romberg (Eds), *Addition and Subtraction: A Cognitive Perspective* (10–24). Hillsdale, NJ: Erlbaum.

Carr, S. B. & Coustan, D. R. (2006). Drugs, alcohol abuse and effects in pregnancy. In E. A. Reece & J. C. Hobbins (Eds), *Clinical Obstetrics: The Foetus and Mother* (88–94). Oxford: Blackwell.

Carroll, J. M. & Snowling, M. J. (2004). Language and phonological skills in children at high risk of reading difficulties. *Journal of Child Psychology and Psychiatry*, 45 (3), 631–640.

Carter, D. B. & Levy, G. D. (1988). Cognitive aspects of early sex-role development: The influence of gender schemas on preschoolers' memories and preferences for sex-typed toys and activities. *Child Development*, 59, 782–792.

Carver C.S., Scheier M.F. & Weintraub J.K. (1989). Assessing coping strategies: A theoretically based approach. *Journal of Personality and Social Psychology*, 56, 267–283.

Case, R. (1985). *Intellectual Development: Birth to Adulthood*. New York: Academic Press.

Case, R. (1992). Neo-Piagetian theories of child development. In R.J. Sternberg & C.A. Berg (Eds) *Intellectual Development* (161–196). New York: Cambridge University Press.

Case, R. (1998). The development of conceptual structures. In W. Damon (Series Ed.) & D. Kuhn & R.S. Siegler (Vol. Eds), *Handbook of Child Psychology: Vol. 2, Cognition, Perception, and Language* (5th Ed.) (745–764). New York: Wiley.

Casella, R. (2002). Where policy meets the pavement: Stages of public involvement in the prevention of school violence. *International Journal of Qualitative Studies in Education*, 15 (3), 349–372.

Cashon, C. H. & Cohen, L. B. (2000). Eight-month-old infants' perception of possible and impossible events. *Infancy*, 1, 429–446.

Caspers, K., Paradiso, S., Yuvuis, R., Troutman, B., Arndt, S. & Philibert, R. (2009). Association between the serotonin transporter promoter polymorphism (5-HTTLPR) and adult unresolved attachment. *Developmental Psychology*, 45, 64–76.

Caspi, A. (2000). The child is father of the man: Personality continuities from childhood to adulthood. *Journal of Personality and Social Psychology*, 78, 158–172.

Caspi, A., Harrington, H., Milne, B., Amell, J. W., Theodore, R. F. & Moffitt, T. E. (2003). Children's behavioural styles at age 3 are linked to their adult personality traits at 26. *Journal of Personality*, 71, 495–514.

Caspi, A. & Moffitt, T. E. (1991). Individual differences are accentuated during periods of social change: The sample case of girls at puberty. *Journal of Personality and Social Psychology*, 61, 157–168.

Caspi, A. & Moffitt, T. E. (2006). Gene-environment interactions in psychiatry: Joining forces with neuroscience. *Nature Reviews: Neuroscience*, 7, 583–590.

Caspi, A. & Silva, P. A. (1995). Temperamental qualities at age three predict personality traits in young adulthood: Longitudinal evidence from a birth cohort. *Child Development*, 66, 486–498.

Catherwood, D. (1993). The haptic processing of texture and shape by 7- to 9-month-old infants. *British Journal of Developmental Psychology*, 11, 299–306.

Catherwood, D. (1993). The robustness of infant haptic memory: Testing its capacity to withstand delay and haptic interference. *Child Development*, 64, 702–710.

Catherwood, D., Skoien, P., Green, V. & Holt, C. (1996). Assessing the primal moments in infant encoding of compound visual stimuli. *Infant Behavior and Development*, 19, 1–11.

Catherwood, D., Cramm, A. & Foster, H. (2003). Asymmetry in infant hemispheric readiness after exposure to a visual stimulus. *Developmental Science*, 6, 62–66.

Cattell, R. B. (1940). A culture-free intelligence test. I. *Journal of Educational Psychology*, 31 (3), 161–179.

Ceci, S. J. & Bruck, M. (1993). Suggestibility of the child witness: An historical review and synthesis. *Psychological Bulletin*, 113, 403–439.

Center for Disease Control and Prevention (2007). Surveillance summaries. *Morbid Mortal Weekly Report*, 56, 1–28.

Cernoch, J. M. & Porter, R.H. (1985). Recognition of maternal axillary odours by infants. *Child Development*, 56, 1593–1598.

Chabert, R., Guitton, M.J., Amram, D., Uziel, A., Pujol, R., Lallemant, J.G. and Puel, J.L. (2006). Early maturation of evoked otoacoustic emissions and medial olivocochlear reflex in preterm neonates. *Pediatric Research*, 59, 305–308.

Chae, S. S. C. (2003). Adaptation of a picture-type creativity test for pre-school children. *Language Testing*, 20 (2), 179–188.

Chatfield, T. (2010). Why playing in the virtual world has an awful lot to teach children. The Guardian, 10 January 2010. Retrieved 15 October 2010 from http://www.guardian.co.uk/technology/2010/jan/10/playing-in-thevirtual-world.

Chen, Z., Sanchez, R. P. & Campbell, T. (1997). From beyond to within their grasp: The rudiments of analogical problem-solving in 10- to 13-month-olds. *Developmental Psychology*, 33, 790–801.

Chisholm, K. (1998). A three-year follow-up of attachment and indiscriminate friendliness in children adopted from Romanian orphanages. *Child Development*, 69, 1092–1106.

Chisholm, K., Carter, M. C., Ames, E. W. & Morison, S. J. (1995). Attachment security and indiscriminately friendly behavior in children adopted from Romanian orphanages. *Development and Psychopathology*, 7, 283–294.

Chiu, C.-Y. P., Schmithorst, V. J., Brown, R. D., Holland, S. K. & Dunn, S. (2006). Making memories: A crosssectional investigation of episodic memory encoding in childhood using fMRI. *Developmental Neuropsychology*, 29 (2), 321–340.

Cho, S.C., Hwang,, J.W., Lyoo, E.K., Yoo, H.J., Kin, B.N. & Kim, J.W. (2008). Patterns of temperament and character in a clinical sample of Koren children with attention- deficit hyperactivity disorder. *Psychiatry and Clinical Neurosciences*, 62, 160–166.

Chugani, H. T., Phelps, M. E. & Johnson, J. C. (1987). Positron emission tomography study of human brain functional development. *Annals of Neurology*, 22, 487–497.

Cichetti, D. & Barnett, D. (1991). Attachment organization in maltreated preschoolers. *Development and Psychopathology*, 4, 397–411.

Cillissen, A. H. N. & Bellmore, A. D. (2004). Social skills and interpersonal perception in early and middle childhood. In P. K. Smith & C. H. Hart (Eds), *Blackwell Handbook of Childhood Social Development* (355–374). Malden, MA: Blackwell.

Cillessen, A. H. N. & Mayeux, L. (2004). From censure to reinforcement: Developmental changes in the association between aggression and social status. *Child Development*, 75, 147–163.

Cillessen, A. H. N., van I. Jzendoorn, H. W., van Lieshout, C. F. M. & Hartup, W. W. (1992). Heterogeneity among peer-rejected boys: Subtypes and stabilities. *Child Development*, 63, 893–905.

Claes, M., Lacourse, E., Bouchard, C. & Perucchini, P. (2003). Parental practices in late adolescence, a comparison of three countries: Canada, France and Italy. *Journal of Adolescence*, 26 (4), 387–399.

Claes, M., Lacourse, E., Ercolani, A.P., Pierro, A., Leone, L. & Presaghi, F. (2005). Parenting, peer orientation, drug use, and antisocial behavior in late adolescence: A crossnational study. *Journal of Youth and Adolescence*, 34 (5), 401–411.

Clark, A. H., Wyon, S. M. & Richards, M. P. M. (1969). Free-play in nursery school children. *Journal of Child Psychology and Psychiatry*, 10, 205–216.

Clark, M. L., Cheyne, J. A., Cunningham, C. E. & Siegel, L. S. (1988). Dyadic peer interaction and task orientation in Attention Deficit Disordered children. *Journal of Abnormal Child Psychology*, 16, 1–15

Clarke-Stewart, A. (1988). The "effects" of infant day care reconsidered: Risks for parents, children and researchers. *Early Childhood Research Quarterly*, 3, 292–318.

Clarke-Stewart, K. A., Goosens, F. A. & Allhusen, V. D. (2001). Measuring infant mother attachment: Is the Strange Situation enough? *Social Development*, 10, 143–69.

Clarkson, T. W., Magos, L. & Myers, G. J. (2003). The toxicology of mercury – current exposures and clinical manifestations. *New England Journal of Medicine*, 349, 1731–1737.

Clements, W.A. & Perner, J. (1994). Implicit understanding of belief. *Cognitive Development*, 9, 377–396.

Coie, J. D., Dodge, K. A. & Coppotelli, H. (1983). Dimensions and types of social status: A cross-age perspective. *Developmental Psychology*, 18, 557–570.

Cole, P.M., Barrett, K.C. & Zahn-Waxler, C. (1992). Emotion displays in two-year-olds during mishaps. *Child Development*, 63 (2), 314–324.

Collaer, M. L. & Hines, M. (1995). Human behavioral sex differences: A role for gonadal hormones during early development? *Psychological Bulletin*, 118, 55–107.

Collishaw, S., Maughan, B., Goodman, R. & Pickles, A. (2004). Time trends in adolescent mental health. *Journal of Child Psychology and Psychiatry*, 45 (8), 1350–1362.

Colombo, J. (2001). The development of visual attention in infancy. *Annual Review of Psychology*, 52, 337–367.

Colwell, J. & Payne, J. (2000). Negative correlates of computer game play in adolescents. *British Journal of Psychology*, 91, 295–310.

Condry, J. & Condry, S. (1976). Sex differences: A study in the eye of the beholder. *Child Development*, 47, 812–819.

Conners, C. K. (1994). The Conners rating scales: Use in clinical assessment, treatment planning and research. In M. Maruish (Ed.), *Use of Psychological Testing for Treatment Planning and Outcome Assessment* (467–497) Hillsdale, NJ: Erlbaum.

Conners, C. K., March, J. S., Frances, A., Wells, K. C. & Ross, R. (2001). Treatment of attention deficit hyperactivity disorder: Expert consensus guidelines. *Journal of Attention Disorders*, 4, 7–128.

Conway, M. (2007). 10,000 *Autobiographical memories: Results of the BBC's National Memory Survey*. Keynote Address to the Annual Conference of the British Psychological Society, York, 21–23 March.

Cook, E. H., Vandenbergh, D. J., Stein, M. A., Cox, N. J., Yan, S., Krasowski, M. D., Uhl, G. R. & Leventhal, B. L. (1995). Molecular genetic analysis of the dopamine transporter in attention-deficit/hyperactivity disorder (ADHD). *American Journal of Human Genetics*, 57 (4), A189.

Cooley, C. H. (1902). *Human Nature and the Social Order*. New York: Scribner.

Copeland, W., Landry, K., Stanger, C. & Hudziak, J. J. (2004). Multi-informant assessment of temperament in children with externalizing behavior problems. *Journal of Clinical Child and Adolescent Psychology*, 33, 547–556.

Corbett, J. A. (1979). Psychiatric morbidity and mental retardation. In F. E. James and R. P. Smith (Eds), *Psychiatric Illness and Mental Handicap* (11–25). London: Gaskell Press.

Corkum, P., Moldofsky, H., Hogg-Johnson, S., Humphries, T. & Tannock, R. (1999). Sleep problems in children with attention-deficit/hyperactivity disorder: Impact of subtype, comorbidity, and stimulant medication. *Journal of the American Academy of Child and Adolescent Psychiatry*, 38, 1285–1293.

Corpus, J. H. & Lepper, M. R. (2007). The effects of person versus performance praise on children's motivation: Gender and age as moderating factors. *Educational Psychology*, 27 (4), 487–508.

Correa, J., Nunes, T. & Bryant, P. (1998). Young children's understanding of division: The relationship between division terms in a noncomputational task. *Journal of Educational Psychology*, 90, 321–329.

Corsaro, W. (1985). *Friendship and Peer Culture in the Early Years*. Norwood, NJ: Ablex.

Costa, P. T. & McCrae, R. R. (1997). Longitudinal stability of adult personality. In R. Hogan, J. Johnson & S. Briggs (Eds), *Handbook of Personality Psychology* (269–290). San Diego, CA: Academic Press.

Cottingham, M. (2005). Developing spirituality through the use of literature in history education. *International Journal of Children's Spirituality*, 10 (1), 45–60.

Courage, M. L., Reynolds, G. D. & Richards, J. E. (2006). Infants' attention to patterned stimuli: Developmental change from 3 to 12 months of age. *Child Development*, 77, 680–695.

Courcier, I. (2007). Teachers' perceptions of personalised learning. *Evaluation & Research in Education*, 20 (2), 59–80.

Cowan, N. (1999). An embedded-processes model of working memory. In A. Miyake & P. Shah (Eds), *Models of Working Memory: Mechanisms of Active Maintenance and Executive Control* (62–101). Cambridge: Cambridge University Press.

Cowan, R. & Daniels, H. (1989). Children's use of counting and guidelines in judging relative number. *British Journal of Educational Psychology*, 59, 200–210.

Cowie, H. (2000). Bystanding or standing by: Gender issues in coping with bullying. *Aggressive Behavior*, 26, 85–97.

Cowie, H., & Sharp, S. (1994). How to tackle bullying through the curriculum. In S. Sharp & P.K. Smith, (Eds), *Tackling Bullying in Your School: A Practical Handbook for Teachers* (41–78). London: Routledge.

Cowie, H. & Wallace, P. (2000). *Peer Support in Action: From Bystanding to Standing By*. London: Sage.

Cowie, H., Naylor, P., Rivers, I., Smith, P.K. & Pereira, B. (2002). Measuring workplace bullying. *Aggression and Violent Behaviour*, 7, 33–51.

Cox, M. J., Owen, M. T., Henderson, V. K. & Margand, N. A. (1992). Prediction of infant-father and infant-mother attachment. *Developmental Psychology*, 28, 474–483.

Craig, C. M. & Lee, D. N. (1999). Neonatal control of sucking pressure: Evidence for an intrinsic tau guide. *Experimental Brain Research*, 124, 371–382.

Crain, W. (2004). *Theories of Development* (5th Ed.). Englewood Cliffs, NJ: Prentice Hall.

Crain, W. (2005). *Theories of Development: Concepts and Applications (5th Ed.)*. Englewood Cliffs, NJ: Pearson Prentice Hall.

Cramer, K., Post, T. & Currier, S. (1993). Learning and teaching ratio and proportion: research implications. In D. T. Owens (Ed.), *Research Ideas for the Classroom: Middle Grades Mathematics* (159–178). New York: Macmillan.

Creasey, G. L., Jarvis, P. A. & Berk, L. E. (1998). Play and social competence. In O. N. Saracho & B. Spodek (Eds), *Multiple Perspectives on Play in Early Childhood Education* (116–143). Albany, NY: State University of New York Press.

Crick, N.R., Casas, J.F. & Mosher, M. (1997). Relational and overt aggression in preschool. *Developmental Psychology*, 33, 589–600.

Crick, N. R., Casas, J. F. & Nelson, D. A. (2002). Toward a more comprehensive understanding of peer maltreatment: Studies of relational victimization. *Current Directions in Psychological Science*, 11, 98–101.

Crick, N.R. & Dodge, K.A. (1994). A review and reformulation of social-information processing mechanisms in children's social adjustment. *Psychological Bulletin*, 115, 74–101.

Crick, N.R. & Dodge, K.A. (1999). 'Superiority' is in the eye of the beholder: A comment on Sutton, Smith and Swettenham. *Social Development*, 8, 128–131.

Crick, N.R. & Grotepeter, J.K. (1995). Relational aggression: Gender and social psychological adjustment. *Child Development*, 66, 710–722.

Crick, N.R., Grotepeter, J.K. & Bigbee, M.A. (2002). Relationally and physically aggressive chidlren's intent attributions and feelings of distress for relational and instrumental peer provocations. *Child Development*, 73, 1134–1142.

Crockenberg, S. (2003). Rescuing the baby from the bathwater: How gender and temperament (may) influence how child care affects child development. *Child Development*, 74, 1034–1038.

Crook, C. (1987). Taste and olfaction. In P. Salapatek & L. Cohen (Eds), *Handbook of Infant Perception: Vol.1: From Sensation to Perception* (237–264). New York: Academic Press.

Crooks T. (2002). Educational assessment in New Zealand schools. *Assessment in Education: Principles, Policy & Practice*, 9 (2), 237–253.

Csibra, G. & Johnson, M. H. (2007). Investigating even-trelated oscillations in infancy. In M. de Haan (Ed.), *Infant EEG and Event-related Potentials* (289–304). Hove: Psychology Press.

Csibra, G., Davis, G., Spratling, M. W. & Johnson, M. H. (2000). Gamma oscillations and object processing in the infant brain. *Science*, 290, 1582–1585.

Cunningham, P. (2006). Early years teachers and the influence of Piaget: Evidence from oral history. *Early Years: An International Journal of Research and Development*, 26 (1), 5–16.

Currie, C., Roberts, C., Morgan, A., Smith, R., Settertobulte, W., Sandal, O. & Barnekow Rasmussen, V. (Eds) (2004) *Young People's Health in Context. Health Behaviour in School-Aged Children (HBSC) study: International Report from the 2001/2002 Survey*. Copenhagen: World Health Organisation. Retrieved 29 April 2009 from http://www.hbsc.org/downloads/IntReport04/HBSCFull-Report0102.pdf.

Currie, D., Kelly, D. & Pomerantz, S. (2006). 'The geeks shall inherit the earth': Girls' agency, subjectivity and empowerment. *Journal of Youth Studies*, 9 (4), 419–436.

Daley, D. (2006). Attention Deficit Hyperactivity Disorder: A review of the essential facts. *Child Care Health and Development*, 32, 193–204.

Daley, D. & Birchwood, J. (2010). ADHD and academic performance: Why does ADHD impact on academic performance and what can be done to support ADHD children in the classroom? *Child Care Health and Development*, 26, 455–464.

Daley, D. & Thompson, M. (2007). Parent training for ADHD in preschool children. *Advances in ADHD*, 2, 11–16.

Danckaerts, M.E., Brensinger, C.M., Ralph, L.N., Seward, D.A., Bilker, W.B. & Siegel, S.J. (2010). Psychiatric health care provider attitudes towards implantable medication. *Psychiatry Research*, 15, (177), 167–171.

Dannemiller, J. L. & Stephens, B. R. (1988). A critical test of infant pattern preference models. *Child Development*, 59, 210–216.

Daurignac, E., Houdé, O. & Jouvent, R. (2006). Negative priming in a numerical Piaget-like task as evidenced by ERP. Journal of Cognitive Neuroscience, 18, 730–736. de Schonen, S. & Mathivet, E. (1990). Hemispheric asymmetry in a face discrimination tasks in infants. *Child Development*, 61, 1192–1205.

Dave, S., Nazareth, I., Senior, R. & Sherr, L. (2008). A comparison of father and mother report of child behaviour on the Strengths and Difficulties Questionnaire. *Child Psychiatry & Human Development*, 39, 399–413.

Davidson, R. J. (1994). Asymmetric brain function, affective style and psychopathology: The role of early experience and plasticity. *Development & Psychopathology*, 6, 741–758.

Davies, D. R. (1986). Children's performance as a function of sex-typed labels. *British Journal of Social Psychology*, 25, 173–175.

Deary, I. J., Whalley, L. J., Lemmon, H., Crawford, J. R. & Starr, J. M. (2000). The stability of individual differences in mental ability from childhood to old age: Follow-up of the 1932 Scottish Mental Survey. *Intelligence*, 28, 357–375.

Deary, I. J., Leaper, S. A., Murray, A. D., Staff, R. T. & Whalley, L. J. (2003). Cerebral white matter abnormalities and lifetime cognitive change: A 67-year follow-up of the Scottish Mental Survey of 1932. *Psychology and Ageing*, 18, 140–148.

Deary, I. J., Whiteman, M. C., Starr, J. M., Whalley, L. J. & Fox, H. C. (2004). The impact of childhood intelligence on later life: Following up the Scottish Mental Surveys of 1932 and 1947. *Journal of Personality and Social Psychology*, 86 (1), 130–147.

Deater-Deckard, K., Pike, A., Petrill, S. A., Cutting, A. L., Huges, C. & O'Connor, T. G. (2001). Nonshared environmental processes in social-emotional development: An observational study of identical twin differences in the preschool period. *Developmental Science*, 4, F1–F6.

DeCasper, A. J. & Fifer, W. P. (1980). Of human bonding: Newborns prefer their mothers' voices. *Science*, 208, 1174–1176.

DeCasper, A. J. & Spence, M. J. (1986). Prenatal maternal speech influences newborns' perceptions of speech sounds. *Infant Behavior and Development*, 9, 133–150.

DeCasper, A. & Lecanuet, J.P., Busnel, M.C., Granier-Deferre, C. & Maugeais, R. (1994). Foetal reactions to recurrent maternal speech. *Infant Behaviour and Development*, 17, 159–164.

De Haan, M. (2008). Brain function. *Encyclopaedia of Infant and Early Development*, 225–236.

De Haan, M. & Johnson, M. H. (2003). *The Cognitive Neuroscience of Development*. London: Psychology Press.

Dehaene, S. (1997). *The Number Sense*. London: Penguin.

Dehaene, S. (1992). Varieties of numerical abilities. *Cognition*, 44, 1–42.

Dehaene, S., DehaeneLambertz, G. & Cohen, L. (1998). Abstract representations of numbers in the animal and human brain. *Trends in Neurosciences*, 21, 355–361.

Dehue, F., Bolman, C. & Völlink, T. (2008). Cyberbullying: Youngsters' experiences and parental perception. *CyberPsychology & Behaviour*, 11, 217–223.

Deisinger, J. A. (2008). Issues pertaining to siblings of individuals with autism spectrum disorders. In A. Rotatori (Ed.), *Autism and Developmental Disabilities: Current Practices and Issues (Advances in Special Education, Volume 18)* (135–155). Bingley: Emerald Group Publishing Limited.

Dejin-Karlsson, E., Hanson, B.S., Estergren, P.O., Sjoeberg, N.-O & Marsal, K. (1998). Does passive smoking in early pregnancy increase the risk of small-for-gestational-age infants? *American Journal of Public Health*, 88, 1523–1527.

Deloache, J. S. & Brown, A. L. (1983). Very young children's memory for the location of objects in a large-scale environment. *Child Development*, 54, 888–897.

Denham, S. A., von Salish, M., Olthof, T., Kochanoff, A. & Caverly, S. (2004). Emotional and social development in childhood. In P. K. Smith & C. H. Hart (Eds), Blackwell *Handbook of Childhood Social Development* (307–328). Malden, MA: Blackwell.

Dennett, D. (1978). *Brainstorms: Philosophical Essays on Mind and Psychology*. Cambridge, MA: Bradford Books/MIT Press.

Department for Children, Schools and Families (2007). *Safe to Learn: Embedding Antibullying Work in Schools*. Nottingham: DCSF Publications.

Department for Education and Employment (2000). *Bullying: Don't Suffer in Silence*. London: The Stationary Office.

Department of Health (2007). www.dh.gov.uk. *Developing a speech and language strategy for the community: Thinking beyond Sure Start to the challenge of the mainstream.*

Derrington, C. (2005). Perceptions of behaviour and patterns of exclusion: Gypsy traveller students in English secondary schools. *Journal of Research in Special Educational Needs*, 5 (2), 55–61.

DeRosier, M. E. (2007). Peer-rejected and bullied children: A safe schools initiative for elementary school students. In J. E. Zins, M. J. Elias & C. A. Maher (Eds), *Bullying, Victimization, and Peer Harassment* (257–276). New York: Haworth.

De Schipper, J.C., Tavecchio, L.W.C., Van Ijzendoorn, M.H., & Van Zeijl, J. (2004). Goodness-of-fit in center day care: relations of temperament, stability and quality of care with the child's problem behavior and well-being in day care. *Early Childhood Research Quarterly*, 19, 257–272.

deVilliers, J.G. & deVilliers, P.A. (2000). Linguistic determinism and the understanding of false beliefs. Children's reasoning and the mind. In P. Mitchell & K.J. Riggs (Eds). *Children's Reasoning and the Mind* (191–228). Hove: Psychology Press/Taylor & Francis UK.

Devine, P. G. (1989). Stereotypes and prejudice: Their automatic and controlled components. *Journal of Personality and Social Psychology*, 56 (1), 5–18.

Devís-Devís, J. (1997). Policy, practice, and reconversion in Spanish educational reform: Teaching and teacher education in physical education. *The Curriculum Journal*, 8 (2), 213–230.

de Wolff, M. S. & van IJzendoorn, M. H. (1997). Sensitivity and attachment: A meta-analysis on parental antecedents of infant attachment. *Child Development*, 68, 571–591.

DfES. (2006). *Disapplication of the National Curriculum (Revised) Guidance*. London: DfES.

Diamantopoulou, S., Rydell, A., Thorell, L. B. & Bohlin, G. (2007). Impact of executive functioning and symptoms of attention deficit hyperactivity disorder on children's peer relations and school performance. *Developmental Neuropsychology*, 32 (1), 521–542.

Diamond, A. (2009a). The interplay of biology and the environment broadly defined. *Developmental Psychology*, 45, 1–8.

Diamond, A. (2009b). All or none hypothesis: A global deficit mode that characterizes the brain and mind. *Developmental Psychology*, 45, 130–138.

Diamond, A., Cruttenden, L. & Neiderman, D. (1994). AB with multiple wells: 1: Why are multiple wells sometimes easier that two wells? Memory or memory+ inhibition. *Developmental Psychology*, 30, 192–205.

Diamond, A., Prevor, M. B., Callender, G. & Druin, D.P. (1997). Prefrontal cortex cognitive deficits in children treated early and continuously for PKU. *Monographs of the Society for Research in Child Development*, 62, 1–205.

Diamond, M. (1982). Sexual identity, monozygotic twins reared in discordant sex roles and a BBC follow-up. *Archives of Sexual Behavior*, 11, 181–186.

Diamond, M. & Sigmundson, H. K. (1997). Sex reassignment at birth. *Pediatric and Adolescent Medicine*, 151, 298–304.

Dinn, W. M., Robbins, N. C. & Harris, C. L. (2001). Adult attention deficit/hyperactivity disorder: Neuropsychological correlates and clinical presentation. *Brain Cognition*, 46, 114–121.

Dion, K. & Berscheid, E. (1974). Physical attractiveness and peer perception among children. *Sociometry*, 37, 1–12.

DiScala, C., Lescohier, I., Barthel, M & Li, G.H. (1998). Injuries to children with attention deficit hyperactivity disorder. *Paediatrics*, 6, 1415–1421.

Dobson, V. & Teller, D. Y. (1978). Assessment of visual acuity in infants. In J. C. Armington, J. Krauskopf & B. R. Wooten (Eds), *Visual Psychophysics and Physiology* (385–396). New York: Academic Press.

Dockett, S. (1998). Constructing understandings through play in the early years. *International Journal of Early Years Education*, 6, 105–106.

Dodge, K. A., Coie, J. D., Pettit, G. S. & Price, J. M. (1990). Peer status and aggression in boys groups: Developmental and contextual analysis. *Child Development*, 61, 1289–1309.

Doherty-Sneddon, G. (2008). The great baby signing debate. *The Psychologist*, 21 (4), 300–303.

Dori, Y. & Herscovitz, O. (2005). Case-based long-term professional development of science teachers. *International Journal of Science Education*, 27 (12), 1413–1446.

Doymus, K. (2008). Teaching chemical equilibrium with the jigsaw technique. *Research in Science Education*, 38 (2), 249–260.

Dozier, M., Stovall, K.C., Albus, K.E. & Bates, B. (2001). Attachment for infants in foster care: The role of caregiver state of mind. *Child Development*, 72, 1467–1477.

Dromi, E. (1987). *Early Lexical Development*. Cambridge: Cambridge University Press.

Duff, F. J., Fieldsend, E., Bowyer-Crane, C., Hulme, C., Smith, G., Gibbs, S. & Snowling, M. J. (2008). Reading with vocabulary intervention: Evaluation of an instruction for children with poor response to reading intervention. *Journal of Research in Reading*, 31 (3) 319–336.

Duncan-Andrade, J. (2007). Gangstas, Wankstas, and Ridas: Defining, developing, and supporting effective teachers in urban schools. *International Journal of Qualitative Studies in Education*, 20 (6), 617–638.

Dunn, J. & Kendrick, C. (1982). *Siblings: Love, Envy and Understanding*. Cambridge, MA: Harvard University Press.

Dunn, L., & Herwig, J. E. (1992). Play behaviors and convergent and divergent thinking skills of young children attending full-day preschool. *Child Study Journal*, 22 (1), 23–38.

Dunphy, E. (2009). Early childhood mathematics teaching: challenges, difficulties and priorities of teachers of young children in primary schools in Ireland. International *Journal of Early Years Education*, 17 (1), 3–16.

Dunsmore, J., Noguchi, R., Garner, P., Casey, E. & Bhullar, N. (2008). Gender-specific linkages of affective social competence with peer relations in preschool children. *Early Education and Development*, 19, 211–237.

DuPaul, G. J., McGoey, K. E., Eckert, T. L. & Vanbrakle, J. (2001). Preschool children with Attention-Deficit/Hyperactivity Disorder: Impairments in behavioural, social, and school functioning. *Journal of the American Academy of Child and Adolescent Psychiatry*, 40, 508–522.

Durkin, K. (1985). Television and sex-role acquisition: Ill effects. *British Journal of Social Psychology*, 24, 191–210.

East Sussex County Council (2008). *Safer Schools Survey (Second Phase November 2008)*. East Sussex County Council.

Eckes, T., Trautner, H.M. & Behrendt, R. (2005). Gender subgroups and intergroup perception: Adolescents' views of own-gender and other-gender groups. *Journal of Social Psychology*, 145 (1), 85–111.

Eckert, M. A., Lombardino, L. J. & Leonard, C. M. (2001). Planar asymmetry tips the phonological playground and environment raises the bar. *Child Development*, 72 (4), 988–1002.

Edelson, D. C. (2001). Learning-for-use: A framework for the design of technology-supported inquiry activities. *Journal of Research in Science Teaching*, 38 (3), 355–385.

Edgardh, K. (2002). Sexual behaviour and early coitarche in a national sample of 17-year-old Swedish boys. *Acta Paediatrica*, 91, 985–991.

Eimas, P. D. (1975). Auditory and phonemic coding of the cues for speech: Discrimination of the [r-l] distinction by young infants. *Perception and Psychophysics*, 18, 341–347.

Eimas, P. D., Siqueland, E. R., Jusczyk, P.W. & Vigorito, J. (1971). Speech perception in infants. *Science*, 171, 303–306.

Eisenberg, L. (1999). Experience, brain and behaviour: The impact of a head start. *Pediatrics*, 103, 1031–1035.

Eisenberg, N., Fabes, R. A., Murphy, B., Maszk, P., Smith, M. & Karbon, M. (1995). The role of emotionality, regulation, and social functioning: A longitudinal study. *Child Development*, 66, 1360–1384.

Eisenberger, N. (2003). Does rejection hurt? An fMRI study of social exclusion. *Science*, 302, 290–292.

Eke, R. & Lee, J. (2004). Pace and differentiation in the Literacy Hour: Some outcomes of an analysis of transcripts. *The Curriculum Journal*, 15 (3), 219–231.

Eley, T.C., Lichtenstein, P. & Stevenson, J. (1999). Sex differences in the etiology of aggressive and nonaggressive anti-social behaviour: Results from two twin studies. *Child Development*, 70, 155–168.

Elias, C. L. & Berk, L. E. (2002). Self-regulation in young children: Is there a role for sociodramatic play? *Early Childhood Research Quarterly*, 17, 1–17.

Elias, M. J. & Schwab, Y. (2006). From compliance to responsibility: Social and emotional learning and classroom management. In C. Evertson & C. S. Weinstein (Eds), *Handbook for Classroom Management: Research, Practice, and Contemporary Issues* (309–341). Mahwah, NJ: Erlbaum.

Elicker, J., Englund, M. & Sroufe, L. A. (1992). Predicting peer competence and peer relationships in childhood from early parent-child relationships. In R. D. Parke & G. W. Ladd (Eds), *Family-peer Relationships: Modes of Linkage* (77–106). Hillsdale, NJ: Erlbaum.

Elkind, D. (1967). Egocentrism in adolescence. *Child Development*, 38 (4), 1025–1034.

Ellis, J. (1996). Prospective memory or the realisation of delayed intentions: A conceptual framework for research. In M. Brandimonte, G.O. Einstein & M.A McDaniel (Eds), *Prospective Memory: Theory and Applications* (1–22). Hillsdale, NJ: Erlbaum.

Ellis, J. & Kvavilashvili, L. (2000). Prospective memory in 2000: Past, present and future directions. *Applied Cognitive Psychology*, 14, S1–S9.

Emde, R. N., Gaensbauer, T. G. & Harmon, R. J. (1976). Emotional expression in infancy: A biobehavioural study. *Psychological Issues: Monograph Series*, 10 (37).

Emde, R. N., Plomin, R., Robinson, J., Corley, R., De-Fries, J., Fulker, D. W., Reznick, J. S., Campos, J., Kagan, J. & Zahn-Waxler, C. (1992). Temperament, emotion, and cognition at fourteen months: The MacArthur longitudinal twin study. *Child Development*, 63, 1437–1455.

Emmerich, W., Goldman, K. S., Kirsh, B. & Sharabany, R. (1977). Evidence for a transitional phase in the development of gender constancy. *Child Development*, 48, 930–936.

Emory, E. K., Emory, U. & Toomey, Kay A. (1988). Environmental stimulation and human foetal responsivity in late pregnancy. In W. P. Smotherman, & S. R. Robinson (Eds), *Behavior of the Foetus* (141–161). Caldwell, NJ: Telford Press.

Epstein, J. L. (1989). The selection of friends: Changes across the grades and in different school environments. In T. J. Berndt & G. W. Ladd (Eds), *Peer Relationships in Child Development* (158–187). New York: Wiley.

Erikson, E.H. (1950). *Childhood and Society*. New York: Norton.

Erikson, E.H. (1963). *Childhood and Society* (2nd Ed.). New York: Norton.

Erikson, E.H. (1968). *Identity, Youth and Crisis*. New York: Norton.

Ericsson, K.A., Krampe, R. Th. & Tesch-Römer, C. (1993). The role of deliberate practice in the acquisition of expert performance. *Psychological Review*, 100, 363–406.

Ericsson, K.A., Nandagopal, K. & Roring, R.W. (2005). Giftedness viewed from the expert performance perspective. *Journal for the Education of the Gifted*, 28 (3), 287–311.

Erikson, P. S., Perfileva, E., Bjork-Erikson T., Alborn, A., Nordborg, C., Peterson, D. & Gage, F. (1998). Neurogenesis in the adult hippocampus. *Nature Medicine*, 4, 1313–1317.

Erzar, T. & Erzar, K. K. (2008). 'If I commit to you, I betray my parents': some negative consequences of the intergenerational cycle of insecure attachment for young adult romantic relationships. *Sexual & Relationship Therapy*, 23(1), 25-35.

Esch, B. E. & Carr, J. E. (2005). Secretin as a treatment for autism: A review of the evidence. *Journal of Autism and Developmental Disorders*, 34 (5), 543–556.

Eysenck, H. J. (1981). *A Model for Personality*. Berlin: Springer.

Fagan, J. F. (1970). Memory in the infant. *Journal of Experimental Child Psychology*, 9, 217–226.

Fagan, J. F. (1973). Infants' delayed recognition memory and forgetting. *Journal of Experimental Child Psychology*, 14, 453–476.

Fagot, B. I. (1977). Consequences of moderate cross-gender behavior in preschool children. *Child Development*, 48, 902–907.

Fagot, B. I. (1978). The influence of sex of child on parental reactions to toddler children. *Child Development*, 49, 459–465.

Fagot, B. I. (1985). Beyond the reinforcement principle: Another step toward understanding sex role development. *Developmental Psychology*, 21, 1097–1104.

Fagot, B. I. & Hagan, R. (1991). Observations of parent reactions to sex-stereotyped behaviors: Age and sex effects. *Child Development*, 62, 617–628.

Fagot, B. I. & Leinbach, M. D. (1993). Gender-role development in young children: From discrimination to labelling. *Developmental Review*, 13, 205–224.

Fagot, B. I., Leinbach, M. D. & O'Boyle, C. (1992). Gender labelling, gender stereotyping, and parenting behaviors. *Developmental Psychology*, 28, 225–230.

Fantuzzo, J., Coolahan, K. & Mendez, J. (1998). Contextually relevant validation of peer play constructs with African American Head Start children: Penn Interactive Play Scale. *Early Childhood Research Quarterly*, 13, 411–431.

Fantz, R. L. (1956). A method for studying early visual development. *Perceptual and Motor Skills*, 6, 13–15.

Fantz, R. L. (1964). Visual experience in infants: Decreased attention to familiar patterns relative to novel ones. *Science*, 146, 668–670.

Faraone, S. V. (2000). Attention deficit hyperactivity disorder in adults: Implications for theories of diagnosis. *Current Directions in Psychological Science*, 9, 33–36.

Faraone, S. V., Sergeant, J., Gillberg, C. & Biederman. (2003). The worldwide prevalence of ADHD: Is it an American condition? *World Psychiatry*, 2 (2), 104–113.

Farrington, D. P. (1993). Understanding and preventing bullying. In M. Tonry & N. Morris (Eds), Crime and Justice: *An Annual Review of Research*, 17 (381–458). Chicago, IL: University of Chicago Press.

Fatimilehin, I.A. (1999). Of jewel heritage: Racial socialization and racial identity attitudes amongst adolescents of mixed African-Caribbean/White parentage. *Journal of Adolescence*, 22 (3), 303–318.

Fearon, R.M., Van Ijzendoorn, M.H., Fonagy, P., Bakermans-Kranenburg, M.J., Schuengel, C. & Bokhorst, C.L. (2006). In search of shared and nonshared environmental factors in security of attachment: A behavior-genetic study of the association between sensitivity and attachment security. *Developmental Psychology*, 42 1026–1040.

Feeney, J.A. & Noller, P. (1996). *Adult Attachment*. Thousand Oaks, CA: Sage.

Feng, Y. & Walsh, C. A. (2001). Protein-protein interactions, cytoskeletal regulation and neuronal migration. *Nature Reviews Neuroscience*, 2, 408–416

Fenson, L., Dale, P., Reznick, J. S., Thal, D., Bates, E., Hartung, J. P., Pethick, S. & Reilly, J. S. (1993). *Macarthur Communicative Development Inventories: User's Guide and Technical Manual*. San Diego, CA: Singular Publishing.

Fenson, L., Dale, P.S., Resnick, J.S., Bates, E., Thale, D.J. & Pethick, S.J. (1994). Variability in early communicative development. *Monographs of the Society for Research in Child Development*, 59 (5), 174–179.

Ferrier, S., Dunham, P. & Dunham, F. (2000). The confused robot: Two-year-olds' responses to breakdowns in conversation. *Social Development*, 9 (3) 337–347.

Field, T. M., Woodson, R. W., Cohen, D., Greenberg, R., Garcia, R. & Collins, K. (1983). Discrimination and imitation of facial expressions by term and preterm neonates. *Infant Behavior and Development*, 6, 485–489.

Field, T. M., Cohen, D., Garcia, R. & Greenberg, R. (1984). Mother-stranger face discrimination by the newborn. *Infant Behavior and Development*, 7, 19–25.

Fifer, W., Monk, C. & Grose-Fifer, J (2001). Prenatal development and risk. In G. Bremner & A. Fogel (Eds), *Blackwell Handbook of Infant Development* (505–542). Oxford: Blackwell.

Fight Crime Invest in Kids (July, 2006). *Cyber Bully: Preteen*. Princeton, NJ: Opinion Research Corporation. Retrieved October 14, 2010 from http://www.fightcrime. org/cyberbullying/cyberbullyingpreteen.pdf.

Filloy, E., & Rojano, T. (1989). Solving equations: The transition from arithmetic to algebra. *For the Learning of Mathematics*, 9, 19–25.

Finlay, D. & Ivinskis, A. (1984). Cardiac and visual responses to moving stimuli presented either successively or simultaneously to the central and peripheral visual fields in 4-month-old infants. *Developmental Psychology*, 20, 29–36.

Fischer, K.W. and Bidell, T.R. (2006). Dynamic development of action and thought. In R.M. Lerner (Ed.), *Handbook of Child Psychology. Vol 1: Theoretical Models of Human Development* (6th Ed.) (313–399). New York:Wiley.

Fischer, M., Barkley, R. A., Fletcher, K. E. & Smallish, L. (1993). The adolescent outcome of hyperactive children: predictors of psychiatric, academic, social, and emotional adjustment. *Journal of the American Academy of Child and Adolescent Psychiatry*, 32, 324–332.

Fitzgerald, D. & White, K. (2003). Linking children's social worlds: Perspective-taking in parent-child and peer contexts. *Social Behaviour and Personality*, 31, 509–522.

Flanagan, C. (1999). *Early Socialisation: Sociability and Attachment*. London: Routledge.

Flavell, J. H., Miller, P. H. & Miller, S. A. (2002). *Cognitive Development*. Upper Saddle River, N.J: Prentice Hall.

Flouri, E. & Buchanan, A. (2002). What predicts good relationships with parents in adolescence and partners in adult life: Findings from the 1958 British birth cohort. *Journal of Family Psychology*, 16 (2), 186–198.

Flouri, E. & Buchanan, A. (2003). The role of mother involvement and father involvement in adolescent bullying behavior. *Journal of Interpersonal Violence*, 18 (6), 634–644.

Flynn, N. (2007). Good practice for pupils learning English as an additional language: Lessons from effective literacy teachers in inner-city primary schools. *Journal of Early Childhood Literacy*, 7 (2), 177–198.

Foley, M., McClowry, S. G. & Castellanos, F. (2008). The relationship between Attention Deficit Hyperactivity Disorder and child temperament. *Journal of Applied Development Psychology*, 29, 157–169.

Fombonne, E. (1999). The epidemiology of autism: A review. *Psychological Medicine*, 29, 769–786.

Fombonne E. (2001). Is there an epidemic of autism? *Pediatrics*, 109, 411–412.

Fombonne, E. (2009). Epidemiology of pervasive developmental disorders. *Pediatric Research*, 65 (6), 591–598.

Fombonne, E. & Cook, E. H. (2003). MMR and autistic enterocolitis: Consistent epidemiological failure to find an association. *Molecular Psychiatry*, 8, 133–134.

Fonzi, A., Schneider, B. H., Tani, F. & Tomada, G. (1997). Predicting children's friendship status from their dyadic interaction in structured situations of potential conflict. *Child Development*, 68, 496–506.

Forman, E. A. & McPhail, J. (1993). Vygotskian perspective on children's collaborative problem-solving activities. In E. A. Forman, N. Minick & C.A. Stone (Eds), *Contexts for Learning* (323–347). New York: Cambridge University Press.

Fox, N., Henderson, H., Rubin, K., Calkins, S. & Schmidt, L. (2001). Continuity and discontinuity of behavioral inhibition and exuberance: Psychophysiological and behavioral influences across the first four years of life. *Child Development*, 72, 1–21.

Franklin, A., Catherwood, D., Alvarez, J. & Axelson, E. (2010) Hemispheric asymmetries in categorial perception of orientation in infants and adults. *Neuropsychologia*, 48, 2648–2657.

Franklin, A. & Davies, I. R. L. (2004). New evidence for infant colour categories. *British Journal of Developmental Psychology*, 22, 349–377.

Franklin, A., Drivonikou, G. V., Bevis, L., Davies, I. R. L., Kay, P. & Regier, T. (2008). Categorical perception of colour is lateralized to the right hemisphere in infants, but to the left hemisphere in adults. *Proceedings of the National Academy of Sciences*, USA, 105, 3221–3225.

Freeman, N.H., Lewis, C. & Doherty, M. (1991). Preschoolers' grasp of a desire for knowledge in falsebelief reasoning: Practical intelligence and verbal report. *British Journal of Developmental Psychology*, 9, 139–157.

Freeman, N. H., Antonuccia, C. & Lewis, C. (2000). Representation of the cardinality principle: Early conception of error in a counterfactual test. *Cognition*, 74, 71–89.

Freud, S. (1949). *An Outline of Psychoanalysis*. New York: Norton. (Translated by J. Stratchey; originally published, 1940).

Freud, S. (1995[1920]). Beyond the pleasure principle. In J. Strachey (Ed.), *The Standard Edition of the Complete Psychological Works of Sigmund Freud*, Vol. XVII. London: The Hogarth Press.

Friedman, S. (1972). Habituation and recovery of visual response in the alert human newborn. *Journal of Experimental Child Psychology*, 13, 339–349.

Friedman, S. & Sigman, M. (Eds) (1981). *Preterm Birth and Psychological Development*. New York: Academic Press.

Friedman, J. M. & Polifka, J. E. (1998). *The Effects of Neurologic and Psychiatric Drugs on the Foetus and Nursing Infant*. Baltimore, MD: John Hopkins University Press.

Frith, U. (1989). *Autism: Explaining the Enigma*. Oxford: Blackwell.

Frosh, S., Phoenix, A. & Pattman, R. (2002). *Young Masculinities*. Basingstoke: Palgrave Macmillan.

Frydman, O. & Bryant, P. E. (1988). Sharing and the understanding of number equivalence by young children. *Cognitive Development*, 3, 323–339.

Frydman, O. & Bryant, P. (1994). Children's understanding of multiplicative relationships in the construction of quantitative equivalence. *Journal of Experimental Child Psychology*, 58, 489–509.

Fullward, W., McDevitt, S. C. & Carey, W. (1978). *Toddler Temperament Scale*. Philadelphia, PA: Department of Educational Psychology, Temple University.

Gaddis, A. & Brooks-Gunn, J. (1985). The male experience of pubertal change. *Journal of Youth and Adolescence*, 14, 61–69. Cited in Berk, L.E. (1998). Development Through the Life-span. Needham Heights, MA: Allyn & Bacon.

Gadow, K. & Nolan, E. (2002). Differences between preschool children with ODD, ADHD, and ODD & ADHD symptoms. *Journal of Child Psychology and Psychiatry*, 43, 191–201. *International Journal of Psychophysiology*, 74, 149–157.

Galanaki, E. (2004). Teachers and loneliness: The children's perspective. *School Psychology International*, 25, 92–105.

Gallese, V., Rochat, M., Cossu, G. & Sinigaglia, C. (2009). Motor cognition and its role in the phylogeny and ontogeny of action and understanding. *Developmental Psychology*, 45, 103–113.

Gallimore, R. & Weisner, R. S. (1977). My brother's keeper: Child and sibling caretaking. *Current Anthropology*, 18, 169–190.

Gallistel, C. R. & Gelman, R. (1992). Preverbal and verbal counting and computation. *Cognition*, 44, 43–74.

Gamliel T., Hoover, J.H., Daughtry D.W. & Imbra C.M. (2003). A qualitative investigation of bullying. The perspectives of fifth, sixth and seventh graders in a USA parochial school. *School Psychology International*, 24, 405–420.

Ganger, J. & Brent M. R. (2004). Reexamining the vocabulary spurt. *Developmental Psychology*, 40 (4), 621–632.

Garcia, J.J.M., Collado, E.N. & Gomez, J.L.G. (2005). Psychological risk and protective factors for antisocial behavior in adolescents. *Actas Espanolas De Psiquiatria*, 33 (6), 366–373.

Gardner, H. (1993). *Multiple Intelligences*. New York: Basic Books.

Gardner, H. (2006). *Changing Minds. The Art and Science of Changing Our Own and Other People's Minds*. Boston, MA: Harvard Business School Press.

Gauthier, I., Williams, P., Tarr, M. J. & Tanaka, J. (1998) Training 'greeble' experts: a framework for studying expert object recognition processes. *Vision Research*, 38, 2401–2428.

Gauze, C., Bukowski, W. M., Aquan-Assee, J. & Sippola, L. K. (1996) Interactions between family environment and friendship and associations with self-perceived well-being during early adolescence. *Child Development*, 67, 2201–2216.

Ge, X., Conger, R.D. & Elder, G.H.Jr. (1996). Coming of age too early: Pubertal influences on girls' vulnerability to psychological distress. *Child Development*, 67, 3386–3400.

Geber, M. & Dean, M. R. C. P. (1957). Gesell tests on *African children. Pediatrics*, 20 (6), 1055–1065.

Gelman, R. & Butterworth, B. (2005). Number and language: How are they related? *Trends in Cognitive Sciences*, 9, 6–10.

Gelman, R. & Gallistel, C. R. (1978). *The Child's Understanding of Number*. Cambridge, MA: Harvard University Press.

Gelman, R. & Meck, E. (1983). Preschoolers' counting: Principles before skill. *Cognition*, 13, 343–359.

Gentile, B., Dolan-Pascoe, B., Twenge, J.M., Maitino, A., Grabe, S & Wells, B.E. (2009). Gender differences in domain-specific self-esteem: A meta-analysis. *Review of General Psychology*, 13 (1), 34–45.

George, R. (2006). A cross-domain analysis of change in students' attitudes toward science and attitudes about the utility of science. *International Journal of Science Education*, 28 (6), 571–589.

George, R. & Clay, J. (2007). Reforming teachers and uncompromising 'standards': Implications for Social Justice in Schools. *FORUM: for Promoting 3-19 Comprehensive Education*, 50 (1), 103–112.

Gerstadt, C. L., Hong, Y. J. & Diamond, A. (1994). The relationship between cognition and action: Performance of 3.5-7 year olds on Stroop-like day-night test. *Cognition*, 53, 129–153.

Gervai, J., Novak, A., Lakatos, K., Toth, I., Danis, I., Ronai, Z., Nemoda, Z., Sasvani-Szekely, M., Bureau, J.F., Bronfman, E. & Lyons-Rubh, K. (2007). Infant genotype may moderate sensitivity to maternal affective communications: attachment disorganization, quality of care, and the DRD4 polymorphism. *Social Neuroscience*, 2, 307–319.

Geschwind, D. H. (2009). Autism: The ups and downs of neurolin. *Biological Psychiatry*, 66 (10), 904–905.

Gesell, A. (1933). Maturation and the patterning of behavior. In C. Murchison (Ed.), *A Handbook of Child Psychology* (2nd Ed. rev.) (209–235) Worcester, MA: Clark University.

Gevensleben, H., Holl, B., Albrecht, B., Schlamp, D., Kratz, O., Studer, P., Wangler, S., Rothenberger, A., Moll, G.H. & Heinrich, H. (2009). Distinct EEG effects related to neurofeedback training in children with ADHD: A randomized controlled trial. *International Journal by Psychophysiology*, 74, 149–157.

Ghetti, S., Edelstein, R. S., Goodman, G. S., Cordon, I. M., Quas, J. A., Alexander, K. W., Redlich, A. D. & Jones, D. P. H. (2006). What can subjective forgetting tell us about memory for childhood trauma? *Memory & Cognition*, 34 (5), 1011–1025.

Ghuman, J. K., Ginsburg, G. S., Subramaniam, G., Ghuman, H. S., Kau, A. S., & Ma, R. (2001). Psychostimulants in preschool children with attention-deficit/hyperactivity disorder: Clinical evidence from a developmental disorders institution. *Journal of the American Academy of Child and Adolescent Psychiatry*, 40, 516–524.

Gibson, E. & Walk, R. D. (1960). The 'visual cliff'. *Scientific American*, 202, 64–71.

Giedd, J. N., Blumenthal, J., Jeffries, N. O., Rajapaske, J. C., Vaituzis, C. & Liu, H. (1999). Development of the corpus callosum during childhood and adolescence: A longitudinal MRI study. *Progress in Neuro-Psychopharmacology and Biological Psychiatry*, 23, 571–588.

Gilbert, S. F. (2000). *Developmental Biology* (6th Ed.). Sunderland, MA: Sinauer.

Giedd, J. N. (2008). The teen brain: Insights from neuroimaging. *Journal of Adolescent Health*, 42 (4), 335–343.

Gillard, D. (2008). Blair's academies: The story so far. FORUM: for Promoting 3-19 *Comprehensive Education*, 50 (1), 11–22.

Gillberg, C., Gillberg, C. I., Rasmussen, P., Kadesjo, B., Soderstrom, H., Rastam, M., Johnson, M., Rothenberger, A. & Niklasson, L. (2004). Coexisting disorders in ADHD – implications for diagnosis and intervention. European *Journal of Adolescent Psychiatry*, 13, 180–192.

Gillies, R. M. (2000). The maintenance of co-operative and helping behaviours in co-operative groups. *British Journal of Educational Psychology*, 70 (1), 97–111.

Ginsberg, H.P. (1997). *Entering the Child's Mind: The Clinical Interview in Psychological Research and Practice*. Cambridge: Cambridge University Press.

Gluckman, P., Hanson, M. & Beedle, A. (2007). Early life events and their consequences for later disease: A life history and evolutionary perspective. *American Journal of Human Biology*, 19, 1–19.

Glutting, J. J., Youngstrom, E. A. & Watkins, M. W. (2005). ADHD and college students: Exploratory and confirmatory factor structures with student and parent data. *Psychological Assessment*, 17 (1), 44–55.

Gogtay, N., Giedd, J. N., Lusk, L., Hayashi, K. M., Greenstein, D., Vaitusis, A. C., Nugent, T. F. III, Herman, D. H., Clasen, L. S., Toga, A. W., Rapoport, J. L. & Thompson, P. M (2004). Dynamic mapping of human cortical development during childhood through early adulthood. *PNAS*, 101, 8174–8179.

Gokiert, R. J., Chow, W., Parsa, B. & Vandenberghe, C. (2007). *Community Cross-cultural Lessons: Early Childhood Developmental Screening and Approaches to Research and Practice*. Community-University Partnership for the Study of Children, Youth, and Families, University of Alberta, Edmonton.

Goldberg, S. (2000). *Attachment and Development*. London: Arnold.

Goldfarb, W. (1947). Variations of adolescent adjustment of institutionally reared children. *American Journal of Orthopsychiatry*, 17, 449–457.

Goldfield, E. C. & Wolff, P.H. (2002). Motor development in infancy. In A. Slater & M. Lewis (Eds), *Introduction to Infant Development* (6–82). Oxford: Oxford University Press.

Golding, J., Prembey, M., Jones, R. & ALSPAC team (2001). ALSPAC – The Avon Longitudinal Study of Parents and Children I. Study Methodology. *Paediatric and Perinatal Epidemiology*, 15, 74–87.

Goldsmiths, H. H., Buss, A. H., Plomin, R., Rothbart, M. K., Thomas, A., Stella, C., Hinde, R. A. & McCall, R. B. (1987). Roundtable: What is temperament? Four Approaches. *Child Development*, 58, 505–529.

Goldsmiths, H. H., Lemery, K. S., Buss, K. A. & Campos, J. J. (1999). Genetic analyses of focal aspects of infant temperament. *Developmental Psychology*, 35, 972–985.

Goleman, D. (1995). *Emotional Intelligence*. New York: Basic Books.

Golombok, S. & Fivush, R. (1994). *Gender Development*. Cambridge: Cambridge University Press.

Golombok, S. & Hines, (2002). Sex differences in social behavior. In P. K. Smith & C. H. Hart (Eds), Blackwell *Handbook of Childhood Social Development* (117–136). Malden: Blackwell.

Göncü, A. & Gaskins, S. (2007). *Play and Development: Evolutionary, Sociocultural and Functional Perspectives*. Hove: Psychology Press.

Goodman, J. (2006). School discipline in moral disarray. *Journal of Moral Education*, 35 (2), 213–230.

Goodman, R. (1997). The Strengths and Difficulties Questionnaire: A research note. *Journal of Child Psychology, Psychiatry, and Allied Disciplines*, 38, 581–586.

Goodman, R. (2000). *Children of the Japanese State*. Oxford: Oxford University Press.

Gopnick, A. & Meltzoff, A. (1987). The development of categorization in the second year and its relation to other cognitive and linguistic developments. *Child Development*, 58, 1523–1531.

Gopnik, A., Slaughter, V., & Meltzoff, A.N. (1994). Changing your views: How understanding visual perception can lead to a new theory of the mind. In C. Lewis & P. Mitchell (Eds), *Children's Early Understanding of Mind: Origins and Development* (157–181). Hillsdale, NJ: Erlbaum.

Gorard, S., Taylor, C. & Fitz, J. (2002). Does school choice lead to 'spirals of decline'? *Journal of Education Policy*, 17 (3), 367–384.

Goswami, U. (2006). The foundations of psychological understanding. *Developmental Science*, 9, 545–550.

Goswami, U. & Bryant, P. (2007). Children's cognitive development and learning. *The Primary Review*, 2/1a, 1–4.

Gottman, J. M. (1986). The world of coordinated play: Same- and cross-sex friendship in young children. In J. M. Gottman & J. G. Parker (Eds), *Conversations of Friends: Speculations on Affective Development* (139–191). Cambridge: Cambridge University Press.

Gouze, K. R. & Nadelman, L. (1980). Constancy of gender identity for self and others in children between the ages of three and seven. *Child Development*, 51, 275–278.

Graber, J.A., Brooks-Gunn, J., Paikoff, R.L. & Warren, M.P. (1994). Prediction of eating problems: an 8 year study of adolescent girls. *Developmental Psychology*, 28, 731–740.

Graber, J. A., Brooks-Gunn, J., Paikoff, R. L. & Warren, M. P. (1994). Prediction of eating problems and disorders: An eight year study of adolescent girls. *Developmental Psychology*, 30 (6), 823–834.

Graham, S. & Juvonen, J. (2001). An attributional approach to peer victimisation. In J. Juvonen & S. Graham (Eds), *Peer Harassment in School. The Plight of the Vulnerable and Victimized* (49–72). New York: Guilford Press.

Graham, S. A. & Kilbreath, C. S. (2007). It's a sign of the kind: Gestures and words guide infants' inductive inferences. *Developmental Psychology*, 43, 1111–1123.

Grattan, M. P., De Vos, E., Levy, J. & McClintock, M. K., (1992). Asymmetric action in the human newborn: Sex differences in patterns of organization. *Child Development*, 63, 273–289.

Greatorex, J. & Malacova, E. (2006). Can different teaching strategies or methods of preparing pupils lead to greater improvements from GCSE to A level performance? *Research Papers in Education*, 21 (3), 255–294.

Gréco, P. (1962). Quantité et quotité: nouvelles recherches sur la correspondance terme-a-terme et la conservation des ensembles. In P. Gréco & A. Morf (Eds), *Structures numeriques elementaires: Etudes d'Epistemꞁ gie Genetique* Vol. 13 (35–52). Paris: Presses Universitairꞁ de France.

Greene, R. W. & Ablon, J. S. (2001). What does the MTA study tell us about effective psychosocial treatments for ADHD. *Journal of Clinical Child Psychology*, 30, 114–121.

Greene, R. W., Biederman, J., Faraone, S. V., Sienna, M., & Garcia-Jetton, J. (1997). Adolescent outcome of boys with Attention Deficit/Hyperactivity Disorder and social disability: Results from a 4-year longitudinal follow-up study. *Journal of Consulting and Clinical Psychology*, 65, 758–767.

Grieg, A., Taylor, J. & MacKay, T. (2007). *Doing Research With Children*. (2nd Ed.). London: Sage.

Griffiths, C. C. B. (2007). Pragmatic abilities in adults with and without dyslexia: A pilot study. *Dyslexia*, 13, 276–296.

Grossmann, K. E. (1985). Die Qualität der Beziehung zwischen Eltern und Kind. Grundlagen einer psychisch gesunden Entwicklung (The quality of the relationship between parents and child: The basis for healthy psychical development.) *Praxis der Psychotherapie und Psychosomatik*, 30, 44–54.

Grossmann, K. E., Grossmann, K. & Schwan, A. (1986). Capturing the wider view of attachment: A reanalysis of Ainsworth's strange situation. In C. E. Izard & P. E. Read (Eds), *Measuring Emotions in Infants and Children* (124–171), Vol. 2. New York: Cambridge University Press.

Grossmann, K., Grossmann, K. E., Fremmer-Bombik, E., Kindler, H., Scheueueu-Englisch, H. & Zimmerman, P. (2002). The uniqueness of the child-father attachment relationship: Fathers' sensitive and challenging play as a pivotable variable in a 16-year longitudinal study. *Social Development*, 11, 307–331.

Gruber, R., Sadeh, A. & Raviv, A. (2000). Instability of sleep patterns in children with attention-deficit/hyperactivity disorder. *Journal of the American Academy of Child and Adolescent Psychiatry*, 39, 495–501.

Guerin, S. & Hennessy, E. (2002). Pupils' definitions of bullying. *European Journal of Psychology of Education*, 17, 249–261.

Gwiazda, J. & Birch, E. E. (2001). Perceptual development: Vision. In E. B. Goldstein (Ed.), *Handbook of Perception* (636–668). Oxford: Blackwell.

Hagekull, B., Bohlin, G. & Lindhagen, K. (1984). Validity of parental reports. *Infant Behaviour and Development*, 7, 77–92.

Hagen, E. H. (2002). Depression as bargaining: The case postpartum. *Evolution and Human Behaviour*, 23, 323–336.

Hahn, W. K. (1987). Cerebral lateralisation of function: From infancy through childhood. *Psychological Bulletin*, 101, 376–392.

Hainline, L. (1998). The development of basic visual abilities. In A. Slater (Ed.), *Perceptual Development: Visual, Auditory and Speech Perception in Infancy* (5–50). Hove: Psychology Press.

Haith, M.M. (1998). Who put the cog in infant cognition? Is rich interpretation too costly? *Infant Behavior & Development*, 21, 167–179.

…usberg, H. (2003). The influence of …nd: A training study. *Development*

…: Its education, health and …r & S. Wheeler. (2005). *The Project …y EBook of Youth: Its Education, Regimen, and Hygiene by G. Stanley Hall*. October, 2005.

Hallam, S. & Ireson, J. (2005). Secondary school teachers' pedagogic practices when teaching mixed and structured ability classes. *Research Papers in Education*, 20 (1), 3–24.

Halliday, J.L., Watson, L.F., Lumley, J., Danks, D.M., & Sheffield, L.J. (1995). New estimates of Down syndrome risks at chorionic villus sampling, amniocentesis and live birth in women of advanced maternal age from a uniquely defined population, *Prenatal Diagnosis*, 15, 455–465.

Halligan, J. (2009). *Ryan's story. In memory of Ryan Patrick Halligan 1989–2003*. Retrieved April 2, 2010 from http://www.ryanpatrickhalligan.org/laws/laws.htm.

Hamilton, C. E. (1994). Continuity and discontinuity of attachment from infancy through adolescence. *Child Development*, 71, 690–694.

Hampel, P. & Petermann, F. (2005). Age and gender effects on coping in children and adolescents. *Journal of Youth and Adolescence*, 34 (2), 73–83.

Hane, A. A., Fox, N. A., Henderson, H. A. & Marshal, I. J. (2008). Behavioural reactivity and approach-withdrawal bias in infancy. *Developmental Psychology*, 44, 1491–1496.

Hanish, L.D. & Guerra, N.G. (2004). Aggressive victims, passive victims, and bullies: Developmental continuity or developmental change? *Merrill-Palmer Quarterly*, 50, 17–38.

Hannon, E. E. & Trehub, S. E. (2005). Metrical categories in infancy and adulthood. *Psychological Science*, 16, 48–55.

Happé, F. (1994). An advanced test of theory of mind: Understanding of story characters' thoughts and feelings by able autistic, mentally handicapped, and normal children and adults. *Journal of Autism and Developmental Disorders*, 24, 129–154.

Happé, F. & Frith, U. (2006). The weak coherence account: Detail-focused cognitive style in autism spectrum disorders. *Journal for Autism Development and Disorder*, 36 (1), 5–25.

Harden, R. M. (2008). Death by PowerPoint – the need for a 'fidget index'. *Medical Teacher*, 30 (9–10), 833–835.

Hariri, A. R. & Forbes, E. E. (2007). Genetics of emotion regulation. In J. J. Gross (Ed.), *Handbook of Emotion Regulation* (110–134). New York: Guilford.

Harlow, H. (1958). The nature of love. *American Psychologist*, 13, 673–685.

Harlow, H. & Harlow, M. (1969). Effects on various mother-infant relationships on rhesus monkey behaviours. In B. M. Foss (Ed.), *Determinants of Infant Behaviour*, Vol. 4 (15–36). London: Methuen.

Harlow, H. & Zimmerman, R. R. (1959). Affectional responses in the infant monkey. Science, 130, 421–432.

Hodges, J. & Tizard, B. (1989). Social and family relationships of ex-institutional adolescents. *Journal of Child Psychology and Psychiatry*, 30, 77–98.

Haroaian, L. (2000). Sexual competency development in sexually permissive and sexually restrictive societies. *Electronic Journal of Human Sexuality*, 3 (1).

Harris, A. (2008). Leading innovation and change: Knowledge creation by schools for schools. *European Journal of Education: Research, Development and Policies*, 43 (2), 219–228.

Harris, G. (1997). Development of taste perception and appetite regulation. In G. Bremner, A. Slater & G. Butterworth (Eds), *Infant Development: Recent Advances* (9–30). Hove: Psychology Press.

Harris, J. R. (1998). *The Nurture Assumption: Why Children Turn Out the Way They Do*. New York: Free Press.

Harrist, A. W., Zaia, A. F., Bates, J. E., Dodge, K. A. & Pettit, G. S. (1997). Subtypes of social withdrawal in early childhood: Sociometric status and social-cognitive differences across four years. *Child Development*, 68, 278–294.

Hart, B. & Risley, T.R. (1995). *Meaningful Differences in the Everyday Experiences of Young American Children*. Baltimore, MD: Brookes.

Hart, K., Brown, M., Kerslake, D., Kuchermann, D. & Ruddock, G. (1985). *Chelsea Diagnostic Mathematics Tests. Fractions 1*. Windsor, UK: NFER-Nelson.

Harter, S. (1987). The determinations and mediational role of global self-worth in children. In N. Eisenberg (Ed.), *Contemporary Topics in Developmental Psychology* (219–242). New York: Wiley Interscience.

Harter, S. (1990). Processes underlying adolescent self-concept formation. In R. Montemayor, G. R. Adams & T. P. Gullotta (Eds), *From Childhood to Adolescence: A Transitional Period?* (205–239). Newbury Park, CA: Sage.

Hartman, R. R., Stage, S. A. & Webster-Stratton, C. (2003). A growth curve analysis of parent training outcomes: examining the influence of child risk factors (inattention, impulsivity, and hyperactivity problems), and parental and family risk factors. *Journal of Child Psychology and Psychiatry and Allied Disciplines*, 44, 388–398.

Hartshorn, K., Rovee-Collier, C., Gerhardstein, P. C., Bhatt, R. S., Wondoloski, T. L., Klein, P., Gilch, J., Wurtzel, N. & Campos-de-Carvalho, M. (1998). Ontogeny of long-term memory over the first year-and-a-half of life. *Developmental Psychobiology*, 32, 69–89.

Hartung, B. & Sweeney, K. (1991). Why adult children return home. *Social Science Journal*, 28, 467–480.

Hartup, W. W. (1989). Social relationships and their developmental significance. *American Psychologist*, 44 (2), 120–126.

Hartup, W. W. (2006). Relationships in early and middle childhood. In A. L. Vangelisti & D. Perlman (Eds), *Cambridge Handbook of Personal Relationships* (171–190). New York: Cambridge University Press.

Hartup, W. W. & Stevens, N. (1999). Friendships and adaptation across the life span. *Current Directions in Psychological Science*, 8, 76–79.

Hasebrink, U., Livingstone, S. & Haddon, L. (2008). *Comparing Children's Online Opportunities and Risks Across Europe: Cross-national Comparisons for EU Kids Online*. London: EU Kids Online (Deliverable D3.2).

Haselager, J. T., Hartup, W. W., van Lieshout, C. F. M. & Riksen-Walraven, J. M. A. (1998). Similarities between friends and nonfriends in middle childhood. *Child Development*, 69, 1198–1208.

Hasselgreen, A. A. H. (2005). Assessing the language of young learners. *Language Testing*, 22 (3), 337–354.

Hatch, J.A. (Ed.) (1995). *Qualitative Research in Early Childhood Settings*. Westport, CT and London: Praeger.

Hatten, M. E. (2002). New directions in neuronal migration. *Science*, 297, 1660–1663.

Hatton, C. & Emerson, E. (2003). Families with a person with intellectual disabilities: Stress and impact. *Current Opinion in Psychiatry*, 16, 497–501.

Hausmann, M., Schoofs, D., Rosenthal, H. E. S. & Jordan, K. (2009). Interactive effects of sex hormones and gender stereotypes on cognitive sex differences: A psychobiosocial approach. *Psychoneuroendocrinology*, 34 (3), 389–401.

Hawley, P.H. (1999). The ontogenesis of social dominance: a strategy-based evolutionary perspective. *Developmental Review*, 19, 97–132.

Hay, D. (2007). Using concept maps to measure deep, surface and non-learning outcomes. *Studies in Higher Education*, 32 (1), 39–57.

Hay, D. & Ross, H. (1982). The social nature of early conflict. *Child Development*, 53, 105–113.

Hay, D., Nash, A. & Pederson, J. (1983). Interactions between six-month-old peers. *Child Development*, 54, 557–562.

Hayne, H. (2004). Infant memory development: Implications for childhood amnesia. *Developmental Review*, 24, 33–73.

Heath, C. & Hindmarsh, J. (1997). Analysing interaction: Video, ethnography and situated conduct. In J. A. Hughes & W. Sharrock (Eds), *The Philosophy of Social Research* (99–121). London: Longman.

Held, R. & Hein, A. (1963). Movement produced stimulation in the development of visually guided behaviour. *Journal of Comparative and Physiological Psychology*, 56, 872–876.

Henderson, H. A., Fox, N. A. & Rubin, K. H. (2001). Temperamental contributions to social behavior: The moderating roles of frontal EEG asymmetry and gender. *Journal of the American Academy of Child and Adolescent Psychiatry*, 40, 68–74.

Henderson, H., Marshall, P., Fox, N. & Rubin, K. (2004). Psychophysiological and behavioral evidence for varying forms and functions of non-social behavior in preschoolers. *Child Development*, 75, 236–250.

Henderson, M., Wight, D., Raab, G., Abraham, C., Buston, K., Hart, G. & Scott, S. (2002). Heterosexual risk behaviour among young teenagers in Scotland. Journal of Adolescence, 25 (5), 483–494.

Hepper, P. G. (1988). Foetal "soap" addiction. *Lancet*, June, 1347–1384.

Hepper, P. G. (1992). Fetal psychology. An embryonic science. In J. G. Nijhuis (Ed.), *Fetal Behaviour. Developmental and Perinatal Aspects* (129–156). Oxford: Oxford University Press.

Hepper, P. G. (1996). Foetal memory does it exist? *Acta Paediatrica*, Supplement 416, 16–20.

Hepper, P. G. (2002). Prenatal development. In Slater, A., & Lewis, M. (2002). *Introduction to Infant Development* (39–60). Oxford: Oxford University Press.

Hepper, P. G. & Leader, L. R. (1996). Foetal habituation. *Fetal and Maternal Medicine Review*, 8, 109–123.

Hernandez-Reif, M., Field, T., del Pino, N. & Diego, M. (2000). Less exploring by mouth occurs in newborns of depressed mothers. *Infant Mental Health Journal*, 21, 204–210.

Hesslinger, B., Thiel, T., Van Elst, L. T., Hennig, J. & Ebert, D. (2001). Attention-deficit disorder in adults with or without hyperactivity: Where is the difference? A study in humans using short echo H-1-magnetic resonance spectroscopy. *Neuroscience Letters*, 304, 117–119.

Hetherington, E.M. & Stanley-Hagan, M. (2002). Parenting in divorced and remarried families. In M.H. Bornstein (Ed.), *Handbook of Parenting* (2nd Ed.), Vol. 3, 287–315. Mahwah, NJ: Erlbaum.

Heuser, L. (2005). We're not too old to play sports: The career of women lawn bowlers. *Leisure Studies*, 24 (1), 45–60.

Hierbert, J. & Tonnessen, L. H. (1978). Development of the fraction concept in two physical contexts: An exploratory investigation. *Journal for Research in Mathematics Education*, 9 (5), 374–378.

Hinde, R. A. (1989). Temperament as an intervening variable. In G. A. Kohnstamm, J. E. Bates & M. K. Rothbart (Eds), *Temperament in Childhood* (27–33). Chichester: Wiley.

Hinde, R. A., Titmus, G., Easton, D. & Tamplin, A. (1985). Incidence of "friendship" and behavior toward strong associates versus nonassociates in preschoolers. *Child Development*, 56, 234–245.

Hinojosa, T., Sheu, C.F. & Michel, G. F. (2003). Infant hand preference for grasping objects contributes to the development of a hand-use preference for manipulating objects. *Developmental Psychobiology*, 43, 328–334.

Hinshaw, S. P. (1994). *Attention Deficits and Hyperactivity in Children*. Thousand Oaks, CA: Sage.

Hinshaw, S. P. & Melnick, S. M. (1995). Peer relationships in boys with attention deficit hyperactivity disorder with and without co-morbid aggression. *Development and Psychopathology*, 7, 267–647.

Holland, R. (2002). *Vouchers Help the Learning Disabled*. Chicago, IL: The Heartland Institute. Retrieved November 6 from http://www.heartland.org/full/9291/Vouchers_Help_the_Learning_Disabled.html.

Hollander, E., Wasserman, S., Swanson, E. N., Chaplin, E., Schapiro, M. L., Zagursky, K. & Novotny, S. (2006). A double-blind placebo-controlled pilot study of olanzapine in childhood/adolescent pervasive developmental disorder. *Journal of Child and Adolescent Psychopharmacology*, 16 (5), 541–548.

Holmes, D. (1990). The evidence for repression: An examination of sixty years of research. In J. Singer (Ed.), *Repression and Dissociation: Implications for Personality, Theory, Psychopathology, and Health* (85–102). Chicago, IL: University of Chicago Press.

Holyoak, K. J., Junn, E. N. & Billman, D. O. (1984). Development of analogical problem-solving skill. *Child Development*, 55, 2042–2055.

Honess, T.M., Charman, E.A., Zani, B., Cicognani, E., Xerri, M.L., Jackson, A.E. & Bosma, H.A. (1997). Conflict between parents and adolescents: Variation by family constitution. *British Journal of Developmental Psychology*, 15, 367–385.

Home Office and Department of Health (1992). *Memorandum of Good Practice on Video Recorded Interviews with Child Witnesses for Criminal Proceedings*. London: HMSO.

Horsthemke, K. & Kissack, M. (2008). Vorleben: Educational practice beyond prescription. *Journal of Curriculum Studies*, 40 (3), 277–288.

Horwitz, S. M., Irwin, J. R., Briggs-Gowan, M. J., Bosson, H. J., Mendoza, J. & Carter, A. S. (2003). Language delay in a community cohort of young children. *Journal of the American Academy of Child & Adolescent Psychiatry*, 42 (8), 932–940.

Howard, J., Jenvey, V. & Hill, C. (2006). Children's categorisation of play and learning based on social context. *Early Child Development and Care*, 176 (3&4), 379–393.

Howe, C. (1993). Peer interaction and knowledge acquisition. *Social Development* (Special issue), 2 (3).

Howe, C. & Mercer, N. (2007). *Children's Social Development, Peer Interaction and Classroom Learning (Primary Review Research Survey 2/1b)*, Cambridge: University of Cambridge Faculty of Education.

Howe, M. L. & Courage, M. L. (1997). The emergence and early development of autobiographical memory. *Psychological Review*, 104, 499–523.

Howes, C. (1983). Patterns of friendship. *Child Development*, 54, 1041–1053.

Howes, C. (1987). Social competence with peers in young children: Developmental sequences. *Developmental Review*, 7, 252–272.

Hsu, C.C., Soong, W.T., Stigler, J.W., Hong, C.C. & Liang, C.C. (1981). The temperamental characteristics of Chinese babies. *Child Development*, 52, 1337–1340.

Hsu, V. C. & Rovee-Collier, C. (2006). Memory reactivation in the second year of life. *Infant Behavior and Development*, 29 (1), 91–107.

Huber, S. G. & Grdel, B. (2006). Quality assurance in the German school system. *European Educational Research Journal*, 5 (3–4), 196–209.

Hudson, B. (2006). User outcomes and children's services reform: Ambiguity and conflict in the policy implementation process. *Social Policy and Society*, 5 (2), 227–236.

Hughes, C. (1999). Identifying critical social interaction behaviors among high school students with and without disabilities. *Behavior Modification*, 23, 41–60.

Hughes, C., Jaffee, S.R., Happe, F., Taylor, A., Caspi, A. & Moffitt, T.E. (2006). Origins of individual differences in theory of mind: From nature to nurture? *Child Development*, 76 (2), 356–370.

Hughes, C., White, A., Sharpen, J. & Dunn, J. (1998). Antisocial, angry, and unsympathetic: 'Hard to manage' preschoolers' peer problems and possible cognitive influences. *Journal of Child Psychology and Psychiatry*, 41, 169–179.

Hughes, J., Cavell, T. & Grossman, P. (1997). A positive view of self: Risk or protection for aggressive children? *Development and Psychopathology*, 9, 75–94.

Hughes, J. & W. Sharrock (Eds), *The Philosophy of Social Research* (99–121). London: Longman.

Hughes, M. (1981). Can preschool children add and subtract? *Educational Psychology*, 3, 207–219.

Hughes, M. W. H., & Longman, D. (2006). *Whole class teaching strategies and interactive technology: Towards a connectionist classroom*. British Educational Research Association Conference, 5th–7th September, 2006 University of Warwick.

Hunting, R. P. & Sharpley, C. F. (1988). Fractional knowledge in preschool children. *Journal for Research in Mathematics Education*, 19 (2), 175–180.

Huston, A. C., Wright, J. C., Marquis, J. & Green, S. B. (1999). How young children spend their time: Television and other activities. *Developmental Psychology*, 35, 912–925.

Hutchings, J., Bywater, T., Daley, D., Gardner, F., Jones, K., Eames, C., Tudor-Edwards, R. & Whitakker, C. (2007). A pragmatic randomised control trial of a parenting intervention in sure start services for children at risk of developing conduct disorder. *British Medical Journal*, 334, 678–682.

Huttenlocher, J., Haight, W., Byrk, A., Seltzer, M. & Lyons, T. (1991). Early vocabulary growth: Relation to language input and gender. *Developmental Psychology*, 27 (2), 236–248.

Huttenlocher, P. R. (1990) Morphometric study of human cerebral cortex development. *Neuropsychologia*, 28, 517–527.

Huttenlocker, P.R. (1994). Synaptogenesis in human cerebral cortex. In G.Dawson & K.W. Fischer (Eds), *Human Behaviour and the Developing Brain* (137–152). New York: Guildford.

Hyde, J.S. (2005). The gender similarities hypothesis. *American Psychologist*, 60 (6), 581–592.

Hyvonen. P. (2008). Teachers' perceptions of boys' and girls' shared activities in the school context: Towards a theory of collaborative play. *Teachers and Teaching: Theory and Practice*, 14 (5–6), 391–409.

Imbo, I. & Vandierendonck, A. (2007). The development of strategy use in elementary school children: Working memory and individual differences. *Journal of Experimental Child Psychology*, 96, 284–309.

Infantino, J. & Little, E. (2005). Students' perceptions of classroom behaviour problems and the effectiveness of different disciplinary methods. *Educational Psychology*, 25 (5), 491–508.

Inhelder, B. & Piaget, J. (1958). *The Growth of Logical Thinking from Childhood to Adolescence*. New York: Basic Books.

Inoue, K., Nadaoka, T., Oiji, A., Morioka, Y., Totsuka, S., Kanbayashi, Y. & Hukui, T. (1998). Clinical evaluation of attention-deficit hyperactivity disorder by objective quantitative measures. *Child Psychiatry and Human Development*, 28, 179–188.

Isabella, R. A. (1993). Origins of attachment: Maternal interactive behavior across the first year. *Child Development*, 64, 605–621.

Isabella, R. A. (1995). The origins of the infant-mother attachment: Maternal behavior and infant development. *Annals of Child Development*, 10, 57–81.

Izard, C. E. (1994). Innate and universal facial expressions: Evidence from developmental and cross-cultural research. *Psychological Bulletin*, 115, 288–299.

James, W. (1890). The Principles of Psychology. New York: Holt.

James, W. (1892; published in 1961). *Psychology: The Briefer Course*. New York: Harper & Row.

Jasinskaja-Lahti, I. & Liebkind, K. (2001). Perceived discrimination and psychological adjustment among Russian-speaking immigrant adolescents in Finland. *International Journal of Psychology*, 36 (3), 174–185.

Jellinek, M. S. & McDermott, J. (2004). Formulation: Putting the diagnosis into a therapeutic context and treatment plan. *Child and Adolescent Psychiatry*, 43 (7), 913–916.

Jensen, P. S., Hinshaw, S. P., Kraemer, H. P. et al. (2001). ADHD comorbidity findings from MTA study: Comparing comorbid subgroups. *Journal of the American Academy of Child and Adolescent Psychiatry*, 40, 147–158

Jerome, A. C., Fujiki, M., Brinton, B. & James, S. L. (2002). Self-esteem in children with specific language impairment. *Journal of Speech, Language and Hearing Research*, 45, 700–714.

Johnson, M. H. (2001). Functional brain development in infancy. In G. Bremner & A. Fogel (Eds), Blackwell *Handbook of Infant Development* (169–190). Oxford: Blackwell.

Johnson, M. H. (2002). The development of visual attention in early infancy: A cognitive neuroscience perspective. In M. H. Johnson, Y. Munakata & R. O. Gilmore (Eds), *Brain Development and Cognition: a Reader* (134–150). Oxford: Blackwell.

Johnson, M.H., Munakata, Y. & Gilmore, R.O. (Eds) (2002). *Brain Development and Cognition: A Reader*. Oxford: Blackwell.

Johnston, C. & Mash, E. J. (2001). Families of children with attention-deficit/hyperactivity disorder: Review and recommendations for future research. Clinical Child and *Family Psychology Review*, 4, 183–207.

Johnston, J. C., Durieux-Smith, A., & Bloom, K. (2005). Teaching gestural signs to infants to advance child development: A review of the evidence. *First Language*, 25 (2), 235–251.

Johnstone, L. (2006). Controversies and debates about formulation. In R. Dallos and L. Johnstone (Eds), *Formulation in Psychology and Psychotherapy*. Abingdon: Taylor & Francis.

Jokela, M., Power, C. & Kivimäki, M. (2009). Childhood problem behaviours and injury risk over the life course. *Journal of Child Psychology and Psychiatry*, 50, (12), 1541–1549.

Jones, J. M. (1997). *Prejudice and Racism* (2nd Ed.). New York: McGraw-Hill.

Jones, K., Daley, D. Hutchings, J., Bywater, T. & Eames, C. (2007). Efficacy of the Incredible years intervention for children with ADHD. *Child Care Health and Development*, 33, 749–756.

Jordan, F. M. & Murdoch, B. E. (1993). A prospective study of the linguistic skills of children with closed-head injury. *Aphasiology*, 7, 503–512.

Jorgensen, K. (1999). Pain assessment and management in the newborn infant. *Journal of Perianesthesia Nursing*, 14, 349–356.

Joseph, J. (2001). Separated twins and the genetics of personality differences: a critique. *American Journal of Psychology*, 114, 1–30.

Jusczyk, P. W., Houston, D. & Goodman, M. (1998). Speech perception during the first year. In A. Slater (Ed.), *Perceptual Development: Visual, Auditory and Speech Perception in Infancy* (357–388). Hove: Psychology Press.

Kadesjo, B., Gillberg, C. & Hagberg, B. (1999). Brief report: Autism and Aspergers syndrome in seven-year old children. *Journal of Autism and Developmental Disorder*, 29, 327–331.

Kadesjo, C., Kadesjo, B., Hagglof, B. & Gillberg, C. (2001). ADHD in Swedish 3- to 7-year-old children. *Journal of the American Academy of Child and Adolescent Psychiatry*, 40, 1021–1028.

Kagan, J. (1989). Temperamental contributions to social behaviour. *American Psychologist*, 44, 668–674.

Kagan, J. (1991). Continuity and discontinuity in development. In S. E. Brauth, W. S. Hall & R. J. Dooling (Eds), *Plasticity of Development* (11–26). Cambridge MA: MIT Press.

Kagan, J. (1994). *Galen's Prophecy*. New York: Basic Books.

Kagan, J. (1998). Biology and the child. In N. Eisenberg (Ed.), *Handbook of Child Psychology, Vol. 3, Social, Emotional, and Personality Development* (5th Ed.) (177–236). New York: Wiley.

Kagan, J. (1999). The concept of behavioral inhibition. In L. A. Schmidt & J. Schulkin (Eds), *Extreme Fear, Shyness, and Social Phobia: Origins, Biological Mechanisms, and Clinical Outcomes* (3–13). New York: Oxford University Press.

Kagan, J. (2003). Behavioral inhibition as a temperamental category. In R. J. Davidson, K. R. Scherer & H. H. Goldsmith (Eds), *Handbook of Affective Science* (320–331). New York: Oxford University Press.

Kagan, J. (2008). In defense of qualitative changes in development. *Child Development*, 79, 1606–1624.

Kagan, J. & Herschkowitz, N. (2005). *A Young Mind in a Growing Brain*. Mahwah, NJ: Erlbaum.

Kagan, J. & Moss, H. A. (1983). *Birth to Maturity: A Study in Psychological Development* (2nd Ed.). Newhanen, CT: Yale University Press.

Kagan, J., Kearsley, R. & Zelazo, P. (1978). *Infancy: Its Place in Human Development*. Cambridge, MA: Harvard University Press.

Kagan, J., Reznick, J. S. & Snidman, N. (1988). Childhood derivatives of high and low reactivity in infancy. *Child Development*, 69, 1483–1493.

Kagan, J., Arcus, D. & Snidman, N. (1993a). The idea of temperament: Where do we go from here? In R. Plomin & G. E. McClearn (Eds), *Nature, Nurture and Psychology* (197–210). Washington DC: American Psychological Association.

Kagan, J., Snidman, N., & Arcus, D. (1993b). On the temperamental qualities of inhibited and uninhibited children. In K. H. Rubin & J. B. Asendorpf (Eds), *Social Withdrawal, Inhibition, and Shyness in Childhood* (19–28). Hillsdale, NJ: Erlbaum.

Kagan, J., Arcus, D., Snidman, N., Feng, W. Y., Hendler, J. & Greene, S. (1994). Reactivity in infants: A cross-national comparison. *Developmental Psychology*, 30, 342–345.

Kaiser, F. (1946). *Der Nürnberger Trichter*. Nuremberg: Sebaldus-Verlag.

Kalter, H. (2003). Teratology in the 20th century: environmental causes of congenital malformations in humans and how they were established. *Neurotoxicology and Teratology*, 25, 131–282.

Kamii, C. & Clark, F. B. (1995). Equivalent fractions: their difficulty and educational implications. *Journal of Mathematical Behavior*, 14, 365–378.

Karmiloff-Smith, A. (1998). Development itself is the key to understanding developmental disorders. *Trends in Cognitive Sciences*, 2, 389–398.

Karmiloff-Smith, A. (1999). The connectionist infant: Would Piaget turn in his grave? In A. Slater & D. Muir (Eds), *The Blackwell Reader in Developmental Psychology* (43–52). Oxford: Blackwell.

Kaufman, B. A. (1994). Day by day: Playing and learning. *International Journal of Play Therapy*, 3 (1), 11–21.

Kaufman, J., Csibra, G. & Johnson, M. H. (2003a). Representing occluded objects in the infant brain. *Proceedings Royal Society London B* (Suppl.), 270, S140–S143.

Kaufman, J., Mareschal, D. & Johnson, M. H. (2003b). Graspability and object perception in infants. *Infant Behaviour and Development*, 26, 516–528.

Kaukiainen, A., Bjorkqvist, K., Lagerspetz, K., Osterman, K., Salmivalli, C., Rothberg, S. & Ahlbo, A. (1999). The relationships between social intelligence, empathy, and three types of aggression. *Aggressive Behaviour*, 25, 81–89.

Kave, G., Knafo, A. & Gilboa, A. (2010). The rise and fall of word retrieval across the lifespan. *Psychology & Aging*, 25 (3), 719–724.

Kaye, K. (1977). Toward the origin of dialogue. In H. R. Schaffer (Ed.). *Studies in Mother-Infant Interaction* (89–117). London: Academic Press.

Kaye, K. & Brazelton, T. B. (1971). *Mother-Iinfant Interaction in the Organisation of Sucking. Society for Research in Child Development*, 1–4 April, Minneapolis, MN.

Kaye, K. & Wells, A. J. (1980). Mothers' jiggling and the burst – pause pattern in neonatal feeding. *Infant Behaviour and Development*, 3, 29–46.

Keating, D. (1980). Thinking processes in adolescence. In J. Adelson (Ed.), *Handbook of Adolescent Psychology* (211–246). New York: Wiley.

Keil, F.C. (2006). Cognitive science and cognitive development. In W. Damon & R. Lerner (Series Eds) & D. Kuhn & R. S. Siegler (Vol. Eds), *Handbook of Child Psychology: Vol. 2: Cognition, Perception, and Language* (609–635). New York: Wiley.

Keil, F. C. (2008). Space – the primal frontier? Spatial cognition and the origins of concepts. *Philosophical Psychology*, 21, 241–250.

Kendrick, W. (1994). *A Thing About Men, and a Thing About Women*. New York: Simon & Schuster.

Kenworthy, L., Yerys, B. E., Anthony, L. G. & Wallace, G. L. (2008) Understanding executive control in autism spectrum disorders in the lab and in the real world. *Neuropsychology Review*, 18 (4), 320–338.

Kessler R.C., Chiu W.T., Demler O. & Walters E.E. (2005). Prevalence, severity, and comorbidity of twelve-month DSM-IV disorders in the National Comorbidity Survey Replication (NCS-R). *Archives of General Psychiatry*, 62 (6), 617–627.

Ketelaars, M.P., van Weerdenburg, M., Verhoeven, L., Cuperus, J.M. & Jansonius, K. (2010). Dynamics of the Theory of Mind construct: A developmental perspective. *European Journal of Developmental Psychology*, 7 (1), 85–103.

Kett, J.F. (1977). *Rites of Passage: Adolescence in America, 1790 to the Present*. New York: Basic Books.

Kieren, T. E. (1993). Rational and fractional numbers: From quotient fields to recursive understanding. In T. Carpenter, E. Fennema & T. A. Romberg (Eds), *Rational Numbers: An Integration of Research* (49–84). Hillsdale, NJ: Erlbaum.

Kisilevsky, B. S., Hains, S.M., Brown, C.C., Lee, C.T., Cowperthwaite, B., Stutzman, S. S., Swansburg, M. L., Lee, K., Xie, X., Huang, H., Ye, H. H., Zhang, K. & Wang, Z. (2009). Foetal sensitivity to properties of maternal speech and language. *Infant Behaviour and Development*, 32, 59–71.

Klapper, J. (2003). Taking communication to task? A critical review of recent trends in language teaching. *Language Learning Journal*, 27 (1), 33–42.

Klaus, M. H., Kennell, J. H. & Klaus, P. H. (1995). *Bonding: Building the Foundations of Secure Attachment and Independence*. Reading, MA: Addison-Wesley.

Klein, C., Wendling, K., Huettner, P., Ruder, H., & Peper, M. (2006). Intra-subject variability in Attention-Deficit Hyperactivity Disorder. *Biological Psychiatry*, 60 (10), 1088–1097.

Klingberg, T., Fernell, E., Olesen, P.J., Johnson, M., Gustafsson, P., Dahlstrom, K., Gillberg, C.G., Forssberg, H. & Westerberg, H. (2005). Computerized training of working memory in children with ADHD – a randomized, controlled trial. *Journal of The American Academy of Child and Adolescent Psychiatry*, 44, 177–186.

Kochanska, G., Gross, J. N., Lin, M. H. & Nichols, K. E. (2002). Guilt in young children: Development, determinants, and relations with a broader system of standards. *Child Development*, 73 (2), 461–482.

Kochenderfer, B.J. & Ladd, G.W. (1996). Peer victimization: Cause or consequence of school maladjustment? *Child Development*, 67, 1305–1317.

Kohlberg, L. (1963). The development of children's orientations towards a moral order I. Sequence in the development of moral thought. *Vita Humana*, 6, 11–33. Reprinted in *Human Development* (2008), 51, 8–20.

Kohlberg, L. (1966). A cognitive-developmental analysis of children's sex-role concepts and attitudes. In E. E. Maccoby (Ed.), *The Development of Sex Differences* (82–173). London: Tavistock.

Kohlberg, L. (1969). Stage and sequence: The cognitive-developmental approach to socialization. In D. A. Goslin (Ed.), *Handbook of Socialization Theory and Research* (347–480). Chicago, IL: Rand McNally.

Kohlberg, L. (1973). The claim to moral adequacy of a highest stage of moral judgment. *The Journal of Philosophy*, 70 (18), 630–646.

Kohlberg, L. (1976). Moral stages and moralization: the cognitive-developmental approach. In T. Lickona (Ed.), *Moral Development and Behavior: Theory, Research and Social Issues* (31–53). New York: Holt, Rinehart and Winston.

Kohlberg, L. (1981). *Essays on Moral Development, Vol 1: The Philosophy of Moral Development*. San Francisco, CA: Harper & Row.

Kohnstamm, G. A. (1989). Temperament in childhood: Cross-cultural and sex differences. In G. A. Kohnstramm, J. E. Bates & M. K. Rothbart (Eds), *Temperament in Childhood* (321–356). Chichester: Wiley.

Kollins, S., Greenhill, L., Swanson, J., Wigal, S., Abikoff, H., McCracken, J., Riddle, M., McGough, J., Vitiello, B., Wigal, T., Skrobala, A., Posner, K., Ghuman, J., Davies, M., Cunningham, C. & Bauzo, A. (2006). Rationale, design, and methods of the Preschool ADHD Treatment Study (PATS). *Journal of the American Academy of Child and Adolescent Psychiatry*, 45, 1275–1283.

Konrad, K., Neufang, S., Hanisch, C., Fink, G. R. & Herpertz-Dahlmann, B. (2006). Dysfunctional attentional networks in children with attention deficit/hyperactivity disorder: Evidence from an event-related functional magnetic resonance imaging study. *Biological Psychiatry*, 59, 643–651.

Kornilaki, E. (1999). *Young Children's Understanding of Multiplicative Concepts. A Psychological Approach*. London: University of London.

Kornilaki, E. & Nunes, T. (2005). Generalising principles in spite of procedural differences: Children's understanding of division. *Cognitive Development*, 20, 388–406.

Kowalski, R.M. & Limber, S.P. (2007). Electronic bullying among middle school students. *Journal of Adolescent Health*, 41, S22–S30.

Kowalski, R., Limber, S. & Agatston, P. (2008). *Cyber Bullying: Bullying in the Digital Age*. Malden, MA: Blackwell.

Krahe, B. & Moller, I. (2004). Playing violent electronic games, hostile attributional style, and aggression-related norms in German adolescents. *Journal of Adolescence*, 27 (1), 53–69.

Kramer, A. F. & Willis, S. L. (2003). Cognitive plasticity and aging. *Psychology of Learning and Motivation*, 43, 267–302.

Krampe, R. Th. & Ericsson, K.A. (1996). Maintaining excellence: Deliberate practice and elite performance in young and older pianists. *Journal of Experimental Psychology: General*, 125, 331–359.

Krebs, G., Squire, S. & Bryant, P. (2003). Children's understanding of the additive composition of number and of the decimal structure: What is the relationship? *International Journal of Educational Research*, 39, 677–694.

Kuczaj, S. (1982). The acquisition of word meaning in the context of the development of the semantic system. In C. Brainerd & M. Pressley (Eds), *Progress in Cognitive Development Research, Volume 2, Verbal Processes in Children* (95–123). New York: Springer.

Kuhl, P. & Rivera-Gaxiola, M. (2008). Neural substrates of language acquisition. *Annual Review of Neuroscience*, 31, 511–534.

Kuhn, D., Nash, S. C. & Brucken, L. (1978). Sex role concepts of two- and three-year-olds. *Child Development*, 49, 445–451.

Kummel, D. A., Seligson, F. H., and Guthrie, H. A. 1996. Hyperactivity: Is candy causal? *Critical Review in Food Science*, 36, 31.

Kumpulainen, K. & Räsänen, E. (2000). Children involved in bullying at elementary school age: Their psychiatric symptoms and deviance in adolescence. An epidemiological sample. *Child Abuse & Neglect*, 24, 1567–1577.

Ladd, G. W. & Burgess, K. B. (1999). Charting the relationship trajectories of aggressive, withdrawn, and aggressive/withdrawn children during early grade school. *Child Development*, 70, 910–929.

Lagerspetz, K., Björkqvist, K., Berts, M. & King, E. (1982). Group aggression among school children in three schools. *Scandinavian Journal of Psychology*, 23, 45–52.

Lahey, B. B., Pelham, W. E., Stein, M. A., Loney, J., Trapani, C., Nugent, K., Kipp, H., Schmidt, E., Lee, S., Cale, M., Gold, E., Hartung, C. M., Willcutt, E. & Baumann (1988). Validity of DSM IV attention deficit/hyperactivity disorder for younger children. *Journal of the American Academy of Child and Adolescent Psychiatry*, 37, 695–702.

Lahey, B. B., Pelham, W. E., Loney, J., Kipp, H., Ehrhardt, A., Lee, S. S., Willcutt, E. G., Hartung, C. M., Chronis, A. & Massetti, G. (2004). Three year predictive validity of DSM-IV attention deficit hyperactivity disorder in children diagnosed at 4–6 years of age. *American Journal of Psychiatry*, 161, 2014–2020.

Lakatos, K., Nemoda, Z., Birkas, E., Ronai, Z., Kovacs, E., Ney, K., Toth, I., Sasvari-Szekely, M. & Gervai, J. (2003). Association of D4 dopamine receptor gene and serotonin transporter promoter polymorphisms with infants' response to novelty. *Molecular Psychiatry*, 8, 90–97.

Lam, V. L. & Leman, P. J. (2003). The influence of gender and ethnicity on children's inferences about toy choice. *Social Development*, 12, 269–287.

Lamb, M. (1987). Introduction: The emergent American father. In M. E. Lamb (Ed.), *The Father's Role: Crosscultural Perspectives* (3–25). Hillsdale, NJ: Erlbaum.

Lamb, M. E. (1997). The development of father-infant relationships. In M. E. Lamb (Ed.), *The Role of the Father in Child Development* (3rd Ed.) (104–120). New York: Wiley.

Lamb, M. E. (1998). Nonparental child care: Context, quality, correlates, and consequences. In I. E. Sigel & K. A. Renninger (Eds), *Handbook of Child Psychology, Vol. 4, Child Psychology in Practice* (5th Ed.) (73–133). New York: Wiley.

Lamb, M. E. (2004). *The Role of the Father in Child Development*. London: Wiley.

Lamon, S. J. (1996). The development of unitizing: Its role in children's partitioning strategies. *Journal for Research in Mathematics Education*, 27, 170–193.

Lane, D. A. (1989). Bullying in school: The need for an integrated approach. In E. Roland & E. Munthe (Eds), *Bullying: An International Perspective* (x–xiv). London: David Fulton.

Langer, A. (2003). Forms of workplace literacy using reflection-with-action methods: A scheme for inner-city adults. *Reflective Practice*, 4 (3), 317–333.

Langlois, J. H. & Downs, A. C. (1980). Mothers, fathers, and peers as socialization agents of sex-typed play behaviors in young children. *Child Development*, 51, 1237–1247.

Lanz, M., Iafrate, R., Rosnati, R. & Scabini, E. (1999). Parent-child communication and adolescent self-esteem in separated, intercountry adoptive and intact non-adoptive families. *Journal of Adolescence*, 22 (6), 785–794.

Larson, R. W. (2001). How US children and adolescents spend time: what it does (and doesn't) tell us about their development. *Current Directions in Psychological Science*, 10, 160–164.

Lavonen, J. Juuti, K., Aksela, M. & Meisalo, V. (2006). A professional development project for improving the use of information and communication technologies in science teaching. *Technology, Pedagogy and Education*, 15 (2), 159–174.

Law, J., Garrett, Z., & Nye, C. (2004). *Speech and language therapy interventions for children with primary speech and language delay or disorder. Cochrane Collaboration Database of Systematic Reviews 2009*, 4, CD004110.

Leach, F. (2003). Learning to be violent: The role of the school in developing adolescent gendered behaviour. *Compare*, 33 (3), 385–400.

Leader, L. R., Baille, P. & Martin, B. (1982). The assessment and significance of habituation to a repeated stimulus by the human foetus. *Early Human Development*, 7, 211–219.

Leaper, C. (1991). Influence and involvement in children's discourse: Age, gender and partner effects. *Child Development*, 62, 797–811.

Leaper, C. (2000). Gender, affiliation, assertion, and the interactive context of parent-child play. *Developmental Psychology*, 36, 381–393.

Leary, M.R. (2008). *Introduction to Behavioural Research Methods* (5th Ed.). Boston, MA: Pearson.

Le Corre, M. & Carey, S. (2007). One, two, three, nothing more: An investigation of the conceptual sources of verbal number principles. *Cognition*, 105, 395–438.

Le Doux, J. (1999). *The Emotional Brain*. London: Phoenix.

Lee, L., Stemple, J., Glaze, L. & Kelchner, L. (2004). Quick screen for voice and supplementary documents for identifying pediatric voice disorders. *Language, Speech, and Hearing Schools*, 35, 318–319.

Leech, D. & Campos, E. (2003). Is comprehensive education really free?: A case-study of the effects of secondary school admissions policies on house prices in one local area. *Journal of the Royal Statistical Society: Series A (Statistics in Society)*, 166 (1), 135–154.

Leinonen, E. & Letts, C. (1997). Why pragmatic impairment? A case study in the comprehension of inferential meaning. *European Journal of Disorders of Communication*, 32, 35–52.

Lemery, K. S., Goldsmith, H. H., Klinnert, M. D. & Mrazek, D. A. (1999). Developmental models of infant and childhood temperament. *Developmental Psychology*, 35, 189–204.

Lenneberg, E. (1967). *Biological Foundations of Language*. New York: Wiley.

Leo, I. & Simion, F. (2009). Face processing at birth: A Thatcher Illusion Study. *Developmental Science*, 12, 492–498.

Lerner, J. V. & Galambos, N. L. (1985). Maternal role satisfaction, mother-infant interaction and child temperament. *Developmental Psychology*, 21, 1157–1164.

Leroux, G., Spiess, J., Zago, L., Rossi, S., Lubin, A., Turbelin, M. R., Mazoyer, B., Tzourio-Mazoyer, N., Houde, O. & Joliot, M. (2009). Adult brains don't fully overcome biases that lead to incorrect performance during cognitive development: An fMRI study in young adults completing a Piaget-like task. *Developmental Science*, 12, 326–338.

Leslie, A.M. (1987). Pretence and representation: The origins of 'theory of mind'. *Psychological Review*, 94, 412–426.

Leslie, A.M. (1994). Pretending and believing: Issues in the theory of ToM. *Cognition*, 50, 211–238.

Leslie, A.M. & Frith, U. (1988). Autistic children's understanding of seeing, knowing, and believing. *British Journal of Developmental Psychology*, 6, 315–324.

Leslie, A.M. & Thaiss, L. (1992). Domain specificity in conceptual development: Neuropsychological evidence from autism. *Cognition*, 43, 225–251.

Lester, B. M., Hoffman, J. & Brazelton, T. B. (1985). The rythmic structure of mother–infant interaction in term and preterm infants. *Child Development*, 56, 15–27.

Levin, J. R. (1976). What have we learned about maximising what children learn? In J. R. Levin and V. L. Allen (Eds), *Cognitive Learning in Children: Theories and Strategies* (105–134). New York: Academic Press.

Levin, J. R. & Nolan, J. F. (2000). Principles of Classroom Management: *A Professional Decision-making Model*. Boston, MA: Allyn and Bacon.

Levin, M.L., Xu, X.H. & Bartkowski, J.P. (2002). Seasonality of sexual debut. *Journal of Marriage and the Family*, 64, 871–884.

Levinson, S. C. (1983). *Pragmatics*. Cambridge: Cambridge University Press.

Levy, S. E., Mandell, D. S. & Schultz, R. T. (2009). Autism. *Lancet*, 374, 1627–1638.

Lewin, C., Somekh, B. & Steadman, S. (2008). Embedding interactive whiteboards in teaching and learning: The process of change in pedagogic practice. *Education and Information Technologies*, 13 (4), 291–303.

Lewis, A. & Mayer, R. (1987). Students' miscomprehension of relational statements in arithmetic word problems. *Journal of Educational Psychology*, 79, 363–371.

Lewis, M. (1975). The development of attention and perception in the infant and young child. In W. M. Cruickshank & D. P. Hallahan (Eds). *Perceptual and Learning Disabilities in Children* (Vol. 2, 137–162). Syracuse, NY: Syracuse University Press.

Lewis, M. (1990). Social knowledge and social development. *Merrill-Palmer Quarterly*, 36, 93–116.

Lewis, M. (1991). Ways of knowing: Objective selfawareness of consciousness. *Developmental Review*, 11, 231–243.

Lewis, M. & Brooks-Gunn, J. (1978). Self-knowledge and emotional development. In M. Lewis & L. A. Rosenblum (Eds), *The Development of Affect* (205–226). New York: Plenum Press.

Lewis, M. & Brooks-Gunn, J. (1979). *Social Cognition and the Acquisition of Self*. New York: Plenum Press.

Li, Z., van Aelst, L. & Cline, H. T. (2000). Rho GTPases regulate distinct aspects of dendritic arbor growth in Xenopus central neurons *in vivo*. *Nature Neuroscience*, 3, 217–225.

Libet, B., Wright, E. W., Feinstein, B. & Pearl, D. K. (1979). Subjective referencing of the timing for a conscious experience. *Brain*, 102, 193–224.

Liben, L. S. & Signorella, M. L. (1993). Gender-schematic processing in children: The role of initial interpretations of stimuli. *Developmental Psychology*, 29, 141–149.

Liddell, C. & Rae, G. (2001). Predicting early grade retention: A longitudinal investigation of primary school progress in a sample of rural South African children. *The British Journal of Educational Psychology*, 71 (3), 413–428.

Liebkind, K. & Jasinskaja-Lahti, I. (2000). Acculturation and psychological well-being among immigrant adolescents in Finland: A comparative study of adolescents from different cultural backgrounds. *Journal of Adolescent Research*, 15 (4), 446–469.

Likierman, H. & Muter, V. (2005). *ADHD and ADD*. Website ADHD Treatment Options – OmniMedicalSearch.com, retrieved 23 July 2010.

Liley, A. W. (1972). The foetus as a personality. *Australian and New Zealand Journal of Psychiatry*, 6, 99–103.

Lindsey, E. W. & Colwell, M. J. (2003). Preschoolers' emotional competence: Links to pretend and physical play. *Child Study Journal*, 33, 39–52.

Lipkin, P. H. (2005). Towards creation of a unified view of the neurodevelopment of the infant. *Mental Retardation and Developmental Disabilities Research Reviews*, 11, 103–106.

Livingstone, S. & Bovill, M. (2001). *Children and Their Changing Media Environment: A European Comparative Study*. Mahwah, MJ: Erlbaum.

Lloyd, B. & Duveen, G. (1992). *Gender Identities and Education: The Impact of Starting School*. London: Harvester Wheatsheaf.

Locke, A., Ginsborg, J. & Peers, I. (2001). Development and disadvantage: Implications for the early years and beyond. *International Journal Language & Communication Disorders*, 37 (1), 3–15.

Locke, J. (1690). *Concerning Human Understanding*. Retrieved October 14, 2010 from http://arts.cuhk.edu.hk/Philosophy/Locke/echu/.

Lodge, C. (2002). *Tutors talking. Pastoral Care in Education*, 20 (4), 35–37.

Loftus, E. F. (1993). The reality of repressed memories. *American Psychologist*, 48 (5), 518–537.

Lorberbaum, J. P., Newman, J. D., Horwitz, A. R., Dubno, J. D., Lydiard, R. B., Hamner, M. B., Bohning, D. E. & George, M. S. (2002). A potential role for thalamocingulate circuitry in human maternal behaviour. *Biological Psychiatry*, 51, 431–445.

Lorenz, K. (1952). *King Soloman's Ring*. New York: Crowell.

Lorenz, K. (1966). *On Aggression*. London: Methuen.

Louis, J., Cannard, C., Bastuji, H., & Challamel, M. J. (1997). Sleep ontogenesis revisited: A longitudinal 24-hour home polygraphic study on 15 normal infants during the first 2 years of life. *Sleep*, 20, 323–333.

Love, J., Harrison, L., Sagi-Schwartz, A., van IJzendoorn, M., Ross, C., Ungerer, J., Raikes, H., Brady-Smith, C., Boller, K., Brooks-Gunn, J., Constantine, J., Kisker, E., Paulsell, D. & Chazan-Cohen, R. (2003). Child care quality matters: How conclusions may vary with context. *Child Development*, 74, 1021–1033.

Lummaa, V., Vuorisalo, T., Barr, R. G. & Lehtonen, L. (1998). Why cry? Adaptive significance of intensive crying in human infants. *Evolution and Human Behaviour*, 19, 193–202.

Lyle, S. & Hendley, D. (2007). Can portfolios support critical reflection? Assessing the portfolios of Schools Liaison Police Officers. *Journal of In-Service Education*, 33 (2), 189–207.

Lyons-Ruth, K., Repacholi, B., McLeod, S. & Silva, E. (1991). Disorganized attachment behavior in infancy: Short-term stability, maternal and infant correlates and risk-related subtypes. *Development and Psychopathology*, 3, 377–396.

Lyons-Ruth, K., Bronfman, E. & Parsons, E. (1999). Maternal frightened, frightening or atypical behavior and disorganized infant attachment patterns. In J. E. Vondna and D. Barnett (Eds), *Atypical Attachment in Infancy and Early Childhood Among Children at Developmental Risk. Monographs of the Society for Research in Child Development*, 64 (3), Serial No. 258, 67–96.

Lytton, H. & Romney, D. M. (1991). Parents' differential socialization of boys and girls: A meta-analysis. *Psychological Bulletin*, 109, 267–296.

Maas, W. (2000). Early detection of speech and language delays in the Netherlands. The case for integrating primary and secondary prevention. *Child: Care, Health and Development*, 26 (2), 150–162.

Maccoby, E. E. (1980). *Social Development, Psychological Growth and the Parent-child Relationship*. New York: Harcourt Brace Jovanovich.

Maccoby, E. E. (1988). Gender as a social category. *Developmental Psychology*, 24, 755–765.

Maccoby, E. E. (1990). Gender and relationships: A developmental account. *American Psychologist*, 45, 513–520.

Maccoby, E. E. (1998). *The Two Sexes: Growing up Apart, Coming Together*. Cambridge, MA: Harvard University Press.

Maccoby, E. E. (2000). Perspectives on gender development. *International Journal of Behavioral Development*, 24, 398–406.

Maccoby, E. E. (2002). Gender and group process: A developmental perspective. *Current Directions in Psychological Science*, 11, 54–58.

Maccoby, E. E. & Jacklin, C. N. (1974). *The Psychology of Sex Differences*. Stanford, CA: Stanford University Press.

Macdonald, H. (2002). Perinatal care at the threshold of viability. *Pediatrics*, 110, 1024–1027.

MacFarlane, A. (1975). Olfaction in the development of social preferences in the human neonate. In *Parent-infant Interaction*. (CIBA Foundation Symposium No. 33) (103–117). Amsterdam: Elsevier.

MacLean, P. D. (Ed.) (1990). *The Triune Brain in Evolution: Role in Paleocerebral Functions*. New York: Plenum.

Madsen, K. C. (1996). Differing perceptions of bullying and their practical implications. *Education and Child Psychology*, 13, 14–22.

Maguire, M. & Dunn, J. (1997). Friendships in early childhood and social understanding. *International Journal of Behavioral Development*, 21, 669–686.

Mahady-Wilton, M.M., Craig, W.M. & Pepler, D.J. (2000). Emotional regulation and display in classroom victims of bullying: Characteristic expressions of affect, coping styles and relevant contextual factors. *Social Development*, 9, 226–246.

Main, M. & Cassidy, J. (1988). Categories of responses to reunion with the parent at age 6: Predictable for infant classifications and stable over a 1-month period. *Developmental Psychology*, 24, 415–426.

Main, M. & Goldwyn, R. (1994). *Adult Attachment and Classification System*. Unpublished manuscript. Berkeley, CA: University of California Press.

Main, M. & Hesse, E. (1990). Parents' unresolved traumatic experiences are related to infant disorganized attachment status: Is frightened and/or frightening parental behavior the linking mechanism? In M. T. Greenberg, D. Cicchetti & E. M. Cummings (Eds), *Attachment During the Preschool Years: Theory, Research and Intervention* (161–182). Chicago, IL: University of Chicago Press.

Main, M. & Solomon, J. (1990). Procedures for identifying disorganized/disoriented infants during the Ainsworth Strange Situation. In M. Greenberg, D. Cicchetti & M. Cummings (Eds), *Attachment in the Preschool Years: Theory, Research and Intervention* (121–160). Chicago, IL: University of Chicago Press.

Main, M., Kaplan, N. & Cassidy, J. (1985). Security in infancy, childhood, and adulthood: A move to the level of representation. In I. Bretherton & E. E. Waters (Eds), *Growing Points of Attachment Theory and Research*. Monographs of the Society for Research in Child Development, 50, 66–104.

Maines, B. & Robinson, G. (1991). Don't beat the bullies! *Educational Psychology in Practice*, 7, 168–172.

Maines, B. & Robinson, G. (1992). *The No-Blame Approach*. Bristol: Lucky Duck.

Maines, B. & Robinson, G. (1998). The no-blame approach to bullying. In D. Shorrocks-Taylor (Ed.), *Directions in Educational Psychology* (281–295). London, Whurr.

Mamede, E., Nunes, T. & Bryant, P. (2005). The equivalence of ordering of fractions in part-whole and quotient situations. In W. Chick & J. L. Vincent (Eds), *Proceedings of the 29th Conference of the International Group for the Psychology of Mathematics Education* (3-281–3-288), Melbourne: PME.

Mamede, E. P. B. d. C. (2007). *The effects of situations on children's understanding of fractions*. Unpublished Ph.D. Thesis, Oxford Brookes University, Oxford.

Mamede, E. (2009). Early years mathematics. The case of fractions. In Durand-Guerrier, V., Soury-Lavergne, S. & Arzarello, F. (Eds), *CERME 6, Proceedings of the Sixth Congress of the European Society for Research in Mathematics Education* (2607–2616). Lyon: Institut National de Recherché Pédagogique.

Mampe, B., Friederici, A. D., Christophe, A. & Wermke, K. (2009). Newborns' cry melody is shaped by their native language. *Current Biology*, 19, 1994–1997.

Mandler, J. M. (2003). Conceptual categorization. In D. H. Rakison & L. M. Oakes (Eds), *Early Category and Concept Development: Making Sense of the Blooming, Buzzing Confusion* (103–131). Oxford: Oxford University Press.

Mandler, J. M. & McDonough, L. M. (1993). Concept formation in infancy. *Cognitive Development*, 8, 291–318.

Mangelsdorf, S. C., Schoppe, S. J. & Buur, H. (2000). The meaning of parental reports: A contextual approach to the study of temperament and behavior problems. In V. J. Molfese & D. L. Molfese (Eds), *Temperament and Personality Across the Life Span* (121–140). Mahwah, NJ: Erlbaum.

Mannuzza, S., Klein, R. G., Bessler, A., Malloy, P. & LaPadula, M. (1993). Adult outcome of hyperactive boys: Educational achievement, occupational rank, and psychiatric status. *Archives of General Psychiatry*, 50, 565–576.

Margison, F. R., McGrath, G., Barkham, M., Mellor-Clark, J., Audin, K., Connell, J. & Evans, C. (2000). Measurement and psychotherapy: Evidence-based practice and practice-based evidence. *British Journal of Psychiatry*, 177, 123–130.

Mariani, M. & Barkley, R. A. (1997). Neuropsychological and academic functioning in preschool children with attention deficit hyperactivity disorder. *Developmental Neuropsychology*, 13, 111–129.

Marland, M. (2002). From 'Form Teacher' to 'Tutor': The Development from the fifties to the seventies. *Pastoral Care in Education*, 20 (4), 3–11.

Marsh, H. W., Craven, R. & Debus, R. (1998). Structure, stability, and development of young children's selfconcepts: A multicohort-multioccasion study. *Child Development*, 69, 1030–1053.

Martin, C. L. (1993). New directions for investigating children's gender knowledge. *Developmental Review*, 13, 184–204.

Martin, C. L. & Halverson, C. F. (1981). A schematic processing model of sex typing and stereotyping in children. *Child Development*, 52, 1119–1134.

Martin, C. L. & Halverson, C. F. (1983). The effects of sex-typing schemas on young children's memory. *Child Development*, 54, 563–574.

Martin, C. L. & Halverson, C. F. (1987). The role of cognition in sex role acquisition. In D. B. Carter (Ed.), *Current Conceptions of Sex Roles and Sex Typing: Theory and Research* (123–137). New York: Praeger.

Martin, C. L., Eisenbud, L. & Rose, H. (1995). Children's gender-based reasoning about toys. *Child Development*, 66, 1453–1471.

Martin, C. L., Fabes, R. A., Evans, S. M. & Wyman, H. (1999). Social cognition on the playground: Children's beliefs about playing with girls versus boys and their relations to sex segregated play. *Journal of Social and Personal Relationships*, 16, 751–771.

Martinussen, R., Hayden, J., Hogg-Johnson, S. & Tannock, R. (2005). A meta-analysis of working memory impairments in children with attention-deficit/hyperactivity disorder. *Journal of the American Academy of Child and Adolescent Psychiatry*, 44, (4), 377–384.

Marzano, R. J. & Marzano, J. S. (2003). The key to classroom management. *Educational Leadership*, 61 (1), 6–13.

Maschietto, M., & Bussi, M. B. (2009). Working with artefacts: Gestures, drawings and speech in the construction of the mathematical meaning of the visual pyramid. *Educational Studies in Mathematics*, 70 (2), 143–157.

Mayseless, O. (2006). *Parenting Representations: Theory, Research and Clinical Implications*. New York: Cambridge University Press.

McBryde, C., Ziviani, J. & Cuskelly, M. (2004). School readiness and factors that influence decision making. *Occupational Therapy International*, 11 (4), 193–208.

McCann, D., Barrett, A., Cooper, A., Crumpler, D., Dalen, L., Grimshaw, K., Kitchin, E., Lok, K., Porteous, L., Prince, E., Sonuga-Barke, Edmund, E.J.B.,Warner, J.O. & Stevenson, J. (2007). Food additives and hyperactive behaviour in 3-year-old and 8/9-year-old children in the community: A randomised, double-blinded, placebo-controlled trial. *The Lancet*, 370, (9598), 1560–1567.

McCartney, K., Harris, M. J. & Bernieri, F. (1990). Growing up and growing apart: A developmental meta-analysis of twin studies. *Psychological Bulletin*, 107, 226–237.

McCarty, M. E. & Ashmead, D. H. (1999). Visual control of reaching and grasping in infants. *Developmental Psychology*, 35, 620–631.

McCarty, M. E., Clifton, R. K. & Collard, R. R. (1999). Problem-solving in infancy: The emergence of an action plan. *Developmental Psychology*, 35, 1091–1101.

McClearn, G. E., Johansson, B., Berg, S., Pedersen, N. L., Ahern, F., Petrill, S. A. & Plomin, R. (1997). Substantial genetic influence on cognitive abilities in twins 80 years old or more. *Science*, 276 (5318), 1560–1563.

McCormick, M. C., McCarton, C., Tonascia, J. & Brooks-Gunn, J. (1993). Early educational intervention for very low birth weight infants: Results from the Infant Health and Development Program. *Journal of Pediatrics*, 123, 527–533.

McCracken, J. T., McGough, J., Shah, B., Cronin, P., Hong, D., Aman, M.G., Arnold, E., Lindsay, R., Nash, P., Hollway, J., McDougle, C. J., Posey, D., Swiezy, N., Kohn, A., Scahill, L., Martin, A., Koenig, K., Volkmar, F., Carroll, D., Lancor, A., Tierney, E., Ghuman, J., Gonzalez, N. M., Grados, M., Vitiello, B., Ritz, L., Davies, M., Robinson, J. & McMahon, D. (2002). Risperidone in children with autism and serious behavioral problems. *New England Journal of Medicine*, 347 (5), 314–321.

McCrink, K. & Wynn, K. (2004). Large number addition and subtraction by 9-month-old infants. *Psychological Science*, 15, 776–781.

McCune-Nicolich, L. & Bruskin, C. (1982). Combinatorial competency in symbolic play and language. In D. J. Pepler & K. H. Rubin (Eds), *The Play of Children: Current Theory and Research* (Vol. 6, 30–45). New York: Karger.

McElhaney, K.B., Antonishak, J. & Allen, J. P. (2008). "They like me, they like me not": Popularity and adolescents' perceptions of acceptance predicting social funcioning over time. *Child Development*, 79, (3), 720–731.

McGee, R., Williams, S. & Feehan, M. (1992). Attention-deficit disorder and age of onset of problem behaviours. *Journal of Abnormal Child Psychology*, 20 (5), 487–502.

McGivern, R.F., Andersen, J., Byrd, D., Mutter, K.L., & Reilly, J. (2002). Cognitive efficiency on a match to sample task decreases at the onset of puberty in children. *Brain and Cognition*, 50, 73–89.

McGregor, H. A. & Elliot, A. J. (2005). The shame of failure: Examining the link between fear of failure and shame. *Personality and Social Psychology Bulletin*, 31 (2), 218–231.

McLaughlin, P. & Simpson, N. (2007). The common first year programme: Some lessons from a construction science course. *Teaching in Higher Education*, 12 (1), 13–23.

McPherson, S., Fairbanks, L., Tiken, S., Cummings, J.I. & Back-Madruga, C. (2002). Apathy and executive function in Alzheimer's disease. *Journal of the International Neuropsychological Society*, 8, 373–381.

Mead, G. H. (1934). *Mind, Self and Society*. Chicago, IL: University of Chicago Press.

Meaney, M. J. (2001). Maternal care, gene expression, and the transmission of individual differences in stress reactivity across generations. *Annual Review of Neuroscience*, 24, 1161–1192.

Mebert, C. J. (1991). Dimensions of subjectivity in parents' ratings of infant temperament. *Child Development*, 62, 352–361.

Medline Plus (2010). http://www.nichd.nih.gov/health/topics/Congenital_Adrenal_Hyperplasia.cfm.

Mehler, J., Jusczyk, P. W., Lambertz, G., Halsted, N., Bertoncini, J. & Amieltison, C. (1988). A precursor of language acquisition in young infants. *Cognition*, 29, 143–178.

Meins, E., Fernyhough, E., Fradley, E. & Tuckey, M. (2001). Rethinking maternal sensitivity: Mothers' comments on infants' mental processes predict security of attachment at 12 months. *Journal of Child Psychology and Psychiatry*, 42, 637–648.

Meins, E., Fernyhough, E., Wainwright, R., Das Gupta, M., Fradley, E. & Tuckey, M. (2002). Maternal mindmindedness and attachment security as predictors of theory of mind understanding. *Child Development*, 73, 1715–1726.

Melhuish, E. C., Mooney, A., Martin, S. & Lloyd, E. (1990). Type of childcare at 18 months—I. Differences in interactional experience. *Journal of Child Psychology and Psychiatry*, 31, 849–859.

Meltzoff, A. N. (1990). Foundations for developing a concept of self: The role of imitation in relating self to other and the value of social mirroring, social modelling, and self practice in infancy. In D. Cicchetti & M. Beeghly (Eds), *The Self in Transition: Infancy to Childhood* (139–164). Chicago, IL: University of Chicago Press.

Meltzoff, A.N. (1995). Understanding the intentions of others: Reenactment of intended acts by 18-month-old children. *Developmental Psychology*, 31, 838–850.

Meltzoff, A. N. & Moore, M. K. (1977). Imitation of facial and manual gestures by human neonates. *Science*, 198, 75–78.

Mennes, M., van den Bergh, B., Lagae, L. & Stiers, P. (2009). Developmental brain alterations in 17 year old boys are related to antenatal maternal anxiety. *Clinical Neurophysiology*, 120, 1116–1122.

Meristo, M., Falkman, K.W., Hjelmquist, E., Tedoldi, M. Surian, L. & Siegal, M. (2007). Language access and theory of mind reasoning: Evidence from deaf children in bilingual and oralist environments. *Developmental Psychology*, 43, (5), 1156–1169.

Merrell, K. W., Gueldner, B. A., Ross, S. W. & Isava, D. M. (2008). How effective are school bullying intervention programs? A meta-analysis of intervention research. *School Psychology Quarterly*, 23, 26–42.

Merriwether, A. M. & Liben, L. S. (1997). Adult's failures on euclidean and projective spatial tasks: Implications for characterizing spatial cognition. *Journal of Adult Development*, 4, 57–69.

Mervis, C. B., Mervis, C. A., Johnson, K. E. & Bertrand, J. (1992). Studying early lexical development: The value of the systematic diary method. In C. Rovee-Collier and L. P. Lipsitt (Eds), *Advances in Infancy Research*, Volume 7 (291–378). New Jersey: Ablex.

Meyer, M. A. (2007). Didactics, sense making, and educational experience. *European Educational Research Journal*, 6 (2), 161–173.

Michie, S. (1984). Why preschoolers are reluctant to count spontaneously. *British Journal of Developmental Psychology*, 2, 347–358.

Middleton, H. (2009). Problem-solving in technology education as an approach to education for sustainable development. *International Journal of Technology and Design Education*, 19 (2), 187–197.

Milgram, S. (1974). *Obedience to Authority; An Experimental View*. Harper Collins.

Miller, K. (1984). Measurement procedures and the development of quantitative concepts. In C. Sophian (Ed.), *Origins of Cognitive Skills. The Eighteenth Annual Carnegie Symposium on Cognition* (193–228). Hillsdale, NJ: Erlbaum.

Milne, R. & Bull, R. (1999). *Investigative interviewing: Psychology and Practice*. Chichester: Wiley.

Milne, R. & Bull, R. (2002). Back to basics: A componential analysis of the original cognitive interview mnemonics with three age groups. *Applied Cognitive Psychology*, 16, 743–753.

Mischel, W. (1966). A social learning view of sex differences in behavior. In E. E. Maccoby. (Ed.), *The Development of Sex Differences* (56–81). London: Tavistock.

Mischel, W. (1970). Sex typing and socialization. In P. H. Mussen (Ed.), *Carmichael's Manual of Child Psychology*, Vol. 2 (3–72). New York: Wiley.

Mishna, F. (2004). A qualitative study of bullying from multiple perspectives. *Children & Schools*, 26, 234–247.

Mo, Z. & Zecevic, N. (2008). Is *Pax6* critical for neurogenesis in the human foetal brain? *Cerebral Cortex*, 18, 1455–1465.

Moffitt, T. E., Caspi, A., Harrington, H., Milne, B. J., Melchior, M., Goldberg, D. & Poulton, R. (2007). Generalized anxiety disorder and depression: Childhood risk factors in a birth cohort followed to age 32. *Psychological Medicine*, 37, 441–452.

Molfese, V., Modglin, A. & Molfese, D. (2003). The role of environment in the development of reading skills: A longitudinal study of preschool and school-age measures. *Journal of Learning Disabilities*, 36, 59–67.

Molina, J. C., Chotro, M. G. & Dominguez, H. D. (1995). Foetal alcohol learning resulting from contamination of the prenatal environment. In J.P. Lecanuet, W.P. Fifer, N. A. Krasnegor & W. P. Smotherman (Eds), *Foetal Development: A Psychobiological Perspective* (419–438). Hillsdale, NJ: Erlbaum.

Money, J. & Ehrhardt, A. A. (1972). Man and Woman/Boy and Girl. Baltimore, MD: Johns Hopkins University Press.

Munroe, R. H., Shimmin, H. S. & Munroe, R. L. (1984). Gender understanding and sex role preference in four cultures. *Developmental Psychology*, 20, 673–682.

Monks, C.P., Smith, P.K. & Swettenham, J. (2004). Aggressors, victims, and defenders in preschool: peer, self-, and teacher reports. *Merrill-Palmer Quarterly*, 49, 453–469.

Monks, C.P. & Smith, P.K. (2006). Definitions of 'bullying'; Age differences in understanding of the term, and the role of experience. *British Journal of Developmental Psychology*, 24, 801–821.

Moni, K., van Kraayenoord, C. & Baker, C. (2002). Students' perceptions of literacy assessment. *Assessment in Education: Principles, Policy & Practice*, 9 (3), 319–342.

Montgomery, A., Bjornstad, G. & Dennis, J. (2006). *Media based behavioural treatments for behaviour problems in children*. Cochrane Database of Systematic Reviews, 1. Art. No.: CD002206. DOI: 10.1002/14651858.

Moore, K. L. & Persaud, T. V. N. (2003). *The Developing Human: Clinically Oriented Embryology*. Philadelphia, PA: Saunders.

Morawska, A. & Sanders, M. R. (2006). Self-administered behavioural family interventions for parents of toddlers. Part 1: efficacy. *Journal of Consulting and Clinical Psychology*, 74, 10–19.

Morgan, K. & Hayne, H. (2006). The effect of encoding time on retention by infants and young children. *Infant Behaviour and Development*, 29, 599–602.

Morgan, S. & Stevens, P. (2008). Transgender identity development as represented by a group of female-to-male transgendered adults. *Issues in Mental Health Nursing*, 29 (6), 585–599.

Mori, L. & Peterson, L. (1995). Knowledge of safety of high and low active-impulsive boys – implications for child injury prevention. *Journal of Clinical Child Psychology*, 24, 370–376.

Morrell, J. & Murray, L. (2003). Parenting and the development of conduct disorder and hyperactive symptoms in childhood: A prospective longitudinal study from 2 months to 8 years. *Journal of Child Psychology and Psychiatry*, 44, 489–508.

Morrongiello, B. A., Fenwick, K. D., Hillier, L., & Chance, G. (1994). Sound localization in newborn human infants. *Developmental Psychobiology*, 27, 519–538.

Morton, J. & Johnson, M. H. (1991). Conspec and Conlearn: A two-process theory of infant face recognition. *Psychological Review*, 98, 164–181.

Müller-Lyer, F. C. (1890). Review (untitled). *The American Journal of Psychology* – Stable URL: http://www.jstor.org/stable/1411109 (Accessed: 16/08/2010), 3(2), 207–208.

Mumtaz, S. & Humphreys, G. (2001). The effects of bilingualism on learning to read English: Evidence from the contrast between Urdu-English bilingual and English monolingual children. *Journal of Research in Reading*, 24 (2), 113–134.

Murray, L. (1992). The impact of post-natal depression on infant development. *Journal of Child Psychology and Psychiatry*, 33, 543–561.

Murray, L. & Stein, A. (1991). The effects of postnatal depression on mother-infant relations and infant development. In M. Woodhead, R. Carr & P. Light (Eds), *Becoming a Person* (144–166). London: Routledge.

Mynard, H., Joseph, S. & Alexander, J. (2000). Peervictimisation and posttraumatic stress in adolescents. *Personality and Individual Differences*, 29 (5), 815–821.

Naito, M. (2003). The relationship between theory of mind and episodic memory: Evidence for the development of autonoetic consciousness. *Journal of Experimental Child Psychology*, 85, 312–336.

Nakagawa, M., Lamb, M. E. & Miyaki, K. (1992). Antecedents and correlates of the Strange Situation behavior of Japanese infants. *Journal of Cross-Cultural Psychology*, 23, 300–310.

Nakano, T., Watanabe, H., Homae, F. & Taga, G. (2009). Prefrontal cortical involvement in young infants' analysis of novelty. *Cerebral Cortex*, 19, 455–463.

Nansel, T.R., Overpeck, M.D., Pilla, R.S., Ruan, W.J., Simmons-Morton, B. & Scheidt, P. (2001). Bullying behaviour among U.S. youth: Prevalence and association with psychosocial adjustment. *Journal of the American Medical Association*, 285, 2094–2100.

Nathanielsz, P. (1999). *Life in the Womb. The Origin of Health and Disease*. Ithaca, NY: Promethan Press.

National Initiative for Autism: Screening and Assessment (2003). *National Autism Plan for Children*. London: National Autistic Society.

Naylor, P., Cowie, H., Cossin, F., de Bettencourt, R. & Lemme, F. (2006). Teachers' and pupils' definitions of bullying. *British Journal of Educational Psychology*, 76, 553–576.

Nazzi, T., Floccia, C. & Bertoncini, J. (1998). Discrimination of pitch contours by neonates. *Infant Behavior and Development*, 21, 779–784.

Nelson, C. A. (2002a). Neural development and lifelong plasticity. In R. M. Lerner, F. Jacobs, & D. Wertleib (Eds), *Handbook of Developmental Science* (Vol. 1, 31–60). Thousand Oaks, CA: Sage.

Nelson, C. A. (2002b). The ontogeny of human memory: A cognitive neuroscience perspective. In M. H. Johnson., Y. Munakata & R. O. Gilmore (Eds), *Brain Development and Cognition: A Reader* (151–178). Oxford: Blackwell.

Nelson, C. A., Thomas, K. M. & de Hann, M. (2006). *Neuroscience of Cognitive Development: The Role of Experience and the Developing Brain*. Hoboken, N.J.: Wiley.

Nelson, E. A. S., Yu, L. M., Wong, D., Wong, H. Y. & Yim, L. (2004). Rolling over in infants: Age, ethnicity, and cultural differences. *Developmental Medicine & Child Neurology*, 46, 706–709.

Nelson, K. and Gruendel, J. (1981). Generalised event representations: Basic building blocks of cognitive development. In M. E. Lamb and A. L. Brown (Eds), *Advances in Developmental Psychology*, Volume 1 (21–46). Hillsdale, NJ: Erlbaum.

Neuman, W.L. (2007). *Basics of Social Research: Qualitative and Quantitative Approaches* (2nd Ed.). London: Pearson.

Newman, C., Atkinson, J. & Braddick, O. (2001). The development of reaching and looking preferences in infants to objects of different sizes. *Developmental Psychology*, 37, 561–572.

Newman, G.E., Herrmann, P., Wynn, K. & Keil, F. C. (2008). Biases towards internal features in infants' reasoning about objects. *Cognition*, 107, 420–432.

Newman, M. (2008). Big or small: Does the size of a secondary school matter? FORUM: for Promoting 3-19 *Comprehensive Education*, 50 (2), 167–176.

Newschaffer, C. J., Croen, L. A., Daniels, J., Giarelli, E., Grether, J. K., Levy, S. E., Mandell, D. S., Miller, L. A. & Pinto-Martin, J. (2007). The epidimiology of autism spectrum disorders. *Annual Review of Public Health*, 28, 235–258.

NHS immunisation statistics, England: 2001–02. Retrieved November 6 from http://www.dh.gov.uk/en/ Publicationsandstatistics/Statistics/StatisticalWorkAreas/ Statisticalhealthcare/DH_4016228.

NICE (2008). *Attention Deficit Hyperactivity Disorder: Diagnosis and Management of ADHD in Children, Young People and Adults*. London: National Institute for Health and Clinical Excellence.

Nichols, S. & Stich, S. (2003). *Mindreading: An Integrated Account of Pretence, Self-awareness and Understanding of Other Minds*. Oxford: Oxford University Press.

Nigg, J. T. (2001). Is ADHD a disinhibitory disorder? *Psychological Bulletin*, 127, 571–598.

Nigg, J. T. (2006). Temperament and developmental psychopathology. *Journal of Child Psychology and Psychiatry*, 47, 395–422.

Nijmeijer, J. S., Minderaa, R. B., Buitelaar, J. K., Mulligan, A., Hartman, C. A. & Hoekstra, P. J. (2008). Attention deficit/hyperactivity disorder and social dysfunctioning. *Clinical Psychology Review*, 28, 692–708.

Nilsson, L., & Hamberger, L. (1990). *A Child is Born*. New York: Delacorte.

Niswander, K. R. & Evans, A. T. (1996). *Manual of Obstetrics*. Boston, MA: Little Brown.

Notaro, P. C. & Volling, B. L. (1999). Parental responsiveness and infant-parent attachment: A replication study with fathers and mothers. *Infant Behaviour and Development*, 22, 345–352.

Novillis, C. F. (1976). An analysis of the fraction concept into a hierarchy of selected subconcepts and the testing of the hierarchical dependencies. *Journal for Research in Mathematics Education*, 7, 131–144.

Nowakowski, R. S. & Hayes, N. L. (2002). General principles of CNS development. In Johnson, M. H., Munakata, Y. & Gilmore, R. O. (Eds), *Brain Development and Cognition: A Reader* (57–82). Oxford: Blackwell.

Noyes, A. (2006). School transfer and the diffraction of learning trajectories. *Research Papers in Education*, 21 (1), 43–62.

Nunes, T. & Bryant, P. (1996). *Children Doing Mathematics*. Oxford: Blackwell.

Nunes, T. & Bryant, P. (2010). Insights from everyday knowledge for mathematics education. In D. Preiss & R. Sternberg (Eds), *Innovations in Educational Psychology* (51–78). New York: Springer.

Nunes, T., Bryant, P., Burman, D., Bell, D. Evans, D. & Hallett, D. (2008a). Deaf children's informal knowledge of multiplicative reasoning. *Journal of Deaf Studies and Deaf Education*, 14, 260–277.

Nunes, T., Bryant, P., Evans, D., Bell, D., Gardner, S., Gardner, A. & Carraher, J. N. (2007a). The contribution of logical reasoning to the learning of mathematics in primary school. *British Journal of Developmental Psychology*, 25, 147–166.

Nunes, T., Bryant, P., Evans, D., Bell, D. & Hallett, D. (2008b). *Developing deaf children's understanding of additive composition*. American Educational Research Association Annual Meetings. 24–28 March, New York.

Nunes, T., Bryant, P., Sylva, K. & Barros, R. (2009). *Development of Maths Capabilities and Confidence in Primary School (No. Research Report DCSF-RR118)*. London: Department for Children, Schools and Families. Retrieved 7 November 2010 from http://publications.dcsf.gov.uk/ eOrderingDownload/DCSF-RB118.pdf.

Nunes, T., Bryant, P., Evans, D. & Bell, D. (2010). The scheme of correspondence and its role in children's mathematics. *British Journal of Educational Psychology, Monographs Series II*, 1(1), 1–18.

Nunes, T. & Moreno, C. (2002). An intervention program to promote deaf pupil's achievement in numeracy. *Journal of Deaf Studies and Deaf Education*, 7, 120–133.

Nunes, T., Bryant, P., Pretzlik, U., Bell, D., Evans, D. & Wade, J. (2007b). La compréhension des fractions chez les enfants. In M. Merri (Ed.), *Activité humaine et conceptualisation*.

Nunes, T., Bryant, P., Pretzlik, U. & Hurry, J. (2006). *Fractions: Difficult but Crucial in Mathematics Learning*. London Institute of Education, London: ESRC-Teaching and Learning Research Programme, Research Briefing Number 13.

Nunes, T. & Schliemann, A. D. (1990). Knowledge of the numeration system among pre-schoolers. In L. S. T. Wood

(Ed.), *Transforming Early Childhood Education: International Perspectives* (135–141). Hillsdale, NJ: Erlbaum.

Nunes, T., Schliemann, A. D. & Carraher, D. W. (1993). *Street Mathematics and School Mathematics*. New York: Cambridge University Press.

O'Brien, M. (1992). Gender identity and sex roles. In V. B. Van Hasselt & M. Hersen (Eds), *Handbook of Social Development: A Lifespan Perspective* (325–345). New York: Plenum Press.

O'Connor, M., Foch, T., Todd, S. & Plomin, R. (1980). A twin study of specific behavioural problems of socialisation as viewed by parents. *Journal of Abnormal Child Psychology*, 8, 189–199.

Offer, D. (1969) *The Psychological World of the Teenager. A Study of Normal Adolescent Boys*. New York: Basic Books.

Ohlsson, S. (1988). Mathematical meaning and applicational meaning in the semantics of fractions and related concepts. In J. Hiebert & M. Behr (Eds), *Number Concepts and Operations in the Middle Grades* (53–92). Reston, VA: National Council of Mathematics Teachers.

Okamoto, Y., Curtis, R., Jabagchourian, J. J. & Weckbacher, L. M. (2006). Mathematical precocity in young children: A neo-Piagetian perspective. *High Ability Studies*, 17 (2), 183–202.

Olive, M. & Liu, Y.J. (2005). Social validity of parent and teacher implemented assessment-based interventions for challenging behaviour. *Educational Psychology*, 25 (2–3), 305–312.

Oliver, L. N., Dunn, J. R., Kohen, D. E. & Hertzman, C. (2007). Do neighbourhoods influence the readiness to learn of kindergarten children in Vancouver? A multilevel analysis of neighbourhood effects. *Environment and Planning A*, 39 (4), 848–868.

Oller, D. K. (1980). The emergence of the sounds of speech in infancy. In G. Yeni-Komshian, J. F. & C. A. Ferguson (Eds), *Child Phonology: 1 Production* (93–112). New York: Academic Press.

Olweus, D. (1993a). *Bullying at School: What We Know and What We Can Do*. Oxford: Blackwell.

Olweus D. (1993b). Victimisation by peers: Antecedents and long-term outcomes. In K.H. Rubin & J.B. Asendorpf (Eds), *Social Withdrawal, Inhibition and Shyness in Childhood* (315–341). Hillsdale, NJ: Erlbaum.

Olweus, D. (1994). Bullying at School: Basic facts and effects of a school-based intervention programme. *Journal of Child Psychology and Child Psychiatry*, 35 (7), 171–1190.

O'Moore, A.M. & Kirkham, C. (2001). Self-esteem and its relationship to bullying behaviour. *Aggressive Behavior*, 27, 269–283.

O'Moore, A.M., Kirkham, C. & Smith, M. (1997). Bullying behaviour in Irish schools: A nationwide study. *The Irish Journal of Psychology*, 18, 141–169.

Onishi, K. H. & Baillargeon, R. (2005, April 8). Do 15-month-old infants understand false beliefs? *Science*, 308, 255–258.

Oortwijn, M., Boekaerts, M. & Vedder, P. (2008). The impact of the teacher's role and pupils' ethnicity and prior knowledge on pupils' performance and motivation to cooperate. *Instructional Science*, 36 (3), 251–268.

The Open University (2003). *U212 Childhood, Video 3, Band 3, Pretend play*. Milton Keynes: The Open University.

Opie, I. (1993). *The People in the Playground*. Oxford: Oxford University Press.

Orekhova, E. V., Stroganova, T. A. & Posikera, I. N. (2001). Alpha activity as an index of cortical inhibition during sustained internally controlled attention in infants. *Clinical Neurophysiology*, 112, 740–749.

Orekhova, E. V., Stroganova, T. A., Posikera, I. N. & Elam, M. (2006). EEG theta rhythm in infants and preschool children. *Clinical Neurophysiology*, 117, 1047–1062.

Orth, U., Trzesniewski, K.H. & Robins, R.W. (2010). Self-esteem development from young adulthood to old age: A cohort-sequential longitudinal study. *Journal of Personality and Social Psychology*, 98 (4), 645–658.

Ortner, T.M. & Sieverding, M. (2008). Where are the gender differences? Male priming boosts spatial skills in women. *Sex Roles*, 59 (3–4), 274–281.

Osborn, M. (2001). Constants and contexts in pupil experience of learning and schooling: Comparing learners in England, France and Denmark. *Comparative Education*, 37 (3), 267–278.

Osborne, J., Simon, S. & Collins, S. (2003). Attitudes towards science: A review of the literature and its implications. *International Journal of Science Education*, 25 (9), 1049–1079.

Oshima, J., Oshima, R., Murayama, I., Inagaki, S., Takenaka, M., Nakayama, H. & Yamaguchi, E. (2004). Design experiments in Japanese elementary science education with computer support for collaborative learning: Hypothesis testing and collaborative construction. *International Journal of Science Education*, 26 (10), 1199–1221.

Osler, A. (2000). Children's rights, responsibilities and understandings of school discipline. *Research Papers in Education*, 15 (1), 49–67.

Ostgard-Ybrandt, H. & Armelius, B.A. (2004). Self-concept and perception of early mother and father behavior in normal and antisocial adolescents. *Scandinavian Journal of Psychology*, 45 (5), 437–447.

Ostoja, E., McCrone, E., Lehn, L., Reed, T. & Sroufe, L. A. (1995). *Representations of close relationships in adolescence: Longitudinal antecedents from infancy through childhood*. Paper presented at the biennial meeting of the *Society for Research in Child Development*, Indianapolis, IN, March.

O'Toole, L. (2008). Understanding individual patterns of learning: Implications for the well-being of students. *European Journal of Education: Research, Development and Policies*, 43 (1), 71–86.

Oxford Dictionaries (2008). *Concise Oxford English Dictionary* (11th Ed., revised). Oxford: Oxford University Press.

Owens, L., Shute, R. & Slee, P. (2000) "I'm in and you're out . . .": Explanations for teenage girls' indirect aggression. *Psychology, Evolution & Gender*, 2, 19–46.

Palmer, E.J. & Hollin, C.R. (2001). Sociomoral reasoning, perceptions of parenting and self-reported delinquency in adolescents. *Applied Cognitive Psychology*, 15 (1), 85–100.

Palmert, M.R., Radovik, S. & Boepple, P.A. (1998). Leptin levels in children with central precocious puberty. *The Journal of Clinical Endocrinology & Metabolism*, 83 (7), 2260–2265.

Pantev, C., Ross, B., Fujioka, T., Trainor, L., Schulte, M. & Schulz, M. (2003). Music and learning-induced cortical plasticity. In G. Avanzini, D. Miciacchi, L. Lopez & M. Majno (Eds), *The Neurosciences and Music: Mutual Interactions and Implications of Developmental Functions*. Annals of the New York Academy of Sciences (438–450).

Papatheodorou, T. (2002). How we like our school to be: Pupils' voices. *European Educational Research Journal*, 1 (3), 445–467.

Pardini, M. & Nichelli, P.F. (2009). Age-related decline in mentalizing skills across adult life span. *Experimental Aging Research*, 35, 98–106.

Parker, J. G. & Asher, S. R. (1987). Peer relations and later personal adjustment: Are low accepted children at risk? *Psychological Bulletin*, 102, 357–389.

Parsons, L. M. & Osherson, D. (2001). New evidence for distinctive brain systems for deductive and probabilistic reasoning. *Cerebral Cortex*, 11, 954–965.

Parten, M. B. (1932). Social participation among preschool children. *Journal of Abnormal and Social Psychology*, 27, 243–269.

Parry, G. (2000). Evidence-based psychotherapy: An overview. In N. Rowland and S. Goss (Eds), *Evidence-based Counselling and Psychological Therapies: Research and Applications* (57–76). London: Routledge.

Parry, G. D., Cape, J. & Pilling, S. (2003). Clinical practice guidelines in clinical psychology and psychotherapy. *Journal of Clinical Psychology and Psychotherapy*, 10, 337–357.

Pascalis, O. & Slater, A. (Eds) (2003). *The Development of Face Processing in Infancy and Early Childhood*. New York: Nova Science.

Pasztor, A. (2008). The children of guest workers: Comparative analysis of scholastic achievement of pupils of Turkish origin throughout Europe. *Intercultural Education*, 19 (5), 407–419.

Paterson, S. J., Brown, J. H., Gsodi, M. K., Johnson, M. H. & Karmiloff-Smith, A. (1999). Cognitive modularity and genetic disorders. *Science Magazine*, 286, 2355–2358.

Patterson, C. J. (1995). Sexual orientation and human development: An overview. *Developmental Psychology,* 31 (Special issue: Sexual orientation and human development), 3–11.

Pauli-Pott, U, Mertesacker, B., Bade, U., Haverkock, A. & Beckmann, D. (2003). Parental perceptions and infant temperament development. *Infant Behavior and Development*, 26, 27–48.

Payne, L. (2007). A 'Children's Government' in England and child impact assessment. *Children & Society*, 21 (6), 470–475.

Pedlow, R., Sanson, A., Prior, M. & Oberklaid, F. (1993). Stability of maternally reported temperament from infancy to 8 years. *Developmental Psychology*, 29, 998–1007.

Pedrosa de Jesus, H. & Coelho Moreira, A. (2009). The role of students' questions in aligning teaching, learning and assessment: A case study from undergraduate sciences. *Assessment & Evaluation in Higher Education*, 34 (2), 193–208.

Pelham, W.E., Wheeler, T., & Chronis, A. (1998). Empirically supported psycho-social treatments for attention deficit hyperactivity disorder. *Journal of Clinical Child Psychology*, 27, 189–204.

Pelkonen, M., Marttunen, M. & Aro, H. (2003). Risk for depression: a 6-year follow-up of Finnish adolescents. *Journal of Affective Disorders*, 77 (1), 41–51.

Pellegrini, A. D. (2006). The development and function of rough-and-tumble play in childhood and adolescence: A sexual selection theory perspective. In A. Göncü, & S. Gaskins (Eds). *Play and Development: Evolutionary, Sociocultural and Functional Perspectives* (77–98). London: Erlbaum.

Pellegrini, A.D. & Bertini, M. (2001). Dominance in early adolescent boys: Affiliative and aggressive dimensions and possible functions. *Merrill-Palmer Quarterly*, 47, 142–163.

Pellegrini, A. D. & Smith, P. K. (1998). Physical activity play: The nature and function of a neglected aspect of play. *Child Development*, 69, 577–598.

Pennington, B. F. (2002). Genes and brain: individual differences and human universals. In M. H. Johnsom, Y. Munakata, R. O. Gilmore (Eds), *Brain Development and Cognition: A Reader* (494–508). Oxford: Blackwell.

Pennington, B. F., McGrath, L. M., Rosenberg, J., Barnard, H., et al. (2008). Gene–environment interactions in reading disability and attention-deficit/hyperactivity disorder. *Developmental Psychology*, 45, 77–89.

Pepler, D. J., Craig, W. M., Zieglier, S. & Charach, A. (1994). An evaluation of an anti-bullying intervention in Toronto schools. *Canadian Journal of Community Mental Health*, 13 (2), 95–110.

Perner, J. (1991). *Understanding the Representational Mind*. Cambridge, MA: MIT Press.

Perner, J., Kloo, D. & Gornik, E. (2007). Episodic memory development: Theory of mind is part of re-experiencing experienced events. *Infant and Child Development*, 16, 471–490.

Perner, J., Leekam, S.R. & Wimmer, H. (1987). Three-year-old's difficulty with false-belief: the case for a conceptual deficit. *British Journal of Developmental Psychology*, 5, 125–137.

Perner, J. & Ruffman, T. (1995). Episodic memory and autonoetic consciousness: Developmental evidence and a theory of childhood amnesia. *Journal of Experimental Child Psychology*, 59 (3), 516–548.

Perner, J., & Ruffman, T. (2005). Infants' insight into the mind: How deep? *Science*, 308, 214–216.

Perring, C. (1997). Medicating children: The case of Ritalin. *Bioethics*, 1, 228–240.

Peskin, J. & Ardino, V. (2003). Representing the mental world in children's social behavior: Playing hide-and-seek and keeping a secret. *Social Development*, 12, 496–512.

Pesonen, A.K., Räikkonen, K., Heinonen, K., Järvenpää, A.L. & Strandberg, R.E. (2006). Depressive vulnerability in parents and their 5-year-old child's temperament: A family system perspective. *Journal of Family Psychology*, 20, 648–655.

Pesonen, A., Raikkonen, K., Strandberg, T., Kelitikan-gas-Jarvinen, L. & Jarvenpaa, A. (2004). Insecure adult attachment style and depressive symptoms: Implications for parental perceptions of infant temperament. *Infant Mental Health Journal*, 25, 99–116.

Peterson, B. S., Pine, D. S., Cohen, P. & Brook, J. S. (2001). Prospective, longitudinal study of tic, obsessivecompulsive, and attention-deficit/hyperactivity disorders in an epidemiological sample. *Journal of the American Academy of Child and Adolescent Psychiatry*, 40, 685–695.

Piaget, J. (1932). *The Moral Judgment of the Child*. London: Kegan Paul, Trench, Trubner and Co.

Piaget, J. (1951). *Play, Dreams and Imitation in Childhood*. London: Routledge & Kegan Paul.

Piaget, J. (1952). *The Child's Conception of Number*. London: Routledge.

Piaget, J. (1952). *The Origins of Intelligence in Children*. London: Routledge & Kegan Paul.

Piaget, J. (1954). *The Construction of Reality in the Child*. New York: Basic Books.

Piaget, J. (1958). *The Growth of Logical Thinking from Childhood to Adolescence*. New York: Basic Books.

Pinel, J. J. (2008). Biopsychology. Boston, MA: Pearson.

Piaget, J. (1962). *Play, Dreams, and Imitation in Childhood*. New York: Norton.

Piaget, J. (1972). *The Child's Conception of the World*. Towota, NJ: Littlefield Adams. (Original work published 1926)

Piaget, J. (1981). *Intelligence and Affectivity*. New York: Basic Books.

Piaget, J. and Inhelder, B. (1956). *The Child's Conception of Space*. London: Routledge.

Piaget, J., Inhelder, B. & Szeminska, A. (1960). *The Child's Conception of Geometry*. New York: Harper & Row.

Pierce, E.W., Ewing, L. J. & Campbell, S. B. (1999). Diagnostic status and symptomatic behaviour of hard to manage preschool children in middle childhood and early adolescence. *Journal of Clinical Child Psychology*, 28, 44–57.

Pikas, A. (1989). The common concern method for the treatment of mobbing. In E. Roland & E. Munthe (Eds), *Bullying: An International Perspective* (91–104). London: David Fulton.

Pilgrim, D. (2001). Disordered personalities and disordered concepts. *Journal of Mental Health*, 10 (3), 253–265.

Pinker, S. (2002). *The Blank Slate: The Modern Denial of Human Nature*. London: Allen Lane.

Pisterman, S., McGrath, P., Firestone, P., Goodman, J. T., Webster, I. & Mallory, R. (1989). Outcome of parentmediated treatment of preschoolers with attention deficit disorder with hyperactivity. *Journal of Consulting and Clinical Psychology*, 57, 628–635.

Pixa-Kettner, U. (2005). Parenting with intellectual disability in Germany: Results of a new nationwide study. *Journal of Applied Research in Intellectual Disabilities*, 21 (4), 315–319.

Plomin, R. & DeFries, J. C. (1980). Genetics and intelligence: Recent data. *Intelligence*, 4 (1), 15–24.

Plomin, R., DeFries, J. C. & Fulker, D. W. (1988). *Nature and Nurture During Infancy and Early Childhood*. Cambridge: Cambridge University Press.

Plomin, R., Emde, R. N., Braungart, J. M., Campos, J., Corley, R., Fulker, D. W., Kagan, J., Reznick, J. S., Robinson, J., Zahn-Waxler, C. & DeFries, J. C. (1993). Genetic change and continuity from fourteen to twenty months: The MacArthur longitudinal twin study. *Child Development*, 64, 1354–1376.

Poli, P., Sbrana, B., Marcheschi, M. & Masi, G. (2003). Self-reported depressive symptoms in a school sample of Italian children and adolescents. *Child Psychiatry & Human Development*, 33 (3), 209–226.

Posada, G., Jacobs, A., Richmond, M. Carbonell, O., Alzate, G., Bustamante, M. & Quiceno, J. (2002). Maternal caregiving and infant security in two cultures. *Developmental Psychology*, 38, 67–78.

Posada, G., Carbonell, O. A., Alzate, G. & Plata, S. J. (2004). Through Colombian lenses: Ethnographic and conventional analyses of maternal care and their associations with secure base behavior. *Developmental Psychology*, 40, 508–518.

Posner, M. I. & Rothbart, M. K. (1981). The development of attentional mechanisms. In J. H. Flowers (ed.), *Nebraska Symposium on Motivation* (Vol. 28, 1–52). Lincoln, NE: University of Nebraska Press.

Pothier, Y. & Sawada, D. (1983). Partitioning: The emergence of rational number ideas in young children. *Journal for Research in Mathematics Education*, 14, 307–317.

Potts, A. (2006). Schools as dangerous places. *Educational Studies*, 32 (3), 319–330.

Power, M. & Prasad, S. (2003). Schools for the future: Inner city secondary education exemplar. *Architectural Research Quarterly*, 7 (3–4), 262–279.

Power, S. & Clark, A. (2000). The right to know: Parents, school reports and parents' evenings. *Research Papers in Education*, 15 (1), 25–48.

Premack, D. & Woodruff, G. (1978) Does the chimpanzee have a 'theory of mind'? *Behavioral and Brain Sciences*, 4, 515–526.

Pressley, M. (1982). Elaboration and memory development. *Child Development*, 53, 296–309.

Prior, M., Sanson, A., Smart, D. & Oberklaid, F. (2000). Does shy-inhibited temperament in childhood lead to anxiety problems in adolescence? *Journal of the American Academy of Child and Adolescent Psychiatry*, 39, 461–468.

Psillos, D. (2004). An epistemological analysis of the evolution of didactical activities in teaching-learning sequences:

The case of fluids. *International Journal of Science Education,* 26 (5), 555–578.

Purves, D. Brannon, E. M., Cabeza, R., Huettel, S. A., LaBar, K. S., Platt, M. L. & Woldorff, M. G. (2008). *Principles of Cognitive Neuroscience.* Sunderland, MA: Sinauer.

Putnam, S. P., Samson, A. V. & Rothbart, M. K. (2000). Child temperament and parenting. In V. J. Molfese & D. L. Molfese (Eds), *Temperament and Personality Across the Life Span* (255–277). Mahwah, NJ: Erlbaum.

Pye, C. (1986). Quiche Mayan speech to children. *Journal of Child Language,* 13, 85–100.

Questions à Gérard Vergnaud (255–262). Toulouse: Presses Universitaires du Mirail.

Quijada, R.E., Montoya, C.M., Laserna, P.A., Toledo, A.P., Marco, E.M. & Rabadan, F.E. (2005). Depression prevalence in adolescents. *Actas Espanolas De Psiquiatria,* 33 (5), 298–302.

Quilgars, D., Searle, B. & Keung, A. (2005). Mental health and well-being. In J. Bradshaw & E. Mayhew (Eds), *The Well-Being of Children in the UK* (134–160). London: Save the Children.

Quinn, P. C. (2002). Categorization. In A. Slater & M. Lewis (Eds), *Introduction to Infant Development* (115–130). Oxford: Oxford University Press.

Quinn, P. C. (2004). Development of subordinate-level categorization in 3- to 7-month-old infants. *Child Development,* 75, 886–899.

Quinn, P. C (2008). In defense of core competencies, quantitative change, and continuity. *Child Development,* 79, 1633–1638.

Quinn, P. C. & Eimas, P. D. (1996). Perceptual cues that permit categorical differentiation of animal species by infants. *Journal of Experimental Child Psychology,* 63, 189–211.

Quinn, P. C. & Johnson, M. H. (2000). Global-before-basic object categorization in connectionist networks and 2-month-old infants. *Infancy,* 1, 31–46.

Quinn, P. C., Westerlund, A. & Nelson, C. A. (2006). Neural markers of categorization in 6-month-old infants. *Psychological Science,* 17, 59–67.

Rahman, A., Lovel, H., Bunn, J., Igbal, A. & Harrington, R. (2004). Mothers' mental health and infant growth: A case-control study from Rawalpindi, Pakistan. *Child: Care, Health, and Development,* 30, 21–27.

Rainey, D. & Murova, O. (2004). Factors influencing education achievement. *Applied Economics,* 36 (21), 2397–2404.

Rakison, D. H. (2000). When a rose is just a rose: The illusion of taxonomies in infat categorization. *Infancy,* 1, 77–90.

Rakison, D. & Butterworth, G. (1998). Infants' use of object parts in early categorization. *Developmental Psychology,* 34, 49–62.

Rakoczy, H., Tomasello, M. & Striano, T. (2004). Young children know that trying is not pretending: A test of the "behaving-as-if" construal of children's early concept of pretense. *Developmental Psychology,* 40, 388–399.

Ramus, F. (2002). Language discrimination by newborns: Teasing apart phonotactic, rhythmic, and intonational cues. *Annual Review of Language Acquisition,* 2, 85–115.

Ramus, F. (2006). Genes, brain, and cognition: A roadmap for the cognitive scientist. *Cognition,* 101, 247–269.

Raskauskas, J. & Stolz, A.D. (2007). Involvement in traditional and electronic bullying among adolescents. *Developmental Psychology,* 43, 564–575.

Rauschecker, J. P. & Henning, P. (2000). Crossmodal expansion of cortical maps in early blindness. In J. Kaas (Ed.), *The Mutable Brain* (243–259). Singapore: Harwood Academics.

Rayner, C. & Hoel, H. (1997). A summary review of literature relating to workplace bullying. *Journal of Community & Applied Psychology,* 7, 181–191.

Read, M. (1968). *Children of their Fathers: Growing up among the Ngoni of Malawi.* New York: Holt, Rinehart and Winston.

Reece, E. A. & Hobbins, J. C. (Eds) (2006). *Clinical Obstetrics: The Foetus and Mother.* Oxford: Blackwell.

Rees, J. M., Lederman, S. A. & Kiely, J. L. (1996). Birth weight associated with lowest neonatal mortality: Infants of adolescent and adult mothers. *Pediatrics,* 98, 1161–1166.

Reid, K. (2006). An evaluation of the views of secondary staff towards school attendance issues. *Oxford Review of Education,* 32 (3), 303–324.

Reijneveld, S. A., van der Wal, M. F., Brugman, E., Hira Sing, R. A. & Verloove-Vanhorick, S. P. (2004). Infant crying and abuse. *The Lancet,* 364, 1340–1342.

Renfrew, C. (1991). *The Bus Story: A Test of Continuous Speech.* Oxford: Headington.

Resnick, L. & Ford, W. W. (1981). *The Psychology of Mathematics for Instruction.* Hillsdale, NJ: Erlbaum.

Resnick, L. B., Nesher, P., Leonard, F., Magone, M., Omanson, S. & Peled, I. (1989). Conceptual bases of arithmetic errors: The case of decimal fractions. *Journal for Research in Mathematics Education,* 20, 8–27.

Retts Syndrome Association UK (2010). *What is Rett Syndrome?* Retrieved November 6 from http://www.rettuk.org/rettuk-public/rettuk/about-rett-syndrome/what-is-rett-syndrome.

Review of Psychotherapy Research (37–56). New York: The Guildford Press.

Reyna, V. F., Holliday, R. E. & Marche, T. (2002). Explaining the development of false memories. *Developmental Review,* 22, 436–489.

Reznick, J. S. & Goldfield, B. A. (1992). Rapid change in lexical development in comprehension and production. *Developmental Psychology,* 28, (3), 406–413.

Rheingold, H. L. & Adams, J. L. (1980). The significance of speech to newborns. *Developmental Psychology,* 16 (5), 397–403.

Richards, C. A. & Sanderson, J. A. (1999). The role of imagination in facilitating deductive reasoning in 2-, 3- and 4-year-olds. *Cognition,* 72, B1–9.

Richardson, K. (1994). Interactions in development. In J. Oates (Ed.), *The Foundations of Child Development* (211–258). Milton Keynes: The Open University/Oxford: Blackwell.

Ricketts, J., Bishop, D. V. M. & Nation, K. (2008). Investigating orthographic and semantic aspects of word learning in poor comprehenders. *Journal of Research in Reading*, 31 (1), 117–135.

Rigby, K. (1994). Psychosocial functioning in families of Australian adolescent schoolchildren involved in bully/victim problems. *Journal of Family Therapy*, 16, 173–187.

Rigby, K. (1997). Attitudes and beliefs about bullying among Australian school children. *The Irish Journal of Psychology*, 18, 202–220.

Rigby, K. (2001). Health consequences of bullying and its prevention in schools. In J. Juvonen & S. Graham (Eds), *Peer Harassment in School. The Plight of the Vulnerable and Victimized* (310–331). New York: Guilford Press.

Rigby, K. (2002a). *New Perspectives on Bullying*. London: Jessica Kingsley.

Rigby, K. (2002b). Bullying. In P.K. Smith & C.H. Hart (Eds), *Blackwell Handbook of Childhood Social Development* (549–568). Oxford: Blackwell.

Ridley, M. (1995). *Animal Behavior: An Introduction to Behavioral Mechanisms, Development and Ecology* (2nd Ed.). Cambridge MA: Blackwell Scientific.

Rittle-Johnson, B., Siegler, R. S. & Alibali, M. W. (2001). Developing conceptual understanding and procedural skill in mathematics: An iterative process. *Journal of Educational Psychology*, 93 (2), 46–36.

Roberts, D. F., Foehr, U. G., Rideout, V. & Brodie, M. (2004). *Kids and Media in America*. Cambridge: Cambridge University Press.

Robertson, J. & Robertson, J. (1989). *Separation and the Very Young*. London: Free Association Books.

Roland, E. (1989). Bullying: The Scandinavian research tradition. In D. P. Tattum & D. A. Lane (Eds), *Bullying in School* (21–32). Stoke-on-Trent: Trentham Books.

Rosch, E. (1978). Principles of categorization. In E. Rosch & B. B. Lloyd (Eds), *Cognition and Categorization* (27–48). Hillsdale, NJ: Erlbaum.

Rose, A.J. & Asher, S.R. (1999). Children's goals and strategies in response to conflicts within a friendship. *Developmental Psychology*, 35, (1), 69–79.

Rose, A. J. & Asher, S. R. (2004). Children's strategies and goals in response to help-giving and help-seeking tasks within a friendship. *Child Development*, 75, 749–763.

Rose, S. A. (1981). Developmental changes in infants' retention of visual stimuli. *Child Development*, 52, 227–233.

Rose, S. A., Feldman, J. F. & Jankowski, J. J. (2004). Infant visual recognition memory. *Developmental Review*, 24, 74–100.

Rose, S. A., Feldman, J. F. & Jankowski, J. J. (2004). The effect of familiarization time, retention interval, and context change on adults' performance in the visual paired comparison task. *Developmental Psychobiology*, 44, 146–155.

Rose, S., Feldman, J. F. & Jamkowski, J. J. (2005). Dimensions of cognition in infancy. *Intelligence*, 32, 245–262.

Rosehan, D. L., Moore, B. S. & Underwood, B. (1976). The social psychology of moral behaviour. In T. Lickona (Ed.). *Moral Development and Behavior* (241–252). New York: Holt, Rinehart & Winston.

Rosenberg, M. (1979). *Conceiving the Self*. New York: Basic Books.

Rosenstein, D. & Oster, H. (1988). Differential facial responsiveness to four basic tastes in newborns. *Child Development*, 59, 1555–1568.

Rosenzweig, M. R. (1984). Experience, memory and the brain. *American Psychologist*, 39, 365–376.

Rosenzweig, M. R. Breedlove, S. M. & Watson, N. V. (2005). *Biological Psychology: An Introduction to Behavioural and Cognitive Neuroscience*. Sunderland, MA: Sinauer.

Rossetti, L. M. (2001). *Communication Intervention – Birth to Three* (2nd Ed.). Albany, NY: Singular Thomson Learning: Delmar Publishing.

Roth, A., Fonagy, P. & Parry, G. (1996). Psychotherapy research, funding, and evidence-based practice. In A. Roth and P. Fonagy (Eds), *What Works for Whom? A Critical Review of Psychotherapy Research* (37–56). New York: The Guildford Press.

Rothbart, M. (2004). Temperament and the pursuit of an integrated developmental psychology. *Merrill-Palmer Quarterly*, 50, 492–505.

Rothbart, M. K. & Bates, J. E. (1998). Temperament. In D. William & N. Eisenberg (Eds), *Handbook of Child Psychology, Vol. 3. Social, Emotional, and Personality Development* (5th Ed.) (105–176). Hoboken, NJ: Wiley.

Rothbart, M., Ahadi, S. & Evans, D. (2000). Temperament and personality: Origins and outcomes. *Journal of Personality and Social Psychology*, 78, 83–116.

Rothbart, M. K., Ahadi, S. A., Hershey, L. L. & Fisher, P. (2001). Investigations of temperament at three to seven years: The children's behavior questionnaire. *Child Development*, 72, 1394–1408.

Rothbart, M. K., Ellis, L. K., Rueda, M. R. & Posner, M. I. (2003). Developing mechanisms of temperamental effortful control. *Journal of Personality*, 71, 1113–1143.

Rothbaum, F., Pott, M., Azuma, H., Miyake, K. & Weisz, J. (2000). The development of close relationships in Japan and the United States: Paths of symbiotic harmony and generative tension. *Child Development*, 71, 1121–1142.

Rovee-Collier, C. K. & Boller, K. (1995). Interference or facilitation in infant memory? In F. N. Dempster & C. J. Brainerd (Eds), *Interference and Inhibition in Cognition* (61–104). San Diego, CA: Academic Press.

Rovee-Collier, C. & Cuevas, K. (2009). Multiple memory systems are unnecessary to account for infant memory development: An ecological model. *Developmental Psychology*, 45, 160–174.

Rovee-Collier, C., Sullivan, M., Enright, M., Lucas, D. & Fagen, J. W. (1980). Reactivation of infant memory. *Science*, 208, 1159–1161.

Rubia K., Smith A., Taylor E. (2007) Performance of children with Attention Deficit Hyperactivity Disorder (ADHD) on a biological marker test battery for impulsiveness. *Child Neuropsychology*, 13 (3), 276–304.

Rubin, J. Z., Provenzano, F. J. & Luria, Z. (1974). The eye of the beholder: Parents' views on sex of newborns. *American Journal of Orthopsychiatry*, 44, 512–519.

Rubin, K., Bukowski, W. & Parker, J. (1998). Peer interactions, relationships and groups. In N. Eisenberg & W. Damon (Eds), *Handbook of Child Psychology, Vol. 3: Social, Emotional and Personality Development* (619–700). New York: Wiley.

Rubin, K., Wojslawowicz, J., Rose-Krasnor, L., Booth-LaForce, C. & Burgess, K. (2006). The best friendships of shy/withdrawn children: Prevalence, stability and relationship quality. *Journal of Abnormal Child Psychology*, 34, 143–157.

Rubin, K. H. (1982). Non-social play in preschoolers: Necessarily evil? *Child Development*, 53, 651–657.

Rubin, K. H., Fein, G. G. & Vandenberg, B. (1983). Play. In E. M. Hetherington (Ed.), *Handbook of Child Psychology: Vol. 4, Socialization, Personality, and Social Development* (4th Ed. 693–744). New York: Wiley.

Rubin, K. H., Hymel, S. & Mills, R. S. L. (1989). Sociability and social withdrawal in childhood: stability and outcomes. *Journal of Personality*, 57, 237–255.

Ruble, D. N. & Stangor, C. (1986). Stalking the elusive schema: Insights from developmental and social-psychological analyses of gender schemas. *Social Cognition*, 4, 227–261.

Ruble, D. N., Balaban, T. & Cooper, J. (1981). Gender constancy and the effects of sex-typed televised commercials. *Child Development*, 52, 667–673.

Ruff, H. A. & Capozzoli, M. C. (2003). Development of attention and distractibility in the first 4 years of life. *Developmental Psychology*, 39, 877–890.

Ruff, H. A. & Rothbart, M. E. (1996). *Attention in Early Development: Themes and Variations*. Oxford: Oxford University Press.

Rummelhart, D. E., McClelland, J. L. & the PDP Research Group (1986). *Parallel Distributed Processing: Explorations in the Microstructure of Cognition. Vol. 1: Foundations*. Cambridge, MA: MIT Press.

Russ, S. W. (2004). *Play in Child Development and Psychotherapy: Toward Empirically Supported Practice*. Hillsdale, NJ: Erlbaum.

Ruthsatz, J., Detterman, D., Griscom, W.S. & Cirullo, B.A. (2008). Becoming an expert in the musical domain: It takes more than just practice. *Intelligence*, 36, 330–338.

Rutter, M. (1970). *The description and classification of infantile autism. Proceedings of the Indiana University Colloquium on Infantile Autism*. Springfield, IL: Charles C. Thomas.

Rutter, M. (1987). Temperament, personality and personality disorder. *British Journal of Psychiatry*, 150, 443–458.

Rutter, M., Kreppner, J. & O'Connor, T. (2001). Specificity and heterogeneity in children's responses to profound institutional privation. *The British Journal of Psychiatry*, 179, 97–103.

Rutter, M., Silberg, J., O'Connor, T. & Simonoff, E. (1999). Genetics and child psychiatry: II empirical research findings. *Journal of Child Psychology and Psychiatry*, 40, 19–55.

Rymer, R. (1992). *Genie: A Scientific Tragedy*. New York: Harper Collins.

Saab, N., van Joolingen, W. R. & van Hout-Wolters, B. H. A. M. (2005). Communication in collaborative discovery learning. *The British Journal of Educational Psychology*, 75 (4), 603–621.

Sachdev, P. (1999). Attention deficit hyperactivity disorder in adults. *Psychological Medicine*, 29, 507–514.

Sacks, H., Schegloff, E. A. & Jefferson, G. (1974). A simplest systematics for the organisation of turn-taking for conversation. *Language*, 50, 696–735.

Saffran, J. R., Loman, M. M. & Robertson, R. R. W. (2000). Infant memory for musical experiences. *Cognition*, 77, B15–B23.

Saida, Y. & Miyashita, M. (1979) Development of fine motor skill in children: Manipulation of a pencil in children aged 2 to 6 years old. *Journal of Human Movement Studies*, 5, 104–113.

Sainsbury, M., Whetton, C. Mason, K. & Schagen, I. (1998). Fallback in attainment on transfer at age 11: Evidence from the Summer Literacy Schools evaluation. *Educational Research*, 40 (1), 73–81.

Salmivalli, C. (2001). Group view on victimisation. Empirical findings and their implications. In J. Juvonen & S. Graham (Eds), *Peer Harassment in School. The Plight of the Vulnerable and Victimized* (398–419). New York: Guilford Press.

Salmivalli, C., Lagerspetz, K., Bjorkqvist, K., Österman, K. & Kaukiainen, A. (1996). Bullying as a group process: Participant roles and their relations to social status within the group. *Aggressive Behaviour*, 22, 1–15.

Salmon, P. (1992). The peer group. In J. C. Coleman (Ed.), *The School Years: Current Issues in the Socialisation of Young People* (2nd Eds). London: Routledge.

Sambeth, A., Pakarinen, S., Ruohio, K., Fellman, V., van Zuijen, T. L. & Huotilainen, M. (2009). Change detection in newborns using a multiple deviant paradigm: A study using magnetoencephalography. *Clinical Neuropsychology*, 120, 530–538.

Sanders, M. R., Calam, R., Durand, M., Liversidge, T. & Carmont, S. A. (2008). Does self-directed and web-based support for parents enhance the effects of viewing a reality television series based on the triple P-Positive Parenting programme? *Journal of Child Psychology and Psychiatry*, 49, 924–932.

Sandstrom, M. J. & Cillessen, A. H. N. (2003). Sociometric status and children's peer experiences: Use of the daily diary method. *Merrill-Palmer Quarterly*, 49, 427–452.

Sanford, K. & Madill, L. (2006). Resistance through video game play: It's a boy thing. *Canadian Journal of Education*, 29, 287–306.

Sarnecka, B. W. & Gelman, S. A. (2004). Six does not just mean a lot: Preschoolers see number words as specific. *Cognition*, 92, 329–352.

Savin-Williams, R. C. & Berndt, T. J. (1990). Friendship and peer relations. In S. S. Feldman & G. R. Elliott (Eds), *At the Threshold: The Developing Adolescent* (277–307). Cambridge, MA: Harvard University Press.

Saxe, G. (1981). Body parts as numerals: A developmental analysis of numeration among the Oksapmin in Papua New Guinea. *Child Development*, 52, 306–316.

Saxe, G., Guberman, S. R. & Gearhart, M. (1987). Social and developmental processes in children's understanding of number. *Monographs of the Society for Research in Child Development*, 52, 100–200.

Sayer, J. (1982). *Biological Politics: Feminist and Antifeminist Perspectives*. London: Tavistock.

Schaaf, R. C. & Miller, L. J. (2005). Occupational therapy using a sensory integrative approach for children with developmental disabilities. *Mental Retardation and Developmental Disability Research Review*, 11, 143–148.

Schaffer, H. & Emerson, P. (1964). The development of social attachments in infancy. *Monographs of the Society for Research in Child Development*, 29 (3), Serial No. 94.

Schiefflin, B. B. & Ochs, E. (1983). A cultural perspective on the transition from prelinguistic to linguistic communication. In R. M. Golinkoff (Ed.), *The Transition From Prelinguistic to Linguistic Communication* (115–131). Hillsdale, NJ: Erlbaum.

Schneider, B.H. (2000). *Friends and Enemies. Peer Relations in Childhood*. London: Arnold.

Schneider, B. H., Atkinson, L., & Tardif, C. (2001). Child-parent attachment and children's peer relations: A quantitative review. *Developmental Psychology*, 37, 87–100.

Schuengel, G., Bakermans-Kranenburg, M. J. & van IJzendoorn, M. H. (1999). Attachment and loss: Frightening maternal behavior linking unresolved loss and disorganized infant attachment. *Journal of Consulting and Clinical Psychology*, 67, 54–63.

Schuetze, P. & Zeskind, P. S. (1997). Relation between reported maternal caffeine consumption during pregnancy and neonatal state and heart rate. *Infant Behavior and Development*, 20, 559–562.

Schulkin, J. (2000). Theory of mind and mirroring neurons. *Trends in Cognitive Sciences*, 4 (7), 252–254.

Schwartz, C. E., Wright, C., Shin, L., Kagan, J. & Raugh, S. (2003). Inhibited and uninhibited infants 'grown up': Adult amygdalar response to novelty. *Science*, 300, 1952–1953.

Schwartz, D., Dodge, K.A., Pettit, G.S. & Bates, J.E. (1997). The early socialisation of aggressive victims of bullying. *Child Development*, 68, 665–675.

Schwartz, D., Proctor, L.J. & Chien, D.H. (2001). The aggressive victim of bullying: Emotional and behavioural dysregulation as a pathway to victimisation by peers. In J. Juvonen & S. Graham (Eds), *Peer Harassment in School. The Plight of the Vulnerable and Victimized* (147–174). New York: Guilford Press.

Sebald, H. (1989). Adolescents' peer orientations: Changes in the support system during the past decades. *Adolescence*, 24, 936–946.

Seeley, J., Small, J., Walker, H., Feil, E., Severson, H., Golly, A. & Forness, S. (2009). Efficacy of the first step to success intervention for students with attention-deficit/hyperactivity disorder. *School Mental Health*, 1 (1), 37–48.

Seidler, F. J., Levin, E. D., Lappi, S. E. & Slotkin, T.A. (1992). Fetal nicotine exposure ablates the ability of postnatal nicotine challenge to release norepinephrine from rat brain regions. *Developmental Brain Research*, 69, 288–291.

Seiffge-Krenke, I. (2000). Causal links between stressful events, coping style, and adolescent symptomatology. *Journal of Adolescence*, 23 (6), 675–691.

Seiffge-Krenke, I. & Beyers, W. (2005). Coping trajectories from adolescence to young adulthood: Links to attachment state of mind. *Journal of Research on Adolescence*, 15 (4), 561–582.

Seiffge-Krenke, I. & Klessinger, N. (2000). Long-term effects of avoidant coping on adolescents' depressive symptoms. *Journal of Youth and Adolescence*, 29 (6), 617–630.

Selman, R. L. (1980). *The Growth of Interpersonal Understanding*. New York: Academic Press.

Selman, R. L. (2003). *The Promotion of Social Awareness: Powerful Lessons from the Partnership of Developmental Theory and Classroom Practice*. New York: Russell Sage.

Sen, M. G., Yonas, A. & Knill, D. C. (2001). Development of infants' sensitivity to surface contour information for spatial layout. *Perception*, 30, 167–176.

Serbin, L. A., Powlishta, K. K. & Gulko, J. (1993). The development of sex typing in middle childhood. *Monographs of the Society for Research in Child Development*, 58, Serial No. 232.

Serketich, W. J. & Dumas, J. E. (1996). The effectiveness of behavioural parent training to modify antisocial behaviour in children: A meta-analysis. *Behaviour Therapy*, 27, 171–186.

Seymour, P. H. K., Aro, M. & Erskine, J. M. (2003). Foundation literacy acquisition in European orthographies. *British Journal of Psychology*, 94, 143–174.

Shaffer, D.R. & Kipp, K. (2010). *Development Psychology: Childhood and Adolescence*. Belmont, CA: Wadsworth.

Shahar, S. (1990). *Childhood in the Middle Ages*. London: Routledge.

Shahin, A.J., Roberts, L.E., Chau, W., Trainer, L.J. & Miller, L. M. (2008). Music training leads to the development of timbre-specific gamma band activity. *NeuroImage*, 41, 113–122.

Sharp, C. (2002). *School starting age: European policy and recent research. Local Government Association Seminar 'When should our children start school?'*. London, 1 November.

Sharp, S. (1996). The role of peers in tackling bullying. *Educational Psychology in Practice*, 11, 17–22.

Shaw, P., Greenstein, D., Lerch, J., Clasen, L., Lenroot, R., Gogtay, N. & Evans, A. (2006). Intellectual ability and cortical development in children and adolescents. *Nature*, 440, 676–679.

Sheridan, M. (2008). *From Birth to Five Years*. Oxford: Routledge.

Shreeve, A., Boddington, D., Bernard, B., Brown, K., Clarke, K., Dean, L., Elkins, T., Kemp, S., Lees, J. Miller, D., Oakley, J. & Shiret, D. (2002). Student perceptions of rewards and sanctions. *Pedagogy, Culture & Society*, 10 (2), 239–256.

Shriberg, E. (1999). Phonetic consequences of speech disfluency. In J. Ohala, Y. Hasegawa, M. Ohala, D. Granveille & A. Bailey (Eds), *Proceedings of the XIVth International Congress on Phonetic Sciences Volume 1* (619–622). Berkeley, CA: Department of Linguistics, University of California at Berkeley.

Shulman, S., Elicker, J. & Sroufe, L. A. (1994). Stages of friendship growth in preadolescence as related to attachment history. *Journal of Social and Personal Relationships*, 11, 341–361.

Siegal, M. & Beattie, K. (1991). Where to look first for children's knowledge of false beliefs. *Cognition*, 38, 1–12.

Siegler, R. S. (1996). *Emerging Minds: The Process of Change in Children's Thinking*. New York: Oxford University Press.

Siegler, R., DeLoache, J. & Eisenberg, N. (2010). *How Children Develop* (3rd Ed.). New York: Worth.

Simmons, R. G. & Blyth, D. A. (1987). *Moving into Adolescence: The Impact of Pubertal Change and School Context*. Hawthorne, NY: Aldine de Gruyter.

Simpson, A. & Riggs, K. J. (2005). Inhibitory and working memory demands of the day-night task in children. *British Journal of Developmental Psychology*, 23, 471–486.

Simpson, S., Vitiello, B., Wells, K., Wigal, T. & Wu, M. (2001). Clinical relevance of the primary findings of the MTA: success rates based on severity of ADHD and ODD symptoms at the end of treatment. *Journal of the American Academy of Child and Adolescent Psychiatry*, 40, 168–179.

Skinner, B.F. (1957). *Verbal Behaviour*. East-Norwalk, CT: Appleton-Century-Crofts.

Slaby, R. G., & Frey, K. S. (1975). Development of gender constancy and selective attention to same-sex models. *Child Development*, 46, 849–856.

Slater, A. & Johnson, S. P. (1999). Visual sensory and perceptual abilities of the newborn: Beyond the blooming, buzzing confusion. In A. Slater & S. P. Johnson (Eds), *The Development of Sensory, Motor and Cognitive Capacities* (121–141). Hove: Psychology Press.

Slater, A. & Lewis, M. (2002). *Introduction to Infant Development*. Oxford: Oxford University Press.

Slater, A. M. & Morison, V. (1985). Shape constancy and slant perception at birth. *Perception*, 14, 337–344.

Slater, A., Morison, V. & Rose, D. (1983). Perception of shape by the newborn baby. *British Journal of Developmental Psychology*, 1, 135–142.

Slater, A. M., Mattock, A. & Brown, E. (1990). Size constancy at birth: Newborn infants reponses to retinal and real size. *Journal of Experimental Child Psychology*, 49, 314–322.

Slobin, D. (1972). Children and language: They learn the same way around the world. *Psychology Today*, July, 71–76.

Smilansky, S. (1968). *The Effects of Sociodramatic Play on Disadvantaged preschool Children*. New York: Wiley.

Smith, A., Taylor, E., Warner Rogers, J., Newman, S. & Rubia, K. (2002). Evidence for a pure time perception deficit in children with ADHD. *Journal of Child Psychology and Psychiatry*, 43, 529–542.

Smith, A. D. (2009). On the use of drawing tasks in neuropsychological assessment. *Neuropsychology*, 23 (2), 231–239.

Smith, S. N. & Miller, R. (2005). Learning approaches: Examination type, discipline of study, and gender. *Educational Psychology*, 25 (1), 43–53.

Smith, P.K. (1997). Bullying in life-span perspective: What can studies of school bullying and workplace bullying learn from each other? *Journal of Community & Applied Psychology*, 7, 249–255.

Smith, P.K. (2004). Bullying: Recent developments. *Child and Adolescent Mental Health*, 9, 98–103.

Smith, P. K. & Levan, S. (1995). Perceptions and experiences of bullying in younger pupils. *British Journal of Educational Psychology*, 65, 489–500.

Smith, P. K., Cowie, H., Olafsson, R. & Liefooghe, A. (2002). Definitions of bullying: a comparison of terms used, and age and sex differences, in a 14-country international comparison. *Child Development*, 73, 1119–1133.

Smith, P. K., Cowie, H., & Sharp, S. (1994). Working directly with pupils involved in bullying situations. In P. K. Smith & S. Sharp (Eds), *School Bullying: Insights and Perspectives* (193–212). London: Routledge.

Smith, P.K., Madsen, K.C. & Moody, J.C. (1999a). What causes the age decline in reports of being bullied at school? Towards a developmental analysis of risks of being bullied. *Educational Research*, 41, 267–285.

Smith, P.K., Mahdavi, J., Carvalho, M., Fisher, S., Russell, S. & Tippett, N. (2008a) Cyberbullying: its nature and impact in secondary school pupils. *Journal of Child Psychology & Psychiatry*, 49, 376–385.

Smith, P.K., Morita, Y., Junger-Tas, J., Olweus, D., Catalano, R. & Slee, P. (1999b). *The Nature of School Bullying: A Cross-national Perspective*. London: Routledge.

Smith, P. K. & Sharp, S. (1994). The problem of school bullying. In P.K. Smith & S. Sharp (Eds), *School Bullying: Insights and Perspectives* (2–19). London: Routledge.

Smith, P.K., Singer, M. Hoel, H. & Cooper, C.L. (2003). Victimization in the school and the workplace: Are there any links? *British Journal of Psychology*, 94, 175–188.

Smith, P. K., & Sloboda, J. (1986). Individual consistency in infant-stranger encounters. *British Journal of Developmental Psychology*, 4, 83–91.

Smith, P.K., Smith, C., Osborn, R. & Samara, M. (2008b). A content analysis of school anti-bullying policies: progress and limitations. *Educational Psychology in Practice*, 24, 1–12.

Smolak, L. (1986). *Infancy*. Englewood Cliffs, NJ: Prentice Hall.

Smorti, A., Menesini, E. & Smith, P.K. (2003). Parents' definitions of children's bullying in a five-country comparison. *Journal of Cross-Cultural Psychology*, 34 (4), 417–432 (2003).

Snow, C. (1994). Beginning from baby-talk: Twenty years of research on input and interaction. In C. Galloway and B. Richards (Eds), *Input and Interaction in Language Acquisition* (3–12). London: Cambridge University Press.

Snowling, M. (2000). *Dyslexia*. Oxford: Blackwell.

Sobel, D. (2000). *Galileo's Daughter. A Drama of Science, Faith and Love*. London: Fourth Estate Limited.

Sokolov, E. N. (1963). *Perception and the Conditioned Reflex*. Oxford: Pergamon.

Solanto, M. V., Abikoff, H., Sonuga-Barke, E., Schachar, R., Logan, G. D., Wigal, T., Hechtman, L., Hinshaw, S. & Turkel, E. (2001). The ecological validity of delay aversion and response inhibition as measures of impulsivity in AD/HD: a supplement to the NIMH multi-modal treatment study of AD/HD. *Journal of Abnormal Child Psychology*, 29, 215–228.

Soltis, J. (2004). The signal functions of early infant crying. *Behavioural and Brain Sciences*, 27, 443–490.

Sonuga-Barke, E. J. S. (2002). Psychological heterogeneity in AD/HD – a dual pathway model of behaviour and cognition. *Behavioural Brain Research*, 130, 29–36.

Sonuga-Barke, E. J. S. (2004). On the reorganization of incentive structure to promote delay tolerance: A therapeutic possibility for AD/HD? *Neural Plasticity*, 11, 23–28.

Sonuga-Barke, E. J. S., Minocha, K., Taylor, E.A & Sandberg, S. (1993). Interethnic bias in teachers ratings of childhood hyperactivity. *British Journal of Developmental Psychology*, 11, 187–200.

Sonuga-Barke, E. J. S., Lamparelli, M., Stevenson, J., Thompson, M. & Henry, A. (1994). Behaviour problems and pre-school intellectual attainment – the associations of hyperactivity and conduct problems. *Journal of Child Psychology and Applied Disciplines*, 35 (5), 949–960.

Sonuga-Barke, E. J. S, Williams, E., Hall, M. & Saxton, T. (1996). Hyperactivity and delay aversion. III: The effects on cognitive style of imposing delay after errors. *Journal of Child Psychology and Psychiatry*, 37, 189–194.

Sonuga-Barke, E. J. S., Daley, D., Thompson, M., Laver-Bradbury, C. & Weeks, A. (2001). Parent-based therapies for preschool attention-deficit/hyperactivity disorder: A randomized, controlled trial with a community sample. *Journal of the American Academy of Child and Adolescent Psychiatry*, 40, 402–408.

Sonuga-Barke, E. J. S., Dalen, L. & Remmington, B. (2003). Do executive deficits and delay aversion make independent contributions to preschool attention deficit/hyperactivity disorder? *Journal of the American Academy of Child and Adolescent Psychiatry*, 42, 1335–1342.

Sophian, C. (1988). Limitations on preschool children's knowledge about counting: Using counting to compare two sets. *Developmental Psychology*, 24, 634–640. 230.

Sowell, E. R., Thompson, P. M., Holmes, C. J., Batth, R., Jernigan, T. L. & Toga, A.W. (1999). Localizing age related changes in brain structure between childhood and adolescence using statistical parametric mapping. *NeuroImage*, 6, 587–597.

Span, S. A., Earlywine, M. & Strybel, T. Z. (2002). Confirming the factor structure of attention deficit hyperactivity disorder symptoms in adult, nonclinical samples. *Journal of Psychopathology and Behavioural Assessment*, 24 (2), 129–136.

Spelke, E. S. (1979). Perceiving bimodally specified events in infancy. *Developmental Psychology*, 15, 626–636.

Spelke, E. (2000). Core knowledge. *American Psychologist*, 55, 1233–1242.

Spielhofer, T., Benton, T. & Schagen, S. (2004). A study of the effects of school size and single-sex education in English schools. *Research Papers in Education*, 19 (2), 133–159.

Sponheim, E. & Skjeldal, O. (1998). Autism and related disorders: Epidemiological findings in a Norwegian study using diagnostic criteria. *Journal of Autism and Developmental Disorder*, 28, 217–227.

Spratt, J., Shucksmith, J., Philip, K. & Watson, C. (2006). Interprofessional support of mental well-being in schools: A Bourdieuan perspective. *Journal of Interprofessional Care*, 20 (4), 391–402.

Sprich, S., Biederman, J., Crawford, M. H., Mundy, E. & Faraone, S. V. (2000). Adoptive and biological families of children and adolescents with ADHD. *Journal of the American Academy of Child and Adolescent Psychiatry*, 39, 1432–1437.

Sroufe, L. A., Carlson, E. & Schulman, S. (1993). Individuals in relationships: Development from infancy through adolescence. In D. C. Funder, R. D. Parke, C. Tomlinson-Keasey & K. Widaman (Eds), *Studying Lives Through Time: Personality and Development* (315–342). Washington, DC: APA.

Stackhouse, J. & Wells, B. (1997). *Children's Speech and Literacy Difficulties: A Psycholinguistic Framework*. London: Singular Publishers.

Stams, G. J. M., Juffer, F. & van Ijzendoorn, M. H. (2002). Maternal sensitivity, infant attachment, and temperament in early childhood predict adjustment in middle childhood: The case of adopted children and their biologically unrelated parents. *Developmental Psychology*, 38, 806–821.

Standards for Education and Training in Psychological Assessment (2006). Position of the Society for Personality Assessment – An Official Statement of the Board of Trustees of the Society for Personality Assessment. *Journal of Personality Assessment*, 87, 355–357.

Stark, R. E. (1980). Stages of speech development in the first year of life. In G. Yeni-Komshian, J. F. & C. A. Ferguson (Eds), *Child Phonology: 1 Production* (73–90). New York: Academic Press.

Stark, R. E. (1981). Infant vocalisation: A comprehensive view. *Infant Mental Health Journal*, 2, 118–128.

Stattin, H. & Magnusson, D. (1990). *Pubertal Maturation in Female Development*, Vol. 2. Hillsdale, NJ: Erlbaum.

Steele, M., Hodges, J., Kaniuk, J., Hillman, S. & Henderson, K. (2003). Attachment representations and adoption: Associations between maternal states of mind and emotion narratives in previously maltreated children. *Journal of Child Psychotherapy*, 29, 187–205.

Steele, M., Marigna, M. R., Tello, J. and Johnston, R. (2000). *Strengthening Families, Strengthening Communities: An Inclusive Programme. Facilitator Manual*. London: Race Equality Unit.

Steffe, L. P., von Glaserfeld, E., Richards, J. & Cobb, P. (1983). *Children's Counting Types: Philosophy, Theory and Application*. New York: Praeger.

Stemmer, B. & Joanette, Y. (1998). The interpretation of narrative discourse of brain-damaged individuals within the framework of a multilevel discourse model. In M. Beeman & C. Chiarello (Eds), *Right Hemisphere Language Comprehension: Perspectives from Cognitive Neuroscience* (329–348). London: Erlbaum.

Stephenson, P., & Smith, D. (1989). Bullying in the junior school. In D. P. Tattum & D. A. Lane (Eds), *Bullying in School* (45–57). Stoke-on-Trent: Trentham Books.

Stern, M., & Karraker, K. H. (1989). Sex stereotyping of infants: A review of gender labelling studies. *Sex Roles*, 20, 501–522.

Stern, W. (1912). *The Psychological Methods of Intelligence Testing*. Baltimore, MD: Warwick & York.

Sternberg, R. J. (1985). *Beyond IQ: A Triarchic Theory of Human Intelligence*. New York: Cambridge University Press.

Stevens, S.E., Sonuga-barke, E.J.B., Kreppner, J.M., Beckett, C., Castle, J., Colvet, E., Groothues, C., Hawkins, A. & Rutter, M. (2008). Inattention/overactivity following early severe institutional deprivation: Presentation and associations in early adolescence. *Journal of Abnormal Child Psychology*, 36, 385–398.

Stevens, V., De Bourdeaudhuij, I. & Van Oost, P. (2002). Relationship of the family environment to children's involvement in bully/victim problems at school. *Journal of Youth and Adolescence*, 31, 419–428.

Stilberg, J., San Miguel, V., Murelle, E., Prom, E., Bates, J., Canino, G., Egger, H. & Eaves, L. (2005). Genetic environmental influences on temperament in the first year of life: The Puerto Rico Infant Twin Study (PRINTS). *Twin Research and Human Genetics*, 8, 328–336.

Stinson, J. & Milter, R. (1996). Problem-based learning in business education: Curriculum design and implementation issues. In L. Wilkerson & W. Gijselaers (Eds), *Bringing Problem-Based Learning to Higher Education: Theory and Practice*. (33–42) San Francisco, CA: Jossey-Bass.

Stormshak, E. A., Bierman, K. L., Bruschi, D., Dodge, K. A. & Coie, J. D. (1999). The relation between behavior problems and peer preference in different classroom contexts. *Child Development*, 79, 169–182.

Stouthamer-Loeber, M. (1986). Lying as a problem behavior in children: A review. *Clinical Psychology Review*, 6, 267–289.

Strachan, T. & Read, A. (2003). *Human Molecular Genetics*. New York: Wiley.

Strauch, B. (2003). *The Primal Teen: What the New Discoveries About the Teenage Brain Tell Us About Our Kids*. New York: Anchor.

Streeter, L. (1976). Language perception of 2-month-old infants shows effects of both innate mechanisms and experience. *Nature*, 259, 39–41.

Streri, A. & Spelke, E. S. (1988). Haptic perception of objects in infancy. *Cognitive Psychology*, 20, 1–23.

Stevenson, C.S., Stevenson, R.J. & Whitmont, S. (2003). A self-directed psychosocial intervention with minimal therapist contact for adults with attention deficit hyperactivity disorder. *Clinical Psychology & Psychotherapy*, 10, 93–101.

Streissguth, A. P., Barr, H. M., Sampson, P. D. & Bookstein, F. L. (1994). Prenatal alcohol and offspring development: the first fourteen years. *Drug and Alcohol Dependence*, 36, 89–99.

Striano, T., Tomasello, M. & Rochat, P. (2001). Social and object support for early symbolic play. *Developmental Science*, 4, 442–455.

Sugawara, M., Sakamoto, S., Kitamura, T., Toda, M. A. & Shima, S. (1999). Structure of depression symptoms in pregnancy and the postpartum period. *Journal of Affective Disorders*, 54, 161–169.

Sugita, Y. (2004). Experience in early infancy is indispensable for colour perception. *Current Biology*, 14, 1267–1271.

Suler, J. (2004). The online disinhibition effect. *Cyber Psychology & Behaviour*, 7, 321–326.

Suomi, S. J. & Harlow, H. F. (1972). Social rehabilitation of isolate-reared monkeys. *Developmental Psychology*, 6, 487–496.

Surbey, M. (1990). Family composition, stress, and human menarche. In F. Bercovitch & T. Zeigler (Eds), *The Socio-endocrinology of Primate Reproduction* (71–97). New York: Liss.

Surian, L. & Leslie, A.M. (1999). Competence and performance in false belief understanding: A comparison of autistic and normal 3-year-old children. *British Journal of Developmental Psychology*, 17, 141–155.

Susman, E. J., Nottleman, E. D., Inoff-Germain, G. E., Loriaux, D. L. & Chrousos, G. P. (1985). The relation of relative hormonal levels and physical development and social–emotional behavior in young adolescents. *Journal of Youth and Adolescence*, 14, 245–264.

Sutherland, P., Badger, R. & White, G. (2002). How new students take notes at lectures. *Journal of Further and Higher Education*, 26 (4), 377–388.

Sutton, J. & Smith, P.K. (1999). Bullying as a group process: An adaptation of the participant role approach. *Aggressive Behaviour*, 25, 97–111.

Sutton, J., Smith, P.K. & Swettenham, J. (1999a). Social cognition and bullying: Social inadequacy or skilled manipulation? *British Journal of Developmental Psychology*, 17, 435–450.

Sutton, J., Smith, P.K. & Swettenham, J. (1999b). Bullying and "Theory of Mind": A critique of the 'social skills deficit' view of anti-social behaviour. *Social Development*, 8, 117–127.

Swanson, J. M., Kraemer, H. C., Hinshaw, S. P., Arnold, L. E., Conners, C. K., Abikoff, H. B., Clevenger, W., Davies, M., Elliott, G. R., Greenhill, L. L., Hechtman, L., Hoza, B., Jensen, P. S., March, J. S., Newcorn, J. H., Owens, E. B., Pelham, W. E., Schiller, E., Severe, J. B., Simpson, S., Vitiello, B., Wells, K., Wigal, T. & Wu, M. (2001). Clinical relevance of the primary findings of the MTA: Success rates based on severity of ADHD and ODD symptoms at the end of treatment. *Journal of the American Academy of Child and Adolescent Psychiatry*, 40, 168–179.

Swanson, J. M., Arnold, L. E., Vitiello, B., Abikoff, H. B., Wells, K. C., Pelham, W. E., March, J. S., Hinshaw, S. P., Hoza, B., Epstein, J. N., Elliott, G. R., Greenhill, L. L., Hechtman, L., Jensen, P. S., Kraemer, H. C., Kotkin, R., Molina, B., Newcorn, J. H., Owens, E. B., Severe, J., Hoagwood, K., Simpson, S., Wigal, T. & Hanley, T. (2002). Response to commentary on the multimodal treatment study of ADHD (MTA): Mining the meaning of the MTA. *Journal of Abnormal Child Psychology*, 30, 327–332.

Swindells, D. & Stagnitti, K. (2006). Pretend play and parents' view of social competence: The construct validity of the Child-Initiated Pretend Play Assessment. *Australian Occupational Therapy Journal*, 53 (4), 314–324.

Swinson, J. & Cording, M. (2002). Assertive discipline in a school for pupils with emotional and behavioural difficulties. *British Journal of Special Education*, 29 (2), 72–75.

Szatmari, P. (2000). The classification of autism, Asperger's syndrome, and pervasive developmental disorder. *Canadian Journal of Psychiatry*, 45, 731–738.

Szatmari, P. (2003). The causes of autism spectrum disorders. *British Medical Journal*, 326, 173–174.

Szücs, D. (2005). The use of electrophysiology in the study of early development. *Infant and Child Development*, 14, 99–102.

Tajfel, H. (1978). *Differentiation Between Social Groups: Studies in the Social Psychology of Intergroup Relations*. London: Academic Press.

Takahashi, K. (1990). Are the key assumptions of the 'strange situation' procedure universal? A view from Japanese research. *Human Development*, 33, 23–30.

Tallon-Baudry, C., Bertrand, O., Peronnet, F. & Pernier, J. (1998). Induced gammaband activity during the delay of a visual short-term memory task in humans. *Journal of Neuroscience*, 18, 4244–4254.

Tanner, J. M. (1990). *Foetus into Man: Physical Growth from Conception to Maturity* (2nd Ed.). Cambridge, MA: Harvard University Press.

Tardif, T., Fletcher, P., Liang, W., Zhang, Z, Kaciroti, N. & Marchman, V. A. (2008). Baby's first 10 words. *Developmental Psychology*, 44 (4), 929–938.

Tarrant, M., North, A. C., Edridge, M. D., Kirk, L. E., Smith, E. A. & Turner, R.E. (2001). Social identity in adolescence. *Journal of Adolescence*, 24 (5), 597–609.

Tasker, M. (2008). Smaller Schools: A conflict of aims and purposes? *FORUM: for Promoting 3–19 Comprehensive Education,* 50 (2), 177–184.

Taylor, E., Sandberg, S., Thorley, G. & Giles, S. (1991). *The Epidemiology of Childhood Hyperactivity*. Oxford: Oxford University Press.

Taylor, J. (2008). *Could you care for a baby?* Sky News. Retrieved 25 October 2010 from http://blogs.news.sky.com/eyewitnessblog/Post:c7fa863b-8ad9-495f-9abfa71db34f5964.

Taylor, J. L., Greenberg, J. S., Seltzer, M. M. & Floyd, F. J. (2008). Siblings of adults with mild intellectual deficits or mental illness: Differential life course outcomes. *Journal of Family Psychology*, 22 (6), 905–914.

Taylor, M. & Carlson, S. M. (1997). The relation between individual differences in fantasy and theory of mind. *Child Development*, 68, 20–27.

Teller, D. Y. (1998). Spatial and temporal aspects of colour vision. *Vision Research*, 38, 3275–3282.

Teller, D. Y. & Bornstein, M. H. (1987). Infant colour vision and colour perception. In P. Salapatek & L. Cohen (Eds), *Handbook of Infant Perception: Vol. 2: From Perception to Cognition* (185–236). Orlando, FL: Academic Press.

Tervo, R. (2003). Identifying patterns of developmental delays can help diagnose neurodevelopmental disorders. *A Pediatric Perspective*, 13 (3), 3–15.

Teuber, H. L. & Rudel, R. G. (1962). Behaviour after cerebral lesions in children and adults. *Developmental Medicine and Child Neurology*, 3, 3–20.

Thapar, A., Holmes, J., Poulton, K. & Harrington, R. (1999). Genetic basis of attention deficit and hyperactivity. *British Journal of Psychiatry*, 174, 105–111.

Thapar, A., Langley, K., Owen, M. J. & O'Donovan, M. C. (2007). Advances in genetic findings on attention deficit/hyperactivity disorder. *Psychological Medicine*, 37, 1681–1692.

Thatcher, R. W. (1991). Maturation of human frontal lobes: Physiological evidence for staging. *Developmental Neuropsychology*, 7, 397–419.

Thatcher, R. W., Lyon, G. R., Rumsey, J. & Krasnegor, J. (1996). *Developmental Neuroimaging*. San Diego, CA: Academic Press.

Thelen, E. & Smith, L. (Eds). (1994). *A Dynamic Systems Approach to the Development of Cognition and Action*. Cambridge, MA: MIT Press.

Thomas, A. & Chess, S. (1977). *Temperament and Development*. New York: Brunner/Mazel.

Thomas, A. & Chess, S. (1990). Continuities and discontinuities in temperament. In L. N. Robins & M. Rutter (Eds), *Straight and Devious Pathways from Childhood to Adulthood* (205–290). New York: Cambridge University Press.

Thomas, A., Chess, S., Birch, H. G., Hertzig, M. E. & Korn, S. (1963). *Behavioral Individuality in Early Childhood*. Oxford: New York University Press.

Thomas, A., Chess, B. & Birch, H. G. (1968). *Temperament and Behaviour Disorders in Children*. New York: New York University Press.

Thompson, P. W. (1993). Quantitative reasoning, complexity, and additive structures. *Educational Studies in Mathematics*, 3, 165–208.

Thompson, P. (1994). The development of the concept of speed and its relationship to concepts of rate. In G. Harel & J. Confrey (Eds), *The Development of Multiplicative Reasoning in the Learning of Mathematics* (181–236). Albany, NY: State University of New York Press.

Thompson, R. A. (2000). The legacy of early attachments. *Child Development*, 71, 145–52.

Thompson, S. K. (1975). Gender labels and early sex role development. *Child Development*, 46, 339–347.

Tizard, B. (1977). *Adoption: A Second Chance*. London: Open Books.

Tizard, B. & Hodges, J. (1978). The effect of early institutional rearing on the development of eight-year-old children. *Journal of Child Psychology and Psychiatry*, 19, 99–118.

Tizard, B. & Hughes, M. (1984). *Young Children Learning: Talking and Thinking at Home and at School*. London: Fontana.

Tizard, B. & Rees, J. (1975). The effect of early institutional rearing on the behaviour problems and affectional relationships of four-year-old children. *Journal of Child Psychology and Psychiatry*, 16, 61–74.

Tobin, J. J., Wu, D. Y. H. & Davidson, D. H. (1998). Komastsudai: A Japanese preschool. In M. Woodhead, D. Faulkner and K. Littleton (Eds), *Cultural Worlds of Early Childhood* (261–278). London: Routledge.

Tocci, S. (2000). *Down Syndrome*. New York: Franklin Watts.

Tomkins, C. A., Bloise, C., Timko, M. & Baumgartner, A. (1994). Working memory and inference revision in brain-damaged and normally ageing adults. *Journal of Speech and Language*, 37, 896–912.

Tomas de Almeida, A.M. (1999). Portugal. In P.K. Smith, Y. Morita, Junger-Tas, J., D. Olweus, R. Catalano & P. Slee (Eds), *The Nature of School Bullying. A Cross-National Perspective* (174–186). London: Routledge.

Tomlinson, S. (2008). Gifted, talented and high ability: Selection for education in a one-dimensional world. *Oxford Review of Education*, 34 (1), 59–74.

Toppelberg, C., & Shapiro, T. (2000). Language disorders: A 10-year research update review. *Journal of American Academy Child & Adolescent Psychiatry*, 39 (2), 143–152.

Traeen, B., Lewin, B. & Sundet, J. M. (1992a). The real and the ideal-gender differences in heterosexual behavior among Norwegian adolescents. *Journal of Community & Applied Social Psychology*, 2 (4), 227–237.

Traeen, B., Lewin, B. & Sundet, J. M. (1992b). Use of birth-control pills and condoms among 17–19-year-old adolescents in Norway-contraceptive versus protective behavior. *Aids Care–Psychological and Socio-Medical Aspects of Aids/Hiv*, 4 (4), 371–380.

Trainor, L. J. & Heinmiller, B. M. (1998). The development of evaluative responses to music: Infants prefer to listen to consonance over dissonance. *Infant Behaviour and Development*, 21, 77–88.

Trainor, L. J., Shahin, A. & Roberts, L. E. (2003). Effects of musical training on auditory cortex in children. In G. Avanzini, C. Faienze, D. Miciacchi, L.Lopez & M. Majno (Eds), The Neurosciences and Music: Mutual Interactions and Implications of Developmental Functions. *Annals NY Academy of Sciences*, 999, 520–521.

Trehub, S. E., Thorpe, L. A. & Morrongiello, B. A., (1985). Infants' perception of melodies: Changes in a single tone. *Infant Behaviour and Development*, 8, 213–223.

Trehub, S. E., Schneider, B. A., Thorpe, L. A. & Judge, P. (1991). Observational measures of auditory sensitivity in early infancy. *Developmental Psychology*, 27, 40–49.

Trudeau, N., Poulin-Dubois, D., and Joanette, Y. (2000). Language development following brain injury in early childhood: A longitudinal case study. *International Journal of Language and Communication Disorders*, 35 (2), 227–249.

Tulving, E. (1983). *Elements of Episodic Memory*. New York: Oxford University Press.

Tversky, A. & Kahneman D. (1973). Availability: A heuristic for judging frequency and probability. *Cognitive Psychology*, 5, 207–232.

Tynes, B., Reynolds, L. & Greenfield, P. M. (2004). Adolescence, race and ethnicity on the Internet: A comparison of discourse in monitored vs. unmonitored chat rooms. *Journal of Applied Developmental Psychology*, 25, 667–684.

Tyler, K. & Jones, B. D. (2002). Teachers' responses to the ecosystemic approach to changing chronic problem behaviour in schools. *Pastoral Care in Education*, 20 (2), 30–39.

Tymms, P., Merrell, C. & Jones, P. (2004). Using baseline assessment data to make international comparisons. *British Educational Research Journal*, 30 (5), 673–689.

Underwood, M. (1997). Peer social status and children's understanding of the expression and control of positive and negative emotions. *Merrill-Palmer Quarterly*, 43, 610–634.

Underwood, M.K. (2002). Sticks and stones and social exclusion: Aggression among girls and boys. In P.K. Smith & C.H. Hart (Eds), *Blackwell Handbook of Childhood Social Development* (533–548). Oxford: Blackwell.

US Department of Education (2001). The 23rd Annual Report to Congress on the Implementation of the Individuals with Disabilities Education Act.

Valkenburg, P. M. & Peter, J. (2007). Preadolescents' and adolescents' online communication and their closeness to friends. *Developmental Psychology*, 43, 267–277.

van den Boom, D. C. (1994). The influence of temperament and mothering on attachment and exploration: An experimental manipulation of sensitive responsiveness among lower-class mothers with irritable infants. *Child Development*, 65, 1457–1477.

Vanderbosch, H. & Van Cleemput, K. (2008). Defining cyberbullying: A qualitative research into the perceptions of youngsters. *Cyberpsychology & Behavior*, 11, 499–503.

Van der Meer, A. L. H., Van der Weel F. R. & Lee D. N. (1996). Lifting weights in neonates: Developing visual control of reaching. *Scandinavian Journal of Psychology*, 37, 424–436.

Van der Meer, A. L. H., Fallet, G. & van der Weel, F. R. (2008). Perception of structured optic flow and random visual motion in infants and adults: A high-density EEG study. *Experimental Brain Research*, 186, 493–502.

van Ijzendoorn, M. H. (1995). The association between adult attachment representations and infant attachment, parental responsiveness, and clinical status: A metaanalysis on the predictive validity of the Adult Attachment Interview. *Psychological Bulletin*, 113, 404–410.

van Ijzendoorn, M. H. & deWolff, M. S. (1997). In search of the absent father-meta-analyses of infant-father attachment: A rejoinder to our discussants. *Child Development*, 68, 604–609.

van Ijzendoorn, M. H. & Kroonenberg, P. M. (1988). Cross-cultural patterns of attachment: A meta-analysis of the Strange Situation. *Child Development*, 59, 147–156.

van Ijzendoorn, M. H., Vereijken, C. M. J. L., Bakermans-Kranenburg, M. J. & Riksen-Walraven, J. M. (2004). Assessing attachment security with the attachment Q Sort: Meta-analytic evidence for the validity of the Observer AQS. Child Development, 75, 1188–1213.

Valkenburg, P. M. & Vroone, M. (2004). Developmental changes in infants' and toddlers' attention to television entertainment. *Communication Research*, 31, 288–311.

Varley, W. H., Levin, J. R., Severson, R. A. & Wolff, P. (1974). Training imagery production in young children through motor involvement. *Journal of Educational Psychology*, 66, 262–266.

Vartia, M. (1996). The sources of bullying – Psychological work environment and organizational climate. *European Journal of Work and Organizational Psychology*, 5, 203–214.

Vaughn, B. E., Bradley, C. F., Joffe, L. S., Seifer, R. & Barglow, P. (1987). Maternal characteristics measured prenatally are predictive of ratings of temperamental "difficulty" on the Carey Infant Temperament Questionnaire. *Developmental Psychology*, 23, 152–161.

Veenman, S., Kenter, B. & Post, K. (2000). Cooperative learning in Dutch primary classrooms. *Educational Studies*, 26 (3), 281–302.

Veenstra-Vanderweele, J. & Cook, E. (2003). Genetics of childhood disorders: Autism. *Journal of the American Academy of Child and Adolescent Psychiatry*, 42, 116–118.

Venezia, M., Messinger, D. S., Thorp, D. & Mundy, P. (2004). The development of anticipatory smiling. *Infancy*, 6 (3), 397–406.

Vergnaud, G. (1982). A classification of cognitive tasks and operations of thought involved in addition and subtraction problems. In T. P. Carpenter, J. M. Moser and T. A Romberg (Eds), *Addition and Subtraction: A Cognitive Perspective* (60–67). Hillsdale, NJ: Erlbaum.

Vergnaud, G. (1983). Multiplicative structures. In R. Lesh & M. Landau (Eds), *Acquisition of Mathematics Concepts and Processes* (128–175). London: Academic Press.

Vergnaud, G. (2009). The theory of conceptual fields. *Human Development*, 52, 83–94.

Verschaffel, L. (1994). Using retelling data to study elementary school children's representations and solutions of compare problems. *Journal for Research in Mathematics Education*, 25, 141–165.

Veugelers, W. & Vedder, P. (2003). Values in teaching. *Teachers and Teaching: Theory and Practice*, 9 (4), 377–389.

Vinther, J. (2005). Cognitive processes at work in CALL. *Computer Assisted Language Learning*, 18 (4), 251–271.

Volkmar, F. R. & Chawarska, K. (2008). Autism in infants: An update. *World Psychiatry*, 7, 19–21.

Von Hofsten, C. (1982). Eye-hand coordination in newborns. *Developmental Psychology*, 18, 450–461.

Von Hofsten, C. (1984). Developmental changes in the organization of pre-reaching movements. *Developmental Psychology*, 20, 378–388.

Voogt, J., Tilya, F. & van den Akker, J. (2009). Science teacher learning of MBL-supported student-centered science education in the context of secondary education in Tanzania. *Journal of Science Education and Technology*, 18 (5), 429–438.

Vygotsky, L.S. (1962). *Thought and Language*. Cambridge, MA: MIT Press.

Vygotsky, L. S. (1978). *Mind and Society: The Development of Higher Mental Processes*. Cambridge, MA: Harvard University Press.

Wachs, T. D. & Bates, J. E. (2001). Temperament. In G. Bremner & A. Fogel (Eds), *Blackwell Handbook of Infant Development* (465–501). Oxford: Blackwell.

Wakefield, A. J., Murch, S. H., Anthony, A., Linnell, J., Casson, D. M., Malik, M., Berelowitz, M., Dhillon, A. P. (1998). Ileal-lymphoide-nodular hyperplasia, non-specific colitis and pervasive developmental disorder in children. *The Lancet*, 351 (9103). Retracted.

Walford, G. (2001). Funding for religious schools in England and the Netherlands. Can the piper call the tune? *Research Papers in Education*, 16 (4), 359–380.

Walker, S., Berthelsen, D. & Irving, K. (2001). Temperament and peer acceptance in early childhood: Sex and social status differences. *Child Study Journal*, 31, 177–192.

Warneken, F. & Tomaselo, M. (2006). Altruistic helping in human infants and young chimpanzees. *Science*, 311, 1301–1303.

Warneken, F. & Tomasello, M. (2009). Varieties of altruism in children and chimpanzees. *Trends in Cognitive Science*, 13, 397–402.

Watkins, M. W., Lei, P. W. & Canivez, G. L. (2007). Psychometric intelligence and achievement: A cross-lagged panel analysis. *Intelligence*, 35 (1), 59–68.

Watson, J.B. (1930). *Behaviorism* (revised edition). Chicago, IL: University of Chicago Press.

Watts, B. & Youens, B. (2007). Harnessing the potential of pupils to influence school development. *Improving Schools*, 10 (1), 18–28.

Watts, T. J. (2008). The pathogenesis of autism. *Clinical Medicine: Pathology*, 1, 99–103.

Weaver, I. C. G. Cervoni, N., Champagne, F. A., D'Alessio, A. C., Sharma, S., Seeki, J. R., Dymov, S., Szyf, M. & Meaney, M. J. (2004). Epigenetic programming by maternal behaviour. *Nature Neuroscience*, 7, 847–854.

Webb, R. & Vulliamy, G. (2007). Changing classroom practice at Key Stage 2: The impact of New Labour's national strategies. *Oxford Review of Education*, 33 (5), 561–580.

Webster-Stratton, C. (2006). *Incredible Years – Trouble-Shooting Guide for Parents of Children Aged 3–8*. London.

Webster-Stratton, C. & Hancock, L. (1998). Parent training for young children with conduct problems. Content, methods and therapeutic process. In C. E. Schaefer (Ed.), *Handbook of Parent Training* (98–152). New York: Wiley.

Wegerif, R., Littleton, K., Dawes, L., Mercer, N. & Rowe, D. (2004). Widening access to educational opportunities through teaching children how to reason together. *International Journal of Research & Method in Education*, 27 (2), 143–156.

Weinraub, M., Clemens, L. P., Sockloff, A., Ethridge, R., Gracely, E. & Myers, B. (1984). The development of sex-role stereotypes in the third year: Relationships to gender labelling, gender identity, sex-typed toy preference, and family characteristics. *Child Development*, 55, 1493–1503.

Wellings, F., Nanchahal, K., Macdowall, W., McManusk S., Erens, B., Mercer, C. H., Johnson, A. M., Copas, A.J., Korovessis, C., Fenton, F.A. & Field, J. (2001). Sexual behaviour in Britain: Early heterosexual experience. *The Lancet*, 358 (9296), 1843–1850.

Wellman, H. & Estes, D. (1986). Early understanding of mental entities: A re-examination of childhood realism. *Child Development*, 57, 910–923.

Wellman, H.M., Cross, D. & Watson, J. (2001). Meta-analysis of theory of mind development: The truth about false belief. *Child Development*, 72 (3), 655–684.

Wentzel, K. R. & Asher, S. R. (1995). The academic lives of neglected, rejected, popular, and controversial children. *Child Development*, 66, 754–763.

Werker, J. F. & Tees, R. C. (1984). Cross-language speech perception: Evidence for perceptual reorganization during the first year of life. *Infant Behaviour and Development*, 7, 49–63.

Werker, J. (1989). Becoming a native listener. *American Scientist*, 77, 54–59.

Wechsler, D. (1992). *Wechsler Intelligence Scale for Children III*. San Antonio, TX: The Psychological Corporation.

Wetz, J. (2009). *Urban Village Schools: Putting Relationships at the Heart of Secondary School Organisation and Design*. London: Calouste Gulbenkian Foundation.

White, B. & Held, R. (1966). Plasticity of sensori-motor development in the human infant. In J. F. Rosenblith & W.

Allinsmith (Eds), *The Causes of Behaviour* (60–70). Boston, MA: Allyn and Bacon.

Whitney, I., Rivers, I., Smith, P. K., & Sharp, S. (1994). The Sheffield project: Methodology and findings. In P. K. Smith & S. Sharp (Eds), *School Bullying: Insights and Perspectives* (20–56). London: Routledge.

Whitney, I. & Smith, P.K. (1993). A survey of the nature and extent of bullying junior/middle and secondary schools. *Educational Research*, 35, 3–25.

WHO (1992). *ICD-10 Classification of Mental and Behavioural Disorders*. Geneva: World Health Organization.

Wigal, T., Greenhill, L., Chuang, S., McGough, J., Vitiello, B., Skrobala, A., Swanson, J., Wigal, S., Abikoff, H., Kollins, S., McCracken, J., Riddle, M., Posner, K., Jaswinder, G., Davies, M., Thorp, B. & Stehli, A. (2006). Safety and tolerability of methylphenidate in preschool children with ADHD. *Journal of the American Academy of Child and Adolescent Psychiatry*, 45, 1294–1303.

Wight, M. & Chapparo, C. (2008). Social competence and learning difficulties: Teacher perceptions. *Australian Occupational Therapy Journal*, 55 (4), 256–265.

Will, J. A., Self, P. A. & Datan, N. (1976). Maternal behavior and perceived sex of infant. *American Journal of Orthopsychiatry*, 46, 135–139.

Williams, M. & Gersch, I. (2004). Teaching in mainstream and special schools: Are the stresses similar or different? *British Journal of Special Education*, 31 (3), 157–162.

Williams, P. & Nicholas, D. (2006). Testing the usability of information technology applications with learners with special educational needs (SEN). *Journal of Research in Special Educational Needs*, 6 (1), 31–41.

Williams, R. (2010). *Parents too busy to help children learn to talk*. The Guardian, 4 January 2010. Retrieved 15 October 2010 from: http://www.guardian.co.uk/society/2010/jan/04/parents-busy-children-learn-talk.

Wilson, J. D. (1972). Recent studies on the mechanism of action of testosterone. *New England Journal of Medicine*, 287, 1284–1291.

Wilson, J. D. (1978). Sexual differentiation. *Annual Review of Physiology*, 40, 279–306.

Wimmer, H. & Perner, J. (1983). Beliefs about beliefs: Representation and constraining function of wrong beliefs in young children's understanding of deception. *Cognition*, 13, 41–68.

Windle, M., Iwawaki, S. & Lerner, R. M. (1988). Cross-cultural comparability of temperament among Japanese and American preschool children. *International Journal of Psychology*, 88, 547–567.

Winkler, I. Haden, G. P., Ladinig, O., Sziller, I. & Honing, H. (2009). Newborn infants detect the beat in music. *Proceedings of the National Academy of Sciences USA*, 106, 2468–2471.

Wolke, D., Woods, S., Stanford, K. & Schulz, H. (2001). Bullying and victimisation of primary school children in England and Germany. Prevalence and school factors. *British Journal of Psychology*, 92, 673–696.

Wolff, P. H. (1966). The causes, controls and organization of behaviour in the neonate. *Psychological Issues*, 5 (No. 17).

Wolff, P. H. (1968). Sucking patterns of infant mammals. *Brain, Behaviour and Evolution*, 1, 354–367.

Wolff, P. H. (1968). The serial organisation of sucking in the young infant. *Paediatrics*, 42, 943–956.

Wong, W. K., Chan, T. W., Chou, C. Y., Heh, J. S. & Tung, S. H. (2003). Reciprocal tutoring using cognitive tools. *Journal of Computer Assisted Learning*, 19 (4), 416–428.

Woods, L. (2006). Children and families: Evaluating the clinical effectiveness of neonatal nurse practitioners: an exploratory study. *Journal of Clinical Nursing*, 15 (1), 35–44.

Woods, R. (2008). When rewards and sanctions fail: A case study of a primary school rule-breaker. International *Journal of Qualitative Studies in Education*, 21 (2), 181–196.

Woolfolk, A., Hughes, M. & Walkup, V. (2008). *Psychology in Education*. Harlow: Pearson Education.

Wynn, K. (1992). Evidence against empiricist accounts of the origins of numerical knowledge. *Mind and Language*, 7, 315–332.

Wynn, K. (1998). Psychological foundations of number: Numerical competence in human infants. *Trends in Cognitive Science*, 2, 296–303.

Xu, F. & Spelke, E. (2000). Large number discrimination in 6-month-old infants. *Cognition*, *74*, B1–B11.

Yakovlev, P.A. & Lecours, I.R. (1967). The myelogenetic cycles of regional maturation of the brain. In A. Minkowski (Ed.), *Regional Development of the Brain in Early Life* (3–70). Oxford: Blackwell.

Ybarra, M.L. & Mitchell, K.J. (2004). Online aggressor/targets, aggressors and targets: a comparison of associated youth characteristics. *Journal of Child Psychology & Psychiatry*, 45, 1308–1316.

Young, R. & Sweeting, H. (2004). Adolescent bullying, relationships, psychological well-being, and gender-atypical behavior: A gender diagnosticity approach. *Sex Roles*, 50, 525–537.

Young, R. D. (1964). Effect of prenatal drugs and neonatal stimulation on later behavior. *Journal of Comparative and Physiological Psychology*, 58, 309–311.

Young, S. (1998). The support group approach to bullying in school. *Educational Psychology in Practice*, 14, 32–39.

Younger, B. A., & Cohen, L. B. (1986). Developmental changes in infants' perceptiom of correlations among attributes. *Child Development*, 57, 803–815.

Zakriski, A. & Coie, J. (1996). A comparison of aggressive-rejected and nonaggressive-rejected children's interpretation of self-directed and other-directed rejection. *Child Development*, 67, 1048–1070.

Zemach, I., Cheng, S. & Teller, D. Y. (2007). Infant colour vision: prediction of infants' spontaneous colour preferences. *Vision Research*, 47, 1368–1381.

Zimmer, E.Z., Fifer, W.P., Kim, Y.-I., Rey, H.R., Chao, C.R. & Myers, M.M. (1993). Response of the premature fetus to stimulation by speech sounds. *Early Human Development*, 33, 207–215.

Zimmerman, C. (2000). The development of scientific reasoning skills. *Developmental Review*, 20, 99–149.

Zimmermann, P. (2004). Attachment representations and characteristics of friendship relations during adolescence. *Journal of Experimental Child Psychology*, 88 (1), 83–101.

Zito, J. M., Safer, D. J., dosReis, S., Gardner, J. F., Boles, M. & Lynch, F. (2000). Trends in the prescribing of psychotropic medications to preschoolers. *Journal of the American Medical Association*, 283, 1025–1030.

Zohar, A. (2006). Connected knowledge in science and mathematics education. *International Journal of Science Education*, 28 (13), 1579–1599.

Zoia, S., Blason, L., D'Ottavio, G., Bulgheroni, M., Pezzetta, E., Scabar, A. & Castiello, U. (2002). Evidence of early development of action planning in the human foetus: A kinematic study. *Experimental Brain Research*, 176, 217–226.

Index